THE HERITAGE OF
WORLD CIVILIZATIONS

VOLUME TWO: SINCE 1500
SEVENTH EDITION

ALBERT M. CRAIG
Harvard University

WILLIAM A. GRAHAM
Harvard University

DONALD KAGAN
Yale University

STEVEN OZMENT
Harvard University

FRANK M. TURNER
Yale University

PEARSON

Prentice
Hall

Upper Saddle River, New Jersey 07458

Library of Congress Cataloging-in-Publication Data

The heritage of world civilizations / Albert M. Craig ... [et al].- 7th ed., combined volume
    p. cm.
  Includes bibliographical references and index.
  ISBN 0-13-192623-3
    1. Civilizations–History–Textbooks.   I. Craig, Albert M.
  CB69.H45 2005
  909'—dc22

2004063382

VP, Editorial Director: Charlyce Jones Owen
Executive Editor: Charles Cavaliere
Associate Editor: Emsal Hasan
Editorial Assistant: Shannon Corliss
Director of Marketing: Heather Shelstad
Marketing Assistant: Cherron Gardner
VP, Director of Production and Manufacturing: Barbara Kittle
Managing Editor: Joanne Riker
Production Editor: Kathleen Sleys
Production Assistants: Marlene Gassler and Kristen Sleys
Editor-in-Chief, Development: Rochelle Diogenes
Development Editor: Barbara Muller
Media Editor: Deborah O'Connell
Prepress and Manufacturing Manager: Nick Sklitsis
Prepress and Manufacturing Buyer: Ben Smith
Creative Design Director: Leslie Osher

Interior and Cover Designer: Laura Gardner
Line Art Coordinator: Scott Garrison
Electronic Artists: Carey Davies, Guy Ruggiero
Director, Image Resource Center: Melinda Reo
Interior Image Specialist: Beth Boyd Brenzel
Cover Image Specialist: Karen Sanatar
Image Permission Coordinator: Michelina Viscusi
Photo Researcher: Sheila Norman
Color Scanning Services: Joe Conti, Greg Harrison, Cory Skidds, Rob Uibelhoer, Ron Walko
Compositor: Preparé, Inc.
Printer/Binder: Courier Companies, Inc.
Cover Printer: Phoenix Color Corp.
Cover Art: Eduardo Abela (1889–1965) ©Copyright. Peasants, Havana. Photo Credit: Snark/Art Resource, NY

Credits and acknowledgments borrowed from other sources and reproduced, with permission, in this textbook appear on the appropriate page within text or on page C-1.

Pearson Education Ltd., London
Pearson Education Australia Pty., Limited, Sydney
Pearson Education Singapore, Pte., Ltd.
Pearson Education North Asia Ltd., Hong Kong

Pearson Education Canada, Ltd., Toronto
Pearson Educación de Mexico, S.A. de C.V.
Pearson Education — Japan, Tokyo
Pearson Education Malaysia, Pte., Ltd.

10 9 8 7 6 5 4 3 2 1

ISBN 0-13-192622-5

Brief Contents

Contents

● ● ● ● ● ● ● ● ● ● ● ●

PART 1 THE BIRTH OF CIVILIZATION 2

CHAPTER 1

CHAPTER 2

••••••• •••••••

PART 2 EMPIRES AND CULTURES OF THE ANCIENT WORLD 80

CHAPTER **5**

Africa: Early History to 1000 C.E. 147

CHAPTER **6**

Republican and Imperial Rome 171

PART 3 CONSOLIDATION AND INTERACTION OF WORLD CIVILIZATIONS 224

CHAPTER

10

Iran and India Before Islam 285

CHAPTER

11

The Formation of Islamic Civilization, 622–945 301

CHAPTER

12

The Byzantine Empire and Western Europe to 1000 323

• • • • • • • • • • • •
PART **4** THE WORLD IN TRANSITION **432**

PART 5 ENLIGHTENMENT AND REVOLUTION IN THE WEST 632

••••••• ••••••

PART 6 INTO THE MODERN WORLD 732

CHAPTER 25

Northern Transatlantic Economy and Society, 1815–1914 737

CHAPTER 26

Latin America from Independence to the 1940s 773

CHAPTER 27

India, the Islamic Heartlands, and Africa: The Challenge of Modernity (1800–1945) 799

CHAPTER **28**

• • • • • • • • • • • •

PART 7 GLOBAL CONFLICT AND CHANGE 866

CHAPTER

32

The West Since World War II   959

CHAPTER

33

East Asia: The Recent Decades   993

Postcolonialism and Beyond 1023

Global Perspective: Democratization, Globalization, and Terrorism 1024

Beyond the Postcolonial Era 1025

Documents

Maps

Preface

The response of the United States to the events of September 11, 2001, including the war in Iraq and Afghanistan have brought upon the world a new awareness of human history in a global context. Prior to the attacks on New York and Washington and the subsequent U.S. intervention in the Middle East, readers in North America generally understood world history and globalism as academic concepts. They now understand them as realities shaping their daily lives and experience. The immediate pressures of the present and of the foreseeable future draw us to seek a more certain and extensive understanding of the past.

The idea of globalization is now a pressing reality on the lives of nations, affecting the domestic security of their citizens, the deployment of armed forces, their standard of living, and the environment. Whether, as Samuel Huntington, the distinguished Harvard political scientist, contends, we are witnessing a clash of civilizations, we have certainly entered a new era in which no active citizen or educated person can escape the necessity of understanding the past in global terms. Both the historical experience and the moral, political, and religious values of the different world civilizations now demand our attention and our understanding. It is our hope that in these new, challenging times *The Heritage of World Civilizations* will provide one path to such knowledge.

The Roots of Globalization

Globalization—that is, the increasing interaction and interdependency of the various regions of the world—has resulted from two major historical developments: the closing of the European era of world history and the rise of technology.

From approximately 1500 C.E. to the middle of the twentieth century, Europeans gradually came to dominate the world through colonization (most particularly in North and South America), state-building, economic productivity, and military power. That era of European dominance ended during the third quarter of the twentieth century after Europe had brought unprecedented destruction on itself during World War II and as the nations of Asia, the Near East, and Africa achieved new positions on the world scene. Their new political independence, their control over strategic natural resources, and the expansion of their economies (especially those of the nations of the Pacific rim of Asia), and in some cases their access to nuclear weapons have changed the shape of world affairs.

Further changing the world political and social situation has been a growing discrepancy in the economic development of different regions that is often portrayed as a problem between the northern and southern hemispheres. Beyond the emergence of this economic disparity has been the remarkable advance of radical political Islamism during the past forty years. In the midst of all these developments, as a result of the political collapse of the former Soviet Union, the United States has emerged as the single major world power.

The second historical development that continues to fuel the pace of globalization is the advance of technology, associated most importantly with transportation, military weapons, and electronic communication. The advances in transportation over the past two centuries including ships, railways, and airplanes have made more parts of the world and its resources accessible to more people in ever shorter spans of time. Over the past century and a half, military weapons of increasingly destructive power enabled Europeans and then later the United States to dominate other regions of the globe. Now, the spread of these weapons means that any nation with sophisticated military technology can threaten other nations, no matter how far away. Furthermore, technologies that originated in the West from the early twentieth century to the present have been turned against the West. More recently, the electronic revolution associated with computer technology and most particularly the internet has sparked unprecedented speed and complexity in global communications. It is astonishing to recall that personal computers have been generally available for less than twenty-five years and the rapid personal communication associated with them has existed for less than fifteen years.

Why not, then, focus only on new factors in the modern world, such as the impact of technology and the end of the European era? To do so would ignore the very deep roots that these developments have in the past. More important, the events of recent years demonstrate, as the authors of this book have long contended, that the major religious traditions continue to shape and drive the modern world as well as the world of the past. The religious traditions link today's civilizations to their most ancient roots. We believe this emphasis on the great religious traditions recognizes not only a factor that has shaped the past, but one that is profoundly and dynamically alive in our world today.

Strengths of the Text

Balanced and Flexible Presentation   In this edition, as in past editions, we have sought to present world history fairly, accurately, and in a way that does justice to its great variety. History has many facets, no one of which can account for the others. Any attempt to tell the story of civilization from a single perspective, no matter how timely, is bound to neglect or suppress some important part of that story.

Historians have recently brought a vast array of new tools and concepts to bear on the study of history. Our coverage introduces students to various aspects of social and intellectual history as well as to the more traditional political, diplomatic, and military coverage. We firmly believe that only through an appreciation of all pathways to understanding of the past can the real heritage of world civilizations be claimed.

The Heritage of World Civilizations, Seventh Edition, is designed to accommodate a variety of approaches to a course in world history, allowing teachers to stress what is most important to them. Some teachers will ask students to read all the chapters. Others will select among them to reinforce assigned readings and lectures.

Clarity and Accessibility   Good narrative history requires clear, vigorous prose. Our goal has been to make our presentation fully accessible to students without compromising on vocabulary or conceptual level. We hope this effort will benefit both teachers and students.

Current Scholarship   As in previous editions, changes in this edition reflect our determination to incorporate the most recent developments in historical scholarship and the expanding concerns of professional historians. To better highlight the dynamic processes of world history, significant new coverage of the Silk Road, Byzantium, the Crusades, Southeast Asia, women in Islam, nineteenth-century European science, the homefront during World War II, student protest and popular music, and recent events in the Middle East has been added to the Seventh Edition.

Content and Organization

The many changes in content and organization in this edition of *The Heritage of World Civilizations* reflect our ongoing effort to present a truly global survey of world civilizations that at the same time gives a rich picture of the history of individual regions:

◆ **Strengthened Global Approach.** The Seventh Edition more explicitly highlights the connections and parallels in global history among regions of the world. Greater emphasis is now placed on cultural exchange, trade, encounter, and the diffusion of ideas. Each chapter now begins with a "Global Perspective" section that succinctly places in a wider, global framework the regions and topics that are to be discussed. In addition, each of the seven parts opens with a two-page global map that visually depicts the key themes in the chapters that follow.

◆ **Expanded and Improved Map Program.** The entire map program for the Seventh Edition has been completely clarified and expanded. Twenty-one maps are new to the Seventh Edition and graphically illustrate key global developments such as trade in the classical world, the spread of Buddhism, the Islamicization of Southeast Asia, the Columbian exchange, world slavery, European global conflicts in the eighteenth century, global migration, the Holocaust, and the so-called "clash of civilizations." Every single map in the text has been redesigned for greater visual appeal and accuracy. All maps are now referenced in the narrative. A listing of all the maps in the text can be found on p. xxiii–xxiv.

◆ **Improved, Streamlined Organization.** To better accommodate typical teaching sequences, the number of chapters has been reduced to 34, with coverage of European society and state-building in the seventeenth and eighteenth centuries now treated in a single chapter. In addition, coverage of Han China (chapter 7) now immediately succeeds coverage of the Rome (chapter 6) making it easier to draw connections and parallels between these two empires. The final chapter has been extensively reorganized to better examine important recent events in the Middle East.

◆ **New Design and Photo Program.** The entire text has been set in a lively and engaging new design. Each of the 34 chapters includes photos never before included in previous editions of the text and the number of illustrations has been increased. Seven new graphs and tables have also been added to the text to help students visualize important data.

Pedagogical Features

This edition retains many of the pedagogical features of previous editions, while providing increased assessment opportunities.

NEW ◆ **Two-page Global Maps** open each of the seven parts of the book. These provide a visual and geographical overview of the key themes presented in the chapters that follow. Introduction and questions help students make connections across time and space.

◆ **Part Timelines** show chronologically the major events in five regions—Europe, the Near East and India, East Asia, Africa, and the Americas—side by side. Appropriate photographs enrich each timeline.

◆ **Religions of the World** essays examine the historical impact of each of the world's great religious traditions: Judaism, Christianity, Islam, Buddhism, and Hinduism.

◆ **Chapter Outlines** open each chapter and help students access important topics for study and review.

NEW ◆ **Global Perspective Essays** introduce the key problems of each chapter and place them in a global and historical context. Questions prompt student to consider the causes, connections, and consequences of the topics they will encounter in the main narrative.

NEW ◆ **Overview Tables** summarize key concepts and reinforce material presented in the main narrative.

◆ **Chronologies** within each chapter help students situate key events in time.

◆ **Documents,** including selections from sacred books, poems, philosophical tracts, political manifestos, letters, and travel accounts, expose students to the raw material of history, providing an intimate contact with peoples of the past. Questions accompanying the source documents direct students toward important, thought-provoking issues and help them relate the documents to the main narrative.

NEW ◆ **Key Terms** are boldfaced in the text, listed (with page reference) at the end of each chapter, and defined in the book's glossary.

◆ **Interactive Maps,** usually one per chapter, prompt students to explore the relationship between geography and history in a dynamic fashion.

NEW ◆ **Chapter Summaries** conclude each chapter, organized by subtopic, and recap important points.

◆ **Chapter Review Questions** help students interpret the broad themes of each chapter. These questions can be used for class discussion and essay topics.

◆ **Documents CD-ROM,** containing over 200 documents in world history, is bound with all new copies of the text. A list of relevant documents found on the CD-ROM is found at the end of each chapter.

A Note on Dates and Transliteration We have used B.C.E. (before the common era) and C.E. (common era) instead of B.C. (before Christ) and A.D. (anno domini, the year of our Lord) to designate dates.

Until recently, most scholarship on China used the Wade-Giles system of romanization for Chinese names and terms. China, today, however, uses another system known as pinyin. Virtually all Western newspapers have adopted it. In order that students may move easily from the present text to the existing body of advanced scholarship on Chinese history, we now use the pinyin system throughout the text.

Also, we have followed the currently accepted English transliterations of Arabic words. For example, today Koran is being replaced by the more accurate Qur'an; similarly Muhammad is preferable to Mohammed and Muslim to Moslem. We have not tried to distinguish the letters 'ayn and hamza; both are rendered by a simple apostrophe (') as in shi'ite.

With regard to Sanskritic transliteration, we have not distinguished linguals and dentals, and both palatal and lingual s are rendered sh, as in Shiva and Upanishad.

Ancillary Instructional Materials

The Heritage of World Civilizations, Seventh Edition, comes with an extensive package of ancillary materials.

For the Instructor

◆ The *Instructor's Manual/Test-Item File* includes chapter outlines, overviews, key concepts, discussion questions, suggestions for useful audiovisual resources, and approximately 1500 test items (essay, multiple choice, true/false, and matching).

◆ The *Instructor Resource CDROM,* compatible with both Windows and Macintosh environments, provides instructors with such essential teaching tools as hundreds of digitized images and maps for classroom presentations, PowerPoint lectures, and other Instructional material. The assets on the IRCDROM can be easily exported into online courses, such as WebCT and Blackboard.

◆ *Test Manager* is a computerized test management program for Windows and Macintosh environments. The program allows instructors to select items from the test-item file to create tests. It also allows online testing.

◆ The *Transparency Package* provides instructors with full color transparency acetates of all the maps, charts, and graphs in the text for use in the classroom.

For the Student

◆ *History Notes* (Volumes I and II) provides practice tests, essay questions, and map exercise to help reinforce key concepts.

◆ *Documents in World History* (Volumes I and II) is a collection of 200 primary source documents in global history. Questions accompanying the documents can be used for discussion or as writing assignments.

DK ◆ Produced in collaboration with Dorling Kindersley, the world's most respected cartography publisher, *The Prentice Hall Atlas of World History* includes approximately 100 maps fundamental to the study of world history—from early hominids to the twenty-first century.

◆ *Reading Critically About History* is a brief guide to reading effectively that provides students with helpful strategies for reading a history textbook.

◆ *Understanding and Answering Essay Questions* suggest helpful analytical tools for understanding different types of essay questions, and provides precise guidelines for preparing well-carfted essay answers.

0 ◆ Prentice Hall is pleased to provide adopters of *The Heritage of World Civilizations* with an opportunity to receive significant discounts when copies of the text are bundled with Penguin Classics titles in world history. Contact your local Prentice Hall representative for details.

Media Resources

OneKey ◆ Prentice Hall's New Online Resource **OneKey** lets instructors and students in to the best teaching and learning resources–all in one place. This all-inclusive online resource is designed to help you minimize class preparation and maximize teaching time. Conveniently organized by chapter, OneKey for *The Heritage of World Civilizations*, Seventh Edition, reinforces what students have learned in class and from the text. Among the student resources available for each chapter are: a complete, media-rich e-book version of *The Heritage of World Civilizations* Seventh Edition; quizzes organized by the main subtopics of each chapter; over 200 primary-source documents; and interactive map quizzes.

For instructors, OneKey includes images and maps from *The Heritage of World Civilizations* Seventh Edition; instructional material; hundreds of primary-source documents; and PowerPoint presentations.

◆ *Prentice Hall One Search with Research Navigator: History 2005* This brief guide focuses on developing critical-thinking skills necessary for evaluating and using online sources. It provides a brief introduction to navigating the Internet with specific references to History web sites. It also provides an access code and instruction on using Research Navigator, a powerful research tool that provides access to three exclusive databases of reliable source material: ContentSelect Academic Journal Database, the New York Times Search by Subject Archive, and Link Library.

◆ The *Companion Website*™ (*www.prenhall.com/craig*) works in tandem with the text and features objectives, study questions, web links to related Internet resources, document exercises, interactive maps, and map labelling exercises.

◆ *World History Document CD-ROM* Bound into every new copy of this textbook is a free World History Documents CD-ROM. This is a powerful resource for research and additional reading that contains more than 200 primary source documents central to World History. Each document provides essay questions that are linked directly to a website where short-essay answers can be submitted oline or printed out. A complete list of documents on the CD-ROM is found at the end of the text.

Pearson Prentice Hall is pleased to serve as a sponsor of the **The World History Association Teaching Prize** and **The World History Association and Phi Alpha Theta Student Paper Prize** (undergraduate and graduate divisions). Both of these prizes are awarded annually. For more information, contact *thewha@hawaii.edu*

Acknowledgments

We are grateful to the many scholars and teachers whose thoughtful and often detailed comments helped shape this as well as previous editions of *The Heritage of World Civilizations*. The Advice and guidance provided by Magnus T. Bernhardsson of Williams College in the revision of the coverage of Islam is especially appreciated. We also thank Tianyuan Tan of Harvard University, who helped with conversion of Chinese words to the pinyin system and Gayle K. Brunelle, California State University (Fullerton), who provided invaluable input on strengthening the book's global approach.

Wayne Ackerson, *Salisbury State University*

Jack Martin Balcer, *Ohio State University*

Charmarie J. Blaisdell, *Northeastern University*

Deborah Buffton, *University of Wisconsin at La Crosse*

Loretta Burns, *Mankato State University*

Gayle K. Brunelle, *California State University, Fullerton*

Chun-shu Chang, *University of Michigan, Ann Arbor*

Mark Chavalas, *University of Wisconsin at La Crosse*

Anthony Cheeseboro, *Southern Illinois University at Edwardsville*

William J. Courteney, *University of Wisconsin*

Samuel Willard Crompton, *Holyoke Community College*

James B. Crowley, *Yale University*

Bruce Cummings, *The University of Chicago*

Stephen F. Dale, *Ohio State University, Columbus*

Clarence B. Davis, *Marian College*

Raymond Van Dam, *University of Michigan, Ann Arbor*

Bill Donovan, *Loyola University of Maryland*

Wayne Farris, *University of Tennessee*

Anita Fisher, *Clark College*

Suzanne Gay, *Oberlin College*

Katrina A. Glass, *United States Military Academy*

Robert Gerlich, *Loyola University*

Samuel Robert Goldberger, *Capital Community-Technical College*

Andrew Gow, *University of Alberta*

Katheryn L. Green, *University of Wisconsin, Madison*

David Griffiths, *University of North Carolina, Chapel Hill*

Louis Haas, *Duquesne University*

Joseph T. Hapak, *Moraine Valley Community College*

Hue-Tam Ho Tai, *Harvard University*

David Kieft, *University of Minnesota*

Frederick Krome, *Northern Kentucky University*

Lisa M. Lane, *Mira Costa College*

Richard Law, *Washington State University*

David Lelyveld, *Columbia University*

Jan Lewis, *Rutgers University, Newark*

James C. Livingston, *College of William and Mary*

Richard L. Moore Jr., *St. Augustine's College*

Beth Nachison, *Southern Connecticut State University*

Robin S. Oggins, *Binghamton University*

Louis A. Perez Jr., *University of South Florida*

Jonathan Perry, *University of Central Florida*

Cora Ann Presley, *Tulane University*

Norman Raiford, *Greenville Technical College*

Norman Ravitch, *University of California, Riverside*

Thomas M. Ricks, *University of Pennsylvania*

Philip F. Riley, *James Madison University*

Thomas Robisheaux, *Duke University*

William S. Rodner, *Tidewater Community College*

David Ruffley, *United States Air Force Academy*

Dankwart A. Rustow, *The City University of New York*

James J. Sack, *University of Illinois at Chicago*

William Schell, *Murray State University*

Marvin Slind, *Washington State University*

Daniel Scavone, *University of Southern Indiana*

Roger Schlesinger, *Washington State University*

Charles C. Stewart, *University of Illinois*

Nancy L. Stockdale, *University of Central Florida*

Carson Tavenner, *United States Air Force Academy*

Truong-buu Lam, *University of Hawaii*

Harry L. Watson, *Loyola College of Maryland*

William B. Whisenhunt, *College of DuPage*

Paul Varley, *Columbia University*

Finally, we would like to thank the dedicated people who helped produce this revision: our acquisitions editor, Charles Cavaliere; our development editor, Barbara Muller; Laura Gardner who created the handsome new design for this edition; Kathleen Sleys, our production editor; and Ben Smith our manufacturing buyer.

A.M.C.
W.A.G.
D.K.
S.O.
F.M.T.

About the Authors

Albert M. Craig is the Harvard-Yenching Research Professor of History at Harvard University, where he has taught since 1959. A graduate of Northwestern University, he took his Ph.D. at Harvard University. He has studied at Strasbourg University and at Kyoto, Keio, and Tokyo universities in Japan. He is the author of *Choshu in the Meiji Restoration* (1961), *The Heritage of Chinese Civilization* (2001), and, with others, of *East Asia, Tradition and Transformation* (1989). He is the editor of *Japan, A Comparative View* (1973) and co-editor of *Personality in Japanese History* (1970). At present he is engaged in research on the thought of Fukuzawa Yukichi. For eleven years (1976–1987) he was the director of the Harvard-Yenching Institute. He has also been a visiting professor at Kyoto and Tokyo Universities. He has received Guggenheim, Fulbright, and Japan Foundation Fellowships. In 1988 he was awarded the Order of the Rising Sun by the Japanese government.

William A. Graham is Albertson Professor of Middle Eastern Studies and Professor of the History of Religion at Harvard University, and Master of Currier House at Harvard University. From 1990–1996 he directed Harvard's Center for Middle Eastern Studies. He has taught for twenty-six years at Harvard, where he received the A.M. and Ph.D. degrees. He also studied in Göttingen, Tübingen, and Lebanon. He is the author of *Divine World and Prophetic World in Early Islam* (1977), awarded the American Council of Learned Societies History of Religions book prize in 1978, and of *Beyond the Written Word: Oral Aspects of Scripture in the History of Religion* (1987). He has published a variety of articles in both Islamic studies and the general history of religion and is one of the editors of the *Encyclopedia of the Qur'an*. He serves currently on the editorial board of several journals and has held John Simon Guggenheim and Alexander von Humboldt research fellowships. *Three Faiths, One God*, co-authored with Jacob Neusner and Bruce Chilton, published in January 2003.

Donald Kagan is Sterling Professor of History and Classics at Yale University, where he has taught since 1969. He received the A.B. degree in history from Brooklyn College, the M.A. in classics from Brown University, and the Ph.D. in history from Ohio State University. During 1958–1959 he studied at the American School of Classical Studies as a Fulbright Scholar. He has received three awards for undergraduate teaching at Cornell and Yale. He is the author of a history of Greek political thought, *The Great Dialogue* (1965); a four-volume history of the Peloponnesian war, *The Origins of the Peloponnesian War* (1969); *The Archidamian War* (1974); *The Peace of Nicias and the Sicilian Expedition* (1981); *The Fall of the Athenian Empire* (1987); and a biography of Pericles, *Pericles of Athens and the Birth of Democracy* (1991); *On the Origins of War* (1995), and *The Peloponnesian War* (2003). He is coauthor, with Frederick W. Kagan of *While America Sleeps* (2000). With Brian Tierney and L. Pearce Williams, he is the editor of *Great Issues in Western Civilization*, a collection of readings. He was awarded the National Humanities Medal for 2002.

Steven Ozment is McLean Professor of Ancient and Modern History at Harvard University. He has taught Western Civiliza-tion at Yale, Stanford, and Harvard. He is the author of eleven books. *The Age of Reform*, 1250–1550 (1980) won the Schaff Prize and was nominated for the 1981 National Book Award. Five of his books have been selections of the History Book Club: *Magdalena and Balthasar: An Intimate Portrait of Life in Sixteenth Century Europe* (1986), *Three Behaim Boys: Growing Up in Early Modern Germany* (1990), *Protestants: The Birth of A Revolution* (1992), *The Burgermeister's Daughter: Scandal in a Sixteenth Century German Town* (1996), and *Flesh and Spirit: Private Life in Early Modern Germany* (1999). His most recent publications are *Ancestors: The Loving Family of Old Europe* (2001), *A Mighty Fortress: A New History of the German People* (2004), and "Why We Study Western Civ," *The Public Interest* 158 (2005).

Steven Ozment is McLean Professor of Ancient and Modern History at Harvard University. He has taught Western Civilization at Yale, Stanford, and Harvard. He is the author of nine books. *The Age of Reform*, 1250–1550 (1980) won the Schaff Prize and was nominated for the 1981 National Book Award. Five of his books have been selections of the History Book Club: *Magdalena and Balthasar: An Intimate Portrait of Life in Sixteenth Century Europe* (1986), *Three Behaim Boys: Growing Up in Early Modern Germany* (1990), *Protestants: The Birth of A Revolution* (1992), *The Burgermeister's Daughter: Scandal in a Sixteenth Century German Town* (1996), and *Flesh and Spirit: Private Life in Early Modern Germany* (1999). His most recent book is *Ancestors: The Loving Family of Old Europe* (2001). A history of Germany, *A Mighty Fortress: A New History of the German People*, published in January 2004.

Frank M. Turner is John Hay Whitney Professor of History at Yale University and Director of the Beinecke Rare Book and Manuscript Library at Yale University, where he served as University Provost from 1988 to 1992. He received his B.A. degree at the College of William and Mary and his Ph.D. from Yale. He has received the Yale College Award for Distinguished Undergraduate Teaching. He has directed a National Endowment for the Humanities Summer Institute. His scholarly research has received the support of fellowships from the National Endowment for the Humanities and the Guggenheim Foundation and the Woodrow Wilson Center. He is the author of *Between Science and Religion: The Reaction to Scientific Naturalism in Late Victorian England* (1974), *The Greek Heritage in Victorian Britain* (1981), which received the British Council Prize of the Conference on British Studies and the Yale Press Governors Award, *Contesting Cultural Authority: Essays in Victorian Intellectual Life* (1993), and *John Henry Newman: The Challenge to Evangelical Religion* (2002). He has also contributed numerous articles to journals and has served on the editorial advisory boards of *The Journal of Modern History, Isis,* and *Victorian Studies.* He edited *The Idea of a University,* by John Henry Newman (1996) and *Reflections on the Revolution in France* by Edmund Burke (2003). Since 1996 he has served as a Trustee of Connecticut College. In 2003, Professor Turner was appointed Director of the Beinecke Rare Book and Manuscript Library at Yale University..

Europe to the Early 1500s

Revival, Decline, and Renaissance

- Revival of Empire, Church, and Towns

- Society

- Growth of National Monarchies

- Political and Social Breakdown

- Ecclesiastical Breakdown and Revival: The Late Medieval Church

- The Renaissance in Italy (1375–1527)

- Revival of Monarchy: Nation Building in the Fifteenth Century

◄ The idealism of a devout Crusader is captured in this thirteenth-century drawing.
British Library, London. The Bridgeman Art Library Ltd..

GLOBAL PERSPECTIVE

The High Middle Ages in Western Europe

With its borders finally secured, Western Europe during the High Middle Ages was able to concentrate on its political institutions and cultural development which had been ignored during the early Middle Ages. For Western Europe, the High Middle Ages were a period of clearer self-definition during which individual lands gained much of the geographic shape we recognize today. Europe also began to escape its relative isolation from the rest of the world which had prevailed since the early Middle Ages. Two factors contributed to this increased engagement: the Crusades and renewed trade along the Silk Road linking China and Europe that the Mongol conquests in Asia made possible.

Under the Song dynasty (960–1279), before Mongol rule, China continued its technological advance. In addition to the printing press, the Chinese invented the abacus and gunpowder. They also enjoyed a money economy unknown in the West. But culturally, these centuries between 1000 and 1300 were closed and narrow by comparison with those of the Tang dynasty. Politically, the Song were far more autocratic. This was also an era of expansion for Chinese trade, and one of the few in Chinese history in which merchants as a group were able to advance in wealth and status. Although the imperial reach of the Song was limited, Chinese culture in this period was more open to outside influences than in any previous era.

In the late twelfth century Japan shifted from civilian to military rule; the Kamakura *bakufu* governed by mounted warriors who were paid with rights to income from land in exchange for their military services. This rise of a military aristocracy marked the beginning of Japan's "medieval," as distinct from its "classical," period. Three Mongol invasions in the thirteenth century also fostered a strong military to resist them. With a civilian court also in existence, Japan actually had a dual government (that is, two emperors and two courts) until the fourteenth century. However, this situation differed greatly from the deep and permanent national divisions developing at this time among the emerging states and autonomous principalities of Western Europe.

Within the many developing autonomous Islamic lands at this time, the teachings of Muhammad created an international culture. Religious identity enabled Muslims to transcend their new and often very deep regional divisions. Similarly, Christianity allowed Englishmen, Frenchmen, Germans, and Italians to think of themselves as one people and to unite in crusades to the Holy Land. As these Crusades got underway in the late eleventh century, Islam too was on the march, penetrating Anatolia and Afghanistan and impinging upon India, where it met a new challenge in Hinduism.

The legacy of the Crusades was mixed. They accomplished few of the goals that originally motivated the European Crusaders; the Holy Land remained under Islamic control, the Crusader kingdoms there collapsed within a few generations of their founding, and the animosity toward Christians fostered by the Crusades resonates even today in the Middle East. Still, the Crusades brought Europeans into more direct and frequent contact with the non-European world than they had known since the heyday of the Roman Empire. Crusaders sampled and sent home products from the Middle East, Asia, and North Africa, creating new tastes in food, art, and even fashion. The resulting growth in demand for these products impelled rising numbers of European merchants to seek these products beyond Europe. Eventually Europeans sought to bypass the Islamic world entirely and secure supplies of Eastern products, especially spices, by going directly to the sources in India and East Asia. By such development European isolation was ended.

THINK AHEAD

◆ How did the High Middle Ages in Europe differ from the Early Middle Ages?

◆ What was the legacy of the Crusades for Europe? In what ways did they signal the start of new relationships between Europe and the wider world?

THE HIGH MIDDLE AGES (FROM THE ELEVENTH through the thirteenth centuries) were a period of political expansion and consolidation and of intellectual flowering and synthesis. The Latin, or Western, church established itself as a spiritual authority independent of secular monarchies, which became more powerful and self-aggrandizing. The parliaments and popular assemblies that accompanied the rise of these monarchies laid the foundations of modern representative institutions.

The High Middle Ages saw a revolution in agriculture that increased food supplies and populations. Trade and commerce revived, towns expanded, protomodern forms of banking and credit developed, and a "new rich" merchant class became ascendant in Europe's cities. Universities sprouted. Contact with the Arab world made possible the discovery of antiquity in the writings of the ancient Greek philosophers. Those sources in turn stimulated the great expansion of Western education and culture during the late Middle Ages and the Renaissance.

The late Middle Ages and the Renaissance, roughly 1300–1500, were a time of both unprecedented calamity and bold new beginnings in Europe. France and England grappled with each other in a bitter conflict known as the Hundred Years' War (1337–1453). Bubonic plague, which contemporaries called Black Death, killed as much as one third of the population in many regions between 1348 and 1350. Thereafter a schism occurred in the church (1378–1417). If that were not calamity enough, in 1453 the Turks captured Constantinople and seemed to be taking dead aim at Western Europe.

The late Middle Ages also witnessed a rebirth that would continue into the seventeenth century. Scholars began to criticize medieval assumptions about the nature of God, humankind, and society. Italian and northern humanists made a full recovery of classical knowledge and languages and ignited new cultural fires that would burn bright throughout Europe. The "divine art" of printing was invented. The **vernacular**, the local language, took its place alongside Latin. In the independent nation-states of Europe, patriotism and incipient nationalism became major forces.

Revival of Empire, Church, and Towns

OTTO I AND THE REVIVAL OF THE EMPIRE

The fortunes of both the old empire and the papacy began to revive when the Saxon Henry I ("the Fowler"; d. 936) became the first non-Frankish king of Germany in 918. Henry rebuilt royal power and left his son and successor Otto I (r. 936–973) in a strong position. Otto maneuvered his own kin into power in Bavaria, Swabia, and Franconia and then invaded Italy and proclaimed himself its king in 951. In 955 he defeated the Hungarians at Lechfeld, securing German borders against new barbarian attacks and earning the title "the Great."

As part of a royal rebuilding program, Otto enlisted the strong hands of the church. Bishops and abbots, men who possessed a sense of universal empire, yet did not marry and found competitive dynasties, were made royal princes and agents of the king. On February 2, 962, Otto, who had long aspired to the imperial crown, gained it from Pope John XII (955–964) after having rescued the pope from his Italian enemies in the previous year. Thereafter, the church came more than ever under royal control and increasingly determined to be free of it.

▲ **Otto I and the Church.** Otto I presents the Magdeburg Cathedral to Christ, as the pope (holding the keys to the kingdom of heaven) watches, a testimony to Otto's guardianship of the Church.
"Christ Enthroned with Saints and Emperor Otto I" (r. 962-973). One from a series of 19 known as the Magdeburg Ivories. Ivory H 5" × W 4$^1/_2$" (12.7 × 11.4 cm).

THE REVIVING CATHOLIC CHURCH

With the royal focus shifted from Germany to Italy, Otto's successors, transfixed by their Italian possessions, allowed their German base to deteriorate. As the German empire began to crumble in the eleventh century, the church, long unhappy with imperial domination, declared its independence by embracing a reform movment that had erupted in a monastic order.

Cluny Reform Movement In a great monastery at Cluny, founded in 910 in east-central France, a reform movement, aimed at freeing the church from secular political influence and control, was born. The reformers of Cluny were aided in their efforts by popular respect for the church that found expression in both religious fervor among laypersons and generous baronial patronage of religious houses. People admired clerics and monks because the church was medieval society's most open institution as far as lay participation was concerned. In the Middle Ages any man could theoretically become pope, since the pope was supposed to be elected by the people and the clergy of Rome. All people were candidates for the church's grace and salvation. The church promised a better life to come to the great mass of ordinary people, who found their present existence brutish and without hope.

The Cluny reformers condemned uncompromisingly the contemporary mixing of religious and secular institutions on the part of the state and the subservience of the clergy to royal authority. They taught that the pope in Rome alone commanded the clergy and demanded a clear demarcation between ecclesiastical and secular authority. They further denounced the transgression of ascetic piety by "secular" parish clergy, who lived openly with concubines in a relationship akin to marriage. Although in narrow religious guise, both the celibacy of the clergy and the separation of church and state found precedents in this powerful monastic reform movement. From Cluny, reformers were dispatched throughout France and Italy in the late eleventh century to save the clergy from wives and the church from the state. In both cases, the pope embraced their reforms.

◀ **Struggle Between Emperor and Pope.** A twelfth-century German manuscript portrays the struggle between Emperor Henry IV and Pope Gregory VII. In the top panel, Henry installs the puppet pope Clement III and drives Gregory from Rome. Below, Gregory dies in exile. The artist was a monk, whose sympathies were with Gregory, not Henry.

Thuringer Universities and Landesbibliothek, Jena: Bos. q. 6, Blatt 79r.

Investiture Struggle: Gregory VII and Henry IV   In 1075 Pope Gregory VII (r. 1073–1085), a fierce advocate of church reform, condemned under penalty of excommunication lay investiture of the clergy in their religious offices at any level. He had primarily in mind the emperor's well-established custom of installing favored bishops to administer his royal estates. This was done by presenting them with the ring and staff of episcopal office at the very same time they received their new secular titles and endowments. Henry IV considered Gregory's action a direct challenge to his ability to administer his realm, while Gregory believed the emperor was usurping the keys to his kingdom. Perceiving that such a measure would weaken royal power vis-à-vis their own, the German princes eagerly supported Gregory's edict.

The lines of battle were quickly drawn. Henry assembled his loyal German bishops at Worms in January 1076 and had them proclaim their independence from Gregory. Gregory promptly excommunicated Henry and absolved all Henry's subjects from loyalty to him. The German princes were delighted, and Henry now faced a general revolt. He had no choice but to come to terms with Gregory. In a famous scene, he prostrated himself outside the pope's castle retreat at Canossa in northern Italy on January 25, 1077. There he reportedly stood barefoot in the snow off and on for three days before the pope gave him absolution. Papal power had reached a pinnacle.

The Investiture Controversy was finally settled in 1122 with the Concordat of Worms. There, the new Emperor Henry V (r. 1106–1125) formally renounced his power to invest bishops with ring and staff. In exchange, the new Pope Calixtus II (r. 1119–1124) recognized the emperor's right to be present and to invest bishops with fiefs before or after their investment with ring and staff by the church. The emperor also effectively retained the right to nominate, or veto, candidates. Despite the continuing cooperation between church and state, which was desirable for both sides, distinctive spheres of ecclesiastical and secular authority had been stipulated to by both sides. In settling the Investiture Controversy in this way, pope and emperor had also set the stage for greater conflicts and division between church and state.

THE CRUSADES

If an index of popular piety and support for the pope in the High Middle Ages is needed, the **Crusades** amply provide it. What the Cluny reform was to the clergy, the Crusades to the Holy Land were to the laity: an outlet for the heightened religiosity of the late eleventh and twelfth centuries.

Late in the eleventh century, the Byzantine Empire was under severe pressure from the Seljuk Turks, and the Eastern emperor, Alexius I Comnenus, appealed for Western aid. At the Council of Clermont in 1095, Pope Urban II responded positively to that appeal, setting the First Crusade in motion. (See Document, "Pope Urban II (r. 1088–1099) Preaches the First Crusade.")

This event has puzzled some historians, because the First Crusade was a very risky venture. But the pope, the nobility, and Western society at large had much to gain by removing large numbers of nobility temporarily from Europe. Too many idle, restless noble youths spent too great a part of their lives feuding with each other and raiding other people's lands. The pope saw that peace and tranquility might more easily be gained at home by sending these factious aristocrats abroad, 100,000 of whom marched off with the First Crusade (see Map 15–1). The nobility, in turn, saw that fortunes could be made in foreign wars. That was especially true for the younger sons of noblemen, who, in an age of growing population and shrinking landed wealth, found in crusading the opportunity to become landowners. Pope Urban may well have also believed that the Crusade would reconcile and reunite Western and Eastern Christianity.

Religion was not the only motive inspiring the Crusaders; hot blood and greed were no less strong. But unlike the later Crusades, which were undertaken for mercenary reasons, the early Crusades were inspired by genuine religious piety and carefully orchestrated by a revived papacy. Popes promised the first Crusaders a plenary indulgence should they die in battle. That was a complete remission of the temporal punishment due them for unrepented mortal sins, and hence a release from suffering for them in purgatory. In addition to this spiritual reward, the prospect of Holy War against the Muslim infidel also propelled the Crusaders. The Crusade to the Holy Land was also a romantic pilgrimage. All these motives combined to make the First Crusade a Christian success.

En route the Crusaders began a general cleansing of Christendom that would intensify during the thirteenth-century papacy of Pope Innocent III. Accompanied by the new mendicant orders of Dominicans and Franciscans, Christian knights attempted to rid Europe of Jews as well as Muslims. Along the Crusaders' routes, especially in the Rhineland, Jewish communities were subjected to pogroms.

The First Victory   The Eastern emperor welcomed Western aid against advancing Islamic armies. However, the Crusaders had not assembled merely to defend Europe's outermost borders against Muslim aggression. Their goal was to rescue the holy city of Jerusalem, which had been in the hands of the Seljuk Turks since the seventh century. To this end, three great armies—tens of thousands of Crusaders—gathered in France, Germany, and Italy and taking different routes reassembled in Constantinople in 1097.

The convergence of these spirited soldiers on the Eastern capital was a cultural shock that deepened antipathy toward the West. The Eastern emperor suspected their motives, and the common people, whose villages they plundered and suppressed, did not consider them to be Christian brothers in a common cause. Nonetheless the Crusaders accomplished what

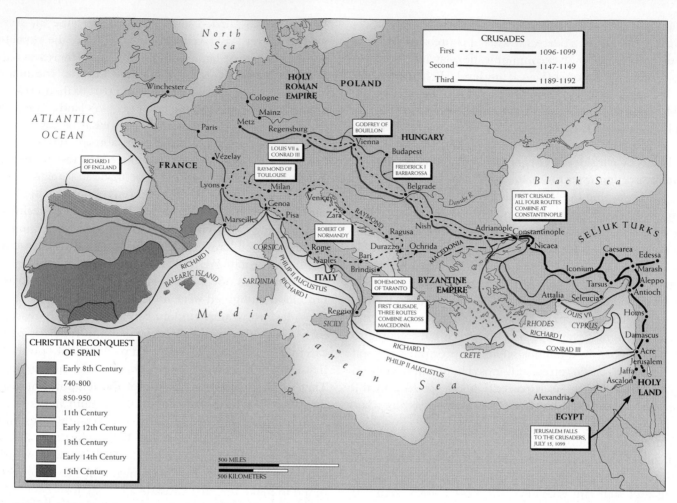

MAP 15–1 The Early Crusades. Routes and several leaders of the Crusades during the first century of the movement are shown. The names on this map do not exhaust the list of great nobles who went on the First Crusade. The even showier array of monarchs of the Second and Third Crusades still left the Crusades, on balance, ineffective in achieving their goals.

no Byzantine army had been able to do. They soundly defeated one Seljuk army after another in a steady advance toward Jerusalem, which they captured on July 15, 1099. The Crusaders owed their victory to superior military discipline and weaponry and were also helped by the deep political divisions within the Islamic world that prevented a unified Muslim resistance.

The victorious Crusaders divided conquered territories into the feudal states of Jerusalem, Edessa, and Antioch, which were apportioned to them as fiefs from the pope. Godfrey of Bouillon, leader of the French-German army, and after him his brother Baldwin, ruled over the kingdom of Jerusalem. The Crusaders, however, remained small islands within a great sea of Muslims, who looked on the Western invaders as savages to be slain or driven out. Once settled in the Holy Land, the Crusaders found themselves increasingly on the defensive. Now an occupying rather than a conquering army, they became obsessed with fortification, building castles and forts throughout the Holy Land, the ruins of which can still be seen today.

Once secure within their new enclaves, the Crusaders ceased to live off the land as they had done since departing Europe and

▲ **Godfrey of Bouillon.**
Bibliotheque Nationale, Paris, France.

increasingly relied on imports from home. As they developed the economic resources of their new possessions, the once fierce warriors were transformed into international traders and businessmen. The Knights Templar, originally a military-religious order, remade themselves into castle stewards and escorts for Western pilgrims going to and from the Holy Land. Through such endeavors, they became very rich, ending up as wealthy bankers and moneylenders.

The Second and Third Crusades   Native resistance broke the Crusaders' resolve around midcentury, and the forty-year plus Latin presence in the East began to crumble. Edessa fell to Islamic armies in 1144. A Second Crusade, preached by Christendom's most eminent religious leader, the Cistercian monk Bernard of Clairvaux (1091–1153), attempted a rescue but met with dismal

failure. In October 1187, Saladin (r. 1138–1193), king of Egypt and Syria, reconquered Jerusalem. Save for a brief interlude in the thirteenth century, the holiest of cities remained thereafter in Islamic hands until the twentieth century.

A Third Crusade in the twelfth century (1189–1192) attempted yet another rescue, led by the most powerful Western rulers: Hohenstaufen emperor Frederick Barbarossa, Richard the Lion-Hearted, king of England, and Philip Augustus, king of France. It became instead a tragicomic commentary on the passing of the original crusading spirit. Frederick Barbarossa accidentally drowned while fording the Saleph River, a small stream, near the end of his journey across Asia Minor. Richard the Lion-Hearted and Philip Augustus reached the outskirts of Jerusalem, only to shatter the Crusaders' unity and chances of victory by their intense personal rivalry. Philip Augustus returned to France and

---

DOCUMENT   Pope Urban II (r. 1088–1099) Preaches the First Crusade

When Pope Urban II summoned the First Crusade in a sermon at the Council of Clermont on November 26, 1095, he painted a most savage picture of the Muslims who controlled Jerusalem. Urban also promised the Crusaders, who responded by the tens of thousands, remission of their unrepented sins and assurance of heaven. Robert the Monk is one of four witnesses who has left us a summary of the sermon.

♦ Is the pope engaging in a propaganda and smear campaign? What images of the enemy does he create and how accurate and fair are they? Did the Christian church have a greater claim to Jerusalem than the people then living there? Does a religious connection with the past entitle one group to confiscate the land of another?

From the confines of Jerusalem and the city of Constantinople a horrible tale has gone forth and very frequently has been brought to our ears, namely, that a race from the kingdom of the Persians [that is, the Seljuk Turks], an accursed race, a race utterly alienated from God, a generation forsooth which has not directed its heart and has not entrusted its spirit to God, has invaded the lands of those Christians and has depopulated them by the sword, pillage and fire; it has led away a part of the captives into its own country, and a part it has destroyed by cruel tortures; it has either entirely destroyed the churches of God or appropriated them for the rites of its own religion. They destroy the altars, after having defiled them with their uncleanness. They circumcise the Christians, and the blood of the circumcision they either spread upon the altars or pour into the vases of the baptismal

font. When they wish to torture people by a base death, they perforate their navels, and dragging forth the extremity of the intestines, bind it to a stake; then with flogging they lead the victim around until the viscera having gushed forth the victim falls prostrate upon the ground. Others they bind to a post and pierce with arrows. Others they compel to extend their necks and then, attacking them with naked swords, attempt to cut through the neck with a single blow. What shall I say of the abominable rape of the women? The kingdom of the Greeks is now dismembered by them and deprived of territory so vast in extent that it can not be traversed in a march of two months. On whom therefore is the labor of avenging these wrongs and of recovering this territory incumbent, if not upon you? …

Jerusalem is the navel of the world; the land is fruitful above others, like another paradise of delights. This the Redeemer of the human race has made illustrious by His advent, has beautified by residence, has consecrated by suffering, has redeemed by death, has glorified by burial. This royal city, therefore, situated at the centre of the world, is now held captive by His enemies, and is in subjection to those who do not know God, to the worship of the heathens. She seeks therefore and desires to be liberated, and does not cease to implore you to come to her aid. From you especially she asks succor, because, as we have already said, God has conferred upon you above all nations great glory in arms.

Accordingly undertake this journey for the remission of your sins, with the assurance of the imperishable glory of the kingdom of heaven.

Translations and reprints from *Original Sources of European History*, Vol. 1 (Philadelphia: Department of History, University of Pennsylvania, 1910), pp. 5–7.

made war on Richard's continental territories. Richard, in turn, fell captive to the Emperor Henry VI while returning to England.

The English paid a handsome ransom for their adventurous king's release. Popular resentment of taxes levied for that ransom became part of the background of the revolt against the English monarchy that led to royal recognition of English freedoms in the Magna Carta of 1215.

The long-term results of the first three Crusades had little to do with their original purpose. Politically and religiously they were a failure. The Holy Land reverted as firmly as ever to Muslim hands. But the Crusades had been a safety valve for violence-prone Europeans. More importantly, they stimulated Western trade with the East, as Venetian, Pisan, and Genoan merchants followed the Crusaders across Byzantium to lucrative new markets. The need to resupply the Christian settlements in the Near East also created new trade routes and reopened old ones long closed by Islamic warships in the Mediterranean.

The Fourth Crusade   It is a commentary on both the degeneration of the original crusading ideal and the Crusaders' true historical importance that a Fourth Crusade transformed itself into a piratical commercial venture controlled by the Venetians. Launched in 1202, 30,000 crusaders arrived in Venice to set sail for Egypt. When they could not pay the price of transport, the Venetians negotiated an alternative venture: the conquest of Zara, a rival Christian port city on the Adriatic. As a shocked world watched, the Crusaders obliged the Venetians. Zara, however, proved to be only their first digression; in 1204, they besieged Constantinople itself.

This stunning event brought Venice new lands and maritime rights that assured its domination of the eastern Mediterranean. Constantinople was now the center for Western trade throughout the Near East. Although its capture embarrassed reigning Pope Innocent III, the papacy was soon sharing the spoils, gleeful at the prospect of extending Roman Christianity East. A confidant of the pope became patriarch of Constantinople and launched a mission to win the Greeks and the Slavs to the Roman Church. Western control of Constantinople continued until 1261, when Eastern emperor Michael Paleologus, helped by the Genoese, who envied their great rival's windfall in the East, finally recaptured the city. This fifty-year plus occupation of Contstantinople did nothing to heal the political and religious divisions between East and West.

TOWNS AND TOWNSPEOPLE

In the eleventh and twelfth centuries, most towns were small and held only about 5 percent of western Europe's population, but they contained the most creative segments of medieval society.

The Chartering of Towns   Towns were originally dominated by feudal lords, both lay and clerical, who granted charters to those who would agree to live and work within them. The charters guaranteed the towns' safety and gave their inhabitants an in-

dependence unknown to peasants who worked the land. The purpose was originally to concentrate skilled laborers who could manufacture the finished goods desired by lords and bishops.

As towns grew and beckoned, many serfs took their skills to the new urban centers. There they found the freedom and profits that could lift an industrious craftsperson into higher social ranks. As this migration of serfs to the towns accelerated, the lords in the countryside offered serfs more favorable terms of tenure to keep them on the land. The growth of towns thus improved the lot of serfs generally.

The Rise of Merchants   Rural society not only gave the towns their craftspeople and day laborers, but the first merchants themselves may also have been enterprising serfs. Certainly, some of the long-distance traders were people who had nothing to lose and everything to gain from the enormous risks of foreign trade. They traveled together in armed caravans and convoys, buying goods and products as cheaply as possible at the source and selling them for all they could get in Western ports (see Map 15–2).

▲ **Foundry in Florence.** Skilled workers were an integral component of the commerce of medieval towns. This scene shows the manufacture of cannons in a foundry in Florence.
Scala/Art Resource, N.Y.

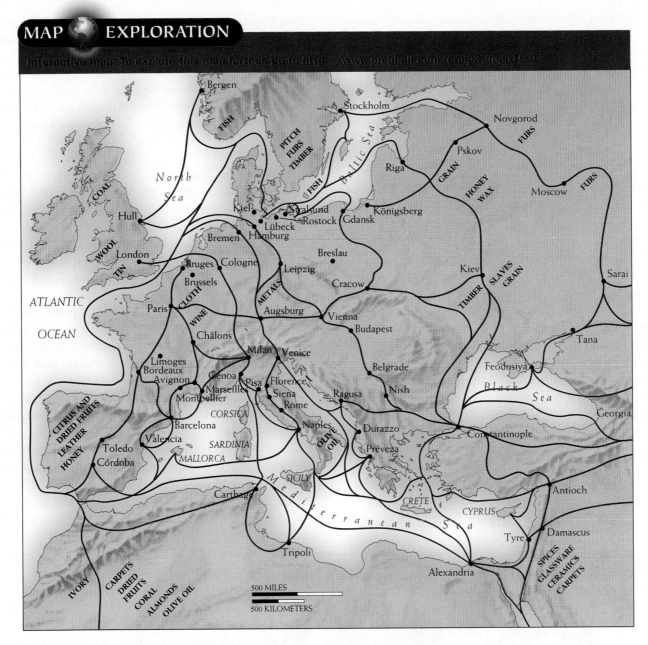

MAP EXPLORATION

Interactive map: To explore this map further, go to http://www.prenhall.com/craig3/map15.2

MAP 15–2 Medieval Trade Routes and Regional Products. Trade in Europe varied in intensity and geographical extent in different periods during the Middle Ages. The map shows some of the channels that came to be used in interregional commerce. Labels tell part of what was carried in that commerce.

At first the merchants were disliked because they were outside the traditional social groups of nobility, clergy, and peasantry. Over time, however, the powerful grew to respect the merchants, and the weak always tried to imitate them, because the merchants left a trail of wealth behind them wherever they went.

As the traders established themselves in towns, they grew in wealth and numbers, formed their own protective associations, and soon found themselves able to challenge traditional seigneurial authority. Merchants especially wanted to end the arbitrary tolls and tariffs regional magnates imposed over the surrounding countryside. Such regulations hampered the flow of commerce on which both merchant and craftsman in the growing urban export industries depended.

Townspeople needed simple and uniform laws and a government sympathetic to their new forms of business activity, not the fortress mentality of the lords of the countryside. The result was often a struggle with the old nobility within and outside the towns. This conflict led towns in the High and late Middle Ages to form their own independent communes and to ally themselves with kings against the nobility in the countryside, a development that would eventually rearrange the centers of power in medieval Europe and dissolve classic feudal government.

Because the merchants were the engine of the urban economy, small shopkeepers and artisans identified far more with them than with aloof lords and bishops, who had been medieval society's traditional masters. The lesser nobility (small knights) outside the towns also recognized the new mercantile economy as the wave of the future. During the eleventh and twelfth centuries, the burgher upper classes increased their economic strength and successfully challenged the old noble urban lords for control of the towns.

New Models of Government   With urban autonomy came new models of self-government. Around 1100 the old urban nobility and the new burgher upper class merged into an urban patriciate. It was a marriage between those wealthy by birth (inherited property) and those whose fortunes came from long-distance trade. From this new ruling class was born the aristocratic town council, which henceforth governed towns.

Enriching and complicating the situation, small artisans and craftspeople also slowly developed their own protective associations or **guilds** and began to gain a voice in government. The towns' opportunities for the "little person" had created the slogan "Town air brings freedom." Within town walls people thought of themselves as citizens with basic rights, not subjects at the mercy of their masters' whim.

Towns and Kings   By providing kings with the resources they needed to curb factious noblemen, towns became a major force in the transition from feudal societies to national governments. Towns were a ready source of educated bureaucrats and lawyers who knew Roman law, the tool for running the state. Money was also to be found in the towns in great quantity, enabling kings to hire their own armies and free themselves from dependence on the nobility. In turn towns won royal political recognition and had their constitutions guaranteed. In France, towns became integrated early into royal government. In Germany, they fell under ever-tighter control by the princes. In Italy, uniquely, towns became genuine city-states during the Renaissance.

Jews in Christian Society   Towns also attracted Jews who plied trades in small businesses. Many became wealthy as moneylenders to kings, popes, and businesspeople. Jewish intellectual and religious culture both dazzled and threatened Christians. These various factors encouraged suspicion and distrust among Christians and led to an unprecedented surge in anti-Jewish sentiment in the late twelfth and early thirteenth centuries.

Schools and Universities   In the twelfth century, Byzantine and Spanish Islamic scholars made it possible for the philosophical works of Aristotle, the writings of Euclid and Ptolemy, the texts of Greek physicians and Arab mathematicians, and the corpus of Roman law to circulate among Western scholars. Islamic scholars wrote thought-provoking commentaries on Greek texts that were subsequently translated into Latin and made available to Western scholars and students. The resulting intellectual ferment gave rise to Western universities as we know them today. The first important one was established in 1158 in Bologna, which became the model for the universities of Spain, Italy, and southern France, and gained renown for the revival of Roman law. The University of Paris, became the model for northern European universities and the study of theology.

In the High Middle Ages the learning process was basic. People assumed that truth was already known and only needed to be properly organized, elucidated, and defended. Students wrote commentaries on authoritative texts, especially those of Aristotle and the church fathers. Teachers did not encourage students to strive independently for undiscovered truth beyond the received knowledge of the experts. Rather, students learned to organize and harmonize the accepted truths of tradition, which were drilled into them.

This method of study, was known as **Scholasticism**. Students summarized and compared the traditional authorities in their field, elaborated their arguments pro and con, and drew the logical conclusions. With

◀ **The University of Bologna** in central Italy was distinguished as the center for the revival of Roman law. This carving on the tomb of a Bolognese professor of law shows students attending one of his lectures.
Scala/Art Resource, N.Y.

OVERVIEW   Medieval Universities

In the twelfth century, Latin translations of ancient texts in law, astronomy, philosophy, and mathematics, and learned commentaries on them by Islamic and Byzantine scholars, reached the West. The resulting intellectual ferment gave rise to the medieval universities. The first university was established at Bologna in Italy in 1158. By 1500, there were almost fifty universities across Europe from Scotland to Poland. Universities helped bring wealth and prestige to towns; graduated professionals, such as lawyers, physicians, and theologians; and provided rulers with trained bureaucrats for their increasingly complex administrations. The following is a list of the medieval universities and the dates of their founding.

University	Country	Date of Founding	University	Country	Date of Founding
Bologna	Italy	1158	Erfurt	Germany	1379
Paris	France	ca. 1150–1160	Heidelberg	Germany	1385
Oxford	England	1167	Ferrara	Italy	1391
Vicenza	Italy	1204	Wurzburg	Germany	1402
Cambridge	England	1209	Leipzig	Germany	1409
Salamanca	Spain	1218	St. Andrews	Scotland	1411
Padua	Italy	1222	Turin	Italy	1412
Naples	Italy	1224	Louvain	Belgium	1426
Toulouse	France	1229	Poitiers	France	1431
Rome	Italy	1244	Caen	France	1437
Siena	Italy	1247	Bourdeaux	France	1441
Piacenza	Italy	1248	Barcelona	Spain	1450
Montpellier	France	1289	Trier	Germany	1450
Lisbon	Portugal	1290	Glasgow	Scotland	1451
Avignon	France	1303	Freiburg	Germany	1455
Orleans	France	1305	Ingolstadt	Germany	1459
Perugia	Italy	1308	Basel	Switzerland	1460
Coimbra	Portugal	1308	Nantes	France	1463
Grenoble	France	1339	Bourges	France	1465
Pisa	Italy	1343	Ofen	Germany	1475
Valladolid	Spain	1346	Tubingen	Germany	1477
Prague	Bohemia	1348	Uppsala	Sweden	1477
Pavia	Italy	1361	Copenhagen	Denmark	1479
Vienna	Austria	1364	Aberdeen	Scotland	1494
Cracow	Poland	1364			

the arrival of Aristotle's works in the West, logic and dialectic became the new tools for disciplining thought and knowledge. Dialectic was the art of discovering a truth by pondering the arguments against it. Together with aspiring philosophers, theologians, and lawyers, even medical students learned their vocation by debating the authoritative texts in their field, not by clinical medical practice.

Abelard   No one promoted the new Aristotelian learning more boldly and controversially than Peter Abelard (1079–1142), the leading philosopher and theologian of his time and the first European scholar to gain a large student audience. He ended up, however, not as an academic superstar, but as an obscure abbot of a monastery in Brittany. That was because his bold subjection of church teaching to Aristotelian logic and critical reasoning made him many powerful enemies at a time when there was no tenure to protect genius and free speech in schools and universities. Accused of multiple transgressions of church doctrine, he wrote an autobiography recounting the "calamities" that befell him over a lifetime. His critics especially condemned his subjective interpretations. He likened the trinitarian bonds among God the Father, the Son, and the Holy Spirit to those created among people by sworn documents and covenants. Rather than a God-begotten cosmic ransom of humankind from the Devil, Christ's crucifixion was said to redeem Christians by virtue of its impact on their hearts and minds when they heard and pondered the story. Abelard's ethical teaching stressed intent: The motives of the doer made an act good or evil, not the deed itself. Inner feelings were also said to be more important for receiving divine forgiveness than the sacrament of penance performed by the priest.

Between his native genius and youthful disrespect for seniority and tradition, Abelard gained powerful enemies in high places. He gave those enemies the opportunity to strike him down when, in Paris, where he was Master of Students at Notre Dame, he seduced the bright, seventeen-year-old niece of a powerful canon (her name was Heloise), who hired Abelard to be her tutor in his home. The passionate affair ended in public scandal, with Heloise pregnant. Unable to marry her officially (university teachers had to be single and celibate), they wed secretly. Intent on punishing Abelard and ending his career, the enraged uncle not only exposed their affair and secret marriage but also hired men to castrate Abelard.

Thereafter both entered cloisters in nearby Paris: Heloise at Argenteuil, Abelard at St. Denis. She continued to love Abelard and relive their passion in her mind, while Abelard became a self-condemning monk's monk, who assured Heloise in his letters that his "love" for her had only been wretched desire. The famous philosopher ended his life as a platitudinous monk. In 1121, a church synod ordered his writings burned. Another synod in 1140 condemned nineteen propositions from his works as heresy. Retracting his teaching, Abelard lived out the remaining two years of his life in the monastery of St. Denis. Heloise lived another twenty years and gained renown for her positive efforts to reform the rules for the cloistered life of women, under which she had suffered so much. Their story is a revelation of contemporary academic and religious life, the relationship of men and women, and the power of a reform-minded and controlling church.

Society
THE ORDER OF LIFE

In the art and literature of the Middle Ages, three basic social groups were represented: those who fought as mounted knights (the landed nobility), those who prayed (the clergy), and those who labored in fields and shops (the peasantry and village artisans). After the revival of towns in the eleventh century, a fourth social group emerged: the long-distance traders and merchants.

Nobles By the late Middle Ages, a distinguishable higher and lower nobility had evolved, living in both town and country. The higher were the great landowners and territorial magnates, long the dominant powers in their regions; the lower were petty landlords, the descendants of minor knights, newly rich merchants, or wealthy farmers.

Arms were the nobleman's profession, waging war his sole occupation. The nobility accordingly celebrated physical strength, courage, and the constant activity of warfare. Warring brought new riches and a chance to gain honor and glory, whereas peace meant boredom and economic stagnation. In the eighth century the adoption of stirrups by mounted knights gave armies the edge.

◀ **Dominicans (left) and Franciscans (right).** Unlike the other religious orders, the Dominicans and Franciscans did not live in cloisters but wandered about preaching and combating heresy. They depended for support on their own labor and the kindness of the laity.
Cliché Bibliothèque Nationale de France, Paris.

No medieval social group was absolutely uniform. Noblemen formed a broad spectrum—from minor vassals without subordinate vassals to mighty barons, the principal vassals of a king or prince, who had many vassals of their own. Dignity and status within the nobility were directly related to the exercise of authority over others; a chief with many vassals far excelled the small country nobleman who was lord over none but himself.

By the late Middle Ages, several factors forced the landed nobility into a steep economic and political decline from which it never recovered. Climatic changes and agricultural failures created large famines, while the great plague (see below) brought about unprecedented population losses. Changing military tactics occasioned by the use of infantry and heavy artillery during the Hundred Years' War made the noble cavalry nearly obsolete. And the alliance of wealthy towns with the king weakened the nobility within their own domains. After the fourteenth century, land and wealth counted for far more than lineage as qualification for entrance into the highest social class.

Clergy Unlike the nobility and the peasantry, the clergy was an open estate: One was a cleric by religious training and ordination, not because of birth or military prowess.

There were two basic types of clerical vocation: regular and secular. The **regular clergy** comprised the orders of monks who lived according to a special ascetic rule (*regula*) in cloisters separated from the world. In the thirteenth century, two new orders—the Franciscans and the Dominicans—gained the sanction of the church. Their members went out into the world to preach the church's mission and to combat heresy.

The **secular clergy**, those who lived and worked directly among the laity in the world (*saeculum*), formed a vast hierarchy. At the top were the wealthy cardinals, archbishops, and bishops who were drawn almost exclusively from the nobility. Below them were the urban priests, the cathedral canons, and the court clerks. Finally, there was the great mass of poor parish priests, who were neither financially nor intellectually much above the common people they served.

During most of the Middle Ages, the clergy were the first estate, and theology was the queen of the sciences. How did the clergy attain such prominence? A lot of it was self-proclaimed. However, there were also popular respect and reverence for the clergy's role as mediator between God and humanity. The priest brought the Son of God down to earth when he celebrated the sacrament of the Eucharist; his absolution released penitents from punishment for sin. It was declared improper for mere laypeople to sit in judgment on such a priest.

Peasants The largest and lowest social group in medieval society was one on whose labor the welfare of all others depended: the agrarian peasantry. Many peasants lived and worked on the manors of the nobility, the vital cells of rural social life. The lord of the manor required a certain amount of produce (grain, eggs, and the like) and services from the peasant families and held both judicial and police powers. He owned and operated the machines that processed crops into food and drink. The lord also had the right to subject his tenants to exactions known as *banalities*. He could, for example, force them to breed their cows with his bull, and to pay for the privilege; to grind their bread grains in his mill; to bake their bread in his oven; to make their wine in his wine press; to buy their beer from his brewery; and even to surrender to him the choice parts of all animals slaughtered on his lands. The lord also collected as an inheritance tax a serf's best animal. Without the lord's permission, a serf could neither travel nor marry outside the manor in which he served.

However, the serfs' status was not chattel slavery. It was to a lord's advantage to keep his serfs healthy and happy; his welfare, like theirs, depended on a successful harvest. Serfs had their own dwellings and modest strips of land, and they lived off the produce of their own labor and organization. They could also market for their own profit any surpluses that remained after the harvest. And serfs could pass their property (their dwellings and field strips) on to their children, along with their worldly goods.

Two basic changes occurred in the evolution of the manor from the early to the later Middle Ages. The first was the increasing importance of the single-family holding. As family farms replaced manorial units, land and property remained in the possession of a single family from generation to generation. Second was the conversion of the serf's dues into money payments, a change made possible by the revival of trade and the rise of the towns. This development, completed by the thirteenth century, permitted serfs to hold their land as rent-paying tenants and to overcome their servile status.

By the mid–fourteenth century, a declining nobility in England and France, faced with the ravages of the great plague and the Hundred Years' War, tried to turn back the historical clock by increasing taxes on the peasantry and restricting their migration to the cities. The response was armed revolt. The revolts of the agrarian peasantry, like those of the urban proletariat, were brutally crushed. They stand out at the end of the Middle Ages as violent testimony to the breakup of medieval society. As growing national sentiment would break its political unity and heretical movements end its nominal religious unity, the peasantry's revolts revealed the absence of medieval social unity.

MEDIEVAL WOMEN

The image and the reality of medieval women are two very different things. The image was strongly influenced by the views of male Christian clergy, whose ideal was the celibate life of chastity, poverty, and obedience. Drawing on both the Bible and classical medical, philosophical, and legal writings predating Christianity, Christian theologians depicted women as physically, mentally,

Virgin and Child, surrounded by angels, by Giovanni Cimabue (1240-1302).
SuperStock, Inc.

and morally weaker than men. On the basis of such assumptions, Christian clergy considered marriage a debased state by comparison with the religious life, and in their writings praised virgins and celibate widows over wives. In marriage, a woman's role was to be obedient to her husband, who, as the stronger, had a duty to protect and discipline her.

This image suggests that medieval women had two basic options in life: to become either a subjugated housewife or a confined nun. In reality, the vast majority of medieval women were neither.

Image and Status   Both within and outside the Church, this image of women is contradicted. Together with the cult of the Virgin Mary, the chivalric romances and courtly love literature of the twelfth and thirteenth centuries put women on pedestals and treated them as superior to men in purity. If the church harbored misogynist sentiments, it also condemned them, as in the case of the thirteenth-century *Romance of the Rose* and other popular bawdy literature.

The learned churchman Peter Lombard (1100–1169) asked why God created Eve from Adam's rib rather than taking her from his head or one of his feet? His answer: God took Eve

from Adam's side because woman was created neither to rule over man nor to be enslaved by him but rather to stand squarely at his side, as a companion and partner in mutual aid and trust. By such insistence on the spiritual equality of men and women and their shared responsibility to one another, the church also helped raise the dignity of women.

Germanic law treated women better than Roman law had done, recognizing basic rights that forbade their treatment as chattel. Unlike Roman women, who as teens married much older men, German women married husbands of similar age. Another practice unknown to the Romans was the groom's conveyance of a portion, or dowry (*dos*), to his bride which became her own in the event of his death. All major Germanic law codes recognized the economic freedom of women: their right to inherit, administer, dispose of, and confer property and wealth on their children. They could also press charges in court against men for bodily injury and rape, the latter receiving punishments ranging from fines, flogging, and banishment to blinding, castration, and death.

Life Choices   The nunnery was an option for single women from the higher social classes. Entrance required a dowry and could be almost as expensive as a wedding, although usually cheaper. Within the nunnery, a woman could rise to leadership as an abbess or a mother superior, exercising a degree of authority denied her in much of secular life. However, the nunneries of the established religious orders remained under male supervision, so that even abbesses had to answer to higher male authority.

In the ninth century, under the influence of Christianity, the Carolingians made monogamy official policy. Heretofore they had practiced polygamy and concubinage and permitted divorce. The result was both a boon and a burden to women. On one hand,

Medieval Marketplace. A fifteenth-century rendering of an 11th- or 12th-century marketplace. Medieval women were active in all trades, but especially in the food and clothing industries.
Scala/Art Resource, N.Y.

wives gained a greater dignity and legal security. On the other hand, a wife's labor as household manager and bearer of children greatly increased. And the Carolingian wife was now also the sole object of her husband's wrath and pleasure. Such demands clearly took their toll. The mortality rates of Frankish women increased and their longevity decreased after the ninth century.

Under such conditions, the cloister became an appealing refuge for women. However, the number of women in cloisters was never very large. In late medieval England no more than 3,500 women entered the cloister.

Working women The vast majority of medieval women were neither housewives nor nuns, but working women. The evidence suggests they were respected and loved by their husbands, perhaps because they worked shoulder by shoulder with them in running the household and often also home-based businesses. Between the ages of ten and fifteen, girls were apprenticed in a trade and learned to be skilled workers much like boys. If they married, they often continued their trade, operating their bake or dress shops next to their husbands' business, or becoming assistants and partners in the shops of their husbands. Women appeared in virtually every "blue-collar" trade, from butcher to goldsmith, but mostly worked in the food and clothing industries. Women belonged to guilds, just like men, and they became craftmasters. By the fifteenth century, townswomen increasingly had the opportunity to go to school and gain vernacular literacy.

Although women did not have as wide a range of vocations as men, their vocational destinies were just as fixed. Unlike men, however, women were excluded from the learned professions of scholarship, medicine, and law by reason of gender alone. Their freedom of movement within a profession was often more regulated than a man's and their wages for the same work were not as great. Still, women remained as prominent and as creative a part of workaday medieval society as men.

Growth of National Monarchies
ENGLAND AND FRANCE: HASTINGS (1066) TO BOUVINES (1214)

William the Conqueror The most important change in English political life was occasioned in 1066 by the death of the childless Anglo-Saxon ruler Edward the Confessor (r. 1042–1066), so named because of his reputation of piety. Edward's mother was a Norman princess, which gave Duke William of Normandy (d. 1087) a hereditary claim to the English throne. The Anglo-Saxon assembly, however, chose instead Harold Godwinsson (ca. 1022–1066). That defiant action brought the swift conquest of England by the powerful Normans. William's forces defeated Harold's army at Hastings on October 14, 1066, and William was crowned king of England in Westminster Abbey within weeks of the invasion.

Thereafter William established a strong monarchy but kept the Anglo-Saxon tax system, the practice of court writs (legal warnings) as a flexible form of central control over localities, and the Anglo-Saxon quasi-democratic tradition of frequent *parleying*—that is, the holding of conferences between the king and lesser powers who had vested interests in royal decisions. The result was a balancing of monarchical and parliamentary elements that remains true of English government today.

Popular Rebellion and Magna Carta William's grandson, Henry II (r. 1154–1189), brought to the throne greatly expanded French holdings through inheritance from his father (Maine, Touraine, and Anjou) and his marriage to Eleanor of Aquitaine (1122–1204), a union that created the so-called Angevin or English-French empire. As Henry II acquired new lands abroad, he became more autocratic at home. The result was strong political resistance from both the nobility and the clergy.

▲ **Battle of Hastings.** William the Conqueror on horseback urging his troops into combat with the English at the Battle of Hastings (October 14, 1066). From the Bayeux Tapestry, about 1073–1083.
Giraudon/Art Resource, N.Y.

DOCUMENT | The English Nobility Imposes Restraints on King John

The gradual building of a sound English constitutional monarchy in the Middle Ages required the king's willingness to share power. He had to be strong but could not act as a despot or rule by fiat. The danger of despotism became acute in England under the rule of King John. In 1215 the English nobility forced him to recognize the Magna Carta, which reaffirmed traditional rights and personal liberties that are still enshrined in English law.

♦ Are the rights protected by the Magna Carta basic ones or special privileges? Do they suggest there was a sense of "fairness" in the past? Does the granting of such rights in any way weaken the king?

A free man shall not be fined for a small offense, except in proportion to the gravity of the offense; and for a great offense he shall be fined in proportion to the magnitude of the offense, saving his freehold [property]; and a merchant in the same way, saving his merchandise; and the villein [a free serf, bound only to his lord] shall be fined in the same way, saving his wainage [wagon], if he shall be at [the king's] mercy. And none of the above fines shall be imposed except by the oaths of honest men of the neighborhood. ...

No constable or other bailiff of [the king] shall take anyone's grain or other chattels without immediately paying for them in money, unless he is able to obtain a postponement at the good will of the seller.

No constable shall require any knight to give money in place of his ward of a castle [i.e., standing guard], if he is willing to furnish that ward in his own person, or through another honest man, if he himself is not able to do it for a reasonable cause; and if we shall lead or send him into the army, he shall be free from ward in proportion to the amount of time which he has been in the army through us.

No sheriff or bailiff of [the king], or any one else, shall take horses or wagons of any free man, for carrying purposes, except on the permission of that free man.

Neither we nor our bailiffs will take the wood of another man for castles, or for anything else which we are doing, except by the permission of him to whom the wood belongs. ...

No free man shall be taken, or imprisoned, or dispossessed, or outlawed, or banished, or in any way injured, nor will we go upon him, nor send upon him, except by the legal judgment of his peers, or by the law of the land.

To no one will we sell, to no one will we deny or delay, right or justice.

James Harvey Robinson, ed., *Readings in European History*, Vol. 1 (Boston: Athenaeum, 1904), pp. 236–237.

Under Henry's successors, the brothers Richard the Lion-Hearted (r. 1189–1199) and John (r. 1199–1216), burdensome taxation in support of foreign Crusades, and a failing war with France turned resistance into outright rebellion. With the full support of the clergy and the townspeople, English barons forced the king's grudging recognition of the **Magna Carta** ("Great Charter") in 1215. (See Document, "The English Nobility Imposes Restraints on King John.")

This famous cornerstone of modern English law put limits on royal power and secured the rights of the privileged to be represented at the highest levels of government in important matters like taxation. The Great Charter enabled the English to avoid both a dissolution of the monarchy by the nobility and the abridgment of the rights of the nobility by the monarchy.

Philip II Augustus Powerful feudal princes dominated France from the beginning of the Capetian dynasty (987) until the reign of Philip II Augustus (1180–1223). During this period the Capetian kings wisely concentrated their limited resources on securing the territory surrounding Paris known as the Île-de-France. By the time of Philip II, Paris had become the center of French government and culture,

and the Capetian dynasty a secure hereditary monarchy. Thereafter, the kings of France were able to impose their will on the French nobles.

The Norman Conquest of England enabled the Capetian kings to establish a truly national monarchy. The Duke of Normandy, who after 1066 was master of England, was also a vassal of the French king in Paris. Capetian kings understandably watched with alarm as the power of their Norman vassal grew.

Philip Augustus faced both an internal and an international struggle, and he succeeded at both. His armies occupied all the English territories on the French coast except for Aquitaine. At Bouvines on July 27, 1214, the French won handily over the English and their German allies. The victory unified France around the monarchy and thereby laid the foundation for French ascendancy in the late Middle Ages.

FRANCE IN THE THIRTEENTH CENTURY: REIGN OF LOUIS IX

Louis IX (r. 1226–1270), the grandson of Philip Augustus, embodied the medieval view of the perfect ruler. He inherited a unified and secure kingdom.

Gothic Cathedral. The portal of Reims Cathedral, where the kings of France were crowned. The cathedral was built in the Gothic style—emblematic of the High and late Middle Ages—that originated in France in the mid–twelfth century. The earlier Romanesque (Roman-like) style from which it evolved is characterized by fortresslike buildings with thick stone walls, rounded arches and vaults, and few windows. The Gothic style, in contrast, is characterized by soaring sturctures, their interiors flooded with colored light from vast expanses of stained glass. Distinctive features of the Gothic style include ribbed, crisscrossing vaulting; pointed rather than rounded arches; and prominent exteriror flying buttresses. The vaulting and the flying buttresses made possible the great height of Gothic buildings. By shifting structural weight from the walls, the buttresses also made possible the large, stained-glass-filled windows. The windows were used much as mosaics had been earlier, to show stories from the Bible, saints' lives, and local events.

Scala/Art Resource, N.Y.

Louis' greatest achievements lay at home. The efficient French bureaucracy became under him an instrument of order and fair play in local government. He sent forth royal commissioners to monitor the royal officials responsible for local governmental administration and ensure justice. These royal ambassadors were received as genuine tribunes of the people. Louis further abolished private wars and serfdom within his own royal domain, gave his subjects the right of appeal from local to higher courts, and made the tax system more equitable. The French people came to associate their king with justice, and national feeling, the glue of nationhood, grew strong during his reign.

During Louis' reign, French society and culture became an example to all of Europe, a pattern that would continue into the modern period. Northern France became the showcase of monastic reform, chivalry, and Gothic art and architecture. Louis' reign also coincided with the golden age of Scholasticism, which saw the convergence of Europe's greatest thinkers on Paris, among them Saint Thomas Aquinas.

THE HOHENSTAUFEN EMPIRE (1152–1272)

While stable governments developed in both England and France during the Middle Ages, the Holy Roman Empire fragmented in disunity and blood feuding (see Map 15–3).

Frederick I Barbarossa   Frederick I Barbarossa (1152–1190), the first of the Hohenstaufens, reestablished imperial authority but also initiated a new phase in the contest between popes and emperors. Never have rulers and popes despised and persecuted one another more than they did during the Hohenstaufen dynasty. Frederick attempted to hold the empire together by stressing feudal bonds, but his reign ended with stalemate in Germany and defeat in Italy. In 1186 his son—the future Henry VI (r. 1190–1197)—married Constance, heiress to the kingdom of Sicily. That alliance became a fatal distraction for the Hohenstaufens. This union of the empire with Sicily left Rome encircled, thereby ensuring the undying hostility of a papacy already thoroughly distrustful of the emperor.

When Henry VI died in September 1197, chaos followed. Germany was thrown into anarchy and civil war. Meanwhile, Henry VI's four-year-old son, Frederick, who had a direct hereditary claim to the imperial crown, had for his own safety been made—fatefully, it would prove—a ward of Pope Innocent III (r. 1198–1215), who proclaimed and practiced as none before him the doctrine of the plenitude of papal power. Innocent had both the will and the means to challenge the Hohenstaufens.

Frederick II   Hohenstaufen support had meanwhile remained alive in Germany, where in December 1212 young Frederick, with papal support, became Emperor Frederick II. But Frederick soon disappointed papal hopes. He was Sicilian and only nine of his thirty-eight years as emperor were spent in Germany. To secure the imperial title for himself and his sons, he gave the German princes what they wanted. The German princes became undisputed lords over their territories, petty kings.

Frederick had an equally disastrous relationship with the papacy, which excommunicated him four times and led the German princes against him, launching the church into European politics on a massive scale. This transformation of the

papacy into a formidable political and military power soon made the church highly vulnerable to criticism from religious reformers and royal apologists.

When Frederick died in 1250, the German monarchy died with him. The princes established an electoral college in 1257 to pick the emperor, and the "king of the Romans" became their puppet. Between 1250 and 1272 the Hohenstaufen dynasty slowly faded into oblivion.

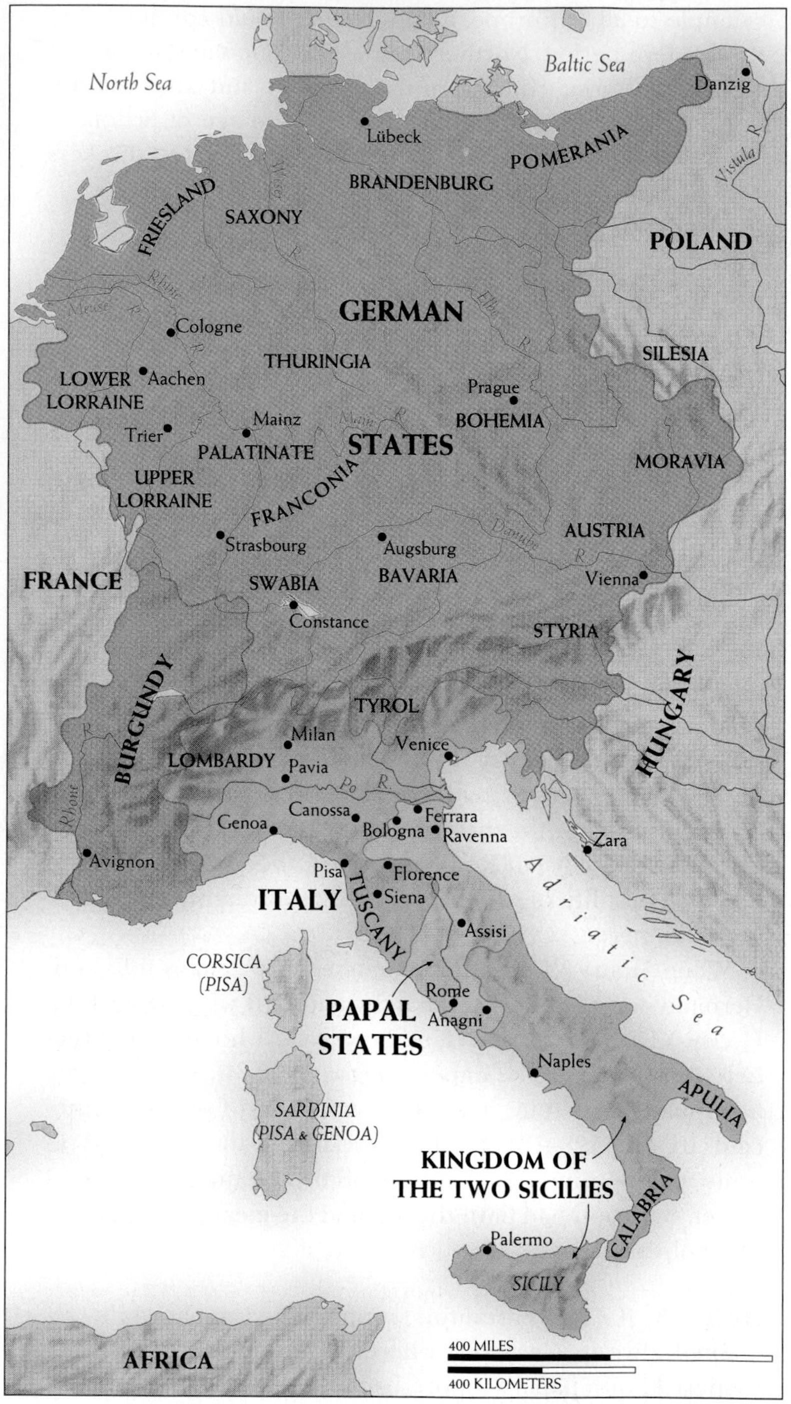

Political and Social Breakdown

HUNDRED YEARS' WAR

The Causes of the War The Hundred Years' War, which began in May 1337 and lasted until October 1453, started when the English king Edward III (r. 1327–1377), the grandson of Philip the Fair of France (r. 1285–1314), claimed the French throne. But the war was more than a dynastic quarrel. England and France were territorial and economic rivals with a long history of prejudice and animosity between them. These factors made the Hundred Years' War a struggle for national identity.

Although France had three times the population of England, was far wealthier, and fought on its own soil, most of the major battles were stunning English victories. The primary reason for these French failures was internal disunity caused by endemic social conflicts. Unlike England, France was still struggling to make the transition from a fragmented feudal society to a centralized modern state.

France's defeats also resulted from incompetent leadership and English military superiority. The English infantry was more disciplined than the French, and English archers could fire six arrows a minute with enough force to pierce an inch of wood or the armor of a knight at 200 yards. Eventually, thanks in part to the inspiring leadership of Joan of Arc (1412–1431), and a sense of national identity and self-confidence, the French were able to expel the English from France. By 1453, all that remained to the English was their coastal enclave of Calais.

Charles forgot his liberator as quickly as he had embraced her. When the Burgundians captured Joan in May 1430, he could have secured her release but did not. The Burgundians and the English wanted her publicly discredited, believing this would demoralize French resistance. She was turned over to the Inquisition in English-held Rouen, where, after ten weeks of interrogation, she was executed on May 30, 1431.

The Hundred Years' War had lasting political and social consequences. It devastated France, but it also awakened French nationalism and hastened the country's transition from a feudal monarchy to a centralized state. In both France and England the burden of the war fell most heavily on the peasantry, who were forced to support it with taxes and services.

MAP 15–3 Germany and Italy in the Middle Ages. Medieval Germany and Italy were divided lands. The Holy Roman Empire (Germany) embraced hundreds of independent territories that the emperor ruled only in name. The papacy controlled the Rome area and tried to enforce its will in the Romagna. Under the Hohenstaufens (mid–twelfth to mid–thirteenth centuries), internal German divisions and papal conflict reached new heights; German rulers sought to extend their power to southern Italy and Sicily.

THE BLACK DEATH

Preconditions and Causes   In the fourteenth century, nine tenths of the population worked the land. The three-field system of crop production increased the amount of arable land and with it the food supply. But as that supply grew, so did the population. It is estimated that Europe's population doubled between the years 1000 and 1300 and began thereafter to outstrip food production. There were now more people than there was food to feed them or jobs to employ them, and the average European faced the probability of extreme hunger at least once during his or her expected thirty-five-year life span.

Between 1315 and 1317, crop failures produced the greatest famine of the Middle Ages. Densely populated urban areas such as the industrial towns of the Netherlands experienced great suffering. Decades of overpopulation, economic depression, famine, and bad health progressively weakened Europe's population and made it highly vulnerable to a virulent bubonic plague that struck with full force in 1348.

The **Black Death**, so called by contemporaries because of the way it discolored the body, was most likely introduced by rats from Black Sea areas, the epidemic following the trade routes from Asia into Europe. Appearing in Sicily in late 1347, it entered Europe through the port cities of Venice, Genoa, and Pisa in 1348, and from there it swept rapidly through Spain and southern France and into northern Europe. Areas that lay outside the major trade routes, like Bohemia, appear to have remained virtually unaffected. Bubonic plague made

CHRONOLOGY
Church and Empire

910	Monastery of Cluny founded
918	Henry I becomes king of Germany
951	Otto I invades Italy
955	Otto I defeats the Hungarians at Lechfeld
962	Otto I crowned emperor by Pope John XII
1077	Gregory VII pardons Henry IV at Canossa
1122	Concordat of Worms settles the investiture controversy
1152–1190	Reign of Frederick Barbarossa
1198–1215	Reign of Innocent III
1214	Collapse of the claims of Otto IV
1220	Frederick II crowned emperor
1232	Frederick II devolves authority to the German princes
1257	The German monarchy becomes elective

numerous reappearances in succeeding decades. It is estimated that western Europe had lost as much as two fifths of its population by the early fifteenth century. (See Map 15–4.)

Popular Remedies   Transmitted by rat- or human-borne fleas, the plague often reached a victim's lungs during the course of the disease. From the lungs, it was spread from person to person by the victim's sneezing and wheezing. Contemporary physicians had little understanding of these processes, so the most rudimentary prophylaxis was lacking. Throughout much of Western Europe, the plague brought with it an obsession with death and dying, engendering a deep pessimism that endured for decades.

Popular wisdom held that a corruption in the atmosphere caused the disease. Some blamed poisonous fumes released by earthquakes. Many wore aromatic amulets as a remedy. According to the contemporary observations of Boccaccio, who recorded the reactions in the *Decameron* (1353), some sought a remedy in moderation and a temperate life, others gave themselves over entirely to their passions (sexual promiscuity ran high within the stricken areas), and still others, "the most sound, perhaps, in judgment," chose flight and seclusion as the best medicine.

One extreme reaction was processions of flagellants, religious fanatics who beat themselves in ritual penance, believing such action would bring divine intervention. The terror created by the flagellants, whose dirty bodies may have transported the disease, became so socially disruptive and threatening that the church finally outlawed such processions.

In some places, Jews were cast as scapegoats. Centuries of Christian propaganda had bred hatred toward Jews, as had their role as society's moneylenders. Pogroms occurred in several cities, sometimes incited by the flagellants.

:ymago mortis

▲ **The Image of Death.** The brevity and fragility of life were favorite themes of late medieval artists, who graphically depicted the horrors of death and death's power to sweep away all human pretensions to pomp and glory.
Corbis/Bettmann.

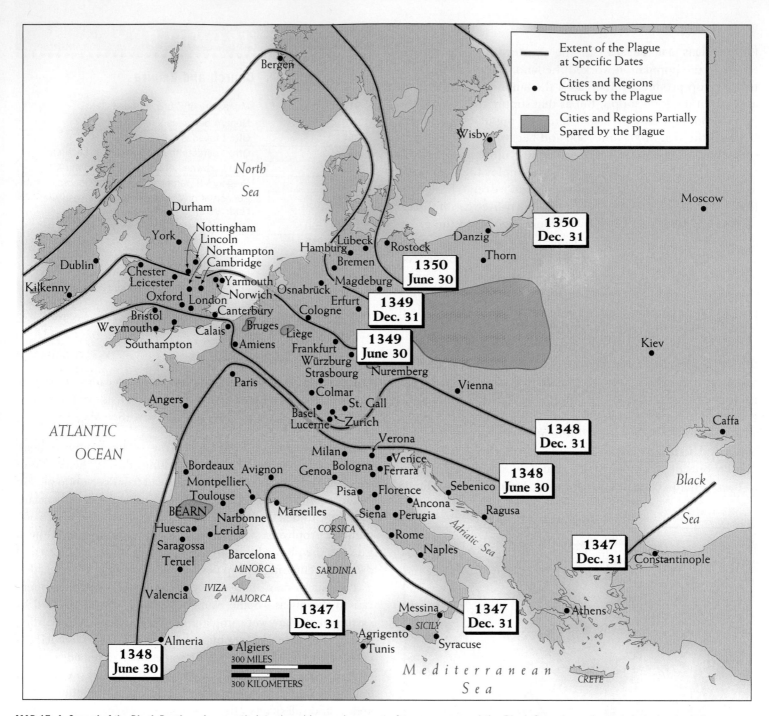

MAP 15–4 Spread of the Black Death. Apparently introduced by sea-borne rats from areas around the Black Sea where plague-infested rodents have long been known, the Black Death had great human, social, and economic consequences. According to one of the lower estimates, it killed 25 million in Europe. The map charts the spread of the plague in the mid–14th century. Generally following trade routes, it reached Scandinavia by 1350, and some believe it then went on to Iceland and even Greenland. Areas off the main trade routes were largely spared.

Social and Economic Consequences

Whole villages vanished in the wake of the plague. Among the social and economic consequences of such high depopulation were a shrunken labor supply and a decline in the value of the estates of the nobility. As the number of farm laborers decreased, wages increased and those of skilled artisans soared. Many serfs chose to commute their labor services by money payments and pursue more interesting and rewarding jobs in skilled craft industries in the cities. Agricultural prices fell because of lowered demand, and the price of luxury and manufactured goods—the work of skilled artisans—rose. The noble landholders suffered the greatest decline in power. They were forced to pay more for finished products and for farm labor, while receiving a smaller return on their agricultural produce. Everywhere rents declined after the plague.

Peasants Revolt To recoup their losses, some landowners converted arable land to sheep pasture, substituting more profitable wool production for labor-intensive grain crops. Others abandoned the farms leasing them to the highest bidder. Landowners also sought to reverse their misfortune by new repressive legislation that forced peasants to stay on their farms while freezing their wages at low levels. In 1351, the English Parliament passed a Statute of Laborers, which limited wages to preplague levels and restricted the ability of peasants to leave the land of their masters. Opposition to such legislation was also a prominent factor in the English peasants' revolt in 1381. In France the direct tax on the peasantry, the *taille*, was increased, and opposition to it helped ignite the French peasant uprising known as the Jacquerie.

Cities Rebound Although the plague hit urban populations hard, the cities and their skilled industries came in time to prosper from its effects. Cities had always protected their interests, passing legislation as they grew to regulate competition from rural areas and to control immigration. After the plague, the reach of such laws extended beyond the cities to include the surrounding lands of nobles and landlords, many of whom now peacefully integrated into urban life.

The omnipresence of death also whetted the appetite for goods that only skilled industries could produce. Expensive cloths and jewelry, furs from the north, and silks from the south were in great demand in the decades after the plague. Initially this new demand could not be met. The basic unit of urban industry, the master and his apprentices (usually one or two), purposely kept its numbers low, jealously guarding its privileges. The first wave of plague turned this already restricted supply of skilled artisans into a shortage almost overnight. As a result, the prices of manufactured and luxury items rose to new heights, which in turn encouraged workers to migrate from the countryside to the city and learn the skills of artisans. Townspeople profited coming and going. As wealth poured into the cities and per capita income rose, agricultural products from the countryside, now less in demand, declined.

There was also gain and loss for the church. It suffered as a landholder and was politically weakened, yet at the same time, it received new revenues from the vastly increased demand for religious services for the dead and the dying, along with new gifts and bequests.

New Conflicts and Opportunities

By increasing the importance of skilled artisans, the plague contributed to new social conflicts within the cities. The economic and political power of local artisans and trade guilds grew steadily in the late Middle Ages, along with the demand for their goods and services. The merchant and patrician classes found it increasingly difficult to maintain their traditional dominance and grudgingly gave guild masters a voice in city government. As the guilds won political power, they encouraged restrictive legislation to protect local industries. The restrictions, in turn, caused conflict between master artisans, who wanted to keep their numbers low and expand their industries at a snail's pace, and the many journeymen, who were eager to rise to the rank of master. To the long-existing conflict between the guilds and the ruling urban patriciate was now added a conflict within the guilds themselves.

Also after 1350, the two traditional "containers" of monarchy—the landed nobility and the church—were put on the defensive as a consequence of the plague. Kings now exploited growing national sentiment in an effort to centralize their governments and economies. At the same time, the battles of the Hundred Years' War demonstrated the military superiority of paid professional armies over the traditional noble cavalry, thus bringing into question the latter's future role. The plague also killed many members of the clergy—perhaps one third of the German clergy fell victim as they dutifully ministered to the sick and dying. This reduction in clerical ranks occurred in the same century that saw the pope move from Rome to Avignon (1309–1377) and the Great Schism (1378–1417) divide the Church into warring factions.

Black Death. Men and women carrying plague victims in coffins to the burial ground in Tournai, Belgium, 1349.
The Granger Collection, New York.

Ecclesiastical Breakdown and Revival: The Late Medieval Church

BONIFACE VIII AND PHILIP THE FAIR

By the fourteenth century popes faced rulers far more powerful than the papacy. When Pope Boniface VIII (r. 1294–1303) issued a bull, *Clericis Laicos,* which forbade lay taxation of the clergy without prior papal approval, King Philip the Fair of France (r. 1285–1314) unleashed a ruthless antipapal campaign. Boniface made a last-ditch stand against state control of national churches on November 18, 1302, when he issued the bull *Unam Sanctam,* which declared that temporal authority was "subject" to the spiritual power of the church.

The French responded with force. Philip sent troops who beat the pope badly and might even have executed him had not an aroused populace liberated the pope and returned him safely to Rome.

There was no papal retaliation. No pope ever again so seriously threatened kings and emperors. Future relations between church and state would henceforth tilt toward state control of religion within particular monarchies.

THE GREAT SCHISM (1378–1417) AND THE CONCILIAR MOVEMENT TO 1449

After Boniface VIII's death, his successor, Clement V (r. 1305–1314), moved the papal court to Avignon on the southeastern border with France, where it remained until Pope Gregory XI (r. 1370–1378) reestablished the papacy in Rome in January 1377. His successor, Pope Urban VI (r. 1378–1389), proclaimed his intention to reform the papal government in the **Curia**. This announcement alarmed the cardinals, most of whom were French. Not wanting to surrender the benefits of a papacy under French influence, the French king, Charles V (r. 1364–1380), supported a schism in the church, known thereafter as the **Great Schism**. On September 20, 1378, thirteen cardinals, all but one of whom was French, elected a cousin of the French king as Pope Clement VII (r. 1378–1397). Clement returned to Avignon. Thereafter allegiance to the two papal courts divided along political lines: Acknowledging Urban VI were England and its allies—the **Holy Roman Empire** (based on the old Roman Empire, mostly

◀ **Papal Authority.** Pope Boniface VIII (r. 1294–1303), who opposed the taxation of the clergy by the kings of France and England, issued one of the strongest declarations of papal authority, the bull *Unam Sanctam.* This statue is in the Museo Civico, Bologna, Italy.
Scala/Art Resource, N.Y.

Germany and Northern Italy), Hungary, Bohemia, and Poland. Supporting Clement VII were France and its orbit—Naples, Scotland, Castile, and Aragon. Only the Roman line of popes, however, is recognized as official by the church.

In 1409 a council at Pisa deposed both the Roman and the Avignon popes and elected its own new pope. But neither Rome nor Avignon accepted its action, so after 1409 there were three contending popes. This intolerable situation ended when the emperor Sigismund (r. 1410– 1437) prevailed on the Pisan pope to summon a legal council of the church in Constance in 1414, a council also recognized by the reigning Roman pope Gregory XII (r. 1406–1415). After the three contending popes had either resigned or been deposed, the council elected a new pope, Martin V (r. 1417–1431), in November 1417, reuniting the church.

Under Pope Eugenius IV (r. 1431–1447), the papacy regained much of its prestige and authority, and in 1460 the papal bull *Execrabilis* condemned all appeals to councils as "completely null and void." But the conciliar movement had planted deep within the conscience of all Western peoples the conviction that the leader of an institution must be responsive to its members and not act against their best interests.

The Renaissance in Italy (1375–1527)

The **Renaissance** is the term used to described the fourteenth and fifteenth-century effort to revive ancient learning. Most scholars agree that it was a transition from the medieval to the modern world. Medieval Europe, especially before the twelfth century, had been a fragmented feudal society with an agricultural economy, its thought and culture dominated by the church. Renaissance Europe, especially after the fourteenth century, was characterized by growing national consciousness and political centralization, an urban economy based on organized commerce and capitalism, and ever greater lay and secular control of thought and culture.

The distinctive features and achievements of the Renaissance are most strikingly revealed in Italy from roughly 1375 to 1527, the year of the infamous sack of Rome by imperial soldiers. What was achieved in Italy during these centuries also deeply influenced northern Europe.

THE ITALIAN CITY-STATE: SOCIAL CONFLICT AND DESPOTISM

Renaissance society took distinctive shape within the cities of late medieval Italy. Italy was the natural gateway between East and West. Venice, Genoa, and Pisa traded uninterruptedly with the Near East throughout the Middle Ages and maintained vibrant urban societies. During the thirteenth and fourteenth centuries, the trade-rich Italian cities became powerful city-states, dominating the political and economic life of the surrounding countryside. By the fifteenth century, the great Italian cities had become the bankers for much of Europe. There were five such major, competitive states in Italy: the duchy of Milan, the republics of Florence and Venice, the Papal States, and the kingdom of Naples (see Map 15–5).

Social strife and competition for political power were so intense within the cities that for survival's sake, most had evolved into despotisms by the fifteenth century. Venice, ruled by a successful merchant oligarchy, was the notable exception. Elsewhere, the new social classes and divisions within society produced by rapid urban growth fueled chronic, near-anarchic conflict.

In Florence, these social divisions produced conflict at every level of society. True stability was not established until the ascent to power in 1434 of Cosimo de' Medici (1389–1464). The wealthiest Florentine and a most astute statesman, Cosimo controlled the city internally from behind the scenes, skillfully manipulating the constitution and influencing elections. His grandson Lorenzo the Magnificent (1449–1492, r. 1478–1492) ruled Florence in almost totalitarian fashion.

Despotism was less subtle elsewhere in Italy. To prevent internal social conflict and foreign intrigue from paralyzing their cities, the dominant groups in many cities cooperated in the hiring of a strongman, known as a *podesta*, to maintain law and order. Because these despots could not depend on the divided populace, they operated through mercenary armies.

Political turbulence and warfare also gave birth to diplomacy, through which the various city-states stayed abreast of foreign military developments and, if shrewd enough, gained power and advantage without actually going to war. Most city-states established resident embassies during the fifteenth century, their ambassadors watchful eyes and ears at rival courts. Renaissance culture was promoted as vigorously by despots as by republicans and by popes as enthusiastically as by humanists.

HUMANISM

Humanism was the scholarly study of the Latin and Greek classics and the ancient Church Fathers, both for their own sake and to promote a rebirth of ancient norms and values. Humanists advocated the ***studia humanitatis***, a liberal arts program that embraced grammar, rhetoric, poetry, history, politics, and moral philosophy.

The first humanists were orators and poets. They wrote original literature in both the classical and the vernacular lan-

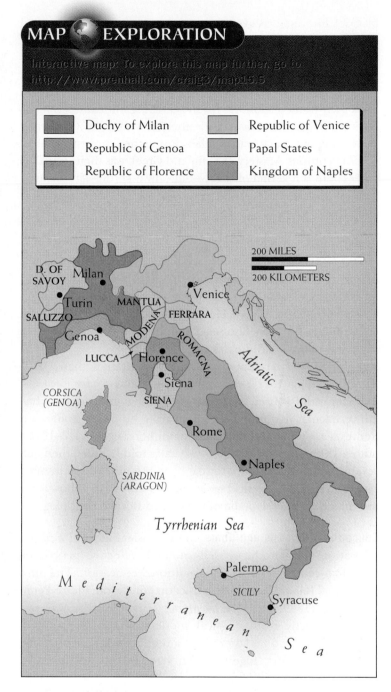

MAP EXPLORATION

Interactive map: To explore this map further, go to http://www.prenhall.com/craig3/map15.5

Duchy of Milan · Republic of Venice · Republic of Genoa · Papal States · Republic of Florence · Kingdom of Naples

MAP 15–5 Renaissance Italy. The city-states of Renaissance Italy were self-contained principalities whose internal strife was monitored by their despots and whose external aggression was long successfully controlled by treaty.

guages, inspired by the newly discovered works of the ancients, and they taught rhetoric within the universities. Their talents were sought as secretaries, speech writers, and diplomats in princely and papal courts.

Classical and Christian antiquity had been studied before the Italian Renaissance—during the Carolingian renaissance of the ninth century, for example. However, the Italian Renaissance of the late Middle Ages was more secular and lay dominated, had broader interests, recovered more manuscripts, and possessed far superior technical skills than earlier rebirths of antiquity.

Unlike their Scholastic rivals, humanists were not content only to summarize and compare the views of recognized authorities on a question but instead went directly to the original source and drew their own conclusions. Avidly searching out manuscript collections, Italian humanists made the full sources of Greek and Latin antiquity available to scholars during the fourteenth and fifteenth centuries. Mastery of Latin and Greek was their surgeon's tool. There is a kernel of truth—but only a kernel—in the arrogant boast of the humanists that the period between themselves and classical civilization was a "dark middle age."

Petrarch, Dante, and Boccaccio   Francesco Petrarch (1304–1374) was the father of humanism. He left the legal profession to pursue his love of letters and poetry. Petrarch celebrated ancient Rome in his writings and tirelessly collected ancient manuscripts; among his finds were letters by Cicero. His critical textual studies, elitism, and contempt for the allegedly useless learning of the Scholastics were shared by many later humanists.

Petrarch was far more secular in orientation than Dante Alighieri (1265–1321), whose *Vita Nuova* and *Divine Comedy*—together with Petrarch's sonnets—form the cornerstones of Italian vernacular literature. Also pioneering humanist studies was Petrarch's student and friend Giovanni Boccaccio (1313–1375), author of the *Decameron*, 100 bawdy tales told by three men and seven women in a country retreat from the plague that ravaged Florence in 1348. An avid collector of manuscripts, Boccaccio assembled an encyclopedia of Greek and Roman mythology.

Educational Reforms and Goals   The classical ideal of a useful education that produces well-rounded, effective people inspired far-reaching reforms in traditional education. The most influential Italian Renaissance tract on education, Pietro Paolo Vergerio's (1349–1420) *On the Morals That Befit a Free Man*, was written directly from classical models. Vittorino da Feltre (d. 1446) directed his students to a highly disciplined reading of ancient authors, together with vigorous physical exercise and games with intellectual pursuits.

Educated and cultured noblewomen also had a prominent place at Renaissance courts, among them Christine de Pisan (1363?–1434). She was an expert in classical, French, and Italian languages and literature and became a well-known woman of letters in the courts of Europe. Her most famous work, *The City of Ladies*, describes the accomplishments of the great women of history.

RENAISSANCE ART

In Renaissance Italy, as later in Reformation Europe, the values and interests of the laity were less subordinated to those of the clergy than previously. In education, culture, and religion,

▲ **Cosimo de' Medici (1389–1464).** Florentine banker and statesman, in his lifetime the city's wealthiest man and most successful politician. This portrait is by Jacopo da Pontormo (1494–1556).
Jacopo Pontormo (1494–1556), "Cosimo de' Medici the Elder, Pater Patriae," (1389–1464). Oil on wood, 87 × 65 cm. Inv. 3574. Uffize, Florence. Photograph © Erich Lessing/Art Resource, N.Y.

medieval Christian values were adjusting to a more this-worldly spirit. Men and women began again to appreciate and even to glorify the secular world, secular learning, and purely human pursuits as ends in themselves.

This perspective on life is especially prominent in the painting and sculpture of the High Renaissance (late fifteenth and early sixteenth centuries), when Renaissance art reached its full maturity. In imitation of Greek and Roman art, painters and sculptors attempted to create harmonious, symmetrical, and properly proportioned figures, portraying the human form with a glorified realism. Whereas Byzantine and Gothic art had been religious and idealized in the extreme, Renaissance art, especially in the fifteenth century, realistically reproduced nature and human beings as a part of nature.

Renaissance artists took advantage of new technical skills and materials developed during the fifteenth century: the use of oil paints, using shading to enhance realism (**chiaroscuro**), and adjusting the size of figures to give the viewer a feeling of continuity with the painting (linear perspective). Compared with their flat Byzantine and Gothic counterparts, Renaissance paintings seem filled with energy and life and stand out from the canvas in three dimensions. The great masters of the High Renaissance included Leonardo da Vinci (1452–1519), Raphael (1483–1520), and Michelangelo Buonarroti (1475–1564).

Leonardo da Vinci   Leonardo personified the Renaissance ideal of the universal person, one who is not only a jack-of-all-trades, but also a master of many. (See Document, "Pico Della Mirandola States the Renaissance Image of Man.") A military engineer and advocate of scientific experimentation, he dissected corpses to learn anatomy and was a self-taught botanist. He foresaw such modern machines as airplanes and submarines. The variety of his interests tended to shorten his attention span, so that he constantly moved from one activity to another. As a painter, his great skill lay in conveying inner moods through complex facial features, such as that seen in the most famous of his paintings, the *Mona Lisa*.

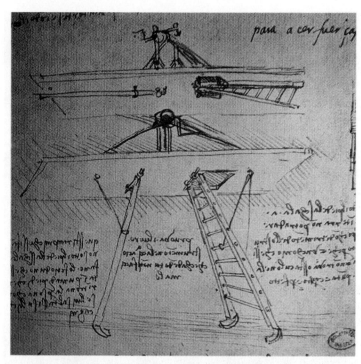

▲ **Aviation Drawings by Leonardo da Vinci (1452–1519).** He imagined a possible flying machine with a retractable ladder for boarding.
David Forbert/SuperStock, Inc.

DOCUMENT   Pico della Mirandola States the Renaissance Image of Man

One of the most eloquent Renaissance descriptions of the abilities of humankind comes from the Italian humanist Pico della Mirandola (1463–1494). In his famed Oration on the Dignity of Man *(ca. 1486), Pico described humans as free to become whatever they choose.*

◆ In what does the dignity of humankind consist? Does Pico reject the biblical description of Adam and Eve's fall? Does he exaggerate a person's ability to choose freely to be whatever he or she wishes? What inspired such seeming hubris during the Renaissance?

The best of artisans [God] ordained that that creature (man) to whom He [God] had been able to give nothing proper to himself should have joint possession of whatever had been peculiar to each of the different kinds of being. He therefore took man as a creature of indeterminate nature and, assigning him a place in the middle of the world, addressed him thus: "Neither a fixed abode nor a form that is thine alone or any function peculiar to thyself have we given thee, Adam, to the end that according to thy longing and according to thy judgment thou mayest have and possess what abode, what form, and what functions thou thyself shalt desire. The nature of all other beings is limited and constrained within the bounds of laws prescribed by Us. Thou, constrained by no limits, in accordance with thine own free will, in whose hand We have placed thee, shalt ordain for thyself the limits of thy nature. We have set thee at the world's center that thou mayest from thence more easily observe whatever is in the world. We have made thee neither of heaven nor of earth, neither mortal nor immortal, so that with freedom of choice and with honor, as though the maker and molder of thyself, thou mayest fashion thyself in whatever shape thou shalt prefer. Thou shalt have the power to degenerate into the lower forms of life, which are brutish. Thou shalt have the power, out of thy soul's judgment, to be reborn into the higher forms, which are divine." O supreme generosity of God the Father, O highest and most marvelous felicity of man! To him it is granted to have whatever he chooses, to be whatever he wills.

From Giovanni Pico della Mirandola, *Oration on the Dignity of Man*, in *The Renaissance Philosophy of Man*, ed. by E. Cassirer et al. Phoenix Books, 1961, pp. 224–225. Reprinted by permission of The University of Chicago Press.

▲ **Raphael's Portrait (ca. 1515) of Baldassare Castiglione (1478–1529)**
Now in the Louvre. Castiglione, author of the *Book of the Courtier*, was Raphael's close friend. The self-restraint and inner calm that he considered the chief qualities of the gentleman are also qualities of Raphael's art, reflected in the portrait's perfect balance and harmony. This painting greatly influenced Rembrandt, who later tried unsuccessfully to buy it.
Reunion des Musées Nationaux/Art Resource, N.Y.

Raphael Raphael, who died young (thirty-seven), is famous for his tender madonnas. Art historians also praise his fresco *The School of Athens*, which depicts Plato and Aristotle surrounded by philosophy and science, as one of the most perfect examples of Renaissance artistic theory and technique.

Michelangelo This melancholy genius also excelled in a variety of arts and crafts. His eighteen-foot godlike sculpture *David* is a perfect example of the Renaissance artist's devotion to harmony, symmetry, and proportion, as well as his extreme glorification of the human form. Four different popes commissioned works by Michelangelo, the best known of which are the frescoes for the Sistine Chapel, painted for Pope Julius II (r. 1503–1513).

His later works mark, artistically and philosophically, the passing of High Renaissance painting and the advent of a new, experimental style known as *mannerism*, which reached its peak in the late sixteenth and early seventeenth centuries. It derived its name from the fact that it permitted the artist to express his own individual perceptions and feelings to paint, compose, or write in a "mannered" or "affected" way. Tintoretto (d. 1594) and especially El Greco (d. 1614) became its supreme representatives.

ITALY'S POLITICAL DECLINE: THE FRENCH INVASIONS (1494–1527)

Autonomous city-states of Italy had always preserved their peace and safety from foreign invasion by cooperation with each other. However, in 1494 Naples, supported by Florence and the Borgia pope Alexander VI (1492–1503), prepared to attack Milan. At this point, the Milanese despot Ludovico il Moro (r. 1476–1499) invited the French to revive their dynastic claim to Naples. But France also had dynastic claims to Milan, and the French appetite for new territory became insatiable once French armies had crossed the Alps and reestablished themselves in Italy.

The French king Charles VIII (r. 1483–1498) responded rapidly to Ludovico's call. Within five months he had crossed the Alps (August 1495) and raced as conqueror through Florence and the Papal States into Naples.

Charles' lightning march through Italy alarmed Ferdinand of Aragon (r. 1479–1516), who was also king of Sicily, and helped to create a counteralliance: the League of Venice, which was able to force Charles to retreat.

The French returned to Italy under Charles's successor, Louis XII (r. 1498–1515), this time assisted by the Borgia pope Alexander VI (1492–1503). Alexander, probably the most corrupt pope in history, sought to secure a political base in Romagna, officially part of the Papal States, for his son Cesare.

Seeing that a French alliance could allow him to reestablish control over the region, Alexander agreed to abandon the League of Venice, which made the league too weak to resist a French reconquest of Milan. Louis successfully invaded Milan in August 1499. In 1500 he and Ferdinand of Aragon divided Naples between themselves, while the pope and Cesare Borgia conquered the Romagna without opposition.

In 1503 Cardinal Giuliano della Rovere became Pope Julius II (1503–1513). He suppressed the Borgias and placed their newly conquered lands in Romagna under papal jurisdiction. After fully securing the Papal States with French aid, Julius changed sides and sought to rid Italy of his former ally, the French invaders. Julius, Ferdinand of Aragon, and Venice formed a Holy League in October 1511, and soon Emperor Maximilian I (r. 1493–1519) and the Swiss joined them. By 1512 the French were in full retreat.

The French invaded Italy again under Louis's successor, Francis I (r. 1515–1547). French armies massacred Swiss soldiers of the Holy League at Marignano in September 1515. That victory won from the Medici pope Leo X (r. 1513–1521) an agreement known as the Concordat of Bologna (August 1516), which gave the French king control over the French clergy and the right to collect taxes from them, in exchange for French recognition of the pope's superiority over church councils. This helped keep France Catholic after the outbreak of the Protestant Reformation. But the new French entry into Italy also led to the first of four major wars with Spain in the first half of the sixteenth century: the Habsburg-Valois wars, none of which France won.

NICCOLÒ MACHIAVELLI

The foreign invasions made a shambles of Italy. One who watched as French, Spanish, and German armies wreaked havoc on his country was Niccolò Machiavelli (1469–1527). The more he saw, the more convinced he became that Italian political unity and independence were ends that justified any means. Machiavelli admired the heroic acts of ancient Roman rulers, what Renaissance people called their *Virtù*. Romanticizing the old Roman citizenry, he lamented the absence of heroism among his compatriots. Such a perspective caused his interpretation of both ancient and contemporary history to be exaggerated.

The juxtaposition of what Machiavelli believed the ancient Romans had been with the failure of contemporary Romans to realize such high ideals made him the famous cynic we know in the popular epithet *Machiavellian*. Only an unscrupulous strongman, he concluded, using duplicity and terror, could impose order on so divided and selfish a people. Machiavelli seems to have been in earnest when he advised rulers to discover the advantages of fraud and brutality. He apparently hoped to see a strong ruler emerge from the Medici family. The Medicis, however, were not destined to be Italy's deliverers. The second Medici pope, Clement VII (r. 1523–1534), watched helplessly as Rome was sacked by the army of Emperor Charles V (r. 1519–1556) in 1527, the year of Machiavelli's death.

Revival of Monarchy: Nation Building in the Fifteenth Century

With the emergence of sovereign rulers after 1450, unified national monarchies progressively replaced fragmented and divisive feudal governance, but the dynastic and chivalric ideals of feudalism did not disappear. Minor territorial princes survived, and representative assemblies even grew in influence in some regions. But by the late fifteenth and early sixteenth centuries, the old problem of the one and the many was being decided clearly in favor of monarchy.

In the feudal monarchy of the High Middle Ages, the basic powers of government were divided between the king and his semi-autonomous vassals. The nobility and the towns acted with varying degrees of unity and success through such evolving representative bodies as the English Parliament, the French Estates

Niccolò Machiavelli. Santi di Tito's portrait of Machiavelli, perhaps the most famous Italian political theorist, who advised Renaissance princes to practice artful deception and inspire fear in their subjects if they wished to succeed.
Scala/Art Resource, N.Y.

General, and the Spanish Cortes to thwart the centralization of royal power. However, as a result of the Hundred Years' War and the schism in the church, the landed nobility and the clergy were in decline in the late Middle Ages. The increasingly important towns now began to ally with the king. Loyal, businesswise townspeople, not the nobility and the clergy, staffed the royal offices, becoming the king's lawyers, bookkeepers, military tacticians, and diplomats. This new alliance between king and town would slowly break the bonds of feudal society and make possible the rise of the modern sovereign state.

In a sovereign state, the powers of taxation, war making, and law enforcement are no longer the local right of semi-autonomous vassals but are concentrated in the monarch and exercised by his chosen agents. Taxes, wars, and laws become national rather than merely regional matters. Only as monarchs were able to act independently of the nobility and the representative assemblies could they overcome the decentralization that had been the basic obstacle to nation building.

Monarchies also began to create standing national armies in the fifteenth century. As the noble cavalry receded and the

CHRONOLOGY

Major Political Events of the Italian Renaissance (1375–1527)

1378–1382	Ciompi revolt in Florence
1434	Medici rule in Florence established by Cosimo de' Medici
1454–1455	Treaty of Lodi allies Milan, Naples, and Florence (in effect until 1494)
1494	Charles VIII of France invades Italy
1495	League of Venice unites Venice, Milan, the Papal States, the Holy Roman Empire, and Spain against France
1499	Louis XII invades Milan (the second French invasion of Italy)
1500	The Borgias conquer Romagna
1512–1513	The Holy League (Pope Julius II, Ferdinand of Aragon, Emperor Maximilian I, and Venice) defeat the French
1513	Machiavelli writes *The Prince*
1515	Francis I leads the third French invasion of Italy
1516	Concordat of Bologna between France and the papacy
1527	Sack of Rome by imperial soldiers

infantry and the artillery became the backbone of armies, mercenary soldiers were recruited from Switzerland and Germany to form the mainstay of the "king's army."

The growing cost of warfare increased the need to develop new national sources of royal income. The expansion of royal revenues was especially hampered by the stubborn belief among the highest classes that they were immune from government taxation. The nobility guarded their properties and traditional rights and despised taxation as an insult and a humiliation. Royal revenues accordingly grew at the expense of those least able to resist and least able to pay. Monarchs had several options. As feudal lords they could collect rents from their royal domain. They might also levy national taxes on basic food and clothing, such as the *gabelle* or salt tax in France and the *alcabala* or 10 percent sales tax on commercial transactions in Spain. Kings could also levy direct taxes on the peasantry and on commercial transactions in towns under royal protection. This they did through agreeable representative assemblies of the privileged classes in which the peasantry did not sit. The French *taille* was such a tax. Sale of public offices and the issuance of high-interest government bonds appeared in the fifteenth century as innovative fund-raising devices. But kings did not levy taxes on the powerful nobility. They turned for loans to rich nobles, as they did to the great bankers of Italy and Germany, bargaining with the privileged classes, who often remained as much the kings' creditors and competitors as their subjects.

MEDIEVAL RUSSIA

In the late tenth century Prince Vladimir of Kiev (r. 972–1015), then Russia's dominant city, received delegations of Muslims, Roman Catholics, Jews, and Greek Orthodox Christians, each group hoping to win the Russians to its religion. Prince Vladimir chose Greek Orthodoxy, which became the religion of Russia, adding a new cultural bond to the long-standing commercial ties the Russians had with the Byzantine Empire.

Vladimir's successor, Yaroslav the Wise (r. 1016–1054), developed Kiev into a magnificent political and cultural center, but after his death, rivalry among princes challenged Kiev's dominance, and it became just one of several national centers.

Mongol Rule (1243–1480)   Mongol (or Tatar) armies (see Chapters 8 and 13) invaded Russia in 1223, and Kiev fell in 1240. Russian cities became tribute-paying principalities of the segment of the Mongol Empire called the ***Golden Horde***, which had its capital at Sarai, on the lower Volga.

Mongol rule further divided Russia from the West but left Russian political institutions and religion largely intact. Thanks to their far-flung trade, the Mongolians brought most Russians greater peace and prosperity than they had enjoyed before.

Russian Liberation   The princes of Moscow cooperated with the Mongols and grew wealthy. They then gradually expanded the principality through land purchases, colonization, and conquest.

In 1380 Grand Duke Dimitri of Moscow (1350–1389) defeated Tatar forces at Kulikov Meadow in a victory that marked the beginning of the decline of Mongolian hegemony. Another century would pass before Ivan III, called Ivan the Great (d. 1505), would bring all of northern Russia under Moscow's control and end Mongol rule in 1480. By the last

◀ **Exterior of a Russian Orthodox Church** in Novgorod, Russia
UNESCO, Ann Ronan/ The Image Works.

quarter of the fifteenth century, Moscow had replaced Kiev as the political and religious center of Russia. In Russian eyes it was destined to become the "third Rome" after the fall of Constantinople to the Turks in 1453.

FRANCE

There were two cornerstones of French nation building in the fifteenth century. The first was the collapse of the English holdings in France following the Hundred Years' War. The second was the defeat of Charles the Bold (r. 1467–1477) and the duchy of Burgundy. Perhaps Europe's strongest political power in the mid–fifteenth century, Burgundy aspired to lead a dominant middle kingdom between France and the Holy Roman Empire. It might have succeeded had not the Continental powers joined together in opposition. When Charles the Bold was killed at Nancy in 1477, the dream of Burgundian empire died with him.

The dissolution of Burgundy ended its constant intrigue against the French king and left Louis XI (r. 1461–1483) free to secure the monarchy. The newly acquired Burgundian lands and his own Angevin inheritance permitted the king to double the size of his kingdom. Louis harnessed the nobility and expanded trade and industry.

A strong nation is a two-edged sword. It was because Louis' successors inherited such a secure and efficient government that France was able to pursue Italian conquests in the 1490s and to fight a long series of losing wars with the Habsburgs in the first half of the sixteenth century. By the mid–sixteenth century France was again a defeated nation and almost as divided internally as it had been during the Hundred Years' War.

SPAIN

Spain, too, became a strong country in the late fifteenth century. Both Castile and Aragon had been poorly ruled, divided kingdoms in the mid–fifteenth century. The marriage of Isabella of Castile (r. 1474–1504) and Ferdinand of Aragon (r. 1479–1516) changed that situation. The two future sovereigns married in 1469, despite strong protests from neighboring Portugal and France, both of which foresaw the formidable European power such a union would create. Castile was by far the richer and more populous of the two, having an estimated 5 million inhabitants to Aragon's population of under 1 million. Castile was also distinguished by its lucrative sheep-farming industry, which was run by a government-backed organization called the *Mesta*, another example of developing centralized economic planning. Although the two kingdoms were dynastically united by the marriage of Ferdinand and Isabella in 1469, each retained its own government agencies—separate laws, armies, coinage, and taxation—and cultural traditions.

Ferdinand and Isabella could do together what neither was able to accomplish alone, namely, subdue their realms, secure their borders, and venture abroad militarily. Townspeople allied themselves with the crown and progressively replaced the nobility within the royal administration. The crown also extended its authority over the wealthy chivalric orders, a further circumscription of the power of the nobility.

Spain had long been remarkable as a place where three religions—Islam, Judaism, and Christianity—coexisted with a certain degree of toleration. This toleration ended dramatically under Ferdinand and Isabella, who made Spain the prime example of state-controlled religion. Ferdinand and Isabella exercised almost total control over the Spanish church as they placed religion in the service of national unity. They appointed the higher clergy and the officers of the Inquisition. The Inquisition, run by Tomás de Torquemada (d. 1498), Isabella's confessor, was a key national agency established in 1479 to monitor the activity of converted Jews (*conversos*) and Muslims (*Moriscos*) in Spain. In 1492 the Jews were exiled and their properties were confiscated. In 1502 nonconverting Moors in Granada were driven into exile. Spanish spiritual life remained largely uniform and regimented, a major reason for Spain's remaining a loyal Catholic country throughout the sixteenth century and providing a base of operation for the European Counter-Reformation.

Ferdinand and Isabella had wide horizons. They contracted anti-French marriage alliances that came to determine much of European history in the sixteenth century. In 1496 their eldest daughter, Joanna, later known as "the Mad" (1479–1555), married Archduke Philip (1478–1506), the son of Emperor Maximilian I (r. 1493–1519). Their son, Charles I, the first ruler over a united Spain, came by his inheritance and election as Emperor Charles V in 1519 to rule over a European kingdom almost equal in size to that of Charlemagne. A second daughter, Catherine of Aragon (1485–1536), married King Henry VIII of England. The failure of this latter marriage became the key factor in the emergence of the Anglican Church and the English Reformation.

The new Spanish power was also evident in Ferdinand and Isabella's promotion of overseas exploration. Their patronage of the Genoese adventurer Christopher Columbus (1451–1506), who discovered the islands of the Caribbean while sailing west in search of a shorter route to the spice markets of the Far East, led to the creation of the Spanish Empire in Mexico and Peru, whose gold and silver mines helped to make Spain Europe's dominant power in the sixteenth century.

ENGLAND

The last half of the fifteenth century was a period of especially difficult political trial for the English. Following the Hundred Years' War, a defeated England was subjected to internal warfare between two rival branches of the royal family, the House of York and the House of Lancaster. This conflict, known to us today as the Wars of the Roses (as York's symbol, according to legend, was a white rose, and Lancaster's a red rose), kept England in turmoil from 1455 to 1485.

The Lancastrian monarchy of Henry VI (r. 1422–1461) was consistently challenged by the Duke of York and his supporters in the prosperous southern towns. In 1461 Edward IV (r. 1461–1483), son of the Duke of York, seized power and, assisted by loyal and able ministers, effectively bent Parliament to his will. His brother and successor was Richard III (r. 1483–1485), whose reign saw the growth of support for the exiled Lancastrian Henry Tudor. Henry returned to England to defeat Richard on Bosworth Field in August 1485.

Henry Tudor ruled as Henry VII (r. 1485–1509), the first of the new Tudor dynasty that would endure until 1603. To bring the rival royal families together and to make the hereditary claim of his offspring to the throne uncontestable, Henry married Edward IV's daughter, Elizabeth of York. He succeeded in disciplining the English nobility through a special and much-feared instrument of the royal will known as the Court of Star Chamber. Henry shrewdly construed legal precedents to the advantage of the crown, using English law to further his own ends. He confiscated so much noble land and so many fortunes that he governed without dependence on Parliament for royal funds, always a cornerstone of strong monarchy. Henry thus began to shape a monarchy that became one of early modern Europe's most exemplary governments during the reign of his granddaughter, Elizabeth I (r. 1558–1603).

Tres Riches Heures du Duc de Berry.

Summary

Medieval Society   In theory, medieval society was divided into three main groups: clergy (those who prayed), nobility (those who fought as mounted warriors), and laborers (peasants and artisans). The rise of merchants, self-governing towns, and universities helped break down this division. By supporting rulers against the nobility, towns gave kings the resources—money and university-trained bureaucrats and lawyers—to build national governments. Much of medieval history involved the struggle by rulers to assert their authority over powerful local lords and the church.

Church and State   The medieval papacy sought to extend its power over both church and state. In the tenth century, the Cluny reform movement increased popular respect for the church and strengthened the papacy. In the Investiture Struggle, the papacy secured the independence of the clergy by enlisting the support of the German princes against the Holy Roman Emperors, thus weakening imperial power in Germany. The First Crusade further strengthened papal prestige. But, by the end of the thirteenth century, kings had become more powerful than popes, and the French king, Philip the Fair, was able to defy the papacy. In the fourteenth century, the Great Schism further weakened papal prestige. Although it was able to fend off a movement to make church councils superior to popes, the papacy never recovered its authority over national rulers.

The Renaissance   The Renaissance, which began in the Italian city-states in the late fourteenth century, marks the transition from the medieval to the modern world. Humanism, the scholarly study of the Greek and Latin classics and the ancient Church fathers, promoted a rebirth of ancient norms and values and the classical ideal of an educated, well-rounded person. The growth of secular values led to a great burst of artistic activity by artists such as da Vinci, Raphael, and Michelangelo. The political weakness of the Italian states invited foreign intervention by France, Spain, and the Habsburgs. The sack of Rome by imperial forces in 1527 marks the end of the Renaissance.

Nation Building   By the fifteenth century, England, France, and Spain had developed into strong national monarchies with centralized bureaucracies and professional armies. Although medieval institutions, such as the English Parliament, in theory limited royal power, in practice monarchs in these countries held unchallenged authority. The Great Schism, the Hundred Years' War, and the Black Death had weakened the church and the nobility, while townspeople supported the kings. A similar process was beginning in Russia where the rulers of Moscow were extending their authority after throwing off Mongol rule. In the Empire, however, regional lords had defeated the emperors' attempts to build a strong central state.

Review Questions

1. How do you account for the success of the Cluny reform movement? Can major features of the modern Catholic Church be found in the Cluny reforms?

2. Was the Investiture Controversy a political or a religious conflict? Summarize the respective arguments of Gregory VII and Henry IV. Is the conflict a precedent for the modern doctrine of the separation of church and state?

3. Why did Germany remain divided while France and England began to coalesce into reasonably strong states during the High Middle Ages?

4. How did the responsibilities of the nobility differ from those of the clergy and the peasantry during the High Middle Ages? How did each social class contribute to the stability of society?

5. Describe the circumstances that gave rise to towns. How did towns change traditional medieval society?

6. How did the Hundred Years' War, the Black Death, and the Great Schism in the church affect the course of history? Which had the most lasting effects on the institutions it touched?

7. Was the church an aggressor or a victim in the late Middle Ages and the Renaissance? How successful was it in its confrontations with Europe's emerging dynastic states?

8. What was "reborn" in the Renaissance? Were the humanists the forerunners of modern secular education and culture, or eloquent defenders of a still-medieval Christian view of the world against the church's secular and pagan critics?

9. Historians find features of modern states developing in Europe during the late Middle Ages and Renaissance. What modern features can you identify in the governments of the Italian city-states and the northern monarchies? In Russia?

Key Terms

Black Death (p. 419)

chiaroscuro (p. 425)

Crusades (p. 405)

Curia (p. 422)

Golden Horde (p. 428)

Great Schism (p. 422)

guilds (p. 410)

Holy Roman Empire (p. 422)

humanism (p. 423)

Magna Carta (p. 416)

mannerism (p. 426)

regular clergy (p. 413)

Renaissance (p. 422)

Scholasticism (p. 410)

secular clergy (p. 413)

studia humanitatis (p. 423)

taille (p. 420)

vernacular (p. 403)

Documents CD-ROM

Mediterranean Civilization after the Fall of Rome

7.6 Launching the Crusades (1095): "It is the Will of God!"

The Formation of European Civilization

10.1 St. Hidegard of Bingen, Know the Ways

10.2 St. Francis of Assisi, "The Rule of St. Francis"

10.3 The Goodman of Paris

10.4 The Love of God

10.5 St. Thomas Aquinas

10.6 Unam Sanctam (1302): Pope Boniface VIII

10.7 "A Most Terrible Plague": Giovanni Boccaccio

Renaissance and Reformation in Europe

13.1 Oration on the Dignity of Man (1486)

13.2 The Soul of Man (1474)

13.3 Castiglione's "Courtier": Prosperity Makes a Gentleman

Eurasian Connections before European Expansion

11.4 The Mongol Khan's Ultimatum to the Nations of Europe

11.5 Kuyuk Khan, Letter to Pope Innocent IV

NOTE: *To learn more about the topics in this chapter, see the Suggested Readings at the end of the book.*

The sixteenth through the eighteenth centuries were a period of great transition in world history, both in terms of social change and in the expansion of trade and migration. The European voyages of discovery and subsequent colonization of the New World created a new transatlantic economy linking the world's oceans for the first time.

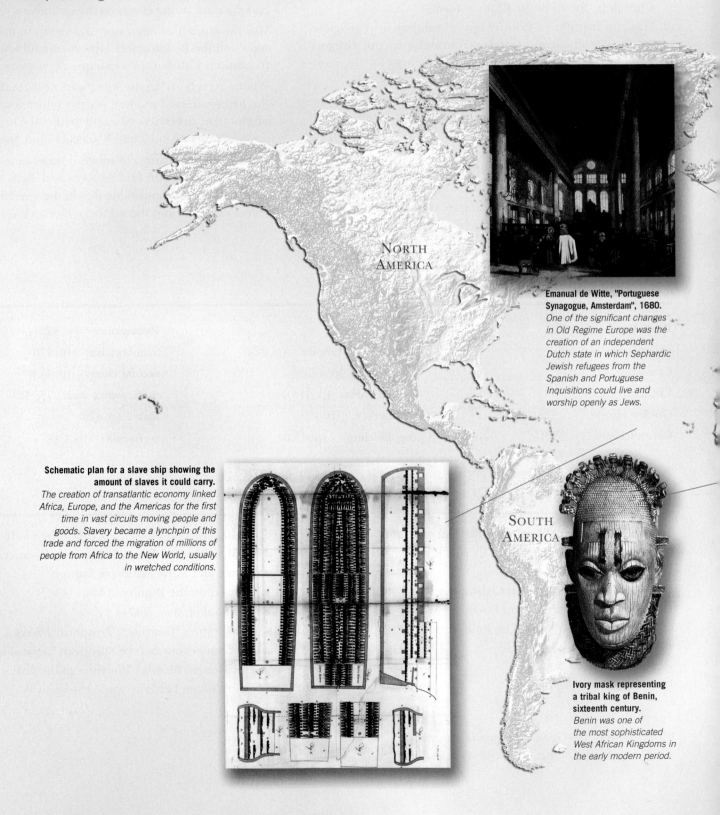

NORTH AMERICA

Emanual de Witte, "Portuguese Synagogue, Amsterdam", 1680.
One of the significant changes in Old Regime Europe was the creation of an independent Dutch state in which Sephardic Jewish refugees from the Spanish and Portuguese Inquisitions could live and worship openly as Jews.

Schematic plan for a slave ship showing the amount of slaves it could carry.
The creation of transatlantic economy linked Africa, Europe, and the Americas for the first time in vast circuits moving people and goods. Slavery became a lynchpin of this trade and forced the migration of millions of people from Africa to the New World, usually in wretched conditions.

SOUTH AMERICA

Ivory mask representing a tribal king of Benin, sixteenth century.
Benin was one of the most sophisticated West African Kingdoms in the early modern period.

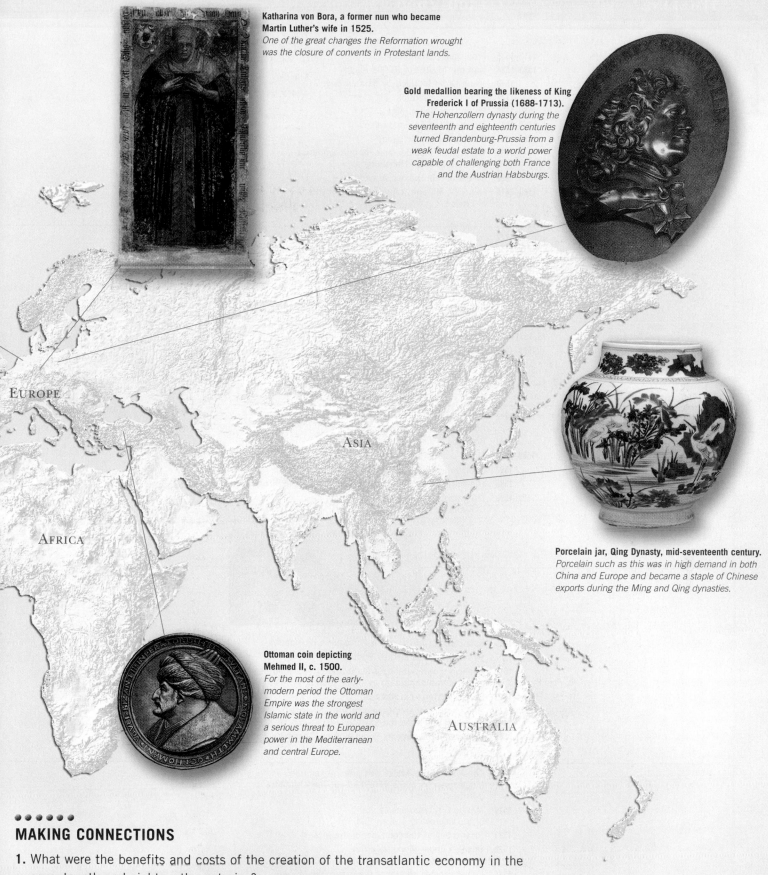

Katharina von Bora, a former nun who became Martin Luther's wife in 1525.
One of the great changes the Reformation wrought was the closure of convents in Protestant lands.

Gold medallion bearing the likeness of King Frederick I of Prussia (1688-1713).
The Hohenzollern dynasty during the seventeenth and eighteenth centuries turned Brandenburg-Prussia from a weak feudal estate to a world power capable of challenging both France and the Austrian Habsburgs.

EUROPE

ASIA

AFRICA

Porcelain jar, Qing Dynasty, mid-seventeenth century.
Porcelain such as this was in high demand in both China and Europe and became a staple of Chinese exports during the Ming and Qing dynasties.

Ottoman coin depicting Mehmed II, c. 1500.
For the most of the early-modern period the Ottoman Empire was the strongest Islamic state in the world and a serious threat to European power in the Mediterranean and central Europe.

AUSTRALIA

MAKING CONNECTIONS

1. What were the benefits and costs of the creation of the transatlantic economy in the seventeenth and eighteenth centuries?

2. How did shifts in the balance of power alter societies around the world between 1500 and 1800?

PART 4

THE WORLD IN TRANSITION

EUROPE

1517–1555	Protestant Reformation
1533–1584	Ivan the Terrible of Russia reigns
1540	Jesuit Order founded by Ignatius Loyola
1543–1727	Scientific Revolution
1556–1598	Philip II of Spain reigns
1558–1603	Elizabeth I of England reigns
1562–1598	French Wars of Religion
1581	The Netherlands declares its independence from the Spanish Habsburgs
1588	Defeat of the Spanish Armada
1589–1610	Henry IV, Navarre, founds Bourbon dynasty of France

▲ Queen Elizabeth I

NEAR EAST/INDIA

1500–1722	Safavid Shi'ite rule in Iran
1512–1520	Ottoman ruler Selim I
1520–1566	Ottoman ruler Suleiman the Magnificent
1525–1527	Babur founds Mughai dynasty in India
1540	Hungary under Ottoman rule
1556–1605	Akbar the Great of India reigns
1571	Battle of Lepanto; Ottomans defeated
ca. 1571–1640	Safavid philosopher-writer Mullah Sadra
1588–1629	Shah Abbas I of Iran reigns

Leaf from "Divan" ▶
by the poet, Hafiz

EAST ASIA

1500–1800	Commercial revolution in Ming-Qing China; trade with Europe; flourishing of the novel
1543	Portuguese arrive in Japan
1568–1600	Era of unification follows end of Warring States Era in Japan
1587	Spanish arrive in Japan
1588	Hideyoshi's sword hunt in Japan
1592–1598	Ming troops battle Hideyoshi's army in Korea

AFRICA

Feluccas ▶
on the Nile

1506	East coast of Africa under Portuguese domination
1507	Mozambique founded by Portuguese
1517	Spanish crown authorizes slave trade to its South American colonies; rapid increase in importation of slaves to the New World
1554–1659	Sa'did Sultanate in Morocco
1575	Union of Bornu and Kanem by Idris Alawma (r. 1575–1610); Kanem-Bornu state the most fully Islamic in West Africa
1591	Moroccan army defeats Songhai army; Songhai Empire collapses

THE AMERICAS

1519	Conquest of the Aztecs by Cortes; Aztec ruler, Montezuma (r. 1502–1519) killed; Tenochtitlán destroyed
1529	Mexico City becomes capital of the viceroyalty of New Spain
1533	Pizarro begins his conquest of the Incas
1536	Spanish under Mendoza arrive in Argentina
1544	Lima becomes capital of the viceroyalty of Peru
1584	Sir Walter Raleigh sends expedition to Roanoke Island (North Carolina)

◀ Algonquin village of Secotton

▲ Aztec drawing of Spanish conquest of Mexico

1618–1648	Thirty Years' War
1640–1688	Frederick William, the Great Elector, reigns in Brandenburg-Prussia
1642–1646	Puritan Revolution in England
1643–1715	Louis XIV of France reigns
1682–1725	Peter the Great of Russia reigns
1688	Glorious Revolution in England
1690	"Second Treatise of Civil Government," by John Locke

◄ Louis XIV of France

1701	Act of Settlement provides for Protestant succession to English throne
1702–1713	War of Spanish Succession
1740–1748	War of Austrian Succession
1756–1763	Seven Years' War
ca. 1750	Industrial Revolution begins in England
1772	First partition of Poland
1789	First French Revolution
1793 and 1795	Last two partitions of Poland

▲ "Evening" by Francis Wheatley

1628–1657	Shah Jahan reigns; builds Taj Mahal as mausoleum for his beloved wife
1646	Founding of Maratha Empire
1648	Delhi becomes the capital of Mughal Empire
1658–1707	Shah Aurangzeb, the "World Conqueror," reigns in India; end of religious toleration toward Hindus; beginning Mughal decline
1669–1683	Last military expansion by Ottomans: 1669, seize Crete; 1670s, the Ukraine; 1683, Vienna

▲ The Taj Mahal

1700	Sikhs and Marathas bring down Mughal Imperial Power
1708	British East India Company and New East India Company merge
1722	Last Safavid ruler forced to abdicate
1724	Rise in the Deccan of the Islamic state of Hyderabad
1725	Nadir Shah of Afganhistan becomes ruler of Persia
1739	Persian invasion of northern India, by Nadir Shah
1748–1761	Ahmad Shah Durrani of Afghanistan invades India
1757	British victory at Plassey, in Bengal

1600	Tokugawa Ieyasu wins battle of Sekigahara, completes unification of Japan
1600–1868	Tokugawa shogunate in Edo
1630s	Seclusion adopted as national policy in Japan
1644–1694	Bashō, Japanese poet
1644–1911	Qing (Manchu) dynasty in China
1661–1722	Kangxi reign in China
1673–1681	Revolt of southern generals in China
1699	British East India Company arrives in China

◄ "White Heron" castle in Jimeji

1701	Forty-seven rō-nin incident in Japan
1716–1733	Reforms of Tokugawa Yoshimune in Japan
1737–1795	Reign of Qianlong in China
1742	Christianity banned in China
1784	American traders arrive in China
1787–1793	Matsudaira Sadanobu's reforms in Japan
1798	White Lotus Rebellion in China

Manchu emperor ▶ Qianlong

1600s	English, Dutch, and French enter the slave trade; slaves imported to sugar plantations in the Caribbean
1619	First African slaves in North America land in Virginia
1652	First Cape Colony settlement of Dutch East India Company
1660–1856	Omani domination of East Africa; Omani state centered in Zanzibar; 1698, takes Mozambique from Portuguese

◄ Slave labor on sugar plantation in Brazil and the West Indies

1702	Asiento Guinea Trade Company founded for slave trade between Africa and the Americas
1700s	Transatlantic slave trade at Its height
1741–1856	United Sultanate of Oman and Zanzibar
1754–1817	Usman Dan Fodio, founder of sultanate in northern and central Nigeria; the Fulani become the ruling class in the region
1762	End of Funj Sultanate in eastern Sudanic region

◄ The Friday Mosque at Shela

1607	The London Company establishes Jamestown Colony (Virginia)
1608	Champlain founds Quebec
1619	Slave labor introduced at Jamestown (Virginia)

1733	Georgia founded as last English colony in North America
1739–1763	Era of trade wars in Americas between Great Britain and the French and Spanish
1763	Peace of Paris establishes British government in Canada
1776–1781	American Revolution
1783–1830	Simón Bolívar, Latin American soldier, statesman
1789	U.S. Constitution
1791	Negro slave revolt in French Santo Domingo
1791	Canada Constitution Act divides the country into Upper and Lower Canada

16

Europe 1500–1650:

Expansion, Reformation, and Religious Wars

◄ THE MIRACLE OF ST. IGNATIUS OF LAYOLA by Peter Poul Rubens. Here, the founder of the Society of Jesus, surrounded by angels and members of the new order, preaches to an aroused assembly.

Erich Lessing/Art Resource, N.Y.

GLOBAL PERSPECTIVE

European Expansion

In the late fifteenth and the sixteenth centuries, Europeans sailed far from their own shores, reaching Africa, southern and eastern Asia, and the New World of the Americas. From Japan to Peru, they now directly confronted for the first time civilizations other than their own and that of Islam, with which they had already been in contact in the form of trade and, more often, military confrontation. A major motivation for the voyages, which began with a reconnaissance of the coast of West Africa, was to find a way to circumvent the monopoly Muslim merchants had over the movement of spices from the Indian Ocean into Europe, a grip that only strengthened with the rise of the Ottomans. A wealthier, more self-confident Europe, now recovered from the devastating plague-induced population decline of the fourteenth century, its taste for Asian spices long since whetted during the Crusades, was ready to go to the sources of those spices itself.

Voyages of exploration also set forth from Ming China, especially between 1405 and 1433, reaching India, the Arabian Gulf, and East Africa. If followed up, they might have prevented Europeans from establishing a presence in the Indian Ocean. The Chinese now faced both serious pressures on their northern and western borders and the problem of administrating a vast, multicultural empire stretching into Central Asia, where non-Chinese rivals had to be kept under control. Moreover, the dominant Neo-Confucian philosophy espoused by the scholar-bureaucrats in the imperial court disdained merchants and commerce, extolling instead a peasant agrarian economy.

These factors led the Chinese to turn inward and abandon overseas trade and exploration precisely at the moment when Europeans were exploring the coast of Africa on their way to the Indian Ocean. It was a fateful choice, because it meant that the Asian power best able to resist the establishment of European commercial and colonial empires in the Indian Ocean, had abdicated that role, leaving a vacuum of power for Europeans to fill. Still, Chinese merchants continued to ply ocean

trade routes and settle as far from home as the Philippines and, in later centuries, the West Coasts of North and South America. Wherever there was commerce in Chinese goods, there were Chinese merchants, albeit now operating without support from their government.

Although parallels may be drawn between the court culture of the Forbidden Palace in Beijing and that of King Louis XIV in seventeenth-century France, the Chinese government with its philosophy of Confucianism remained more unified and patriarchal than its counterparts in the West. The Chinese, at first, readily tolerated other religions, warmly embracing Jesuit missionaries, doing so in part because political power in China was not bound to a particular religion. The Japanese were also admirers of the Jesuits, who arrived in Japan with the Portuguese in 1543. The admiration was mutual, leading to three hundred thousand Christian converts by 1600. Tolerance of Christianity did not last as long in Japan as in China. Hideyoshi, in his drive for internal unity, banned Christianity in the late sixteenth century. Nonetheless China and Japan, as well as many Islamic societies, including the Ottomans and the Mughals, demonstrated more tolerance for foreign religions, such as Christianity, than did the West for Islam, or Asian religious traditions.

THINK AHEAD

◆ Why did the Europeans launch voyages of exploration in the fifteenth and sixteenth centuries? What role did the Crusades and the rise of the Ottoman Empire play in this enterprise?

◆ Why did the Chinese voyages of exploration under the Ming come to a halt? What were the consequences for the history of the Indian Ocean?

◆ How did the Chinese and Japanese react to the introduction of Christianity?

IN THE SECOND DECADE OF THE SIXTEENTH CENTURY, a powerful religious movement began in Saxony in Germany and rapidly spread throughout northern Europe, deeply affecting society and politics as well as the spiritual lives of men and women. Attacking what they believed to be burdensome superstitions and corrupt practices that robbed people of both their money and their peace of mind, Protestant reformers led a revolt against the medieval church. In a short period of time, hundreds of thousands of people from all social classes set aside the beliefs of centuries and adopted a more simplified religious practice.

The Protestant Reformation challenged aspects of the Renaissance, especially its tendency to follow classical sources in glorifying human nature and its loyalty to traditional religion. Protestants were more impressed by the human potential for evil than by the inclination to do good, and encouraged parents, teachers, and magistrates to be firm disciplinarians. On the other hand, Protestants also embraced many Renaissance values, especially humanist educational reforms and in the study of ancient languages. Here they found tools to master Scripture and challenge the papacy.

Protestantism was not the only reform movement to grow out of the religious grievances and reforms of the late Middle Ages. Within the church itself a reform was emerging that would give birth to new religious orders, rebut Protestantism, and win back a great many of its converts.

As different groups identified their political and social goals with either Protestantism or Catholicism, a hundred years of bloody opposition between Protestants and Catholics darkened the second half of the sixteenth century and the first half of the seventeenth. The political conflict that had previously been confined to central Europe and a struggle for Lutheran rights and freedoms then shifted to Western Europe—to France, the Netherlands, England, and Scotland—and became a struggle for Calvinist recognition. In France Calvinists fought Catholic rulers for the right to form their own communities, practice their chosen religion openly, and exclude from their lands those they deemed heretical. During the Thirty Years' War (1618–1648), international armies of varying religious persuasions clashed in central and northern Europe. By 1649 English Puritans had overthrown the Stuart monarchy and the Anglican Church.

For Europe the late fifteenth and the sixteenth centuries were a period of unprecedented territorial expansion. Permanent colonies were established in the Americas and the exploitation of the New World's human and mineral resources begun. Imported American gold and silver spurred scientific invention and a new weapons industry. The new bullion helped create an international traffic in African slaves as rival tribes eagerly sold their captives to the Portuguese. Slaves came in ever-increasing numbers to work the mines and the plantations of the New World as replacements for faltering American natives.

The Discovery of a New World

The discovery of the Americas dramatically expanded the horizons of Europeans, both geographical and intellectual. Knowledge of the New World's inhabitants and exploitation of its mineral and human wealth set new cultural and economic forces in motion throughout Western Europe. Beginning with the successful voyages of the Portuguese and Spanish in the fifteenth century, commercial supremacy progressively shifted from the Mediterranean and Baltic Seas to the Atlantic seaboard, setting the stage for global expansion (see Map 16–1).

The Portuguese Chart the Course Seventy-seven years before Columbus, who sailed under the flag of Spain, set foot in the Americas, Prince Henry "the Navigator" (1394–1406), ruler of a stong and united Portugal, captured the West African Muslim city of Ceuta at the mouth of the Mediterranean Sea.

There began the Portuguese exploration of the African coast, first in search of Guinea gold and slaves, and by century's end a sea route to Asia's spice markets. Topping the list of spices were pepper and cloves as they both preserved and enhanced the dull diet of most Europeans. Initially the catch of raiders, African slaves were soon taken effortlessly by Portuguese traders in direct exchanges with tribal chiefs, who readily swapped their captured enemies for horses, corn, and finished goods (cloth and brassware). Over the second half of the fifteenth century, Portuguese ships delivered 150,000 slaves to Europe.

Before there was a sea route to the Orient, spices could only be obtained through the Venetians, who bought or bartered them from Eastern Muslim merchants. This was a powerful Venetian-Mameluke (Turkish) monopoly the Portuguese resolved to beat by going directly to the source by sea. Overland

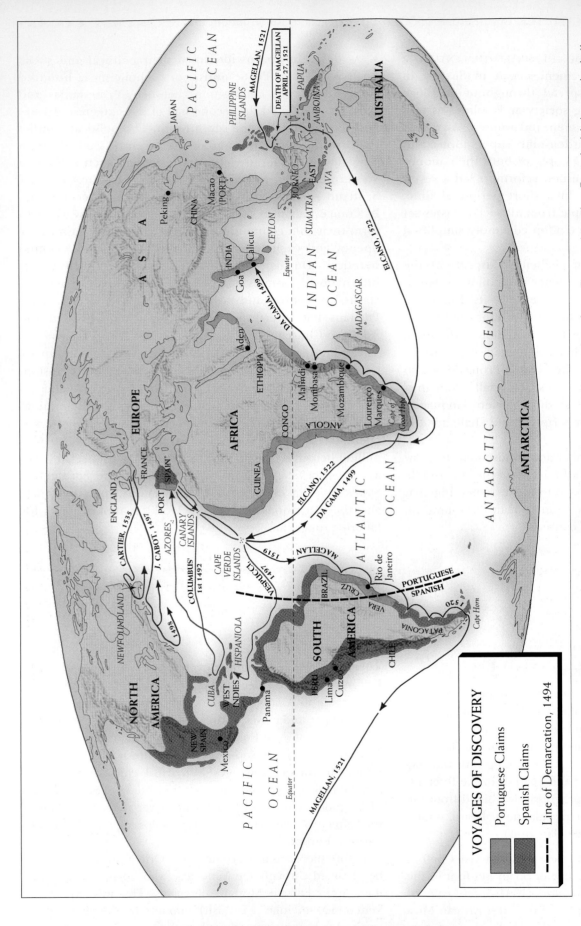

MAP 16–1 European Voyages of Discovery and the Colonial Claims of Spain and Portugal in the Fifteenth and Sixteenth Centuries.   The map dramatizes Europe's global expansion in the fifteenth and sixteenth centuries.

routes to India and China had long existed, but their transit had become too difficult and unprofitable by the fifteenth century. The route by sea posed a different obstacle and risk: fear of the unknown, making the first voyages of exploration slow and tentative. Venturing down the African coast Portuguese square riggers were turned out into the deep ocean by cape after cape, and the farther out they sailed to round them, the greater the sailors' fear that they would not have the sail power to return home. Each cape successfully rounded became a victory and a lesson, allowing the crews to discover the rigging and the skills they would need to cross the oceans to the Americas and the Orient.

In addition to spice markets, the voyages of discovery also sought allies against Western Europe's archenemies, the Muslims.

In 1455, a very self-interested pope gave the Portuguese explorers virtual carte blanche from the coast of Guinea to the Indies, granting them all the spoils of war: land, goods, and slaves. The church expected mass conversions in the wake of conquest, a Christian coup as well as mercantile advantage. The explorers also kept an eye out for a reportedly friendly Eastern potentate known as Prester John. Rumored to be a potential Christian ally against the Muslim infidel, he was real enough for Vasco da Gama to carry a letter of introduction to him from the Portuguese king, when he sailed East in 1497.

Bartholomew Dias pioneered the eastern Portuguese Empire after safely rounding the Cape of Good Hope at the tip of Africa in 1487. A decade later, in 1498, Vasco da

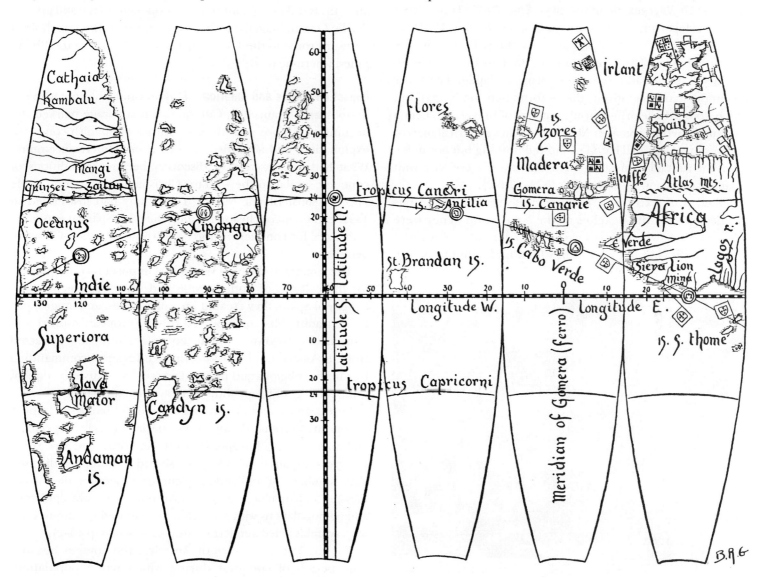

▲ **Martin Behaim's "Globe Apple."** What Columbus knew of the world in 1492 was contained in this map by Nuremberg geographer Martin Behaim (1440–1507), creator of the first spherical globe of the earth. The ocean section of Behaim's globe is reproduced here. Departing the Canary Islands (in the second section from the right), Columbus expected his first major landfall to be Japan, or what he calls Cipangu (in the second section from the left). When he landed at San Salvador, he thought he was on an outer island of Japan; after reaching Cuba, he believed it to be Japan. Only slowly did it dawn on him that these new lands had never before been seen by Europeans.

From Admiral of the Ocean Sea by Samuel Eliot Morison. Copyright 1942 © renewed 1970 by Samuel Eliot Morison. By permission of Little, Brown and Company, Boston, MA.

Gama stood on the shores of India. When he returned to Portugal, he carried a cargo worth sixty times the cost of the voyage. Later, the Portuguese established successful colonies in Goa and Calcutta, whence they successfully challenged the Arabs and the Venetians for control of the European spice trade.

The Portuguese had concentrated their explorations on the Indian Ocean. Initially following in their wake, the Spanish turned out into the Atlantic Ocean, believing they could find a shorter route to the East Indies by sailing due West. Rather than beating the Portuguese to Asia, Columbus instead discovered the Americas—although he did not know that on his first voyage.

The Spanish Voyages of Christopher Columbus Thirty-three days after departing the Canary Islands, on October 12, 1492, Columbus landed in San Salvador (Watlings Island) in the eastern Bahamas. Thinking he was in the East Indies, he mistook his first landfall as an outer island of Japan. The error was understandable given the information he relied on: Marco Polo's thirteenth-century account of his years in China and Nuremberg mapmaker Martin Behaim's spherical map of the presumed world. That map showed nothing but ocean between the west coast of Europe and the east coast of Asia, with Cipangu, or Japan, in between (see Map 16-2).

Naked and extremely friendly natives met Columbus and his crew on the beaches of the New World. They were Taino Indians, who spoke a variant of a language known as Arawak. Believing the island on which he landed to be the

▲ **Magellan's Global Circumnavigation.** An imaginative portrayal of Portuguese explorer Ferdinand Magellan's circumnavigation of the globe amid fires, monsters, mythological figures, guided by a naked angel with a harp and halo.
The Mariners' Museum, Newport News, VA.

East Indies, Columbus called the native people who met him Indians, a name that stuck even after it was known that he had actually discovered a new continent. The natives' generosity amazed Columbus, as they freely gave his men all the corn and yams they desired, along with many sexual favors. "They never say no," Columbus marveled, as he observed how easily they could be enslaved by the Spanish.

On the heels of Columbus, Amerigo Vespucci (1451–1512), after whom America is named, and Ferdinand Magellan (1480–1521) carefully explored the coastline of South America. Their travels proved that the new lands discovered by Columbus were not the outermost territory of the Far East, but an entirely unknown continent that opened on the still greater Pacific Ocean. Magellan, who was continuing the search for a westward route to the Indies, made it all the way to the Philippines, where he died.

Impact on Europe and America Unknowingly to those who undertook and financed it, Columbus's first voyage marked the beginning of more than three centuries of Spanish conquest, exploitation, and administration of a vast American empire. What began as voyages of discovery became expeditions of conquest similar to the warfare Christian Aragon and Castile waged against Islamic Moors. Those wars had just ended in 1492, and their conclusion imbued the early Spanish explorers with a zeal for conquering and converting other non-Christian peoples.

The voyages to the New World had important consequences for the cultures of both Europe and America. Much to the benefit of Spain, they created Europe's largest and longest surviving trading bloc and spurred other European countries to undertake their own colonial ventures. The wealth extracted from its American possessions financed Spain's commanding role in the religious and political wars of the sixteenth century, while fueling a Europe-wide economic expansion.

European expansion also had a profound biological impact. Europeans introduced numerous species of fruits, vegetables, and animals from Europe, into the Americas, and vice versa. European expansion also led to a spread of European diseases. Vast numbers of indigenous American peoples died from measles and smallpox, which broke out in massive epidemics among populations with no natural or acquired immunity. Likewise, syphillis killed a million Europeans (see Map 16–2).

For the native peoples of America, the voyages began a long period of conquest during which native populations were devastated by warfare, new diseases, and slave labor. In both South and North America, Spanish rule left a lasting footprint of Roman Catholicism, economic dependency, and hierarchical social structure, all of which is still visible today (see Chapter 18).

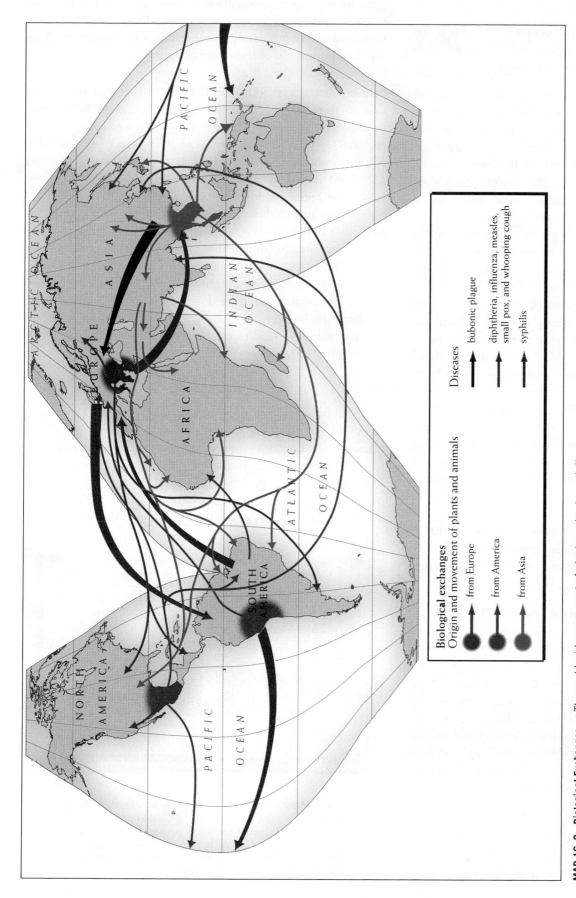

MAP 16–2 Biological Exchanges. The world-wide movement of plants, animals, and diseases.

Biological exchanges
Origin and movement of plants and animals

○→ from Europe

○→ from America

○→ from Asia

Diseases

↑ bubonic plague

↑ diphtheria, influenza, measles, small pox, and whooping cough

↑ syphilis

The Reformation

The **Reformation** was the sixteenth-century religious movement that sought to reform the Church and led to the establishment of Protestantism. It began in Germany.

Religion and Society   The Reformation broke out first in the free imperial cities of Germany and Switzerland. There were about sixty-five such cities, and each was in a sense a little kingdom unto itself. Most had Protestant movements, but with mixed success and duration. Some quickly turned Protestant and remained so. Some were Protestant only for a short time. Others developed mixed confessions, frowning on sectarianism and aggressive proselytizing, letting Catholics and Protestants coexist.

What seemed a life-and-death struggle with higher princely or royal authority was not the only conflict cities were experiencing. They also suffered deep internal social and political divisions. Certain groups favored the Reformation more than others. In many places, guilds like that of the printers, whose members were prospering both socially and economically and who had a history of conflict with local authority, were in the forefront of the Reformation. Evidence suggests that people who felt pushed around and bullied by either local or distant authority—a guild by an autocratic local government, a city or region by a prince or king—perceived in the Protestant movement an ally, at least initially.

Social and political experience thus coalesced with the larger religious issues in both town and countryside. When Martin Luther and his comrades wrote, preached, and sang about a priesthood of all believers, scorned the authority of ecclesiastical landlords, and ridiculed papal laws as arbitrary human inventions, they touched political as well as religious nerves in German and Swiss cities. This was also true in the villages, for the peasants on the land also heard in the Protestant sermon and pamphlet a promise of political liberation and even a degree of social betterment.

Popular Movements and Criticism of the Church   The Protestant Reformation could also not have occurred without the monumental crises of the late medieval church and the Renaissance papacy. For many people, the church had ceased to provide a viable foundation for religious piety. Laity and clerics alike began to seek a more heartfelt, idealistic, and often—in the eyes of the pope—increasingly heretical religious piety. The late Middle Ages were marked by independent lay and clerical efforts to reform local religious practice and by widespread experimentation with new religious forms that shared a common goal of religious simplicity in imitation of Christ.

A variety of factors contributed to the growth of lay criticism of the church. The laity in the cities were becoming increasingly knowledgeable about the world and those who controlled their lives. They traveled widely—as soldiers, pilgrims, explorers, and traders. New postal systems and the printing press increased the information at their disposal. The new age of books and libraries raised literacy and heightened curiosity. Laypersons were increasingly able to take the initiative in shaping the cultural life of their communities.

Secular Control over Religious Life   On the eve of the Reformation, Rome's international network of church offices began to fall apart in many areas, hurried along by a growing sense of regional identity—incipient nationalism—and local secular administrative competence. The late medieval church had permitted important ecclesiastical posts ("benefices") to be sold to the highest bidders and had not enforced residency requirements in parishes. Rare was the late medieval German town that did not have complaints about the maladministration, concubinage, or fiscalism of its clergy, especially the higher clergy (bishops, abbots, and prelates).

City governments also sought to restrict the growth of ecclesiastical properties and clerical privileges and to improve local religious life by bringing the clergy under the local tax code and by endowing new clerical positions for well-trained and conscientious preachers.

THE NORTHERN RENAISSANCE

The scholarly works of northern humanists created a climate favorable to religious and educational reforms. Northern humanism was initially stimulated by the importation of Italian learning through such varied intermediaries as students who had studied in Italy, merchants, and the Brothers of the Common Life. The northern humanists tended to come from more diverse social backgrounds and to be more devoted to reli-

▲ **Gutenberg Bible.** The printing press made possible the diffusion of Renaissance learning. But no book stimulated thought more at this time than did the Bible. With Gutenberg's publication of a printed Bible in 1454, scholars gained access to a dependable, standardized text, so that Scripture could be discussed and debated as never before.
The Pierpont Morgan Library/Art Resource/N.Y.

gious reforms than were their Italian counterparts. They were also more willing to write for lay audiences.

The growth of schools and lay education combined with the invention of cheap paper to create a mass audience for printed books. In response, Johann Gutenberg (d. 1468) invented printing with movable type in the German city of Mainz around 1450. Thereafter, books were rapidly and handsomely produced on topics both profound and practical. By 1500, printing presses operated in at least 60 German cities and in more than 200 throughout Europe. A new medium now existed for politicians, humanists, and reformers alike.

The most famous of the northern humanists was Desiderius Erasmus (1466–1536), the "prince of the humanists." Idealistic and pacifistic, Erasmus gained fame as both an educational and a religious reformer. He aspired to unite the classical ideals of humanity and civic virtue with the Christian ideals of love and piety. He believed that disciplined study of the classics and the Bible, if begun early enough, was the best way to reform both individuals and society. He summarized his own beliefs with the phrase *philosophia Christi*, a simple, ethical piety in imitation of Christ. He set this ideal against what he believed to be the dogmatic, ceremonial, and factious religious practice of the late Middle Ages. To promote his own religious beliefs, Erasmus edited the works of the Church Fathers and made a Greek edition of the New Testament (1516), which became the basis for a new, more accurate Latin translation (1519). Martin Luther later used both these works as the basis for his famous German translation.

The best known of early English humanists was Sir Thomas More (1478–1535), a close friend of Erasmus. It was while visiting More that Erasmus wrote his most famous work, *The Praise of Folly* (1511), an amusing and profound exposé of human self-deception that was quickly translated from the original Latin into many vernacular languages. More's *Utopia* (1516), a criticism of contemporary society, depicts an imaginary society based on reason and tolerance that requires everyone to work and has rid itself of all social and political injustice. Although More would remain staunchly Catholic, humanism in England, as in Germany, paved the way for the English Reformation. A circle of English humanists, under the direction of Henry VIII's minister Thomas Cromwell, translated and disseminated late medieval criticisms of the papacy and many of Erasmus's satirical writings as well.

Whereas in Germany, England, and France, humanism helped the Protestants, in Spain it entered the service of the Catholic Church. Here the key figure was Francisco Jiménez de Cisneros (1437–1517), a confessor to Queen Isabella, and after 1508 Grand Inquisitor—a position from which he was able to enforce the strictest religious orthodoxy. Jiménez was a conduit for humanist scholarship and learning. He founded the University of Alcalá near Madrid in 1509, printed a Greek edition of the New Testament, and translated many religious

tracts that aided clerical reform and control of lay religious life. His greatest achievement, taking fifteen years to complete, was the Complutensian Polyglot Bible, a six-volume work that placed the Hebrew, Greek, and Latin versions of the Bible in parallel columns. Such scholarly projects and internal church reforms joined with the repressive measures of Ferdinand and Isabella to keep Spain strictly Catholic.

MARTIN LUTHER AND GERMAN REFORMATION TO 1525

Unlike France and England, late medieval Germany lacked the political unity to enforce "national" religious reforms during the late Middle Ages. There were no lasting Statutes of Provisors and Praemunire, as in England, nor a Pragmatic Sanction of Bourges, as in France, both limiting papal jurisdiction and taxation on a national scale. What happened on a unified national level in England and France occurred only locally and piecemeal within German territories and towns. As popular resentment of clerical immunities and ecclesiastical abuses, especially over the selling of indulgences, spread among German cities and towns, an unorganized "national" opposition to

▲ **John Tetzel.** A contemporary caricature depicts John Tetzel, the famous indulgence preacher. The last lines of the jingle read: "As soon as gold in the basin rings, right then the soul to heaven springs." It was Tetzel's preaching that spurred Luther to publish his ninety-five theses.
Courtesy Stiftung Luthergedenkstaten in Sachsen-Anhalt/Lutherhalle, Wittenberg.

Rome formed. German humanists had long given voice to such criticism, and by 1517 it was pervasive enough to provide a solid foundation for Martin Luther's reform.

Luther (1483–1546) was the son of a successful Thüringian miner. He was educated in Mansfeld, Magdeburg (where the Brothers of the Common Life were his teachers), and Eisenach. Between 1501 and 1505 he attended the University of Erfurt, where the nominalist teachings of William of Ockham and Gabriel Biel (d. 1495) prevailed. After receiving his master of arts degree in 1505, Luther registered with the law faculty, following his parents' wishes, but he never began the study of law. To the disappointment of his family, he instead entered the Order of the Hermits of Saint Augustine in Erfurt on July 17, 1505. This decision had apparently been building for some time and was resolved during a lightning storm in which Luther, terrified and crying out to Saint Anne for assistance (Saint Anne was the patron saint of travelers in distress), promised to enter a monastery if he escaped death.

Ordained in 1507, Luther pursued a traditional course of study. In 1510, he journeyed to Rome on the business of his order, finding there justification for the many criticisms of the church he had heard in Germany. In 1511, he moved to the Augustinian monastery in Wittenberg, where he earned his doctorate in theology in 1512. Thereafter, he became a leader within the monastery, the new university, and the spiritual life of the city.

Justification by Faith Alone Reformation theology grew out of a problem then common to many of the clergy and the laity: the failure of traditional medieval religion to provide either full personal or intellectual satisfaction. Luther was especially plagued by the disproportion between his own sense of sinfulness and the perfect righteousness that God required for salvation, according to medieval theology. Traditional church teaching and the sacrament of penance proved no consolation. Luther wrote that he came to despise the phrase "righteousness of God," for it seemed to demand of him a perfection he knew neither he nor any other human being could ever achieve. His insight into the meaning of "justification by faith alone" was a gradual process that extended between 1513 and 1518. The righteousness that God demands, he concluded, did not result from many religious works and ceremonies but was given in full measure to those who believe and trust in Jesus Christ, who alone is the perfect righteousness satisfying to God. To believe in Christ meant to stand before God clothed in Christ's sure righteousness.

The Attack on Indulgences An **indulgence** was a remission of the temporal penalty imposed by priests on penitents as a "work of satisfaction" for their mortal sins. According to medieval theology, after the priest absolved a penitent of guilt for the sins, the penitent remained under an eternal penalty, a punishment God justly imposed for sin. After absolution, however, this eternal penalty was said to be transformed into a temporal penalty, a manageable "work of satisfaction" that the penitent might perform here and now (for example, through prayers, fasting, almsgiving, retreats, and pilgrimages). Penitents who defaulted on such prescribed works of satisfaction could expect to suffer for them in purgatory.

At this point, indulgences, which had earlier been given to Crusaders who did not complete their penances because they had fallen in battle, became an aid to laity, made genuinely anxious by their belief in a future suffering in purgatory for neglected penances or unrepented sins. In 1343, Pope Clement VI (r. 1342–1352) had proclaimed the existence of a "treasury of merit," an infinite reservoir of good works in the church's possession that could be dispensed at the pope's discretion. On the basis of this declared treasury, the church sold "letters of indulgence," which covered the works of satisfaction owed by penitents. In 1476, Pope Sixtus IV (r. 1471–1484) extended indulgences also to cover purgatory.

Originally, indulgences had been given only for the true self-sacrifice of going on a Crusade to the Holy Land. By Luther's time, they were regularly dispensed for small cash payments (very modest sums that were regarded as a good work of almsgiving). They were presented to the laity as remitting not only their own future punishments, but also those of their dead relatives presumed to be suffering in purgatory.

In 1517, Pope Leo X (r. 1513–1521) revived a plenary Jubilee Indulgence that had first been issued by Pope Julius II (r. 1503–1513), whose proceeds were to be used to rebuild St. Peter's Basilica in Rome. Such an indulgence promised forgiveness of all outstanding unrepented sins upon the completion of certain acts. That kind of indulgence was subsequently preached on the borders of Saxony in the territories of the future Archbishop Albrecht of Mainz, who was much in need of revenues because of the large debts he had incurred in order to hold, contrary to church law, three ecclesiastical appointments. The selling of the indulgence was a joint venture by Albrecht, the Augsburg banking house of Fugger, and Pope Leo X, with half the proceeds going to the pope and half to Albrecht and his creditors. The famous indulgence preacher John Tetzel (d. 1519) was enlisted to preach the indulgence in Albrecht's territories because he was a seasoned professional who knew how to stir ordinary people to action. As he exhorted on one occasion:

> Don't you hear the voices of your dead parents and other relatives crying out, "Have mercy on us, for we suffer great punishment and pain. From this you could release us with a few alms. … We have created you, fed you, cared for you, and left you our temporal goods. Why do you treat us so cruelly and leave us to suffer in the flames, when it takes only a little to save us?"[1]

[1] *Die Reformation in Augenzeugen Berichten*, ed. by Helmar Junghans (Dusseldorf: Karl Rauch Verlag, 1967), p. 44

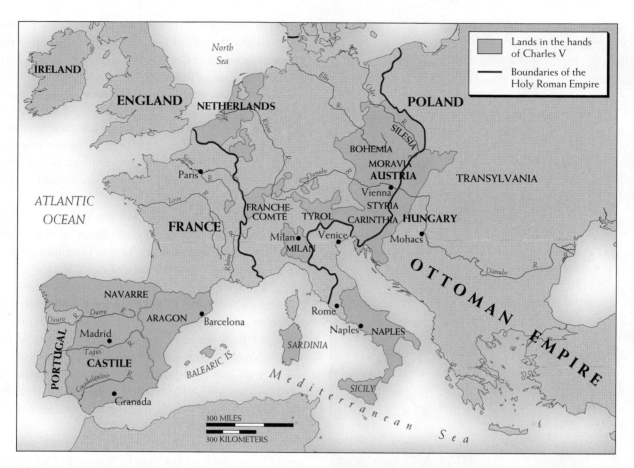

MAP 16–3 The Empire of Charles V.   Dynastic marriages and good luck concentrated into Charles's hands rule over the lands shown here, plus Spain's overseas possessions. Crowns and titles rained down on him; election in 1519 as emperor gave him new burdens and responsibilities.

When Luther, according to tradition, posted his ninety-five theses against indulgences on the door of Castle Church in Wittenberg, on October 31, 1517, he protested especially against the impression created by Tetzel that indulgences actually remitted sins and released the dead from punishment in purgatory. Luther believed these claims went far beyond the traditional practice and seemed to make salvation something that could be bought and sold.

Election of Charles V   Luther's **ninety-five theses** made him famous overnight. They were embraced by humanists and other proponents of reform, but they prompted official proceedings against him. In October, he was called before the general of the Dominican order in Augsburg. As sanctions were being prepared against Luther, however, Emperor Maximilian I died (January 12, 1519), and this event, fortunate for the Reformation, turned attention away from heresy in Saxony to the contest for a new emperor.

The pope backed the French king, Francis I. However, Charles I of Spain, a youth of nineteen, succeeded his grandfather and became Emperor Charles V. (See Map 16–3.) Charles was assisted by both a long tradition of Habsburg imperial rule and a massive Fugger campaign chest, which secured the votes of the seven electors. The electors, who traditionally enhanced their power at every opportunity, wrung new concessions from Charles for their votes. The emperor agreed to a revival of the Imperial Supreme Court and the Council of Regency and promised to consult with a diet of the empire on all major domestic and foreign affairs that affected the empire. These measures also helped the development of the Reformation by preventing unilateral imperial action against the Germans, something Luther could be thankful for in the early years of the Reformation.

Luther's Excommunication and the Diet of Worms   In the same month in which Charles was elected emperor, Luther entered a debate in Leipzig (June 27, 1519) with the Ingolstadt professor John Eck. During this contest, Luther challenged the infallibility of the pope and the inerrancy of church councils, appealing for the first time to the sovereign authority of Scripture alone. He burned all his bridges to the old church when he further defended certain teachings of John Huss that had been condemned by the Council of Constance.

▲ **A Catholic Portrayal of Martin Luther Tempting Jesus (1547).**
Reformation propaganda often portrayed the pope as the Antichrist or
the devil. Here Catholic propaganda turns the tables on the
Protestant reformers by portraying a figure of Martin Luther as the
devil (note the monstrous feet and tail under his academic robes).
Versuchung Christi, 1547, Gemälde, Bonn, Landschaftsverband Rheinland/Rheinisches
Landesmuseum, Bonn. Inv. Nr. 58.3.

In 1520, Luther described the pillars of his reform in three
pamphlets. The *Address to the Christian Nobility of the German
Nation* urged the German princes to force reforms on the
Roman church, especially to curtail its political and economic
power in Germany. The *Babylonian Captivity of the Church* examined the traditional seven sacraments of the church, arguing
that only two, baptism and the Eucharist, were biblical, and
exalted the authority of Scripture, church councils, and secular princes over that of the pope. The *Freedom of a Christian*
summarized the new theology for the laity, describing a "happy
union" between the soul and Christ by faith alone, in which
everything the soul had (sin, death, and damnation) became
Christ's and everything Christ had (purity, life, and heaven)
became the believer's.

In April 1521, Luther defended his religious teaching
before the imperial **Diet of Worms**, over which newly elected

Emperor Charles V presided. Ordered to recant, Luther
declared that he could not act against Scripture, reason, and
his own conscience. On May 26, 1521, he was placed under the
imperial ban and thereafter became an "outlaw" to secular as
well as religious authority. For his own protection, friends hid
him in a secluded castle, where he spent almost a year, from
April 1521 to March 1522. During his stay, he translated the
New Testament into German, using Erasmus's new Greek text
and Latin translation, and he attempted, by correspondence,
to oversee the first stages of the Reformation in Wittenberg.

Imperial Distractions: France and the Turks   The Reformation
was greatly helped in these early years by the emperor's war
with France and the advance of the Ottoman Turks into eastern Europe. Against both adversaries Charles V, who also remained a Spanish king with dynastic responsibilities outside
the empire, needed German troops, and to that end he promoted friendly relations with the German princes. Between
1521 and 1559, Spain (the Habsburg dynasty) and France (the
Valois dynasty) fought four major wars over disputed territories in Italy and along their borders. In 1526, the Turks overran Hungary at the Battle of Mohacs; in Western Europe the
French-led League of Cognac formed against Charles for the
second Habsburg-Valois war.

Thus preoccupied, the emperor agreed through his representatives at the German Diet of Speyer in 1526 that each German territory was free to enforce the Edict of Worms (1521)
against Luther "so as to be able to answer in good conscience
to God and the emperor." That concession, in effect, gave the
German princes territorial sovereignty in religious matters and
gave the Reformation time to put down deep roots. Later, in
1555, the Peace of Augsburg would enshrine such local
princely control over religion in imperial law.

How the Reformation Spread   In the late 1520s and on into the
1530s, the Reformation passed from the hands of the theologians and pamphleteers into those of the magistrates and
princes. In many cities, the magistrates quickly followed the lead
of the Protestant preachers and their sizable congregations in
mandating the religious reforms they preached. In numerous
instances, magistrates had themselves worked for decades to
bring about basic church reforms and thus welcomed the
preachers as new allies. Reform now ceased to be merely slogans
and became laws that all townspeople had to obey.

The religious reform became a territorial political movement
as well led by the elector of Saxony and the prince of Hesse, the
two most powerful German Protestant rulers. Like the urban
magistrates, the German princes quickly recognized the political
and economic opportunities offered them by the demise of the
Roman Catholic Church in their regions. Soon they, too, were
pushing Protestant faith and politics onto their neighbors. By the

1530s, Protestant cities and lands formed powerful defensive alliances and prepared for war with the Catholic emperor.

The Peasants' Revolt

In its first decade, the Protestant movement suffered more from internal division than from imperial interference. By 1525, Luther had become as much an object of protest within Germany as was the pope. Original allies, sympathizers, and fellow travelers declared their independence from him. Like the German humanists, the German peasantry also had at first believed Luther to be an ally. Since the late fifteenth century, the peasantry had been organized against efforts by territorial princes to override their traditional laws and customs and to subject them to new regulations and taxes. (See Document, "German Peasants Protest Rising Feudal Exactions.") Peasant leaders, several of whom were convinced Lutherans, saw in Luther's teaching about Christian freedom and his criticism of monastic landowners a point of view close to their own. They openly solicited Luther's support of their political and economic rights, including their revolutionary request for release from serfdom.

Lutheran pamphleteers made Karsthans, the burly, honest peasant who earned his bread by the sweat of his brow and sacrificed his comfort for the well-being of others, a symbol of the simple life God desired all people to live. Lutherans were not, however, social revolutionaries. Luther believed the freedom of the Christian to be an inner release from guilt and anxiety, not the right to create an egalitarian society by violent revolution. When the peasants revolted against their landlords in 1524–1525, Luther predictably condemned them as "un-Christian" and urged the princes to crush their revolt. An estimated 70,000 to 100,000 peasants may have died by the time the revolt was put down. Had Luther supported the peasants' revolt, not only would he have contradicted his own teaching, he would surely also have ended any chance of the survival of his reform beyond the 1520s.

Luther and the Jews

Also controversial is Luther's stand toward the Jews. In 1523, as part of a heady program of civic reform, he published a pamphlet entitled, "Jesus Christ was Born a Jew." Therein, he urged Christians to be kinder and gentler to German Jews in the hope that "some" or "many" might assimilate to Christian society and eventually convert to the new reformed Christianity. By the late 1530s, Luther's Protestant reform was only one among many and even faltering, and some Christians in Bohemia and Moravia, he was told, were even converting to Judaism. He tells the story of three rabbis even coming to him in Wittenberg in the hope of "finding a new Jew in me." Was his kindness to Jews to be repaid by Jewish proselytization of the great reformer himself? From that suspicion on, he regretted his 1523 pamphlet and viewed the Jews as just another in a long history of foreign predators threatening German Christians. He took his anger at Jews out in several new pamphlets published in the

late 1530s and early 1540, in which he urged German princes forcibly to remove nonconverting Jews to a land of their own as France, Spain, and Bohemia had already done. Although far short of making Judaism a capital crime, as imperial law had done with Anabaptism in 1529, Luther's proposals ran along a similar line: assimilation or exile. Fortunately, the shocked and disappointed Jews had a protector in Emperor Charles V, and Luther's colleagues had no heart to replace traditional Christian watchful waiting on the Jews with forced conversions and exile. In Hesse and Saxony around this time, rulers tightened traditional restrictions on Jews. Had Luther been willing, he might have softened these restrictions or prevented them altogether as expectant Jewish leaders had asked him to do.

ZWINGLI AND THE SWISS REFORMATION

Although Luther's was the first, Switzerland and France had their own independent reform movements almost simultaneously with Germany's. Switzerland was a loose confederacy of thirteen autonomous cantons or states and allied areas (see Map 16–4). Some became Protestant, some remained Catholic, and a few managed to effect a compromise. The two preconditions of the Swiss Reformation were the growth of national sentiment and a desire for church reform.

▲ **Execution of a Peasant Leader.** The punishment of a peasant leader in a village near Heilbronn. After the defeat of rebellious peasants in and around the city of Heilbronn, Jacob Rorbach, a well-to-do peasant leader from a nearby village, was tied to a stake and slowly roasted to death.
© Badische Landesbibliothek

The Reformation in Zurich Ulrich Zwingli (1484–1531), the leader of the Swiss Reformation, was widely known for opposition to the sale of indulgences and religious superstition. The people's priest in Zurich, he made the city his base for reform. Zwingli's reform guideline was simple and effective: whatever lacked literal support in Scripture was to be neither believed nor practiced. After a public disputation in January 1523, based on his Scripture test, Zurich became, to all intents and purposes, a Protestant city and the center of the Swiss Reformation. Its harsh discipline in pursuit of its religious ideals made it one of the first examples of a "puritanical" Protestant city.

The Marburg Colloquy Landgrave Philip of Hesse (1504–1567) sought to unite Swiss and German Protestants in a mutual defense pact, a potentially significant political alliance. His efforts were spoiled, however, by theological disagreements between Luther and Zwingli over the nature of Christ's presence in the Eucharist. Zwingli maintained a symbolic interpretation of Christ's words, "This is my body". Christ, he argued, was only spiritually, not bodily, present in the bread and wine of the Eucharist. Luther, to the contrary, insisted that Christ's human nature could share the properties of his divine nature; hence, where Christ was spiritually pre-sent, he could also be bodily present, for his was a special nature (***transubstantiation***).

Philip of Hesse brought the two Protestant leaders together in his castle in Marburg in early October 1529, but they were unable to work out their differences on this issue. Luther left thinking Zwingli a dangerous fanatic. The disagreement splintered the Protestant movement theologically and politically.

ANABAPTISTS AND RADICAL PROTESTANTS

The moderate pace and seemingly small ethical results of the Lutheran and Zwinglian reformations discontented many people, among them some of the original co-workers of Luther and Zwingli. Many desired a more rapid and thorough implementation of primitive Christianity and accused the major reformers of going only halfway. The most important of these radical groups were the Anabaptists, the sixteenth-century ancestors of the modern Mennonites and Amish. The Anabaptists were especially distinguished by their rejection of infant baptism and their insistence on only adult baptism (*Anabaptism* derives from the Greek word meaning "to rebaptize"), believing that baptism as a consenting adult conformed to Scripture and was more respectful of human freedom.

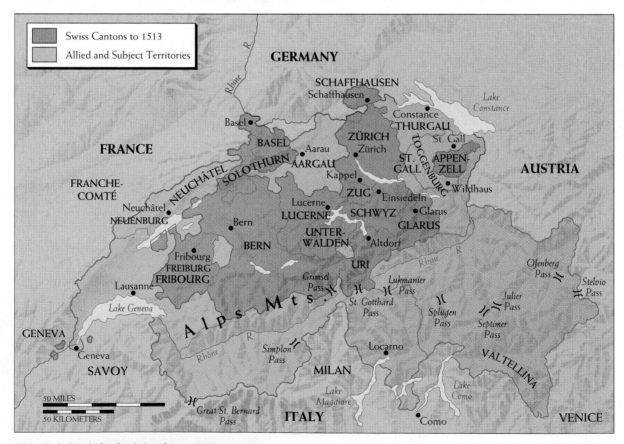

MAP 16–4 The Swiss Confederation. While nominally still a part of the Holy Roman Empire, Switzerland grew from a loose defensive union of the central "forest cantons" in the thirteenth century to a fiercely independent association of regions with different languages, histories, and religions in the sixteenth century.

DOCUMENT   German Peasants Protest Rising Feudal Exactions

In the late fifteenth and early sixteenth centuries, German feudal lords, both secular and ecclesiastical, tried to increase the earnings from their lands by raising demands on their peasant tenants. As the lords restricted the traditional freedoms and property rights of peasants, massive revolts occurred in southern Germany in 1525. The following, representative statement of peasant grievances, summarized in twelve articles, came from the town of Memmingen.

> ◆ Are the peasants more interested in material than in spiritual freedom? Which of their demands are the most revolutionary, and which are the least problematic for their lords to grant? Why do some centuries exhibit greater social and political equality than others?

1. It is our humble petition and desire that in the future each community should choose and appoint a pastor, and that we should have the right to depose him should he conduct himself improperly …

2. We are ready and willing to pay the fair tithe of grain … The small tithes [of cattle], whether [to] ecclesiastical or lay lords, we will not pay at all, for the Lord God created cattle for the free use of man …

3. We … take it for granted that you will release us from serfdom as true Christians, unless it should be shown us from the Gospel that we are serfs.

4. It has been the custom heretofore that no poor man should be allowed to catch venison or wildfowl or fish in flowing water, which seems to us quite unseemly and unbrotherly as well as selfish and not agreeable to the Word of God …

5. We are aggrieved in the matter of woodcutting, for the noblemen have appropriated all the woods to themselves …

6. In regard to the excessive services demanded of us which are increased from day to day, we ask that this matter be properly looked into so that we shall not continue to be oppressed in this way …

7. We will not hereafter allow ourselves to be further oppressed by our lords, but will let them demand only what is just and proper according to the word of the agreement between the lord and the peasant. The lord should no longer try to force more services or other dues from the peasant without payment …

8. We are greatly burdened because our holdings cannot support the rent exacted from them … We ask that the lords may appoint persons of honor to inspect these holdings and fix a rent in accordance with justice …

9. We are burdened with a great evil in the constant making of new laws … In our opinion we should be judged according to the old written law …

10. We are aggrieved by the appropriation … of meadows and fields which at one time belonged to a community as a whole. These we will take again into our own hands …

11. We will entirely abolish the due called Todfall [that is, *heriot* or *death tax*, by which the lord received the best horse, cow, or garment of a family upon the death of a serf] and will no longer endure it, nor allow widows and orphans to be thus shamefully robbed against God's will, and in violation of justice and right …

12. It is our conclusion and final resolution, that if any one or more of the articles here set forth should not be in agreement with the Word of God, as we think they are, such article we will willingly retract.

Translations and Reprints from the Original Sources of European History, Vol. 2 (Philadelphia: Department of History, University of Pennsylvania, 1897).

Anabaptists physically separated from society to form a more perfect community in imitation of what they believed to be the example of the first Christians. Due to the close connection between religious and civic life in this period, the political authorities viewed such separatism as a threat to basic social bonds.

At first Anabaptism drew its adherents from all social classes. But as Lutherans and Zwinglians joined with Catholics in opposition to it, a more rural, agrarian class came to make up the great majority of Anabaptists. In 1529 rebaptism became a capital offense throughout the Holy Roman Empire. It has been estimated that from 1525 to 1618, between one and five thousand men and women were executed for rebaptizing themselves as adults.

JOHN CALVIN AND THE GENEVAN REFORMATION

Calvinism was the religious ideology that inspired or accompanied massive political resistance in France, the Netherlands, and Scotland. Believing in both divine predestination and the individual's responsibility to create a godly society, Calvinists became zealous reformers. In a famous and controversial study, *The Protestant Ethic and the Spirit of Capitalism* (1904), the German sociologist Max Weber argued that this combination of religious confidence and self-disciplined activism produced an ethic congenial to emergent capitalism, bringing Calvinism and later Puritanism into close association with the development of modern capitalist societies.

Political Revolt and Religious Reform in Geneva   Whereas in Saxony religious reform paved the way for a political revolution against the emperor, in Geneva a political revolution against the local prince-bishop laid the foundation for religious change. In late 1533 the Protestant city of Bern sent Protestant reformers to Geneva and by the summer of 1535, after much internal turmoil, the Protestants triumphed. On May 21, 1536, the city voted officially to adopt the Reformation: "to live according to the Gospel and the Word of God … without … any more masses, statues, idols, or other papal abuses."

John Calvin (1509–1564), a reform-minded humanist and lawyer, arrived in Geneva after these events, in July 1536. The local Protestant reformer persuaded him to stay and assist the Reformation. Before a year had passed, Calvin had drawn up articles for the governance of the new church, as well as a catechism to guide and discipline the people. As a result of the strong measures proposed to govern Geneva's moral life, many suspected the reformers of trying to create a "new papacy." In February 1538 they were exiled from the city.

Calvin went to Strasbourg, a model Protestant city, where he became pastor to the French exiles. During his two years in Strasbourg he wrote biblical commentaries and a second edition of his masterful *Institutes of the Christian Religion*, which many consider the definitive theological statement of the Protestant faith. He also married and participated in the ecumenical discussions urged on Protestants and Catholics by Charles V. Most important, he learned from the Strasbourg

▲ **A Portrait of the Young John Calvin.**
Bibliotheque Publique et Universitaire, Geneva.

reformer Martin Bucer (1491–1551) how to implement the Protestant Reformation successfully.

Calvin's Geneva   In 1540 Geneva elected officials favorable to Calvin and he was invited to return. Within months of his arrival, new ecclesiastical ordinances were implemented that allowed the magistrates and the clergy to cooperate in matters of internal discipline.

Calvin and his followers were motivated above all by a desire to make society godly. The "elect," Calvin taught, should live a manifestly God-pleasing life, if they are truly God's elect. The majesty of God demanded nothing less. The consistory, a judicial body composed of clergy and laity, became his instrument of power. It enforced the strictest moral discipline, meting out punishments for a broad range of moral and religious transgressions, and became unpopular with many Genevans.

After 1555 the city's magistrates were all devout Calvinists, and Geneva became home to thousands of exiled Protestants who had been driven out of France, England, and Scotland. Refugees (more than five thousand), most of them utterly loyal to Calvin, came to make up over one third of the population of Geneva. From this time until his death in 1564, Calvin's position in the city was greatly strengthened and the magistrates were very cooperative.

POLITICAL CONSOLIDATION OF THE LUTHERAN REFORMATION

By 1530 the Reformation was in Europe to stay. It would, however, take several decades and major attempts to eradicate it before all would recognize this fact. With the political triumph of Lutheranism in the empire by the 1550s, Protestant movements elsewhere gained a new lease on life.

Expansion of the Reformation   In the 1530s German Lutherans formed regional consistories, which oversaw and administered the new Protestant churches. These consistories replaced the old Catholic episcopates. Under the leadership of Philip Melanchthon (1497–1560), Luther's most admired colleague, educational reforms were enacted that provided for compulsory primary education, schools for girls, a humanist revision of the traditional curriculum, and catechetical instruction of the laity in the new religion.

The Reformation also dug in elsewhere. Introduced into Denmark by Christian II (r. 1513–1523), Lutheranism became the state religion under Christian III (r. 1536–1559). In Sweden, Gustavus Vasa (r. 1523–1560), supported by a nobility greedy for church lands, confiscated church property and subjected the clergy to royal authority at the Diet of Vesteras (1527). In politically splintered Poland, Lutherans, Calvinists, and others found room to practice their beliefs. The absence of a central political authority made Poland a model of religious pluralism and toleration in the second half of the sixteenth century.

Reaction Against Protestants: The "Interim"   Charles V made abortive efforts in 1540–1541 to enforce a compromise agreement between Protestants and Catholics. As these and other conciliar efforts failed, he turned to a military solution. In 1547 imperial armies crushed the Protestant Schmalkaldic League.

The emperor established puppet rulers in Saxony and Hesse and issued as imperial law the Augsburg Interim, a new order that Protestants everywhere must readopt Catholic beliefs and practices. But the Reformation was too entrenched by 1547 to be ended even by brute force. Confronted by fierce Protestant resistance and weary from three decades of war, the emperor was forced to relent.

The Peace of Augsburg in September 1555 made the division of Christendom permanent. This agreement recognized in law what had already been well established in practice: *cuius regio, eius religio,* meaning that the ruler of a land would determine the religion of the land. Lutherans were permitted to retain all church lands forcibly seized before 1552. Those discontented with the religion of their region were permitted to migrate to another.

Calvinism was not recognized as a legal form of Christian belief and practice by the Peace of Augsburg. Calvinists remained determined not only to secure the right to worship publicly as they pleased, but also to shape society according to their own religious convictions. They organized to lead national revolutions throughout northern Europe.

THE ENGLISH REFORMATION TO 1553

Late medieval England had a well-earned reputation for defending the rights of the crown against the pope. It was, however, the unhappy marriage of King Henry VIII (r. 1509–1547) that ensured the success of the English protest against the church.

The King's Affair   Henry had married Catherine of Aragon (d. 1536), a daughter of Ferdinand and Isabella of Spain, and the aunt of Emperor Charles V. By 1527 the union had produced only one surviving child, a daughter, Mary Tudor. Henry was justifiably concerned about the political consequences of leaving only a female heir. People in this period believed it unnatural for women to rule over men. At best, a woman ruler meant a contested reign; at worst, turmoil and revolution. Henry even came to believe that his union with Catherine, who had had numerous miscarriages and stillbirths, had been cursed by God, because before their marriage Catherine had briefly been the wife of his late brother, Arthur.

By 1527 Henry, thoroughly enamored of Anne Boleyn (ca. 1504–1536), one of Catherine's ladies in waiting, decided to put Catherine aside and marry Anne. This he could not do in Catholic England without papal annulment of the marriage to Catherine. And therein lay a problem. In 1527 the reigning pope, Clement VII (r. 1523–1534), was a prisoner of Charles V, Catherine's nephew. Even if this had not been the case, it would have been virtually impossible for the pope to grant an annulment of the marriage. Not only had it survived for eighteen years, but it had also been made possible in the first place by a special papal dispensation required because Queen Catherine had previously been the wife of Henry's brother, Arthur.

After Cardinal Wolsey (1475–1530), Lord Chancellor of England since 1515, failed to secure the annulment, Thomas Cranmer (1489–1556) and Thomas Cromwell (1485–1540), both of whom harbored Lutheran sympathies, became the king's closest advisers. Finding the way to a papal annulment closed, Henry's new advisers struck a different course: Why not simply declare the king supreme in English spiritual affairs as he was in English temporal affairs? Then the king could settle his own affair.

Reformation Parliament   In 1529 Parliament convened for what would be a seven-year session that earned it the title of "Reformation Parliament." It passed a flood of legislation that harassed and finally placed royal reins on the clergy. In January 1531 the clergy publicly recognized Henry as head of the church in England "as far as the law of Christ allows." In 1533 Parliament passed the Submission of the Clergy, effectively placing canon law under royal control and thereby the clergy under royal jurisdiction.

CHRONOLOGY

Progress of Protestant Reformation on the Continent

1517	Luther posts ninety-five theses against indulgences
1519	Charles I of Spain elected Holy Roman emperor (as Charles V)
1519	Luther challenges infallibility of pope and inerrancy of church councils at Leipzig Debate
1521	Papal bull excommunicates Luther for heresy
1521	Diet of Worms condemns Luther
1521–1522	Luther translates the New Testament into German
1524–1525	Peasants' Revolt in Germany
1529	Marburg Colloquy between Luther and Zwingli
1530	Diet of Augsburg fails to settle religious differences
1531	Formation of Protestant Schmalkaldic League
1536	Calvin arrives in Geneva
1540	Jesuits, founded by Ignatius of Loyola, recognized as order by pope
1546	Luther dies
1547	Armies of Charles V crush Schmalkaldic League
1555	Peace of Augsburg recognizes rights of Lutherans to worship as they please
1545–1563	Council of Trent institutes reforms and responds to the Reformation

◀ Tudor Succession. An allegorical depiction of the Tudor succession by the painter Lucas de Heere (1534–1584). On Henry VIII's right stands his Catholic daughter Mary (1533–1558) and her husband Philip II of Spain. They are accompanied by Mars, the god of war. Henry's son, Edward VI (r. 1547–1553), kneels at the king's left. Elizabeth I (1558–1603) is shown standing in the foreground attended by Peace and Plenty, allegorical figures of what her reign brought to England.

Sudeley Castle National Museums & Galleries of Wales.

CHRONOLOGY

Main Events of the English Reformation

1529	Reformation Parliament convenes
1532	Parliament passes the Submission of the Clergy, an act placing canon law and the English clergy under royal jurisdiction
1533	Henry VIII weds Anne Boleyn
1534	Act of Succession makes Anne Boleyn's children legitimate heirs to the English throne
1534	Act of Supremacy declares Henry VIII the only supreme head of the Church of England
1535	Thomas More executed for opposition to Acts of Succession and Supremacy
1535	Publication of Coverdale Bible
1539	Henry VIII imposes the Six Articles, condemning Protestantism and reasserting traditional doctrine
1547	Edward VI succeeds to the throne
1549	First Act of Uniformity imposes Book of Common Prayer on English churches
1553–1558	Mary Tudor restores Catholic doctrine
1558–1603	Elizabeth I fashions an Anglican religious settlement

In January 1533 Henry wed the pregnant Anne Boleyn, with Thomas Cranmer officiating. In 1534 Parliament ended all payments by the English clergy and laity to Rome and gave Henry sole jurisdiction over high ecclesiastical appointments. The Act of Succession in the same year made Anne Boleyn's children legitimate heirs to the throne, and the Act of Supremacy declared Henry "the only supreme head in earth of the church of England."

The Protestant Reformation Under Edward VI   Despite his political break with Rome, Henry remained decidedly conservative in his religious beliefs, and Catholic doctrine remained prominent in a country seething with Protestant sentiment. Henry forbade the English clergy to marry and threatened to execute clergy caught twice in concubinage. The Six Articles of 1539 reaffirmed transubstantiation, denied the Eucharistic cup to the laity, declared celibate vows inviolable, provided for private Masses, and ordered the continuation of auricular confession.

Edward VI (r. 1547–1553), Henry's son by his third wife, Jane Seymour, became king at age ten. Under his regents, England enacted much of the Protestant Reformation. Henry's Six Articles and laws against heresy were repealed, and clerical marriage and Communion with the cup were sanctioned. An Act of Uniformity imposed Thomas Cranmer's Book of Common Prayer on all English churches, which were stripped of their images and altars. His forty-two-article confession of faith set forth a moderate Protestant doctrine.

These changes were short-lived because in 1553 Catherine of Aragon's daughter, Mary Tudor (d. 1558), succeeded to the throne and restored Catholic doctrine and practice with a single-mindedness that rivaled that of her father. It was not until the reign of Anne Boleyn's daughter, Elizabeth I (r. 1558–1603), that a lasting religious settlement was worked out in England.

CATHOLIC REFORM AND COUNTER-REFORMATION

The Protestant Reformation did not take the medieval church completely by surprise. There were many internal criticisms and efforts at reform before there was a **Counter-Reformation** in reaction to Protestant successes.

Sources of Catholic Reform   Before the Reformation began, ambitious proposals had been made for church reform. But sixteenth-century popes, mindful of how the Councils of Constance and Basel had stripped the pope of his traditional powers, quickly squelched such efforts to bring about basic changes in the laws and institutions of the church. Despite such papal foot-dragging, the church was not without its reformers. Many new religious orders sprang up in the sixteenth century to lead a broad revival of piety within the church.

Ignatius of Loyola and the Society of Jesus   Of the various reform groups, none was more instrumental in the success of the Counter-Reformation than the Society of Jesus, the new order of Jesuits. Organized by Ignatius of Loyola in the 1530s, it was officially recognized by the church in 1540. Within a century the society had more than fifteen thousand members scattered throughout the world, with thriving missions in India, Japan, and the Americas.

Ignatius of Loyola (1491–1556) was a heroic figure. A dashing courtier and caballero in his youth, he began his spiritual pilgrimage in 1521 after having been seriously wounded in the legs during a battle with the French. During a lengthy and painful convalescence, he read Christian classics. So impressed was he with the heroic self-sacrifice of the church's saints and their methods of overcoming mental anguish and pain that he underwent a profound religious conversion. Henceforth, he too would serve the church as a soldier of Christ.

After recuperating, Ignatius applied the lessons he had learned during his convalescence to a program of religious and moral self-discipline that came to be embodied in the *Spiritual Exercises.* This psychologically perceptive devotional guide contained mental and emotional exercises designed to teach one absolute spiritual self-mastery. A person could shape his or her own behavior, even create a new religious self, through disciplined study and regular practice.

Whereas in Jesuit eyes Protestants had distinguished themselves by disobedience to church authority and by religious innovation, the exercises of Ignatius were intended to teach

▲ **The Ecstasy of Saint Teresa of Avila** by Gianlorenzo Bernini (1598–1680). Catholic mystics like Saint Teresa and Saint John of the cross helped revive the traditional piety of medieval monasticism. © Scala/Art Resource, N.Y.

good Catholics to submit without question to higher church authority and spiritual direction. Perfect discipline and self-control were the essential conditions of such obedience. To these were added the enthusiasm of traditional spirituality and mysticism and uncompromising loyalty to the church's cause above all else. (See Document, "Ignatius of Loyola's 'Rules for Thinking with the Church.'") This potent combination helped counter the Reformation and win many Protestants back to the Catholic fold, especially in Austria and Germany.

The Council of Trent (1545–1563)   The broad success of the Reformation and the insistence of the emperor Charles V forced Pope Paul III (r. 1534–1549) to call a general council of the church to reassert church doctrine. The pope also appointed a

DOCUMENT | Ignatius of Loyola's "Rules for Thinking with the Church"

As leaders of the Counter-Reformation, the Jesuits attempted to live by and instill in others the strictest obedience to church authority. The following are some of the eighteen rules included by Ignatius in his Spiritual Exercises *to give Catholics positive direction. These rules also indicate the Catholic reformers' refusal to compromise with Protestants.*

♦ Would Protestants find any of Ignatius's "rules" acceptable? Might any of them be controversial among Catholic laity as well as among Protestant laity?

In order to have the proper attitude of mind in the Church Militant we should observe the following rules:

1. Putting aside all private judgment, we should keep our minds prepared and ready to obey promptly and in all things the true spouse of Christ our Lord, our Holy Mother, the hierarchical Church.

2. To praise sacramental confession and the reception of the Most Holy Sacrament once a year, and much better once a month, and better still every week. ...

3. To praise the frequent hearing of Mass. ...

4. To praise highly the religious life, virginity, and continence; and also matrimony, but not as highly. ...

5. To praise the vows of religion, obedience, poverty, chastity, and other works of perfection and supererogation. ...

6. To praise the relics of the saints ... [and] the stations, pilgrimages, indulgences, jubilees, Crusade indulgences, and the lighting of candles in the churches.

7. To praise the precepts concerning fasts and abstinences ... and acts of penance. ...

8. To praise the adornments and buildings of churches as well as sacred images. ...

9. To praise all the precepts of the church. ...

10. To approve and praise the directions and recommendations of our superiors as well as their personal behaviour. ...

11. To praise both the positive and scholastic theology. ...

12. We must be on our guard against making comparisons between the living and those who have already gone to their reward, for it is no small error to say, for example: "This man knows more than St. Augustine"; "He is another Saint Francis, or even greater." ...

13. If we wish to be sure that we are right in all things, we should always be ready to accept this principle: I will believe that the white that I see is black, if the hierarchical Church so defines it. For I believe that between ... Christ our Lord and ... His Church, there is but one spirit, which governs and directs us for the salvation of our souls.

From *The Spiritual Exercises of St. Ignatius*, trans. by Anthony Mottola. Copyright © 1964 by Doubleday, a division of Bantam, Doubleday, Dell Publishing Group, Inc., pp. 139–141. Used by permission of Doubleday, a division of Random House, Inc.

---

reform commission, whose report, presented in February 1537, bluntly criticized the fiscality and simony[2] of the papal Curia (court) as the primary source of the church's loss of esteem. The report was so critical that Pope Paul attempted unsuccessfully to suppress its publication, Protestants reprinted and circulated it widely.

The long-delayed council met in 1545 in the imperial city of Trent in northern Italy. There were three sessions, spread over eighteen years, with long interruptions due to war, plague, and politics. Unlike the general councils of the fifteenth century, Trent was strictly under the pope's control, with high Italian prelates prominent in the proceedings.

The council's most important reforms concerned internal church discipline. The selling of church offices and other religious goods was forbidden. Trent strengthened the authority of local bishops so they could effectively discipline popular religious

[2] The sin of selling of sacred or spiritual things, in this instance church offices.

practice. Bishops who resided in Rome were forced to move to their appointed seats of authority. They had to preach regularly and conduct annual visitations. Parish priests were required to be neatly dressed, better educated, strictly celibate, and active among their parishioners. To train better priests, Trent also called for the establishment of a seminary in every diocese.

The Council did not make a single doctrinal concession to the Protestants, however. In the face of Protestant criticism, the Council of Trent reaffirmed the traditional scholastic education of the clergy; the role of good works in salvation; the authority of tradition; the seven sacraments; **transubstantiation**; the withholding of the Eucharistic cup from the laity; clerical celibacy; the reality of purgatory; the veneration of saints, relics, and sacred images; and the granting of letters of indulgence.

Rulers initially resisted Trent's reform decrees, fearing a revival of papal political power within their lands. But in time the new legislation took hold, and parish life revived under the guidance of a devout and better-trained clergy.

The Reformation's Achievements

Although politically conservative, the Reformation brought about far-reaching changes in traditional religious practices and institutions in many lands. By the end of the sixteenth century, what had disappeared or was radically altered was often dramatic.

Religion in Fifteenth-Century Life   In the fifteenth century, on the streets of the great cities of central Europe that later turned Protestant (for example, Zurich, Strasbourg, Nuremberg, or Geneva), the clergy and the religious were everywhere. They made up 6 to 8 percent of the total urban population, and they exercised considerable political as well as spiritual power. They legislated and taxed; they tried cases in special church courts; and they enforced their laws with threats of excommunication.

The church calendar regulated daily life. About one third of the year was given over to some kind of religious observance or celebration. There were frequent periods of fasting. On almost a hundred days out of the year a pious Christian could not, without special dispensation, eat eggs, butter, fat, or meat.

Monasteries and especially nunneries were prominent and influential institutions. The children of society's most powerful citizens resided there. Local aristocrats were closely identified with particular churches and chapels, whose walls recorded their lineage and proclaimed their generosity. On the streets, friars from near and far begged alms from passersby. In the churches the Mass and liturgy were read entirely in Latin. Images of saints were regularly displayed, and on certain holidays their relics were paraded about and venerated.

There was a booming business at local religious shrines. Pilgrims gathered there by the hundreds, even thousands, many sick and dying, all in search of a cure or a miracle, but also for diversion and entertainment. Several times during the year special preachers arrived in the city to sell letters of indulgence.

Many clergy walked the streets with concubines and children, although they were sworn to celibacy and forbidden marriage. The church tolerated such relationships upon payment of penitential fines.

People everywhere could be heard complaining about the clergy's exemption from taxation and, in many instances, also from the civil criminal code. People also grumbled about having to support church offices whose occupants actually lived and worked elsewhere. Townspeople also expressed concern that the church had too much influence over education and culture.

Religion in Sixteenth-Century Life   In these same cities after the Reformation had firmly established itself, few changes in politics and society were evident. The same aristocratic families governed as before, and the rich generally got richer and the poor poorer. But overall numbers of clergy fell by two thirds and religious holidays shrunk by one third. Monasteries and nunneries were nearly absent. Many were transformed into hospices for the sick and poor or into educational institutions, their endowments also turned over to these new purposes. A few cloisters remained for very devout old monks and nuns, who could not be pensioned off or who lacked families and friends to care for them. But these remaining cloisters died out with their inhabitants.

In the churches, which had also been reduced in number by at least a third, worship was conducted almost completely in the vernacular. In some, particularly those in Zwinglian cities, the walls were stripped bare and whitewashed to make sure the congregation meditated only on God's Word. The laity observed no obligatory fasts. Indulgence preachers no longer appeared. Local shrines were closed down, and anyone found openly venerating saints, relics, and images was subject to fine and punishment.

Copies of Luther's translation of the New Testament, or more often excerpts from it, could be found in private homes, and meditation on them was encouraged by the new clergy. The clergy could marry, and most did. They paid taxes and were punished for their crimes in civil courts. Domestic moral life was regulated by committees composed of roughly equal numbers of laity and clergy, over whose decisions secular magistrates had the last word.

Not all Protestant clergy remained enthusiastic about this new lay authority in religion. And the laity themselves were also ambivalent about certain aspects of the Reformation. Over half of the original converts returned to the Catholic fold before the end of the sixteenth century. Whereas half of Europe could be counted in the Protestant camp in the mid–sixteenth century, only a fifth would be there by the mid–seventeenth century.[3]

FAMILY LIFE IN EARLY MODERN EUROPE

Changes in the timing and duration of marriage, family size, and infant and child care suggest that family life was under a variety of social and economic pressures in the sixteenth and seventeenth centuries. The Reformation was only one factor in these changes and not the major one.

Later Marriages   Between 1500 and 1800, men and women in Western Europe and England married at later ages than they had in previous centuries: men in their mid- to late twenties, and women in their early to mid-twenties. The canonical, or church-sanctioned, age for marriage remained fourteen for men and twelve for women. The church also recognized as valid free, private exchanges of vows between a man and a woman otherwise qualified. After the Reformation, which condemned such clandestine unions, both Protestants and

---

[3] Geoffrey Parker, *Europe in Crisis, 1598–1648* (Ithaca, NY: Cornell University Press, 1979), p. 50.

▲ **A Young Couple in Love** (ca. 1480) by an anonymous artist.
Bildarchiv Preussischer Kulturbesitz.

Catholics required parental consent and public vows in church before a marriage could be deemed fully licit.

Late marriage in the West reflected the difficulty couples had supporting themselves independently. It simply took the average couple a longer time than before to prepare themselves materially for marriage. In the sixteenth century, one in five women never married, and these, combined with the estimated 15 percent who were widows, constituted a large unmarried female population. A later marriage was a marriage of shorter duration, since couples who married in their thirties did not spend as much time together as couples who married in their twenties. And because women who bore children for the first time at advanced ages had higher mortality rates, late marriage meant more frequent remarriage for men. As evidenced by the rapid growth of orphanages and foundling homes between 1600 and 1800, delayed marriage also increased premarital sex and the number of illegitimate children.

Arranged Marriages Marriage tended to be "arranged" in the sense that the parents met and discussed the terms of the marriage before the prospective bride and bridegroom became directly party to the preparations. But the wealth and social standing of the bride and the bridegroom were not the only

things considered when youth married. By the fifteenth century, it was usual for the future bride and bridegroom to have known each other and to have had some prior relationship. Also, their emotional feeling for one another was respected by parents. Parents did not force total strangers to live together, and children had a legal right to protest and resist a coerced marriage, which was by definition invalid. The best marriage was one desired by the bride and groom and their families.

Family Size The West European family was conjugal, or nuclear, consisting of a father and a mother and two to four children who survived into adulthood. This nuclear family lived within a larger household, including in-laws, servants, laborers, and boarders. The average husband and wife had six to seven children, a new birth about every two years. Of these, an estimated one third died by age five, and one half by their teens. Rare was the family, at any social level, that did not experience infant mortality and child death.

Birth Control Artificial birth control (sponges, acidic ointments) has existed since antiquity. The church's condemnation of coitus interruptus (male withdrawal before ejaculation) during the thirteenth and fourteenth centuries suggests the existence of a contraceptive mentality, that is, a conscious, regular effort at birth control. Early birth control measures, when applied, were not very effective, and for both historical and moral reasons the church opposed them. According to Saint Thomas Aquinas, a moral act must aid and abet, never frustrate, nature's goal and the natural end of sex was the birth of children and their godly rearing within the bounds of holy matrimony and the community of the church.

Wet Nursing The church allied with the physicians of early modern Europe on another intimate family matter. Both condemned women who hired wet nurses to suckle their newborn children. The practice was popular among upper-class women and a reflection of their social standing. The practice appears to have increased the risk of infant mortality by exposing infants to a strange and shared milk supply from women who were often not as healthy as the infants' own mothers and lived under less sanitary conditions. But nursing was distasteful to some upper-class women, whose husbands also preferred that they not do it. Among women, vanity and convenience appear to have been motives for hiring a wet nurse, while for husbands, even more was at stake. Because the church forbade sexual intercourse to lactating women, a nursing wife often became a reluctant lover. In addition, nursing had a contraceptive effect (about 75 percent effective). Some women prolonged nursing their children to delay a new pregnancy, and some husbands cooperated in this form of family planning. For other husbands, however, especially noblemen and royalty who desired an abundance of male heirs, nursing seemed to rob them of offspring and jeopardize their patrimony—hence their support of hired wet nurses.

Loving Families?   The traditional Western European family had features that seem cold and distant. Children between the ages of eight and thirteen were routinely sent from their homes into apprenticeships, school, or employment in the homes and businesses of relatives, friends, and occasionally strangers. The emotional ties between spouses also seem to have been as tenuous as those between parents and children. Widowers and widows often married again within a few months of their spouses' deaths, and marriages with extreme disparity in age between partners suggest limited affection.

In response to modern-day criticism, an early modern parent might well have asked, "What greater love can parents have for their children than to equip them well for a worldly vocation?" A well-apprenticed child was a self-supporting child, and hence a child with a future. In light of the comparatively primitive living conditions, contemporaries also appreciated the purely utilitarian and humane side of marriage and understood when widowers and widows quickly remarried. Marriages with extreme disparity in age, however, were no more the norm in early modern Europe than the practice of wet nursing, and they received just as much criticism and ridicule.

The Wars of Religion

After the Council of Trent adjourned in 1563, Catholics began a Jesuit-led counteroffensive against Protestants. At the time of John Calvin's death in 1564, Geneva had become both a refuge for Europe's persecuted Protestants and an international school for Protestant resistance, producing leaders fully equal to the new Catholic challenge.

Genevan Calvinism and the reformed Catholicism of the Council of Trent were two equally dogmatic, aggressive, and irreconcilable church systems. Calvinists may have looked like "new papists" to critics when they dominated cities like Geneva, but when as minorities they found their civil and religious rights denied in the empire and elsewhere, they became true firebrands and revolutionaries.

Calvinism adopted a presbyterian organization that magnified regional and local religious authority. Boards of presbyters, or elders, representing the many individual Calvinist congregations, directly shaped the policy of the church at large. By contrast, the Counter-Reformation sponsored a centralized episcopal church system, hierarchically arranged from pope to parish priest and stressing absolute obedience to the person at the top. The high clergy—the pope and his bishops—not the synods of local churches, ruled supreme. Calvinism attracted proponents of political decentralization who opposed totalitarian rulers, whereas Catholicism remained congenial to proponents of absolute monarchy determined to maintain "one king, one church, one law."

The wars of religion were both internal national conflicts and truly international wars. Catholic and Protestant subjects struggled to control France, the Netherlands, and England. The Catholic governments of France and Spain conspired and finally sent armies against Protestant regimes in England and the Netherlands. The outbreak of the Thirty Years' War in 1618 made the international dimensions of the religious conflict especially clear; before it ended in 1648, the war drew every major European nation directly or indirectly into its deadly net.

FRENCH WARS OF RELIGION (1562–1598)

When Henry II (r. 1547–1559) died accidentally during a tournament in 1559, his sickly fifteen-year-old son, Francis II (d. 1560), came to the throne under the regency of the queen mother, Catherine de Médicis (1519–1589). With the monarchy so weakened, three powerful families began to compete to control France. They were the Bourbons, whose power lay in the south and west; the Montmorency-Châtillons, who controlled the center of France; and the Guises, who were dominant in eastern France. The Guises were by far the strongest, and the name of *Guise* was interchangeable with militant, ultra-Catholicism. The Bourbon and Montmorency-Châtillon families, in contrast, developed strong Huguenot sympathies, largely for political reasons. (French Protestants were called **Huguenots** after Besançon Hughes, the leader of Geneva's political revolt against the Savoyards in the late 1520s.) The Bourbon Louis I, prince of Condé (d. 1569), and the Montmorency-Châtillon admiral Gaspard de Coligny (1519–1572) became the political leaders of the French Protestant resistance.

Often for quite different reasons, ambitious aristocrats and discontented townspeople joined Calvinist churches in opposition to the Guise-dominated French monarchy. In 1561 over two thousand Huguenot congregations existed throughout France. Although they made up only about a fifteenth of the population, Huguenots held important geographic areas and represented the more powerful segments of French society. Over two fifths of the French aristocracy became Huguenots. Many apparently hoped to establish within France a principle of territorial sovereignty akin to that secured within the Holy Roman Empire by the Peace of Augsburg (1555). Calvinism thus indirectly served the forces of political decentralization.

Catherine de Médicis and the Guises   Following Francis II's death in 1560, Catherine de Médicis continued as regent for her second son, Charles IX (r. 1560–1574). Fearing the Guises, Catherine, whose first concern was always to preserve the monarchy, sought allies among the Protestants. Early in 1562 she granted Protestants freedom to worship publicly outside towns—although only privately within them—and to hold synods, or church assemblies. In March of the same year this royal toleration ended when the Duke of Guise surprised a Protestant congregation worshiping illegally at Vassy in Champagne and proceeded to massacre several score—an event that marked the beginning of the French wars of religion. Perpetually caught between fanatical Huguenot and Guise extremes, Queen Catherine always sought to play the one side against the other. She wanted a Catholic France but not a Guise-dominated monarchy.

On August 22, 1572, four days after the Huguenot Henry of Navarre had married Charles IX's sister—another sign of growing Protestant power in the queen mother's eye—the Huguenot leader Coligny, who increasingly had the king's ear, was wounded by an assassin's bullet. Catherine had apparently been a part of this Guise plot to eliminate Coligny. After its failure, she feared both the king's reaction to her complicity and the Huguenot response under a recovered Coligny. Catherine convinced Charles that a Huguenot coup was afoot, inspired by Coligny, and that only the swift execution of Protestant leaders could save the crown from a Protestant attack on Paris. On the eve of Saint Bartholomew's Day, August 24, 1572, Coligny and three thousand fellow Huguenots were butchered in Paris. Within three days an estimated twenty thousand Huguenots were executed in coordinated attacks throughout France.

▲ **The St. Bartholemew's Day Massacre.** In this notorious event, here depicted by the contemporary Protestant painter François Dubois, three thousand Protestants were slaughtered in Paris and an estimated twenty thousand others died throughout France. The massacre transformed the religious struggle in France from a contest for political power into an all-out war between Protestants and Catholics.

Le Massacre de la St–Barthelemy, entre 1572 et 1584. Oil on wood, 94 × 154 cm. Musée Cantonal des Beaux Arts, Lausanne. Photo: J.–C. Ducret Musee Cantonal des Beaux–Arts, Lausanne.

This event changed the nature of the struggle between Protestants and Catholics both within and beyond the borders of France. It was thereafter no longer an internal contest between Guise and Bourbon factions for French political influence, nor was it simply a Huguenot campaign to win basic religious freedoms. Henceforth, in Protestant eyes, it became an international struggle to the death for sheer survival against an adversary whose cruelty justified any means of resistance.

The Rise to Power of Henry of Navarre   Henry III (r. 1574–1589), who was Henry II's third son and the last Valois king, found the monarchy wedged between a radical Catholic League, formed in 1576 by Henry of Guise, and vengeful Huguenots. Like the queen mother, Henry III sought to steer a middle course, and in this effort he received support from a growing body of neutral Catholics and Huguenots who put the political survival of France above its religious unity. Such *politiques*, as they were called, were prepared to compromise religious creeds to save the nation.

In the mid-1580s the Catholic League, supported by the Spanish, became completely dominant in Paris. Henry III failed to rout the league with a surprise attack in 1588 and had to flee Paris. Forced by his weakened position into guerrilla tactics, the king had both the Duke and the Cardinal of Guise assassinated. The Catholic League reacted with a fury that matched the earlier Huguenot response to the Massacre of Saint Bartholomew's Day. The king was now forced to strike an alliance with his Protestant cousin and heir, Henry of Navarre, in April 1589.

As the two Henrys prepared to attack Paris, however, a fanatical Dominican friar murdered Henry III. Thereupon the Bourbon Huguenot Henry of Navarre became Henry IV of France (r. 1589–1610).

Henry IV came to the throne as a *politique*, weary of religious strife and prepared to place political peace above absolute religious unity. He believed that a royal policy of tolerant Catholicism would be the best way to achieve such peace. On July 25, 1593, he publicly abjured the Protestant faith and embraced the traditional and majority religion of his country. "Paris is worth a Mass," he is reported to have said.

The Edict of Nantes   Five years later, on April 13, 1598, Henry IV's famous Edict of Nantes proclaimed a formal religious settlement. In 1591 he had already assured the Huguenots of at least qualified religious freedoms. The Edict of Nantes made good that promise. It recognized and sanctioned minority religious rights within what was to remain an officially Catholic country. This religious truce—and it was never more than that—granted the Huguenots, who by this time numbered well over a million, freedom of public worship, the right of assembly, admission to public offices and universities, and permission to maintain fortified towns. Most of the new freedoms, however,

were to be exercised within their own localities. Concession of the right to fortify towns reveals the continuing distrust between French Protestants and Catholics. The edict only transformed a long hot war between irreconcilable enemies into a long cold war. To its critics, it created a state within a state.

A Catholic fanatic assassinated Henry IV in May 1610. Although Henry is best remembered for the Edict of Nantes, the political and economic policies he put in place were equally important. They laid the foundations for the transformation of France into the absolutist state it would become in the seventeenth century. Ironically, in pursuit of the political and religious unity that had escaped Henry IV, his grandson Louis XIV (r. 1643–1715), calling for "one king, one church, one law," would later revoke the Edict of Nantes in 1685 (see Chapter 20). This action would force France and Europe to learn again by bitter experience the hard lessons of the wars of religion. Rare is the politician who learns from the lessons of history rather than repeat its mistakes.

IMPERIAL SPAIN AND THE REIGN OF PHILIP II (1556–1598)

Until the English defeated his mighty Armada in 1588, no one person stood larger in the second half of the sixteenth century than Philip II of Spain. During the first half of his reign, attention focused on the Mediterranean and Turkish expansion. On October 7, 1571, a Holy League of Spain, Venice, and the pope defeated the Turks at Lepanto in the largest naval battle of the sixteenth century. Before the engagement ended, thirty thousand Turks had died and over one third of the Turkish fleet was sunk or captured.

Revolt in the Netherlands   The spectacular Spanish military success in southern Europe was not repeated in northern Europe when Philip attempted to impose his will within the Netherlands and on England and France. The resistance of the Netherlands especially proved the undoing of Spanish dreams of world empire.

The Netherlands were the richest area in Europe (see Map 16–5). The merchant towns of the Netherlands were Europe's most independent, however; many, like magnificent Antwerp, were also Calvinist strongholds. A stubborn opposition to the Spanish overlords formed under William of Nassau, the Prince of Orange (r. 1533–1584). Like other successful rulers in this period, William of Orange was a *politique* who placed the Netherlands' political autonomy and well-being above religious creeds. He personally passed through successive Catholic, Lutheran, and Calvinist stages.

The year 1564 saw the first fusion of political and religious opposition to Spanish rule, the result of Philip II's unwise insistence that the decrees of the Council of Trent be enforced throughout the Netherlands. A national covenant was drawn

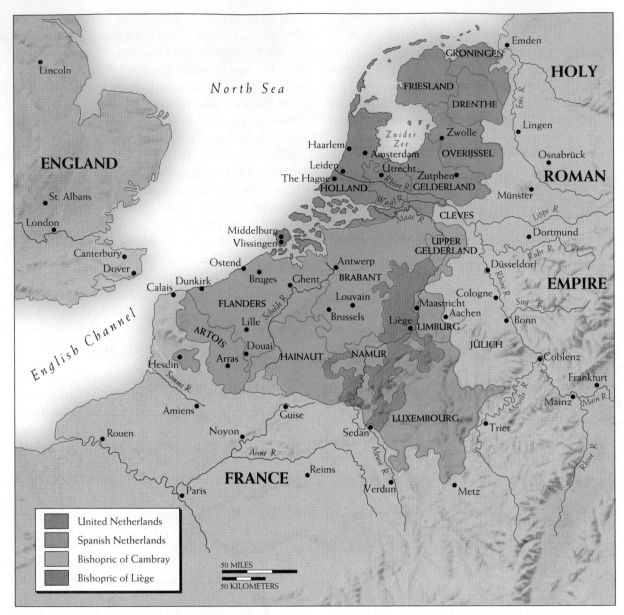

MAP 16–5 The Netherlands During the Reformation. The northern provinces of the Netherlands—the United Provinces—were mostly Protestant in the second half of the sixteenth century. The southern provinces—the Spanish Netherlands—made peace with Spain and remained largely Catholic.

up called the Compromise, a solemn pledge to resist the decrees of Trent and the Inquisition.

Philip dispatched the Duke of Alba (1508–1582) to suppress the revolt. His army of ten thousand men marched northward from Milan in 1567 in a show of combined Spanish and papal might. A special tribunal, known to the Spanish as the Council of Troubles and among the Netherlanders as the Council of Blood, reigned over the land. Several thousand suspected heretics were publicly executed before Alba's reign of terror ended.

William of Orange had been an exile in Germany during these turbulent years. He now emerged as the leader of a broad movement for the Netherlands' independence from Spain.

After a decade of persecution and warfare, the ten largely Catholic southern provinces (what is roughly modern Belgium) came together in 1576 with the seven largely Protestant northern provinces (what is roughly the modern Netherlands) in unified opposition to Spain. This union, known as the Pacification of Ghent, declared internal regional sovereignty in matters of religion. It was a Netherlands version of the Peace of Augsburg.

After more fighting, in January 1579 the southern provinces formed the Union of Arras and made peace with Spain. The northern provinces responded with the formation of the Union of Utrecht and continued the struggle. Spanish preoc-

The Milch Cow. This sixteenth-century satirical pain- ►
ting depicts the Netherlands as a land all the great
powers of Europe wish to exploit. Elizabeth of
England is feeding her (England had long-standing
commerical ties with Flanders); Philip II of Spain is
attempting to ride her (Spain was trying to reassert
its control over the entire region); William of Orange
is trying to milk her (he was the leader of the anti-
Spanish rebellion); and the king of France holds her
by the tail (France hoped to profit from the rebellion
at Spain's expense).

The "Milch Cow." Rijksmuseum, Amsterdam.

cupation with France and England in the 1580s permitted the
northern provinces to drive out all Spanish soldiers by 1593. In
1596 France and England formally recognized the independence of these provinces. However, the northern provinces did
not formally conclude peace with Spain until 1609, when the
Twelve Years' Truce concluded their virtual independence.
But Spain did not fully recognize that independence until the
Peace of Westphalia in 1648.

ENGLAND AND SPAIN (1558–1603)

Elizabeth I   Elizabeth I (r. 1558–1603), the daughter of Henry
VIII and Anne Boleyn, was perhaps the most astute politician of
the sixteenth century in both domestic and foreign policy. She
repealed the anti-Protestant legislation of her predecessor Mary
Tudor and guided a religious settlement through Parliament
that prevented England from being torn asunder by religious
differences in the sixteenth century, as the Continent was.

Catholic extremists hoped to replace Elizabeth with the
Catholic Mary Stuart, Queen of Scots. But Elizabeth acted
swiftly against Catholic assassination plots and rarely let emo-
tion override her political instincts.

Elizabeth dealt cautiously with the Puritans, Protestants who
sought to "purify" the national church of every vestige of "pop-
ery" and to make its Protestant doctrine more precise. The
Puritans had two special grievances: (1) the retention of
Catholic ceremony and vestments within the Church of England, and (2) the continuation of the episcopal system of
church governance.

▲ **Elizabeth I (1558–1603) Standing on a Map of England
in 1592.** An astute, if sometimes erratic, politician in
foreign and domestic policy, Elizabeth was one of the
most successful rulers of the sixteenth century.

National Portrait Gallery, London/SuperStock.

Sixteenth-century Puritans were not separatists, however. They worked through Parliament to create an alternative national church of semi-autonomous congregations governed by representative presbyteries (hence, Presbyterians), following the model of Calvin and Geneva. The more extreme Puritans wanted every congregation to be autonomous, a law unto itself, with no higher control. They came to be known as Congregationalists. Elizabeth refused to tolerate this group, whose views she considered subversive.

Deterioration of Relations with Spain A series of events led inexorably to war between England and Spain, despite the sincere desires of both Philip II and Elizabeth to avoid it. Following Spain's victory at Lepanto in 1571, England signed a mutual defense pact with France. Also in the 1570s, Elizabeth's famous seamen, John Hawkins (1532–1595) and Sir Francis Drake (?1545–1596), began to prey regularly on Spanish shipping in the Americas. Drake's circumnavigation of the globe between 1577 and 1580 was one in a series of dramatic demonstrations of English ascendancy on the high seas. In 1585 Elizabeth signed a treaty that committed English soldiers to the Netherlands. These events made a tinderbox of English-Spanish relations. The spark that finally touched it off was Elizabeth's reluctant execution of Mary, Queen of Scots (1542–1587) on February 18, 1587, for complicity in a plot to assassinate Elizabeth. Philip II ordered his Armada to make ready.

On May 30, 1588, a mighty fleet of 130 ships bearing 25,000 sailors and soldiers under the command of the Duke of Medina-Sidonia set sail for England. But the day belonged completely to the English. The barges that were to transport Spanish soldiers from the galleons onto English shores were prevented from leaving Calais and Dunkirk. The swifter English and Netherlands ships, assisted by an "English wind," dispersed the waiting Spanish fleet, over a third of which never returned to Spain. The Armada's defeat gave heart to Protestant resistance everywhere. Spain never fully recovered from it. By the time of Philip's death on September 13, 1598, his forces had been rebuffed by the French and the Dutch. His seventeenth-century successors were all inferior leaders who never knew responsibilities equal to Philip's; nor did Spain ever again know such imperial grandeur. The French soon dominated the Continent, while the Dutch and the English whittled away Spain's overseas empire.

Elizabeth died on March 23, 1603, leaving behind her a strong nation poised to expand into a global empire.

THE THIRTY YEARS' WAR (1618–1648)

The Thirty Years' War in the Holy Roman Empire was the last and most destructive of the wars of religion. Religious and political differences had long set Catholics against Protestants and Calvinists against Lutherans. What made the Thirty Years' War so devastating was the now entrenched hatred of the various sides and their seeming determination to sacrifice all for their territorial sovereignty and religious beliefs. As the conflicts multiplied, virtually every major European land became involved either directly or indirectly. When the hostilities ended in 1648, the peace terms shaped much of the map of northern Europe as we know it today (see Map. 16–6).

Fragmented German During the second half of the sixteenth century, Germany was an almost ungovernable land of 360 autonomous political entities. The Peace of Augsburg (1555) had given each a significant degree of sovereignty within its own borders. Each levied its own tolls and tariffs and coined its own money, practices that made land travel and trade between the various regions difficult, if not impossible. Many of these little "states" also had great power pretensions. Political decentralization and fragmentation characterized Germany as the seventeenth century opened; it was not a unified nation like Spain, England, or even strife-torn France.

Religious Division Religious conflict accentuated the international and internal political divisions (see Map 16–6). The Holy Roman Empire was about equally divided between Catholics and Protestants, the latter having perhaps a slight numerical edge by 1600 (see Map 16–7). The terms of the Peace of Augsburg (1555) had attempted to freeze the territorial holdings of the Lutherans and the Catholics. In the intervening years, however, the Lutherans had gained political control in many Catholic areas, as had the Catholics in a few previously Lutheran areas. There was also religious strife between liberal and conservative Lutherans and between Lutherans and the growing numbers of Calvinists.

As elsewhere in Europe, Calvinism was the political and religious leaven within the Holy Roman Empire. Unrecognized as a legal religion by the Peace of Augsburg, Calvinism established a strong foothold within the empire when Elector Frederick III (r. 1559–1576), a devout convert to Calvinism, made it the official religion within the Palatinate in 1559. By 1609 Palatine Calvinists headed a Protestant defensive alliance supported by Spain's sixteenth-century enemies: England, France, and the Netherlands.

If the Calvinists were active within the Holy Roman Empire, so also were their Catholic counterparts, the Jesuits. Staunchly Catholic Bavaria, supported by Spain, became militarily and ideologically for the Counter-Reformation what the Palatinate was for Protestantism. From Bavaria, the Jesuits launched successful missions throughout the empire. In 1609 Maximilian, Duke of Bavaria (1573–1651), organized a Catholic League to counter a new Protestant alliance that had been formed by the Calvinist Elector Palatine, Frederick IV (r. 1583–1610). When the league fielded a great army under the command of Jean't Senclaes, Count of Tilly, (1559–1632), the stage was set, internally and internationally, for the Thirty

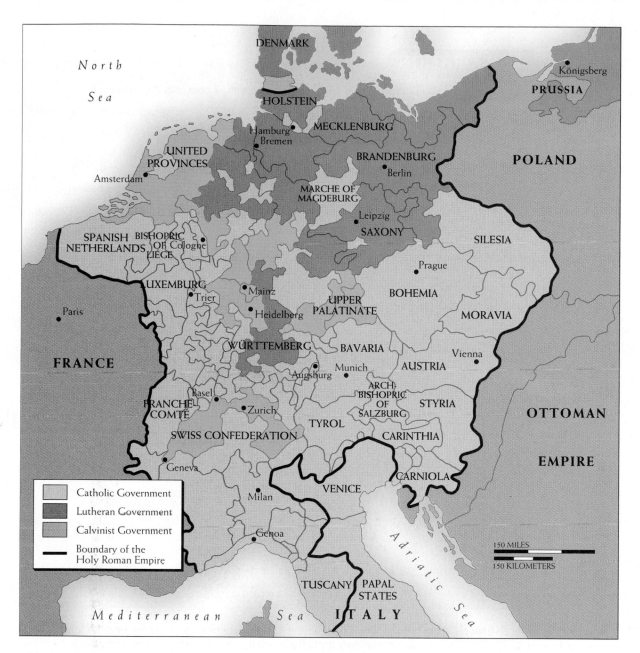

MAP 16–6 The Holy Roman Empire ca. 1618.   On the eve of the Thirty Years' War the empire was politically and religiously fragmented, as this somewhat simplified map reveals. Lutherans dominated the north and Catholics the south, while Calvinists controlled the United Provinces and the Palatinate and also had an important presence in Switzerland and Brandenburg.

Years' War, the worst European catastrophe since the Black Death of the fourteenth century.

The Treaty of Westphalia   In 1648 all hostilities within the Holy Roman Empire were brought to an end by the Treaty of Westphalia. It firmly reasserted the major feature of the religious settlement of the Peace of Augsburg (1555), as rulers were again permitted to determine the religion of their lands. The treaty also gave the Calvinists their long-sought legal

recognition while still denying it to sectarians. The independence of the Swiss Confederacy and the United Provinces of Holland, long recognized in fact, now became law.

By confirming the territorial sovereignty of Germany's many political entities, the Treaty of Westphalia perpetuated German division and political weakness into the modern period. However, two German states attained international significance during the seventeenth century: Austria and Brandenburg-Prussia. The petty regionalism within the

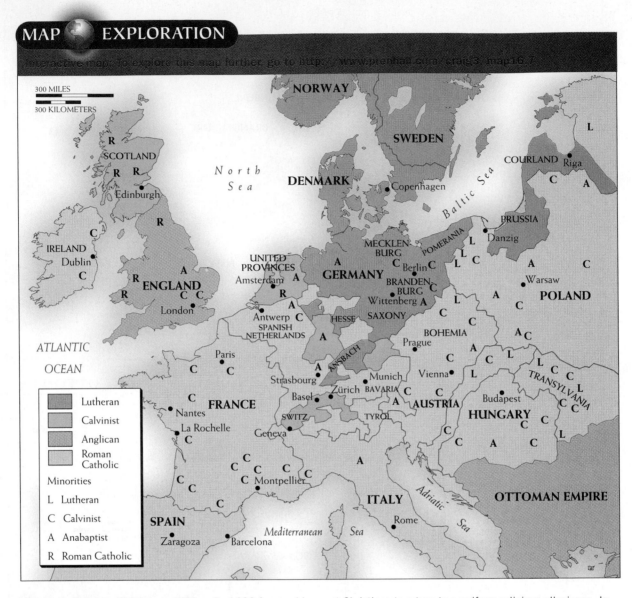

Interactive map: To explore this map further, go to http://www.prenhall.com/craig3_map16.7

MAP 16–7 Religious Division ca. 1600.   By 1600 few could expect Christians to return to a uniform religious allegiance. In Spain and southern Italy Catholicism remained relatively unchallenged, but note the existence elsewhere of large religious minorities, both Catholic and Protestant.

empire also reflected on a small scale the drift of larger European politics. During the seventeenth century distinctive nation-states, each with its own political, cultural, and religious identity, reached maturity and firmly established the competitive nationalism of the modern world.

Superstition and Enlightenment: The Battle Within

Religious reform and warfare permanently changed religious institutions in major European lands. They also moved intellectuals to rethink human nature and society. One side of that reconsideration was dark and cynical, perhaps because the peak years of religious warfare had also been those of the great European witch hunts. Another side, however, was brilliantly skeptical and constructive, reflecting the growing scientific movement of the years between 1500 and 1700.

WITCH HUNTS AND PANIC

Nowhere is the dark side of early modern thought and culture better seen than in the witch hunts and panics that erupted in almost every Western land. Between 1400 and 1700, courts sentenced an estimated 70,000 to 100,000 people to death for harmful magic (*maleficium*) and diabolical witchcraft. In addition to inflicting

OVERVIEW   The Religious Divisions of Europe

The Reformation permanently shattered the religious unity of Western Europe that had existed since the fifth century C.E. It also gave rise to more than a century of warfare, in which Catholics fought Protestants, and Protestants fought each other all in the name of faith. By 1648 when the Treaty of Westphalia ended the Thirty Years' War, Europe remained divided into regions that were mostly Catholic, those that were mostly Protestant, and those areas with large religious minorities. Most of these divisions have persisted to the present day.

Country	Religion
Scotland	Calvinist
England	Protestant (Anglicans, Calvinists, and Anabaptists); a declining Catholic minority
Ireland	Mostly Catholic but with a Protestant minority (Anglicans and Calvinists) mainly in the north
France	Catholic, but with substantial numbers of Calvinists
Belgium	Catholic
Netherlands	A Calvinist majority, but with a large Catholic minority
Spain	Catholic
Portugal	Catholic
Sandinavia	Lutheran
Switzerland	Almost evenly divided between Catholics and Protestants (both Calvinists and Lutherans)
Italy	Catholic
Austria	Catholic
Germany	The north was predominately Protestant (Lutheran, Calvinist, Anabaptist); the south and the Rhineland were mostly Catholic; but each area had religious minorities
Hungary	Mostly Catholic, but with a large Calvinist minority
Poland	Catholic
Lithuania	Catholic
Latvia	Lutheran
Estonia	Lutheran
Croatia	Catholic
Slovenia	Catholic
Bohemia (modern Czech Republic)	Catholic
Slovakia	Catholic

harm on their neighbors, witches were said to attend mass meetings known as *sabbats*, to which they were believed to fly. They were also accused of indulging in sexual orgies with the devil, who appeared in animal form, most often as a he-goat. Still other charges against them were cannibalism (especially the devouring of small Christian children) and a variety of ritual acts and practices, often sexual, that denied or perverted Christian beliefs.

Why did great witch panics occur in the second half of the sixteenth and early seventeenth centuries? The misfortune created by religious division and warfare were major factors. Some argue that the Reformation spurred the panics by ridiculing the traditional church defenses against the devil and demons, compelling people to protect themselves by searching out and executing witches. Political consolidation by secular governments

and the papacy probably played a greater role, with both aggressively conforming their realms and eliminating competition for the loyalty of their subjects.

Village Origins   The roots of witch beliefs are found in both popular and elite culture. In village societies, feared and respected "cunning folk" helped people cope with natural disasters and disabilities by magical means. For local people, these were important services that kept village life moving forward in times of calamity.

The possession of magical powers, for good or ill, made one an important person within village society. Claims to such powers were often made by those who were most in need of security and influence, particularly women, and especially old, impoverished single or widowed women. In village society witch beliefs may also have been a way to defy urban Christian society's attempts to impose its orthodox beliefs, laws, and institutions on the countryside. Under church persecution local fertility cults, whose customary semipagan practices were intended to ensure good harvests, acquired the features of diabolical witchcraft.

Influence of the Clergy   Popular belief in magic was the essential foundation of the witch hunts. Had ordinary people not believed that "gifted persons" could help or harm by magical means, and had they not been willing to make accusations against them, the hunts would never have occurred. The contribution of learned, Christian society was equally great. The Christian clergy also practiced magic, that of the holy sacraments, transforming bread and wine into the body and blood of Christ, and eternal punishments for sins into temporal ones. And they also exorcised demons.

In the late thirteenth century the church declared its magic the only legitimate magic. Since such power was not human, the theologians reasoned, it came either from God or from the devil.

That from God was properly exercised within and by the church. Any who practiced magic outside and against the church did so on behalf of the devil. From such reasoning grew allegations of "pacts" between non-Christian magicians and Satan. Attacking accused witches became a way for the church to extend its spiritual hegemony, especially in new areas being conformed by church and state to higher Christian society. As spiritual authorities revered and feared by villagers or townspeople, local cunning folk posed an obstacle to that mission. To accuse, try, and execute witches was a declaration of moral and political authority over a village or territory.

Why Women?   Roughly 80 percent of the victims of witch hunts were women, most single and between forty-five and sixty years of age. This suggests that misogyny fueled the witch hunts. Inspired by male hatred and sexual fear of women, and occurring at a time when women were also breaking out from under male control, witch hunts were simply a conspiracy of males against females.

Older single women claiming supernatural powers, may, however, have been vulnerable for more basic social reasons. As a dependent social group ever in need of public assistance, they were natural targets for the peculiar "social engineering" of the witch hunts. Because of their economic straits, more women than men laid claim to the supernatural powers that made them influential in village society. Such women thus found themselves on the front lines in disproportionate numbers when the church declared war against those who practiced magic without its special blessing. Also, many of these women were midwives an activity that which associated them with the deaths of beloved mothers and infants during childbirth; this misfortune made them targets of local resentment and accusations. Both the church and their neighbors were prepared to think and say the worst about them, a deadly combination.

End of the Witch Hunts   Many factors helped end the witch hunts. The emergence of a more scientific worldview made it difficult to believe in the powers of witches. In the seventeenth century mind and matter came to be viewed as two independent realities, making it harder to believe that words and thoughts could impact physical things. A witch's curse was merely words. With advances in medicine, the rise of insurance companies, and the availability of lawyers, people could protect themselves when physical affliction and natural calamity struck. Witch hunts also tended to get out of hand. Tortured witches sometimes alleged having seen leading townspeople at sabbats; even the judges themselves! At this point the trials ceased to serve the interests of those conducting them. They not only became dysfunctional but threatened anarchy as well.

WRITERS AND PHILOSOPHERS

By the end of the sixteenth century, many could no longer embrace either old Catholic or new Protestant absolutes. Intellectually as well as politically, the seventeenth century would be a period of transition, one already well prepared by the humanists and scientists of the Renaissance and post-Renaissance (see Chapter 22), who reacted strongly against medieval intellectual traditions.

The writers and philosophers of the late sixteenth and the seventeenth centuries were aware that they lived in a period of transition. Some embraced the emerging new science wholeheartedly (Hobbes and Locke), some tried to straddle the two ages (Cervantes and Shakespeare), and still others ignored or opposed the new developments that seemed mortally to threaten traditional values (Pascal).

Miguel de Cervantes Saavedra   Spanish literature of the sixteenth and seventeenth centuries was influenced by the peculiar religious and political history of Spain in this period. Spain was dominated by the Catholic Church, whose piety was strongly promoted by the state. The intertwining of Catholic piety and Spanish political power underlay literary preoccupation with medieval chivalric virtues—in particular, honor and loyalty.

Generally acknowledged to be the greatest Spanish writer of all time, Cervantes (1547–1616) was preoccupied in his work with the strengths and weaknesses of religious idealism. He was the son of a nomadic physician. Having received only a smattering of formal education, he educated himself by insatiable reading in vernacular literature and immersion in the school of life. As a young man, he worked in Rome for a Spanish cardinal. In 1570 he became a soldier and was decorated for gallantry at Lepanto (1571). He conceived and began to write his most famous work, *Don Quixote,* in 1603, while languishing in prison after conviction for theft.

The first part of *Don Quixote* appeared in 1605, and a second part in 1615. If, as many argue, the intent of this work was

to satirize the chivalric romances so popular in Spain, Cervantes failed to conceal his deep affection for the character he had created as an object of ridicule, Don Quixote. Don Quixote, a none-too-stable middle-aged man, is driven mad by reading too many chivalric romances. He comes to believe that he is an aspirant to knighthood and must prove his worthiness. To this end, he acquires a rusty suit of armor, mounts an aged horse, and chooses for his inspiration a quite unworthy peasant girl whom he fancies to be a noble lady to whom he can, with honor, dedicate his life.

Don Quixote's foil in the story—Sancho Panza, a clever, worldly wise peasant who serves as his squire—watches with bemused skepticism, but also with genuine sympathy, as his lord does battle with a windmill (which he mistakes for a dragon) and repeatedly makes a fool of himself as he gallops across the countryside. The story ends tragically with Don Quixote's humiliating defeat by a well-meaning friend, who, disguised as a knight, bests Don Quixote in combat and forces him to renounce his quest for knighthood. The humiliated Don Quixote does not, however,

▲ **Miguel de Cervantes Saavedra (1547–1616),** the author of Don Quixote, considered by many to be Spain's greatest writer.
Art Resource, N.Y.

come to his senses as a result. He returns sadly to his village to die a shamed and broken-hearted old man.

Throughout *Don Quixote*, Cervantes juxtaposed the down-to-earth realism of Sancho Panza with the old-fashioned religious idealism of Don Quixote. Cervantes admired the one as much as the other. He wanted his readers to remember that to be truly happy, men and women need dreams, even impossible ones, just as much as a sense of reality.

William Shakespeare   There is much less factual knowledge about William Shakespeare (1564–1616), the greatest playwright in the English language, than one would expect of such an important figure. He apparently worked as a schoolteacher for a time and in this capacity acquired his broad knowledge of Renaissance learning and literature. His work shows none of the Puritan distress over worldliness. He took the new commercialism and the bawdy pleasures of the Elizabethan Age in stride and with amusement. In politics and religion, he was a man of his time and not inclined to offend his queen.

That Shakespeare was interested in politics is apparent from his history plays and the references to contemporary political events that fill all his plays. He seems to have viewed government simply, however, through the character of the individual ruler, whether Richard III or Elizabeth Tudor, not in terms of ideal systems or social goals. By modern standards he was a political conservative, accepting the social rankings and the power structure of his day and demonstrating unquestioned patriotism.

Shakespeare knew the theater as one who participated in every phase of its life. A member and principal dramatist of a famous company of actors known as the King's Men, he was a playwright, actor, and part owner of a theater. His work brought together in an original synthesis the best past and current achievements in the dramatic arts. He particularly mastered the psychology of human motivation and passion and had a unique talent for psychological penetration.

Shakespeare wrote histories, comedies, and tragedies. The tragedies are considered his unique achievement. Four of these were written within a three-year period: *Hamlet* (1603), *Othello* (1604), *King Lear* (1605), and *Macbeth* (1606). The most original of the tragedies, *Romeo and Juliet* (1597), transformed an old popular story into a moving drama of "star-cross'd lovers."

In his lifetime and ever since, Shakespeare has been immensely popular with both audiences and readers. As Ben Jonson (1572–1637), a contemporary classical dramatist who created his own school of poets, put it in a tribute affixed to the *First Folio* edition of Shakespeare's plays (1623): "He was not of an age, but for all time."

Blaise Pascal   Blaise Pascal (1623–1662) was a French mathematician and a physical scientist widely acclaimed by his contemporaries. Torn between the continuing dogmatism and the

new skepticism of the seventeenth century, he aspired to write a work that would refute two groups: the Jesuits, whose casuistry (i.e., confessional tactics designed to minimize and even excuse sinful acts) he considered a distortion of Christian teaching, and the skeptics, who either denied religion altogether (atheists) or accepted it only as it conformed to reason (deists). Pascal never realized such a definitive work, and his views on these matters exist only in piecemeal form. He wrote against the Jesuits in his *Provincial Letters* (1656–1657), and he left behind a provocative collection of reflections on humankind and religion that was published posthumously under the title *Pensées*.

Pascal was early influenced by the Jansenists, seventeenth-century Catholic opponents of the Jesuits. Although good Catholics, the Jansenists shared with the Calvinists Saint Augustine's belief in the total sinfulness of human beings, their eternal predestination by God, and their complete dependence on faith and grace for knowledge of God and salvation.

Pascal believed that reason and science, although attesting to human dignity, remained of no avail in religion. Here only the reasons of the heart and a "leap of faith" could prevail. Pascal saw two essential truths in the Christian religion: A loving God, worthy of human attainment, exists, and human beings, because they are corrupted in nature, are utterly unworthy of God. Pascal believed that the atheists and deists of the age had spurned the lesson of reason. For him, rational analysis of the human condition attested to humankind's utter mortality and corruption and exposed the weakness of reason itself in resolving the problems of human nature and destiny. Reason should rather drive those who truly heed it to faith and dependence on divine grace.

Pascal made a famous wager with the skeptics. It is a better bet, he argued, to believe that God exists and to stake everything on his promised mercy than not to do so; if God does exist, everything will be gained by the believer, whereas the loss incurred by having believed in God should he prove not to exist is, by comparison, very slight.

Pascal was convinced that belief in God measurably improved earthly life psychologically and disciplined it morally, regardless of whether God proved in the end to exist. He thought that great danger lay in the surrender of traditional religious values. Pascal urged his contemporaries to seek self-understanding by "learned ignorance" and to discover humankind's greatness by recognizing its misery. Thereby he hoped to counter what he believed to be the false optimism of the new rationalism and science.

Baruch Spinoza   The most controversial thinker of the seventeenth century was Baruch Spinoza (1632–1677), the son of a Jewish merchant of Amsterdam. Spinoza's philosophy caused his excommunication by his own synagogue in 1656. In 1670 he published his *Treatise on Religious and Political Philosophy*, a work that criticized the dogmatism of Dutch Calvinists and championed freedom of thought. During his lifetime, both Jews and Protestants attacked him as an atheist.

Spinoza's most influential writing, *Ethics*, appeared after his death in 1677. Religious leaders universally condemned it for its apparent espousal of pantheism. God and nature were so closely identified by Spinoza that little room seemed left either for divine revelation in Scripture or for the personal immortality of the soul, denials equally repugnant to Jews and to Christians.

The most controversial part of *Ethics* deals with the nature of substance and of God. According to Spinoza there is only one substance, which is self-caused, free, and infinite, and God is that substance. From this definition, it follows that everything that exists is in God and cannot even be conceived of apart from him. Such a doctrine is not literally pantheistic, because God is still seen to be more than the created world that he, as primal substance, embraces. Nonetheless, in Spinoza's view, statements about the natural world are also statements about divine nature. Mind and matter are seen to be extensions of the infinite substance of God; what transpires in the world of humankind and nature is a necessary outpouring of the Divine.

Such teaching clearly ran the danger of portraying the world as eternal and human actions as unfree and inevitable, the expression of a divine fatalism. Such points of view had been considered heresies by Jews and Christians because these views deny the creation of the world by God and destroy any voluntary basis for personal reward and punishment.

Thomas Hobbes Thomas Hobbes (1588–1679) was the most original political philosopher of the seventeenth century. Although he never broke with the Church of England, he came to share basic Calvinist beliefs, especially the low view of human nature and the ideal of a commonwealth based on a covenant, both of which find eloquent expression in his political philosophy.

Hobbes was an urbane and much traveled man and one of the most enthusiastic supporters of the new scientific movement. During the 1630s he visited Paris, where he came to know Descartes; after the outbreak of the Puritan Revolution (see Chapter 20) in 1640, he lived as an exile in Paris until 1651. Hobbes also spent time with Galileo (see Chapter 22) in Italy and took a special interest in the works of William Harvey. Harvey was a physiologist famed for the discovery of how blood circulated through the body; his scientific writings influenced Hobbes's own tracts on bodily motions.

Hobbes was driven to the vocation of political philosophy by the English Civil War (see Chapter 20). In 1651 his *Leviathan* appeared. Its subject was the political consequences of human passions, and its originality lay in (1) its making natural law, rather than common law (i.e., custom or precedent), the basis of all positive law, and (2) its defense of a representative theory of absolute authority against the theory of the divine right of kings. Hobbes maintained that statute law found its justification only as an expression of the law of nature and that rulers derived their authority from the consent of the people.

Hobbes viewed humankind and society in a thoroughly materialistic and mechanical way. Human beings are defined as a collection of material particles in motion. All their psychological processes begin with and are derived from bare sensation, and all their motivations are egotistical, intended to increase pleasure and minimize pain.

Despite this seemingly low estimate of human beings, Hobbes believed much could be accomplished by the reasoned use of science. All was contingent, however, on the correct use of that greatest of all human powers, one compounded of the powers of most people: the commonwealth, in which people are united by their consent in one all-powerful person.

The key to Hobbes' political philosophy is a brilliant myth of the original state of humankind. According to this myth, human beings in the natural state are generally inclined to a "perpetual and restless desire of power after power that ceases only in death."[4] As all people desire—and in the state of nature have a natural right to—everything, their equality breeds enmity, competition, and diffidence, and the desire for glory begets perpetual quarreling—"a war of every man against every man."[5]

Whereas earlier and later philosophers saw the original human state as a paradise from which humankind had fallen, Hobbes saw it as a corruption from which only society had delivered people. Contrary to the views of Aristotle and of Christian thinkers like Thomas Aquinas, Hobbes saw human beings not as sociable, political animals, but as self-centered beasts, laws unto themselves, utterly without a master unless one is imposed by force.

According to Hobbes, people escape the impossible state of nature only by entering a social contract that creates a commonwealth tightly ruled by law and order. The social contract obliges every person, for the sake of peace and self-defense, to agree to set aside personal rights to all things. We should impose restrictions on the liberty of others only to the degree that we would allow others to restrict our own.

Because words and promises are insufficient to guarantee this state, the social contract also establishes the coercive force necessary to compel compliance with the covenant. Hobbes believed that the dangers of anarchy were far greater than those of tyranny, and he conceived of the ruler's power as absolute and unlimited. There is no room in Hobbes's political philosophy for political protest in the name of individual conscience, nor for resistance to legitimate authority by private individuals—features of *Leviathan* criticized by his contemporary Catholics and Puritans alike.

---

[4] *Leviathan*, Parts I and II, ed. by H. W. Schneider (Indianapolis, IN: Bobbs-Merrill, 1958), p. 86.
[5] Ibid., p. 106.

John Locke   John Locke (1632–1704) has proved to be the most influential political thinker of the seventeenth century.[6] His political philosophy came to be embodied in the so-called Glorious Revolution of 1688–1689 (Chapter 20). Although he was not as original as Hobbes, his political writings were a major source of the later Enlightenment criticism of absolutism, and they gave inspiration to both the American and French Revolutions.

Locke's two most famous works are the *Essay Concerning Human Understanding* (1690) (discussed in Chapter 22) and *Two Treatises of Government* (1690). Locke wrote *Two Treatises of Government* against the argument that rulers were absolute in their power. Rulers, Locke argued, remain bound to the law of nature, which is the voice of reason, teaching that "all mankind [are] equal and independent, [and] no one ought to harm another in his life, health, liberty, or possessions,"[7] inas-much as all human beings are the images and property of God. According to Locke, people enter social contracts, empowering legislatures and monarchs to "umpire" their disputes, precisely to preserve their natural rights, and not to give rulers an absolute power over them.

"Whenever that end [namely, the preservation of life, liberty, and property for which power is given to rulers by a commonwealth] is manifestly neglected or opposed, the trust must necessarily be forfeited and the power devolved into the hands of those that gave it, who may place it anew where they think best for their safety and security."[8] From Locke's point of view, absolute monarchy was "inconsistent" with civil society and could be "no form of civil government at all."[9]

---

[6] Locke's scientific writings are discussed in Chapter 24.

[7] *The Second Treatise of Government*, ed. by T. P. Peardon (Indianapolis, IN: Bobbs-Merrill, 1952), chap. 2, sects. 4–6, pp. 4–6.

[8] Ibid., chap. 13, sect. 149, p. 84.

[9] Ibid.

Ships of a Portuguese Explorer.

Summary

Voyages of Discovery   In the late fifteenth century, Europe began to expand around the globe. Driven by both mercenary and religious motives, the Portuguese pioneered a sea route around Africa to India and the Far East, and the Spanish discovered the Americas. Social, political, and biological consequences were immense for Europeans, Native Americans, Africans, and Asians. In time, a truly global world would emerge.

The Reformation   The Reformation began in Germany with Martin Luther's attack on indulgences in 1517. Despite the opposition to the Reformation of Emperor Charles V, Luther had the support of many German princes. The Reformation shattered the religious unity of Europe. In Switzerland, Zwingli and Calvin launched their own versions of Protestantism. In England, Henry VIII repudiated papal authority when the pope refused to grant him a divorce. The different protestant sects were often as hostile to each other as they were to Catholicism. The Reformation also led to far-reaching changes in religious practices and social attitudes, including steps toward the advancement of women.

The Roman Catholic Church also acted to reform itself. The Council of Trent tightened church discipline and reaffirmed traditional doctrine. The Jesuits converted many Protestants back to Catholicism.

The Wars of Religion   The religious divisions of Europe led to more than a century of warfare from the 1520s to 1648. The chief battlegrounds were in France, the Netherlands, and Germany. When the Thirty Years' War ended in 1648, Europe was permanently divided into Catholic and Protestant areas.

Superstition and Enlightenment   The Reformation led to both dark and constructive views of human nature. Perhaps the darkest view was the witch crazes that erupted across Europe. Thousands of innocent people, mostly women, were persecuted and executed as witches between 1400 and 1700 by both Catholic and Protestant authorities.

In literature and philosophy, however, these years witnessed an outpouring of creative thinking. Among the greatest writers of the age were Cervantes, Shakespeare, Pascal, Spinoza, Hobbes, and Locke.

Review Questions

1. What impact did European expansion have on the societies of both the Old and New Worlds?

2. What were the main problems of the church that contributed to the Protestant Reformation? Why was the church unable to suppress dissent as it had earlier?

3. How did the theologies of Luther, Zwingli, and Calvin differ? Were their differences only religious, or did they have political consequences for the Reformation as well?

4. Why did the Reformation begin in Germany and not in France, Italy, England, or Spain?

5. What was the Catholic Reformation? Did the Council of Trent alter the character of traditional Catholicism?

6. Why did Henry VIII break with the Catholic Church? Was the "new" religion he established really Protestant?

7. Were the wars of religion really over religion? Explain.

8. Henry of Navarre (later Henry IV of France), Elizabeth I, and William of Orange have been called *politiques*. What does that term mean, and how might it apply to each?

9. Why was England more successful than other lands in resolving its internal political and religious divisions peacefully during the sixteenth and seventeenth centuries?

10. "The Thirty Years' War is the outstanding example in European history of meaningless conflict." Evaluate this statement and provide specific reasons.

Key Terms

Counter-Reformation (p. 454)

Diet of Worms (p. 447)

Huguenot (p. 459)

indulgences (p. 445)

ninety-five theses (p. 446)

Reformation (p. 443)

transubstantiation (p. 450, 456)

Documents CD-ROM

Renaissance and Reformation in Europe
13.4 Martin Luther
13.5 Luther vs. Erasmus: A Reformer's Attack on Free Will
13.6 John Calvin and the Genevan Reformation
13.7 Council of Trent: The Catholic-Reformation
13.8 The Society of Jesus

European Explorations and Expansion
14.2 Vasco da Gama, Journey to India

14.4 "Cut Off Their Ears, Hands and Noses!": Gaspar Correa
14.5 Christopher Columbus
14.9 The Prospects of Christian Conversion: Saint Francis Xavier

From Old Regime to Revolution
18.1 "The Mortal God": Leviathan (1651)

NOTE: *To learn more about the topics in this chapter, see the Suggested Readings at the end of the book.*

CHRISTIANITY

Christianity is based on the teaching of Jesus of Nazareth, a Jew who lived in Palestine during the Roman occupation. His simple message of faith in God and self-sacrificial love of one's neighbor attracted many people. The Roman authorities, perceiving his large following as a threat, crucifed him. After Jesus' crucifixion, his followers proclaimed that he had been resurrected from the dead and that he would return in glory, to defeat sin, death, and the devil, and take all true believers with him to heaven—a radical vision of judgment and immortality that has driven Christianity's appeal since its inception. In the teachings of the early church, Jesus became the Christ, the son of God, the long-awaited Messiah of Jewish prophecy. His followers called themselves Christians.

Christianity proclaimed the very incarnation of God in a man, the visible presence of eternity in time. According to early Christian teaching, the power of God's incarnation in Jesus lived on in the preaching and sacraments of the church under the guidance of the Holy Spirit. According to the Christian message, in Jesus, eternity has made itself accessible to every person here and now and forevermore.

The new religion attracted both the poor and powerless and the socially rising and well-to-do. For some, the gospel of Jesus promised a better material life. For others, it imparted a sense of spiritual self-worth regardless of one's place or prospects in society.

In the late second century the Romans began persecuting Christians as "heretics" (because of their rejection of the traditional Roman gods) and as social revolutionaries (for their loyalty to a lord higher than the emperor of Rome). At the same time dissenting Christians, particularly sects claiming direct spiritual knowledge of God apart from Scripture, internally divided the young church, To meet these challenges the church established effective weapons against state terrorism and Christian heresy: an ordained clergy, a hierarchical church organization, orthodox creeds, and a biblical canon (the New Testament). Christianity not only gained legal status within the Roman Empire, but also, by the fourth century, most favored religious status thanks to Emperor Constantine's embrace of it.

After the fall of the Western Roman Empire in the fifth century C.E., Christianity became one of history's great success stories. Aided by the enterprise of its popes and the example of its monks, the church cultivated an appealing lay piety centered around the Lord's Prayer, the Apostles' Creed, veneration of the Virgin, and the sacrament of the Eucharist. Clergy became both royal teachers and bureaucrats within the kingdom of the Franks. Despite a growing schism between the Eastern (Byzantine) and Western churches, and a final split in 1054, by 1000 the church held real economic and political power. In the eleventh century reform-minded prelates put an end to presumptuous secular interference in its most intimate spiritual affairs by ending the lay investiture of clergy in their spiritual offices. For several centuries thereafter the church remained a formidable international force, able to challenge kings and emperors and inspire crusades to the Holy Land.

By the fifteenth century the new states of Europe had stripped the church of much of its political power. It was thereafter progressively confined to spiritual and moral authority. Christianity's

▲ **Pentecost.** This exquisite enamel plaque, from the Mosan school that flourished in France in the eleventh and twelfth centuries, shows the descent of the Holy Spirit upon the apostles, fifty days after the resurrection of Jesus, on the ancient Jewish festival called the "feast of weeks," or Pentecost.
Courtesy Metropolitan Museum of ART.

Female Bishop. Women are entering the ministry and priesthood of many Christian denominations. The first woman bishop of the Episcopal Church of North America is here shown consecrating the Eucharist. The Church of England has also voted to admit women to the priesthood.
Ira Wyman/Corbis/Sygma.

greatest struggles ever since have been not with kings and emperors over political power, but with materialistic philosophies and worldly ideologies, matters of spiritual and moral hegemony within an increasingly pluralistic and secular world. Since the sixteenth century a succession of humanists, skeptics, Deists, Rationalists, Marxists, Freudians, Darwinians, and atheists have attempted to explain away some of traditional Christianity's most basic teachings. In addition, the church has endured major internal upheavals. After the Protestant Reformation (1517–1555) made the Bible widely available to the laity, the possibilities for internal criticism of Christianity multiplied geometrically. Beginning with the split between Lutherans and Zwinglians in the 1520s, Protestant Christianity has fragmented into hundreds of sects each claiming to have the true interpretation of Scripture. The Roman Catholic church, by contrast, has maintained its unity and ministry throughout perilous times, although present-day discontent with papal authority threatens the modern Catholic church almost as seriously as the Protestant Reformation once did.

Christianity has remained remarkably resilient. It possesses a simple, almost magically appealing gospel of faith and love in and through Jesus. In a present-day world whose religious needs and passions still run deep, evangelical Christianity has experienced a remarkable revival. The Roman Catholic church, still troubled by

challenges to papal authority, has become more pluralistic than in earlier periods. The pope has become a world figure, traveling to all continents to represent the church and advance its position on issues of public and private morality. A major ecumenical movement emerging in the 1960s has promoted unprecedented cooperation among evangelical Christian denominations. Everywhere Christians of all stripes are politically active, spreading their divine, moral, and social messages. Meanwhile, old hot-button issues, such as the ordination of women, are being overtaken by new ones, particularly the marriage of gay men and women and the removal of clergy who do not maintain the moral discipline of their holy orders.

◆ Over the century what have been some of the chief factors attracting people to Christianity?

◆ What forces have led to disunity among Christians in the past; what factors cause tensions among modern Christians?

Africa
ca. 1000–1800

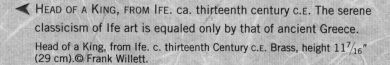

◄ HEAD OF A KING, FROM IFE. ca. thirteenth century C.E. The serene classicism of Ife art is equaled only by that of ancient Greece.

Head of a King, from Ife. c. thirteenth Century C.E. Brass, height $11^{7}/_{16}$" (29 cm).© Frank Willett.

Africa, 1000–1800

Developments in African history from 1000 to 1800 varied markedly by region. Because of trade, the North African coast and the Sahel, because of trade, were oriented toward the Mediterranean and the *dar-al-Islam*. The East African coast, also under Islamic influence was integrated into the Indian Ocean basin, while Sub-Saharan Africa was culturally diverse. It is important to remember that Africa, unlike China, India, or Japan, is a continent home to many societies with different histories, languages, religions, and cultures. Africa is also much larger than Europe, which some geographers view more as a peninsula of a vast Eurasian continent than as a continent in its own right, and more ethnically and culturally diverse.

Along the Mediterranean, the key new factor in African history at this time was the Ottomans' imperial expansion into Egypt and the Magrehb. Their long hegemony in the Mediterranean, altered the political configuration of the Mediterranean world. Merchants and missionaries carried Islam and Arabian cultural influences across the Sahara from North Africa and the Middle East to the Sudan, where Muslim conversion played a growing social and political role, especially among the ruling elites who profited most from brokering trade between their lands and the Islamic north. Islam provided a shared arena of expression for at least some classes and groups in societies over a vast area from Egypt to Senegambia. In Africa as elsewhere, the successful diffusion of Islam and Arabian culture depended upon their modification through a process of syncretism to create a distinctive African form of Islam faithful to tenets of the religion, but differing in its observances and customs from those of the Arabian cultural sphere, especially in attitudes toward women and relationships between the sexes.

At the same time, most Africans from the Sahara south clung to their older traditions. In central and southern Africa, except along the east coast, and in the West African forests, there was little or no evidence of Islam beyond individual Muslims involved in trade. On the east coast, however, Islam influenced the development of the Swahili culture and language, a

unique blend of African, Indian, and Arabian traditions, and Islamic traders linked the region to India, China, and the Indies. In sub-Saharan Africa, the spread of Islam took place almost entirely through peaceful means.

Along the Atlantic and Indian Ocean coasts of Africa, the key development of the fifteenth century was the appearance of ships from Christian Europe and the traders and missionaries they carried. First the Portuguese and later the Dutch, Spaniards, and other Europeans came by sea in search of commerce and eventually spheres of influence. The strength of African societies and the geographical and ecological dangers to Europeans venturing into the interior meant, however, that most of the trade between the African interior and Europeans on both the east and west coasts remained in the hands of Africans for generations after the first arrival of the Europeans. Even before Europeans themselves penetrated into the interior, however, the trade in slaves, weapons, and gold that they fostered disrupted traditional political and social structures and greatly altered African societies that had not yet even seen a European. The European voyages of discovery of the fifteenth and sixteenth centuries were especially important for Africa, therefore, presaging the continent's involvement in a new, expanding and, by the eighteenth century, European-dominated global trading system. This system generally exploited rather than bolstered African development, as the infamous Atlantic slave trade and the South African experience illustrate.

THINK AHEAD

◆ Which parts of Africa were most influenced by Islam?

◆ Where in Africa was Islam concentrated? How did Islam spread? What does this reveal about the relationship between commerce and cultural diffusion?

◆ What impact did the arrival of Europeans have on African societies?

THE HISTORY OF AFRICA IN THE FIRST HALF OF THE second millennium C.E. varied considerably for different parts of the continent. Many African regions were little influenced by outsiders; others were strongly influenced by Europe and the Islamic world.

The Atlantic slave trade was the major phenomenon that affected almost all of Africa between the fifteenth and nineteenth centuries and is treated in Chapter 18. However, in this chapter we cannot overlook its importance in disrupting and reconfiguring African economies, social organization, and political life

We begin with Africa above the equator, where the influence of Islam increased and where substantial empires and kingdoms developed. Then we discuss west, east, central, and southern Africa and the effects of first Arab-Islamic and then European influence in these regions.

North Africa and Egypt

As we saw in Chapter 13, Egypt and other North African societies played a central role in Islamic and Mediterranean history after 1000 C.E. From Tunisia to Egypt, Sunni religious and political leaders and their Shi'ite, especially Isma'ili, counterparts struggled for the minds of the masses. By the thirteenth century, however, the Shi'ites had become a small minority of the Muslim population of Mediterranean Africa. In Egypt a Sunni revival confirmed the Sunni character of Egyptian religiosity and legal interpretation: In general, a feisty regionalism characterized states, city-states, and tribal groups north of the Sahara and along the lower Nile. No single power controlled them for long. Regionalism persisted even after 1500, when most of North Africa came under the influence—and often direct control—of the Ottoman Empire centered in Istanbul and felt the pressure of Ottoman–European naval rivalry in the Mediterranean.

By 1800 the nominally Ottoman domains from Egypt to Algeria were effectively independent. In Egypt the Ottomans had established direct rule after their defeat of the Mamluks in 1517, but by the seventeenth and eighteenth centuries, power had passed to Egyptian governors descended from the former ruling Mamluks. These Mamluk governors survived until the rise of Muhammad Ali in the wake of the French invasion of 1800 (see Chapter 27). The Mediterranean coastlands between Egypt and Morocco were officially Ottoman provinces, or regencies. By the eighteenth century, however, Algiers was a separate, locally run principality with an economy based on piracy. Tripoli (in modern Libya) was ruled by a family of hereditary, effectively independent rulers, and Tunisia was virtually independent of its nominal Ottoman overlords.

Morocco, ruled by a succession of *Sharifs* (leaders claiming descent from the family of the Prophet Muhammad), was the only North African sultanate to remain fully independent after 1700. The most important *Sharifian* dynasty was that of the Sa'dis (1554–1659). One major reason for Morocco's independence was that its Arab and Berber populations united after 1500 to oppose the Portuguese and the Spaniards.

The Spread of Islam South of the Sahara

Islamic influence in sub-Saharan Africa began as early as the eighth century and by 1800 affected most of the Sudanic belt and the coast of East Africa as far south as modern Zimbabwe. The process was mostly peaceful, gradual, and partial. Islam

▲ **Feluccas on the Nile.** These lateen-rigged sailing vessels are the traditional riverboats of Egypt and are still in use today.
Hisham F. Ibrahim/Getty Images, Inc.-Photodisc.

▲ **The Great Mosque in Timbuktu.** This mud and wood building is typical of western Sudanese mosques. The distinctive tower of the mosque was a symbol of the presence of Islam, which came to places like Timbuktu in central and West Africa by way of overland trade routes.
Werner Forman/Art Resource, N.Y.

rarely penetrated beyond the ruling or commercial classes and tended to coexist or blend with indigenous ideas and practices. Nevertheless, agents of Islam brought commercial and political changes as well as the Qur'an, new religious practices, and literate culture, which proved as important for subsequent history as any other development. Many innovations, from architecture and technology to intellectual life and administrative practice, depended on writing and literacy, two major bases for developing large-scale societies and cultures.

Comparison of the spread of Islam in West and central Africa with that in East Africa is instructive. In East Africa, Muslim traders moving down the coastline with the ancient monsoon trade routes had begun to "Islamize" ports and coastal regions even before 800 C.E. From the thirteenth century on, Islamic trading communities and city-states developed along the coast from Mogadishu to Kilwa.

By contrast, in the western and central parts of the continent, Islam penetrated south of the Sahara into the Sudan by overland routes, primarily from North Africa and the Nile valley. Yet as in East Africa, its agents were traders, chiefly Berbers who plied the desert routes (see Chapter 5) to trading towns such as Awdaghast on the edge of the Sahel, as early as the eighth century. From there Islam spread south to centers such as Kumbi and beyond, southeast across the Niger, and west

into Senegambia. Another source for the gradual spread of Islam into the central and western Sudan were Egypt and the Nilotic Sudan. Its agents were primarily emigrants from the east seeking new land; migrating Arab tribal groups in particular came west to settle in the central sub-Saharan Sahel.

Some Muslim conversion in the western and central Sudan came early, again virtually always through the agency of Muslim traders. The year 985 marks the first time a West Africa royal court—that of the kingdom of Gao, east of the Niger bend—officially became Muslim (see Chapter 5 and below). The Gao rulers did not, however, try to convert their subjects. By contrast, as we shall see later in the chapter, the rulers of the later kingdom of Ghana long maintained their indigenous traditions even though they traded with Muslims and had Muslim advisors.

From the 1030s zealous militants known as Almoravids (see Chapter 13) began an overt conversion campaign that extended to the western Sahel and Sahara. This movement eventually swept into Ghana's territory, taking first Awdaghast and finally Kumbi in 1076. Thereafter, the forcibly converted Soninke ruling group of Ghana spread Islam among their own populace and farther south in the savannah. Here they converted Mande-speaking traders, who brought Islam south into the forests. Farther west, the Fulbe rulers of Takrur along the Senegal became Muslim in the 1030s and propagated their new faith among their subjects. The Fulbe, or Fulani, remained important carriers of Islam over the next eight centuries as they migrated gradually into new regions as far east as Lake Chad, where some rulers were Muslim as early as 1100.

Major groups in West Africa strongly resisted Islamization, especially the Mossi kingdoms founded in the Volta region at Wagadugu around 1050 and Yatenga about 1170.

Sahelian Empires of the Western and Central Sudan

As we noted in Chapter 5, substantial states had risen in the first millennium C.E. in the Sahel regions just south of the Sahara proper.[1] From about 1000 to 1600, four of these developed into relatively long-lived empires: Ghana, Mali, and Songhai in the western Sudan, and Kanem-Bornu in the central Sudan.

GHANA

Ghana established the model for later empires of the Sahel region of the western Sudan. It was located well north of modern Ghana (and unrelated to it except by name) in the region between the inland Niger Delta and the upper Senegal to the

[1] S. K. and R. J. McIntosh, *Prehistoric Investigations at Jenne, Mali* (1980), pp. 41–59, 434–461; R. Oliver, *The African Experience* (New York: Harper-Collins, 1991), pp. 90–101.

DOCUMENT   Ghana and Its People in the Mid–Eleventh Century

The following excerpt is from the geographical work of the Spanish Muslim geographer al-Bakri (d. 1094). In it he describes customs of the ruler and people of the capital of Ghana as he carefully gleaned them from other Arabic sources and travelers (he never visited West Africa himself, it seems).

◆ How did the ruler of Ghana deal with the differing religious groups in his capital?

Ghana is a title given to their kings; the name of the region is Awkar, and their king today, namely in the year 460 [1067–8], is Tanka Manin. ... This Tanka Manin is powerful, rules an enormous kingdom, and possesses great authority.

The city of Ghana consists of two towns situated on a plain. One of these towns, which is inhabited by Muslims, is large and possesses twelve mosques, in one of which they assemble for the Friday prayer. There are salaried imams and muezzins, as well as jurists and scholars. In the environs are wells with sweet water, from which they drink and with which they grow vegetables. The king's town is six miles distant from this one and bears the name of Al-Ghaba. Between these two towns there are continuous habitations. The houses of the inhabitants are of stone and acacia (*sunt*) wood. The king has a palace and a number of domed dwellings all surrounded with an enclosure like a city wall (*sur*). In the king's town, and not far from his court of justice, is a mosque where the Muslims who arrive at his court ... pray. Around the king's town are domed buildings and groves and thickets where the sorcerers of these people, men in charge of the religious cult, live. In them too are their idols and the tombs of their kings. ...

All of them shave their beards, and women shave their heads. The king adorns himself like a woman [wearing necklaces] round his neck and [bracelets] on his forearms, and he puts on a high cap (*tartur*) decorated with gold and wrapped in a turban of fine cotton. He sits in audience or to hear grievances against officials (*mazalim*) in a domed pavilion around which stand ten horses covered with gold-embroidered materials. Behind the king stand ten pages holding shields and swords decorated with gold, and on his right are the sons of the [vassal] kings of his country wearing splendid garments and their hair plaited with gold. The governor of the city sits on the ground before the king and around him are ministers seated likewise. ... When the people who profess the same religion as the king approach him they fall on their knees and sprinkle dust on their heads, for this is their way of greeting him. As for the Muslims, they greet him only by clapping their hands.

Their religion is paganism and the worship of idols (*dakakir*). When their king dies they construct over the place where his tomb will be an enormous dome of saj wood. Then they bring him on a bed covered with a few carpets and cushions and place him beside the dome. At his side they place his ornaments, his weapons, and the vessels from which he used to eat and drink, filled with various kinds of food and beverages.

From J. F. P. Hopkins, trans.; N. Levtzion and J. F. P. Hopkins, eds., *Corpus of Early Arabic Sources for West African History*. Reprinted with permission of Cambridge University Press, pp. 79–80.

north. A Ghanaian kingdom originated as early as 400–600 C.E., but Ghana emerged as a regional power only near the end of the first millennium and flourished for about two centuries. Its capital, Kumbi (or Kumbi Saleh), on the desert's edge, was well sited for the Saharan and Sahelian trade networks. Ghana's major population group was the Soninke. (*Ghana* is the Soninke term for "ruler.")

The Ghanaian rulers were matrilineally descended (through the previous king's sister). They ruled through a council of ministers. The reports we have, especially from the eleventh-century Muslim writer al-Bakri (see Document, "Ghana and Its People in the Mid–Eleventh Century."), indicate that the king was supreme judge and held court regularly to hear grievances. The royal ceremonies reported to have been held in Kumbi Saleh were embellished with the full trappings of regal wealth and power appropriate to a king held to be divinely blessed if not semidivine himself.

Ghana's power rested on a solid economic base. Tribute from the empire's many chieftaincies and taxes on royal lands and crops supplemented duties levied on all incoming and outgoing trade. This trade, both north–south between the Sahara and the savannah and especially east–west through the Sahel between Senegambia and more easterly trading towns like Gao on the Niger Bend, involved a variety of goods—notably imported salt, cloth, and metal goods such as copper—probably in exchange for gold and perhaps kola nuts from the south. The regime apparently also controlled the gold (and, presumably, the slave) trade that originated in the savannah to the south and west, in the tributary regions of the Bambuk and Galam regions of the middle Senegal and its southern tributary, the Faleme, and in the Boure region of the upper Niger and its tributaries.

Although the king and court of Ghana did not convert to Islam, they made elaborate arrangements to accommodate

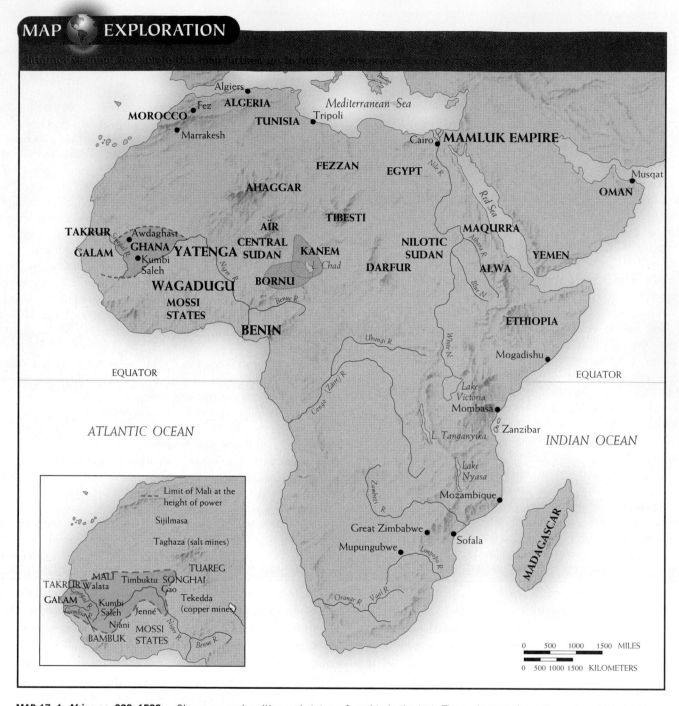

MAP EXPLORATION

MAP 17–1 Africa ca. 900–1500.   Shown are major cities and states referred to in the text. The main map shows the region of West Africa occupied by the empire of Ghana from ca. 990 to ca. 1180. The inset shows the region occupied by Mali between 1230 and 1450.

Muslim traders and government servants in their own settlement a few miles from the royal preserve in Kumbi Saleh. Muslim traders were prominent in the court, literate Muslims administered the government, and Muslim legists advised the ruler. In Ghana's hierarchical society, slaves were at the bottom; farmers and draftsmen above them; merchants above them; and the king, his court, and the nobility on top.

A huge, well-trained army secured royal control and enabled the kings to extend their sway in the late tenth century to the Atlantic shore and to the south (see Map 17–1). Ghanaian troops captured Awdaghast, the important southern terminus of the trans-Saharan trade route to Morocco, from the Berbers in 992. The empire was, however, vulnerable to attack from the desert fringe, as Almoravid Berber forces proved in 1054 when they took Awdaghast in a single raid.

▲ **The Great Mosque at Jenne.** Jenne was one of the important commercial centers controlled by the empire of Mali in the 13th and 14th centuries. Ann Stalcup.

Ghana's empire was probably destroyed in the late twelfth century by the anti-Muslim Soso people from the mountains southeast of Kumbi Saleh, a Malinke clan who had long been part of the Ghanaian Empire. Their brief ascendancy between 1180 and 1230 apparently spelled the end of the once great transregional power centered at Kumbi.[2]

MALI

With Ghana's collapse and the Almoravids' failure to build a new empire below the Sahara (largely because of their focus on North Africa), the western Sudan broke up into smaller kingdoms. The former Ghanaian provinces of Mande and Takrur were already independent before 1076, and in the early twelfth century Takrur's control of the Senegal valley and the gold-producing region of Galam made it briefly the strongest state in the western Sudan. Like Ghana, however, it was soon eclipsed, first by the brief Soso ascendancy and then by the rise of Mali.

In the mid–thirteenth century the Keita ruling clan of a Ghanaian successor kingdom, Mali, forged a new and lasting empire. This empire seems to have been built on the same economic base as that of Ghana and Takrur earlier: monopolization of the lucrative north–south gold trade. The Keita kings dominated enough of the Sahel to control the flow of West African gold from the Senegal regions and the forest lands south of the Niger to the trans-Saharan trade routes, and the influx of copper and salt in exchange. Because they were farther south, in the fertile land along the Niger, than their Ghanaian predecessors had been, they were better placed to control all trade on the upper Niger and to add to it the Gambia and Senegal trade to the west. They also used captives for plantation labor in the Niger inland delta to produce surplus food for trade.

Agriculture and cattle farming were the primary occupations of Mali's population and, together with the gold trade, the mainstays of the economy. Rice was grown in the river valleys and millet in the drier parts of the Sahel. Together with beans, yams, and other agricultural products, this made for a plentiful food supply. Fishing flourished along the Niger and elsewhere. Cattle, sheep, and goats were plentiful. The chief craft specialties were metalworking (iron and gold) and weaving of cotton grown within the empire.

[2] D. Conrad and H. Fisher, "The Conquest That Never Was: Ghana and the Almoravids, 1076," *History in Africa 9* (1982): 1–59; 10 (1983): 53–78.

Mansa Musa, King of Mali. The fourteenth century Catalan Atlas shows King Mansa Musa of Mali, seated on a throne. A rider on a camel approaches him.
The Granger Collection.

The Malinke, a southern Mande-speaking people of the upper Niger region, formed the core population of the new state. They apparently lived in walled urban settlements typical of the western savannah region. Each walled town was surrounded by its own agricultural land, held perhaps 1,000 to 15,000 people, and presumably had enough arable land within its walls to deal with siege. Each was linked to neighboring cities by trade and possibly intermarriage.

The Keita dynasty had converted early to Islam (ca. 1100) and even claimed descent from Muhammad's famous muezzin (the person who calls the faithful to worship), Bilal, a former black slave from Abyssinia whose son was said to have settled in the Mande-speaking region. During Mali's heyday in the thirteenth and fourteenth centuries, its kings often made the pilgrimage to Mecca. From their travel in the central Islamic lands, they brought back with them not only military aids, such as large Barbary war horses, but also new ideas about political and military organization. Through Muslim traders' networks, Islam also connected Mali to other areas of Africa, especially those to the east.

Mali's imperial power was built largely by the Keita King Sundiata (or Sunjaata, r. 1230–1255). Sundiata and his successors exploited their agricultural resources, significant population growth, and Malinke commercial skills to build an empire even more powerful than that of Ghana. Sundiata extended his control west to the Atlantic coast and east beyond Timbuktu. By controlling the commercial entrepôts of Gao, Walata, and Jenne, he dominated the Saharan as well as the Niger trade. He built his capital, Niani, into a major city. Niani was located on a tributary of the Niger in the savannah at the edge of the forest in a gold- and iron-rich region. It had access to the forest trade products of gold, kola nuts, and palm oil; it

was easily defended by virtue of its surrounding hills; and it was readily reached by river.

The empire that Sundiata and his successors built ultimately encompassed three major regions and language groups of Sudanic West Africa: (1) the Senegal region (including Takrur), occupied by speakers of the West Atlantic Niger-Kongo language group (including Fulbe, Tukulor, Wolof, Serer); (2) the central Mande states between Senegal and Niger, occupied by the Niger-Kongo-speaking Soninke and Mandinke peoples; and (3) the peoples of the Niger in the Gao region who spoke Songhai, the only Nilo-Saharan language west of the Lake Chad basin. Mali was less a centralized bureaucratic state than the center of a vast sphere of influence that included provinces and tribute-paying kingdoms. Many individual chieftaincies were independent but recognized the sovereignty of the supreme, sacred *mansa*, or "emperor," of the Malian realms.

The greatest Keita king proved to be Mansa Musa (r. 1312–1337), whose pilgrimage through Mamluk Cairo to Mecca in 1324 became famous. He paid out or gave away so much gold in Cairo alone that he started massive inflation lasting over a decade. He returned with many Muslim scholars, artists, and architects. At home, he consolidated Mali's power, securing peace for most of his reign throughout his vast dominions. Musa's devoutness as a Muslim fostered the spread of Islam in the empire and beyond. Under his rule, Timbuktu became famous for its *madrasas* and libraries, and for its poets, scientists, and architects, making it the leading intellectual center of sub-Saharan Islam and a major trading city of the Sahel—roles it retained long after Mali's imperial sway ended.

Mali's dominance waned after Musa, evidently as the result of rivalries for the throne. Eventually the empire withered, and after 1450 a new Songhai power in Gao to the east ended Mali's imperial authority.

SONGHAI

Evidence suggests that as early as the eleventh or twelfth century there was a Songhai kingdom around Gao, on the eastern arc of the great bend of the Niger. In 1325 Mansa Musa brought this kingdom and the Gao region under the control of Mali and the Malinke. Mali's domination ended with the rise of a dynasty in Gao known as the Sunni or Sonni around 1375. The kingdom became an imperial power, under the greatest Sunni ruler, Sonni Ali (r. 1464–1492). Thereafter the Songhai Empire for more than a century was arguably the most powerful state in Africa (see Map 17–2). With a strong military built around a riverboat flotilla and cavalry, Sonni Ali took Jenne and Timbuktu. He pushed the Tuareg Berbers

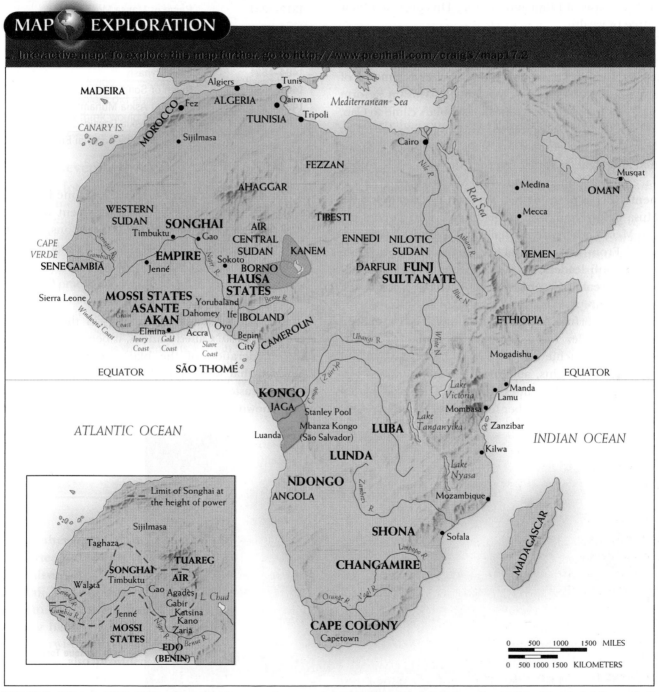

MAP 17–2 Africa ca. 1500–1800.   Important towns, regions, peoples, and states. The inset shows the empire of Songhai at its greatest extent in the early 16th century.

from a wider region of vassal chieftaincies. Islamic acculturation progressed most rapidly in the core territories under direct rule.

Civil strife, largely over the royal succession, weakened the Kanuri state in the later fourteenth and fifteenth centuries. After 1400 the locus of power shifted from Kanem proper westward, to the land of Bornu, southwest of Lake Chad. Here, at the end of the fifteenth century, a new Kanuri empire arose almost simultaneously with the collapse of the Askia dynasty of the Songhai Empire at Gao. Near the end of the sixteenth century firearms and Turkish military instructors enabled the Kanuri leader Idris Alawma (r. ca. 1575–1610) to unify Kanem and Bornu. He set up an avowedly Islamic state and extended his rule even into Hausaland, between Bornu and the Niger River. The center of trading activity as well as political power and security now shifted from the Niger Bend east to the territory under Kanuri control.

Deriving its prosperity from the trans-Saharan trade, Idris Alawma's regional empire survived for nearly a century. It was finally broken up by a long famine, repeated Tuareg attacks, lack of strong leadership, and loss of control over trade to smaller, better-organized Hausa states. The ruling dynasty held out until 1846, but by 1700 its power had been sharply reduced by the growing Hausa states to the west in what is now northern Nigeria. Their real power came only in the nineteenth century with their unification under the Fulani sultanate of Sokoto (see Chapter 27).

The Eastern Sudan

The Christian states of Maqurra and Alwa in the Nilotic Sudan, or Nubia, lasted for more than 600 years from their early-seventh-century beginnings and maintained political, religious and commercial contact with Egypt, the Red Sea world, and much of the Sudan.

After 1000 C.E. Maqurra and Alwa continued treaty relations with their more powerful northern Egyptian neighbors. However, the Mamluks intervened repeatedly in Nubian affairs, and Arab nomads constantly threatened the Nubian states.

CHRONOLOGY

Central Sudanic Empires

ca. 1100–1500	Kanuri empire of Kanem
ca. 1220s–1400	Height of empire of Kanem
1221–1259	Reign of Mai Dunama Dibbalemi
1575–1846	Kanuri empire of Kanem-Bornu
1575–1610	Reign of Idris Alawma, major architect of the state

From late Fatimid times onward, both Maqurra and Alwa were increasingly subject to immigrating Muslim Arab, tribesmen and to traders and growing Muslim minorities. The result was a long-term intermingling of Arabic and Nubian cultures and the creation of a new Nilotic Sudanese people and culture.

A significant factor in the gradual disappearance of Christianity in Nubia was its elite character there and its association with the foreign Egyptian world of Coptic Christianity. Maqurra became officially Muslim at the beginning of the fourteenth century, although Christianity survived until late in the same century. The Islamization of Alwa came somewhat later, most effectively under the long-lived Funj sultanate that replaced the Alwa state.

The Funj state flourished between the Blue and White Niles and to the north along the main Nile from just after 1500 until 1762. The Funj were originally cattle nomads who apparently adopted Islam soon after setting up their kingdom. During the late sixteenth and the seventeenth centuries, the Funj developed an Islamic society whose Arabized character was unique in sub-Saharan Africa. A much reduced Funj state held out until an Ottoman Egyptian invasion in 1821.

The Forestlands—Coastal West and Central Africa

WEST AFRICAN FOREST KINGDOMS: THE EXAMPLE OF BENIN

Many states, some with distinct political, religious, and cultural traditions, had developed in the southern and coastal regions of West Africa several centuries before the first Portuguese reports in 1485. Even those states like Asante or the Yoruba kingdoms of Oyo and Ife, which reached their height only after 1500, had much earlier origins. Benin, the best known of these forest kingdoms, reflects, especially in its art, the sophistication of West African culture before 1500.

Benin State and Society   The Edo speakers of Benin have occupied the southern Nigerian region between Yorubaland and the Ibo peoples east of the lower Niger for millennia. Traditional Edo society is organized according to a patrilineal system emphasizing primogeniture. The village is the fundamental political unit, and authority is built around the organization of males into age-grade units.[3]

According to archaeological evidence, the local traditions of the Edo culture of Benin were closely linked to those of Ife, one of the most prominent Yoruba states northwest of Benin. Some kind of distinct kingdom of Benin likely existed as early

[3] A. F. C. Ryder, *Benin and the Europeans, 1485–1897* (New York: Longman, 1969), p. 1. Ryder's work is a basic reference for the following brief summary about Benin.

as the twelfth century, and traditional accounts of both Ife and Edo agree that an Ife prince was sent to rule in Benin around 1300. There are indications that the power of the king, or *oba*, at this time was sharply limited by the Edo leaders who invited the foreign ruler. These leaders were known as the *uzama*, an order of hereditary indigenous chiefs. According to tradition, the fourth *oba* managed to wrest more control from these chiefs and instituted something of the ceremonial authority of absolute monarchy. However, only in the fifteenth century, with King Ewuare, did Benin become a royal autocracy and a large state of major regional importance.

Ewuare rebuilt the capital—known today as Benin City—and named it and his kingdom Edo. He apparently established a government in which he had sweeping authority, although he exercised it in light of the deliberations of a royal council. Ewuare formed this council not only from the palace *uzama*, but also from the townspeople. He gave each chief specific administrative responsibilities and rank in the government hierarchy. Ewuare and his successors developed a tradition of military kingship and engaged in major wars of expansion, both into Yorubaland to the west and Ibo country east across the Niger River. They also claimed for the office of *oba* an increasing ritual authority that presaged more radical developments in the king's role.

In the seventeenth century the *oba* was transformed from a military leader into a religious figure with supernatural powers. Human sacrifice, specifically of slaves, seems to have accompanied the cult of deceased kings and became even more frequent later, in the nineteenth century. The succession by primogeniture was discontinued, and the *uzama* chose *obas* from any branch of the royal family.

Benin Art   The lasting significance of Benin, however, lies in its court art, especially its famous brass sculptures. The splendid terra-cotta, ivory, and brass statuary sculpture of Ife-Benin are among the glories of human creativity. These magnificent sculptures seem to be wholly indigenous African products, and some scholars trace their artistic and technical lineage to the sculptures of the Nok culture of ancient West Africa (see Chapter 5).

The best sculptures before the sixteenth century and the coming of the Portuguese are cast bronze plaques depicting legendary and historical scenes. These were mounted in the royal palace in Benin City. There are also brass heads, apparently of royalty, that resemble the many life-size terra-cotta and brass heads found at Ife. The heads at Ife are held to represent the Oni, or religious chief of ancient Ife, or particular ancestors, who are thereby reverently remembered by their descendants.

Similar sculptures have been found both to the north and in the Niger Delta. Recent excavations east of the Niger at Igbo-Ukwu have unearthed stunning terra cottas and bronzes

▲ **Benin Plaque.** Some of the world's finest works of art were made by the artists of Benin and Ife, though much is still unknown about them. Rarely found elsewhere in Africa, bronze panels like the plaque shown here, possibly inspired by European illustrated books, adorned the royal palace, and are considered examples of "court art." The figures are typical of the Benin style in their proportions of head to body—about one to four—perhaps emphasizing the head's importance as a symbol of life and behavior.

Benin Plaque. Brass. Lost wax W. Africa 16th-17th C.A.D. Hillel Burger/Peabody Museum, Harvard University © President and Fellows of Harvard College. All rights reserved.

that belong to the same general artistic culture, which is dated as early as the ninth century. These artifacts testify to the high cultural level attained in traditional African societies that had little or no contact with the extra-African world.

EUROPEAN ARRIVALS ON THE COASTLANDS

Along the coasts of West and central Africa, many important changes occurred between 1500 and 1800. Those wrought by the burgeoning Atlantic slave trade are the most famous (see Chapter 18). Of comparable importance are changes connected with trade in West African gold and other commodities and the effects associated with the importation and spread in West and central Africa of food crops, such as maize, peanuts, squash, sweet potatoes, cocoa, and cassava (manioc) from the Americas. The gradual involvement of Africa in the emerging global economic system paved the way for eventual colonial domination of the continent, especially its coastal regions, by the Europeans. The European names for segments of the coastline—the Grain (or Pepper) Coast, the Ivory Coast, the Gold Coast, and the Slave Coast—identify the main exports that could be extracted by ship.

Senegambia   In West Africa, Senegambia—which takes its name from the Senegal and Gambia Rivers—was one of the earliest regions affected by European trade. Its interior had long been involved in both trans-Saharan trade and east–west trade in the Sahel and the savannah, especially in the heydays of the empires of Ghana, Mali, and Songhai. Senegambia's maritime trade with European powers, like the older overland trade, was primarily in gold and products such as salt, cotton goods, hides, and copper. For roughly a century Senegambian states also provided slaves for European purchase; indeed, perhaps a third of all African slaves exported during the sixteenth century came from Senegambia. Thereafter, however, the focus of the slave trade shifted south and east along the coast (see Chapter 18). Over time, Portuguese-African mulattos and the British came to control the Gambia River trade, while the French won the Senegal River markets.

The Gold Coast   The Gold Coast, like Senegambia, was one of the West African coastal districts most affected by the arrival of international maritime trade. The name derives from the region's

Benin Bronze Plaque. From the palace of the Obas of Benin it dates to the Edo period of Benin culture, 1575–1625. It depicts two Portuguese males, perhaps a father and son, holding hands. It is likely that they represent the traders or government officials who came to the African coasts in increasing numbers from the end of the 15th century on.
Werner Forman, Art Resource, N.Y.

importance after 1500 as the outlet for the more southern of West Africa's gold fields in the forestland of Akan. Here, beginning with the Portuguese at Elmina in 1481, but primarily after 1600, European states and companies built coastal forts to protect their trade and to serve as depots for inland goods. The trade in gold, kola nuts, and other commodities seems to have encouraged the growth of larger states in the region, perhaps because they could better handle and control the overland commerce.

The intensive contact of the Gold Coast with Europeans also led to the importation and spread of American crops, notably maize and cassava. The success of these crops in West and central Africa likely contributed to substantial population growth in the sixteenth and seventeenth centuries.

The Gold Coast escaped the ravages of the slave trade for some decades; it was even an importer of slaves until long after 1500. Slaves, however, became big business here in the late seventeenth century, especially in the Accra region. The economy was so disrupted by the slave trade that gold mining declined sharply. Eventually more gold came into the Gold Coast from the sale of slaves than went out from its mines (see Chapter 18).

CENTRAL AFRICA

The vast center of the subcontinent is bounded by swamps in the north, coastal rain forests to the west, highlands to the east, and deserts in the south. Before 1500 these natural barriers impeded international contact and trade with the interior. They also shaped the two-pronged route by which Bantu peoples and languages moved, over many centuries, from western and west-central Africa south into the Zaire basin and east around the equatorial forest into the lakes of highland East Africa. In the tropical central area, regional interaction in

CHRONOLOGY	
Benin	
ca. 1100–1897	Benin state
ca. 1300	First Ife king of Benin state
1440–1475	Reign of Ewuare

movements of peoples and in trade and culture had always been the norm. Here as elsewhere in Africa, however, large as well as small political, economic, and social units could be found. Peoples such as the Lunda and the Luba, for example, on the southern savannah below the rain forest, carved out sizable kingdoms by the fifteenth century and expanded their control over neighboring areas into the eighteenth century.

The Portuguese came to the western coastal regions looking for gold and silver but found none. Ultimately, their main export was slaves. These slaves were taken, first for gang labor to the Portuguese sugar plantations on Sao Thomé island in the Gulf of Guinea and then, in vast numbers to perform similar plantation labor in Brazil. In the 1640s the Dutch briefly succeeded the Portuguese as the major suppliers of African slaves to English and French plantations in the Caribbean.

The Kongo Kingdom   Kongo was the major state with which the Portuguese dealt after coming to central Africa in 1483. Dating from probably the fourteenth century, the Kongo kingdom was located on a fertile, well-watered plateau south of the lower Zaïre River valley, between the coast and the Kwango River in the east. Here, astride the border between forest and grassland, the Kongo kings had built a central government based on a pyramid structure of tax or tribute collection. The king's, authority was tied to acceptance of him as a kind of spiritual spokesman of the gods or ancestors. By 1600 Kongo was half the size of England and boasted a high state of specialization in weaving and pottery, salt production, fishing, and metalworking.

The Portuguese brought Mediterranean goods, preeminently luxury textiles from North Africa, to trade for African goods. Such luxuries augmented the prestige and wealth of the ruler and his elites. However, slaves became the primary export that could be used to obtain foreign luxuries. Meanwhile, imports such as fine clothing, tobacco, and alcohol did nothing to replace the labor pool lost to slavery.

At first the Portuguese put time and effort into education and Christian proselytizing, but the need for more slaves eventually outweighed these concerns. Regional rulers sought to procure slaves from neighboring kingdoms, as did Portuguese traders who went inland themselves. As the demand grew,

---

CHRONOLOGY

Central Africa

1300s	Kongo kingdom founded
1483	Portuguese come to central African coast
ca. 1506–1543	Reign of Affonso I as king of Kongo
1571	Angola becomes Portuguese proprietary colony

---

local rulers increasingly attacked neighbors to garner slaves for Portuguese traders (see Chapter 18 .).

The Kongo ruler Affonso I (r. ca. 1506–1543), a Christian convert, at first welcomed Jesuit missionaries and supported conversion. But in time he broke with the Jesuits and encouraged traditional practices, even though he himself remained a Christian. Affonso had constant difficulty curbing the more exploitative slaving practices and independent-minded provincial governors, who often dealt directly with the Portuguese, undermining royal authority. (See Document, "Affonso I Writes to the King of Portugal.") Affonso's successor finally restricted Portuguese activity to Mpinda harbor and the Kongo capital of Mbanza Kongo (São Salvador). A few years later, Portuguese attempts to name the Kongo royal successor caused a bloody uprising against them that led in turn to a Portuguese boycott on trade with the kingdom.

Thereafter, disastrous internal wars shattered the Kongo state. Slavery apparently contributed significantly to provincial unrest. Independent Portuguese traders and adventurers soon did their business outside of government channels and tried to manipulate the Kongo kings.

Kongo, however, enjoyed renewed vigor in the seventeenth century. The Kongo kings, all descended from Affonso, ruled as divine-right monarchs at the apex of a complex sociopolitical pyramid that rose from district headmen through provincial governors to the court nobility and king. Royal power came to depend on a guard of musket-armed hired soldiers. The financial base of the kingdom rested on tribute from officials and taxes and tolls on commerce. Christianity, the state religion, was accommodated to the traditional ancestor cult, magic, and sorcery. Sculpture, iron and copper technology, and dance and music flourished.

Angola   To the south, in Portuguese Angola, the experience was even worse than in Kongo. The Ndongo kingdom flourished among the Mbundu people during the sixteenth century, though the Portuguese tried and failed to make Angola a proprietary colony (the first white colonial enterprise in black Africa). By the end of the 1500s Angola was exporting thousands of slaves yearly through the port of Luanda. In less than a century the hinterland had been depopulated. New internal trade in salt and the spread of American food crops such as maize and cassava (which became part of the staple diet of the populace) produced some positive changes in the interior, but in the coastal region the Portuguese brought catastrophe.

East Africa
Swahili Culture and Commerce

The participation of East African port towns in the lucrative South Seas trade was ancient. Arabs, Indonesians, and even some Indians had trafficked there for centuries. Many had

DOCUMENT | Affonso I of Kongo Writes to the King of Portugal

In 1526 Affonso, the Christian African king of Kongo, wrote to the Portuguese monarch ostensibly to complain about the effects of slaving on the Kongo people and economy. But the real issue was that the Portuguese were circumventing his own royal monopoly on the inland slave trade. One of the insidious effects of the massive demand of the Atlantic trade for slaves was the ever-increasing engagement in it of African monarchs, chieftains, and merchants.

◆ How had the introduction of Portuguese merchants and European goods upset the social and political situation in Kongo? How had these goods tempted Affonso's subjects into the slave trade? How did Affonso wish to change the relationship of his people to Portugal? Was the king more worried about human rights or his economic losses?

Sir, Your Highness [of Portugal] should know how our Kingdom is being lost in so many ways that it is convenient to provide for the necessary remedy, since this is caused by the excessive freedom given by your factors and officials to the men and merchants who are allowed to come to this Kingdom to set up shops with goods and many things which have been prohibited by us, and which they spread throughout our Kingdoms and Domains in such an abundance that many of our vassals, whom we had in obedience, do not comply because they have the things in greater abundance than we ourselves; and it was with these things that we had them content and subjected under our vassalage and jurisdiction, so it is doing a great harm not only to the service of God, but the security and peace of our Kingdoms and State as well.

And we cannot reckon how great the damage is, since the mentioned merchants are taking every day our natives, sons of the land and the sons of our noblemen and vassals and our relatives, because the thieves and men of bad conscience grab them wishing to have the things and wares of this Kingdom which they are ambitious of; they grab them and get them to be sold; and so great, Sir, is the corruption and licentiousness that our country is being completely depopulated, and Your Highness should not agree with this nor accept it as in your service. And to avoid it we need from those [your] Kingdoms no more than some priests and a few people to teach in schools, and no other goods except wine and flour for the holy sacrament. That is why we beg of Your Highness to help and assist us in this matter, commanding your factors that they should not send here either merchants or wares, because it is *our will that in these Kingdoms there should not be any trade of slaves nor outlet for them.**

Concerning what is referred above, again we beg of Your Highness to agree with it, since otherwise we cannot ... remedy such an obvious damage. Pray Our Lord in His mercy to have Your Highness under His guard and let you do for ever the things of His service. I kiss your hands many times. ...

From *The African Past*, trans. by J. O. Hunwick, reprinted in Basil Davidson (Grosset and Dunlap, The Universal Library), pp. 191–193. Reprinted by permission of Curtis Brown Ltd. Copyright © 1964 by Basil Davidson.

*Emphasis in the original

---

been absorbed into what had become, during the first millennium C.E., from Somalia south, a predominantly Bantu-speaking population. From the eighth century onward Islam traveled with Arab and Persian sailors and merchants to these southerly trading centers of what the Arabs called the land of the *Zanj*, or "Blacks" (hence "Zanzibar"). Conversion to Islam, however, occurred only along the coast. In the thirteenth century Muslim traders from Arabia and Iran began to dominate the coastal cities from Mogadishu to Kilwa. By 1331 the traveler Ibn Battuta writes of Mogadishu as a thoroughly Islamic port and of the ruler and inhabitants of Kilwa as Muslims. He also notes that towns there had mosques for the faithful.[4] (See Document, "Visiting Mogadishu and Kilwa [1331].")

By this time a common language called **Swahili**, or *Kiswahili*, from the Arabic *sawahil*, "coastlands," had developed from the interaction of Bantu and Arabic speakers along the coast. Its structure is Bantu, its vocabulary has a strong admixture of Arabic, and it is written in Arabic script.

Current theory suggests that, like the language, Swahili culture is basically African with a large contribution by Arab, Persian, and other extra-African elements. This admixture created a new consciousness and identity. Today, the many coastal peoples who share Swahili language join African to Persian, Indian, Arab, and other ancestry.

Swahili language and culture probably developed first in the northern towns of Manda, Lamu, and Mombasa, then farther south along the coast to Kilwa. They remained localized largely along the coast until recently. Likewise, the spread of Islam was largely limited to the coastal civilization, with the

---

[4] *Travels in Asia and Africa, 1325–1354*, trans. and selected by H. A. R. Gibb (New York: Robert M. McBride, 1929), pp. 110–113.

possible exception of the Zambezi valley, where Muslim traders penetrated upriver. This contrasts with the Horn of Africa, where Islamic kingdoms developed both in the Somali hinterland and on the coast.

Swahili civilization reached its apogee in the fourteenth and fifteenth centuries. The harbor trading towns were the administrative centers of the local Swahili states, and most of them were sited on coastal islands or easily defended peninsulas. To these ports came merchants from abroad and from the African hinterlands. These towns were impressive. Stone mosques, fortress-palaces, harbor fortifications, fancy residences, and commercial buildings have their own distinctive cast, which combines African and Arabo-Persian elements.

The Swahili states' ruling dynasties were probably African in origin, with an admixture of Arab or Persian blood. Swahili coastal centers boasted an advanced, cosmopolitan culture; by comparison, most of the populace in the small villages lived in mud and sometimes stone houses and earned their living by farming or fishing. Society seems to have consisted of three principal groups: the local nobility, the commoners, and resident foreigners engaged in commerce. Slaves constituted a fourth class, although their local extent (as opposed to their sale) is disputed.

The flourishing trade of the coastal centers was fed mainly by export of inland ivory. Other exports included gold, slaves, turtle shells, ambergris, leopard skins, pearls, fish, sandalwood, ebony, and cotton cloth. The chief imports were cloth, porcelain, glassware, glass beads, and glazed pottery. Certain exports tended to dominate particular ports: cloth, sandalwood, ebony, and ivory at Mogadishu, ivory at Manda, and gold at Kilwa (brought up the coast from Sofala, still farther south). Cowrie shells were a common currency in the inland trade, but coins minted at Mogadishu and Kilwa from the fourteenth century on were increasingly used in the major trading centers.

THE PORTUGUESE AND THE OMANIS OF ZANZIBAR

The original Swahili civilization declined in the sixteenth century primarily because the trade that had originally made everything possible waned with the arrival of the Portuguese and their destruction of both the old oceanic trade (in particular, the Islamic commercial monopoly) and the main Islamic city-states along the eastern coast. Decreases in rainfall or invasions of Zimba peoples from inland regions may also have contributed to the decline.

Nevertheless, the Portuguese undoubtedly intended to gain control of the South-Seas trade (see Chapter 18). In Africa, as everywhere, they saw the **Moors** (the Spanish and Portuguese term for Muslims) as their implacable enemies and viewed the struggle to wrest the commerce and the parts of Africa and Asia from Islamic control as a Christian crusade.

▲ **Swahili Mosque.** The Friday Mosque at Shela on the southeastern coast of Lamu Island, Kenya. This fine example of Late Swahili architecture dates to the early 19th century. It is the only surviving pre-20th-century mosque in the region with a minaret. Swahili settlements on Lamu Island date to about the 15th century and enjoyed a period of substantial wealth that reached its zenith in the nineteenth century.
Embassy of Kenya.

The initial Portuguese victories along the African coast led to the submission of many small Islamic ports and states. Still, there was no concerted effort to spread Christianity beyond the fortified settlements established in places like Sofala, Zanzibar, Mozambique, and Mombasa. Thus the long-term cultural and religious consequences of the Portuguese presence were slight.

The Portuguese did, however, cause widespread economic decline on the east coast. When the inland Africans refused to cooperate with them, the formerly heavy gold trade up the Zambezi from Sofala dried up. The militant Portuguese presence also sharply reduced Muslim coastal shipping from India and Arabia. Ottoman efforts in the late sixteenth century failed to defeat the Portuguese, but after 1660 the strong eastern Arabian state of Oman raided the African coast with impunity. In 1698 the Omanis took Mombasa and ejected the Portuguese everywhere north of Mozambique.

Under the Omanis, Zanzibar became a new and major power center in East Africa. Their control of the coastal ivory

DOCUMENT | **Visiting Mogadishu and Kilwa (1331)**

Ibn Battuta (d. 1369 or 1377), a native of Tangier, became one of history's most famous travelers through his voluminous and entertaining writings about his years of journeying from West and East Africa to India and China. In the following two excerpts from his description of his trip down the East African coast in 1331, he describes first the daily proceedings at the grievance and petitions court presided over by the Sultan of Mogadishu, then the generosity of the Sultan of Kilwa. The East Africans referred to their Sultan as "Shaikh" (a term used also for any religiously learned man). A qadi is a judge; a faqih, a jurisconsult or legal scholar; a wazir, a government minister; an amir, a military commander; and a sharif, a descendant of the Prophet Muhammad (which carries special social status).

◆ What Muslim values and practices do the two reports seem to describe? Does Ibn Battuta as a Muslim, but also as an Arab outsider to the African Muslim societies he is visiting, seem to approve or disapprove of what he reports?

Mogadishu

When it is Saturday, the people come to the door of the shaikh (the local term for the Sultan), and they sit in covered halls outside the house. The *qadi*, the *faqihs*, the *sharifs*, the men of piety, the shaikhs and the men who have performed the pilgrimage enter the second council room. They sit on wooden platforms prepared for the purpose. The *qadi* is on a platform by himself and each group on a platform reserved for them which nobody shares with them. Then the shaikh sits in his council and sends for the *qadi* who sits on his left. Then enter the *faqihs* and their leaders sit in front of him while the rest of them salute and go away. Then the *sharifs* enter, their leaders sit before him, the rest of them salute and go away. If they are guests, they sit on his right. Then enter the shaikhs and those who have performed the pilgrimage, and their great ones sit and the rest salute and go away. Then enter the *wazirs* and *amirs*; the heads of the soldiers, rank upon rank, they salute and go. Food is brought and the *qadi*, the

sharifs and whoever is sitting in that session eat with the shaikh and the shaikh eats with them. If he wishes to honour one of the leaders of his *amirs*, he sends for him that he should eat with them. The rest of the people eat in the dining hall and their eating is according to precedence in the manner of their entrance before the shaikh. Then the shaikh goes into his house and the *qadi*, the *wazirs*, the private secretary, and four of the leading *amirs* sit for hearing litigation between the members of the public and hearing the cases of people with complaints. In a matter connected with the rules of the *shari'a* [religious law] the *qadi* passes judgement; in a matter other than that, the members of the council pass judgement, that is, the ministers and the *amirs*. In a matter where there is need of consultation with the sultan, they write about it to him and he sends out the reply to them immediately on the back of the note in accordance with his view. And such is always their custom.

The Sultan of Kilwa

When I arrived, the Sultan was Abu al-Muzaffar Hasan surnamed Abu al-Mawahib [the Father of Gifts] on account of his numerous charitable gifts. He frequently makes raids into the Zanj country, attacks them and carries off booty, of which he reserves a fifth, using it in the manner prescribed by the Koran. That reserved for the kinsfolk of the Prophet is kept separate in the Treasury, and, when *sharifs* come to visit him, he gives it them. They come to him from Iraq, the Hijaz, and other countries. I found several *sharifs* from the Hijaz at his court, among them Muhammad ibn Jammaz, Mansur ibn Labida ibn Abi Nami and Muhamma ibn Shumaila ibn Abi Nami. At Mogadishu I saw Tabl ibn Kubaish ibn Jammaz, who also wished to visit him. This Sultan is very humble: he sits and eats with beggars, and venerates holy men and descendants of the Prophet.

From Said Hamdun and Noël King, ed. and trans., *Ibn Battuta in Black Africa*, (Princeton, NJ: Markus Wiener, rev. ed., 1994), pp. 20–21. Reprinted by permission of Markus Wiener Publishers, Inc.

and slave trade seems to have fueled a substantial recovery of prosperity by the later eighteenth century. Zanzibar itself benefited from the introduction of clove cultivation in the 1830s; cloves became its staple export thereafter. (The clove plantations became also the chief market for a new, devastating internal slave trade, which flourished in East Africa into the late nineteenth century even as the external trade in slaves was crushed.) Omani African sultans dominated the east coast until 1856. Thereafter, Zanzibar and its coastal holdings became independent under a branch of the same family that ruled in Oman. Zanzibar passed eventually to the British when they, the

Germans, and the Italians divided East Africa in the late 1880s. Still, the Islamic imprint on the whole coast survives today.

Southern Africa
SOUTHEASTERN AFRICA: "GREAT ZIMBABWE"

At about the same time that the east-coast trading centers were beginning to flourish, a different kind of civilization was enjoying its heyday farther south, in the rocky, savannah-woodland watershed between the Limpopo and Zambezi Rivers, in modern

▲ **Great Zimbabwe.** The most impressive of 300 such stone ruins in modern Zimbabwe and neighboring countries. These sites give clear evidence of the advanced Iron Age mining and cattle-raising culture that flourished in this region between about 1000 and 1500 C.E. The people, thought to have been of Bantu origins, apparently had a highly developed trade in gold and copper with outsiders, including Arabs on the east coast. As yet, all too little is known about this impressive society.

Werner Forman/Art Resource, N.Y.

southern Zimbabwe. This civilization was a purely African one sited far enough inland never to have felt the impact of Islam. It was founded in the tenth or eleventh century by Bantu-speaking Shona people, who still inhabit the same general area today. It seems to have become a large and prosperous state between the late thirteenth and the late fifteenth centuries. We know it only through the archaeological remains of an estimated 150 settlements in the Zambezi-Limpopo region.

The most impressive of these ruins, and the apparent capital of this ancient Shona state, is known today as "Great Zimbabwe"—a huge, sixty-odd-acre site encompassing two major building complexes. One—the so-called acropolis—is a series of stone enclosures on a high hill. It overlooks another, much larger enclosure that contains many ruins and a circular tower, all surrounded by a massive wall some thirty-two feet high and up to seventeen feet thick. The acropolis complex may have contained a shrine, whereas the larger enclosure was appar-

ently the royal palace and fort. The stonework reflects a wealthy and sophisticated society. Artifacts from the site include gold and copper ornaments, soapstone carvings, and imported beads, as well as glass and porcelain of Chinese, Syrian, and Persian origins.

The state itself seems to have had partial control of the increasing gold trade between inland areas and the east-coast port of Sofala. Its territory lay east and south of substantial gold-mining enterprises. We can speculate that this large settlement was the capital city of a prosperous empire and the residence of a ruling elite. Its wider domain was made up mostly of smaller settlements whose inhabitants lived by subsistence agriculture and cattle raising and whose culture was different from that of the capital.

We are not sure why Great Zimbabwe civilization flourished. The evidence suggests first general population growth and increasing economic prosperity in the Zambezi-Limpopo region before 1500 C.E. Even earlier Iron Age sites farther south suggest that other large state entities may have preceded the heyday of Great Zimbabwe proper. The specific impetus for Great Zimbabwe may have been a significant immigration around 1000 C.E. of Late Iron Age Shona speakers who brought with them mining techniques and farming innovations, along with their ancestor cults. Improved farming and animal husbandry could have led to substantial population growth. The gold trade between the inland gold mining areas and Sofala may also have expanded. Great Zimbabwe may have been the chief beneficiary of this trade. This hypothesis links the flourishing of Zimbabwe to that of the East African coast from about the thirteenth century.

However, without new sources, we may never know why this impressive civilization developed and dominated its region for nearly 200 years. The reasons for its demise are also obscure. It appears that the northern and southern sectors of the state split up, and people moved away from Great Zimbabwe, probably because the farming and grazing land there was exhausted. The southern successor kingdom was known as Changamire, which became powerful from the late 1600s until about 1830. The northern successor state, stretched along the middle and lower course of the Zambezi, was known to the first Portuguese sources as the kingdom ruled by the Mwene Mutapa, or "Master Pillager," the title of its sixteenth-century ruler, Mutota, and his successors.

THE PORTUGUESE IN SOUTHEASTERN AFRICA

The Portuguese destroyed Swahili control of both the inland gold trade and the multifaceted overseas trade. Their chief object was to obtain gold from the Zambezi region of the interior. However, because the gold production of the entire region

◀ **Carving from Great Zimbabwe.** This carving (steatite, 40.5 cm high) is thought to represent a mythical eagle that carries messages from man to the gods. It dates to ca. 1200–1400 C.E.
Werner Forman Archive/Art Resource, N.Y.

was small and because they encountered repeated difficulties trying to control it, the Portuguese derived little lasting profit from the enterprise. When they had problems sustaining the Zambezi gold trade by trying simply to supplant the Swahili merchants on the coast, they established fortified posts up the Zambezi and meddled in the regional politics of the Shona who controlled the region. This tactic led to ongoing strife between the invaders and the Shona kingdoms. In the 1690s the Changamire Shona dynasty conquered the northern Shona territory and pushed the Portuguese out of gold country.

All along the Zambezi, however, a lasting and destabilizing consequence of Portuguese intrusion was the creation of quasi-tribal chiefdoms. These were led by mixed-blood Portuguese landholders, or *prazeros*, descended from the first Portuguese estate holders along the Zambezi, who had built up huge estates. Their descendants eventually formed a few clanlike groups of mixed-blood members (from unions with Africans, Indian immigrants, or other estate families). By the end of the eighteenth century, they controlled vast land holdings, commanded armies (often made up largely of slaves), and were a disruptive force in the region because they were too strong for either the Portuguese or the regional African rulers to control. They remind us of how diverse the peoples of modern Africa are.

SOUTH AFRICA: THE CAPE COLONY

In South Africa the Dutch planted the first European colonials almost inadvertently, yet the consequences of their action were to be ultimately as grave and far-reaching as any European incursion onto African soil. The first Cape settlement was built in 1652 by the Dutch East India Company as a resupply point and way station for Dutch vessels on their way back and forth between the Netherlands and the East Indies. The support station grew gradually into what became by century's end a large settler community (the population of the colony in 1662, including slaves, was 392; by 1714 it had reached 3,878).[5] These settlers were the forebears of the Afrikaners of modern South Africa.

[5] R. Elphick and H. Giliomee, *The Shaping of South African Society, 1652–1820* (Cape Town: Longman, 1979), p. 4.

CHRONOLOGY	
East and Southeast Africa	
900–1500	"Great Zimbabwe" civilization
ca. 1200–1400	Development of Bantu Kiswahili language
ca. 1300–1600	Height of Swahili culture
1698	Omani forces take Mombasa, oust Portuguese from East Africa north of the port of Mozambique
1741–1856	United sultanate of Oman and Zanzibar

Cape Town, with European Ships in its harbor. The colony relied on shipping for commercial links with the outside world.
National Archives of South Africa.

CHRONOLOGY	
Southern Africa	
1652	First Cape Colony settlement of Dutch East India Company
1795	British replace Dutch as masters of Cape Colony

The colony also imported slaves from all along the southern-seas trade routes, including India, East Africa, and Madagascar. Slavery set the tone for relations between the emergent, and ostensibly "white," Afrikaner population and the "coloreds" of other races. Free or not, the latter were eventually all too easily identified with slave peoples.

After the first settlers spread out around the Company station, nomadic white livestock farmers, or *Trekboers*, moved more widely afield, leaving the richer, but limited, farming lands of the coast for the drier interior tableland. There they contested still wider groups of Khoikhoi cattle herders for the best grazing lands. To this end, they developed military techniques—notably the "commando," a collective civilian punitive raid—to secure their way of life by force where necessary. Again the Khoikhoi were the losers. By 1700 they were stripped almost completely of their own pasturages, and their way of life was destroyed. More and more Khoikhoi took up employment in the colonial economy, among the Trekboers as well as the settled colonists. Others moved north to join with other refugees from Cape society (slaves, mixed bloods, and some freedmen) to form raiding bands operating along the frontiers of Trekboer territory close to the Orange River. The disintegration of Khoikhoi society continued in the eighteenth century, accelerated sharply by smallpox—a European import against which this previously isolated group had no immunity.

Many of the less powerful Khoikhoi people of the region were gradually incorporated into the new colonial economy. The local Khoikhoi (see Chapter 5) were almost exclusively pastoralists; they had neither traditions of strong political organization nor an economic base beyond their herds. At first they bartered livestock freely to Dutch ships and then to the Company settlement for iron, copper, and tobacco. However, when settlers began to displace the Khoikhoi in the southwestern Cape, conflicts ensued. The results were the consolidation of European landholdings and a breakdown of Khoikhoi society. Dutch military success led to even greater Dutch control of the Khoikhoi by the 1670s. Treated as free persons, they became the chief source of colonial wage labor—labor in ever-greater demand as the colony grew.

OVERVIEW Major African States, 1000–1800

North Africa	Sahel	Eastern Sudan	West and Central Africa	East Africa	Southern Africa
Morocco	Ghana	Maqurra	Benin	Zanzibar	"Great Zimbabwe"
Algiers	Mali	Alwa	Kongo		
Tunis	Songhai	Funj			
Tripoli	Kanem				
Egypt					

The Cape society in this period was thus a diverse one. The Dutch Company officials (including Dutch Reformed ministers), the emerging Afrikaners (both settled colonists and Trekboers), the Khoikhoi, and the slaves played differing roles in the emerging new society radiating from Capetown. Intermarriage and cohabitation of masters and slaves added to the social complexity, despite laws designed to check such mixing.

Accommodation of nonwhite minority groups within Cape society went on apace; the slow emergence of *Afrikaans*, a new vernacular language of the colonials, shows that the Dutch immigrants themselves were also subject to acculturation processes. By the time of English domination after 1795, the sociopolitical foundations—and the bases of *apartheid*—of modern South Africa were firmly laid.

Feluccas on the Nile at Luxor.

Summary

North Africa   Developments in African history from 1000 to 1800 varied from region to region. In North Africa, the key new factor was the imperial expansion of the Ottoman Empire as far west as Morocco. But regionalism soon rendered Ottoman authority in North Africa purely nominal.

Empires of the Sudan   Several substantial states arose south of the Sahara: Ghana, Mali, Songhai, and Kanem. The ruling elites of these states converted to or were heavily influenced by Islam, although most of their populations clung to their older traditions. Much of the wealth of these states was tied to their control of the trans-Saharan trade routes. Farther south, in the coastal forestlands of Central Africa, another substantial kingdom arose in Benin, famous for its brass sculptures.

East Africa   On the east coast, Islam influenced the development of the distinctive Swahili culture and language, and Islamic traders linked the region to India and East Asia.

The Coming of the Europeans   The key development of the fifteenth century was the arrival of European traders, missionaries, and warships. The Portuguese and later Europeans came in search of commerce, converts to Christianity, and spheres of influence. Their arrival disrupted indigenous African culture and political relations and presaged Africa's involvement in and exploitation by a new, expanding global trading system dominated by Europeans.

⋮ Review Questions

1. Why did Islam succeed in sub-Saharan and East Africa? What role did warfare play in its success? What role did trade have in it?

2. What was the importance of the empires of Ghana, Mali, and Songhai to world history? Why was the control of the trans-Saharan trade so important to these kingdoms? What was the importance of Islamic culture to them? Why did each of these empires break up?

3. What was the impact of the Portuguese on East Africa? On Central Africa? How did European coastal activities affect the African interior?

4. Why did Ottoman influence decline in northern Africa in the eighteenth century?

5. How did the Portuguese and Dutch differ from or resemble the Arabs, Persians, and other Muslims who came as outsiders to sub-Saharan Africa?

6. Discuss the diversity of Cape society in South Africa before 1800. Who were the Trekboers and what was their conflict with the Khoikhoi? How was the basis for apartheid formed in this period?

Key Terms

Afrikaans   (p. 498)
apartheid   (p. 498)
Moors   (p. 493)

oba   (p. 489)
Swahili   (p. 492)

Trekboers   (p. 497)
uzama   (p. 489)

Documents CD-ROM

Eurasian Connections before European Expansion
11.1 Mansa Musa: The "King Who Sits on a Mountain of Gold"
11.3 Ibn Battuta in Mali

NOTE: To learn more about the topics in this chapter, see the
Suggested Readings at the end of the book.

European Explorations and Expansion
14.1 Kilwa, Mombasa, and the Portuguese: Realities of Empire
14.3 The Portuguese in Africa and India: Duarte Barbosa

18

Conquest and Exploitation

The Development of the Transatlantic Economy

- Periods of European Overseas Expansion

- Mercantilist Theory of Economic Exploitation

- Establishment of the Spanish Empire in America

- Economies of Exploitation in the Spanish Empire

- Colonial Brazil and Slavery

- French and British Colonies in North America

- Slavery in the Americas

- Africa and the Transatlantic Slave Trade

◀ JOHN SINGLETON COPLEY, AMERICAN, 1738–1815. *WATSON AND THE SHARK*, 1778. In several respects, this painting illustrates the interconnectedness of the eighteenth-century transatlantic world. Copley is an American artist working in London. The action occurs in a Spanish colony during a commercial venture. The person being rescued is an English subject who will become a rich merchant. The boat holds a cross section of races and cultures from Africa, Europe, and the Americas that characterized the world of the plantation economies.

Oil on canvas, $72^{1}/_{4} \times 90^{3}/_{8}$ in. Gift of Mrs. George von Lengerke Meyer. Courtesy, Museum of Fine Arts, Boston. Reproduced with permission © Museum of Fine Arts, Boston. All Rights Reserved.

GLOBAL PERSPECTIVE

The Atlantic World

The contact between the native peoples of the American continent and the European explorers of the fifteenth and sixteenth centuries transformed world history. In the Americas, the native peoples—whose ancestors had migrated from Asia millennia before—had established a wide variety of civilizations. Some of their most remarkable architectural monuments and cities were constructed during the very centuries when European civilizations were reeling from the collapse of Roman power. Until European exploration, the civilizations of the Americas and the civilizations of Eurasia and Africa had had no significant contact with each other.

Within half a century of the landing of Columbus, millions of America's native peoples in Florida, the Caribbean islands, Mesoamerica, and South America had encountered Europeans intent on conquest, exploitation, and religious conversion. The Europeans' rapid conquest was the result of several factors—their advanced weapons and navies; the new diseases they brought with them; and internal divisions among the Native Americans. Thereafter, Spain and Portugal dominated Latin America, and England, France, and Holland set out to settle North America. The Europeans imported their own food crops, such as wheat and apples, while also taking advantage of American plants, such as potatoes, corn, and tobacco.

In both North and South America, Europeans established economies of exploitation. They were generally determined to do little labor themselves. In Latin America, they developed various institutions to extract native labor. They established a long corridor of slave-labor plantation systems from the Mid-Atlantic English colonies through the Caribbean and into Brazil. Except for tobacco, the crops grown derived largely from the Old World. So did the slaves, forcibly imported from Africa and sold in America to plantation owners who preferred them to less easily controlled white indentured servants and less hardy indigenous laborers who lacked the Africans' immunity to European diseases. The slave trade corroded the political and social structures of African societies while drawing the economies and peoples of Europe, Africa, and the Americas into a vast worldwide web of production based on slave labor

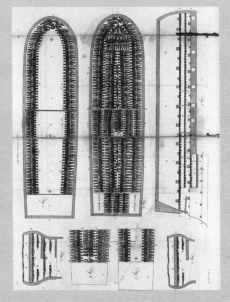

that some historians have suggested in its efficient organization and use of labor set the stage for the Industrial Revolution.

The impact of slavery in the Americas was not limited to the lives of the black slaves. Whites in the New World numbered about 12 million in 1820, compared to some 6 million blacks. However, up to that time only about 2 million whites had migrated there, compared to some 11 million or more Africans forcibly imported as slaves. Such numbers reveal the effects of brutal slave working conditions and the high mortality and sharply reduced birthrates of the slave population relative to those of the free white population.

None of the statistics, however, enables us to assess adequately the role of slavery in the history of the Americas or, more particularly, the United States. The United States actually imported only slightly more than a quarter as many slaves as did Brazil or the British and French Caribbean regions together, yet the consequences of the forced migration of just over half a million Africans have been and remain massive. Consider just the American Civil War and the endurance of societal racism and inequality or, more positively, the African contribution to American industrial development, language, music, literature, and artistic culture. The impact of the Atlantic slave trade has been and continues to be felt at both ends of the original "trade."

THINK AHEAD

◆ Why was the Spanish Empire an empire based on economies of exploitation? How was the labor of non-European peoples drawn into the economy of this empire?

◆ How and why did the plantation economy develop? Why did it rely on African slaves for its labor? What were the consequences of the slave trade for Africa? What were the consequences for Africans forced to migrate and their descendants in the Americas?

◆ Why do we think of the plantation economy as a global, rather than regional system of production? Why was it the "engine" of Atlantic basin trade?

THE LATE-FIFTEENTH-CENTURY EUROPEAN encounter with the American continents changed the world. The more than two and a half centuries of European domination and government that followed the encounter made the Americas a region where European languages, legal and political institutions, trade, and religion prevail. These developments in the Americas gave Europe more influence over other world cultures and civilizations than it would otherwise have achieved.

Within decades of the European voyages of discovery, Native Americans, Europeans, and Africans began to interact in a manner unprecedented in human history. The Native Americans of North and South America encountered bands of European conquerors and European Roman Catholic missionaries. Technological and military superiority as well as political divisions among the Native Americans allowed the Europeans to realize their material and religious ambitions. By the middle of the sixteenth century Europeans had begun to import black Africans into the American continents as chattel slaves, converting them to Christianity in the process. Consequently, by the close of the sixteenth-century Europe, the Americas, and Africa had become linked in a vast transatlantic economy that extracted material and agricultural wealth from the American continents largely on the basis of the nonfree labor of impressed Native Americans and imported African slaves.

The next century would see English and French colonists settling in North America and the Caribbean, introducing different political values and, through the English, Protestantism. These North American colonists would also become part of the transatlantic economy, and many would become economically involved directly or indirectly with African slavery. They too would interact with the Native Americans of North America, sometimes destroying their cultures, sometimes converting them to Christianity, and always drawing them into the transatlantic economy as they exploited the American wilderness.

Beginning in the sixteenth century the importation of African slaves and the use of slave labor were fundamental to the plantation economy that eventually extended from Maryland to Brazil. The slave trade intimately connected the economy of certain sections of Africa to the transatlantic economy. The slave trade had a devastating effect on the African people and cultures involved in it, but it also enriched the Americas with African culture and religion.

Periods of European Overseas Expansion

It may be useful to see the establishment of this vast new transatlantic economy in the larger context of European overseas expansion. That expansion loosed the forces that created the transatlantic economy.

Since the late fifteenth century, European contacts with the rest of the world have gone through four distinct stages. The first was that of the European discovery, exploration, initial conquest, and settlement of the Americas and commercial expansion elsewhere in the world. By the close of the seventeenth century Spain governed South America, except for Portuguese-ruled Brazil. French and British colonies had been established in North America. France, Britain, the Netherlands, and Spain controlled various islands in the Caribbean. The French, British, and Dutch held outposts in Asia.

The second era was one of colonial trade rivalry among Spain, France, and Great Britain. The Anglo-French side of the contest has often been compared to a second Hundred Years' War. During this second period both the British colonies of the North American seaboard and the Spanish colonies of Mexico and Central and South America emancipated them-selves from European control. This era may be said to have closed during the 1820s (see Chapter 23).

The third stage of European contact with the non-European world occurred in the nineteenth century when European governments carved new formal empires in Africa and Asia. Those nineteenth-century empires also included new areas of European settlement such as Australia, New Zealand, and South Africa. The bases of these empires were trade, national honor, racial theories, religious expansion, and military superiority (see Chapter 25).

The last period of European empire occurred during the mid–twentieth century with the decolonization of peoples who had previously been under European colonial rule (see Chapters 32 and 33).

During the four and a half centuries before decolonization, Europeans exerted political dominance over much of the rest of the world that was out of all proportion to Europe's size or population. Europeans frequently treated other peoples as social, intellectual, and economic inferiors. They ravaged existing cultures because of greed, religious zeal, or political ambition. These actions significantly affect the contemporary relationship between Europe and its former colonies. What allowed the Europeans to exert such influence and domination for so long

Batavia. The Dutch established a major trading ▶
base at Batavia in the East Indies in the
seventeenth century. Its geographical position
allowed the Dutch to dominate the spice trade.
Batavia is now Djakarta, capital of modern-day
Indonesia.
Bildarchiv Preussicher Kulturbesitz.

over so much of the world was not any innate cultural superiority, but a technological supremacy related to naval power and gunpowder. Ships and guns allowed the Europeans to exercise their will almost wherever they chose.

Mercantilist Theory of Economic Exploitation

The early modern European empires of the sixteenth through the eighteenth centuries—empires based on commerce—existed primarily to enrich trade. Extensive trade rivalries sprang up around the world. The protection of these empires required naval power. Spain dominated the largest of these empires and constructed elaborate naval, commercial, and political structures to exploit and govern it. Finally, these empires depended largely on slave labor. Indeed, the Atlantic slave trade was a major way in which European merchants enriched themselves. That trade in turn forcibly brought the peoples of Africa into the life and culture of the New World.

To the extent that any formal economic theory lay behind the conduct of these empires, it was mercantilism, that practical creed of hard-headed business people. The terms *mercantilism* and *mercantile system* (coined by later opponents) designate a system in which governments heavily regulate trade and commerce in hope of increasing individual national wealth. Economic writers of the time believed that a nation had to gain a favorable trade balance of gold and silver bullion. A nation was truly wealthy only if it amassed more bullion than its rivals.

From beginning to end, the economic well-being of the home country was the primary concern of mercantilist writers. Colonies existed to provide markets and natural resources for the indus-

▲ As this painting of the Custom House Quay in London suggests, trade form European empires and the tariffs imposed on it were expected to generate revenue for the home country. But behind many of the goods carried in the great sailing ships in the harbor and landed on these docks lay the labor of African slaves working on the plantations of North and South America.
Samuel Scott, "Old Custom House Quay" Collection. V&A Images, the Victoria and Albert Museum. London.

| Buccaneers Prowl the High Seas

Piracy was a major problem for transatlantic trade. There was often a fine line between freewheeling, buccaneering pirates operating for their own gain and privateers who in effect worked for various European governments who wanted to penetrate the commercial monopoly of the Spanish Empire. Alexander Exquemelin was a ship's surgeon who for a time plied his trade on board a pirate ship and then later settled in Holland. He wrote an account of those days in which he emphasizes the careful code of conduct among the pirates themselves and the harshness of their behavior to both wealthy ships they captured and poor farmers and fishermen whom they robbed and virtually enslaved.

♦ How did the restrictive commercial policy of the Spanish Empire encourage piracy and privateering? Was there a code of honor among the pirates? What kinds of people may have suffered most from piracy? To what extent did pirates have any respect for individual freedom? How romantic was the real world of pirates?

When a buccaneer is going to sea he sends word to all who wish to sail with him. When all are ready, they go on board, each bringing what he needs in the way of weapons, powder and shot.

On the ship, they first discuss where to go and get food supplies. … The meat is either [salted] pork or turtle … Sometimes they go and plunder the Spaniards' *corrales*, which are pens where they keep perhaps a thousand head of tame hogs. The rovers … find the house of the farmer … [whom] unless he gives them as many hogs as they demand, they hang … without mercy. …

When a ship has been captured, the men decide whether the captain should keep it or not: if the prize is better than their own vessel, they take it and set fire to the other. When a ship is robbed, nobody must plunder and keep the loot to himself. Everything taken … must be shared …, without any man enjoying a penny more than his faire share. To prevent deceit, before the booty is distributed everyone has to swear an oath on the Bible that he has not kept for himself so much as the value of sixpence … And should any man be found to have made a false oath, he would be banished from the rovers, and never be allowed in their company. …

When they have captured a ship, the buccaneers set the prisoners on shore as soon as possible, apart from two or three whom they keep to do the cooking and other work they themselves do not care for, releasing these men after two or three years.

The rovers frequently put in for fresh supplies at some island or other, often … lying off the south coast of Cuba. … Everyone goes ashore and sets up his tent, and they take turns to go on marauding expedition in their canoes. They take prisoner … poor men who catch and set turtles for a living, to provide for their wives and children. Once captured, these men have to catch turtle for the rovers as long as they remain on the island. Should the rovers intend to cruise along a coast where turtle is abound, they take the fishermen along with them. The poor fellows may be compelled to stay away from their wives and families four or five years, with no news whether they are alive or dead.

From John Exquemelin, *The Buccaneers of America*, Alexis Brown, trans. Penguin Books © 1969. pp. 70–72.

tries of the home country. In turn, the home country furnished military security and political administration for the colonies. For decades both sides assumed that the colonies were the inferior partner in the relationship. The mercantilist statesmen and traders regarded the world as an arena of scarce resources and economic limitation. They assumed that one national economy could grow only at the expense of others. The home country and its colonies were to trade exclusively with each other. To that end, they tried to forge trade-tight systems of national commerce through navigation laws, tariffs, bounties to encourage production, and prohibitions against trading with the subjects of other monarchs. National monopoly was the ruling principle.

Mercantilist ideas were always neater on paper than in practice. By the early eighteenth century, mercantilist assumptions were far removed from the economic realities of the colonies. The colonial and home markets simply did not mesh. Spain could not produce enough goods for South America. Economic production in the British North American colonies challenged English manufacturing and led to British attempts to limit certain colonial industries, such as iron and hat making.

Colonists of different countries wished to trade with each other. English colonists could buy sugar more cheaply from the French West Indies than from English suppliers. The traders and merchants of one nation always hoped to break the monopoly of another. For all these reasons, the eighteenth century became the "golden age of smugglers."[1] The governments could not control the activities of all their subjects. Clashes among colonists could and did lead to war between governments. Consequently, the problems associated with the European mercantile empires led to conflicts around the world. (See Document, "Buccaneers Prowl the High Seas.")

[1] Walter Dorn, *Competition for Empire, 1740–1763* (New York: Harper, 1940), p. 266.

This brief overview of the periods of the European empire and of mercantile theory should provide a clearer context for understanding the character of the conquest of America and the establishment of the transatlantic economy.

Establishment of the Spanish Empire in America

CONQUEST OF THE AZTECS AND THE INCAS

Within twenty years of the arrival of Columbus (1451–1506), Spanish explorers in search of gold had claimed the major islands of the Caribbean and brutally suppressed the native peoples. These actions presaged what was to occur on the continent. The Caribbean islands became the staging areas for the further exploration and conquest of other parts of the Americas.

In 1519 Hernán Cortés (1485–1547) landed in Mexico with about 500 men and a few horses. He opened communication with nearby communities and then with Moctezuma II (1466–1520), the Aztec emperor. Moctezuma may initially have believed Cortés to be the god Quetzalcoatl, who, according to legend, had been driven away centuries earlier but had promised to return. Whatever the reason, Moctezuma hesitated to confront Cortés, attempting at first to appease him with gifts of gold that only whetted Spanish appetites. Cortés succeeded in forging alliances with some subject peoples and, most importantly, with Tlaxcala, an independent state and traditional enemy of the Aztecs. His forces then marched on the

▲ **Spanish Conquest of Mexico.** A sixteenth-century Aztec drawing depicts a battle during the Spanish conquest of Mexico.
Corbis–Bettmann. Archivo Iconografico. S. A./Corbis.

Aztec capital of Tenochtitlán (modern Mexico City), where Moctezuma welcomed him. Cortés soon seized Moctezuma, making him a prisoner in his own capital. Moctezuma died in unexplained circumstances, and the Aztecs' wary acceptance of the Spaniards turned to open hostility. The Spaniards were driven from Tenochtitlán and nearly wiped out, but they ultimately returned and laid siege to the city. The Aztecs, under their last ruler, Cuauhtemoc (ca. 1495–1525), resisted fiercely but were finally defeated in late 1521. Cortés razed Tenochtitlán, building his own capital over its ruins, and proclaimed the Aztec Empire to be New Spain.

In 1532, largely inspired by Cortés's example in Mexico, Francisco Pizarro (ca. 1478–1541) landed on the western coast of South America to take on the Inca Empire, about which he knew almost nothing. His force included about 200 men armed with guns, swords, and horses, the military power of which the Incas did not understand. Pizarro lured the Inca ruler Atahualpa (ca. 1500–1533) into a conference and then seized him. The imprisoned Atahualpa tried to ransom himself with a hoard of gold, but instead of releasing him Pizarro treacherously had him garroted in 1533. The Spaniards fought their way to Cuzco, the Inca capital, and captured it, effectively ending the Inca Empire. The Spanish faced insurrections, however, and fought among themselves for decades. Effective royal control was not established until the late 1560s.

The conquests of Mexico and Peru are among the most dramatic and brutal events in modern world history. Small military forces armed with advanced weapons and in alliance with indigenous enemies of the ruling Aztecs and Incas subdued, in a remarkably brief time, thise two advanced, powerful peoples. The spread of European diseases, especially smallpox, among the Native Americans also aided the conquest. The native populations had long lived in isolation, and many of them succumbed to the new diseases. But beyond the drama and bloodshed, these conquests, as well as those of other Native American peoples, marked a fundamental turning point. Whole civilizations with long histories and a record of enormous social, architectural, and technological achievement were effectively destroyed. Native American cultures endured, accommodating to European dominance, but there was never any doubt about which culture had the upper hand.

THE ROMAN CATHOLIC CHURCH IN SPANISH AMERICA

The Spanish conquest of the West Indies, Mexico, and the South American continent opened that vast region to the Roman Catholic faith. Roman Catholic priests followed in the steps of the explorers and conquerors. As it had in the Castilian reconquest of the Iberian Peninsula from the Moors, religion played a central role in the conquest of the New World. In this respect the crusade against Islamic civilization in Spain and

OVERVIEW   The Columbian Exchange

The same ships that that carried Europeans and Africans to the Americas also transported animals, plants, and diseases that had never before appeared in the New World. There was a similar transport back to Europe and Africa. Historians call this cross-continental flow "the Columbian exchange." The overall result was an ecological transformation that continues to shape the world.

To the Americas

Animals	pigs, cattle, horses, goats, sheep, chickens
Plants	apples, peaches, pears, apricots, plums, oranges, mangos, lemons, olives, melons, almonds, grapes, bananas, cherries, sugar cane, rice, wheat, oats, barley, onions, radishes, okra, dandelions, cabbage, and other green vegetables
Diseases	smallpox, influenza, bubonic plague, typhoid, typhus, measles, chicken pox, malaria, and diphtheria

From the Americas

Animals	turkeys
Plants	maize, tomatoes, sweet peppers, chilis, potatoes, sweet potatoes, squash, pumpkins, manioc (tapioca), beans, cocoa, peanuts, pecans, pineapples, guavas, avocados, blueberries, and tobacco
Diseases	syphilis

the crusade against the indigenous religions of the Americas were closely related. In both cases the Castilian monarchy received approval from church authorities for a policy of military conquest on the grounds of converting non-Christians to the Christian faith and eradicating their indigenous religious practices. The mission of conversion justified military conquest and the extension of political control and dominance. As a consequence of this policy, the Roman Catholic Church in the New World was always a conservative force working to protect the political power and prestige of the conquerors and the interests of the Spanish authorities.

The relationship between political authority and the propagation of religious doctrine was even closer in the New World than on the Iberian Peninsula. The papacy recognized that it could not from its own resources support so extensive a missionary effort, the full requirements for which became clear only after the conquests of Mexico and Peru. The papacy therefore turned over much of the control of the church in the New World directly to the Spanish monarchy. There was thus always a close relationship between the political and economic goals of the monarchy and the role of the church. The zeal of both increased early in the sixteenth century as the papacy and the Habsburg monarchy fought the new enemy of Protestantism, which they were determined should have no foothold in America. As a consequence, the Roman Catholicism that spread throughout the Spanish domains of America took the form of the increasingly zealous faith associated with the Counter-Reformation.

During the sixteenth century the Roman Catholic Church, represented more often than not by the mendicant orders such as the Franciscans and Dominicans, and later by the newly formed Jesuits, sought to convert the Native Americans. In the early decades these conversions often occurred shortly before the Spanish exterminated Native Americans or after they had conquered them. The conversion effort also involved attempts to eradicate surviving Indian religious practices. The Roman Catholic authorities tended to tolerate some residual Indian ceremonies in the sixteenth century but worked to prohibit them during the seventeenth century. Thus religious conversion represented, among other things, an attempt to destroy still another part of the Native American culture. Furthermore, conversion did not bring acceptance; even until late in the eighteenth century, there were few Native American Christian priests.

Real tension, however, existed between the early Spanish conquerors and the mendicant friars who sought to minister to the Native Americans. Without conquest the church could not convert the Native Americans, but the priests often deplored the harsh conditions imposed on the native peoples. By far the most effective and outspoken clerical critic of the Spanish conquerors was Bartolomé de Las Casas (1474–1566), a Dominican. He contended that conquest was not necessary for conversion. One result of his campaign was new royal regulations after 1550.

DOCUMENT · A Contemporary Describes Forced Indian Labor at Potosí

The Potosí range in Bolivia was the site of the great silver-mining industry in the Spanish Empire. The vast wealth of the region became legendary almost as soon as mining commenced there in the 1540s. Native Americans, most of whom were forced laborers working under the mita *system of conscription, did virtually all of the work underground. This description, written by a Spanish friar in the early seventeenth century, portrays both the large size of the enterprise and the harsh conditions that the Native Americans endured. At any one time only one third of the 13,300 conscripted Native Americans were employed. The labor force was changed every four months.*

> ◆ How efficient does the description suggest the mines were? What would have been the likely effects of working so long underground surrounded by burning candles?

According to His Majesty's warrant, the mine owners on this massive range have a right to the *mita* [conscripted labor] of 13,300 Indians in the working and exploitation of the mines, both those which have been discovered, those now discovered, and those which shall be discovered. It is the duty of the Corregidor [municipal governor] of Potosí to have them rounded up and to see that they come in from all the provinces between Cuzco over the whole of El Collao and as far as the frontiers of Tarija and Tomina. ...

The *mita* Indians go up every Monday morning to the locality of Guayna Potosí which is at the foot of the range; the Corregidor arrives with all the provincial captains or chiefs who have charge of the Indians assigned them, and he there checks off and reports to each mine and smelter owner the number of Indians assigned him for his mine or smelter; that keeps him busy till 1 P.M., by which time the Indians are already turned over to these mine and smelter owners.

After each has eaten his ration, they climb up the hill, each to his mine, and go in, staying there from that hour until Saturday evening without coming out of the mine; their wives bring them food, but they stay constantly underground, excavating and carrying out the ore from which they get the silver. They all have tallow candles, lighted day and night; that is the light they work with, for as they are underground, they have need of it all the time. ...

These Indians have different functions in the handling of the silver ore; some break it up with bar or pick, and dig down in, following the vein in the mine; others bring it up; others up above keep separating the good and the poor in piles; others are occupied in taking it down from the range to the mills on herds of llamas; every day they bring up more than 8,000 of these native beasts of burden for this task. These teamsters who carry the metal do not belong to the *mita*, but are mingados—hired.

From Antonio Vázquez de Espinosa, *Compendium and Description of the Indies* (ca. 1620), trans. by Charles Upson Clark (Washington, DC: Smithsonian Institution Press, 1968), p. 62, quoted in Helen Delpar, ed., *The Borzoi Reader in Latin American History* (New York: Alfred A. Knopf, 1972), pp. 92–93.

Another result of Las Casas's criticism was the emergence of the "**Black Legend**," according to which all Spanish treatment of the Native Americans was unprincipled and inhumane. Those who created this view of Spanish behavior drew heavily on Las Casas's writings. Although substantially true, the "Black Legend" nonetheless exaggerated the case against Spain. Certainly the rulers of the native empires—as the Aztec demands for sacrificial victims attest—had often themselves been exceedingly cruel to their subject peoples.

By the end of the sixteenth century the church in Spanish America had become largely an institution upholding the colonial status quo. Although individual priests did defend the communal rights of Indian tribes, the colonial church prospered as the Spanish elite prospered through its exploitation of the resources and peoples of the New World. The church became a great landowner through crown grants and through bequests from Catholics who died in the New World. The monasteries took on an economic as well as a spiritual life of their own. Whatever its concern for the spiritual welfare of the Native Americans, the church remained one of the indications that Spanish America was a conquered world. Those who spoke for the church did not challenge Spanish domination or any but the most extreme modes of Spanish economic exploitation. The church at best only modestly moderated the forces exploiting human labor and material wealth. By the end of the colonial era in the late eighteenth century, the Roman Catholic Church had become one of the single most conservative forces in Latin America and would continue to be so for at least the next century and a half.

Economies of Exploitation in the Spanish Empire

The colonial economy of Spanish America was an economy of exploitation in two senses. First, the organization of labor within the Spanish Empire in one situation after another involved structures of highly dependent servitude or slavery. Second, the resources of the continent were exploited in mercantilist fashion for the economic advantage of Spain.

The Silver Mines of Potosí. Worked by conscripted Indian laborers under extremely harsh conditions, these mines provided Spain with a vast treasure in silver.

Hulton/Corbis-Bettmann.

VARIETIES OF ECONOMIC ACTIVITY

The early *conquistadores* ("conquerors") had primarily been interested in gold, but by the middle of the sixteenth century silver mining provided the chief source of metallic wealth. The great silver mining centers were Potosí in present-day Bolivia and smaller sites in northern Mexico. The Spanish crown was particularly interested in mining because it received one fifth (the *quinto*) of all mining revenues. The crown thus maintained a monopoly over the production and sale of mercury, which was required for separating silver from the other impurities in the ore. Silver mining was a flourishing source of wealth for the Spanish until the early seventeenth century, when the industry underwent a recession because of lack of new investment and the increasing costs involved in deeper mines. Nonetheless, silver predominated during the colonial era and experienced a major boom, especially in Mexico, during the eighteenth century. Its production for the benefit of Spaniards and the Spanish crown epitomized the wholly extractive economy on which Latin American colonial life was based.

The activities associated with this extractive economy—mining the ore, smelting it, harvesting wood to feed the smelters' fires—required labor. From the initial contact with America, there were too few Spanish colonists to provide the needed labor. Furthermore, the social status and expectations of those colonists who did come to the Americas made them unlikely to provide wage labor. Consequently, the Spaniards looked first to the native Indian population and then to black African slaves. Indian labor dominated on the continent and African labor in the Caribbean. (See Document, "A Contemporary Describes Forced Indian Labor at Potosi.")

Encomienda   The Spanish devised a series of institutions to exploit Native American labor. The first was the *encomienda*, a formal grant by the crown of the right to the labor of a specific number of Native Americans for a particular time. An *encomienda* usually involved a few hundred Native Americans but might grant the right to the labor of several thousand. The *encomienda* was first used on Hispaniola but spread to the continent as the conquest took place. *Encomienda* as an institution persisted in some parts of Latin America well into the eighteenth century but had generally declined by the middle of the sixteenth. Some Native Americans substituted payments in kind or cash for labor.

The Spanish crown disliked the *encomienda* system. The monarchy was distressed by reports from concerned clergy that the Native Americans were being mistreated under the system and feared that *encomienda* holders were attempting to transform themselves into a powerful independent nobility in the New World.

Repartimiento   The passing of the *encomienda* led to another arrangement of labor servitude, the *repartimiento*, which was largely copied from the draft labor practices of the Incas. *Repartimiento*, in an adaptation of the Incan *mita*, required adult male Native Americans to devote a set number of days of labor annually to Spanish economic enterprises. In the mines of Potosí, the *repartimiento* was known as the *mita*. The time limitation on *repartimiento* led some Spanish managers to use their workers in an extremely harsh manner, under the assumption that more fresh workers would soon be appearing on the scene. Native Americans sometimes did not survive their days of labor rotation.

The Crueltes usd by the Spaniards on the Indians

▲ **The Cruelties Used by the Spaniards on the Indians,** from a 1599 English edition of *The Destruction of the Indies* by Bartolomé de las Casas. These scenes were copied from a series of engravings produced by Theodore de Bry that accompanied an earlier edition. British Library.

The Hacienda Outside the mines, the major institution using dependent labor in the Spanish colonies was the *hacienda*. This institution, which dominated rural and agricultural life in Spanish colonies on the continent, developed when the crown, partly to counter the extension of the *encomienda*, made available grants of land. These grants led to the establishment of large landed estates owned by *peninsulares*, whites born in Spain, or Creoles, whites born in America. The crown thus continued to use the resources of the New World for patronage without directly impinging on the Native Americans because the grazing that occurred on the *haciendas* required far less labor than did the mines. The establishment of *haciendas* represented the transfer of the principle of the large unit of privately owned land, which was characteristic of Europe and especially of Spain, to the New World. Such estates would become one of the most important features of Latin American life. Laborers on the *hacienda* usually stood in some relation of formal servitude to the owner. Furthermore, they were usually required to buy goods for everyday living on credit from the owner. They were rarely able to repay the resulting debts and thus could not move to work for new landowners. This system was known as *debt peonage*. There were two major products of the *hacienda* economy: foodstuffs for mining areas and urban centers, and leather goods used in vast quantities on mining machinery. Both farming and ranching were thus subordinate to the mine economy.

THE DECLINE OF THE NATIVE AMERICAN POPULATION

The conquest and the economy of exploitation and forced labor (and the introduction of European diseases) produced extraordinary demographic consequences for the Indian population. Beginning in the sixteenth century Native Americans had begun to die off in huge numbers. The pre-Columbian population of America is a matter of great controversy, but conservative estimates put the Indian population at the time of Columbus's discovery at well over 50 million. In New Spain (Mexico) alone, the population probably declined from approximately 25 million to fewer than 2 million within the first century after the conquest. Similar depopulation of native peoples appears to have occurred elsewhere in Spanish America during approximately the same period. Thereafter the Indian population began to expand slowly. Whatever the exact figures, the precipitous drop eliminated the *conquistadores'* easy supply of exploitable labor.

COMMERCIAL REGULATION AND THE FLOTA SYSTEM

Because Queen Isabella of Castile (r. 1474–1504) had commissioned Columbus, the technical legal link between the New World and Spain was the crown of Castile. Its powers both at home and in America were subject to few limitations.

Smallpox. Introduced by Europeans to the Americas, ▶ smallpox had a devastating effect on Native American populations. It swept through the Aztec capital of Tenochtitlán soon after the Spaniards arrived, contributing to the fall of the city. This illustration of the effect of the plague in the Aztec capital is from a postconquest history known as the Florentine Codex compiled for Spanish church authorithies by Aztec survivors.

Sixteenth century drawing of smallpox victims. Atzec original codex Florentino. Courtesy President and Fellows of Harvard College. Courtesy Peabody Museum of Archeology and Ethnology, Harvard University, photograph by Hillel Burger.

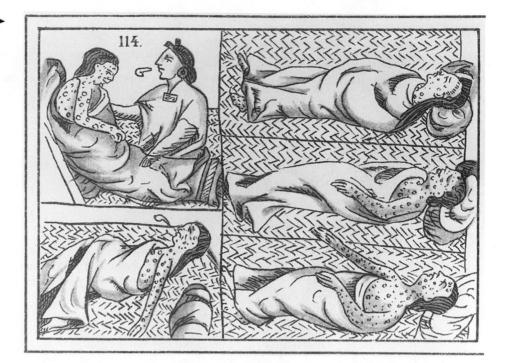

Government of America was assigned to the Council of the Indies, which, in conjunction with the monarch, nominated the viceroys of New Spain and Peru. These viceroys were the chief executives in the New World and carried out the laws promulgated by the Council of the Indies. Each of the viceroyalties included subordinate judicial councils known as *audiencias*. There were also a variety of local officers, the most important of which were the *corregidores*, who presided over municipal councils. These offices provided the monarchy with a vast array of opportunities for patronage, usually bestowed on persons born in Spain. Virtually all political power flowed from the top of this political structure downward; in effect, there was little or no local initiative or self-government (see Map 18–1).

The colonial political structures existed largely to support the commercial goals of Spain. Spanish control of its American empire involved a system of monopolistic trade regulation that was more rigid in appearance than in practice. The trade monopoly was often breached. The Casa de Contratación (House of Trade) in Seville regulated all trade with the New World. Cádiz was the only Spanish port to be used for the American trade. In America there were similarly specific ports for trade both to Spain and with non-Spanish merchants. The latter trade was highly restricted. The Casa de Contratación was the single most influential institution of the Spanish Empire, and its members worked closely with the Consulado (Merchant Guild) of Seville and other groups involved with the American commerce in Cádiz. The entire organization was geared to benefit the Spanish monarchy and these privileged merchant groups.

A complicated system of trade and bullion fleets administered from Seville provided the key for maintaining the trade monopoly. Each year a fleet of commercial vessels (the *flota*) controlled by Seville merchants, escorted by warships, carried merchandise from Spain to a few specified ports in America. These included Portobello, Veracruz, and Cartagena. There were no authorized ports on the Pacific coast. Areas far to the south, such as Buenos Aires, received goods only after the shipments had been unloaded at one of the authorized ports. After selling their wares, the ships were loaded with silver and gold bullion, usually wintered in heavily fortified Caribbean ports, and then sailed back to Spain. The flota system always worked imperfectly, but trade outside it was illegal. Regulations prohibited the Spanish colonists within the American empire from trading directly with each other and from building their own shipping and commercial industry. Foreign merchants were also forbidden to breach the Spanish monopoly.

Colonial Brazil and Slavery

Spain and Portugal originally had rival claims to the Americas. In 1494, by the Treaty of Tordesillas, the pope divided the seaborne empires of Spain and Portugal by drawing a line west of the Cape Verde Islands. In 1500 a Portuguese explorer landed on the coast of what is present-day Brazil, which extended east of the papal line of division, and thus Portugal gained a major hold on the South American continent.

Portugal had fewer human and material resources to devote to its New World empire than did Spain. The crown granted captaincies to private persons that permitted them to attempt

Interactive map: To explore this map further, go to http://www.prenhall.com/craig3/map18.1

MAP 18–1   Viceroyalties in Latin America in 1870. Spain organized its vast holdings in the New World into Viceroyalties, each of which had its own governor and other administrative officials.

to exploit the region. The native people in the lands that Portugal governed lived for the most part in small, nomadic groups. In this they differed from the native peoples of Spanish America, with their centralized empires, cities, and organized political structures. As a result, labor practices in the two regions were also different. The Portuguese imported Africans as slaves rather than using the Native Indian population, as did the Spanish in most areas.

By the mid–sixteenth century, sugar production had gained preeminence in the Brazilian economy, although some minerals were discovered and some cattle raised. Because sugar cane was grown on large estates (*fazendas*) with African slave labor, the dominance of sugar meant also the dominance of slavery.

Toward the close of the seventeenth century, sugar prices declined and the economy suffered. In the early eighteenth century, however, significant deposits of gold were discovered in southern Brazil. Immigrants from Portugal joined the ensuing gold rush, and economic activity moved suddenly toward the south. This shift, however, did not reduce Brazil's reliance on slave labor. In fact, the expansion of gold mining also led to the increased importation of African slaves. Nowhere, except perhaps in the West Indies, was slavery as important as it was in Brazil, where it persisted until 1888.

The taxation and administration associated with gold mining brought new, unexpected wealth to the eighteenth-century Portuguese monarchy, allowing it to rule without recourse to the Cortés or traditional parliament for taxation. Through trans-

atlantic trade the new wealth generated from Brazilian gold also filtered into all the major trading nations, which could sell their goods to Portugal as well as profit from the slave trade.

As in the Spanish Empire, the Portuguese crown attempted to establish a strong network of regulation around Brazilian trade. Brazil, however, required less direct control by the Portuguese than the Spanish Empire required from Spain, and as a result, Brazil's colonial settlers may have felt less resentment toward the Portuguese government than the settlers of the Spanish Empire felt toward the Spanish administrators. In Brazil, where the basic unit of production was the plantation, there were fewer large cities than in Spanish America. The crown's determination in Spanish America to have precious metals sent to Spain required a vast colonial administration. The sugar plantations of Brazil, in contrast, did not require such direct administration. Consequently, the Portuguese were willing to allow more local autonomy than was Spain. More local officials were allowed to serve in the government in Brazil than in Spanish America, where the administration was dominated by officials born in Spain. In Spanish America the use of Indian labor, which was important to the colonial economy, required government supervision. Brazil, less dependent on Indian labor, felt no such constraints. Indeed, the Portuguese government condoned policies whereby Indian tribes were driven into the back country or exterminated. Throughout the eighteenth century the Portuguese government also favored the continued importation of slaves.

Sugar plantations of Brazil and the West Indies were a major source of the demand for slave labor. Slaves are here shown grinding sugar cane and refining sugar, which was then exported to the consumer markets in Europe.
© Hulton-Deutsch Collection/Corbis.

◀ **Native Americans** in the Saint Lawrence region of North America were drawn into the transatlantic economy through interaction with French fur traders in the early 17th century. This illustration shows Samuel de Champlain, the founder of New France, assisting his Huron allies in an attack on the Iroquois in part of an ongoing struggle for control of valuable fur grounds. The palm trees in the background suggest that the artist was unfamiliar with the region.

Samuel de Champlain "Voyages...," Paris, 1613. Illustration opp. pg. 322. Early battle with the Iroquois. Rare Books Division, the New York Public Library, Astor Lenox and Tilden Foundation.

French and British Colonies in North America

French explorers had pressed down the St. Lawrence river valley in Canada during the seventeenth century. French fur traders and Roman Catholic Jesuit missionaries had followed in their wake, with the French government supporting the missionary effort. By the end of the seventeenth century a significant but sparsely populated French presence existed in Canada. Trade rather than extensive settlements characterized the French effort. The largest settlement was Quebec, founded in 1608. Some French settlers married Native American women; the absence of a drive to permanently claim land reduced conflict between the French and the Native Americans. It was primarily through the fur trade that French Canada functioned as part of the early transatlantic economy.

For most readers of this volume, the story of the founding of the English-speaking colonies along the Atlantic seaboard is relatively familiar, but it needs to be set in the larger world context. Beginning with the first successful settlement in Jamestown, Virginia, in 1607 and ending with the establishment of Georgia in 1733, the eastern seaboard of the United States became populated by a series of English colonies. Other nations, including the Dutch and Swedes, had founded settlements, but all of them were eventually taken over during the seventeenth century by the English.

A wide variety of reasons led to the founding of the English colonies. Settlement for enrichment from farming and trade accounted for some settlements, such as Virginia and New Amsterdam (after 1664, New York). Others, such as the Carolinas, were developed by royal favorites who were given vast land tracts. James Oglethorpe founded Georgia as a refuge for English debtors. But the pursuit of religious liberty constituted the major driving force of the Pilgrim and Puritan founders of Massachusetts, the Baptist Roger Williams in Rhode Island, the Quaker William Penn in Pennsylvania, and the Roman Catholic Lord Baltimore in Maryland.

With the exception of Maryland, these colonies were Protestant. The Church of England dominated the southern colonies. In New England, varieties of Protestantism associated with or derived from Calvinism were in the ascendancy. In their religious affiliations, the English-speaking colonies manifested two important traits derived from the English experience. First, much of their religious life was organized around self-governing congregations. Second, their religious outlook derived from those forms of Protestantism that were suspicious of central political authority and especially of potentially despotic monarchs. In this regard, their cultural and political outlook differed sharply from the cultural and political outlook associated with the Roman Catholicism of the Spanish Empire. In a sense the values of the extreme Reformation and Counter-Reformation confronted each other on the two American continents.

The English colonists had complex interactions with the Native American populations. Unlike the Spanish to the south or the French to the north, they had only modest interest in missionary enterprise. As in South America, new diseases imported from Europe took a high death toll among the native population. Unlike Mexico and Peru, however, North America had no large Native American cities. The Native American populations were far more dispersed, and intertribal animosity was intense. The English often encountered well-organized resistance, as from the Powhatan conspiracy in Virginia and the Pequots in New England. The most powerful of the Native American groups was the Iroquois Nation, organized in the early eighteenth century in New York. The Iroquois battled successfully against other tribes and long negotiated successfully with both the Dutch and the English. The English also often used one tribe against another, and the Native Americans also tried to use the English or the French in their own conflicts. The outcome of these struggles between the English settlers and the Native Americans was rarely full victory for either side, but rather mutual exhaustion, with the Native Americans temporarily retreating beyond the reach of English settlements and the English temporarily restraining their initial claims. From the late seventeenth century through the American Revolution, however, the Native Americans of North America were drawn into the Anglo-French Wars that were fought in North America as well as Europe. Indeed, Native American alliances became important for the Anglo-French conflict on the Continent, which was intimately related to their rivalry over transatlantic trade (see Chapter 20).

The largest economic activity throughout the English-speaking colonies was agriculture. From New England through the Middle Atlantic states there were mostly small farms tilled by free white labor; from Virginia southward it was the plantation economy, dependent on slavery. During the early eighteenth century the chief products raised on these plantations were tobacco, indigo, rice, and sugar. Although slavery was a dominant institution in the South, all of the colonies included slaves. The principal port cities along the seaboard—Boston, Newport, New York, Philadelphia, Baltimore, and Charleston—resembled small provincial English cities. They were primarily trading centers through which goods moved back and forth between the colonies and England and the West Indies. The commercial economies of these cities were all related to the transatlantic slave trade.

Until the 1760s the political values of the Americans resembled those of their English counterparts. The colonials were thoroughly familiar with events in England. They sent many of their children there to be educated. They were monarchists but, like their English counterparts, suspicious of monarchical power. Their politics involved vast amounts of patronage and individual favors. Their society was clearly hierarchical, with an elite that functioned like a colonial aristocracy and many ordinary people who were dependent on that aristocracy. Throughout the colonies during the eighteenth century, the Anglican Church grew in influence and membership. The prosperity of the colonies might eventually have led them to separate from England, but in 1750 few people thought that would occur.

Both England and France had important sugar islands in the Caribbean. England held Jamaica and Barbados, and

France held Saint Domingue (Haiti), Guadeloupe, and Martinique. The plantations on these islands were worked by African slaves, and the trade and commerce of the northern British colonies were closely related to meeting the needs of these islands.

▲ **Roanoke.** The first successful English colonies in North America in the 17th century were preceded by two failed efforts on Roanoke Island in what is now North Carolina in the late 16th century. John White accompanied both attempts, the second as governor. White was a perceptive and sensitive observer whose watercolor paintings provide invaluable information about Native American life in the coastal Carolina region at the time of contact. This painting shows the Algonquian village of Secoton. The houses were bark covered. In the lower left is a mortuary temple. The dancers in the lower right are performing a fertility ceremony. The man sitting in the platform in the upper right is keeping birds away from the corn crop.
The Bridgeman Art Library International Ltd.

Slavery in the Americas

Black slavery was the final mode of forced or subservient labor in the New World. Unlike the labor exploitation of Native Americans discussed earlier in this chapter, black slavery extended throughout not only the Spanish Empire but also Portuguese Brazil and the English-speaking colonies of North America.

ESTABLISHMENT OF SLAVERY

As the numbers of Native Americans in South America declined due to disease and exploitation, the Spanish and the Portuguese turned to the labor of imported African slaves.

By the late sixteenth century, in the islands of the West Indies and the major cities of South America, black slaves equaled or surpassed the white European population.

On much of the South American continent dominated by Spain, the number of slaves declined during the late seventeenth century, and the institution became less fundamental there than elsewhere. Slavery continued to prosper, however,

Slave Auction Notice. Africans who survived the voyage across the Atlantic were immediately sold into slavery in the Americas. This slave-auction notice relates to a group of slaves whose ship had stopped at Charleston, South Carolina, and then landed elsewhere in the region to auction its human cargo. Notice the concern to assure potential buyers that the slaves were healthy.
Corbis-Bettmann.

in Brazil and in the Caribbean. Later, starting with the importation of slaves to Jamestown in 1619, slavery spread into the British North American colonies and became a fundamental institution there.

One of the forces that led to the spread of slavery in Brazil and the West Indies was the cultivation of sugar. Sugar cane required a large investment in land and equipment, and only slave labor could provide enough workers for the extremely profitable sugar plantations. As the production of sugar expanded, so did the demand for slaves, and more slaves were imported.

By the close of the seventeenth century the Caribbean islands were the world center for sugar production. As the European appetite for sugar continued to grow, the slave population continued to expand. By 1725 black slaves may have constituted almost 90 percent of the population of Jamaica. The situation was similar throughout the West Indies. There and elsewhere, in Brazil and the southern British colonies, prosperity and slavery went hand in hand. The wealthiest and most prized of the colonies were those that raised consumer staples, such as sugar, rice, tobacco, or cotton, by slave labor.

THE PLANTATION ECONOMY AND TRANSATLANTIC TRADE

The **plantation economy** was comprised of plantations that stretched from Maryland through the West Indies and into Brazil. They formed a vast corridor of slave societies in which social and economic subordination was based on both involuntary servitude and race. This kind of society, in its total dependence on slave labor and racial differences, was something novel in world history; it had not existed before the European discovery and exploitation of the Americas. The social and economic influence of plantation slavery touched not only the plantation societies themselves, but also West Africa, western Europe, and New England. It persisted from the sixteenth century through the second half of the nineteenth century, ending with the British effort to outlaw the slave trade during the first half of the nineteenth century, the Latin American Wars of Independence, the Emancipation Proclamation of 1862 in the United States, and the Brazilian emancipation of 1888. Every society in which it existed still contends with its long-term effects.

The slave trade was part of the larger system of transatlantic trade that linked Europe, Africa, and the European colonies in South America, the Caribbean, and North America. In this system the Americas supplied labor-intensive raw materials like tobacco, sugar, coffee, precious metals, cotton, and indigo. Europe supplied manufactured goods like textiles, liquor, guns, metal wares, and beads, not to mention various forms of cash, including even gold. And Africa supplied gold, ivory, wood, palm oil, gum, and other products, as well as the slaves who provided the labor to create the American products. By the eighteenth century slaves were the predominant African export.

SLAVERY ON THE PLANTATIONS

The plantations in the Americas to which the African slaves eventually arrived were always in a fairly isolated rural setting. Their products, however, were agricultural goods produced for an external overseas market that was part of a larger integrated transatlantic economy. The plantation might raise food for its owners and their slaves, but the main production—whether sugar, tobacco, or, later, cotton and coffee—was intended for export. In turn, plantation owners imported from other parts of the world virtually all the finished or manufactured goods they used or consumed.

The life conditions of plantation slaves differed from colony to colony. Most owners possessed relatively few slaves, and vast slaveholdings were the exception. Black slaves living in Portuguese areas had the fewest legal protections. In the Spanish colonies the church attempted to provide some small protection for black slaves but devoted much more effort toward protecting the Native Americans. Slave codes were developed in the British and the French colonies during the seventeenth century, but they provided only the most limited protection. Virtually all slave owners feared a slave revolt; slave-related legislation and other regulations were intended to prevent such an event. Slave laws favored the master rather than the slave. Masters were permitted to punish slaves by whipping and other harsh corporal punishment. Furthermore, slaves were often forbidden to gather in large groups lest they plan a revolt. In most slave-owning societies, the marriages of slaves were not recognized by law. The children of slaves continued to be slaves and were owned by the owner of the parents. Slave families could be separated by the owner or after the owner's death.

The daily life of most slaves during these centuries was one of hard agricultural labor, poor diet and clothing, and inadequate housing. The death rate among slaves was high. Their welfare and their lives were sacrificed to the ongoing expansion of the plantations that made their owners wealthy and that produced goods demanded by consumers in Europe. Scholars have argued that slaves in one area or another had a better existence than others, but it is generally accepted that slaves in all plantation societies suffered under difficult conditions. The specifics of those conditions may have varied, but they were not significantly better in one place than another.

The African slaves who were transported to the Americas were, like the Native Americans, converted to Christianity: in the Spanish domains to Roman Catholicism, and in the English colonies to various forms of Protestantism. In both cases, they became largely separated from African religious outlooks. Although some African practices survived in muted forms, and slaves did manage to mix Christianity with African religion, the conversion of Africans to Christianity nonetheless represented another example of the crushing of a set of non-European cultural values in the context of the New World economies and social structures.

The European settlers in the Americas and the slave traders were also prejudiced against black Africans. Many Europeans thought Africans were savage or less than civilized. Others looked down on them simply because they were slaves. These attitudes had been shared by both Christians and Muslims in the Mediterranean world, where slavery had long existed. Furthermore, many European languages and European cultures attached negative connotations to the idea and image of blackness. In virtually all plantation societies, race was an important element in keeping black slaves subservient. Although racial thinking in regard to slavery became more important in the nineteenth century, the fact that slaves were differentiated from the rest of the population by race as well as by their status as chattel property was fundamental to the system.

Africa and the Transatlantic Slave Trade

It was the establishment of plantations demanding the use of slave labor that drew Africa and its peoples into the heart of the transatlantic economy. As Native American peoples were decimated by conquest and European diseases or proved unsatisfactory as plantation laborers, colonial entrepreneurs began to look elsewhere for people to work their plantations. First the Portuguese, and then the Spanish, Dutch, French, and English (others would follow, including Americans) turned to west, central, and, to a lesser degree, southeastern Africa for an ample supply of slaves. Thus the Atlantic slave trade was not overtly the result of racist principles, but of the economic needs of the colonial powers and their willingness to exploit weaker peoples to satisfy them. However, this willingness was based on the tacit racist assumption that non-European, nonwhite tribal peoples were subhuman and could be enslaved for European purposes.

The Portuguese, who were the principal carriers throughout most of the history of the trade, had a virtual monopoly until the Dutch broke it in the 1640s and briefly became the chief carriers. The French and the English came into the trade only in the late seventeenth century, yet during the eighteenth century, which saw the greatest shipments, they carried almost half the total traffic. Americans, too, were latecomers but avid slavers who managed to make considerable profits before and even after Britain and the United States outlawed slaving in 1807.

If gold and the search for a sea route to Asia brought the first European ships to Africa, slaves were the main commodity for which they returned for a long time. Slaving was an important part of the massive new overseas trade that financed much European and American economic development that so dramatically changed the West during the nineteenth century. The success of this trade, bought at the price of immense human suffering, helped propel Europe and some of its colonial offshoots in the Americas into world dominance.

THE BACKGROUND OF SLAVERY

Slavery seems to have been one of the tragic facts of human societies as far back as we can trace its history. Although linked to warfare and the age-old practice of taking captives, it cannot be fully explained by military or economic necessity.

Virtually every premodern state around the globe depended on slavery to some extent (see Map 18–2). The Mediterranean and African worlds were no exception, in both the pre-Islamic and the Islamic periods. Slave institutions in sub-Saharan Africa were ancient and included traffic with the Mediterranean world. The Islamic states of southwestern Asia and North Africa continued and even increased this traffic, importing slaves from both the Sudan and Horn of Africa as well as the East African coast,

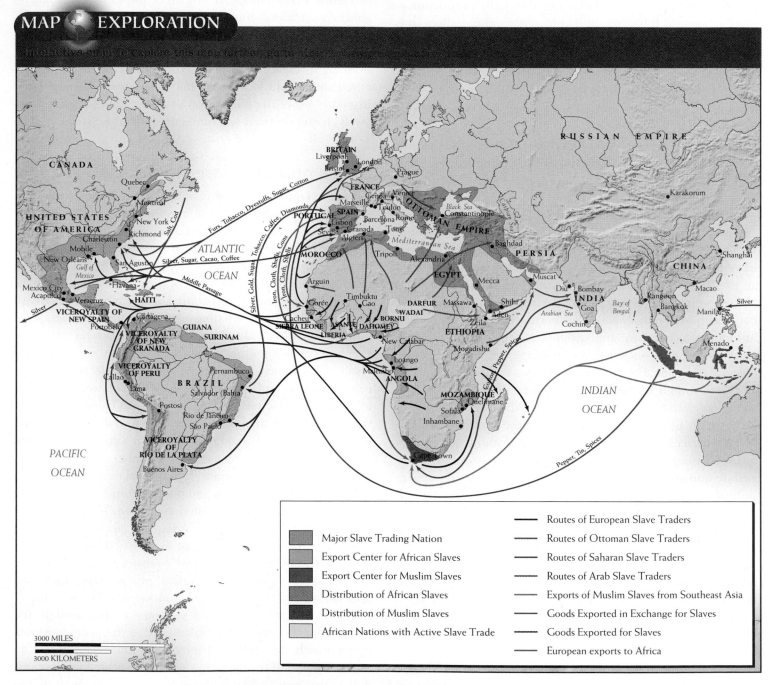

MAP 18–2 The Slave Trade, 1400–1860. Slavery is an ancient institution and complex slave-trading routes were in existence in Africa, the Middle East, and Asia for centuries, but it was the need to supply labor for the plantations of the Americas that led to the greatest movement of peoples across the face of the earth.

although they took fewer slaves from Africa than from eastern Europe and Central Asia. Central Asia, for example, was the source of most of the (largely Turkish) slave-soldier dynasties that came to rule many Islamic states from India to North Africa. (Hence it is not surprising that the word *slave* is derived ultimately from *Slav*.) Both Mediterranean Christian and Islamic peoples were using slaves—mostly Greeks, Bulgarians, Turkish prisoners of war, and Black Sea Tartars, but also Africans—well before the voyages of discovery opened sub-Saharan sources of slaves for the new European colonies overseas.

Not all forms of slavery were as dehumanizing as the chattel slavery that came to predominate (with the sanction of Christian authorities) during the colonization of the Americas. Islamic law, for example, although permitting slavery, also ameliorated it. All slavery, however, involved the forceful exploitation and degradation of some human beings for the profit of others, the denial of basic freedoms, and sometimes the sundering, often violently, of even the closest family ties.

Africa suffered immense social devastation when it was the chief supplier of slaves to the world. The societies that were built to a great extent on the exploitation of African slavery also suffered enduring consequences, not the least of which, many believe, is racism.

SLAVERY AND SLAVING IN AFRICA

The trade that long before the fifteenth century supplied African slaves to the Islamic lands of the Mediterranean and to southwestern and southern Asia has conventionally been termed the "Oriental" slave trade. The savannahs of the Sudan and the Horn of Africa were the two prime sources of slaves for this trade. The trade managed by Europeans, conventionally called the "Occidental" slave trade, can be traced at least to the thirteenth century, when Europeans established sugar cane plantations on Cyprus soon after Muslim forces had driven them out of the Holy Land. In Cypress, as later in Brazil and the Caribbean islands, slaves proved an especially profitable workforce for the labor-intensive process of sugar production. This industry subsequently spread westward to Crete and Sicily and, in the fifteenth century, to the Portuguese Atlantic islands of Madeira and São Thomé.

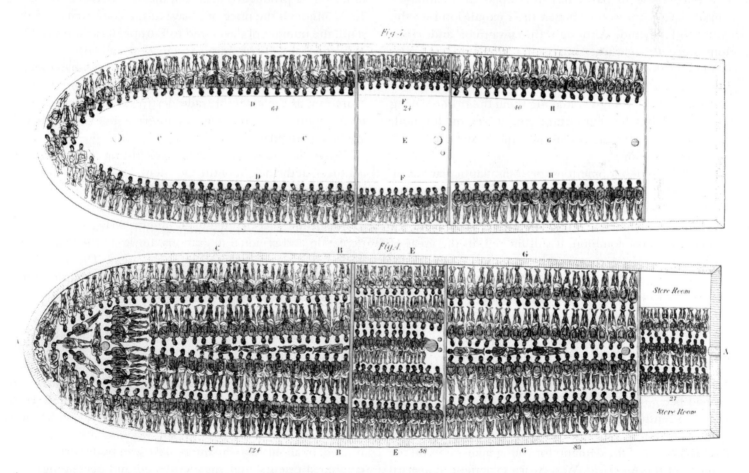

▲ **Slave Ship.**   Loading plan for the main decks of the 320-ton slave ship *Brookes*. The *Brookes* was only 25 feet wide and 100 feet long, but as many as 609 slaves were crammed on board for the nightmarish passage to the Americas. The average space allowed each person was only about 78 inches by 16 inches.

Photographs and Prints Division, Schomburg Center for Research in Black Culture, The New York Public Library, Astor, Lenox, and Tilden Foundations.

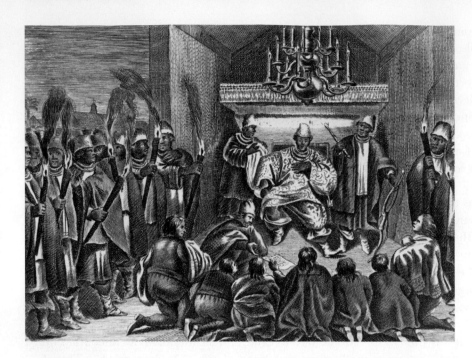

King Alfonzo I of the Congo holds an audience with European ambassadors who kneel before him.
Courtesy of the Library of Congress.

The Portuguese in particular developed the plantation system of slave labor as they began their expansion into the Atlantic and beyond. Although the savannah and Horn regions were the earliest sources for this trade, voyages beginning in the fifteenth century by first the Portuguese and then other Europeans opened the western coasts of Africa as far south as Angola, making them the prime slaving areas. A third but less important source region for both Occidental and Oriental trades was the eastern coast of Africa below the Horn.

Before the full development of the transatlantic slave trade by about 1650, slavery and slave trading had been no more significant in Africa than anywhere else in the world.[2] Indigenous African slavery resembled that of other premodern societies. It was apparently most common, if still limited, in the areas of the savannah and Horn, presumably because these areas were involved in external slave trading. In the western and central Sudan, slavery came largely to be regulated by Islamic norms, but in the Horn, specifically in Ethiopia, slavery was practiced in both Christian and Muslim communities. Estimates suggest that about 10,000 slaves per year, most of them female, were taken from sub-Saharan Africa through the Oriental trade.

By about 1650 the newer Occidental slave trade of the Europeans had become as large as the Oriental trade and for the ensuing two centuries far surpassed it. It affected adversely all of Africa, disrupting especially western and central African society. As a result of the demand for young male slaves on the plantations of the Americas, West Africa experienced a sharp

drain on its productive male population. Between 1640 and 1690, although the price of a slave at the coast remained constant, the number of slaves sold to European carriers doubled, indicating the increasing participation of Africans in the expanding trade. With the growing demand for slaves came an increase in internal warfare in western and central Africa. Moreover, as the external trade destroyed the regional male-female population balance, an internal market for female slaves in particular arose.

These developments accelerated during the eighteenth century—at the height of the Occidental trade. It was also during this period that African states and slave traders were most heavily involved as regulators and suppliers of the trade. Slave prices at times accelerated accordingly. Owing to population depletion and regional migrations, however, the actual number of sold slaves declined in some areas. The population declined sharply in the coastal and inland areas hardest hit by the ravages of the trade in the later eighteenth century and continued to decline in places even until 1850.

As European nations, followed by nations in the Americas, slowly began to outlaw slaving and slavery in the nineteenth century, occidental demand slowed and prices for slaves sank. The result was that the oriental and internal trades increased. Slave exports from East Africa and the Sudan and Horn increased significantly after about 1780, and indigenous African slavery, predominantly of women, also expanded. Indeed, by about 1850 the internal African trade surpassed the combined oriental and (now outlawed and decreasing) occidental trade. This traffic was dominated by the same figures—merchants, warlords, and rulers—who had previously profited from external trade.

[2] The summary follows closely that of P. Manning, *Slavery and African Life: Occidental, Oriental, and African Slave Trades* (Cambridge: Cambridge University Press, 1990), pp. 127–140.

Slave dealing in the streets of Zanzibar. ➤
Slaving was a part of East African trade
for centuries.
Corbis-Bettmann.

Indigenous African slavery began a real decline only at the end of the nineteenth century, in part because of the dominance of European colonial regimes and in part because of internal changes. The formal end of African indigenous slavery occurred over a long period, beginning in 1874 in the Gold Coast and ending only in 1928 in Sierra Leone.

THE AFRICAN SIDE OF THE TRANSATLANTIC TRADE

Africans were actively involved in the transatlantic slave trade. Except for the Portuguese in central Africa, European slave traders generally obtained their human cargoes from private or government-sponsored African middlemen at coastal forts or simply at anchorages along the coast. A system of forts built by Europeans mostly between 1640 and 1750, for example, dominated the Gold Coast. This situation was the result of both the desire and ability of Africans to control inland trade and the vulnerability of Europeans to tropical disease (a new European arrival stood a less than 50 percent chance of surviving a year on the tropical African coast). Thus it was largely African middlemen who undertook the actual capture or procurement of slaves and the difficult, dangerous task of marching them to the coast. These middlemen were generally either wealthy merchants who could mount slaving expeditions inland or the agents of African chieftaincies or kingdoms who sought to profit from the trade. (See Document, "A Slave Trader Describes the Atlantic Passage.")

The media of exchange were varied. At first they usually involved mixed barter for goods that ranged from gold dust or firearms to beads and alcohol. As time went on they came increasingly to involve some form of monetary payment. This exchange drained productive resources (human beings) in return for nonproductive wealth.

The chief western and central African slaving regions provided different numbers of slaves at different times, and the total number of exported slaves varied sharply between periods. When one area was unable to produce sufficient numbers to meet demand (whether as a result of depopulation of choice areas, local warfare, or changing state policies), the European traders shifted their buying to other points. Thus, between 1526 and 1550 the major sources of the slaves for the Atlantic trade were the Kongo-Angola region (34 percent), the Guinea coast of Cape Verde (25.6 percent), and Senegambia (23.5 percent).[3] By contrast, between 1761 and 1810 the French drew some 52 percent of their slaves from Angola and 24 percent from the Bight of Benin, but only 4.8 percent from Senegambia, whereas the British relied most heavily on the Bight of Biafra and central Africa.[4] Traders naturally went where population density and the presence of active African merchant or state suppliers promised the best numbers and prices, although prices do not seem to have varied radically in a given period.

THE EXTENT OF THE SLAVE TRADE

The slave trade varied sharply in extent from period to period. Only about 3 percent of the total Occidental trade occurred before 1600, and only about 14 percent between 1600 and 1700. The period of greatest activity, 1701–1810, accounted for

[3] Philip Curtin, *The Atlantic Slave Trade: A Census* (Madison: University of Wisconsin Press, 1969), p. 101.
[4] Curtin, *The Atlantic Slave Trade*, pp. 101, 129; James A. Rawley, *The Transatlantic Slave Trade: A History* (New York: W. W. Norton, 1981), p. 129.

DOCUMENT | A Slave Trader Describes the Atlantic Passage

During 1693 and 1694 Captain Thomas Phillips carried slaves from Africa to Barbados on the ship Hannibal. *The financial backer of the voyage was the Royal African Company of London, which held an English crown monopoly on slave trading. Phillips sailed to the west coast of Africa, where he purchased the Africans who were sold into slavery by an African king. Then he set sail westward.*

◆ Who are the various people described in this document who in one way or another were involved in or profited from the slave trade? What dangers did the Africans face on the voyage? What contemporary attitudes could have led this ship captain to treat and think of his human cargo simply as goods to be transported? What are the grounds of his self-pity for the difficulties he met?

Having bought my complement of 700 slaves, 480 men and 220 women, and finish'd all my business at Whidaw [on the Gold Coast of Africa], I took my leave of the old king and his cappasheirs [attendants], and parted, with many affectionate expressions on both sides, being forced to promise him that I would return again the next year, with several things he desired me to bring from England. ... I set sail the 27th of July in the morning, accompany'd with the East-India Merchant, who had bought 650 slaves, for the Island of St. Thomas ... from which we took our departure on August 25th and set sail for Barbadoes.

We spent in our passage from St. Thomas to Barbadoes two months eleven days, from the 25th of August to the 4th of November following: in which time there happened such sickness and mortality among my poor men and Negroes. Of the first we buried 14, and of the last 320, which was a great detriment to our voyage, the Royal African Company losing ten pounds by every

slave that died, and the owners of the ship ten pounds ten shillings, being the freight agreed on to be paid by the charterparty for every Negro delivered alive ashore to the African Company's agents at Barbadoes. ... The loss in all amounted to near 6500 pounds sterling.

The distemper which my men as well as the blacks mostly died of was the white flux, which was so violent and inveterate that no medicine would in the least check it, so that when any of our men were seized with it, we esteemed him a dead man, as he generally proved. ...

The Negroes are so incident to the small pox that few ships that carry them escape without it, and sometimes it makes vast havock and destruction among them. But tho' we had 100 at a time sick of it, and that it went thro' the ship, yet we lost not above a dozen by it. All the assistance we gave the diseased was only as much water as they desir'd to drink, and some palm-oil to annoint their sores, and they would generally recover without any other helps but what kind nature gave them. ...

But what the small pox spar'd, the flux swept off, to our great regret, after all our pains and care to give them their messes in due order and season, keeping their lodgings as clean and sweet as possible, and enduring so much misery and stench so long among a parcel of creatures nastier than swine, and after all our expectations to be defeated by their mortality. ...

No gold-finders can endure so much noisome slavery as they do who carry Negroes; for those have some respite and satisfaction, but we endure twice the misery; and yet by their mortality our voyages are ruin'd, and we pine and fret ourselves to death, and take so much pains to so little purpose.

From Thomas Phillips, *"Journal," A Collection of Voyages and Travels*, Vol. VI, ed. by Awnsham and John Churchill (London, 1746), as quoted in Thomas Howard, ed., *Black Voyage: Eyewitness Accounts of the Atlantic Slave Trade* (Boston: Little, Brown and Company, 1971), pp. 85–87.

---

over 60 percent of the total, and even the final half century of slaving until 1870 accounted for over 20 percent of the total. Despite moves by European nations to abolish slaving in the early 1800s, the Portuguese still transported more than a million slaves to Brazil between 1811 and 1870. In fact, more slaves landed in the Americas in these final years of the trade than during the entire seventeenth century.[5] We would do well to remember how long it actually took the "modern" occidental world to abolish the trade in African slaves.

The overall number of African slaves exported during the occidental trade—effectively, between 1451 and 1870—is still debated

and must be seen in the larger context of all types of slaving in Africa in the same period. A major unknown—for both the occidental and the oriental trades—is the number of slaves who died under the brutal conditions to which they were subjected when captured and transported overland and by sea. The most reliable estimates pertain only to those slaves who actually landed abroad, and these estimates are more reliable for the occidental trade than for the older, smaller, and more dispersed oriental trade. Those who actually reached an American or Old World destination in the occidental trade totaled more than 11 million souls.

Recent scholarship estimates that at a minimum Africa lost some 13 million people to the Atlantic trade alone during its four centuries of existence. Another 5 million or

[5] Rawley, *The Transatlantic Slave Trade*, p. 429; Curtin, *Atlantic Slave Trade*, p. 268.

LANGUAGE	Estimated Slave Imports into the Americas and Old World by Region, 1451–1870				
British North America	523,000	French Caribbean	1,655,000	Brazil (Portuguese)	4,190,000
Spanish America	1,687,000	Dutch Caribbean	500,000	Old World	297,000
British Caribbean	2,443,000	Danish Caribbean	50,000	**Total**	**11,345,000**

Figures as calculated by James A. Rawley, *The Transatlantic Slave Trade: A History* (New York: W. W. Norton, 1981), p. 428, based on his and other more recent revisions of the careful but older estimates of Philip D. Curtin, *The Atlantic Slave Trade: A Census* (Madison: University of Wisconsin Press, 1969), especially pp. 266, 268.

more were lost to the oriental trade. Finally, the occidental trade spurred an apparently huge increase in internal slavery, and according to the estimate of one expert, an additional 15 million people were enslaved within African societies themselves.[6]

CONSEQUENCES OF THE SLAVE TRADE FOR AFRICA

The statistics in the previous section hint at the massive impact slave trading had on African life and history. Still, the question of the actual effects remains difficult and disputed. Modern scholarship has tended to emphasize the importance for African history of the coming of the maritime European powers in general and the Atlantic slave trade in particular. Regarding the slave trade, it is safe to say that the impact was considerable, however much that general conclusion must be qualified in the light of particular cases. (See Document, "Olaudah Equiano Recalls His Experience at the Slave Market in Barbados.") Consider some examples.

We do not know for certain if the Atlantic trade brought net population loss or gain to specific areas of West Africa. The wide and rapid spread of maize and cassava cultivation in forest regions after these plants had been imported from the Americas may have fueled African population increases that offset regional human loss through slaving. We know, however, that slaving took away many of the strongest young men in many areas and, in the oriental trade zones, most of the young women.

Similarly, we do not know if more slaves were captured as byproducts of local wars or from pure slave raiding, but we do know they were captured and removed from their societies.

Nor do we know if slaving always inhibited development of trade or perhaps sometimes stimulated it because commerce in a range of African products—from ivory to wood and hides—often accompanied that in slaves. Still, we do know that in general, the exchange of productive human beings for money or goods that were generally not used to build a productive economy was a great loss for African society as a whole.

Finally, because we do not yet have accurate estimates of the total population of Africa at different times over the four centuries of the Atlantic slave trade, we cannot determine with certainty its demographic impact. We can, however, make some educated guesses. If, for example, tropical Africa had possibly 50 million inhabitants in 1600, it would then have had 30 percent of the combined population of the Americas, the Middle East, Europe, and Africa. If in 1900, after the depredations of the slave trade, it had 70 million inhabitants, its population would have dropped to only slightly more than 10 percent of the combined population of the same world regions. Accordingly, current best estimates indicate that overall

▲ **Slave Coffle.** This 18th-century print shows bound African captives being forced to a slaving port. It was largely African middlemen who captured slaves in the interior and marched them to the coast. North Wind Picture Archives.

[6] Manning, *Slavery African and Life*, pp. 37, 170–171.

Job ben Solomon. Captured by Mandingo enemies and sold to a Maryland tobacco planter, Job ben Solomon accomplished the nearly impossible feat of returning to Africa as a freeman. By demonstrating his talents as a Muslim scholar, including his ability to write the entire Qur'an from memory, he astonished his owners and eventually convinced them to let him go home.

"The Fortunate Slave," An Illustration of African Slavery in the early 18th century by Douglas Grant (1968). From "Some Memoirs of the Life of Job," by Thomas Bluett 1734. Photo by Robert D. Rubic/Precision Chromes, Inc., Rare Books Division, the New York Public Library/Art Resource, NY, Lenox and Tilden Foundations.

African population growth suffered significantly as a result of the devastating numbers of people lost to enslavement or to the increased warfare and decreased birthrate tied to the slave trade. Figures like these also give some idea of slavery's probable impact on Africa's ability to keep up with the modern industrializing world.[7]

It is important to remember that even in West and central Africa, which bore the brunt of the Atlantic trade, its impact and the response to it were so varied in different places and times that even accurate overall statistics could be misleading for particular cases. In a few cases, kingdoms such as Dahomey

[7] On all of the preceding points regarding probable impact of the trade, see Manning, *Slavery and African Life*, pp. 126–148, 168–176.

(the present Republic of Benin) seem to have sought and derived immense economic profit for a time by making slaving a state monopoly. Other kingdoms, such as Benin, sought to stay almost completely out of slaving and derived no gain from it. In many instances, including the rise of Asante power or the fall of the Yoruba Oyo Empire, it now appears that increased slaving was in part a result as well as a cause of regional instability and change. Increased warfare meant increased prisoners to be enslaved and a surplus to be sold off; however, whether slaving gave good cause for war is still a major question in each regional context.

Similarly, if one can establish, as seems evident, a major increase in indigenous slavery as a result of the external trade to occident and orient during the centuries in question, we have to assume major social consequences for African society as a whole, but the specific consequences would differ according to the specifics of regional situations. For example, in West Africa relatively more men were taken as slaves than women, whereas in the Sahelian Sudanic regions relatively more women than men were taken. In the west the loss of so many men increased the pressures for polygamy and possibly the regional use of women slaves as well, whereas in the Sahelian Sudanic regions the loss of women may have stimulated polyandry and reduced the birthrate significantly.

CHRONOLOGY

Conquest of the Americas and the Transatlantic Slave Trade

1494	The Treaty of Tordesillas divides the seaborne empires of Spain and Portugal
1500	The Portuguese arrive in Brazil
1519–1521	Hernan Cortés conquers the Aztec Empire
1531–1533	Francisco Pizarro conquers the Inca Empire
1607	Jamestown, Virginia, first permanent English settlement in North America founded
1608	The French found Quebec
1619	First African slaves brought to British North America
1650	Transatlantic slave trade becomes bigger than the older oriental slave trade
1700s	Over 6 million slaves imported from Africa to the Americas
1807	Slavery abolished in British domains
1808	The importation of slaves abolished in the United States
1874–1928	Indigenous African slavery abolished
1888	Slavery abolished in Brazil

| # Olaudah Equiano Recalls His Experience at the Slave Market in Barbados

Olaudah Equiano composed one of the most popular and influential slave narratives of the late eighteenth and early nineteenth centuries. He had led a remarkable life. Born in West Africa in what is today Nigeria, he spent his early life among the Ibo. He was captured and sold into slavery, making the dreaded Atlantic crossing described in the previous document. In the passage that follows, he recounts his arrival in Barbados and the experience of cultural disorientation, sale into slavery, and seeing Africans separated from their families. Equiano's life did not end in slavery, the most destructive aspects of which he also described in vivid detail. He achieved his freedom and then led an adventuresome life on various commercial and military ships plying the Caribbean, the Atlantic, and the Mediterranean. He also made a trip to the Arctic Ocean. Equiano's account consequently describes not only the life of a person taken from Africa and sold into American slavery, but also the life of a person who, once free, explored the entire transatlantic world. His autobiographical narrative, which first appeared in 1789 and displayed Equiano's wide reading, served two purposes for the antislavery campaign that commenced in the second half of the eighteenth century. First, it provided a firsthand report of the slave experience in crossing from Africa to America. Second, his powerful rhetoric and clear arguments demonstrated that, if free, Africans could achieve real personal independence. Many defenders of slavery had denied that Africans possessed the character and intelligence to be free persons.

◆ What were the fears of the Africans on the slave ship as they approached the port? How were older slaves in Barbados used to calm their fears? How did the sale of slaves proceed? What happened to African families in the process of the sale?

At last, we came in sight ... of Barbados, ... and we soon anchored ... off Bridgetown. Many merchants and planters now came on board. ... They put us in separate parcels, and examined us attentively. They also made us jump, and pointed to the land, signifying we were to go there. We thought by this we should be eaten by these ugly men, as they appeared to us; and when, soon after we were all put down under the deck again, there was much dread and trembling among us, and nothing but bitter cries to be heard all the night from these apprehension, insomuch that at last the white people got some old slaves from the land to pacify us. They told us we were not to be eaten, but to work, and were soon to go on land, where we should see many of our country people. This report eased us much.... We were conducted immediately to the merchant's yard, where we were all pent up together like so many sheep in a fold, without regard to sex or age. As every object was new to me, everything filled me with surprise ... and indeed I thought these people were full of nothing but magical arts. ... We were not many days in the merchant's custody before we were sold after their usual manner which was this: On a signal given (as the beat of a drum), the buyers rush at once into the yard where the slaves are confined, and make choice of that parcel they like best. The noise and clamour with which this is attended, and the eagerness visible in the countenances of the buyers, serve not a little to increase the apprehension of the terrified Africans, who may well be supposed to consider them as the ministers of that destruction to which they think themselves devoted. In this manner, without scruple, relations and friends separate, most of them never to see each other again. I remember in the vessel in which I was brought over, in the men's apartment, there were several brothers who, in the sale, were sold in different lots; and it was very moving on this occasion to see and hear their cries at parting.... Surely this is a new refinement in cruelty, which, while it has no advantage to atone for it, thus aggravates distress, and adds fresh horrors even to the wretchedness of slavery.

From *The Interesting Narrative of the Life of Olaudah Equiano or Gustavus Vassa, The African, Written by Himself* (first published 1789), as quoted in Henry Louis Gates Jr., and William L. Andrews, eds., *Pioneers of the Black Atlantic: Five Slave Narratives from the Enlightenment, 1772–1815* (Washington, DC: Counterpoint, 1998), pp. 221–223.

Even though slavery existed previously in Africa, the scale of the Atlantic trade was unprecedented and hence had an unprecedented impact on indigenous social, political, and economic realities. In general, the slave trade measurably changed patterns of life and balances of power in the main affected areas, whether by stimulating trade or warfare (or at least raiding for new supplies), by disrupting previous market and political structures, by substantially increasing slavery inside Africa, or by disturbing the male-female ratio (and hence the workforce balance and birthrate patterns) and consequently the basic social institution of monogamous marriage.

If the overseas slave trade did not substantially and irrevocably change every region it touched, at the least it siphoned indigenous energy into ultimately counterproductive or destructive directions. This, in turn, meant the inhibition of true economic development, especially in central and coastal West Africa. The Atlantic slave trade must by any standard be described as one of the most tragic aspects of European involvement in Africa.

Slave Ship.

Summary

European Conquest of the New World   The contact between the native peoples of the American continents and the European explorers of the fifteenth and sixteenth centuries transformed world history. In the Americas, the native peoples had established a wide variety of civilizations. Some of their most remarkable architectural monuments and cities were constructed during the centuries when European civilizations were feeble in comparison. Until the European explorations, the civilizations of the Americas, and Eurasia, and Africa had had no significant contact with each other.

Within half a century of the landing of Columbus, millions of America's native peoples had encountered Europeans intent on conquest, exploitation, and religious conversion. Because of their advanced weapons, navies, and the new diseases they brought with them, as well as internal divisions among the Native Americans, the Europeans achieved a rapid conquest.

The Transatlantic Economy   In both North and South America, economies of exploitation were established. In Latin America, various institutions were developed to extract native labor. From the Mid-Atlantic English colonies through the Caribbean and into Brazil, slave-labor plantation systems were established. The slaves were forcibly imported from Africa and sold in America to plantation owners. The economies and peoples of Europe, Africa, and the Americas were thus drawn into a vast worldwide web of production based on slave labor.

Slavery   The impact of slavery in the Americas was not limited to the life of the black slaves. Whites in the New World numbered about 12 million in 1820, compared to some 6 million blacks. However, only about 2 million whites had migrated there, compared to some 11 million or more Africans forcibly imported as slaves. Such numbers reveal the effects of brutal slave conditions and the high mortality and low birthrates of slave populations.

None of these statistics, however, enables us to assess the role that slavery has played in the Americas or, in particular, the United States. The United States actually received only a bit more than a quarter as many slaves as did Brazil alone or the British and French Caribbean regions together, yet the forced migration of Africans as slaves into the United States had profound consequences. Consider just the American Civil War and the endurance of racism and inequality or, more positively, the African contribution to American industrial development, language, music, literature, and artistic culture. The Atlantic slave trade's impact continues to be felt at both ends of the original "trade."

Review Questions

1. How were small groups of Spaniards able to conquer the Aztec and Inca Empires?

2. What was the basis of the mercantilist theory of economics? What was the relationship between the colonial economies and those of the homelands?

3. Describe the economies of Spanish America and Brazil. What were the similarities and differences between them and the British and French colonies in the Caribbean and North America? What role did the various colonies play in the transatlantic economy?

4. Why did forced labor and slavery develop in tropical colonies? How was slavery in the Americas different from slavery in earlier societies?

5. What was the effect of the transatlantic slave trade on West African societies? On East Africa? What role did Africans themselves play in the slave trade?

Key Terms

Black Legend   (p. 508)

conquistadores   (p. 509)

debt peonage   (p. 510)

encomienda   (p. 509)

hacienda   (p. 510)

mercantilism   (p. 504)

peninsulares   (p. 510)

plantation economy   (p. 516)

repartimiento   (p. 509)

Documents CD-ROM

European Explorations and Expansion
14.7 Bartolomé de las Casas: Persecutor Turns Protector
14.8 The British Encounter Maoris: A Sailor's Impressions

Trade and Exploitation Across the Atlantic
15.1 The "Black Legend" of Spain: Bartolomé de las Casas

15.2 "Our Kingdom Is Being Lost": Nzinga Mbemba (Afonso I)
15.3 Olaudah Equiano, The Life of Olaudah Equiano, or Gustavus Vassa, The African
15.4 Commerce, Slavery, and Religion in North Africa
15.5 Thomas Nelson, Slavery and the Slave of Brazil

NOTE: *To learn more about the topics in this chapter, see the Suggested Readings at the end of the book.*

CHAPTER 19

East Asia in the Late Traditional Era

LATE IMPERIAL CHINA

- Ming (1368–1644) and Qing (1644–1911) Dynasties

JAPAN

- Warring States Era (1467–1600)

- Tokugawa Era (1600–1868)

KOREA AND VIETNAM

- Korea

- Vietnam

- Southeast Asia

◄ MOTHER BATHING HER SON. Woodblock print (37.8 × 25.7 cm) by Kitagawa Utamaro (1753–1806). Utamaro was so popular a master of his genre that publishers hired unknown artists to produce fakes in his name. This led him to sign some works "the genuine Utamaro." He boasted of his high fees, comparing himself to a great courtesan and his imitators to streetwalkers. Note the tub's skillful design, the mothers wooden clog and her simple yet elegant kimono. A second kimono hangs to dry at the upper-right corner.

East Asia in the Late Traditional Era

Why did the West, and not East Asia or anywhere else, open the door to modernity? Why did an industrial revolution not develop within the sophisticated commercial economies of Japan and China? The answer, obviously, must be found within Western history. Still, a few comparisons with the West may illuminate aspects of premodern East Asia.

1. The sociologist Max Weber saw Western capitalism as inspired by the Protestant ethic—which he found lacking in India, China, and Catholic Europe. But is the East Asian family–centered ethic of frugality, savings, and hard work not a "Protestant" ethic or sorts? And if a deeper Calvinist anxiety about salvation is required, then why has East Asia achieved such explosive growth since World War II?

2. Was the scientific revolution of the seventeenth century critical to the industrial revolution? Some historians say that revolution was well under way before science made a substantial contribution.

3. The self-educated technicians of England who invented the water loom and steam engine reaped enormous honors and rewards. In China and Japan no patents protected inventors and no economists wrote of inventors as the benefactors of society. Wealth and honors were reserved for officials and gentry, who were literary and political in orientation and despised those who worked with their hands. (Of course, in earlier dynasties, Chinese had been brilliantly inventive without patent protection.)

4. Bureaucracy is sometimes viewed as a key component of modernity. Bureaucracy does for administration what the assembly line does for production: it breaks complex tasks into simple ones, to achieve huge gains in efficiency. In the West bureaucracies appeared only in recent centuries. They strengthened monarchies and nation-states against landed aristocrats; they represented the triumph of ability over hereditary privilege. Chinese bureaucrats shared many of the same virtues. They were an elite of talent educated in the Confucian classics as British officials were ed-

ucated in those of Greece and Rome. But they were somehow different. They had wielded power for at least a millennium, and were a segment of the landed gentry class in a country from which hereditary aristocrats had long since disappeared. Despite their talent, in the nineteenth century they would constitute a major obstacle to modernity.

Putting aside comparisons with Europe, we also note the difference between Chinese and Japanese attitudes toward outside civilizations. When the Jesuits tried to introduce science, the Chinese response was occasional curiosity and general indifference. A few Jesuits were appointed as interpreters or court astronomers, or were used to cast cannons for China's armies. The Chinese lack of interest in foreign cultures can be explained by the coherence of China's core institutions: the emperor, bureaucracy, examination system, Confucian schools, and gentry. These were so deeply rooted and highly appreciated as to constitute a closed system. In contrast, despite a national policy of seclusion, Japanese reached out for Dutch medicine and science—as they had earlier reached out for Chinese Neo-Confucianism. In the middle of the nineteenth century, this greater openness helps explain their rapid advance.

That Vietnam and Korea did not achieve industrial revolutions requires less explanation. They were smaller and less commercially developed than China or Japan. Vietnam was preoccupied with wars and its expansion to the south. In Korea—sometimes called the "hermit Kingdom," the elites were open only to Chinese culture and engaged in endless factional struggles.

THINK AHEAD

◆ What features of Japan or China, other than those mentioned above, bear on their lack of progress from commerce to industry? Are there still other factors treated in the chapters on Europe that are also relevant?

◆ Why was Tokugawa Japan more open to Western learning that Qing China? Was population a plus, a minus, or a factor that did not matter?

ONE DIFFICULTY IN COMPARING EAST ASIAN countries is that although they shared many cultural elements, their institutions and history were so different. Their cultural affinity is immediately apparent if we look at Chinese, Japanese, Korean, and Vietnamese paintings side by side. Less visible, but no less basic, was a range of social values shared at least by their elites. To the extent that it was based on Confucianism, the similarity may have been greatest in the mid–nineteenth century, when Japan, Korea, and Vietnam had become more Confucian than ever before.

But when we compare their histories and institutions, the similarities diminish. China and Japan were furthest apart. Each had gone its own way. Korea and Vietnam, even while forging an identity in reaction to China, were more directly influenced by China in their history and closer to China in their culture and institutions.

For China, the Ming (1368–1644) and Qing dynasties (1644–1911) were just two more centralized bureaucratic regimes of a kind that had been in place for centuries. In the Tang (618–907) the Chinese had forged a pattern of government so efficient and closely geared to the deeper familial and educational constitution of the society that, thereafter, they rebuilt it after each dynastic breakdown. This pattern continued during the Ming and the Qing, giving their histories a recognizable cyclical cast, even though they are also replete with historical trends that cut across dynastic lines.

Japanese political history, in contrast, is not cyclical. Each period of Japanese history reflects a new and different configuration. The centralized governments of the Nara and early Heian gave way to a manorial social order in which a powerful, local warrior class emerged. From this "feudal" class arose first the Kamakura *bakufu,* and then the Ashikaga. These in turn were followed by an era of Warring States and then a lengthy period of centralized "feudalism." Superficially at least, Japan's history was more like that of Europe than of China. Neither Europe nor Japan ever found a pattern of rule that worked so well, was so satisfactory to the rulers, and was so deeply embedded in the institutions of the society that it was re-created over and over again. In fact, from a Japanese or European point of view, that is not how history works.

This chapter underlines the dynamism of both China and Japan during these late centuries. "Late traditional society" does not mean "late static society." In both countries the society became more integrated and the apparatus of government more sophisticated than ever before. These advances shaped Chinese and Japanese responses to the West during the nineteenth century. Even Korea and Vietnam did not lack dynamism, but we must also note that during these centuries the West was transformed. In fact, Greece and Rome apart, most of what seems important in Western history— the Renaissance, the Reformation, the Scientific Revolution, the formation of nation-states, the Industrial Revolution, the Enlightenment, and the democratic revolution—happened while the Ming and the Qing dynasties were reigning in China. As we view East Asia from the perspective of Europe, it appears to have been caught in a tar pit of slow motion. But it was actually the West that had accelerated.

LATE IMPERIAL CHINA
Ming (1368–1644) and Qing (1644–1911) Dynasties

The Ming and the Qing were China's last dynasties. The first was Chinese, the second a dynasty of conquest in which the ruling house and an important segment of the military were foreign (Manchus). They were nevertheless remarkably similar in their institutions and pattern of rule, so much so that historians sometimes speak of "Ming-Qing despotism" as if it were a single system. The two dynasties are also coupled as a result of certain demographic and economic trends that began during the Ming and continued through the Qing.

LAND AND PEOPLE

China's population doubled from about 60 or 90 million in 1368 at the start of the Ming dynasty to about 125 million in 1644 at its end. The population then tripled during the early and middle Qing dynasty, reaching about 410 million people several decades into the mid–nineteenth century. This population density stimulated the growth of commerce and gave new prominence to the scholar-gentry class.

An increase in the food supply paralleled population growth. During the Ming, the spread of Song agricultural technology and new strains of rice accounted for 40 percent of the higher yields, and newly cultivated lands accounted for the rest. During the Qing, half the increased food supply was due to new lands and the other half to better seeds, fertilizers, and irrigation. New crops introduced from America during the late Ming, such as maize, sweet potatoes, and peanuts (which could be planted on dry sandy uplands and did not compete with rice), also bolstered the food supply. By the nineteenth century maize was grown in all parts of China.

In north China the population had declined from 32 million to 11 million during the Mongol conquests. The Ming government repopulated its open lands, resettling villages, building water control systems, and reopening the Grand Canal in 1415. The movement of people to the north continued until the nineteenth century. In the north, most farmers owned the land they worked and at times used hired labor. The land consisted mainly of irrigated dry fields, and the chief crops were millet, sorghum, and wheat.

South and southwest China also saw an influx of migrants from the densely populated lower Yangzi region, many settling in hilly or mountainous border areas that were agriculturally marginal. The White Lotus Rebellion of 1796–1804 occurred in such a recently settled area far from centers of governmental authority. The Miao Wars of the late eighteenth century also were precipitated by the movement of Chinese settlers into southwestern uplands previously left to the slash-and-burn agriculture of the Miao tribes. Other Chinese crossed over to Taiwan or emigrated overseas. During the Qing dynasty, large Chinese mercantile communities became established in Southeast Asia.

The Yangzi basin, meanwhile, became even more densely populated. The lower Yangzi region and the delta, well supplied with waterways, had long been the rice basket of China, but from the late Ming agricultural cash crops, such as silk and cotton, predominated. Cotton was so widely grown in the delta that food had to be brought in from other areas by the early nineteenth century. In the lower Yangzi absentee landlords owned almost half of the land. A typical landlord's holdings were subdivided among tenants, who paid fixed rents in kind. South China also had extensive absentee landlordism, but far more land was owned collectively by clans, which managed the land and distributed rents among their members.

There are many unanswered questions regarding the population growth during these six centuries. Was there a decline in the death rate and, if so, why? Or was it simply that new lands and technology enabled more mouths to be fed? Did the population oblige by promptly increasing? Certainly the Ming-Qing era was the longest continuous period of good government in Chinese history. The good years of Ming rule were longer than such periods in earlier dynasties, and the transition to Qing rule was quicker and less destructive. How much did these long periods of good government contribute to the population growth? Epidemic disease was not absent. In the great plagues from 1586 to 1589 and from 1639 to 1644, as many as 20 to 30 percent of the people died in the most populous regions of China, and in

specific counties and villages the figure was often higher. Another epidemic occurred in 1756 and a cholera epidemic from 1820 to 1822. The growth of China's population more than overcame such losses. Because of the growth in agriculture and population, most accounts view the eighteenth century as the most prosperous in Chinese history. But by the early nineteenth century the Chinese standard of living may have begun to decline. An ever increasing population was no blessing.

CHINA'S THIRD COMMERCIAL REVOLUTION

Commerce in China flourished between 300 B.C.E. and 220 C.E. (the late Zhou through the Han dynasties), only to decline in the centuries of disunity that followed. In Chapter 7 we read Sima Qian's description of wealthy Han merchants. Between 850 and 1250 (late Tang through Song) commerce again surged, only to contract during the Mongol conquest. At the end of the Mongol dynasty, warlords confiscated merchant wealth. Early Ming emperors, isolationist and agrarian in orientation, restricted the use of foreign goods, required licenses for junks, and attempted to encase foreign trade within the constraints of the tribute system. The early Ming also operated government monopolies that stifled enterprise and depressed the southeastern coastal region by their restrictions on maritime trade and shipping. In the mid–sixteenth century commerce started to grow again, buoyed by the surge of population and agriculture and aided by a relaxation of government controls. If the growth during the Han and Song dynasties may be called, respectively, China's first and second commercial revolutions, then the expansion between 1500 and 1800 was the third. This revolution was partly the extension to other parts of China of changes begun earlier in the Yangzi area, but it had new features as well. By the early nineteenth century China was the most highly commercialized nonindustrial society in the world.

One stimulus to commerce was imported silver, which played the role in the Ming-Qing economy that copper cash had played in the Song dynasty. The Chinese balance of trade was favorable. Beginning in the mid–sixteenth century silver from mines in western Japan entered China, and, from the 1570s, Spanish galleons sailing from Acapulco to China via Manila brought in Mexican and Peruvian silver. In exchange, Chinese silks and porcelains were vended in the shops of Mexico City. The late Ming court also opened silver mines in Guizhou and Yunnan provinces. In the eighteenth century copper mines were opened in south China. Also, private Shaanxi banks opened branches throughout China to facilitate the transfer of funds from one area to another and extend credit for trade. Eventually they opened offices in Singapore, Japan, and Russia, as well.

As in Europe, so in China, the influx of silver and the overall increase in liquidity led to inflation and commercial growth. The price of land rose steadily. During the sixteenth century the thirty or forty early Ming taxes on land that were

◀ **"Fishermen on Autumn River,"** a Ming dynasty scroll painting by Dai Qin (1390–1460).

Tai Chin, "Fisherman on an Autumn River," (1390–1460). Painting. Ink and color on paper. 18 1/8 × 291 1/4 in. (46 × 740 cm). Courtesy of Freer Gallery of Art, Smithsonian Institution, Washington, D.C.

payable in grain, labor service, and cash were consolidated into one tax payable in silver, the so-called Single Whip Reform. To obtain the silver, farmers sold their grain in the market, and some switched from grain to cash crops. Moreover, by the early nineteenth century there were six times as many farm families as in the mid–fourteenth century.

Urban growth between 1500 and 1800, responding to flourishing local markets, was mainly at the level of intermediate market towns. These towns grew more rapidly than the population as a whole and provided the link between the local markets and the larger provincial capitals and cities such as Beijing, Hangzhou, or Guangzhou. The commercial integration of local, intermediate, and large cities was not entirely new, having occurred during the Song dynasty in the lower Yangzi region. But now it spread over all of China. Interregional trade also gained. Where Song trade between regions was mainly in luxury goods such as silk, lacquerware, porcelains, medicines, and paintings, early Qing traders also dealt in staples, such as grain, timber, salt, iron, and cotton. Not that China developed a national economy. Seven or eight regional economies, each the size of a large European nation, were still the focus for most economic activity. But a new level of trade developed among them, especially where water transport made such trade economical. A final feature of eighteenth-century Chinese economic life was the so-called "putting out" system in textiles, under which merchant capitalists organized and financed each stage of production from fiber to dyed cloth.

Women and the Commercial Revolution The Confucian family ideal changed little during the Ming and Qing dynasties. A woman was expected first to obey her parents, then her husband, and finally her son—when he became the new family head. Physically, women became more restricted. Footbinding, which had begun among the elite during the Song dynasty,

spread through the upper classes during the Ming and to some commoners during the mid to late Qing. Most girls were subjected to this cruel and deformative procedure. Even in villages, women with big—that is to say, normal —feet were sometimes considered unmarriageable. One exception to the rule was the Hakka people of south China. Hakka women with unbound feet worked in the fields alongside their male kinsmen. Another exception was the Manchus. One Manchu (Qing) emperor even issued an edict banning footbinding, but the Chinese ignored it.

As population grew and the size of the average landholding shrank, more women worked at home, spinning, weaving, and making other products for the burgeoning commercial markets. As their contribution to the household income grew, their voice in household decisions often became larger than Confucian doctrines would suggest. But at the same time, women's property rights—to inheritance and control of dowries—became more limited than in previous dynasties. Furthermore, the same commercial revolution increased the

▲ **Foot Binding.** As a young girl her arches were broken and her feet forced into iron training shoes. As a maiden, her deformed feet are encased in silk slippers and she walks with a slow and swaying gait, a thing of beauty.
AP WideWorld Photos.

DOCUMENT | The Thin Horse Market

In China, ancestors without descendants to perform the rites ran the danger of becoming hungry ghosts or wandering spirits. Consequently, having a son who would continue the family line was an act of filial piety. If a wife failed to produce an heir, an official, merchant, or wealthy landowner might take a concubine and try again. Or he might do so simply because he was able to, because it gave him pleasure, and because it was socially acceptable. For a poor peasant household, after a bad harvest and faced with high taxes, the sale of a comely daughter often seemed preferable to the sale of ancestral land.

♦ Concubines usually had no choice in the matter, but neither did many brides in premodern China. Was a woman better off as the wife of a poor peasant, experiencing hardship, hunger, and want, or as the concubine in a wealthy household with servants, good food, and the likelihood that her children would receive an education? What does the following passage tell us about attitudes toward women in premodern China?

Upwards of a hundred people in Yangzhou earn a living in the "thin horse" business. If someone shows an interest in taking a concubine, a team of a broker, a drudge, and a scout stick to him like flies. Early in the morning, the teams gather to wait outside the doors of potential customers, who usually give their business to the first team to arrive. Any teams coming late have to wait for the next opportunity. The winning team then leads their customer to the broker's house. The customer is then served tea and seated to wait for the women. The broker leads out each of them, who do what the matchmaker tells them to do. After each of her short commands, the woman bows to the customer, walks forward, turns toward the light so the customer can see her face clearly, draws back her sleeves to show him her hands, glances shyly at him to show her eyes, says her age so he can hear her voice, and finally lifts her skirt to reveal whether her feet are bound. An experienced customer could figure out the size of her feet by listening to the noise she made as she entered the room.

If her skirt made noise when she walked in, she had to have a pair of big feet under her skirt. As one woman finishes, another comes out, each house having at least five or six. If the customer finds a woman to his liking, he puts a gold hairpin in her hair at the temple, a procedure called "inserting the ornament." If no one satisfies him, he gives a few hundred cash to the broker or the servants.

If the first broker gets tired, others will willingly take his place. Even if a customer has the stamina to keep looking for four or five days, he cannot finish visiting all the houses. Nevertheless, after seeing fifty to sixty white-faced, red-dressed women, they all begin to look alike and he cannot decide which are pretty or ugly. It is like the difficulty of recognizing a character after writing it hundreds or thousands of times. Therefore, the customer usually chooses someone once his mind and eyes can no longer discriminate. The owner of the woman brings out a piece of red paper on which are listed the "betrothal presents," including gold jewelry and cloth. Once he agrees to the deal, he is sent home. Before he even arrives back at his lodgings, a band and a load of food and wine are already waiting there. Before long, presents he was to send are prepared and sent back with the band. Then a sedan chair and all the trimmings—colorful lanterns, happy candles, attendants, sacrificial foods—wait outside for the customer's arrangement. The cooks and the entertainer for the wedding celebration also arrive together with foods, wine, candy, tables, chairs, and tableware. Without the customer's order, the colorful sedan chair for the girl and the small sedan chair for her companion are dispatched to get the girl. The new concubine performs the bowing ceremony with music and singing and considerable clamor. The next morning before noon the laborers ask for rewards from the man, then leave to prepare another wedding for another customer in the same manner.*

Reprinted with the permission of The Free Press, a division of Simon & Schuster Adult Publishing Group, from *Chinese Civilization: A Sourcebook,* Second Edition by Patricia Buckley Ebrey. Copyright © 1993 by Patricia Buckley Ebrey. All rights reserved.

* A horse market is for the sale of horses. A "thin horse" market is the market for concubines. The name implies a measure of criticism.

number of rich townsmen who could afford concubines and patronize tea houses, restaurants, and brothels. (See Document, "The Thin Horse Market.")

POLITICAL SYSTEM

One might expect these massive demographic and economic changes to have produced, if not a bourgeois revolution, at least some profound change in the political superstructure of China. They did not. Government during the Ming and Qing was much like that of the Song or Yuan, only improved and made stronger. Historians sometimes describe it as the "perfected" late imperial system. This system, they argue, was able to contain and use the new economic energies that destroyed the weaker late feudal polities of Europe. The sources of strength of the perfected Ming-Qing system were the spread of education, Confucianism ideology, stronger emperors, better government finances, more competent officials, and a larger gentry class with an expanded role in local society.

Role of Confucianism Confucian teachings were more widespread in late imperial China than ever before. There were more schools in villages and towns. Academies preparing candidates for the civil service examinations multiplied. Publishing flourished, bookstores abounded, and literacy outpaced population growth. The Confucian view of society was patriarchal. The family, headed by the father, was the basic unit. The emperor, the son of heaven and the ruler-father of the empire, stood at its apex. In between were the district magistrates, the "father-mother officials." The idea of the state as the family writ large was not just a matter of metaphor but carried with it duties and obligations that were binding at every level.

The sociopolitical worldview of Confucianism was also buttressed by Neo-Confucian metaphysics, which gave a unitary character to Ming and Qing culture. This is not, of course, to deny the existence of different schools of Confucian thought. The vitality of late Ming thinkers was especially notable. Still, in comparison to Europe, where religious philosophies were less involved with the state and where a revolution in science was reshaping both religious and political doctrines, the greater unity and integration of the Chinese worldview cannot be denied.

Emperor In Ming-Qing times the emperor was stronger than ever. The Secretariat of high officials that had coordinated government affairs during the Song and the Yuan was abolished by the first Ming emperor, who himself made all important and many unimportant decisions. His successors, often aided by Grand Secretaries, continued this pattern of direct, personal rule. During the late fourteenth and fifteenth centuries the emperor was the bottleneck official, without whose active participation the business of government would bog down.

Then, during the sixteenth and early seventeenth centuries, a series of emperors appeared who were not interested in government. One spent his days on wine, women, and sports; another on Daoist rites; and still another emperor, who never learned to write, passed his days making furniture. During this era Grand Secretaries or eunuchs exercised the emperor's authority. But the Qing reestablished the pattern of personal government by emperors.

Emperors wielded despotic powers at their courts. They had personal secret police and prisons where those who gave even minor offense might be tortured. Even high officials might suffer the humiliating, and sometimes fatal, punishment of having their bared buttocks beaten with bamboo rods at court—a practice inherited from the Mongols. The dedication and loyalty even of officials who were mistreated attest to the depth of their Confucian ethical formation. One censor who had served three emperors ran afoul of a powerful eunuch. The eunuch obtained an imperial order and had the official tortured to death in 1625. In his deathbed notes to his sons, the official blamed the villain for his agonies but wrote that he welcomed death because his body belonged to his "ruler-father." An earlier mid–sixteenth century incident involved Hai Rui, the most famous censor of the Ming period:

> Hai presented himself at the palace gate to submit a memorial denouncing some of the emperor's notorious idiosyncrasies. The emperor flew into a rage and ordered that Hai not be permitted to escape. "Never fear, sire," the eunuch go-between told the emperor. "He has said goodbye to his family, has brought his coffin with him, and waits at the gate!" Shih-tsung [the emperor] was so taken aback by this news that he forgave Hai for his impertinence.[1]

During the Qing the life-and-death authority of emperors did not diminish, but officials were generally better treated. As foreign rulers, the Manchu emperors took care not to alienate Chinese officials.

The Forbidden Palace in Beijing, rebuilt when the third Ming emperor moved the capital from Nanjing to Beijing, was an icon of the emperor's majesty. Unlike the Kremlin, which consists of an assortment of buildings inside a wall, the entire palace complex in Beijing focused on the single figure of the ruler. Designed geometrically its massive outer and inner walls, and vast courtyards, and halls progress stage by stage to the raised area of the audience hall. During the Tang, emperors sat together with their grand councilors while discussing matters of government. In the Song, officials stood in his presence. By the Ming, the emperor sat on an elevated dais above the officials, who knelt before him. Behind the audience hall were the emperor's private chambers and his harem. In 1425 the palace had 6300 cooks serving 10,000 persons daily. These numbers later increased. By the seventeenth century there were 9,000 palace ladies and perhaps 70,000 eunuchs. The glory of the emperor extended to his family, whose members were awarded vast estates in North China.

Bureaucracy A second component of the Ming-Qing system was the government itself. The formal organization of offices was little different from that in the Tang or the Song. At the top were the military, the censorate, and the administrative branch, and beneath the administration were the six ministries and the web of provincial, prefectural, and district offices. But government was better financed than during earlier dynasties. The productivity of China became steadily greater, whereas the apparatus of government grew only slowly. Government finances had ups and downs, but as late as the 1580s huge surpluses were still accumulated at both the central and the provincial levels.

[1] C. O. Hucker, *China's Imperial Past* (Stanford, CA: Stanford University Press, 1975), p. 206.

These surpluses probably braked the process of dynastic decline. Only during the last fifty years of the Ming did soaring military expenses bankrupt government finances.

Then, in the second half of the seventeenth century the Manchus reestablished a strong central government and restored the flow of taxes to levels close to those of the Ming. In fact, revenues were so ample that early in the eighteenth century the emperors were able to freeze taxes on agriculture at the 1711 level and fix quotas for each province.

This contributed to the general prosperity of the eighteenth century but led to problems during the nineteenth century. Because agricultural productivity continued to rise, even though local officials collected some of the surplus, fixed quotas meant a declining share of the product. Both cultivators and gentry probably benefited from the new wealth, with the latter obtaining the larger share.

If the Ming-Qing system can be spoken of as perfected, the good government it brought to China was largely a product of the ethical commitment and the exceptional ability of its officials. No officials in the world today approach in power or prestige those of the Ming and the Qing. When the Portuguese arrived early in the sixteenth century, they called these officials "mandarins." (This term began as a Sanskrit word for "counselor" that became Hindi, entered Malay, and was then picked up by the Portuguese and adopted by other Europeans.) As in the Song, the rewards of an official career were so great that the competition to enter it was intense. As population grew and schools increased, entrance became evermore competitive. (See Document, "The Seven Transformations of an Examination Candidate.")

After being screened at the district office, a candidate took the county examination. If he passed he became a member of the gentry. He gained the cap and sash of the scholar and exemption from state labor service. Even this examination required years of arduous study. About half a million passed each year. The second hurdle was the provincial examination held every third year. Only one in a hundred or more was successful. The final hurdle was the metropolitan examination, also held triennially. During the Ming fewer than ninety passed each year. As in earlier dynasties, regional quotas were set to prevent the Yangzi region from dominating the officialdom.

Gentry A final component in the Ming-Qing system—if not new, at least vastly more significant than in earlier dynasties—was the **gentry** class. It was an intermediate layer between the elite bureaucracy above and the village below. The lowest level of bureaucratic government was the office of the district magistrate. Although the population increased sixfold during the Ming and the Qing, the number of district magistrates increased only from 1,171 to 1,470. Thus the average district, which had had a population of 50,000 in the early Ming and 100,000 in the late Ming, had two or three times that number by the early nineteenth century. The district magistrate came to his district as an outsider. The "law of avoidance," designed to prevent conflicts of interest, prevented him from serving in his home province. His office compound had a large staff of secretaries, advisers, specialists, clerks, and runners; but even then, he could not govern such a large population directly. To govern effectively, the magistrate had to obtain the cooperation of the local literati or gentry.

By *gentry* we do not mean a rural elite, like English squires. The Chinese gentry was largely urban, living in market towns or district seats. Socially and educationally, its members were of the same class as the magistrate—a world apart from clerks, runners, or village headmen. They usually owned land, which enabled them to avoid manual labor and to send their chil-

◀ **Examination Stalls.** The dilapidated remains of the examination stalls at Nanjing. Doors to individual cubicles can be seen to the right and left of the three-story gate. Thousands of such cubicles made up the old examination stalls. Those who passed the exams governed China.
Corbis-Bettmann.

DOCUMENT | The Seven Transformations of an Examination Candidate

The Chinese civil service examination was a grueling ordeal. Like a chess tournament, it required physical strength. Chinese critics said, "To pass the provincial examination a man needed the spiritual strength of a dragon-horse, the physique of a donkey, the insensitivity of a wood louse, and the endurance of a camel." The following selection is by a seventeenth-century writer who never succeeded in passing.

◆ Is the style of this passage overdone or effective? What is distinctively Chinese about it?

When he first enters the examination compound and walks along, panting under his heavy load of luggage, he is just like a beggar. Next, while undergoing the personal body search and being scolded by the clerks and shouted at by the soldiers, he is just like a prisoner. When he finally enters his cell and, along with the other candidates, stretches his neck to peer out, he is just like the larva of a bee. When the examination is finished at last and he leaves, his mind in a haze and his legs tottering, he is just like a sick bird that has been released from a cage. While he is wondering when the results will be announced and waiting to learn whether he passed or failed, so nervous that he is startled even by the rustling of the trees and the grass and is unable to sit or stand still, his restlessness is like that of a monkey on a leash. When at last the results are announced and he has definitely failed, he loses his vitality like one dead, rolls over on his side, and lies there without moving, like a poisoned fly. Then, when he pulls himself together and stands up, he is provoked by every sight and sound, gradually flings away everything within his reach, and complains of the illiteracy of the examiners. When he calms down at last, he finds everything in the room broken. At this time he is like a pigeon smashing its own precious eggs. These are the seven transformations of a candidate.

From I. Miyazaki, *China's Examination Hell*, trans. by C. Schirokauer. Copyright © 1976 Weatherhill, pp. 57–58.

---

dren to private academies. As absentee landlords whose lands were worked by sharecroppers, they were often exploitative; rebels at the end of the Ming attacked landlords as they did government offices. But the gentry were also local leaders. They represented community interests, which they interpreted conservatively, vis-à-vis the bureaucracy. They also performed quasi-official functions on behalf of their communities: maintaining schools and Confucian temples; repairing roads, bridges, canals, and dikes; and writing local histories.

The gentry class was the matrix from which officials arose; it was the local upholder of Confucian values. During the mid–nineteenth century, at a time of crisis, it would become the sustainer of the dynasty.

Pattern of Manchu Rule

The collapse of the Ming dynasty in 1644 and the establishment of Manchu rule was less of a break than might be imagined. First, the transition was short. Second, the Manchus, unlike the Mongols, were already partially Sinicized at the time of the conquest. They had been vassals of the Chinese state during the Ming, organized by tribal units into commanderies. Even before entering China, they had had the experience of ruling over Chinese who had settled in Manchuria to the north of the Great Wall.

In the late sixteenth century an able leader unified the Manchurian tribes and proclaimed a new dynasty. While still based in Mukden (more recently, Shenyang), the dynasty established a Confucian government with six ministries, a censorate, and other Chinese institutions. When the Ming collapsed and rebel forces took over China, the Manchus presented themselves as the conservative upholders of the Confucian order. The Chinese gentry preferred the Manchus to Chinese rebel leaders, whom they regarded as bandits. After the Manchu conquest, a few scholars and officials became famous as Ming loyalists. Most, however, served the new dynasty. The Qing as a Chinese dynasty dates from 1644, when the capital was moved from Shenyang (Mukden) to Beijing. All of south China was taken by 1659, with the aid of Ming generals who switched their allegiance to the new regime.

As a tiny fraction of China's population, the Manchus adopted institutions to maintain themselves as an ethnically separate elite group. One was their military organization. The basic unit was the banner—the unit took the name of its flag. There were eight Manchu banners, eight Mongol, and eight Chinese. There were more companies (of 300 men each) in the Manchu banners than in either of the other two; together with their steppe allies, the Mongols, the Manchu troops outnumbered Chinese troops by more than two to one. Furthermore, the Chinese banners were mainly Manchurian Chinese, who had been a part of the regime from its inception. Manchu garrison forces were segregated and were not under the jurisdiction of Chinese officials. They were given stipends and lands to cultivate. They were forbidden to marry Chinese, their children had to study Manchu, and they were not permitted to practice

Emperor Qianlong. The great Manchu emperor Qianlong
(r. 1736–1795).

Unidentified Artist. The emperor of Ch'ien Lung (1736–1795) as a Young Man.
Colors on silk. H. 63 1/2 in. W. 30 1/2 in. © Metropolitan Museum of Art,
Rogers Fund, 1942. (42.141.8). Photograph © 1980 the Metropolitan
Museum of Art.

first the distinction between the banners and the Chinese military
was critical. Later, as the dynasty became Sinicized and accepted,
the ethnic basis of its military strength became less important.

The second institutional feature of Manchu government was
what has been termed "dyarchy": the appointment of two persons, one Chinese and one Manchu, to each key post in the central government. Early in the dynasty the Chinese appointments
were often bannermen or bondservants who were personally
loyal to the Manchus. At the provincial level Manchu governor-
generals oversaw Chinese governors. Most officials and virtually
all district magistrates beneath the governors were Chinese.

A particular strength of the Manchu dynasty was the long
reigns of two extremely able emperors, Kangxi (1661–1722)
and Qianlong (1736–1795). Kangxi was born in 1654, ten
years after the start of the dynasty. He ascended the throne at
the age of seven, began to rule at thirteen, and held sway until
his death in 1722. He was a man of great vigor. He rose at dawn
to read memorials (official documents) before beginning his
daily routine of audiences with officials. He sired thirty-six sons
and twenty daughters by thirty consorts. He presided over
palace examinations. Well versed in the Confucian classics, he
won the support of scholars by his patronage of the *Ming History*, a new dictionary, and a 5,000-volume encyclopedia.

Kangxi also displayed an interest in European science: He
studied with Jesuit court astronomers whom the Qing had inherited from the Ming. He opened four ports to foreign trade and
carried out public works, improving the dikes on the Huai and

CHRONOLOGY

Late Imperial China

Ming Dynasty 1368–1644

1368–1398	Reign of first Ming emperor; Chinese armies invade Manchuria, Mongolia, and eastern Central Asia
1402–1424	Reign of third Ming emperor; Chinese armies invade Vietnam and Mongolia
1405–1433	Voyages of Zheng He to India and Africa
1415	Grand Canal reopened
1472–1529	Wang Yangming, philosopher
1592–1598	Chinese army battles Japanese army in Korea

Qing (Manchu) Dynasty 1644–1911

1668	Manchuria closed to Chinese immigrants (by Willow Palisade)
1661–1722	Reign of Kangxi
1681	Suppression of revolts by Chinese generals
1683	Taiwan captured
1689	China and Russia sign Treaty of Nerchinsk
1736–1795	Reign of Qianlong
1793	Macartney mission

footbinding. In 1668 northern and central Manchuria were
cordoned off by a willow palisade as a Manchu strategic tribal
territory and closed to Chinese immigrants.

In addition to the Manchu banners, there were also Chinese
constabulary forces known as "armies of the green standard." At

Yellow Rivers and dredging the Grand Canal. During his reign he made six tours of China's southern provinces. Kangxi, in short, was a model emperor. But he was also responsible for the various policies that sought to preserve a separate Manchu identity. Like Kublai Khan (r. 1271–1294) before him, he built a summer palace on the plains of Manchuria, where he hunted, hawked, and rode horseback with the freedom of a steppe lord.

Qianlong began his reign in 1736, fourteen years after the death of his grandfather Kangxi, and ruled until 1795. During his reign the Qing dynasty attained its highest level of prosperity and power. Like Kangxi, he was vigorous, wise, conscientious, careful, and hard-working. He visited south China on inspection tours. He patronized scholars on a grand scale: His *Four Treasures* of the classics, treating history, letters, and philosophy, put 15,000 copyists to work for almost fifteen years. (But he also carried out a literary inquisition against works critical of Manchu rule.)

Only in his last years did Qianlong lose his grip and permit a court favorite to practice corruption on an almost unprecedented scale. In 1796 the White Lotus Rebellion broke out. Qianlong's successor put down the rebellion and permitted the corrupt court favorite to take his own life. The ample financial reserves that had existed throughout the eighteenth century were never reestablished. China nevertheless entered the nineteenth century with its government intact and with a peaceful and stable society. There were few visible signs of what was soon to come.

MING-QING FOREIGN RELATIONS

Ming   Some scholars have contended that post-Song China was not an aggressive or imperialist state. They cite its inability to resist foreign conquest; the civility, self-restraint, and gentlemanliness of its officials; and the Song adage that good men should not be used to make soldiers just as good iron is not used to make nails. The early Ming convincingly disproves this contention. The first Ming emperor (r. 1368–1398) oversaw the vigorous expansion of China's borders. At his death, China controlled the northern steppe from Hami at the gateway of Central Asia to the Sungari River in Manchuria and had regained control of the southern tier of Chinese provinces as well. The Mongols were expelled from Yunnan in 1382 (see Map 19–1).

During the reign of the third Ming emperor (1402–1424) China became even more aggressive. The emperor sent troops into northern Vietnam, which became a Chinese province for two decades. He also personally led five expeditions into the Gobi Desert in pursuit of Mongol troops.

Whenever possible, the third emperor and his successors "managed" China's frontiers with the tribute system. In this system the ambassadors of vassal kings acted out their political subordination to the universal ruler of the celestial kingdom. An ambassador approached the emperor respectfully, performed the kowtow (kneeling three times and each time bowing his head to the floor three times), and presented his gifts. In return, the vassal kings were sent seals confirming

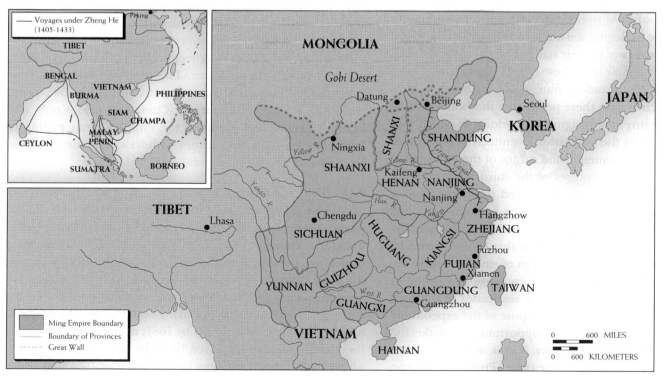

MAP 19–1 Ming Empire and the Voyages of Zheng He.   The inset map shows the voyages of Zeng He to Southeast Asia and India. Some ships of his fleet even reached East Africa. (Zheng himself didn't.)

Qianlong's Edict to King George III of England

The Chinese emperor rejected the requests of the 1793 Macartney mission for change in the restrictive Canton system. His edict reflects the Chinese sense of their superiority to other peoples and their belief that China was the "central kingdom" of the world.

> ◆ What philosophical principles underlie the emperor's sense of superiority?

You, O King, are so inclined toward our civilization that you have sent a special envoy across the seas to bring to our Court your memorial of congratulations on the occasion of my birthday and to present your native products as an expression of your thoughtfulness. On perusing your memorial, so simply worded and sincerely conceived, I am impressed by your genuine respectfulness and friendliness and greatly pleased. ...

The Celestial Court has pacified and possessed the territory within the four seas. Its sole aim is to do its utmost to achieve good government and to manage political affairs, attaching no value to strange jewels and precious objects. The various articles presented by you, O King, this time are accepted by my special order to the office in charge of such functions in consideration of the offerings having come from a long distance with sincere good wishes. As a matter of fact, the virtue and prestige of the Celestial Dynasty having spread far and wide, the kings of the myriad nations come by land and sea with all sorts of precious things. Consequently there is nothing we lack, as your principal envoy and others have themselves observed. We have never set much store on strange or ingenious objects, nor do we need any more of your country's manufactures. ...

Reprinted by permission of the publisher from *China's Response to the West: A Documentary Survey, 1839–1923,* by Ssu-yu Teng and John K. Fairbank, pp. 24–27, 155–156, 240–241. Cambridge, MA: Harvard University Press. Copyright © 1954, 1979 by the President and Fellows of Harvard College. Reprinted by permission of Harvard University Press. Copyright renewed 1982 by Ssu-yu Teng and John K. Fairbank.

Buddhism as superstitions but argued that Confucianism as a rational philosophy complemented Christianity, just as Aristotle's teaching complemented Christian theology in Europe. They handled the problem of the Confucian rites of ancestor worship by interpreting them as secular and nonantagonistic to Christianity. A few high court officials were converted. Kangxi was sympathetic to the scholarly personalities of the Jesuits and appreciated the cannon they cast but was unsympathetic to their religion: "I had asked [the Jesuit] Verbiest why God had not forgiven his son without making him die, but though he had tried to answer I had not understood him.[2]

Meanwhile, their Franciscan and Dominican rivals had reported to Rome that the Jesuits condoned the Confucian rites. The ensuing debate was long and complex, but in the end, papal bulls issued in 1715 and 1742 decided against the Jesuits and forbade Chinese Christians to participate in the family rites of ancestor worship. Thereupon the emperor banned Christianity in China, churches were seized, missionaries were forced to flee, and congregations declined.

Other Europeans came to China to trade. The Portuguese came first in the early sixteenth century but behaved badly and were expelled. They returned in midcentury and were permitted to trade on a tiny peninsula at Macao that was walled off from China. They were followed by Dutch from the East Indies (Indonesia), by the British East India Company in 1699, and by Americans in 1784.

At first the Westerners mingled with ships from Southeast Asia in a fairly open multiport pattern of trade. Then, during the early eighteenth century, the more restrictive "Canton system" evolved. Westerners could trade only at Guangzhou—or

[2] D. Spence, *Emperor of China: Self-Portrait of K'ang-Hsi* (New York: Alfred A. Knopf, 1974), p. 84.

◄ **Western Factories in Canton (Guangzhou) c. 1800–1815.** A factory was a trading post, not a manu-factory. This street scene shows many Chinese mingling with a few westerners wearing tall hats. The factories were built on river banks outside the city walls. Western merchants were not allowed to bring their wives to China, they were tightly controlled by Chinese merchant guilds, and communicated with the Chinese in pidgin (that is to say business) English.
The Henry Francis du Pont Winterthur Museum, Inc.

"Canton" as it was known to Westerners. They were barred from entering the city proper but were assigned land outside its walls along the river. They could not bring their wives to China. They were subject to the harsh dispositions of Chinese law. They were under the control of official merchant guilds. Nevertheless, the trade was profitable to both sides.

The British East India Company developed a triangular commerce among China, India, and Britain that enabled the English to drink tea and wear silk. Private fortunes were built. For China this trade produced a huge influx of specie, and the Chinese officials in charge grew immensely wealthy. Chafing under the various restrictions, the British government in 1793 sent the Macartney mission to China to negotiate the opening of other ports, fixed tariffs, representation at Beijing, and so on. The emperor Qianlong graciously permitted Lord Macartney (1736–1806) to present his gifts—which the Chinese described as tribute, even though Macartney refused to perform the kowtow—but he turned down Macartney's requests. (See Document, "Qianlong's Edict to King George III of England.") Western trade remained encapsulated at Guangzhou, distant from Beijing and little noted elsewhere in China.

MING-QING CULTURE

One thing that can be said of Ming-Qing culture, like population or agricultural productivity, is that there was more of it. Whether considering gentry, scholar officials, or a professionalized class of literati, their numbers and works were far greater than in previous dynasties. Even local literary figures or philosophers were likely to publish their collected works or have them published by admiring disciples. Bookstores came of age in the Ming, selling the Confucian classics; commentaries on them; collections of Tang and Song poetry; and also colored prints, novels, erotica, and model answers for the civil service examinations.

Chinese culture had begun to turn inward during the Song in reaction to Buddhism. This tendency was accelerated by the Chinese antipathy to Mongol rule and continued into the Ming and Qing, when Chinese culture became virtually impervious to outside influences. Even works on mathematics and science translated into Chinese by the Jesuits left few traces in Chinese scholarly writings. Chinese cultural self-sufficiency, of course, reflected a tradition and a social order that had stood the test of time, but it also indicated a closed system of ideas with weaknesses that would become apparent in the nineteenth century. Orthodox thought during these five centuries was Zhu Xi Neo-Confucianism. From the mid- to the late Ming, some perturbations were caused by the Zen-like teachings of the philosopher Wang Yangming (1472–1529), whose activism caused him to be jailed, beaten, and exiled at one point in an otherwise illustrious official career.

Several other original thinkers' refusal to accept bureaucratic posts under the Qing won them plaudits during the anti-Manchu nationalism of the early twentieth century, but they had only a limited influence on their own times. The

▲ **Ming Dynasty Ink Painting by Wu Wei (1479–1508).** The seated human figure is a part of the tranquility of nature. Nature, densely concentrated at the left and lower portions of the painting, stretches off into space in the middle and upper-right portion.
Wu Wei, "Scholar Seated Under a Tree," China. Ink + traces of colour on silk. 14.7 × 8.25. Chinese and Japanese Special Fund. © 1996. All rights reserved. Courtesy of Museum of Fine Arts, Boston.

most interesting was Gu Yanwu, who wrote on both philology and statecraft. He used philology and historical phonetics to get at the original meanings of the classics and contrasted their practical ethics with the "empty words" of Wang Yangming. Gu's successors extended his philological studies, developing empirical methods for textual studies, but lost sight of their implications for politics. The Manchus clamped down on unorthodox thought, and the seventeenth-century burst of creativity guttered out into a narrow, bookish, conservative scholasticism. Not until the end of the nineteenth century did thinkers draw from these studies the kind of radical inferences that philological studies of the Bible had produced in Europe.

Ming and Qing Chinese esteemed most highly, and not without reason, the traditional categories of high culture: painting, calligraphy, poetry, and philosophy. Porcelains of great beauty were also produced. In the early Ming the blue-on-white glazes predominated. During the later Ming and Qing more decorative wares with enamel painted over the glaze became widespread. The pottery industry of Europe was begun during the sixteenth century to imitate these wares, and Chinese and Japanese influences have dominated Western ceramics down to the present. Chinese today, however, look back and see the novel as the characteristic cultural achievement of the Ming and Qing.

The novel in China grew out of plot-books used by earlier storytellers. Like the stories, Chinese novels consisted of episodes strung together, and chapters in early novels often ended with an admonition to the reader not to miss the next exciting development. Ming and Qing novels were usually written by scholars who had failed the examinations, which may account for their caustic comments on officials. As most novels were written in colloquial Chinese, which was not quite respectable in the society of scholars, their authors wrote under pseudonyms.

Two collections of lively short stories are available in English: *Stories from a Ming Collection* and *The Courtesan's Jewel Box*. Many other stories were pornographic. In fact, the Ming may have invented the humorous pornographic novel. One example available in English is *The Carnal Prayer Mat*. This genre was suppressed in China during the Qing and rediscovered in Japanese collections in the twentieth century.

DOCUMENT | A Star in Heaven

Among the officials whose stories are told in The Scholars *is Fan Chin, thin and sallow with a grizzled beard and threadbare linen gown, who finally passes the county examination at the age of fifty-four. On his return home, he is given a feast and advice by his domineering father-in-law, Butcher Hu. But when Fan Chin asks Hu for money to travel to the provincial examination, he gets the following reaction.*

◆ Why did a satire such as *The Scholars* not undermine the premises on which Qing society rested?

Butcher Hu spat in his face and let loose a stream of abuse. "Don't forget who you are!" he bellowed. "Just passing one examination and you become like a toad thinking to dine on the flesh of a swan. I hear you passed the examination not because of your essay, but because the examiner took pity on your old age. Now, like a fool, you aspire to be an official. Don't you know that those who have passed the higher examination are all stars in heaven! Haven't you seen the Changs in the city? Those officials all have tons of money and generously proportioned faces and ears. Now look at you with your protruding mouth and monkey chin. Piss on the ground and take a good look at yourself in the puddle! A miserable creature like you can't even hope to swallow a swan's fart! Forget it!

[Fan Chin takes the examination anyway. When he returns home, he discovers that his family has been hungry for two days. Fan goes to the market to sell a chicken. In the meantime, heralds on horseback arrive to proclaim he has passed the provincial examination. Returning home, Fan sees the posted announcement and falls into a dead faint. When revived, he begins ranting incoherently. A herald suggests that Butcher Hu, whom Fan fears, bring him to his senses with a slap. Butcher Hu demurs.]

"He may be my son-in-law," he said, "but now he has become a member of the gentry, a star in heaven. How can I hit a star in heaven? I've heard from Buddhist priests that whoever strikes a star in heaven will be carried away by the King of Hell, struck one hundred times with an iron rod, consigned to the eighteenth hell, and never return to human form again. I wouldn't dare do it."

[Eventually Butcher Hu slaps him, and Fan recovers in time to receive a visit from a member of the local gentry, who is wearing "an official's gauze cap, sunflower-coloured gown, gilt belt and black shoes." "Sir," he says to Fan, "although we live in the same district, I regret that we have never become acquainted." After paying his respects, the visitor presents Fan with fifty taels of silver and a more appropriate house. Soon others give him land, goods, money, rice, and servants. The chapter ends with the maids cleaning up under the supervision of Fan Chin's wife after several days of feasting. Fan Chin's mother enters the courtyard.]

"You must be very careful," the old lady warned her daughter-in-law and the maids. "These things all belong to someone else, so don't break them."

The maids replied:" How can you say they belong to others, madam? They all belong to you."

"Oh no! How could our house have such things?" she said with a smile. "How can you talk of their belonging to others?" the maids replied in unison. "And not only these things, but all of us and the house, too, belong to you."

When the old lady heard this, she picked up the bowls and dishes of fine porcelain and the cups and chopsticks inlaid with silver and examined them one by one. She burbled: "These things are all mine." Laughing wildly, she fell over backward, choked on phlegm, and lost consciousness.

If you want to know what became of the old lady, please read the next chapter.

Translation by Shang Wei.

Short descriptions of several major novels may convey something of their flavor:

1. *The Romance of the Three Kingdoms*, published in 1522, tells of the political and military struggles in China in the aftermath of the Han dynasty. Like Shakespeare, the author, whose identity is uncertain, used a historical setting to create a dramatic world in which human character determines the outcome of events. More than twenty editions had appeared by the end of the Ming, and the novel was also extremely popular in Japan and Korea.

2. *All Men Are Brothers* (also translated as *The Water Margin*) tells of 108 bandit heroes who flee government repression during the late northern Song, establish a hideout on a mountain amid marshes, and like Robin Hood, avenge the wrongs perpetrated by corrupt officials. Separate episodes tell why each had to leave society and of their many daring and funny adventures. Of all Chinese novels, this was the most popular. It was officially banned as subversive during the Qing but was widely read nonetheless.

3. *The Golden Lotus* is a pornographic novel about the sexual adventures of an urban merchant. It gives vivid descriptions of individual women and satirical descriptions of venal officials and greedy monks. In the end the hero dies of his excesses and his family—all six wives and their children—disintegrates. The early English translation of this novel had long passages in Latin to protect those whose minds were not disciplined by the study of that language. Despite its literary merits, the book, like all of its genre, was proscribed during the era of Mao Zedong. In the recent decade it has become available again.

4. *The Dream of the Red Chamber* (also translated as *The Story of the Stone*) is generally considered China's greatest novel. It tells the story of a youth growing up in a wealthy but declining family during the early Qing. Critics praise its subtlety and psychological insight. Anthropologists mine the novel for information on the Chinese extended family and for its depiction of social relations. Like other Ming and Qing novels, it was recognized as a respectable work of art only during the twentieth century, after Western novels entered China.

5. *The Scholars* is a social satire of the early Qing that pokes fun at scholars and officials. (See Document, "A Star in Heaven.")

JAPAN

The two segments of "late traditional" Japan could not be more different. The Warring States era (1467–1600), really the last phase of Japan's medieval history, saw the unleashing of internal wars and anarchy that scourged the old society from the bottom up. Within a century all vestiges of the old manorial or estate system had been scrapped and virtually all of the Ashikaga lords had been overthrown. The Tokugawa era (1600–1868) that followed saw Japan reunited and stable, with a more competent government than ever. The culture was also brilliantly transformed, preparing it for the challenge it would face during the mid–nineteenth century.

Warring States Era (1467–1600)

War is the universal solvent of old institutions. Nowhere in history was this clearer than in Japan between 1467 and 1600. In 1467 a dispute arose over who would be the next Ashikaga shōgun. The dispute led to war between two territorial lords who supported the respective contenders. Other lords used the opportunity to gain territory at the expense of weaker neighbors, and wars raged throughout Japan for eleven years. Most of Kyoto was destroyed in the fighting, and the authority of the Ashikaga *bakufu* came to an end. This first war ended in 1477, but the fighting resumed and continued for more than a century.

WAR OF ALL AGAINST ALL

Even before 1467 the Ashikaga equilibrium had been precarious. Regional **daimyo** lords had relied on their relationship to the *bakufu* to hold their stronger vassals in check, while relying on these vassals to preserve their independence against strong neighbors. The collapse of *bakufu* authority after 1467 pulled the linchpin from the system. It left the regional lords standing alone, removing the last barrier to internecine wars.

The regional lords, however, were too weak to stand alone. A region was a hodgepodge of competing jurisdictions. Lands might be "public," or in estates, and some were starting to look like private fiefs. Revenues might be paid to nobles in Kyoto, to regional lords, or to local samurai strongmen. Most regions contained military bands that were not the vassals of the daimyo. Several daimyo had lands in the territories of other lords. Occasionally vassals were militarily more powerful than their daimyo lords. Some local vassals commanded bands of village warriors. Once the regional daimyo were forced to stand alone, they became prey to the stronger among their vassals as well as to neighboring states.

By the end of the sixteenth century all Ashikaga daimyo had fallen, with one exception in remote southern Kyushu. In their place emerged hundreds of little "Warring States daimyo," each with his own warrior band. In one prefecture along the Inland Sea, the remains of 200 hillside castles of such daimyo have been identified. The constant wars among these men were not unlike those of the early feudal era in Europe.

---

[3] G. Elison and B. L. Smith, eds., *Warlords, Artists, and Commoners* (Honolulu: Hawaii University Press, 1981), p. 57.

Daimyo Castle. Construction of the "White Heron" castle in Himeji was begun during the Warring States era and was completed shortly after 1600. During the Tokugawa peace, it remained as a monument to the glory of the daimyo. Today it can be seen from the "bullet train." Japan Airlines Photo.

A Japanese term for "survival of the fittest"—"the strong eat and the weak become the meat"—is often applied to this century of warfare. Of the daimyo bands, the most efficient in revamping their domain for military ends survived. The less ruthless, who clung to old ways, were defeated and absorbed. It was an age, as one Warring States general put it, "when only muscle counts." Another said, "The warrior doesn't care if he's called a dog or beast, the main thing is winning.[3]

Early in this period, when there were hundreds of small states, castles were built on a bluff above a river or on a mountainside with natural defenses against surprise attacks. Inuyama Castle, today a thirty-minute bus ride from Nagoya, is the most impressive surviving example.

As fighting continued, hundreds of local states gave way to tens of regional states. The castles of such regional states were often located on plains, and as castle towns grew up around them, merchants flocked to supply the needs of their growing soldiery. Eventually, alliances of these regional states fought it out, until in the late sixteenth century all of Japan was brought under the hegemony of a single lord. Oda Nobunaga (1534–1582) completed the initial unification of central Honshu and would have finished the job had a treacherous vassal not assassinated him in 1582. Toyotomi Hideyoshi (1536–1598), who had begun life as a lowly foot soldier, completed the unification in 1590. After his death his vassal generals once again went to war, and it was only with the victory of Tokugawa Ieyasu (1542–1616) at the Battle of Sekigahara in 1600 that true unifi-

cation was finally achieved. Ieyasu's unification of 1600 superficially resembled that of the Minamoto in 1185 but was in fact based on a sweeping transformation of Japan's society.

FOOT SOLDIER REVOLUTION

During the Warring States period, the foot soldier replaced the aristocratic mounted warrior as the backbone of the military in Japan. Soldiers were still called *samurai*. They were still the vassals of daimyo or, sometimes, the vassals of vassals of daimyo, but their numbers, social status, and techniques of warfare changed dramatically. As a result, Japanese society changed from what it had been only a century earlier.

The changes began on the land. Ashikaga daimyo had diverted more and more land revenues for their own use, but Warring States daimyo took them all. Public lands and estates, including those of the imperial house, were seized and converted into fiefs. Soldiers were paid stipends from the revenues of the daimyo's lands, and important vassals, usually the officers or commanders of the daimyo's army, were awarded fiefs of their own. The governance of fiefs was essentially private, in the hands of the fief holder.

Inheritance patterns changed to fit the new circumstances. Multigeniture—the division of a warrior's rights to revenues from land among his children—was not appropriate to a society with a hereditary military class. It had impoverished the Kamakura vassals. To protect the integrity of the warrior's household economy, multigeniture had begun to give way to single inheritance during the Ashikaga period. After 1467 single inheritance became universal. As the fief was often passed to the most able son, not necessarily the eldest, the pattern is usually called *unigeniture* rather than *primogeniture*.

With larger revenues, Warring States daimyo built bigger armies. They recruited mainly from the peasantry. Some of the new soldiers moved to the castle town of the daimyo. Others lived on the land or remained in their villages, farming in peace and fighting in war. The growth of the military class had begun earlier. Accounts of twelfth-century battles tell of fighting by tens of hundreds of warriors, sometimes more. Scroll paintings of the Heiji wars corroborate these figures. By the fourteenth century battles involved thousands or tens of thousands of troops. By the late sixteenth century hundreds of thousands were deployed in major campaigns. Screen paintings show massed troops in fixed emplacements with officers riding about on horseback. Of course, special cavalry strike forces were still used.

In the mid–fourteenth century a new weapon was developed: a thrusting spear with a thick shaft and a heavy chisel-like blade. Held in both hands, it could penetrate medieval armor as a sword could not. It could also be swung about like a quarterstaff. It was used by soldiers positioned at intervals of three feet, in a pincushion tactic to impale charging cavalry. The weapon spelled the end of the aristocratic warrior in Japan, just as the pikes used by Swiss soldiers ended knighthood in northern Europe during the fifteenth century. After 1467 this spear became the principal weapon of Warring States Japan. Not surprisingly, its spread coincided with the recruitment of peasant soldiers, for it required only short training. By the early sixteenth century it was every warrior's dream to be the "number one spearman" of his lord. Even generals trained in its use. One famous general wrote that "one hundred spearmen are more effective than ten thousand swords."

A second change in military technology was the introduction of the musket by the Portuguese in the mid–sixteenth century. Warring States generals quickly adopted it. Its superiority was proved in the Battle of Nagashino in 1575, in which Oda Nobunaga and Tokugawa Ieyasu used spear and musket platoons against the cavalry of a famous military tactician. Massing 3,000 muskets behind a bamboo barrier-fence and firing in volleys, Nobunaga decimated the forces of his enemy. As individual combat gave way to mass armies, warfare became pitiless, cruel, and bloody.

How, then, should one characterize the society that emerged from the Warring States? Does the word *feudal* apply, with its suggestion of lords and vassals and manorial life on the fiefs of aristocratic warriors? In some respects, it does: By the late sixteenth century all warriors in Japan were part of a pyramid of vassals and lords headed by a single overlord; warriors of rank held fiefs and vassals of their own.

In other respects Japan resembled postfeudal Europe. First, most of the military class were soldiers, not aristocrats. Even though they were called samurai and were vassals, they were something new. They were not given fiefs but were paid with stipends of so many bales of rice. Second, unlike, say, feudal England, where the military class was about one quarter of 1 percent of the population, in mid-sixteenth-century Japan it may have reached 7 or 8 percent. It was more of a size with the mercenary armies of Europe during the fifteenth or sixteenth centuries. Third, the recruitment of village warriors added significantly to the power of Warring States daimyo but gave rise to problems as well. Taxes became harder to collect. Local samurai were often involved in uprisings. When organized by Pure Land Buddhist congregations, these uprisings sometimes involved whole provinces. Again, the parallels with postfeudal Europe seem closer. Fourth, even in a feudal society, not everything is feudal. The commercial growth of the Kamakura and Ashikaga periods continued through the dark decades of the Warring States era.

FOREIGN RELATIONS AND TRADE

Japanese pirate-traders plied the seas of East (see Map 19–1) Asia during the fifteenth and sixteenth centuries. To halt their depredations, the Ming emperor invited the third Ashikaga shōgun to trade with China. An agreement was reached in 1404 and the shōgun was appointed the "King of Japan." During the next century and a half, periodic "tribute missions" were sent to China. The opening of official trade channels did not, however, end piracy. It stopped only after Japan was reunified at the close of the sixteenth century.

The content of the trade reflected the progress of Japanese crafts. Early Japanese exports to China were raw materials such as raw copper, sulfur, or silver, but by the sixteenth century manufactured goods were rising in importance and included swords, spears, wine bottles, folding fans, picture scrolls, screen paintings, ink slabs, and the like. In exchange, Japan received copper cash, porcelains, paintings, books, and medicines.

After establishing his hegemony over Japan, Hideyoshi permitted only ships with his vermilion seal to trade with China, a policy the Tokugawa continued. Between 1604 and 1635 over 350 ships went to China in this "vermilion-seal trade." Then, in 1635, the imposition of seclusion ended Japan's foreign trade: No Japanese could leave Japan; the construction of large ships was prohibited; trade with the continent was limited to a small community of Chinese merchants in Nagasaki, and to quiet trading with China and Korea through the Ryukyu and Tsushima Islands.

Overlapping Japan's maritime expansion in the seas of East Asia was the arrival of European ships. Portuguese pirate-traders made their way to Goa in India, to Malacca, to Macao in China, and arrived in Japan in 1543. Spanish galleons came

▲ **Arrival of the Portuguese in Japan.** Portuguese merchants arrived in Japan in 1543 from India and the East Indies. Their crews were multiethnic, and they brought Jesuit priests as well.

"Arrival of the Portuguese in Japan" Detail—central section of the boat. 1954–1618. Screen. Paint, gold, paper. Museo Soares Dos Reis, Porto, Portugal. Bridgemann-Giraudon/Art Resource, N.Y.

in 1587 via Mexico and the Philippines. These eastern and western waves of Iberian expansion were followed by the Dutch and the English after the turn of the century.

The Portuguese, from a tiny country with a population of 1.5 million, were motivated by a desire for booty and profits and by religious zeal. Their ships were superior. Taking advantage of the Chinese ban on maritime commerce, they became important as shippers. They carried Southeast Asian goods and Japanese silver to China and Chinese silk to Japan and then used their profits to buy Southeast Asian spices for the European market. The Portuguese, initially at least, found it easier to trade with the daimyo of a disunited Japan than to deal with the authorities of a united China. A few Kyushu daimyo, thinking to attract Portuguese traders, even converted to Christianity.

Traders brought with them Jesuit missionaries. The Society of Jesus had been founded in 1540 to act as soldiers in the pope's campaign against the Reformation. Only nine years later Saint Francis Xavier (1506–1552) arrived in Japan. He soon wrote back that the Japanese were "the best [people] who have yet been discovered." Another Jesuit wrote that the Japan-

ese "are all white, courteous, and highly civilized, so much so that they surpass all other known races of the world." The Japanese, for their part, also appeared to admire the Jesuits for their asceticism, devoutness, and learning.

As they had attempted to convert scholar-officials in China, so the Jesuits in Japan directed their efforts toward the samurai. Moving to Kyoto, they won the favor of Nobunaga, who was engaged in campaigns against warrior monks on Mount Hiei and against Pure Land strongholds in Osaka. Portuguese and Christian objects became fashionable. Painters produced "Southern Barbarian screens" that depicted the "black ships" of the Portuguese. Christian symbols were used on lacquer boxes and saddles. Nobunaga himself occasionally wore Portuguese clothes and a cross and said he might become a Christian if only the Jesuits would drop their insistence on monogamy. Christian converts increased from a few in the early years to 130,000 in 1579, and to about 300,000 in 1600. That is to say, in the late sixteenth century a higher percentage of Japanese were Christian than today.

It is difficult to explain why Christianity met with greater success in Japan than in other Asian lands. When introduced, it was seen as a new Buddhist sect. There seemed little difference to the Japanese between the cosmic Buddha of Shingon and the Christian God, between the paradise of Amida and the Christian heaven, or between prayers to Kannon—the female *bodhisattva* of mercy—and to the Virgin Mary. The Japanese also noted the theological similarity between the pietism of the Pure Land sect and that of Christianity. To Japanese ears, the passage in Romans 10:13, "whosoever shall call upon the name of the Lord shall be saved," was reminiscent of the Pure Land practice of invoking the name of Amida. The Jesuits, too,

CHRONOLOGY

Warring States Japan and the Era of Unification (1467–1600)

1467–1568	Battles throughout Japan
1543	Portuguese arrive in Japan
1568	Oda Nobunaga takes Kyoto and partially unifies Japan
1575	Battle of Nagashino
1582	Nobunaga assassinated
1588	Hideyoshi starts sword hunt
1590	Hideyoshi completes unification
1592, 1597–1598	Hideyoshi sends armies to Korea
1597	Hideyoshi bans Christianity
1598	Hideyoshi dies, his generals battle for succession
1600	Battle of Sekigahara; Tokugawa reunifies Japan

noted these parallels and felt that the devil had established these sects in Japan to test their faith. Xavier, who, despite his admirable personal characteristics, was narrow-minded, referred to the historical Buddha and Amida as "two demons." Although this intolerance gave rise to certain tensions and animosities, Christianity spread, and to no small measure as a result of the personal example of the Jesuits.

The fortunes of Christianity began to decline in 1597, when Hideyoshi banned Christianity and had six Spanish Franciscans and twenty Japanese converts crucified in Nagasaki. Hideyoshi was aware of Spanish colonialism in the Philippines, and it was said that a Spanish pilot had boasted that merchants and priests represented the first step toward the conquest of Japan. Sporadic persecutions continued until 1614, when Tokugawa Ieyasu began a serious movement to extirpate the foreign religion. Faced with torture, some Christians recanted. More than 3,000 others were martyred.

The last resistance was an uprising near Nagasaki in 1637 and 1638 in which 37,000 Christians died. After that, Christianity survived in Japan only as a hidden religion with secret rites and devotions to "Maria-Kannon," the mother of Jesus represented or disguised as the Buddhist goddess of mercy holding a child in her arms. A few of these "hidden Christians" reemerged in the later nineteenth century. Otherwise, apart from muskets and techniques of castle building, all that remained of the Portuguese influence were certain loan words that became a permanent part of the Japanese language: *pan* for bread, *birōdo* for velvet, *kasutera* for sponge cake, *karuta* for playing cards, and *tempura* for that familiar Japanese dish.

Tokugawa Era (1600–1868)
POLITICAL ENGINEERING AND ECONOMIC GROWTH DURING THE SEVENTEENTH CENTURY

From 1467 to 1590 Japan's energies were absorbed in ever bigger wars. But after the unifications of 1590 and 1600 Japan's leaders sought to create a peaceful, stable, orderly society. Like a great tanker that requires many times its own length to come about, Japan made this transition slowly. Many of the values and habits of mind of the Warring States era continued into the seventeenth century. By the middle or late seventeenth century, however, its society and political system had been radically reengineered. Vigorous economic and demographic growth had also occurred. This combination of political and economic change made the seventeenth century a period of great dynamism.

Hideyoshi's Rule   One pressing problem faced by Japan's unifiers was how to cope with an armed peasantry. In war, village warriors fought for their lord: The benefit they offered the

lord was greater than their cost. In peace, only the cost remained: their resistance to taxation and the threat of local uprisings. Accordingly, in the summer of 1588 Hideyoshi ordered a "sword hunt" to disarm the peasants. Records of the collected weaponry exist for only one county of 3400 households in Kaga, a domain on the Sea of Japan: 1,073 swords, 1,540 short swords, 700 daggers, 160 spears, 500 suits of armor, and other miscellaneous items. Once the hunt was completed, the 5 percent of the population who remained samurai used their monopoly on weapons to control the other 95 percent.

Hideyoshi next moved to freeze the social classes. Samurai were prohibited from quitting the service of their lord. Peasants were barred from abandoning their fields to become townspeople. This policy was continued by the Tokugawa after 1600, and by and large succeeded. Samurai, farmers, and townspeople tended to marry within their respective classes, and each class developed a unique cultural character. The authorities even attempted to dictate lifestyles, prescribing who could ride in palanquins, who could wear silk, and who was permitted to build fancy gates in front of their houses.

But to grasp the class structure of Tokugawa society, we must note the vast range of social gradations within each class. A farmer who was a landlord and a district official was a more important figure than most lower samurai and lived in a different social world from a landless "water-drinking" peasant too poor to buy tea. A townsman could be the head of a great wholesale house, or a humble street peddler or clog mender. A samurai could be an elder, a key decision maker of his domain, with an income of thousands of bushels of rice and several hundred vassals of his own, or an impecunious foot soldier who stood guard at the castle gate.

Having disarmed the peasantry, Hideyoshi ordered cadastral surveys on his own lands and on those of his vassals. The surveys defined each parcel of land by location, size, soil quality, product, and cultivator's name. For the first time, an attempt was made to standardize the rods used to measure land and the boxes used to measure quantities of rice. These standards marked the beginning of the detailed record keeping that characterized the Tokugawa era. Hideyoshi's survey laid the foundations for a systematic land tax. Based on these surveys, domains and fiefs were henceforth ranked in terms of their assessed yield.

Establishment of Tokugawa Rule   Bedazzled by his own power and military successes, and against all the evidence of Warring States political behavior, Hideyoshi assumed that his vassals would honor their sworn oaths of loyalty to his heir. He was especially trustful of his great ally Tokugawa Ieyasu, whose domains were larger than his own. His trust was misplaced. After his death in 1598, Hideyoshi's former vassals, paying little attention to his heir, broke apart into two opposing camps and fought a great battle in 1600 from which the alliance headed by Tokugawa Ieyasu emerged victorious. Ieyasu was wise, effective in maintaining alliances, and a master strategist, but above all patient. In comparing the three unifiers, the Japanese tell the story that when a cuckoo failed to sing, Nobunaga said, "I'll kill it if it doesn't sing"; Hideyoshi said, "I'll make it sing"; but Ieyasu sat down and said, "I'll wait until it sings."

Like the Minamoto of twelfth-century Kamakura, Ieyasu spurned the Kyoto court and established his headquarters in Edo (today's Tokyo), in the center of his military holdings in eastern Japan (see Map 19–3). He took the title of shōgun in 1603 and called his government the *bakufu*. In Edo he built a great castle, surrounded by massive fortifications of stone and con-

centric moats. The inner portion of these moats and stone walls remains today as the Imperial Palace. Ieyasu then used his military power to reorganize Japan.

Ieyasu's first move was to confiscate the lands of his defeated enemies and to reward his vassals and allies. During the first quarter of the seventeenth century the *bakufu* confiscated the domains of 150 daimyo, some of former enemies and some for infractions of the Tokugawa legal code, and transferred 229 daimyo from one domain to another. The transfers completed the work of Hideyoshi's sword hunt by severing long-standing ties between daimyo and their disarmed former village retainers. When a daimyo was transferred to a

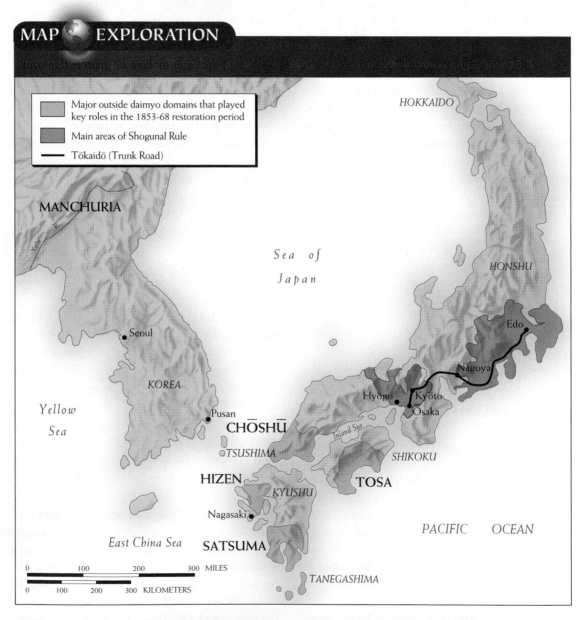

MAP 19–3 Tokugawa Japan and the Korean Peninsula.   The area between Edo and Osaka in central Honshu was both the political base of the Tokugawa *bakufu* and its rice basket. The domains that would overthrow the Tokugawa *bakufu* in the late 19th century were mostly in outlying areas of southwestern Japan.

Edo Castle Edo first became a castle town in the mid-15th century. Tokugawa Ieyasu made the castle his residence and headquarters in 1590, and, after his great victory in 1600, rebuilt and extended it. This early Edo period screen painting shows (upper right) the keep or inner citadel, which was not rebuilt after a fire in 1657. Korean envoys (bottom center) enter the castle grounds. They have brought tiger skins and other gifts. Onlookers gawk at their unfamiliar garb. Warriors (top, far right) practice archery. The inner castle compounds shown in the painting were only the central part of an elaborate system of moats, stone-block ramparts, and gates. In 1868, after the Meiji Restoration, the Edo Castle was renamed the Tokyo (Eastern Capital) Castle, and became the residence of the emperor.
Courtesy: Albert Craig.

new fief, he took his samurai retainers with him. During the second quarter of the seventeenth century transfers and confiscations ended and the system settled down.

The reshuffling of domains had not been random. The configuration that emerged was, first, of a huge central Tokugawa domain. It contained the following: most of the domains of "house daimyo"—those who had been Tokugawa vassals before 1600; the fiefs of the 5,000 Tokugawa bannermen (upper samurai); and the lands that furnished the stipends of the other 17,000 Tokugawa direct retainers (middle and lower samurai). Then, strategically placed around the Tokugawa heartland were the domains of the "related daimyo." These domains had been founded by the second and third sons of early shōgun and furnished a successor to the main Tokugawa line when a shōgun had no heir. Beyond the related daimyo was a second tier of "outside daimyo" who had fought as allies of Tokugawa Ieyasu in 1600 but became his vassals only after the battle was over.

Finally, at the antipodes of the system were those outside daimyo who had been permitted to survive despite having fought against the Tokugawa in 1600. Their domains were drastically reduced. They remained the "enemies" within the system, although they had submitted and become Tokugawa vassals after 1600. Thus, the entire layout of domains constituted a defensive system, with the staunchest Tokugawa supporters nearest to the center.

The Tokugawa also established other systemic controls. Legal codes regulated the imperial court, temples and shrines, and daimyo. Military houses were enjoined to use men of ability and to practice frugality. They were prohibited from engaging in drinking parties, wanton revelry, sexual indulgence, habitual gambling, or the ostentatious display of wealth. Only with *bakufu* consent could daimyo marry or repair their castles.

A second control was a hostage system, firmly established by 1642, that required the wives and children of daimyo to reside permanently in Edo and the daimyo themselves to spend every second year in Edo. Like the policy of Louis XIV (r. 1643–1715) at Versailles, this requirement transformed feudal lords into courtiers. The palatial Edo compounds of the daimyo contained hundreds or thousands of retainers and servants and occupied much of the city.

A third key control, established during the 1630s, was the national policy of seclusion. Seclusion was no barrier to cultural imports from China and Korea. But except for small Chinese and Dutch trading contingents at Nagasaki, no foreigners were permitted to enter Japan, and on pain of death, no Japanese were allowed to go abroad. Nor could oceangoing ships be built. This policy was strictly enforced until 1854. Like the case of a watch, seclusion enclosed the workings of the entire system. Cut off from substantial outside political contacts, for Japanese, Japan became the world.

An interesting parallel can be drawn between Europe and Tokugawa Japan. Between the fifteenth and eighteenth centuries France moved from a late feudal pattern toward ever greater centralization, whereas Germany moved toward a decentralized order of many independent states. In Japan these two tendencies were delicately balanced. On the one hand, representing the forces of centralization, was the *bakufu*, which

Daimyo. A daimyo seated in a palanquin carried by commoner porters. The screen at the side is rolled up so that he can observe the sights of Edo. Surrounding the palanquin are several dozen of his samurai retainers. In the right foreground are Edo townsmen. Courtesy Albert Craig.

governed its own domain and also administered the controls over the whole system. Its offices were staffed by its vassals—its highest councils by house daimyo and high-ranking bannermen, and lesser posts by lower ranking vassals of ability. The pool of rank was always larger than that of the available posts.

On the other hand, representing decentralization were the domains of the 260 or so daimyo. Except for the house daimyo, they were excluded from service in the *bakufu*. Their domain governments, like miniature *bakufu*, were staffed by their samurai vassals. Each domain had its own autonomous military, finances, judiciary, schools, paper money, and so on. This balance between centralization and decentralization has led Japanese scholars to label the Tokugawa polity the "*bakufu*-domain system."

The Seventeenth-Century Economy   The political dynamism of the period from Hideyoshi through the first century of Tokugawa rule was matched by economic growth. By the late sixteenth century there existed a backlog of agricultural techniques, the spread of which had been impeded by regionalism and wars: methods of water control and irrigation that made double-cropping easier, better tools, new seed strains, the use of bony fish or of night soil from cities as fertilizers, and so on. During the seventeenth century these techniques were widely applied. Resources no longer needed for war were allocated to land reclamation. The result was a doubling of agricultural production, as well as a doubling of population from 12 million in 1600 to 24 million in 1700. The production of agricultural byproducts—cotton, silk, indigo, lumber, dyes, *sake*, and so on—also grew, especially in central Japan and along the shores of the Inland Sea.

Peace also sustained growth in commerce. The merchants in Warring States Japan, like geese who lay golden eggs, had always been at risk. They had to pay for security; they operated within cramped regional economies. On coming to power, Nobunaga and Hideyoshi knew that political unification alone was not enough. They recognized that prosperity would make their rule easier and, acknowledging the enterprise of merchants, they abolished the medieval guilds and freed Japan's central markets from monopolistic restrictions. The result was a burgeoning of trade and the formation of a national market network atop the domain economies. As this network expanded during the seventeenth century, economic functions became more differentiated and efficient. The economic chain that began with a local buyer might extend to a merchant house in a regional port, to coastal shippers, to warehousers in Osaka or Edo, and then to great wholesale houses.

Seclusion ended much foreign trade. One might expect the sharp decline in trade to have dampened Japan's domestic economy. Instead, commerce continued to grow for the remainder of the seventeenth century.

To explain this growth, we must look at the tax system and the pattern of consumption in the castle towns and Edo. Tokugawa tax policy was based on land, not commerce. Taxes took about one third of the peasant's production. It was a heavier tax rate than that in neighboring China and bespeaks the effective grasp that the military class had on Japanese society. Most taxes were paid in grain. Even as late as the mid–nineteenth century, only a third was collected in money payments. Thus, the 87 percent of the population who lived in the countryside paid almost one third of the country's agricultural wealth to the 5 percent in the military class. The remaining 8 percent of townspeople also lived off the tax flow by providing goods and services for samurai. This distribution of benefits was mirrored in the three-area city planning common to all castle towns: a large parklike area with castle, trees, stone walls, and moats for the daimyo and his government; an extensive samurai quarter; and a meaner townspeople's quarter. Moreover, just as the castle towns were the consumption centers of the regional tax economies, so was Edo the national consumption center and a super-castle town. It had the same three-area layout, although on a far grander scale. When the daimyo of Kaga, from a great domain on the Japan Sea, was in attendance at Edo, he was served by 8,000 samurai. When he returned to his domain, 4,000 stayed on in Edo to manage the Kaga estates: 267 acres of houses and gardens, barracks, schools, warehouses, and so on. One of these estates, with its magnificent red gate still intact, is today the main campus of Tokyo University. Other daimyo had establishments proportional to their domains. By 1700 Edo had a population of about 1 million.

To support their Edo establishments, the daimyo sold tax rice in Osaka. The "kitchen of Japan," Osaka became the redistribution center from which competing fleets of coastal shippers brought to Edo food, clothing, lumber, oil, and other supplies. By 1700 Osaka's population was about 400,000. Kyoto, rebuilt after its destruction in the early Warring States period, was almost as big. It continued as a center of handicraft production. It also was the location of the "captive" imperial court, which, after suffering penury during the Warring States era, was given support lands equivalent in revenues to those of a small daimyo.

The system of alternate-year attendance at Edo contributed to the development of overland transportation. The most traveled grand trunk road was the Tōkaidō Road between Edo and Kyoto (see Map 19–3). The artist Hiroshige (1797–1858) made a series of woodblock prints that depicted the scenery at its fifty-three post stations. The post stations had official inns for traveling daimyo and requisitioned supplies and horses as a tax obligation from adjacent villages. These stations often grew into thriving local towns.

The growth of a national economy led to a richness and diversity in urban life. Townsmen governed their districts. Samurai city managers watched over the city as a whole. Public schools, police, and companies of firefighters provided public services—a proverb of the time was "Fires are the flowers of Edo." But there were also servants, cooks, messengers, restaurant owners, priests, doctors, teachers, sword sharpeners, book lenders, instructors in the martial arts, prostitutes, and bathhouse attendants. In the world of popular arts there were woodblock printers and artists, book publishers, puppeteers, acrobatic troupes, storytellers, and **Kabuki** and **Nō** actors. Merchant establishments included money changers, pawnbrokers, peddlers, small shops, single-price retail establishments like the House of Mitsui, and great wholesale merchants. Merchant households furnished the raw materials for the personae of Edo fiction: the skinflint merchant who pinches every penny, the profligate son who runs through an inheritance to an inevitable bankruptcy, an erring wife, or the clerk involved in a hopeless affair with a prostitute. (See Document, "The Virtuous Wife.")

EIGHTEENTH AND EARLY NINETEENTH CENTURIES

By the late seventeenth century the political engineering of the Tokugawa state was complete. After that, few major new laws were enacted, and few important changes were made in governing institutions. In the economy, too, from the early eighteenth century, dynamic growth gave way to slower growth within a high-level equilibrium. In the words of some historians, the society

The Commercial District of Osaka, the "kitchen" of Tokugawa Japan. Warehouses bear the crests of their merchant houses. Ships (upper right) loaded with rice, cotton goods, *sake*, and other goods are about to depart for Edo (Tokyo). Their captains vied with one another to arrive first and get the best price.
Courtesy Albert Craig.

had become "frozen," "unchanging," or "strangely preserved." Yet changes of a different kind were under way.

The Forty-Seven Rōnin The eighteenth century began with high drama. In the spring of 1701 a daimyo on duty at Edo Castle drew his sword and slightly wounded a *bakufu* official who had insulted him. Even to unsheath a sword within the castle was punishable by death. On the same day the daimyo was ordered to commit *harakiri* (literally, to cut his stomach), and his domain was confiscated. Fearing an attempt at revenge, the *bakufu* police kept an eye on the daimyo's retainers—now *rōnin*, or "masterless samurai." The retainers dissembled, working at lowly jobs, staying at home with their families, or leading lives of drunkenness and debauchery.

Twenty-one months later, on a snowy night in January, forty-seven of the retainers gathered in Edo, attacked the residence of the *bakufu* official, took his head, and then surrendered to the authorities. Their act struck the imagination of the citizenry of Edo and was widely acclaimed. But the *bakufu* council, after deliberating for two months, ordered all forty-seven to commit *harakiri*. The incident embodied the perennial theme of duty versus human feelings. Writers of Kabuki drama and puppet theater quickly took up the incident, and to this day it has been reworked into novels, movies, and television scripts. Just as in Western theater there have been different Hamlets, so have there been many characterizations of Ōishi Kuranosuke, the leader of the band of forty-seven.

Viewed historically, three points may be noted about the incident. First, in a similar situation the more practical samurai of the Warring States period would have forgotten their former lord and rushed to find a new one. Loyalty was highly valued because disloyalty was a live option. But this was no longer true in the Tokugawa era. With the authority of the daimyo backed by that of the shōgun, there was no room for disloyalty. So loyalty became deeply internalized and was viewed almost as a religious obligation. It was also easier for Tokugawa samurai to be loyal unto death because, for the most part, there was so little likelihood in an era of peace that such a loyalty would be called for. In any case, in 1701 it was this Tokugawa species of absolute loyalty that moved the forty-seven rōnin.

Second, the incident tells something of the state in Tokugawa Japan. The 1615 "Laws for the Military Houses" contains the passage: "Law is the basis of the social order. Reason may be violated in the name of law, but law may not be violated in the name of reason. Those who break laws deserve heavy punishments.[4] One Tokugawa law forbade private vendettas. So, despite the moral purity of their act—which all recognized, even those who condemned them to death—the forty-seven

"virtuous warriors" had to die. The state was above ethics. Their death sentence was a bureaucratic necessity.

Third, loyalty and idealism were not a monopoly of the males. In the drama, at least, samurai wives and daughters displayed the same heroic spirit of self-sacrifice.

Cycles of Reform Most political history of late Tokugawa Japan is written in terms of alternating cycles of laxity and reform. Even during the mid–seventeenth century the expenses of the *bakufu* and daimyo states were often greater than their income. In part, the reason was structural: Taxes were based on agriculture in an economy that was becoming commercial. In part, it was simple mathematics: After the samurai were paid their stipends, not enough was left for the expenses of domain governments and the costs of the Edo establishments. In part, it was the toll of extraordinary costs, such as a *bakufu* levy, the wedding of a daimyo's daughter, or the rebuilding of a castle after a fire. And finally, in part, it was a growing taste for luxury among daimyo and retainers of rank.

Over the years a familiar pattern emerged. To make ends meet, domains would borrow from merchants. Then, as finances became even more straitened, a reformist clique of officials would appear, take power, retrench the domain's finances, eliminate extravagance, and return the domain to a more frugal and austere way of life. Debts would be repaid or repudiated. A side effect of reform was the depression of the local merchant economy. But no one likes to practice frugality forever. So, after some of the goals of the reform had been achieved, a new clique would take over the government and a new round of spending would begin. The *bakufu* carried out three great reforms on Tokugawa lands:

1716–1733	Tokugawa Yoshimune	17 years
1787–1793	Matsudaira Sadanobu	6 years
1841–1843	Mizuno Tadakuni	2 years

The first two were long and successful; the third was not. Its failure set the stage for the ineffective response of the *bakufu* to the West in the mid–nineteenth century. Daimyo domains also carried out reforms. Some were successful, enabling them to respond more effectively to the political crisis of the mid–nineteenth century.

Bureaucratization The balance between centralization and decentralization lasted until the end of the Tokugawa era. Not a single domain ever tried to overthrow the *bakufu* hegemony. Nor did the *bakufu* ever try to extend its control over the domains. But bureaucracy grew steadily both within the *bakufu* and within each domain. One development was the extension of public authority into areas that had been private. In 1600 most samurai fiefs were run by their samurai fief holders. They collected the taxes, often at a heavier rate than the do-

---

[4] R. Tsunoda, W. T. de Bary, and D. Keene, eds., *Sources of the Japanese Tradition* (New York: Columbia University Press, 1958), p. 336.

▲ **Bridal Procession.** The bridal procession of Yohime, the 21st daughter of the 11th Tokugawa shōgun, approaches the Edo mansion of the Kaga daimyo. The red gate (upper right), built in 1827 for this occasion, is today an entrance to the main campus of Tokyo University. The 11th shōgun had twenty-eight sons and twenty-seven daughters by his more than forty concubines. Of his children, thirteen sons and twelve daughters survived to maturity. This woodblock print by Kunisada is a "national treasure."
Courtesy Albert Craig.

main set, and appointed fief stewards to oversee the fiefs. By 1850, however, district officials administered all but the largest of samurai fiefs. They collected the standard domain taxes and forwarded their income to the samurai. In periods of retrenchment, samurai were often paid only half the amount due.

Along with the growth of bureaucracy was the proliferation of administrative codes and government by paperwork. Surviving domain archives house room after room of records of every imaginable kind, mostly from the late eighteenth and early nineteenth centuries: records of births, adoptions, name changes, samurai ranks, fief registers, stipend registers, land and tax registers, court proceedings, domain history, and so on. Administrative codes for the *bakufu* exchequer, for example, grew from a single page during the seventeenth century to forty pages in the late Tokugawa. They define among other things an elaborate structure of offices and suboffices, their jurisdictional boundaries, and detailed instructions about how many copies of each document should be made and to which offices they should be forwarded.

Of course, bureaucratization had limits. Only samurai could aspire to official posts. They came to the office wearing their two swords. Decision-making posts were limited to upper ranking samurai. In periods of financial crises—endemic in the late Tokugawa—a demand arose for men of ability, and middle- or lower-middle-ranking samurai joined domain decision making by becoming staff assistants to bureaucrats of rank.

The Later Tokugawa Economy   By 1700 the economy approached the limit of expansion within the available technology. The population, an important index, reached 26 million early in the eighteenth century and was at the same figure in the mid–nineteenth century, a period during which the population of China more than doubled. Within this constant figure were various smaller movements. Population declined during epidemics in the 1750s and the 1760s, and during famines in the 1780s. The northeast never fully recovered. Southwestern Japan along the Inland Sea gained in population. Central Japan stayed even; it was more urban, and like most premodern cities, Tokugawa cities had higher death rates.

After 1700 taxes became stabilized and land surveys were few. Evidence suggests little increase in grain production and only slow growth in agricultural byproducts. Some families, to raise their standard of living, made conscious efforts to limit their size. Contraception and abortion were commonplace, and infanticide (euphemistically called *mabiki*, the term for thinning out rice shoots in a paddy) was practiced in hard times. But periodic disease, shortages of food, and late marriages among the poor were more important factors. A study of one rural village showed the daughters of poor farmers marrying at twenty-two and having an average of 4.6 children, whereas for the daughters of rich farmers the figures were nineteen and 6.2. A study of another domain showed that the size of the average farm household declined from 7 to 4.25 members.

During the Tokugawa some farmers remained independent small cultivators, but others became landlords or tenants. By the mid–nineteenth century tenants worked about a quarter of all cultivated lands. Most landlords were small, lived in their villages, and often were village leaders. They were not at all like the Chinese gentry. The misery of the lower stratum of rural society contributed to an increase in peasant uprisings during the late eighteenth and early nineteenth centuries. Authorities had no difficulty in quelling them, although some involved thousands of protestors and were locally destructive. No uprising in Japan even remotely approached those of late Manchu China.

Commerce grew slowly during the late Tokugawa. In the early eighteenth century it was reencased within guilds. Merchants paid set fees, usually not especially high, in return for monopoly privileges in central marketplaces. Guilds were also reestablished in the domains, and some domains established domain-run monopolies on products such as wax, paper, indigo, or sugar. The problem facing domain leaders was how to tax profits without injuring the competitive standing of domain exports. Most late Tokugawa commercial growth was in countryside industries—*sake*, soy sauce, dyes, silks, or cotton—and was especially prominent in central and western Japan. Some were organized and financed by city merchants under the putting-out system. Others competed with city merchants, shipping directly to end markets to circumvent monopoly controls. The expansion of labor in such rural industries contributed to the population shrinkage in late Tokugawa cities.

The largest question about the Tokugawa economy concerns its relation to Japan's amazing industrialization, which began later in the nineteenth century. Some scholars have suggested that Japan had a "running start." Others have stressed Japanese backwardness in comparison with European late developers. The question is still unresolved.

TOKUGAWA CULTURE

If the *Tale of Genji* represents the classical culture of the aristocratic Heian court, and if Nō drama or an ink painting by Sesshō represents the austere samurai culture of medieval Japan, then a satire by Saikaku (1642–1693), a drama by Chikamatsu (1653–1724), or a woodblock print of a beauty by Utamaro (1753–1806) may be taken to represent the new urban culture of the Tokugawa era. In such works, one discerns a new secular consciousness, an exquisite taste put to plebeian ends, occasional vulgarities, and a sense of humor only occasionally encountered in the earlier Japanese tradition.

But there was more to Tokugawa culture than the arts and literature of the townspeople. Two hundred and fifty years of peace and prosperity provided a base for an ever more complex culture and a broader popular participation in cultural life. In the villages Buddhism became more deeply rooted; new folk religions proliferated; by the early nineteenth century most well-to-do farmers could read and write. The aristocratic culture of the ranking samurai houses also remained vigorous. Nō plays continued to be staged. The medieval tradition of black ink paintings was continued by the Kanō school and other artists.

The Ashikaga tradition of restraint, simplicity, and naturalness in architecture was extended. The imperial villa in Katsura outside of Kyoto has its roots in medieval architecture and to this day inspires Japanese architects. The gilded and colored screen paintings that had surged in popularity during Hideyoshi's rule developed further, culminating in the powerful works of Ogata Kōrin (1658–1716).

Zen Buddhism, having declined during the Warring States period, was revitalized by the monk Hakuin (1686–1769). One of the great cultural figures of the Tokugawa era, Hakuin was also a writer, a painter, a calligrapher, and a sculptor. His autobiographical writings have been translated as *The Embossed Tea Kettle*.

Some scholars have argued that Tokugawa urban culture had a double structure. On the one hand were the samurai, serious and high-minded, who produced a vast body of Chinese-style paintings, poetry, and philosophical treatises. On the other hand was the culture of the townspeople: lowbrow, irreverent, secular, satirical, and often scatological. The samurai esteemed Song-style paintings of mountains or waterfalls, often adorned with quotations from the Confucian classics or Tang poetry. The townspeople collected prints of local beauties, actors, courtesans, and scenes from everyday life. Samurai moralists saw money as the root of evil. Merchants saw it as their goal in life; in Osaka, they even held an "abacus festival," at which their adding machines were consecrated to the gods of wealth and commerce.

In poetry, too, a double structure appeared. Bashō (1644–1694) was born a samurai but gave up his status to live as a wandering poet. He is famous for his travel journal, *The Narrow Road of Oku*, and especially for his haiku, little word-picture poems:

> Such stillness—
> The cries of the cicadas
> Sink into the rocks.

> A crow perches
> On a leafless branch
> An autumn evening.

Or, on visiting a battlefield of the past, he wrote:

> The summer grass
> All that is left
> Of a warrior's dream.[5]

[5] D. Keene, ed., *Anthology of Japanese Literature* (New York: Grove Press, 1955), p. 371. Used by permission of Grove/Atlantic, Inc.

DOCUMENT | The Virtuous Wife

The three-generation stem family, composed of the older parents, their eldest son and his "bride," and their children, was the ideal during the Edo period. The principal family bond was between the parents and their elder son. The son's "bride," at least until she produced children of her own, was less than a full family member, as the adage "the womb is borrowed" suggests. Kaibara Ekken (1630–1714), an early Confucian moralist, propounded an ethic appropriate to such a family in his Greater Learning for Women. *It reflects the "wisdom" of his age.*

◆ Can people accept and practice any ethic that serves their society? Or are some ethics more "natural" than others? How did a girl raised in Tokugawa society feel? Could she embrace Ekken's teachings? Or does the following passage suggest, at least obliquely, that some human feelings are universal and difficult to deny?

Girl's Instruction

Seeing that it is a girl's destiny, on reaching womanhood, to go to a new home, and live in submission to her father-in-law, it is even more incumbent upon her than it is on a boy to receive with all reverence her parents' instructions. Should her parents, through their tenderness, allow her to grow up self-willed, she will infallibly show herself capricious in her husband's house, and thus alienate his affection; while, if her father-in-law be a man of correct principles, the girl will find the yoke of these principles intolerable. She will hate and decry her father-in-law, and the end of these domestic dissensions will be her dismissal from her husband's house and the covering of herself with ignominy. Her parents, forgetting the faulty education they gave her, may, indeed, lay all the blame on the father-in-law. But they will be in error; for the whole disaster should rightly be attributed to the faulty education the girl received from her parents.

The Infirmities of Woman

The five worst infirmities that afflict the female are indocility, discontent, slander, jealousy, and silliness. Without any doubt, these five infirmities are found in seven or eight out of every ten women, and it is from these that arises the inferiority of women to men. A woman should cure them by self-inspection and self-reproach.

The Wife's Miscellaneous Duties

A woman has no particular lord. She must look to her husband as her lord, and must serve him with all worship and reverence, not despising or thinking lightly of him. The great lifelong duty of a woman is obedience. In her dealings with her husband, both the expression of her countenance and style of her address should be courteous, humble, and conciliatory, never peevish and intractable, never rude and arrogant—that should be a woman's first and chiefest care. When the husband issues his instructions, the wife must never disobey them. In doubtful cases she should inquire of her husband, and obediently follow his commands. If ever her husband should inquire of her, she should answer to the point—to answer in a careless fashion would be a mark of rudeness. Should her husband be roused at any time to anger, she must obey him with fear and trembling, and not set herself up against him in anger and forwardness. A woman should look on her husband as if he were Heaven itself, and never weary of thinking how she may yield to her husband and thus escape celestial castigation.

Kaibara Ekken, *Greater Learning for Women* in K. Hoshino, *The Way of Contentment* (London: John Murray, 1913, reprinted 1979), pp. 33–34, 44–45.

Contrast Bashō's sense of the transience of life with the worldliness humor of the townsman:

> From a mountain temple
> The snores of a monk and
> the voice of the cuckoo.
>
> Showing a love-letter
> to her mother
>
> From a man she doesn't love.
> Even the most virtuous woman
> will undo her sash
> For a flea.[6]

[6] R. H. Blyth, *Japanese Humor* (Tokyo: Japanese Travel Bureau, 1957), p. 141.

This is not to say, of course, that townspeople did not write proper haiku as well.

Literature and Drama   Is cultural creativity more likely during periods of economic growth and political change or during periods of stability? The greatest works of literature and philosophy of Tokugawa Japan were produced between 1650 and 1725, just as the initial political transformation was being completed but the economy was still growing and the society was not yet set in its ways.

One of the major literary figures and certainly the most entertaining was Ihara Saikaku (1642–1693), who is generally credited with having re-created Japanese fiction. Saikaku was heir to an Osaka merchant house. He was raised to be its master, but after his wife died he let the head clerk manage the

◀ **Kabuki Theater.** One of Edo's three Kabuki theaters during the 1790s. The male actors provide the drama—even female roles are played by men. The audience eats, drinks, and smokes while watching the action. Note the mix of social classes: Day laborers at center-left sit on boards while well-to-do merchants occupy more expensive seats in the right and left foreground. At bottom-center an artisan cadges a light for his pipe. Several boxes to his left, another pours a drink. A reprint of a three-panel woodblock print by Utagawa Toyokuni (1769–1825) from the late 1790s.

Toyokuni Utagawa. Interior of a Theater. Nineteenth Century © Musee Grimet, Paris, France. Giraudon/Art Resource, N.Y.

business and devoted himself to poetry, theater, and the pleasure quarters. At the age of forty he wrote and illustrated *The Life of an Amorous Man,* the story of a modern and bawdy Prince Genji who cuts a swath through bathhouse girls, shrine maidens, courtesans, and boy actors. The overnight success of the work led to a sequel, *The Life of an Amorous Woman,* the tale of a woman undone by passion and of her downward spiral through the minutely graded circles of the Osaka demimonde. Saikaku also wrote more than twenty other works, including *The Japanese Family Storehouse,* which humorously chronicles the contradictions between the pursuit of wealth and the pursuit of pleasure.

A second major figure of Osaka culture at the turn of the century was the dramatist Chikamatsu Monzaemon (1653–1724). Born a samurai in Echizen province, Chikamatsu entered the service of a court aristocrat in Kyoto and then, in 1705, moved to Osaka to write for both the Kabuki and the puppet theater. Kabuki had begun early in the seventeenth century as suggestive skits and erotic dances performed by troupes of actresses. In 1629 the *bakufu* forbade women to perform on the stage. By the 1660s Kabuki had evolved into a more serious drama with male actors playing both male and female roles. Actors entered the stage on a raised runway or "flower path" through the audience. Famous actors took great liberties in interpreting plays, to roars of approval from the audience. There was a ready market for woodblock prints of actors in their most famous roles—like posters of rock musicians today, but done with incomparably greater artistry.

The three main types of Kabuki plays were dance pieces, which were influenced by the tradition of the Nō; domestic dramas; and historical pieces. Chikamatsu wrote all three. In contrast to Saikaku's protagonists, the men and women in Chikamatsu's dramas struggle to fulfill the duties and obligations of their stations in life. Only when their passions become uncontrollable, which is generally the case, do the plays end in

tragedy. The emotional intensity of the ending is heightened by the restraint shown by the actors before they reach their breaking point. In some plays the hero and heroine leave duty behind and, hoping for felicity in the next world, set out on a flight to death. Indeed, this ending was banned by *bakufu* authorities when the excessive popularity of the drama led to its imitation in real life.

It is interesting to compare Kabuki and the Nō drama. Nō is like early Greek drama in that the chorus provides the narrative line. In Nō, the stylization of action is extreme. In Kabuki, as in Elizabethan drama, the actors declaim their lines in the dramatic realism demanded by the commoner theatergoers of seventeenth-century Japan. But to convey the illusion of realism required some deviation from it. As Chikamatsu himself noted about Kabuki: "Many things are said by the female characters which real women could not utter. … It is because they say what could not come from a real woman's lips that their true emotions are disclosed." For him, "Art is something that lies in the slender margin between the real and the unreal.[7] Yet, for all that Chikamatsu was concerned with the refinements of his craft and the balance between emotional expressiveness and unspoken restraints, he never talked of the mysterious "no mind" as the key to an actor's power. His dramas are a world removed from the religiosity of the medieval Nō.

In the early eighteenth century Kabuki was displaced in popularity by the puppet theater (Bunraku). Many of Chikamatsu's plays were written for this genre. The word "*puppet*" does not do justice to the half-life-sized human figures, which rival Nō masks in their artistry. Manipulated by a team of three, a puppet does not only kneel and bow or engage in swordplay but can mimic brushing a tear from the eye with its kimono sleeve or threading a needle. In the late eighteenth century the puppet theater, in turn, declined, and as the center of cul-

---

[7] Tsunoda, de Bary, Keene, *Japanese Tradition,* p. 448.

ture shifted from Osaka to Edo, Kabuki again blossomed as Japan's premier form of drama.

Confucian Thought   The most important change in Tokugawa intellectual life was that the ruling elite abandoned the religious teachings of Buddhism in favor of the more secular worldview of Confucius, opening many avenues for further changes. (See Document, "A Tokugawa Skeptic.") The reworking occurred slowly. During the seventeenth century samurai were enjoined never to forget the arts of war and to be ever ready to die for their lord. One samurai in his deathbed poem lamented dying on *tatami*—with his boots off, as it were. In this period, most samurai were illiterate and saw book learning as unmanly. Nakae Tōju (1608–1648), a samurai and a Confucian scholar, recounted that as a youth he swaggered around with his friends during the day and studied secretly at night so as not to be thought a sissy. Schools, too, were slow to develop. One Japanese scholar has noted that in 1687 only four domains had proper domain schools; in 1715, only ten.

The great figures of Tokugawa Confucianism lived during the same years as Saikaku and Chikamatsu, in the late seventeenth and early eighteenth centuries. They are great because they succeeded in the difficult task of adapting Chinese Confucianism to fit Japanese society. One problem, for example, was that in Chinese Confucianism there was no place for a shōgun, whereas in the Japanese tradition of sunline emperors there was no room for the Mandate of Heaven. Most Tokugawa thinkers handled this discrepancy by saying that Heaven gave the emperor its mandate and that the emperor then entrusted political authority to the shōgun. One philosopher suggested that the divine emperor acted for Heaven and gave the mandate to the shōgun. Neither solution was very comfortable, for, in fact, the emperor was as much a puppet as those in the Osaka theater.

Another problem was the difference between China's centralized bureaucratic government and Japan's "feudal" system of lord-vassal relationships. Samurai loyalty was clearly not that of a scholar-official to the Chinese emperor. Some Japanese thinkers solved this problem rather ingeniously by saying that it was China that had deviated from the feudal society of the Chou sages, whereas in Japan, Tokugawa Ieyasu had re-created just such a society.

A third problem concerned the "central flowery kingdom" and the barbarians around it. No philosopher could quite bring himself to say that Japan was the real middle kingdom and China the barbarian, but some argued that centrality was relative, and still others suggested that China under barbarian Manchu rule had lost its claim to universality. These are just a few of a large range of problems related to Japanese political organization, Shinto, and to Japanese family practices. By the early eighteenth century these problems had been addressed,

and a revised Confucianism acceptable for use in Japan had come into being.

Another point to note is the continuing vitality of Japanese thought—Confucian and otherwise—into the mid–nineteenth century. This vitality is partly explained by the disputes among different schools of Confucianism and partly, perhaps, by Japan's lack of an examination system. The best energies of its samurai youth were not channeled into writing the conventional and sterile "eight-legged essay" that was required in the Chinese examination system. Official preferment—within the constraints of Japan's hereditary system—was often obtained by writing a proposal for domain reforms, although this could sometimes lead to punishments as well.

The vitality was also a result of the rapid expansion of schools from the early eighteenth century. By the early nineteenth century every domain had its own official school and a school on its Edo estate. Commoner schools (*terakoya*), in which reading, writing, and the rudiments of Confucianism were taught, grew apace. In the first half of the nineteenth century private academies also appeared throughout the country. By the late Tokugawa era about 40 to 50 percent of the male population and 15 to 20 percent of the female population was literate—a far higher rate than in most of the world, and on a par with European late developers.

Other Developments in Thought   For Tokugawa scholars, the emotional problem of how to deal with China was vexing. Their response was usually ambivalent. They praised China as the teacher country and respected its creative tradition. They studied its history, philosophy, and literature, and began a tradition of scholarship on China that has remained powerful to this day. But they also sought to retain a separate Japanese identity. Most scholars dealt with this problem by adapting Confucianism to fit Japan. But two schools—never in the mainstream of Tokugawa thought, but growing in importance during the eighteenth and early nineteenth centuries—arrived at more radical positions. The schools of National Studies and Dutch Studies were diametrically opposed in most respects but alike in criticizing the Chinese influence on Japanese life and culture.

National Studies began as philological studies of ancient Japanese texts. One source of its inspiration was Shinto; another was the Neo-Confucian School of Ancient Learning. Just as the School of Ancient Learning had sought to discover the original, true meanings of the Chinese classics before they were contaminated by Song metaphysics, so the scholars in the National Studies tradition tried to find in the Japanese classics the original true character of Japan before it had been contaminated by Chinese ideas. On studying the *Record of Ancient Matters*, *The Collection of Myriad Leaves*, or *The Tale of Genji*, they found that the early Japanese spirit was free, spontaneous,

CHRONOLOGY

Tokugawa Era (1600–1868)

1600	Tokugawa Ieyasu reunifies Japan
1615	"Laws of Military Houses" issued
1639	Seclusion policy adopted
1642	Edo hostage system in place
1644–1694	Bashō, poet
1653–1724	Chikamatsu Monzaemon, dramatist
1701	The forty-seven rōnin avenge their lord
1853, 1854	Commodore Matthew Perry visits Japan

clean, lofty, and honest, in contrast to the Chinese spirit, which they characterized as rigid, cramped, and artificial. Some writings of this school appear to borrow the anti-Confucian logic of Daoism.

A second characteristic of National Studies was its reaffirmation of Japan's unique creation, and by extension, the uniqueness of its emperor. Motoori Norinaga (1730–1801) wrote of Shinto creationism as the "Right Way":

> Heaven and Earth, all the gods and all phenomena, were brought into existence by the creative spirits of two deities. ... This ... is a miraculously divine act the reason for which is beyond the comprehension of the human intellect.
>
> But in foreign countries where the Right Way has not been transmitted, this act of divine creativity is not known. Men there have tried to explain the principle of Heaven and earth and all phenomena by such theories as the yin and yang, the hexagrams of the Book of Changes, and the Five Elements. But all of these are fallacious theories stemming from the assumptions of the human intellect and they in no wise represent the true principle.
>
> The "special dispensation of our Imperial Land" means that ours is the native land of the Heaven-Shining Goddess who casts her light over all countries in the four seas. Thus our country is the source and fountainhead of all other countries, and in all matters it excels all the others.[8]

National Studies became influential during the late Tokugawa era. It had a small but not unimportant influence on the Meiji Restoration. Its doctrines continued thereafter as one strain of modern Japanese ultranationalism. Its most enduring achievement was in Japanese linguistics. Even today, scholars admire Motoori's philology. Moreover, in an age when the

prestige of things Chinese was overwhelming, Motoori helped redress the balance by appreciating and giving a name to the aesthetic sensibility found in the Japanese classics. The phrase he used was *mono no aware*, which means, literally, "the poignancy of things."

But National Studies had several weaknesses that prevented it from becoming the mainstream of Japanese thought. First, even the most refined sensibility is no substitute for philosophy. In its celebration of the primitive, National Studies ran headlong into the greater rationality of Confucian thought. Second, National Studies was chiefly literary, and apart from its enthusiasm for the divine emperor, it had little to offer politically in an age when political philosophy was central in both the domain and the *bakufu* schools.

A second development was Dutch Studies. After Christianity had been proscribed and the policy of seclusion adopted, all Western books were banned in Japan. Some knowledge of Dutch was maintained among the official interpreters who dealt with the Dutch at Nagasaki. The ban on Western books (except for those propagating Christianity) was ended in 1720 by the shōgun Tokugawa Yoshimune (r. 1716–1745), following the advice of a scholar whom he had appointed to reform the Japanese calendar.

During the remainder of the eighteenth century, a school of "Dutch medicine" became established in Japan. Japanese pioneers early recognized that Western anatomy texts were superior to Chinese. The first Japanese dissection of a corpse occurred in 1754. In 1774 a Dutch translation of a German anatomy text was translated into Japanese. By the mid–nineteenth century there were schools of Dutch Studies in the main cities of Japan, and instruction was available in some domains as well. Fukuzawa Yukichi (1835–1901), who studied Dutch and Dutch science during the mid-1850s at a school begun in 1838 in Osaka, wrote in his *Autobiography* of the hostility of his fellow students toward Chinese learning:

> Though we often had discussions on many subjects, we seldom touched upon political subjects as most of us were students of medicine. Of course, we were all for free intercourse with Western countries, but there were few among us who took a serious interest in that problem. The only subject that bore our constant attack was Chinese medicine. And by hating Chinese medicine so thoroughly, we came to dislike everything that had any connection with Chinese culture. Our general opinion was that we should rid our country of the influences of the Chinese altogether. Whenever we met a young student of Chinese literature, we simply felt sorry for him. Particularly were the students of Chinese medicine the butt of our ridicule.[9]

---

[8] Tsunoda, de Bary, Keene, *Japanese Tradition*, pp. 521, 523.

[9] E. Kiyooka, trans., *The Autobiography of Fukuzawa Yukichi* (New York: Columbia University Press, 1966), p. 91.

DOCUMENT   A Tokugawa Skeptic

Confucian teachings, while hardly scientific, placed a premium on rational argument. Some scholars used this rationalism to attack Buddhism. Others directed their attack against superstitions and explanations of natural phenomena that they found wanting. The following passages by Miura Baien (1723–1789), the son of a Kyushu doctor, exemplify such a rationalism.

◆ Does modern science answer the kind of question that Baien is raising? Are some superstitions in modern societies still vulnerable to his critique?

Why do a pair of dark things on the forehead see; why do a pair of holes in the head hear? Why don't eyes hear, why don't ears see? When most people come to these points they just leave them alone, but I simply can't leave them alone. ... They refer the question to past authority, and when they find a book that deals with it, they accept whatever answer it gives. I can't convince myself entirely in that way. When they discuss the natural world, they do so in a wild, hit-or-miss manner; when they talk of life and death, they do so in an absurd or obscure manner. Though their evidence may be flimsy and their arguments preposterous, this does not disturb people at all.

[It is] a human peculiarity ... to view everything as human. Take, for example, children's picture books, *The Betrothal of Rats* or *Monsters and Goblins*. Rats are never kept as rats in their true shape; instead all of them are turned into human forms. The bridegroom appears in the book in ceremonial robes with a pair of swords, while the bride is shown with a flowing gown on and snowy cap of cotton, and is carried in a palanquin with an escort of footmen and young guards. In the book of *Monsters and Goblins*, no cases are found of an umbrella turning into a tea-mortar, or of a broom changing into a bucket. But all monsters and goblins are given eyes and noses and hands and feet, so as to look like members of the human family. ...

It is such an imagination as this that populates heaven with a supreme God, and earth with gods of wind and thunder. Monstrous in form, they all move by foot, and do their work by hand. Wind is put in bags, thunder is beaten out on drums. If they are real bags, how are they made? And there must be skin to make a drum. If such imaginings are carried further, the sun will be unable to go on revolving unless it gets feet, and nature will be helpless in her work unless she has hands.

R. Tsunoda, W. T. de Bary, and D. Keene, eds., *Sources of the Japanese Tradition* (New York: Columbia University Press, 1960), pp. 490, 493–494.

While medicine was the primary occupation of those who studied Dutch, some knowledge of Western astronomy, geography, botany, physics, chemistry, and arts also entered Japan. Works on science occasionally influenced other thinkers as well. Yamagata Bantō (1748–1821) was a rich and scholarly Osaka merchant who devised a rationalistic philosophy based on a synthesis of Neo-Confucianism and Western science. After studying a work on astronomy, he wrote in 1820 that conditions on other planets "varied only according to their size and their proximity to the sun." Bantō also speculated that "grass and trees will appear, insects will develop; if there are insects, fish, shellfish, animals and birds will not be absent, and finally there will be people too." Bantō qualified his argument with the naturalistic supposition that Mercury and Venus would probably lack human life, "since these two planets are near to the sun and too hot." He contrasted his rational arguments regarding evolution with the "slap-dash" arguments of Buddhists and Shintoists.[10]

From the late eighteenth century the Japanese began to be aware of the West, and especially of Russia, as a threat to Japan. In 1791 a concerned scholar wrote *A Discussion of the Military Problems of a Maritime Nation*, advocating a strong navy and coastal defenses. During the early nineteenth century such concerns mounted. A sudden expansion in Dutch Studies occurred after Commodore Matthew Perry's visits to Japan in 1853 and 1854. During the 1860s Dutch Studies became Western Studies, as English, French, German, and Russian were added to the languages studied at the *bakufu* Institute for the Investigation of Barbarian Books. In sum, Dutch Studies was not a major influence on Tokugawa thought. It cannot begin to compare with Neo-Confucianism. But it laid a foundation on which the Japanese built quickly when the need arose.

KOREA AND VIETNAM

A feature of world history, noted earlier, is the spread of heartland civilizations into their surrounding areas. In East Asia the heartland civilization was that of China; the surrounding areas that were able to take in Chinese learning were Japan, Korea,

[10] M. Jansen, ed., *Changing Japanese Attitudes Toward Modernization* (Princeton, NJ: Princeton University Press, 1965), p. 144.

and Vietnam. Like the Japanese, Koreans and Vietnamese learned to write using Chinese ideographs. They partially modeled their governments on those of China. They accepted Chinese Buddhism and Confucianism, and with them Chinese conceptions of the universe, state, and human relationships. The Confucian definitions of the relations between ruler and minister, father and son, and husband and wife were emphasized in Korea and Vietnam as they were in China. But at the same time, Koreans and Vietnamese, who spoke non-Chinese tongues, saw themselves as separate peoples, and gradually came to take pride in their independence. In Europe, Germany might be a parallel case: It became civilized by borrowing the heartland Graeco-Christian culture of the Mediterranean area, but it kept its original tongue and elements from its earlier culture.

Korea

A range of mountains along its northern rim divides the Korean peninsula from Manchuria, making it a distinct geographical unit. Mountains continue south through the eastern third of Korea, while in the west and south are coastal plains and broad river valleys. The combination of mountains, rice paddies, and sea makes Korea a beautiful land. The traditional name for Korea may be translated as the "land of the morning calm." Two further geographical factors affected Korean history. One was that the northwestern corner of Korea was only 300 miles from the northeastern corner of historical China: close enough for Korea to be vulnerable to invasions by its powerful neighbor but far enough away so that most of the time China found it easier to treat Korea as a tributary than to control it directly. The other factor was that the southern rim of Korea was just one hundred miles distant from the Japanese southern island of Kyushu across the Tsushima Straits.

EARLY HISTORY

During its old and new stone ages, Korea was peopled by Tungusic tribes moving south from northeast Asia. They spoke an Altaic tongue—distantly related to Japanese and to Manchurian, Mongolian, and Turkic. They lived by hunting, gathering, and fishing, and, like other early peoples of northeast Asia, made comb-patterned pottery and practiced an ani-

◀ **Glazed Pot.** Celadon glazes spread from China to Korea during the Koryo period (918–1392). Pots such as this late-12th- or early-13th-century ewer are prized by collectors around the world for their graceful contours and detail. Melon-shaped Ewer, Stoneware. Koryo dynasty, ca. 12th century H. 9" × Diam. 19 1/2". Korea. The Avery Brundage Collection/Asian Art Museum of San Francisco.

mistic religion. During the first millennium B.C.E. agriculture, bronze and iron were introduced, transforming their primitive society. But Koreans were still ruled by tribal chiefdoms in 108 B.C.E. when the Han emperor Wudi sent an army into north Korea to menace the flank of the Hunnish (Xiongnu) empire that spread across the steppe to the north of China. Wudi built a Chinese city—near the present-day capital of North Korea—which survived into the fourth century C.E., and established commanderies and prefectures to administer the land.

Between the fourth and seventh centuries three archaic states emerged from earlier tribal confederations. Silla, one of the three, aided by armies from Tang China, conquered the other two in the seventh century. The Tang armies wanted to stay and rule Korea, but after battles with Silla troops they withdrew, and Silla was recognized by China in 675 as an autonomous tribute state. The period of Silla rule may be likened to Nara Japan: Korea borrowed Chinese writing, established some government offices on the Chinese model, sent annual embassies to the Tang court, and took in Chinese Buddhism and Chinese arts and philosophies. Yet within the Silla government, birth mattered more than scholarship and rule by aristocrats continued, while in village Korea, the worship of nature deities was only lightly touched by the Buddhism that spread among the ruling elites.

Silla underwent a normal end-of-dynasty decline, and in 918 a warlord general founded a new dynasty, the Koryo. The English word "Korea" is derived from this dynastic name. This was a creative period. Korean scholars advanced in their mastery of Chinese principles of government. New genres of poetry and literature appeared. Korean potters made celadon vases rivaling those of China. The craft of history advanced: The earliest surviving history of Korea was compiled in 1145. Printing using moveable metallic type was invented during the thirteenth century. But most important of all was the growth of Buddhism. Temples, monasteries, and nunneries were built throughout the land, and Buddhist arts flourished. During the thirteenth century, Buddhist scholars produced in classical

Chinese a printed edition of the Tripitaka, a huge compendium of sutras and other sacred writings.

Despite cultural advances, the Koryo state was weak. For one thing, the Koryo economy was undeveloped: Trade was by barter, money did not circulate, and Chinese missions commented on the extravagance of officials in the capital and the squalor of commoners and slaves in Korea's villages. For another, the dynasty was aristocratic from the start, and as centuries passed, private estates and armies arose, and civil officials were replaced by military men. For still another, frequent incursions from across Korea's northern border weakened the state. The cost of wars with the Mongols was particularly high. The Koryo court survived as long as it did by becoming in succession the tributary of the Song, Liao, Chin, and Mongol dynasties.

THE CHOSON ERA: LATE TRADITIONAL KOREA

In 1392, a Koryo general, Yi Songgye, switched his allegiance from the Mongols to the rising Ming state, deposed the Koryo king, and founded a new dynasty. It lasted for 518 years until 1910; its amazing longevity was directly related to the stability of Ming-Qing China.

After seizing power, Yi carried out an extensive land reform and strengthened his government by absorbing into his officialdom members of the great Koryo families. During the Yi or Choson period, these elite families, known as *yangban*, monopolized education, official posts, and land. Beneath them were the commoners known as "good people," tax-paying free subjects of the king. Beneath the commoners and constituting perhaps one third of the population were government and private slaves. Korean scholars argue that they were not like slaves in other lands, since there were no slave auctions, and, following Confucian teachings, husbands were not separated from their wives. But Korean slaves were nonetheless property. They were often attached to land, they could be given as gifts, and their children were slaves to be used as their owners willed.

Early Choson culture showed many signs of vigor. Lyrical poetry and then prose reached new heights. In 1443, a group of scholars under King Sejong—who was regarded as a sage—invented a simple alphabet for the transcription of Korean without the burden of Chinese ideographs. Such was the prestige of Chinese writing that the simple alphabet was not used until modern times. The most important intellectual trend during the Choson era was the gradual movement of the *yangban* away from Buddhism and their acceptance of Neo-Confucianism. By the late fifteenth century, Korean philosophers were making original contributions to the philosophy of this school, contributions that later became influential in Japan.

But at mid-dynasty, invasions dealt a severe blow to the well-being of Choson society. Hideyoshi, having brought all of Japan under his control, decided to conquer China; for him, the path to China was through Korea. His samurai armies devastated Korea twice, once in 1592 and again in 1596. The invasions ended with his death in 1598. On both occasions the Ming court sent troops to aid its tributary, but the rescuing Chinese armies, in turn, devastated the land almost as much as had the Japanese. A third disaster occurred in 1627 and 1637 when Manchu troops invaded pro-Ming Korea, laying waste to the northwest and to Seoul. The result of these multiple incursions was a drop in taxable land to about a quarter of its late-sixteenth-century level. Behind this statistic lay a grim reality of famine, death, and misery.

Had the late-sixteenth-century Choson government been stronger, it might have recovered. But from the end of the fifteenth century cliques of officials had begun to fight among themselves, and their partisan struggles intensified during the centuries that followed. On the surface, the struggles took the form of debates over issues relating to the king or queen. In actuality, they were bitter contests between the growing numbers of educated sons of *yangban* families over a limited number of official positions. Many in the losing factions were executed—at times dismembered—or imprisoned. As the struggles became more fierce, the effectiveness of government declined, except for a brief recovery during the early eighteenth century. High officials in Seoul used their power to garner private agricultural estates, and established local academies to prepare their own kinsmen for the official examinations.

From the mid–seventeenth century on, Korea offers a mixed picture. Literacy rose and a new popular fiction of fables, romances, and novels appeared. Women writers became important for the first time. Among some *yangban* there was a philosophic reaction against what was perceived as the emptiness of Neo-Confucianism. Calling for "practical learning" to effect a renewal of Korean society, scholars criticized the Confucian classics and outlined plans for administrative reforms and the encouragement of commerce. Unfortunately, their recommendations were not adopted, and the society continued its decline. More Koreans died in the famine

CHRONOLOGY

Korea

108 B.C.E.–4th century C.E.	Chinese rule in northern Korea
4th century C.E.–675	Three archaic states
675–918	Silla
918–1392	Koryo
1392–1910	Choson
1592, 1596	Japanese invasions of Korea
1627, 1637	Manchu invasions of Korea
1671	Famine

of 1671 than during Hideyoshi's invasions. Overtaxation, drought, floods, pestilence, and famine became commonplace. Robberies occurred in daytime Seoul, and bandits plagued the countryside. Disgruntled officials led peasants in month-long revolts in 1811 and 1862. Because of the concentration of officials, wealth, and military power at Seoul and because of Manchu support for the ruling house, neither revolt succeeded in toppling the dynasty, but the revolts left Korea with neither the will nor the means to meet the challenges it would soon face.

Vietnam

EARLY VIETNAM

Vietnam has been likened to two baskets on a carrying pole. One basket is the Red River basin, centering on Hanoi in the north, the other the delta of the Mekong centering on Saigon (today Ho Chi Minh City) in the south. The carrying pole is the narrow mountainous strip of central Vietnam with little river valleys opening to the South China Sea (see Map 19–4). Until the late fifteenth century, Vietnamese inhabited only the northern half of what is today Vietnam, that is to say, the basin of the Red River, which flows from west to east and empties into the Gulf of Tongking. Unlike other Southeast Asian peoples, whose culture was either Indic or Islamic, Vietnamese higher culture came from China.

Central Vietnam and part of the southeastern coast was inhabited by the Chams, a people ethnically closer to Indonesians than to Vietnamese. The Chams were a sea-faring people, who engaged in trade and piracy. They early became Hindu-Buddhist and later Muslim. They were united in the kingdom of Champa and waged intermittent wars against the Vietnamese to their north. Southern Vietnam, that is to say the Mekong River delta, was ruled by Hindu-Buddhist Cambodian empires and inhabited mainly by Cambodians.

The political history of the Vietnamese in the Red River basin began in 208 B.C.E. when a renegade Han dynasty general formed the state of Nan Yueh. Its capital was near the present-day Chinese city of Guangzhou. It ruled over peoples in both southeastern China and the Red River basin. In Vietnamese, the Chinese ideograph *Yueh* is read "Viet." The name "Vietnam," literally, "Viet to the south," is derived from the name of this early state. Nan Yueh lasted for about a century until 111 B.C.E., when the armies of Han Wudi conquered it and brought it under Chinese control. After that, the Red River basin was ruled by China for more than one thousand years.

For the first seven centuries, Vietnam was a Chinese military commandery—like those established in Korea and other border regions to govern non-Chinese "barbarian" populations. The administrative center was initially a fort with a Chinese governor and Chinese troops. The governor ruled indirectly through local Vietnamese chiefs or magnates. In 39 C.E. the Trung sisters led a revolt against Chinese rule—the husband of one had been executed by the Chinese. The sisters later became national heroes. As a fifteenth-century Vietnamese poet put it:

> All the male heroes bowed their heads in submission;
> Only the two sisters proudly stood up to avenge the country.[11]

But in that age there was little sense of "country," and the only consequence of the revolt was a further strengthening of Chinese controls.

Vietnamese society advanced during the centuries of Chinese rule. Early Vietnamese had a matrilineal tribal society, practiced slash-and-burn agriculture, and moved their settlements when their lands became exhausted. New agricultural techniques, introduced from China, made possible permanent settlements and denser populations. Tribal organization gave way to village society, and matrilineal to patrilineal descent—though women continued to enjoy a higher status than in China. Buddhism entered, replacing or mingling with earlier animistic beliefs. Chinese officials sometimes married Vietnamese women, and a Sino-Vietnamese social elite arose in the capital. The influence of Chinese higher culture was largely confined to this elite.

During the Tang dynasty (618–907), Vietnam was still treated as a border region, but Chinese administration became stronger. Elements of Chinese law and, possibly, the Chinese land and tax system were introduced at this time. Also, the Red River basin was divided into provinces, which the Chinese referred to collectively as **Annam**, the "pacified south." When the French came to Vietnam in the nineteenth century, they picked up the term and called the north Vietnamese *Annamese*.

Since it was during the Tang that Japan and Korea also took in Chinese learning, one can ask whether Vietnam was a parallel case. In some regards it was. In all three societies Buddhism entered, flourished in the capitals, and gradually percolated into local areas, where it absorbed elements from earlier indigenous religions. In all three, other aspects of China's higher culture affected mainly the elites of the society, while an older way of life continued in villages with only small changes. But where Japanese and Korean rulers reached out for Chinese learning and technology and used it for their own ends, the Vietnamese had it thrust upon them. In the ninth century the Japanese devised a phonetic syllabary for the transcription of their language, and by the year 1000 were writing works such as *The Tale of Genji*—reflecting a new culture in which native and Chinese elements were fused. In Vietnam, where both the rulers and the written language were Chinese, no such transformation occurred.

[11] K. W. Taylor, *The Birth of Vietnam* (1983). p. 334.

OVERVIEW   The Religions of Southeast Asia

The countries of Southeast Asia, the area between India and China, have been influenced by Indian, Chinese, Muslim, and, since the sixteenth century, Western culture and religion. Hinduism, Buddhism, Islam, and Christianity were brought to the area by invaders, merchants, and missionaries. Their presence is reflected in the religious makeup of the countries of Southeast Asia in the twenty-first century. While most of these countries are predominately Buddhist, Muslim, or Christian, most of them also include many adherents of other religions.

Predominately Buddhist	Burma
	Thailand, but with a significant Muslim minority
	Cambodia
	Laos
	Vietnam, but with a large Roman Catholic, minority
	Singapore includes Muslim, Christian, and Hindu minorities
Predominately Muslim	Indonesia; but the island of Bali is Hindu, and there is a large Christian minority
	Malaysia, but with Hindu, Buddhist, and Christian minorities
	Brunei
Predominately Christian	Philippines, but with a sizeable Muslim minority

THE SECOND MILLENNIUM: POLITICS AND SOCIETY

Ten major revolts occurred during the thousand years of Chinese rule—a not unusual number for a Chinese border region with a non-Chinese population. The last revolt, which took place in 939, when China was weak, led to the establishment of

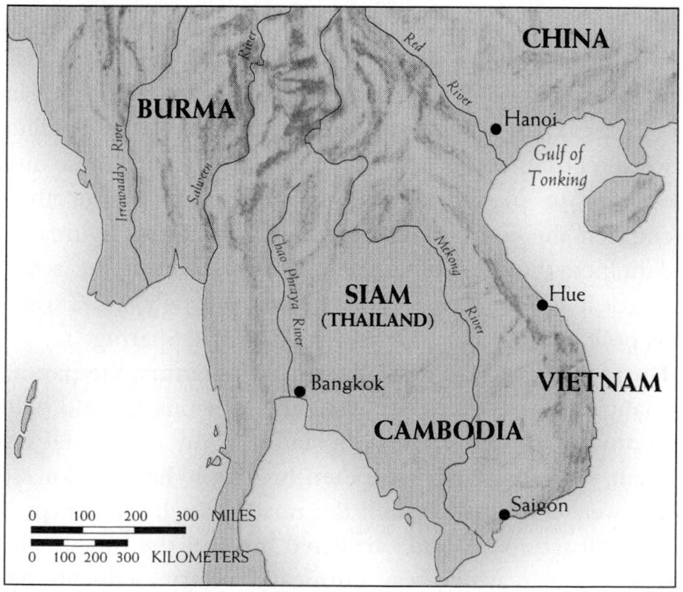

MAP 19–4 Vietnam and Neighboring Southeast Asia.

an independent Vietnamese government. Vietnam never again became a part of China.

The history of Vietnam's second millennium is conventionally broken into dynastic blocks named after the ruling family:

Ly	1009–1225
Tran	1225–1400
Le	1428–1787
Nguyen	1802–1880s

Vietnamese dynasties, however, were not the strong, centralized, bureaucratic states found in Chinese history. From the beginnings of dynasties, there were tensions between the center and periphery. At the center were the social elites who ruled the population of the Red River delta. At the periphery were magnates—powerful local figures who controlled upland peoples. Of these peripheral areas, the province of Thanh Hoa, one hundred miles south of the Hanoi capital, was of particular importance with magnates who were usually autonomous and often opposed the dynasty. Both center and periphery maintained military forces and sometimes engaged in wars. Often, several independent states coexisted during the timespan of a single "dynasty."

Chinese invasions also affected Vietnamese history. Most Chinese dynasties, as they expanded, attempted to reconquer the "south" that had once been ruled by China. Such invasions were repelled—though Ming armies occupied Vietnam for twenty years from 1407. But rather than defying China altogether, Vietnamese rulers found it easier to accommodate: Every Vietnamese dynasty became a "tributary" of China and sent missions that professed the Vietnamese ruler's submission to the Chinese emperor. In official communications with the Chinese "emperor," the Vietnamese rulers styled themselves as "kings," indicating their subordinate status.

Such submission, however, was purely formal. Within Vietnam, Vietnamese rulers styled themselves as "emperors" and claimed their mandate to rule came directly from Heaven, separate but equal to the mandate received by the Chinese emperor. They also denied the universality of the Chinese imperium by referring to China not as the Middle Kingdom but as the Northern Court—their own government being the Southern Court. In 1076, a Vietnamese general fighting Chinese troops wrote the following poem:

> The Southern emperor rules the Southern land
> Our destiny is writ in Heaven's Book
> How dare you bandits trespass on our soil
> You shall meet your undoing at our hands[12]

One should note that the poem was in Chinese, Vietnam's only written language, and couched in the terminology of Chinese political thought.

Two momentous developments occurred in Vietnam during the fifteenth century. The first was the increased use of Chinese institutions and culture as an advanced technology to strengthen government. The reforms of Le Thanh Tong (1442–1497), an immensely talented early Le dynasty ruler, were especially notable. He divided his realm into thirteen provinces and then into prefectures, counties, and departments. He weakened the nobility by holding civil service examinations for the selection of officials and set up nine ranks of civil and military officials. He established schools, introduced Neo-Confucian learning, and promoted public works. He registered the population and reinstituted a Chinese-type land tax. Over decades such reforms would break down, until another reformer came along, but nonetheless, Chinese culture had a more lasting influence than Chinese arms.

The second development, after years of conflict, was the destruction of the Champa state by the same Le Thanh Tong in 1471. To help rule the culturally alien Chams, he promulgated in 1483 a Confucian-tinged legal code that remained in effect through most of the dynasty. He also established colonies of Vietnamese soldier-peasants along the coast of the former kingdom. Thus began the centuries-long movement of Vietnamese into the central and southern portions of what is today Vietnam. Vietnamese historians label this movement "the march to the south," but it might be more apt to call it a "drift." Le Thanh Tong's suc-

cessors were unable to hold together the territories he had conquered. Autonomous Vietnamese states arose in the area, which impeded the passage of settlers to the south during the sixteenth and early seventeenth centuries.

Demography and politics became entwined. During the late Le dynasty, the north was actually ruled by the Trinh family, and central Vietnam was ruled, from 1558, by the Nguyen family, whose capital was in the city of Hue. The two states fought during the early 1600s, but in 1673 agreed on a truce: They would separately rule the two parts of the country while paying lip service to the Le dynasty. In the mid–seventeenth century the Mekong delta was sparsely populated, mostly by Cambodians and Chams. The post-Ming diaspora of Chinese throughout Southeast Asia began during the seventeenth century. By the century's end substantial numbers of Chinese immigrants had settled and formed communities in the Mekong delta. Some became Saigon merchants, selling rice to Chinese merchants in Singapore. Today about a million partially assimilated Chinese live in southern Vietnam and play a major role in its economy. Vietnamese also began to move south. The Nguyen court in Hue extended its rule to Saigon in 1698, when it sent an official to settle a dispute between Chinese and Cambodians. By 1757 the Nguyen had extended their control over the entire Mekong delta westward to the Gulf of Siam. Political control facilitated the further movement of Vietnamese to the south, though they remained a minority in southern Vietnam throughout the eighteenth century.

During the late eighteenth century wars broke out again between the Nguyen and the north. By 1802 the Nyugen had defeated the opposing armies, unified the country, and established a new dynasty. It kept its capital at Hue. In coming to power the new emperor had been aided by French advisors and adventurers, several of whom were rewarded with high official posts. The Nguyen dynasty, nonetheless, became more Chinese than any previous dynasty. It adopted the law codes of Manchu China and established institutions such as the Six Boards, Hanlin Academy, Censorate, and a hierarchy of civil and military officials recruited by examinations. The reasons for these initiatives were to placate Confucian scholars in the north, to strengthen the court, and to weaken the military figures who had helped the dynasty's rise. From the time of the second emperor it also became anti-French and strongly anti-Christian in its policies. (See Document, "On Husband-Sharing.")

During the first half of the nineteenth century, Vietnam was probably governed better than in any previous era and better than any other Southeast Asian state. By any traditional standard, it was governed competently. But it had weaknesses. There were tensions between the north, which was overpopulated, well schooled, and furnished most of the official class, and the south, which was ethnically diverse, educationally backward, and poorly represented in government. Trade and

---

[12] S. T. Huynh, *The Heritage of Vietnamese Poetry* (1979), p. 3. Reprinted by permission. Yale University Press.

DOCUMENT | On Husband-Sharing

The position of women in Vietnam may have been higher than in China, but Vietnamese officials still had concubines when they could afford them. The eighteenth-century poet Ho Xuang Huong gives her view on the subject.

◆ Should this poem be read as a criticism of the prevailing Confucian ethos?

One rolls in warm blankets,
The other freezes:

Down with this husband-sharing!
You're lucky ever to have him,
He comes perhaps twice a month,
Or less.
Ah—to fight for—this!
Turned to a half-servant, an unpaid maid!
Had I known
I would have stayed single.

From *A Thousand Years of Vietnamese Poetry* by Nguyen Ngoc Bich. Copyright © 1975 by The Asia Society. Reprinted by permission.

---

artisanal industries were less developed than in China and Japan, only small amounts of specie circulated, and periodic markets were more common than market towns. The government rested on a society composed largely of self-sufficient villages. In sum, Vietnam entered the second half of the nineteenth century even less prepared than China or Japan for the challenges it would soon face.

Southeast Asia

The historical civilizations of Southeast Asia were shaped by four movements. One was the movement of peoples and languages from north to south. Ranges of mountains rising in Tibet and South China extend southward, dividing Southeast Asia into river valleys. The Mon and Burmese peoples had moved from the southeast slopes of the Tibetan plateau into the Upper Irrawaddy by 500 B.C.E., and continued south along the Irrawaddy and Salween Rivers, founding the kingdom of Pagan in 847 C.E. Thai tribes moved south from China down the valley of the Chao Phraya River somewhat later, founding the kingdoms of Sukhothai (1238–1419) and Ayutthaya (1350–1767). Even today Thai-speaking tribes are still to be found in several south China provinces. The Vietnamese, too, arose in the north and moved into present-day central and south Vietnam only in recent historical times.

A second movement was the Indianization of Southeast Asia (see Chapters 4 and 13). Between the first and fifteenth centuries Indian traders and missionaries crossed the Bay of Bengal and established outposts throughout Southeast Asia. As Hinduism and Buddhism spread through the region, Indian-type states with god-kings were established, and Indian scripts, legal codes, literature, drama, art, and music were adopted by the indigenous peoples. Today, Burma, Thailand, and Cambodia retain an Indian-type of Buddhism; on the walls of Bangkok temples are painted scenes from the great Hindu epic, the *Mahabharata.*

A third movement of considerable dynamism was of Arab and Indian traders who sailed across the Indian Ocean to dominate trade with the Spice Islands (the Moluccas of present-day Indonesia) between the thirteenth and fifteenth centuries (see Chapter 13). Settling on the coasts and islands of Southeast Asia, they married into local ruling families and spread the teachings of Islam. Local rulers who converted became sultans. Today Malaysia and Indonesia are predominantly Muslim. The majestic Buddhist temple at Borobudur in central Java is a monument of an earlier age, submerged today in a sea of Islamic practice. Only the Hindu island of Bali to the east of Java retains the Indian religion that once covered the entire Indonesian archipelago.

A fourth movement was the Chinese **diaspora**. The emigration of Chinese to most parts of the world but especially to Southeast Asia began as a trickle and gathered momentum after 1842, after the post-Opium War treaties. Most Chinese went, initially, as indentured labor to work on plantations. But in time many moved to cities and opened shops. The mercantile ethos of Chinese was more advanced than that of peoples to the south. Even today the casual visitor to Bangkok sees shopkeepers sitting in front of their shops reading Chinese newspapers. Their children became educated. Some went into banking or law. In most of Southeast Asia the urban economies were largely developed and controlled by Chinese. This created resentments and, occasionally, anti-Chinese riots. To appease the powers that be, Chinese companies routinely appointed non-Chinese politicians or generals to their boards of directors. The greatest concentrations of Chinese, apart from Singapore (three quarters of the population), were in Malaysia, Indonesia, and Thailand. Assimilation occurred at a steady but generational pace.

Fisherman on an Autumn River.

Summary

China   China's last two imperial dynasties were the Ming (1368–1644) and the Qing or Manchus (1644–1911). Although China could not match the dynamism of the West during these years, its society became more integrated and its government more sophisticated. The population reached 410 million, cities grew, and commerce expanded. Chinese government depended on the Confucian bureaucracy and the gentry class. Under the Manchus, China expanded to the east and annexed Taiwan. There also was growing trade with the West, especially Britain, but it was conducted under highly restricted terms by Chinese officials.

Japan   After more than a century of civil war among the warrior aristocracy (the Warring States era, 1467–1600), the Tokugawa shōguns (1600–1868) restored order. Their government controlled the aristocracy and encouraged economic growth. Christianity, which had made many converts in Japan, was driven underground, and Japan was closed to the outside world except for a small Dutch presence at Nagasaki. Japanese drama, literature, and art flourished, as did commercial life.

Korea and Vietnam   China considered both Korea and Vietnam to be tributary states, and both countries adopted Chinese Confucian culture and forms of government while preserving their political independence.

Southeast Asia   Southeast Asian civilizations have been heavily influenced by the movement of peoples, religions (especially Hinduism and Buddhism), and the Chinese diaspora, which increased in the nineteenth century.

Review Questions

1. What factors led to economic growth in late traditional China?

2. Did Manchu rule resemble Mongol rule, or was it different? Explain. In what regards were other manchus, Kangxi and Qianlong, indistinguishable from the Chinese emperors?

3. Ming-Qing foreign relations set the stage for China's nineteenth-century encounter with the West. How would you describe the setting?

4. How did military technology in Japan change during the fifteenth and sixteenth centuries? Was unification the consequence or would it have happened anyway?

5. Contrast the dynamism of social engineering in seventeenth-century Japan with the high-level equilibrium of the eighteenth and early nineteenth centuries. How did these influence changes in Japanese thought?

6. In what sense was Chinese culture a "technology" used by Japan, Korea, and Vietnam for state building? Why were the results in each country so different?

7. Why can Southeast Asian civilizations be described as syncretistic?

Key Terms

Annam (p. 566)

daimyo (p. 545)

diaspora (p. 564)

gentry (p. 536)

Kabuki (p. 553)

Nō play (p. 553)

National Studies (p. 559)

yangban (p. 563)

Documents CD-ROM

Imperial China and the Diffusion of East Asian Civilization
9.6 Thai Civilization: Southeast Asia

Late Traditional Asia
16.1 Matteo Ricci, Journals
16.2 Dynastic Change in China Tears a Family Apart
16.3 Ceremonial for Visitors: Court Tribute
16.4 Taisuke Mitamura, The Palace Eunuchs of Imperial China

16.5 Letter to King George: China and Great Britain
16.6 Japan Encounters the West
16.7 The Laws for the Military House (Buke Shohatto), 1615

East Asia Responds to the West
21.7 President Filmore, "Letter to the Emperor of Japan"

NOTE: *To learn more about the topics in this chapter, see the Suggested Readings at the end of the book.*

State Building
and Society
in Early Modern Europe

Vie des bords de la Neva en descendant la riviere entre le Palais
d'hyver de Sa Majesté Imperiale & les batimens de l'Academie des Sciences

◄ Throughout the age of the splendor at the court of Louis XIV
millions of French peasants endured lives of poverty and
hardship.
Erich Lessing/Art Resource, N.Y.

State Building and Society in Early Modern Europe

By the second quarter of the eighteenth century, the major European powers were not yet nation-states in which the citizens felt themselves united by a shared sense of community, culture, language, and history. They were still monarchies in which the personality of the ruler and the personal relationships of the great noble families considerably influenced public affairs. As yet they differed little in political and social structures from many other societies in the world, and still lagged behind India, China, and some parts of the Islamic world in population density and urbanization. However, industry and military technology were beginning to reverse the global balance of power between Europe and Asia.

These European states displayed certain problems that also characterized the governments of China and Japan during the same epochs. In particular, as in Japan, the problem of a balance between centralization and decentralization arose in virtually all the European states. In France, Russia, and Prussia, the forces of centralization proved quite strong. In Austria the forces of decentralization were powerful. England achieved a rather delicate balance. Furthermore, as in Tokugawa, Japan, European states of the eighteenth century generally saw an increase in legal codification and in the growth of bureaucracy. Only in Prussia did the military influence on society resemble that in Japan.

The role of the personality of the monarch in Europe bore some resemblance to that of certain Manchu emperors in China, such as Kangxi (1662–1722) and Qianlong (r. 1736–1795). Louis XIV and Peter the Great had no less influence on their nations than did these great Manchu emperors. All of them built up military strength and fostered innovation. However, although European rulers developed state bureaucracies, none of them put together so brilliant a group of trained civil servants as those who administered China. The roots of the Chinese civil service went back centuries, and Chinese civil servants, unlike those in Europe, tended to resist modernization of the Chinese government and economy for both practical and ideological reasons. Civil servants in Europe, perhaps because they rose to power simultaneously with Europe's industrialization, tended to foster rather than obstruct modernization, which posed no threat to their power or worldview.

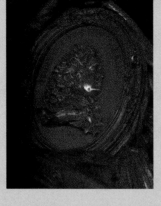

The global commercial empires of France, Spain, and England gave rise to fierce commercial rivalries. The drive for empire and commercial supremacy propelled these states into contact with Africa, Latin America, India, China, and Japan. Spain and Portugal had long exploited Latin America as their own monopoly, an arrangement that England challenged in the eighteenth century. China's lack of interest in dominating the Indian Ocean opened the way for European adventurers and traders in India. France and England fought for commercial supremacy in India, and by the 1760s England had, in effect, conquered the subcontinent. The slave trade between Africa and the New World flourished throughout the eighteenth century. European merchants and navies also sought to penetrate East Asia, although their success was limited until the advent of nineteenth-century "gunboat diplomacy." As this term implies, European success in Africa, Asia, and the Indian Ocean was always closely linked to its sophisticated military technology, and especially the construction of sturdy ships able to carry heavy cannons. As a result of these developments, European commerce dominated the world for the next two centuries. Europe and its colonists extracted labor and other natural resources from virtually all the other continents of the world. These assets in turn only widened the growing gap in wealth and power that separated Europe from the rest of the world in the nineteenth and twentieth centuries.

Consequently, by the mid–eighteenth century, the European states that just two centuries earlier lagged behind China in wealth and technology, had made their power and influence felt throughout the world. Beginning in the early eighteenth century, the political power of the European states became linked to a qualitatively different economic base than any seen elsewhere in the world. That political and economic combination allowed Europe to dominate the world from the 1750s to the Second World War.

THINK AHEAD

◆ How did European states resemble those in other parts of the world in the mid-eighteenth century? How did they differ?

◆ What was the relationship between military technology, especially naval power, and the growth of European colonial empires?

ETWEEN THE EARLY SEVENTEENTH AND MID–TWENTIETH centuries no region so dominated other parts of the world politically, militarily, and economically as Europe. Such had not been the situation before that time and would not be the situation after World War II. However, for approximately three and a half centuries northwestern Europe became the chief driving force in one world historical development after another. Two broad factors accounted for this situation.

First, by the mid–eighteenth century five major states had come to dominate European politics and would continue to do so until at least World War I. They were Great Britain, France, Austria, Prussia, and Russia. These states established their dominance at the expense of Spain, Portugal, the United Provinces of the Netherlands, Poland, Sweden, and the Ottoman Empire. Equally essential to their rise was the weakness of the Holy Roman Empire after the Peace of Westphalia (1648).

Commencing in the late seventeenth century these five successful states entered upon over a hundred years of warfare among themselves. These wars were fought first in Europe and then in Europe and the European colonial empires, making them the first extensive world wars. These conflicts produced the most extensive European impact on the non-European world since the early sixteenth century when the Spanish had conquered the civilizations of Mexico and Peru.

The second factor in the dominance of Europe on the world scene was that during these decades the peoples living primarily in northwestern Europe undertook a series of economic advances that laid the foundation for the social and economic transformation of the world. Europeans began for the first time in their history to achieve a more or less stable food supply. For reasons still much debated, the population of Europe commenced a major period of growth. New inventions in the manufacture of textiles transformed Europe's productive capacity, and the invention of the steam engine, powered by coal as a fuel, opened the way for moving manufacturing from the countryside to cities. Furthermore, the production of iron greatly expanded. These developments, known collectively as the Industrial Revolution, gave Europe a productive capacity previously unknown in human history. That state of economic advance provided Europeans with the tools to dominate much of the world both economically and militarily.

European Political Consolidation
TWO MODELS OF EUROPEAN POLITICAL DEVELOPMENT

In the second half of the sixteenth century, changes in European military organization, weapons, and tactics sharply increased the cost of warfare. Because traditional sources of state income could not finance these growing military costs, monarchs sought new revenues. Monarchies that succeeded in building a secure financial base independent of the support of noble estates, diets, or assemblies achieved what later became known as absolute rule. The French monarchy was the most successful example of such centralized government. The English monarchy, by contrast, failed to make itself absolute, but rather by the end of the seventeenth century could govern only with and through Parliament. These differing paths of political development led to the two distinct models of government—**absolutism** in France and **parliamentary monarchy** in England—that shaped subsequent political development in Europe.

TOWARD PARLIAMENTARY GOVERNMENT IN ENGLAND

When Elizabeth I died in 1603 without children, the English crown passed to James VI of Scotland, the son of Mary Queen of Scots, who became James I of England, the first of the Stuart dynasty. In their pursuit of adequate income, Stuart monarchs of seventeenth-century England threatened the local political interests and economic well-being of the nobility and the landed and commercial elites represented in Parliament. These groups in turn over the course of the decades invoked traditional English liberties to effectively resist the monarchs. Furthermore, **Puritans** in the Church of England, whose Protestant religious views derived from John Calvin, wished to see a more radical reformation carried out in England. While attempting to rule as much as possible without Parliament, both James I (r. 1603–1625) and his son Charles I (r. 1625–1649) also resisted the Puritan demands and at the same time favored peaceful relations with the Roman Catholic powers Spain and France. (See Document, "King James I

DOCUMENT | King James I Defends Popular Recreation Against the Puritans

The English Puritans believed in strict observance of the Sabbath, disapproving any sports, games, or general social conviviality on Sunday. James I thought these strictures prevented many Roman Catholics from joining the Church of England. In 1618, he ordered the clergy of the Church of England to read the Book of Sports *from their pulpits. In this declaration, he permitted people to engage in certain sports and games after church services. His hope was to allow innocent recreations on Sunday while encouraging people to attend the Church of England. Despite the king's good intentions, the order offended the Puritans. The clergy resisted his order and he had to withdraw it.*

◆ What motives of state might have led James I to issue this declaration? How does he attempt to make it favorable to the Church of England? Why might so many clergy have refused to read this statement to their congregations?

With our own ears we heard the general complaint of our people, that they were barred from all lawful recreation and exercise upon the Sunday's afternoon, after the ending of all divine service, which cannot but produce two evils: the one the hindering of the conversion of many [Roman Catholic subjects], whom their priests will take occasion hereby to vex, persuading them that no honest mirth or recreation is lawful or tolerable in our religion, which cannot but breed a great discontentment in our people's hearts, especially as such as are peradventure upon the point of turning [to the Church of England]: the other inconvenience is, that this prohibition barreth the common and meaner sort of people from using such exercises as may make their bodies more able for war, when we or our successors shall have occasion to use them; and in place thereof sets up filthy tipplings and drunkenness, and breeds a number of idle and discontented speeches in their ale-houses. For when shall the common people have leave to exercise, if not upon the Sundays and holy days, seeing they must apply their labor and win their living in all working days? ...

[A]s for our good people's lawful recreation, our pleasure likewise is, that after the end of divine service our good people be not disturbed, ... or discouraged from any lawful recreation, such as dancing, either men or women; archery for men, leaping, vaulting, or any other such harmless recreation, or from having of Hay-games, Whitsun-ales, and Morris-dances; and the setting up of May-poles and other sports therewith used; ... but withal we do here account still as prohibited all unlawful games to be used upon Sundays only, as bear and bull-baitings ... and at all times in the meaner sort of people by law prohibited, bowling.

And likewise we bar from this benefit and liberty all such known as recusants [Roman Catholics], either men or women, as will abstain from coming to church or divine service, being therefore unworthy of any lawful recreation after the said service, that will not first come to the church and serve God; prohibiting in like sort the said recreations to any that, though [they] conform in religion [i.e., members of the Church of England], are not present in the church at the service of God, before their going to the said recreations.

Excerpt pp. 400–403 from *Documents of the Christian Church*, 2nd ed. edited by Henry Bettenson. Copyright © 1963. Reprinted by permission of Oxford University Press.

Defends Popular Recreation Against the Puritans.") Consequently the first two Stuarts confronted a combined political and religious opposition to their efforts to make the English monarchy the supreme power in the land. Many of the same political leaders who saw themselves defending traditional English liberties against the monarchy also saw themselves as having to protect the Protestant Reformation in England.

By 1642 the conflict between Charles I and Parliament over religion and arbitrary taxation erupted into civil war. In 1645 the parliamentary and Puritan forces triumphed. Disputes continued, and in 1649 a rump Parliament from whom any opposing members had been removed voted for the execution of Charles I. Thereafter, Parliament abolished the monarchy, the House of Lords, and the established Church of England. What replaced them was a Puritan republic led by Oliver Cromwell (1599–1658), the victorious general in the civil war.

Cromwell himself soon encountered difficulties with Parliament and from 1653 onward governed as a military dictator.

After Cromwell died in 1658, disillusionment with Puritan strictness and political uncertainty led to the restoration of the Stuart monarchy under Charles II (r. 1660–1685). The restored monarch would have extended very considerable religious toleration, but the restored Parliament dominated by conservative members of the Church of England imposed a restrictive religious code on the land. Thereafter the Church of England found itself opposed by both Protestant Non-Conformists and Roman Catholics. Charles II in 1670 entered a secret treaty with Louis XIV of France to oppose the Dutch. As a result of that treaty, Charles again attempted to extend religious toleration. Parliament resisted by passing a Test Act that required all officials to take an oath, which no Roman Catholic could in good conscience take.

Charles I ruled for several years without calling Parliament, but once he began a war with Scotland, he needed revenues that only Parliament could supply.
Musée du Louvre, Pans/Superstock.

Oliver Cromwell. His model army defeated the royalists in the English Civil War. After the execution of Charles I in 1649, Cromwell dominated the short-lived English republic, conquered Ireland and Scotland, and ruled as Lord Protector from 1653 until his death in 1658.
Stock Montage, Inc./Historical Pictures Collection.

James, Duke of York, Charles's brother, was a Roman Catholic and became monarch in 1685. Immediately he extended toleration to both Roman Catholics and the Protestant Non-Conformists. In June 1688 James II (r. 1685–1688) imprisoned seven Anglican bishops who had refused to publicize his suspension of laws against Catholics. Under the guise of a policy of enlightened toleration, James was actually seeking to subject all English institutions to the power of the monarchy.

The English political classes had hoped that James would be succeeded by Mary (r. 1689–1694), his Protestant eldest daughter. She was the wife of William of Orange (1650–1702), stadtholder of the Netherlands, great-grandson of William the Silent (1533–1584), and the leader of European opposition to Louis XIV. But on June 20, 1688, James II's Catholic second wife gave birth to a son. There was now a Catholic male heir to the throne. The Parliamentary opposition invited William to invade England to preserve its "traditional liberties," that is, the Anglican Church and parliamentary government.

THE "GLORIOUS REVOLUTION"

William of Orange arrived with his army in November 1688 and was received without opposition by the English people. James fled to France, and Parliament in 1689 proclaimed William III and Mary II the new monarchs, thus completing the bloodless **Glorious Revolution**. William and Mary, in turn, recognized a Bill of Rights that limited the powers of the monarchy and guaranteed the civil liberties of the English privileged classes. Henceforth, England's monarchs would be subject to law and would rule by the consent of Parliament, which was to be called into session every three years. The Bill of Rights also prohibited Roman Catholics from occupying the English throne. The Toleration Act of 1689 permitted worship by all Protestants but outlawed Roman Catholics and those who denied the Christian doctrine of the Trinity.

CHRONOLOGY

England

1603	James VI of Scotland becomes James I of England
1625	Charles I becomes king of England
1629	Charles I dissolves Parliament and embarks on eleven years of personal rule
1640	April–May, Short Parliament; November, Long Parliament convenes
1642	Outbreak of the Civil War
1649	Charles I executed
1649–1660	Various attempts at a Puritan Commonwealth
1660	Charles II restored to the English throne
1670	Secret Treaty of Dover between France and England
1672	Parliament passes the Test Act
1685	James II becomes king of England
1688	Glorious Revolution
1689	William III and Mary II come to the throne of England
1701	Act of Settlement provides for Hanoverian Succession
1702–1714	Queen Anne, the last of the Stuarts
1714	George I of Hanover becomes king of England
1721–1742	Ascendancy of Sir Robert Walpole

The measure closing this century of strife was the Act of Settlement in 1701. This bill provided for the English crown to go to the Protestant House of Hanover in Germany if Anne (r. 1702–1714), the second daughter of James II and the heir to the childless William III, died without issue. Thus, at Anne's death in 1714, the Elector of Hanover became King George I of England (r. 1714–1727), the third foreigner to occupy the English throne in just over a century.

Under the Hanoverians, Britain achieved political stability and economic prosperity during the first quarter of the eighteenth century. Robert Walpole (1676–1745) eventually became George I's chief minister. Walpole's ascendancy from 1721 to 1742 was based on royal support, his ability to handle the House of Commons, and his iron-fisted control of government patronage. He maintained peace abroad and promoted the status quo at home. Britain's foreign trade spread from New England to India. Agriculture became more productive. Because the dominant economic groups were represented in Parliament, they were willing to pay the taxes to support a powerful military force, particularly a strong navy. As a result, Great Britain became not only a European power of the first order, but also eventually a world power.

The power of the British monarchs and their ministers had real limits. Parliament could not wholly ignore popular pressure. Even with the extensive use of patronage, many members of Par-

liament maintained independent views. Newspapers and public debate flourished. Free speech could be exercised, as could freedom of association. There was no large standing army. Walpole's enemies could and did openly oppose his policies in a fashion impossible on the Continent. Consequently, the English state embodied both very considerable military power and political liberty. British political life became the model for all progressive Europeans who questioned the absolutist political developments of the Continent. Furthermore, many of the political values that had emerged in the British Isles during the seventeenth century also took deep root among their North American colonies.

RISE OF ABSOLUTE MONARCHY IN FRANCE: THE WORLD OF LOUIS XIV

The French monarchy trod a very different political path. Louis XIV (r. 1643–1715) came to the throne at the age of five. During his childhood Cardinal Mazarin (1602–1661), his chief

▲ **Louis XIV of France** (r. 1643–1715) was the dominant European monarch in the second half of the 17th century. The powerful centralized monarchy he created established the prototype for the mode of government later termed absolutism.
Bridgemann-Giraudon/Art Resource, N.Y.

minister, tried to impose direct royal administration on France. These efforts aroused a series of widespread rebellions among French nobles between 1649 and 1652 known as the Fronde (after the slingshot used by street boys).

YEARS OF PERSONAL RULE

On the death of Mazarin in 1661 Louis XIV assumed personal control of the government at the age of twenty-three. Convinced by the Fronde that heavy-handed policies could endanger the monarchy, Louis concentrated unprecedented authority in the monarchy, but he took care not to intrude excessively on local social and political institutions. He appointed no chief minister. Rebellious nobles would now be challenging the king directly; they could not claim to be resisting only a bad minister.

Louis ruled through powerful councils that controlled foreign affairs, the army, domestic administration, and economic regulations. Each day he spent hours with the chief ministers of these councils, whom he chose from families long in royal service or from among people just beginning to rise in the social structure. Unlike the more ancient noble families, they had no real or potential power bases in the provinces and depended solely on the king for their standing in both government and society.

More than any other monarch of the day, Louis XIV used the physical setting of his court to exert political control. The palace at Versailles, built between 1676 and 1708 on the outskirts of Paris, became Louis' permanent residence after 1682. It was a temple to royalty, architecturally designed and artistically decorated to proclaim the glory of the Sun King, as

CHRONOLOGY

France

1649–1652	The Fronde, a revolt of nobility and townspeople against the crown
1661	Louis assumes personal rule
1667	Louis XIV invades Flanders
1672	France invades the United Provinces
1678–1679	Peace of Nijmwegen
1682	Louis establishes his court at Versailles
1685	Edict of Nantes revoked
1689–1697	Nine Years' War between France and the League of Augsburg
1697	Peace of Ryswick
1702–1714	War of the Spanish Succession
1713	Treaty of Utrecht between England and France
1714	Treaty of Rastadt between the emperor and France

Louis was known. A spectacular estate with magnificent fountains and gardens, it housed thousands of the more important nobles, royal officials, and servants. Moments near the king were important to most court nobles because they were effectively excluded from the real business of government. The king's rising and dressing were times of rare intimacy, when nobles could whisper their special requests in his ear. Fortunate nobles held his night candle as they accompanied him to his bed.

An important source for Louis's concept of royal authority was his devout tutor, the political theorist Bishop Jacques-Bénigne Bossuet (1627–1704). In direct contrast to the English Puritan challenges to royal authority, Bossuet defended what he called the "**divine right of kings**." He cited examples of Old Testament rulers divinely appointed by and answerable only to God. Medieval popes had insisted that only God could judge a pope; so Bossuet argued that only God could judge the king. Although kings might be duty bound to reflect God's will in their rule, yet as God's regents on earth they could not be bound to the dictates of mere nobles and parliaments. Such assumptions lay behind Louis XIV's alleged declaration: "*L'état, c'est moi*" ("I am the state").

Louis was determined to unify France religiously. In October 1685 he revoked the Edict of Nantes (1598) which had extended protections to the Huguenots. (See Document, "Louis XIV Revokes the Edict of Nantes.") Protestant churches and schools were closed, Protestant ministers exiled, nonconverting laity forced to be galley slaves, and Protestant children ceremonially baptized by Catholic priests. The revocation prompted the emigration of more than a quarter million people, who formed new communities and joined the resistance to France in England, Germany, Holland, and the New World.

As will be seen later in the chapter, Louis used most of the wealth and authority he had amassed to lead France into a long series of wars that ultimately weakened the nation by the time of his death in 1715. Yet despite those failures he had established a model of strong centralized monarchy that other monarchs in central and eastern Europe would copy. They believed Louis had been more successful than the Stuart monarchs of Great Britain, who by the early eighteenth century could rule only with and through Parliament.

RUSSIA ENTERS THE EUROPEAN POLITICAL ARENA

The emergence of Russia as an active European power was a wholly new factor in European politics. Previously, Russia had been considered part of Europe only by courtesy, and before 1673 it did not send permanent ambassadors to Western Europe. Geographically and politically, it lay on the periphery. Hemmed in by Sweden on the Baltic and by the Ottoman Empire on the Black Sea, Russia had no warm-water ports.

Believing a country could not be under one king and one law unless it was also under one religious system, Louis XIV stunned much of Europe in October 1685 by revoking the Edict of Nantes, which had protected the religious freedoms and civil rights of French Protestants since 1598.

> ◆ What specific actions does this declaration order against Protestants? Do.es it offer any incentives for Protestants to convert to Catholicism?

Art. 1. Know that we ... with our certain knowledge, full power and royal authority, have by this present, perpetual and irrevocable edict, suppressed and revoked the edict of the aforesaid king our grandfather, given at Nantes in the month of April, 1598, in all its extent ... together with all the concessions made by [this] and other edicts, declarations, and decrees, to the people of the so-called Reformed religion, of whatever nature they be ... and in consequence we desire ... that all the temples of the people of the aforesaid so-called Reformed religion situated in our kingdom ... should be demolished forthwith.

Art. 2. We forbid our subjects of the so-called Reformed religion to assemble any more for public worship of the above-mentioned religion. ...

Art. 3. We likewise forbid all lords, of whatever rank they may be, to carry out heretical services in houses and fiefs ... the penalty for ... the said worship being confiscation of their body and possessions.

Art. 4. We order all ministers of the aforesaid so-called Reformed religion who do not wish to be converted and to embrace the Catholic, Apostolic, and Roman religion, to depart from our kingdom and the lands subject to us within fifteen days from the publication of our present edict ... on pain of the galleys.

Art. 5. We desire that those among the said [Reformed] ministers who shall be converted [to the Catholic religion] shall continue to enjoy during their life, and their wives shall enjoy after their death as long as they remain widows, the same exemptions from taxation and billeting of soldiers, which they enjoyed while they fulfilled the function of ministers. ...

Art. 8. With regard to children who shall be born to those of the aforesaid so-called Reformed religion, we desire that they be baptized by their parish priests. We command the fathers and mothers to send them to the churches for that purpose, on penalty of a fine of 500 livres or more if they fail to do so; and afterwards, the children shall be brought up in the Catholic, Apostolic, and Roman religion. ...

Art. 10. All our subjects of the so-called Reformed religion, with their wives and children, are to be strongly and repeatedly prohibited from leaving our aforesaid kingdom ... or of taking out ... their possessions and effects. ...

The members of the so-called Reformed religion, while awaiting God's pleasure to enlighten them like the others, can live in the towns and districts of our kingdom ... and continue their occupation there, and enjoy their possessions ... on condition ... that they do not make public profession of [their religion].

S. Z. Ehler and John B. Morrall, eds. and trans., *Church and State Through the Centuries: A Collection of Historic Documents* (New York: Biblo and Tannen, 1967), pp. 209–213. Reprinted by permission of Biblo and Tannen Booksellers and Publishers.

Its chief outlet for trade to the west was Archangel on the White Sea, which was ice-free for only part of the year.

BIRTH OF THE ROMANOV DYNASTY

The second half of the sixteenth century had witnessed enormous political turmoil during the last half of the reign of Ivan IV (r. 1533–1584), later known as Ivan the Terrible. A period known as the Time of Troubles followed his death. In 1613, hoping to end the uncertainty, an assembly of nobles elected as tsar a seventeen-year-old boy named Michael Romanov (r. 1613–1645). Thus began the dynasty that ruled Russia until 1917. Though a new dynasty had been established, Russia remained weak and impoverished. The *boyars*, the old nobility, controlled the bureauacracy, while the *streltsy*, or guards of the Moscow garrison, persistently posed the danger of mutiny.

PETER THE GREAT

In 1682, another boy—ten years old at the time—ascended the fragile Russian throne as co-ruler with his half brother. His name was Peter (r. 1682–1725), and Russia would never be the same after him. He and his sickly brother, who died in 1696, had come to power on the shoulders of the *streltsy*, who expected to be rewarded for their support. Like Louis XIV, the dangers and turmoil of his youth convinced Peter of two things: First, the power of the tsar must be made secure from the jealousy of the *boyars* and the greed of the *streltsy*; second, the military power of Russia must be increased.

Northwestern Europe, particularly the military resources of the maritime powers, fascinated Peter I, who eventually became known as Peter the Great. In 1697, he made a famous visit in transparent disguise to Western Europe. There he

CHRONOLOGY

Rise of Russian Power

1533–1584	Reign of Ivan the Terrible
1584–1613	Time of Troubles
1613	Michael Romanov becomes tsar
1682	Peter the Great becomes tsar as a boy
1689	Peter assumes personal rule
1697	European tour of Peter the Great
1698	Peter suppresses the *streltsy*
1700	The Great Northern War opens between Russia and Sweden; Russia defeated at Narva by Charles XII
1703	Saint Petersburg founded
1709	Russia defeats Sweden at Poltava
1718	Death of Alexis, son of Peter the Great
1721	Peace of Nystad ends the Great Northern War
1721	Peter establishes control over the Russian church
1722	The Table of Ranks
1725	Peter dies, leaving an uncertain succession

spent his happiest moments inspecting shipyards, docks, and the manufacture of military hardware in England and the Netherlands. Peter returned to Moscow determined to copy the technology he had seen abroad, for he knew warfare would be necessary to make Russia a great power. But he also understood his goal would require him to confront the long-standing power and traditions of the Russian nobles.

Taming the *Streltsy* and *Boyars* In 1698, before Peter's return from abroad, the *streltsy* had rebelled. On his return, Peter brutally suppressed the revolt with private tortures and public executions, in which his own ministers took part. Approximately a thousand of the rebels were put to death, and their corpses remained on public display to discourage future disloyalty.

Peter then built a new military establishment that would serve the tsar and not itself. He introduced effective and ruthless policies of conscription, drafting an unprecedented 130,000 soldiers during the first decade of the eighteenth century and almost 300,000 troops by the end of his reign. He adopted policies for the officer corps and general military discipline patterned on those of West European armies.

Peter also determined to make a sustained attack on the *boyars* and their attachment to traditional Russian culture. After his European journey, he personally shaved the long beards of the court *boyars* and sheared off the customary long hand-covering sleeves of their shirts and coats, which had made them the butt of jokes among other European courts.

Peter became highly skilled at balancing one group against another, while never completely excluding any, as he set about to organize Russian government and military forces along the lines of the more powerful European states.

Developing a Navy In the mid-1690s, Peter oversaw the construction of ships to protect his interests in the Black Sea against the Ottoman Empire. In 1695, he began a war with the Ottomans. Part of the reason for Peter's trip to Western Europe in 1697 was to learn how to build still better warships, this time for combat on the Baltic. The construction of a Baltic fleet, largely constructed on the Finnish coast, was essential in the Great Northern War with Sweden (1700–1721), a struggle that over the years accounted for many of Peter's major steps toward Westernizing his realm. When the Great Northern War came to a close in 1721, the Peace of Nystad confirmed the Russian conquest of Estonia, Livonia, and part of Finland. Henceforth, Russia possessed ice-free ports and a permanent influence on European affairs.

Founding St. Petersburg At one point, the domestic and foreign policies of Peter the Great intersected. This was at the site on the Gulf of Finland where he founded his new capital city of St. Petersburg in 1703. There he built government structures and compelled the *boyars* to construct town houses. He thus imitated those European monarchs who had copied Louis XIV by constructing smaller versions of Versailles. The founding of St. Petersburg went beyond establishing a central imperial court, however; it symbolized a new Western orientation of Russia and Peter's determination to hold his position on the Baltic coast.

The Case of Peter's Son Aleksei and Reforms of Peter the Great's Final Years Other reforms arose from Peter's family difficulties. Peter's son Aleksei had been born to his first wife whom he had divorced in 1698. Peter was jealous of the young man, who had never demonstrated strong intelligence or ambition. Increasingly distrustful of his son, Peter became convinced by late 1717 that his court opponents looked to Aleksei as a focus for possible sedition while Russia remained at war with Sweden. Peter undertook an investigation during which he personally interrogated Aleksei, who was eventually condemned to death and died under mysterious circumstances on June 26, 1718.

The interrogations surrounding Aleksei had revealed greater degrees of court opposition than Peter had suspected. Recognizing he could not eliminate his numerous opponents the way he had attacked the *streltsy* in 1698, Peter undertook radical administrative reforms designed to bring the nobility and the Russian Orthodox Church more closely under the authority of persons loyal to the tsar.

Vüe des bords de la Neva en descendant la riviere entre le Palais
d'hyver de Sa Majesté Imperiale & les batimens de l'Academie des Sciences

Administrative Colleges   In December 1717 Peter reorganized his domestic administration to sustain his own personal authority and to fight rampant corruption. To achieve this goal, Peter looked to Swedish institutions called *colleges*—bureaus of several persons operating according to written instructions rather than departments headed by a single minister. These colleges, eight of which he imposed on Russian administration, were to look after matters such as the collection of taxes, foreign relations, war, and economic affairs. Each college was to receive advice from a foreigner. Peter used his appointive power to balance the influence in these colleges between nobles and persons he was certain would be personally loyal to himself.

Achieving Secular Control of the Church   Peter also moved to suppress the independence of the Russian Orthodox Church where some bishops and clergy had displayed sympathy for the tsar's son. In 1721, Peter simply abolished the position of *patriarch*, the bishop who had been head of the church. In its place he established a government department called the *Holy Synod* which consisted of several bishops headed by a layman called the *procurator general*. This body would govern the church in accordance with the tsar's secular requirements.

Table of Ranks   In 1722 Peter published a **Table of Ranks** intended to draw the nobility into state service. That table equated a person's social position and privileges with his rank in the bureaucracy or the military, rather than with his lineage among the traditional landed nobility, many of whom contin-

ued to resent the changes Peter had introduced into Russia. Peter thus made the social standing of individual *boyars* a function of their willingness to serve the central state.

For all the numerous decisive actions Peter had taken since 1717, he still had not settled on a successor. Consequently, when he died in 1725, there was no clear line of succession to the throne. For more than thirty years, soldiers and nobles again determined who ruled Russia. Peter had laid the foundations of a modern Russia, but not the foundations of a stable state.

THE HABSBURG EMPIRE AND THE PRAGMATIC SANCTION

After 1648 the Habsburg family retained a firm hold on the title of Holy Roman Emperor, but the power of the emperor depended less on force of arms than on the cooperation he could elicit from the various political bodies in the empire. These included large German units (such as Saxony, Hanover, Bavaria, and Brandenburg) and scores of small German cities, bishoprics, principalities, and territories of independent knights. While establishing their new dominance among the German states, the Habsburgs also began to consolidate their power and influence within their hereditary possessions outside the Holy Roman Empire, which included the Crown of Saint Wenceslas, encompassing the kingdom of Bohemia (in modern Czechoslovakia) and the duchies of Moravia and Silesia; and the Crown of Saint Stephen, which ruled Hungary, Croatia, and Transylvania. In each of their many territories, the Habsburgs ruled by virtue of a different title and needed the cooperation of the local nobility, which was not always forthcoming. They repeatedly had to bargain with nobles in one part of Europe to maintain their position in another.

Despite these internal difficulties, Leopold I (r. 1658–1705) managed to resist the advances of the Turks into central Europe, which included a siege of Vienna in 1683, and to thwart the aggression of Louis XIV. He achieved Ottoman recognition of his sovereignty over Hungary in 1699 and extended his territorial holdings over much of the Balkan Peninsula and western Romania (see Map 20–1).

In the early eighteenth century the Habsburg emperor Charles VI (r. 1711–1740) had no male heir, and there was only a weak precedent for a female ruler of the Habsburg domains. Charles feared that on his death the Austrian Habsburg lands might fall prey to the surrounding powers. Determined to prevent that disaster and to provide his domains with the semblance of legal unity, he devoted most of his reign to seeking the approval of his family, the estates of his realms, and the major foreign powers for a document called the *Pragmatic Sanction.*

This instrument provided the legal basis for a single line of inheritance within the Habsburg dynasty through Charles VI's daughter Maria Theresa (1740–1780). After extracting various concessions from Charles, the nobles of the various Habsburg domains and the other European rulers did likewise. Consequently, when Charles VI died in October 1740, he believed that he had secured legal unity for the Habsburg Empire and a safe succession for his daughter. Despite the Pragmatic Sanction, however, his failure to provide his daughter with a strong army or a full treasury left her inheritance open to foreign aggression. Less than two months after his death, the fragility of the foreign agreements became apparent. In December 1740 Frederick II of Prussia invaded the Habsburg province of Silesia. Maria Theresa had to fight for her inheritance.

THE RISE OF PRUSSIA

The rise of Prussia occurred within the German power vacuum created by the Peace of Westphalia. It is the story of the extraordinary Hohenzollern family, which had ruled Brandenburg since 1417. Through inheritance the family had acquired a series of territories, most of which were not contiguous with Brandenburg. By the late seventeenth century, however, the scattered Hohenzollern holdings represented a block of territory within the Holy Roman Empire second in size only to that of the Habsburgs.

Beginning in the mid–seventeenth century, Hohhenzollern rulers forged their geographically separated holdings into a powerful state by collecting taxes simply on their own authority and then building an army which allowed them to continue to enforce their will without the approval of the nobility.

There was, however, a political and social tradeoff between the Hohenzollerns and their various nobles. These **Junkers,** or

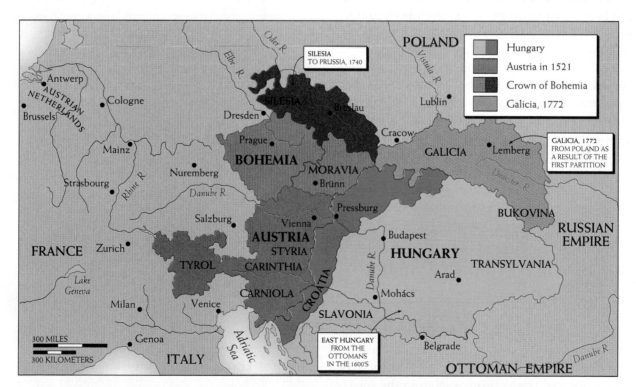

MAP 20–1 The Austrian Habsburg Empire, 1521–1772. The empire had three main units—Austria, Bohemia, and Hungary. Expansion was mainly eastward: eastern Hungary from the Ottomans (17th century) and Galicia from Poland (1772). Meantime, Silesia was lost after 1740, but the Habsburgs remained Holy Roman Emperors.

German noble landlords, were allowed almost complete control over the serfs on their estates. In exchange for their obedience to the Hohenzollerns, the *Junkers* received the right to demand obedience from their serfs. Furthermore taxes fell most heavily on the backs of the peasants and the urban classes. As the years passed, *Junkers* increasingly dominated the army officer corps, and this became even more pronounced during the eighteenth century. All officials and army officers took an oath of loyalty directly to the Hohenzollern rulers. The army and the Elector thus came to embody the otherwise absent unity of the state. The army made Prussia a valuable potential ally. As a result of providing aid to the Habsburg emperor in 1701, the Hohenzollerns were permitted the title of "King" in Prussia, one of their parcels of territory that lay inside Poland and outside the authority of the Holy Roman Emperor.

Frederick William I (r. 1713–1740) of Prussia organized the bureaucracy along military lines. The Prussian military grew from about 39,000 in 1713 to over 80,000 in 1740, making it the third- or fourth-largest army in Europe. Prussia's population, in contrast, ranked thirteenth in size. Separate laws applied to the army and to civilians. Laws, customs, and royal attention made the officer corps the highest social class of the state. Military service thus attracted the sons of *Junkers*. In this fashion the army, the *Junker* nobility, and the monarchy became forged into a single political entity. Military priorities and values dominated Prussian government, society, and daily life as in no other state in Europe. It has often been said that whereas other nations possessed armies, the Prussian army possessed its nation.

Although Frederick William I built the best army in Europe, he avoided conflict. His army was a symbol of Prussian power and unity, not an instrument for foreign adventures or aggression. At his death in 1740 he passed to his son Frederick II (Frederick the Great, r. 1740–1786) this superb military machine, but not the wisdom to refrain from using it. Almost immediately on coming to the throne, Frederick II upset the Pragmatic Sanction and invaded Silesia (see Map 20–2). He thus crystallized the Austrian-Prussian rivalry for the control of Germany that would dominate central European affairs for over a century.

European Warfare: From Continental to World Conflict

Without exception the emergence of Great Britain, France, Russia, the Habsburg Empire, and Prussia as the major European powers involved warfare. Whereas religious zeal had largely fueled the European wars of the Reformation era, dynastic and commercial rivalry drove wars from the reign of the Louis XIV through the conclusion of the Seven Years' War in 1763. Each round of warfare was geographically more wide-

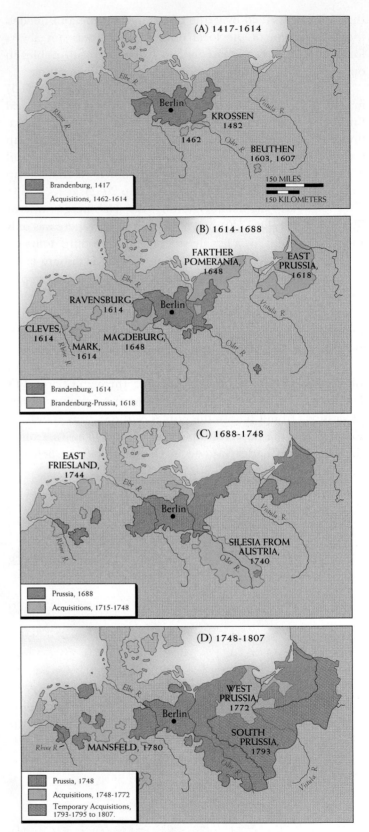

MAP 20–2 Expansion of Brandenburg-Prussia. In the 17th century Brandenburg-Prussia expanded mainly by acquiring dynastic titles in geographically separated lands. In the 18th century it expanded through aggression to the east, seizing Silesia in 1740 and various parts of Poland in 1772, 1793, and 1795.

OVERVIEW   Great Powers and Declining Powers in Europe

In the seventeenth and eighteenth centuries, five European states—Britain, France, Austria, Prussia, and Russia—became European great powers and remained so until and, in every case except Austria, even after the end of World War I in 1918. At the same time, four other states that had been major European powers declined permanently into secondary status. The table below lists the main strengths of the rising powers and the main sources of weakness of the declining states.

Five Great Powers

State	Government	Strengths
Britain	Constitutional Monarchy	Commercial and financial resources; navy; colonial empire; overseas trade; intellectual liberty; growing industry; religious toleration
France	Absolute Monarchy	Army; large population; cultural preeminence; colonial empire; intellectual vibrancy
Austria	Absolute Monarchy	Imperial prestige; dynastic loyalty: army
Prussia	Absolute Monarchy	Army; efficient bureaucracy
Russia	Absolute Monarchy	Army; large population; extensive natural resources; imperial control over church and state

Four Declining Powers

State	Government	Weaknesses
Spain	Absolute Monarchy	Stagnant economy; inefficient government; weak military; enforced religious and intellectual conformity
Ottoman Empire	Absolute Monarchy	Backward economy; unstable government; resistance to change; outmoded military
Sweden	Constitutional Monarchy	Small population; weak economy
Netherlands	Republic	Divided government; small population; declining economy

spread than the last, and eventually these wars became genuinely worldwide. Through these conflicts the European powers extended their military and political presence to match their expanding commercial presence in the Americas and in Asia. At the same time, through their conflicts with each other the European powers developed the military weapons and naval prowess that they also turned against non-European peoples. Thus these European wars are important for both their political and technological character.

THE WARS OF LOUIS XIV

By the late 1660s France had become superior to any other European nation in administrative bureaucracy, armed forces, and national unity. Louis XIV could afford to raise and maintain a large and powerful army and was in a position to dominate Europe.

Commencing in 1667, Louis XIV led France into four major wars of expansion each with a widening scope (see Map 20–3). In 1667 and then again in 1672 Louis invaded Flanders. His second war during which he was allied with England led the Dutch to rally around the leadership of William Prince of Orange, the future William III of England. He forged an alliance with the Holy Roman Emperor, Spain, Lorraine, and Brandenburg against Louis, by then regarded as a menace to the whole of Western Europe, Catholic and Protestant alike. Louis' second war ended inconclusively with the Peace of Nijmwegen, signed with different parties in successive years (1678, 1679).

In 1681 Louis' forces occupied the free city of Strasbourg, prompting new defensive coalitions to form against him. One of these, the League of Augsburg, grew to include England, Spain, Sweden, the United Provinces, and the major German states including the Habsburg emperor. One of the chief reasons that in 1688 William of Orange consented to become monarch of England was to draw that nation and its wealth into the coalition against France. Between 1689 and 1697 the League of Augsburg and France battled each other on European fronts in the Nine Years' War, while England and France struggled to control North America. The Peace of Ryswick, signed in September 1697, secured Holland's borders and thwarted Louis' expansion into Germany.

Then on November 1, 1700, Charles II of Spain (r. 1665–1700) died without direct heirs. He left his entire inheritance to Louis'

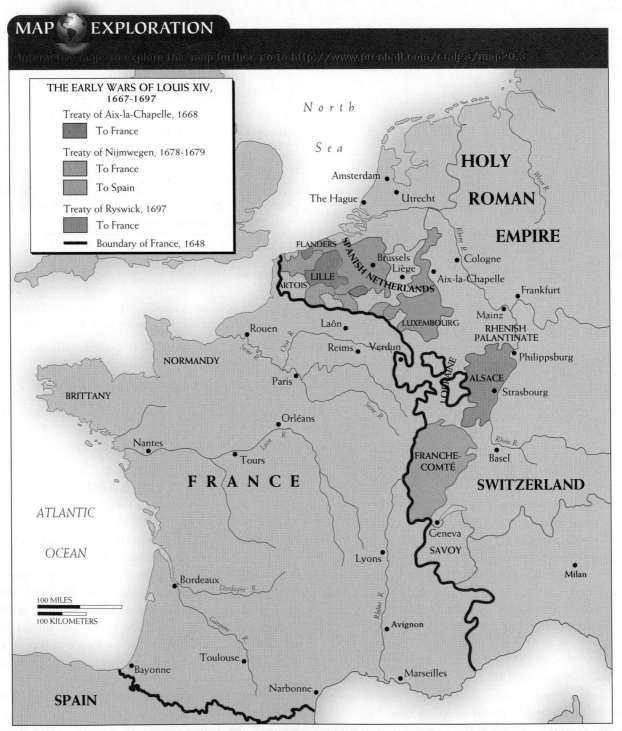

MAP EXPLORATION

Interactive map to explore this map further, go to http://www.prenhall.com/craig3/map20.3

THE EARLY WARS OF LOUIS XIV, 1667-1697

Treaty of Aix-la-Chapelle, 1668
  To France

Treaty of Nijmwegen, 1678-1679
  To France
  To Spain

Treaty of Ryswick, 1697
  To France
  —— Boundary of France, 1648

MAP 20–3 The Early Wars of Louis XIV. This map shows the territorial changes resulting from Louis XIV's first three major wars (1667–1697).

grandson Philip of Anjou, who became Philip V of Spain (r. 1700–1746). Spain and the trade with its American empire appeared to have fallen to France. In September 1701 England, Holland, and the Holy Roman Empire formed the Grand Alliance to preserve the balance of power by once and for all securing Flanders as a neutral barrier between Holland and France and by gaining for the emperor his fair share of the Spanish inheritance.

The War of the Spanish Succession (1701–1714) soon enveloped Western Europe. (see Map 20–4) France finally made peace with England at Utrecht in July 1713 and with Holland and the emperor at Rastadt in March 1714. Philip V remained king of Spain, but England got Gibraltar, making it a Mediterranean power. Louis also formally recognized the right of the House of Hanover to accede to the English throne. At the conclusion of this long war, France was economically and politically exhausted. The European wars of the next generation occurred not only in Europe but also throughout the European overseas empires.

The Eighteenth-Century Colonial Arena

The Treaty of Utrecht established the boundaries of empire during the first half of the eighteenth century. Except for Brazil, which was governed by Portugal, Spain controlled all of mainland South America, as well as Florida, Mexico, and California in North America. Spain also ruled Cuba and half of Hispaniola. The British Empire consisted of the colonies along the North Atlantic seaboard, Nova Scotia, Newfoundland, Jamaica, and Barbados. Britain also possessed a few trading stations on the Indian subcontinent. The Dutch controlled

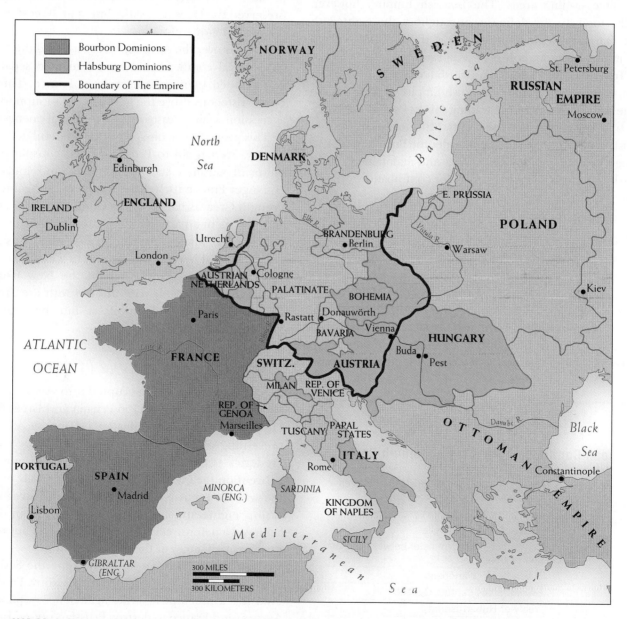

MAP 20–4 Europe In 1714.   The War of the Spanish Succession ended a year before the death of Louis XIV. The Bourbons had secured the Spanish throne, but Spain had forfeited its possessions in Flanders and Italy.

Surinam, or Dutch Guiana, in South America; various trading stations in Ceylon and Bengal; and, most important, the trade with Java in what is today Indonesia.

The French had also established an empire in America and southern Asia. It covered the Saint Lawrence River valley; the Ohio and Mississippi river valleys; Saint Domingue (Haiti), Guadeloupe, and Martinique in the West Indies; and trading stations in India and West Africa. The economy of their West Indian islands resembled those of the Spanish and the British. Their holdings in Canada were sparsely populated, Quebec being the largest settlement, and the economy was based on agriculture and the fur trade. French and English settlers in North America clashed throughout the eighteenth century.

Each of the powers sought to make its imperial holdings into impenetrable trading areas. The Spanish Empire, however, especially stood on the defensive throughout the eighteenth century. The Spanish government lacked the capacity to maintain a commercial monopoly over its sprawling territory.

The Treaty of Utrecht gave the British a thirty-year *asiento*, or contract, to furnish slaves to the Spanish Empire and the right to send one ship each year to the trading fair at Portobello. Nothing but friction arose from these rights. Much to the chagrin of the British, the Spanish government under the Bourbons took its own alleged trading monopoly seriously and maintained coastal patrols which searched English vessels for contraband.

WAR OF JENKINS'S EAR

In 1731, during one such search, there was a fight, and an English captain named Robert Jenkins had his ear cut off by the Spaniards. Thereafter, he preserved his ear in a jar of brandy. This incident was of little importance until 1738, when Jenkins appeared before the British Parliament, reportedly brandishing his ear as an example of Spanish atrocities to British merchants in the West Indies. British commercial interests put great pressure on Parliament to do something about Spanish

CHRONOLOGY

European Conflicts of the Mid-Eighteenth Century

1739	Outbreak of War of Jenkins's Ear between England and Spain
1740	War of the Austrian Succession commences
1748	Treaty of Aix-la-Chapelle
1756	Convention of Westminster between England and Prussia
1756	Seven Years' War opens
1759	British forces capture Quebec
1763	Treaty of Hubertusburg
1763	Treaty of Paris

interference in their trade. Robert Walpole could not resist these pressures, and in late 1739 Great Britain went to war with Spain. This might have been a relatively minor clash, but as a result of the Prussian invasion of Silesia, it became the opening encounter in a series of worldwide European wars.

THE WAR OF THE AUSTRIAN SUCCESSION (1740–1748)

In December 1740, as noted earlier in the chapter, the new king of Prussia, Frederick II, ignored the Pragmatic Sanction and seized the Austrian province of Silesia. In response to the Prussian aggression, the young Maria Theresa of Austria recognized Hungary as the most important of her crowns and promised the Magyars considerable local autonomy. She thus preserved the Habsburg state, but at great cost to the power of the central monarchy.

The war over the Austrian succession and the British-Spanish commercial conflict could have remained separate disputes. What united them was the role of France. There aggressive court aristocrats drove the government to support the Prussian aggression against Austria, the traditional enemy of France.

This proved to be one of the most fateful decisions in world history. French aid to Prussia helped consolidate a new and powerful German state that could, and indeed later did, endanger France itself. The French move against Austria also brought Great Britain into the Continental war against France and Prussia in an attempt to assure that Belgium remained in the friendly hands of Austria. In 1744 the British-French conflict expanded beyond the Continent when France decided to support Spain against Britain in the New World. The war ended in military stalemate in 1748 with the Treaty of Aix-la-Chapelle. Prussia retained Silesia, but the treaty was a truce rather than a permanent peace.

THE SEVEN YEARS' WAR (1756–1763)

Before the rivalries again erupted into war, a dramatic shift of alliances took place. In 1756 Prussia and Great Britain signed the Convention of Westminster, a defensive alliance aimed at preventing the entry of foreign troops into the Germanies. Frederick feared invasions by both Russia and France. The convention meant that Great Britain, the ally of Austria since the wars of Louis XIV, had now joined forces with Austria's major eighteenth-century enemy. Later in 1756 Austria achieved a defensive alliance with France. Thus the traditional European alliances of the previous century were reversed.

In August 1756, what would become the Seven Years' War opened when Frederick II invaded Saxony. Frederick considered this a preemptive strike against a conspiracy by Saxony, Austria, and France to destroy Prussian power. In the spring of 1757 France and Austria made a new alliance dedicated to the

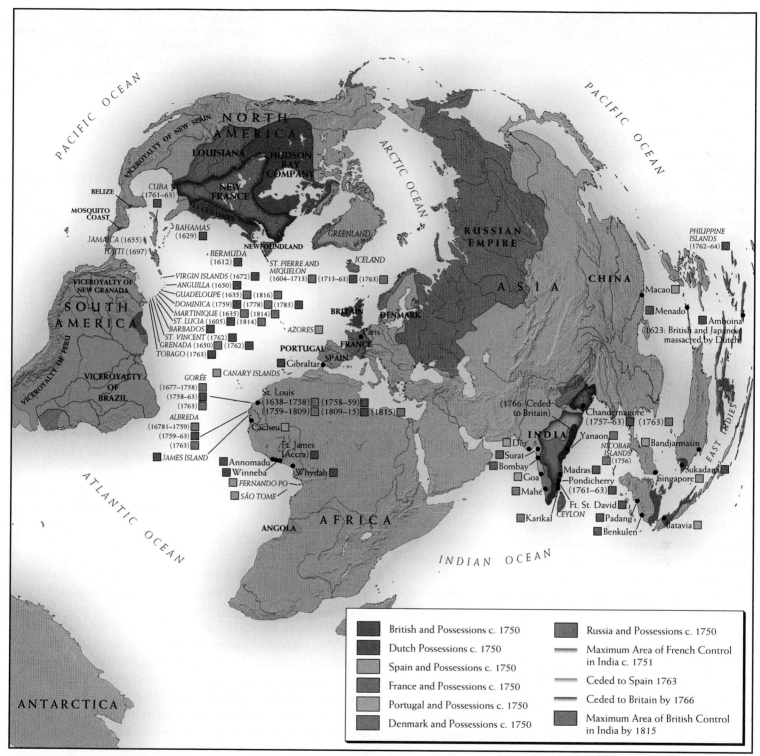

MAP 20–5 The Colonial Arena. The acquisition of overseas colonies by European powers led to intense rivalries on a global scale. Territories frequently changed hands during the eigteenth century.

destruction of Prussia. They were eventually joined by Sweden, Russia, and the smaller German states. Two factors, in addition to Frederick's strong leadership (it was after this war that he came to be called Frederick the Great), saved Prussia—British financial aid and the death in 1762 of Empress Elizabeth of

Russia (r. 1741–1762). Her successor Tsar Peter III (d. 1762), a fervent admirer of Frederick, immediately made peace with Prussia, thus allowing Frederick to hold off Austria and France. The Treaty of Hubertusburg of 1763 closed the Continental conflict with no significant changes in prewar borders.

More impressive to the rest of Europe than the survival of Prussia were the victories of Great Britain in every theater of conflict. The architect of victory was William Pitt the Elder (1708–1778). Although Pitt had previously criticized British involvement with the Continent, once he was named secretary of state in charge of the war in 1757 he reversed himself and pumped huge financial subsidies to Frederick the Great. But North America was Pitt's real concern. Put simply, he wanted all of North America east of the Mississippi for Great Britain, and that was exactly what he won as he directed unprecedented resources into the overseas colonial conflict. In what Americans know as the French and Indian War, the French government was unwilling and unable to direct similar resources against the English in America. In September 1759 the British took Quebec City. Montreal fell the next year. The French empire in Canada was coming to an end.

Pitt's colonial vision, however, was global. The French West Indies fell to the British fleets. On the Indian subcontinent the British forces under Robert Clive (1725–1774) defeated the French in 1757 at the Battle of Plassey. This victory opened the way for the eventual conquest of all India by the British East India Company. Never had any other European power experienced such a complete worldwide military victory. Never had a European military victory affected so many non-Europeans.

The Treaty of Paris of 1763 was somewhat less triumphant. Pitt was no longer in office. George III (r. 1760–1820) had succeeded to the British throne and by 1762 had replaced Pitt with a new minister who was responsible for the peace settlement, in which Britain received all of Canada, the Ohio river valley, and the eastern half of the Mississippi river valley. France retained footholds in India at Pondicherry and Chan-

dernagore and regained the West Indies sugar islands of Guadeloupe and Martinique.

The midcentury wars among European powers resulted in a new balance of power on the European continent and the high seas (see Map 20-5). Great Britain gained a world empire, and Prussia was recognized as a great continental power. With the surrender of Canada, France retreated from North America and thus opened the way for a continent largely dominated by the English language and Protestantism. By contrast, Latin America remained dominated by the Spanish and Portuguese languages and Roman Catholicism. For many years, West Africa would continue to furnish slaves to the economies of both Americas. On the subcontinent of Asia the foundations were laid for almost two centuries of British dominance.

By the mid–eighteenth century, the European states that just two centuries earlier had only started to settle the Americas and to engage in limited long-range trade had made their power and influence felt throughout the world. As those wars of the midcentury came to an end, the political power of the European states became linked to a qualitatively different economic base than any seen elsewhere in the world. That political and economic combination allowed Europe to dominate the world from the 1750s to the Second World War.

The Old Regime

During the turmoil of the French Revolution and its aftermath, it became customary to refer to the patterns of social, political, and economic relationships that had existed in France before 1789 as the *ancien régime*, or the **Old Regime**. The term has come to be applied generally to the life and institutions of all prerevolutionary Continental Europe. Politically, it meant the rule of theoretically absolute monarchies with growing bureaucracies and aristocratically led armies. Economically, the Old Regime was characterized by food shortages, the predominance of agriculture, slow transport, a low level of iron production, comparatively unsophisticated financial institutions, and, in some cases, competitive commercial overseas empires. Socially, men and women saw themselves less as individuals than as members of distinct corporate bodies that possessed certain privileges or rights as a group.

MAINTENANCE OF TRADITION

Few persons outside the political, commercial, and intellectual elite actually wanted change or innovation. This was especially true of social relationships. Both nobles and peasants repeatedly called for the restoration of traditional or customary rights. The nobles asserted what they considered their ancient rights against the intrusion of the expanding monarchical bureaucracies. The peasants, through petitions and revolts, called for the revival or the maintenance of the customary manorial rights that allowed them access to particular lands, courts, or grievance procedures.

Except for the early industrial development in Britain, the economy was also predominantly traditional. The quality and quantity of the grain harvest remained crucial for most of the population and the gravest concern for governments.

HIERARCHY AND PRIVILEGE

The medieval sense of hierarchy became more rigid during the century. Several cities retained sumptuary laws forbidding persons in one class or occupation from dressing like their social superiors. These laws were largely ineffective. What really enforced the hierarchy was the corporate nature of social relationships.

Each state or society was considered a community composed of numerous smaller communities. Eighteenth-century Europeans did not enjoy what Americans regard as individual rights. Instead, persons enjoyed such rights and privileges as were guaranteed to whatever communities or groups of which they were a part. The "community" might include the village, the municipality, the nobility, the church, the guild, a university, or the parish. In turn, each of these bodies enjoyed certain privileges—some great, some small. The privileges might involve exemption from taxation or degrading punishment, the right to practice a trade or craft, the right of one's children to pursue a particular occupation, or, for the church, the right to collect the tithe.

ARISTOCRACY

The eighteenth century was the great age of the aristocracy. The nobility constituted approximately 1 to 5 percent of the population of any given country. In every European state, it was the single wealthiest sector of the population; possessed the widest degree of social, political, and economic power; and dominated polite society. Land provided the aristocracy with its largest source of income, but the influence of aristocrats was felt in every area of life. Across the Continent, to be an aristocrat was a matter of birth and legal privilege, but in almost every other respect, aristocrats differed markedly from country to country. The smallest, wealthiest, best defined, and most socially responsible aristocracy resided in Great Britain. As one moved eastward across Europe the aristocracy became more numerous, not always wealthy, but possessing increasing degrees of arbitrary, repressive power over those below them in the social structure.

Throughout the century, in a European-wide *aristocratic resurgence*, the various nobilities sought to protect their social position and privileges against the expanding power of the monarchies and the growing wealth of commercial groups. First, all nobilities attempted to restrict entry into their ranks and institutions.

Second, they also attempted to monopolize appointments to the officer corps of the armies, the bureaucracies, the government ministries, and the church. The nobles thus hoped to control the power of the monarchies.

Third, the nobles attempted to use institutions they already controlled against the monarchies. These institutions included the British Parliament, the French *parlements*, local aristocratic estates, and provincial diets.

Fourth, the aristocracies pressed the peasantry for higher rents or long-forgotten feudal dues. This was part of an effort by the nobility to shore up its position by appealing to tradition and reasserting old privileges that had lapsed. To contemporaries, this aristocratic resurgence was one of the most fundamental political facts of the day.

THE LAND AND ITS TILLERS

Land was the economic basis of eighteenth-century life in Europe as it was throughout the rest of the world. Well over three fourths of all Europeans lived on the land, and most never traveled more than a few miles from their birthplaces. With the exception of the nobility and the wealthier landowners, the dwellers on the land were poor, and by any modern standard, their lives were hard.

PEASANTS AND SERFS

Those people who worked the land were subject to immense influence and in some cases direct control by the landowners. This situation prevailed in different degrees for free peasants, such as English tenants and most French cultivators, and for the serfs of Germany, Austria, and Russia, who were legally bound to a particular plot of land and a particular lord. In all cases, the class that owned the land also controlled the local government and the courts.

▲ **Road Work.** Eighteenth-century France had some of the best roads in the world, but they were often built with forced labor. French peasants were required to work part of each year on such projects. This system, called the *corvée*, was not abolished until the French Revolution in 1789.
Joseph Vernet, "Construction of a Road." Louvre, Paris, France/Bridgemann-Giraudon/Art Resource, N.Y.

Landlord power increased as one moved from west to east. Most French peasants owned some land, but a few were serfs. However, nearly all peasants were subject to certain feudal dues and to forced labor on the lord's estate for a certain number of days each year. Because French peasants rarely owned enough land to support their families, they were also subject to feudal dues attached to the plots of land they rented.

In Prussia and Austria, despite attempts by the monarchies late in the century to improve the lot of the serfs, the landlords continued to exercise almost complete control over them. Moreover, throughout Continental Europe the burden of state taxation fell on the tillers of the soil. Many peasants, serfs, and other agricultural laborers were forced to undertake supplemental work to pay the tax collector. Through various legal privileges and the ability to demand further concessions from the monarchs, the landlords escaped the payment of numerous taxes. They also presided over the manorial courts.

The condition of the serfs was the worst in Russia. The Russian custom of reckoning one's wealth by the number of owned "souls" (that is, male serfs) rather than by the size of an estate reveals the contrast between Russia and eastern Europe. Russian serfs were, in effect, regarded merely as economic commodities. Their services were attached to an individual lord rather than to a particular plot of land. Russian landlords could demand as many as six days a week of labor, and like Prussian and Austrian landlords, they could punish their serfs or even exile them to

Siberia. Although serfs had little recourse against their lords, custom, tradition, and law did provide a few protections. For example, the marriages of serfs, unlike those of most slaves throughout the world, were legally recognized. The landlord could not disband the family of a serf. (See Document, "Russian Serfs Lament Their Condition.")

The Russian monarchy itself contributed to the degradation of the serfs. Peter the Great (r. 1682–1725) gave whole villages to favored nobles. Catherine the Great (r. 1762–1796) confirmed the authority of the nobles over their serfs in exchange for the nobility's political cooperation. This situation led to considerable unrest. There were well over fifty peasant revolts between 1762 and 1769. They culminated between 1773 and 1774 in Pugachev's rebellion, during which all of southern Russia was in ferment. Emelyan Pugachev (1726–1775) promised the serfs land and freedom. The rebellion was brutally suppressed, and any thought of liberalizing the condition of the serfs was set aside for a generation.

Pugachev's was the largest peasant uprising of the eighteenth century. Smaller peasant revolts or disturbances occurred in Bohemia in 1775, in Transylvania in 1784, in Moravia in 1786, and in Austria in 1789. Western Europe was more tranquil, but England experienced numerous enclosure riots. Rural rebellions were violent, but the peasants and serfs normally directed their wrath against property rather than persons. The rebels usually sought to reassert traditional or customary rights against

DOCUMENT | Russian Serfs Lament Their Condition

As with other illiterate groups in European history, it is difficult to recapture the voices of Russian serfs. The following verses from "The Slaves' Lament," a popular ballad from the era of the Pugachev Rebellion (1773–1775), indicate the serfs were aware of how the legislation of that era which favored the landowning classes affected their lives. The verses embody the resentment that Pugachev's Rebellion ignited. Note how the verses suggest that the tsar may be more favorable to serfs than their landowners are. Pugachev claimed to be Tsar Peter III, and many Russian serfs believed him and thus considered him a liberator from landlord tyranny. Throughout this ballad, serfs present themselves as slaves.

◆ What specific complaints about landlords are expressed in these verses? What charges indicate that serfs may believe their situation has worsened? What hope do they seem to place in the tsar? What idealized picture of the world do the serfs believe they would themselves create?

O woe to us slaves living for the masters!
We do not know how to serve their ferocity!
Service is like a sharp scythe;
And kindness is like the morning dew.
* * * * *
Brothers, how annoying it is to us
And how shameful and insulting
That another who is not worthy to be equal with us
Has so many of us in his power.
* * * * *
And if we steal from the lord one half kopeck,
The law commands us to be killed like a louse.
And if the master steals ten thousand,
Nobody will judge who should be hanged.
The injustice of the Russian sheriffs has increased:
Whoever brings a present is right beyond argument.
They have stopped putting their trust in the Creator for
   authority,
And have become accustomed to own us like cattle.
All nations rebuke us and wonder at our stupidity,

That such stupid people are born in Russia.
And indeed, stupidity was rooted in us long ago,
as each honour here has been given to vagrants.
The master can kill the servant like a gelding;
The denunciation by a slave cannot be believed.
Unjust judges have composed a decree
That we should be tyrannically whipped with a knout for
   that.
* * * * *
Better that we should agree to serve the tsar.
Better to live in dark woods
Than to be before the eyes of these tyrants;
They look on us cruelly with their eyes
And eat us as iron eats rye. No one wants to serve the
   tsar
But only to grind us down to the end.
And they try to collect unjust bribes,
And they are not frightened that people die cruelly.
* * * * *
Ah brothers, if we got our freedom,
We would not take the lands or the fields for ourselves.
We would go into service as soldiers, brothers,
And would be friendly among ourselves,
Would destroy all injustice
And remove the root of evil lords.
* * * * *
They [the landlords] sell all the good rye to the
   merchants,
And give us like pigs the bad.
The greedy lords eat meat at fast time,
And even when meat is allowed, the slaves
must cook meatless cabbage soup.
O brothers, it is our misfortune
always to have rye kasha.
The lords drink and make merry,
And do not allow the slaves even to burst out laughing.

From Paul Dukes, trans. and ed., Russia under Catherine the Great: Select Documents on Government and Society (Oriental Research Partners, 1978), pp. 115–117. Reprinted by permission of Oriental Research Partners.

practices they perceived as innovations. In this respect, the peasant revolts were conservative in nature.

FAMILY STRUCTURES AND THE FAMILY ECONOMY

In preindustrial Europe, the household was the basic unit of production and consumption. That is to say, very few productive establishments employed more than a handful of people not belonging to the owner's family. These rare establishments were located in cities. But most Europeans lived in rural areas. There,

as well as in small towns and cities, the household mode of organization predominated on farms, in artisans' workshops, and in small merchants' shops. With that mode of economic organization, there developed what is known as the *family economy*.

THE FAMILY ECONOMY

Throughout Europe people thought and worked in terms of sustaining the economic life of the family, and family members saw themselves as working together in an interdependent

goods and income produced went to the benefit of the household rather than to the individual family member. Depending on their ages and skills, everyone worked. The need to survive poor harvests or economic slumps meant that no one could be idle.

The family economy also dominated the life of skilled urban artisans. The father was usually the chief craftsman. He generally had one or more servants in his employ, but he would also expect his children to work in the enterprise. His eldest child was usually trained in the trade. His wife often sold the wares or had a small shop. The wife of a merchant also often ran the husband's business, especially when he traveled to purchase new goods. In any case, everyone in the family was involved. If business was poor, family members would look for employment elsewhere, not to support themselves but to help the family unit survive.

WOMEN AND THE FAMILY ECONOMY

The family economy established many of the chief constraints on the lives and the personal experiences of women in preindustrial society. Most of the historical research that has been undertaken on this subject relates to Western Europe. There, a woman's life experience was largely the function of her capacity to establish and maintain a household. For women, marriage was an institution of economic necessity as well as

▲ **Emelyan Pugachev** (1726–1775) led the largest peasant revolt in Russian history. In this contemporary propaganda picture he is shown in chains. An inscription in Russian and German was printed below the picture decrying the evils of revolution and insurrection.
Bildarchiv Preussischer Kulturbesitz.

rather than an independent or individualistic manner. The goal of the family household was to produce or secure through wages enough food to support its members. In the countryside, that effort virtually always involved farming. In cities and towns, artisan production or working for another person was the usual pattern. Almost everyone lived within a household because ordinary people could rarely support themselves independently. Indeed, except for members of religious orders, people living outside a household were viewed with great suspicion as potentially criminal or disruptive or, at least, potentially dependent on the charity of others.

Marriage and the family within this economy meant that everyone in the household had to work. On a farm, much of the effort went directly into raising food or producing other agricultural goods that could be exchanged for food. In Western Europe, however, few people had enough land to support their households from farming alone. For this reason, one or more family members might work elsewhere and send wages home. For example, the father or older children might be migrant workers, perhaps many miles from home. The burden of the farm work would then fall on the wife and the younger children. This was not uncommon. Within this family economy, all of the

▲ **Women's Work.** During the 18th century, with their employment opportunities tightly restricted, many unmarried women and widows served as governesses to children of the aristocracy and other wealthier groups in Europe.
Chardin, Jean-Baptiste-Simeon: "The Governess" (#6432), National Gallery of Canada, Ottawa.

Farm Family. Painted by the English artist ▶ Francis Wheatley (1747–1801) near the close of the 18th century, this scene is part of a series illustrating a day in the life of an idealized farm family. Note the artist's assumptions about the division of labor by gender. Men work in the fields, women work in the home or look after the needs of men and children. As other illustrations in this chapter show, many 18th-century women in fact worked outside the home, but considerable social pressure was developing at this time to restrict them to domestic roles. This painting and the others in the series are thus more prescriptive than descriptive, intended in part to persuade their viewers that women belonged in their separate family sphere. Many, perhaps most, families living in the countryside could not maintain the closeness that these paintings extol. To survive, many had to send members to work on other farms or even to other regions.

Francis Wheatley (RA) (1747–1801), "Evening," signed and dated 1799, oil on canvas, 17 1/2 × 21 1/2 in. (44.5 × 54.5 cm), Yale Center for British Art, Paul Mellon Collection, Bridgmann Art Library (B1977.14.118)

one that fulfilled sexual and psychological needs. A woman outside a household was highly vulnerable. Unless she was an aristocrat or a member of a religious order, she could probably not support herself by her own efforts alone. Consequently, much of a woman's life was devoted first to aiding the maintenance of her parents' household and then to getting her own household to live in as an adult. In most cases, bearing and rearing children were subordinate to these goals.

As a child, certainly by the age of seven, a girl was expected to begin to contribute to the household work. On a farm, she might look after chickens or water animals or carry food to adult men and women working the land. In an urban artisan's household, she would do some form of light work, perhaps involving cleaning or carrying and later sewing or weaving. The girl would remain in her parents' home as long as either she made a real contribution to the family enterprise or her labor elsewhere was not more valuable to the family. An artisan's daughter might not leave home until marriage because she could learn increasingly valuable skills from her parents.

The labor of the much larger number of girls growing up on farms quickly became of little value to the family. These girls would then leave home, usually by the age of twelve or fourteen. They might go to another farm but were more likely to migrate to a nearby town or city. They would rarely travel more than thirty miles from their parents' household and would then normally become servants in the household of an employer. (See Document, "Priscilla Wakefield Demands More Occupations Be Opened to Women.")

Having migrated from home, the young woman's chief goal was to accumulate a dowry. Her savings would allow her to make the necessary contribution to form a household with her husband. Marriage within the family economy was a joint economic undertaking, and the wife was expected to make an immediate contribution of capital for the establishment of the household. A young woman might well work for ten years or more to accumulate a dowry. This practice meant that marriage was usually postponed until a woman's mid- to late twenties.

Within the marriage, earning enough money or producing enough farm goods to ensure an adequate food supply was always the dominant concern. Domestic duties, childbearing, and child rearing were subordinate to economic survival. Consequently, couples would often practice birth control, usually through *coitus interruptus*, or withdrawal of the male before ejaculation. Young children were often placed with wet nurses so the mother could continue to contribute to the household economy. The wet nurse, in turn, was contributing to her own household. The child would be fully reintegrated into its family when it was weaned and would be expected to aid the family at an early age. (See Document, "An Edinburgh Physician Describes the Dangers of Childbirth.")

A married woman's work was in many ways a function of her husband's occupation. If the peasant household possessed enough land to support itself, the wife spent much of her time

| **Priscilla Wakefield Demands More Occupations Be Opened to Women**

At the end of the eighteenth century, several English women writers began to demand a wider life for women. Priscilla Wakefield was among such authors. She was concerned that women found themselves able to pursue only occupations that paid poorly. Often they were excluded from work on the grounds of their alleged physical weakness. She also believed that women should receive equal wages for equal work. Many of the issues she raised have yet to be adequately addressed on behalf of women.

> ◆ From reading this passage, what do you understand to have been the arguments at the end of the eighteenth century to limit the kinds of employment that women might enter? Why did women receive lower wages for work similar to or the same as that done by men? What occupations traditionally filled by men does Wakefield believe women might also pursue?

Another heavy discouragement to the industry of women, is the inequality of the reward of their labor, compared with that of men; an injustice which pervades every species of employment performed by both sexes.

In employments which depend on bodily strength, the distinction is just; for it cannot be pretended that the generality of women can earn as much as men, when the produce of their labor is the result of corporeal exertion; but it is a subject of great regret, that this inequality should prevail even where an equal share of skill and application is exerted. Male stay-makers, mantua-makers, and hair-dressers, are better paid than female artists of the same professions; but surely it will never be urged as an apology for this disproportion, that women are not as capable of making stays, gowns, dressing hair, and similar arts, as men; if they are not superior to them, it can only be accounted for upon this principle, that the prices they receive for their labor are not sufficient to repay them for the expense of qualifying themselves for their business; and that they sink under the mortification of being regarded as artisans of inferior estimation. ...

Besides these employments which are commonly performed by women, and those already shown to be suitable for such persons as are above the condition of hard labor, there are some professions and trades customarily in the hands of men, which might be conveniently exercised by either sex. —Watchmaking requiring more ingenuity than strength, seems peculiarly adapted to women; as do many parts of the business of stationer, particularly, ruling account books or making pens. The compounding of medicines in an apothecary's shop, requires no other talents than care and exactness; and if opening a vein occasionally be a indispensable requisite, a woman may acquire the capacity of doing it, for those of her own sex at least, without any reasonable objection. ... Pastry and confectionery appear particularly consonant to the habits of women, though generally performed by men; perhaps the heat of the ovens, and the strength requisite to fill and empty them, may render male assistants necessary; but certain women are most eligible to mix up the ingredients, and prepare the various kinds of cakes for baking. —Light turnery and toy-making depend more upon dexterity and invention than force, and are therefore suitable work for women and children. ...

Farming, as far as respects the theory, is commensurate with the powers of the female mind: nor is the practice of inspecting agricultural processes incompatible with the delicacy of their frames if their constitution be good.

From Priscilla Wakefield, *Reflections on the Present Condition of the Female Sex* (1798), (London, 1817), pp. 125–127, as quoted in Bridget Hill, ed., *Eighteenth-Century Women: An Anthology*. Copyright © 1984 George Allen & Unwin, pp. 227–228.

---

literally carrying things for her husband—water, food, seed, harvested grain, and the like. But few peasants had such adequate landholdings. If the husband had to do work other than farming, such as fishing or migrant labor, the wife might do the plowing, planting, and harvesting. In the city, the wife of an artisan or merchant often acted as a business manager. She might manage the household finances and participate in the trade or business. When her husband died, she might take over the business, perhaps hiring an artisan.

Finally, if economic disaster struck the family, more often than not it was the wife who took the lead in sending off family members to find work elsewhere or even to beg in the streets.

In all phases of life within the family economy, women led active, often decisive roles. Industriousness rather than idleness was their lot in life. Finding a functional place in the household was essential to their well-being, but once that place had been found, their function was essential to the ongoing well-being of the household.

The Revolution in Agriculture

The main goal of traditional European peasant society was to ensure the stability of the local food supply. That supply was never certain and became more uncertain the farther east one traveled. A failed harvest meant not only hardship, but also death from either outright starvation or protracted debility. Food was often harder to find in the country than in cities because city governments usually stored reserve supplies of grain.

English Children. Few children in the 18th century were as privileged as these in this landed English family. Most began working to help support their families as soon as they were physically able. It was during the 18th century, however, that Europeans apparently began to view childhood as a distinct period in human development. Even though Arthur Devis has painted these children to look something like little adults, he has included various toys associated with chidhood.

Arthur Devis (c. 1711–1787), "Children in an Interior," © 1742–1743, oil on canvas, 39 × 49 3/4 in. (99.0 × 125.5 cm), Yale Center for British Art, Paul Mellon Collection, B1978.43.5.

Poor harvests also played havoc with prices. Smaller supplies or larger demand raised grain prices. Even small increases in the cost of food could squeeze peasant or artisan families. If prices increased sharply, many of those families fell back on poor relief from their local government or the church. What made the situation of food supply and prices so difficult was the peasants' sense of helplessness before the whims of nature and the marketplace. Despite differences in rural customs throughout Europe, peasants resisted changes that they felt might endanger the sure supply of food, which they generally believed traditional cultivation practices ensured.

During the century, historians now believe, bread prices slowly but steadily rose, spurred largely by population growth. This put pressure on all of the poor. The prices rose faster

---

DOCUMENT | An Edinburgh Physician Describes the Dangers of Childbirth

Death in childbirth was a common occurrence throughout Europe until the twentieth century. This brief letter from an Edinburgh physician illustrates how devastating infectious diseases could be to women at the time of childbirth.

◆ How does this passage illustrate a health danger that only women confronted? How might the likelihood of the death of oneself or a spouse in childbirth have affected one's attitudes toward children? How does this passage illustrate limitations on knowledge about disease in the eighteenth century?

We had puerperal fever in the infirmary last winter. It began about the end of February, when almost every woman, as soon as she was delivered, or perhaps about twenty-four hours after, was seized with it; and all of them died, though every method was tried to cure the disorder. What was singular, the women were in good health before they were brought to bed, though some of them had been long in the hospital before delivery. One woman had been dismissed from the ward before she was brought to bed; came into it some days after with her labor upon her; was easily delivered, and remained perfectly well for twenty-four hours, when she was seized with a shivering and the other symptoms of the fever. I caused her to be removed to another ward; yet notwithstanding all the care that was taken of her she died in the same manner as the others.

From a letter to Mr. White from a Dr. Young of Edinburgh, 21 November 1774, cited in C. White, *Treatise on the Management of Pregnant and Lying-In Women* (London, 1777), pp. 45–46, as quoted in Bridget Hill, ed., *Eighteenth-Century Women: An Anthology.* Copyright © 1984 George Allen & Unwin, p. 102.

Grain production lay at the heart of 18th-century farming. In this engraving farm workes can be seen threshing wheat, winnowing the grain, and finally putting the grain in bags so it can be carried to a mill and ground into flour. In many cases the mill would be owned by the local landlord, who would charge peasants for its use.
Art Resource/Bildarchiv Preussischer Kulturbesitz.

than urban wages and brought no appreciable advantage to the small peasant producer. On the other hand, the rise in grain prices benefited landowners and those wealthier peasants who had surplus grain to sell.

The increasing price of grain allowed landlords to improve their income and lifestyle. They began a series of innovations in farm production that is known as the *agricultural revolution*.

New Crops and New Methods This movement began during the sixteenth and seventeenth centuries in the Low Countries, where Dutch landlords and farmers devised better ways to build dykes and to drain land so that they could farm more extensive areas. They also experimented with new crops, such as clover and turnips, that would increase the supply of animal fodder and replenish the soil.

These methods were extensively adopted in England during the early eighteenth century. There, new methods of farming, new crops, and new modes of landholding eventually led to greater productivity. This advance in food production was necessary for an industrial society to develop. It ensured adequate food for the cities and freed surplus agricultural labor for industrial production. The changing modes of agriculture sponsored by the landlords undermined the assumptions of traditional peasant production. Farming now took place not only to provide the local food supply but also to earn the landlord a handsome profit.

Enclosure Replaces Open-Field Method Many of the agricultural innovations, which were adopted only slowly, were incompatible with the existing organization of land in Britain.

Small cultivators who lived in village communities still farmed most of the soil. Each farmer tilled an assortment of unconnected strips. The two- or three-field systems of rotation left much land fallow and unproductive each year. Animals grazed on the common land in the summer and on the stubble of the harvest in the winter. Until at least the middle of the eighteenth century the decisions about which crops would be planted were made communally. The entire system discouraged improvement and favored the poorer farmers, who needed the common land and stubble fields for their animals. The village method made it almost impossible to increase pasture land and with it the size of herds and the production of manure for fertilizer. Traditional methods aimed to produce a steady, but not a growing, supply of food.

In 1700 approximately half the arable land in Britain was farmed by this open-field method. By the second half of the century the rising price of wheat encouraged landlords to consolidate or enclose their lands to increase production. The **enclosures** were intended to use land more rationally and to raise profits. The process involved the fencing of common lands, the reclamation of previously untilled waste, and the transformation of strips into block fields. These procedures disrupted the economic and social life of the countryside. Riots often ensued. Because many British farmers either owned their strips or rented them in a manner that amounted to ownership, the larger landlords usually had to resort to parliamentary acts to legalize the enclosure of the land, which they owned but rented to the farmers. Because the large landowners controlled Parliament, such measures passed easily. Between 1761 and 1792, almost 500,000 acres were enclosed through parliamentary act, as compared with 75,000 acres between 1727 and 1760. In 1801 a general enclosure act streamlined the process.

The enclosures have remained controversial. By permitting the extension of both farming and innovation, they increased food production on larger agricultural units. However, they also disrupted the small traditional communities. They forced off the land some independent farmers, who had needed the common pasturage, and very poor cottagers, who had lived on the reclaimed waste land. However, the enclosures did not depopulate the countryside. In some counties where the enclosures took place, the population increased. New soil had come into production, and services subsidiary to farming also expanded.

POPULATION EXPANSION

Agricultural improvement was both a cause and a result of an immense expansion in the population of Europe. The current population explosion seems to have had its origins in the eighteenth century. Exact figures are lacking, but the best estimates suggest that in 1700 Europe's population, excluding the

European provinces of the Ottoman Empire, was between 100 million and 120 million people. By 1800 the figure had risen to almost 190 million, and by 1850 to 260 million. The population of England and Wales rose from 6 million in 1750 to over 10 million in 1800. France grew from 18 million in 1715 to approximately 26 million in 1789. Russia's population increased from 19 million in 1722 to 29 million in 1766. Such extraordinary sustained growth put new demands on all resources and considerable pressure on existing social organization.

The population expansion occurred across the Continent in both the country and the cities. Only a limited consensus exists about the causes of this growth. There was a clear decline in the death rate. There were fewer wars and somewhat fewer epidemics in the eighteenth century. Hygiene and sanitation also improved. But changes in the food supply itself may have been the chief reason for sustained population growth. One contributing factor was improved and expanding grain production. Another, even more important, was the introduction in the eighteenth century of widespread cultivation of a New World tuber, the potato. Enough potatoes could be raised on a single acre to feed one peasant's family for an entire year. With this more certain food supply, more children could be reared, and more could survive.

The Eighteenth-Century Industrial Revolution

AN EVENT IN WORLD HISTORY

In the second half of the eighteenth century the European economy began very slowly to industrialize. This development, more than any other single factor, distinguished Europe and eventually North America from the rest of the world for the next two centuries. While this economic development was occurring, people did not call it a *revolution*. That term came to be applied to the experience of British technological advances in productivity only after the French Revolution, when Continental writers contended that what had taken place in Britain was the economic equivalent of the political events in France. From this comparison arose the concept of an *industrial* revolution. The process, however, was revolutionary less in its pace, which was on the whole rather slow, than in its implications for the future of European society.

The European **Industrial Revolution** of the eighteenth century constituted the achievement of sustained economic growth. Previously, production had been limited. The economy of a province or a country might grow but soon reached a plateau. However, since the late eighteenth century the economy of Europe has expanded relatively uninterruptedly. Depressions and recessions, however disruptive, have been

temporary, and even during such economic downturns the Western economy has continued to grow.

At considerable social cost and dislocation, industrialism produced more goods and services than ever before in human history. Industrialism in Europe eventually overcame the economy of scarcity. The new means of production demanded new kinds of skills, new discipline in work, and a large labor force. The produced goods met immediate consumer demand and created new demands. In the long run, industrialism clearly raised the standard of living; the poverty in which most Europeans had always lived was overcome. Industrialization provided human beings greater control over the forces of nature than they had ever known.

Over time the wealth produced by industrialism upset the political and social structures of the Old Regime and led to political and social reforms. The economic elite of the emerging industrial society would eventually challenge the political dominance of the aristocracy. Industrialization also undermined traditional communities and, along with the growth of cities, displaced many people. These processes repeated themselves virtually everywhere that industrialization occurred during the next two centuries.

The consumer products of the industrializing businesses gave Europeans vast amounts of new goods to sell throughout the world and thus encouraged more international trade in which Western nations supplied the finished goods in exchange for raw materials. As a consequence, the prosperity of other areas of the globe became economically dependent on European and American demand. The wealth achieved through this uneven commerce allowed Europeans to dominate world markets for almost two centuries.

Furthermore, by the early nineteenth century iron and steel production and the new technologies of manufacture allowed European states and later the United States to build more powerful military forces, especially navies, than those of Africa, Latin America, or Asia. Both the economic and the military dominance of the West arose directly from the industrial achievement.

Much of the history of the non-Western world from the middle of the eighteenth century to the present can be understood in terms of how the nonindustrialized nations initially reacted to the penetration of their world by Europeans and Americans made wealthy and powerful through industrialized economies. Africa and Latin America became generally dependent economies. Japan, by the middle of the nineteenth century, decided it must imitate the European pattern and did so successfully. China did not make that decision and became indirectly ruled by Europeans. The Chinese revolutions of the twentieth century have largely represented efforts to achieve real self-direction. Southeast Asia and the Middle East became drawn into the network of resource supply to the West; they

OVERVIEW   Why the Industrial Revolution Began in Britain

Great Britain was the home of the Industrial Revolution, and until the middle of the nineteenth century, it maintained the industrial leadership of Europe. Several factors contributed to the early industrialization of Britain.

Natural Resources	Britain had extensive deposits of coal and iron ore.
Infrastructure	Britain had an extensive network of roads and canals that facilitated the shipment of raw materials and goods.
Society	1. The predominance of London: London was the largest city in Europe and the social, commercial, financial, and political center of Britain. It was thus both an enormous market for consumer goods itself and created a demand for these goods in the rest of Britain, which sought to emulate London fashions.
	2. The prevalence of newspapers: Newspapers thrived in Britain, and advertisements in them increased consumer demand for goods.
	3. Wealth in Britain brought status: British society was relatively mobile. Wealthy merchants and entrepreneurs could rise socially, enter the aristocracy, and enjoy political influence.
Government, Financial Institutions, and Empire	1. The rule of law: Britain had a stable government that guaranteed property rights.
	2. Britain was a free trade area. No internal tolls inhibited the shipment of goods and raw materials within Britain.
	3. Britain had a sound system of banking and public credit that created a stable climate for investing in commerce and industry.
	4. Taxes were collected efficiently and fairly. No class was exempt from paying taxes.
	5. The colonial empire: British colonies were both a market for British goods and sources of raw materials for British manufacturers.

could achieve movement toward economic independence only through imitation or, like Arab nations in the early 1970s, by refusing to supply oil to the West. The process of industrialization that commenced in small factories in eighteenth-century Europe has changed the world more than any other single development in the last two centuries.

INDUSTRIAL LEADERSHIP OF GREAT BRITAIN

Great Britain was the home of the Industrial Revolution and, until the late nineteenth century, remained the industrial leader of Europe and the world (see Map 20–6). Several factors contributed to the early start of industrialization in Britain. Britain was the single largest free-trade area in Europe, with good roads and waterways without tolls or other internal trade barriers. There were rich deposits of coal and iron ore. The political structure was stable, and property was absolutely secure. A sound system of banking and public credit created a good investment climate. Taxation in Britain was heavy, but it received legal approval from Parliament. Taxes were efficiently and fairly collected, largely from indi-

rect taxes with all regions and persons from all classes paying the same taxes. Besides satisfying domestic consumer demand, the British economy also benefited from the demand for goods from the North American colonies. Finally, British society was relatively mobile. Persons who had money or could earn it could rise socially.

New Methods of Textile Production   Although eighteenth-century European society was devoted primarily to agriculture, small-scale household manufacturing permeated the countryside. The same peasants who tilled the land in spring and summer often spun thread or wove textiles in winter. Under the domestic or *putting-out system*, agents of urban textile merchants took wool or other unfinished fiber to the homes of peasants, who spun it into thread. The agent then transported the thread to other peasants, who wove it into the finished product. The merchant sold the wares. In literally thousands of peasant cottages from Ireland to Austria stood either a spinning wheel or a hand loom. Sometimes the spinners or weavers owned their own equipment, but more often than not, by the middle of the

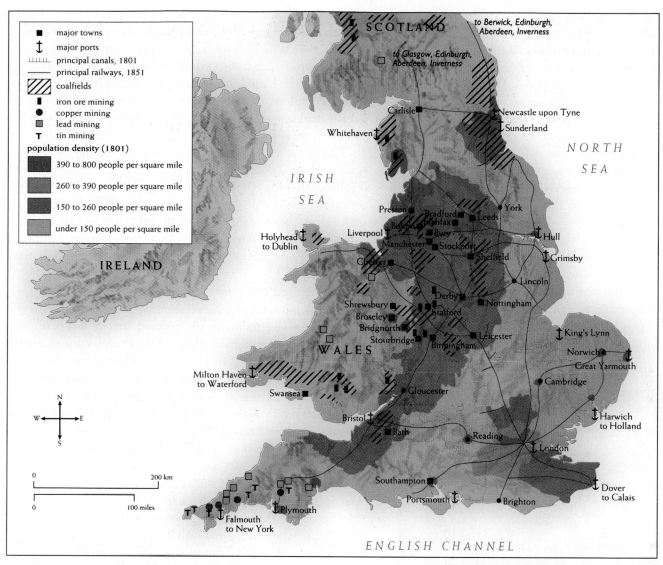

MAP 20–6 The Industrial Revolution in Britain.   Richly endowed with coal and iron ore, possessing many natural ports, and a network of navigable waterways, Britain exploited these advantages to become the world's first industrial nation.

century, the merchant capitalist owned the machinery as well as the raw material.

What must be kept constantly in mind is that eighteenth-century industrial development took place within this rural setting. The peasant family living in a one- or two-room cottage, not the factory, was the basic unit of production. The family economy, rather than the industrial factory economy, characterized the century.

By midcentury production bottlenecks had developed within the domestic system. The demand for cotton textiles was growing more rapidly than production. This demand arose particularly in Great Britain, whose growing population wanted cotton textiles, as did its colonies in North America. The most famous inventions of the Industrial Revolution were devised in response to this consumer demand for cotton textiles.

Cotton textile weavers had the technical capacity to produce enough fabric to satisfy demand. However, the spinners could not produce as much thread as the weavers needed and could use. This imbalance had been created during the 1730s by John Kay's invention of the flying shuttle, which increased the productivity of the weavers. Thereafter, manufacturers and merchants offered prizes for the invention of a machine to eliminate this bottleneck. In about 1765 James Hargreaves (d. 1778) invented the **spinning jenny**. Initially this machine allowed 16 spindles of thread to be spun, but by the close of the century it included as many as 120 spindles.

The spinning jenny broke the bottleneck between the productive capacity of the spinners and the weavers, but it was still a piece of machinery that was used in the cottage. The invention that took cotton textile manufacture from the home to the factory was Richard Arkwright's (1732–1792) **water frame**, patented in 1769. It was a water-powered device designed to permit the production of a purely cotton fabric rather than a cotton fabric containing linen fiber for durability. Eventually Arkwright lost his patent rights, and other manufacturers were able to use his invention freely. As a result, numerous factories sprang up in the countryside near streams that provided the necessary water power. From the 1780s onward the cotton industry could meet an ever-expanding demand. Between 1780 and 1800 cotton output increased by 800 percent. By 1815 cotton composed 40 percent of the value of British domestic exports, and by 1830 just over 50 percent.

The Steam Engine The new technology in textile manufacture vastly increased cotton production and revolutionized a major consumer industry. But the invention that more than any other enabled industrialization to grow on itself and expand into one area of production after another was the steam engine. This machine provided for the first time in human his-

tory a steady and essentially unlimited source of inanimate power. Unlike engines powered by water or wind, the steam engine, driven by the burning of coal, was a portable source of industrial power that did not fail or falter as the seasons of the year changed. Unlike human or animal power, the steam engine depended on mineral energy that never tired. Finally, the steam engine could be applied to many industrial and, eventually, transportation uses.

The first practical engine using steam power was invented by Thomas Newcomen (1663–1729) in the early eighteenth century. It was large, inefficient in its use of energy, and practically untransportable. Nonetheless, English mine operators used it to pump water out of coal and tin mines. By the late eighteenth century almost a hundred Newcomen machines were operating in the mining districts of England.

During the 1760s James Watt (1736–1819) began to experiment with a model of a Newcomen machine at the University of Glasgow. He gradually understood that if the condenser were separated from the piston and the cylinder, much greater efficiency would result. In 1769 he patented his new invention, but his design required exceedingly precise metalwork. Watt soon found a partner in Matthew Boulton (1728–1809), a toy manufacturer in Birmingham, the city with the most skilled metalworkers in Britain. Watt and Boulton in turn consulted with John Wilkinson (1728–1808), a cannon manufacturer, to find ways to drill the precise metal cylinders required by Watt's design. In 1776 the Watt steam engine found its first commercial application pumping water from mines.

The use of the steam engine spread slowly because until 1800 Watt retained the exclusive patent rights and was reluctant to modify the engine. Boulton eventually persuaded him to adapt the engines for use in running cotton mills. By the early nineteenth century the steam engine had become the prime mover for all industry. With its application to ships and then to wagons on iron rails, it also revolutionized transportation.

▲ **Blacksmith Shop.** During the 18th century, most goods were produced in small workshops, such as this English blacksmith shop shown in a painting by Joseph Wright of Derby (1734–1797), or in the homes of artisans. Not until very late in the century, with the early stages of industrialization, did a few factories appear.
Joseph Wright of Derby, "The Blacksmith's Shop," signed and dated 1771, oil on canvas, 50 1/2 × 41 in. (128.3 × 104.0 cm). Yale Center for British Art, Paul Mellon Collection.

CHRONOLOGY

Major Inventions in the Textile-Manufacturing Revolution

1733	John Kay's flying shuttle
1765	James Hargreaves's spinning jenny (patent 1770)
1769	James Watt's steam engine patent
1769	Richard Arkwright's water frame patent
1787	Edmund Cartwright's power loom

Iron Production   The manufacture of high-quality iron has been basic to modern industrial development. It constitutes the chief element of all heavy industry and land or sea transport and is the material out of which most productive machinery itself has been manufactured. During the early eighteenth century British iron-makers produced less than 25,000 tons annually. Three factors held back the production of the metal. First, charcoal rather than coke was used to smelt the ore. Charcoal, which is derived from wood, was becoming scarce, and it did not burn at as high a temperature as coke, which is derived from coal. Second, until the perfection of the steam engine, insufficient blasts could be achieved in the furnaces. Finally, the demand for iron was limited. The elimination of the first two problems eliminated the third.

In the course of the century, British ironmakers began to use coke, and the steam engine provided new power for the blast furnaces. Coke was abundant because of Britain's large coal deposits. The steam engine both improved iron production and increased the demand for iron.

In 1784 Henry Cort (1740–1800) introduced a new method for melting and stirring the molten ore. Cort's process produced a purer iron. He also developed a rolling mill that continually shaped the still-molten metal into bars, rails, or other forms. Previously, the metal had been pounded into these forms.

All of these innovations achieved a better, more versatile, and cheaper product. The demand for iron grew as its price went down. By the early nineteenth century annual British iron production amounted to over a million tons. The lower cost of iron in turn lowered the cost of steam engines and allowed them to be used more widely.

European Cities
PATTERNS OF PREINDUSTRIAL URBANIZATION

Remarkable changes occurred in the pattern of city growth between 1500 and 1800. In 1500 there were approximately 156 cities within Europe (excluding Hungary and Russia) with a population greater than 10,000. Only four of those cities—Paris, Milan, Venice, and Naples—had more than 100,000 inhabitants. By 1800 approximately 363 cities had 10,000 or more inhabitants, and 17 of those had populations larger than 100,000. The percentage of the European population living in urban areas had risen from just over 5 percent to just over 9 percent. The urban concentration had also shifted from southern Mediterranean Europe to the north.

URBAN CLASSES

Social divisions were as marked in the cities of the eighteenth century as they were in the industrial centers of the nineteenth.

Dress Shop. Consumption of all forms of consumer goods increased greatly in the 18th century. This engraving illustrates a shop, probably in Paris. Here women, working apparently for a woman manager, are making dresses and hats to meet the demands of the fashion trade.
Bildarchiv Preussischer Kulturbesitz.

The expansion of the European population further stimulated change and challenge to tradition, hierarchy, and corporateness. The traditional economic and social organization (the family economy) had presupposed a stable or declining population. A larger population created the need for new ways to solve old problems. The social hierarchy had to accommodate more people. Corporate groups, such as the guilds, had to confront an expanded labor force. New wealth meant that birth would cease to determine social relationships.

The eighteenth century furthermore witnessed the beginning of industrial production in response to the demands for consumer goods by the expanding population. New inventions greatly increasing productive capacity first appeared in the English textile industry. Thereafter industrial modes of production spread to the manufacture of iron. The steam engine provided a portable source of energy allowing factories to be moved from the countryside into cities.

Industrialization also affected Europe's relations with much of the non-European world. For the first time in history, major changes in one region of Europe left virtually no corner of the globe untouched. By the close of the eighteenth century, a movement toward world interconnectedness and interdependence had begun.

Review Questions

1. By the end of the seventeenth century, England and France had different systems of government with different religious policies. What were the main differences? Similarities? Why did each nation develop as it did?

2. How and why did Russia emerge as a great power? Discuss the character of Peter the Great. How were his domestic reforms related to his military ambitions? What were his methods of reform? To what extent did he succeed?

3. What were the main points of conflict between Britain and France in North America, the West Indies, and India? What were the results of these conflicts by 1763? Which countries emerged stronger from the Seven Years' War and why?

4. Why were so many people living in the European countryside dependent upon the aristocracy?

5. How would you define the term *family economy*? In what ways were the lives of women constrained by the family economy in preindustrial Europe? What active roles were possible for women?

6. What caused the agricultural revolution? How did technological innovations help change European agriculture? To what extent did the English aristocracy contribute to the agricultural revolution? What were some of the reasons for peasant revolts in Europe in the eighteenth century?

7. What factors led to the Industrial Revolution of the eighteenth century? What were some of the technological innovations and why were they important? Why did Great Britain take the lead in the Industrial Revolution? How did the consumer contribute to the Industrial Revolution?

8. Describe city life during the eighteenth century. Were all European cities of the same character? What changes had taken place in the distribution of population in cities and towns? Compare the lifestyle of the upper class with those of the middle and lower classes.

9. What was the status of European Jews in the Old Regime? How were they made to live as a people apart from the rest of the European population? What were the sources of prejudice against Jews in Europe?

Key Terms

absolutism   (p. 573)

agricultural revolution   (p. 596)

aristocratic resurgence   (p. 589)

boyars   (p. 578)

divine right of kings   (p. 578)

domestic or putting-out system   (p. 598)

enclosures   (p. 596)

family economy   (p. 592)

ghettos   (p. 603)

Glorious Revolution   (p. 575)

Industrial Revolution   (p. 597)

Junkers   (p. 581)

Old Regime   (p. 588)

parliamentary monarchy   (p. 573)

Pragmatic Sanction   (p. 581)

Puritans   (p. 573)

spinning jenny   (p. 599)

streltsy   (p. 578)

Table of Ranks   (p. 580)

water frame   (p. 600)

Documents CD-ROM

From Old Regime to Revolution

18.2 The Ideal Absolute State (1697): Jean Domat

18.3 The Sighs of Enslaved France (1690): Pierre Jurieu

18.5 "What is the Third Estate?" (January 1789): The Abbè Sieyès

NOTE: *To learn more about the topics in this chapter, see the Suggested Readings at the end of the book.*

21

The Last Great Islamic Empires 1500–1800

ISLAMIC EMPIRES

- The Ottoman Empire

- The Safavid Shi'ite Empire

- Mughals

ISLAMIC ASIA

- Central Asia: Islamization and Isolation

- Power Shifts in the Southern Seas

◄ Firdawsi (ca. 935–1020), born Abu ol-Qasem Mansur, composed one of the world's great epic poems, the *Shah-nameh*, or *Book of Kings*, an account of Persia's sovereigns, historical and legendary, up to the Muslim conquest of 652. The *Shah-nameh* was recited and illustrated for centuries, but it was under the patronage of Tahmasp I, the second Safavid shah, that the most brilliant known manuscript of the royal history of Persia was undertaken. In 1522, two years before ascending the throne, Shah Tahmasp, still in his teens, directed painters and calligraphers to begin their labors on the unique work of art shown here. Firdawsi is visible in the lower-left corner in this episode from the poem and Tahmasp is believed to be the young man on the far right. The scene harmoniously combines various sophisticated and refined-features of classical Persian painting.

By permission of the Houghton Library, Harvard University, the Houghton Shahnama, ed., Martin Bernard Dickson (Cambridge, MA: Harvard University Press, 1981), vol. 1,45.

The Last Great Islamic Empires

Islamic vitality between 145 and 1650 was exemplified by the three mighty empires and prosperous societies of the Ottomans, Safavids, and Mughals. All three built vast bureaucracies using Islamic ideology, but even more their own imperial vigor to legitimize their rule. They also built arguably the greatest cities in the world of their time and patronized the arts to stimulate important new traditions of Islamic literature, calligraphy, painting, and architecture. Yet they were profoundly conservative societies. Economically they remained closely tied to agricultural production and taxation based on land. Perhaps because they were such powerful, wealthy, and successful societies, they did not undergo the kind of social or religio-political revolutions that rocked the Western world after 1500. Thus, much like the societies of China and Japan in the same period, they did not experience the sort of generative changes in material and intellectual life that the still comparatively underdeveloped Western world experienced in the sixteenth, seventeenth, and eighteenth centuries (although their intellectual culture was vibrant and diverse). There was no compelling challenge to traditional Islamic ideals of societal organizations and human responsibility, even though many Islamic movements of the eighteenth century did call for communal and personal reform.

As one historian has put it, the striking growth of Islamic societies and cultures in this age was "not one of *origination*, but rather one of *culmination* in a culture long already mature." Even in their heydays, these empires produced much scientific work, but no scientific revolution; much art, architecture, and literature of high quality, but none that departed radically in concept or inspiration from previous traditions; political consolidation and also expansion, but no conquest of significant new markets or territories; commercial prosperity, but no beginnings of a real commercial or industrial revolution. By the latter half of this period, all were in economic, political, and military decline. By contrast, the West, having lagged behind the Islamic world in economic, social, and cultural development as well as political and military might dur-ing the Middle Ages and much of the early modern period, was by the eighteenth century in the midst of an industrial (and military) revolution and finally poised to challenge successfully the Islamic empires.

Thus it is not surprising that European expansionism impinged fatefully in these three centuries upon Africa, India, Indonesia, and the heartland culture of the Islamic world, rather than the reverse. Neither the great imperial Islamic states, the smaller Islamic sultanates and emirates, the diverse Hindu kingdoms, nor the varied African states (let alone the smaller societies of Africa, the Americas, and the South Pacific) fared well in their encounters with Europeans during this age. The growing European domination of the seas allowed Europeans to contain as well as to bypass the major Islamic lands in their quest for commercial empires.

Industrial development and military technology joined economic wealth and political stability by the late 1700s to give the West global military supremacy for the first time. Before 1800 the Europeans were able to bring only minor Islamic states under colonial administrations. However, the footholds they gained in Africa, India, and Southeast Asia laid the groundwork for rapid colonial expansion after 1800. The age of the last great Muslim empires was the beginning of the first great modern European empires. The colonialism of the nineteenth century accompanied the relentless advance of Western industrial, commercial, and military power that held sway until the mid-twentieth century.

THINK AHEAD

- How did the trajectory of development differ between the Islamic empires and Europe in the period from 1500–1800?

- Why, after centuries as the "underdog," was Europe by the end of the eighteenth century finally able to challenge the power of the Islamic empires?

- Why was the Islamic world, more than China and Japan, increasingly subject to European intrusion during the early modern period?

Between 1450 and 1650 islamic culture and statecraft blossomed. The creation of three powerful empires and several strong regional states was the culmination of long processes in Islamic history. During this time the ideal of a universal Muslim caliphate yielded to the reality of multiple secular, albeit distinctively "Islamic," sultanates.

The simultaneous growth of the Ottoman, Safavid, and Mughal Empires, sometimes called the "gunpowder empires," marked the global apogee of Islamic culture and power. By about 1600 the Ottoman Turks controlled Asia Minor, the Fertile Crescent, the Balkans, Crimean Europe, the Islamic Mediterranean, and Arabia; the Persian

Safavids ruled all of greater Iran; and descendants of Timur—the Timurid line known as the Mughals—governed Afghanistan and most of the Indian subcontinent. Around these empires were arrayed Muslim khanates of Central Asia and Russia, sultanates of Southeast Asia and East Africa, the Sharifian state of Morocco, and regional empires of the Sudan in which Islam played a significant role (see Map 21–1).

In 1600 Islamic civilization seemed as strong and vital as that of Western Europe, China, or Japan, yet Islamic military preeminence and economic and political strength were declining. By the late seventeenth century Islamic military power was almost everywhere in retreat before the rising tide of

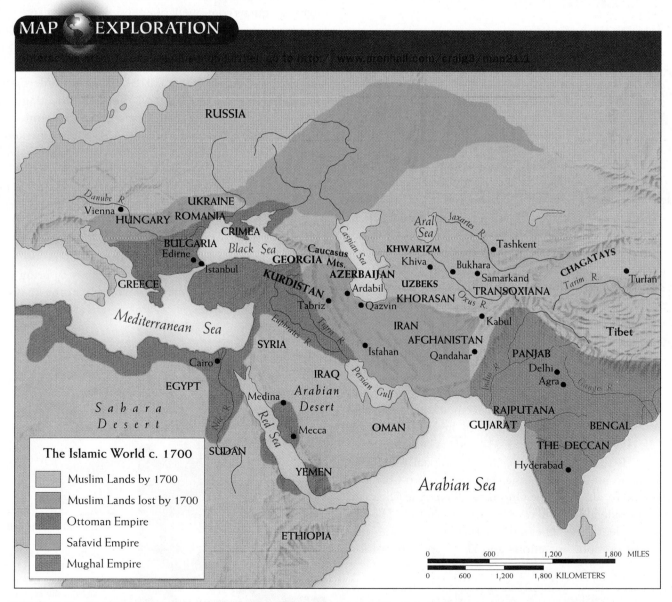

MAP 🌐 EXPLORATION

Interactive version of this map is available. Go to http://www.prenhall.com/craig3/map21.1

The Islamic World c. 1700

- Muslim Lands by 1700
- Muslim Lands lost by 1700
- Ottoman Empire
- Safavid Empire
- Mughal Empire

MAP 21–1 The Islamic World ca. 1700. The three rival "gunpowder" empires—the Safavid, Mughal, and Ottoman, empires—dominated the Islamic heartlands. Despite variations, the three empires demonstrated somewhat similar organizational structures.

Western European military and economic trading expansion and empire building, even though Islamic cultural life flourished and Islam continued to enjoy widesbread acceptance globally between 1500 and 1800.

Hindus were the chief religious group the Muslims displaced. Islam never ousted the Indian Buddhist cultures of Burma, Thailand, and Indochina. Islam did, however, win most of Malaysia, Sumatra, Java, and the "Spice Islands" of the Moluccas. By the end of the fifteenth century, Islam had also spread along the East African coast.

In this chapter we focus first on the three major Islamic empires of the period and then turn briefly to the smaller Islamic political and cultural centers of Central Asia and the coastlands of southern Asia and the Indies where European power was having an impact on what had been a virtual Muslim monopoly on maritime trade.

ISLAMIC EMPIRES

The Ottoman Empire

ORIGINS AND DEVELOPMENT OF THE OTTOMAN STATE BEFORE 1600

The Ottomans were a Turkish dynasty that rose to prominence as one of various groups of western Oghuz Turks from the steppes of Central Asia who came to Anatolia as settlers and Muslim frontier warriors.[1] The Ottomans reached Anatolia (Asia Minor) in the time of the Seljuks of Rum (1098–1308), who were the first western Turks to have founded a lasting state there (see Chapter 13). By about 1300, the newcomers had built one of several small military states along the Byzantine-Seljuk frontier in western Anatolia. In the fourteenth century several vigorous leaders expanded their territories east into central Anatolia and west across the Dardanelles (in 1356) onto European soil in the Byzantine lands of Macedonia and modern Bulgaria (see Map 21–1). Exchanging grants of revenue-producing conquered land (*timars*) for military service, the Ottomans built both a formidable fighting force and a loyal military aristocracy.

By 1402 the center of Ottoman rule had shifted northwest to Edirne on the Balkan Peninsula itself. Ottoman control then extended northwest as far as the Danube and east across central Anatolia. Only encircled Constantinople formed an alien pocket within these dominions, and it finally fell in 1453 to Sultan Mehmed II, "the Conqueror" (r. 1451–1481). Constantinople, now renamed "Istanbul," became the Ottoman capital. After hundreds of years proud Byzantium, the center of Eastern Christendom, was no more, although the Ottomans allowed the Christian patriarch to preside in Istanbul over the Eastern church. The fall of Constantinople, or the "liberation of Istanbul," was both the culmination of previous war efforts and also a springboard for Ottoman European ambitions. As their expansionist and extraordinary conquests continued, often justified in the name of Islam, they became in Christian European eyes the scourge of God.

By 1512 Ottoman rule was secure in virtually all of southeastern Europe and north of the Black Sea in most of the Ukraine. Under Selim I (r. 1512–1520) and Süleyman, "the Lawgiver" (known in the West as "Süleyman the Magnificent," r. 1520–1566), this sovereignty was greatly expanded. Selim subjugated the Egyptian Mamluks (1517) and annexed Syria-Palestine, most of North Africa, the Yemen, and western Arabia, including Mecca and Medina. Selim also nullified the Shi'ite threat from Iran in the east (see below). Süleyman extended Ottoman control over Kurdistan and Georgia (in the Caucasus), as well as Mesopotamia and Iraq. He also advanced Ottoman borders in eastern Europe. Having won much of Hungary and nearly taken Vienna by siege in 1526–1529, he was able by battle and treaty to bring virtually all of Hungary under direct Ottoman rule in the 1540s.

◄ **The Fall of Constantinople in 1453.** Turkish forces under the leadership of Sultan Mehmed II "the Conqueror," extinguish the last remnants of the Byzantine Empire.
Sonia Halliday Photographs.

---

[1] The Ottomans, sometimes called *Osmanlis*, are named after Osman (1259–1326), also rendered *Othman* or *Uthman*, a *ghazi* said to have founded the dynasty when he set up a border state about 1288 on the Byzantine frontier in northwestern Anatolia.

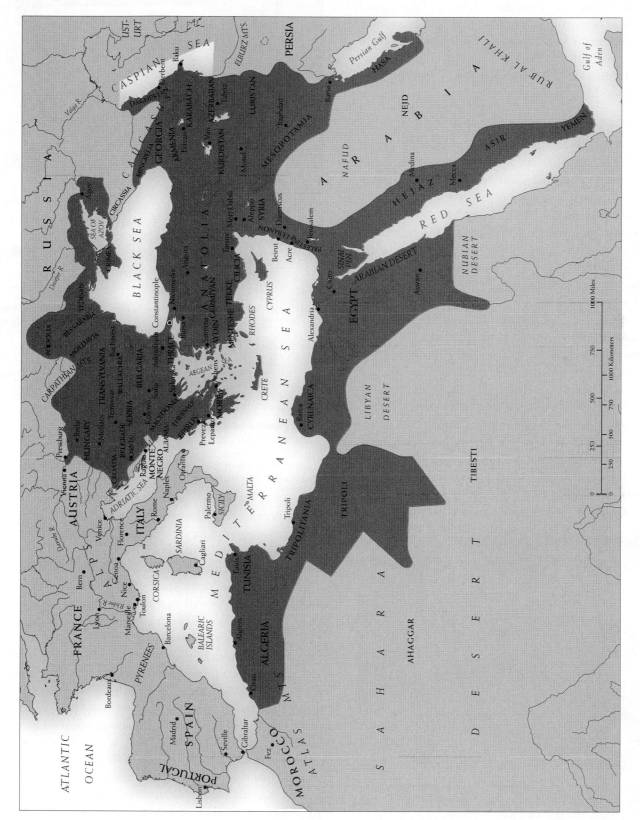

MAP 21–2 The Ottoman Empire at its Zenith. This large and multiethnic empire spanned three continents and lasted for more than 400 years.

The Ottoman ruler could now claim to be the Abbasid heir and caliph for all Muslims. This claim was symbolized by the addition (begun by Selim I, after the Mamluk conquest in 1517) of the title "Protector of the Sacred Places [Mecca and Medina]" to that of emperor, *padishah*. At this point, Ottoman military might was unmatched by any state in the world, except possibly China. It controlled a large geographical area—home to numerous linguistic and ethnic groups—making the Ottoman an empire in every sense of the word.

THE "CLASSICAL" OTTOMAN ORDER

Mehmed II was the true founder of the Ottoman order. He replaced the tribal chieftains with loyal servants of the ruler; he initiated a tradition of formal governmental legislation with his **Qanun-name** *("Lawbook")*; and he organized the *ulama* into a hierarchy under a single "Sheikh of Islam." In the next century Süleyman earned his title "Lawgiver" by his legislation touching all aspects of life and all social ranks, his reconciliation of customary law and **Shari'a**, religious law, and his efforts to regularize both law and bureaucracy.

The entire Ottoman state was organized as one vast military institution. All members, whatever their function, held military ranks as the standing "army" of the state under the hereditary leadership of the Sultan. This centralized state was supported by the productivity of its Muslim and non-Muslim subjects, such as Jewish and Armenian merchants. The ruling class were Muslims, shared the common Ottoman culture, and had to give utter allegiance to the sultan. The state organization included the palace and three other functional divisions: the administrative or ruling institution, the military institution, and the religious or learned institution. The palace included the sultan, his **harem**, his ministers, and servants. The privy council, headed by the grand vizier, together with the chancery, the imperial treasury, and the remain-

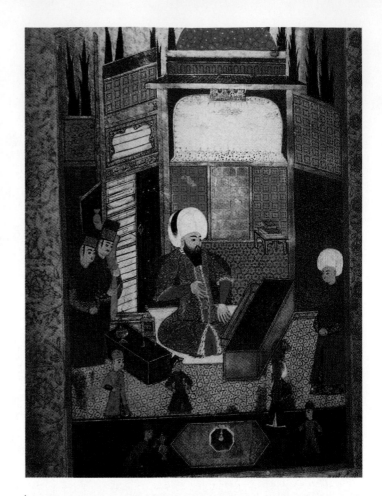

▲ **Süleyman the Lawgiver.** Süleyman giving advice to the Crown Prince, Mehmed Khan. From a contemporaneous Ottoman miniature.
Suleyman I (Kanuni); Shehzade by Talikizade Suphi. Folio 79a of the Talikizade Shehnamesi, Library at the Topkapi Palace Museum, A3592, Photograph courtesy of Talat Halman.

▲ **Topkapi Palace, Istanbul.** Inside the imperial harem, a sanctuary from the outside world, this elegant room was used to entertain the Sultan who watched the proceedings from his large throne.
Tony Souter © Dorling Kindersley.

ing civil bureaucracy, formed the backbone of the ruling or administrative institution. Although men held the keys to power, women also had certain important roles, most often concealed to the public eye. Traditional Turkish customs assumed that power was vested collectively in the family. Women had some ceremonial functions; they also played vital roles in court polities, especially in selection of officers and in negotiating economic policy.

Several measures helped ensure the ongoing strength of the sultan at the apex of the ruling institution. Young Ottoman princes were given administrative and leadership training in the provinces, which kept them from being sheltered in the palace and gave them experience of life outside the capital. Stability of succession was traditionally guaranteed by the practice of fratricide in the ruling family, which, legalized formally in Mehmed II's *Qanun-name*, continued until the late sixteenth century. Thus the succession was theoretically left to God, the strongest aspirant to the sultanate having to assert himself and seize power, after which he was expected to execute his brothers to eliminate future competing claims to the throne.

The Ottomans co-opted the legal-religious and educational-intellectual roles of the religious scholars, or *ulama*, for the service of the state, making them an arm of the government under a single religious authority, the **Grand Mufti** or "Shaykh of Islam." This highly organized branch of the state was open only to Muslim men and included the entire system of courts and judges. It was based on a comprehensive network ranging from local mosque schools to the four elite madrasas built around the Süleymaniye Mosque in Istanbul during Süleyman's reign. Scholars' ranks within the graded hierarchy of the *ulama* reflected the level of schooling and teaching they had attained.

While the *ulama* were thus under state control, the state itself was formally committed to maintaining the divinely ordained *Shari'a*, and the *ulama* enjoyed great esteem. This structure may account for the fact that whereas the *ulama* in both Safavid Iran and Mughal India often differed with their rulers, the Ottoman *ulama* usually functioned tamely as part of the state apparatus.

Although the religious establishment upheld the supremacy of the *Shari'a* and the sultan recognized its authority, the functional law of the land was the highly organized state administrative law—the practical code, or *Qanun*, established by the ruler. The *Shari'a* as interpreted by the *ulama* theoretically governed the *Qanun*, and often the sultan formally applied traditional religious norms in his regulations. The conformity of these regulations to the *Shari'a* sometimes came from the genuine piety of a particular administrator or ruler and was sometimes only a pious fiction, something also true for Safavid Iran and Mughal India.

The key ingredient to Ottoman power, however, was the military. The Ottoman rulers kept its loyalty by two means: checks on the power of the old landed aristocracy by careful registry and control of *timar* lands, and the use of slave soldiers with allegiance only to the sultan. The army was based originally on the provincial cavalry whose officers were supported with *timar* land revenues in lieu of cash wages. The state held all conquered agricultural land as its direct property, granting peasants hereditary land use but not ownership. Careful records were kept of the revenue due on all lands, and as long as the state was strong, so too was its control over productive land and the cavalry-gentry whom *timar* revenues supported. But even as early as 1400 the Ottoman rulers tried to reduce the cavalry-gentry's preeminence by employing specialized infantry troops of well-trained and well-paid slave soldiers (equipped, unlike the cavalry, with firearms) whose loyalty was to the sultan alone.

To sustain the quality of these slave troops, the Ottomans developed a unique institution: the provincial slave levy, or ***devshirme***. This institution selected young Christian boys from the provincial peasantry to be raised as Muslims; most came from the Balkan peasantry. They were trained to serve in both army and bureaucracy at all levels, from provincial officer to grand vizier. The most famous slave corps was the **Janissaries**, the elite infantry troops of the empire. Muslim boys were not allowed into the slave corps, although some parents tried to buy them a place in what offered the most promising careers in the empire. Until 1572 marriage was forbidden to the slave soldiers, which further ensured loyalty and prevented hereditary claims on office.

AFTER SÜLEYMAN: CHALLENGES AND CHANGE

The reign of Süleyman marked the peak of Ottoman prestige and power. Further territorial gains were made in the seventeenth century, and the Ottoman state long remained a major force in European and Asian politics. However, beginning with the reign of Süleyman's weak son, Selim II (1566–1574), the empire was plagued by military corruption, governmental decentralization, and maritime setbacks. Economically there were agricultural failures, commercial imbalances, and inflation. Yet culturally and intellectually, the seventeenth and eighteenth centuries were periods of impressive accomplishments and lively activity. Overall, these ensuing two centuries witnessed a seesaw pattern between decline and vitality.

▲ **Devshirme.** An Ottoman portrayal of the *Devshirme*. This miniature painting from about 1558 depicts the recruiting of young Christian children for the Sultan's elite Janissary corps.

Arifi, "Suleymanname," Topkapi Palace Museum, II 1517, fol. 31b, photograph courtesy of Talat Halman.

Political and Military Developments   The post-Süleyman era began on a sour note with the loss of territory in the Caucasus and Mesopotamia to the Persian Safavids (1603). By this time the Ottoman military apparatus was already weakened, partly from fighting two-front wars with the Safavids and the Habsburgs and partly because of European advances in military and naval technology. The Janissaries became increasingly disruptive. By 1600 they had largely replaced the provincial cavalry as new warfare styles made cavalry obsolete. By 1600 Muslims were allowed into the Janissary corps, marriage was possible, and the *devshirme* was declining in use (it ended just over a century later). During the seventeenth century, the Janissaries became increasingly corrupt as they tampered with politics, trying to influence decision making and even dynastic succession. Finally, the increasing employment of mercenaries resulted in peacetime in the release of masses of unemployed armed men

---

DOCUMENT | The Distinctiveness of Ottoman Identity and Culture

Presiding over a pluralistic culture, the Ottoman Turks, themselves a people from the periphery of the central Islamic lands, developed a distinctive "Ottoman" identity and culture that was most evident in their ruling elite. The following selections from members of that elite describe some of the values and qualities they saw as important to Ottoman identity. In the first, Mustafa Ali (d. 1600), a major historian, intellectual, and official of the Ottoman state, lists the special divine favors granted the Ottoman rulers. In the second, another historian, Kinalizade Ali, adopts an ancient political saying attributed to Aristotle and others to describe the prerequisites for an ordered polity under the Shari'a.

♦ Compare the two passages. What common themes emerge?

1. The Gifts of Divine Favor Given the Ottoman Dynasty

The first gift: They reside all by themselves in a palace like unique jewels in the depth of the oyster-shell, and totally sever all relations with relatives and dependents. The slave girls and slave pages that have access to their honored private quarters (harem), who are evidently at least three to four thousand individuals, are all strangers and the person of the monarch is like a single gem in their midst . . .

The second gift: Their religious convictions being immaculate and their character like a shining mirror, it has never happened that a single member of that noble family ever swerved from the road of orthodoxy or that one valiant sultan befriended himself with an unseemly doctrine.

The third gift: The Lord, the Creator and Protector, has always hidden that great race under His protection and it has never been heard that the plague would have entered their flourishing palace or that an individual belonging to that blemishless progeny would have been struck by the horror of the pestilence and would have died of it.

The fourth gift: Whenever they conquered a province and, destroying and eradicating its castles and estates, were confronted with the necessity of appointing a magistrate and assigning a substantial force on their own authority they considered it a sign of weakness, like Alexander the Great, to appoint again one of the great of that province and to assign him certain revenues; may [that province] be as far away as can be, they would opt to send one of the attendants of their Gate of Happiness [there] as sanjaq begi, and to Yemen and Ethiopia and to very remote places like Algeria a begler-begi. No such absolute power was given to the earlier sovereigns.

The fifth gift: The various special troops in their victory-oriented army and the various tools of war and battle use that are given to them were not available to the brawny fists of anyone of the countless armies [of previous times]. To their attacks going downward and going upward are the same, to their victory-imprinted military music low and high notes are of the same level and equal. In their eyes, as it were, the conquest of a castle is like destroying a spider's web, and in their God-assisted hands to beat the enemies is clearly like pulling out a hair from the beard of a decrepit old man.

The sixth gift: The coherence of the figures in the registers of their revenues and the order of the recordings in the ledgers of their expenses are so strict that they and their salaried classes are free of worries. Consequently, their income exceeds their necessary expenses, their gain is larger than [the expenses for] the important affairs of state.

2. The Need of Authority to Uphold the Shari'a

There can be no royal authority without the military
There can be no military without wealth
The subjects produce the wealth
Justice preserves the subjects' loyalty to the sovereign
Justice requires harmony in the world
The world is a garden, its walls are the state
The Holy Law [Shari'a] orders the state
There is no support for the Holy Law except through royal authority.

Selection 1 from Andreas Tietze, *Mustafa Ali's Counsel for Sultans of 1581*, Verlag Der Osterreichischen Akademie Der Wissenshaften, Vienna, 1979, pp. 38–39. Selection 2 from Cornell H. Fleischer, *Bureaucrat and Intellectual in the Ottoman Empire: The Historian Mustafa Ali (1541–1600)*, Princeton University Press, 1986, p. 262.

into the countryside, which led to the sacking of provincial towns, banditry, and revolts, which disrupted society.

Murad IV (r. 1623–1640) introduced reforms and ruled with an iron hand, but his death left again a weak central authority. The Koprülüs, father and son, two capable viziers (r. 1656–1676), briefly renewed strong administrative control and military success, but thereafter the central institutions decayed.

Economic Developments Financing the Ottoman state grew ever more difficult. The increase in the Janissary corps from 12,000 to 36,000 men between the early 1500s and 1600 drained state coffers. Inflation grew as the coinage was debased. In contrast to the mercantilist and protectionist policies of European powers, the Ottomans discouraged exports and encouraged imports since too many exports would have raised domestic prices. This damaged the economy in the long run. The population doubled in the sixteenth century, and unemployment grew after 1600. Increased decentralization paved the way for the rise of provincial notables (*ayan*), who became virtually independent in the eighteenth century. Tax farming also went hand-in-glove with the rise of large private estates. New taxes were imposed and old emergency levies regularized, and taxes were required in cash rather than in kind and increasingly on a communal rather than an individual basis.

Culture and Society The seventeenth and eighteenth centuries were an era of genuine vitality in poetry, prose, music, painting, cartography, historiography, astronomy, and other fields. The Ottoman patronage of the arts and sciences was one way to assert the Ottoman claim to Islamic and universal authority. The seventeenth century saw especially lively intellectual exchange, both religious and secular. But it was also a time when the *ulama* became an aristocratic and increasingly corrupt elite. Major religious posts became hereditary sinecures for sons and other relatives of a handful of families who had produced prominent *ulama*, and the pasts were often sold or leased. (See Document, "The Distinctiveness of Ottoman Identity and Culture.")

In literature and the arts, the seventeenth and eighteenth centuries were highly productive. Of the many individuals who were learned in many fields, Katib Chelebi (d. 1657) was the most illustrious; he wrote histories, social commentary, geographies, and encyclopedic works. Other important writers were the great historian of the Ottomans, Na'ima (d. 1716), the tireless traveler and travel writer Evliya Chelebi (d. ca. 1685), and probably the greatest Ottoman poet, Nedim (d. 1730). Ottoman art had been highly eclectic in the first century after Mehmed II, but in the latter sixteenth century a more conservative turn produced distinctively Ottoman artistic and architectural forms. The greatest name here is that of the imperial master architect Sinan (d. 1678). The first half of the eighteenth century was the

CHRONOLOGY

The Ottoman Empire

ca. 1280	Foundation of early Ottoman principality in Anatolia
1356	Ottomans cross Dardanelles into Europe
1451–1481	Rule of Sultan Mehmed II, "the Conqueror"
1453	Fall of Constantinople to Mehmed the Conqueror
1512–1520	Rule of Selim I
1517	Ottoman conquest of Egypt, assumption of claim to Abbasid caliphal succession from Mamluks
1520–1566	Rule of Süleyman, "the Lawgiver"
1526–1529	First Ottoman siege of Vienna
1578	Death of Ottoman master architect, Sinan
1656–1676	Governance of Koprülüs as viziers
1683	Second Ottoman siege of Vienna
1699	Treaty of Karlowitz, loss of Hungarian and other European territory
1774	Loss of Crimea to Russia; Tsar becomes formal protector of Ottoman Orthodox Christians
1918	End of empire

golden age of Ottoman poetry and art; it also saw the first Ottoman printing press and the beginning of strong European influence in the arts, architecture, and manners. In the popular sphere, the now classical form of Turkish theater (in which two men play male and female parts) began as early as the sixteenth century, perhaps under Jewish immigrant influence.

Socially, the period saw the consolidation of Ottoman society as a multi-ethnic and multireligious state. The empire encompassed a dizzying array of languages, religions, and ethnic identities. All subjects, both Muslim and non-Muslim, were organized into small communities called **millets** that were responsible for their community members from the cradle to the grave. The millets thus administered their educational, charitable, and judicial affairs and assisted the central government to collect taxes. Typically the millets were headed by a religious leader and enjoyed some degree of internal autonomy. Thus early on the Ottoman Empire proved to be a haven for a number of minority groups especially Jews. Considerable immigration of Jews into Ottoman societies following their expulsion from Spain during the Spanish Inquisition (1492) had brought new craftsmen, physicians, bankers, scholars, and even entertainers. The large Christian population of the empire was generally well treated, but in the eighteenth and nineteenth centuries they began to suffer from increasing taxes and other discrimination. As a result the Christians looked as never before to Christian Europe and Russia for liberation.

Still, state policy encouraged just treatment of all subjects; for example, "rescripts of justice" (mostly against the malpractices of tax collectors) were often issued. Although royal decrees reserved special privileges for Muslims, they seldom affected mass behavior. In the eighteenth century, however, relations between Muslims and non-Muslims deteriorated, in part because of the remarkable rise in the economic and social status of non-Muslims—in particular the rich mercantile middle class. Non-Muslims virtually monopolized foreign trade, and in the eighteenth century European countries gave many of them citizenship, which allowed them the trade privileges granted to foreign governments by the sultan.

One of the major social institutions of later Ottoman society, the coffeehouse, flourished from the mid–sixteenth century on. Probably originally a Sufi institution that came with coffee to the Mediterranean from the Yemen, the Ottoman coffeehouse rapidly became a major common space for socializing. Here people gathered to drink coffee, play games, watch puppet shows, read books, discuss public affairs, and even engage in political agitation. Despite bans by the sheikh of Islam because of the stimulant qualities of coffee, both the coffee habit and coffeehouses, like the similarly new imported habit of cigarette smoking, could not be suppressed. Different types of coffeehouses developed, each identified by its focus: music, theater, recitation, poetry, or Janissary or other professional affiliation (e.g., firefighting). The coffeehouse stimulated the development of a common Ottoman urban culture among lower and middle classes.

THE DECLINE OF OTTOMAN MILITARY AND POLITICAL POWER

After their failure in 1683 to take Vienna, the Ottomans were driven out of Hungary and Belgrade and never again seriously threatened Europe. In 1774 Russia took the Crimea and became the formal protector of the Orthodox Christians of the Islamic empire (1774). Whereas in the seventeenth century the Ottoman Empire was a relatively self-contained empire, by the mid–eighteenth century the empire was more dependent on the international system. Previously its economic growth had been based on conquest and the control of land as a source of wealth. But as soon as its expansion was stopped, the Ottoman Sultans were not fully prepared to adjust to changes in an increasingly West-European world economy that was increasingly geared towards capitalist accumulation and industrialisation. Henceforth, the Ottomans were prey to the West, never regaining their earlier power and influence before their collapse in 1918.

Outflanked by Russia to the north and by European sea power to the south and west, the Ottomans were blocked in the east by their implacable Shi'ite foes in Iran. They could not sustain the level of external trade needed to support their expensive wars, especially when, in the eighteenth century, Italian, British, and Dutch traders obtained special concessions for their trade in the Persian Gulf and Red Sea that Ottoman merchants did not have. Ultimately, their dependence on an agrarian-age economy proved insufficient to face the rising commercial and industrial powers of Europe.

The Safavid Shi'ite Empire

ORIGINS

As noted in Chapter 13, Iranian history changed under the Safavid dynasty after 1500. The Safavids had begun in the fourteenth century as hereditary Turkish spiritual leaders of a Sunni Sufi order, in the northwestern Iranian province of Azerbaijan. In the fifteenth century the Safavid order evolved a new and militant Shi'ite ideology. By claiming descent from the seventh imam of the Twelver Shia (see Chapter 13), the Safavid spiritual masters (*shaykhs* and **pirs**) became the focus of Shi'ite religious allegiance. Many adherents were won to the order and to Shi'ism from among the Turkoman tribesmen of eastern Anatolia, northern Syria, and northwestern Iran. These mounted warriors were called *Kizilbash* ("Red Heads") because of their distinctive red uniform hats which signaled their allegiance to the twelve Shi'ite imams and their Safavid master.

The growing strength of the Safavids brought about conflict with the dominant Sunni Turkoman groups in the region around Tabriz. The Safavids emerged victorious in 1501 under the leadership of the young Safavid master-designate Isma'il. Recognized as a divinely appointed representative of the "hidden" imam (see Chapter 11), Isma'il extended his sovereignty over the southern Caucasus, Azerbaijan, the Tigris-Euphrates valley, and all of western Iran by 1506 (see Map 21–3). Unified under a common religious identity and in league with Babur, the Timurid ruler of Kabul, the Safavids by 1512 had taken from the Uzbek Turks all of eastern Iran from the Oxus River south to the Arabian Sea. But the Uzbeks, however, became implacable foes of the Safavids and throughout the ensuing century often forced them to fight a debilitating two-front war, against Uzbeks in the east and Ottomans in the west.

A strong central rule now united traditional Iranian lands for the first time since the heyday of the Abbasid caliphate. It was a regime based on the existing Persian bureaucratic institutions, which in turn were based on Seljuk institutions. Shah Isma'il ruthlessly enforced Shi'ite conformity, which slowly took root across the realm—perhaps bolstered by a rising Persian self-consciousness in the face of the Sunni Ottomans, Arabs, Uzbeks, and Mughals who surrounded Iran. In the latter part of his reign, Shah Isma'il began to develop a more centralized bureaucracy at the expense of his Sufi enthusiasts. The shah was determined to rule not merely as a leader of a Sufi religious movement but also to govern, both culturally and politically, as a reconsturction of the historic Iranian monarchy. Although the shah had loyal tribal and religious support within his domain, Isma'il had tenu-

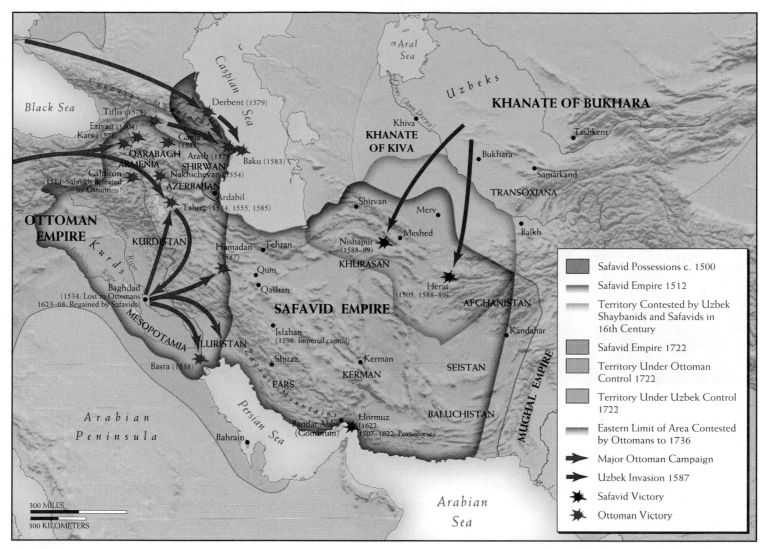

MAP 21–3 The Safavid Empire.   The Safavid Empire had a difficult time maintaining a cohesive state in the face of numerous invasions from both north and west.

ous ties with his neighbors, especially the leaders of the Ottoman Empire, who vigorously ensured that this Sufi inspired Shi'ite monarchy would not spread further into Ottoman terrain.

In 1514 the better-armed Ottoman army of Selim I soundly defeated the Safavid forces at Chaldiran, near Salmas, marking the beginning of an extended series of Ottoman-Safavid conflicts over the next two centuries. Chaldiran also marked the beginning of Kizilbash disaffection with Shah Isma'il and consequent efforts to take over power from the Safavids. Furthermore, this defeat gave the Ottomans control of the Fertile Crescent and forced the Safavids to move their capital and their focus eastward, first to Qazwin, and then to Isfahan.

SHAH ABBAS I

Isma'il's successor, Tahmasp I (r. 1524–1576), survived repeated attacks by both Ottomans and Uzbeks, in part through the strength of Shi'ite religious feeling and the alle-giance of the Iranian bureaucracy. A few years later, however, the greatest Safavid ruler Shah Abbas I (r. 1588–1629) brought able leadership to the Safavid domains. He regained provincial land for the state and used the revenue to pay for new troops from his Caucasian territories, thereby providing a counterweight to the sometimes unruly Kizilbash, who (like the old Ottoman cavalry) were supported by land revenue assignments. Shah Abbas not only pushed the Ottomans out of Azerbaijan and Iraq but also turned back new Uzbek invasions in Khorasan. He also sought alliances with the Ottomans' European enemies. This latter tactic, used by several Safavid rulers, reflects the deep military and economic divisions the new militant Persian Shi'ism had brought to the Islamic world. Abbas also broke the century-long Portuguese monopoly on trade along Persian shores and opened trade with English and Dutch commercial companies. His reign brought considerable prosperity to Iran, symbolized by the

Shah Abbas I. Shah Abbas I receiving a diplomatic embassy from the Turks in 1609.

Staatliche Museen zu Berlin/Bildarchiv Preussischer Kulturbesitz-Museum für Islamic Kunst.

magnificent capital he built at Isfahan which epitomized Safavid grandeur and aspirations—symbolized most vividly in its regal central square, the Maydan-i Shah.

The most enduring aspect of Safavid consolidation of power in Iran was the replacement of Sunni Islam with Shi'ite Islam as the official religion. Because Twelver Shi'ism was not grounded

The Shah's Mosque (Masjid-i Shah) in Isfahan, Iran. During its heyday as the Safavid capital, Isfahan was given the lofty epithet "half of the world." Its elegant architecture with its lavish use of ceramic tiles, reflect the majestic Safavid self-image.

Corbis-Bettmann.

in Iranian religious tradition, the Safavid Shahs imported religious scholars (*ulama*) primarily from today's Lebanon and Syria, placing them squarely in the service of the state to give legitimacy to the government. The Safavids discouraged pilgrimage to Mecca but instead emphasized visits to Karbala, or to the shrine of Husayn, the grandson of the Prophet Muhammad. Eventually, however, the relations between the government and the *ulama* became strained. By the seventeenth century, the *ulama* withdrew from political participation and refused to bestow direct legitimacy on the Shah.

SAFAVID DECLINE

After Shah Abbas, the empire rarely again enjoyed able leadership. This led finally to its decline and collapse, the chief causes of which were (1) continued two-front pressure from Ottoman and Uzbek armies, (2) economic decline, and (3) the increasing power and bigotry of the Shi'ite *ulama*. The conservative *ulama* not only introduced a Shi'ite legalism but also emphasized their own authority as interpreters of the law over that of the monarch. They also persecuted religious minorities and encouraged hatred of Sunni Muslims.

One result of Shi'ite exclusivism was tribal revolts among the Sunni Afghans. In the end, an Afghan leader captured Isfahan and forced the abdication of Husayn I (1694–1722). Safavid princes managed to retake control of western Iran, but the empire's greatness was past. A revived, but officially Sunni, monarchy under the talented Kizilbash tribal leader Nadir Shah (r. 1736–1747) and several successors restored much of Iran's lost territories. However, Nadir Shah's military ventures, which included an invasion of North India and the conquest of Delhi, sapped the empire's finances. After his autocratic and despotic reign, Iran could not regain stability for another half century.

CULTURE AND LEARNING

In the long run, the most impressive aspect of Safavid times, besides the conversion of Iran to Shi'ism, was the cultural and intellectual renaissance of the sixteenth and seventeenth centuries. The traditions of painting, with their origins in the powerful miniatures of the preceding century—notably those from Herat after 1450, exemplified by the work of the painter Bihzad (1440–1514) in late Timurid times—were cultivated and modified in Safavid times. Portraiture and scenes from everyday life became popular. Among the most developed crafts were ceramic tile, porcelain, and carpets. The magnificent architecture of Isfahan, especially evident in the exquisite gardens and grand arches and domes constructed in Shah Abbas's time gives breathtaking evidence of the developed sense of proportion, color, and design of Safavid taste. So impressive and ambitious was the scope of Isfahan that it became known as being "half the world," a lofty epithet which offers the notion that it was the quintessence of the religious and imperial Iranian world. It marks a high point in the lavish use of ceramic tiles to decorate both the facades and, especially the great domes, of major buildings.

In intellectual life, the *Ishraqi* or "illuminationist" school of theological-philosophical thought brought together the mystical bent of Persian Islamic thought and the long Islamic traditions of Aristotelianism and Platonism in the form of Shi'ite religious speculation into the nature of divine truth and its accessibility to human reason and imagination. The illuminationists' two key ideas were the concept of transcendence and the notion of a "realm of images." They conceived of transcendence in terms of a divine light identified with the Light

Safavid Art. *Woman with a Veil* by Riza Abbasi ca. 1595. During Safavid times, Persian artists started to depict everyday life and people in their art. Opaque watercolor, ink, and gold on paper 34.2 × 21.5 cm. Arthur M. Sackler Gallery, Smithsonian Institution, Washington, D.C. Lent by the Art and History Trust, LTS 1995. 2.80.

of Truth, which was expressed most fully in Muhammad and the Shi'ite imams. The realm of images was a sphere of being in which the attuned spirit could experience true visions. These ideas reconceived human experience of the Divine in a way that transcended logic and had to be experienced individually. At stake were basic notions of the human psyche and the larger cosmos. The most prominent exponent of the *Ishraqi* school was Mulla Sadra (d. 1640).

The lasting legacies of Safavid rule were the firmly Shi'ite character of the whole Iranian region and the Persian culture that was elaborated largely under Safavid patronage in literature, theology, philosophy, painting, crafts, and architecture. The Safavid age also saw a distinctively Shi'ite piety develop. It focused on commemorating the suffering of the imams and loyalty to the Shi'ite *ulama*, who alone provided guidance in the absence of the hidden imam (see Chapter 11).

The Mughals

ORIGINS

In the early sixteenth century, invaders from beyond the Oxus River to the northwest, in the age-old pattern of Indian history, began a new era in the subcontinent: They ended the political fragmentation that by 1500 had reduced the Delhi sultanate to only one among many Indian states. These invaders were Chaghatay Turks descended from Timur (Tamerlane) and known to history as the **Mughals** (a Persianate form of *Mongol*). In 1525–1527 the founder of the Mughal dynasty, Babur, marched on India, replaced the last sultan of Delhi, and then defeated a Rajput confederacy. Before his death in 1530 he ruled

CHRONOLOGY

The Safavid Empire

1334	Death of Safi al-Din, founder of Safavid Sufi order
ca. 1500	Rise of Safavids under Shah Isma'il
1501–1510	Safavid conquest of greater Iran; Shi'ite state founded
1588–1629	Rule of Shah Abbas I
1722	Forced abdication of last Safavid ruler
1736–1747	Rule of the Sunni Afshar leader, Nadir Shah; revival of Sunni monarchy in Iran
1739	Nadir Shah invades northern India, sacks Delhi

DOCUMENT | A Diplomatic Exchange between Shah Abbas I and Jahangir (1622)

In the 16th and 17th centuries, the central Islamic regions regained their cultural and political vitality within a new imperial framework. The so-called "Gunpowder Empires": the Ottoman Empire, the Safavid Empire, and the Mughal Empire of Delhi, made lasting political and social contributions and were centers of power and prosperity. Yet they were also geopolitical rivals. In this diplomatic exchange, the Safavid emperor Shah Abbas I (1571–1629) and the Mughal emperor Jahangir (1569–1627) discuss the recent capture of the city of Kandahar in today's Afghanistan by Safavid forces. Underneath the ornate and polite language customary of such diplomatic exchanges lies a serious security question for both empires. The Iranian control of Kandahar blocked the Mughal Empire from Central Asian trade; instead it turned to trading on the seas, eventually developing a successful merchant marine.

◆ How would you characterize the tone of the letters? What is Jahangir's biggest concern regarding the Iranian seizure of Kandahar?

Since Kandahar was under the control of those appointed by your exalted dynasty, we considered them as our own and did not harass them, waiting for you to attend to the transference in a spirit of cooperativeness and brotherliness, like your mighty fathers and forefathers. When you neglected this, we repeatedly requested it by letter and message, by allusion and openly, thinking that perhaps in His Majesty's exalted view this miserable territory was not worth contending over and that he would order it given over to the representatives of this family, resulting in the elimination of the taunts of enemies and detractors and cutting-short the long tongues of the envious and fault-finders. This matter was put into abeyance, and when

this was learned among friends and enemies and no reply either positive or negative was received from you, it occurred to us to take a hunting tour in Kandahar, thinking perhaps by this means my renowned brother's appointees, in view of the close and amicable relations that exist between us, would greet our retinue and meet us, and once again the firm foundations of amity on both sides would be apparent to the world and cause a cessation to the prattle of the envious and detractors. We set out on this tour without arms or armaments. . . .

We arrived in the vicinity of the fortress and once again summoned the above-mentioned nobleman. Having said to him what advice had to be said, we sent him off and ordered our divinely assisted soldiers not to set foot near the fortress for ten days. Our advice profited not. They persisted in their opposition. Since it was impossible to have more forbearance than this, the *Qizilbash* [Turcoman nomadic] army, despite the lack of armaments, occupied itself with the subjugation of the fortress; and in a short period of time they had reduced towers and ramparts to the ground and brought the defenders to the point of asking for amnesty. Maintaining the connection of affection that has been observed from olden days between these two exalted lines and treading the path of brotherliness that was again so strongly reaffirmed in the days of that monarch's princehood between Your Majesty and our regal self that it was the object of jealousy of all rulers on the face of the earth, we pardoned their faults as required by innate manliness, enveloped them in favor, and sent them off to that exalted court. ... Truly the basis of inherited and acquired amity and friendship on our part is too strong and firm to be damaged by the occurrence of some events ... that happen by destiny. "Between us and thee there will be no custom of

an empire stretching from the Oxus to Bihar, and the Himalaya to the Deccan. But the real founder of the Mughal Empire and the greatest Indian ruler since Ashoka (ca. 264–223 B.C.E.) was Akbar "the Great" (r. 1556-1605). Indeed, he was as great a ruler as, if not greater than, his famous contemporaries, Elizabeth I (r. 1558–1603), Charles V (r. 1519–1556), and Süleyman.

AKBAR'S REIGN

Akbar began his reign, like so many other illustrious rulers, with an impressive record of military success. He added North India and the northern Deccan to the Mughal dominions. Even more significant, however, were his governmental reforms, cultural patronage, and religious toleration. He completely reorganized the central and provincial governments and rationalized the tax system. His marriages with Rajput princesses and his appointment of Hindus to positions of power eased Muslim-Hindu tensions. So did his cancellation of

the poll tax on non-Muslims (1564) and his efforts to reduce the power of the more literalist, "hard-line" *ulama*. Under his leadership the Mughal Empire became a truly Indian empire.

Akbar was a religious eclectic who showed not only tolerance of all faiths but also unusual interest in different religious traditions. He frequently brought together representatives of all faiths—Jain and Buddhist monks, Brahmans, *ulama*, Parsis (Zoroastrians), and Jesuits—to discuss religion. These debates took place in a special hall in Akbar's magnificent palace complex at Fatehpur Sikri outside the Mughal capital, Agra.

THE LAST GREAT MUGHALS

Akbar's three immediate successors were Jahangir (r. 1605–1627), Shah Jahan (r. 1628–1658), and Awrangzeb (r. 1658–1707). They left behind significant achievements, but the problems of sustaining an Indian empire took their toll on Mughal power. The reigns of Jahangir and Shah Jahan

cruelty; there will be nothing but the path of love and fidelity." It is hoped that on your part too such pleasing conduct will be followed and that you will disregard certain trivial matters. If there has been any anxiety, please be so kind as to do away with it. Keep the garden of eternal spring of unity and concord green and fresh, and concentrate your exalted mind upon affirming the bases of agreement and concord, which maintain the harmony of persons and nations. Know that all our protected realm belongs to you, and kindly inform anyone you wish that it will be turned over to him without opposition. . . . More would be long-windedness. May your highly exalted banner be always and ever embraced by divine protection.

Reply from the Mughal Emperor

. . . That shah of Jamshedian might, whose army is like the stars, whose court is like the celestial sphere, who is worthy of the crown of the Chosroë's, scion of the Alavid house, offspring of the Safavid family, has, without provocation or cause, caused to wither the garden of amity, friendship, brotherliness, and unity, which should not have been clouded by the dust of contention until the end of time. Apparently the custom of unity and loyalty between rulers of the world used to be so firmly founded upon fraternal amity that they swore on each other's heads, and with such perfect spiritual intimacy and corporeal comradeship that a spirit could not come between them—much less territory or property. … "Alas for our unbounded love." The arrival of your amicable letter apologizing for "touring and hunting" in Kandahar … has assured us of the health of your angelic self. Roses of joy and glee have blossomed in the face of the auspicious age. May it not be hidden from the world-adorning mind of that exalted brother that until the arrival of your messenger … at this magnificent court no expression of a desire for Kandahar had ever been made. During the time we were occupied by a hunting tour of the happy vale of Kashmir, the temporal rulers of the Deccan short-sightedly stepped off the highway of obedience and subservience and took the path of rebellion. It was therefore incumbent upon our imperial mind to chastise the shortsighted, and the victory-emblazoned banners descended to the seat of the sultanate, Lahore; and we assigned our worthy son Shahjahan an invincible army to go against the wretches. … At that point news arrived that that brother had come to conquer Kandahar—something that had never occurred to us. We were astonished. What could have caused him to go there himself in conquest, disregarding our friendship and brotherliness? Although the informants were reliable, we could not believe it. After the news was verified … we immediately ordered Abdul-Aziz Khan not to cross our brother, for the fraternal link was still strong, and we would not trade our degree of unity and loyalty for all the world. It would have been appropriate, given our friendship, to wait until the emissary arrived, for an amicable settlement of the claim might have been made. To have committed such an outrage before the emissary's arrival—upon whose shoulders will the people of the world lay the blame for breaking pacts and oaths and a breach of manliness and virtue? May God keep and preserve you at all times.

From *The Middle East and Islamic Reader* by Marvin Gettlemen and Stuart Schar © 2003 by Marvin Gettlemen and Stuart Schar. reprinted by permission of Grove Press.

were arguably the golden age of Mughal culture, notably in architecture and painting. But the burdens imposed by new building, by military campaigns, and by the erosion of Akbar's administrative and tax reforms led to economic decline. Jahangir set a fateful precedent in permitting English merchants to establish a trading post, or "factory," at Surat on the western coast in Gujarat. Shah Jahan brought the Deccan wholly under Mughal control but lost Kandahar to Safavid forces in 1648. (See Document, "A Diplomatic Exchange Between Shah Abbas I and Jahangir.") His wars further strained the Mughal economy. No less a burden on the treasury were his elaborate building projects, the most magnificent of which was the Taj Mahal (built 1632–1653), the unparalleled tomb that he built for his beloved consort, Mumtaz.

With Shah Jahan, religious toleration retreated; under his son, Awrangzeb, a narrow religious fanaticism all but reversed Akbar's earlier policies. The resulting internal disorder and instability hastened the decline of Mughal power. Awrangzeb persecuted non-Muslims, destroying Hindu temples, reimposing the poll tax (1679), and alienating the Raj-put leaders, whose forebears Akbar had so carefully cultivated. His intransigent policies coincided with and perhaps contributed to the spread of the militant reformism of the Sikh movement throughout the Punjab and the rise of Hindu Maratha nationalism in western India.

SIKHS AND MARATHAS

In the late sixteenth and early seventeenth centuries the Sikhs, who trace their origins to the irenic teachings of Guru Nanak (d. 1538), developed into a distinctive religious movement. Neither Muslim nor Hindu, they had their own scripture, ritual, and moralistic and reformist ideals. (See Document, "Guru Arjun's Faith.") Awrangzeb earned their lasting enmity by persecution that culminated in the

The Taj Mahal, built between 1632 and 1647 in Agra, by Shah Jahan, as a tomb for his beloved consort, is arguably the greatest monumental tomb ever built. Its setting amidst gardens and pools alludes to paradise, and its great dome seems suspended like the rising sun over the horizon.

Trevor Wood/Getty Images, Inc.-Stone AllStock.

of North India by Nadir Shah in 1739; the invasions (1748–1761) by the Afghan tribal leader Ahmad Shah Durrani (r. 1747–1773), "founder of modern Afghanistan"; and the British victories over Bengali forces at Plassey in Bengal (1757) and over the French on the southeastern coast (1740–1763). By 1819 the dominance of the British East India Company had eclipsed Mughal as it did Maratha and almost all regional Indian power, even though the Mughal line did not officially end until 1858.

martyrdom of their ninth leader, or guru, Teg Bahadur, in 1675. Thereafter, the tenth and last Sikh guru, Gobind Singh (d. 1708), developed the Sikhs into a formidable military force. Awrangzeb and his successors had to contend with repeated Sikh uprisings.

The Hindu Marathas, led by the charismatic Shivaji (d. 1680), rose in religious and nationalistic fervor to found their own regional empire about 1646. On Shivaji's death, the Maratha state controlled the mountainous western coast, and its army was the most disciplined force in India. Despite Awrangzeb's subsequent defeat of the Marathas and his conquest of the entire south of India, the Marathas continued to fight him. After his death they brought about a confederation of almost all the Deccan states under their leadership. While formally acknowledging Mughal sovereignty, the Marathas actually controlled far more of India after about 1740 than did the Mughals.

POLITICAL DECLINE

In addition to the Rajput, Sikh, and Maratha wars, other factors sealed the fate of the once great Mughal empire after Awrangzeb's death in 1707: the rise in the Deccan of the powerful Islamic state of Hyderabad in 1724; the Persian invasion

Jahangir and Shaykh Husain. Jahangir showing preference to the Chishti Sufi *shaykh* and saint Husain over three temporal rulers: the Ottoman emperor, the King of England, and a Hindu prince. The Timurid emperor presents a book to Shaykh Husain, the descendant of the great Chishti saint Mu'inuddin, while ignoring the temporal rulers in the lower-left corner. The artist copied the likeness of King James I from an English portrait given to Jahangir by Sir Thomas Roe, the British ambassador from 1615 to 1619. The magnificent floral borders to the miniature (ca. 1615–1618) were added in 1727 by Muhammad Sadiq.

Bichitr, *Jahangir Preferring a Sufi Shakikh to Kings*, ca. 1660–70, Album Page; Opaque watercolor, gold and ink on paper, 25.3 × 18.1 cm. Courtesy of the Freer Gallery of Art, Smithsonian Institution, Washington, D.C.

CHRONOLOGY

India: The Mughals and Contemporary Indian Powers

1525–1527	Rule of Babur, founder of Indian Timurid state
1538	Death of Guru Nanak, founder of Siteh religious tradition
1556–1605	Rule of Akbar "the Great"
1605–1627	Rule of Jahangir
1628–1658	Rule of Shah Jahan, builder of the Taj Mahal
1646	Founding of Maratha Empire
1658–1707	Rule of Awrangzeb
1680	Death of Maratha leader, Shivaji
1708	Death of tenth and last Sikh guru, Gobind Singh
1724	Rise of Hyderabad state
1739	Iranian invasion of North India under Nadir Shah
1757	British East India Company victory over Bengali forces at Plassey

RELIGIOUS DEVELOPMENTS

The period from about 1500 to 1650 was of major importance for Indian religious life. Akbar's eclecticism mirrored the atmosphere of the sixteenth century in India. A number of religious figures preached a spiritually or mystically oriented piety that transcended the legalism of both the *ulama* and the Brahmans and rejected caste distinctions. In these ideas, we can see both Muslim Sufi and Hindu *bhakti* influences at work. We mentioned in Chapter 13 two forerunners of such reformers, Ramananda and Kabir. Guru Nanak, the spiritual father of the Sikh movement, took up Kabir's ideas and preached faith and devotion to one loving and merciful God. He opposed narrow allegiance to particular creeds or rites and excessive pride in external religious observance. Nanak's hymns of praise contain both Hindu and Muslim ideas and imagery. Dadu (d. 1603) preached a similar message. He was born a Muslim but, like Kabir and Nanak, strove to get people to go beyond either Muslim or Hindu allegiance to a more spiritual love and service of God.

There was also an upsurge of *bhakti* devotionalism that amounted to a Hindu revival. It was epitomized by the Bengali Krishna devotee Chaitanya (d. ca. 1533), who stressed total devotion to Lord Krishna. The forebears of present-day Hare Krishna devotees, his followers spread widely his ecstatic public praise of God and his message that all are equal in God's sight. The other major figure in Hindu devotionalism in this era was Tulasidas (d. 1623), whose Hindi retelling of the story of the Sanskrit *Ramayana* remains among the most popular works of Indian literature. Tulasidas used the story of Rama's adventures to present *bhakti* ideas that remain as alive in current everyday Hindu life as do his verses.

Muslim eclectic tendencies came primarily from the Sufis. By 1500 many Sufi retreat centers had been established in India. Sufis' enthusiastic forms of worship and their inclination to play down the externals of religion proved particularly congenial to Indian sensibilities. Such Sufis were, however, often opposed by the more puritanical *ulama*, many of whom held powerful positions as royal advisers and judges. To check puritan bigotry among the *ulama*, Akbar named himself the supreme spiritual authority in the empire and then ordered that toleration be the law of the land.

After Akbar's death the inevitable reaction set in. It was summed up in the work of the Indian leader of the central Asian Sufi order of the Naqshbandiya, Ahmad Sirhindi (d. 1624). He sought to purge Sufism of its extreme tendencies and of all popular practices not sanctioned by the schools of law. He crusaded against any practices that smacked of Hindu influence and also against tolerant treatment of the Hindus themselves. Among Akbar's royal successors, Awrangzeb, as noted above, was known for his strictures against non-Muslims. His intolerance has often been unfairly exaggerated, but in the end its spirit won the day. The possibilities for Hindu-Muslim rapprochement that had emerged in Akbar's time waned, presaging the communal strife that has so marred southern Asian history in recent times.

ISLAMIC ASIA

Central Asia: Islamization and Isolation

We can trace the solid footing of Islam in Central Asia to the post-Timur era of the fifteenth century. Even in the preceding century, as the peoples of western Central Asia had begun to shift from nomadic to settled existence, the familiar pattern of Islamic diffusion from trading and urban centers to the countryside had set in. Islamization by Sunni Sufis, traders, and tribal rulers went on apace thereafter, even as far as western China and Mongolia. It was slowed only in the late sixteenth century by the conversion of the tribes of Mongolia proper to the Buddhism of the Tibetan lamas. Thus, after 1500 the Safavid Shi'ite realm was bounded by Sunni states in India, Afghanistan, Anatolia, Mesopotamia, Transoxiana, and western Turkestan (Khwarizm, the region between the Aral and Caspian Seas). In these last two areas, the most important states were those founded by Uzbek and Chaghatay Turks, both of whom were ruled by Muslim descendants of Genghis Khan.

UZBEKS AND CHAGHATAYS

During the fifteenth century Timur's heirs had ruled Transoxiana and most of Iran (see Chapter 13). To the north, above the Jaxartes River (Syr Darya) and the Aral Sea, a new steppe khanate had been formed by the unification in 1428 of assorted clans of Turks and Mongols known as the Uzbeks. In time, an Uzbek leader who was descended from Genghis Khan, Muhammad Shaybani (d. 1510), invaded Transoxiana (1495–1500). There he founded a new Uzbek Islamic empire that replaced Timurid rule, which shifted south to Kabul and eventually India, as described earlier. Muhammad's line continued Uzbek rule in Transoxiana at Bukhara into the eighteenth century, while another Uzbek line ruled the independent khanate of Khiva in western Turkestan from 1512 to 1872.

Of the other Central Asian Islamic states after 1500, the most significant was that of the Chaghatay Turks. The Chaghatays had been the successors of Genghis Khan in the whole region from the Aral Sea and the Oxus River to Yuan China. After 1350 Timur's invasion broke up their khanate. From about 1514 a revived Chaghatay state flourished in eastern Turkestan—the Tarim basin and the territory north of it, between Tashkent in the west and the Turfan oasis in the east. Although the Chaghatay rulers lasted until 1678 in one part of the Tarim basin, their real power was lost after about 1555 to various Khoja princes, Sunni zealots who claimed to be *Sharifs* (descendants of the Prophet).

CONSEQUENCES OF THE SHI'ITE RIFT

On the face of it, the Ottoman, Mughal, Safavid, and Central Asian Islamic states had much in common: Muslim faith and culture, similar systems of taxation and law, the Persian language, and Turkish rulers. Yet the deep religious division between the Shi'ite Safavids and all their Sunni neighbors proved stronger than their common bonds. The result was a serious geographic division that isolated Central Asian Muslims in particular.

Shi'ite-Sunni political competition was sharpened by Safavid militancy, to which the Sunni states responded in kind. Attempts to form alliances with non-Muslim states, previously unheard of in the Islamic world, became a commonplace of Shi'ite political strategy. The Sunnis also resorted to such tactics: The Ottomans, for example, made common cause with Protestants against their Catholic Habsburg enemies. Although trade continued, the presence of a militant Shi'ite state astride the major overland trade routes of the larger Islamic world hurt the international flow of Islamic commerce.

▲ **The great central square of the Registan**, in Samarkand, with the 17th-century Shir Dar Madrasa on the right and the 15th-century Ulugh Beg Madrasa on the left. Samarkand and other major Central Asian cities were centers of Islamic culture and learning as well as political power.
Michel Gotin/Ouzebekistan.

DOCUMENT | Guru Arjun's Faith

These lines are from the pen of the fifth guru of the Sikh community, Arjun (d. 1606). In them he repeated the teaching of Kabir, a fifteenth-century Indian saint whose teachings are included with those of Guru Nanak and other religious poets in the Sikh holy scripture, the Adi Granth. This teaching focuses on the error of clinging to a doctrinaire communalist faith, be it that of the Hindus or of the Muslims.

◆ Why might syncretic teachings, such as those of the Sikhs, have been appealing in seventeenth-century India?

I practice not fasting, nor observe the [month of]
  Ramazan:
I serve Him who will preserve me at the last hour.
The one Lord of the earth is my God,
Who judgeth both Hindus and Muslims.
I go not on a pilgrimage to Mecca, nor worship at
  Hindu places of Pilgrimage.
I serve the one God and no other.
I neither worship as the Hindus, nor pray as the
  Muslims.
I take the Formless God into my heart, and there make
  obeisance unto Him.
I am neither a Hindu nor a Muslim.
The soul and the body belong to God whether He be
  called Allah or Ram.
Kabir hath delivered this lecture.
When I meet a true guru or pir, I recognize my own Master.

From Max Arthur Macauliffe, *The Sikh Religion*, 6 vols. (Oxford: Clarendon Press, 1909), p. 422.

The Safavid Shi'ite schism also ruptured the shared cultural traditions of the "Abode of Islam." This rupture was especially reflected in the fate of Persian literary culture. As a result of its ever stronger association with Shi'ite religious ideas after the rise of the Safavids, Persian made little further progress as a potential common language alongside Arabic—let alone above it—in Sunni lands. Outside Iran it was destined to remain a language of high culture, the court, and bureaucracy, where it (much like French in eighteenth and nineteenth century Europe) was the mark of the educated and cultural person: Persian language and mastery of the Persian classics defined to a great extent what it meant to be an Ottoman or Mughal "gentlemen." In India, Urdu became the common Muslim idiom (see Chapter 13), and in Ottoman and Central Asian lands, one or another Turkic tongue was spoken in everyday life. The Persian classics inspired Persian learning among educated Sunnis, but Safavid Persian literature was largely ignored.

Central Asia was ultimately the Islamic region most decisively affected by the Shi'ite presence in Iran. Combined with the growing pressure of Christian Russian power from the West, the militant Shi'ism of Iran isolated Central Asia from the rest of the Muslim world. Political and economic relations with other Islamic lands became increasingly difficult after 1500, as did religious and cultural interchange. However healthy Islam remained in this region, its contact with the original Islamic heartlands (and even with India) shrank. Contact came primarily through a few pilgrims, members of Sufi orders, *ulama*, and students. Central Asian Islam mostly developed in isolation, a large but peripheral area to the Islamic mainstream communities.

Power Shifts in the Southern Seas
SOUTHERN-SEAS TRADE

Along the southern rim of Asia, from the Red Sea and East Africa to Indonesia and the South China Sea, the first half of the second millennium witnessed the gradual spread of Islamic religion and culture into new regions and among new peoples. In ports in Java, Sumatra, the Malay Peninsula, South India, Gujarat, East Africa, Madagascar, and Zanzibar, Islamic traders established thriving communities. Their enclaves in these cities often became the dominant presence. Initially the Muslims' economic stature attracted especially the socially and religiously mobile peoples of these cosmopolitan centers; many of them also found the ideas and practices of Islam compelling. Typically this first stage of conversion was followed by Islam's transmission to surrounding areas and finally to inland centers. In this transmission, Sufi orders and their preachers and holy men played the main role. However, conquest by Muslim coastal states quickened the process in Indonesia and East Africa.

The international trade network that the Muslims inherited in the southern seas was ancient. Before 1200 much of the trade in these waters had been dominated by Hindu or Buddhist kingdoms on the Malay Peninsula or Sumatra (see Chapter 13). Arab traders had also been active at least in the Indian Ocean. Hindu culture had been carried, along with an

OVERVIEW   Major Islamic States, ca. 1600

The fifteenth to the eighteenth centuries were the age of the last great Islamic empires. These states dominated the Islamic world, which stretched from Morocco on the Atlantic coast of North Africa across the Near East and along the eastern coast of Africa to the southeast Asian islands that today make up the Republic of Indonesia. Despite these political divisions and the religious divide between Sunni and Shi'ite Muslims, in many respects the Islamic world formed a single cultural unit.

State	Location	Islamic Tradition
Ottoman Empire	Balkans, Anatolia, North Africa, Syria, Iraq, Arabia	Sunni
Safavid Empire	Iran, Afghanistan, Caucasus	Shi'ite
Mughal Empire	India	Sunni
Uzbeks	Central Asia: Kiva, Bokhara	Sunni
Chaghatays	Central Asia: Tukistan	Sunni
Acheh	Sumatra	Sunni

Indonesian language, as far as Madagascar in the first millennium C.E. Hindus were the chief religious group the Muslims displaced. In the East, Islam never ousted the Indian Buddhist cultures of Burma, Thailand, and Indochina, although Muslim traders lived in their ports. Islam did, however, gradually win most of Malaysia, Sumatra, Java, and the "Spice Islands" of the Moluccas—always the coastal areas first, then the inland regions.

CONTROL OF THE SOUTHERN SEAS

The Portuguese reached the East African coast in 1498. In the following three centuries, the history of the lands along the trade routes of the southern Asian seas, from the shores of East Africa to Indonesia and Malaysia, was bound closely not only with Islamic religious, cultural, and commercial networks, but also with the rising power of Christian Western Europe (see Map 21–4). The key attractions of these diverse lands were their commercial and strategic possibilities.

In the sixteenth century the Europeans began to displace by armed force the Muslims who, by 1500, had come to dominate the maritime southern rim of Asia. European success was based on two key factors. One was that their naval and commercial ventures were backed by national support systems. The other, for a time at least, was their superior warships. This combination enabled the Portuguese to carve out a major power base in the early sixteenth century along the west coast of India at the expense of the Muslims who dominated Indian maritime trade. They did so through superior naval power, and by exploiting indigenous rivalries and terrorizing all who opposed them.

However, in the southern-seas trade centers, Islamization continued, even in the face of Christian proselytizing and growing European political and commercial presence. The Muslims, unlike most of the European Christians, never kept aloof from the native populations and were largely assimilated everywhere. They rarely abandoned their faith, which proved generally attractive to new peoples they encountered. The result was usually an Islamized and racially mixed population.

As a result, while European gunboat imperialism had considerable military and economic success, often at the expense of Islamic

CHRONOLOGY

The Southern Seas: Arrival of the Europeans

1498	The Portuguese come to the East African coast and to the west coast of India
1500–1512	The Portuguese establish bases on west Indian coast, replace Muslims as Indian Ocean power
early 1500s	Muslim sultanates replace Hindu states in Java, Sumatra
1524–1910	State of Acheh in northwestern Sumatra
1600s	Major increase in Islamization and connected spread of Malay language in the archipelago
1641	Dutch conquest of Malacca
ca. 1800	Dutch replace Muslim states as main archipelago power
1873–1910	War between Holland and Acheh

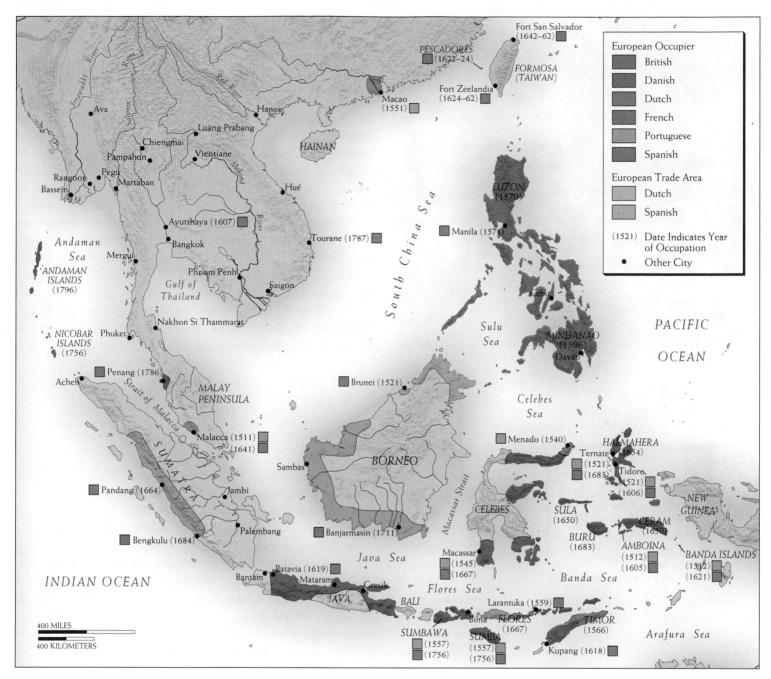

MAP 21–4 European Commercial Penetration of Southeast Asia. Beginning with the Portuguese and Spanish in the sixteenth century, and then the Dutch in the seventeenth, European powers established commercial bases throughout Southeast Asia, often cooperating with local rulers.

states, European culture and Christianity made little headway against Islam. From East Africa to the Pacific, only in the northern Philippines did a substantial population become largely Christian.

THE INDIES: ACHEH

The history of the Indonesian archipelago has always revolved around the international demand for its spices, peppers, and other produce. By the fifteenth century the coastal Islamic states were

centered on the trading ports of the Malay Peninsula, the north shores of Sumatra and Java, and the Moluccas, or "Spice Islands." The last great Hindu kingdom of inland Java was defeated by an Islamic coalition of states in the early 1500s. Several substantial Islamic sultanates arose in the sixteenth and seventeenth centuries, even as Europeans were carving out their own economic empires in the region. The most powerful of these Islamic states was Acheh, in northwestern Sumatra (ca. 1524–1910).

◀ **A European Footprint in South-East Asia.** The Dutch Square in Malacca, Malaysia.
Mart Nieuwland/OmniPhoto Communications, Inc.

In its early years Acheh provided the only counterweight to the Portuguese presence across the straits in Malacca (Malaysia). Although the Acheh sultans were unable to drive out the better armed invaders, neither could the Portuguese subdue them. Despite Portuguese control of Indies commerce, Acheh managed to dominate the pepper trade of Sumatra and to thrive until the end of the sixteenth century. In the first half of the seventeenth century the sultanate controlled both coasts of Sumatra and parts of the Malay Peninsula. Meanwhile, the Dutch had replaced the Portuguese in the business of milking the Indies of their wealth, and by the eighteenth century they were doing it just as ruthlessly and more efficiently. In the early twentieth century the Dutch finally won full control in the region, but only after nearly forty years of intermittent war with Acheh (1873–1910).

Turkish Emperor Süleyman I.

Summary

The Last Islamic Empires   The period from 1500 to 1800 marks the cultural and political blossoming of the last Islamic empires and their sharp decline. The Islamic vitality in the first half of this period was exemplified in the Ottoman, Safavid, and Mughal Empires. All three built vast bureaucracies and arguably the greatest cities in the world of their time. They patronized the arts. Yet they were conservative societies. Economically they remained tied to agricultural production and taxation based on land. They did not undergo the social or religio-political revolutions that rocked the West after 1500 or changes in material and intellectual life similar to that experienced in the Western world during the same period. There was no compelling challenge to traditional Islamic ideals, even though numerous Islamic movements of the eighteenth century did call for reform.

Decline   By the latter half of this period, all these empires were in economic, political, and military decline, even if intellectual and artistic vigor held on.

Thus, it is not surprising that European expansionism impinged in these three centuries upon Africa, India, Indonesia, and the Islamic heartland, rather than the reverse. None of the Islamic states fared well in their encounters with Europeans during this age. Europeans' growing domination of the world's seas allowed them to contain or to bypass the major Islamic lands in their quest for commercial empires.

By the late 1700s, industrial development joined economic wealth and political stability to give the West global military supremacy for the first time. Before 1800, the Europeans were able to bring only minor Islamic states under colonial administrations. However, the footholds they gained in Africa, India, and Southeast Asia laid the groundwork for rapid colonial expansion after 1800. The age of the last great Muslim empires was the beginning of the first great modern European empires.

Review Questions

1. Why did the Ottoman Empire expand so rapidly into Europe? Why did the empire fail to hold certain areas in Europe?

2. Why did the Safavid Empire succeed in Iran? What role did Islamic religion have in this development? Who were the major foes of this empire?

3. What were the most important elements that united all Islamic states? Why was there a lack of unity between these states from 1500 to 1800? How and why were the European powers able to promote division among these various states?

4. What were Akbar's main policies toward the Hindu population? Why did he succeed and his followers fail in this area? What were his main governmental reforms?

5. How and why did the Sikhs develop into a formidable military power? Why did they become separatist in their orientation to the larger Indian world?

6. What were the main tenets of the Ishraqi or "illumination" school of theological-philosophical thought? Define the concepts of "transcendence" and a "realm of images."

7. Compare the Sunni-Shi'ite split within the Islamic world (1500–1800) with that of the Protestant-Catholic split within the Christian world during that same period. For example, can we compare relations between England and Spain in the sixteenth century to those between the Ottomans and the Safavids? Explain.

8. Why were outside powers attracted to the southern-seas lands? Why did the European powers triumph in the struggle to control this area?

Key Terms

ayan (p. 617)

devshirme (p. 615)

Grand Mufti (p. 614)

harem (p. 613)

Janissaries (p. 615)

millets (p. 617)

Mughals (p. 622)

padishah (p. 613)

pirs (p. 618)

Qanun (p. 615)

Qanun-name (p. 613)

Shari'a (p. 613)

Documents CD-ROM

Islamic Empires

12.2 Süleyman "The Lawgiver" and the Advantages of Islam: Oiger de Busbecq

12.3 Women in Ottoman Society: Oigier de Busbecq

12.4 The Ottomans: Empire-builders at the Crossroads of Three Continents

12.5 The Safavid Shi'ite Empire of Persia

12.6 Shah Abbas the Great: The Resurgence of the Persian Empire

12.7 Mughal Apogee: Akbar the Enlightened

NOTE: *To learn more about the topics in this chapter, see the Suggested Readings at the end of the book.*

Between approximately 1750 and 1850 extraordinary changes occurred in Western civilization. Although of immediate significance primarily for the nations of Europe and the Americas, these developments produced in the long run an immense impact throughout the world. Europe became the great exporter of ideas and technologies that in time transformed one area of human experience after another.

NORTH AMERICA

The death of General Warren at the Battle of Bunker Hill, June 17, 1775. *The art of the eighteenth century in Europe mirrored the contrasts of the age, at once reflecting the confidence and rationality of the Enlightenment, and the romantic passions of revolutions that shattered the institutions of the Old Regime.*

Portrait of the Marquis de Pompal. *He insisted that Libson be reconstructed according to rational principles after the earthquake that destroyed the city.*

SOUTH AMERICA

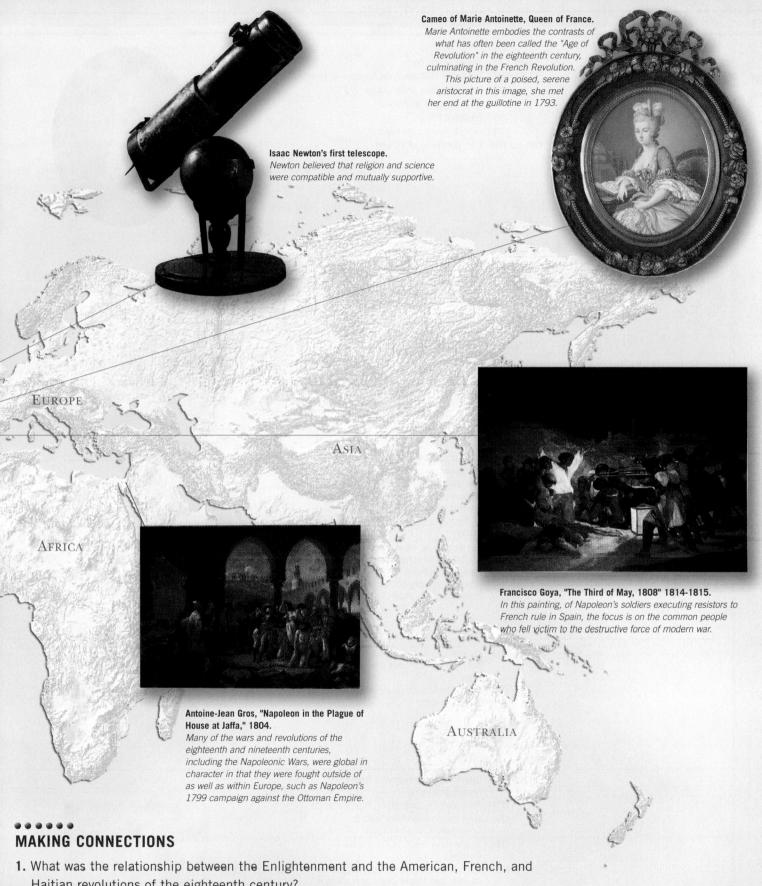

Cameo of Marie Antoinette, Queen of France.
Marie Antoinette embodies the contrasts of what has often been called the "Age of Revolution" in the eighteenth century, culminating in the French Revolution. This picture of a poised, serene aristocrat in this image, she met her end at the guillotine in 1793.

Isaac Newton's first telescope.
Newton believed that religion and science were compatible and mutually supportive.

EUROPE

ASIA

AFRICA

Francisco Goya, "The Third of May, 1808" 1814-1815.
In this painting, of Napoleon's soldiers executing resistors to French rule in Spain, the focus is on the common people who fell victim to the destructive force of modern war.

Antoine-Jean Gros, "Napoleon in the Plague of House at Jaffa," 1804.
Many of the wars and revolutions of the eighteenth and nineteenth centuries, including the Napoleonic Wars, were global in character in that they were fought outside of as well as within Europe, such as Napoleon's 1799 campaign against the Ottoman Empire.

AUSTRALIA

●●●●●●
MAKING CONNECTIONS

1. What was the relationship between the Enlightenment and the American, French, and Haitian revolutions of the eighteenth century?

2. Is it ironic that ideas and technologies that contributed to an awakening of European power also fostered critiques that non-European peoples would employ against Western dominance?

PART 5

ENLIGHTENMENT AND REVOLUTION IN THE WEST

EUROPE

1756–1763	Seven Years' War
1762–1796	Catherine II, "the Great," reigns in Russia
1763	Peace of Paris Seven Years' War
1772	First partition of Poland
1783	Peace of Paris
1789	French Revolution begins
1793 and 1795	Last partitions of Poland

◄ *July 14, 1789, Bastille prison, Paris*

Sir Isaac Newton ▶

NEAR EAST/ INDIA

1757	British victory at Plassey, in Bengal
1761	English oust French from India
1772–1784	Warren Hastings' administration in India
1772–1833	Ram Mohan Roy, Hindu reformer in India
1794–1925	Qajar shahs in Iran
1805–1849	Muhammad Ali in Egypt

▲ *Muhammad Ali*

EAST ASIA

1753–1806	Kitagawa Utamaro, Tokugawa era artist
1787–1793	Matsudaira Sadanobu's reforms in Japan
1789	White Lotus Rebellion in China
1823–1901	Li Hongzhang, powerful Chinese governor-general
1853	Commodore Perry negotiates treaty of friendship with Japan

◄ *Commodore Perry meets Japanese royal commissioner*

AFRICA

1754–1817	Usman Dan Fodio, founder of Sultanate in northern and central Nigeria
1762	End of Funj sultanate in eastern Sudanic region

THE AMERICAS

1759–1788	Spain reorganizes government of its American Empire
1776	American Declaration of Independence
1791	First ten amendments to U.S. Constitution (Bill of Rights) ratified
1791	Negro slave revolt in French Santo Domingo
1794	Canada Constitutional Act divides the country into Upper and Lower Canada

The "Boston Massacre" of ▶
March 5, 1770 by Paul Revere

1804–1814 Napoleon's empire
1814–1815 Congress of Vienna
1830–1848 Louis Philippe reigns in France
1832 First British Reform Act
1837–1901 Queen Victoria of England
1848 Revolutions across Europe

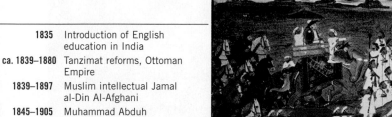

1835 Introduction of English education in India
ca. 1839–1880 Tanzimat reforms, Ottoman Empire
1839–1897 Muslim intellectual Jamal al-Din Al-Afghani
1845–1905 Muhammad Abduh

◄ *British colonial rule in India (1880)*

1835–1908 Empress Dowager Cixi
1839–1842 Opium War; 1842, Treaty of Nanjing grants Hong Kong to the British and allows them to trade in China
1844 Similar treaties made between China and France and the United States

Armed Chinese junk ▶
during the
Opium War

1804 Fulani Jihad into Hausa lands
1806 British take Cape Colony from the Dutch
1817–1828 Zulu chief Shaka reigns
1830–1847 French invasion of Algeria
1830s Dutch settlers, the Boers, expand northward from Cape Colony
1848–1885 Sudanese Madhi, Muhammad Ahmad

1804 Haitian independence
1808–1824 Wars of independence in Latin America
1822 Brazilian independence
1847 Mexican War

Simón Bolívar ▶

22

The Age of European Enlightenment

- The Scientific Revolution

- The Enlightenment

- The Enlightenment and Religion

- The Enlightenment and Society

- Enlightened Absolutism

◄ JOSEPH WRIGHT OF DERBY, *AN EXPERIMENT ON A BIRD IN THE AIR-PUMP* (1768). The air-pump, devised by the pioneering English natural philosopher Robert Boyle in the 1650s, stood for over a century as a major symbol of the new experimental science championed by the Royal Society of London. The instrument permitted air to be pumped out of a spherical glass jar to create a vacuum for the purpose of demonstrating the qualities of air and air pressure. By the middle of the 18th century many provincial English scientific societies possessed effective models such as the one portrayed here. Wright, who lived near Derby in an early industrial region of England, was a close friend of manufacturers and other persons interested in science. In this dramatically lit painting, Wright portrays the excited interest of fashionable upper-class audiences in experimental science.

National Gallery, London, Great Britain. The Bridgemann Art Gallery.

The European Enlightenment

Of all the movements of modern European thought, the most influential are the Scientific Revolution and the Enlightenment. A direct line of intellectual descent exists from those movements to the science and social criticism of the present day. Wherever modern science and technology are pursued and their effects felt, the spirit of the Enlightenment persists. From the eighteenth century to the present, the writers of the Enlightenment provided a pattern for intellectuals who wished to make their societies more rational, scientific, and secular, and thus "modern." Moreover, the Enlightenment model of society has become so influential in the West and, via the West in the rest of the world that it has become synonymous with "modern," so that societies worldwide are judged to be modernized to the extent that their economies are industrialized and their societies scientific and secular.

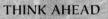

The Enlightenment writers valued emotions and passions as well as reason, but they used reason as a weapon for reform and the basis for a more productive economic life. In the two centuries since the Enlightenment, such a use of critical reason has become a mark of reforming and progressive social and intellectual movements. The Enlightenment writers first used reason against Christianity, but reason came to be used against other world religions as well, leading to the tendency in the modern world to view science and religion in potential conflict, and less scintifically advanced societies as inherently culturally backward. This particular view of modernization tends to make the European and later North American experience the necessary pattern for all advanced society. This outlook originated with the majority of Enlightenment writers themselves. A minority of those writers as with many present-day commentators questioned whether even a rational, critical, and economically productive Europe should be the pattern for all human societies.

In terms of political thought the heritage of the Enlightenment was complex with different strands of political thought often in tension or outright conflict with each other. One strand of Enlightenment political thought contributed to constitutionalism and modes of government in which the power and authority of the central government stand sharply circumscribed. Montesquieu, for example, influenced the Constitution of the United States and the numerous constitutions that document later influenced. Another strand of Enlightenment political thought, found in Voltaire, contributed to the growth of strong central governments which was the case with enlightened absolutism. Advocates of this method of government believed that a monarch or strong central bureaucracy could formulate and impose rational solutions to political and social problems. Still another strand of political thought, arising from Rousseau, led to the socialist concern with inequality of wealth. Because of the complexity of Enlightenment political thought, modern governments displaying liberalism, socialism, and bureaucratic centralism may find roots in eighteenth-century thinkers. Modern political movements finding themselves essentially at odds with the Enlightenment heritage are those attached radical islamic groups who define themselves in opposition to most Western values.

Much of what has been best about the Western cultural legacy to global culture derives from the Enlightenment, although it is important to remember that, as we observed in Chapter 18, the eighteenth century, the era of the Enlightenment, also gave rise to European colonial empires and plantation economies based on slavery. Europeans' treatment of non-Europeans, as well as their warfare against each other in this era often belied the principles of the Enlightenment. By the same token, some of the most admirable principles of Western culture, including advocacy of democracy and human rights, can be traced to Enlightenment roots.

THINK AHEAD

◆ How did Enlightenment values as well as Enlightenment admiration of science become one of the chief defining qualities of societies regarded as advanced, progressive, and modern?

◆ How has the political thought of the Enlightenment influenced the development of modern political philosophies and modern governments?

NO SINGLE INTELLECTUAL FORCE DURING the past three centuries has so transformed every region of the world as has Western science and the technology that has flowed from its understanding of nature. Although throughout the world today there has arisen much interest in nontraditional methods of healing, the impact of Western science on every area of human life remains a dominant force. Furthermore, the attainment of scientific knowledge, often for the purposes of military advantage as well as medical and economic advance, has become a goal of most modern states.

The impact of science could make itself felt first in Europe and then elsewhere only as the conviction came to spread that change and reform were both possible and desirable. This attitude is now commonplace, but it came into its own in Europe only after 1700. The capacity and even eagerness to embrace change, especially change as justified on the grounds of science, represents one of the primary intellectual inheritances from that age. The movement of people and ideas that fostered such thinking is called the *Enlightenment.* Its leading voices combined confidence in the human mind inspired by the Scientific Revolution and faith in the power of rational criticism to challenge the intellectual authority of tradition and revealed religion. Its writers believed that human beings could comprehend the operation of physical nature and mold it to the ends of material and moral improvement. The rationality of the physical universe became a standard against which the customs and traditions of society could be measured and criticized. Such criticism penetrated every corner of contemporary society. As a result, the spirit of innovation and improvement came to characterize modern Western society. This outlook would become perhaps the most important European cultural export to the rest of the world.

The Scientific Revolution

The sixteenth and seventeenth centuries witnessed a sweeping change in the scientific view of the universe. From being considered the center of the universe, the Earth was now seen as only another planet orbiting about the sun. The sun itself became one of millions of stars. This transformation led to a vast rethinking of moral and religious matters as well as of scientific theory. Science and the scientific method became so impressive and so influential that they set a new standard for evaluating knowledge in the Western world.

The process that established the new view of the universe is normally termed the ***Scientific Revolution.*** The revolution-in-science metaphor must be used carefully, however. Not everything associated with the "new" science was necessarily new. Sixteenth- and seventeenth-century natural philosophers were often reexamining and rethinking theories and data from the ancient world and the late middle ages. Moreover, the word *revolution* normally denotes rapid, collective political change involving large numbers of people. The Scientific Revolution was *not* rapid. It was a complex movement with many false starts and brilliant people suggesting wrong as well as useful ideas. Nor did it involve more than a few hundred people who labored in widely separated studies and crude laboratories located in Poland, Italy, Bohemia, France, and Great Britain. Furthermore, the achievements of the new science were not simply the function of isolated brilliant scientific minds. The leading figures of the Scientific Revolution often drew upon the aid of artisans and craftspeople to help them construct new instruments for experimentation and to carry out their experiments. Thus, the Scientific Revolution involved a reappropriation of older knowledge as well as new discoveries. Additionally, because the practice of science involves social activity as well as knowledge, the revolution also saw the establishment of new social institutions to support the emerging scientific enterprise.

From the early seventeenth century through the end of the twentieth century science achieved greater cultural authority in the Western world than any other form of intellectual activity, and the authority and application of scientific knowledge became one of the defining characteristics of modern Western civilization. Although new knowledge emerged in many areas during the sixteenth and seventeenth centuries, including medicine, chemistry, and natural history, the scientific achievements that most captured the learned imagination and persuaded people of the cultural power of natural knowledge were those that occurred in astronomy.

NICOLAUS COPERNICUS REJECTS AN EARTH-CENTERED UNIVERSE

Nicolaus Copernicus (1473–1543) was a Polish astronomer who enjoyed a high reputation during his life. He had been educated first in Cracow and later in Italy. He had not been known for strikingly original or unorthodox thought. In 1543, the year of his death, Copernicus published *On the Revolutions of the Heavenly Spheres*. Copernicus's book was "a revolution-making rather than a revolutionary text."[1] What Copernicus did was to provide an intellectual springboard for a complete criticism of the then-dominant view of the position of the Earth in the universe.

The Ptolemaic System   At the time of Copernicus, the standard explanation of the place of the Earth in the heavens was the **Ptolemaic system**. It combined the mathematical astronomy of Ptolemy, contained in his work entitled the *Almagest* (150 C.E.), with the physical cosmology of Aristotle. Over the centuries, commentators on Ptolemy's work had developed several alternative Ptolemaic systems, on the basis of which they made mathematical calculations relating to astronomy. Most of these writers assumed that the Earth was the center of the universe, an outlook known as *geocentricism*. Drawing upon Aristotle, these commentators assumed that above the Earth lay a series of concentric spheres, probably fluid in character, one of which contained the moon, another the sun, and still others the planets and the stars. At the outer regions of these spheres lay the realm of God and the angels. The Earth had to be the center because of its heaviness. The stars and the other heavenly bodies had to be enclosed in the spheres so that they could move, since nothing could move unless something was actually moving it. The state of rest was presumed natural; motion required explanation. This was the astronomy found in such works as Dante's *Divine Comedy*.

Numerous problems were associated with the Ptolemaic model, and these had long been recognized. The most important was the observed motions of the planets. At certain times the planets actually appeared to be going backwards. The Ptolemaic model accounted for these motions primarily through *epicycles*. The planet moved uniformly about a small circle (an epicycle), while the center of the epicycle moved uniformly about a larger circle (called a deferent), with the Earth at or near its center. The combination of these two motions, as viewed from the Earth, was meant to replicate the changing planetary positions among the fixed stars—and did so to a high degree of accuracy. The circles employed in Ptolemaic systems were not meant to represent the actual paths of anything; that is, they were not orbits. Rather, they were the components of purely mathematical models meant to predict planetary positions. Other intellectual, but nonobservational difficulties related to the immense speed at which the spheres had to move around the Earth. To say the least, the Ptolemaic systems were cluttered. They were effective, however, as long as one assumed Aristotelian physics.

[1] Thomas S. Kuhn, *The Copernican Revolution: Planetary Astronomy in the Development of Western Thought* (New York: Vintage, 1959), p. 135.

Copernicus's Universe   Copernicus's *On the Revolutions of the Heavenly Spheres* challenged the Ptolemaic picture in the most conservative manner possible. Copernicus adopted many elements of the Ptolemaic model but transferred them to a *heliocentric* (sun-centered) model which assumed that the Earth moved about the sun in a circle. Copernicus's model, which retained epicycles, was actually no more accurate than Ptolemy's. However, Copernicus could claim certain advantages over the ancient model. In particular, the epicycles were smaller. The retrograde motion of the planets now stood explained as a result of an optical illusion arising from an observer viewing the planets from a moving Earth. The order of the planets from the sun became more clearly intelligible when it was understood as a result of their increasing periods of revolution based on the planets' increasing distance from the sun.

The repositioning of the Earth had not been Copernicus's goal. Rather, Copernicus appears to have set out to achieve new intelligibility and mathematical elegance to astronomy. The means of doing so was to reject Aristotle's cosmology and to remove the Earth from the center of the universe. His system was no more accurate than the existing ones for predicting the location of the planets. He had used no new evidence. The major impact of his work was to provide another way of confronting some of the difficulties inherent in Ptolemaic astronomy. The Copernican system did not immediately replace the old astronomy, but it allowed other people who were also discontented with the Ptolemaic view to think in new directions. Indeed, for at least a century, the Copernican system was embraced by a distinct minority of natural philosophers and astronomers.

TYCHO BRAHE AND JOHANNES KEPLER

The next major step toward the conception of a sun-centered system was taken by the Danish astronomer Tycho Brahe (1546–1601). He spent most of his life opposing Copernicus and advocating a different kind of Earth-centered system. He suggested that the moon and the sun revolved around the Earth and that the other planets revolved around the sun. However, in attacking Copernicus, he gave the latter's ideas more publicity. More important, his major weapon against Copernican astronomy was a series of new astronomical observations made with the naked eye. Brahe constructed the most accurate tables of observations that had been drawn up for centuries.

When Brahe died, these tables came into the possession of Johannes Kepler (1571–1630), a German astronomer. Kepler was a convinced Copernican, but for philosophical, not scientific, reasons. Kepler was deeply influenced by Renaissance Neo-Platonists who, following upon Plato's (ca. 428–ca. 328 B.C.E.) association of knowledge with light, honored the sun. These Neo-Platonists were also determined to discover mathematical harmonies that would support a sun-centered universe. After much work, Kepler discovered that to keep the sun at the cen-

named Galileo Galilei (1564–1642) first turned a telescope on the heavens. He saw stars where none had been known to exist, mountains on the moon, spots moving across the sun, and moons orbiting Jupiter. The heavens were far more complex than anyone had formerly suspected. None of these discoveries proved that the earth orbited the sun, but they did suggest the complete inadequacy of the Ptolemaic system. It simply could not accommodate these new phenomena. Some of Galileo's colleagues at the University of Padua were so unnerved that they refused to look through the telescope, because it revealed the heavens to be different from the teachings of the church and from Ptolemaic theories. (See Document, "Galileo Discusses the Relationship of Science to the Bible.")

Galileo publicized his findings and arguments for the Copernican system in numerous works, the most famous of which was his *Dialogues on the Two Chief Systems of the World* (1632). This book brought down on him the condemnation of the Roman Catholic Church. He was compelled to recant his opinions. However, he is reputed to have muttered after the recantation, "*E pur si muove*" ("It [the earth] still moves").

Galileo's most important achievement was to articulate the concept of a universe totally subject to mathematical laws. More than any other writer of the century, he argued that nature in its most minute details displayed mathematical

▲ **Tycho Brahe** in the Uranienburg observatory on the Danish island of Hven (1587). Brahe made the most important observations of the stars since antiquity. Kepler used his data to solve the problem of planetary motion in a way that supported Copernicu's sun-centered view of the universe. Ironically, Brahe himself had opposed Copernicus's view.

Bildarchiv Preussischer Kulturbesitz.

ter of things, he must abandon the Copernican concept of circular orbits. The mathematical relationships that emerged from a consideration of Brahe's observations suggested that the orbits of the planets were elliptical. Kepler published his findings in 1609 in a book entitled *On the Motion of Mars*. He had solved the problems of planetary orbits by using Copernicus's sun-centered universe and Brahe's empirical data.

Kepler had, however, also defined a new problem. None of the available theories could explain why the planetary orbits were elliptical. That solution awaited the work of Sir Isaac Newton.

GALILEO GALILEI

From Copernicus to Brahe to Kepler, there had been little new information about the heavens that might not have been known to Ptolemy. However, in 1609 an Italian scientist

▲ **Newton's Telescope.** Behind it is a copy of *Principia Mathematica*, his most famous work.

© James A. Sugar/Corbis.

DOCUMENT · Galileo Discusses the Relationship of Science to the Bible

The religious authorities were often critical of the discoveries and theories of sixteenth- and seventeenth-century science. For years before his condemnation by the Roman Catholic Church in 1633, Galileo had contended that scientific theory and religious piety were compatible. In his Letter to the Grand Duchess Christiana *(of Tuscany), written in 1615, he argued that God had revealed truth in both the Bible and physical nature and that the truth of physical nature did not contradict the Bible if the latter were properly understood. Galileo encountered difficulties regarding this letter because it represented a layman telling church authorities how to read the Bible.*

◆ Why does Galileo see a difference between the text of scripture and the knowledge of nature achivied through the senses? To which does he seem to give priority? Why might church authorities have difficulty with his arguments? Why might some Roman Catholic authorities think he was behaving as a Protestant might believe?

The reason produced for condemning the opinion that the Earth moves and the sun stands still is that in many places in the Bible one may read that the sun moves and the Earth stands still. ...

With regard to this argument, I think in the first place that it is very pious to say and prudent to affirm that the holy Bible can never speak untruth—whenever its true meaning is understood. But I believe nobody will deny that it is often very abstruse, and may say things which are quite different from what its bare words signify. ...

This being granted, I think that in discussions of physical problems we ought to begin not from the authority of scriptural passages, but from sense-experiences and necessary demonstrations; for the holy Bible and the phenomena of nature proceed alike from the divine Word, the former as the dictate of the Holy Ghost and the latter as the observant executrix of God's commands. It is necessary for the Bible, in order to be accommodated to the understanding of every man, to speak many things which appear to differ from the absolute truth so far as the bare meaning of the words is concerned. But Nature, on the other hand, is inexorable and immutable; she never transgresses the laws imposed upon her, or cares a whit whether her abstruse reasons and methods of operation are understandable to men. For that reason it appears that nothing physical which sense-experience sets before our eyes, or which necessary demonstrations prove to us, ought to be called in question (much less condemned) upon the testimony of biblical passages which may have some different meaning beneath their words. For the Bible is not chained in every expression to conditions as strict as those which govern all physical effects; nor is God any less excellently revealed in Nature's actions than in the sacred statements of the Bible. ...

From this I do not mean to infer that we need not have an extraordinary esteem for the passages of holy Scripture. On the contrary, having arrived at any certainties in physics, we ought to utilize these as the most appropriate aids in the true exposition of the Bible and in the investigation of those meanings which are necessarily contained therein for these must be concordant with demonstrated truths. I should judge the authority of the Bible was designed to persuade men of those articles and propositions which, surpassing all human reasoning, could not be made credible by science, or by any other means than through the very mouth of the Holy Spirit. ...

But I do not feel obliged to believe that the same God who has endowed us with senses, reason, and intellect has intended to forgo their use and by some other means to give us knowledge which we can attain by them.

regularity. Copernicus had thought that the heavens conformed to mathematical regularity; Galileo saw this regularity throughout all physical nature. He believed that the smallest atom behaved with the same mathematical precision as the largest heavenly sphere.

Galileo stood as one of the foremost champions of the application of mathematics to scientific investigation and of the goal of reducing phenomena to mathematical formulas. However, earlier in the century the English philosopher Francis Bacon had advocated a method based solely on empiricism. As the century passed, both empirical induction and mathematical analysis proved fundamental to scientific investigation.

FRANCIS BACON: THE EMPIRICAL METHOD

Bacon (1561–1626) was an Englishman of almost universal accomplishment. He was a lawyer, a high royal official, and the author of histories, moral essays, and philosophical discourses. Traditionally, he has been regarded as the father of **empiricism** and of experimentation in science. Much of this reputation was actually unearned. Bacon was not a natural philosopher, except in the most amateur fashion. His real accomplishment was setting an intellectual tone and helping to create a climate conducive to scientific work.

In books such as *The Advancement of Learning* (1605), the *Novum Organum* (1620), and the *New Atlantis* (1627), Bacon attacked the scholastic belief that most truth had already been discovered and only required explanation, as well as the scholastic reverence for authority in intellectual life. He believed that scholastic thinkers paid too much attention to tradition and to the knowledge of the ancients. He urged contemporaries to strike out on their own in search of a new understanding of nature. He wanted seventeenth-century Europeans to have confidence in themselves and their own abilities rather than in the people and methods of the past. Bacon was one of the first major European writers to champion the desirability of innovation and change.

Bacon believed that human knowledge should produce useful results—deeds rather than words. In particular, knowledge of nature should be brought to the aid of the human condition. These goals required the modification or abandonment of scholastic modes of learning and thinking. Bacon contended, "The [scholastic] logic now in use serves more to fix and give stability to the errors which have their foundation in commonly received notions than to help the search after truth."[2] Scholastic philosophers could not escape from their syllogisms to examine the foundations of their thought and intellectual presuppositions. Bacon urged that philosophers and investigators of nature examine the evidence of their senses before constructing logical speculations. In a famous passage, he divided all philosophers into "men of experiment and men of dogmas" and then observed:

> The men of experiment are like the ant, they only collect and use; the reasoners resemble spiders, who make cobwebs out of their own substance. But the bee takes a middle course: it gathers its material from the flowers of the garden and of the field, but transforms and digests it by a power of its own. Not unlike this is the true business of philosophy.[3]

By directing natural philosophy toward an examination of empirical evidence, Bacon hoped that it would achieve new knowledge and thus new capabilities for humankind.

Most of the people in Bacon's day, including the intellectuals, thought that the best era of human history lay in antiquity. Bacon dissented vigorously from that view. He looked to a future of material improvement achieved through the empirical examination of nature. His own theory of induction from empirical evidence was unsystematic, but his insistence on appealing to experience influenced others whose methods were more productive. He and others of his outlook received almost daily support from the reports not only of European explorers, but also of ordinary seamen who now sailed all over the world and could describe wondrous cul-

tures, as well as plants and animals, unknown to the European ancients.

Bacon believed that science had a practical purpose and its goal was human improvement. Some scientific investigation does have this character. Much pure research does not. Bacon, however, linked science and material progress in the public mind. This was a powerful idea and has continued to influence Western civilization to the present day. It has made science and those who can appeal to the authority of science major forces for change and innovation. Thus, though not making any major scientific contribution himself, Bacon directed investigators of nature to a new method and a new purpose. As a person actively associated with politics, Bacon also believed that the pursuit of new knowledge would increase the power of governments and monarchies. Again, his thought in this area opened the way for the eventual strong linkage between governments and the scientific enterprise.

ISAAC NEWTON DISCOVERS THE LAWS OF GRAVITATION

The question that continued to perplex seventeenth-century scientists who accepted the theories of Copernicus, Kepler, and Galileo was how the planets and other heavenly bodies moved in an orderly fashion. The Ptolemaic and Aristotelian answer had been the spheres and a universe arranged in the order of the heaviness of its parts. Many unsatisfactory theories had been set forth to deal with the question. It was this issue of planetary motion that the Englishman Isaac Newton (1642–1727) addressed and, in so doing, established a basis for physics that endured for more than two centuries.

In 1687 Newton published *The Mathematical Principles of Natural Philosophy*, better known by its Latin title of *Principia Mathematica*. Much of the research and thinking for this great work had taken place more than fifteen years earlier. Galileo's mathematical bias permeated Newton's thought, as did his view that inertia applied to bodies both at rest and in motion. Newton reasoned that the planets and all other physical objects in the universe moved through mutual attraction, or gravity. Every object in the universe affected every other object through gravity. The attraction of gravity explained why the planets moved in an orderly, rather than a chaotic, manner. Newton had found that "the force of gravity towards the whole planet did arise from and was compounded of the forces of gravity towards all its parts, and towards every one part was in the inverse proportion of the squares of the distances from the part."[4] Newton proved this relationship mathematically; he made no attempt to explain the nature of gravity itself.

---

[2] Quoted in Franklin Baumer, *Main Currents of Western Thought*, 4th ed. (New Haven, CT: Yale University Press, 1978), p. 281.

[3] Quoted in Baumer, p. 288.

[4] Quoted in A. Rupert Hall, *From Galileo to Newton, 1630–1720* (London: Fontana, 1970), p. 300.

▲ **Sir Isaac Newton** discovered the mathematical and physical laws governing the force of gravity. Newton believed that religion and science were compatibile and mutually supportive, and that the study of nature gave one a better understanding of the Creator. This portrait of Newton is by Sir Godfrey Kneller.

Sir Godfrey Kneller, *Sir Isaac Newton*, 1702. Oil on canvas. The Granger Collection.

Newton was a great mathematical genius, but he also upheld the importance of empirical data and observation. Like Francis Bacon, he believed that one must observe phenomena before attempting to explain them. The final test of any theory or hypothesis for him was whether it described what was actually observed. Newton was a great opponent of the rationalism of the French philosopher René Descartes (1596–1650), which he believed included insufficient guards against error. Consequently, as Newton's own theory of universal gravitation became increasingly accepted, so, too, was Baconian empiricism.

WOMEN IN THE WORLD OF THE SCIENTIFIC REVOLUTION

The absence of women in the emergence of the new science of the seventeenth century has been a matter of much historical speculation. What characteristics of early modern European intellectual and cultural life worked against extensive contributions by women? Why have we heard so little of the activity by women that did actually occur in regard to the new science?

The same factors that had long excluded women from participating in most intellectual life continued to exclude them from working in the emerging natural philosophy. Traditionally, the institutions of European intellectual life had all but excluded women. Both monasteries and universities had been institutions associated with celibate male clerical culture. Except for a few exceptions in Italy, women had not been admitted to either medieval or early modern European universities; they would continue to be excluded from them until the end of the nineteenth century. Women could and did exercise much influence over princely courts where natural philosophers, such as Galileo, sought patronage, but they usually did not determine those patronage decisions or benefit from them. Queen Christina of Sweden was an exception by engaging René Descartes to provide the regulations for a new science academy. When various scientific societies were founded, women were not admitted to membership. In that regard, there were virtually no social spaces that might have permitted women easily to pursue science.

Yet a few isolated women from two different social settings did manage to engage in the new scientific activity—noblewomen and women from the artisan class. In both cases, they could do so only through their husbands or other men in their families.

The social standing of certain noblewomen allowed them to command the attention of ambitious natural philosophers who were part of their husband's social circle. Margaret Cavendish (1623–1673) actually made significant contributions to the scientific literature of the day. After she had been privately tutored and become widely read, her marriage to the duke of Newcastle introduced her into a circle of natural philosophers. She understood the new science, quarreled with the ideas of Descartes and Hobbes, and criticized the Royal Society for being more interested in novel scientific instruments than in solving practical problems. Her most important works were *Observations upon Experimental Philosophy* (1666) and *Grounds of Natural Philosophy* (1668). She was the only woman in the seventeenth century to be allowed to visit a meeting of the Royal Society of London.

Women associated with artisan crafts actually achieved greater freedom in pursuing the new sciences than did noblewomen. Traditionally, women had worked in artisan workshops, often with their husbands; and might take over the business when their spouse died. In Germany, much astronomy occurred in these settings, with women assisting their fathers or husbands. One such German female astronomer, Maria Cunitz, published a book on astronomy that many people thought her husband had written until he added a preface supporting her sole authorship. Elisabetha and Johannes Hevelius constituted a wife-and-husband astronomical team, as did Maria Winkelmann and her husband Gottfried Kirch. In each case, the wife served as the assistant to an artisan astronomer. Although Winkelmann discovered a comet in 1702, not until 1930 was the discovery ascribed to her rather than to her husband. Nonetheless, contemporary philosophers did recognize her abilities and understanding of astronomy. Winkelmann had worked jointly with her husband who was the official astronomer of the Berlin Academy of Sciences and was responsible for establishing an official calendar published by the Academy. When her husband died in 1710, Winkelmann applied for permission to continue the work, basing her application for the post on the guild's tradition of allowing women to continue their husband's work, in this case the completion of observations required for creating an accurate calendar. After much debate, the Academy formally rejected her application on the grounds of her gender, although its members knew of her ability and previous accomplishments. Years later, she returned to the Berlin Academy as an assistant to her son, who had been appointed astronomer. Again, the Academy insisted that she leave, forcing her to abandon astronomy. She died in 1720.

Such policies of exclusion, however, did not altogether prevent women from acquiring knowledge about the scientific endeavors of the age. Margaret Cavendish had composed a *Description of a New World, Called the Blazing World* (1666) to introduce women to the new science. Other examples of scientific writings for a female audience were Bernard de Fontenelle's *Conversations on the Plurality of Worlds* and Francesco Algarotti's *Newtonianism for Ladies* (1737). During the 1730s, Emilie du Châtelet aided Voltaire in his composition of an important French popularization of Newton's science. Her knowledge of mathematics was more extensive than his and crucial to his completing his book.

Still, with only a few exceptions, women were barred from science and medicine until the late nineteenth century, and not until the twentieth century did they enter these fields in any significant numbers. Not only did the institutions of science exclude them, but also, the ideas associated with medical practice, philosophy, and biology suggested that women and their minds were essentially different from, and inferior to, men and theirs. By the early eighteenth century, despite isolated precedents of women pursuing natural knowledge, reading scientific literature, and engaging socially with natural philosophers, it had become a fundamental assumption of European intellectual life that the pursuit of natural knowledge was a male vocation.

JOHN LOCKE

John Locke (1632–1704) attempted to achieve for philosophy a lawful picture of the human mind similar to that which Newton had presented of nature. Locke's three most famous works were the *Essay Concerning Human Understanding* (1690), *Two Treatises of Government*, and his *Letter Concerning Toleration* (1689). Each of them sounded philosophical themes that later

▲ **John Locke** (1632–1704), defender of the rights of the people against rulers who think their power absolute.
By courtesy of the National Portrait Gallery, London.

writers of the Enlightenment found welcome. No other philosopher had so profound an impact on European and American thought during the eighteenth century.

In the *Essay Concerning Human Understanding*, Locke envisioned the human mind as being blank at the time of an individual's birth. In Locke's view, contrary to that of much medieval philosophy, there are no innate ideas (i.e., ideas people are born with); all knowledge is derived from actual sense experience. Each individual mind grows through experience as it confronts the world of sensation. Human ideas are either simple (that is, passive receptions from daily experience) or complex (that is, products of sustained mental exercise). What people know is not the external world in itself, but the results of the interaction of their minds with the outside world. Locke's thinking thus represented an early form of behaviorism. Human nature is changeable and can be molded by modifying the surrounding physical and social environment. Locke also, in effect, rejected the Christian view that human beings were creatures permanently flawed by original sin. Human beings do not need to wait for the grace of God or other divine aid to better their lives. They can take charge of their own destiny.

OVERVIEW   Major Figures in the Scientific Revolution

The Scientific Revolution was a major turning point in Western culture. Although the Scientific Revolution never involved more than a few hundred people, the ideas they formulated and publicized gradually overturned the theological and religious modes of thought that were central to the medieval worldview. Humankind and life on Earth became the focus of Western thinking, and Western intellectuals developed more self-confidence in their capacity to shape the world and their own lives. Below is a list of the major scientific thinkers of the sixteenth and seventeenth centuries and their most important accomplishments.

Nicolaus Copernicus (1473–1543)	Argued that the Earth moved around the sun. His combination of mathematical astronomy with empirical observation and data became the model of scientific thought.
Tycho Brahe (1546–1601)	Compiled accurate tables of astronomical observations.
Johannes Kepler (1571–1601)	Used Brahe's data to argue that the orbits of the planets were elliptical.
Galileo Galilei (1564–1642)	First astronomer to use a telescope. Argued that mathematical laws governed the universe.
Francis Bacon (1561–1626)	Argued that scientific thought must conform to empirical evidence. Championed innovation and change.
René Descartes (1596–1650)	Invented analytical geometry. Argued that the world was governed by mathematical laws that could be deduced by reason.
Isaac Newton (1642–1727)	Explained the effect of gravity mathematically and established a theoretical basis for physics that endured until the late nineteenth century.
John Locke (1632–1704)	Argued that human nature was a blank slate that could be molded by modifying the environment. Human beings could thus take charge of their own destiny without divine aid.

Locke wrote *Two Treatises of Government* during the reign of Charles II (r. 1660–1685). Locke argued that rulers are not absolute in their power. They remain bound to the law of nature. That law is the voice of reason, teaching that human beings are equal and independent and that they should not harm one another or disturb one another's property because all persons are the images and property of God. According to Locke, people enter political contracts, empowering legislatures and monarchs to judge their disputes in order to preserve their natural rights (which include the possession of property) but not to give rulers an absolute power over them. Locke also contended that a monarch who violated the trust that had been placed in him could be overthrown. This argument reappeared in the American Declaration of Independence in 1776. But in eighteenth-century Europe it was Locke's argument against absolutism and in favor of limited government that was most influential. Like his philosophy, it opened a wider arena for individual action.

Locke's *Letter Concerning Toleration* contended that each person was responsible for his own religious salvation. Governments existed to protect property and the civil order. Matters only became confused when governments undertook to legislate on religion and require conformity to a single church. Yet Locke himself drew the line in England against toleration of Roman Catholics and Unitarians. During the eighteenth century, however, the logic of his argument was extended to advocate toleration for those faiths as well.

The Enlightenment

The movement that came to be known as the **Enlightenment** included a number of writers living at different times in various countries. Its early exponents, known as the *philosophes*, popularized the rationalism and scientific ideas of the seventeenth century. They worked to expose contemporary social and political abuses and argued that reform was necessary and possible. The advancement of their cause and ideas was anything but steady. They confronted vested interests, political oppression, and religious condemnation. Yet by midcentury they had brought enlightened ideas to the European public in a variety of formats.

Voltaire. Philosopher, dramatist, poet, historian, and popularizer of scientific ideas, Voltaire (1694–1778) was the most famous and influential of the 18th-century philosophers. His sharp satire and criticism of religious institutions opened the way for a more general critique of the European political and social status quo.
Nicholas de Largilliere/Art Resource/Bildarchiv Preussischer Kulturbesitz.

Slaughterhouses and Butchering Tools from the 18th Century. The *Encyclopedia* included hundreds of illustrations of the work of skilled artisan. Here is illustrated the work of butchers in a slaugherhouse and the implements of their labors.
Corbis/Bettman.

VOLTAIRE

One of the earliest and by far the most influential of the *philosophes* was François Marie Arouet, known to posterity as Voltaire (1694–1778). During the 1720s Voltaire had offended the French authorities by certain of his writings. He was arrested and briefly imprisoned. Later he went to England, visiting its best literary circles, observing its tolerant intellectual and religious climate, relishing the freedom he felt in its moderate political atmosphere, and admiring its science and economic prosperity. In 1733 he published *Letters on the English*, which appeared in French the next year. The book praised the virtues of the English and indirectly criticized the abuses of French society. In 1738 he published *Elements of the Philosophy of Newton*, which popularized the thought of the great scientist. Both works enhanced his reputation.

Thereafter, Voltaire lived part of the time in France and part near Geneva, just across the French border, where the royal authorities could not bother him. His essays, history, plays, stories, and letters made him the literary dictator of Europe. He turned the bitter venom of his satire and sarcasm against one evil after another in French and European life. His most famous satire is *Candide* (1759), in which he attacked war, religious persecution, and what he regarded as unwarranted optimism about the human condition. Like most *philosophes*, Voltaire believed that human society could and should be improved. But he was never certain that reform, if achieved, would be permanent. The optimism of the Enlightenment constituted a tempered hopefulness rather than a glib certainty. Pessimism was an undercurrent in most of the works of the period.

THE *ENCYCLOPEDIA*

The midcentury witnessed the publication of the *Encyclopedia*, one of the greatest monuments of the Enlightenment. Under the heroic leadership of Denis Diderot (1713–1784) and Jean le Rond d'Alembert (1717–1783), the first volume appeared in 1751. When completed in 1772, it numbered seventeen volumes of text and eleven of plates. The *Encyclopedia* was the product of the collective effort of more than one hundred authors, and its editors had solicited articles from all the major French *philosophes*. The project reached fruition only after numerous attempts to censor it and to halt its publication. The *Encyclopedia* set forth the most advanced critical ideas in religion, government, and philosophy. This criticism often had to be hidden in obscure articles or under the cover of irony. The articles represented a collective plea for freedom of expression. However, the large volumes also provided important information on manufacturing, canal building, ship construction, and improved agriculture. (See Document: "The *Encyclopedia* Praises Mechanical Arts and Artisans.")

Between 14,000 and 16,000 copies of various editions of the *Encyclopedia* were sold before 1789. The project had been

DOCUMENT | The *Encyclopedia* Praises Mechanical Arts and Artisans

The leading intellectuals and men of letters of the day wrote the articles of the Encyclopedia. *Yet the concrete reality of contemporaneous economic life in towns and the countryside fill its pages. Two of the most remarkable features of the* Encyclopedia *are the vast quantity of information it included in numerous articles about the mechanical arts and, in these articles, engravings that portrayed eighteenth-century French artisans in their workplace. The editors of the* Encyclopedia *believed disseminating such information was necessary to aid the spirit of improvement and to promote economic growth. In the "Preliminary Discourse," which served as a general introduction to the* Encyclopedia, *d'Alembert explained the importance of the mechanical arts and the way the authors had explored these arts and the workshops where they were practiced.*

♦ How does d'Alembert defend the importance of the mechanical arts? Why does he think they have not always received proper attention and appreciation? How did the authors of the *Encyclopedia* familiarize themselves with such work? What kind of conversation might have occurred between one of those authors and a skilled artisan operating his machinery?

The mechanical arts, which are dependent upon manual operation and are subjugated ... to a sort of routine, have been left to those among men whom prejudices have placed in the lowest class. Poverty has forced these men to turn to such work more often than taste and genius have attracted them to it. Subsequently it became a reason for holding them in contempt. ... However, the advantage that the liberal arts have over the mechanical arts ... is sufficiently counterbalanced by the quite superior usefulness which the latter for the most part have for us. It is this very usefulness which

reduced them perforce to purely mechanical operations in order to make them accessible to a larger number of men. But while justly respecting great geniuses for their enlightenment, society ought not to degrade the hands by which it is saved. ...

Too much has been written on the sciences; not enough has been written well on the mechanical arts. ... Thus everything impelled us to go directly to the workers.

We approached the most capable of them. ... We took the trouble of going into their shops, of questioning them, of writing at their dictation, of developing their thoughts and of drawing therefrom the terms peculiar to their professions, of setting up tables of these terms and of working out definitions for them, of conversing with those from whom we obtained memoranda, and (an almost indispensable precaution) of correcting through long and frequent conversations with others what some of them imperfectly, obscurely, and sometimes unreliably had explained. There are some artisans who are also men of letters, and we would be able to cite them here; but their numbers are very small. Most of those who engage in the mechanical arts have embraced them only by necessity and work only by instinct. ...

But there are some trades so unusual and some operations so subtle that unless one does the work oneself, unless one operates a machine with one's own hands, and sees the work being created under one's own eyes, it is difficult to speak of it with precision. Thus several times we had to get possession of the machines, to construct them, and to put a hand to the work. It was necessary to become apprentices, so to speak, and to manufacture some poor object ourselves in order to learn how to teach others the way good specimens are made.

From *Emile on Education* by Jean-Jaques Rousseau, translated by Allan Bloom. Copyright © 1979 by Basic Books, Inc. Reprinted by permission of Basic Books, a member of Perseus Books, LLC.

designed to secularize learning and to undermine the intellectual assumptions remaining from the Middle Ages and the Reformation. The articles on politics, ethics, and society ignored concerns about divine law and concentrated on humanity and its immediate well-being. The encyclopedists looked to antiquity rather than to the Christian centuries for their intellectual and ethical models. The future welfare of humankind lay not in pleasing God or following divine commandments, but rather in harnessing the power of the earth and its resources and in living at peace with one's fellow human beings. The good life was to be achieved through the application of reason to human relationships.

With the publication of the *Encyclopedia*, enlightened thought became more fully diffused over the Continent. Enlightened ideas penetrated German and Russian intellectual and political circles.

The Enlightenment and Religion

Throughout the century, in the eyes of the *philosophes*, the chief enemy of the improvement of humankind and the enjoyment of happiness was the church. The hatred of the *philosophes* for the church and Christianity was summed up in Voltaire's cry of "Crush the Infamous Thing." Almost all varieties of Christianity, but especially Roman Catholicism, invited the criticism of the *philosophes*. Intellectually, the churches perpetuated a religious rather than a scientific view of humankind and physical nature. The clergy taught that human beings were basically sinful and that they required divine grace to become worthy creatures. The doctrine of original sin in either its Catholic or its Protestant formulation suggested that meaningful improvement in human nature was impossible. Religious concerns turned human interest away from this world to the world to come. For the *philosophes*, the concept of predestination suggested that the fate of the human soul after death bore little or no relationship to virtuous living. Through their disagreements over obscure doctrines, the various churches favored the politics of intolerance and bigotry that in the past had caused human suffering, torture, and war.

DEISM

The *philosophes* believed that religion should be reasonable and lead to moral behavior. The Newtonian worldview had convinced many writers that nature was rational. Therefore, the God who had created nature must also be rational, and the religion through which that God was worshiped should be rational. Moreover, Lockean philosophy, which limited human knowledge to empirical experience, cast doubt on whether divine revelation was possible. These considerations gave rise to a movement for enlightened religion known as *deism*.

The title of one of its earliest expositions, *Christianity Not Mysterious* (1696) by John Toland, indicates the general tenor of this religious outlook. Toland and later writers wished to consider religion a natural and rational, rather than a supernatural and mystical, phenomenon. In this respect the deists differed from Newton and Locke, who had regarded themselves as distinctly Christian. Newton had believed that God might interfere with the natural order, whereas the deists regarded God as resembling a divine watchmaker who had set the mechanism of nature to work and then let them operate without intervention.

There were two major points in the deists' creed. The first was a belief in the existence of God, which they thought could be empirically deduced from the contemplation of nature.

Because nature provided evidence of a rational God, that Deity must also favor rational morality. Consequently, the second point in the deists' creed was a belief in life after death, when rewards and punishments would be meted out according to the virtue of the life a person led on this earth.

Deism was empirical, tolerant, reasonable, and capable of encouraging virtuous living. It was the major positive religious component of the Enlightenment. Voltaire declared:

> The great name of Deist, which is not sufficiently revered, is the only name one ought to take. The only gospel one ought to read is the great book of Nature, written by the hand of God and sealed with his seal. The only religion that ought to be professed is the religion of worshiping God and being a good man.[5]

If such a faith became widely accepted, it would overcome the fanaticism and rivalry of the various Christian sects. Religious conflict and persecutions would end. There would also

[5] Quoted in J. H. Randall, *The Making of the Modern Mind*, rev. ed. (New York: Houghton Mifflin, 1940), p. 292.

CHRONOLOGY	
Major Publication Dates of the Enlightenment	
1687	Newton's *Principia Mathematica*
1690	Locke's *Essay Concerning Human Understanding*
1696	Toland's *Christianity Not Mysterious*
1733	Voltaire's *Letters on the English*
1738	Voltaire's *Elements of the Philosophy of Newton*
1748	Montesquieu's *Spirit of the Laws*
1750	Rousseau's *Discourse on the Moral Effects of the Arts and Sciences*
1751	First volume of the *Encyclopedia* edited by Diderot and d'Alembert
1755	Rousseau's *Discourse on the Origin of Inequality*
1762	Rousseau's *Social Contract*
1763	Voltaire's *Treatise on Tolerance*
1776	Smith's *Wealth of Nations*
1779	Lessing's *Nathan the Wise*
1792	Wollstonecraft's *A Vindication of the Rights of Woman*

be little or no necessity for a priestly class to foment fanaticism, denominational hatred, and bigotry.

TOLERATION

A primary social condition for such a life was the establishment of religious toleration. Voltaire took the lead in championing this cause. In 1762 the political authorities in Toulouse ordered the execution of a Huguenot named Jean Calas (1698–1762). He stood accused of having murdered his son to prevent him from converting to Roman Catholicism. Calas had been viciously tortured and publicly strangled without ever having confessed his guilt. The confession would not have saved his life, but it would have given the Catholics good propaganda to use against Protestants.

Voltaire learned of the case only after Calas's death. He made the dead man's cause his own. In 1763 he published a *Treatise on Tolerance* and hounded the authorities for a new investigation. Finally, in 1765 the judicial decision against the unfortunate man was reversed. For Voltaire, the case illustrated the fruits of religious fanaticism and the need for rational reform of judicial processes. Somewhat later in the century the German playwright and critic Gotthold Lessing (1729–1781) wrote *Nathan the Wise* (1779) as a plea for toleration not only of different Christian sects, but also of religious faiths other than Christianity. All of these calls for toleration stated, in effect, that human life should not be subordinated to religion. Secular values and considerations were more important than religious ones.

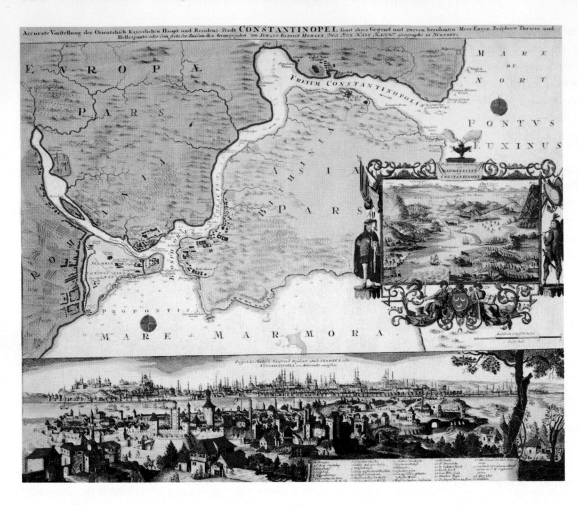

Map of Turkey and View of Constantinople. Few Europeans visited the Ottoman Empire. What little they know about it came from reports of travellers and from illustrations such as this view of Constantinople the Empire's Capital.
© Historical Picture Archive/Corbis.

ISLAM IN ENLIGHTENMENT THOUGHT

Islam, except in the Balkan Peninsula, had few adherents in eighteenth-century Europe. Although European merchants traded with the Ottoman Empire or with those parts of South Asia where Islam prevailed, most Europeans came to know what little they did know about the Islamic world and Islam as a religion through books—the religious commentaries of Christian missionaries, histories, and the reports of travelers—that with rare exceptions were hostile to Islam and deeply misleading.

Islam continued to be seen as a rival to Christianity. European writers repeated what other Christian critics had said for centuries. They portrayed Islam as a false religion and Muhammed as an impostor and a false prophet because he had not performed miracles. Furthermore, they also attacked Islam as an exceptionally carnal or sexually promiscuous religion because of its teaching that heaven was a place of sensuous delights, its permission for a man to have more than one wife, Muhammed's own polygamy, and the presence of harems in the Islamic world.

Christian authors also ignored the Islamic understanding of the life and mission of Muhammed. They referred to Islam as Muhammedanism, thus implying that Muhammed was divine rather than a human being with whom God had chosen to communicate. For Muslims, the suggestion that Muhammed was divine is blasphemous.

Several European universities did endow professorships for the study of Arabic during the seventeenth century. But these university scholars generally agreed with theological critics that Islam too often embodied religious fanaticism. Even relatively well-informed works based on considerable knowledge of Arabic and Islamic sources, such as Barthélemy d'Herbelot's *Bibliothèque orientale* (*Oriental Library*), a reference book published in 1697, Simon Ockley's *History of the Saracens* (1718), and George Sale's introduction to the first full English translation of the Qur'an (1734) were largely hostile to their subject. All these books continued to be reprinted and remained influential well into the nineteenth century, demonstrating how little disinterested information was available to Europeans about Islam.

Enlightenment philosophes spoke with two voices regarding Islam. Voltaire indicated his opinion along with that of many of his contemporaries in the title of his 1742 tragedy, *Fanaticism, or Mohammed the Prophet.* Although he sometimes spoke well of the Qur'an, Voltaire declared in a later historical work, "We must suppose that Muhammed, like all enthusiasts, violently impressed by his own ideas, retailed them in good faith, fortified them with fancies, deceived himself in deceiving others, and finally sustained with deceit a doctrine he believed to be good."[6] Thus for Voltaire, Muhammed and Islam in general represented simply one more example of the religious fanaticism he had so often criticized among Christians.

Some Enlightenment writers, however, spoke well of the Islamic faith. The deist John Toland, who opposed prejudice against both Jews and Muslims, contended that Islam derived from early Christian writings and was thus a form of Christianity. These views so offended most of his contemporaries that Toland became known as a "Mohametan" Christian. Edward Gibbon (1737–1794), who blamed Christianity for contributing to the fall of the Roman Empire, wrote with respect of Muhammed's leadership and Islam's success in conquering so vast a territory in the first century of its existence. Other commentators approved of Islam's tolerance and the charitable work of Muslims.

Some philosophes criticized Islam on cultural and political grounds. In *The Persian Letters* (1721), supposedly written by two Muslim Persians visiting Europe, Charles Louis de Secondat, baron de Montesquieu (1689–1755), who became a major political philosopher, used Islamic culture as a foil to criticize his own European society. But by the time he wrote his more influential *Spirit of the Laws* (1748), discussed more fully later in this chapter, Montesquieu associated Islamic society with the passivity that he ascribed to people subject to political despotism. Like other Europeans, Montesquieu believed the excessive influence of Islamic religious leaders prevented the Ottoman Empire from adapting itself to new advances in technology.

One of the most positive commentators on eighteenth-century Islam was a woman. Between 1716 and 1718, Lady Mary Wortley Montagu (1689–1762) lived in Constantinople with her husband, the British ambassador to Turkey. She wrote a series of letters about her experiences there that were published the year after her death. In these *Turkish Embassy Letters*, she praised much about Ottoman society and urged the English to copy the Turkish practice of vaccination against smallpox. Unlike European males, Montagu had access to the private quarters of women in Istanbul. In contrast to the constraints under which English women found themselves, she thought upper-class Turkish women were remarkably free and well treated by their husbands despite having to wear clothing that completely covered them in public. In fact, Montagu thought the anonymity these coverings bestowed allowed Turkish women to move freely about Istanbul. She also considered the magnificent Ottoman architecture better than anything in Western Europe. Montagu repeatedly criticized the misinformation that prevailed in Europe about the Ottoman Empire and declared that many of the hostile comments about Islam and Islamic morality were simply wrong.

Yet the European voices demanding fairness and expressing empathy for Islam were rare throughout the eighteenth century. As one historian has commented, "The basic Christian attitude was still what it had been for a millennium: a rejection of the claim of Muslims that Muhammad was a prophet and the Qur'an the word of God, mingled with a memory of periods of fear and conflict, and also, a few thinkers and scholars apart, with legends, usually hostile and often contemptuous."[7]

Nor were Muslims very curious about the Christian West. Only a handful of people from the Ottoman Empire visited Western Europe in the eighteenth century, and no Islamic writers showed much interest in contemporary European authors. The Ulama, the Islamic religious establishment, reinforced these attitudes. They taught that God's revelations to Muhammad meant Islam had superceded Christianity as a religion and therefore there was little to be learned from the Christian culture of Europe.

The Enlightenment and Society

Although the *philosophes* wrote much about religion, humanity was the center of their interest. As one writer in the *Encyclopedia* observed, "Man is the unique point to which we must refer everything, if we wish to interest and please amongst considerations the most arid and details the most dry."[8] The *philosophes* believed that the application of human reason to society would reveal laws in human relationships similar to those found in physical nature. Although the term did not appear until later, the idea of social science originated with the Enlightenment. The purpose of discovering social laws was to remove the inhumanity that existed through ignorance of them.

MONTESQUIEU AND "THE SPIRIT OF THE LAWS"

Charles Louis de Secondat, Baron de Montesquieu, was a French noble of the robe and a magistrate. His work *The Spirit of the Laws* (1748), perhaps the single most influential book of the century, exhibits the internal tensions of the Enlightenment. Montesquieu pursued an empirical method, taking illustrative examples from the political experience of both ancient and modern nations. From them he concluded that no single set of political laws could apply to all peoples at all times and in all places. Rather, the good political life depended on the relationship of many political variables. Whether a monarchy or a republic was the best form of government depended on the size of the political unit and its population, its social and religious customs, economic structure, traditions, and climate. Only a careful examination and evaluation of these elements

---

[6] Quoted in Theodore Besterman, *Voltaire* (New York: Harcourt, Brace, & World, 1969), p. 409.

[7] A. Hourani, *Islam in European Thought* (Cambridge: Cambridge University Press, 1991), p. 136.
[8] Quoted in F. L. Baumer, *Main Currents of Western Thought*, 4th ed. (New Haven, CT: Yale University Press, 1978), p. 374.

could reveal what mode of government would prove most beneficial to a particular people. A century later such speculations would have been classified as sociology.

As far as France was concerned, Montesquieu believed in a monarchy whose power was tempered and limited by various intermediary institutions, including the aristocracy, the towns, and the other corporate bodies that enjoyed particular liberties that the monarch must respect. These corporate bodies might be said to represent various segments of the general population and thus of public opinion. In France he regarded the *parlements*, judicial courts dominated by aristocrats like himself, as the major example of an intermediary association. Their role was to limit the power of the monarchy and thus to preserve the liberty of the subjects. In championing these aristocratic bodies and the general role of the aristocracy, Montesquieu was a political conservative. He adopted that stance, however, in the hope of achieving reform, for he considered the oppressive and inefficient absolutism of the monarchy responsible for the degradation of French life.

One of Montesquieu's most influential ideas was that of division of power. He took Great Britain for his model of a government with power wisely separated among different branches. There he believed he had found a system in which executive power resided in the king, legislative power in the Parliament, and judicial power in the courts. He thought any two branches could check and balance the power of the other. His perception of the eighteenth-century British constitution was incorrect, because he failed to see how patronage and electoral corruption allowed a handful of aristocrats to dominate the government. Moreover, he was also unaware of the emerging cabinet system, which meant that the executive power was slowly becoming a creature of the Parliament. Nevertheless, the analysis illustrated Montesquieu's strong sense of the need to limit the exercise of power through a constitution and for legislatures, not monarchs, to make laws. Although Montesquieu set out to defend the political privileges of the French aristocracy, his ideas had a profound and enduring effect on the liberal democracies of the next two centuries.

ADAM SMITH ON ECONOMIC GROWTH AND SOCIAL PROGRESS

The most important economic work of the Enlightenment was Adam Smith's (1723–1790) *Inquiry into the Nature and Causes of the Wealth of Nations* (1776). Smith, who was for a time a professor at Glasgow, believed that economic liberty was the foundation of a natural economic system. As a result, he urged that the mercantile system of England—including the navigation acts, the bounties, most tariffs, special trading monopolies, and the domestic regulation of labor and manufacture—be abolished. These regulations were intended to preserve the wealth of the nation, to capture wealth from other nations, and to maximize the work available for the nation's laborers. Smith argued, however, that they hindered the expansion of wealth and production. The best way to encourage economic growth, he maintained, was to unleash individuals to pursue their own selfish economic interests. As self-interested individuals sought to enrich themselves by meeting the needs of others in the marketplace, the economy would expand. Consumers would find their wants met as manufacturers and merchants competed for their business.

It was a basic assumption of mercantilism that the earth's resources are limited and scarce, so that one nation can acquire wealth only at the expense of others. Smith's book challenged this assumption. He saw the resources of nature—water, air, soil, and minerals—as boundless. To him, they demanded exploitation for the enrichment and comfort of humankind. In effect, Smith was saying that the nations and peoples of Europe need not be poor.

Smith is usually regarded as the founder of *laissez-faire* economic thought and policy, which favors a limited role for the government in economic life. *The Wealth of Nations* was, however, a complex book. Smith was no simple dogmatist. For example, he did not oppose all government activity touching

▲ **Montesquieu.** Charles de Secondat, Baron de Montesquieu (1689–1755) was the author of *The Spirit of the Laws,* possibly the most influential work of political thought of the 18th century.
Hulton/UPI/Corbis-Bettmann
© Stefano Bianchetti/Corbis.

Printing Shops. Shops such as this were the productive centers for the book trade and newspaper publishing which spread the ideas of the Enlightenment.
The Granger Collection.

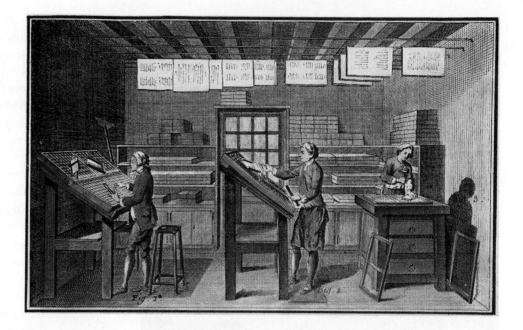

the economy. The state, he argued, should provide schools, armies, navies, and roads. It should also undertake certain commercial ventures, such as the opening of dangerous new trade routes that were economically desirable, but too expensive or risky for private enterprise.

Within *The Wealth of Nations*, Smith, like other Scottish thinkers of the day, embraced an important theory of human social and economic development, known as the *four-stage theory*. According to this theory, human societies can be classified as hunting and gathering, pastoral or herding, agricultural, and commercial. The hunters and gatherers have little or no settled life. Pastoral societies are groups of nomads who tend their herds and develop some private property. Agricultural or farming societies are settled and have clear-cut property arrangements. Finally, in the commercial state there exist advanced cities, the manufacture of numerous items for wide consumption, extensive trade between cities and the countryside, as well as elaborate forms of property and financial arrangements. Smith and other Scottish writers described the passage of human society through these stages as a movement from barbarism to civilization.

The four-stage theory implicitly evaluated the later stages of economic development and the people dwelling in them as higher, more progressive, and more civilized than the earlier ones. A social theorist using this theory could thus very quickly look at a society and, on the basis of the state of its economic development and organizations, rank it in terms of the stage it had achieved. In point of fact, the commercial stage, the highest rank in the theory, described society as it appeared in northwestern Europe. Thus, Smith's theory allowed Europeans to look about the world and always find themselves dwelling at the highest level of human achievement. This outlook served as one of the major justifications in the minds of Europeans for their

economic and imperial domination of the world during the next century. They repeatedly portrayed themselves as bringing a higher level of civilization to people elsewhere who, according to the four-stage theory, lived in lower stages of human social and economic development. Europeans thus imbued with the spirit of the Enlightenment presented themselves as carrying out a civilizing mission to the rest of the world.

ROUSSEAU

Jean-Jacques Rousseau (1712–1778) held a different view of political power. Rousseau was a strange, isolated genius who never felt comfortable with the other *philosophes*. Yet perhaps more than any other writer of the mid–eighteenth century, he transcended the thought and values of his own time. Rousseau had a deep antipathy toward the world and the society in which he lived. It seemed impossible for human beings living according to contemporary commercial values to achieve moral, virtuous, or sincere lives. In 1750, in his *Discourse on the Moral Effects of the Arts and Sciences*, he contended that civilization and enlightenment had corrupted human nature. Human beings in the state of nature had been more dignified. In 1755, in a *Discourse on the Origin of Inequality*, Rousseau blamed much of the evil in the world on maldistribution of property.

In both works, Rousseau directly challenged the social fabric of the day. He questioned the concepts of material and intellectual progress and the morality of a society in which commerce and industry were regarded as the most important human activities. He felt that the real purpose of society was to nurture better people. Rousseau's vision of reform was much more radical than that of other contemporary writers.

Rousseau carried these same concerns into his political thought. His most extensive discussion of politics appeared in

Rousseau. The writings of Jean-Jacques Rousseau (1712–1778) raised some of the most profound social and ethical questions of the Enlightenment. This portrait by Maurice Quentin was made ca. 1740.
Bildarchiv Preussischer Kulturbesitz
Maurice Quentin de la Tour/Bildarchiv Preussicher Kulturbesitz.

The Social Contract (1762). Compared to Montesquieu's *The Spirit of the Laws, The Social Contract* is an abstract book. It does not propose specific reforms but outlines the kind of political structure that Rousseau believed would overcome the evils of contemporary politics and society.

In the tradition of John Locke, most eighteenth-century political thinkers regarded society as a collection of independent individuals pursuing personal, selfish goals. These writers wished to liberate these individuals from the undue bonds of government. Rousseau picked up the stick from the other end. His book opens with the declaration, "All men are born free, but everywhere they are in chains."[9] The rest of the volume constitutes a defense of the chains of a properly organized society over its members. Rousseau suggested that society is more important than its individual members, because they are what they are only as a result of their relationship to the larger community. Independent human beings living alone can achieve little. Through their relationship to the larger community, they become moral creatures capable of significant action. The question then becomes what kind of community allows people to behave morally. Rousseau sought to project the vision of a society in which each person could maintain personal freedom while also behaving as a loyal member of the larger community. He drew on the traditions of Plato and Calvin to define freedom as obedience to law. In his case, the law to be obeyed was that created by the general will. This concept normally indicated the will of the majority of voting citizens who acted with adequate information and under the influence of virtuous customs and morals. Such democratic participation in decision making would bind the individual citizen to the community. Rousseau believed that the general will must always be right and that to obey the general will was to be free. This argument led him to the notorious conclusion that some people must be forced to be free. His politics thus constituted a justification for radical direct democracy and for collective action against individual citizens.

Rousseau had, in effect, assaulted the eighteenth-century cult of the individual and the fruits of selfishness. He stood at odds with the commercial spirit that was transforming society. Adam Smith wanted people to be prosperous; Rousseau wanted them to be good even if it meant they might remain poor. He saw human beings not as independent individuals, but as creatures enmeshed in necessary social relationships. He believed that loyalty to the community should be encouraged. As one device to that end, he suggested a civic religion based on deism. Such a shared tolerant religious faith would unify society. Rousseau's chief intellectual inspiration arose from his study of Plato and the ancient Greek *polis*. Especially in Sparta, he thought he had discovered human beings dwelling in a moral society inspired by a common purpose. He hoped that modern human beings might also create such a moral commonwealth in which virtuous living would not become subordinate to commercial profit.

ENLIGHTENED CRITICS OF EUROPEAN EMPIRE

Most European thinkers associated with the Enlightenment favored the extension of European empires across the world. Like the Scottish writers who embraced the four-stage theory, they believed that the extension of the political structures and economies of northwestern Europe amounted to the spread of progress and civilization. The Scottish commentators and their followers were not without their criticisms of European civilization, but on the whole they believed it superior.

There were, however, a few minority Enlightenment voices who criticized the European empires. The topic that most frequently allowed such criticism were discussions of the European conquest of the Americas, the treatment of Native Amer-

[9] Jean-Jacques Rousseau, *The Social Contract and Discourses*, trans. by G. D. H. Cole (New York: Dutton, 1950), p. 3.

DOCUMENT   Denis Diderot Condemns European Empires

Denis Diderot was one of the most prolific writers of the Enlightenment. He is most famous as editor of the Encyclopedia. *Some of his writings were published without being directly attributed to him. Among these were his contributions to Abbé G. T. Raynal's* History of the Two Indies, *published in various changing editions after 1772. Diderot's contributions appear to have been made in 1780. The entire* History *was critical of the European colonial empires that had arisen since the Spanish encounter with the New World. Diderot was particularly concerned to condemn the inhumane treatment of the native populations of the Americas, the greed displayed by all Europeans, and the establishment of various forms of forced labor.*

◆ What is the basis for Diderot's view that Europeans have behaved tyrannically? How does he portray the behavior of Europeans once they have left their own native countries and find themselves in foreign areas? What are the specific social results he associates with European greed?

Let the European nations make their own judgment and give themselves the name they deserve … Their explorers arrive in a region of the New World unoccupied by anyone from the Ole World, and immediately bury a small strip of metal on which they have engraved these words: *This country belongs to us.* Any why does it belong to you? … You have no right to the natural products of the country where you land, and you claim a right over your fellow-men. Instead of recognizing this man as a brother you only see him as a slave, a beast of burden. Oh my fellow citizens! You think like that and you behave like that; and you have ideas of justice, a morality, a holy religion … in common with whose whom you treat so tyrannically. This reproach should especially be addressed to the Spaniards.

****

Beyond the Equator a man is neither English, Dutch, French, Spanish, nor Portuguese. He retains only those principles and prejudices of his native country which justify or excuse his conduct. He crawls when he is weak; he is violent when strong; he is in a hurry to acquire, in a hurry to enjoy, and capable of every crime which will lead him most quickly to his goals. He is a domestic tiger returning to the forest; the thirst for blood takes hold of him once more. This is how all the Europeans, every one of them, indistinctly, have appeared in the countries of the New World. There they have assumed a common frenzy—the thirst for gold.

****

The Spaniard, the first to be thrown up by the waves onto the shores of the New World, thought he had no duty to people who did not share his color, customs, or religion. He saw in them only tools for his greed, and he clapped them in irons. These weak men, not used to work, soon died in the foul air of the mines, or in other occupations which were virtually as lethal. Then people called for slaves from Africa. Their number has gone up as more land has been cultivated. The Portuguese, Dutch, English, French, Danes, all the nations, free or subjected, have without remorse sought to increase their fortune in the sweat, blood and despair of these unfortunates. What a horrible system!

Denis Diderot, *Political Writings*, John Hope Mason and Robert Wokler, eds., (Cambridge: Cambridge University Press, 1998), pp. 177, 178, 186

---

icans, and the enslavement of Africans on the two American continents. The most important of these critics were Denis Diderot and two German philosophers, Immanuel Kant (1724–1804) and Johann Gottfried Herder (1744–1803). (See Document: "Denis Diderot Condemns European Empires.")

What sets of ideas allowed these figures from the Enlightenment to criticize empire? As Sankar Muthu has recently written, "The first and most basic idea is that human beings deserve some modicum of moral and political respect simply because of the fact that they are human."[10] In other words, the Enlightenment critics of empire argued for the existence of a form of shared humanity which the sixteenth-century European conquerors and their successors in the Americas and in other areas of imperial conquest had ignored. Immanuel Kant, the German philosopher, wrote, "When America, the Negro countries, the Spice Islands, the Cape, and so forth were discovered, they were to them [the Europeans], countries belonging to no one, since they counted the inhabitants as *nothing.*"[11] Kant, Denis Diderot, and the German philosopher of history Herder rejected this dismissive outlook and the harsh policies that had flowed from it. They believed no single definition of human nature could be made the standard throughout the world and then used to dehumanize people whose appearance or culture differed from that standard.

A second of these critical ideas was the conviction that the people whom Europeans had encountered in the Americas had actually possessed cultures that should have been respected and understood rather than being destroyed. Some Europeans in the early years of the encounter with America had actually argued that the native peoples were human, but that their way of life was so low, they could not be treated a being equally human with Europeans.

[10] Sankar Muthu, *Enlightenment Against Empire* (Princeton: Princeton University Press, 2003), p. 268. This section draws primarily from this excellent recent book.
[11] Quoted in Muthu, *Enlightenment Against Empire*, p. 267.

DOCUMENT | Rousseau Argues for Separate Spheres for Men and Women

Rousseau published Émile, *a novel about education, in 1762. In it he made one of the strongest and most influential arguments of the eighteenth century for distinct social roles for men and women. Furthermore, he portrayed women as fundamentally subordinate to men. See page 657 for a contemporary rebuttal.*

◆ How does Rousseau move from the physical differences between men and women to an argument for distinct social roles and social spheres? What would be the proper kinds of social activities for women in Rousseau's vision? What kind of education would he think appropriate for women?

There is no parity between the two sexes in regard to the consequences of sex. The male is male only at certain moments. The female is female her whole life or at least during her whole youth. Everything constantly recalls her sex to her; and, to fulfill its functions well, she needs a constitution which corresponds to it. She needs care during her pregnancy; she needs rest at the time of childbirth; she needs a soft and sedentary life to suckle her children; she needs patience and gentleness, a zeal and an affection that nothing can rebuff in order to raise her children. She serves as the link between them and their father; she alone makes him love them and gives him the confidence to call them his own. How much tenderness and care is required to maintain the union of the whole family! And, finally, all this must come not from virtues but from tastes, or else the human species would soon be extinguished.

The strictness of the relative duties of the two sexes is not and cannot be the same. When woman complains on this score about unjust man-made inequality, she is wrong. This inequality is not a human institution—or, at least, it is the work not of prejudice but of reason. It is up to the sex that nature has charged with the bearing of children to be responsible for them to the other sex. Doubtless it is not permitted to any one to violate his faith, and every unfaithful husband who deprives his wife of the only reward of the austere duties of her sex is an unjust and barbarous man. But the unfaithful woman does more; she dissolves the family and breaks all the bonds of nature. ...

Once it is demonstrated that man and woman are not and ought not be constituted in the same way in either character or temperament, it follows that they ought not to have the same education. In following nature's directions, man and woman ought to act in concert, but they ought not to do the same things. The goal of their labors is common, but their labors themselves are different, and consequently so are the tastes directing them. ...

The good constitution of children initially depends on that of their mothers. The first education of men depends on the care of women. Men's morals, their passions, their tastes, their pleasures, their very happiness also depend on women. Thus the whole education of women ought to relate to men. To please men, to be useful to them, to make herself loved and honored by them, to raise them when young, to care for them when grown, to counsel them, to console them, to make their lives agreeable and sweet—these are the duties of women at all times, and they ought to be taught from childhood. So long as one does not return to this principle, one will deviate from the goal, and all the precepts taught to women will be of no use for their happiness or for ours.

From *Émile; or, On Education,* by Jean-Jacques Rousseau, by Allan Bloom, trans. Copyright ©1979 by Basic Books, a member of Perseus Books L.L.C.

In the late eighteenth century Herder directly rejected such a view, "'European culture' is a mere abstraction, an empty concept. Where does or did it actually exist in its entirety? In which nation? In which period? ... Only a misanthrope could regard European culture as the universal condition of our species. The culture of man is not the culture of the European; it manifests itself according to time and place in every people."[12] For Herder, human beings living in different societies possessed the capacity as human beings to develop in culturally different fashions. He thus strongly embraced an outlook later known as cultural relativism.

A third idea, closely related to the second, was that human beings may develop distinct cultures possessing intrinsic values that cannot be directly compared. The reason they may not be compared one to the detriment of another is that each culture possesses deep inner social and linguistic complexities which make any simple comparison impossible. Indeed, Diderot, Kant, and Herder argued that one fundamental aspect of humanity is the ability to develop a variety of distinctly different cultures.

These arguments critical of empire often involved criticism of New World slavery and were part of the antislavery movement to be discussed in a later chapter. Whereas the antislavery arguments took strong hold in both Europe and America from the late eighteenth century onward, the arguments critical of empire did not. They stand generally isolated from the rest of Enlightenment political thought and would not be strongly revived until new anticolonial voices were raised in Europe and the non-European world at the close of the nineteenth century.

[12] F. M. Barnard, *Self-direction and Political Legitimacy: Rousseau and Herder* (Oxford: Clarendon Press, 1988), p. 227

DOCUMENT | Mary Wollstonecraft Criticizes Rousseau's View of Women

Mary Wollstonecraft published A Vindication of the Rights of Woman *in 1792, thirty years after Rousseau's* Émile *had appeared. She criticized and rejected Rousseau's argument for distinct and separate spheres for men and women as defending the continued bondage of women to men and as hindering the wider education of the entire human race.*

♦ What specific criticisms does Wollstonecraft direct against Rousseau's views? Why does Wollstonecraft put so much emphasis on a new kind of education for women?

The most perfect education … is such an exercise of the understanding as is best calculated to strengthen the body and form the heart. Or, in other words, to enable the individual to attain such habits of virtue as will render it independent. In fact, it is a farce to call any being virtuous whose virtues do not result from the exercise of its own reason. This was Rousseau's opinion respecting men: I extend it to women. …

I may be accused of arrogance; still I must declare what I firmly believe, that all the writers who have written on the subject of female education and manners from Rousseau to Dr. Gregory [a Scottish physician], have contributed to render women more artificial, weak characters, than they would other wise have been; and, consequently, more useless members of society. …

… Strengthen the female mind by enlarging it, and there will be an end to blind obedience; but, as blind obedience is ever sought for by power, tyrants and sensualists are in the right when they endeavour to keep women in the dark, because the former only wants slaves, and the latter a play-thing. The sensualist, indeed, has been the most dangerous of tyrants, and women have been duped by their lovers, as princes by their ministers, whilst dreaming that they reigned over them.

… Rousseau declares that a woman should never, for a moment, feel herself independent, that she should be governed by fear to exercise her natural cunning, and made a coquettish slave in order to render her a more alluring object of desire, a sweeter companion to man, whenever he chooses to relax him-

self. He carries the arguments, which he pretends to draw from the indications of nature, still further, and insinuates that truth and fortitude, the corner stones of all human virtue, should be cultivated with certain restrictions, because, with respect to the female character, obedience is the grand lesson which ought to be impressed with unrelenting rigour.

What nonsense! When will a great man arise with sufficient strength of mind to put away the fumes which pride and sensuality have thus spread over the subject! If women are by nature inferior to men, their virtues must be the same in quality, if not in degree, or virtue is a relative idea; consequently, their conduct should be founded on the same principles, and have the same aim.

Connected with man as daughters, wives, and mothers, their moral character may be estimated by their manner of fulfilling those simple duties; but the end, the grand end of their exertions should be to unfold their own faculties and acquire the dignity of conscious virtue. …

But avoiding … any direct comparison of the two sexes collectively, or frankly acknowledging the inferiority of women, according to the present appearance of things, I shall only insist that men have increased that inferiority till women are almost sunk below the standard of rational creatures. Let their faculties have room to unfold, and their virtues to gain strength, and then determine where the whole sex must stand in the intellectual scale. …

… I … will venture to assert, that till women are more rationally educated, the progress of human virtue and improvement in knowledge must receive continual checks. …

The mother, who wishes to give true dignity of character to her daughter, must regardless of the sneers of ignorance, proceed on a plan diametrically opposite to that which Rousseau has recommended with all the deluding charms of eloquence and philosophical sophistry: for his eloquence renders absurdities plausible, and his dogmatic conclusions puzzle, without convincing, those who have not ability to refute them.

From Mary Wollstonecraft, *A Vindication of the Rights of Woman*, ed. by Carol H. Poston. Copyright © 1975 W. W. Norton & Co., Inc., pp. 21, 22, 24–26, 35, 40, 41.

WOMEN IN THE THOUGHT AND PRACTICE OF THE ENLIGHTENMENT

Women, especially in France, helped significantly to promote the careers of the *philosophes*. In Paris the salons of women such as Marie-Thérèse Geoffrin (1699–1777), Julie de Lespinasse (1733–1776), and Claudine de Tencin (1689–1749) gave the *philosophes* access to useful social and political contacts and a receptive environment for their ideas. These women were well connected to major political figures who could help protect the *philosophes* and secure them pensions. The marquise de Pom-

padour (1721–1764), the mistress of Louis XV, for example, played a key role in overcoming efforts to censor the *Encyclopedia*. She also helped block the circulation of works attacking the *philosophes*.

Nonetheless, the *philosophes* were on the whole not strong feminists. Although many criticized the education women received as overly religious and tended to reject ascetic views of sexual relations, the *philosophes* advocated no radical changes in the social condition of women.

Montesquieu, for example, maintained in general that the status of women in a society was the result of climate, the political

Enlightenment Salon. The salon of Mme. Marie-Thérèse Geoffrin (1699–1777) was one of the most important gathering spots for Enlightenment writers during the middle of the 18th century. Well-connected women such as Mme. Geoffrin were instrumental in helping the *philosophes* they patronized to bring their ideas to the attention of influential people in French society and politics.

Chateaux de Malmaison et Bois-Preau, Rueil-Malmaison. Bridgemann-Giraudon/Art Resource, N.Y.

regime, culture, and women's physiological nature. He believed women were not naturally inferior to men and should have a wider role in society. He was well aware of the personal, emotional, and sexual repression women endured in his day. Yet there were limits to his willingness to consider change in women's social role. He retained a traditional view of marriage and family and expected men to dominate those institutions. Furthermore, although he supported the right of women to divorce and opposed laws that directly oppressed them, he upheld the ideal of female chastity.

The views about women expressed in the *Encyclopedia* were less generous. The editors, Diderot and d'Alembert, recruited men almost exclusively as contributors and saw no need to include many articles by women. Most of the articles that dealt with women specifically or that discussed women in connection with other subjects often emphasized their physical weakness and inferiority, usually attributed to menstruation or childbearing. Contributors disagreed on the social equality of women. Some favored it, others opposed it, and still others were indifferent. The articles conveyed a general sense that women were reared to be frivolous and unconcerned with important issues. The encyclopedists discussed women primarily in a family context—as daughters, wives, and mothers—and considered motherhood their most important occupation. On sexual behavior, the encyclopedists upheld an unquestioned double standard.

In contrast to the articles, however, illustrations in the *Encyclopedia* showed women deeply involved in the economic activities of the day. The illustrations also showed the activities of lower- and working-class women, about whom the articles have little to say.

Rousseau urged a traditional role for women. In his novel *Émile* (1762) he declared that women should be educated for a position subordinate to men, emphasizing especially women's function in bearing and rearing children. He portrayed them as weaker and inferior to men in virtually all respects except perhaps for their capacity for feeling and giving love. He excluded them from political life. Women were assigned the domestic sphere alone. Many of these attitudes were not new—some have roots as ancient as Roman law—but Rousseau's powerful presentation and the influence of his other writings gave them new life, including in the legislation of the French Revolution. (See Document: "Rousseau Argues for Separate Spheres for Men and Women.")

Paradoxically, despite these views and his own ill treatment of the many women who bore his many children, Rousseau achieved a vast following among women in the eighteenth century. He is credited with persuading thousands of upper-class women to breast-feed their own children rather than putting them out to wet nurses. One explanation for this influence is that his writings, although they did not advocate liberating women or expanding their social or economic roles, did stress the importance of their emotions and subjective feelings. He portrayed the domestic life and the role of wife and mother as a noble and fulfilling vocation, giving middle- and upper-class women a sense that their daily occupations had purpose. He assigned them a degree of influence in the domestic sphere that they could not have competing with men outside it.

In 1792 in *A Vindication of the Rights of Woman*, Mary Wollstonecraft (1759–1797) brought Rousseau before the judgment of the rational Enlightenment ideal of progressive knowledge. Wollstonecraft (who, like so many women of her day, died shortly after childbirth of puerperal fever) accused Rousseau and others after him who upheld traditional roles for women of attempting to narrow women's vision and limit their experience. She argued that to confine women to the separate domestic sphere because of their supposed physiological limitations was to make them the sensual slaves of men. Confined in this separate sphere, as the victims of male tyranny, they could never achieve their own moral or intellectual identity. Denying good education to women would impede the progress of all humanity. Wollstonecraft was demanding for women the kind of intellectual liberty that male writers of the Enlightenment had been championing for men for more than a century. (See Document, "Mary Wollstonecraft Criticizes Rousseau's View of Women.")

Enlightened Absolutism

During the last third of the century it seemed that several European rulers had embraced many of the reforms set forth by the *philosophes. Enlightened absolutism* is the term used to describe this phenomenon. The phrase indicates monarchical government dedicated to the rational strengthening of the central absolutist administration at the cost of lesser centers of political power. The monarchs most closely associated with it—Frederick II of Prussia, Joseph II of Austria, and Catherine II of Russia—often found that the political and social realities of their realms caused them to moderate both their enlightenment and their absolutism. Frederick II corresponded with the *philosophes*, invited Voltaire to his court, and even wrote history and political tracts. Catherine II, who was a master of what would later be called public relations, consciously sought to create the image of being enlightened. She read the works of the *philosophes*, became a friend of Diderot and Voltaire, and made frequent references to their ideas, all in the hope that her nation might seem more modern and Western. Joseph II continued numerous initiatives begun by his mother, Maria Theresa, and imposed a series of religious, legal, and social reforms that contemporaries believed he had derived from suggestions of the *philosophes*.

Despite such appearances, the relationship between these rulers and the writers of the Enlightenment was more complicated. The rulers did wish to see their subjects enjoy better health, more accessible education, a more rational political administration, and economic prosperity. In many of these policies, they were more advanced than the rulers of western Europe. However, the humanitarian and liberating zeal of the Enlightenment directed only part of their policies. Frederick II, Joseph II, and Catherine II were also determined to play major diplomatic and military roles in Europe. In no small measure they sought the rational economic and social integration of their realms, so they could achieve military strength. After the Seven Years' War all the states of Europe understood that they would require stronger armed forces, which meant they needed new revenues. The search for new revenues and for more political support for their rule led these monarchs to make "enlightened" reforms. Consequently, they and their advisers used rationality to pursue many goals admired by the *philosophes* but also to further what the *philosophes* considered irrational militarism.

JOSEPH II OF AUSTRIA

No eighteenth-century ruler so embodied rational, impersonal force as the emperor Joseph II of Austria. He was the son of Maria Theresa (r. 1740–1780) and co-ruler with her from 1765 to 1780. During the next ten years he ruled alone. He lived very simply, sleeping on straw and eating little but beef. He lively in a town house in Vienna rather than the elaborate royal palace on the outskirts of the city. He prided himself on a narrow, passionless rationality, which he sought to impose by his own will on the various Habsburg domains. Despite his eccentricities and cold personality, Joseph II genuinely and sincerely wished to improve the lot of his peoples. His well-intentioned efforts led to a series of aristocratic and peasant rebellions from Hungary to the Austrian Netherlands.

Of all the rising states of the eighteenth century, Austria was the most diverse in its people and problems. The Habsburgs never succeeded in creating either a unified administrative structure or a strong aristocratic loyalty. The price of preserving the monarchy during the War of the Austrian Succession (1740–1748) had been guarantees of considerable aristocratic independence, especially in Hungary.

During and after the conflict, however, Maria Theresa had strengthened her powers in Austria and Bohemia. Through major administrative reorganization she imposed a much more efficient system of tax collection that extracted funds even from the clergy and the nobles, and she established several central councils to deal with governmental problems. She was particularly concerned about bringing all educational institutions into the service of the crown so that she could have enough educated officials, and she expanded primary education on the local level.

Maria Theresa was also concerned about the welfare of the peasants and serfs. The extension of the authority of the royal bureaucracy over that of the local nobilities helped the peasants, as did the empress's decrees limiting the services that landowners could demand from them. This concern arose from her desire to assure a good military recruitment pool. In all these policies and in her general desire to stimulate prosperity and military strength by royal initiative, Maria Theresa anticipated the policies of her son.

Joseph II, however, was more determined, and his projected reforms were more wide ranging than his mother's. He was ambitious to expand at the expense of Poland, Bavaria, and the Ottoman Empire. But his greatest ambition was to change the authority of the Habsburg emperor over his various realms. He sought to overcome the pluralism of the Habsburg holdings by increasing the power of the central monarchy in areas of political and social life that Maria Theresa had wisely not disturbed. In particular, Joseph sought to lessen Hungarian autonomy. He refused to have himself crowned king of Hungary and even had the Crown of Saint Stephen sent to Vienna. He thus avoided having to guarantee existing or new Hungarian privileges in a coronation oath. He reorganized local government in Hungary to increase the authority of his own officials, and he required the use of the German language in all governmental matters. But the Magyar nobility resisted, and in 1790 Joseph had to rescind most of his centralizing measures.

Another target of Joseph's assertion of royal absolutism was religion. In October 1781 Joseph extended freedom of worship to Lutherans, Calvinists, and the Greek Orthodox. They were permitted to have their own churches, sponsor schools, enter skilled trades, and to hold academic appointments and positions in the public service. From 1781 through 1789 Joseph relieved the Jews of certain taxes and signs of personal degradation and gave them the right of private worship.

Despite these benefits the Jews still did not enjoy general legal rights equal to those of other Habsburg subjects.

Above all, Joseph sought to bring the various institutions of the Roman Catholic Church directly under his control. He forbade direct communication between the bishops of his realms and the pope. He regarded most orders of monks and nuns as unproductive. Consequently, he dissolved over 600 monasteries and confiscated their lands, although he excepted certain orders that ran schools or hospitals. He also dissolved the traditional Roman Catholic seminaries, which he believed taught priests too great a loyalty to the papacy and too little concern for their future parishioners. In their place he sponsored eight general seminaries that emphasized parish duties. In effect, Joseph's policies made Roman Catholic priests the employees of the state and ended the influence of the church as an independent institution in Habsburg lands. In many respects, the ecclesiastical policies of Joseph II, known as *Josephinism*, prefigured those of the French Revolution.

Toward serfdom and the land, Joseph II again pursued policies initiated by Maria Theresa to more far-reaching ends. During his reign he introduced reforms that touched the heart of rural society. He abolished the legal status of serfdom defined in terms of servitude to another person. He gave peasants much more personal freedom. They could marry, engage in skilled work, or have their children trained in such skills without permission of the landlord. The procedures of the manorial courts were reformed, and avenues of appeal to royal officials were opened. Joseph also encouraged landlords to change land leases, so that it would be easier for peasants to inherit them or to transfer them to another peasant without bringing into doubt the landlord's title of ownership. Joseph believed that reducing traditional burdens would make the peasant tillers of the land more productive and industrious.

In 1789 Joseph proposed a new and daring system of land taxation. All proprietors were to be taxed, regardless of social status. No longer were the peasants alone to bear the burden of taxation. He commuted compulsory service into a monetary tax, split between the landlord and the state. The decree was drawn up, but resistance from the nobles delayed its implementation. Then in 1790 Joseph died, and the decree never went into effect. However, his measures had stirred up turmoil throughout the Habsburg realms. Peasants revolted over disagreements about the interpretation of their newly granted rights. The nobles of the various realms protested the taxation scheme.

On Joseph's death, the crown went to his brother Leopold II (r. 1790–1792). Although sympathetic to Joseph's goals, Leopold had to repeal many of the most controversial decrees, such as that changing taxation.

▲ **Catherine the Great** ascended to the Russian throne after the murder of her husband. She tried initially to enact major reforms, but she never intended to abandon absolutism. She assured the nobility of their rights and by the end of her reign had imposed press censorship.
The Granger Collection.

CATHERINE THE GREAT OF RUSSIA

Joseph II never grasped the practical necessity of cultivating political support for his policies. Catherine II (r. 1762–1796), who had been born a German princess, understood only too well the fragility of the Romanov dynasty's power base.

After the death of Peter the Great in 1725, the court nobles and the army had determined the Russian succession. As a result, the crown fell into the hands of people with little talent until 1741, when Peter's daughter Elizabeth came to the throne. At her death in 1762 Elizabeth was succeeded by Peter III, one of her nephews. He was a weak and possibly insane ruler who had been married in 1745 to a young German princess, the future Catherine the Great. Catherine had neither love nor loyalty for her demented husband. After a few months of rule Peter III was deposed and murdered with Catherine's approval, if not aid. On his deposition she was immediately proclaimed empress.

CHRONOLOGY

Russia from Peter the Great Through Catherine the Great

1725	Death of Peter the Great
1741–1762	Elizabeth
1762	Peter III
1762	Catherine II (the Great) becomes empress
1767	Legislative Commission summoned
1768	War with Turkey
1771–1774	Pugachev's Rebellion
1772	First Partition of Poland
1774	Treaty of Kuchuk-Kainardji ends war with Turkey
1775	Reorganization of local government
1783	Russia annexes the Crimea
1785	Catherine issues the Charter of the Nobility
1793	Second Partition of Poland
1795	Third Partition of Poland
1796	Death of Catherine the Great

Catherine's familiarity with the Enlightenment and the general culture of Western Europe convinced her that Russia must make major reforms if it were to remain a great power Since she had come to the throne through a palace coup, she understood that any major reform must enjoy wide political and social support.

Consequently, in 1767 Catherine summoned a Legislative Commission to advise her on revising the law and government of Russia. There were over 500 delegates drawn from all sectors of Russian life. Before the commission convened, Catherine wrote a set of *Instructions*, containing ideas drawn from the political writings of the *philosophes*. The revision of Russian law, however, did not occur for more than half a century. In 1768 Catherine dismissed the commission before several of its key committees had reported. Yet the commission had gathered a vast amount of information about the conditions of local administration and economic life throughout Russia. The inconclusive debates and the absence of programs from the delegates themselves suggested that most Russians saw no alternative to an autocratic monarchy. Catherine herself had no intention of departing from absolutism.

Catherine proceeded to carry out limited reforms on her own authority. She supported the rights and local power of the nobility. In 1775 she reorganized local government to solve problems brought to light by the Legislative Commission. She put most local offices into the hands of nobles rather than creating a royal bureaucracy. In 1785 Catherine issued the Charter of the Nobility, which guaranteed many noble rights and privileges. She issued a similar charter to the towns of her realms. In part, the empress had to favor the nobles. There were too few educated subjects in her realm to establish an independent bureaucracy, and the treasury could not afford an army strictly loyal to the crown. So Catherine wisely made a virtue of necessity. She strengthened the stability of her crown by a convenient alliance with her nobles and urban leaders.

Catherine continued the Russian drive for warm-water ports (see Map 22–1). This led to warfare with the Turks between 1768 and 1774, when the Treaty of Kuchuk-Kainardji gave Russia a direct outlet on the Black Sea, free navigation rights in its waters, and free access through the Bosphorus. Moreover, the Crimea became an independent state, which Catherine painlessly annexed in 1783.

MAP 22–1 Expansion of Russia, 1689–1796. The overriding territorial aim of the two most powerful Russian monarchs of the 18th century, Peter the Great (in the first quarter of the century) and Catherine the Great (in the last half of the century) was to secure navigable outlets to the sea in both the north and the south for Russia's vast empire; hence Peter's push to the Baltic Sea and Catherine's to the Black Sea. Russia also expanded into Central Asia and Siberia during this time period.

THE PARTITION OF POLAND

These Russian military successes made the other states of eastern Europe uneasy. Their anxieties were allayed by the First Partition of Poland (see Map 23–2). The Russian victories along the Danube River in what is today Romania were most unwelcome to Austria, which had its own ambitions there. At the same time, the Ottoman Empire was pressing Prussia for aid against Russia. Frederick the Great made a proposal to Russia and Austria that would give each something it wanted, prevent conflict among them, and save appearances. After long, complicated, secret negotiations, the three powers agreed that Russia would abandon the Danubian provinces in return for a large chunk of Polish territory with almost 2 million inhabitants. As a reward for remaining neutral, Prussia annexed most of the Polish territory between East Prussia and Prussia proper, which allowed Frederick to unite two previously separate sections of his realm. Finally, Austria took Galicia, with its important salt mines, and other Polish territory with over 2.5 million inhabitants. The Polish state had lost approximately one third of its territory.

There were two additional partitions of Poland by Russia and Prussia, and one more by Austria. They occurred in 1793 and 1795 and removed Poland from the map of Europe until 1919. The great powers contended that they were saving themselves, and by implication the rest of Europe, from Polish anarchy. The argument was plausible to some contemporaries because of the fears spurred by the French Revolution. However, the truth was that the political weakness of Poland made the country and its resources a rich field for plunderous aggression.

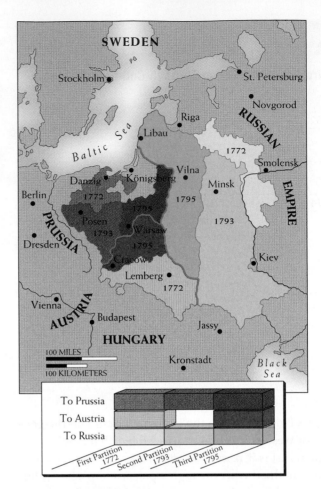

MAP 22–2 Partitions of Poland, 1772, 1793, and 1795. The callous eradication of Poland from the map displayed 18th-century power politics at its most extreme. Poland, without a strong central government, fell victim to the strong absolute monarchies of central and eastern Europe.

Galileo.

Summary

The Scientific Revolution   The scientific ideas of the sixteenth and seventeenth centuries changed the way Western intellectuals thought about the world and humankind. Instead of a view of nature and humanity based on Scripture and Divine Revelation, Western thinkers came to rely on mathematical laws, empirical data, and experimentation. Copernicus, Kepler, and Galileo overturned the ancient idea, sanctioned by the Bible, that the Earth was the center of the universe and that the sun and the planets revolved around it. Galileo and Descartes maintained that the world was governed by mathematical laws. Francis Bacon urged the necessity for observation and experimentation. Newton showed the effects of gravity and established an enduring basis for physics. Locke argued that human beings are shaped by their sense experiences and are hence creatures of their environment subject to reform and possible progress.

The Enlightenment   The Enlightenment *philosophes* used reason as a basis for reform and to advocate progressive social, economic, and political movements. Voltaire attacked religious intolerance and advocated strong central government to impose rational solutions to social and political problems. Montesquieu and other *philosophes* argued for limited, constitutional government. Rousseau wished to reform society in the name of virtue rather than material happiness. He maintained that in the pursuit of virtue the needs of society were more important than those of the individual. The spirit of the Enlightenment continues to pervade Western society.

Enlightened Absolutism   Enlightened absolutism was a form of monarchical government dedicated to the rational strengthening of the central government. Many of the reforms enlightened monarchs imposed were influenced by the ideas of the *philosophes*, but the chief goal of these rulers was to increase their own authority and military strength, as witnessed by the partitions of Poland among Russia, Prussia, and Austria at the end of the eighteenth century. The most important enlightened monarchs were Frederick II of Prussia, Joseph II of Austria, and Catherine the Great of Russia.

Review Questions

1. What was the Scientific Revolution? What were the major contributions of Copernicus, Brahe, Kepler, Galileo, Bacon, and Newton? Do you think they regarded themselves as revolutionaries?

2. Define the Enlightenment. Is it best seen as a single movement or a series of related movements? What was the relationship of the Enlightenment to the New Science? How did the Enlightenment further the idea of progress and the superiority of European civilization?

3. Why did the *philosophes* believe they must comment so extensively on religion? Why did they criticize Christianity?

Why did some of them champion Deism? What were the differing views of the philosophes toward Islam?

4. Was there a single Enlightenment view of politics? Why could writers so dedicated to reform have so many different political paths to achieve reform? Why did some Enlightenment writers argue for the superiority of European culture? Why did others criticize European empires?

5. Define enlightened absolutism. What were the similarities in the policies of Frederick the Great, Joseph II, and Catherine the Great? To what extent do their policies actually seem to stem from the ideas of the Enlightenment *philosophes*?

Key Terms

deism   (p. 648)

empiricism   (p. 642)

Enlightenment   (p. 646)

laissez-faire   (p. 652)

philosophes   (p. 646)

Ptolemaic system   (p. 640)

Scientific Revolution   (p. 639)

Documents CD-ROM

New Science and Englightenment

17.1 The Heliocentric Statement (ca. 1520): Nicolaus Copernicus

17.2 "I Think, Therefore I Am": Discourse on Method (1637)

17.3 "I Learn and Teach from the Fabric of Nature": On the Circulation of the Blood (1628)

17.4 Isaac Newton

17.5 Francis Bacon

17.6 On Universal Toleration: Voltaire

17.7 "The Greatest Happiness of the Greatest Number": On Crimes and Punishments (1764)

17.8 An Inquiry Into the Nature and Causes of the Wealth of Nations: Adam Smith

17.9 What Is Enlightenment? (1784): Immanuel Kant

NOTE: *To learn more about the topics in this chapter, see the Suggested Readings at the end of the book.*

Revolutions in the Transatlantic World

- Revolution in the British Colonies in North America

- Revolution in France

- Wars of Independence in Latin America

- Toward the Abolition of Slavery in the Transatlantic Economy

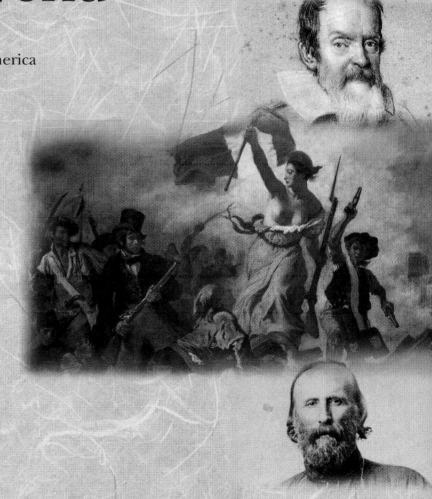

◄ This print of 1774 illustrates rowdy Bostonians tormenting a tarred and feathered exciseman or tax collector who had attempted to collect taxes imposed by the British Parliament. They are forcing tea down his throat while other Bostonians pour the contents of tea boxes into the harbor. On the tree in the back is a copy of the Stamp Act posted upside down. That act had been passed by Parliament in 1765 but repealed a year later after widespread American protest.
The Granger Collection.

The Transatlantic Revolutions

The revolutions and the crusade against slavery that occurred throughout the transatlantic world between 1776 and 1824 transformed the political, social, and economic life of three continents. First in North America, than in France and other parts of Europe, and finally in South America bold political experiments challenged colonial government, monarchies and aristocratic governments and laid the foundations for modern liberal democracy. These revolutions and the effort to abolish slavery owed much to the philosophical inspiration of the Enlightenment and bear witness to the immense influence of the Enlightenment in world history.

As a result of the events of this age of transatlantic revolution the largest republic since ancient times was established in North America. In Europe the absolutist governments were overthrown across the continent by the impact of the French Revolution and the armies of Napoleon. Slaves on Haiti overthrew the French colonial regime and established the first black republic. By the close of the first quarter of the nineteenth century wars of independence across Latin America had closed the era of European empire with the establishment of republics everywhere except Brazil.

No less important this era witnessed the beginning of an international effort to bring about the abolition of the slave economies that had long dominated the transatlantic economy.

The expanding forms of political liberty found their counterparts in an economic life freed from the constraints of the old colonial empires and eventually from the economies based on plantation slave labor. The new American republic constituted a vast free trade zone with its commerce and ports open to the entire world.

For the first time since the encounter with Europe, all of Latin America could trade freely with its own peoples and those of the rest of the world.

In Europe the reforms of the French Revolution and the new Napoleonic Code of law removed many regional economic barriers and led to more standard weights and measures.

National law formed the framework for economic activity. The movement to abolish slavery fostered a wage economy of free laborers. That kind of economy generated its own set of problems and social dislocation, including a sort of sharecropping serfdom for many former slaves, but it was nonetheless an economy of free human beings who were the chattel of no other human being.

Finally, the age of transatlantic revolutions saw the emergence of nationalism as a political force. All of the revolutions, because of their popular political base, had given power to the idea of nations defined by their own character and historical past rather than by dynastic rulers. Americans saw themselves as forming a new kind of nation. The French had demonstrated the power of a nation fully mobilized for military purposes. In turn the aggression of France had aroused national sentiment, especially in Great Britain, Spain, and Germany. The new nations of Latin America also sought to define themselves by their heritage and historical experience rather than by their past in the Spanish and Portuguese empires.

These various revolutions, their political doctrines, and their social and economic departures provided examples to peoples elsewhere in the world. But even more important, the transformations of the transatlantic revolutions and eventual abolition of slavery meant that new political classes and newly organized independent nations would become actors on the world scene. Europeans would have to deal with a score of new nations in the Americas. The rest of the world confronted new nations freed from the direction and authority of European powers. In turn, the political changes in Europe meant that those nations and their relationships with the rest of the world would be directed by a broader range of political groups and forces than in the past. Ironically, however, by the close of the nineteenth century several of the European nations as well as the United States that had become liberal democratic states would commence a new wave of colonialism throughout Africa and Asia and would impose new economic dominance on the republics of Latin America.

THINK AHEAD

- What is the relationship between the Enlightenment and the transatlantic revolutions? Between the Enlightenment and the crusade against slavery?

- How did the transatlantic revolutions fundamentally alter the relationship between Europe and the Americas?

- What is the relationship between the transatlantic revolutions and nationalism? Why did such a relationship exist?

ETWEEN 1776 AND 1824 A WORLD-TRANSFORMING series of revolutions occurred in France and the Americas. In half a century the peoples of the two American continents established their independence of European political control. In Europe the French monarchy collapsed from the forces of aristocratic resistance and popular revolution. All the revolutionary leaders sought to establish new governments based largely, though never entirely, on Enlightenment principles.

From start to finish these revolutions were connected. The financial pressures from the Seven Years' War (1756–1763) had led Britain, Spain, and France to undertake a search for revenue that politically destabilized the Americas and France itself. Once the American Revolution began, France aided the colonists, thus exacerbating its own financial problem. In turn the French Revolution and the ensuing Napoleonic Wars created situations in Spain and Portugal to which the colonial elites in Latin America responded by seeking independence. Thus the transatlantic revolutions, despite their individual characters and developments, were interconnected events in world history. Furthermore, the era witnessed the commencement of a vast international crusade, first to abolish the slave trade and then to abolish slavery in the transatlantic world. The same Enlightenment ideas that inspired many of the revolutionaries also inspired the opponents of slavery as did religious convictions. The political and economic dislocations of the revolutionary era helped the antislavery forces achieve their goals. The political, social, and economic life of the transatlantic world would never be the same again.

Revolution in the British Colonies in North America

RESISTANCE TO THE IMPERIAL SEARCH FOR REVENUE

After the Treaty of Paris in 1763 ended the Seven Years' War, the British government faced two imperial problems (Map 23–1). The first was the sheer cost of empire, which the British felt they could no longer carry alone. The second was that the defeat of the French required the British to organize a vast expanse of new territory: all of North America east of the Mississippi, with its French settlers and, more important, its Indian possessors.

The British drive for revenue began in 1764 with the Sugar Act, which attempted to produce more revenue from imports into the colonies by the rigorous collection of what was actually a reduced tax on sugar. Smugglers were to be tried in admiralty courts without juries. The next year, Parliament passed the Stamp Act, which put a tax on legal documents and certain other items such as newspapers. The British considered these taxes legal and just because they had been approved by Parliament and because the revenue was to be spent in the colonies. The Americans responded that they alone through their assemblies had the right to tax themselves and that they were not represented in Parliament. Furthermore, the Americans feared that if colonial government were financed from Britain, they would cease to control it.

In October 1765 the Stamp Act Congress met in America and drew up a protest to the Crown. (See Document, "The Stamp Act Congress Addresses George III.") There was much disorder in the colonies, particularly in Massachusetts, led by groups known as the Sons of Liberty. The colonists agreed to boycott British goods. In 1766 Parliament repealed the Stamp Act but, through the Declaratory Act, claimed the power to legislate for the colonies.

AMERICAN POLITICAL IDEAS

The political ideas of the American colonists had largely arisen from the struggle of seventeenth-century English aristocrats and gentry against the absolutism of the Stuart monarchs. The American colonists believed that the English Revolution of 1688 had established many of their own fundamental political liberties. The colonists claimed that, through the measures imposed from 1763 to 1776, George III (r. 1760–1820) and the British Parliament were attacking those liberties and dissolving the bonds of moral and political allegiance that had formerly united the two peoples. Consequently, the colonists employed a theory that had originally been developed to justify an aristocratic rebellion in England to support their own popular revolution.

These Whig political ideas, largely derived from John Locke (1632–1704), were only a part of the English ideological heritage that affected the Americans. Throughout the eighteenth century they had become familiar with a series of British political writers called the *Commonwealthmen*. These writers held republican political ideas that had their intellectual roots in the most radical thought of the Puritan revolution. They had relentlessly criticized

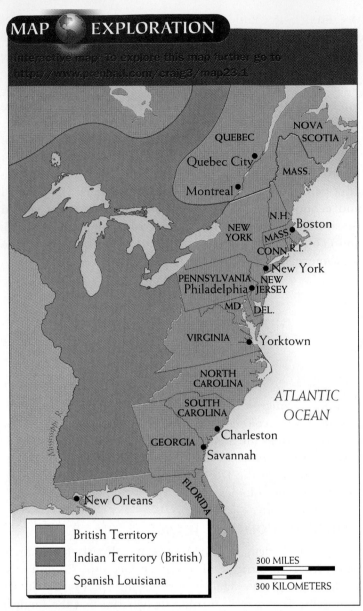

MAP EXPLORATION

Interactive map: To explore this map further go to
http://www.prenhall.com/craig3/map23.1

QUEBEC

NOVA
SCOTIA

Quebec City

MASS.

Montreal

N.H.

NEW
YORK   MASS.   Boston

CONN. R.I.

New York

PENNSYLVANIA   NEW
Philadelphia JERSEY

MD.   DEL.

VIRGINIA   Yorktown

NORTH
CAROLINA   ATLANTIC
OCEAN
SOUTH
CAROLINA

Charleston
GEORGIA
Savannah

FLORIDA

New Orleans

	British Territory
	Indian Territory (British)
	Spanish Louisiana

300 MILES

300 KILOMETERS

MAP 23–1 North America in 1763.   In the year of the victory over France, the English colonies lay along the Atlantic seaboard. The difficulties of organizing authority over the previous French territory in Canada and west of the Appalachian Mountains would contribute to the coming of the American Revolution.

the government patronage and parliamentary management of Robert Walpole (1676–1745) and his successors. They argued that such government was corrupt and that it undermined liberty. They regarded much parliamentary taxation as simply a means of financing political corruption. They also attacked standing armies as instruments of tyranny. In Great Britain this republican political tradition had only a marginal impact. Most Britons regarded themselves as the freest people in the world. In the colonies, however, these radical books and pamphlets were read widely and were often accepted at face value. The policy of Great Britain toward America after the Treaty of Paris made many colonists believe that the worst fears of the Commonwealthmen were coming true.

CRISIS AND INDEPENDENCE

In 1767 Charles Townshend (1725–1767) led Parliament to regulate and tax colonial imports. The colonists again resisted. The ministry sent over its own customs agents to administer the laws. To protect these new officers, the British sent troops to Boston in 1768. The obvious tensions resulted, and in March 1770 British troops killed five citizens in the Boston Massacre. In that same year Parliament repealed the Townshend duties except for the one on tea.

In May 1773 Parliament allowed the East India Company to import tea directly into the American colonies. Although the law lowered the price of tea, it retained the tax without the colonists' consent. In some cities the colonists refused to permit the tea to be unloaded; in Boston, a shipload of tea was thrown into the harbor, an event known since as the Boston Tea Party.

The British ministry of Lord North (1732–1792) was determined to assert the authority of Parliament over the resistant colonies. In 1774 Parliament passed a series of laws known in American history as the Intolerable Acts. These measures closed the port of Boston, reorganized the government of Massachusetts, allowed troops to be quartered in private homes, and removed the trials of royal customs officials to

▲ **"Boston Massacre."** This view of the Boston Massacre of March 5, 1770 by Paul Revere owes more to propaganda than fact. There was no order to fire and the innocent citizens portrayed here were really an angry, violent mob.

The Granger Collection, New York.

DOCUMENT | The Stamp Act Congress Addresses George III

In 1765 the Stamp Act Congress met to protest the British imposition of taxes on the colonies. American leaders believed Great Britain had no right to impose such taxation. Their argument was that they were not and could not be represented in Parliament and that they were subject to the taxation only of their own assemblies. Later clauses implied that the taxation would prevent the colonists from purchasing manufactured goods from Britain and demanded the repeal of the act.

♦ Why does the Congress insist on the same rights for subjects born in the colonies as those born in England? On what grounds does the Congress declare that Parliament may not levy taxes in the colonies? Why is the Congress so concerned about what courts may try cases arising from the Stamp Act?

The Members of this Congress, sincerely devoted, with the warmest sentiments of affection and duty to His Majesty's person and government ... and with minds deeply impressed by a sense of the present and impending misfortunes of the British colonies on this continent; having considered as maturely as time will permit, the circumstances of the said colonies, esteem it our indispensable duty to make the following declarations of our humble opinion, respecting the most essential rights and liberties of the colonists, and of the grievances under which they labor, by reason of several late acts of Parliament.

1. That His Majesty's subjects in these colonies, owe the same allegiance to the crown of Great Britain, that is owing from his subjects born within the realm, and all due subordination to that august body the Parliament of Great Britain.

2. That His Majesty's liege subjects in these colonies are entitled to all the inherent rights and liberties of his natural born subjects, within the kingdom of Great Britain.

3. That it is inseparably essential to the freedom of a people, and the undoubted right of Englishmen, that no taxes be imposed on them but with their own consent, given personally, or by their representatives.

4. That the people of these colonies are not, and cannot, be represented in the House of Commons in Great Britain.

5. That the only representatives of the people of these colonies are persons chosen therein by themselves, and that no taxes ever have been, or can be constitutionally imposed on them, but by their respective legislatures.

6. That all supplies to the crown being free gifts of the people, it is unreasonable and inconsistent with the principles and spirit of the British constitution, for the people of Great Britain to grant to His Majesty the property of the colonists.

7. That trial by jury, is the inherent and invaluable right of every British subject in these colonies.

8. That the late act of Parliament entitled, *An act for granting and supplying certain stamp duties, and other duties, in the British colonies and plantations, in America, etc.* by imposing taxes on the inhabitants of these colonies, and the said act, and several other acts, by extending the jurisdiction of the courts of admiralty beyond its ancient limits, have a manifest tendency to subvert the rights and liberties of the colonists.

From *Journal of the First Congress of the American Colonies ... 1765* (New York, 1845), pp. 27–29, as quoted in Oscar Handlin, ed., *Readings in American History*. Copyright ©1957 Alfred A. Knopf, pp. 116–117.

England. In the same year Parliament approved the Quebec Act, which extended the boundaries of Quebec to include the Ohio river valley. The Americans regarded the Quebec Act as an attempt to prevent the extension of their mode of self-government westward beyond the Appalachian Mountains.

During these years committees of correspondence, composed of citizens critical of Britain, had been established throughout the colonies. In September 1774 these committees organized the First Continental Congress in Philadelphia. This body hoped to persuade Parliament to restore self-government in the colonies and to abandon its attempt at direct supervision of colonial affairs. Conciliation, however, was not forthcoming. By April 1775 the battles of Lexington and Concord had been fought. In June the colonists were defeated at the Battle of Bunker Hill.

The Second Continental Congress gathered in May 1775. It still sought conciliation with Britain but soon undertook the government of the colonies. By August 1775 George III had declared the colonies in rebellion. During the winter Thomas Paine's (1737–1809) pamphlet *Common Sense* galvanized public opinion in favor of separation from Great Britain. A colonial army and navy were organized. In April 1776 the Continental Congress opened American ports to the trade of all nations. Finally, on July 4, 1776, the Continental Congress adopted the Declaration of Independence. Thereafter, the War of the American Revolution continued until 1781, when the forces of George Washington

(1732–1799) defeated those of Lord Cornwallis (1738–1805) at Yorktown. Early in 1778, however, the war had widened into a European conflict when Benjamin Franklin (1706–1790) persuaded the French government to support the rebellion. In 1779 the Spanish also came to the aid of the colonies. The 1783 Treaty of Paris concluded the conflict, and the thirteen American colonies had established their independence.

As the crisis with Britain unfolded during the 1760s and 1770s, the American colonists came to see themselves as first preserving traditional English liberties against a tyrannical Crown and corrupt Parliament and then as developing a new sense of liberty. By the mid-1770s the colonists had embraced republican political ideals. They would govern themselves through elected assemblies without any monarchical authority. The Constitutional Convention met in 1787. After the constitution was adopted in 1788, Americans would insist on a bill of rights specifically protecting civil liberties. The Americans would reject the aristocratic social hierarchy that had existed in the colonies. They would embrace democratic ideals, even if the franchise remained limited. They would assert the equality of white male citizens not only before the law but also in ordinary social relations. They would reject social status based on birth and inheritance and assert the necessity of liberty for all citizens to improve their social standing and economic lot by engaging in free commercial activity. They did not free their slaves nor did they address the rights of women or Native Americans, but the American Revolution produced a society freer than any the world had seen, one that would expand the circle of political and social liberty. The American Revolution was a genuinely radical movement, the influence of which would increase as Americans moved across the continent and as other peoples began to question traditional European government. The political and social values of the American Revolution would inspire the wars of independence in Latin America and, to a lesser extent, both liberal and radical political movements in Europe.

Revolution in France

The French monarchy emerged from the Seven Years' War both defeated and deeply in debt. The later French support for the American Revolution exacerbated the financial difficulties. Given the economic vitality of France, the government debt was neither overly large nor disproportionate to the debts of other European powers. The problem was the government's inability to collect sufficient taxes to service and repay the debt.

Between 1786 and 1788 Louis XVI (r. 1774–1792) appointed several different ministers to deal with the financial crisis. All failed to persuade the aristocracy and the church to pay more taxes. As these negotiations dragged on, the parlement of Paris declared that only the Estates General could institute new taxes. The Estates General had not met since 1614. Consequently, in July 1788, Louis XVI agreed to convene the Estates General the next year.

REVOLUTIONS OF 1789

The Estates General Becomes the National Assembly The Estates General had three divisions: the First Estate of the clergy, the Second Estate of the nobility, and the **Third Estate**, representing everyone else in the kingdom. Before the Estates General met at Versailles in May 1789, there had been much public debate over its organization. The monarchy had agreed that the Third Estate should have twice as many members as either the nobility or the clergy. Then there arose the question of how voting should be organized. The nobility wanted all votes to be taken by Estate, which would have allowed the nobles and clergy to outvote the Third Estate. The Third Estate wanted each member to vote individually so that, with its larger membership, it would dominate.

From the beginning the Third Estate, composed largely of local officials, professional men, and lawyers, refused to sit as a separate order as the king desired. For several weeks there was a standoff. Then, on June 1 the Third Estate invited the clergy and the nobles to join it in organizing a new legislative body. A few of the lower clergy did so. On June 17 that body declared itself the National Assembly.

Three days later, finding themselves accidentally locked out of their usual meeting place, the National Assembly moved to a nearby tennis court, where its members took the famous Tennis

---

CHRONOLOGY	
The American Revolution	
1760	George III becomes king
1763	Treaty of Paris concludes the Seven Years' War
1764	Sugar Act
1765	Stamp Act
1766	Sugar Act repealed and Declaratory Act passed
1767	Townshend Acts
1770	Lord North becomes George III's chief minister
1770	Boston Massacre
1773	Boston Tea Party
1774	Intolerable Acts
1774	First Continental Congress
1775	Second Continental Congress
1776	Declaration of Independence
1778	France enters the war on the side of America
1781	British forces surrender at Yorktown
1783	Treaty of Paris concludes War of the American Revolution

Court Oath to continue to sit until they had given France a constitution. Louis XVI ordered the National Assembly to desist, but shortly afterward most of the clergy and many nobles joined the assembly. On June 27 the king capitulated and formally requested the First and Second Estates to meet with the National Assembly, where voting would occur by head rather than by order. Government by the privileged orders thus ended, and the National Assembly became the National Constituent Assembly.

Fall of the Bastille   Two new factors soon intruded. First, Louis XVI attempted to regain the initiative by mustering troops near Versailles and Paris. This was the beginning of a steady, and consistently poorly executed, royal attempt to halt the revolution. Most of the National Constituent Assembly wished to create some form of constitutional monarchy, but from the start Louis's refusal to cooperate thwarted that effort.

The second new factor was the populace of Paris. The mustering of royal troops created anxiety in the city, where there

had been several bread riots. By June the Parisians were organizing a citizen militia and collecting arms.

On July 14 around 800 people, mostly small shopkeepers, tradespeople, artisans, and wage earners, marched to the Bastille in search of weapons for the militia. This great fortress had once held political prisoners. Through miscalculations and ineptitude by the governor of the fortress, the troops in the Bastille fired into the crowd, killing ninety-eight people and wounding many others. The crowd then stormed the fortress, released its seven prisoners, none of whom was there for political reasons, and killed several soldiers and the governor. They found no weapons.

This was the first of many crucial *journées*, or days when the populace of Paris would redirect the course of the revolution. The fall of the Bastille signaled that the political future of the nation would not be decided solely by the National Constituent Assembly. As the news spread, similar disturbances took place in the provincial cities. A few days later Louis XVI,

▲ **Storming of the Bastille.** On July 14, 1789, crowds stormed the Bastille, a prison in Paris. This event, whose only practical effect was to free a few prisoners, marked the first time the populace of Paris redirected the course of the revolution.
Anonymous, France, 18th century. "Seige of the Bastille, 14 July, 1789." Obligatory mention of the following: Musee de la Ville de Paris, Musee Carnavalet, Paris, France. Bridgeman-Giraudon/Art Resource, N.Y.

again bowing to events, came to Paris and recognized both the new elected government of the city and its National Guard. The citizens of Paris were, for the time being, satisfied.

The Great Fear and Surrender of Feudal Privileges

As popular urban disturbances erupted in various cities, a movement known as the *Great Fear* swept across much of the French countryside. Peasants were reclaiming rights and property that they had lost through the aristocratic resurgence of the last quarter century, as well as venting their anger against the injustices of rural life. The Great Fear, which was an intensification of peasant disturbances that had begun during the spring, witnessed the burning of châteaux, the destruction of records and documents, and the refusal by peasants to pay feudal dues.

On the night of August 4, 1789, aristocrats in the National Constituent Assembly attempted to halt the disorder in the countryside. By prearrangement, liberal nobles and churchmen rose in the assembly and surrendered hunting and fishing rights, judicial authority, tithes, and special exemptions. In a sense, these nobles gave up what they had already lost and what they could not have regained without civil war. Later, many would also be compensated for their losses. Nonetheless, after August 4 all French citizens were subject to the same and equal laws.

Declaration of the Rights of Man and Citizen

On August 27, 1789, the assembly issued the *Declaration of the Rights of Man and Citizen*. This declaration drew together much of the political language of the Enlightenment and was also influenced by the Declaration of Rights adopted by Virginia in America in June 1776. The French declaration proclaimed that all men were "born and remain free and equal in rights." Their natural rights were "liberty, property, security, and resistance to oppression." Governments existed to protect those rights. All political sovereignty resided in the nation and its representatives. All citizens were to be equal before the law and were to be "equally admissible to all public dignities, offices and employments, according to their capacity, and with no other distinction than that of their virtues and talents." There were to be due process of law and presumption of innocence until proof of guilt. Freedom of religion was affirmed. Taxation was to be apportioned equally according to capacity to pay. Property constituted "an inviolable and sacred right."[1]

Louis XVI stalled before ratifying both the declaration and the aristocratic renunciation of feudalism. His hesitations fanned suspicions that he might try to resort to force. Moreover, bread shortages continued. On October 5 several thousand Parisian women marched to Versailles, demanding more bread. This was one of several occasions when women played a major role in the actions of the Parisian crowd. (See Document,

"French Women Petition to Bear Arms".) On this day they milled about the palace, and many stayed the night. Under this pressure the king agreed to sanction the decrees of the assembly. The Parisians believed that the king had to be kept under the watchful eye of the people. Consequently they demanded that Louis and his family return to Paris. The monarch had no real choice. On October 6, 1789, his carriage followed the crowd into the city, where he and his family settled in the palace of the Tuileries. The National Constituent Assembly soon followed. Thereafter, both Paris and France remained relatively stable and peaceful until the summer of 1792.

RECONSTRUCTION OF FRANCE

Once established in Paris, the National Constituent Assembly set about reorganizing France. Throughout its proceedings the Assembly was determined to protect property and to limit the impact on national life of small-property owners as well as of the unpropertied elements of the nation. While championing civic equality before the law, the Assembly spurned social equality and extensive democracy. The Assembly thus charted a general course that, to a greater or lesser degree, nineteenth-century liberals across Europe and in other areas of the world would follow.

Political Reorganization

The Constitution of 1791, the product of the National Constituent Assembly's deliberations, established a constitutional monarchy. There was a unicameral Legislative Assembly vested with powers of war and peace. The monarch could delay but not halt legislation. The system of voting was complex and restricted. Only about 50,000 citizens of the French nation of 26 million could actually elect or serve in the Legislative Assembly.

The exclusion of women from both voting and holding office did not pass unnoticed. In 1791 Olympe de Gouges (d. 1793), a butcher's daughter who became a major radical in Paris, composed a *Declaration of the Rights of Woman*, which she ironically addressed to Queen Marie Antoinette (1755–1793). Much of the document reprinted the *Declaration of the Rights of Man and Citizen*, adding the word *woman* to the various original clauses. That strategy demanded that women be regarded as citizens and not merely as daughters, sisters, wives, and mothers of citizens. Olympe de Gouges further outlined rights that would permit women to own property and require men to recognize the paternity of their children. She called for equality of the sexes in marriage and improved education for women. She declared, "Women, wake up; the tocsin of reason is being heard throughout the whole universe; discover your rights."[2] Her demands illustrated how the public listing of

---

[1] Quoted in Georges Lefebvre, *The Coming of the French Revolution*, trans. by R. R. Palmer (Princeton, NJ: Princeton University Press, 1967), pp. 221–223.

[2] Quoted in Sara E. Melzer and Leslie W. Rabine, eds., *Rebel Daughters: Women and the French Revolution* (New York: Oxford University Press, 1992), p. 88.

Women's March. The women of Paris marched to Versailles on October 5, 1789. The following day the royal family was forced to return to Paris with them. Henceforth, the French government would function under the constant threat of mob violence.

Anonymous, 18th century C.E. "To Versailles, to Versailles." The Women of Paris going to Versailles, 7 October, 1789. French, Musee de la Ville de Paris, Musee Carnavalet, Paris, France. Photograph copyright Bridgeman-Giraudon/Art Resource, N.Y.

rights in the *Declaration of the Rights of Man and Citizen* created universal civic expectations even among those it did not cover.

The National Constituent Assembly abolished the ancient French provinces, such as Burgundy, and replaced them with eighty-three departments (*départements*) of generally equal size named after rivers, mountains, and other geographical features. The ancient judicial courts, including the seigneurial courts and the *parlements*, were suppressed and replaced by established uniform courts with elected judges and prosecutors. Legal procedures were simplified, and the most degrading punishments abolished.

Economic Policy   In economic matters the National Constituent Assembly suppressed the guilds and liberated the grain trade. The assembly established the metric system to provide the nation with uniform weights and measures. These policies of economic freedom and uniformity disappointed both peasants and urban workers caught in the cycle of inflation. By the decrees of 1790 the Assembly placed the burden of proof on the peasants to rid themselves of the residual feudal dues for which compensation was to be paid. On June 14, 1791, the Assembly enacted the Chapelier Law forbidding worker associations, thereby crushing the attempts of urban workers to protect their wages. Peasants and workers were to be left to the mercy of the free marketplace.

The National Constituent Assembly decided to pay the troublesome royal debt by confiscating and then selling the lands of the Roman Catholic Church in France. The Assembly then authorized the issuance of **assignats**, or government bonds, the value of which was guaranteed by the revenue to be generated from the sale of church property. When the *assignats* began to circulate as currency, the Assembly issued even larger quantities of them to liquidate the national debt. However, within a few months the value of *assignats* began to fall. Inflation increased and put new stress on the lives of the urban poor.

Civil Constitution of the Clergy   In July 1790 the National Constituent Assembly issued the Civil Constitution of the Clergy, which transformed the Roman Catholic Church in France into a branch of the secular state. This measure reduced the number of bishoprics, made borders of dioceses conform to those of the new departments, and provided for the election of priests and bishops, who henceforth became salaried employees of the state. The Assembly consulted neither the pope nor the French clergy about these broad changes. The king approved the measure only with the greatest reluctance.

The Civil Constitution of the Clergy was the major blunder of the National Constituent Assembly. The measure roused immense opposition within the French church, even from bishops who had long championed Gallican liberties over papal domination. Faced with this resistance, the Assembly unwisely ruled that all clergy must take an oath to support the Civil Constitution. Only seven bishops and about half the clergy did so. In reprisal, the assembly designated the clergy who had not taken the oath as "refractory" and removed them from their clerical functions. Refractory priests immediately attempted to celebrate Mass.

In February 1791 the pope condemned not only the Civil Constitution of the Clergy but also the *Declaration of the Rights of Man and Citizen*. That condemnation marked the opening of a Roman Catholic offensive against liberalism in Europe and revolution throughout the world that continued for over a century. Within France itself, the pope's action meant that religious devotion and revolutionary loyalty became incompatible for many people. French citizens quickly divided between those who supported the constitutional priests and those who resorted to the refractory clergy. Louis XVI and his family favored the latter.

Counterrevolutionary Activity   In the summer of 1791 the queen and some nobles who had already left the country persuaded Louis XVI also to flee. The escape failed when Louis, along with his family, was recognized and stopped in the town of Varennes. On June 24 soldiers escorted the royal family back to Paris. Thereafter, the leaders of the National Constituent Assembly knew that the chief counterrevolutionary sat on the French throne.

Two months later, on August 27, 1791, Emperor Leopold II of Austria (r. 1790–1792), who was the brother of Marie Antoinette, and Frederick William II (r. 1786–1797), the king of Prussia, issued the Declaration of Pillnitz. The two monarchs promised to intervene in France to protect the royal family and to preserve the monarchy if the other major European powers agreed. The latter provision rendered the statement meaningless because Great Britain would not have given its consent. In France, however, the revolutionaries felt surrounded by aristocratic and monarchical foes.

Near its close in September 1791 the National Constituent Assembly forbade any of its own members to sit in the Legislative Assembly then being elected. This new body met on October 1 to confront immense problems.

A Second Revolution

Since the earliest days of the revolution, various clubs of politically like-minded persons had organized themselves in Paris. The best organized were the *Jacobins*, whose name derived from the fact that the group met in a former Dominican (Jacobin) monastery located in the Rue St. Jacques. The Paris club was linked to other local clubs in the provinces. In the Legislative Assembly a group of Jacobins known as the *Girondists* (because many of them came from the department of the Gironde) assumed leadership.[3] They led the Legislative Assembly on April 20, 1792, to declare war on Austria, by this time governed by Francis II (r. 1792–1835) and allied to Prussia.

End of the Monarchy   The war radicalized the revolution and led to what is usually called the *second revolution*, which overthrew the constitutional monarchy and established a republic. The war initially went poorly, and the revolution seemed in

---

[3] The Girondists are also frequently called the *Brissotins* after Jacques-Pierre Brissot (1754–1793), who was their chief representative in early 1792.

◀ **Capture of Louis XVI.** One of the key events of the French Revolution was the unsuccessful attempt by Louis XVI and his family to escape the country in June 1791. They were recognized and captured in the French city of Varennes and then returned to Paris under armed escort.
© Corbis-Bettmann.

DOCUMENT | French Women Petition to Bear Arms

The issue of women serving in the revolutionary French military appeared early in the revolution. In March 1792 Pauline Léon presented a petition to the National Assembly on behalf of more than 300 Parisian women asking the right to bear arms and train for military service for the revolution. Similar requests were made during the next two years. Some women did serve in the military, but in 1793 legislation specifically forbade it on the grounds that women belonged in the domestic sphere and that military service would lead them to abandon family duties.

◆ "Citoyenne" is the feminine form of the French word for citizen. How does this petition seek to challenge the concept of citizenship in the French *Declaration of the Rights of Man and Citizen?* How do these petitioners relate their demand to bear arms to their role as women in French society? How do the petitioners relate their demands to the use of all national resources against the enemies of the revolution?

Patriotic women come before you to claim the right which any individual has to defend his life and liberty.

… We are citoyennes [female citizens], and we cannot be indifferent to the fate of the fatherland.

… Yes, Gentlemen, we need arms, and we come to ask your permission to procure them. May our weakness be no obstacle; courage and intrepidity will supplant it, and the love of the fatherland and hatred of tyrants will allow us to brave all dangers with ease. …

No, Gentlemen, We will [use arms] only to defend ourselves the same as you; you cannot refuse us, and society cannot deny the right nature gives us, unless you pretend the *Declaration of Rights* does not apply to women and that they should let their throats be cut like lambs, without the right to defend themselves. For can you believe the tyrants would spare us? … Why then not terrorize aristocracy and tyranny with all the resources of civic effort and the pure zeal, zeal which cold men can well call fanaticism and exaggeration, but which is only the natural result of a heart burning with love for the public weal? …

… If, for reasons we cannot guess, you refuse our just demands, these women you have raised to the ranks of citoyennes by granting that title to their husbands, these women who have sampled the promises of liberty, who have conceived the hope of placing free men in the world, and who have sworn to live free or die—such women, I say, will never consent to concede the day to slaves; they will die first. They will uphold their oath, and a dagger aimed at their breasts will deliver them from the misfortunes of slavery! They will die, regretting not life, but the uselessness of their death; regretting moreover, not having been able to drench their hands in the impure blood of the enemies of the fatherland and to avenge some of their own!

But, Gentlemen, let us cast our eyes away from these cruel extremes. Whatever the rages and plots of aristocrats, they will not succeed in vanquishing a whole people of united brothers armed to defend their rights. We also demand only the honor of sharing their exhaustion and glorious labors and of making tyrants see that women also have blood to shed for the service of the fatherland in danger.

Gentlemen, here is what we hope to obtain from your justice and equity:

1. Permission to procure pikes, pistols, and sabres (even muskets for those who are strong enough to use them), within police regulations.

2. Permission to assemble on festival days and Sundays on the Champ de la Fédération, or in other suitable places, to practice maneuvers with these arms.

3. Permission to name the former French Guards to command us, always in conformity with the rules which the mayor's wisdom prescribes for good order and public calm.

From "French Women Petition to Bear Arms" in *Women in Revolutionary Paris 1789–1795*, trans. by Darline Gay Levy, Harriet Branson Applewhite, and Mary Durham Johnson. ©1979 by the Board of Trustees of the University of Illinois. Used with permission of the authors and the University of Illinois Press.

danger. Late in July, under radical working-class pressure, the government of Paris passed from the elected council to a committee, or commune, of representatives from the sections (municipal wards) of Paris. On August 10, 1792, a large crowd invaded the Tuileries and forced Louis XVI and Marie Antoinette to take refuge in the Legislative Assembly itself. During the disturbance several hundred of the royal Swiss guards and many Parisians died. Thereafter, the royal family was imprisoned in comfortable quarters, but the king was suspended from his political functions.

The Convention and the Role of Sans-Culottes During the first week of September, in what are known as the September Massacres, the Paris Commune summarily killed about 1,200 people in the city jails. Many were aristocrats or priests, but most were simply common criminals. The crowd had assumed that the prisoners were all counterrevolutionaries. The Paris Commune then compelled the Legislative Assembly to call for the election, by universal manhood suffrage, of a new assembly to write a democratic constitution. That body, called the **Convention** after its American counterpart of 1787, met on September 21, 1792.

As its first act the Convention declared France a republic, that is, a nation governed by an elected assembly without a king. The second revolution had been the work of Jacobins more radical than the Girondists and of the people of Paris known as the *sans-culottes*. The name of the latter means "without breeches," and was derived from the long trousers that, as working people, they wore instead of aristocratic knee breeches. The *sans-culottes* were shopkeepers, artisans, wage earners, and a few factory workers. The politics of the Old Regime had ignored them, and the policies of the National Constituent Assembly had left them victims of unregulated economic liberty. (See Document, "A Pamphleteer Describes a Sans-Culotte.")

The *sans-culottes*, whose labor and military service were needed for the war effort, generally knew what they wanted. They sought immediate price controls for relief from food shortages and rising prices. They believed that all people had a right to subsistence

and profoundly resented most forms of social inequality. They felt intense hostility toward the aristocracy and the original leaders of the revolution, whom they believed simply wanted to take over the social privileges of the aristocracy. They did not demand the abolition of property, but advocated a community of relatively small-property owners. They were antimonarchical, strongly republican, and suspicious even of representative government.

In contrast, the Jacobins were republicans who sought representative government. Their hatred of the aristocracy did not extend to a general suspicion of wealth. Basically, the Jacobins favored an unregulated economy. However, from Louis XVI's flight to Varennes onward, the more extreme Jacobins began to cooperate with leaders of the Parisian *sans-culottes* and the Paris Commune to overthrow the monarchy. Once the Convention began its deliberations, these advanced Jacobins, known as the Mountain because of their seats high in the assembly hall, worked with *sans-culottes* to carry the revolution forward and win the war.

In December 1792 Louis XVI was put on trial as mere "Citizen Capet." (Capet was the family name of medieval forebears of the royal family.) The Girondists sought to spare his life, but the Mountain defeated the effort. By a narrow majority, Louis

▲ **Execution of Louis XVI.** On January 21, 1793, the Convention executed Louis XVI.
Execution of Louis XVI. Aquatint. French, 18th century. Musée de la Ville de Paris, Musée Carnavalet, Paris. France. Giraudon/Art Resource, N.Y.

DOCUMENT | A Pamphleteer Describes a Sans-Culotte

This document from 1793 describes a sans-culotte as a hardworking, useful, patriotic citizen who sacrifices himself to the war effort. It contrasts those virtues with the lazy and unproductive luxury of the noble and the self-interested plottings of the politician.

> ◆ What social resentments appear in this description? How could these resentments create solidarity among the sans-culottes to defend the revolution? How does this document relate civic virtue to work? Where does this document suggest that the sans-culotte may need to confront enemies of the republic?

A *sans-culotte* you rogues? He is someone who always goes on foot, who has no millions as you would all like to have, no chateaux, no valets to serve him, and who lives simply with his wife and children, if he has any, on a fourth or fifth story.

He is useful, because he knows how to work in the field, to forge iron, to use a saw, to use a file, to roof a house, to make shoes, and to shed his last drop of blood for the safety of the Republic.

And because he works, you are sure not to meet his person in the Café de Chartres, or in the gaming houses where others conspire and game; nor at the National theatre ... nor in the literary clubs. ...

In the evening he goes to his section, not powdered or perfumed, or smartly booted in the hope of catching the eye of the citizenesses in the galleries, but ready to support good proposals with all his might, and to crush those which come from the abominable faction of politicians.

Finally, a *sans-culotte* always has his sabre sharp, to cut off the ears of all enemies of the Revolution; sometimes he even goes out with his pike; but at the first sound of the drum he is ready to leave for the Vendée, for the army of the Alps or for the army of the North. ...

From "Reply to an Impertinent Question: What Is a Sans-culotte?" April 1793. Reprinted in Walter Markov and Albert Soboul, eds., *Die Sansculotten von Paris*, and republished trans. by Clive Emsley in Merryn Williams, ed., *Revolutions: 1775–1830* (Baltimore, MD: Penguin Books, in association with the Open University, 1971), pp. 100–101.

---

was convicted of conspiring against the liberty of the people and the security of the state. Condemned to death, he was beheaded on January 21, 1793.

The next month, the Convention declared war on Great Britain, Holland, and Spain. France was now at war with virtually all Europe. Civil war soon followed. In March 1793 aristocratic officers and priests commenced a royalist revolt in the Vendée in western France and roused much local popular support. The Girondists had led the country into the war but had proved themselves incapable either of winning it or of suppressing the enemies of the revolution at home. The Mountain stood ready to take up the task.

THE REIGN OF TERROR AND ITS AFTERMATH

The **Reign of Terror** is the name given to the months of quasijudicial executions and murders stretching from the autumn of 1793 to the midsummer of 1794. The Terror can be understood only in the context of the internal and external wars, on the one hand, and the revolutionary expectations of the Convention and the *sans-culottes*, on the other.

Committee of Public Safety In April 1793 the Convention established a Committee of General Security and a Committee of Public Safety to perform the executive duties of the government.

The latter committee eventually enjoyed almost dictatorial power. The committee conceived of their task as saving the revolution from mortal enemies at home and abroad. They generally enjoyed a working political relationship with the *sans-culottes* of Paris, but it was an alliance of expediency for the committee.

The major problem was to secure domestic support for the war. In early June 1793 the Parisian *sans-culottes* invaded the Convention and secured the expulsion of the Girondist members. That gave the Mountain complete control. On June 22 the Convention approved a fully democratic constitution but suspended its operation until after the war emergency. August 23 saw a *levée en masse*, or general military requisition of population, which conscripted males into the army and directed economic production for military purposes. On September 29 a maximum on prices was established in accord with *sans-culottes*' demands. During these same months the armies of the revolution also crushed many of the counterrevolutionary disturbances in the provinces.

The Society of Revolutionary Republican Women Revolutionary women established their own distinct institutions to fight the internal enemies of the revolution. In May 1793 Pauline Léon and Claire Lacombe founded the Society of Revolutionary Republican Women. Its members and other women filled the galleries of the Convention to hear the debates and cheer their favorite

CHRONOLOGY

The French Revolution

1789

May 5	Estates General opens at Versailles
June 17	Third Estate declares itself the National Assembly
June 20	National Assembly takes the Tennis Court Oath
July 14	Fall of the Bastille
July	Great Fear spreads in the countryside
August 4	Nobles surrender their feudal rights in a meeting of the National Constituent Assembly
August 27	*Declaration of the Rights of Man and Citizen*
October 5–6	Parisian women march to Versailles and force Louis XVI and his family to return to Paris

1790

July 12	Civil Constitution of the Clergy adopted
July 14	New constitution accepted by the king

1791

June 20–24	Louis XVI and his family attempt to flee France and are stopped at Varennes
August 27	Declaration of Pillnitz
October 1	Legislative Assembly meets

1792

April 20	France declares war on Austria
August 10	Tuileries palace stormed, and Louis XVI takes refuge in the Legislative Assembly
September 2–7	September Massacres
September 21	Convention meets, and monarchy abolished

1793

January 21	Louis XVI executed
February 1	France declares war on Great Britain
March	Counterrevolution breaks out in the Vendée
April 6	Committee of Public Safety formed
June 22	Constitution of 1793 adopted but not put into operation
July	Robespierre enters Committee of Public Safety
August 23	*Levée en masse* proclaimed
September 29	Maximum prices set on food and other commodities
October 16	Queen Marie Antoinette executed
November 10	Cult of Reason proclaimed; revolutionary calendar beginning in September

1794

May 7	Cult of the Supreme Being proclaimed
June 8	Robespierre leads the celebration of Festival of the Supreme Being
July 27	Ninth of Thermidor and fall of Robespierre
July 28	Robespierre executed

1795

August 22	Constitution of the Year III adopted, establishing the Directory

speakers. The Society became increasingly radical, however. Its members sought stricter controls on the price of food and other commodities, worked to ferret out food hoarders, and brawled with working market women thought to be insufficiently revolutionary. The women of the Society also demanded the right to wear the revolutionary cap or cockade usually worn only by male citizens. By October 1793 the Jacobins in the Convention had begun to fear the turmoil the Society was causing and banned all women's clubs and societies.

There were other examples of repression of women in 1793. Olympe de Gouges, author of the *Declaration of the Rights of Woman*, opposed the Terror and accused certain Jacobins of corruption. She was tried and guillotined in November 1793. In the same year women were formally excluded from the French army and from attending the galleries of the Convention.

The Republic of Virtue   The pressures of war made it relatively easy to dispense with legal due process. However, the people in the Convention and the Committee of Public Safety also believed they had made a new departure in world history. They had established a republic in which civic virtue rather than aristocratic and monarchical corruption might flourish.

Dechristianization   The most dramatic departure of the republic of virtue was an attempt to dechristianize France. In October 1793 the Convention proclaimed a new calendar dating from the first day of the French Republic. There were twelve months of thirty days with names associated with the seasons and climate. Every tenth day, rather than every seventh, was a holiday. Many of the most important events of the next few years became known by their dates on the revolutionary calendar.[4]

In November 1793 the convention decreed the Cathedral of Notre Dame to be a Temple of Reason. The legislature then sent trusted members, known as deputies on mission, into the provinces to enforce dechristianization by closing churches, persecuting clergy and believers, and occasionally forcing priests to marry. This religious policy roused much opposition and deeply separated the French provinces from the revolutionary government in Paris.

Progress of the Terror   During late 1793 and early 1794 Maximilien Robespierre (1758–1794) emerged as the chief figure on the Committee of Public Safety. The Jacobin Club provided his primary forum and base of power. A shrewd and sensitive politician, he had opposed the war in 1792, believing it to be a measure that might aid the monarchy. He largely depended on the support of the *sans-culottes* of Paris but continued to dress as he had before the revolution and opposed dechristianization as a

---

[4] From summer to spring, the months on the revolutionary calendar were *Messidor, Thermidor, Fructidor, Vendémiaire, Brumaire, Frimaire, Nivose, Pluviose, Ventose, Germinal, Floréal,* and *Prairial.*

Revolutionary Calendar. To symbolize the beginning of a new era in human history, French revolutionary legislators established a new calendar. This calendar for Year Two (1794) proclaims the indivisible unity of the revolution and the goals of Liberty, Equality, and Fraternity.
Art Resource/Bildarchiv Preussischer Kulturbesitz.

political blunder. For him, the republic of virtue meant whole-hearted support of republican government and the renunciation of selfish gains from political life. He once told the Convention:

> If the mainspring of popular government in peace-time is virtue, amid revolution it is at the same time virtue and terror: virtue, without which terror is fatal; terror, without which virtue is impotent. Terror is nothing but prompt, severe, inflexible justice; it is therefore an emanation of virtue."[5]

The Reign of Terror manifested itself through a series of revolutionary tribunals established by the Convention during the summer of 1793. The tribunals were to try the enemies of the Republic, but the definition of enemy remained uncertain and shifted as the months passed. The first victims were Marie Antoinette, other members of the royal family, and aristocrats, who were executed in October 1793. They were followed by Girondist politicians who had been prominent in the Legislative Assembly.

By early 1794 the Terror had moved to the provinces, where the deputies-on-mission presided over the summary execution of thousands of people who had allegedly supported internal opposition to the revolution. In Paris during the late winter of 1794 Robespierre turned the Terror against republican political figures of the left and right. On March 24 he secured the execution of certain extreme *sans-culottes* leaders. Shortly thereafter he moved against more conservative republicans. Robespierre thus exterminated the leadership from both groups that might have threatened his own position. Finally, on June 10 he secured passage of a law that permitted the revolutionary tribunal to convict suspects without hearing substantial evidence.

In May 1794, at the height of his power, Robespierre, considering the worship of reason too abstract for most citizens, abolished it and established the Cult of the Supreme Being. He did not long preside over this new religion. On June 26 he made an ill-tempered speech in the Convention, declaring the existence of a conspiracy among other leaders of the government against him and the revolution. Such accusations against unnamed persons had usually preceded his earlier attacks. On July 27 (the Ninth of Thermidor) members of the Convention, by prearrangement, shouted him down when he rose to speak. Robespierre was arrested that night and executed the next day.

The Reign of Terror soon ended, having claimed as many as 40,000 victims. Most were peasants and *sans-culottes* who had rebelled against the revolutionary government. By the late summer

---

[5] Quoted in Richard T. Bienvenu, *The Ninth of Thermidor: The Fall of Robespierre* (New York: Oxford University Press, 1968), p. 38.

of 1794 those provincial uprisings had been crushed, and the war against foreign enemies was also going well. Those factors, combined with the feeling in Paris that the revolution had consumed enough of its own children, brought the Terror to an end.

The Thermidorian Reaction: End of the Terror and Establishment of the Directory   The tempering of the revolution, called the **Thermidorian Reaction**, began in July 1794. It destroyed the machinery of terror and set up a new constitutional regime. The influence of generally wealthy middle-class and professional people replaced that of the *sans-culottes*. Many of the people responsible for the Terror were removed from public life. The Paris Jacobin Club was closed, and provincial Jacobin clubs were forbidden to correspond with each other.

The Thermidorian Reaction also involved still further political reconstruction. In place of the fully democratic constitution of 1793, which had never gone into effect, the Convention issued the Constitution of the Year III. It was a conservative document that provided for a bicameral legislative government heavily favoring property owners. The executive body, consisting of a five-person Directory, was elected by the upper legislative house, known as the Council of Elders.

By the Treaty of Basel of March 1795, the Convention concluded peace with Prussia and Spain. With the war effort succeeding, the Convention severed its ties with the *sans-culottes*. True to their belief in an unregulated economy, the Thermidorians repealed the ceiling on prices. When food riots resulted during the winter of 1794–1795, the Convention put them down to prove that the era of the *sans-culottes journées* had ended. On October 5, 1795 (13 Vendémiaire) the sections (municipal units, each with its own assembly) of Paris rebelled against the Convention. For the first time in the history of the revolution, artillery was turned against the people of Paris. A general named Napoleon Bonaparte (1769–1821) commanded the cannon and with what he termed a "whiff of grapeshot" dispersed the crowd. Other enemies of the Directory would be more difficult to disperse.

THE NAPOLEONIC ERA

Napoleon Bonaparte was born in 1769 to a poor family of lesser nobles in Corsica. Because France had annexed Corsica in 1768, he went to French schools, pursued a military career, and in 1785 obtained a commission as a French artillery officer. He strongly favored the revolution and was a fiery Jacobin. In 1793 he played a leading role in recovering the port of Toulon from the British. As a reward the government appointed him a brigadier general. His defense of the new regime on 13 Vendémiaire won him another promotion and a command in Italy. By October 1797 he had crushed the Austrian army in Italy and concluded on his own initiative the Treaty of Campo Formio, which took Austria out of the war.

Soon all of Italy and Switzerland lay under French domination.

In November 1797 the triumphant Bonaparte returned to Paris to be hailed as a hero and to confront France's only remaining enemy, Britain. Judging it impossible to cross the Channel and invade England at that time, he chose to capture Egypt from the Ottoman Empire. He thus hoped to drive the British fleet from the Mediterranean, cut off British communication with India, damage British trade, and threaten the British Empire. But the invasion of Egypt was a failure. Admiral Horatio Nelson (1758–1805) destroyed the French fleet at Aboukir on August 1, 1798. The French army could then neither accomplish anything of importance in the Near East nor get home. The French invasion of Egypt had alarmed Russia, which had its own ambitions in the Near East. The Russians,

▲ **Napoleon.** In December 1799 Napoleon seized power and established himself as First Consul. The title of "Consul" came from the ancient Roman Republic; by 1894 Napoleon would assume the title of "Emperor" as the French Republic gave way to the Napoleonic Empire. The simplicity of this modest military dress as First Consul also gave way to flowing imperial robes.
© Historical Picture Archive/CORBIS.

the Austrians, and the Ottomans joined Britain to form the Second Coalition. In 1799 the Russian and Austrian armies defeated the French in Italy and Switzerland and threatened to invade France.

Having heard of these misfortunes, Napoleon abandoned his army in Egypt and returned to France in October 1799. On November 10, 1799 (19 Brumaire) his troops overthrew the Directory. Bonaparte issued the Constitution of the Year VII in December 1799, establishing himself as the First Consul. The constitution received overwhelming approval from the electorate in a largely rigged plebiscite. The establishment of the **Consulate**, in effect, closed the revolution in France. (See Document, "Napoleon Describes Conditions Leading to the Consulate.")

The Consulate in France (1799–1804)   Bonaparte quickly justified the public's confidence by achieving peace with France's enemies. Russia had already left the Second Coalition. A campaign in Italy brought another victory over Austria at Marengo in 1800. The Treaty of Lunéville early in 1801 took Austria out of the war and confirmed the earlier settlement of Campo Formio. Britain was now alone and, in 1802, concluded the Treaty of Amiens, which temporarily brought peace to Europe.

Bonaparte also restored peace and order at home. Although he used generosity, flattery, and bribery to win over some of his enemies, issued a general amnesty, and employed persons from all political factions, Bonaparte was ruthless and efficient in suppressing political opposition. He established a highly centralized administration in which all departments

---

DOCUMENT | Napoleon Describes Conditions Leading to the Consulate

In late 1799 various political groups in France became convinced that the constitution that had established the Directory could not allow France to achieve military victory. They also feared domestic unrest and new outbreaks of the radicalism that had characterized the French Revolution during the mid-1790s. With the aid of such groups Napoleon Bonaparte seized power in Paris in November 1799. Thereafter, under various political arrangements, he governed France until 1814. He later gave his own version of the situation that brought him to power.

◆ What are the factors that Napoleon outlines as having created a situation in which the government of France required change? In his narration how does he justify the use of military force? How does he portray himself as a savior of political order and liberty?

On my return to Paris I found division among all authorities, and agreement upon only one point, namely, that the Constitution was half destroyed and was unable to save liberty.

All parties came to me, confided to me their designs, disclosed their secrets, and requested my support; I refused to be the man of a party.

The Council of Elders summoned me; I answered its appeal. A plan of general restoration had been devised by men whom the nation has been accustomed to regard as defenders of liberty, equality, and property; this plan required an examination, calm, free, exempt from all influence and all fear. Accordingly, the Council of Elders resolved upon the removal of the Legislative Body to Saint-Cloud; it gave me the responsibility of disposing the force necessary for its independence. I believe it my duty to my fellow citizens, to the soldiers perishing in our armies, to the national glory acquired at the cost of their blood, to accept the command. …

I presented myself to the Council of Five Hundred, alone, unarmed, my head uncovered, just as the Elders had received and applauded me; I came to remind the majority of its wishes, and to assure it of its power.

The stilettos which menaced the deputies were instantly raised against their liberator; twenty assassins threw themselves upon me and aimed at my breast. The grenadiers of the Legislative Body whom I had left at the door of the hall ran forward, placed themselves between the assassins and myself. One of these brave grenadiers had his clothes pieced by a stiletto. They bore me out.

At the same moment cries of "Outlaw" were raised against the defender of the law. It was the fierce cry of assassins against the power destined to repress them.

They crowded around the president, uttering threats, arms in their hands; they commanded him to outlaw me. I was informed of this; I ordered him to be rescued from their fury, and six grenadiers of the Legislative Body secured him. Immediately afterwards some grenadiers of the Legislative Body charged into the hall and cleared it.

The factions, intimidated, dispersed and fled. …

Frenchmen, you will doubtless recognize in this conduct the zeal of a soldier of liberty, a citizen devoted to the Republic. Conservative, tutelary, and liberal ideas have been restored to their rights through the dispersal of the rebels who oppressed the Councils. …

From J. H. Stuart, *A Documentary Survey of the French Revolution* (New York: Macmillan, 1951), pp. 763–765.

were managed by prefects directly responsible to the central government in Paris. He employed secret police. He stamped out, once and for all, the royalist rebellion in the west and moved against other royalist plots.

Napoleon also alleviated the hostility of French Catholics. In 1801 he concluded a concordat with Pope Pius VII (r. 1800–1823), to the shock and dismay of his anticlerical supporters. The concordat declared that "Roman Catholicism is the religion of the great majority of French citizens." This was merely a statement of fact and fell far short of what the pope had wanted—religious dominance for the Roman Catholic Church. Both refractory and constitutional clergy were forced to resign. Their replacements received their spiritual investiture from the pope, but the state named the bishops and paid their salaries and the salary of one priest in each parish. In return, the church gave up its claims to its confiscated property. The clergy had to swear an oath of loyalty to the state, and the Organic Articles of 1802, which were actually distinct from the concordat, established the supremacy of state over church. Similar laws were applied to the Protestant and Jewish religious communities as well, reducing still further the privileged position of the Catholic Church.

In 1802 another plebiscite appointed Napoleon consul for life, and he soon produced still another new constitution, which granted him what amounted to full power. He transformed the basic laws and institutions of France on the basis of both liberal principles derived from the Enlightenment and the early years of the revolution and conservative principles going back to the Old Regime, on the one hand, and the spirit that had triumphed at Thermidor, on the other. This was especially true of the Civil Code of 1804, usually called the Napoleonic Code. However, these laws stopped far short of the full equality advocated by liberal rationalists. Fathers were granted extensive control over their children and men over their wives. Labor unions were still forbidden, and the rights of workers were inferior to those of their employers.

In 1804 Bonaparte seized on a bomb attack on his life to make himself emperor. He argued that the establishment of a dynasty would make the new regime secure and make further attempts on his life useless. Still another new constitution, ratified by a plebiscite, was promulgated, designating Napoleon Emperor of the French instead of First Consul of the Republic. Napoleon summoned the pope to Notre Dame to take part in the coronation. But at the last minute the pope agreed that Napoleon should actually crown himself. The emperor had no intention of allowing anyone to think that his power and authority depended on the approval of the church. Henceforth he was called Napoleon I.

Napoleon's Empire (1804–1814)   Between his coronation as emperor and his final defeat at Waterloo (1815), Napoleon conquered most of Europe in military campaigns that astonished the world. France's victories changed the map of Europe, ended the Old Regime and its feudal trappings in western Europe, and forced the eastern European states to reorganize themselves to resist Napoleon's armies. Everywhere, Napoleon's advance unleashed the powerful force of nationalism.

◄ **William Pitt and Napoleon.** In this early 19th-century cartoon, England, personified by a caricature of William Pitt, and France, personified by a caricature of Napoleon, are carving out their areas of interest around the globe. Cartoon by Gillray/Corbis-Bettmann.

William Napier was a British officer during the Napoleonic Wars. In this passage, he describes his experiences in a battle that took place in 1811 in Spain.

◆ What were Napier's expectations of his men? of his officers? How does he explain the difficulties that his troops had in responding to his orders? How does he indicate his contempt for bad officers and yet a certain understanding that in war a person's character may display different faces?

I arrived [with two companies] just in time to save Captain Dobbs, 52nd, and two men who were cut off from their regiment. The French were gathering fast about us, we could scarcely retreat, and Dobbs agreed with me that boldness would be our best chance; so we called upon the men to follow, and, jumping over a wall which had given us cover, charged the enemy with a shout which sent the nearest back. …

Only the two men of the 52nd followed us, and we four arrived unsupported at a second wall, close to a considerable body of French, who rallied and began to close upon us. Their fire was very violent, but the wall gave cover. I was, however, stung by the backwardness of my men, and told Dobbs I would save him or lose my life by bringing up the two companies; he entreated me not, saying I could not make two paces from the wall and live. Yet I did go back to the first wall, escaped the fire, and, reproaching the men gave them the word again, and returned to Dobbs, who was now upon the point of being taken; but again I returned alone! The soldiers had indeed crossed the wall in their front, but kept edging away to the right to avoid the heavy fire. Being now maddened by this second failure, I made another attempt, but I had not made

ten paces when a shot struck my spine, and the enemy very ungenerously continued to fire at me when I was down. I escaped death by dragging myself by my hands—for my lower extremities were paralyzed—towards a small heap of stones which was in the midst of the field, and thus covering my head and shoulders.… However, Captain Lloyd and my company, and some of the 52nd, came up at that moment, and the French were driven away.

The excuses for the soldiers were—1st That I had not made allowance for their exertions in climbing from the ravine up the hill-side with their heavy packs, and they were very much blown. 2nd Their own captains had not been with them for a long time, and they were commanded by two lieutenants, remarkable for their harsh, vulgar, tyrannical dispositions, and very dull bad officers withall; and one of them exhibited on this occasion such miserable cowardice as would be incredible if I had not witnessed it. I am sure he ordered the men not to advance; and I saw him leading them the second time to the right. This man was lying down with his face on the ground; I called to him, reproached him, bad him remember his uniform; nothing would stir him; until losing all patience I threw a large stone at his head. This made him get up, but when he got over the wall he was wild, his eyes staring and his hand spread out. He was a duellist, and had wounded one of the officers some time before. I would have broken him, but before I recovered my wound sufficiently to join, he had received a cannon-shot in the leg, and died at the old, desolate, melancholy mill below Sabugal. Everything combined to render death appalling, yet he showed no signs of weakness. Such is human nature, and so hard it is to form correct opinions of character!

Quoted in H. A. Bruce, *Life of Sir William Napier* (London: John Murray, 1864), 1:55–57.

The Treaty of Amiens with Britain (1802) could not last. Napoleon intervened militarily to extend French influence in Europe. The British issued an ultimatum. When Napoleon ignored it, Britain declared war, in May 1803. William Pitt the Younger (1759–1806) returned to office as prime minister in 1804 and began to construct the Third Coalition. By August 1805 he had persuaded Russia and Austria to move once again against French aggression. On October 21, 1805, Lord Nelson destroyed the combined French and Spanish fleets at the Battle of Trafalgar just off the Spanish coast. Nelson was killed, but the British lost no ships. Trafalgar put an end to the French hope of invading Britain and guaranteed British control of the sea.

On land, however, the story was different. Between mid-October 1805 and July 1807 Napoleon had defeated the armies of Austria, Prussia, and Russia in stunning victories.

The most famous of the victories was that of Austerlitz on December 2, 1805. Through these campaigns he forced Austria to withdraw from northern Italy, where Napoleon himself was recognized as king. He replaced the ancient Holy Roman Empire with the Confederation of the Rhine. On July 7, 1807, Napoleon and Emperor Alexander I (r. 1800–1825) of Russia concluded the Treaty of Tilsit, which confirmed France's gains in central and eastern Europe. Prussia and Russia became allies of Napoleon.

Napoleon knew that he could not be genuinely secure until he had defeated Britain. Unable to compete with the British navy, he adopted economic warfare to cut off all British trade with the European continent. He thus hoped to cripple British commercial and financial power, cause domestic unrest and revolution, and drive the British from the war. On November

21, 1806, he had issued the Berlin Decrees forbidding his allies to import British goods. The Milan Decree of 1807 attempted to halt neutral nations, such as the United States, from trading with Britain. Nonetheless, the British economy survived because of its access to the growing markets of North and South America and the eastern Mediterranean. Known as the Continental System, Napoleon's policies harmed the European economies and roused resentment against France.

The Wars of Liberation   In 1807, as part of the strategy of crippling the British economy, a French army invaded the Iberian Peninsula to force Portugal to abandon its traditional alliance with Britain. The army stayed in Spain to protect lines of supply and communication. When a revolt broke out in Madrid in 1808, Napoleon deposed the Bourbons and placed his brother Joseph (1768–1844) on the Spanish throne. Attacks on the privileges of the church increased public outrage.

In Spain Napoleon faced a kind of warfare not vulnerable to his usual tactics. Guerrilla bands cut communications, killed stragglers, destroyed isolated units, and then disappeared. The British landed an army under Sir Arthur Wellesley (1769–1852), later the Duke of Wellington, to support the Spanish insurgents. Thus began the long peninsular campaign

that would drain French strength and play a critical role in Napoleon's eventual defeat. (See Document, "A Commander Recalls an Incident in Spain.")

Encouraged by the French troubles in Spain, the Austrians renewed the war in 1809. The French army nonetheless marched swiftly into Austria and won the battle of Wagram. The resulting peace deprived Austria of much territory and 3.5 million subjects. Another spoil of victory was the Archduchess Marie Louise (1791–1847), Francis I's eighteen-year-old daughter, whom Napoleon married for dynastic purposes after divorcing his wife Josephine de Beauharnais (1763–1814), who had borne him no children.

The Franco-Russian alliance concluded at Tilsit was faltering. The Continental System had harmed the Russian economy. Napoleon's organization of a Polish state, the Grand Duchy of Warsaw, on the Russian doorstep and its enlargement in 1809 after the battle of Wagram angered Alexander I. Napoleon's annexation of Holland in violation of the Treaty of Tilsit, his recognition of the French Marshal Bernadotte as the future king of Sweden (r. 1818–1844), and his marriage to an Austrian princess further disturbed the tsar. At the end of 1810 Russia withdrew from the Continental System and began to prepare for war (see Map 23–2).

Determined to stifle the Russian military threat, Napoleon amassed an army of over 600,000 men, including over 400,000

◀ **Goya y Lucientes, Francisco de Goya. *The Third of May, 1808*, 1814–1815.** Napoleon sent troops into Spain in 1807 after the king of Spain had agreed to aid France against Portugal, which was assisting Britain. By early 1808 Spain had essentially become an occupied nation. On May 2 riots took place in Madrid between French troops and Spanish civilians. In response to the riots, the French marshall Joachim Murat ordered numerous executions, especially of artisans and clergy, during the night of May 2 and 3.

Francisco de Goya, "Los fusilamientos del 3 de Mayo, 1808" 1814. Oil on canvas, 8'6" × 11'4". © Museo Nacional Del Prado, Madrid.

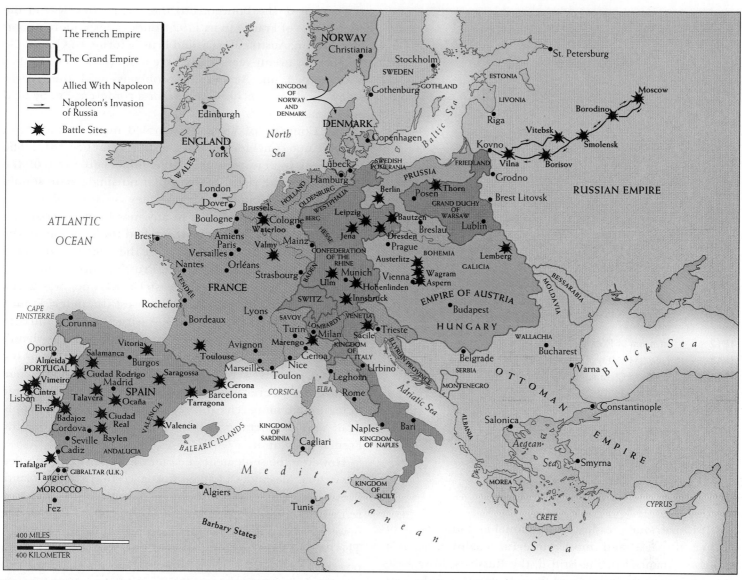

MAP 23–2 Napoleonic Europe in late 1812. By mid-1812 the areas shown in peach were incorporated into France, and most of the rest of Europe was directly controlled by or allied with Napoleon. But Russia had withdrawn from the failing Continental System, and the decline of Napoleon was about to begin.

non-French soldiers drawn from his empire and allies. He intended the usual short campaign crowned by a decisive battle, but the Russians retreated before his advance. His vast superiority in numbers—the Russians had only about 160,000 troops—made it foolish for them to risk a battle. Instead, they destroyed all food and supplies as they retreated. The so-called Grand Army of Napoleon could not live off the country, and Russia was too vast for supply lines. Terrible rains, fierce heat, shortages of food and water, and the courage of the Russian rear guard eroded the morale of Napoleon's army.

In September 1812 Russian public opinion forced the army to stand and fight. At Borodino, not far west of Moscow, the bloodiest battle of the Napoleonic era cost the French 30,000 casualties and the Russians almost twice as many. Yet the Russian army was not destroyed. Napoleon had won nothing substantial. By October, after occupying Moscow, the Grand Army was forced to retreat. By December Napoleon realized that the Russian fiasco would encourage plots against him at home. He returned to Paris, leaving the remnants of his army to struggle westward. Perhaps only as many as 100,000 lived to tell the tale of their terrible ordeal. Even as the news of the disaster reached the west, the total defeat of Napoleon was far from certain. He was able to suppress his opponents in Paris and raise another 350,000 men.

CHRONOLOGY

Napoleonic Europe

1797	Napoleon concludes Treaty of Campo Formio
1798	Nelson defeats French navy at Aboukir
1799	Consulate established
1801	Concordat between France and papacy
1802	Treaty of Amiens
1803	War renewed between France and Britain
1804	Execution of Duke of Enghien; Napoleonic Civil Code issued; Napoleon crowned emperor
1805	Nelson defeats French fleet at Trafalgar (October 21); Austerlitz (December 2)
1806	Continental System established by Berlin Decrees
1807	Treaty of Tilsit
1808	Beginning of Spanish resistance to Napoleonic domination
1809	Wagram; Napoleon marries Archduchess Marie Louise of Austria
1812	Invasion of Russia
1813	Leipzig (Battle of the Nations)
1814	Treaty of Chaumont (March) establishes Quadruple Alliance; Congress of Vienna convenes (September)
1815	Napoleon returns from Elba (March 1); Waterloo (June 18); Holy Alliance formed (September 26); Quadruple Alliance renewed (November 20)
1821	Napoleon dies on Saint Helena

In 1813 patriotic pressure and national ambition brought together the last and most powerful coalition against Napoleon. Financed by the British, the Russians drove westward to be joined by Prussia and then Austria. From the west Wellington marched his peninsular army into France. Napoleon waged a skillful campaign in central Europe and defeated the allies at Dresden. In October, however, he met decisive defeat at Leipzig from the combined armies of his enemies, in what the Germans called the Battle of the Nations. At the end of March 1814 the allied army marched into Paris. Napoleon abdicated and went into exile on the island of Elba off the coast of northern Italy.

THE CONGRESS OF VIENNA AND THE EUROPEAN SETTLEMENT

Once Napoleon was removed, the allies began to pursue their own separate ambitions. The key person in achieving eventual agreement among the allies was Robert Stewart, Viscount Castlereagh (1769–1822), the British foreign secretary. Even before the victorious armies had entered Paris, he achieved the Treaty of Chaumont on March 9, 1814, providing for the restoration of the Bourbons to the French throne and the contraction of France to its 1792 frontiers. Even more important, Britain, Austria, Russia, and Prussia formed a Quadruple Alliance for twenty years to preserve whatever settlement they later agreed on. Remaining problems—and there were many—and final details were left for a conference to be held at Vienna.

The Congress of Vienna assembled in September 1814 but did not conclude its work until November 1815. The four great powers conducted the important work of the conference. The victors agreed that no single state should be allowed to dominate Europe. They constructed a series of states to serve as barriers to any new French expansion (see Map 23–3). Thus, they established the kingdom of the Netherlands, including Belgium in the north, and added Genoa to Piedmont in the south. Prussia, whose power was increased by acquisitions in eastern Europe, was given important new territories in the west to deter French aggression along the Rhine River. Austria was given full control of northern Italy to prevent a repetition of Napoleon's conquests there. Most of Napoleon's arrangements in the rest of Germany were left untouched. The Holy Roman Empire was not revived. The Congress established the rule of legitimate monarchs and rejected any hint of the republican and democratic politics that had flowed from the French Revolution.

However, the settlement of eastern Europe sharply divided the victors. Alexander I wanted Russia to govern all of Poland. Prussia was willing if it received all of Saxony. Austria, however, refused to surrender its share of Poland or to see Prussian power grow and Russia penetrate deeper into central Europe. The Polish-Saxon question enabled France to rejoin the great powers. The French Foreign Minister Talleyrand (1754–1838) suggested that the weight of France, added to that of Britain and Austria, might bring Alexander to his senses. When news of a secret treaty among the three leaked out, the tsar agreed to become ruler of a smaller Poland, and Frederick William III of Prussia (r. 1797–1840) agreed to settle for part of Saxony. Thereafter, France was included as a fifth great power in all deliberations.

Napoleon's escape from Elba on March 1, 1815, further restored unity among the victors. He promised a liberal constitution and a peaceful foreign policy, but the allies declared him an outlaw (a new device under international law) and sent their armies to crush him. Wellington, with the crucial help of the Prussians, defeated Napoleon at Waterloo in Belgium on June 18, 1815. Napoleon again abdicated and was exiled to Saint Helena, a tiny Atlantic island off the coast of Africa, where he died in 1821.

The Hundred Days, as the period of Napoleons' return is called, made the peace settlement somewhat harsher for

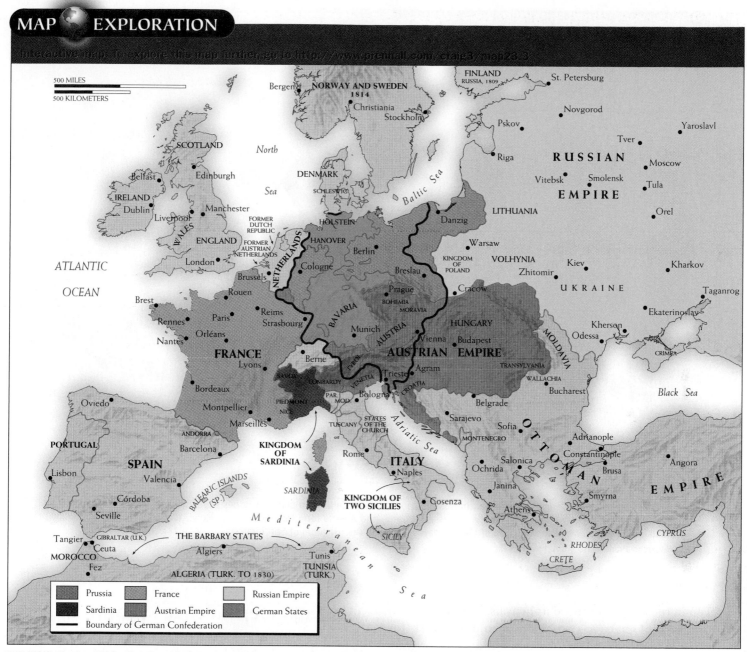

MAP EXPLORATION

Interactive maps: To explore the map further, go to http://www.prenhall.com/craig3/map23.3

MAP 23–3 Europe 1815, after the Congress of Vienna.   The Congress of Vienna achieved the post-Napoleonic territorial adjustments shown on the map. The most notable arrangements dealt with areas along France's borders (the Netherlands, Prussia, Switzerland, and Piedmont) and in Poland and northern Italy.

France, but the other main outlines of the Vienna Settlement remained in place. The Quadruple Alliance between England, Austria, Prussia, and Russia was renewed on November 20, 1815. Henceforth, it was as much a coalition for the maintenance of peace as for the pursuit of victory over France. A coalition with such a purpose had not previously existed in European international relations. Its existence and later operation represented an important new departure in European affairs. Unlike the situation in the eighteenth century, certain European powers were determined to prevent the outbreak of future war. The statesmen at Vienna, unlike their eighteenth-century counterparts, had seen the armies of the French Revolution change major frontiers of the European states and overturn the political and social order of much of the Continent. They had seen unprecedented military destruction. They were determined

Political Cartoon of the Congress of Vienna. In this cartoon depiction, Talleyrand simply watches which way the wind is blowing, Castlereagh hesitates, while the monarchs of Russia, Prussia, and Austria form the dance of the Holy Alliance. The King of Saxony holds onto his crown and the republic of Geneva pays homage to the Kingdom of Sardinia.
Bildarchiv Preussischer Kulturbesitz.

to prevent a recurrence of those upheavals. The shared purpose of the diplomats was to establish a framework for future stability, not to punish a defeated France. The great powers through the Vienna Settlement framed international relations in such a manner that the major powers would respect that settlement and not as in the eighteenth century use military force to change it.

The Congress of Vienna succeeded in preventing future French aggression and in arranging an acceptable settlement for Europe that produced a long-lasting peace. Its work has been criticized for failing to recognize and provide for the great forces that would stir the nineteenth century—nationalism and democracy—but such criticism is inappropriate. The settlement, like all such agreements, was aimed at solving past ills, and in that it succeeded. The Vienna Settlement remained essentially intact for almost half a century and spared Europe a general war until 1914.

Wars of Independence in Latin America

The wars of the French Revolution, particularly those of Napoleon, sparked movements for independence throughout Latin America. Between 1804 and 1824 France was driven from Haiti, Portugal lost control of Brazil, and Spain was forced to withdraw from all of its American empire except for Cuba and Puerto Rico. Three centuries of Iberian colonial government over the South American continent ended.

EIGHTEENTH-CENTURY DEVELOPMENTS

Spain was one of the defeated powers in 1763. Charles III (r. 1759–1788) and the government circles in Spain were convinced that the American colonial system had to be changed. After 1765 the monarch abolished the monopolies of Seville and Cádiz and permitted other Spanish commercial centers to trade with America. He also opened more

OVERVIEW   The Vienna Settlement

The Congress of Vienna met from September 1814 to November 1815 to redraw the map of Europe after the defeat of Napoleon. With few exceptions, the borders the Congress agreed on remained in place until the 1850s and beyond. The statesmen at Vienna wanted to prevent another outbreak of the wars that had followed the French Revolution. The main principles behind their deliberations were a determination to confine France, which they saw as the home of revolution, within its traditional boundaries: legitimacy, by which they meant the restoration of Europe's traditional monarchs to their thrones; and compensation—the idea that the states that had defeated Napoleon deserved to be "compensated" for their expenditure of lives and treasure with new territory. Below is a summary of what the statesmen at Vienna achieved.

France	was reduced to its 1792 frontiers and ringed along its borders with a series of strengthened states to discourage French aggression. Thus, Prussia was given the Rhineland along France's eastern frontier; the Kingdom of the Netherlands was created to the north of France by combining Belgium and Holland; and the Kingdom of Sardinia on France's southern border was strengthened by the addition of the great port of Genoa.
Italy	Austria was compensated by becoming the dominant power in Italy and by being given Lombardy and Venetia. The Papal States were reconstituted, and the legitimate Italian rulers were restored to their thrones: the House of Savoy in Piedmont-Sardinia, the Bourbons in the Two Sicilies and Lucca; the Habsburgs in Tuscany, Modena, and Parma. Most of these rulers depended on Austrian support. The old republics of Venice and Genoa, which Napoleon had abolished, were not restored.
Germany	The Holy Roman Empire was not revived. Instead, it was replaced by a loose Germanic Confederation of mostly monarchical states under the presidency of Austria. Prussia was compensated by receiving two-thirds of Saxony, which had been an ally of Napoleon.
Scandinavia	Denmark, another ally of Napoleon, had to cede Norway as compensation to Sweden, which had lost Finland to Russia.
Poland	Poland was not restored as an independent state. It remained divided among Prussia, Austria, and Russia. Russia was compensated by being given the largest share of Poland.
Britain	was compensated with a number of former French and Dutch colonies. It also became the dominant naval power in the Mediterranean by annexing Malta in the central Mediterranean and the Ionian Islands at the mouth of the Adriatic.

South American and Caribbean ports to trade and authorized commerce between American ports. In 1776 he organized a fourth viceroyalty in the region of the Río de la Plata, which included much of present-day Argentina, Uruguay, Paraguay, and Bolivia. Charles III also attempted to make tax collection more efficient and to eliminate bureaucratic corruption. To achieve those ends, he introduced into the empire *intendents*, who were royal bureaucrats loyal only to the Crown.

These reforms, which took place during the same years as the unsuccessful British effort to reorganize its authority in its North American colonies, largely succeeded in returning the empire to direct Spanish control. Many **peninsulares**, whites born in Spain, went to the New World to fill new posts at the expense of **Creoles**, whites born in America. Expanding trade likewise brought more Spanish merchants to Latin America. The economy retained its export orienta-

tion, and economic life continued to be organized for the benefit of Spain. There matters stood until the early nineteenth century.

FIRST MOVEMENTS TOWARD INDEPENDENCE

Haiti achieved independence from France in 1804, following a slave revolt that commenced in 1794 led by Toussaint L'Ouverture (1744–1803) and Jean-Jacques Dessalines (ca. 1756–1806). Haiti's revolution involved the popular uprising of a repressed social group, which proved to be the great exception in the Latin American drive for liberty from European masters. Generally speaking, on the South American continent it was the Creole elite—merchants, landowners, and professional people—who led the movements against Spain and Portugal. Few Indians, blacks, mestizos, mulattos, or slaves became involved or benefited from the end of Iberian rule. Indeed, the Haitian slave revolt haunted

▲ **Toussaint L'Ouverture.** L'Ouverture (1744–1803) began the revolt that led to Haitian independence in 1804.
Historical Pictures Collection/Stock Montage, Inc.

the Creoles, as did an Indian revolt in the Andes in 1780 and 1781. The Creoles were determined that political independence from Spain and Portugal should not cause social disruption or the loss of their social and economic privileges. In this respect the Creole revolutionaries were not unlike American revolutionaries in the Southern colonies who wanted to reject British rule but keep their slaves, or French revolutionaries who wanted to depose the king but not extend liberty to the French working class.

Creole complaints resembled those of the American colonists against Great Britain. Latin American merchants wanted to trade more freely within the region and with North American and European markets. They wanted commercial regulations that would benefit them rather than Spain.

Creoles also feared that Spanish imperial regulations might affect landholdings, access to commissions in the army, local government policy, and the treatment of slaves and Indians in ways that would harm their interests. They also deeply resented Spanish policies favoring *peninsulares* for political patronage, including appointments in the colonial government, church, and army. They believed the *peninsulares* improperly secured all the best positions. Seen in this light,

the royal patronage system represented another device with which Spain extracted wealth and income from America for its own people rather than its colonial subjects.

From the 1790s onward Spain suffered military reverses in the wars associated with the French Revolution and Napoleon, and the commercial situation turned sharply against the inhabitants of the Spanish Empire. The military pressures led the Spanish monarchy into a desperate search for new revenues, including increased taxation and the confiscation of property in the American Empire. The policies harmed the economic life of the Creole elite.

Creole leaders had read the Enlightenment *philosophes* and regarded their reforms as potentially beneficial to the region. They were also well aware of the events and the political philosophy of the American Revolution. But something more than reform programs and revolutionary example was required to transform Creole discontent into revolt against the Spanish government. That transforming event occurred in Europe when Napoleon toppled the Portuguese monarchy in 1807 and the Spanish government in 1808 and then placed his own brother on the thrones of both countries. The Portuguese royal family fled to Brazil and established its government there. But the Bourbon monarchy of Spain seemed wholly vanquished.

The Creole elite feared that a liberal Napoleonic monarchy in Spain would impose reforms in Latin America harmful to their economic and social interests and would drain the region of the wealth and resources needed for Napoleon's wars. To protect their interests, various Creole juntas, or political committees, between 1808 and 1810 claimed the right to govern different regions of Latin America. After the establishment of these local juntas, the Spanish would not again directly govern the continent and after ten years of politically and economically exhausting warfare were to recognize the permanence of Latin American independence.

SAN MARTÍN IN RÍO DE LA PLATA

The first region to assert its independence was the Río de la Plata, or modern Argentina. As early as 1806 the citizens of Buenos Aires had fought off a British invasion and thus had learned that they could look to themselves rather than Spain for effective political and military action. In 1810 the junta in Buenos Aires not only thrust off Spanish authority but also sent liberation forces against Paraguay and Uruguay. The armies were defeated, but Spain nonetheless soon lost control in the two areas. Paraguay asserted its own independence. Uruguay was eventually absorbed by Brazil.

Undiscouraged by these early defeats, the Buenos Aires government remained determined to liberate Peru, the greatest stronghold of royalist power and loyalty on the continent. By 1814 José de San Martín (1778–1850), the leading general of

had forced Ferdinand VII (r. 1813–1833) to accept a liberal constitution. Conservative Mexicans feared that the new liberal monarchy would attempt to impose liberal reforms on Mexico. Therefore, for the most conservative of reasons, they rallied to a former royalist general, Agustín de Iturbide (1783–1824), who in 1821 declared Mexico independent of Spain. Shortly thereafter, Iturbide was declared emperor. His own regime did not last long, but an independent Mexico, governed by persons determined to resist any significant social reform, had been created.

Great Britain was highly sympathetic to the independence movements in the different regions of Latin America. By breaking the hold of the Spanish empire the movement toward independence opened the markets of the continent to British trade and investment. Consequently in 1823 Great Britain supported the American Monroe Doctrine that prohibited further colonization and intervention by European powers in America. Britain soon recognized the Spanish colonies as independent states. Through the rest of the century, British commercial interests dominated Latin America.

BRAZILIAN INDEPENDENCE

Brazilian independence, in contrast to that of Spanish Latin America, came relatively simply and peacefully. As already noted, the Portuguese royal family, along with several thousand government officials and members of the court, took refuge in Brazil in 1807. Their arrival immediately transformed Rio de Janeiro into a court city. The prince regent Joao (r. 1816–1826) addressed many of the local complaints, equivalent to those of the Spanish Creoles. In 1815 he made Brazil a kingdom, which meant that it was no longer to be regarded merely as a colony of Portugal. This transformation was in many respects long overdue because Brazil was far larger and more prosperous than Portugal itself. Then in 1820 a revolution occurred in Portugal, and its leaders demanded Joao's return to Lisbon. They also demanded the return of Brazil to colonial status. Joao, who had become Joao VI in 1816, returned to Portugal but left his son Pedro (r. 1822–1831) as regent in Brazil, encouraging him to be sympathetic to the political aspirations of the Brazilians. In September 1822 Pedro embraced Brazilian independence against the recolonializing efforts of Portugal. By the end of the year he had become emperor of an independent Brazil, which remained a monarchy until 1889. Thus in contrast to virtually all other nations of Latin America, Brazil achieved independence in a way that left no real dispute as to where the center of political authority lay.

Another factor aided the peaceful transition to independence in Brazil. The political and social elite there were determined to preserve slavery against the forces (to be discussed in the next section) that were challenging that institution. The

CHRONOLOGY

The Wars of Latin American Independence

1759–1788	Charles III of Spain carries out imperial reforms
1776	Organization of Viceroyalty of Río de la Plata
1780–1781	Revolt of Indians in the Andes
1794	Toussaint L'Ouverture leads slave revolt in Haiti
1804	Independence of Haiti
1807	Portuguese royal family flees to Brazil
1808	Spanish monarchy falls to Napoleon
1808–1810	Creole Committees organized to govern much of Latin America
1810	Buenos Aires junta sends forces to liberate Paraguay and Uruguay
1811	Miguel Hidalgo y Costilla leads rebellion in New Spain and is executed
1811–1815	José María Morelos y Pavón leads rebellion in New Spain and is executed
1814	San Martín organizes army
1815	Brazil declared a kingdom
1816	Bolívar invades Venezuela
1817	San Martín occupies Santiago, Chile
1820	Revolution in Spain
1821 February 24	New Spain declares independence
June 29	Bolívar captures Caracas, Venezuela
July 28	San Martín liberates Peru
1822 July 26–27	San Martín and Bolívar quarrel at Guayaquil; San Martín goes into exile in Europe
September 7	Dom Pedro declares Brazilian independence
1824	Battle of Ayacucho—final Spanish defeat

wars of independence elsewhere had led to the abolition of slavery or moved the independent states closer to abolition. Any attempt to gain independence from Portugal through warfare might have caused social as well as political turmoil that would open the slavery question.

Toward the Abolition of Slavery in the Transatlantic

ECONOMY

In 1750 almost no one seriously questioned the institution of slavery; by 1888 slavery no longer existed in the transatlantic economy. This vast transformation of economic and social life occurred as the result of an international effort, first to abolish the slave trade and then to abolish the institution of slavery itself. At no previous time in world history had a society actually attempted to abolish slavery. Its eventual abolition in the transatlantic world stands as

the Río de la Plata forces, had organized and led a disciplined army in a daring march over the Andes Mountains. By early 1817 he had occupied Santiago in Chile, and established the Chilean independence leader Bernardo O'Higgins (1778–1842) as supreme dictator. San Martín then constructed a naval force that in 1820 transported his army to Peru. The next year, he drove royalist forces from Lima and assumed the title of Protector of Peru (Map 23–4).

SIMÓN BOLÍVAR'S LIBERATION OF VENEZUELA

While San Martín had been liberating the southern portion of the Continent, Simón Bolívar (1783–1830) had been pursuing a similar task in the north. In 1810, as a firm advocate of both independence and republicanism, Bolívar had helped organize a liberating junta in Caracas, Venezuela. Between 1811 and 1814 civil war broke out throughout Venezuela as both royalists, on the one hand, and slaves and *llaneros* (Venezuelan cowboys), on the other, challenged the authority of the repub-

▲ **Simón Bolívar.** Bolívar was the liberator of much of Latin America. He inclined toward a policy of political liberalism.
SuperStock Inc.

lican government. (See Document, "Bolívar Denounces Spanish Rule in Latin America.") Bolívar had to go into exile. In 1816, with help from Haiti, he launched a new invasion against Venezuela. He first captured Bogotá, capital of New Granada (including modern Colombia, Bolivia, and Ecuador), as a base for attacking Venezuela. By the summer of 1821 his forces had captured Caracas, and he had been named president.

A year later, in July 1822, the armies of Bolívar and San Martín joined to liberate Quito. At a famous meeting in Guayaquil the two leaders sharply disagreed about the future political structure of Latin America. San Martín believed that monarchies were required; Bolívar maintained his republicanism. Not long thereafter San Martín quietly retired from public life and went into exile in Europe. Meanwhile, Bolívar purposefully allowed the political situation in Peru to fall into confusion, and in 1823 he sent troops to establish his control. On December 9, 1824, at the Battle of Ayacucho, the Spanish royalist forces suffered a major defeat at the hands of the liberating army. The battle marked the conclusion of Spain's effort to retain its American empire.

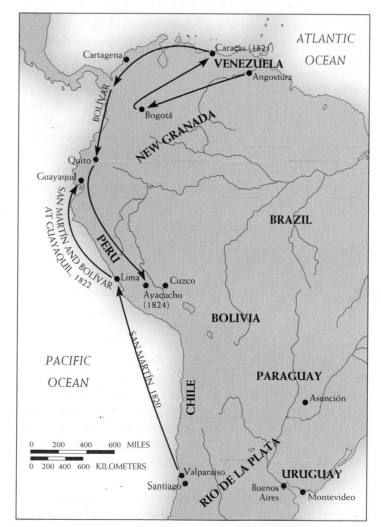

MAP 23–4 The Independence Campaigns of San Martín and Bolívar.

DOCUMENT | Bolívar Denounces Spanish Rule in Latin America

In September 1815 Simón Bolívar published a long statement, often called The Jamaica Letter, in which he explained the political and economic difficulties under which the Creole elite of the Spanish Empire had lived. He defined Americans as referring to those persons in Latin America who were neither Indian nor European by birth. He also implicitly excluded black slaves. Consequently his attack on Spain was voiced on behalf of the white population of the South American continent who had been born there and who demanded rights of political participation and economic freedom.

♦ Why does Bolívar describe the Creole elite as having lived in a permanent political infancy? What are the economic disadvantages that he describes, and why had those become more burdensome in the half century before he wrote this letter? How had Spanish economic regulation prevented the Creole elite from achieving positions of responsibility in Latin America? How does this document compare with others concerned with movements of independence and nationalism? See "The Stamp Act Congress Addresses George III" (earlier in this chapter), "Mazzini Defines Nationality" (Chapter 25), "The Pan-Slavic Congress Calls for the Liberation of Slavic Nationalities" (Chapter 25), "William Gladstone Pleads for Irish Home Rule" (Chapter 26), and "Gandhi on Passive Resistance and Swaraj" (Chapter 28).

The role of the inhabitants of the American hemisphere has for centuries been purely passive. Politically they were non-existent. We are still in a position lower than slavery, and therefore it is more difficult for us to rise to the enjoyment of freedom. ... We have been harassed by a conduct which has not only deprived us of our rights but has kept us in a sort of permanent infancy with regard to public affairs. If we could at least have managed our domestic affairs and our internal administration, we could have acquainted ourselves with the processes and mechanics of public affairs. ...

Americans today, and perhaps to a greater extent than ever before, who live within the Spanish system occupy a position in society no better than that of serfs destined for labor, or at best they have no more status than that of mere consumers. Yet even this status is surrounded with galling restrictions, such as being forbidden to grow European crops, or to store products which are royal monopolies, or to establish factories of a type the [Spanish] Peninsula itself does not possess. To this add the exclusive trading privileges, even in articles of prime necessity, and the barriers between American provinces, designed to prevent all exchange of trade, traffic, and understanding. In short, do you wish to know what our future held?—simply the cultivation of the fields of indigo, grain, coffee, sugar cane, cacao, and cotton; cattle raising on the broad plains; hunting wild game in the jungles; digging in the earth to mine its gold—but even these limitations could never satisfy the greed of Spain.

So negative was our existence that I can find nothing comparable in any other civilized society, examine as I may the entire history of time and the politics of all nations. Is it not an outrage and a violation of human rights to expect a land so splendidly endowed, so vast, rich, and populous, to remain merely passive?

As I have just explained, we were cut off and, as it were, removed from the world in relation to the science of government and administration of the state. We were never viceroys or governors, save in the rarest of instances; seldom archbishops and bishops; diplomats never; as military men, only subordinates; as nobles, without royal privileges. In brief, we were neither magistrates nor financiers and seldom merchants. ...

*From Harold A. Bierck Jr., ed., Selected Writings of Bolívar, Vol. 1.
Copyright © 1951 The Colonial Press, pp. 110–112.*

INDEPENDENCE IN NEW SPAIN

The drive for independence in New Spain, which included present-day Mexico as well as Texas, California, and the rest of the southwestern United States, clearly illustrates the socially conservative outcome of the Latin American colonial revolutions. As elsewhere, a local governing junta was organized. But before it had undertaken any significant measures, a Creole priest, Miguel Hidalgo y Costilla (1753–1811), issued a call for rebellion to the Indians in his parish. They and other repressed groups of black and mestizo urban and rural workers responded. Father Hidalgo set forth a program of social change, including hints of land reform. Soon he stood at the head of a rather unorganized group of 80,000 followers and marched on Mexico City. Both Hidalgo's forces and the royalist army that opposed them committed numerous atrocities. In July 1811 he was captured and executed. Leadership of his movement then fell to José María Morelos y Pavón (1765–1815), a mestizo priest. Far more radical than Hidalgo, he called for an end to forced labor and for substantial land reforms. He was executed in 1815, ending five years of popular uprising.

In 1820, however, the conservative political groups in Mexico, both Creole and Spanish, found their recently achieved security challenged from an unexpected source. A revolution in Spain

---

one of the most permanent achievements of the forces unleashed by the eighteenth-century Enlightenment and revolutions.

The eighteenth-century crusade against slavery in the plantation economy that stretched from Maryland south to Brazil (see Chapter 18) originated among writers of the Enlightenment and religious critics of slavery. Although some authors associated with the Enlightenment, including John Locke, were reluctant to question slavery or even defended it, the general Enlightenment rhetoric of equality stood in sharp contrast to the radical inequality of slavery. Montesquieu satirized slavery in *The Spirit of the Laws*. Adam Smith's emphasis in *The Wealth of Nations* on free labor and the efficiency of free markets undermined economic defenses of slavery. Much eighteenth-century literature idealized primitive peoples living in cultures very different from those of Europe and portrayed them as embodying a lost human virtue. This literature allowed some Europeans to look upon African slaves in the Americas as having been betrayed and robbed of an original innocence. In such a climate, slavery, once considered the natural and deserved result of some deficiency in slaves themselves, grew to be regarded as undeserved and unacceptable. Other Enlightenment ethical thinking led reformers to believe that by working against slavery, for virtually the first time defined as an unmitigated evil, they would realize their own highest moral character.

▲ **Spanish Slave Ship.** After 1807 the British Royal Navy patrolled the West African coast attempting to intercept slave-trading ships. In 1846 the British ship HMS *Albatross* captured a Spanish slave ship, the *Albanoz*, and freed the slaves. A British officer depicted the appalling conditions in the slavehold in this watercolor.
The Granger Collection, N.Y.

The initial religious protest against slavery originated among English Quakers, a radical Protestant religious group founded by George Fox in the seventeenth century. By the early eighteenth century it had solidified itself into a small, but relatively wealthy, sect in England. Members of Quaker congregations at that time actually owned slaves in the West Indies and participated in the transatlantic slave trade. During the Seven Years' War (1756–1763), however, many Quakers experienced economic hardship. Furthermore, the war created other difficulties for the English population as a whole. Certain Quakers decided that the presence of the evil of slavery in the world explained these troubles. They then sought to remove this evil from their own lives and from the lives of their congregations by taking action against the whole system of slavery that characterized the transatlantic economy.

Just as the slave system was a transatlantic affair, so was the crusade against it. There were Quaker communities in America, and soon Quakers in both Philadelphia and England wrote and organized against the institution. By the earliest stages of the American Revolution small groups of reformers, usually spearheaded by Quakers, had established an antislavery network. The turmoil of the American Revolution and the founding of the American republic gave these groups the occasion for some of their earliest successes. Emancipation gradually, but nonetheless steadily, spread among the northern states. In 1787 the Continental Congress forbade slavery in the newly organized Northwest Territory north of the Ohio River.

Despite these American developments, Great Britain became and remained the center for the antislavery movement. In 1772 a decision by the chief justice affirmed that slaves brought into Great Britain could not forcibly be removed. During the early 1780s the antislavery reformers in Great Britain decided to work toward ending the slave trade rather than the institution of slavery itself. The horrors of the slave trade caught the public's attention in 1783 when the captain of the slave ship *Zong* threw more than 130 slaves overboard in order to collect insurance. Soon after, groups from the Church of England and the English Quakers formed the Society for the Abolition of the Slave Trade. The most famous of the new leaders was William Wilberforce, who, each year for the rest of his life, introduced a bill to end the slave trade.

For the reformers, attacking the trade rather than the institution appeared a less radical and more achievable reform. To many, the slave trade appeared a more obvious crime than the holding of slaves, which seemed a more passive act. Furthermore, attacking slavery itself involved serious issues of property rights, which might alienate potential supporters of the abolition of the slave trade. The antislavery groups also believed that if the trade were ended, planters would have to treat their remaining slaves more humanely.

While the British reformers worked for the abolition of the slave trade, slaves themselves in certain areas took matters into their own hands. Indeed, the largest emancipation of slaves to occur in the eighteenth century came on the island of Saint Domingue (Haiti), France's wealthiest colony, as a result of the slave revolt of 1794 led by Toussaint L'Ouverture and Jean-Jacques Dessalines (see page 000). The revolt in Haiti and Haiti's eventual independence in 1804 stood as a warning to slave owners throughout the West Indies. Other slave revolts occurred, such as those in Virginia led by Gabriel Prosser in 1800 and by Nat Turner in 1831, in South Carolina led by Denmark Vesey in 1822, in British-controlled Demarra in 1823 and 1824, and in Jamaica in 1831. Each of these was brutally suppressed.

For complicated economic reasons some British West Indies planters began to consider abolition of the slave trade useful to their interests. Within the West Indies themselves the planters were experiencing soil exhaustion and competition from newly tilled islands opened for sugar cultivation. Some older plantations were being abandoned while others operated with low profitability. With the new islands there was a glut of sugar on the market, and as a consequence the price was falling. Under these conditions some British West Indies planters, for reasons that had nothing to do with religion or enlightened humanitarianism, began to favor curtailing the slave trade. Without new slaves competing French planters would lack the labor they needed to exploit their islands.

Then, during the Napoleonic Wars, the British captured a number of the valuable French islands. In 1805 to protect the planters of the older British West Indies islands, the British Cabinet forbade the importation of slaves into the newly acquired French islands. By 1807 the abolition sentiment was strong enough for Parliament to pass Wilberforce's often proposed measure prohibiting slave trading from any British port.

Thereafter the suppression of this trade became one of the fundamental pillars of nineteenth-century British foreign policy. The British navy maintained a squadron of ships around the coast of West Africa to halt slave traders. Although the French and Americans also patrolled the West African coast, neither was deeply committed to ending the slave trade. Nonetheless, in 1824 the American Congress had made slave trading a capital offense.

Leaders of the Latin American wars of independence, disposed by Enlightenment ideas to disapprove of slavery, had sought the support of slaves by promises of emancipation. Once free of Spanish domination, the newly independent nations slowly freed their slave populations in order to maintain good relations with Great Britain from whom they needed economic support. Despite the gradual nature of this abolition, slavery would disappear from all nations of Latin America by the middle of the century with the important exception of Brazil.

Having slowly recognized that the abolition of the slave trade had not actually improved the lot of slaves, British reformers in 1823 adopted as a new goal the gradual emancipation of slaves and founded the Abolition Society. The savagery with which West Indian planters put down slave revolts in 1823 and 1824 and again in 1831 strengthened the resolve of the antislavery reformers. By 1830 the reformers abandoned the goal of gradual abolition and demanded immediate complete abolition of slavery. In 1833, following the passage of the Reform Bill in Great Britain, they achieved that goal when Parliament abolished the right of British subjects to hold slaves. In the British West Indies, 750,000 slaves were freed within a few years.

The other old colonial powers in the New World tended to be much slower in their abolition of slavery. Portugal did little or nothing about slavery in Brazil, and when that nation became independent, its new government continued slavery. Portugal ended slavery elsewhere in its American possessions in 1836; the Swedes, in 1847; the Danes, in 1848, but the Dutch not until 1863. France had witnessed a significant antislavery movement throughout the first half of the century but did not abolish slavery in its West Indian possessions until the revolutions of 1848.

Despite all of these considerable achievements of the antislavery movement, during the first thirty years of the nineteenth century the institution of slavery actually revived and achieved new footholds in the transatlantic world. These areas included the lower south of the United States for the cultivation of cotton, Brazil for the cultivation of coffee, and Cuba for the cultivation of sugar. World demand for those products made the slave system economically viable in those regions. Slavery would end in the United States only after American abolitionists brought it to the center of American politics in the 1850s and the Civil War was fought during the next decade. In Cuba it would persist until 1886, and full emancipation would occur in Brazil only in 1888. (See Chapters 25, 26, and 27.)

The emancipation crusade, like slave trading itself, drew Europeans into African affairs. In 1787 the British established a colony for poor free blacks from Britain in Sierra Leone, which actually succeeded only after the British navy began to settle Africans rescued from captured slave-trading ships. The French established a smaller experiment at Libreville in Gabon. The most famous and lasting attempt to settle former black slaves in Africa was the establishment of Liberia through the efforts of the American Colonization Society after 1817. Liberia became an independent republic in 1847. All of these efforts to move former slaves back to Africa had only modest success, but they did affect the future of West Africa itself.

Other antislavery reformers were less interested in establishing outposts for settlement of former slaves than in transforming the African economy itself. These reformers attempted to spread both Christianity and free trade to Africa, hoping to exchange British manufactured goods, particularly textiles, for tropical goods produced by Africans. These commercial efforts of the antislavery movement marked the first serious intrusions of European powers well beyond the coast of West Africa into the heart of the continent.

After the American Civil War finally halted any large-scale demand for slaves from Africa, the antislavery reformers began to focus on ending the slave trade in East Africa and the Indian Ocean. This new drive against slavery and the slave trade in Africa itself became one of the rationales for European interference in Africa during the second half of the century and served as one of the foundations for the establishment of the late-century colonial empires.

Liberty Leading the People.

Summary

The Transatlantic Revolutions   The revolutions and the crusade against slavery that occurred throughout the transatlantic world between 1776 and the 1830s transformed three continents. In North America, in France and other parts of Europe, and in South America, political experiments challenged government and the rule of monarchies and aristocracies. The foundations of modern liberal democracy were laid. The largest republic since ancient times had been established in North America. In Latin America, republicanism triumphed everywhere except Brazil. Never again could government be undertaken in these regions without some form of participation by the governed.

Economic and Social Liberalization   The expanding forms of political liberty found their counterparts in an economic life freed from the constraints of the old colonial empires and the slavery that marked their plantations. The new American republic constituted a vast free trade zone. Its commerce was open to the world. And for the first time since the encounter with Europe, Latin America could trade freely among its own peoples and those of the rest of the world. In France and Europe, where the Napoleonic armies had carried the doctrines of the rights of man, economic life had been rationalized and freed from the domination of local authorities and local weights and measures. National law formed the framework for economic activity. The movement to abolish slavery fostered a wage economy of free laborers. That kind of economy would generate its own set of problems and social dislocation, but it was nonetheless an economy of free human beings.

Nationalism   Finally, the age of transatlantic revolutions saw the emergence of nationalism as a political force. All of the revolutions, because of their popular political base, had given power to the idea of nations defined by their own character and historical past rather than by dynastic rulers. The Americans saw themselves as forming a new kind of nation. The French had demonstrated the power of a nation mobilized for military purposes. In turn, the aggression of France had aroused national sentiment, especially in Great Britain, Spain, and Germany. The new nations of Latin America also sought to define themselves by their heritage and historical experience rather than by their past in the Spanish and Portuguese Empires.

These various revolutions, their political doctrines, and their social and economic departures provided examples to peoples elsewhere in the world. But even more important, the transatlantic revolutions and eventual abolition of slavery meant that new political classes and independent nations would become actors on the world scene. Europeans would have to deal with a score of new nations in the Americas. The rest of the world confronted new nations freed from the direction and authority of European powers. The political changes in Europe meant that those nations and their relationships with the rest of the world would be directed by a broader range of groups than in the past.

Review Questions

1. Discuss the American Revolution in the context of transatlantic history. To what extent were the colonists influenced by their position in the transatlantic economy? To what extent were they influenced by European ideas and political developments? How did their demands for liberty compare and contrast with the ideas of liberty championed during the French Revolution?

2. How was the Estates General transformed into the National Assembly? How does the *Declaration of the Rights of Man and Citizen* reflect the social and political values of the eighteenth-century Enlightenment? What were the chief ways in which France and its government were reorganized in the early years of the revolution? Why has the Civil Constitution of the Clergy been called the greatest blunder of the National Assembly?

3. Why were some political factions dissatisfied with the constitutional settlement of 1791 in France? What was the revolution of 1792 and why did it occur? What were the causes of the Reign of Terror and what political coalitions made it possible?

4. How did Napoleon rise to power? What were his major domestic achievements? Did his rule more nearly fulfill or betray the ideals of the French Revolution? Why did Napoleon decide to invade Russia? Why did he fail? What were the major outlines of the peace settlement achieved by the Congress of Vienna?

5. What political changes took place in Latin America in the twenty years between 1804 and 1824? What were the main reasons for Creole discontent with Spanish rule? Who were some of the primary leaders of Latin American independence and why were they successful? How were the movements to Latin American independence influenced by the American and French Revolutions? What were the factors that made the Latin American wars of independence different from those two revolutions?

6. A motto of the French Revolution was "liberty, equality, and fraternity." How might one compare the American Revolution, the French Revolution, and the Latin American wars of independence in regard to the achievement of these goals? Which groups in each country or region benefited from the revolution and which gained little or nothing from the changes?

7. What intellectual and religious factors contributed to the rise of the antislavery movement? To what extent did nonhumanitarian forces contribute to it? What opposition did it meet? Why did slavery receive a new lease on life during the same years that the antislavery movement emerged?

Key Terms

assignats (p. 674)

Consulate (p. 681)

Convention (p. 675)

Creoles (p. 689)

Jacobins (p. 675)

levée en masse (p. 677)

peninsulares (p. 689)

Reign of Terror (p. 677)

sans-culottes (p. 676)

Thermidorean Reaction (p. 680)

Third Estate (p. 670)

Documents CD-ROM

From Old Regime to Revolution
18.4 Declaration of Independence: Revolutionary Declarations
18.6 The Tennis Court Oath (June 20, 1789)

18.7 Declaratíon of the Rights of Man and Citizen
18.8 Edmund Burke, Reflections on the Revolution in France

NOTE: *To learn more about the topics in this chapter, see the Suggested Readings at the end of the book.*

Political Consolidation in Nineteenth-Century Europe and North America, 1815–1880

- The Emergence of Nationalism in Europe

- Early-Nineteenth-Century Political Liberalism

- Efforts to Liberalize Early-Nineteenth-Century Political Structures

- Testing the New American Republic

- The Canadian Experience

- Midcentury Political Consolidation in Europe

- Unrest of Nationalities in Eastern Europe

- Racial Theory and Anti-Semitism

◄ In 1848, Ana Ipatescu helped to lead Transylvanian
revolutionaries against Russian rule. Transylvania is part of
present day Romania. The revolutions of 1848 in Estern Europe
were primarily rising of nationalist groups. Although generally
repressed in the revolutions of that year, subject nationalities
would prove a source of political upheaval and unrest in region,
throughout the rest of the century ultimately providing the
spark for the outbreak of World War I.
The Art Archive/Picture Desk, Inc./Kobal Collection.

European and North American Political Consolidation

The movement toward strong, centralized national states in Europe and North America during the nineteenth century had counterparts elsewhere in the world. In Asia during this same period, Japan sought to imitate the military and economic power of the European states. Late nineteenth-century Latin America enjoyed one of its most successful and stable periods. The governments of that region established centralized regimes on the basis of relatively prosperous economies. In the United States the Civil War established the power of the central federal government over that of the individual states. The role of the war in the forging of a single American nation was similar to the role that military force played in the unifications of Italy and Germany and the suppression of the Paris Commune.

In Italy and Germany many people regarded the triumph of nationalism as a positive achievement. However, the last half of the century also saw various national and ethnic groups use the power of the national state to repress or dominate other groups. Examples include the Hungarian treatment of smaller subject nationalities and the British treatment of the Irish. To some extent, this phenomenon can be explained by the geographical borders of the new nations that were carved out of former European monarchies and empires, such as the Austro-Hungarian Empire. In many cases, the boundaries ignored the reality that many, perhaps most, regions were home to more than one ethnic group, with religions, languages, and ethnicities different from those of their rulers and the governing class. In the premodern world, loyalty to a ruling dynasty, rather than shared history, language, or ethnicity, was the primary determinant of group identity or membership in a polity above the local level. People saw themselves first as members of a tribe, clan, village, or town, and second as the subjects of a ruler who might not even speak their language and whose authority often impinged very little on their daily lives. Thus ethnic or linguistic minorities posed less of an obstacle to monarchical rulers than to governments of nation-states, where national identity is often based on shared language and ethnicity. This problem has continued to bedevil national states in Europe and elsewhere in the world into the modern era and is an important cause for many recent conflicts in regions as diverse as eastern Europe, Asia, and Africa.

Elsewhere around the globe during the nineteenth century strong central governments often simply repressed minority populations, especially indigenous peoples, or allowed them fewer rights of civic participation and protection. In almost all cases the repression of minority groups generated social and political problems that haunted the twentieth century. Native Americans failed to gain rights in Latin America. In the United States the westward movement brought warfare against Native Americans, and legislation facilitated the segregation of American black citizens. In Canada, English speakers fared better than French speakers. In Australia, Aborigines were killed or forcibly relocated in many regions before and after that country's government gained sovereignty from England.

Finally, the emergence of strong European nation-states set the stage for the transfer of their rivalries from Europe to other areas of the globe. The militarily and economically strong states of Europe soon turned to foreign adventures that subjugated vast areas of Africa and Asia. This imperialism led many colonized peoples to become aware that only strong nationalistic movements of their own could eventually end subjugation by the militarily stronger Europeans. Consequently, during the first quarter of the twentieth century, the nationalistic principle that less than fifty years earlier had dominated European politics began to influence the politics of the peoples on whom Europeans had imposed their government and administration. As these former colonies achieved independence and established their own nation-states, however, their governments experienced problems similar to those of the European nations in balancing the demands for unity of the majority with the rights of the diverse ethnic and religious minorities inhabiting their territory.

THINK AHEAD

- What role has military and economic power played in strengthening nation-states?

- Why do most nation-states have ethnic minorities? Why have these minorities tended to be oppressed?

- How did the rivalry among the European nation-states affect other regions of the world? What relationship did it have on the development of nationalism outside of Europe?

DURING THE NINETEENTH CENTURY TWO fundamental long-term developments occurred in the northern transatlantic world that would have a profound impact over the decades in every culture on the face of the earth. First, in both Europe and North America there took place a process of political consolidation that made the nation-states of that region the strongest of the period. Second, and directly contributing to that political strength, there emerged in Europe and North America powerful, new industrial economies with a new kind of society no longer based primarily on the land. As a direct result of this political consolidation and industrialization, the nations of the northern transatlantic became the world's major military powers. By the close of the nineteenth century and well into the twentieth this political and military power allowed the

nations of Europe and the United States to exert unprecedented political, military, and economic influence around the globe. It was on the basis of that power that many people in Europe and North America came to claim superiority over people dwelling in other cultures and other regions. Moreover, the manner in which Europeans and to a lesser extent Americans developed sets of ideas to explain what was happening politically and economically in their region would later be used by peoples elsewhere in the world as they responded to the worldwide power that the northern transatlantic powers exerted.

The present chapter will examine the process of political consolidation in the northern transatlantic world while Chapter 25 will explore the social changes that occurred there in the nineteenth century. Although we will consider the two processes separately, each contributed to the other.

The Emergence of Nationalism in Europe

Nationalism proved to be the single most powerful European political ideology of the nineteenth and early twentieth centuries. As a political idea, **nationalism** is based on the relatively modern concept that a nation is composed of people who are joined together by the bonds of common language, customs, culture, and history, and who, because of those bonds, should share the same government. That is to say, political and ethnic boundaries should coincide. This idea came into its own in Europe during the late eighteenth and early nineteenth centuries. Early-nineteenth-century nationalists directly opposed the principle upheld at the Congress of Vienna in 1814–1815 that legitimate monarchies or family dynasties, rather than ethnicity, should provide the basis for political unity. Nationalists naturally protested multinational states such as the Austrian or Russian Empires, which embraced a wide variety of diverse ethnic groups who were often hostile to each other. Nationalists also objected to peoples of the same ethnic group, such as Germans and Italians, dwelling in political units smaller than that of the ethnic nation. Consequently, nationalists challenged both the domestic and the international order of the Vienna settlement.

CREATING NATIONS

Nationalists actually created nations in the nineteenth century. During the first half of the century a group of nationalistically minded writers using the printed word spread a nationalistic concept of the nation. They were frequently historians who chronicled a people's past or writers and literary scholars who established a national literature by collecting and publishing earlier writings in the people's language. In effect, they gave a people a sense of their past and a literature of their own. In time schoolteachers, by imparting a nation's official language and history, spread nationalistic ideas. The language to be used in the schools and in government offices was always a point of contention for nationalists. In France and Italy official versions of the national language were imposed in the schools and replaced local dialects. In parts of Scandinavia and eastern Europe nationalists attempted to resurrect from earlier times what they regarded as purer versions of the national language. Often these resurrected languages were virtually invented by modern scholars or linguists. This process of establishing national languages led to far more linguistic uniformity within European nations than had existed before the nineteenth century. In most countries spoken and written proficiency in the official printed language became a path to social and political advancement and employment within government bureaucracies. The growth of a uniform language helped to persuade people who had not

Creating Nations. The proclamation of the German Empire in the Hall of Mirrors at Versailles, January 18, 1871 after the defeat of France in the Franco-Prussian War (see pages 721–724). Kaiser Wilhelm I is standing at the top of the steps under the flags; Otto von Bismarck is in the center in a white uniform. The new nation possessed enormous economic resources and nationalistic ambitions.

Bildarchiv Preussicher Kulturbesitz/Original: Friedrichsruher Fassung, Bismarck-Museum.

thought of themselves as constituting a nation that they were a nation. Yet even in 1850, perhaps less than half of the inhabitants of France, for example, spoke official French.

MEANING OF NATIONHOOD

Nationalists used a variety of arguments and metaphors to express what they meant by nationhood. Some argued, for example, that gathering Italians into a unified Italy or Germans into a unified Germany, thus eliminating the petty dynastic states that governed those regions, would promote economic and administrative efficiency. Some nationalists claimed that nations, like biological species in the natural world, were distinct creations of God. Other nationalists claimed a place for their nations in the divine order of things. Throughout the nineteenth century, for example, Polish nationalists portrayed Poland as the suffering Christ among nations, thus implicitly suggesting that Poland, like Christ, would experience resurrection and a new life (see Document, "Mazzini Defines Nationality").

A significant difficulty for nationalism was, and is, determining which ethnic groups could be considered nations, with claims to territory and political autonomy. In theory, any of them could, but in reality nationhood came to be associated with groups that were large enough to support a viable economy, that had a history of significant cultural association, that possessed a cultural elite that could nourish and spread the national language, and that could conquer other peoples to establish and protect their own independence. Throughout the century many smaller ethnic groups claimed to fulfill these criteria but could not effectively achieve either independence or recognition. They could and did, however, create domestic unrest within the political units they inhabited. Such was the situation in Europe. A similar situation, though in many ways quite different, prevailed for a time in the United States, where by the middle of the century leaders of many Southern states began to make statements that resembled those of nationalist leaders in Europe. One can view the defeat of the Confederate States of America, discussed later in this chapter, as an example of the military failure of a region to establish itself as a kind of nationality.

REGIONS OF NATIONALISTIC PRESSURE IN EUROPE

During the nineteenth century nationalists challenged the political status quo in six major areas of Europe. England had brought Ireland under direct rule in 1800, allowing the Irish to elect members to the British Parliament in Westminster. Irish nationalists, however, wanted independence or at least self-government. The "Irish problem" would haunt British politics for the next two centuries. German nationalists sought political unity for all German-speaking peoples, challenging the multinational Austrian Empire and pitting Prussia and Austria against each other. Italian nationalists sought to unify the peninsula and drive out the Austrians. Polish nationalists struggled, primarily against Russia, to restore Poland as an independent nation. In eastern Europe a host of national groups, including Hungarians, Czechs, Slovenes, and others, sought either autonomy or formal recognition within the Austrian Empire. Finally, in the Balkans national groups, including Serbs, Greeks, Albanians, Romanians, and Bulgarians, sought independence from Ottoman and Russian control. Although there were never simultaneous disturbances in all six areas, any one of them could erupt into turmoil. In each area, nationalist activity ebbed and flowed. The dominant governments often thought they needed only to repress the activity or ride it out until stability returned. During the century, however, nationalists changed the political map and political culture of Europe in a way that the Confederate States of America failed to do in the mid-nineteenth-century United States.

| **Mazzini Defines Nationality**

No political force in the nineteenth century was stronger than nationalism. It replaced dynastic political loyalty with loyalty based on ethnicity. In 1835 the Italian nationalist and patriot Giuseppe Mazzini (1805–1872) explained his understanding of the concept. Note how he combined a generally democratic view of politics with a religious concept of the divine destiny of nations.

• What specific qualities of a people does Mazzini associate with nationalism? How and why does Mazzini relate nationalism to divine purposes? How does this view of nationality relate to the goals of liberal freedom? How does it compare to other perspectives on nationalism and independence movements, for example, "Parnell Calls for Home Rule for Ireland" and, "Herzl Calls for the Establishment of a Jewish State" in this chapter?.

The essential characteristics of a nationality are common ideas, common principles and a common purpose. A nation is an association of those who are brought together by language, by given geographical conditions or by the role assigned them by history, who acknowledge the same principles and who march together to the conquest of a single definite goal under the rule of a uniform body of law.

The life of a nation consists in harmonious activity (that is, the employment of all individual abilities and energies comprised within the association) towards this single goal. …

But nationality means even more than this. Nationality also consists in the share of mankind's labors which God assigns to a people. This mission is the task which a people must perform to the end that the Divine Idea shall be realized in this world; it is the work which gives a people its rights as a member of Mankind; it is the baptismal rite which endows a people with its own character and its rank in the brotherhood of nations. …

Nationality depends for its very existence upon its sacredness within and beyond its borders.

If nationality is to be inviolable for all, friends and foes alike, it must be regarded inside a country as holy, like a religion, and outside a country as a grave mission. It is necessary too that the ideas arising within a country grow steadily, as part of the general law of Humanity which is the source of all nationality. It is necessary that these ideas be shown to other lands in their beauty and purity, free from any alien mixture, from any slavish fears, from any skeptical hesitancy, strong and active; embracing in their evolution every aspect and manifestation of the life of the nation. These ideas, a necessary component in the order of universal destiny, must retain their originality even as they enter harmoniously into mankind's general progress.

The people must be the basis of nationality; its logically derived and vigorously applied principles its means; the strength of all its strength; the improvement of the life of all and the happiness of the greatest possible number its results; and the accomplishment of the task assigned to it by God its goal. This is what we mean by nationality.

From *Absolutism to Revolution, 1648–1848*, 2nd ed., Herbert H. Rowen, ed. Copyright © 1969. Reprinted by permission of Prentice Hall, Upper Saddle River NJ

Early-Nineteenth-Century Political Liberalism

In the present-day United States, the word *liberal* carries meanings and connotations that have little or nothing to do with its significance for nineteenth-century Europeans. European conservatives of the last century saw liberals as more radical than they actually were; present-day Americans often think of nineteenth-century liberals as more conservative than they were. In any case, the term *liberal* as used in present-day American political rhetoric has virtually no relationship to its nineteenth-century counterpart.

POLITICS

European **liberalism** derived from the Enlightenment, the example of English liberties, and the so-called principles of 1789 as embodied in the French *Declaration of the Rights of Man and Citizen*. Liberal political figures sought to establish a framework of legal equality, religious toleration, and freedom of the press. They sought to limit the arbitrary power of the government against the persons and property of individual citizens. They generally believed that the legitimacy of government emanated from the freely given consent of the governed expressed through elected representative or parliamentary bodies. Most important, free government required that state or crown ministers be responsible to the representatives of the nation rather than to the monarch.

These goals were limited. Such responsible government, however, existed in none of the major European countries in 1815. Even in Great Britain the ministers were at least as responsible to the monarch as to the House of Commons. The people who espoused these changes in government tended to be those who were excluded from the existing political processes, but whose wealth and education made them believe

A CONVENTION OF HEMMERS AND STITCHERS HELD AT LYNN, FEB 28, FOR ADOPTING A LIST OF PRICES; MRS. E. HALL, PRESIDING.—(See page 284.)

◀ **Female Activism.** Women's gatherings, like the first women's rights convention in Seneca Falls in 1848 and this meeting of strikers in Lynn in 1860, were indicators of widespread female activism.

Lynn Museum.

such exclusion was unjustified. Liberals were often academics, members of the learned professions, and people involved in the rapidly expanding commercial and manufacturing sectors. They believed in and were products of the career open to talent. The existing monarchical and aristocratic regimes often failed to recognize sufficiently their new status and to provide for their economic and professional interests.

Although European liberals wanted broader political participation, they were not Democrats. Second only to their hostility to the privileged aristocracies was their general contempt for the lower, unpropertied classes. Liberals transformed the eighteenth-century concept of aristocratic liberty into a new concept of privilege based on wealth and property instead of birth. By midcentury this widely shared attitude meant that throughout Europe, liberals had separated themselves from both the rural and the urban working class. In the first half of the nineteenth century political liberals did not generally support the extension of political rights to women, but liberal political principles provided women with strong arguments to do so, as seen for example in the *Declaration of Female Independence* issued by the Seneca Falls convention in the United States in 1848.

ECONOMICS

The economic goals of the liberals also furthered their separation from the working class. Here, the Enlightenment and the economic thought deriving from Adam Smith set the pattern. The manufacturers of Great Britain, the landed and manufacturing middle class of France, and the commercial interests of Germany and Italy wanted to be able to manufacture and sell goods freely. They thus favored the removal of international tariffs as well as internal barriers to trade. To that end, liberals across the Continent and those who imitated them outside of Europe favored the rapid construction of railways from the 1830s onward.

European economic liberals opposed the old paternalistic legislation that established wages and labor practices by government regulation or by guild privileges. Labor was simply one more commodity to be bought and sold freely. Liberals sought an economic structure in which people were free to use their talents and property to enrich themselves. The liberals contended that this would lead to more goods and services for everyone at lower prices. Economic liberty was to provide the basis for material progress.

The economic goals of European liberals found many followers outside Europe among groups that favored the expansion of free trade, new transport systems, and a free market in labor. In the United States people of this outlook often attacked slavery as an inefficient, paternalistic institution. In Latin America political liberals sought to remove paternalistic legislation that had protected Native Americans during the centuries of the Spanish Empire.

RELATIONSHIP OF NATIONALISM AND LIBERALISM

Nationalism was not necessarily or logically linked to liberalism, and some conservative nationalists, for example, ignored the rights of national minorities. Liberalism and nationalism, however, were often complementary. Behind the concept of a people joined naturally together by the bonds of common language, customs, culture, and history lurked the idea of popular sovereignty. The idea of the career open to talent could be applied to suppressed national groups who were not permitted to realize their cultural or political potential. The efficient government and administration required by commerce and industry would mean replacing the small German and Italian states with larger political units. Moreover, nationalist groups in one country could gain the sympathy of liberals in other nations by espousing representative government and political liberty.

LIBERALISM AND NATIONALISM IN MODERN WORLD HISTORY

The wars of the French Revolution in Europe had demonstrated by the early nineteenth century that the ideals of political liberalism could easily spread across dynastic borders. In time those liberal ideals as well as those of nationalism would spread around the globe. It is for this reason that what began as a European development is so important not just for Europe but also for global history. The concept of the rights of man and citizen could be used during the wars of independence in Latin America to challenge Spanish government. By the close of the nineteenth century those same ideals could be turned against the colonial government that Europeans imposed on Africa and Asia. Furthermore, the belief that people should have the right to govern themselves would inspire the settlers who spread across both the United States and Canada as well as those who came to live in Australia and New Zealand. Similarly, the belief that individual ethnic groups should constitute independent nations became a major political idea whereby peoples living under European colonial government during the late nineteenth and even more importantly the twentieth century would challenge the right of Europeans and later Americans to govern them or to dominate their lives informally through economic power. Thus the political developments in Europe during the early nineteenth century would produce a profound impact around the globe during the next century.

Efforts to Liberalize Early-Nineteenth-Century European Political Structures

European nations certainly did not move toward liberal political structures rapidly or without considerable conflict. Indeed after the Congress of Vienna most conservatives hoped that they had established walls against liberal advances. Three examples will indicate the different experiences that different European liberals confronted early in the nineteenth century.

RUSSIA: THE DECEMBRIST REVOLT OF 1825 AND THE AUTOCRACY OF NICHOLAS I

In the process of driving Napoleon's army across Europe and then occupying defeated France, many officers in the Russian army were introduced to the ideas of the French Revolution and the Enlightenment. They realized how economically backward and politically stifled Russia was. Under these conditions, groups within the officer corps formed secret societies. These societies were small and divided in their goals; they agreed only that the government of Russia must change. Sometime during 1825 they seem to have decided to carry out a coup d'état in 1826.

Other events intervened. In late November 1825 Tsar Alexander I suddenly and unexpectedly died. His death created two crises. The first was a dynastic one: Alexander had no direct heir. His brother Constantine stood next in line to the throne. However, Constantine, who was the commander of Russian forces in Poland, had renounced any claim to be tsar. Through a series of secret instructions made public only after his death, Alexander had named his younger brother, Nicholas (r. 1825–1855), as the new tsar. Once Alexander was dead, the legality of these instructions became uncertain. Constantine acknowledged Nicholas as tsar, and Nicholas acknowledged Constantine. This family muddle continued for about three weeks, during which Russia actually had no ruler, to the astonishment of Europe. Then, in early December, the army command reported to Nicholas the existence of a conspiracy among certain officers. Able to wait no longer, Nicholas had himself declared tsar.

The second crisis now unfolded—a plot by junior officers to rally the troops under their command to the cause of reform. On December 26, 1825, the army was to take the oath of allegiance to Nicholas, who was less popular than Constantine and was regarded as more conservative. Nearly all of the regiments did so. But the Moscow regiment, whose chief officers, surprisingly, were not secret society members, marched into the Senate Square in Saint Petersburg and refused to swear allegiance. Rather, they called for Constantine and a constitution. Attempts to settle the situation peacefully failed. Late in the afternoon Nicholas ordered cavalry and artillery to attack the insurgents. Five of the plotters were executed, and over one hundred other officers were exiled to Siberia.

The immediate result of the revolt was the crushing of liberalism as even a moderate political influence in Russia. Nicholas I also manifested extreme conservatism in foreign affairs. Russia under Nicholas became the policeman of Europe, ever ready to provide troops to suppress liberal and nationalist movements. Except for a modest experiment early in the twentieth century tsarist Russia would never know genuinely liberal political structures.

▲ **Decembrist Revolt.** When the Moscow regiment refused to swear allegiance to Nicholas, he ordered the cavalry and artillery to attack them. Although a total failure, the Decembrist Revolt came to symbolize the yearnings of all Russian liberals in the 19th century for a constitutional government.

The Insurrection of the Decembrists at Senate Square, St. Petersburg on 14th December, 1825 (w/c on paper) by Russian School (19th century). Private Collection/Bridgeman Art Library.

REVOLUTION IN FRANCE (1830)

In 1824 Louis XVIII (r. 1814–1824), the Bourbon restored to the throne of France by the Congress of Vienna, died. He was succeeded by his brother, Charles X (r. 1824–1830). The new king considered himself a monarch by divine right and he also moved to restore lands that the French aristocrats had lost during the revolution. He also pressed other conservative measures through the Chamber of Deputies. Opposition soon developed. After elections in 1827 Charles began to govern somewhat less conservatively, but French liberals wanted a genuinely constitutional regime. Matters came to a head in 1829 when Charles abandoned efforts to accommodate liberals and appointed an ultraroyalist ministry, but his efforts backfired.

In 1830 Charles X called for new elections, in which the liberals scored a stunning victory. Instead of attempting to accommodate the new Chamber of Deputies, the king and his ministers decided to undertake a royalist seizure of power. In June and July 1830 the ministry had sent a naval expedition against Algeria. On July 9 reports of its victory, and the consequent foundation of a French empire in North Africa, reached Paris. On July 25, 1830, under the euphoria of this foreign diversion, Charles X issued the Four Ordinances, which restricted freedom of the press, dissolved the recently elected Chamber of Deputies, and called for new elections under a franchise restricted to the wealthiest people in the country.

Liberal newspapers immediately called on the nation to reject the monarch's actions. The laboring populace of Paris, burdened since 1827 by an economic downturn, took to the

Liberty Leading the People. by Eugene Delacroix is a famous ➤ evocation of the Revolution of 1830.
Giraudon/Art Resource, N.Y.

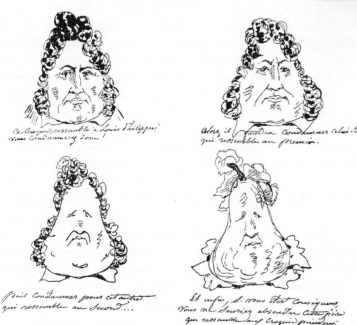

▲ **Cartoons of Louis Philippe.** Despite laws forbidding disrespect to the government, political cartoonists had a field day with Louis Philippe. Here, an artist emphasizes the king's resemblance to a pear and in the process attacks restraints on freedom of the press.
Corbis-Bettmann.

streets and erected barricades. The king called out troops, and over 1,800 people died during the ensuing battles in the city. On August 2 Charles X abdicated and left France for exile in England. The liberals in the Chamber of Deputies named a new ministry composed of constitutional monarchists. They proclaimed Louis Philippe (r. 1830–1848), the Duke of

Orléans, the head of the liberal branch of the royal family, the new monarch. Under what became known as the **July Monarchy**, Louis Philippe was called the king of the French rather than of France. The king had to cooperate with the Chamber of Deputies; he could not dispense with laws on his own authority. The revolutionary tricolor replaced the white flag of the Bourbons. The Charter, or constitution, was regarded as embodying the rights of the people rather than a concession granted by the monarch. Catholicism was recognized only as the religion of the majority of the people, not the official religion. Censorship was abolished. The franchise, though still restricted, was extended. Socially, however, the Revolution of 1830 proved quite conservative. The landed oligarchy retained its economic, political, and social influence. Money became the path to power and influence in the government. There was much corruption. Most important, the liberal monarchy displayed scant sympathy for the lower and working classes.

THE GREAT REFORM BILL IN BRITAIN (1832)

The passage of the **Great Reform Bill**, which became law in 1832, was the result of events different from those that occurred on the Continent. In Britain the forces of conservatism and reform compromised with each other. As a result, during the century Great Britain became for most people the exemplary liberal state not only of Europe but also of the world.

English determination to maintain the union with Ireland caused the first step in the reform process. England's relationship to Ireland was not unlike that of Russia's to Poland or Austria's to Hungary. The Act of Union in 1800 between England

and Ireland suppressed the separate Irish parliament. The Irish now sent representatives to the British parliament at Westminster, but only Protestant Irishmen could be elected to represent overwhelmingly Catholic Ireland.

During the 1820s, under the leadership of Daniel O'Connell (1775–1847), Irish nationalists organized the Catholic Association to agitate for **Catholic emancipation**, as the movement for legal rights for Roman Catholics was known. In 1828 O'Connell was elected to Parliament but could not legally take his seat. The British ministry of the Duke of Wellington (1769–1852) realized that henceforth Ireland might elect a predominantly Catholic delegation to Parliament. If they were not seated, civil war might erupt. Consequently, in 1829 Wellington and Robert Peel (1788–1850) steered the Catholic Emancipation Act through Parliament. Roman Catholics could now become members of Parliament. This measure, together with the repeal in 1828 of restrictions against Protestant nonconformists, ended the monopoly held by members of the Church of England on British political life.

Catholic emancipation alienated many of Wellington's Tory supporters. In the election of 1830 many supporters of parliamentary reform were returned to Parliament. Even some Tories believed that parliamentary reform was necessary because they had concluded that Catholic emancipation could have been passed only by a corrupt House of Commons. The Wellington ministry soon fell. The Tories were badly divided, and King William IV (r. 1830–1837) turned to the Whigs under the leadership of Earl Grey (1764–1845) to form a government.

The Whig ministry soon presented the House of Commons with a major reform bill that had two broad goals. The first was to replace "rotten" boroughs, which had few voters, with representatives for the previously unrepresented manufacturing districts and cities. The second was to increase the number of voters in England and Wales. In 1831 the House of Commons narrowly defeated the bill. Grey called for a new election, in which a majority in favor of the bill was returned to the Commons. The House of Commons passed the reform bill, but the House of Lords rejected it. Mass meetings were held throughout the country, and riots broke out in several cities. Finally, William IV agreed to create enough new peers to give a third reform bill a majority in the House of Lords. Under this pressure, the measure became law in 1832.

The Great Reform Act expanded the size of the English electorate, but it was not a democratic measure. The electorate was increased by over 200,000 persons, or by almost 50 percent. The basis of voting, however, remained a property qualification. Some working-class voters actually lost the vote when their old franchise rights were abolished. New urban boroughs gave the growing cities a voice in the House of Commons. Yet the passage of the Reform Act did not, as it was once thought, constitute the triumph of the middle-class interest in England. For every new urban electoral district, a new rural district was also drawn. It was expected that the aristocracy would dominate the rural elections.

Although passed with much turmoil and conflict, the Great Reform Act established the foundations for long-term political stability in Britain. During the 1840s a major working-class political movement known as **Chartism** would bring the demands of industrial workers into the political process. Despite the tensions created by Chartism, British political structures maintained themselves. Throughout the second half of the nineteenth century Great Britain continued to symbolize the confident liberal state. A large body of ideas emphasizing competition and individualism was accepted by the members of all classes. Even the leaders of trade unions during these years asked only to receive some of the fruits of prosperity and to prove their own social respectability. Parliament itself continued to provide an institution that permitted the absorption of new groups and interests into the existing political processes.

The most important example of the opening of parliamentary processes was the Second Reform Act passed by a Conservative government in 1867. It increased the number of voters from approximately 1,430,000 to 2,470,000. Britain had taken a major step toward democracy. Benjamin Disraeli (1804–1881), who led the Conservatives in the House of Commons, thought significant portions of the working class would eventually support Conservative candidates who were responsive to social issues. He also thought the growing suburban middle class would become more conservative.

Gladstone and Disraeli   The election of 1868, however, which followed the Second Reform Act, dashed Disraeli's hopes. William Gladstone (1809–1898) became the new prime minister. His ministry of 1868–1874 witnessed the culmination of classical British liberalism. Gladstone introduced competitive examinations into the civil service, abolished the purchase of army officers' commissions, and introduced the secret ballot. He opened Oxford and Cambridge universities to students of all religious denominations and, by the Education Act of 1870, made the British government responsible for establishing and running elementary schools, which had been supported by the various churches.

The liberal policy of creating popular support for the nation by extending political liberty and reforming abuses had its conservative counterpart in concern about social reform. Disraeli succeeded Gladstone as prime minister in 1874. Whereas Gladstone looked to individualism, free trade, and competition to solve social problems, Disraeli believed the state should protect weaker citizens. In his view, paternalistic legislation would alleviate class antagonism. His most important measures were the Public Health Act of 1875, which consolidated and extended previous sanitary legislation, and the Artisans Dwelling Act of 1875, through which the government became actively involved in providing housing for the working class.

◀ **A House of Commons Debate.** William Ewart Gladstone, standing on the right, is attacking Benjamin Disraeli, who sits with legs crossed and arms folded. Gladstone served in the British Parliament from the 1830s through the 1890s. Four times the Liberal Party prime minister, he was responsible for guiding major reforms through Parliament. Disraeli regarded as the founder of modern British conservatism, served as prime minister from 1874 to 1880.

Mary Evans Picture Library.

The Irish Question Ireland remained a major issue for the British government. From the late 1860s onward, Irish nationalists had sought to achieve **home rule** for Ireland, by which they meant more Irish control of local government. Their demands of the British government very much resembled the demands that first the Hungarians and then the Czechs made toward the Habsburg government, which will be considered later in this chapter. The Irish, like the Hungarians and Czechs in the Habsburg Empire, proved a profoundly disruptive force in British politics.

The leader of the Irish movement for home rule was Charles Stewart Parnell (1846–1891). (See Document, "Parnell Calls for Home Rule for Ireland.") By 1885 Parnell had organized eighty-five Irish members of the House of Commons into a tightly disciplined party that often voted as a bloc. In the election of 1885 the Irish Party emerged holding the balance of power between the English Liberals and Conservatives. The Irish could decide which party would take office. In December 1885 Gladstone announced support for home rule for Ireland, and Parnell gave his votes to the formation of a Liberal ministry. However, the issue split the Liberal Party. In 1886 a group known as the Liberal Unionists joined with the Conservatives to defeat Gladstone's Home Rule Bill. Gladstone called for a new election, which the Liberals lost. They remained permanently divided. The new Conservative ministry of Lord Salisbury (1830–1903) attempted to reconcile the Irish to the English government through public works and administrative reform. The policy had only marginal success.

▲ **Charles Stewart Parnell (1846–1891).** The Irish statesman entered the British Parliament in 1875, becoming leader of the Home Rule Federation in 1879.

Getty Images, Inc./Houlton Archive photos.

Since 1800, Ireland had been governed as part of Great Britain, sending representatives to the British parliament in Westminster. Throughout the century, there had been tension and violent conflict between the Irish and their English governors. Agitation for home rule whereby the Irish would directly control many of their own affairs reached a peak in the 1880s. Charles Stewart Parnell was the chief leader for the cause of Irish nationalism during that decade. His program at the time was home rule for Ireland, by which he meant Irish administration of Irish domestic affairs in the context of a continuing ill-defined union with England. In 1885, he made a speech in which he outlined the resentments the Irish had felt toward the English since the Act of Union of 1800. He also drew direct parallels between the relationship of Ireland to England and that of Hungary to Austria. The efforts toward achieving home rule failed during the nineteenth century.

◆ How does Parnell say the Act of Union affected Irish sentiment toward England? What parallel does he draw with Hungary and Austria? Why might Parnell be regarded as a moderate nationalist?

It is not possible for human intelligence to forecast the future in the matter; but we can point to this—we can point to the fact that under 85 years of parliamentary connection with England, Ireland has become intensely disloyal and intensely disaffected; that notwithstanding the Whig policy of so-called conciliation, alternative conciliation and coercion... that disaffection has broadened, deepened and intensified from day to day. Am I not, then, entitled to assume that one of the roots of this disaffection and feeling of disloyalty is the assumption by England of the management of our affairs. It is admitted that the present system can't go on, and what are you going to put in its place? My advice to English statesmen considering this question would be this—trust the Irish people altogether or trust them not at all. ... Whatever chance the English rulers may have of drawing to themselves the affection of the Irish people lies in destroying the abominable system of legislative union between the two countries by conceding fully and freely to Ireland their right to manage her own affairs. It is impossible for us to give guarantees, but we can point to the past; we can show that the record of English rule is a constant series of steps from bad to worse, that the condition of English power is more insecure and more unstable at the present moment than it has ever been. We can point to the example of other countries; of Austria and of Hungary—to the fact that Hungary having been conceded self-government became one of the strongest factors in the Austrian empire. We can show the powers that have been freely conceded in the colonies [such as Canada and Australia have led to loyalty]... I am confident that the English statesman who is great enough... to carry out these teachings... to give Ireland full legislative liberty, full power to manage her own domestic concerns will be regarded in the future by his countrymen as one who has removed the greatest peril to the English empire—a peril, I firmly believe, which if not removed will find some day... an opportunity of revenging itself to the destruction of the British empire for the misfortunes, the oppressions, and the misgovernment of our country.

From Charles Stewart Parnell, "Speech at Wicklow," October 5, 1885, as quoted in Raymond Phineas Stearns, *Pageant of Europe: Sources and Selections from the Renaissance to the Present Day* (New York: Harcourt, Brace and Company, 1948), pp. 634–635.

In 1892 Gladstone returned to power and sponsored a second Home Rule Bill that passed the House of Commons but was defeated in the House of Lords. With the failure of this bill, further action on the Irish question was suspended until a Liberal ministry passed the third Home Rule Bill in the summer of 1914. However, the implementation of home rule was suspended for the duration of World War I.

As already noted, the Irish question affected British politics much the way that the nationalities problem affected Austria. Normal British domestic issues could not be adequately addressed because of the political divisions created by Ireland. The split of the Liberal Party hurt the cause of further social and political reform. The people who could agree about reforms could not agree on Ireland, and Ireland seemed more important. Because the two traditional parties failed to deal with the social questions, by the turn of the century a newly organized Labour Party began to fill the vacuum.

1848: YEAR OF REVOLUTIONS IN EUROPE

In 1848 a series of liberal and nationalistic revolutions and revolts spread across Europe. No single factor caused this general revolutionary groundswell; rather, similar conditions existed in several countries. Severe food shortages had prevailed since 1846 due to poor harvests. The commercial and industrial economy was in recession, with widespread unemployment. However, the dynamic for change in 1848 originated not with the working classes but with the political liberals, who were generally drawn from the middle classes. Throughout the Continent liberals were pushing for more representative governments, civil liberty, and unregulated economic life.

MAP 24–1 Centers of Revolution in 1848–1849. The revolution that toppled the July monarchy in Paris in 1848 soon spread to Austria and many of the German and Italian states. Yet by the end of 1849, most of these uprisings had been suppressed.

To put additional pressure on their governments, the liberals began to appeal for the support of the urban working classes, even though the goals of the two groups were different. The working classes sought improved employment and better working conditions rather than political reform for its own sake. The liberals refused to follow political revolution with social reform and thus isolated themselves from their temporary working-class allies. Once separated from potential mass support, the liberal revolutions became an easy prey to the armies of reactionary governments. As a result, the revolutions of 1848 failed to establish genuinely liberal or national states.

What are known in European history as the Revolutions of 1848 were confined to the Continent, where the results were important for the individual nation-states. In France the monarchy of Louis Philippe was overthrown and briefly replaced by a republic. In 1851 the republic was in turn overthrown in a military coup led by Louis Napoleon, a nephew of the first Napoleon. Thereafter Louis Napoleon created the Second Empire and took the title of Napoleon III. In Prussia and the Austrian Empire short-lived revolutions brought political liberals and nationalists to the fore, but in each case those revolutions were suppressed by the military. The same was true of efforts by Italian nationalists to thrust off Austrian rule of Italy.

From the standpoint of world history, however, the chief importance of the failed liberal and national Revolutions of 1848 was the emergence on the European continent of strongly conservative governments that would dominate the scene for the next quarter century. The turmoil of 1848 through 1850 ended the era of liberal revolution that had begun in 1789. Liberals and nationalists had discovered that rational argument and local insurrections would not help them to achieve their goals. The working class also adopted new tactics and organization. The era of the riot and urban insurrection was ending. In the future, workers would turn to trade unions and political parties to achieve their political and social goals. Finally, after the Revolutions of 1848, the political initiative in Europe passed for a time to the conservative political groups.

The defeat of liberal political forces in 1848 and the triumph of conservative powers also influenced the modernization of Japan. Within a few years Japan would emerge from its long self-imposed isolation. After the Meiji Restoration the new leaders of Japan looked to European examples of successful modern nations. The nation they would most clearly copy was the conservative, militaristic Germany that emerged after the defeat of the liberals of 1848.

Testing the New American Republic
TOWARD SECTIONAL CONFLICT

While the nations of Western Europe very slowly embraced political liberalism, the United States of America was continuing its bold republican political experiment. By the first quarter of the century, however, serious sectional tensions had arisen, the most important of which related to the presence of black slavery in the Southern states.

The Constitutional Convention of 1788 had debated the sectional difference in a dispute over what proportion of the slave population, if any, would be counted in determining how many seats the Southern states were allotted in the House of Representatives. A compromise allowed the slave-holding states to count three fifths of their slaves when calculating their population for representation in Congress. The Constitution also forbade any federal attempt to prevent the importation of slaves before 1808. Between 1788 and 1808 thousands of slaves were imported into the United States.

The westward movement, however, meant that slavery could not permanently be ignored. The Ordinance of 1787, passed by Congress under the Articles of Confederation, had prohibited slavery in the Northwest Territory, which embraced the future states of Ohio, Indiana, Illinois, Michigan, and Wisconsin. Territory south of the Ohio River and beyond the Mississippi River

Textile Mill. In New England, as in Europe, textile manufacturing was the first of the highly mechanized industries. American and European textile mills closely resembled each other because those in America had been copied from European and most particularly English technology.

The Granger Collection, N.Y.

was, however, open to slavery, and there it spread. By 1820 the number of slave and free states was evenly divided; this meant an equal number of senators from slave and free states. That year, Missouri was admitted as a slave state and Maine as a free one. It was also decided that in the future no slave states would be carved out of land north of the southern border of Missouri. For the time being, this Missouri Compromise ended congressional debate over slavery. Nonetheless, the economies of the North and the South were rapidly diverging.

Northern Economic Development Family farms, free labor, commerce, and early industrialization in textiles characterized the economy of the Northern states. Northern farmers tended primarily to produce foodstuffs for their local communities. The farms were relatively small and worked by families. Farm laborers were free. Similarly, free laborers worked in the towns, on the ships, and in the factories of the North. The political spokesmen for the North tended to favor tariffs to protect their young industries from cheaper foreign competition. In this favoring of tariffs, many Americans whose political views otherwise often resembled European liberals differed from their European counterparts.

The North was the site of the earliest textile factories in the United States. Samuel Slater had established the first textile mill in Rhode Island in 1790. He had learned how to manufacture textiles in the new mills of industrializing Great Britain. His transfer of that technology to America illustrates how important British and European advances were transported to the United States. Much of the early industrialization of the

United States depended on such technological transfers. By the second decade of the nineteenth century the North had hundreds of cotton factories. These mills used cotton that was produced in the South, but most Southern cotton was sold overseas, mainly to the growing British textile industry.

During the second quarter of the century innovations in transportation led to the fuller integration of different parts of the Northern economy. Canals were built to link the major rivers with manufacturing and agricultural markets. The most famous was the Erie Canal, which connected the Hudson River to the Great Lakes. Other canals linked the Great Lakes to the Ohio River. Major efforts were undertaken to make the Ohio, Mississippi, and Missouri Rivers navigable, which allowed steamboats to transport goods. But by the late 1840s, in America as in Europe, the major transportation innovation was the railroad. Most of the railways linked the Northeast and the West and fostered the commercial agriculture of the Midwest. Its products were sold in the Northeast and exported from Northern ports. Hence, the development of east–west railways undermined the older river-based trade routes along the Ohio and down the Mississippi. Few major lines ran north and south, so former ties between the sections based on the rivers weakened. The building of the early railways also aided the development of the Northern coal and iron industries. The further expansion of railways at midcentury caused new sectional tensions, as it became clear the railways could open for settlement vast territories and could thus also open a national debate over the future of slavery. That prospect sharpened the sectional debate and led to civil war.

Rivers, canals, and railways allowed the upper Midwest to develop into a rich area for agriculture. In this sense much of the Northern economy was as rural and agricultural as the Southern. What most distinguished the two regions was free versus slave labor. The Southern economy depended on slavery and could expand only if slavery were allowed to expand as well.

The Southern Economy   The overwhelmingly rural economy of the American South was dependent on cotton and slavery. In those respects, the Southern economy resembled the economies of many Latin American countries, which were based on exporting a single crop or natural resource and on slave labor. The South had to export goods, primarily raw cotton, either to the North or to Europe, primarily to Great Britain, to maintain its standard of living.

Cotton was king. The invention of the cotton gin by Eli Whitney (1765–1825) in 1793 made cotton cultivation much more profitable because the seed no longer had to be laboriously picked out of the new cotton by hand. The industrial revolution in textiles kept cotton prices high, and the expansion in world population kept the demand for cotton cloth steady. The South profited from growing the cotton, New England

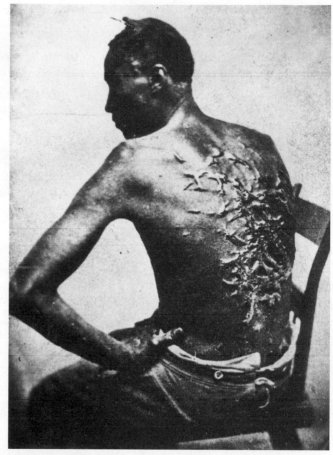

Scars of Slavery This Louisiana slave named Gordon was photographed in 1863 after he had escaped to Union lines during the Civil War. He bears the permanent scars of the violence that lay at the heart of the slave system. Few slaves were so brutally marked, but all lived with the threat of beatings if they failed to obey.
National Archives and Records Administrations.

from shipping it, and other parts of the North from supplying the manufactured goods the South needed. The South had virtually no incentive to diversify its agriculture.

Slavery in the American South   Slavery was abolished in the North by the early nineteenth century largely in response to the egalitarian values of the American Revolution. In any case, slavery had never been fundamental to the Northern economy. But in the South, the expansion of the cotton empire in the Mississippi Delta in the early nineteenth century gave slavery a new lease on life. Although most Southern families never owned slaves and relatively few slave owners had possessed more than a few slaves, the institution of slavery survived for many reasons. For one, it was economically viable, and no one could devise a way politically or socially acceptable to white Southerners to abolish it. No less important was the strong commitment to the protection of private property, which included slaves,

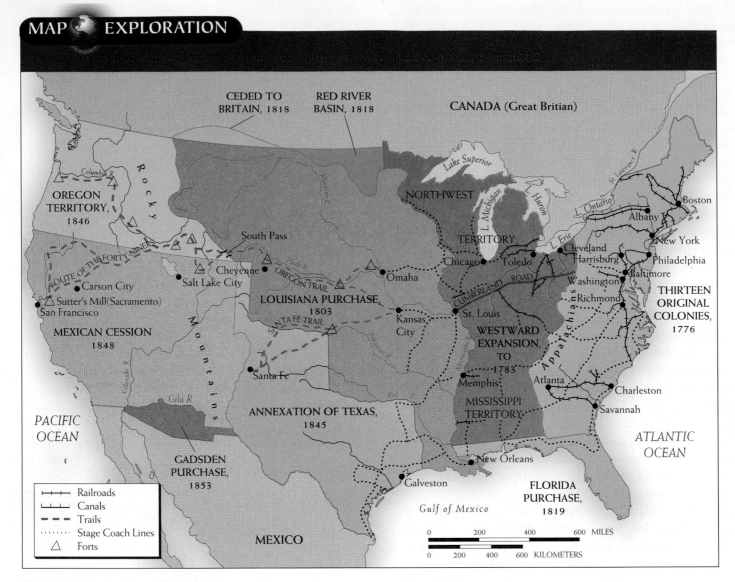

MAP 24–2 Nineteenth-Century North America. During the nineteenth century the United States expanded across the entire North American continent. The revolutionary settlement had provided most of the land east of the Mississippi. The single largest addition thereafter was the Louisiana Purchase of 1803. The annexation of Texas, and later the Mexican Cession following the Mexican War, added the major Southwestern territories. The borders of the Oregon Territory were settled through long, difficult negotiations with Great Britain.

throughout American society in both the North and the South. Perhaps the most basic reason for the endurance of slavery after the early nineteenth century, however, was racist thinking that saw blacks as fundamentally inferior to whites. Such thinking was not peculiar to the South, but it functioned there as one more argument against abolishing slavery.

What was the life of an American slave like? All American slaves were nonwhite, the descendants of Africans who had been forcibly captured and shipped in the most wretched of conditions to the United States (see Chapter 17). Despite much miscegenation among Africans and their white slave

owners and Native Americans, the various slave codes defined as black virtually anyone who had African antecedents. Slaves were regarded as chattel property; that is, they could be sold, given away, or even gambled away like any other piece of property. They had no recourse to law or constitutional protections and could be, and often were, treated badly by their masters. Whipping and beating were permitted. State laws protected slaves from extreme violence but were laxly enforced; slaves lived with no serious protection from the law or legal authorities. Their standard of living was generally poor. Although owners wanted to see their slave investments reproduce themselves, slaves suffered from overwork and from diseases associated with poor nutrition, sanitation, and housing.

Slaves worked primarily in the fields, where they plowed, hoed, and harvested cotton, rice, sugar, tobacco, or corn. They were usually organized into work gangs supervised by white overseers. This work was, like all farming, seasonal, but during planting or harvest seasons, labor would persist from sunrise to sunset. Children would work in the fields as helpers. Older or more privileged slaves might work in the house, cleaning, cooking, or taking care of children.

Recent scholarship has emphasized how the slave communities helped preserve the family life and inner personalities of the slaves. Some elements of African culture persisted in the slave communities. African legends were passed on orally. Religion proved extraordinarily important. Slaves also adopted for their own cultural needs the Old Testament stories of the Jews' liberation from Egypt. They also often combined elements of African religion with evangelical Protestantism. Yet despite these efforts to preserve a sense of community and even of family, marriages and family lives of slaves had no legal recognition. The integrity of the slave family could be violated at the master's whim or changing economic circumstances. White masters and their sons often sexually exploited black slave women. Because slaves were property, they could be sold for profit or transported when the owner moved to a different region. Consequently, families could be, and were, separated by sale or perhaps after an owner's death. Many young children were reared and cared for by other slaves to whom they were not related. In a world of white dominance, the institutions, customs, and religions of the slave community were the only means black slaves had to protect the autonomy of their own personalities.

THE ABOLITIONIST MOVEMENT

During the 1830s a militant antislavery movement emerged in the North. Its leaders and followers refused to accept what they regarded as the moral compromise of living in a nation that tolerated slavery. Abolitionists such as William Lloyd Garrison, editor of the *Liberator*, condemned the Union and the Constitution as structures that perpetuated slavery. Former slaves who had escaped slavery, such as Frederick Douglass and Sojourner Truth, and freeborn black Americans, such as Daniel A. Payne, also joined the cause. (See Document, "Daniel A. Payne Denounces American Slavery.") The antislavery movement, which was initially only one of many American reform movements, gained new adherents during the 1840s as the question of extending slavery into the new territories came to the fore in 1847 toward the end of the Mexican War (1846–1848). That military victory added significant new territory in the Southwest and California, in addition to Texas, which had been annexed in 1845. Through negotiations with

Britain the United States also acquired the vast Oregon Territory in the Northwest in 1846 (see Map 24–2).

Victory in the Mexican War opened debate on the extension of slavery into the huge new territory it created. Southerners feared that the changing climate of national debate and the opening of territories where slavery might be prohibited would give the South a minority status and thus eventually overturn its political and social culture. Northerners came to believe that a slave-power conspiracy controlled the federal government. The Compromise of 1850 temporarily restored political calm and stability and reassured the South; but many Northerners came to believe that the compromise only demonstrated the strength of the slave-power conspiracy in Washington.

In 1854 the introduction of the Kansas-Nebraska Bill renewed the formal national political debate over slavery and galvanized the antislavery forces. The principle of the bill, introduced by Stephen A. Douglas (1813–1861), was that of popular sovereignty. The people of each new territory would decide whether slavery was to be permitted within its borders. Douglas was thus willing to repeal the Missouri Compromise, which had prohibited slavery in most of the Louisiana Territory. Popular sovereignty meant that every newly organized territory had to debate slavery. In 1854 the new Republican Party was organized largely in opposition to the Kansas-Nebraska Bill. Not everyone, however, was willing just to argue. For example, John Brown went to Kansas, where armed conflict had already broken out, and carried out virtual guerrilla warfare against slaveholding settlers. During 1854 "Bleeding Kansas" was in a state of civil war.

In 1857, in the Dred Scott decision, the Supreme Court effectively repealed the Missouri Compromise by declaring that Congress could not prohibit slavery in the territories. The decision further declared that slaves did not become free by living in free states and that slaves did not have rights that others were bound to respect. For radical antislavery Northerners, the decision raised the most serious questions about the morality of the Union itself, and it demonstrated again a Southern conspiracy to protect slavery. Thereafter, slavery dominated national political debate.

In 1859 John Brown seized the federal arsenal at Harpers Ferry, Virginia, as part of an effort to foment a possible slave rebellion. He was captured, tried, and hanged, further increasing sectional polarization. Radical Southerners feared more than ever a Northern conspiracy to attack the institution of slavery, while Northern radicals feared that the South would use the federal government to protect slavery. Thus the politics of both sections became radicalized.

The Republican Party had become the party that opposed slavery, although most Republicans did not favor outright abolition. In 1858 Abraham Lincoln (1809–1865) ran against Stephen Douglas for the U.S. Senate in Illinois. Lincoln lost but made a national reputation for himself in the debates leading up to the election. In 1860 Lincoln, the Republican candidate,

ROAD TO SELF-GOVERNMENT

The British government, operating in the more liberal political climate following the first Reform Act (1832), was determined to avoid another North American revolution. Consequently, it sent the Earl of Durham (1792–1840) to Canada with extensive powers to make reforms. In 1839 his *Report on the Affairs of British North America* advocated responsible government for Canada. Durham contended that both Canadian provinces should be united into one political unit. He thought that such political unification would eventually lead to a thoroughly English culture throughout Canada which would overwhelm the French influence in Quebec. He also believed that most Canadian affairs should be in the hands of a Canadian legislature and that only foreign policy and defense should remain under British control. In effect, Durham wanted Canadians generally to govern themselves, so that English culture would dominate. His policy was carried out in the Canada Act of 1840, which gave the nation a single legislature composed of two houses.

The Durham *Report* established the political pattern that the British government would, to a greater or lesser extent, follow with its other English-speaking colonies during the nineteenth century. Britain sought to foster responsible self-government in Australia, New Zealand, and South Africa. The Canadian experience thus had a considerable impact throughout the world. But, until well into the twentieth century, the British government, like other Western imperial powers, also generally believed that nonwhite peoples, such as those of India, required direct British colonial administration.

KEEPING A DISTINCTIVE CULTURE

Canadians did learn to exercise self-government, but distinct English and French cultures continued to exist. Within the legislature there were almost always tradeoffs between the eastern and western sections of the nation. Furthermore, during the American Civil War, fears arose that the American republic might seek to invade or dominate Canada. One response to this fear was an attempt to unite the Maritime Provinces in 1862. Those discussions led to broader considerations of the desirability for a stronger federation among all the parts of Canada.

The result of those debates and discussions was the British North America Act of 1867, which created a Canadian federation. Canadians hoped to avoid what they regarded as flaws in the constitution of the United States. The Canadian system of government was to be federal, but with much less emphasis on states' rights than in the United States. Canadians established a parliamentary mode of government but also chose to retain the presence of the British monarchy in the person of the governor-general as head of state. The person who was most responsible for establishing this new government and who led it for most of the period between 1867 and 1891 was John A. MacDonald (1815–1891).

Midcentury Political Consolidation in Europe

During the same period that the United States and Canada established themselves as strong unified political entities in North America, major political consolidation occurred in Europe that would have an enormous impact on the rest of the world. As has so often been true in modern European history, war made change possible. In this case a conflict disrupted the international balance that had prevailed since 1815 and quickly unleashed forces that upset the political situation in several of the involved states. The war itself was in some respects less important than the political consequences that flowed from it during the next decade.

THE CRIMEAN WAR

The Crimean War (1854–1856), named after the Black Sea peninsula on which it was largely fought, originated from a long-standing rivalry between Russia and the Ottoman Empire. Russia wanted to extend its influence over the Ottoman provinces of Moldavia and Walachia (now in Romania). In 1853 Russia went to war against the Ottomans on the pretext that the Ottomans had given Roman Catholic France, instead of Orthodox Russia, the right to protect Christians and Christian shrines in the Holy Land. The next year France and Great Britain supported the Ottoman Empire to protect their interests in the eastern Mediterranean, while Austria and Prussia remained neutral. The war quickly bogged down after the French and the British invaded the Crimea. In March 1856 a peace conference in Paris concluded a treaty highly unfavorable to Russia.

The Crimean War shattered the image of an invincible Russia that had prevailed since the close of the Napoleonic Wars. It also shattered the power of the Concert of Europe to settle international disputes on the Continent. The major European powers were no longer willing to cooperate to maintain the existing borders between themselves and their neighbors. For the next twenty-five years instability prevailed in European affairs, allowing a largely unchecked adventurism in foreign policy.

ITALIAN UNIFICATION

Italian nationalists had long wanted to unite the small absolutist principalities of the peninsula into a single state but could not agree on how to do it. Romantic republicans such as Giuseppe Mazzini (1805–1872) and Giuseppe Garibaldi (1807–1882) sought to drive out the Austrians by popular

Crimea. A view of a crowded British camp at a harbor on the Black Sea during the Crimean war. The ill-equipped and poorly commanded armies suffered more fatalities from disease and starvation then they did from combat.

Getty Images. Inc.Hulton Archive Photos.

military force and then to establish a republic. They not only failed but also frightened more moderate Italians. The person who eventually achieved unification was Count Camillo Cavour (1810–1861), the prime minister of Piedmont.

Piedmont (officially styled the "Kingdom of Sardinia"), in northwestern Italy, was the most independent state on the peninsula (see Map 24–3). It had unsuccessfully fought against Austria in 1848 and 1849. Following the second defeat, King Charles Albert (r. 1831–1849) abdicated in favor of his son, Victor Emmanuel II (r. 1849–1878). In 1852 the new monarch chose Cavour—a moderate liberal in economics and a strong monarchist who rejected republicanism—as his prime minister.

Cavour believed that if Italians proved themselves to be efficient and economically progressive, the great powers might decide that Italy could govern itself. He worked for free trade, railway construction, credit expansion, and agricultural improvement. He also fostered the Nationalist Society, which established chapters in other Italian states to press for unification under the leadership of Piedmont. Cavour furthermore believed that Italy could be unified only with the aid of France.

Cavour joined the French and British side in the Crimean War to be able to raise the question of Italian unification at the

peace conference. There he gained no specific rewards but did achieve the sympathy of Napoleon III (r. 1852–1870) of France. In 1858 Cavour and the French emperor met and plotted to start a war with Austria.

During the winter and spring of 1859 tension grew between Austria and Piedmont as the latter mobilized its army. In late April war erupted, and France came to Piedmont's aid. On June 4 the Austrians were defeated at Magenta, and on June 24, at Solferino in Lombardy. Fearing too extensive a Piedmontese victory, Napoleon III concluded a separate peace with Austria on July 11 at Villafranca. Piedmont received Lombardy, but the Veneto remained under Austrian control. Cavour felt betrayed by France, but nonetheless the war had driven Austria from most of northern Italy. Later that summer Parma, Modena, Tuscany, and the Romagna voted to unite with Piedmont.

At this point the forces of romantic republican nationalism compelled Cavour to pursue the complete unification of northern and southern Italy. In May 1860 Garibaldi landed in Sicily with more than 1,000 troops. He captured Palermo and prepared to attack the mainland. By September the city and kingdom of Naples, probably the most corrupt example of Italian absolutism, lay under his control. To forestall a republican victory Cavour rushed troops south to confront Garibaldi.

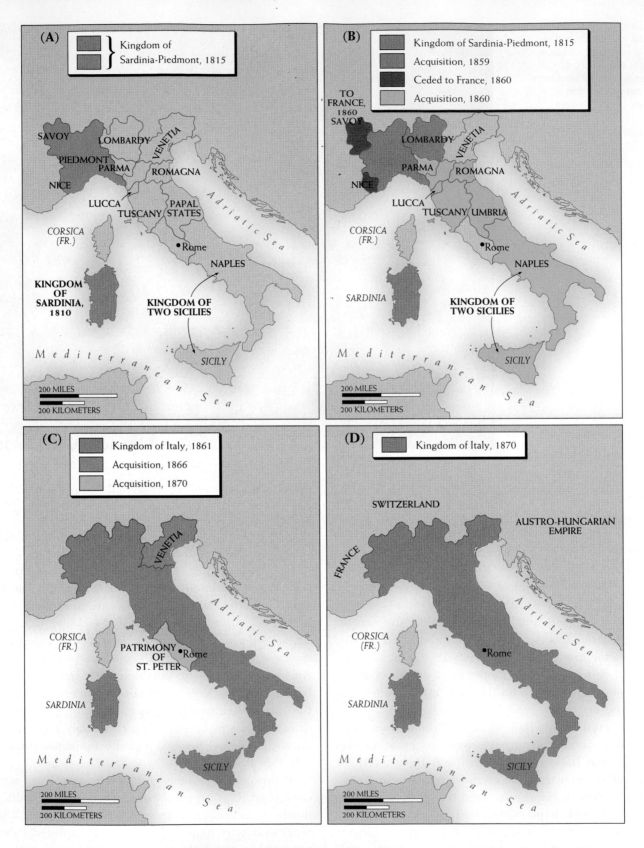

MAP 24–3 The Unification of Italy.   Beginning with the association of Sardinia and Piedmont by the Congress of Vienna in 1815, unification was achieved through the expansion of Piedmont between 1859 and 1870. Both Cavour's statesmanship and the campaigns of ardent nationalists played large roles.

OVERV

The unificat
tical develop
World War I
significant national
the balance of pow
many replaced Fr
achieved unificatio

Italy	1855
	1858
	1859
	1860
	1861
	1866
	1870
Germany	1862
	1863
	1866
	1870
	1871

In 1867 Hanover, H
all of which had sup
annexed by Prussia,
these newly incorpora
stein and the rest of
River, constituted the
was its undisputed lead

THE FRANCO-PRU
AND THE GERMAN

Bismarck now awaited
by bringing the states
ation. The occasion a
surrounding the possi
becoming king of Spai
idea of a second state

Giuseppe Garibaldi. The charismatic leader can be seen on the right urging on his troops in the rout of Neapolitan forces at Calatafimi, Sicily in 1860. The Grager Collection, New York.

On the way Cavour's troops conquered the Papal States except for the area around Rome, which remained under the direct control of the pope.

Garibaldi's nationalism won out over his republicanism, and he unhappily accepted the Piedmontese domination. In late 1860 Naples and Sicily voted to join the northern union forged by Piedmont. In March 1861 Victor Emmanuel II was proclaimed king of Italy. Three months later Cavour died. The new state was governed by the conservative constitution promulgated in 1848 by Charles Albert. Italy gained the Veneto in 1866 as a result of the war between Austria and Prussia, and Rome in 1870 as a result of the Franco-Prussian War.

GERMAN UNIFICATION

A united German nation was the single most important political development in Europe between 1848 and 1914. Germany was united by the conservative army and monarchy of Prussia and by Prussia's conservative prime minister; who sought to outflank the Prussian liberals.

William I (r. 1861–1888) regarded the Prussian army as his first concern. In 1860 his war minister and chief of staff proposed to enlarge the army and to increase the period of conscription from two to three years. The Prussian parliament, created by the constitution of 1850, refused to approve the necessary taxes. A deadlock continued for two years between the monarch and the Parliament dominated by liberals.

CHRONOLOGY

German and Italian Unification

1854	Crimean War opens
1855	Cavour leads Piedmont into war on side of France and England
July 20 1856	Treaty of Paris concludes Crimean War
1858	Secret conference between Louis Napoleon and Cavour
1859	War of Piedmont and France against Austria
1860	Garibaldi lands his forces in Sicily and conquers southern Italy
1861 June 6 March 17	Proclamation of the Kingdom of Italy; Death of Cavour
1862	Bismarck becomes prime minister of Prussia
1864	Danish War
1866	Austro-Prussian War; Veneto ceded to Italy
1867	North German Confederation formed
1870 June 6 July 12	Crisis over Hohenzollern candidacy for the Spanish throne
July 13	Bismarck publishes edited press dispatch
July 19	France declares war on Prussia
September 1	France defeated at Sedan and Napoleon III captured
September 4	French Republic proclaimed
October 2	Italian state annexes Rome
1871 January 18	Proclamation of the German Empire at Versailles
March 18 May 28	Paris Commune
May 10	Treaty of Frankfurt between France and Germany

Bismarck In Septeml
person who, more tha
next thirty years of
(1815–1898). Bismarc
look was deeply infor
ues, including admira
the army. After being
minister in 1862, Bism
eral parliament. He c
permitted the govern
ously granted taxes. T
spent, despite the pa
army and most of the
tion of the constitutic
tained the liberal maje
find some way to attra
als and toward the mo
about uniting Germa
of Prussia. The tactic
from domestic matter

DOCUMENT   Herzl Calls for the Establishment of a Jewish State

In 1896 Theodor Herzl published his pamphlet The Jewish State. *Herzl had become convinced that only the establishment of a separate state for Jews would halt the outbreaks of anti-Semitism that characterized late-nineteenth-century European political and cultural life. Following the publication of this pamphlet, Herzl began to organize the Zionist movement among Jews in both eastern and western Europe.*

◆ Why does Herzl define what he calls the Jewish Question as a national question? What objections does he anticipate to the founding of a Jewish state? Why does he believe that a Jewish state will prevent anti-Semitism?

The idea which I develop in this pamphlet is an age-old one: the establishment of a Jewish State.

The world resounds with outcries against the Jews, and this is what awakens the dormant idea. …

I believe I understand anti-Semitism, a highly complex movement. I view it from the standpoint of a Jew, but without hatred or fear. I think I can discern in it the elements of vulgar sport, of common economic rivalry, of inherited prejudice, of religious intolerance—but also of a supposed need for self-defense. To my mind, the Jewish Question is neither a social nor a religious one, even though it may assume these and other guises. It is a national question, and to solve it we must first of all establish it as an international political problem which will have to be settled by the civilized nations of the world in council.

We are a people, one people.

Everywhere we have sincerely endeavored to merge with the national communities surrounding us and to preserve only the faith of our fathers. We are not permitted to do so….:

And will some people say that the venture is hopeless, because even if we obtain the land and the sovereignty only the poor people will go along? They are the very ones we need first! Only desperate men make good conquerors.

Will anybody say, Oh yes, if it were possible it would have been done by now?

It was not possible before. It is possible now. As recently as a hundred, even fifty years ago it would have been a dream. Today it is all real. The rich, who have an epicurean acquaintance with all technical advance, know very well what can be done with money. And this is how it will be: Precisely the poor and plain people, who have no idea of the power that man already exercises over the forces of Nature, will have the greatest faith in the new message. For they have never lost their hope of the Promised Land. …

Now, all this may seem to be a long-drawn-out affair. Even in the most favorable circumstances it might be many years before the founding of the State is under way. In the meantime, Jews will be ridiculed, offended, abused, whipped, plundered, and slain in a thousand different localities. But no; just as soon as we begin to implement the plan, anti-Semitism will immediately grind to a halt everywhere. …

From Theodor Herzl, *The Jewish State*. © 1970 The Herzl Press, pp. 27, 33, 109, as quoted in William W. Hallo, David B. Ruderman, and Michael Stanislawski, eds., *Heritage: Civilization and the Jews Source Reader*. © 1984 Praeger, pp. 234–235.

200 MILES

200 KILOM

N
S

Amsterdam

BELGIUM
Brussels

Sedan

Verdun

FRAN

MAP 24–4
used diplom
strong natior

his appeal in particular to the economically poor Jews who lived in the ghettos of eastern Europe and the slums of Western Europe. The original call to **Zionism** thus combined a rejection of the anti-Semitism of Europe with a desire to establish some of the ideals of both liberalism and socialism in a state outside Europe.

Racial thinking and revived anti-Semitism were part of a wider late-century aggressive nationalism. Previously, nationalism had been a literary and liberal movement. From the 1870s onward, however, nationalism became a movement with mass

support, well-financed organizations, and political parties. Nationalists tended to redefine nationality in terms of race and blood. The new nationalism opposed the internationalism of both liberalism and socialism. The ideal of nationality was used to overcome the pluralism of class, religion, and geography. The nation and its duties replaced religion for many secularized people. It sometimes became a secular religion in the hands of state schoolteachers, who were replacing the clergy as the instructors of youth. This aggressive, racist nationalism would prove to be the most powerful ideology of the early twentieth century.

Summary

Garibaldi.

Nationalism   Nationalism is the modern concept that people who share the same customs, culture, language, and history should also share the same government. It became the most powerful European political ideology of the nineteenth and early twentieth centuries. Nationalists challenged both the domestic and the international order of the Vienna settlement in the decades after 1815.

Liberalism   Politically, nineteenth-century liberals sought to establish constitutional governments that recognized civil liberties and made the executive responsible to a legislature elected by men of wealth and property. Economically, liberals wanted a laissez-faire economy with minimal government involvement. People should be free to use their talents and property to enrich themselves without the state intervening to protect the working classes or the poor. Liberals often supported nationalists' efforts to create a single national state that could function as a more efficient economic unit. Although efforts to liberalize tsarist Russia failed, liberalism largely triumphed in France after the Revolution of 1830 and in Britain after the passage of the Great Reform Bill. The British were, however, unable to resolve the problem of Irish nationalism in the nineteenth century.

Italian and German Unification   With French assistance, Piedmont and its premier Count Camillo Cavour managed to unite most of the Italian peninsula by 1860. The new Kingdom of Italy was formed from the northern Italian duchies, Austrian Lombardy, the Papal States, and the Kingdom of the Two Sicilies. Austrian Venetia was added in 1866, and Italy occupied Papal Rome in 1870.

German unification was achieved by Prussia under the leadership of Otto von Bismarck between 1864 and 1871. In three victorious wars against Denmark, Austria, and France, Bismarck forged the German states into a German Empire dominated by Prussia. Germany was henceforth the dominant power on the European continent.

North America   In the United States, westward expansion and war against Mexico brought vast new territories under the republic from the Mississippi River to the Pacific, but sectional conflict between North and South over economic issues and slavery led to the outbreak of the Civil War in 1861. Northern victory led to the abolition of slavery, the creation of a continent-wide free labor market, and enormous economic development that would make the United States the world's leading industrial power in the twentieth century.

Canada in these years achieved self-government from Britain and created a united Canadian federation in 1867. However, Canada remained part of the British Empire and retained its connection with the British monarchy.

Eastern Europe   Nationalism created problems for the three eastern European empires: Germany, Russia, and Austria, but Habsburg Austria faced the greatest challenge from nationalism because it was a dynastic, not a national, state. Eleven different nationalities made up the Habsburg Monarchy, each with its own national aspirations. In 1867 the Habsburgs worked out the *Ausgleich*, or Compromise, with the Magyars, by which Hungary became an autonomous kingdom under the Habsburg emperor. Thereafter the Habsburg monarchy became known as Austria-Hungary. However, Czechs, Croats, and other Slavs in the monarchy became increasingly dissatisfied.

Racism and Anti-Semitism   In the late nineteenth century, biological determinism, the concept that some peoples or races were inherently superior to others, took root in Western thought. In Germany, Austria, and France, some nationalists used the concept of race to blame the Jews for their countries' economic and political problems. Part of the Jewish response was the launching of the Zionist movement to found a separate Jewish state.

Review Questions

1. Define nationalism. What were the goals of nationalists? What were the difficulties they confronted in realizing those goals? Why was nationalism a special threat to the Austrian Empire? What areas saw significant nationalist movements between 1815 and 1830? Which were successful and which unsuccessful?

2. What were the tenets of liberalism? Who were the liberals and how did liberalism affect the political developments of the early nineteenth century? What relationship does liberalism have to nationalism?

3. Compare and contrast the movement toward political liberalism between 1815 and 1830 in Russia, France, and Great Britain.

4. What economic differences between the American North and the South gave rise to sectional conflict? Why was slavery the core issue in that conflict? How did the westward movement contribute to making slavery so important an issue?

5. Why was it so difficult to unify Italy? What were the contributions of Mazzini, Cavour, and Garibaldi to Italian unification?

6. Who was Otto von Bismarck and why did he try to unify Germany? What was Bismarck's method of unification and why did he succeed? What effect did the unification of Germany have on the rest of Europe?

7. How did British politicians handle the Irish Question? What were the parallels between England's relationship with Ireland and the nationality problem of the Austrian Empire?

8. What were the origins of the modern idea of racial theory? Who were its major proponents? How did the rise of such a theory change European anti-Semitism?

Key Terms

anti-Semitism   (p. 727)

Ausgleich   (p. 725)

Catholic emancipation   (p. 708)

Chartism   (p. 708)

Great Reform Bill   (p. 707)

home rule   (p. 709)

July Monarchy   (p. 707)

kleindeutsch   (p. 722)

liberalism   (p. 703)

nationalism   (p. 701)

racism   (p. 726)

Zionism   (p. 728)

Documents CD-ROM

Nationalism and Imperialism

20.1 Program of the Serb Society of National Defense [Narodna Odbrana]

20.2 Irish National Identity and Destiny: Three Views

20.3 Fustel de Coulanges, "What Is a Nation?" A reply to Mr. Mommsen, Professor in Berlin

NOTE: *To learn more about the topics in this chapter, see the Suggested Readings at the end of the book.*

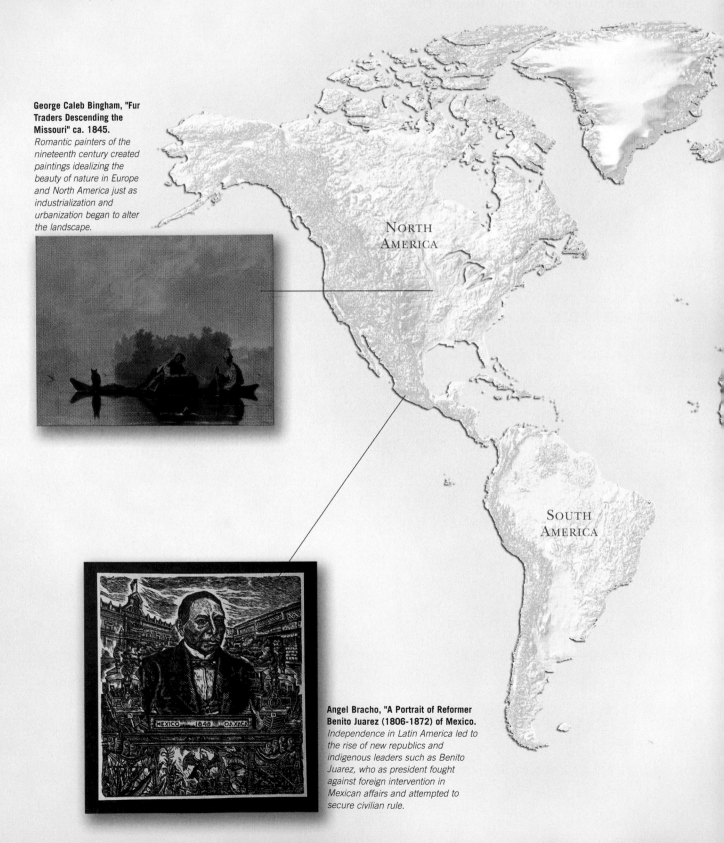

PART 6

INTO THE MODERN WORLD

Between approximately 1850 and 1945 the nations of Europe achieved an unprecedented measure of political, economic, and military power across the globe. The century may thus quite properly be regarded as the European era of world history. But no less impressive than the vast reach of European influence was its brevity. By 1945 much of Europe, from Britain to the Soviet Union, literally lay in ruins.

George Caleb Bingham, "Fur Traders Descending the Missouri" ca. 1845.
Romantic painters of the nineteenth century created paintings idealizing the beauty of nature in Europe and North America just as industrialization and urbanization began to alter the landscape.

NORTH AMERICA

SOUTH AMERICA

Angel Bracho, "A Portrait of Reformer Benito Juarez (1806-1872) of Mexico.
Independence in Latin America led to the rise of new republics and indigenous leaders such as Benito Juarez, who as president fought against foreign intervention in Mexican affairs and attempted to secure civilian rule.

A nineteenth–century painting of Florence Nightingale in the Selimiye Barracks.
The work of Florence Nightingale during and after the Crimean War helped create the modern nursing profession.

Twentieth-century Japanese woodblock print.
Japan more than any other East Asian society eagerly industrialized, yet traditional culture, including the art of woodblock printing, endured as well.

EUROPE

ASIA

AFRICA

AUSTRALIA

Three carved wooden African figures of colonial officials.
These figures are carved using traditional African woodmaking techniques, but their subject matter represents the reality of European colonization in nineteenth-century Africa.

French Indochina.
The city hall of Saigon, Vietnam reflects the colonial legacy of the French Empire.

MAKING CONNECTIONS

1. How special were the circumstances that allowed Western Europe and America to achieve global power?

2. How did technology and new ideas about equality and democracy transform societies in Asia, Africa, and South America?

EUROPE

1852–1870	The Second French Empire, under Napoleon III
1854–1856	The Crimean War
1861	Italy unified
1861	Emancipation of Russian serfs
1866	Austro-Prussian War; creation of Dual Monarchy of Austria-Hungary in 1867
1870–1871	Franco-Prussian War; German Empire proclaimed in 1871
1873	Three Emperors League

◄ Karl Marx

▲ German Empire proclaimed

NEAR EAST/ INDIA

1857–1858	Sepoy Rebellion: India placed directly under the authority of the British government in 1858
1869	Suez Canal completed; 1875, British purchase controlling interest
1869–1948	Mohandas (Mahatma) Gandhi
1876–1949	Muhammad Ali Jinnah, "founder of Pakistan"

"Mahatma" Gandhi ►

EAST ASIA

1850–1873	Taiping and other rebellions
1853–1854	Commodore Perry "opens" Japan to the West, ending seclusion policy
1859	French seize Saigon
1860s	Establishment of treaty ports in China
1864	French protectorate over Cambodia
1868	Meiji Restoration in Japan
1870s	Civilization and Enlightenment movement in Japan
1870s–1890s	Self-Strengthening movement in China

The empress ► dowager Cixi

AFRICA

1856–1884	King Mutasa of Buganda reigns
1870	British protectorate in Zanzibar
1879–1880	Henry M. Stanley gains the Congo for Belgium
1880s	Mahdist revival and uprising in Sudan
1880	French protectorate in Tunisia and the Ivory Coast

THE AMERICAS

1854	Kansas-Nebraska Act
1856	Dred Scott Decision
1859	Raid on Harper's Ferry
1860	Abraham Lincoln elected U.S. president
1861–1865	U.S. Civil War
1862–1867	French invasion of Mexico
1863	Emancipation Proclamation in United States
1865–1877	Reconstruction
1865–1870	Paraguayan War
1879–1880	Argentinian conquest of the desert

◄ Abraham Lincoln

1882	Triple Alliance
1890	Bismarck dismissed by Kaiser Wilhelm II
1902	Entente Cordiale
1905	January 22, "Bloody Sunday"
1905	Revolution in Russia
1914	War begins in Europe

◀ Bloody Sunday

1882	English occupation of Egypt
1886	India National Congress formed
1889–1964	Jawaharlal Nehru
1899	Ottoman sultan Abdulhamid II grants concession to Kaiser Wilhelm II to extend railway to Baghdad ("Berlin-to-Badhdad" Railway)
1908	"Young Turk" Revolt

1889	Meiji Constitution in Japan
1894–1895	Sino-Japanese War; Japan gets Taiwan as colony
1898–1900	Boxer Rebellion in China
1904–1905	Russo-Japanese War
1910	Japan annexes Korea
1911	Republican Revolution begins in China; Qing dynasty overthrown

Promulgation ▶
of the
Meiji Constitution

1884–1885	International Conference in Berlin to prepare rules for further acquisition of African territory; the Congo Free State declared
1884	German Southwest Africa
1885	British control Nigeria and British East Africa
1894	French annex Dahomey
1899	German East Africa; British in Sudan
1899–1902	Boer War
1900	Nigeria a British Crown colony
1907	Orange Free State and the Transvaal join with Natal and Cape Colony to form the Union of South Africa
1911	Liberia becomes a virtual U.S. protectorate
1914	Ethiopia the only independent state in Africa

◀ European exploitation of Africa

1880s	Slavery eliminated in Cuba and Brazil
1898	Spanish-American War
1901	Theodore Roosevelt elected U.S. president
1910–1917	Mexican Revolution
1912	Woodrow Wilson elected U.S. president

◀ Slavery in Brazil

25

Northern Transatlantic Economy and Society, 1815–1914

- European Factory Workers and Urban Artisans

- Nineteenth-Century European Women

- Jewish Emancipation

- European Labor, Socialism, and Politics to World War I

- North America and the New Industrial Economy

- The Emergence of Modern European Thought

- Islam and Late-Nineteenth-Century European Thought

◀ GIUSEPPE PELLIZZA DA VOLPEDO, *IL QUARTO STATO (THE FOURTH ESTATE)*, 1901. Giuseppe Pellizza da Volpedo (1868–1907) was a powerfully committed Italian socialist artist. The title of his painting is taken from the French socialist Jean Jaurés who believed that workers would soon displace the traditional three estates of the clergy, aristocracy, and commoners. Pellizza and other artists embracing *social realism* moved painting away from nostalgic, sentimental depictions of peasants to images of industrial or farm laborers experiencing hunger, poverty, and awakening political consciousness.

Oil on canvas, 283 cm × 550 cm. Civica Galleria d'Arte Moderna-Milano. Photo by Marcello Saporetti.

GLOBAL PERSPECTIVE

The Building of Northern Transatlantic Supremacy

Between 1850 and 1914 Europe had more influence throughout the world than it had before or has had since. Although Europe and North America together were the most industrially advanced regions of the world, the preponderance of economic power lay with Europe. Its industrial base was more advanced than that of any other region, including the still-developing United States. European banks exercised vast influence across the globe. Europeans financed the building of railways in Africa, Asia, and the Americas. Financial power brought political influence. The armaments industry gave European armies and navies predominant power over the peoples of Africa and Asia, whereas the United States began to exercise such power only as a result of the Spanish-American War. These economic developments established a pattern that still persists. First European, and later American, banks, companies, and corporations penetrated the economies and societies of Asia, Africa, and Latin America. These nonpolitical groups often expected their own governments to protect their interests. Thus, what started as commercial contact often evolved into the exercise of direct political influence even over nations that had never been European colonies.

During these years European culture was probably also enjoying its greatest influence. Capital cities in Latin America, especially Buenos Aires and Montevideo, adopted European-style architecture. Paris became synonymous with high fashion. Paris, London, and Vienna were world intellectual centers. The rest of the world regarded advanced industrial and urban civilization of Europe as a model, in part because more non-Europeans were visiting and studying in Europe than ever before. During this period many American artists and writers flocked to Europe to absorb its culture. Another cultural feature of Western Europe and the United States that affected the rest of the world during the era was the emerging role of women. In particular, the demand for the entrance of women into the political process and the professions became a hallmark of the twentieth century. On both sides of the Atlantic, women assumed leadership roles in social reform movements.

The nation that most clearly understood the nature of European power and sought to imitate it was Japan. After the Meiji restoration (1868), Japanese administrators came to Europe to study the new technology, political structures, and military organizations. The Japanese political and military reorganization that resulted proved sufficiently successful to allow them to defeat Russia in 1905, providing the first example of a non-European nation using Western weapons, organizations, and economic power to defeat a European nation. In the twentieth century other non-European nations found ways to import or manufacture technology that permitted them to challenge European and later American hegemony. Indeed, today the proliferation of weaponry usually developed in the United States or Europe has allowed regional powers to challenge Western dominance. This destabilizing arms trade began in the second half of the nineteenth century.

In contrast to Japan, China, India, the countries of the Middle East, and Africa were overwhelmed by the economic and military power of Europe. In time, however, the peoples of those lands under European domination embraced the ideologies of revolutionary protest, most particularly those of nationalism and socialism. As people from the colonial world came to work or study in Europe, they encountered ideas and criticisms that were most effective against European and Western culture. They adapted those ideas to their own cultural contexts and then turned them against their colonial governors.

Europeans eventually turned their military power against each other in 1914. World War I destroyed the late-nineteenth-century European self-confidence. At home, the Bolsheviks brought revolution to Russia. Abroad after the war, anticolonial movements began to grow, especially in India, in a manner that most Europeans in 1900 could not have imagined. In turn, those movements found many sympathetic supporters in Europe as a result of the spread of ideas regarding social justice and public policy. Furthermore, because the political and economic systems of the world had become so interconnected during the second half of the nineteenth century, the influence and impact of the European conflict could not be limited to Europe. The United States again was drawn into World War I and was never again able to avoid worldwide responsibilities.

THINK AHEAD

- What was the relationship between nineteenth century Europe's economic power and its political hegemony in around the globe?

- How did European colonies use ideologies fostered in Europe against their colonial rulers?

URING THE NINETEENTH CENTURY NORTHWESTERN Europe and the United States developed major industrial economies. These economies produced more goods and services than ever before in world history. This economic achievement undergirded the enormous international political power exerted by the industrial nations of the West from that time to the present.

The first half of the nineteenth century witnessed in Europe and to a lesser extent in the United States the emergence of a new kind of industrial labor force. These laborers worked in factories rather than in their homes or in small artisan workshops. More often than not the new industrial working class dwelled in cities. The presence and growth of this new labor force were the most important social developments of the century and would produce a vast influence on European and American political life. It was out of the social and political experience of this work force that the political movement known as socialism arose.

In the second half of the nineteenth century European and American political, economic, and social life assumed many characteristics of our present-day world. In Europe nation-states with large electorates, political parties, centralized bureaucracies, and universal military service emerged. In the United States the politics associated with the Progressive movement brought the presidency to the center of American political life. On both sides of the North Atlantic, business adopted large-scale corporate structures, and the labor force organized itself into trade unions. The number of white-collar laborers grew as urban life became predominant throughout Western Europe. But even as new vast cities arose in the United States, farming continued to spread across the central Midwest and upper Southwest. During this period, too, women began to assert new political awareness and to become politically active in both Europe and America.

During these same years Europe quietly became dependent on the resources and markets of the rest of the world. Farms in the United States, Canada, Latin America, Australia, and New Zealand supplied food to much of the world. Consequently climate changes in Kansas, Argentina, or New Zealand might now affect the European economy. However, before World War I the dependence was concealed by Europe's industrial, military, and financial supremacy. At the time Europeans assumed their supremacy to be natural, but the twentieth century would reveal it to have been temporary. Nevertheless, while it prevailed, Europeans dominated most of the other peoples of the earth and displayed extreme self-confidence. Toward the close of the nineteenth century the United States, having achieved the status of a major industrial power as well as an agricultural supplier, now entered the world stage as a military power, defeating Spain in the Spanish-American War in 1898. With that victory, the United States also acquired its first colonial territories.

During these same decades a number of major new sets of ideas arose. Theories of evoution in biology, relativity in physics, the irrational philosophy, and psychoanalysis in psychology came to the fore shaping much of the intellectual outlook for the next century.

European Factory Workers and Urban Artisans

Although the seeds of industrial production had been sown in the eighteenth century, it was only in the nineteenth century that much of Europe headed toward a more fully industrial society. By 1830 only Great Britain had already attained that status, but new factories and railways were beginning to be constructed elsewhere in Europe. However, what characterized the second quarter of the century was less the triumph of industrialism than the final gasps of those economic groups that opposed it and were displaced by it. Intellectually, the period saw the formulation of the major creeds supporting and criticizing the new society.

The specter of poor harvests still haunted Europe. The worst such experience of the century was the Irish famine of 1845 to 1847. Perhaps as many as half a million Irish peasants with no land or small plots simply starved when disease blighted the potato crop. Hundreds of thousands emigrated. By midcentury, the revolution in landholding had led to greater agricultural production. It also resulted in a vast uprooting of people from the countryside into cities and from Europe into the rest of the word. The countryside thus provided many of the workers for the new factories, as well as people with few economic skills who slowly emigrated to cities in hope of finding work.

In much of northern Europe both artisans and factory workers underwent a process of *proletarianization*. This term indicates the entry of workers into a wage economy and their gradual loss of significant ownership of the means of production, such as tools and equipment, and control over the conduct of their own trades. The process occurred rapidly wherever the factory system arose. The factory owner provided the financial capital to construct the factory, purchase the machinery, and secure the raw materials. The factory workers contributed their labor for a wage. Those workers also submitted to factory discipline, which meant that work conditions became largely determined by the demands for smooth operation of the machines. Closing of factory gates to late workers, fines for lateness, dismissal for drunkenness, and public scolding of faulty laborers constituted attempts to enforce regularity on humans that would match the regularity of cables, wheels, and pistons. The factory workers had no direct say over the quality of the product or its price. It should be noted that for all their difficulties, factory conditions were often better than those of textile workers who resisted the factory mode of production. In particular, English hand-loom weavers, who continued to work in their homes, experienced decades of declining trade and growing poverty in their unsuccessful competition with power looms.

Urban artisans in the nineteenth century experienced proletarianization more slowly than factory workers, and machinery had little to do with the process. The emergence of factories in itself did not harm urban artisans. Many even prospered from the development. For example, the construction and maintenance of the new machines generated demand for metal workers, who consequently did well. The actual erection of factories and the expansion of cities benefited all craftsmen in the building trades, such as carpenters, roofers, joiners, and masons. The lower prices for machine-made textiles aided artisans involved in the making of clothing, such as tailors and hatters, by reducing the costs of their raw materials. Where the urban artisans encountered difficulty, and found their skills and livelihood threatened, was in the organization of production.

In the eighteenth century a European town or city workplace had usually consisted of a few artisans laboring for a master, first as apprentices and then as journeymen, according to established guild regulations and practices. The master owned the workshop and the larger equipment, and the apprentices and journeymen owned their tools. The journeyman could expect to become a master. This guild system had allowed considerable worker control over labor recruitment and training, production pace, product quality, and price.

In the nineteenth century the situation of the urban artisan changed. It became increasingly difficult for artisans to continue to exercise corporate or guild direction and control over their trades. The French Revolution had outlawed such organizations in France. Across Europe, political and economic liberals disapproved of labor and guild organizations and attempted to make them illegal.

Other destructive forces were also at work. The masters often found themselves under increased competitive pressure from larger, more heavily capitalized establishments or from the possibility of the introduction of machine production into a previously craft-dominated industry. In many workshops masters began to follow a practice, known in France as *confection*, whereby goods such as shoes, clothing, and furniture were produced in standard sizes and styles rather than by special orders for individual customers. This practice increased the division of labor in the workshop. Each artisan produced a smaller part of the uniform final product. Consequently, less skill was required of each artisan, and the particular skills possessed by a worker became less valuable. Masters also

◀ **Industrial Labor and Pro-Slavery Arguments.** The condition of European industrial workers entered the political debates on both sides of the Atlantic. This 1841 proslavery cartoon from the United States contrasts allegedly healthy, well-cared-for African American slaves with unemployed British factory workers living in poverty. American proslavery advocates also frequently made the comparison between supposed contented Southern slaves and miserable Northern "wages slaves."
Courtesy of the Library of Congress.

A French Physician Describes a Working-Class Slum in Lille Before the Public Health Movement

The work of medical doctors frequently carried them into working-class areas of industrial cities rarely visited by the middle class. Louis Villermé was such a French physician. He described the slums and living conditions of industrial workers. The passage here, published in 1840, describes a particularly notorious section of Lille, a major cotton-manufacturing town in northern France.

◆ What does this physician find most disturbing about the scene he describes? How is his description designed to evoke concern from a middle-class reader? How might the conditions described have led the poor of France toward socialism or radical politics? How would addressing the problems described have increased the role of government?

The poorest live in the cellars and attics. These cellars … open onto the streets or courtyards, and one enters them by a stairway which is very often at once the door and the window. … Commonly the height of the ceiling is six or six and a half feet at the highest point, and they are only ten to fourteen or fifteen feet wide.

It is in these somber and sad dwellings that a large number of workers eat, sleep, and even work. The light of day comes an hour later for them than for others, and the night an hour earlier.

Their furnishings normally consist, along with the tools of their profession, of a sort of cupboard or a plank on which to deposit food, a stove … a few pots, a little table, two or three poor chairs, and a dirty pallet of which the only pieces are a straw mattress and scraps of a blanket.…

In their obscure cellars, in their rooms, which one would take for cellars, the air is never renewed, it is infected; the walls are plastered with garbage. … If a bed exists, it is a few dirty, greasy planks; it is damp and putrescent straw; it is a coarse cloth whose color and fabric are hidden by a layer of grime; it is a blanket that resembles a sieve. … The furniture is dislocated, worm-eaten, covered with filth. Utensils are thrown in disorder all over the dwelling. The windows, always closed, are covered by paper and glass, but so black, so smoke-encrusted, that the light is unable to penetrate … everywhere are piles of garbage, of ashes, of debris from vegetables picked up from the streets, of rotten straw; of animal nests of all sorts; thus, the air is unbreathable. One is exhausted, in these hovels, by a stale, nauseating, somewhat piquante odor, odor of filth, odor of garbage.…

And the poor themselves, what are they like in the middle of such a slum? Their clothing is in shreds, without substance, consumed, covered, no less than their hair, which knows no comb, with dust from the workshops. And their skin? … It is painted, it is hidden, if you wish, by indistinguishable deposits of diverse exudations.

From Louis René Villermé, *Tableau de l'état et de soie* (Paris, 1840), as quoted and trans. in William H. Sewell Jr., *Work and Revolution in France: The Language of Labor from the Old Regime to 1848.* Copyright © 1980 Cambridge University Press, p. 224.

---

attempted to increase production and reduce their costs for piecework. Those attempts often led to work stoppages or strikes. Migrants from the countryside or small towns created, in some cases, a surplus of relatively unskilled workers who were willing to work for lower wages or under less favorable and protected conditions than traditional artisans. The dilution of skills and lower wages, caused not by machinery but by changes in the organization of artisan production, made it much more difficult for urban journeymen ever to hope to become masters with their own workshops where they would be in charge. Increasingly, these artisans became lifetime wage laborers whose skills were simply bought and sold in the marketplace. (See Document, "A French Physician Describes a Working-Class Slum in Lille Before the Public Health Movement.")

In the United States defenders of slavery frequently compared what they claimed to be the protected situation of slaves living on plantations with the plight of factory workers in both Europe and the northern United States. They argued that a free market in wage labor left workers worse off than slaves. But the situation in the European labor market as in the American North was much more complicated than the defenders of slavery contended.

Nineteenth-Century European Women
WOMEN IN THE EARLY INDUSTRIAL REVOLUTION

The industrial economy ultimately produced an immense impact on the home and the family life of women. First, it took virtually all productive work out of the home and allowed many families to live on the wages of the male spouse alone. That transformation prepared the way for a new concept of gender-determined roles in the home and in general domestic life. Women came to be associated with domestic duties such as housekeeping, food preparation, child rearing and nurturing, and household management. The man came to be associated almost exclusively with breadwinning. Children were reared to match these gender patterns. Previously, this domestic division of labor had prevailed only among the relatively small middle and gentry class. During the nineteenth century it came to characterize the working class as well. Second, industrialization created new modes of employment that allowed many young women to earn enough money to marry or, if necessary, to support themselves independently. Third, industrialism, although fostering more employment for women, lowered the skills required of them.

Because the early Industrial Revolution had begun in textile production, women and their labor were deeply involved from the start. While both spinning and weaving were still domestic industries, women usually worked in all stages of production. Hand spinning was virtually always a woman's task. When spinning was moved into factories and involved large machines, however, men displaced women. The higher wages commanded by male cotton-factory workers allowed many women to stop working or to work only to supplement their husbands' wages.

With the next generation of machines in the 1820s, unmarried women rapidly became employed in the factories. However, their jobs tended to require less skill than most work done by men and than women had previously exercised in the home production of textiles. There was thus a certain paradox in the impact of the factory on women. Many new jobs opened to them, but those jobs were less skilled than those that had been available to them before. Moreover, the women in the factories were almost always young and single or widows. At marriage or perhaps at the birth of the first child, a woman usually found that her husband earned enough money for her to leave the factory. Factory owners also disliked employing married women because of the likelihood of pregnancy, the influence of husbands, and the duties of child rearing.

In Britain and elsewhere by midcentury, industrial factory work accounted for less than half of all employment for women. The largest group of employed women in France continued to work on the land. In England they were domestic servants. Domestic industries, such as lace glove and garment making and other kinds of needlework, employed many women. Their conditions of labor were almost always harsh,

OVERVIEW Major European Cities in 1914

Between 1850 and the outbreak of World War I, European cities from Britain to Russia grew rapidly as rural populations moved to the cities in search of jobs, stimulation, and social opportunities. The tables below show the growth of seven major European cities between 1850 and 1910 and list fourteen other European cities whose populations had grown to exceed 500,000 by 1914.

The Growth of Major Cities	1850	1880	1914
Berlin	419,000	1,122,000	2,071,000
Birmingham	233,000	437,000	840,000
Frankfurt	65,000	137,000	415,000
London	2,685,000	4,470,000	7,256,000
Madrid	281,000	398,000	600,000
Paris	1,053,000	2,269,000	2,888,000
Vienna	444,000	1,104,000	2,031,000

Cities with More than 500,000 People, 1914		
Amsterdam	Hamburg	Munich
Barcelona	Istanbul	Naples
Brussels	Liverpool	St. Petersburg
Budapest	Manchester	Warsaw
Glasgow	Moscow	

whether they worked in their homes or in sweated workshops. Generally all work done by women commanded low wages and involved low skills. They had virtually no way to protect themselves from exploitation. The charwoman was a common sight across the Continent and symbolized the plight of working women.

One of the most serious problems facing working women was the uncertainty of employment. Because they virtually always found themselves in the least skilled jobs and trades, their employment was never secure. Much of their work was seasonal. This was one reason so many working-class women feared they might be compelled to turn to prostitution. On the other hand, cities and the more complex economy did allow a greater variety of jobs. Movement to cities and entrance into the wage economy also gave women wider opportunities for marriage. Cohabitation before marriage seems to have been common. Parents did not arrange marriages as frequently as in the past. Marriage also generally meant that a woman would leave the work force to live on her husband's earnings. If all went well, that arrangement might improve her situation, but if the husband became ill or died, or deserted her, she would have to reenter the market for unskilled labor at a much advanced age.

Nonetheless, many of the traditional practices associated with the family economy survived into the industrial era. As a young woman came of age, both family needs and her desire to marry still directed what she would do with her life. The most likely early occupation for a young woman was domestic service. A girl born in the country normally migrated to a nearby town or city for such employment, often living initially with a relative. As in the past, she would attempt to earn enough in wages to give herself a dowry so she might marry and establish her own household. If she became a factory worker, she would probably live in a supervised dormitory. Such dormitories were one of the ways factory owners attracted young women workers, by convincing parents that their daughters would be safe. The life of young women in the cities seems to have been more precarious than it had been earlier. There seem to have been fewer family and community ties. There were also perhaps more available young men. These men, who worked for wages rather than in the older apprenticeship structures, were more mobile, so relationships between men and women were often more fleeting. In any case, illegitimate births increased. That is to say, fewer women who became pregnant before marriage found the father willing to marry them.

Marriage in the wage industrial economy was also different. It still involved the starting of a separate household, but the structure of gender relationships within the household was different. Marriage was less an economic partnership: The husband might be able to support the entire family. The wage economy and the industrialization that separated workplace

Women in Textile Factories. As textile production became increasingly automated in the 19th century, textile factories required fewer skilled workers and more unskilled attendants. To fill these unskilled positions, factory owners turned increasingly to unmarried women and widows, who worked for lower wages than men and were less likely to form labor organizations.
Bildarchiv Preussischer Kulturbesitz.

and home made it difficult for women to combine domestic duties with work. When married women worked, it was usually in the nonindustrial sector of the economy. More often than not children rather than the wife were sent to work, which may help explain the increase of fertility within marriages, since children in the wage economy tended to be an economic asset. Married women worked outside the home only when family needs or illness or the death of a spouse really required them to do so.

Within the home, the domestic duties of working-class women were an essential factor in the family wage economy. Homemaking came to the fore when a life at home had to be organized that was separate from the place of work. Wives were primarily concerned with food and cooking, but they often also were in charge of the family's finances. The role of the mother expanded when the children still living at home became wage earners. She was then providing home support for her entire wage-earning family. She created the environment to which the family members returned after work. The longer period of home life of working children may also have strengthened the affection between those children and their hardworking, homebound mothers.

SOCIAL DISABILITIES CONFRONTED BY ALL WOMEN

During the early nineteenth century virtually all European women faced social and legal disabilities in property rights, family law, and education. By the close of the century each area had shown improvement. In this period European women, like European men, led lives that reflected their social rank. Yet within each rank, the experience of women was distinct from that of men. Women remained, generally speaking, economically dependent and legally inferior, whatever their social class. Their position thus resembled that of women around the world in that all women found their lives circumscribed by traditional social customs and expectations. (See Document, "English Women Industrial Workers Explain Their Economic Situation.")

Women and Property Until the last quarter of the century in most European countries no married women, whatever their social class, could own property in their own names. In effect, upon marriage women lost to their husbands' control any property they owned or that they might inherit or earn by their own labor. Their legal identities were subsumed into their husbands', and they had no independent standing before the law. The courts saw the theft of a woman's purse as a theft of her husband's property. Because European society was based on private property and wage earning, these disabilities put married women at a great disadvantage, limiting their freedom to work, save, and relocate.

Reform of women's property rights came slowly. By 1882 Great Britain allowed married women to own property in their own right. In France, however, a married woman could not even open a savings account in her own name until 1895, and

---

DOCUMENT | English Women Industrial Workers Explain Their Economic Situation

In 1832, there was much discussion in the British press about factory legislation. Most of that discussion was concerned with the employment of children, but the Examiner *newspaper made the suggestion that any factory laws should not only address the problem of child labor, but also, in time, eliminate women from employment in factories. That article provoked the following letter to the editor, composed by or on behalf of women factory workers, which stated the necessity of such employment for women and the unattractive alternatives.*

> ◆ What reasons do these women give to prove the necessity of their holding manufacturing jobs? What changes in production methods have led women from the home to the factory? How does the situation of these women relate to the possibility of their marrying?

Sir, Living as we do, in the densely populated manufacturing districts of Lancashire, and most of us belonging to that class of females who earn their bread either directly or indirectly by manufactories, we have looked with no little anxiety for your opinion on the Factory Bill. ... You are for doing away with our services in manufactories altogether. So much the better, if you had pointed out any other more eligible and practical employment for the surplus female labour, that will want other channels for a subsistence. If our competition were withdrawn, and short hours substituted, we have no doubt but the effects would be as you have stated, "not to lower wages, as the male branch of the family would be enabled to earn as much as the whole had done," but for the thousands of females who are employed in manufactories, who have no legitimate claim on any male relative for employment or support, and who have, through a variety of circumstance, been early thrown on their own resources for a livelihood, what is to become of them?

In this neighbourhood, hand-loom has been almost totally superseded by power-loom weaving, and no inconsiderable number of females, who must depend on their own exertions, or their parishes for support, have been forced, of necessity into the manufactories, from their total inability to earn a livelihood at home.

It is a lamentable fact, that, in these parts of the country, there is scarcely any other mode of employment for female industry, if we except servitude and dressmaking. Of the former of these, there is no chance of employment for one-twentieth of the candidates that would rush into the field, to say nothing of lowering the wages of our sisters of the same craft; and of the latter, galling as some of the hardships of manufactories are (of which the indelicacy of mixing with the men is not the least), yet there are few women who have been so employed, that would change conditions with the ill-used genteel little slaves, who have to lose sleep and health, in catering to the whims and frivolities of the butterflies of fashion.

We see no way of escape from starvation, but to accept the very tempting offers of the newspapers, held out as baits to us, fairly to ship ourselves off to Van Dieman's Land [Tasmania] on the very delicate errand of husband hunting, and having safely arrived at the "Land of Goshen," jump ashore, with a "Who wants me?" ...

The Female Operatives of Todmorden

From *The Examiner*, February 26, 1832, as quoted in Ivy Pinchbeck, *Women Workers and the Industrial Revolution, 1750–1850* (New York: Augustus M. Kelley, 1969), pp. 199–200.

not until 1907 were married women granted possession of their own wages. In 1900 Germany allowed women to take jobs without their husbands' permission, but a German husband retained control of most of his wife's property except for her wages. Similar laws prevailed elsewhere in Europe.

Family Law European family law also worked to the disadvantage of women. Legal codes required wives to obey their husbands. The Napoleonic Code and the remnants of Roman law made women legal minors throughout Europe. Divorce was difficult for most of the century. In England until 1857 divorce required an act of Parliament. Most nations did not permit divorce by mutual consent. French law forbade divorce between 1816 and 1884. Thereafter the chief recognized legal cause for divorce was cruelty and injury, which had to be proven in court. In Great Britain adultery was the usual cause for divorce, but a woman had to prove her husband's adultery plus

other offenses, whereas a man only had to prove his wife's adultery. In Germany only adultery or serious maltreatment was recognized as grounds for divorce. Across Europe extra-marital sexual relations of husbands were more tolerated than those of wives. Everywhere, divorce required legal hearings and proof, making the process expensive and all the more difficult for women who did not control their own property.

The authority of husbands also extended to children. A husband could take children away from their mother and give them to someone else to rear. Only the husband, in most countries, could permit his daughter to marry. In some countries he could virtually force his daughter to marry the man of his choice. In cases of divorce and separation, the husband normally assumed authority over children no matter how he had treated them previously.

The sexual and reproductive rights of women, which have been so widely debated recently, could hardly be discussed in

▲ **Middle-Class Family.** Family was central to the middle-class conception of a stable and respectable social life. This portrait of the Bellelli family is by Degas. Notice that the husband and father sits at his desk, suggesting his association with business and the world outside the home, whereas the wife and mother stands with their children, suggesting her domestic role.

Edgar Degas (1834–1917), "The Bellelli Family" c. 1858–60. Musee d'Orsay, Paris, France. Photograph Copyright Bridgeman-Giraudon/Art Resource, N.Y.

the nineteenth century. Both contraception and abortion were illegal. The law on rape normally worked against women. Wherever they turned—whether to physicians or lawyers—women confronted an official or legal world populated and controlled by men.

Educational Barriers　Throughout the nineteenth century women had less access to education than men, and what was available to them was inferior. Not surprisingly, the percentage of illiterate women exceeded that of men. Most women were educated only enough for the domestic careers they were expected to follow.

University and professional education remained reserved for men until at least the third quarter of the century. The University of Zurich opened its doors to women in the 1860s. The University of London admitted women for degrees in 1878. Women were not awarded degrees at Oxford until 1920 or at Cambridge until 1921. They could not attend Sorbonne lectures until 1880. Just before the turn of the century universities and medical schools in the Austrian Empire allowed women to matriculate, but Prussian universities did not until after 1900. Russian women did not attend universities before 1914, but other institutions that awarded degrees were open to them. Italian universities were more open to both women students and women instructors than similar institutions elsewhere in Europe.

The absence of a system of private or public secondary education for women prevented most of them from gaining the qualifications they needed to enter a university whether or not the university prohibited them. Considerable evidence suggests that educated, professional men feared the competition of women. Women who attended universities and medical schools were sometimes labeled political radicals.

By 1900 men in the educated elites also feared the challenge educated women posed to traditional gender roles in the home and workplace. Restricting their access to secondary and university education helped bar women from social and economic advancement. Women would benefit only marginally from the expansion of professional employment that occurred during the late nineteenth and early twentieth centuries. Although a few women did enter the professions, especially medicine, most nations prevented women from becoming lawyers until after World War I.

Schoolteaching at the elementary level, which was seen as a female job because of its association with the nurturing of children, became a professional haven for women. Trained at institutions that were equivalent to normal schools, women schoolteachers were regarded as educated, but not as university educated. Secondary education remained largely the province of men.

The few women who pioneered in the professions and on government commissions and school boards or who dispersed birth control information faced grave social obstacles, personal humiliation, and often outright bigotry. These women and their male supporters were challenging that clear separation of life into male and female spheres that had emerged in middle-class European society during the nineteenth century. Women themselves often hesitated to support feminist causes or expanded opportunities for themselves because they had been so thoroughly acculturated into the recently stereotyped roles. Many women saw a real conflict between family responsibilities and feminism.

NEW EMPLOYMENT PATTERNS FOR WOMEN

During the late nineteenth century two major developments affected the economic lives of women. The first was an expansion in the variety of jobs available outside the better paying learned professions. The second was a withdrawal of married women from the work force. These two seemingly contradictory developments require explanation.

Availability of New Jobs　The expansion of governmental bureaucracies, the emergence of corporations and other large-scale businesses, and the expansion of retail stores opened many new employment opportunities for women. The need for elementary schoolteachers, usually women, grew with compulsory education laws. Technological inventions and innovations, such as the typewriter and eventually the telephone exchange, also fostered female employment. Women by the

---

CHRONOLOGY

Major Dates in Late-Nineteenth-Century and Early-Twentieth-Century Women's History

1857	Revised English divorce law
1865	University of Zurich admits women for degrees
1869	John Stuart Mill's *The Subjection of Women*
1878	University of London admits women as candidates for degrees
1882	English Married Woman's Property Act
1894	Union of German Women's Organizations founded
1901	National Council of French Women founded
1903	British Women's Social and Political Union founded
1907	Norway permits women to vote on national issues
1910	British suffragettes adopt radical tactics
1918	Vote extended to some British women
1918	Weimar constitution allows German women to vote
1920–1921	Oxford and Cambridge Universities award degrees to women
1922	French Senate defeats bill extending vote to women
1928	Britain extends vote to women on same basis as men

Women Working at a Telephone Exchange. The invention of the telephone opened new employment opportunities for women.
Mary Evans Picture Library.

thousands became secretaries and clerks for governments and private businesses. More thousands became shop assistants.

Although these jobs did open new and often better employment opportunities for women, they nonetheless required low-level skills and involved minimal training. They were occupied primarily by unmarried women or widows. Few women had prominent positions.

Employers continued to pay women low wages because they assumed, often knowing better, that a woman did not need to support herself independently but could expect additional financial support from her father or husband. Consequently, a woman who did need to support herself independently could rarely find a job paying an adequate income or a position that paid as well as one held by a man who was supporting himself independently.

Withdrawal from the Labor Force   Most of the women filling these new service positions were young and unmarried. After marriage, or certainly after the birth of her first child, a woman normally withdrew from the labor force. She either did not work or she worked at home. This pattern was not new, but it had become more common by the end of the nineteenth century. The industrial occupations that women had filled in the mid–nineteenth century, especially textile and garment making, were shrinking. Those industries thus offered fewer jobs for either married or unmarried women. Employers in offices and retail stores preferred young, unmarried women whose family responsibilities would not interfere with their work. The

decline in the number of births also meant that fewer married women were needed to look after other women's children.

The real wages paid to male workers increased during this period, thus reducing families' need for a second income. Also, thanks to improving health conditions, men lived longer than before, and so wives were less likely to be thrust into the work force by an emergency. Smaller families also lowered the need for supplementary wages. Working children stayed longer at home and continued to contribute to the family's wage pool.

Finally, the cultural dominance of the middle class, with its generally idle wives, established a pattern of social expectations. The more prosperous a working-class family became, the less involved in employment its women were supposed to be. Indeed, the less income-producing work a wife did, the more prosperous and stable the family was considered.

Yet behind these generalities stands the enormous variety of social and economic experience late-nineteenth-century women actually encountered. As might be expected, social class largely determined these individual experiences.

LATE-NINETEENTH-CENTURY WORKING-CLASS WOMEN

Although less dominant than earlier in the century, the textile industry and garment making continued to employ many women. The German clothing-making trades illustrate the kind of vulnerable economic situation that women could encounter as

Women Laundry Workers. Although new opportunities opened to them in the late 19th century, many working-class women, like these women ironing in a laundry, remained in traditional occupations. As the wine bottle suggests, alcoholism was a problem for women as well as men engaged in tedious work. The painting is by Edgar Degas (1834–1917).
Reunion des Musees Nationaux/Art Resource, N.Y.

a result of their limited skills and the organization of the trade. The manufacture of mass-made clothes in Germany was designed to require minimal capital investment by manufacturers and to protect them from significant risk. A major manufacturer would arrange to produce clothing through a putting-out system. He would purchase the material and then put it out for tailoring. The clothing was made not in a factory but usually in independently owned, small sweatshops or by workers in their homes.

In Berlin in 1896 there were more than 80,000 garment workers, mostly women. When business was good, employment for these women was high. If business became poor, however, less and less work was put out, idling many of them. In effect, the workers who actually sewed the clothing carried much of the risk of the enterprise. Some women did work in factories, but they too were subject to layoffs. Furthermore, women in the clothing trade were nearly always in positions less skilled than those of the male tailors or the male middlemen who owned the workshops.

The expectation of separate social and economic spheres for men and women and the definition of women's chief work as pertaining to the home contributed mightily to the exploitation of women workers outside the home. Because their wages were regarded merely as supplementing their husbands', they became particularly vulnerable to the economic exploitation that characterized the German putting-out system for clothing production. Women were nearly always treated as casual workers in Europe.

THE RISE OF POLITICAL FEMINISM

As can be seen from the previous discussion, liberal society and its values neither automatically nor inevitably improved the lot of women. In particular, it did not give them the vote or access to political activity. Male liberals feared that granting the vote to women would benefit political conservatives, because women were thought to be unduly controlled by the clergy. Consequently, anticlerical liberals often had difficulty working with feminists.

Obstacles to Achieving Equality   But women were also often reluctant to support feminist causes. Political issues relating to gender were only one of several priorities for many women. Some were sensitive to their class and economic interests. Others subordinated feminist political issues to national unity and nationalistic patriotism. Still others would not support particular feminist organizations because of differences over tactics. The various social and tactical differences among women often led to sharp divisions within the feminists' own ranks. Except in England, it was often difficult for working-class and middle-class women to cooperate. Roman Catholic feminists were uncomfortable with radical secularist feminists.

Although liberal society and law presented women with many obstacles, they also provided feminists with many of their intellectual and political tools. As early as 1792 in Britain, Mary Wollstonecraft (1759–1797), in *The Vindication of the Rights of*

Women, had applied the revolutionary doctrines of the rights of man to the predicament of the members of her own sex (see Chapter 22). John Stuart Mill (1806–1873), with his wife Harriet Taylor (1804–1858), had applied the logic of liberal freedom to the position of women in *The Subjection of Women* (1869). The arguments for utility and efficiency so dear to middle-class liberals could be used to expose the human and social waste implicit in the inferior role assigned to women.

Furthermore, the socialist criticism of capitalist society often, though by no means always, included a harsh indictment of the social and economic position to which women had been relegated. The earliest statements of feminism arose from critics of the existing order and were often associated with people who had unorthodox opinions about sexuality, family life, and property. This hardened resistance to the feminist message, especially on the Continent.

These difficulties prevented Continental feminists from raising the kind of massive public support or mounting the large demonstrations that feminists in Great Britain and the United States could. Everywhere in Europe, however, including Britain, the feminist cause was badly divided over both goals and tactics.

Votes for Women in Britain
Europe's most advanced women's movement was in Great Britain. There Millicent Fawcett (1847–1929) led the moderate National Union of Women's Suffrage Societies. She believed Parliament would grant women the vote only when convinced that women would be respectable and responsible in their political activity. In 1908 this organization could rally almost half a million women in London. Fawcett was the wife of a former Liberal Party cabinet minister and economist. Her tactics were those of English liberals.

Emmeline Pankhurst (1858–1928) led a different and much more radical branch of British feminists. Pankhurst's husband had been active in both labor and Irish nationalist politics. Irish nationalists had developed numerous disruptive political tactics. Early labor politicians had also sometimes had confrontations with police over the right to hold meetings. In 1903 Pankhurst and her daughters founded the Women's Social and Political Union. For several years they and their followers, known derisively as **suffragettes**, lobbied publicly and privately for women's suffrage. By 1910, having failed to move the government, they turned to the violent tactics of arson, window breaking, and sabotage of postal boxes. They marched en masse on Parliament. The Liberal government of Herbert Asquith (1852–1928), prime minister from 1908 to 1916, imprisoned many of the demonstrators and force-fed those who went on hunger strikes in jail. The government refused to extend the franchise. Only in 1918, and then as a result of their contribution to the war effort, did some British women receive the vote.

Political Feminism on the Continent
The contrast of France and Germany shows how advanced the British women's movement was. In France, when Hubertine Auclert (1848–1914) began campaigning for the vote in the 1880s, she stood virtually alone. During the 1890s several women's organizations emerged. In 1901 the National Council of French Women (CNFF) was organized among upper-middle-class women, but it did not support the vote for women for several years. French

Women's Suffrage. The creator of this poster cleverly reveals the hypocrisy and foolishness of denying the vote to women.
Private collection/Bridgeman Art Library.

Roman Catholic feminists, such as Marie Mauguet (1844–1928), supported the franchise. Almost all French feminists, however, rejected violence: They were also never able to organize mass rallies. The leaders of French feminism believed that the vote could be achieved through careful legalism. In 1919 the French Chamber of Deputies granted the vote to women, but in 1922 the French Senate defeated the bill. French women did not receive the right to vote until 1944 at the end of World War II.

In Germany feminist awareness and action were even more underdeveloped. German law actually forbade German women from political activity. Because no group in the German Empire enjoyed extensive political rights, women were not certain that they would benefit from demanding them. Any such demand would be regarded as subversive of both the state and society.

In 1894 the Union of German Women's Organizations (BDFK) was founded. By 1902 it was calling for the right to vote, but it was largely concerned with improving women's social conditions, their access to education, and their right to other protections. The group also worked to see women admitted to political or civic activity on the municipal level. Their work usually included education, child welfare, charity, and public health. The German Social Democratic Party supported women's suffrage, but that Socialist party was so disdained by the German authorities and German Roman Catholics that this support only made suffrage more suspect in their eyes. Women received the vote in Germany only in 1918 under the constitution of the Weimar Republic. Before World War I, only in Norway (1907) could women vote on national issues.

Jewish Emancipation

One of the most important social changes to occur throughout Europe during the nineteenth century was the emancipation of European Jews from the narrow life of the ghetto into a world of equal or nearly equal citizenship and social status. This transformation represented one of the major social impacts of political liberalism on European life.

EARLY STEPS TO EQUAL CITIZENSHIP

Emancipation, slow and never fully completed, began in the late eighteenth century and continued throughout the nineteenth. It moved at different paces in different countries. In 1782 Joseph II (r. 1765–1790), the Habsburg emperor, issued a decree that placed the Jews of his empire under more or less the same laws as Christians. In France the National Assembly recognized Jews as French citizens in 1789. During the Napoleonic Wars Jewish communities in Italy and Germany were allowed to mix on a generally equal footing with the Christian population.

These various steps toward political emancipation were frequently limited or partially repealed with changes in rulers or governments. Even in countries that granted them political rights, Jews could not own land and could be subject to discriminatory taxes. Nonetheless, by the first half of the nineteenth century Jews in Western Europe and to a much lesser extent in central and eastern Europe had begun to acquire equal or nearly equal citizenship.

In Russia, however, the traditional modes of prejudice and discrimination continued unabated until World War I. Jews were treated as aliens under Russian rule. The government undermined Jewish community life, limited publication of Jewish books, restricted areas where Jews might live, required internal passports from Jews, banned them from many forms of state service and from many institutions of higher education. The police and others were allowed to conduct **pogroms**—organized riots—against Jewish neighborhoods and villages.

BROADENED OPPORTUNITIES

After the revolutions of 1848, and especially in Western Europe, the situation of European Jews improved for several decades. Throughout Germany, Italy, the Low Countries, and Scandinavia, Jews were allowed full rights of citizenship. After 1858 Jews in Great Britain could sit in Parliament. In Austria-Hungary full legal rights were extended to Jews in 1867. From approximately 1850 to 1880 there was relatively little organized or overt prejudice toward Jews. They entered the professions and other occupations once closed to them. They participated fully in the literary and cultural life of their nations. They were active in the arts and music. They became leaders in science and education. Jews intermarried freely with non-Jews as legal prohibitions against such marriages were repealed during the last quarter of the century.

Outside of Russia, Jewish political figures served in the highest offices of the state. Politically they tended to be aligned with liberal parties because such groups had championed equal rights. Later in the century, especially in eastern Europe, many Jews became associated with the Socialist parties.

The prejudice that had been associated with religious attitudes toward Jews seemed to have dissipated, although it still appeared in rural Russia and eastern Europe. From these regions hundreds of thousands of European Jews immigrated to the United States. Almost anywhere in Europe Jews might encounter prejudice on a personal level. But in Western Europe, including England, France, Italy, Germany, and the Low Countries, the Jewish populations seem to have felt relatively secure from the old dangers of legalized persecution and discrimination.

That began to change during the last two decades of the nineteenth century. In the 1870s anti-Semitic sentiments

Dedication of a New Synagogue. The social life of Europe became transformed in numerous ways during the 19th century. Beyond the expansion of cities and the rise of industrial society, there also occurred numerous changes in religious life. One of the most important of these was the gradual emancipation of European Jews from sharply restricted lives in urban ghettos to fuller political participation and social assimilation. This painting by G. E. Opitz portrays the dedication of a new synagogue in Alsace in 1820.

The Jewish Museum, N.Y./Art Resource, N.Y.

attributing the economic stagnation of that decade to Jewish bankers and financial interests began to be voiced. In the 1880s organized anti-Semitism erupted in Germany as it did in France in the 1890s. As we saw in the previous chapter, those developments gave birth to Zionism, the movement to establish a Jewish state in Palestine. However, Zionism was initially a minority movement within the Jewish community. Most Jewish leaders believed the attacks on Jewish life to be temporary recurrences of older prejudice; they felt that their communities would remain safe under the legal protections that had been extended during the century. That analysis would be proved disastrously wrong during the 1930s and 1940s.

European Labor, Socialism, and Politics to World War I

THE WORKING CLASSES IN THE LATE NINETEENTH CENTURY

After 1848 European workers ceased taking to the streets to voice their grievances in the form of riots. They also stopped trying to revive the old paternalistic guilds. After midcentury the labor force accepted the fact of modern industrial production and its general downgrading of skills and attempted to receive more benefits from that system. Workers turned to new institutions and ideologies. Chief among them were trade unions, democratic political parties, and socialism.

Trade Unions Trade unionism came of age as legal protections were extended to unions throughout the second half of the century. Unions became fully legal in Great Britain in 1871

and were allowed to picket in 1875. In France the Third Republic fully legalized unions in 1884. After 1890 they could function in Germany with little disturbance. Initially, most trade unions were slow to enter the political process directly. As long as the traditional governing classes looked after labor interests, members of the working class rarely sought office themselves.

The midcentury organizational efforts of the unions aimed to improve the wages and working conditions of skilled workers. By the close of the century large industrial unions for unskilled workers were also being organized. They confronted extensive opposition from employers, and were often recognized only after long strikes. In the decade before 1914 strikes were common throughout Europe as the unions attempted to raise wages to keep up with inflation. However, despite the advances of unions and the growth of their membership in 1910 to approximately 3 million in Britain, 2 million in Germany, and 977,000 in France, they never included a majority of the industrial labor force. The unions did represent a new collective fashion in which workers could associate to confront the economic difficulties of their lives and attain better security.

Democracy and Political Parties The democratic franchise gave workers direct political influence, which meant they could no longer be ignored. Except for Russia, all the major European states adopted broad-based, if not perfectly democratic, electoral systems. Democracy brought new modes of popular pressure to bear on all governments. It meant that discontented groups could now voice their grievances and advocate their programs within government rather than from outside it.

The advent of democracy witnessed the formation for the first time in Europe of organized mass political parties, such as had existed throughout the nineteenth century in the United States. In the liberal European states with narrow electoral bases, most voters had been men of property who understood what they had at stake in politics. Organization had been minimal. The expansion of the electorate brought into the political processes many people whose level of political consciousness and interest was low. This electorate had to be organized and taught the nature of power and influence in the liberal democratic state. The organized political party—with its workers, newspapers, offices, social life, and discipline—was the vehicle that mobilized the new voters. The largest single group in these mass electorates was the working class. The democratization of politics presented the Socialists with opportunities and required the traditional ruling class to vie with them for the support of the new voters.

MARXIST CRITIQUE OF THE INDUSTRIAL ORDER

During the 1840s Karl Marx (1818–1883) produced the most influential of all critiques of the newly emerged industrial order. His analysis became very important because later in the century it was adopted by the leading Socialist political party in Germany, which in turn influenced most other European Socialist parties including a small group of exiled Russian Socialists led by V. I. Lenin. Marx was born in the Rhineland. His Jewish middle-class parents sent him to the University of Berlin, where he became deeply involved in radical politics. During 1842 and 1843 he edited the radical *Rhineland Gazette*. Soon the German authorities drove him into exile—first in Paris; then in Brussels; and finally, after 1849, in London.

In 1844 Marx met Friedrich Engels (1820–1895), another young middle-class German, whose father owned a textile factory in Manchester, England. The next year, Engels published *The Condition of the Working Class in England*, which presented a devastating picture of industrial life. The two men became fast friends. Late in 1847 they were asked to write a pamphlet for a newly organized and ultimately short-lived secret Communist league. *The Communist Manifesto*, published in German, appeared early in 1848. Marx, Engels, and the league had adopted the name *Communist* because the term was more self-consciously radical than *Socialist*. *Communism* implied the outright abolition of private property rather than some less extensive rearrangement of society. The *Manifesto* itself was a work of fewer than fifty pages. It would become the most influential political document of modern European history, but that development lay in the future. At the time it was simply one more political tract. Moreover, neither Marx nor his thought had any effect on the revolutionary events of 1848.

▲ **Karl Marx.** Marx's Socialist philosophy eventually triumphed over most alternative versions of socialism in Europe, but his monumental work has been subject to varying interpretations, criticisms, and revisions that continue to this day.
Bildarchiv Preussischer Kulturbesitz.

In *The Communist Manifesto* Marx and Engels contended that human history must be understood rationally and as a whole. According to their analysis, history is the record of humankind's coming to grips with physical nature to produce the goods necessary for survival. That basic productive process determines the structures, values, and ideas of a society. Historically, the organization of the means of production has always involved conflict between the classes who owned and controlled the means of production and those classes who worked for them. That necessary conflict has provided the engine for historical development; it is not an accidental byproduct of mismanagement or bad intentions. Consequently, only a radical social transformation, not piecemeal reforms, can eliminate the social and economic evils inherent in the very structures of production. Such a revolution will occur as the inevitable outcome of the development of capitalism.

In Marx's and Engels's eyes, during the nineteenth century the class conflict that had characterized previous Western history had become a struggle between the bourgeoisie and the proletariat, or between the middle class and the workers. The character of capitalism ensured the sharpening of the struggle.

Capitalist production and competition would steadily increase the size of the unpropertied proletariat. Large-scale mechanical production crushed both traditional and smaller industrial producers into the ranks of the proletariat. As the business structures grew larger and larger, smaller middle-class units would be squeezed out by the competitive pressures. Competition among the few remaining gigantic concerns would lead to more intense suffering by the proletariat. As the workers suffered increasingly from the competition among the ever-enlarging firms, they would foment revolution and finally overthrow the few remaining owners of the means of production. For a time the workers would organize the means of production through a dictatorship of the proletariat, which would eventually give way to a propertyless and classless communist society.

This proletarian revolution was inevitable, according to Marx and Engels. The structure of capitalism required competition and consolidation of enterprise. Although the class conflict involved in the contemporary process resembled that of the past, it differed in one major respect. The struggle between the capitalistic bourgeoisie and the industrial proletariat would culminate in a wholly new society that would be free of class conflict. The victorious proletariat, by its very nature, they contended, could not be a new oppressor class: "The proletarian movement is the self-conscious, independent movement of the immense majority, in the interest of the immense majority."[1] The result of the proletarian victory would be "an association, in which the free development of each is the condition for the free development of all."[2] The victory of the proletariat over the bourgeoisie represented the culmination of human history. For the first time, one group of people would not be oppressing another. Marx's analysis was conditioned by his own economic environment. The 1840s had seen much unemployment and deprivation. Capitalism, however, did not collapse as he predicted, nor did the middle class during the rest of the century or later become proletarianized. Rather, more and more people came to benefit from the industrial system. Nonetheless, within a generation Marxism had captured the imagination of many Socialists and large segments of the working class. Its doctrines were allegedly based on the empirical evidence of hard economic fact. This much proclaimed scientific aspect of

Marxism helped the ideology, as science became more influential during the second half of the century. Marx had made the ultimate victory of socialism seem certain. His works also suggested that the path to socialism lay with revolution rather than reform. As Marxist thought permeated the international Socialist movement during the next seventy-five years,

it would provide the ideological basis for some of the most momentous and ultimately repressive political movements in the history of virtually the entire modern world.

GERMANY: SOCIAL DEMOCRATS AND REVISIONISM

That the thought of Karl Marx ultimately came to exercise such vast influence was the result of his ideas becoming adopted by the German Social Democratic Party (SPD). Founded in 1875, the SPD suffered twelve years of persecution by Otto von Bismarck (1815–1898), who believed socialism would undermine German politics and society. In 1878 there was an attempt to assassinate Emperor William I (r. 1861–1888). Bismarck unfairly blamed the Socialists and steered antisocialist laws through the Reichstag, the German Parliament. These measures suppressed the organization, meetings, newspapers, and other public activities of the SPD. Nonetheless, the SPD steadily polled more votes in elections to the Reichstag.

When repression failed, Bismarck enacted social welfare legislation to wean German workers from socialist loyalties. These measures provided health insurance, accident insurance, and old age and disability pensions. The German state itself thus organized a system of social security that did not change the system of property holding or politics.

In 1891, after forcing Bismarck's resignation, Emperor William II (r. 1888–1918) allowed the antisocialist legislation to expire. The SPD then had to decide how to operate as a legalized party. Their new direction was announced in the Erfurt Program of 1891. In good Marxist fashion, the program declared the imminent doom of capitalism and the necessity of socialist ownership of the means of production. However, these goals were to be achieved by legal political participation rather than by revolutionary activity. Since the revolution was inevitable, it was argued, the immediate task of Socialists was to improve workers' lives. In theory, the SPD was vehemently hostile to the German Empire, but in practice the party functioned within its institutions.

This situation of the SPD, however, generated the most important internal socialist challenge to the orthodox Marxist analysis of capitalism and the socialist revolution. Eduard Bernstein (1850–1932) wrote what was regarded as his socialist heresy. Bernstein, who was familiar with the British **Fabians**, questioned whether Marx and his later orthodox followers had been correct in their pessimistic appraisal of capitalism and the necessity of revolution. In *Evolutionary Socialism* (1899), Bernstein pointed to the rising standard of living in Europe, the ongoing power of the middle class, and the opening of the franchise to the working class. He argued that a humane socialist society required not revolution, but more democracy and social reform. Bernstein's doctrines,

---

[1] Robert C. Tucker, ed., *The Marx-Engels Reader* (New York: W. W. Norton, 1972), p. 353.
[2] Ibid.

known as *revisionism*, were widely debated among German Socialists and were finally condemned as theory, although the party actually pursued a peaceful, reformist program. His critics argued that evolution toward social democracy might be possible in liberal, parliamentary Britain but not in authoritarian, militaristic Germany with its basically powerless Reichstag. Therefore, the German SPD continued to advocate revolution.

The German debate over revisionism became important for the later history of Marxist socialism. The German SPD was, as noted, the most successful prewar Socialist party. Its rejection of an ideology of reform socialism in favor of revolutionary socialism influenced all Socialists who looked to the German example. Most significant, Lenin adopted this position, as did the other leaders of the Russian Revolution. Thereafter, wherever Soviet Marxism was influential, the goal of its efforts would be revolution rather than reform.

GREAT BRITAIN: THE LABOUR PARTY AND FABIANISM

No form of socialism made significant progress in Great Britain, the most advanced industrial society of the day. The members of the growing trade unions normally supported Liberal Party candidates. The "new unionism" of the late 1880s and the 1890s organized the dock workers, the gas workers, and similar unskilled groups. Employer resistance to unions heightened class antagonism. In 1892 Keir Hardie (1856–1915) became the first independent worker elected to Parliament. In 1893 the Socialist Independent Labour Party was founded, but it remained ineffective.

In 1901, however, a decision by the House of Lords (Britain's supreme court) removed the legal protection previously accorded union funds. The Trades Union Congress responded by launching the Labour Party, which sent twenty-nine members to Parliament in the election of 1906. Their goals did not yet encompass socialism. The British labor movement also became more militant. In scores of strikes, workers fought for wages to meet the rising cost of living. The government intervened to mediate these strikes, which in 1911 and 1912 involved the railways, the docks, and the mines.

British socialism itself remained primarily the preserve of intellectuals. The Socialists who exerted the most influence were from the Fabian Society, founded in 1884. The society took its name from Q. Fabius Maximus (d. 203 B.C.E.), the Roman general who defeated Hannibal by waiting before attacking. Its name thus indicated a gradualist approach to social reform. Its leading members were Sydney Webb (1859–1947) and Beatrice Webb (1858–1943), H. G. Wells (1866–1946), and George Bernard Shaw (1856–1950). Many of the Fabians were civil servants who believed that the problems of industry, the expansion of ownership, and the state

direction of production could be solved and achieved gradually, peacefully, and democratically. They sought to educate the country to the rational wisdom of socialism. They were particularly interested in collective ownership on the municipal level, or so-called gas-and-water socialism.

RUSSIA: INDUSTRIAL DEVELOPMENT AND THE BIRTH OF BOLSHEVISM

Following its defeat in the Crimean War, the tsarist government in Russia had undertaken a series of major internal reforms. The most important of these was the emancipation of the serfs in 1861. That measure was extremely complicated and in effect required serfs to pay for their land. The poverty of the emancipated serfs became a political cause for groups of urban revolutionaries in Russia who succeeded

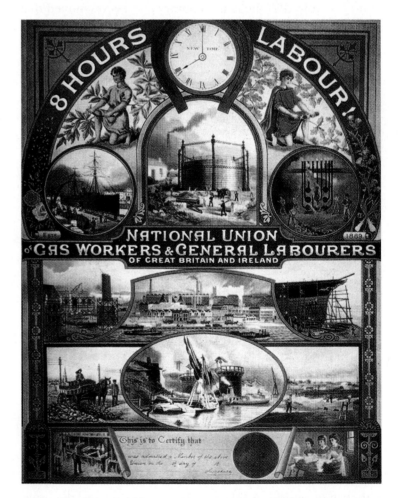

▲ **Trade Union Membership Certificate.** Trade unions continued to grow in late-century Great Britain. The effort to curb the unions eventually led to the formation of the Labour Party. The British unions often had quite elaborate membership certificates, such as this one for the National Union of Gas Workers and General Labourers of Great Britain and Ireland.

The Granger Collection.

Beatrice and Sidney Webb. These most influential British Fabian Socialists, shown in a photograph from the late 1920s, wrote many books on governmental and economic matters, served on special parliamentary commissions, and agitated for the enactment of socialist policies.

UPI/Corbis/Bettmann.

in assassinating Tsar Alexander II (r. 1855–1881) in 1881. Thereafter, the government pursued a policy of general political repression.

At the same time in the late nineteenth century the tsarist government was determined to make Russia an industrial power. It favored the growth of heavy industries, such as railways, iron, and steel. A small, but significant, industrial proletariat arose. By 1900 Russia had approximately 3 million factory workers. Their working and living conditions were bad by any standard.

New political departures accompanied this economic development. In 1901 the Social Revolutionary Party was founded. It opposed industrialism and looked to the communal life of rural Russia as a model for the economic future. In 1903 the Constitutional Democratic Party, or Cadets, was formed. Liberal in outlook, the Cadets were drawn from people who participated in the *zemstvos* (local governments). They wanted a parliamentary regime with responsible ministries, civil liberties, and economic progress. The Cadets hoped to model themselves on the Liberal parties of Western Europe.

Lenin's Early Thought and Career   The situation for Russian Socialists differed radically from that in other major European countries. Russia had no representative political institutions and only a small working class. The compromises and accommodations achieved elsewhere were meaningless in Russia, where socialism in both theory and practice had to be revolutionary. The Russian Social Democratic Party had been established in 1898. It was Marxist, and its members greatly admired the German SPD, but tsarist repression meant that it had to function in exile.

The leading late-nineteenth-century Russian Marxist was Georgii Plekhanov (1857–1918), based in Switzerland. His chief disciple was Vladimir Illich Ulyanov (1870–1924), who took the name of Lenin. The future leader of the communist revolution was the son of a high bureaucrat. His older brother had been executed in 1887 for participating in a plot against Alexander III (r. 1881–1894). In 1893 Lenin moved to Saint Petersburg, where he briefly practiced law. Soon he, too, was drawn to the revolutionary groups among the factory workers. In 1895 he was exiled to Siberia. After his release in 1900, Lenin spent most of the next seventeen years in Switzerland.

In Switzerland Lenin became deeply involved in the organizational and policy disputes of the exiled Russian Social Democrats. They all considered themselves Marxists but quarreled about the proper nature of a Marxist revolution in primarily rural Russia and the structure of their own party. The Social Democrats were modernizers who favored further industrial development. Most believed that Russia must develop a large proletariat before the revolution could come. This same majority hoped to mold a mass political party like the German SPD.

CHRONOLOGY

Major Dates in the Development of Socialism

1864	International Working Men's Association (the First International) founded
1875	German Social Democratic Party founded
1876	First International dissolved
1878	German antisocialist laws passed
1884	British Fabian Society founded
1889	Second International founded
1891	German antisocialist laws permitted to expire
1891	German Social Democratic Party's ErfurtProgram
1895	French *Confédération Générale du Travail* founded
1899	Eduard Bernstein's *Evolutionary Socialism*
1902	Formation of the British Labour party
1902	Lenin's *What Is to Be Done?*
1903	Bolshevik-Menshevik split

DOCUMENT | Darwin Defends a Mechanistic View of Nature

In the closing paragraphs of On the Origin of Species *(1859), Charles Darwin contrasted the view of nature he championed with that of his opponents. He argued that an interpretation of organic nature based on mechanistic laws was actually nobler than an interpretation based on divine creation. In the second edition, however, Darwin added the term Creator to these paragraphs.*

> ◆ Why does Darwin believe a mechanistic creation suggests no less dignity than creation by God? How does the insertion of the term Creator change this passage? What is the grandeur that Darwin finds in his view of life?

Authors of the highest eminence seem to be fully satisfied with the view that each species has been independently created. To my mind it accords better with what we know of the laws impressed on matter by the Creator, that the production and extinction of the past and present inhabitants of the world should have been due to secondary causes, like those determining the birth and death of the individual. When I view all beings not as special creations, but as the lineal descendants of some few beings which lived long before the first bed of the Cambrian [geological] system was deposited, they seem to me to become ennobled. …

It is interesting to contemplate a tangled bank, clothed with many plants of many kinds, with birds singing on the bushes, with various insects flitting about, and with worms crawling through the damp earth, and to reflect that these elaborately constructed forms, so different from each other, and dependent upon each other in so complex a manner, have all been produced by laws acting around us. These laws, taken in the largest sense, being Growth with Reproduction; Inheritance which is almost implied by reproduction; Variability from the indirect and direct action of the conditions of life, and from use and disuse: a Ratio of Increase so high as to lead to a Struggle for Life, and as a consequence to Natural Selection, entailing Divergence of Character and the Extinction of less-improved forms. Thus, from the war of nature, from famine and death, the most exalted object which we are capable of conceiving, namely the production of the higher animals, directly follows. There is grandeur in this view of life, with its several powers, having been originally breathed by the Creator into a few forms or into one; and that, whilst this planet has gone cycling on according to the fixed law of gravity, from so simple a beginning endless forms most beautiful and most wonderful have been, and are being evolved.

Charles Darwin, *On the Origin of Species and the Descent of Man* (New York: Modern Library, n.d.), pp. 373–374.

from the design of the universe and the whole concept of fixity in nature or the universe at large. The world was a realm of flux. The idea that physical and organic nature might be constantly changing allowed people to believe that society, values, customs, and beliefs should also change.

In 1871, in *The Descent of Man*, Darwin applied the principle of evolution by natural selection to human beings. Darwin was hardly the first person to treat human beings as animals, but he contended that humankind's moral nature and religious sentiments, as well as its physical frame, had developed naturalistically largely in response to the requirements of survival. Neither the origin nor the character of humankind, in Darwin's view, required the existence of a god for their explanation. Not since Copernicus had removed the earth from the center of the universe had the pride of Western human beings received so sharp a blow.

Darwin's theory of evolution by natural selection was controversial from the moment *On the Origin of Species* appeared. It encountered criticism from both the religious and the scientific communities. By the end of the century, scientists widely accepted the concept of evolution, but not yet Darwin's mechanism of natural selection. The acceptance of the latter really

dates from the 1920s and 1930s, when Darwin's theory was combined with modern genetics.

THE REVOLUTION IN PHYSICS

By the late 1870s, discontent arose over the belief of many physical scientists that their mechanistic models, solid atoms, and absolute time and space actually described the real universe.

In 1883, Ernst Mach (1838–1916) published *The Science of Mechanics*, in which he urged that scientists consider their concepts descriptive not of the physical world, but of the sensations experienced by the scientific observer. Scientists could describe only the sensations, not the physical world that underlay those sensations. In line with Mach, the French scientist Henri Poincaré (1854–1912) urged that the theories of scientists be regarded as hypothetical constructs of the human mind rather than as true descriptions of nature. In 1911, Hans Vaihinger (1852–1933) suggested the concepts of science be considered "as if" descriptions of the physical world. By World War I, few scientists believed they could portray the "truth" about physical reality. Rather, they saw themselves as recording the observations of instruments and as offering useful hypothetical or symbolic models of nature.

X Rays and Radiation   Discoveries in the laboratory paralleled the philosophical challenge to earlier physical science. In December 1895, Wilhelm Roentgen (1845–1923) published a paper on his discovery of X rays, a form of energy that penetrated various opaque materials. Major steps in the exploration of radioactivity followed within months of the publication of his paper.

In 1896, Henri Becquerel (1852–1908) discovered that uranium emitted a similar form of energy. The next year, J. J. Thomson (1856–1940), at Cambridge University, formulated the theory of the electron. The interior world of the atom had become a new area for human exploration. In 1902, Ernest Rutherford (1871–1937) explained the cause of radiation through the disintegration of the atoms of radioactive materials. Shortly thereafter, he speculated on the immense store of energy present in the atom.

Theories of Quantum Energy, Relativity, and Uncertainty   The discovery of radioactivity and discontent with the existing mechanical models led to revolutionary theories in physics. In 1900, Max Planck (1858–1947) pioneered the articulation of the quantum theory of energy, according to which energy is a series of discrete quantities, or packets, rather than a continuous stream. In 1905, Albert Einstein (1879–1955) published his first epochmaking papers on **relativity** in which he contended that time and space exist not separately, but rather as a combined continuum. Moreover, the measurement of time and space depends on the observer as well as on the entities being measured.

In 1927, Werner Heisenberg (1901–1976) set forth his uncertainty principle, according to which the behavior of subatomic particles is a matter of statistical probability rather than of exactly determinable cause and effect. Much that had seemed unquestionable about the physical universe had now become ambiguous.

The mathematical complexity of twentieth-century physics meant science would rarely again be successfully popularized. At the same time, through applied technology and further research in chemistry, physics, and medicine, science affected daily living more than ever before. Scientists from the late nineteenth century onward became the most successful group of Western intellectuals in gaining the financial support of governments and private institutions for the pursuit of their research. They did so by relating the success of science to the economic progress, military security, and the health of their nations. Science, through research, medicine, and technological change, has thus affected modern life more significantly than any other intellectual activity.

FRIEDRICH NIETZSCHE AND THE REVOLT AGAINST REASON

During the second half of the century, philosophers began to question the adequacy of rational thinking to address the human situation. No writer better exemplified this new attitude than the German philosopher Friedrich Nietzsche (1844–1900). His books remained unpopular until late in his life, when his brilliance had deteriorated into insanity. He was wholly at odds with the values of the age and attacked Christianity, democracy, nationalism, rationality, science, and progress. He sought less to change values than to probe their sources in the human character. He wanted not only to tear away the masks of respectable life, but also to explore how human beings made such masks.

His first important work was *The Birth of Tragedy* (1872) in which he urged that the nonrational aspects of human nature are as important and noble as the rational characteristics. He insisted on the positive function of instinct and ecstasy in human life. To limit human activity to strictly rational behavior was to impoverish human life. In this work, Nietzsche regarded Socrates as one of the major contributors to Western decadence because of the Greek philosopher's appeal for rationality. In Nietzsche's view, the strength for the heroic life and the highest artistic achievement arise from sources beyond rationality.

In later works, such as the prose poem *Thus Spake Zarathustra* (1883), Nietzsche criticized democracy and Christianity. Both would lead only to the mediocrity of sheepish masses. He announced the death of God and proclaimed the coming of the *Overman* (Übermensch), who would embody heroism and greatness. The term was frequently interpreted as some mode of superman or superrace, but such was not Nietzsche's intention. He was critical of contemporary racism and anti-Semitism. He sought a return to the heroism that he associated with Greek life in the Homeric age. He thought the values of Christianity and of bourgeois morality prevented humankind from achieving life on a heroic level.

Two of Nietzsche's most profound works are *Beyond Good and Evil* (1886) and *The Genealogy of Morals* (1887). Both are difficult books. Nietzsche sought to discover not what is good and what is evil, but the social and psychological sources of the judgment of good and evil. He declared, "There are no moral phenomena at all, but only a moral interpretation of phenomena."[5] He dared to raise the question of whether morality itself was valuable: "We need a critique of moral values; the value of these values themselves must first be called in question."[6] In Nietzsche's view, morality was a human convention that had no independent existence. For Nietzsche, this discovery liberated human beings to create life-affirming values instead. Christianity, utilitarianism, and middle-class respectability could, in good conscience, be abandoned. Human beings could create a new moral order that would glorify pride, assertiveness, and strength rather than meekness, humility, and weakness.

[5] *The Basic Writings of Nietzsche*, ed. and trans. by Walter Kaufman (New York: The Modern Library, 1968), p. 275.
[6] Ibid., p. 456.

THE BIRTH OF PSYCHOANALYSIS

A determination to probe beneath surface or public appearance united the major figures of late-nineteenth-century science, art, and philosophy. They sought to discern the undercurrents, tensions, and complexities that lay beneath the calm surfaces of hard atoms, respectable families, rationality, and social relationships. No intellectual development more exemplified this trend than psychoanalysis through the work of Sigmund Freud (1856–1939).

Development of Freud's Early Theories   Freud was born into an Austrian Jewish family that settled in Vienna. He planned to become a lawyer but soon moved to the study of physiology and medicine. In 1886, he opened his medical practice in Vienna, where he lived until driven out by the Nazis in 1938. Freud conducted all his research and writing from the base of his medical practice. His earliest medical interests had been psychic disorders, to which he sought to apply the critical method of science. In late 1885, he had studied in Paris with Jean-Martin Charcot (1825–1893), who used hypnosis to treat cases of hysteria. In Vienna, he collaborated with another physician, Josef Breuer (1842–1925), and in 1895 they published *Studies in Hysteria.*

In the mid-1890s, Freud abandoned hypnosis and allowed his patients to talk freely and spontaneously about themselves. He found that they associated their particular neurotic symptoms with experiences related to earlier experiences, going back to childhood. He also noted that sexual matters were significant in his patients' problems. For a time, he thought that perhaps sexual incidents during childhood accounted for their illnesses.

By 1897, however, Freud had rejected this view. In its place he formulated a theory of infantile sexuality, according to which sexual drives and energy already exist in infants and do not simply emerge at puberty. For Freud, human beings are sexual creatures from birth through adulthood. He thus questioned in the most radical manner the concept of childhood innocence. He also portrayed the little acknowledged matter of sexuality as one of the bases of mental order and disorder.

Freud's Concern with Dreams   During the same decade, Freud also examined the psychic phenomena of dreams. Romantic writers had taken dreams seriously, but few psychologists had examined them scientifically. Freud believed the seemingly irrational content of dreams must have a reasonable, scientific explanation. His research led him to reconsider the general nature of the human mind. He concluded that dreams allow unconscious wishes, desires, and drives that had been excluded from everyday conscious life to enjoy freer play in the mind. "The dream," he wrote, "is the [disguised] fulfillment of a [suppressed, repressed] wish."[7] During the waking hours,

the mind represses or censors certain wishes, which are as important to the individual's psychological makeup as conscious thought is. In fact, Freud argued, unconscious drives and desires contribute to conscious behavior. Freud developed these concepts and related them to his idea of infantile sexuality in his most important book, *The Interpretation of Dreams,* published in 1900.

Freud's Later Thought   In later books and essays, Freud developed a new model of the internal organization of the mind as an arena of struggle and conflict among three entities: the id, the superego, and the ego. The **id** consists of amoral, irrational, driving instincts for sexual gratification, aggression, and general physical and sensual pleasure. The **superego** embodies the external moral imperatives and expectations imposed on the personality by society and culture. The **ego** mediates between the impulses of the id and the asceticism of the superego and allows the personality to cope with the inner and outer demands of its existence. Consequently, everyday behavior displays the activity of the personality as its inner drives are partially repressed through the ego's coping with external moral expectations, as interpreted by the superego.

Despite his interest in the nonrational forces in human life and thought, Freud was a son of the Enlightenment. Like the *philosophes,* he was a realist who wanted human beings to live free of fear and illusions by rationally understanding themselves and their world. He saw the personalities of human beings as being determined by finite physical and mental forces in a finite world. He was hostile to religion and spoke of it as an illusion. Freud, like the writers of the eighteenth century, wished to see civilization and humane behavior prevail. More fully than those predecessors, however, he understood the immense sacrifice of instinctual drives required for rational civilized behavior. It has been a grave misreading of Freud to see him as urging humankind to thrust off all repression. He did indeed believe that excessive repression could lead to mental disorder, but he also believed civilization and the survival of humankind required some repression of sexuality and aggression. Freud thought the sacrifice and struggle were worthwhile, but he was pessimistic about the future of civilization in the West.

Islam and Late-Nineteenth-Century European Thought

The few late-nineteenth-century European thinkers who wrote about Islam interpreted it in terms of the growing contemporary scientific outlook as a historical religious phenomenon without any reference to the supernatural. Islam, like the other great world religions, was seen as a product of a particular culture and the same kind of analysis was applied to the

---

[7] *The Basic Writings of Sigmund Freud,* trans. by A. A. Brill (New York: The Modern Library, 1938), p. 235.

Qur'an. In the works of scholars such as the influential French writer Ernest Renan (1823–1892), Islam was, like Judaism, a manifestation of the ancient Semitic mentality, which had given rise to a powerful monotheistic vision. Renan, and sociologists such as the German Max Weber, also dismissed Islam as a religion and culture incapable of developing science and closed to new ideas.

However, Renan's views were opposed in a French journal by Jamal al-din Al-Afghani (1839– 1897), an Egyptian intellectual, who argued that over time Islam, which had arisen six hundred years after Christianity, would eventually produce cultures as modern as those in Europe. Al-Afghani was one of the rare Islamic writers who directly contested a European thinker.

The European racial and cultural outlooks that denigrated nonwhite peoples and their civilizations were also directed toward the Arab world. European authors who championed white racial superiority looked to India and the Aryan civilization that was supposed to have risen there and later influenced northern European life as the source of Europe's cultural superiority.

Christian missionaries reinforced these anti-Islamic attitudes. They blamed Islam for Arab economic backwardness, for mistreating women, and for condoning slavery. They also often came into conflict with Islamic religious authorities. Because the penalty for abjuring Islam is death, the missionaries made few converts among Muslims. So they turned their efforts to founding schools and hospitals, hoping these Christian foundations would eventually lead some Muslims to Christianity. Few Muslims converted, but these institutions did educate young Arabs in Western science and medicine, and

many of their students became leaders in the Middle East. Eventually, as missionary families came to live for long periods of time among Arabs, they became more sympathetic to Arab political aspirations.

Within the Islamic world, and especially in the decaying Ottoman Empire, as political leaders continued to champion Western scientific education and technology, they confronted a variety of responses from religious thinkers. Some of these thinkers sought to combine modern thought with Islam. For example, the Salafi, or the salafiyya movement, believed there was no inherent contradiction between science and Islam. They believed Muhammad had wisely and properly addressed the issues of his day, and a reformed Islamic faith could do so again. The Arab world should cease direct imitation of the West and modernize itself on the basis of a pure, restored Islamic faith. The Salafi emphasized a rational reading of the Qur'an and saw Ottoman decline as the result of Muslim religious error. This outlook, which had originally sought to reconcile Islam with the modern world, eventually led many Muslims in the twentieth century to oppose Western influence.

Other Islamic religious leaders simply rejected the West and modern thought. They included the Mahdist movement in Sudan, the Sanussiya in Libya, and the Wahhabi movement in the Arabian peninsula (see chapter 27). Such religious-based opposition was strongest in those portions of the Middle East where the European presence was least direct, which is to say outside of Morocco, Algeria, Egypt, and Tunisia, which for all intents and purposes were under the control of Western powers by 1900, and Turkey, where Ottoman leaders had long been deeply involved with the West.

Summary

Workers During the course of the nineteenth century, European workers underwent a process of proletarianization as the process of industrialization spread across the Continent. To protect their interests, European workers joined trade unions and socialist parties, such as the Labour Party in Britain. The Marxist critique of modern capitalism strongly influenced European socialism when the German Social Democratic Party adopted the thought of Karl Marx. In Russia, Lenin founded the Bolsheviks as an elite Marxist party that advocated the overthrow of the tsarist regime through a revolution of workers and peasants.

Women Laundry Workers.

Women Nineteenth-century women were divided along class lines. Unlike working-class women, most women of the upper and middle classes adopted a cult of domesticity and did not work outside the home. Most jobs available to women were low paying and insecure. Women of all classes faced social, political, and legal disabilities that were only gradually improved in the late nineteenth and early twentieth centuries. Before World War I, only Norway allowed women to vote, and few women could earn university degrees or enter the professions.

Jewish Emancipation   With the exception of Russia, European countries had abolished their legal restrictions on Jews by the mid-nineteenth century. Jews became more fully integrated into European political and economic life. After 1880, however, anti-Semitism increased as Jews were blamed for economic and social problems.

The United States   By 1914, the United States had become the world's leading industrial power. However, despite the creation of a mass industrial work force, socialism did not take root in the United States. Under presidents Theodore Roosevelt and Woodrow Wilson, the Progressive movement enacted a number of social and political reforms. The United States also embarked on a more aggressive foreign policy with the Spanish-American War, the acquisition of a colonial empire, interventions in Latin America, and, under Wilson, participation in World War I.

Modern European Through   In 1850, learned Europeans regarded the physical world as rational, mechanical, and dependable. By the first decades of the twentieth century philosophers, scientists, psychologists, and artists began to portray physical reality, human nature, and society in ways that seem familiar to us today. Physicists probed the mysteries of the atom. The theories of evolutionary biology contended that human nature is part of the order of nature and does not stand apart from nature. Traditional morality and the primacy of reason were challenged by Nietzsche and Freud. Within the Islamic world, modern European thought produced a variety of often conflicting responses.

Review Questions

1. What were the chief factors accounting for the proletarianization of the European labor force? How much of the change in the situation of workers was a result of technology and how much of the change in their organization?

2. How would you describe living conditions in European cities during the late nineteenth century? What factors contributed to those conditions? How did urban reform emerge?

3. How did the class position of a European woman determine much of her experience? How did industrialization change the social experience of working-class women? What were the social factors that limited the opportunities of women regardless of their class? Why did women grow discontented with their lot? What factors led to change? To what extent had they improved their position by 1914? Was the emancipation of women inevitable? How did women approach their situation differently from country to country?

4. What were the major characteristics of Jewish emancipation in the nineteenth century? How did late-century economic developments contribute to increasing prejudice against Jews?

5. How did the ideas of Karl Marx come to dominate so much late-nineteenth-century European socialism?

6. What was the status of the working-class groups in the United States and Europe in 1860? What improvements if any had been achieved by 1914?

7. What caused the emergence of trade unions and organized mass political parties in Europe?

8. How did the American Progressives, as reformers, differ from the various European Socialists? Why were the debates of "opportunism" and "revisionism" important to the Socialist parties? Why were there so many disputes among Socialists?

9. Assess the value of industrialism for Russia. Were the tsars wise in attempting to modernize their country or would they have been better off leaving it as it was? How did Lenin's view of socialism differ from that of Socialists in Western Europe? Why did socialism not emerge as a major political force in the United States?

10. What were the major changes in science in the late nineteenth century? How did both Darwin and Einstein challenge assumptions of earlier science? How may both Nietzsche and Freud be seen to challenge confidence in human rationality?

11. What were the chief characteristics of Western attitudes toward Islam in the nineteenth century? How did Islamic thinkers respond to modern Western thought.

Key Terms

Bolsheviks   (p. 756)

Duma   (p. 757)

ego   (p. 768)

Fabians   (p. 754)

id   (p. 768)

Marxism   (p. 753)

Mensheviks   (p. 756)

natural selection   (p. 765)

pogroms   (p. 750)

proletarianization   (p. 739)

relativity   (p. 767)

revisionism   (p. 754)

soviets   (p. 757)

suffragettes   (p. 749)

superego   (p. 768)

Documents CD-ROM

The Industrial Revolution

19.1 Sybil (1845) Benjamin Disraeli

19.2 Women Miners in the English Coal Pits

19.3 Sadler Report: Child Labor

19.4 A Defense of the Factory System (1835): Andrew Ure

19.5 The Chartist Demands (1838)

19.6 Luddism: An Assault on Technology

19.7 Utopian Socialism (1816): Robert Owen

19.8 Karl Marx and Friedrich Engels

NOTE: *To learn more about the topics in this chapter, see the Suggested Readings at the end of the book.*

26

Latin America from Independence to the 1940s

- Independence Without Revolution

- Economy of Dependence

- Search for Political Stability

- Three National Histories

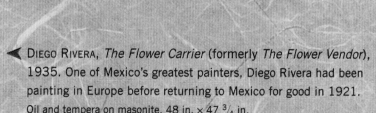

◄ DIEGO RIVERA, *The Flower Carrier* (formerly *The Flower Vendor*), 1935. One of Mexico's greatest painters, Diego Rivera had been painting in Europe before returning to Mexico for good in 1921.

Oil and tempera on masonite, 48 in. × 47 ³/₄ in. (121.92 cm × 121.29 cm) San Francisco Museum of Modern Art. Albert M. Bender Collection, Gift of Albert M. Bender in memory of Caroline Walter.

Latin American History

Since the early nineteenth century, Spanish- and Portuguese-speaking America stretching from the Rio Grande to Cape Horn has posed a paradox. Languages, religion, economic ties, and many political institutions render the area part of the Western world. Yet the economics, politics, and social life of Latin America have developed differently from other parts of the West. Exceedingly rich in natural resources, possessing gold, silver, nitrates, and oil, the region has been plagued with extreme poverty. As other Western nations have moved toward liberal democracy and social equality, the states of Latin America have had millions of citizens living in situations of marked inequality and social dependence. For over a century and a half, the political life of Latin America has been characterized by uncertain democracy, authoritarian regimes, and a general tendency toward instability. Three major explanations have been set forth to account for these difficulties which have led to so much tragedy and human suffering.

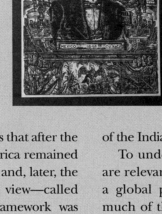

The first and most widely accepted view contends that after the wars of independence the new states of Latin America remained economically and culturally dependent on Europe and, later, the United States. In effect, proponents of this view—called **dependency theory**—argue that the colonial framework was never abolished. Under Spanish and Portuguese rule, Latin America's wealth was extracted and exported for the benefit of those powers. After independence, the creole elite turned toward foreign investors, first British and then American, to finance economic development and to provide the technology for mining, transport, and industry. As a result, Latin America became dependent on wealthy foreign powers for investment and for markets. These foreign powers, more interested in strong governments that would protect their interests than in developing the economies and political structures of the Latin American states, threw their support behind dictators whose policies impoverished their people and suppressed democratic dissent.

A second explanation emphasizes the Iberian heritage. Its advocates contend that Latin America should be viewed as a region on the periphery of the Western world in the same manner that Spain, Portugal, and Italy lie on the Mediterranean periphery of Europe. All of these Latin nations, dominated by Roman Catholicism, have had similar unstable and often authoritarian governments. They have frequently tended toward some version of dictatorship, uneven development, anticlericalism, and social cleavage between urban and rural areas and between wealthy middle-class or landed elites and poor peasant populations. Viewed in this Iberian-Mediterranean context, Latin America seems less puzzling than when it is viewed in the context of northern Europe.

A third explanation emphasizes conscious political, economic, and cultural decisions the Latin American **creole** elite took after independence. This explanation contends that the elite, including the army officers who won the wars, sought to enrich themselves and to maintain their positions at the cost of all other segments of the population, who in many of these countries differed ethnically and racially from the elite. These officers, landowners, and urban middle-class leaders aligned their national economies with the industrializing regions of Europe and North America, with which they aligned themselves culturally as well, thus differentiating themselves from the lower classes and indigenous peoples and culture. They also adopted European liberal political and economic ideologies to justify unlimited exploitation of economic resources on the basis of individualist enterprise. They then used the wealth generated by this exploitation to maintain their power. They embraced European concepts of progress to dismiss the legitimacy of the culture and communal values of the Indians or the peasants.

To understand the region and its past, all three viewpoints are relevant. In addition, it helps to view Latin America within a global perspective. Beginning in the nineteenth century much of the region, like much of Asia and Africa, was drawn into an integrated worldwide economic system dominated by Europe and North America. Many nations in Latin America and elsewhere developed narrow economies based on the export of one or a few raw materials or semifinished products. They were vulnerable to fluctuations in worldwide demand for these products and to political and economic interference from Europe and North America. The results were often economic turbulence and political instability.

By THE MID-1820S, LATIN AMERICANS HAD DRIVEN out their colonial rulers and broken the colonial trade monopolies (see Map 26–1). Although rich in natural resources, the region did not achieve widespread prosperity and long-lasting political stability for more than a century after independence. The wars of independence had not been popular grass-roots movements. They had originated with the creole elite, who were seeking to resist the imposition of European liberalism by Napoleon or, later, the Spanish liberals. In effect, the wars had been fought to break the colonial trade monopolies and to preserve the existing social structure. The military leaders of the wars held much of the political power in the new nations the wars had created.

The wars also destroyed much of the economic infrastructure of the region. Mines had been flooded, livestock depleted, and the work force disrupted. Whereas previously colonial Latin America had been dependent on Spain for its exports and financial credits, it now became dependent on Great Britain and later on the United States.

Latin America shares many cultural features with Europe and North America. Its languages are primarily European, although much of its population speaks Native American languages. Its primary religion is Roman Catholicism. Its nations have often adopted the constitutional traditions of Europe and the United States. Many of its elite have studied abroad. Despite these important similarities, however, the economic and political development of Latin America has been different from that of much of Europe or the United States.

The reasons for these differences have long puzzled historians. Why has Latin America been less stable and less prosperous than Europe and North America? The answers appear to lie in the role Latin America played in the integrated global economic system that began to develop in the nineteenth century, just when it achieved political independence. This system prevented Latin Americans from achieving economic independence. The region's leaders thought they could best satisfy the economic interests of their nations by providing raw materials to the world economy. Most Latin American nations consequently developed export economies devoted to raw materials or semifinished goods. Unfortunately, this decision made their export products vulnerable to worldwide fluctuations in demand. They were also susceptible to undue influence from foreign business and banking interests and to political interference by the governments of the United States and Europe.

Latin America had much in common with other regions of the world—Africa and Asia, for example—during the nineteenth and early twentieth centuries. In all three regions, particular nations or areas would specialize in a particular niche in the increasingly integrated world economy. In Asia and Africa vast plantations produced products such as rubber; in Latin America plantations might produce sugar or coffee. In all three regions huge mining industries extracted resources such as copper, phosphates, gold, and diamonds. Virtually all such enterprises were dominated by Europeans or North Americans. Filling a particular niche by supplying a particular raw product might bring initial prosperity but provided too narrow an economic base for sustained economic well-being. In contrast, the economic advance of the United States and Europe was largely due to their ability to exploit niche economies around the globe.

Independence Without Revolution

IMMEDIATE CONSEQUENCES OF LATIN AMERICAN INDEPENDENCE

The wars of independence left Latin America by the late 1820s liberated from direct European control, but economically exhausted and politically unstable (see Map 26–1). Only Brazil tended to prosper immediately after independence. In contrast, the new republics of the former Spanish empire felt themselves weak and vulnerable. Because the wars of independence had been largely civil wars, the new governments knew that many of their populations might welcome their collapse. Economic life on the continent contracted, and in 1830 over-

all production was lower than it had been in 1800. Difficult terrain over vast distances made interregional trade difficult, and few institutions fostered it. The old patterns of overseas trade had been disrupted. There was an absence of funds for investment. Many wealthy *peninsulares* returned to Spain or departed for Cuba. Consequently, Latin American governments and businesses looked to Britain for protection, markets, and capital investment.

Independence itself also created several new sources of discontent. There was much disagreement about the character of the future government, even among those who had most wanted to oust the Spanish. Certain institutions, such as the Roman Catholic Church, that had enjoyed a privileged status

Interactive map to explore this map further, go to http://www.prenhall.com/craig3_map26.1

CANADA (Great Britian)

UNITED STATES

ATLANTIC

OCEAN

San Antonio

MEXICO
1821

Gulf of Mexico

Mexico City

Veracruz

CUBA (Spain)

HAITI 1804

PUERTO (Spain)
RICO

BR. HONDURAS

Guatemala

Caribbean Sea

UNITED PROVINCES OF
CENTRAL AMERICA
1823–1839

Panama

Caracas

TRINIDAD

BR. GUIANA

DUTCH GUIANA

FR. GUIANA

Bogotá

GRAN
COLOMBIA
1819–1830

GALAPAGOS IS.

Quito

Amazon R.

PACIFIC

PERU
1821

INDEFINITE BOUNDARY

EMPIRE OF BRAZIL
1822

Lima

Andes

Bahia

BOLIVIA
1825

OCEAN

Sucre

PARAGUAY
1811

Rio de Janeiro

Mountains

Asunción

CHILE
1818

URUGUAY 1828

Santiago

Buenos
Aires

Montevideo

UNITED PROVINCES
OF LA PLATA
1816

500 MILES

500 KILOMETERS

MAP 26–1 Latin America In 1830   By 1830 most of Latin America had been liberated from Europe. This map shows the initial borders of the states of the region with the dates of their independence. The United Provinces of La Plata formed the nucleus of what later became Argentina.

in the colonial period sought to maintain those privileges under new and often unfriendly governments. Indian communities, which had also been somewhat protected by paternalistic colonial policies, found themselves subject to new exploitation once Indians were made equal citizens under the law. Major disagreements arose between the creole elites of different regions of the new nations. The agricultural hinterlands resented the predominance of the port cities, whose merchants set the terms of trade. Investors or merchants from one Latin American nation found themselves in conflict with those of others over transport tariffs on rivers or over mining regulations. Civilians often became rivals of the military for political authority.

ABSENCE OF SOCIAL CHANGE

Yet no matter what the actual or potential conflict among various groups in the literate political and economic elites might be, they all opposed substantial social reform. The creole victors in the wars of independence granted equal rights to all persons, and except for Brazil, the independent states had abolished slavery by 1855. However, the right to vote depended on a property qualification, and peasants remained dependent on and often subservient to their landlords. The racial codes of the colonial empires disappeared, but not the racial prejudice. Although mestizos, mulattos, and even Indians who achieved economic success were assimilated into the higher ranks of the social structure, persons of white or nearly white complexion tended to constitute the elite of Latin America. The creole elite generally discriminated against the peoples of color in their midst. Most important, no major changes in landholding accompanied the wars of independence; the ruling classes of all the newly independent nations protected the interests of landholders.

Except for Mexico in 1910, no Latin American nation, from the wars of independence until the 1950s, experienced a fundamental revolution that overthrew the social and economic structures dating from the colonial period. The absence of such social revolution, which would necessarily have involved changes in landholding, is perhaps the single most important factor in Latin American history during the first century of independence. The rise and fall of political regimes represented quarrels among the elite and did not substantially change the structures or expectations of everyday life for most of the population. Throughout the social structure there was no mutually shared trust or allegiance to the political system.

CONTROL OF THE LAND

Most Latin Americans during the nineteenth century lived in the countryside. Agriculture continued to be dominated by large *haciendas*, or plantations. The landowners virtually ruled these estates as small domains. They were nearly a law unto

▲ **A Chilean Cattle Estate.** The great landowners of Latin America ruled their huge estates as small domains.
Sergio Larrain/Magnum Photos Inc.

themselves. The *latifundia* (the large rural estates) actually grew larger during the nineteenth century. Confiscated church lands and conquered Indian territories augmented existing estates or led to the establishment of new ones. These estates might include tens of thousands of acres yet be attended by a relatively sparse work force. Work was labor intensive because little machinery was available; virtually none was manufactured in Latin America. Herding and stock raising produced salted meat, leather, tallow, and wool for the export market. For some products—salted meats, for example—there was a limited manufacturing stage in Latin America. Other agricultural exports included cereal crops, tobacco, sugar, coffee, and cacao.

Landowners constituted a society of their own. Their families intermarried. They sometimes formed friendships or family alliances with members of the wealthy urban classes who were involved in export commerce or the law. Younger sons might enter the army or the church. The landowners served in the various postindependence national parliaments or congresses. Their wealth, literacy, and social connections made them the rulers of the countryside, and the army would protect them from any social uprising.

The landowners lived well and comfortably, although often on isolated estates. Most of the rural work force were socially and economically dependent on them. In Brazil slavery persisted until 1888. Although it was once argued that slavery in Roman Catholic Latin America was more paternalistic and less harsh than elsewhere, that view has long been abandoned among scholars who now believe Latin American slavery was as harsh as that in North America and perhaps more so. In other rural areas many people lived as virtual slaves. **Debt peonage** was widespread and often tied a peasant to the land like a European serf. A peon would become indebted to his landlord and could never repay the debt. Later in the nineteenth century the new lands that were opened were generally organized as large holdings with tenants rather than as small landholdings with independent farmers. This was markedly different from both the United States and Canada. Poor roads and limited railways made internal travel difficult and kept many people on the land. Little effort was made to provide even a primary education, leaving millions of Latin American peasants ignorant, lacking any significant technological skills, and incapable of improving their condition or of protesting or escaping their bondage to the land and its owners.

The second half of the nineteenth century witnessed a remarkable growth in Latin American urban life. There was some movement from the countryside to the city and an influx of European immigrants as well as some from Asia. The creole elite favored European immigration, which increased the size of the white population; Asian immigration was a source of inexpensive labor. Throughout this period there arose a political and social trade-off between the urban and rural elites. Each more or less permitted the other to pursue its economic self-interest, to profit from the commodity export economy through commerce or production, and to repress any discontent. Nonetheless, the growth of the urban centers shifted political influence from the countryside to the cities and gave rise to an urban working class and all the social discontents associated with vast numbers of relatively poor people working in difficult situations. Urban growth in Latin America created social and political difficulties not unlike those that arose in Europe and the United States at about the same time.

SUBMISSIVE POLITICAL PHILOSOPHIES

The political philosophies embraced by the educated and propertied creole elites also discouraged any real challenge to the social order. The political ideas associated with European liberalism, which flourished in Latin America immediately after independence, supported republican government but also limited the franchise to property holders. Thus in Latin America, as in Europe, liberalism protected property and tended to ignore the social problems of the poor and propertyless. In addition, the creole elite frequently exhibited racial prejudice toward the mulatto, mestizo, and Indian populations.

Economic liberalism and the need for British investment led to the championing of free trade. During the decades immediately after independence, Latin America actually exported less than it had under colonial rule. The region achieved a trade balance by exporting precious metals. Because these metals often came from stocks mined years earlier, this in effect amounted to a flight of capital. The general economic view was that Latin America would produce raw materials for export in exchange for manufactured goods imported from Europe, and especially from Britain.

For most of the nineteenth century the landed sector of the economy dominated because cheap imports from abroad and a shortage of local capital discouraged indigenous attempts at industrialism. Latin American liberals championed the extension of great landed estates and all the forms of social dependence associated with them. The produce of the new land could contribute raw materials or lightly processed goods for export to pay for the import of finished goods. Liberals thus favored confiscating land owned by the church and the Indian communities, because these groups did not exploit their lands in a progressive manner, according to the liberals.

During the second half of the century, **positivism**—the political ideas stemming from the French positivist philosopher Auguste Comte (1798–1857)—swept across Latin America. Comte and his followers, had advocated the cult of science and technological progress. This highly undemocratic outlook suggested that either technocrats or dictatorial governments could best achieve modernization. It was especially popular among military officers and influenced the ongoing Latin American struggle between civilian and military elites. The great slogan of Latin American positivism, emblazoned on the flag of the Brazilian republic, was "Order and Progress." Social or political groups that created disorder or challenged the existing social order were by definition unprogressive.

Toward the close of the century the military forces in various countries—following the model of European armies, especially Germany's—became more professionalized. Their new training often made the officer corps the most important educated elite in a country. Their education and attachment to the armies they served gave them considerable influence, generally of a conservative character.

Finally, the late-nineteenth-century European theories of "scientific" racism were used to preserve the Latin American social status quo and the dominance of those of white or more nearly white complexions. Racial theory could attribute the economic backwardness of the region to its vast nonwhite or mixed-blood population. This explanation, of course, shifted responsibility for the economic difficulties of Latin America away from the mostly white governing elites toward Indians, blacks, **mestizos**, and **mulattos**, who had long been exploited or repressed.

This conservative intellectual heritage continued to affect twentieth-century political thought. First, it can be seen in the ongoing tendency of military groups in Latin America to view themselves as the guarantors of order. These groups were ready to intervene in political affairs and seize control from civilians to protect the status quo or to thwart social change. Second, it can be seen in the way the political elites of Latin America naturally and actively opposed communism after the Russian Revolution. Although many Latin American nations had small organized Communist parties, governments used the fear of communism to resist virtually all political movements—Communist or not—that advocated social reform or questioned property arrangements. From the 1920s onward, in Latin America as in Europe, the fear of communism brought support to conservative governments, whether civilian or military. Communism would become an even more powerful issue throughout the region after the successful Cuban Revolution of 1957 installed an actual Soviet-dominated Communist state in Latin America.

Economy of Dependence

The wars of independence destroyed the Spanish and Portuguese colonial trade monopolies. Where previously only a few dozen ships called annually at any port, hundreds laden with goods from all over the world could now drop anchor. Consequently, Latin America had many new trading partners, but it remained heavily dependent on non-Latin American economies. Trade was free and the nations were politically independent, but other nations continued to shape Latin American economic life in the most fundamental manner.

One of the chief reasons for this dependence on foreign trading partners was the absence of large internal markets. Had such markets existed during the colonial period itself, the newly independent nations might have been able to trade with each other rather than primarily with nations outside the region. Trade after independence flowed in the same direction that trade had flowed before independence because Europe remained the source of imports of finished goods. Furthermore, then as now, geographical barriers hindered internal trade. The jungles of the Amazon and the Andes Mountains prevented any easy east–west trade. No road systems allowed goods to travel between countries or even easily within them, and there was little domestic investment in transport. European and American investments in railways generally facilitated exports rather than internal trade.

NEW EXPLOITATION OF RESOURCES

As previously noted, the wars of independence sharply disrupted the Latin American economy. In both Mexico and Peru, mines were flooded; machinery was in disrepair; labor was dispersed. Agricultural production was also disrupted. Between 1825 and 1850 the new nations attempted to set their economic houses in order, but with mixed results. Capital financing to restore the mining industry and establish new industries was totally inadequate. Virtually no domestic industries existed to manufacture heavy equipment or build ships. Both to restore old industries, such as mining, and to have access to modern transport, such as steamships and railroads, Latin Americans had to turn to Europe and North America. For many decades Britain exercised the predominant economic influence over Latin America. Britain had sought to break the old colonial monopoly. Once it was gone, the British rapidly established their own economic dominance. This desire to pour manufactured goods into Latin America also led Britain and other nations to discourage the development of manufacturing industries there. Europeans and Americans had no desire to see competitors emerge. Foreign investment did help revive the mining industry in Mexico, Peru, and Chile, but mining produces raw materials, not manufactured goods.

▲ **Brazilian Coffee** being loaded onto a British ship. Most Latin American countries developed an export economy based on the exchange of agricultural products, raw materials, and semifinished goods for finished goods and services from abroad. Until recently, the coffee industry dominated both the political and economic life of Brazil. Corbis-Bettmann.

To pay for imports and foreign services, Latin American nations turned to the production of agricultural commodities for which there was great European demand. This shift meant that the rural areas of Latin America and the commercial centers serving agriculture became politically and economically more important than many of the old colonial urban centers. The production of wheat, beef, hides, hemp, coffee, cocoa, and other foodstuffs for the export market also raised the value of land and led governments to expand into previously unsettled territory and to confiscate the lands of the church. Because so much land was available, agricultural production was increased by putting more land under cultivation rather than by finding more efficient ways to farm areas already under cultivation. So much wealth could be accumulated through land speculation and land development that little incentive existed for alternative investments in manufacturing. It would also have been difficult, if not impossible, for new Latin American industries to compete with the cheap goods imported from more established industrial economies abroad.

After 1850 the Latin American republics became, relatively speaking, more prosperous. Chile exported copper and nitrates as well as wheat. Peru exported guano to be used as fertilizer. Coffee was becoming king in Venezuela, Brazil, Colombia, and Central America. Sugar continued to be produced in the West Indies as well as in Cuba, which remained under Spanish control. Argentina supplied hides and tallow. But this limited prosperity and recovery were based on the export of agricultural commodities or extracted minerals or nonreplenishable resources, such as guano, and the importation of finished goods from abroad.

Yet the period from approximately 1870 through 1930 came to be seen as a kind of golden age for the Latin American economy. There was more prosperity than ever before, especially in Chile, Argentina, Brazil, and Mexico. The export economy seemed to foster genuine economic growth. The economies of the Latin American nations grew because industrial production in Europe and the United States created a demand for more exports. The Latin American export economy also allowed large quantities of new products to be imported from Europe and the United States. Both the exports and the imports drew Latin America more deeply than ever into the world economy.

There were three broad varieties of late-nineteenth-century Latin American exports. First were foodstuffs raised in Latin America that were more or less like those that could be raised in Europe, chiefly wheat and beef products, for which Argentina became the great exporter. Second were distinctly tropical products, such as bananas, sugar, and coffee. Third were natural resources, including metals, of which copper was the most important; minerals, such as nitrates; and, later, oil. (See overview on page 793.)

Both the trading patterns for these goods and the internal improvements in Latin American production deeply and inextricably linked the economy of the region to Europe and, after 1900, to the United States. Europeans and North Americans provided capital and the technological and managerial skills to build bridges, roads, railroads, steam lines, and new mines. Most of the transport system was constructed to service the existing export economy rather than to foster the development of alternative forms of domestic economic development. Furthermore, whenever the economy of Europe or the United States floundered, Latin America was hurt. The region could not control its own economic destiny. A decline in the prices of commodities and raw materials could, of course, force Latin America to reduce the amount of goods it imported, harming its European and North American trading partners. But the major economic difficulties almost always struck Latin America first and lasted there longest.

INCREASED FOREIGN OWNERSHIP AND INFLUENCE

During the late nineteenth century the relative prosperity of the export sector increased the degree of dependence. The growing European demand generated by spreading industrialism gave Latin Americans a false sense of the long-term security of their export markets. The vast profits to be made through mining and agricultural exports discouraged investment in local industry, except as it served the export economy. Land still remained the most favored form of domestic investment. Foreigners saw no reason to capitalize local industry that might replace goods being imported. By late in the century the wealthy classes in Latin America had, in effect, lost control and even ownership of some of the most valuable sectors of their economy. For example, in 1901 British and other foreign investors owned approximately 80 percent of the Chilean nitrate industry. Foreigners also owned and operated most of the steamship lines and railroads.

The European and American economic penetration of Latin America was more subtle than that experienced by India or China, but it was no less real. Foreign ownership was not the only indication of economic dependence. Foreign powers used their political and military influence to protect their economic interests. Britain was the dominant power until the turn of the century. Its diplomats and military and naval officers were frequently involved directly or indirectly in the domestic political affairs of the Latin American nations. From the Spanish American War of 1898 onward the United States began to exercise more direct influence in the region. In 1903, to facilitate its plans to build a canal across the Isthmus of Panama, the United States participated in the rebellion that allowed Panama to separate from Colombia. There were numerous

Finally, petroleum began to replace other natural products as an absolute percentage of world trade. This shift meant that petroleum-exporting countries, such as Mexico, gained a greater share of export income.

ECONOMIC CRISES AND NEW DIRECTIONS

The Great Depression turned the difficult economic conditions of the 1920s into a genuine crisis. Commodity prices virtually collapsed. The economic decline in Europe and the United States also lessened the demand for Latin American products. The republics of Latin America could not repay their debts to foreign banks, and a number of them suspended interest payments. Those decisions in turn worsened the economic crisis in the more developed creditor nations. The depression led eventually to the beginning of a new economic era in Latin America. The new era, which really began after the conclusion of World War II, was marked by strong economic nationalism and a determination to create sectors of the various national economies that were not wholly dependent on events and wealth outside Latin America. These various drives toward economic independence have had mixed success, but they date only from the turmoil of the depression.

Where did industrialism fit into this general picture of a dependent economy, or what is sometimes termed a *neo-colonial economy*? The brief answer is, almost always, on the periphery of the export sector. Until the 1940s major industrialization did not occur in Latin America. There were, however, significant earlier developments. Before World War I light manufacturing was done in connection with preparing exports, such as beef processing in Argentina. Light manufactured goods such as textiles were also produced. With the depression, however, it became necessary to substitute domestically manufactured goods for those traditionally imported from abroad. Various nations pursued different policies of what was called *import substitution*, but all of these policies were undertaken because of the collapse of the export economy rather than because of any independent decision to industrialize. In that regard, the effort to industrialize was itself a result of being dependent.

By the mid-1940s there were three major varieties of manufacturing in Latin America. First, there were industries that, as in the past, transformed raw materials for export. They included sugar and other food processing, tin and copper mining, and petroleum refining. Second, there were industries addressing local demands, such as power plants, textiles, foundries, machine shops, and food companies. Third, there were industries depending generally on the transformation of imported materials. These industries were basically assembly plants whose owners could take advantage of inexpensive

United States and Latin America. U.S. influence and investments in Latin America grew rapidly after 1900 and surpassed those of Britain by the 1920s. As this cartoon illustrates, the United States tended to regard its southern neighbors as at best junior and dependent partners. Corbis-Bettmann.

other instances of U.S. military intervention in the Caribbean and in Central America. By the 1920s U.S. investments had become dominant as a result of two decades of "Dollar Diplomacy." During that decade, largely as a result of economic dislocations arising from World War I, the United States generally replaced Great Britain as the dominant trading partner of Latin American nations. The role of the United States remains controversial, but from a structural standpoint it was just one more example of a dominant foreign power treating Latin America as a junior and dependent economic partner.

The United States interventions were one cost to Latin America of being a dependent economy. More significant costs, however, arose from fundamental shifts in world trade that were brought on by World War I and continued through the 1920s. First, the overall amount of trade carried on by European countries decreased, particularly during the war, when traditional trading partners divided into two warring camps. Second, during the 1920s world prices of agricultural commodities dropped steadily. Latin American nations had to produce more goods to pay for their imports, and no easy or rapid adjustment was possible. Third, various synthetic products manufactured in Europe or North America replaced the natural products long supplied by Latin American producers. Most important among these products were synthetic nitrates.

labor. None of this manufacturing was particularly sophisticated, and none of it involved heavy industry. Not until the 1950s would significant steel production, for example, occur in the region.

Search for Political Stability

The new states of independent Latin America, unlike the British colonies of North America, had little or no experience in self-government. The Spanish empire had been ruled directly by the monarchy and by Spanish-born royal bureaucrats. Spain had persistently discriminated against the creole elite as well as against mulattos, mestizos, and Indians. This monarchical or paternalistic heritage survived in two forms. First, many traditionalists and conservatives favored the establishment of monarchies in Latin America, including José de San Martín (1778–1850). Monarchy was briefly established in Mexico. In Brazil, an emperor from the Portuguese royal family governed until 1889.

The second heritage of the colonial monarchy was the proclivity of the Latin American political elites to tolerate or actively to support strong executives. Few of the early republic constitutions endured or established a stable political life. They were frequently suspended or rewritten, so that a strong leader could consolidate his own power. Such figures, who appeared throughout Latin America during the nineteenth century, were called *caudillos*. They usually came from the army officer corps or enjoyed strong ties to the army. Whatever constitutional justification they provided for themselves, the real basis of their rule was force and repression. *Caudillos* might support conservative causes, such as protection of the church or strong central government, or they might pursue liberal policies, such as the confiscation of church land, the extension of landed estates, and the development of education.

Initially, such dictatorial government was accepted simply to ensure political stability when republican regimes floundered. In many countries the early years of independence saw internal conflicts among regions. In this situation, a national *caudillo* might reach a compromise with various regional *caudillos* that allowed them to retain substantial local control.

These strongmen also encountered little opposition because of their repressive policies. Later in the century the new relative prosperity of expanding economies quieted potential discontent. The dictators became more skilled at both repression and patronage. The political and social elites also rallied to their support when, around the turn of the century, the young labor movement called strikes.

Even when *caudillos* were forced from office and parliamentary government was more or less restored, the regimes that replaced them were neither genuinely liberal nor democratic. Parliamentary governments usually ruled by courtesy of the military and in the economic interest of the existing elites. No matter who ruled, the life of the overwhelming mass of the population changed little. Except for the Mexican Revolution of 1910, Latin American politics was run by and for the elite.

Three National Histories

Three Latin American nations possess over 50 percent of the land, people, and wealth of the region. They are Argentina, Mexico, and Brazil. Their national histories illustrate the more general themes of Latin American history.

ARGENTINA

Argentine history from independence to World War II can be divided into three general eras. From the rebellion against Spain in 1810 until midcentury, the question of which region of the nation would dominate political and economic life was foremost. From 1853 until 1916 Argentina experienced extraordinary economic expansion and large-scale immigration from Europe, which transformed its society and its position in the world. From 1916 to 1943 Argentines failed to establish a democratic state and struggled with the ramifications of an economy they did not really control.

Buenos Aires Versus the Provinces In 1810 the junta in Buenos Aires had overturned Spanish government in the viceroyalty of Río de la Plata. However, the other regions of the viceroyalty refused to accept the leadership of the province and city of Buenos Aires. Paraguay, Uruguay, and Upper Peru (Bolivia) went their separate ways. Conflicts between Buenos Aires and the remaining provinces dominated the first seventy years of Argentine history. It was the story of *porteños*, as the inhabitants of Buenos Aires were called, versus provincials. Eventually Buenos Aires established its primacy because of its capacity to dominate trade on the Río de la Plata and its control of the international customhouse, which assured revenue.

Between 1821 and 1827 Bernardino Rivadavia (1780–1845) worked to create a liberal political state but could not overcome the centrifugal forces of regionalism. His major accomplishment was a commercial treaty in 1823 that established Great Britain as a dominant trading partner. Thus began a deep intermeshing of trade and finance between the two nations that would continue for over a century. After Rivadavia's resignation in 1827 came the classical period of *caudillo* rule in Argentina. The strongman of the province of Buenos Aires was Juan Manuel de Rosas (1793–1877). In 1831 he negotiated the Pact of the Littoral, whereby Buenos Aires was put in charge of foreign relations, trade, and the customhouse, while the other provinces were left to run their own internal affairs. Within Buenos Aires, Rosas set up what amounted to dictatorial rule. He tolerated

Juan Manuel de Rosas (1793–1877), a *caudillo* of Buenos Aires from 1827 to 1852.
Corbis-Bettmann.

no dissent, no civil liberties, and no political power distinct from his own. One of his devices was the secret *Mazorca* (ear of corn) association, which terrorized his opponents. His major policies were expansion of trade and agriculture, suppression of the Indians, and nationalism. In Argentine history Rosas symbolized government by a single strong figure.

Expansion and Growth of the Republic   Rosa's success in strengthening Buenos Aires bred resentment in other provinces. In 1852 Justo José de Urquiza (1800–1870), the *caudillo* of the state of Entre Rios, overthrew Rosas. The next year a federal constitution was promulgated for the Argentine Republic. Buenos Aires remained aloof until the republic conquered the province in 1859. Disputes continued. In 1880 the city of Buenos Aires was made a distinct federal province, separate from its rich hinterland. Provincials had hoped that this arrangement would lessen the influence of the city; however, the economic prosperity of the end of the century simply gave the capital new prominence.

The Argentine economy was overwhelmingly agricultural, the chief exports at midcentury being animal products. Internal transportation was poor and the country was sparsely populated. Technological advances changed this situation during the last quarter of the century. In 1876 the first refrigerator ship, *La Frigiorique,* steamed into Buenos Aires. Henceforth, it would be possible to transport large quantities of Argentine beef to Europe. Furthermore, at about the same time it became clear that wheat farming could be extended throughout the pampas. In 1879 and 1880 a government army under General (and later President) Julio Roca (president 1880–1886, 1898–1904) carried out a major campaign against the Indian population known as the *Conquest of the Desert.* The British soon began to construct and manage railways to carry wheat from the interior to the coast, where it would be loaded on British and other foreign steamships. Government policy made the purchase of land by wealthy Argentines simple and cheap. The owners, in turn, rented the land to tenants. The predominance of both large landowners and foreign business interests thus continued throughout the most significant economic transformation in Argentine history.

The development of the pampas and the vastly increased production of beef and wheat made Argentina one of the wealthiest nations of Latin America and a major agricultural rival of the United States. The opening of land, even if only for tenant farming and not ownership, encouraged hundreds of thousands of Europeans, particularly from Spain and Italy, to emigrate to Argentina. The immigrants also provided workers for the food-processing, service, and transportation industries in Buenos Aires. By 1900 the new economic life and the thousands of new citizens had drastically changed Argentina. It became much more urbanized and industrialized. More people had reason to be politically discontent. Moreover, the children of the nineteenth-century immigrants often became the strongest Argentine nationalists during the twentieth century.

The prosperity of economic expansion quieted most political opposition for some time. The conservative landed oligarchy continued to govern under presidents who sought to perpetuate a strong export economy. Like similar groups elsewhere, they ignored the social questions raised by urbanization and industrialization. However, they also ignored the political aspirations of the urban middle and professional classes, whose members wanted a greater share in political life and an end to political corruption. In 1890 these groups founded the Radical Party, which for many years achieved few successes. However, in 1912 the conservative government expanded the franchise and provided for the secret ballot.

Four years later, Hipólito Irigoyen (1850–1933), leader of the Radical Party, was elected president (first term 1916–1922). Without significant support in the legislature, his presidency brought fewer changes than might have been expected. He remained neutral in World War I, so Argentina could trade with both sides. Nonetheless, the war put great pressure on the economy, and much labor agitation resulted.

Although previously sympathetic toward labor, Irigoyen as president used troops against strikers. The most violent labor clash occurred in January 1919, when troops quelled a general strike in Buenos Aires during what became known as the *Semana Trágica*, or Tragic Week. Thereafter, the Radical Party attempted to consolidate support among conservatives and pursued policies that benefited landowners and urban business interests. This was possible because of the close relationship between agricultural producers and processors and because both the landed and the middle classes wanted to resist concessions to the working classes.

The Military in Ascendence   By the end of the 1920s the one-time reformist Radical Party had become corrupt and directionless. The worldwide commodity depression hurt exports. In 1930 the military staged a coup against the aged Irigoyen, who had returned to the presidency in 1928. The officers eventually returned power to conservative civilians, and Argentina remained heavily dependent on the British export market. U.S. interests also began to establish plants in Argentina, removing still more economic activity from Argentine control.

Throughout the 1930s a right-wing nationalistic movement, *nacionalismo*, arose among writers, political journalists, and a few active politicians. This movement resembled the Fascist political movements then active in Europe. Its supporters were angered by British and American domination of the economy, equating their influence with imperialism. In politics the movement's supporters rejected liberalism and spread the fear of international communism. They also exhibited a strong anti-Semitic spirit and warmly supported the Roman Catholic Church. *Nacionalismo* was associated with a relatively progressive social policy rooted in the social values of the late-nineteenth-century papacy of Leo XIII. It advocated social reforms

▲ **Eva Perón** was as influential as her husband, Juan Perón, during his years in power in the late 1940s and early 1950s. She was especially effective in attracting popular support for his government. They are shown here in a reception line in 1951.
Corbis-Bettmann.

that recognized the needs of workers and the poor but that also sought to promote social harmony rather than Communist revolution or Socialist reconstruction of the economy. The various writers who set forth these ideas also looked back to Rosas as a role model for Argentine politics. In effect these groups were anti-imperialistic, socially concerned, authoritarian, and sympathetic to the rule of a modern *caudillo*. The pressures that came to the fore as a result of World War II gave these attitudes and their supporters influence that they had not previously enjoyed.

The war closed almost all of Europe to Argentine exports, creating a sudden economic crisis. The country's leadership seemed incapable of responding to the crisis, and in 1943 the military again seized control. Its leaders had lost patience with politicians more interested in patronage than in patriotism. Many of the officers were children of immigrants and were fiercely nationalistic. They regarded liberal politics as a system that permitted politicians to look after themselves. Some officers had become deeply impressed by the Fascist and Nazi movements and their rejection of European liberal politics. The officers also shared the Fascist and Nazi hostility to Britain. They contended that the government must address social questions, industrialize the country, and liberate it from foreign economic control. In all these respects, they echoed the *nacionalistas*.

Between 1943 and 1946 Juan Perón (1895–1974), one of the colonels involved in the 1943 coup, forged this social discon-

CHRONOLOGY	
Argentina	
1810	Junta in Buenos Aires overthrows Spanish government
1827–1852	Era of Rosas's dictatorial government
1876	Ship refrigeration makes possible export of beef around the world
1879–1880	General Roca carries out Conquest of the Desert against the Indian population
1914–1918	Argentina remains neutral in World War I
1930s	Period of strong influence of nationalist military
1943–1956	Era of Juan and Eva Perón

DOCUMENT | Eva Perón Explains the Sources of Her Popularity

The Perónist movement in Argentina drew broad support from workers and the poor. The movement involved a cult of personality around both Perón and his wife, Eva. In 1951 Eva Perón published a book entitled My Mission in Life (La Razón de mi Vida). *Here she explains how she sought to relate to her husband's political supporters.*

♦ Why was Eva Perón's accepting the name "Evita" a political act? How did her use of this name separate her from the ruling elites of Argentina? What is the role she projects for herself in her relationship to various social groups in Argentina? Do you believe her discussion of herself to be sincere or politically opportunistic?

When I chose to be "Evita," I chose the path of my people. ...

Only the people call me "Evita." Only the *descamisados* [the "unshirted," as Perón's working-class followers were termed] learned to call me so. ...

I appeared to them thus the day I went to meet the humble of my land, telling them that I preferred being "Evita" to being the wife of the president, if that "Evita" could help to mitigate some grief, or dry a tear.

If a man of the government, a leader, a politician, an ambassador, who normally calls me "Señora," should call me "Evita," it would sound as strange and out of place to me as if a street-urchin, a workingman, or a humble person of the people should call me "Señora." ...

Now, if you ask me which I prefer, my reply would be immediately that I prefer the name by which I am known to the people.

When a street-urchin calls me "Evita," I feel as though I were the mother of all urchins, and of all the weak and the humble of my land.

When a working man calls me "Evita," I feel glad to be the companion of all the workingmen of my country and even of the whole world.

When a woman of my country calls me "Evita," I imagine myself her sister, and that of all the women of humanity,

And so, almost without noticing it, I have classified in these three examples the principal activities of "Evita" relating to the humble, the workers, and women.

The truth is that, without any artificial effort, at no personal cost, as though I had been born for all this, I feel myself responsible for the humble as though I were the mother of all of them; I fight shoulder to shoulder with the workers as though I were another of their companions from the workshop or factory; in front of the women who trust in me, I consider myself something like an elder sister, responsible to a certain degree for the destiny of all of them who have placed their hopes in me.

And certainly I do not deem this an honor but a responsibility. ...

Yes. I confess that I have an ambition, one single, great personal ambition: I would like the name of "Evita" to figure somewhere in the history of my country.

From Sara Castro-Klarén, Sylvia Malloy, and Beatriz Sarlo, *Women's Writing in Latin America: An Anthology.* Selection trans. by Ethel Cherry. Copyright © 1991 by Westview Press. Reprinted by permission of Westview Press.

---

tent and these authoritarian political attitudes into a remarkable political movement known as **Perónism**. It was authoritarian, initially militaristic, anti-Communist, and socially progressive. Perón understood better than his fellow officers that political power could be exerted by appeals to the Argentine working class, particularly in Buenos Aires. He gained the support of the trade unions that were opposed to communism. In 1945 he had been arrested by other military leaders, but he was freed when it became clear that he alone could silence working-class discontent. In 1946 he made himself the voice of working-class democracy, even though after his election to the presidency he created an authoritarian regime that only marginally addressed industrial problems. He was greatly aided by his wife, the former actress Eva Duarte (1919–1952). She enjoyed charismatic support among trade-union members and the working class. (See Document, "Eva Perón Explains the Sources of Her Popularity.")

Perón became the most famous of the postwar Latin American dictators, but his power and appeal were rooted in the antiliberal attitudes that had been fostered by the corruption and aimlessness of Argentine politics during the depression. He was the supreme twentieth-century embodiment of the *caudillo*. He was ousted in 1956, but long-term stability would elude Argentine politics after his departure.

MEXICO

The heritage of Mexican independence was a combination of the thwarted social revolution led by Father Hidalgo and José María Morelos between 1811 and 1815 and the conservative political coup carried out in 1820 by the creole elite against a potentially liberal Spanish crown. For the first century of independence conservative forces held sway, but in 1910 the Mexican people launched the most far-reaching revolution in Latin American history.

▲ **Benito Juarez** led *La Reforma*, a mid-nineteenth century movement opposed to the autocracy of Santa Anna. Juarez is portrayed with the tools of an engineer in front of a background of railway building to suggest his dedication to economic progress and modernization in Mexico.

Portrait of Benito Juarez. Oil on canvas, 1941. Presidential collection of portraits of Mexican Presidents. Corbis-Bettmann.

Turmoil Follows Independence   The years from 1820 to 1876 were a time of political turmoil, economic floundering, and national humiliation. Newly independent Mexico attempted no liberal political experiments. Its first ruler was Agustín de Iturbide (1783–1824), who ruled until 1823 as an emperor. After this unsuccessful effort to adopt monarchical rule, Mexico was governed by a succession of presidents, most of whom were *caudillos* from the army or depended on the army for support. The strongest of these figures was Antonio López de Santa Anna (1795–1863), a general and a political opportunist always willing to modify his principles and policies to attain or retain power. Usually he supported conservative political and social interests. He ruled in a thoroughly dictatorial manner. More than once he was driven from office, but he inevitably returned until finally exiled in 1855.

The midcentury movement against Santa Anna's autocracy was called *La Reforma*. In theory, its supporters were liberal, but Mexican liberalism was associated primarily with anticlericalism, confiscation of church lands, and opposition to military influence on national life and politics. *La Reforma* aimed to produce political stability, civilian rule, and an economic policy that would attract foreign capital and immigrants. Having deposed Santa Anna, the leaders of the reform movement passed legislation to break up large landed estates, particularly those owned by the church, and to promote the establishment of small farms. However, the actual content of the laws permitted existing large landowners to purchase additional land cheaply and thus made great estates even larger. The legislative attack on privileges of the church led to further civil war between 1857 and 1860. In January 1861 Benito Juárez (1806–1872) entered Mexico City as the temporary victor.

Political instability was matched by economic stagnation. After 1820 many Spanish officials and merchants fled Mexico, taking with them large quantities of gold and silver. The mines that had produced Mexico's colonial wealth were in poor condition, and the country lacked the investment capital or technological knowledge to repair them. The inefficiencies of the *hacienda* system left farming in a backward condition. Cheap imports of manufactured goods spelled the end of domestic industries. Transportation was primitive. The government's remedy for these weaknesses was massive foreign borrowing; as a result, interest payments became one of the largest portions of the national budget.

Foreign Intervention   Political weakness and economic disarray invited foreign intervention. The territorial ambitions of the United States impinged on Mexico in two ways. In 1823 the Mexican government allowed Stephen F. Austin (1793–1836) to begin the colonization of Texas. During the next decade, the policies of Santa Anna stirred resentment among the Texas settlers, and in 1835 they rebelled. The next year Santa Anna destroyed the defenders of the Alamo but was decisively defeated at the battle of San Jacinto. Texas became an independent republic that was annexed by the United States in 1845. Border clashes between Mexican and U.S. forces enabled President James Polk to launch a war against Mexico in 1846 that saw the United States army occupy Mexico City. Through the treaty of Guadalupe Hidalgo (1848), the United States gained a vast portion of Mexican territory, including what is now New Mexico, Arizona, and California.

Further foreign intervention occurred as a direct result of Juárez's liberal victory in 1861. Mexican conservatives and clerics invited the Austrian Habsburg Archduke Maximilian (1832–1867) to become the emperor of Mexico. Napoleon III (r. 1852–1870) of France, who portrayed himself as a defender of the Roman Catholic Church, provided support for this imperial venture. In May 1862 French troops invaded Mexico, and two years later Maximilian became emperor. He disappointed his conservative supporters by accepting much of the former government's liberal policy toward the church but was unable to gain support from other segments of the population. By 1867 Juárez had organized strong resistance forces. He captured the unhappy emperor and executed him. The Mexicans had been victorious, but their vulnerability to foreign powers had again been exposed.

Díaz and Dictatorship   Once restored to office, the liberal leaders continued their measures against the church but failed to rally significant popular support. Consequently, in 1876 Porfirio Díaz (1830–1915), a liberal general, led a revolt on the grounds that he was restoring a true republic. Except for four years in the

▲ **Porfirio Díaz (1830–1915).** From 1876 to 1911 Díaz ran one of the most successful dictatorships in Latin American history.
Brown Brothers.

1880s, when a surrogate held office, Díaz retained the presidency until 1911. He maintained what became one of the most successful dictatorships in Latin American history by giving almost every political sector something it wanted. He allowed landowners to purchase public land cheaply; he favored the army, whose support he required; and he made peace with the church by not enforcing anticlerical measures. Later, he freely used repression against opponents to diffuse their political activity and bribery to cement the loyalty of his supporters. Wealthy Mexicans grew even richer under Díaz, and Mexico became a respectable member of the international financial community. Unprecedented quantities of foreign capital flooded the nation. Foreign companies, especially from the United States, invested heavily in what, by 1900, appeared to be a thoroughly stable country.

Yet problems remained. The peasants wanted land and resented the ever-growing power of the landlords. Because food production actually declined during the Díaz regime, many Mexicans were malnourished. Labor unrest and strikes afflicted the textile and mining industries. Like other Latin American rulers, and governments in Europe and the United States, Díaz used military force against workers. Due to inflation, real wages for the working class declined in the first decade of this century. The Panic of 1907 in the United States disrupted the Mexican economy. By 1910 the so-called *Pax Porfiriana* was unraveling.

Revolution   In 1908 the elderly Díaz announced that he would not seek reelection. Although he later changed his mind and was reelected in 1910, his first announcement spurred public discussion of Mexico's political and social future. In 1910 Díaz was opposed by Francisco Madero (d. 1913), a wealthy landowner and moderate liberal. Madero's campaign slogan was "Effective Suffrage—No Reelection," which ironically Díaz himself had coined two generations earlier. Díaz won, but Madero then led an insurrection that drove the dictator into European exile by May 1911.

Shortly thereafter, Madero was elected president. He recognized the rights of trade unions to organize and to strike, but he was unwilling to undertake significant agrarian reform that might have changed the pattern of landholding. He ended by being distrusted both by conservatives, who wanted little or no change from the days of Díaz, and by reformist leaders, who thought the time had come for extensive social and political restructuring. Far more radical leaders emerged, calling for social change. Pancho Villa (1874–1923) in the north and Emiliano Zapata (1879–1919) in the south rallied mass followings of peasants who demanded fundamental structural changes in rural landholding. In late 1911 Zapata proclaimed his Plan of Ayala, which in effect set forth a program of large-scale peasant confiscation of land. Much of the struggle during the next ten years would be between supporters and opponents of such agrarian reform. (See Document, "Emiliano Zapata Issues the Plan of Ayala.")

Madero found himself squeezed between the conservative supporters of the deposed Díaz and the radical peasant revolutionaries. No one trusted him, and in early 1913 he was overthrown by General Victoriano Huerta (1854–1916), who had the help of the United States and was assassinated not long

▲ **Orgy—The Night of the Rich,** a mural by the Mexican artist Diego Rivera (1886–1957), casts a scornful eye on the Europeanized decadence of Mexico's elite in the early 20th century.

Mural, 2.05 × 1.54 cm, Court of Fiestas, Level 3, North Wall, Secretaria de Educación Pública, Mexico City, Mexico Schalkwijk/Art Resource, NY © Estate of Diego Rivera.

thereafter. Huerta, who was basically a dictator, failed to quash the peasant rebellion. His attacks against the forces of Zapata involved considerable loss of life. In the meantime, Venustiano Carranza (1859–1920), a wealthy landowner, joined Villa's cause. He soon put himself at the head of a large Constitutionalist Army—so called because it advocated the restoration of constitutional government in opposition to the political dictatorship of Huerta—that initially received the support of both Zapata and Villa. Huerta's government collapsed on August 15, 1914, when Constitutionalist forces entered Mexico City. Thereafter disputes erupted between Carranza and Villa and then between Carranza and Zapata. These conflicts arose both from simple political rivalry and from Carranza's refusal to embrace the kind of radical agrarian reform the two peasant leaders sought. Carranza eventually won out, thanks to his political skills and the effectiveness of his army.

Carranza's political skills also helped him build a broad base and edge out both Villa and Zapata as the chief leader of the revolution. One particularly skillful move followed an attempt by President Woodrow Wilson (1856–1924) of the United States to support Carranza by sending U.S. Marines to Veracruz in April 1914. Carranza shrewdly denounced the United States for this action, thus casting himself in the role of patriot and nationalist, and the Marines departed. In another skillful move, he addressed himself to the concerns of urban industrial workers as well as the land hunger of rural peasants, successfully separating the two groups. This division ultimately doomed the effort to implement an agrarian revolution. Carranza made many promises, especially about agrarian reform, that he had little or no intention of carrying out.

Beginning in early 1915 Carranza's military forces began an ultimately successful campaign against Villa and Zapata. The peasant leaders still commanded regional support but could not win control of the nation. During 1916 Carranza confronted U.S. military intervention along the border that continued until early 1917, when the United States became involved in World War I in Europe. Throughout the turmoil in Mexico, the government of the United States attempted to protect American interests. These activities involved ongoing diplomatic initiatives with the various groups in Mexico as well as the threat of military action.

By 1917, after years of deadly and destructive civil war, Carranza's forces were sufficiently confident to write a constitution. The Constitution of 1917 set forth a program for ongoing social revolution—never pursued with any vigor— and political reform. Perhaps its two most famous provisions were Articles 27 and 123. Article 27 provided for the government, on behalf of the nation, to become the owner of water and mineral rights and other subsoil property rights. This article abrogated all prerevolutionary contracts with foreign companies in regard to oil and minerals. Together with other

▲ **The Mexican Revolution.** The forces of Emiliano Zapata march on Xochimilco in 1914. Women fought alongside men and played other prominent roles during the Mexican Revolution.
UPI/Corbis-Bettman.

provisions, it meant that peasant villages could reclaim land they had lost over the past half century. Article 123 guaranteed certain rights for the organization of labor. Many years would pass before all the provisions of the constitution could be enforced, but from 1917 onward it provided the ongoing goals of the revolution and the ideals toward which Mexican governments were expected to strive.

Carranza and his immediate subordinates were much more conservative than either Villa or Zapata. They recognized the agrarian problem but were cautious about changing existing property arrangements.

Carranza and his chief supporters were associated with northwestern Mexico and admired the economic development they had seen in California. They were determined to modernize Mexican political life and attract capital investment; Mexican leaders would share these goals from that time onward. Thus despite all the radical rhetoric associated with the revolution and the vast upheaval among peasants that it

involved, the Mexican Revolution saw the victory of a more or less middle-class political and economic elite who would attempt to govern the country through enlightened paternalism. Although turmoil would persist for many years, with Carranza's victory the general direction of Mexican political life had been established.

The decade after 1917 witnessed both confusion and consolidation. In 1919 Zapata was lured into an ambush and killed. Carranza was assassinated in 1920. Three years later Villa was also assassinated. In this turmoil, Carranza's generals provided stability. During the 1920s military leaders drawn from Carranza's revolutionary Constitutionalist Army served as presidents. They moved cautiously and hesitated to press land redistribution too quickly. They were opposed by the Roman Catholic Church, which at one point suspended all services for more than two years. In 1929 Plutarco Elías Calles (1877–1945) organized the **PRI**, the Institutional Revolutionary Party, which quickly became the most important political

DOCUMENT   Emiliano Zapata Issues the Plan of Ayala

By November 1911 the Díaz regime had fallen in Mexico, and Francisco Madero was attempting to establish a moderately liberal government. He was confronted by a major popular peasant revolution led in the valley of Morelos by Emiliano Zapata. On November 28 the rebel leader set forth his opposition to Madero and announced sweeping goals of land reform. Zapata never took dominant control of the Mexican Revolution, but the radical economic demands of his Plan of Ayala would influence the course of Mexican social development for the next thirty years.

◆ Why did Zapata place so much emphasis on collective ownership of natural resources? What is Zapata's vision of future economic life? Who would be the winners and losers from his proposed policies?

... be it known: that the lands, woods, and water usurped by the *hacendados* [great landowners] ... henceforth belong to the towns or citizens in possession of the deeds concerning these properties of which they were despoiled through the devious action of our oppressors. The possession of said properties shall be kept at all costs, arms in hand. The usurpers who think they have right to said goods may state their claims before special tribunals to be established upon the triumph of the Revolution.

... the immense majority of Mexico's villages and citizens own only the ground on which they stand. They suffer the horrors of poverty without being able to better their social status in any respect, or without being able to dedicate themselves to industry or agriculture due to the fact that the lands, woods, and water are monopolized by a few. For this reason, through prior compensation, one-third of such monopolies will be expropriated from their powerful owners in order that the villages and citizens of Mexico may obtain *ejidos* [agricultural communities], colonies, town sites, and rural properties for sowing or tilling, and in order that the welfare and prosperity of the Mexican people will be promoted in every way.

The property of those *hacendados* ... who directly or indirectly oppose the present plan shall be nationalized, and two-thirds of their remaining property shall be designated for war indemnities—pensions for the widows and orphans of the victims that succumb in the struggle for this plan.

From James W. Wilkie and Albert L. Michaels, eds., *Revolution in Mexico: Years of Upheaval, 1910–1940.* Copyright © 1969 by Alfred A. Knopf, p. 46.

---

force in the nation and remains so today. The Mexican political system became one dominated by a single party within which most political debate occurred, rather than a system dominated by a single strong leader. Despite external criticism and internal tensions, the PRI has overseen the longest period of political stability experienced by any other Latin American nation in the twentieth century.

In 1934 Lázaro Cárdenas (1895–1970) was elected president. More than any of the other leaders to emerge after the revolution, he moved directly to fulfill the promises and programs of 1917. He turned tens of millions of acres of land over to peasant villages. In 1938, when Mexico was the third largest producer of petroleum, he expropriated the oil industry. His nationalization policy established PeMex, which remains the Mexican national oil company. Cárdenas left other mineral industries in private and generally foreign hands. His extensive reforms went through smoothly because he worked through bureaucratic and administrative means.

With the election of Manuel Ávila Camacho (1897–1955) in 1940, the era of revolutionary politics ended. Thereafter, the major issues in Mexico were those generally associated with postwar economic development. But unlike other Latin American nations, Mexico, because of its revolution, could confront those issues with a democratic perspective and a sense of collective social responsibility, no matter how imperfectly those goals might be realized.

CHRONOLOGY	
Mexico	
1820–1823	Agustín de Iturbide rules unsuccessfully as emperor
1833–1855	Santa Anna dominates Mexican political scene
1846–1848	Mexico defeated by United States and loses considerable territory
1861	Victory of liberal forces under Juárez
1862–1867	French troops led by Archduke Maximilian of Austria unsuccessfully invade Mexico
1876–1911	Era of Porfirio Díaz
1911	Beginning of Mexican Revolution
1911	Zapata proclaims Plan of Ayala
1917	Forces of Carranza proclaim constitution
1929	Institutional Revolutionary Party organized

BRAZIL

Postcolonial Brazil, the largest Latin American country, differed in several important respects from other newly independent nations in the region. Its language and colonial heritage were Portuguese rather than Spanish. For the first sixty-seven years of its independence it had a relatively stable monarchical government. And most distinctively, it retained the institution of slavery until 1888.

Brazil had moved directly from being part of the Portuguese monarchy to becoming an independent empire in 1822. The first emperor, Pedro I (r. 1822–1831), while serving as regent for his father, the king of Portugal, had put himself at the head of the independence movement. Although he granted Brazil a constitution in 1823, Pedro's high-handed rule and his patronage of Portuguese courtiers rather than Brazilians led to his forced abdication in 1831. Brazilians then took hold of their own destinies.

After a decade of political uncertainty under a regency, Pedro II (r. 1831–1889), the fifteen-year-old son of Pedro I, assumed direct power in 1840 and governed Brazil until 1889. Pedro II made wise and shrewd use of patronage. He established a reputation as a constitutional monarch by asking leaders of both the conservative and the liberal political parties to form ministries. Consequently, Brazil enjoyed remarkable political stability. However, the government took few initiatives to develop the economy.

The Slavery Issue The great divisive issue in Brazil's social and political life was slavery. Sugar production remained the mainstay of the economy until the middle of the nineteenth century. Most sugar plantations were located in the coastal provinces of the northeast. Their owners were conservative and resistant to changes in production. Soil exhaustion and inefficient farming methods made profits impossible without the cheap labor of slaves. From about 1850 coffee cultivation began to spread in the southern provinces, marking a key shift in Brazilian agriculture. Coffee would soon become the nation's most important product. Coffee producers also used slave labor and wanted to retain slavery, but their profits were much larger than those of the sugar producers, so a transition to free labor would have been easier for them. Coffee planters also tended to see themselves as being on the side of economic progress. Hence, people investing in coffee were more open to emancipation than those who had invested in sugar.

As early as 1826 the Brazilian government had made a treaty with Great Britain, agreeing to suppress the slave trade. For many years Brazil refused to honor these treaty provisions, but by 1850 had virtually ceased importing slaves, putting the sugar planters on the defensive and freeing the capital once spent on slaves for investments in coffee. The end of slave imports effectively doomed the institution of slavery because

▲ **Antislavery Print.** Slavery lasted longer in Brazil than in any other nation in North or South America. Antislavery groups ciculated prints such as this one pubblished in France to illustrate the brutality of slave life in Brazil.
The Granger Collection, N.Y.

the birthrate among slaves was too low for the slave population to reproduce itself. It was nonetheless one thing to face this technical inevitability and another to abolish slavery.

The Paraguayan War of 1865–1870 postponed consideration of the slave question. This conflict, which pitted Brazil, Argentina, and Uruguay against Paraguay, originated in border disputes and in larger commercial conflicts about ongoing Paraguayan access to the ports on the lower Plate River, in particular Montevideo. The conflict became a long, exceedingly destructive struggle because the dictator of Paraguay, Francisco Solano López (1827–1870), mobilized his entire country into a war of attrition and refused to surrender. His death in battle in 1870 finally ended the war, but only after more than half (and perhaps a larger portion) of the adult male population of Paraguay had been killed. The victorious powers installed a friendly government in Paraguay, which sold off state lands to foreign speculators.

The end of the war returned slavery to the forefront of Brazilian politics. Brazil and the Spanish colonies of Puerto Rico and Cuba were now the only slaveholding countries in the hemisphere. The emperor favored gradual emancipation. A law of 1871 set the stage for such emancipation by freeing slaves owned by the crown and by decreeing legal freedom for future children of slaves. The law actually had little effect because it required the children of slaves to work on plantations until the age of twenty-one. However, throughout the 1870s and 1880s the abolition movement grew in Brazil. Public figures from across the entire political spectrum called for an end to slavery. (See Document, "A Brazilian Liberal Denounces Slavery.") Abolitionists helped slaves to escape.

DOCUMENT   A Brazilian Liberal Denounces Slavery

Critics sharply attacked slavery in Brazil from the mid–nineteenth century onward. The first major attempt to emancipate slaves occurred in 1871. That law proposed gradual emancipation by liberating the children of slaves. The abolitionist movement continued to grow resulting in the final emancipation of slaves in Brazil in 1888. In 1883 Joaquim Nabuco, a major leader of the abolitionist movement, published O Abolicionismo, *which stands as one of the chief examples of Brazilian antislavery literature. Although not quoted in the passage below, Nabuco drew extensive parallels between the slavery of Brazil and that which had existed in the United States before the Civil War. Here Nabuco seeks to demonstrate the manner in which the continuation of slavery prevents commercial economic development in Brazil and inhibits the country from embracing the progressive forces of the day. Note the manner in which Nabuco has absorbed the ideas of the eighteenth-century Enlightenment and nineteenth-century European liberalism.*

> • What are the values and outlooks that Nabuco associates with the expansion of commerce? Why does he see slavery as undermining those values? How and why does he see slavery inhibiting progressive social and intellectual forces? In this passage, what are possible arguments against slavery that Nabuco does not raise?

Slavery does not permit the existence of a true working class, nor is it compatible with the wage system and the personal dignity of the artisan. ... [T]here can be no strong, respected, and intelligent working class where the employers of labor are accustomed to order slaves about. ...

Slavery and industry are mutually exclusive terms, like slavery and colonization. The spirit of the former, spreading through a country, kills every one of the human faculties from which industry springs—initiative, inventiveness, individual energy, and every one of the elements that industry requires—the formation of capital, an abundance of labor, technical education of the workers, confidence in the future. ...

... [C]ommerce, in the absence of industry and free labor, can function only as an agent of slavery, buying whatever it offers and selling whatever it needs. This is why in Brazil commerce does not develop or open new perspectives for the country.... Slavery distrusts commerce, as it distrusts any agency of progress, whether it is a business man's office, a railroad station, or a primary school; yet slavery needs commerce. ... But so long as slavery endures, commerce must always be the servant of a class, and not an independent national agent. ...

Of the classes whose growth slavery artificially stimulates, none is more numerous than that of government employees.... Officeholding is ... the asylum of the descendants of formerly rich and noble families that have squandered the fortunes made from slavery. ... But officeholding is also our political olive tree, that shelters all those young men of brains and ambition but no money who form the great majority of our talented people. ...

Among the forces of progress and change around which slavery has created a vacuum as hostile to its interests, the press is notable—and not only the newspaper but the book, and everything that concerns education. ... The slave hut and the school are poles that repel each other. ...

Among the forces whose emergence slavery has impeded is public opinion, the consciousness of a common destiny. Under slavery there cannot exist that powerful force called public opinion, that simultaneously balances and offers a point of support to the individuals who represented the most advanced throughout of the country. Just as slavery is incompatible with spontaneous immigration, so will it prevent the influx of new ideas. Itself incapable of invention, it will have nothing to do with progress.

Joaquim Nabuco, *O Abolicionismo* (São Paulo, 1938), excerpted from Benjamin Keen, trans., as reprinted in Benjamin Keen, ed., *Readings in Latin-American Civilization 1492 to the Present* (Boston: Houghton Mifflin Company, 1955), pp. 339–343.

The army, many of whose officers held political views associated with positivism, resented having to enforce laws protecting slavery. In 1888 Pedro II was in Europe for medical treatment, and his daughter was regent. She favored abolition rather than gradual emancipation. When Parliament in that year passed a law abolishing slavery without any compensation to the slave owners, she signed it, thus ending slavery in Brazil.

A Republic Replaces Monarchy The abolition of slavery brought to a head other issues that in 1889 caused the collapse of the monarchy. Planters who received no financial compensation for their slaves were resentful. Roman Catholic clerics were disaffected by disputes with the emperor over education. Pedro II was unwell; his daughter, the heir to the throne, was unpopular and distrusted. The officer corps of the army had been dissatisfied with what it regarded as insufficient political influence since its victory in the Paraguayan War. In November 1889 the army sent Pedro II into exile in France.

The Brazilian republic lasted from 1891 to 1930. Like the monarchy, it was dominated by a small group of wealthy persons, the most dominant of whom were the coffee planters. The political arrangement that allowed the republic to function smoothly was an agreement among the state governors. The president was to be chosen alternately from the states of São Paulo and Minas Gerais. In turn, the other eighteen governors had considerable local political latitude. Fixed elections and patronage kept the system in operation. Literacy replaced property as the qualification for voting, leaving few people qualified to vote. There was consequently little organized opposition and, for that matter, little political life at all within the republic.

From the 1890s onward the coffee industry dominated both the political and the economic life of the nation. Around 1900 Brazil was producing over three fourths of the world's coffee. The crop's success led almost inevitably to overproduction. To meet this problem, the government devised policies for maintaining high prices that required large loans from foreign banks. High world coffee prices encouraged competition from other Latin American producers, which in turn required more price supports in Brazil. In addition to the international loans, maintaining the price of coffee required considerable payments to the government from all of the non-coffee-related sectors of the economy. These sectors in turn felt exploited by the coffee interests. As a result of these arrangements, throughout the life of the republic Brazil remained essentially a country producing a single product for export and few goods for internal consumption.

Economic Problems and Military Coups   The end of slavery, the expansion of coffee production, and the beginning of a slow growth of urban industry attracted foreign immigrants to Brazil. They tended to settle in the cities and constituted the core of the early industrial labor force. In Brazil, as elsewhere, World War I caused major economic disruption. Urban labor discontent appeared. There was a general strike in São Paulo in 1917, with the inevitable military action against the strikers. The failure to address urban and industrial social problems and the political corruption of the republic led to attempted military coups in 1922 and 1924. Both revolts failed to bring down the republic, but they indicated profound discontent with a political structure designed primarily to protect the producers of a single agricultural commodity. The revolts also demonstrated that certain segments of the military were determined to change the political system. They wanted a modern nation that was not dependent on a single exportable product and a political system that depended on more than corruption and recognized interests besides those of the coffee planters.

Coffee had ruled as the economic "king" of the Brazilian republic, and its collapse brought the republic down with it. In 1929 coffee prices hit record lows; currency exchange rates fell; and foreign loans were unavailable. Millions of bags of coffee

OVERVIEW   Latin America's Dependent Economy

After independence, most Latin American nations relied on export economies that sold raw materials or semifinished goods, such as animal hides and leather, to the world's economy. Most manufactured goods were imported, primarily from Britain. This created a dependent economy in which Latin American prosperity depended on other nations' paying high prices for its raw materials. What made this dependence even more precarious was that most Latin American nations depended on one or two products for their export earnings. When prices for these products fell or collapsed, as they did during the Great Depression of the 1930s, Latin America had little else to trade, and its prosperity plummeted. The following table shows the main products of the principal Latin American countries between the 1820s and 1930.

Argentina	animal products (meat, leather, wool), grain
Bolivia	tin, silver
Brazil	coffee, sugar, rubber
Chile	copper
Colombia	coffee, cattle
Ecuador	bananas
Mexico	silver, cattle, oil
Peru	nitrates, silver
Uruguay	animal products (meat, leather)
Venezuela	coffee, cattle

▲ **Vargas and the Military.** Getulio Vargas became ruler of Brazil in 1930 through a military coup. Here he stands with his military supporters. One of the purposes of such pictures was to remind the public that any serious opposition might be put down by the military.
UPI/Corbis-Bettmann.

lay in warehouses. Government reserves were depleted in an unsuccessful attempt to hold up the price of coffee and to pay for imports no longer being funded by coffee exports. The economic structure of the republic lay in shambles. In October 1930 a military coup installed Getulio Vargas (1883–1954) in the presidency. Vargas governed Brazil until 1945.

The Vargas years represent a major turning point in Brazilian history. Vargas was initially supported by the reform elements in the military, by professional middle-class groups, and by urban workers. In office, he moved first to the right and then to the left and then back again. He was an experimentalist and pragmatist who primarily wanted to hold on to power and to make Brazil a modern nation. Vargas was able to recognize the new social and economic groups shaping Brazilian political life. First with constitutionalism and then with dictatorship, he attempted to allow the government to act on behalf of those groups without allowing them to influence or direct the government in a genuinely democratic manner. However, despite the personal power that accrued to him, he did not form his own political party or movement as Perón would later do in Argentina or as the Mexican revolutionaries had done. Rather, Vargas attempted to function like a ringmaster direct-

ing the various forces in Brazilian life. His failure to establish a genuinely stable institutional political framework for a Brazil that included many interest groups besides the coffee planters has influenced Brazil to the present day.

Vargas and his supporters sought to lessen dependence on coffee by fostering industries that would produce domestically goods that had previously been imported from abroad. They thus attempted to create internal suppliers for goods needed in the internal Brazilian economy. The policy succeeded, and by the mid-1930s domestic manufacturing was increasing. These years mark the real beginning of Brazilian manufacturing. In the constitution of 1934 Vargas established a legal framework for labor relations. The structures were paternalistic but included an eight-hour day and a minimum wage. The constitution also asserted government responsibility to protect mineral and water rights.

In the Brazilian context these measures appeared reformist, if not necessarily liberal, and marked a departure from government policy dominated by the coffee oligarchy and politics by patronage. However, in the late 1930s Vargas confronted major political opposition from both the Brazilian Communist Party (founded in 1922) and a new right-wing movement called *Integralism*. In 1937, facing these political opponents, Vargas assumed personal dictatorial power. His regime thereafter was repressive. He claimed to have established an **Estado Novo** ("new state"). He wrapped himself in the flag of nationalism and order and presented himself as the protector of national stability against factions that would foster instability and of the national interest against international opponents.

Like the European dictators of the same era, Vargas used censorship, secret police, and torture against his political opponents. He also used his newly assumed power to diversify and modernize the economy. In 1940 a five-year plan provided more state direction for the economy. His government favored the production of goods from heavy industry that would be used in Brazil itself. To maintain the support of workers and trade unions, the state also issued a progressive labor code. Siding with the Allies in World War II, Brazil built up large reserves of foreign currency through the export of foodstuffs. This economic activity and imposed political stability allowed the government to secure foreign loans for still further economic development. By the end of the war Brazil was becoming the major Latin American industrial power.

Participation in World War II on the side of the Allies had led many in Brazil to believe that they should not remain subject to a dictatorship. This attitude was widespread in the military, which had fought in Europe and established close contact with the United States. In 1945 Vargas promised that he would lead the nation toward democracy and hold presidential as well as congressional elections. His actions, however, suggested that he planned to manipulate the elections. In response, the military carried out a coup, and Vargas retired temporarily from political life.

The new regime, which was democratic, continued the general policy of economic development through foreign-financed industrialization. The state, however, assumed a much smaller role. When in 1950 Vargas was elected president, his return to office was anticlimactic. He was by then an elderly man, well past his prime. Yet in 1953 he established Petrobas, a state-owned petroleum exploration company. His presidency remained controversial. There was much criticism of him and of the corruption of his appointments. A member of his staff became involved in the assassination of a prominent civilian journalist. The military demanded that Vargas resign. Instead he took his own life in 1954, leaving a public testament in which he presented himself as the protector of the poor and of the broad national interest.

In the decade after Vargas's death, Brazil remained a democracy, although a highly unstable one. The government itself began to undertake vast projects such as the enormously costly construction of the new capital of Brasília, begun in 1957. Located far inland, Brasília required the creation of a vast road system. With Brasília under way, the government of Juscelino Kubitschek (1902–1976), who had supported the building of the new capital, fostered the establishment of a large automobile industry. The rapid growth of cities and the expansion of a working class radicalized political life. The political system could not readily accommodate itself to the concerns of workers and the urban poor. Widespread poverty and illiteracy continued to plague both the cities and the countryside. In a structural problem created by the constitution of 1946, the presidency was controlled by urban voters, whereas the congress was controlled by rural voters.

By the early 1960s, when President João Goulert (1918–1977) took office, Brazilian political life was in turmoil. Goulert's predecessors, including Vargas, had always attempted to balance interests or to move among various political forces without firmly favoring a single sector. After months of wavering, however, Goulert committed himself to a policy favored by the left. In 1964 he announced his support for land reform. Peasants had already tried to seize land and landowners had fought them. Political conservatives and moderates expected some favors to urban radicals, which they might have tolerated, but vigorously resisted any hint of significant political or land reform in the countryside. Goulert also questioned the authority of the military hierarchy. Moreover, Brazil faced economic problems: Both industrial and farm production had fallen from the levels achieved in 1960, fostering discontent. In March 1964 the military, claiming to protect Brazil from communism, seized control of the government, ending its post–World War II experiment with democracy.

CHRONOLOGY

Brazil

1822	Brazil becomes an independent empire
1840	Pedro II assumes personal rule
1840s and 1850s	Spread of coffee cultivation
1865–1870	Paraguayan War
1871	First law curbing slavery
1888	Slavery abolished
1889	Fall of the monarchy
1917	General strike in São Paulo
1929	Collapse of coffee prices
1930–1945	Vargas era
1957	Construction of Brasília begins
1964	Military takes control of the government

Diego Rivera, *Sugar Cane*, 1931.

Summary

Economic Dependence   In the 1820s, Latin America threw off Spanish and Portuguese rule, but the traditional elites—landowners, military officers, the church—remained in control. A series of strongmen called *caudillos* dominated most Latin American republics. Nor did independence bring economic prosperity. Because Latin American economies remained dependent on producing agricultural commodities for export, foreign nations, particularly Britain, dominated Latin American economic life. When commodity prices collapsed during the Great Depression, Latin American economies were devastated. The crisis did, however, lead to the beginnings of manufacturing in many Latin American countries in an effort to avoid dependence on imports.

Argentina   After independence, Buenos Aires came to dominate Argentina economically and politically. Agricultural exports, the growth of industry, and large-scale European immigration contributed to a strong export economy. However, urban social discontent and the growth of nationalism in the 1930s led to military intervention in politics and the corporatist dictatorship of Juan Perón from 1946 to 1956.

Mexico   In the first decades after independence Mexico was politically and economically unstable. Mexico lost half its territory to the United States and was invaded by France in the 1860s. The long-lasting dictatorship of Porfirio Díaz brought political stability but led to increasing discontent. The Mexican Revolution that began in 1911 produced cautious social and economic reform under the one-party rule of the PRI, the Institutional Revolutionary Party, which remained in power until the end of the century.

Brazil   Brazil was a stable constitutional monarchy after independence until 1889. It also retained slavery until 1888. The establishment of a republic did not change Brazil's economic dependence on coffee exports, however, and the collapse of coffee prices in 1929 led to the dictatorship of Getulio Vargas. Although politically repressive, Vargas instituted social reforms and promoted industrial development, which continued to expand in the decade after his death in 1954.

Review Questions

1. What was the condition of the Latin American economies after independence? What was their relation to Britain? Why were most Latin American states slow to develop an industrial base? What role did their economies play in the worldwide economy that developed in the nineteenth century?

2. Did the structure of Latin American societies change after independence? What role did the traditional elites play in the economic and political life of their nations? What was the condition of the mass of the population?

3. How did European and United States investment in Latin America affect the region economically? Politically?

4. Why did so many Latin American nations find it difficult to develop stable political regimes? What role did the military play?

5. What was the effect of increased European immigration on Argentina? How did the Argentine elite cope with growing urbanization and industrialization? Why was Juan Perón able to seize and hold power?

6. Did Mexico experience a real revolution in the early twentieth century? How does this experience distinguish Mexico from other Latin American countries? What caused the turmoil?

7. Why was the Brazilian experience of independence and early nationhood different from that of Spanish-speaking Latin America? What was the role of coffee in Brazil's economy? How did the Vargas regime change the Brazilian economy? Why did Brazilian democracy end in a military coup in 1964?

Key Terms

caudillo   (p. 782)

creole   (p. 774)

debt peonage   (p. 778)

dependency theory   (p. 774)

Estado Novo   (p. 795)

import substitution   (p. 781)

La Reforma   (p. 786)

mestizos   (p. 778)

mulattos   (p. 778)

nacionalismo   (p. 784)

neo-colonial economy   (p. 781)

Perónism   (p. 785)

positivism   (p. 778)

PRI   (p. 789)

Documents CD-ROM

Nationalism and Imperialism

20.7 Francisco García Calderó, "The North American Peril"

NOTE: *To learn more about the topics in this chapter, see the Suggested Readings at the end of the book.*

27

India, the Islamic Heartlands, and Africa
The Challenge of Modernity (1800–1945)

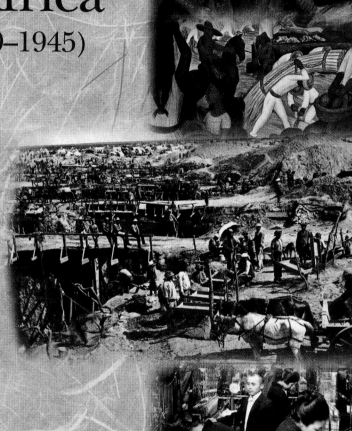

THE INDIAN EXPERIENCE
- British Dominance and Colonial Rule

- From British Crown Raj to Independence

THE ISLAMIC EXPERIENCE
- Islamic Responses to Declining Power and Independence

- Western Political and Economic Encroachment

- The Western Impact

- Islamic Responses to Foreign Encroachment

THE AFRICAN EXPERIENCE
- New States and Power Centers

- Islamic Reform Movements

- Increasing European Involvement

- African Resistance to Colonialism: The Rise of Nationalism

◄ IMPERIAL PROCESSION. A *durbar*, or state reception, showing a procession of Indian and British officials riding lavishly decorated elephants graphically captures the encounter between India, Africa, and the Islamic heartlands with western Europe in the late nineteenth and early twentieth centuries.

"Panorama of Durbar Procession". By permission of the British Library.

India and the Encounter with the Modern West

The century and a half that began in 1800 was bleak for the fortunes of the Indian subcontinent, Africa, and the Islamic societies of the Middle East and elsewhere. For centuries there had been a rough but long-term, balance in advances and setbacks in material and intellectual culture, commercial development, and political stability among the major cultural regions of the world. Suddenly, over a period of 150 years, Europe, long a relative backwater in world history, came to dominate the rest of the world.

The Middle East, Africa, Iran, Central Asia, India, and Indonesia-Malaysia, along with Central and South America—later the so-called "Third World" of "developing nations"—were most drastically affected by European imperialism and colonialism. Notwithstanding indigenous developments in these regions, the overarching and decisive development of this era was new and unprecedented domination of the world's economy, intellectual life, and political and military history by a single segment of the global community. Certainly the histories of the less "developed" nations of the world ("developed" in the sense of evolving toward European-style economic, political, and cultural systems) in this age have their own internal dynamics; in fact, many smaller African or South American societies were not even directly affected by Western dominance until recently. Still, the impact of Western military, economic, and cultural power and influence was considerable. While not synonymous with "progress" as Westerners and modernization theorists have often liked to believe, it has been, nevertheless, a hallmark of the "modern" age in most of Asia, Africa, and South America. Whether by rejection, adaptation and syncretism, or outright imitation, peoples worldwide had to contend with the immense power of the West.

The vitality of so many of the cultures and traditions that bore the brunt of the Western onslaught has been striking. Arab, Iranian, Indian, African, and other encounters with Western material and intellectual domination produced dif-

ferent and often very creative responses and initiatives. These have borne full fruit in political, economic, and intellectual independence only since 1945, although most began much earlier. For example, modern Islamic reform and resurgence began in the eighteenth century, although it has only recently become a major global factor. Indian national, as opposed to regional, consciousness developed from the late eighteenth century onward in response to British imperial and colonial domination, even though it led to national union and independence only after World War II. Ironically, exposure of the indigenous elite to European political and social philosophies gave future leaders of colonial independence drives vital intellectual ammunition with which to develop ideologies of self-rule. Creative thinkers like Mohandas K. Gandhi (b. 1869) merged these European philosophies with ideas drawn from their own cultures to create distinctive new ideologies that could inspire sympathizers from the West as well as their own indigenous followers to oppose European imperialism and oppression of all kinds. African nationalist leaders such as Julius Nyerere (b. 1922) and Nelson Mandela similarly found creative ways to merge European nationalist models with indigenous cultural ones.

Certainly one result of the imperial-colonial experience almost everywhere has been to sharpen the cultural self-consciousness and self-confidence of those peoples most negatively affected by Western dominance. The imperial-colonial experiences of the Third World nations may well prove to have been not only ones of misery and reversal, but also of transition to positive development and resurgence, despite the problems that plague many of these nations.

THINK AHEAD

◆ How did Western domination affect the Indian subcontinent, Asia, and the Islamic heartlands in the nineteenth century?

◆ How did these societies eventually develop ideologies of resistance that helped them achieve independence?

THE ENCROACHMENT OF THE EUROPEAN NATIONS ON the rest of the world from the late fifteenth century onward brought radical, often devastating changes. In the West itself, spiritual and material disruption accompanied the Renaissance, the Reformation, the Enlightenment, and the Industrial and Scientific Revolutions. When Western expansion brought the ideas and innovations of these watershed European developments to Asia and Africa, the challenges and changes that ensued came much more rapidly than they had in the West. Furthermore, this development occurred simultaneously with the spread of European military and economic power, which provided a context for both virulent resistance and cautious adaptation.

To speak of these complex processes under the rubric of "modernization" still does not reflect the acute differences between the relatively lengthy and gradual processes of change in Western Europe and the more rapid and disruptive changes that European imperialism and colonialism brought to other parts of the world. Nor does it do justice to the degree to which the West appropriated the very concept of "modernity." Although every advanced society in any age has presumably viewed its culture as "modern," the dominance of the West in recent centuries has identified modernity with a novel set of ideas and institutions that evolved in Europe between the Renaissance and the early twentieth century and was then gradually exported to, or imposed upon, other societies around the globe. The expression "the impact of modernity" refers to how "modern" Western civilization affected traditional cultures.

The consequences of the spread of Western culture have been so massive that today non-Western peoples are often seen as merely its passive recipients. The American or European view of the world often reflects a simplistic dualism that enhances Western self-esteem by portraying the "modern" West on one side and the "backward" "Orient" on the other, as though all of the world outside Europe, North America, and their most Westernized offshoots were some monolithic, archaic entity. Popular Western stereotypes of the Arab, the African, the Indian, the Chinese, and so on reinforce the Westerner's sense of being the true "modern" of recent history.

As parochial as such chauvinistic generalizations are, these generalizations may nonetheless have a certain grim historical core, as suggested by the crises that many non-Western cultures experienced under the material and spiritual impact of Western modernity and its agents. The impingement of the West has been a major element in the recent history of African, Asian, and Indian civilizations. Not all non-Western societies have had equal success in either retaining or reasserting their precolonial independence and identity, nor in responding creatively to the ongoing challenges of Western-style modernity. The spectrum of postimperial or postcolonial experience ranges from the largely positive response of Japan or the mixed experience of China to the painful and often destructive experiences of most African societies, with India, Iran, South America, and the Middle East somewhere in between.

Nevertheless, in all of these Third World areas, Western modernity entered cultures that had flourishing social, religious, and political traditions of their own. These traditions did not simply melt away on the arrival of the Westerners. Rather, a profound transformation took place that sought to delicately balance the unforeseen challenges of modernity with the familiarity of tradition. That transformation reverberates to this day. It took place throughout Asia and Africa as these continents also became the sites of a fierce European competion for their raw materials and influence. The "great game" and the "scramble for colonies" would permanently alter the cultural, economical and political landscape in both Asia and Africa and in Europe as well.

THE INDIAN EXPERIENCE

British Dominance and Colonial Rule

In the eighteenth century Britain became the dominant power in the southern seas, overshadowing Portugal and Holland. In India the British defeated the French and regional Indian powers for domination of the subcontinent (see Chapter 21). By the early nineteenth century they had built the largest European colonial empire in the Afro-Asian world. India, the greatest traditional civilization of Africa or Asia to come under direct European colonial rule, was the "jewel in the crown" of that empire.

BUILDING THE EMPIRE: THE FIRST HALF OF THE NINETEENTH CENTURY

Penetrating the multi-ethnic, multilingual, and multiconfessional area known as India was not a simple task for Britain but required a multipronged approach. In order for British imperial plans to succeed, the British gradually had to secure the economic and cultural basis for their control. This involved identifying how to be able to extract as many natural resources as possible with minimal costs and also how to convince various stratas of Indian society and the various ethnic groups that cooperation with the British imperial enterprise was in their best interests.

As early as half a century before the British Crown asserted direct rule over India in 1858, the British wielded effective imperial control through the East India Company. As the Company's pressure on smaller states to pay "subsidies" for military "protection" brought ever more of them to either collapse or rebellion, the British annexed more territory. Those areas not annexed were recognized as independent princely states. Ranging in size from less than a square mile to more than 80,000 square miles (Hyderabad), these independent states retained their status only as long as they remained faithfully allied to Britain and contributed money to their common "defense." Members of Indian elites often colluded with the British against local rulers. The state of Mysore, the Maratha confederation, and the Sikhs of the Panjab were overpowered between 1797 and 1853. The India that resulted was a mixture of small and large tributary states and provinces that the British administered directly.

The economic impact of Company rule was extensive. To pay the debts incurred by their military actions, the Company's administrators organized and exploited Indian land revenues. Squeezed by these demands, many peasants deserted their land; by the 1830s land revenues were in sharp decline. In addition, demand for Indian indigo, cotton, and opium in the China and British trade also slacked off in the 1830s, and famines brought widespread suffering. The economic and social reforms (1828–1836) of Governor General Lord William Bentinck (1774–1839) were not sufficient to turn things around substantially.

Company rule, especially in the early nineteenth century, also affected the physical face of India. Company policies encouraged settled agriculture and small commodity production at the expense of the nomadic and pastoralist cultures that had been a major presence across North and central India. British "pacification" involved the clearing of land to deny natural cover to military enemies and the often forced settlement of peasants as pioneer farmers in new regions. Early in the nineteenth century European entrepreneurs also undertook massive commercial logging operations. These activities caused extensive deforestation throughout the subcontinent. This ecological destruction was a major by product of the transformation of India into a more homogeneous peasant farming society that provided a better base for colonial administration.[1]

The Indians were by no means passive in the face of this misuse of their lands and peoples. The first half of the nineteenth century saw almost constant revolt in one place or another. The revolts included peasant movements of noncooperation, Muslim farm workers' attacks on British and Hindu estate owners, grain riots, and tribal warfare. They culminated in a watershed event, the Indian Uprising of 1857 (the so-called Sepoy Mutiny or Rebellion). Thus the commonly accepted image of this era as one of general tranquillity prior to a "mutiny" against British custodianship turns out to have been a product of British propaganda.

The immediate trigger of the Uprising of 1857 was the concern among Bengal troops that animal grease on newly issued rifles exposed them to ritual pollution. Behind this issue, however, lay a variety of grievances, including the recent addition of Sikhs, Gurkhas, and lower caste soldiers to the army; the deteriorating economic conditions of many of the Hindu troops' higher caste relatives back home; outrage at excessive tax rates, especially among troops from Meerut; and anger at the 1856 British annexation of the rich princely state of Awadh (home to many of the troops). One can also see in the revolt the desire to recover and rebuild a pre-British political order in North India. The revolt was not an all-India affair. It centered on Delhi, where the last Mughal emperor joined in the rebel cause, and involved uprisings in other cities and towns from Chittagong in Bengal to Lahore and even Peshawar in the Panjab. Uprisings in the countryside around Delhi and Lucknow involved the peasantry.

Because their real power bases in Bengal and the Panjab were not destroyed, nor their ability to communicate and move new troops impaired, the British eventually won the day. With their forces augmented by Sikhs from the Panjab and Gurkhas from Nepal, they overcame the internally divided Indian opposition. By autumn 1857, the revolt was broken, often with great brutality, and it was finished before the end of the year. In the next year the East India Company was dissolved, and India came under direct rule of the British crown.

The "Mutiny" of 1857 was not a nationalist revolution, but rather a series of anti-foreigner, anti-British spontaneous uprisings. Still, it presaged the rise of an effective unified response and highlighted underlying resentment of the burdens of for-

---

[1] C. A. Bayly, *Indian Society and the Making of the British Empire* (Cambridge: Cambridge University Press, 1988), pp. 138–146.

▲ **The Indian Mutiny of 1857.** The mutinous Sepoy cavalry attacking a British infantry division at the battle of Cawpore. Although the uprising was suppressed it was not easily forgotten. In its aftermath the British reorganized the government of India.
The Granger Collection, New York.

eign domination that were to grow increasingly oppressive for Indians of all regions and religions over the ensuing ninety years of Crown rule, known as the **raj**.

BRITISH-INDIAN RELATIONS

The overall impact of British presence on the Indian masses, under both Company and Crown rule, was brutal but impersonal, in that it was largely economic. India was effectively integrated into Britain's economy, becoming a market for British goods and providing Britain with raw materials and other products. Britain's involvement in India's internal affairs included politics, education, the civil-service infrastructure, communications, and transportation, but the consequences of its domination and exploitation of India's labor and resources were especially far-reaching.

British cultural imperialism was never a major nor even an official policy of the East India Company. In fact, like Warren Hastings (1732–1818), governor general of the Company from 1774 to 1785, many Britons expressed interest in and some openness to Indians and their culture. A few mixed and even intermarried with Indians. The Company itself required many of its India officers to learn Persian and Sanskrit. Nor did it try to propagate Christianity or impose Western culture; indeed, it opposed Christian missionary activity in India until the 1830s and 1840s, partly because the caste system enabled the implementation of imperial policy. Nonetheless the British-Indian relationship had a paternalistic and patronizing dimension, both before and after the events of 1857. Even with the improved access of Indians to English education and to civil-service positions of greater responsibility in the late nineteenth and early twentieth centuries, the fundamental imbalance between overlords and subjects remained and was frequently expressed in racial terms. The ethos of the British rulers included the understanding that they had the task of governing an inferior "race" that could not

A Tea Planter on His Estate. One of the symbols of the *raj*, the great tea plantations of Sri Lanka and northeastern India—especially those of Assam—were major sources of wealth for the British overlords. They were also partly responsible for the deforestation of much of the subcontinent that occurred under British colonial rule in the nineteenth century.

Hulton/Corbis-Bettmann.

handle the job by itself. Even Indians whose university degrees or army training gave them impeccable British qualifications were never accepted as true equals. From army to civil-service ranks, the upper echelon of command was British; the middle and lower echelons of administration were Indian.

Despite this unequal relationship, British ideas and ways of doing things influenced a small but powerful Indian elite in both their business and political life and their manners and customs. Conversion to Christianity was rare, but Christian and secular values associated with the European Enlightenment—the ideals of British liberalism, for example—influenced Hindu and Muslim educated classes.

In the nineteenth century, probably the most influential and controversial member of the Indian elite to engage the British on their own ground was Ram Mohan Roy (1772–1833). Roy, a Bengali Hindu, rose to the top of the native ranks of East India Company service and became a strong voice for reform, both of Hindu life and practice and of British colonial policy where it deviated from European and Christian ideals. The spiritual father of the Brahmo Samaj (1828), a Hindu reform movement opposed to "barbarous" practices that ranged from *sati* (immolation of widows on their husbands' funeral pyres) to "idol worship" and Brahmanic "ritualism," Roy was an avowed modernist who wanted to meld the best of European-Christian morality and thought with the best of Hindu piety and thought. He was quick to oppose autocratic and unfair British legal and commercial practices and campaigned in India and in England to reform the Company's policies. He was influenced by the Christian Scriptures and the great thinkers of European civilization and drew upon them in his Hindu reform efforts. His wide-ranging writings and public campaigns for education, political involvement, and social progress and against the "backward" practices and ideas of many of his Hindu compatriots alienated most of the leading Hindu thinkers and activists of his age, but twentieth-century Indians have often seen him as a visionary.

The cultural relationship between Britain and India was not, of course, a one-way affair. During the Company era, and

An Eighteenth Century *Sati* Scene from South Decca India. A *Sati*, or *sutee* was the act of a Hindu widow cremating herself on a pyre with her dead husband.

Los Angeles County Museum of Art.

DOCUMENT Macaulay Writes on Indian Education

The decision in 1835 to encourage English-language study and the British school curriculum in Indian schools was hotly disputed by both the English and the Indians. In the end it bred a new generation of elite Indians prepared to act as advocates for their nation, as well as a class of bureaucrats for the British raj. *It also worked to the advantage of Hindus because Muslims tended to reject English schooling and lost ground in the long run. This famous position paper by Thomas Babington Macaulay expresses the thinking of the "Anglicists," who prevailed over the "Orientalists," and reveals British prejudices about the superiority of Western culture over Indian culture.*

◆ When Macaulay writes "that English is better worth knowing than Sanscrit or Arabic," is he making an objective judgment or is he engaging in "cultural imperialism"? From your perspective, which are the laudable, and which the problematic, intentions and goals of the writer?

We now come to the gist of the matter. We have a fund to be employed as government shall direct for the intellectual improvement of the people of this country. The simple question is, what is the most useful way of employing it?

All parties seem to be agreed on one point, that the dialects commonly spoken among the natives of this part of India contain neither literary nor scientific information, and are, moreover, so poor and rude that, until they are enriched from some other quarter, it will not be easy to translate any valuable work into them. It seems to be admitted on all sides that the intellectual improvement of those classes of the people who have the means of pursuing higher studies can at present be affected only by means of some language not vernacular amongst them.

What then shall that language be? One-half of the committee maintain that it should be the English. The other half strongly recommend the Arabic and Sanscrit. The whole question seems to me to be, which language is the best worth knowing? …

To sum up what I have said, I think it clear that we are free to employ our funds as we choose; that we ought to employ them in teaching what is best worth knowing; that English is better worth knowing than Sanscrit or Arabic; that the natives are desirous to be taught English, and are not desirous to be taught Sanscrit or Arabic; that neither as the languages of law, nor as the languages of religion, have the Sanscrit and Arabic any peculiar claim to our engagement; that it is possible to make natives of this country thoroughly good English scholars; and that to this end our efforts ought to be directed. In one point I fully agree with the gentlemen to whose general views I am opposed. I feel with them, that it is impossible for us, with our limited means, to attempt to educate the body of the people. We must at present do our best to form a class who may be interpreters between us and the millions whom we govern; a class of persons, Indian in blood and color, but English in taste, in opinions, in morals, and in intellect. To that class we may leave it to refine the vernacular dialects of the country, to enrich those dialects with terms of science borrowed from the Western nomenclature, and to render them by degrees fit vehicles for conveying knowledge to the great mass of the population.

From *Sources of Indian Tradition*, ed. by William Theodore de Bary. Copyright © 1958 by Columbia University Press. Reprinted with permission of the publisher.

---

increasingly after 1858, Britons at home became aware of India and Indians. The image that came to them, however, was filtered through the experience of other Britons who had spent time in the subcontinent and were not always either sympathetic or objective interpreters. Even many of those officers of the Company who made India a career developed little interest in Indians beyond what they needed to know to extract economic gain from them. Others, however, studied Indian cultures and languages and got to know at least some of the Indian elite as friends. However, after the implementation of direct Crown rule in 1858, a stricter social segregation of white rulers from Indian subjects set in.

Despite the keen interest in Indian culture that many of them had, the British, much more than their Central Asian Mughal predecessors, treated Indians all too often as backward heathens in need of the "civilizing" influences of their own "enlightened" culture, law, political system, education, and reli-

gion. A vivid example of this dismissive attitude to Indian culture is evident in the argument of the nineteenth-century British historian and statesman Lord Macaulay (1800–1859) in favor of an English-language curriculum in Indian schools. (See Document, "Macaulay Writes on Indian Education.")

Most Indians resented their subordinate status. The nationalist movement at the end of the nineteenth century extended to the grass-roots level—among tribal groups, peasant farmers, and home or small-industry workers. Whatever their status, the distrust and animosity most Indians felt toward their foreign rulers continued to grow.[2]

---

[2] See, for example, Bayly, *Indian Society and the British Empire*, pp. 169–199; David Arnold, "Rebellious Hillmen: The Gudem-Rampa Risings, 1839–1924," in Ranajit Guha, ed., *Subaltern Studies* (Delhi: Oxford University Press, 1982), pp. 88–142; Ranajit Guha, *Elementary Aspects of Peasant Insurgency in Colonial India* (New Delhi, 1984); cf. Eric Stokes, *The Peasant and the Raj: Studies in Agrarian Society and Peasant Rebellion in Colonial India* (Cambridge: Cambridge University Press, 1978).

◀ **Faces of the Raj.** A tennis party at the Residency, Kapurkala, Panjab, ca. 1894.
Hulton/Corbis-Bettman.

From British Crown Raj to Independence

THE BURDEN OF CROWN RULE

The Revolt of 1857 had numerous consequences beyond the transfer of the administration of India from the East India Company to the British Crown. The bloody conflict exacerbated mutual fear and hatred. Before the revolt, the British had maintained a largely native army under British officers. After the revolt, they tried to maintain a ratio of at least one British to three Indian soldiers. Because the army was financed by Indian, not British, revenues, it imposed a huge economic burden on India, diverting one third of its total annual revenues to pay for its own military occupation.

British economic policies and accelerating population growth put great strains on India's poor. Cheap British machine-produced goods were exchanged for Indian raw materials and the products of its home industries, harming or destroying Indian craft industries and forcing multitudes into poverty or onto the land. Industrialization, which might have provided work for India's unemployed masses, was avoided. During the Civil War in the United States (1861–1865), which interrupted Britain's source of cotton from the U.S. South, there was a shift from food to cotton farming in India. This shift intensified the effects of a drought in the 1870s, leading to widespread famine. Many peasants were forced to emigrate to Britain's dominions in South Africa, where they worked as indentured servants.

The Revolt of 1857 also created a poisonous distrust of Indians within the British colonial administration. **Cantonments** segregating white masters from "untrustworthy" natives became the rule in Indian towns and cities. Despite the just intentions expressed in royal statements and the opening of the civil ser-

vice, at least nominally, to Indian candidates, the *raj* discouraged equality between Indian and Britisher. One bright exception to this trend was the tenure (1880–1884) of the Marquess of Ripon (1827–1909) as viceroy of India. Ripon fought to erase legal racial discrimination by allowing Indian judges to try British as well as Indian citizens. His efforts earned him the hatred of most of his British compatriots in India, but he was an example to emerging Indian leaders of the best that British egalitarianism could produce. Although his British foes managed by agitation to dilute his measures, in doing so they unwittingly gave Indians a model for political agitation of their own.[3]

INDIAN RESISTANCE

Indians soon took up political activism. Late in the nineteenth century they founded the institutions that would help overcome traditional regionalism, build national feeling, and ultimately end colonial rule. In 1885 Indian modernists formed the Indian National Congress to reform traditional Hindu and Muslim practices that were out of line with their liberal ideals and to change British Indian policies that were equally out of line with British democratic ideals. Other Indians agitated for the rejection of British rule altogether. The Muslim League developed as a counterbalance to the Hindu-dominated Congress. The League eventually made common cause with the Congress in the quest for home rule but ultimately worked for, and gained, a separate independent Muslim state, Pakistan. Heavy-handed and erratic British policies in legal administration, political representation, and taxation strengthened the growing desire for nationhood and independence.

---

[3] Stanley Wolpert, *A New History of India*, 2nd ed. (New York: Oxford University Press, 1982), pp. 256–257.

▲ **The Cotton Trade.** Cotton was one of the most important natural resources in the nineteenth century. These pictures depict workers and slaves loading and gathering cotton in India and North America. Courtesy of Library of Congress.

Indian internal divisions were a major obstacle to independence. These divisions included the many language groups and subject princely states of the subcontinent. These, however, were not the only divisions or even the most critical. For much of British rule, every Indian politician was first a representative of his own region or state and second an Indian nationalist. Furthermore, the educated Indian elite had little in common with the masses of farmers and laborers beyond antagonism to foreign rule, making unified resistance or political action difficult. Mistrust and conflict among Hindus, Muslims, Sikhs, and Jains also impeded concerted political action.

Nonetheless, a nationalist movement with many subbranches took root. There were three principal elements within the independence movement that led to the creation of India and Pakistan in 1947.

The first consisted of those in the National Congress organization who sought gradual reform and progress toward Indian self-governance, or *svarāj*. This position did not preclude outright opposition to the British, but it did mean trying to deal with the colonial rulers to change the system from within wherever possible. Among the proponents of this approach were G. K. Gokhale (1866–1915), the champion of moderate, deliberate, peaceful work toward self-determination; the spiritual and political genius

Mohandas K. Gandhi (1869–1948); and his follower Jawaharlal Nehru (1889–1964), who became the first prime minister of India. Gandhi was the principal Indian leader after World War I and directed the all-India drive that finally forced the British out. An English-trained lawyer, Gandhi drew on not only his own native Hindu (and Jain and Buddhist) heritage, but also on the ideas of Western liberal and Christian thinkers like Henry David Thoreau (1817–1862) and Leo Tolstoy (1828–1910). In the end, Gandhi became a world figure as well as an Indian leader. (See Document, "Gandhi on Passive Resistance and Svarāj.")

The second element consisted of the militant Hindu nationalists, whose leader, the extremist B. G. Tilak (1856–1920), stressed the use of Indian languages and a revival of Hindu culture and learning. Tilak also subscribed to an anti-Muslim, Hindu communalist vision of Indian "self-governance." Where earlier in the nineteenth century foreign ideas had stimulated a Hindu renaissance and various reform movements, the Hindu extremists now looked to a return to traditional Indian values and self-sufficiency. Although their movement dissipated in the common resistance effort after 1914, their religious and political ideas still influence Indian political life, as witnessed

▲ **The "Great Soul,"** "Mahatma" Mohandas K. Gandhi, father of the modern state of India. UPI/Corbis-Corbis-Bettmann.

DOCUMENT   Gandhi on Passive Resistance and Svarāj

Gandhi's powerful thinking and prose were already evident in his Hind Svarāj, or Indian Home Rule of 1909. This work was to remain his basic manifesto. The following excerpts reflect important points in his philosophy. Svadeshī refers to reliance only on what one produces at home (rather than on foreign goods).

◆ How does Gandhi relate the ideas of passive resistance and svarāj to his theory of Indian self-rule? What are the advantages and disadvantages of his strategy for effecting political and social change? How does this document compare with others concerned with movements of independence and nationalism? See "The Stamp Act Congress Addresses George III" (Chapter 23) and "Mazzini Defines Nationality" (Chapter 24).

Passive resistance is a method of securing rights by personal suffering; it is the reverse of resistance by arms. When I refuse to do a thing that is repugnant to my conscience, I use soul-force. For instance, the government of the day has passed a law which is applicable to me. I do not like it. If by using violence I force the government to repeal the law, I am employing what may be termed body-force. If I do not obey the law and accept the penalty for its breach, I use soul-force. It involves sacrifice of self.

Everybody admits that sacrifice of self is infinitely superior to sacrifice of others. Moreover, if this kind of force is used in a cause that is unjust, only the person using it suffers. He does not make others suffer for his mistakes. ...

... The real meaning of the statement that we are a law-abiding nation is that we are passive resisters. When we do not like certain laws, we do not break the heads of law-givers but we suffer and do not submit to the laws. ...

If man will only realize that it is unmanly to obey laws that are unjust, no man's tyranny will enslave him. This is the key to self-rule or home-rule. ...

Let each do his duty. If I do my duty, that is, serve myself, I shall be able to serve others. Before I leave you, I will take the liberty of repeating:

1. Real home-rule is self-rule or self-control.

2. The way to it is passive resistance: that is soul-force or love-force.

3. In order to exert this force, *Svadeshī* in every sense is necessary.

4. What we want to do should be done, not because we object to the English or because we want to retaliate, but because it is our duty to do so. Thus, supposing that the English remove the salt-tax, restore our money, give the highest posts to Indians, withdraw the English troops, we shall certainly not use their machine-made goods, nor use the English language, nor many of their industries. It is worth noting that these things are, in their nature, harmful; hence we do not want them. I bear no enmity towards the English but do towards their civilization. In my opinion, we have used the term *Svadeshī* without understanding its real significance. I have endeavored to explain it as I understand it, and my conscience testifies that my life henceforth is dedicated to its attainment.

by the resurgence of Hindu extremist groups in recent years and the communal strife, especially of Hindus with Muslims.

Muslims made up the third element but there were many divergent regional and even sectarian Muslim constituencies. Generally their leaders could be brought to make common cause only by the fear that as a minority they stood to lose what power they had in a Hindu-majority, all-India state. Muslims had been slower than the Hindus to take up British ideas and education and thus lagged behind the Hindu intelligentsia in numbers and influence with the British or other Indians. Because of the prominence of Muslims in the 1857 Revolt, the British were at first much less inclined to foster their advancement than that of Hindus. Nonetheless, the Muslims, distrusting the largely Hindu National Congress after its founding in 1885, sought rapprochement with the British at first, rather than risk being submerged in Hindu-led movements of opposition.

The man who did the most to win back respect and a voice for the Muslims in India under the Crown was Sayyid Ahmad Khan (1817–1898). A long-time supporter of modernist ideas and of cooperation with the British, he could also be sharply critical of their mistakes in India. His opposition to Muslim participation in the National Congress foreshadowed the tensions and conflict in Hindu-Muslim relations. He was also the founder of the Muslim educational initiative that led to the creation of the Muhammadan Anglo-Oriental College at Aligarh, which became the center for modernist Muslim attempts to integrate Muslim faith with modern Western thought and learning. It is still a major Muslim intellectual center in India today.

CHRONOLOGY

India

1774–1785	Administration of Warren Hastings
1772–1833	Ram Mohan Roy, Hindu reformer
1817–1898	Sayyid Ahmad Khan, Muslim reformer
1835	Introduction of English education
1857–1858	Sepoy Revolt, or "Mutiny," followed by direct Crown rule as a British colony
1885	Indian National Congress formed
1869–1948	Mohandas K. Gandhi
1873–1938	Muhammad Iqbal
1876–1949	Muhammad Ali Jinnah
1889–1964	Jawaharlal Nehru
1947	Independence and partition

▲ **The Founding Father of Pakistan.** Muhammad Ali Jinnah was the President of India's Muslim League who in the 1930s advanced the "two nations" theory and made the first formal demand for a separate Muslim homeland. His ideas led to the establishment of Pakistan. AP Wide World Photos.

HINDU-MUSLIM FRICTION ON THE ROAD TO INDEPENDENCE

In the twentieth century the rift between Muslims and Hindus in the subcontinent grew wider, despite periods of cooperation against the British. Arguments for coexistence with Hindus floundered, and Muslim fears of loss of communal identity and rights grew. In the end the great Indo-Muslim poet, thinker, and "spiritual father of Pakistan," Muhammad Iqbal (1873–1938), and the "founder of Pakistan," Muhammad Ali Jinnah (1876–1949), helped move Muslims to separatism.

The independence of India and Pakistan from Western domination was achieved only with suffering and violence. Blood was spilled in the long battle with the British, in communal violence among Indians themselves, in the violence between Hindus and Muslims that accompanied partition in 1947, and in the subsequent (and still festering) dispute over Kashmir between India and Pakistan. Still, the victory of 1947 gave the peoples of the subcontinent, Indians and Pakistanis, at last a sense of participation in the world of nations on their own terms instead of on those dictated by a foreign power. The British influence was in some ways a good one. The British left a legacy of administrative and political unity and egalitarian and democratic ideals that Indian nationalists turned to their own uses.

THE ISLAMIC EXPERIENCE
Islamic Responses to Declining Power and Independence

The eighteenth century saw the weakening of the great Muslim empires and the increasing ascendancy of the West in international trade, military-political power, imperialist expansion, industrial specialization and productivity, and technological progress. The diverse Islamic peoples and states were thrust from positions of global power into a struggle for survival. As with India, the decline of Islamic preeminence was due both to the rise of the modern West and to internal problems.

By the eighteenth century all of the largest Muslim empires—Mughal, Ottoman, Safavid, Moroccan, and Central Asian—had declined politically, militarily, and economically in relation to Western European empires. They had grown increasingly decentralized, were less stable economically and politically, and were increasingly dominated by entrenched hereditary elites. Furthermore, the circumnavigation of the globe meant that it was no longer necessary to cross through the Middle East to get from Europe to Asia and back. For millennia, the Middle East benefited commercially from its geographic middle-man status. The shift in trade routes, however, resulted in changes in Middle Eastern and Mediterranean economies that caused them to become more peripheral to the world economy now centered on Western Europe. Yet once the various European nations had established a foothold in South and Southeast Asia, they turned their attention in the early nineteenth century to the Islamic heartlands in the Middle East. The Middle East became enmeshed in European

Linking Asia and Europe. The opening of the Suez Canal in 1869 was a major engineering achievement. It also became a major international waterway benefiting all maritime states reducing the distance from London to Bombay in half.

Index Stock Imagery, Inc.

imperial competition for its industrial resources such as oil, and most of the area came under Western political and economic domination. The interaction between the people of the Middle East and these new imperial powers was varied. There were some examples of cooperation and accommodation, but for the most part, the prevailing tone in the nineteenth century was one of conflict.

Ultimately, the fundamental question that engrossed Muslim reformers, politicians, and intellectuals was the basis of European ascendancy. Was the secular learning and technological superiority of Europe something transferable to the Middle East or other non European regions? Could the once dominant Islamic word regain its vitality by importing European values and education as well as technology? Could the Islamic tradition of values itself be adapted or reformed to support and foster the kind of societal progress that Europe seemed to have managed without succombing to secularization entirely?

During the eighteenth and nineteenth centuries a variety of reform movements sought to revive Islam as a comprehensive guide for living and to purify it of the effects of many of the more stultifying developments in Islamic societies during the preceding centuries. In the major urban areas such as Cairo, Istanbul, and Damascus, influential reformers such as Muhammad Ali (see below) and the sultan Mahmud II proposed adaptionist reform that sought to reengineer the armies, institutions, and soceieties of the Middle East to conform to the political reality of European domination. In these same urban settings, a variety of intellectuals sought to redefine what it meant to be Muslim in a modern age by emphasizing the malleability of the religion in relation to contemporary society. The most famous of such reform efforts was *Tanzimat* (see below) in the Ottoman Empire. In the more rural areas, where

neither urban Muslim ideas nor European power had penetrated to the same extent, other reformers stressed rejection of more flexible forms of Islam and of any western or other values that might be held up as models.

The most famous of these movements that emphasized a strict construction of what "true" Islam entails was that of the **Wahhabis**, the followers of Ibn Abd al-Wahhab (1703–1792) in Arabia. It sought to combat excesses of popular and Sufi piety, such as saint worship, visitations to saints' tombs, and faith in the intercession of Sufi masters and saints. It also sought to break the stranglehold of the *ulama*'s conformist interpretations of legal and religious issues, favoring instead the exercise of independent judgment. The only authorities were to be the Qur'an and the traditions of the Prophet, not the scholastic edifices of the traditional schools of legal and theological interpretation. Allied with a local Arab prince, Sa'ud, the Wahhabi movement swept much of the Arabian Peninsula. It was crushed in the early nineteenth century by Egyptian military forces acting for the Ottoman regime. Still, the movement finally saw victory under a descendant of Sa'ud at the onset of this century and is the guiding ideology of present-day Saudi Arabia.

Other Muslim reform movements reflected similar revivalist and even militantly pietist responses to Islamic decadence and decline. Examples include that of Usman Dan Fodio in Africa in the late eighteenth century (discussed later in this chapter) and the Muslim Brotherhood in modern Egypt (see Chapter 34). Such groups call for a pristine Islam divested of the authoritarianism of the medieval legal schools, *ulama* theological conformity, and degenerate Sufi orders. Furthermore, these movements inspired a noncritical nostalgia for a time when Islamic societies were in ascendance and even dominating. This memory still rallies movements from Africa to Indonesia and seems to offer a viable alternative to the depressing status quo. In Islamic societies everywhere it has provided a response to the challenge of Western-style "modernity" and a model for cultural and religious life.

Western Political and Economic Encroachment

From the late 1700s until World War II the political fortunes of Arab, Turkish, Persian, Indian, Southeast Asian, and African Islamic states were increasingly dictated from outside by Western powers—including Britain, Russia, Germany, and France—and were at the mercy of the rivalries among them.

Western governments extracted capitulations favorable to their own economic and political interests from indigenous governments in exchange for promises of military protection or other considerations. These capitulations granted commercial concessions, protection, and "extraterritorial" legal status to European merchant enclaves. Such concessions (the earliest had been granted in the sixteenth century) had originally been reciprocal and had also served the commercial purposes of Muslim rulers and merchants. However, they eventually provided Western powers with pretexts for direct intervention in Ottoman, Iranian, Indian, and African affairs. The Ottoman Empire, like the Mughal Empire, suffered from internal disunity; its provincial rulers, or *pashas*, were virtually independent. This, combined with the increasing economic problems facing all the agrarian societies of Asia and Africa, made it easy for the Western powers—with their rapidly industrializing economies and increasingly effective militaries—to take control almost at will. Repeated Ottoman diplomatic and military defeats made that once great imperial power "the sick man of Europe" after 1800; similar weakness allowed Westerners to control the destinies of Indian and Iranian states and principalities.

The event that marked symbolically the onset of European domination of the Islamic heartlands was Napoleon Bonaparte's (1769–1821) invasion of Egypt in 1798 (see Chapter 23). The ease with which the French army was able to invade Egypt and topple the local government was suggestive of the weakened military status of the Middle East and the wider Muslim world. It also demonstrated the technical advances of European field artillery and infantry rifles. Eventually the French were forced by Britain, Russia, and the Ottomans to evacuate Egypt in 1801, but the invasion heralded a new era of European imperialism in the region. The British had already wrested control over India and the Persian Gulf from the French; they now became the preeminent European power in the eastern Mediterranean as well. The French continued to contest British ascendancy in the larger Middle Eastern area, but Russia presented the most serious nineteenth-century challenge to Britain's colonial empire.

Russia, which had already won control of the Black Sea from the Ottomans, sought to gain as much territory and influence in the Iranian and Central Asian regions as possible. Afghanistan, an independent kingdom established by Ahmad Shah Durrani (r. 1737–1773), acted as a buffer that prevented Russia from penetrating into British India. In the Iranian and Ottoman regions, however, Russia and Britain struggled for supremacy. The Crimean War of 1854–1856 (see Chapter 24) was one result of this conflict.

The Western Impact

Beyond the overt political and commercial impact of the West, Western political ideology, culture, and technology proved to be critical factors for change in Islamic societies. Outside of India, this effect was most strongly felt in Egypt, Lebanon, North Africa, and Anatolia (modern Turkey), as we shall see. Of all the Islamic states, including those in Africa and India, the ones least and last affected by Western "modernity" were Iran, Afghanistan, and the Central Asian khanates. The Iranian case deserves at least brief attention.

Iran The rulers of Iran from 1794 to 1925 were the Qajar shahs, a Turkoman dynasty whose absolutist reign was not unlike that of the Safavids. However, unlike the Safavids, the Qajars did not make religious claims to descent from the Shi'ite *imams*. Under Qajar rule, in marked contrast to Safavid rule, the *ulama* of the Shi'ite community became less and less strongly connected with the state apparatus. This period also saw the emergence of a Shi'i traditionalist doctrine that encouraged all Shi'ites, in the absence of a living *imam*, to choose a **mujtahid**—a qualified scholarly guide—from among the *ulama* and follow him in all matters requiring religious-legal interpretation. As a result, the *ulama* gained strength as an independent power in the state. As the guardians of law and faith, they were often the chief critics of the government (not least for its attempts to admit Western influences) and exponents of the people's grievances.

A prime demonstration of *ulama* power occurred when the Qajar Shah granted a fifty-year monopoly on tobacco sales to a British corporation in 1890. In 1891 the leading authority in the *ulama* spearheaded a tobacco boycott to protest the concession. This popular action, the first successful mass protest in modern Iranian history, was also supported by modernist-nationalist opponents of the Qajar regime who had strong connections to Iran's commercial, or **bazaari**, middle classes. In the face of such widespread opposition, the shah had to rescind the concession. On the one hand, this was a stunning victory for the power of public opinion and a symbolic triumph over the penetration of Western commercial interests in Iran. Yet ironically this action only made Iran more dependent on Western capital. The Iranian government was forced to pay an exorbitant compensation of around £500,000 sterling to the British corporation, which necessitated a foreign loan from a British bank. This was Iran's first foreign debt, and caused it to be more reliant on Western institutions thereafter.

Subject as it was to the machinations of outsiders, such as Russia, Britain, and France, Iran inevitably felt the impact of Western ideas about education, science, law, and government. This occurred especially in the latter half of the century, when younger Iranian intellectuals began to warm to Western liberalism on economic, social, and political issues. As in other Islamic countries, the seeds of a new, secular nationalism were being sown where, previously, sectarian or communalist religious sentiments had held sway. It coincided and worked with a growing desire for a voice in government. An uneasy alliance of Iranian modernists with conservative *ulama* proved, on occasion, an effective counterforce to Qajar absolutism, as in the tobacco boycott and in at least the early stages of the effort to force the Qajars to accept a constitution in 1906–1911. Yet such alliances did not bridge the inherent ideological divisions of the two groups, as subsequent twentieth-century history would demonstrate all too clearly.

▲ **Muhammad Ali (1769–1849).** The famous viceroy of Egypt is depicted as an equestrian in this portrait.
Hulton/Corbis-Bettmann.

Islamic Responses to Foreign Encroachment

As the Iranian case shows, Western impingement on the Islamic world in the nineteenth and twentieth centuries elicited varied responses. Every people or state had a different experience, according to its particular circumstances and history. Yet there were at least three typical styles of reaction: (1) a tendency to emulate Western ideas and institutions; (2) the attempt to join Western innovations with traditional Islamic institutions; and (3) a traditionalist rejection of things Western in favor of either the status quo or a return to a purified Islamic community, or *Umma*. Of course, none of these styles was confined to one class or group in Islamic societies, and none was uniform within a country or across political, ethnic, and cultural boundaries.

EMULATION OF THE WEST

The career of the virtually independent Ottoman viceroy Muhammad Ali (ca. 1769–1849), pasha of Egypt from 1805 to 1849, exemplifies a strategy of emulation. Ali, who arrived in Alexandria as part of an Albanian regiment of Ottoman forces sent to fight the French in 1801, set out to rejuvenate Egypt's failing agriculture, introduce modern mechanized industry, modernize the army with European help, and introduce European education and culture in government schools. Although he ultimately failed to make Egypt as powerful as the European states of his day, Muhammad Ali did set his country on the path to becoming a distinct modern national state. Although his successors' financial and political catastrophes led the British to occupy Egypt (1882–1922), he is rightly called "the father of modern Egypt."

Efforts to appropriate Western experience and success were made by several Ottoman sultans and viziers after the devastating defeat of the Turks by Russia in 1774. Most notable were the reforms of Selim III (r. 1762–1808), Mahmud II (r. 1808–1839), and the so-called Tanzimat, or beneficial "legislation" (literally, "[re-]ordering") era, from about 1839 to 1880. Selim made serious efforts at economic, administrative, and military reform. He brought European officers in to train new military corps that were to supplant the conservative Janissaries. Mahmud's reforms were much like those of Muhammad Ali. Most important were his destruction of the Janissary corps, tax and bureaucratic reforms, and encouragement of Western military and educational methods among the Ottoman elites. Like Selim and Muhammad Ali, he was less interested in promoting European enlightenment ideas about citizen rights and equity than in building a stronger, more modern centralized government, which often resulted in the consolidation of political power among a select few.

The Tanzimat reforms, introduced by several liberal Ottoman ministers of state, continued the efforts of Selim and Mahmud to bring the Ottoman state into line with

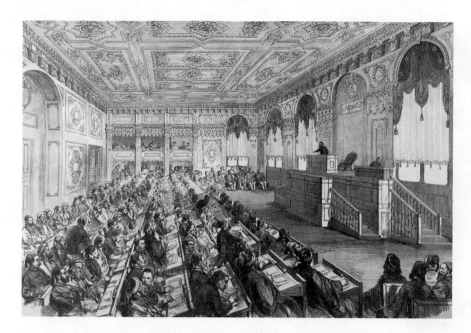

◀ **Tanzimat.** In the nineteenth century the Ottoman Empire went through a series of reforms to bolster its military and economic standing. Here the Turkish parliament debates political reform in Istanbul.
Mary Evans Picture Library Ltd.

ideals espoused by the European states. They were also intended to give European powers less cause to intervene in Ottoman affairs and to regenerate domestic confidence in the state.

The nineteenth-century Ottoman reforms failed to save the empire or truly to revive it as an economically sound, culturally vibrant, or militarily and politically powerful state. Nevertheless, they paved the way for the rise of Turkish nationalism, the "Young Turk" revolution of 1908, and ultimately the nationalist revolution of the 1920s that produced modern Turkey. (Ironically and tragically, this development simultaneously frustrated similar nationalist aspirations among old Ottoman minorities like the Greeks, the Armenians, and the Kurds.)

The creation of the Turkish republic out of the ashes of the Ottoman state after World War I is probably the most extreme example of an effort to modernize and nationalize an Islamic state on a Western model though others would argue that it is the most succesful case of integration. This state was largely the child of Mustafa Kemal (1881–1938), known as "Atatürk" ("father of the Turks"), its founder and first president (1922–1938). Atatürk led Turkey through an intensive period of reform that sought to eliminate vestiges of the ottoman past and orient Turkey even more towards the west. His wide-ranging reforms were based on six principles that Atatürk defined as the foundation of the doctrine known as "Kemalism." These were: reformism, secularism, republicanism, nationalism, (the "statism"), and populism. Though these major reforms ranged from the introduction of a European-style code of civil law to the abolition of the caliphate, Sufi

orders, Arabic script, and the Arabic call to prayer, Atatürk attempted to inculcate pride in the idea of a modern secular Turkish nation that appealed to all segments of society. On the surface, Atatürks reforms constituted a truly radical attempt to secularize an Islamic state and to separate religious from political and social institutions. Yet at the same time, his reforms were largely a continuation of the tranformation that had begun in the Ottman era and had essentially the same goal as the Tanzimat movement, i.e., to make Turkey more responsive to the challenges of modernity. In the intervening years, Turkey has maintained its independence, reaffirmed its commitment to democratic government, and emerged with a unique, but still distinctly, Islamic identity. (See Document, Taha Hussein "The Future of Culture in Egypt.")

INTEGRATION OF WESTERN AND ISLAMIC IDEAS

The attempt to join modernization with traditional Islamic institutions and ideas is exemplified in the thought of famous Muslim intellectuals, such as Jamal al-Din al-Afghani (1839–1897), Muhammad Abduh (1845–1905), and Muhammad Iqbal (1873–1938). These thinkers argued for a progressive Islam rather than a materialist Western secularism as the best answer to life in the modern world.

Afghani is best known for his emphasis on the unity of the Islamic world, or **pan-Islamism**, and on a populist, constitutionalist approach to political order. His ideas and his charismatic personality influenced political activist movements in Egypt, Iran, Ottoman Turkey, and elsewhere.

Kemal Atatürk This 1928 photograph shows Atatürk (right) giving instruction in the Latin alphabet. It reflects the personal engagement of Mustafa Kemal in the many reform efforts he instituted.
Historical Pictures Collection/Stock Montage Inc.

His Egyptian disciple, Muhammad Abduh, sought to modernize Muslim education. He argued that a firm, revealed Qur'anic base could be combined harmoniously with modern science and its open questioning of reality. Through his efforts as Grand Mufti and head of state education, he introduced modernist reforms that affected even the curriculum of the most venerable traditionalist institution of higher learning in the Islamic world, the great al-Azhar school in Cairo.

Muhammad Iqbal, the most celebrated Indian Muslim thinker of the twentieth century, argued for a modernist revival of Muslim faith focused on purifying and uplifting the individual self above enslavement either to reason or to traditionalist conformity. Often credited with the original idea of a separate Muslim state in the Indian subcontinent (today's Pakistan), Iqbal still felt that Islam was essentially nonexclusivist and supranationalist:

> The truth is that Islam is not a church. It is a state conceived as a contractual organism. ... and animated by an ethical ideal which regards man not as an earth-rooted creature, defined by this or that portion of the earth, but as a spiritual being understood in terms of

a social mechanism, and possessing rights and duties as a living factor in that mechanism[4]. ...

Although Iqbal's poetry and essays excited Muslim fervor and dynamism, it is difficult to say how great his actual impact on Islamic political and social life really was.

WOMEN AND REFORM IN THE MIDDLE EAST

Though the discussion of reform, religion, and modernity in the Middle East was dominated by men, there were also a number of Middle Eastern women who started to address the status of women in modern society. Most important were those women who demanded politcal involvement for women in their country's affairs: the Iranian women who confronted their fathers and brothers in the Iranian Parliament in December, 1911, concerning the possibility that the men might capitulate to the Russian-British demands to remove the American reforming administrator, Morgan Schuster; the Egyptian women who upon their return with their politician husbands in 1919 from Paris, where the latter had been humiliated as the Egyptian delegation, or *Wafd*, by the Versailles powers, threw off their veils and declared themselves the new Egyptian women; or the Palestinian women who convened in 1929 a Women's Congress of Palestine to address the political issues that ensued after the Wailing Wall riots of the same year. It is also noteworthy that there emerged in the late nineteenth and early twentieth century a number of journal and magazines that were devoted to women's concerns. These mainly focused on traditional issues such as cooking, parenting, and fashion, but there were other journals that sought to enlarge the domain of women and their role in the public sphere. Some articles stressed that women were an essential part of society and should not be excluded from participation in commerce and politics. Some movements or demonstrations likewise carried forward such concerns. For example, the Egyptian Feminist Union was founded in 1923 by Huda Sha'rawi (1879–1947) to fight for women's suffrage, reform of marriage laws, and equal access to education. In a well-publicized gesture, Sha'rawi and her colleague Saize Nabrawi made a dramatic gesture to highlight the objective of the feminist movement. Standing in the midst of Cairo's bustling train station they publicly removed their veils to emphasize that women should no longer be concealed from the rest of society. Sha'rawi's act, like that of the women returned from Versailles in 1919, indicated that, the veil was symbolic of the inadequate public status of women in Egypt and other Middle Eastern countries. For those outside the Middle East today, veiling is often seen as the most important gender issue. Many Middle Eastern feminists stress, however, that women's inequality

---

[4] Quoted in K. Cragg and R. M. Speight, eds., *Islam from Within* (Belmont, CA: Wadsworth, 1980), p. 213.

DOCUMENT   Taha Hussein "The Future of Culture in Egypt"

Taha Hussein (1889–1973) was the Egyptian Minister of Education 1950–1952 and leading Arab intellectual. He was born in a poor village in upper Egypt and became blind by the age of three. He studied at the important Al-Azhar University and eventually finished his doctorate at the Sorbonne in Paris. Hussein, like so many intellectuals around the world at this time, was very concerned with nationalism and how to reconcile the challenges of modernity with traditional thought and practice. In his writings, he argued that Egypt was part of Mediterranean civilization and that Egypt should follow European ideas in its quest to build up a modern nation. In the following piece, "The Future of Culture in Egypt" written in 1938, Hussein argues that Egypt had historical connections to Europe. Westernization thus constituted a return to Egypt's real roots.

◆ What is Hussein trying to achieve by emphasizing Egypt's historic ties to Europe?

The subject to be treated in this discourse is the future of culture in Egypt, now that our country has regained her freedom through the revival of the constitution and her honor through the realization of independence. We are living in an age characterized by the fact that freedom and independence do not constitute ends in themselves, but are merely means of attaining exalted, enduring, and generally practical goals. …

I know of nothing that causes me more worry than this newly won independence and freedom of ours. I fear that they may beguile us into thinking that we have come to the end of the road when in fact we have just reached the beginning. …

I do not want us feel inferior to the Europeans because of our cultural shortcomings. This would cause us to despise ourselves and admit that they are not treating us unjustly when they are being arrogant. It is obnoxious for a man who is sensitive to dignity and honor to be compelled to acknowledge that he is not yet deserving of them. Let us keep this disgrace from ourselves and

the nation. The way to do it is to take hold of our affairs with determination and vigor from today on, discard useless words for meaningful action, and establish our new life on a sound, constructive basis. …

At the outset we must answer this fundamental question: Is Egypt of the East or of the West? Naturally, I mean East or West in the cultural, not the geographical sense. It seems to me that there are two distinctly different and bitterly antagonistic cultures on the earth. Both have existed since time immemorial, the one in Europe, the other in the Far East. …

The Egyptian mind had no serious contact with the Far Eastern mind; nor did it live harmoniously with the Persian mind. The Egyptian mind has had regular, peaceful, and mutually beneficial relations only with the Near East and Greece. In short, it has been influenced from earliest times by the Mediterranean Sea and the various peoples living around it. …

In order to become equal partners in civilization with the Europeans, we must literally and forthrightly do everything that they do; we must share with them the present civilization, with its pleasant and unpleasant sides, and not content ourselves with words or mere gestures. Whoever advises any other course of action is either a deceiver or is himself deceived. Strangely enough we imitate the West in our everyday life, yet hypocritically deny the fact in our words. If we really detest European life, what is to hinder us from rejecting it completely? And if we genuinely respect the Europeans, as we certainly seem to do by our wholesale adoption of their practices, why do we not reconcile our words with our actions? Hypocrisy ill becomes those who are proud and anxious to overcome their defects.

From *The Future of Culture in Egypt*, by Tâhâ Hussein, trans. by Sidney Glazer, Washington, D. C.: American Council of Learned Societies, 1954, pp. 1–5, 7–9, 15–17, 20, 25. No. 9 in ACLS Near Eastern Translation Project, copyright 1954. Reprinted in *The Islamic World*, eds. William H. McNeill and Marilyn Robinson Waldon, The University of Chicago Press 1973.

is rooted in wide-ranging cultural, political, and economicial structures that need to be addressed long before the issue of the veil.

PURIFICATION AND REVIVAL OF ISLAM

A third kind of Muslim reaction to Western domination has emphasized Islamic values and ideals to the exclusion of "outside" forces. This approach has involved either the kind of reformist revivalism already seen in Wahhabism or the kind of conservatism often associated with Sunni or Shi'ite "establishment" *ulama*, as in the case of Iran since 1979. Both conservative and revivalist Muslim thinkers share the conviction that it is within, not outside, the Islamic tradition that answers to the

questions facing Muslims in the modern world are to be found.

Traditionalist conservatism is much harder to pin down as the ethos of particular movements and organized groups than is reformist revivalism. Whereas Muslim revivalism (today commonly called "Islamism") usually focuses on Qur'an and Prophetic example as the sole authorities for Islamic life, Muslim conservatism commonly champions those forms of Islamic life and thought embodied in traditional law, theology, and even Sufism. It is seen in the legalistic tendencies that have often resurfaced when Islamic norms have been threatened by the breakdown of traditional society and the rise of secularism. Although such conservatism has often been associated with the most reactionary forces in Islamic society, it has often also

CHRONOLOGY

Islamic Lands

1703–1792	Ibn Abd al-Wahhab
1737–1773	Rule of Ahmad Shah Durrani, founder of modern Afghanistan
1794–1925	Qajar shahs of Iran
1798	Invasion of Egypt by Napoleon Bonaparte
1805–1849	Rule of Muhammad Ali in Egypt
ca. 1839–1880	Era of the Tanzimat reforms of the Ottoman Empire
1839–1897	Jamal al-Din al-Afghani
1845–1905	Muhammad Abduh
1882–1922	British occupation of Egypt
1908	"Young Turk" revolution
1922–1938	Mustafa Kemal, "Atatürk" in power

served to preserve basic Muslim values while allowing for gradual change in a way that reformist revivalism could not accept. Where conservatives have formed alliances with governments or simply been co-opted by them, the credibility of the establishment *ulama* has often been destroyed. This is because the masses of Muslims have been increasingly attracted to Islamist agendas for change.

NATIONALISM

Nationalism is a product of modern European history (see Chapter 24). Although not merely a response to Western encroachment, nationalist movements in the Islamic world have been either largely stimulated by Western models or produced in direct reaction to Western imperialist exploitation and colonial occupation. During the late nineteenth century, many intellectuals in Asia or Africa grappled with the question of identity and whether or not their ethnic or linguistic group constituted a distinct nation or whether they were part of a larger whole. (See Document, Taha Hussein "The Future of Culture in Egypt.") The answer was not always self-evident and in fact quite complicated given the mosaic of ethnicities, religions, and language groups across Africa and Asia. Yet the often arbitrary or artificial division of the colonial world by European administrators eventually demanded an answer to these questions in Asia and Africa. In the European capitals new "nations" were created and drawn on the map in the African and Asian continents, especially after World War I. These new nations, such as Nigeria, Lebanon, Congo, or Iraq, reflected realities and interests of imperialism rather than actual facts on the gound. In due time, these borders have taken on an aura of legitimacy. However, forging nations from artificial parameters has proven to be a difficult and some-

times violent process. As in India, nationalism has been an important aspect of the response to Western domination in the Islamic heartlands. In Turkey in the 1920s it took a secularist form; in Libya, Iran, and elsewhere since the 1970s and 1980s it has taken an Islamic-revivalist form. As an Afro-Asian phenomenon, it will reappear in the next section and in Chapter 34.

THE AFRICAN EXPERIENCE

The century and a half between 1800 and 1945 saw striking change throughout Africa, but especially in sub-Saharan Africa. North Africa and Egypt were more closely bound up in the politics of the Ottoman Empire and Europe throughout this period. Except for South Africa below the Transvaal, tropical and southern Africa did not come under colonial control until after 1880. Before then, internal developments—first, demographic and power shifts and then the rise of Islamic reform movements—overshadowed the increasing European presence in the continent.

New States and Power Centers

SOUTHERN AFRICA

In the south, below the Limpopo River, the first quarter of the nineteenth century saw devastating internal warfare, depopulation, and forced migrations of many Bantu peoples in what is known as the **mfecane**, or "crushing" era. Likely brought on by a population explosion and perhaps fueled by increasing economic competition, the *mfecane* was marked by the rapid rise of sizable military states among the northern Nguni-speaking Bantu. Its result was a period of warfare and chaos; widespread

CHRONOLOGY

Southern Africa

ca. 1800–1818	Dingiswayo, Nguni Zulu king, forms new military state
1800–1825	The *mfecane* among the Bantu of southeastern Africa
1806	British take Cape Colony from the Dutch
ca. 1818–1828	Shaka's reign as head of the Nguni state; major warfare, destruction, and expansion
ca. 1825–1870	Sotho kingdom of King Mosheshwe in Lesotho region
1835–1841	Great Trek of Boers into Natal and north onto the high veld beyond the Orange
1843	British annexation of Natal province
1852–1860	Creation of the Orange Free State and South African Republic

▲ **Mosheshwe,** king and founder of Lesotho. Not all of the Bantu peoples followed the militaristic example of Shaka. Mosheshwe, prince of a subtribe of the Sotho Bantus, fought off Zulu attacks and led his people to a mountain stronghold in southern Africa, where, through diplomacy and determination, he founded a small nation that has endured to the present. The kingdom became the British protectorate of Basutoland in 1868. In 1966 it achieved independence as the kingdom of Lesotho under Mosheshwe's great-grandson, King Mosheshwe II.

Courtesy of the Library of Congress.

depopulation by death and emigration; and the creation of new, multitribal, multilingual Bantu states in the regions of modern Zimbabwe, Mozambique, Malawi, Zambia, and Tanzania.

The Nguni warrior-king Dingiswayo formed the first of the new military states between about 1800 and 1818. The most important state was formed by his successor, Shaka, leader of the Nguni-speaking Zulu nation and kingdom (ca. 1818–1828). Shaka's brutal military tactics led to the Zulu conquest of a vast dominion in southeastern Africa and the virtual depopulation of some 15,000 square miles. Refugees from Shaka's "total war" zone fled north into Sotho-speaking Bantu territory or south to put increasing pressure on the southern Nguni peoples. Virtual chaos ensued, both north and south of Zululand.

The net result, beyond widespread suffering and death, was the creation of many new diverse states. Some people tried to imitate the unique military state of Shaka; others fled to mountainous areas; others even went west into the Kalahari and built up new, largely defensive states. The most famous of these was Lesotho, the Sotho kingdom of King Mosheshwe,

which survived as long as he lived (from the 1820s until 1870). Mosheshwe defended his people from the Zulu and held off the Afrikaners, missionaries, and British until his death.

The new state building spawned by the *mfecane* was nullified by Boer expansion and British annexation of the Natal province (1843). These developments stemmed from the **Great Trek** of Boer *voortrekkers*, which took place between 1835 and 1841. This migration brought about 6,000 Afrikaners from the eastern Cape Colony northeastward into the more fertile regions of southern Africa, Natal, and especially the high veld above the Orange River. It resulted in the creation after 1850 of the Afrikaner republics of the Orange Free State between the Orange and Vaal Rivers and the South African Republic north of the Vaal.

EAST AND CENTRAL AFRICA

Farther north in East and East Central Africa, increasing external trade was the basis for the formation of several strong regional states. In the Lakes region, peoples such as the Nyamwezi to the east of Lake Tanganyika and the Baganda west of Lake Victoria gained regional power from as early as the late eighteenth century through trade with the Arab-Swahili eastern coast and the states of the eastern Congo to the west. The chief traffic in this east–west commerce across central Africa involved slaves; ivory; copper; and, from the outside, Indian cloth, firearms, and other manufactured goods.

WEST AFRICA

In West Africa the slave trade was only slowly curtailed. European demand for other products, however—notably palm oil and gum arabic—became more important by the 1820s. In the first half of the century *jihad* (holy struggle) movements of the Fulbe (or Fulani) and others shattered the stability of the western savannah and forest regions from modern Senegal and Ghana through southern Nigeria. Protracted wars and dislocation resulted in the rise of regional kingdoms, such as those of Asante and Dahomey (modern Benin), which flourished before succumbing to internal dissension and the colonial activities of Britain and France.

Islamic Reform Movements

The expansive vitality of Islam was one of the significant agents of change in sub-Saharan Africa before the European rush for colonies in the 1880s. It has remained a factor on the wider African scene ever since. In 1800 Islam was already a long-established tradition from West Africa across the Sudan to the Red Sea and along the East African coast, as well as over all of Arabic-speaking North Africa. It had long been widespread in the southern Sahara and northern Sahel

▲ **Elephant tusks in Central Africa.** Ivory was a prized possession used for decorative purposes and jewelry.
National Museum of African Art/Smithsonian Institution.

and was common among merchant classes in various parts of West Africa. Islam was the law of the land in states such as the sultanate of Zanzibar on the eastern coast and the waning Funj sultanate on the Blue Nile in the eastern Sudan. Even so, the rural populace were still often semipagan, or wholly pagan, and even the ruling and urban elites of the towns were frequently only nominally Muslim.

The nineteenth century is notable for the number and strength of a series of militant Islamic revivalist and reform movements of *jihad*. Aimed at a more truly Muslim society and wider allegiance to Muslim values, these movements both fixed and spread Islam as a lasting part of the African scene. The West African *jihad* movements originated in the seventeenth century with the activities of militant, reformist Sufi brotherhoods that had penetrated West Africa from the north, especially through Mauritania. These movements eventually spread to other regions and flourished, especially in the eighteenth century among widely dispersed groups of people.

The most important *jihad* movement came at the beginning of the nineteenth century and was led by a Fulbe Muslim scholar from Hausa territory in the central Sahel. Usman Dan Fodio (1754–1817) was influenced by the reformist ideas that spread throughout the Muslim world in the eighteenth century, from India to Saudi Arabia and Africa. Shortly after 1804 he gathered an immense army of fervent supporters and conquered most of the Hausa lands of modern Nigeria, bringing

an explicitly Islamic order to the area. Dan Fodio left behind an impressive sultanate centered on the new capital of Sokoto and governed by one of his sons, Muhammad Bello, until 1837. In his wake the Fulbe became the ruling class in the Hausa regions, and Islam spread into the countryside, where it still predominates. (See Document, "Usman Dan Fodio on Evil and Good Government.")

Other nineteenth-century reform movements had similar success both in gaining at least ephemeral political power and in spreading a revivalist, reformist Islamic message among the masses. Most notable alongside several West African *jihad* movements were the Sanusi movement of Libya and the eastern Sahara (after about 1840) and the famous

CHRONOLOGY

Central Africa

1754–1817	Usman Dan Fodio, Fulbe leader of major Islamic *jihad* movement
1810	Dan Fodio founds Islamic sultanate in lands of former Hausa states of northern and central Nigeria
1817–1837	Reign at Sokoto of Muhammad Bello, son of Dan Fodio

Mahdist uprising of the eastern Sudan (1880s and 1890s). The Libyan movement provided the focus for resistance to the Italian invasion of 1911. The Sudanese Muhammad Ahmad (1848—1885) condemned the widespread corruption of basic Islamic ideals and declared himself the awaited deliverer, or Mahdi, in 1881. He led the northern Sudan in

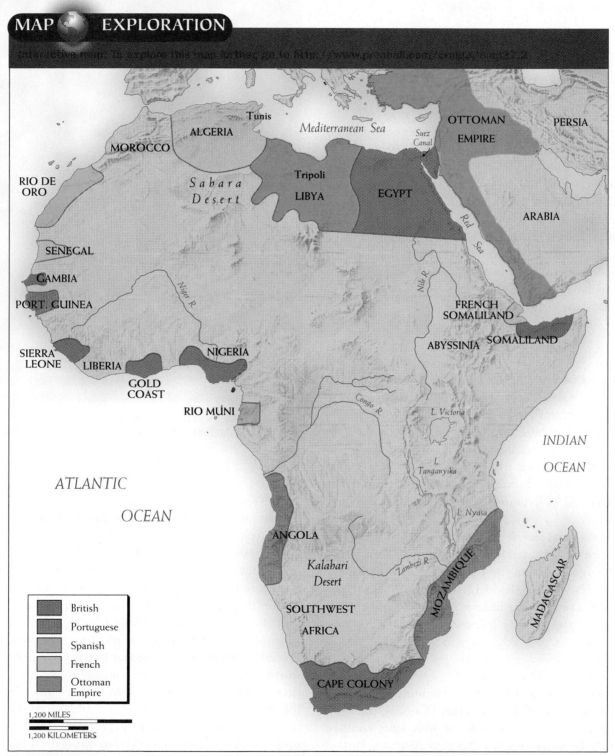

MAP EXPLORATION

Interactive map: To explore this map further, go to http://www.prenhall.com/craig/map27.2

MAP 27–1 Imperial Expansion in Africa up to 1880.   Until the 1880s only a few European countries held colonies in Africa, mostly on the fringes of the continent. A comparison of this map with Map 27–2 shows how rapidly the situation changed.

rebellion against Ottoman-Egyptian control, defeating even the British forces from Egypt under Charles George Gordon (1833–1885) at Khartoum. His successor governed the Sudan until the British finally destroyed the young Islamic state in 1899. In the Caucasus, Islamic reform movements merged into resistance with Russian expansion, led most notably by Imam Shamil (c. 1797–1871).

Increasing European Involvement

During the nineteenth century, the growing involvement of Europe in African affairs led to European domination of the continent's politics and economy. Before the mid-1800s the actual penetration of white outsiders had largely been limited to coastal areas, although their slave trade had affected areas further inland (see Chapter 17 and Map 27–1). This changed drastically as, first, trading companies, explorers, and missionaries and, finally, colonial troops and governments moved into Africa. Ironically, the gradual elimination of the slave trade (primarily through Britain's efforts) was accompanied by increased European exploration and increased Western Christian missionizing, which ushered in imperial and colonial ventures that had even more disastrous consequences than slaving for Africa's future.

Exploration

The nineteenth-century European explorers—mostly English, French, and German—gradually uncovered for Westerners the great "secrets" of Africa: the sources and courses of the Niger, Nile, Zambezi, and Congo Rivers; natural wonders, such as Mount Kilimanjaro and Lake Tanganyika; and fabled places like Timbuktu. The history of European exploration is one of fortune hunting, self-promotion, violence, and mistakes as well as patience, perseverance, bravery, and dedication.

The explorers stimulated European interest in Africa and opened the way for traders, missionaries, and finally soldiers and governors from the Christian West. One of the greatest explorers was Dr. David Livingstone (1813–1873). Livingstone was a missionary in love with and dedicated to Africa and its peoples as were few other Westerners before or after him.

CHRISTIAN MISSIONS

The latter nineteenth century saw a mounting influx of Christian missionaries, both Protestant and Catholic (by 1900, some 10,000). These vied—sometimes with one another, sometimes with Muslims—for the souls of Africans. Part of their motivation for coming to Africa was to eradicate the

▲ **Challenging the Czar.** A Muslin separatist movement led by Imam Shamil established an independent state in 1834 that lasted for 25 years in the Caucasus region of Dagestan.
Getty Images Inc. – Hulton Archive Photos.

remaining slave trade, especially the one in East Africa run by Arabs from Zanzibar.

The missionaries came to know the African peoples far better than did the explorers. Their accounts of Africa contained, to be sure, chauvinistic and misleading descriptions of the "degraded" state of African culture and religion, but they did bring real knowledge of and interest in Africa to Europe. Their translation work and mission schools also brought alphabetic culture and literacy to the African tribal world. Although their settlements, often in remote areas, provided European governments with convenient pretexts for intervention in the affairs of African tribes and states, the missionaries themselves were more often idealists than opportunists and often worked in opposition to the colonial officers. Half of those who went into the tropical regions succumbed to indigenous diseases, such as malaria, yellow fever, and sleeping sickness. If they were often paternalistic and virtual instruments of the imperialism of their home countries, they also sought to provide Africans with medicine and education. Through the ideals of their faith, they provided Africans—sometimes intentionally, sometimes inadvertently—with a weapon of principle to use against their European exploiters. African Christian churches, for example, later played a leading role in the resistance to apartheid in South Africa, despite white Christian oppression and collusion with racism in that country and elsewhere in Africa (see Chapter 34). As this discussion suggests, the role of Christian missionaries in the European domination of Africa was not simple or by any means wholly positive.

THE COLONIAL "SCRAMBLE FOR AFRICA"

Before 1850 the only significant conflict between Europeans and Africans over European attempts to take African territory was in South Africa and Algeria. In South Africa, as we have noted, the Boers came into conflict with Bantu tribes after leaving the British-ruled Cape Colony on their Great Trek to find new lands. The French invaded Algeria in 1830, settled Europeans on choice farmlands, and fought native resistance fighters. Over most of the continent, however, the European presence was felt with real force only from the 1880s. Yet by World War I virtually all of Africa (Ethiopia and Liberia were the only exceptions) was divided into a patch-

work of large territories ruled by European colonial administrations (see Map 27–3).

This foreign takeover of Africa was supported by mounting European popular and commercial interest fueled by the publicity given African exploration and missionary work. The European desire for the industrial markets and natural resources of Africa, together with intra-European competition for power and prestige, pushed one European state after another to claim whatever segments of Africa they could.

The superior economic, technological, and military power the West commanded made this wholesale takeover possible. In particular, European technical expertise opened up the interior of the continent in the late nineteenth century. Except for the Nile and the Niger, all the great African rivers have impassable waterfalls only a short way inland from the sea, where the coastal plains rise sharply to the largely highland interior. Steamboats above the falls and railroads around them (or where no navigable rivers ran) opened the African interior to commercial and colonial exploitation.

Great Britain and France were the vanguard of the European nations that sought to include African lands in their imperial domains. The British had the largest involvement. On one axis, it ranged from South Africa (begun when they took the Cape Colony from the Dutch in 1795) to their effective protectorate in Egypt (from 1882). On another axis, it extended from trading interests in West Africa to colonies such as Sierra Leone and Gambia, set up in 1807, to protectorate rule, as in the Niger districts after 1885, and to

◄ **A Missionary Visit to a Zulu Kraal.** The 19th-century European American enthusiasm for working toward "the evangelization of the world in our time" found one of its major outlets in missionary efforts in Africa.
Courtesy of the Library of Congress.

DOCUMENT | Usman Dan Fodio on Evil and Good Government

Following in the tradition of the Wahhabis in Arabia and virtually all previous Islamic reform movements, Dan Fodio (1754–1817) stressed adherence to Muslim norms as expressed in the Shari'a, the Divine Law. In the two excerpts that follow, he enumerated some of the evils of the previous Hausa rulers and their "law," and then listed five principles of proper Islamic government.

◆ What does the first principle of good government, that "authority shall not be given to one who seeks it," mean? What abuses by government listed by Dan Fodio might be most appalling to the average Muslim? Why?

One of the ways of their government [that is, of the Hausa or Habe kings] is succession to the emirate by hereditary right and by force to the exclusion of consultation. And one of the ways of their government is the building of their sovereignty upon three things: the people's persons, their honour, and their possessions; and whomsoever they wish to kill or exile or violate his honour or devour his wealth they do so in pursuit of their lusts, without any right in the Shari'a. One of the ways of their government is their imposing on the people monies not laid down by the Shari'a, being those which they call janghali and kurdin ghari and kurdin salla. One of the ways of their governments is their intentionally eating whatever food they wish, whether it is religiously permitted or forbidden, and wearing whatever clothes they wish, whether religiously permitted or forbidden, and drinking what beverages [ta'am] they wish, whether religiously permitted or forbidden, and riding whatever riding beasts they wish, whether religiously permitted or forbidden, and taking what women they wish without marriage contract, and living in decorated palaces, whether religiously permitted or forbidden, and spreading soft (decorated) carpets as they wish, whether religiously permitted or forbidden. ...

And I say—and help is with God—the foundations of government are five things: the first is that authority shall not be given to one who seeks it. The second is the necessity for consultation. The third is the abandoning of harshness. The fourth is justice. The fifth is good works. And as for its ministers, they are four. (The First) is a trustworthy wazir to wake the ruler if he sleeps, to make him see if he is blind, and to remind him if he forgets, and the greatest misfortune for the government and the subjects is that they should be denied honest wazirs. And among the conditions pertaining to the wazir is that he should be steadfast in compassion to the people, and merciful towards them. The second of the ministers of government is a judge whom the blame of a blamer cannot overtake concerning the affairs of God. The third is a chief of police who shall obtain justice for the weak from the strong. The fourth is a tax collector who shall discharge his duties and not oppress the subjects. ...

From translation of Usman Dan Fodio's *Kitab al-Farq* by M. Hiskett, *Bulletin of the School of Oriental and African Studies*, London, 1960, Part 3, p. 558. Reprinted by permission of Oxford University Press, Oxford, Great Britain.

---

a Zanzibar-based sphere of influence in East Africa in the 1870s (and finally a protectorate for Zanzibar in 1890).

The British long resisted African colonial involvement and then chose "indirect" as preferable to "direct" colonial administration. Their rule was only slightly more enlightened than that of the French, who had earlier carved out a colonial empire under their direct control. The French had long had government-supported trading outposts in Senegal and other parts of West Africa. After a bitter struggle (1830–1847) they conquered Algeria, creating the first major European colony in Africa. Tunisia and the Ivory Coast became French protectorates in the 1880s, Dahomey was bloodily annexed in 1894, and French Equatorial Africa was proclaimed in 1910.

Beginning in the mid-1880s the major European powers sought mutual agreement to their claims on particular segments of Africa. Leopold II of Belgium (r. 1865–1909) and Otto von Bismarck (1815–1898) in Germany established their own claims to parts of Africa. France and England set about consolidating their African interests. Italy, too, eventually took African colonial territory in Eritrea, Somaliland, and Libya, but

CHRONOLOGY

Colonial Africa

1830	French invasion of Algeria
1890	British protectorate in Zanzibar
ca. 1880	French protectorate in Tunisia and Ivory Coast
1880s–1890s	Mahdist uprising in eastern Sudan
1882	British protectorate in Egypt
1894	French annexation of Dahomey
1910	French colony of Equatorial Africa

Ethiopia used its newly modernized army to defeat an Italian invasion in 1896. Italy finally conquered Ethiopia in 1935. The **scramble for Africa** was largely over by the outbreak of World War I. After the war Germany lost its African possessions to other colonial powers. Europe's colonies in Africa did not gain independence until the changes in the worldwide balance of power and in attitudes toward colonial rule that followed World War II (see Chapter 34).

European colonial rule in Africa is one of the uglier chapters of modern history. If German, French, Belgian, Portuguese, and Boer rule was notoriously brutal and produced worse atrocities, Britain also had its share of misrule and exploitation. The paternalistic attitudes of late-nineteenth-century Europe and America amounted in the end to sheer racism when applied in Africa. The regions with large-scale white settlement produced the worst exploitation at the

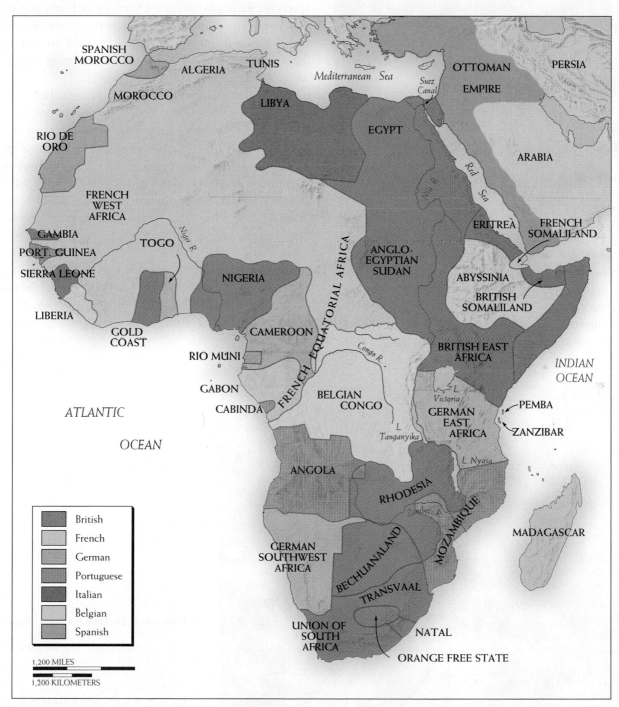

MAP 27–2 Partition of Africa, 1880–1914. By 1914 the only countries in Africa that remained independent were Liberia and Abyssinia (Ethiopia). The occupying powers included most large European states.

▲ **European Exploitation of Africa.** Photograph of white foremen and black laborers in a gold-mining company of South Africa (undated). © Hulton-Deutch Collection/Corbis.

African Resistance to Colonialism: The Rise of Nationalism

African states were not, however, simply passive objects of European manipulation and conquest. Many astute native rulers sought, by diplomacy, trade, and warfare, to use the European presence to their own advantage. Some, like the Bagandan king Mutesa in the 1870s (in what is today Uganda), succeeded for some time. Direct armed resistance was always (even for Ethiopia) doomed because of European technological superiority. Nevertheless, such resistance was widespread and continued into the twentieth century in many places. In the end, however, other factors ended most foreign rule on African soil.

Most important was the rise of nationalism across Africa, especially after World War I. However little the colonial partition of Africa reflected native linguistic, racial, or cultural divisions, it still influenced both nationalist movements and the eventual shape of African states. The "national" consciousness of the diverse peoples of a given colonial unit was fueled by common opposition to foreign rule. It was also fed by the use of a common European tongue and through the assimilation of European thought and culture by a growing educated native elite. These elites were typically educated in mission schools and sometimes foreign universities. Their ranks gradually increased in the early twentieth century. From them came the leaders of Africa's nationalist movements between the two world wars and of Africa's new independent nations after World War II.

expense of vastly greater native populations. Everywhere, white minorities exercised disproportionate power over the lives of black or brown majorities. The worst legacy of the European presence was the white racist state of modern South Africa, which only ended in 1994. No Western nation can have a clear conscience about its involvement in Africa.

◀ **Mutesa of Bugand and His Court.** Noted for his cunning and diplomatic skill and for his autocratic and often cruel conduct, Mutesa was one of the few African rulers who was able to maintain a powerful and successful army and court, which enabled him to deal effectively with Egyptian and British efforts to encroach on his sphere of influence.
Brown Brothers.

OVERVIEW   Colonialism, 1815–1914

Between the end of the Napoleonic Wars and the outbreak of World War I, European powers, the United States, and Japan extended their rule over much of the Near East, Africa, Asia, and the Pacific. The imposition of foreign rule was often the result of conquest, but it also occurred through purchase or the imposition of a "protectorate" in which a local ruler kept his title but ceded real power, especially over foreign affairs, defense, and finances, to colonial advisors or officials. By 1914, except for the Latin American republics, only Liberia and Abyssinia (Ethiopia) in Africa, the Ottoman Empire in the Near East, and Iran, Afghanistan, Thailand, and China had escaped some form of colonial rule. The following table lists the countries and territories that the Western powers and Japan acquired or dominated as protectorates between 1815 and 1914. In addition, older possessions, such as British India and the Portuguese colonies of Angola and Mozambique, were also increased during these hundred years.

Near East And North Africa

Britain	Aden (in Yemen), Bahrain, Cyprus, Egypt, Kuwait, Oman, Qatar, United Emirates
France	Algeria, Morocco, Tunisia
Italy	Rhodes, Libya

Africa

Belgium	Congo (Zaire)
Britain	Botswana, Ghana, Kenya, Lesotho, Malawi, Nigeria, Somaliland, Sudan, Swaziland, Uganda, Zambia, Zanzibar, Zimbabwe, Zululand (in South Africa)
France	Benin, Burkina Faso, Central African Republic, Chad, Congo, Djibouti, Ivory Coast, Madagascar, Mali, Mauretania, Niger
Germany	Burundi, Cameroons, Namibia, Rwanda, Tanganyika (Tanzania), Togo
Italy	Eritrea, Somalia

Asia

Britain	Brunei, Hong Kong, Malaysia, Myanmar (Burma), Nepal, Papua, Singapore
France	Cambodia, Laos, Vietnam
Germany	New Guiana, Tientsin (in China)
Japan	Korea, Okinawa, Taiwan
Netherlands	Acheh
Russia	Amur Territories (from China), Central Asia, Chechnya
United States	Philippines

Pacific

Britain	Fiji, Tonga, Solomons
France	New Caledonia, Tahiti
Germany	Carolines, Marianas
United States	Guam, Hawaii, Midway, Wake

The severest indigenous critiques of the Western treatment of Africa often drew on Western religious and political ideals. The African leaders of the twentieth century learned well from the West and used their learning to help end Western domination. The process culminated in the creation of over forty self-governing African nations after 1945 (see Chapter 34). African independence movements were eventually based on modern nationalist models from Europe and America rather than ancient ones derived from native tradition. The nationalist and independence movements typically sought to eject the colonial intruders and not to return to an earlier status quo. Their aim was to take over and to run for themselves the Western institutions that colonialism had introduced. This legacy from the West is still visible today.

Miners Excavating Diamonds in South Africa.

Summary

Western Encroachment   The century and a half that began in 1800 was a bleak one for the Indian subcontinent, Africa, and the Islamic societies. For centuries there had been a rough balance in material and intellectual culture, commerce, and political stability among the major cultural regions of the world. Suddenly, over 150 years, the European sector of the global community came to dominate the rest of the world.

The Middle East, Africa, Iran, Central Asia, India, and Indonesia-Malaysia, along with Central and South America—what is today referred to as "the Third World" of "developing nations"—were most drastically affected by European imperialism and colonialism. Regardless of indigenous developments in these regions, the decisive development of this era was unprecedented domination by a single segment of the global community. Western dominance, sometimes positive, often sordid and ugly, was by no means synonymous with "progress," as Westerners have often liked to think. Nevertheless, it has been a hallmark of the "modern" age in most of Asia, Africa, and South America.

Indigenous Reactions   The vitality of so many of the cultures and traditions that bore the brunt of the Western onslaught has been striking. Arab, Iranian, Indian, African, and other encounters with Western material and intellectual domination produced different responses and initiatives. These have borne full fruit in political, economic, and intellectual independence only since 1945; however, most began much earlier, some even well before 1800. For example, modern Islamic reform and resurgence began in the eighteenth century, although it has become a major global factor only in recent years. Indian national consciousness also developed from the eighteenth century onward in response to British domination, even though it led to national union and independence only after World War II.

One result of the imperial-colonial experience almost everywhere has been the sharpening of cultural self-consciousness and self-confidence among those peoples most negatively affected by Western dominance. The imperial-colonial experiences of the Third World nations may well prove to have been not only ones of misery and reversal, but also of transition to positive development and resurgence, despite the looming economic, educational, and demographic problems that plague many of them.

Review Questions

1. What does the "impact of modernity" mean to traditional Afro-Asian-Indian cultures? What patterns of reaction can you discern? Why was the West able to impose itself on these cultures?

2. Why was India called the "jewel in the crown" of the British Empire? How did the British gain control of India? What policies did they follow in government and economics?

3. What kinds of political activism against British rule can you cite from Indian history after 1800? What kinds of success or failure did they have?

4. How was the Islamic world internally divided after 1800? How did those divisions influence the coming of European powers?

5. How did nationalism affect European control in south Asia, Africa, and the Middle East? How and when did its various manifestations arise? Were there any successful "national states" from these regions before 1945?

6. Discuss the new African states and power centers of sub-Saharan Africa before 1870. Why did no modern state develop in the area? How did Islam affect the development of new entities? What role did trade play?

7. What were the three main interests of Europeans in the "Dark Continent"? Why were native Africans unable to stop the "scramble for Africa"?

8. What was the role of African nationalism in resisting foreign control?

Key Terms

bazaari (p. 811)

cantonments (p. 816)

Great Trek (p. 817)

mfecane (p. 816)

mujtahid (p. 816)

pan-Islamism (p. 813)

raj (p. 802)

Scramble for Africa (p. 824)

Wahhbis (p. 810)

Documents CD-ROM

Nationalism and Imperialism
20.4 Lord William Bentinck, Comments on Ritual Murder and the Limits of Religious Toleration
20.5 The Scramble for Africa
20.6 Rudyard Kipling

Decolonization
27.1 Mohandas K. Gandhi
27.2 Gandhi and Nehru: "Two Utterly Different Standpoints": Jawaharlal Nehru

NOTE: To learn more about the topics in this chapter, see the Suggested Readings at the end of the book.

ISLAM

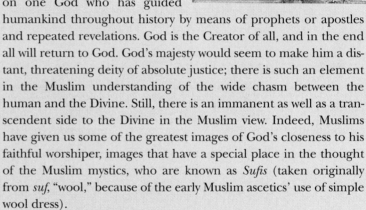

The Islamic tradition is one of the youngest major world religions. Since its inception during the lifetime of the Prophet Muhammad (632 B.C.E.) it has grown, like the Christian and Buddhist traditions, into a worldwide community not limited by national boundaries or defined in racial or ethnic terms. It began among the Arabs but spread widely. Islam's historical heartlands are those Arabic-, Turkic-, and Persian-speaking lands of the Near East between Egypt and Afghanistan. However, today more than half of its faithful live in Asia east of Karachi, Pakistan; and more Muslims live in sub-Saharan Africa than in all of the other Arab lands. There are also growing Muslim minorities in the United States and Europe.

The central vision of Islam is a just and peaceful society where people can freely worship God. It focuses on a human community of worshipers who recognize the absolute sovereignty and one-ness of God and strive to do God's will. Muslims believe that divine will is found first in his revealed word, the Qur'an; then as elaborated and specified in the actions and words of his final prophet, Muhammad; and finally as interpreted and extended in the scriptural exegesis and legal traditions of the Muslim community over the past thirteen and a half centuries.

The Muslim vision thus centers on one God who has guided humankind throughout history by means of prophets or apostles and repeated revelations. God is the Creator of all, and in the end all will return to God. God's majesty would seem to make him a distant, threatening deity of absolute justice; there is such an element in the Muslim understanding of the wide chasm between the human and the Divine. Still, there is an immanent as well as a transcendent side to the Divine in the Muslim view. Indeed, Muslims have given us some of the greatest images of God's closeness to his faithful worshiper, images that have a special place in the thought of the Muslim mystics, who are known as *Sufis* (taken originally from *suf*, "wool," because of the early Muslim ascetics' use of simple wool dress).

Muslims understand God's word in the Qur'an and the elaboration of that word by tradition to be a complete prescription for human life. Thus Islamic law is not law in the Western sense of civil, criminal, or international systems. Rather, it is a comprehensive set of standards for the moral, ritual, social, political, economic, aesthetic, and even hygienic and dietary dimensions of life. By being faithful to God's law the Muslim hopes to gain salvation on the Last Day, when human history shall end and all of God's creatures who have ever lived will be resurrected and called to account for their thoughts and actions during their lives on earth. Some will be saved, but others will be eternally damned.

Thus *Islam*, which means "submission [to God]," has been given as a name to the religiously defined system of life that Muslims have sought to institute wherever they have lived. Muslims have striven to organize their societies and political realities around the ideals represented in the traditional picture of the Prophet's community in Medina and Mecca. This approach necessitated compromise in which power was given to temporal rulers and accepted by Muslim religious leaders as long as those rulers protected God's Law, the *Shari'ah*. The ideal of a single international Muslim community, or *Umma*, has never fully been realized politically, but it remains an ideal.

▲ **Muhammad and Ali.** This sixteenth century Persian miniature shows the prophet Muhammad and his kinsman Ali purifying the Ka'ba in Mecca of pagan idols. The Ka'ba is the geographical point toward which all Muslims face when performing ritual prayer.
Art Resource/Bildarchiv Preussischer Kulturbesitz.

Friday Congregational Worship. Every Friday at the noon hour of daily worship, Muslims are enjoined to gather in as large a congregation as possible to worship together and listen to a weekly preaching in the major mosque in their town or city. Here at a mosque in Jakarta, Indonesian Muslims are seen in the midst of worship rites. More Muslims live in Indonesia than in any other country.

Getty Images, Inc. — Photodisc.

Many movements of reform over the centuries have called for greater adherence to rigorist interpretations of Islamic law and greater dominance of piety and religious values in sociopolitical as well as individual life. The most famous of these movements, that of the Wahhabis in eighteenth-century Arabia, remains influential in much of the Muslim world, including Saudi Arabia. The Wahhabis' puritanical zeal in fighting what they consider "innovations" in many regional Islamic contexts, such as Shi'ism, Sufi traditions, and all more liberal forms of Islamic practice, continues to the present day. Wahhabism has had considerable success in the past half century and was apparently the spawning ground of the extremist views of Osama bin Laden's al-Qaeda terrorist movement, which is largely Arab in its ethnic makeup and which has turned from fighting Muslim states it regards as un-Islamic to opposing what it considers the U.S. intrusion into the Arab Islamic world and its unpopular foreign policy in the region. While meainstream Muslims everywhere reject bin Laden's extremism, Wahhabi zealotry has adherents on the fringes of Islamic communities around the world. In this respect, Islam is not unlike Christianity, Judaism, Hinduism, or other major religions, each of which has over its history spawned literalists, zealots, and extremists, who have urged violence in the name of their version of their parent faith.

The major sectarian, or minority, groups among Muslims are those of the Shi'ites, who have held out for an ideal of a temporal ruler who is also the spiritual heir of Muhammad and God's designated deputy on earth. Most Shi'ites, notably those of Iran, hold that after eleven designated blood descendants of the prophets had each failed to be recognized by the majority of Muslims as the rightful leader, or *Imam*, the twelfth disappeared and remains to this day physically absent from the world, although not dead. He will come again at the end of time to vindicate his faithful followers.

Muslim piety takes many forms. The common duties of Muslims are central for Muslims everywhere: faith in God and trust in his Prophet; regular performance of ritual worship (*Salat*); fasting during daylight hours for thirty days in Ramadan (the ninth month of the lunar year); giving one's wealth to the needy (*zakat*); and at least once in a lifetime, if able, making the pilgrimage to Mecca and its environs (*Hajj*). Other more regional or popular, but ubiquitous, practices are also important. Celebration of the Prophet's birthday indicates the exalted popular status of Muhammad, even though any divine status for him is strongly rejected theologically. Recitation of the Qur'an permeates all Muslim practice, from daily worship to celebrations of all kinds. Visitation of saints' tombs is a prominent form of popular devotion. Sufi chanting or even ecstatic dancing are also practiced by Muslims around the world.

Muslims vary enormously in their physical environment, language, ethnic background, and cultural allegiances. What binds them now as in the past are not political allegiances but religious affinities and a shared heritage of religious faith and culture. How these allegiances and sensibilities will fare in the face of global challenges will be an important factor in shaping the world of the twenty-first century.

- How has the ideal of a single, international Muslim community influenced Islamic history? World history?

- What impact have reform movements had on Islam since its inception? What impact do they have today?

28

Modern East Asia

MODERN CHINA (1839–1949)

- Close of Manchu Rule

- From Dynasty to Warlordism (1895–1926)

- Cultural and Ideological Ferment: The May Fourth Movement

- Nationalist China

MODERN JAPAN (1853–1945)

- Overthrow of the Tokugawa Bakufu (1853–1868)

- Building the Meiji State (1868–1890)

- Growth of a Modern Economy

- The Politics of Imperial Japan (1890–1945)

- Japanese Militarism and German Nazism

◀ COMMODORE MATTHEW PERRY MEETING JAPANESE OFFICIALS AT KURIGAHAMA IN 1853. At the right are two emissaries of the Bakufu; at the left is Perry's Chinese translator, who speaks English and communicates with the Japanese in written Chinese. Perry's ships are visible in the background along with smaller Japanese craft.
U.S. Naval Academy Museum.

Modern East Asia

From the late nineteenth century most countries wanted to become modern. They coveted the wealth and power of the West. But what does it mean to be modern?.

Three stages may be noted in Japan's development as the world's first and most advanced, non-Western modernizer: preconditions, westernization, and assimilation.

Even before contact with the modern West, Japan had some of the preconditions needed for industrialization: a fairly literate people, an ethic of duty and hard work, a market economy, secular thought, some bureaucracy, and a protonationalism. In sum, an adequate base for an "external modernization."

Building on these preconditions, Japan westernized after 1868, adopting a range of new institutions: post offices, banks, custom houses, hospitals, police forces, joint stock companies, universities with faculties of science and engineering, and so on. Japanese thinkers brought in modern ideas and values: Spencer and Guizot, Turgenev and Tolstoi, Adam Smith and Marx. Japanese writers began experimenting with new forms.

Little by little Japan *assimilated* what it had borrowed. The *zaibatsu* combines were modern, with the most recent technologies, yet their business organizations were unlike those of the West. The spare beauty of traditional architecture was transferred to the glass, steel, concrete, and stone of the modern. A new literature, completely Japanese yet also completely modern, appeared.

Japan may serve as a useful model in that its modernization—as analyzed in terms of the above three stages—has gone further than that in any other non-Western country. We note the absence in India or the Islamic world of comparable preconditions. After the end of colonialism, countries in these areas had to create the necessary preconditions even as they borrowed the new technologies. The difficulty explains their limited success. In Africa the dearth of preconditions was even more pronounced.

China, like Japan but unlike countries of South Asia, the Middle East or Africa, had many of the necessary preconditions—they might be called East Asia preconditions—in place. But when it came to westernization, the government by Confucian literati that had long been China's outstanding asset became its greatest liability. It took decades to topple the dynasty and to advance beyond Confucian ideas.

Then, the maelstrom of the May Fourth Movement, intellectual change occurred at a furious pace. But new doctrines alone could not provide a stable polity. Nationalism emerged as the common denominator of Chinese thought. The nationalists (or Guomindang) drew on it at the Huangpu Academy, during the march north, and in the Nanjing government. But other groups could also appeal to it. The Chinese Communists won out by 1949.

It is beguiling to view the CCP cadres as a new class of literati operating the machinery of a monolithic, centralized state, with the teachings of Marx and Lenin replacing those of Confucius, and local party organization replacing the Confucian gentry. But this interpretation is too simple. Communism stressed science, materialism, and class conflict. It broke with the Chinese past.

Communism itself was also modified in China. Marx had predicted that socialist revolutions would break out in advanced economies where the contradictions of capitalism were sharpest. Lenin had shifted the emphasis from spontaneous revolutions by workers to the small but disciplined revolutionary party, the vanguard of the proletariat. He thereby changed communism into what it has been ever since: a movement capable of seizing power only in backward nations. At the level of doctrine, Mao Zedong modified Lenin's ideas only slightly—by theorizing that "progressive" peasants were a part of the proletariat. But he went beyond this theory in practice, virtually ignoring city workers while relying on China's villages for recruits for his armies, who were then indoctrinated using Leninist techniques.

Yet, the organizational techniques that were so effective in creating a party and army would prove less so for economic development. It soon became clear that mass mobilization was no substitute for individual incentives.

THINK AHEAD

◆ What are the preconditions necessary for modernization along Western lines? Why are they so important?

◆ Compare and contrast the process of modernization in Japan and China in the twentieth century. Which country was more successful? Why?

FROM THE MID–NINETEENTH CENTURY, THE West was the expanding, aggressive, imperialistic force in world history. Its industrial goods and gunboats reached every part of the globe. It believed in free trade and had the military might to impose it on others. It was the trigger for change throughout the world. But the response to the Western impact depended on the internal array of forces in each country. In fact, the "response to the West" was only one small, though vital, part of the history of each country. Still, Japan and China were both relatively successful in their responses, for although each was subject to "unequal treaties," neither became a colony.

The two countries were also similar in that their governing elites were educated in Confucianism. Unlike the otherworldly religions of Buddhism, Islam, or Christianity, Confucianism was just secular enough to crumble in the face of the more powerful secularism of nineteenth-century science and the doctrines associated with it. In both Japan and China, although much more rapidly in Japan, the leading intellectuals abandoned Confucianism in favor of Western secular doctrines. To be sure, many Confucian values, deeply embedded in the societies, survived the philosophies of which they had once been a part. In fact, one of the "breakdown products" of the Confucian sociopolitical identity was a strong new nationalism in both China and Japan.

But there the similarities end. In most other respects, modern Japan and China could hardly be more different. Perhaps the difference was only to be expected, given the pattern of recurrent dynasties in China's premodern history and of feudal evolution in Japan's.

The coming of Commodore Matthew Perry (1794–1858) in 1853–1854 precipitated a rapid political change in Japan. Within fifteen years the old Tokugawa regime had collapsed, and the Japanese were building a modern state. Economic growth followed. By 1900 Japan had defeated China and within five years would defeat tsarist Russia in war. Sustained economic growth continued during the early twentieth century. After the Great Depression, Japan, like Italy and Germany, became an aggressive and militarized state and was eventually defeated in World War II. But after the war Japan reemerged more stable, more productive, and with a stronger parliamentary government than before.

The Chinese polity, in contrast, easily weathered the Opium War (1839–1842), an event of considerably greater magnitude than Perry's visit to Japan. The hold of tradition in China was remarkable, as was the effectiveness of traditional remedies in dealing with political ills. Only in its relations with the Western powers did traditional patterns not work. In one sense the strength of tradition was China's weakness, for it took seventy years after the Opium War to overthrow the dynasty. Only then were Chinese able to begin the modernization that Japanese had started in 1868, and even then they were unsuccessful. Along with warlordism and the other problems that had accompanied the dissolution of past dynasties, new ills arose from the rending of the very fabric of the dynastic pattern. To these was added the unprecedented experience of being confronted by nations more powerful than itself. That China in some sense "failed" during this modern century is not a Western view imposed on China; it is the view the Chinese themselves hold.

MODERN CHINA (1839–1949)

China's modern century was not the century in which it became modern as much as it was the century in which it encountered the modern West. Its first phase, from the Opium War to the fall of the Qing or Manchu dynasty (1912), was remarkably little affected by Western impact. Indeed, it was only during the decade before 1912 that the Confucian tradition began to be discarded in favor of new ideas from the West. The second phase of China's modern history, from 1912 to the establishment of a Communist state in 1949, was a time of turmoil and suffering. The fighting incidental to the collapse of the dynasty gave way to decades of warlord rule; to partial military unification and continual military campaigns; to war with Japan; and then, while most countries were returning to peace, to four bitter years of civil war.

Close of Manchu Rule

THE OPIUM WAR

The eighteenth-century three-country trade—British goods to India, Indian cotton to China, and Chinese tea to Britain—was in China's favor. The silver flowing into China spurred the monetization of Chinese markets. Then the British replaced cotton with Indian opium. By the 1820s the balance of trade was reversed, and silver began to flow out of China.

A crisis arose in the 1830s when the British East India Company lost its monopoly on British trade with China. The opium trade became wide open. To check the evil of opium and outflow of specie, the Chinese government banned opium in 1836, closing the dens where it was smoked and executing Chinese

◄ **The Opium War, 1840.** Armed Chinese junks were no match for British warships. The war ended in 1842 with the Treaty of Nanjing.
Hulton-Deutsch Collection/Corbis.

dealers. In 1839 the government sent Imperial Commissioner Lin Zexu (1785–1850) to Guangzhou (Canton) to superintend the ban. He continued the crackdown on Chinese dealers and destroyed over 20,000 chests—a six-month supply—of opium belonging to foreign merchants. This action led to a confrontation between the Chinese and the British. (See Document, "Commissioner Lin Urges Morality on Queen Victoria.")

War broke out in November 1839 when Chinese war junks clashed with a British merchantman. The following June sixteen British warships arrived at Guangzhou, and for the next

◄ **Burning Opium.** Lin Zexu burns British opium in Guangzhou in 1839, at the start of the Opium War. Chinese soldiers guard the scene.
Cambridge University Press.

two years the British bombarded forts, fought battles, seized cities, and attempted negotiations. The Chinese troops, with their antiquated weapons and old-style cannon, were ineffective. The war was finally ended in August 1842 by the Treaty of Nanjing, the first of the "unequal treaties."

The treaty not only ended the "tribute system" but also provided Britain with a superb deep-water port at Hong Kong, a huge indemnity, and the opening of five ports: Guangzhou, Shanghai, Xiamen (Amoy), Ningbo, and Fuzhou. British merchants and their families could reside in the ports and engage in trade; Britain could appoint a consul for each city; and British residents gained extraterritoriality, under which they were subject to British and not Chinese law. The treaty also contained a "most-favored-nation" clause, a provision that any further rights gained by any other nation would automatically accrue to Britain as well. The treaty with Britain was followed in 1844 by similar treaties with the United States and France. The American treaty permitted churches in treaty ports, and the French treaty permitted the propagation of Catholicism.

After the signing of the treaties, Chinese imports of opium rose from 30,000 chests to 87,000 in 1879. Thereafter, imports declined to 50,000 chests in 1906, and ended during World War I. But other kinds of trade did not grow as much as had been hoped, and Western merchants blamed the lack of growth on artificial restraints imposed by Chinese officials. They also complained that, despite the treaties, Guangzhou remained closed to trade. The Chinese authorities, for their part, were incensed by the export of coolies to work under harsh conditions in Cuba and Peru. A second war broke out in 1856, which continued sporadically until Lord Elgin

DOCUMENT | **Commissioner Lin Urges Morality on Queen Victoria**

In 1839 the British in China argued for free trade and protection for the legal rights of their citizens. The Chinese position was that behind such lofty arguments, the British were pushing opium.

◆ What does this document suggest about the Qing dynasty's view of China's place in the world in 1839? Does the dynasty still view China as a universal empire? Do Lin's arguments leave Victoria any ground to stand on?

A communication: magnificently our great Emperor soothes and pacifies China and the foreign countries, regarding all with the same kindness. If there is profit, then he shares it with the peoples of the world; if there is harm, then he removes it on behalf of the world. This is because he takes the mind of heaven and earth as his mind.

The kings of your honorable country by a tradition handed down from generation to generation have always been noted for their politeness and submissiveness. We have read your successive tributary memorials saying, "In general our countrymen who go to trade in China have always received His Majesty the Emperor's gracious treatment and equal justice," and so on. Privately we are delighted with the way in which the honorable rulers of your country deeply understand the grand principles and are grateful for the Celestial grace. For this reason the Celestial Court in soothing those from afar has redoubled its polite and kind treatment. The profit from trade has been enjoyed by them continuously for two hundred years. This is the source from which your country has become known for its wealth. But after a long period of commercial intercourse, there appear among the crowd of barbarians both good persons and bad, unevenly. Consequently there are those who smuggle opium to seduce the Chinese people and so cause the spread of the poison to all provinces. Such persons who only care to profit themselves, and disregard their harm to others, are not tolerated by the laws of heaven and are unanimously hated by human beings. His Majesty the Emperor, upon hearing of this, is in a towering rage …

We find that your country is sixty or seventy thousand *li* [three *li* make one mile, ordinarily] from China. Yet there are barbarian ships that strive to come here for trade for the purpose of making a great profit. The wealth of China is used to profit the barbarians. That is to say, the great profit made by barbarians is all taken from the rightful share of China. By what right do they then in return use the poisonous drug to injure the Chinese people? Even though the barbarians may not necessarily intend to do us harm, yet in coveting profit to an extreme, they have no regard for injuring others. Let us ask, where is your conscience? I have heard that the smoking of opium is very strictly forbidden by your country; that is because the harm caused by opium is clearly understood. Since it is not permitted to do harm to your own country, then even less should you let it be passed on to the harm of other countries—how much less to China!

Suppose there were people from another country who carried opium for sale to England and seduced your people into buying and smoking it; certainly your honorable ruler would deeply hate it and be bitterly aroused. We have heard heretofore that your honorable ruler is kind and benevolent. Naturally you would not wish to give unto others what you yourself do not want.

Now we have set up regulations governing the Chinese people. He who sells opium shall receive the death penalty and he who smokes it also the death penalty. Now consider this: if the barbarians do not bring opium, then how can the Chinese people resell it, and how can they smoke it? The fact is that the wicked barbarians beguile the Chinese people into a death trap. How then can we grant life only to those barbarians? He who takes the life of even one person still has to atone for it with his own life; yet is the harm done by opium limited to the taking of one life only? Therefore in the new regulations, in regard to those barbarians who bring opium to China, the penalty is fixed at decapitation or strangulation. This is what is called getting rid of a harmful thing on behalf of mankind.

[However] all those who within the period of the coming one year (from England) or six months (from India) bring opium to China by mistake, but who voluntarily confess and completely surrender their opium, shall be exempt from their punishment. This may be called the height of kindness and the perfection of justice.

Reprinted by permission of the publisher from Ssu-Yu Teng and John K. Fairbank, *China's Response to the West* (Cambridge, MA: Harvard University Press). Copyright 1954, 1979 by the President and Fellows of Harvard College.

(1811–1863), the British commander, together with a French contingent, captured Beijing in 1860. A new set of conventions and treaties provided for indemnities, the opening of eleven new ports, the stationing of foreign diplomats in Beijing, the propagation of Christianity anywhere in China, and the legalization of the opium trade.

While the British fought China for trading rights, the Russians were encroaching on China's northern frontier. During the 1850s Russia established settlements along the Amur River. In 1858 China signed a treaty ceding the north bank of the Amur to Russia, and in 1860 China gave Russia the Maritime Province between the Ussuri River and the Pacific.

REBELLIONS AGAINST THE MANCHU

Far more immediate a threat to Manchu rule than foreign gunboats and unequal treaties were the Taiping, Nian, and Muslim Rebellions that convulsed China between 1850 and 1873 (see Map 28–1). The torment and suffering they caused were unparalleled in world history. Estimates of those killed during the twenty years of the **Taiping Rebellion** range from 20 to 30 million. If one adds in losses due to other rebellions, droughts, and floods, China's population dropped by 60 million and did not recover to prerebellion levels until almost the end of the dynasty in 1912.

The Taipings were begun by Hong Xiuquan (1814–1864), a schoolteacher from a poor family in a minority Hakka group in the southern province of Kwangtung. Hong had four times failed to pass the civil service examinations. He became ill and saw visions. Influenced by Protestant tracts he had picked up in Guangzhou, Hong announced that he was the younger brother of Jesus and that God had told him to rid China of evil demons—including Manchus, Confucians, Daoists, and Buddhists. He formed an Association of God Worshipers. His followers cut off their queues as a sign of resistance to the Manchus, who called them "long-haired rebels." The Taipings

began by attacking local Confucian temples, arousing the opposition of the gentry. They were soon joined by peasants, miners, and workers. Hong proclaimed the Heavenly Kingdom of Great Peace in 1851 and two years later took Nanjing and made it his capital. The fighting spread until the Taipings controlled most of the Yangzi basin; their expeditions eventually entered sixteen of the eighteen Chinese provinces. By that time their army numbered almost a million.

The Taiping ideology joined Old Testament Christianity with an ancient text often used by reformers, the *Zhou Rites*. The puritanical ethics of the Taipings came from the former, and the notion of sharing property equally came from the latter. The Taipings prohibited opium, tobacco, alcohol, gambling, adultery, prostitution, and footbinding. They upheld filial piety. They maintained that women were men's equals and appointed them to administrative and military posts. In short, like earlier rebels, the Taipings combined moral reform, religious fervor, and a vision of a transformed egalitarian society.

The movement had several weaknesses. Most Taiping leaders were too poorly educated to govern effectively, and the Taipings could not draw on the gentry. When the Taiping area was divided into kingdoms, dissension broke out. The Taipings

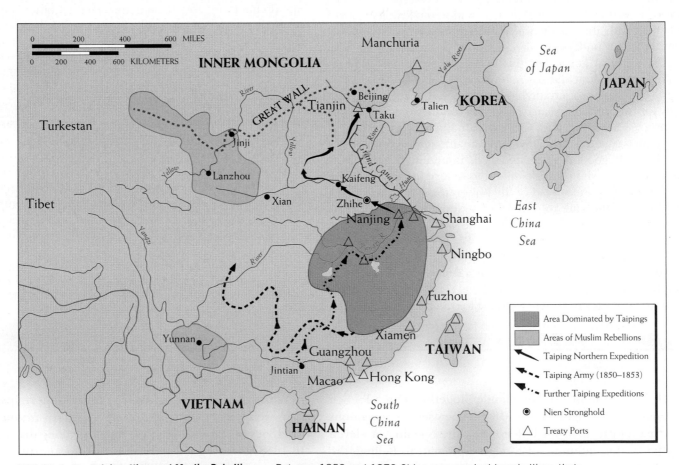

MAP 28–1 The Taiping, Nian, and Muslim Rebellions.   Between 1850 and 1873 China was wracked by rebellions that almost ended the Manchu dynasty. The dynasty was saved by Chinese "gentry armies."

failed to cultivate the secret societies, which were also anti-Manchu. They also failed to cultivate Westerners, who had been neutral before the 1860 treaty settlements and aided the Manchus thereafter. In addition, many Taiping ideals remained unfulfilled; for example, land was not redistributed, and, although Taiping teachings emphasized frugality and the sanctity of monogamous marriage, Hong lived with many concubines in the midst of luxury.

The other rebellions were of lesser note, but longer duration. The Nian were located north of the Taipings along the Huai River. They began as bandits who lived in walled villages, were organized in secret societies, and lived by raiding the surrounding countryside. Eventually they built an army, collected taxes, and ruled 100,000 square miles. The Qing court feared that the Nian would join forces with the Taipings. An even longer revolt was of Muslims against Chinese in the southwest and the northwest. One rebel set up an Islamic kingdom with himself as sultan. Like the Taiping Rebellion, these various rebellions took advantage of the weakened state of the dynasty and occurred in areas that had few officials and no Qing military units.

Against these rebellions, the Manchu Banners and the Chinese Army of the Green Standard proved helpless: The one was useful only for defense, the other only against civilians. The first effective step was taken against the rebellions when, in 1852, the court sent Zeng Guofan (1811–1872) to Hunan Province in south-central China to organize a local army. Zeng was a product of the Confucian examination system and had served in Beijing. He saw the Manchu government, of which he was an elite member, as the upholder of morality and the social order, and Chinese rebels as would-be destroyers of that order. Arriving in Hunan, he recruited members of the gentry as officers. They were of the class that, since the late Ming, had been growing in importance and performing many local government functions, in some cases organizing local militia. Not only were they Confucian, but as landlords they had the most to lose from rebel rule. They recruited soldiers from their local areas. Zeng's "Hunan Braves" stopped the Taipings' advance.

Until 1860 the Qing court was dominated by Manchu conservatives who limited Zeng's role and dragged their feet in upholding the treaties. In 1860 the conservatives lost their footing when the British and the French occupied Beijing. A reform government replaced the conservatives, began internal changes, adopted a policy of cooperation with the Western powers, and put Zeng in charge of suppressing the rebellions. Zeng appointed other able officials to raise regional armies. Li Hongzhang (1823–1901), with his Anhwei Army, was especially effective. Foreigners and Shanghai merchants gave their support. Revenues from the customs service and foreign ships and weapons were essential to Zeng's armies. The Taipings collapsed when Nanjing was captured in 1864 after protracted fighting. Zeng and Li suppressed the Nian by 1868, and the

Muslim rebellion was put down five years later. Scholar-officials, relying on local gentry, had saved the dynasty.

SELF-STRENGTHENING AND DECLINE (1874–1895)

The two decades after the suppression of the midcentury rebellions illustrate the dictum that there is no single "correct" view of history. In comparison, for example, with the late Song or the late Ming, the last decades of the nineteenth century look good. In view of the dynasty's advanced stage of administrative decentralization, the Chinese resiliency and capacity to rebuild after unprecedented destruction were impressive. Even on its borders the Manchu state was able to maintain or regain some territories while losing others. But if we ask instead how effective China's response was to the West, or if we compare China's progress with that of Japan, then China during the same decades looks almost moribund. Historians often call these years the period of "self-strengthening," after a catch phrase in vogue at the time. This term is not inappropriate, as the list of new initiatives taken during the period is long. Yet, since the firepower of Western naval forces doubled each decade, the forces that China faced at the end of the century were vastly more formidable than those of the Opium War. Despite self-strengthening, China was relatively weaker at the end of the period than at the start.

In 1895 Li Hongzhang met with Itō Hirobumi (1838–1909) of Japan to negotiate a peace treaty after China's defeat in the Sino-Japanese War. Itō asked with uncharacteristic bluntness: "Ten years ago when I was at Tianjin, I talked about reform with the Grand Secretary [Li]. Why is it that up to now not a single thing has been changed or reformed?" Li replied: "Affairs in my country have been so confined by tradition that I could not accomplish what I desired … Now in the twinkling of an eye ten years have gone by, and everything is still the same. I am even more regretful. I am ashamed of having excessive wishes and lacking the power to fulfill them." Itō responded blandly: "The providence of heaven has no affection, except for the virtuous."[1] Considering that Li was the single most powerful figure in China during these decades, Itō's puzzlement was not surprising.

The Court at Beijing The situation at the court partly explains China's inability to act effectively. Prince Gong (1833–1898) and the empress dowager (1835–1908) were co-regents for the young emperor. For a Manchu noble, Prince Gong was a man of ideas. After signing the treaties of 1860 he established in 1861 a new office directly under the Grand Council to handle the court's relations with foreign diplomats in Beijing.

---

[1] S. Y. Teng and J. K. Fairbank, *China's Response to the West* (Cambridge, MA: Harvard University Press, 1954), p. 126.

The following year he established a school to train Chinese in foreign languages. Over time, however, his position at the court grew weaker. Outmaneuvered by the empress dowager, he was ousted in 1884.

The empress dowager was the daughter of a Manchu official. She had become an imperial concubine and had produced the only male child of the former emperor. She was educated, clever, petty, strong-willed, and narrow-minded. She did not oppose change, except by circumstance, nor did she favor it. She had no conception of how to reform China. Her single goal was to gather political power into her own hands. She acquired this by forging a political machine of conservative bureaucrats, military commanders, and eunuchs, and by maintaining a balance between the court and the regional strength of the powerful governors general. The result was a court barely able to survive, too weak to govern effectively, and not inclined to do more than approve of initiatives taken at the provincial level.

Regional Governments The most vital figures during these decades were a handful of governors general whose names are legend: Zeng Guofan, Li Hongzhang, Zuo Zongtang (1812–1885), and Zhang Zhidong (1837–1909). Each had a staff of 200 or 300 and an army and was in charge of two or

▲ **The Empress Dowager Cixi (1835–1908).** She manipulated the levers of power at the Manchu court in Beijing.
Hulton Picture Library/Corbis-Bettmann.

three provinces. They were loyal to the dynasty that they had restored in the face of almost certain collapse, and in return for their allegiance they were allowed great autonomy.

Their first task was reconstruction. The rebellions in central China had destroyed the mulberry trees on which the silkworms fed and those in the northwest, the irrigation systems. Millions were hungry or homeless. The leaders' response to these ills was massive and effective. Just as they had mobilized the gentry to suppress the rebellions, now they obtained their cooperation in rebuilding. They set up refugee centers and soup kitchens, reduced taxes in the devastated Yangzi valley, reclaimed lands gone to waste, began water-control projects, and built granaries. By the early 1890s considerable well-being had been restored to China's late dynastic society.

Their second task was self-strengthening—the adoption of Western arms and technology. The governors general were keenly aware of China's weakness. To strengthen China, they built arsenals and shipyards during the 1860s and 1870s, and during the 1870s and 1880s they began commercial ventures as well. The China Merchants Steam Navigation Company was established in 1872, the Kaiping Coal Mine in 1876, and then a telegraph company, short stretches of railways, and cotton mills. The formula applied in running these enterprises was "official supervision and merchant operation." The major decisions were made by scholar-officials like Zeng, but day-to-day operations were left to the merchants. This division of labor led to contradictions. The Steam Navigation Company, for example, was funded partly by the government because private capital was inadequate.

Li Hongzhang awarded the company a monopoly on shipments of the rice paid in taxes and official cargos to Tianjin and won tariff concessions for the company as well. For a time these advantages enabled it to compete successfully with foreign lines. But Li also used company ships to transport his troops; he took company funds to reward his political followers; and he interfered in the company by hiring and firing managers. Under these conditions, both investors and managers took their profits quickly and did not reinvest in the line. Soon British lines once again dominated shipping in China's domestic waters.

Treaty Ports Conditions in the **treaty ports**, of which there were fourteen by the 1860s, were different from the rest of China. The ports were little islands of privilege where foreigners lived in mansions staffed with servants, raced horses at the track, participated in amateur theatricals, drank (in Shanghai, at the longest bar in the world), and went to church on Sunday. But the ports were also islands of security, under the rule of foreign consuls, where capital was safe from confiscation, trade was free, and "squeeze" (extortion by officials) was the exception and not the rule. Foreign companies naturally located in the ports. The Hong Kong and Shanghai Bank, for example, was funded in 1865 by British interests to finance international trade and to make loans to Chinese firms and banks. Chinese merchants were also attracted by these conditions and located their businesses on rented lands in the foreign concessions. Joint ventures, such as steamboats on the Yangzi, were also begun by Chinese and foreign merchants. Well into the twentieth century the foreign concessions (treaty-port lands leased in perpetuity by foreigners) remained the vital sector of China's modern economy.

The effects of the treaty ports and of Western imperialism on China were largely negative. Under the low tariffs mandated by the treaties, Chinese industries had little protection from imports. Native cotton spinning was almost destroyed by imports of yarn—although the cloth woven from the yarn remained competitive with foreign cloth. Chinese tea lost ground to Indian tea and Chinese silk to Japanese silk, as these countries developed products of standard quality and China did not. China found few products to export: pig bristles, soybeans, and vegetable oils. The level of foreign trade stayed low, and China's interior markets were affected only slightly.

By the 1870s the foreign powers had reached an accommodation with China. They counted on the court to uphold the treaties; in return, they became a prop for the dynasty during its final decades. By 1900, for example, the court's revenues from customs fees were larger than those from any other source, including the land tax. The fees were collected by the Maritime Customs Service, a notably efficient and honest treaty-port institution headed by an Irishman, Sir Robert Hart (1835–1911), who saw himself as serving the Chinese government. In 1895 the Maritime Customs Service had 700 Western and 3,500 Chinese employees.

THE BORDERLANDS: THE NORTHWEST, VIETNAM, AND KOREA

China's other foreign relations were with fringe lands inhabited by non-Chinese but which China claimed by right of past conquest or as tributaries. Often distant from the pressing concerns of Chinese government, the tributaries were nonetheless the mirrors in which China saw reflected its own self-image as a universal empire. During the late nineteenth century this image was strengthened in the northwest but dealt a fatal blow in Vietnam and Korea.

The Northwest In the northwest, China confronted tsarist Russia. Both countries had been expanding onto the steppe since the seventeenth century (see Chapter 20). Both had firearms. Caught in a pincers between them, the once proud, powerful, and independent nomadic tribes were gradually rendered impotent. Conservatives at the Manchu court ordered Zuo Zongtang, who had suppressed Muslim rebels within China, to suppress a Muslim leader who had founded

an independent state in Chinese Turkestan (the Tarim basin, a part of the old Silk Road). Zuo led his army across 3,000 miles of deserts, and by 1878 had reconquered the area, which was subsequently renamed Xinjiang, or the "New Territories." A treaty signed with Russia in 1881 also restored most of the Ili region in western Mongolia to Chinese control. These victories strengthened court conservatives who wished to take a stronger stance toward the West.

Vietnam To the south was Vietnam, which had retained its independence from China since 935. It saw itself as an independent and separate state, but it used the Chinese writing system, modeled its laws and government on those of China, and traded with China within the framework of the tribute system. China, more simply, saw Vietnam as a tributary that could be aided or punished as necessary.

During the 1840s the second emperor of the Nguyen dynasty, which had begun in 1802, moved to reduce French influences and suppress Christianity. Thousands were killed, including French and Vietnamese priests. The French responded by seizing Saigon and the three provinces of Cochin China in 1859, establishing a protectorate over Cambodia in 1864, and taking three more provinces in 1867 and Hanoi in 1882. China, flush with confidence after its victories in Central Asia, in 1883 sent in troops to aid its tributary. The result was a two-year war in which French warships ranged the coast of China, attacking shore batteries and sinking ships. In 1885 China was forced to sign a treaty abandoning its claims to Vietnam. By 1893 France had brought together Vietnam, Cambodia, and Laos to form the Federation of Indochina, which remained a French colony until 1940.

Korea A third area of contention was Korea. Unlike Vietnam, Korea saw itself as a tributary of China. Even at his own court the Korean ruler styled himself as a king and not an emperor. It was the only rim area of China that accepted the tribute system on Chinese terms.

During the last decades of the long (1392–1910) Choson dynasty, the Korean state was weak. It hung on to power, in part, by enforcing a policy of seclusion almost as total as that of Tokugawa Japan, which won it the name of the Hermit Kingdom. Its only foreign ties were its tribute relations with China and its trade and occasional diplomatic missions to Japan. In 1876 Japan "opened" Korea to international relations, using much the same tactics that Perry had used twenty-two years earlier against Japan. Japan then contended with China for influence in Korea's internal politics. Conservatives and moderate reformers in Korea looked to China for support. Radical reformers, weaker and fewer in number, looked to Japan, arguing that only sweeping changes such as those that had been made in Japan would enable Korea to survive. The radicals, however, were soon suppressed.

"Open Door" Cartoon. An American view of the "open door." The combination of high self-esteem and negative attitudes toward foreigners at the turn of the century was not a Chinese monopoly. Corbis-Bettmann.

In 1893 a popular religious sect unleashed a rebellion against the weak and corrupt Seoul government. When the government requested Chinese help to suppress the rebellion, China sent troops, but Japan sent more, and in 1894 war broke out between China and Japan. China and the Western powers expected an easy Chinese victory, but they had not understood the changes occurring within Japan. Japan won handily. Neither Chinese fleet nor Chinese armies were a match for the discipline and the superior tactics of the Japanese units. It was after this war that Taiwan became Japan's first colony. The defeat by Japan convinced many throughout China that basic changes were inevitable.

From Dynasty to Warlordism (1895–1926)

China was ruled by officials who had mastered the Confucian classics and the historical and literary tradition that had developed alongside them. This intellectual formation was highly resistant to change. For most officials living in China's interior, the foreign crises of the nineteenth century were "coastal phenomena" that, like bee stings, were painful for a time but

then forgotten. Few officials realized the magnitude of the foreign threat.

China's defeat in 1895 by Japan, another Asian nation and one for which China had had little regard, came as a shock. The response within China was a new wave of reform proposals. (See Document, "Liang Qichao Urges the Chinese to Reform.") The most influential thinker was Kang Youwei (1858–1927), who described China as "enfeebled" and "soundly asleep atop a pile of kindling." For this state of affairs, Kang blamed the "conservatives." They did not understand, Kang argued, that Confucius himself had been a reformer and not simply a transmitter of past wisdom. Confucius had invented the idea of a golden age in the past in order to persuade the rulers of his own age to adopt his ideas. All of history, Kang continued, was evolutionary—a march forward from absolute monarchy to constitutional monarchy to democracy. Actually, Kang was not well-versed in Western ideas; he equated the somewhat mystical Confucian virtue of humanity (*ren*) with electricity and ether. Nonetheless, his reinterpretation of the essentials of Confucianism removed a major barrier to the entry of Western ideas into China.

In 1898 the emperor himself became sympathetic to Kang's ideas and, on June 11, launched "one hundred days of reform." He took as his models not past Chinese monarchs, but Peter the Great (r. 1682–1725) and the Japanese Meiji emperor (r. 1867–1912). Edicts were issued for sweeping reforms of China's schools, railroads, police, laws, military services, bureaucracy, post offices, and examination system. But the orders were implemented in only one province; conservative resistance was nationwide. Even at the court, the empress dowager regained control and ended the reforms. Kang and most of his associates fled to Japan. One reformer who remained behind was executed.

The response of the Western powers to China's 1895 defeat has been described as "carving up the melon." Each nation tried to define a sphere of interest, which usually consisted of a leasehold along with railway rights and special commercial privileges. Russia gained a leasehold at Port Arthur; Germany acquired one in Shandung. Britain got the New Territories adjoining Jiulong (Kowloon) at Hong Kong. New ports and cities were opened to foreign trade. The United States, busy acquiring the Philippines and Guam, was in a weaker position in China. So it enunciated an "open-door" policy: equal commercial opportunities for all powers and the preservation of the territorial integrity of China.

There was in China at this time a religious society known as the **Boxers**. The Chinese name translates more literally as the "Righteous and Harmonious Fists." The Boxers had rituals, spells, and amulets which they believed made them impervious to bullets. They rebelled first in Shandung in 1898, and, gaining court support, entered Beijing in 1900. The court declared war on the treaty powers, and there followed a two-month siege of the foreign legation quarter. Pent-up resentments against

DOCUMENT | Liang Qichao Urges the Chinese to Reform (1896)

Next to Kang Youwei, Liang Qichao (1873–1929) was the most influential thinker of late Qing China.

◆ What kind of reform program is Liang advocating? Compare his response to the challenge of the West with that by a Japanese commentator in "A Japanese View of the Inventiveness of the West," later in this chapter.

On the *Harm of not Reforming.* Now here is a big mansion which has lasted a thousand years. The tiles and bricks are decayed and the beams and rafters are broken. It is still a magnificently big thing, but when wind and rain suddenly come up, its fall is foredoomed. Yet the people in the house are still happily playing or soundly sleeping and as indifferent as if they have seen or heard nothing. Even some who have noted the danger know only how to weep bitterly, folding their arms and waiting for death without thinking of any remedy. Sometimes there are people a little better off who try to repair the cracks, seal up the leaks, and patch up the ant holes in order to be able to go on living there in peace, even temporarily, in the hope that something better may turn up. These three types of people use their minds differently, but when a hurricane comes they will die together ... A nation is also like this ...

India is one of the oldest countries on the great earth. She followed tradition without change; she has been rendered a colony of England. Turkey's territory occupied three continents and had an established state for a thousand years; yet, because of observing the old ways without change, she has been dominated by six large countries, which have divided her territory ... The Moslems in central Asia have usually been well known for their bravery and skill in warfare, and yet they observe the old ways without changing. The Russians are swallowing them like a whale and nibbling them as silkworms eat mulberry leaves, almost in their entirety.

The age of China as a country is equal to that of India and the fertility of her land is superior to that of Turkey, but her conformity to the defective ways which have accumulated and her incapacity to stand up and reform make her also like a brother of these two countries. ... Whenever there is a flood or drought, communications are severed, there is no way to transport famine relief, the dead are abandoned to fill the ditches or are disregarded, and nine out of ten houses are emptied. ... The members of secret societies are scattered over the whole country, waiting for the chance to move. Industry is not developed, commerce is not discussed, the native goods daily become less salable. ... "Leakage" [i.e., squeeze] becomes more serious day by day and our financial sources are almost dried up. Schools are not well-run and students, apart from the "eight-legged" essays, do not know how to do a thing. The good ones are working on small researches, flowery writing, and miscellaneous trifles. Tell them about the vast oceans, they open their eyes wide and disbelieve it.

Reprinted by permission of the publisher from by Ssu-Yu Teng and John K. Fairbank, *China's Response to the West* (Cambridge, MA: Harvard University Press). Copyright 1954, 1979 by the President and Fellows of Harvard College.

---

decades of foreign encroachments fueled support for the rebellion. Eventually an international force captured Beijing, won a huge indemnity, and obtained the right to maintain permanent military forces in the capital. In the aftermath of the Boxer Rebellion, the Russians occupied Manchuria.

The defeat of the Boxers convinced even conservative Chinese leaders of the futility of clinging to old ways. A more powerful reform movement began, with the empress dowager herself in its vanguard. But as the movement gained momentum, the dynasty could not stay far enough in front and eventually was overrun.

Execution of Boxers. The rebels, arms bound behind, lie headless. Chinese ➤ soldiers watch. In the 1900 siege of the foreign legations in Beijing, 76 foreigners were killed by the Boxers. Twelve years later, the dynasty fell.
Neg./Transparency no. 336289. (Photo Copied by P. Goldberg). Courtesy Dept. of Library Services, American Museum of Natural History.

Educational reforms began in 1901. Women, for the first time, were admitted as students to newly formed schools. In place of Confucianism, the instructors taught science, mathematics, geography, and an anti-imperialist version of Chinese history that fanned the flames of nationalism. Western doctrines, such as classical economics, liberalism, socialism, anarchism, and social Darwinism, were also introduced into China. Most entered via translations from Japanese, and in the process the modern vocabulary coined by Japanese scholars was implanted in China. By 1906 there were 8,000 Chinese students in Japan, which had become a hotbed of Chinese reformist and revolutionary societies.

Military reforms were begun by Yuan Shikai (1859–1916), whose New Army drew on Japanese and Western models. Young men from gentry families, spurred by patriotism, broke with the traditional Chinese animus against military careers and joined the New Army as officers. Their loyalty was to their commanders and to their country, not to the dynasty.

Political reforms began with a modification of the examination system to accommodate the learning at the new schools. Then in 1905 the examination system was abolished altogether. Henceforth, officials were to be directly recruited from the graduates of the schools and those who had studied abroad. Provincial assemblies were formed in 1909, and a consultative assembly with some elected members was established in Beijing in 1910. These representative bodies were intended to rally the new gentry nationalism in support of the court, but they became forums for the expression of interests at odds with those of the dynasty.

In sum, during the first decade of the twentieth century the three vital components of the imperial system—Confucian education, the bureaucracy, and the gentry—had been discarded or modified in ways that even a few decades earlier would have been unimaginable.

These changes sparked the 1911 revolution. It began with an uprising in Sichuan province against a government plan to nationalize the main railways. The players were:

1. Gentry who stood to lose their investments in the railways.

2. Qing military commanders, who broke with Beijing, declaring their provinces independent.

3. Sun Zhongshan (or Sun Yat-sen) (1866–1925), a republican revolutionary. Born a peasant, he had learned English and become a Christian in Hawaii, then studied medicine in Guangzhou and Hong Kong. He organized the Revolutionary Alliance in Tokyo in 1905 and was associated with the Nationalist Party (Guomindang) formed in 1912.

4. Yuan Shikai, who was called on by the court to preserve the dynasty. Instead, he arranged for the last child emperor to abdicate, for Sun to step aside, and declared himself president of the new Republic of China.

▲ **Sun Zhongshan (or Sun Yat-Sen) (1866–1925),** father of China's 1911–12 republican revolution.
Brown Brothers.

The Nationalists won the election called in 1913. Yuan thereupon had their leader assassinated, crushed the military governors who supported them, and forced Sun Zhongshan and other revolutionaries to flee again to Japan. Yuan emerged as the uncontested ruler of China. Mistaking the temper of the times, he proclaimed a new dynasty with himself as emperor. The idea of yet another dynasty met implacable opposition from all quarters, forcing Yuan to abandon the attempt. He died three months later in June 1916. After Yuan, China fell into the hands of warlord armies. The years until the late twenties were a time of agony, frustration, and travail for the Chinese people. But they were also a time of intense intellectual ferment.

Cultural and Ideological Ferment: The May Fourth Movement

In the century after the Opium War, China's leading thinkers responded to the challenge of the West in terms of four successive modes of thought:

1. During the 1840s and the 1850s, and into the 1860s, the key event in China was the Taiping Rebellion. The success of gentry Confucianism in putting down the rebellion and in reestablishing the social order underlined for most Chinese the effectiveness, vitality, and validity of traditional doctrines.

2. From the 1860s to the 1890s, the dominant intellectual modality was "*ti-yong* reformism." The essence (*ti*) was to remain Chinese, but useful contrivances (*yong*) could be borrowed from the West. This formula enabled a restabilized

DOCUMENT   Chen Duxiu's "Call to Youth" in 1915

Struggle, natural selection, and organic process are the images used by Chen Duxiu. How different from those of Confucianism!

◆ How does Chen's "Call to Youth" relate to the political conditions in China in 1915?

The Chinese compliment others by saying, "He acts like an old man although still young." Englishmen and Americans encourage one another by saying, "Keep young while growing old." Such is one respect in which the different ways of thought of the East and West are manifested. Youth is like early spring, like the rising sun, like trees and grass in bud, like a newly sharpened blade. It is the most valuable period of life. The function of youth in society is the same as that of a fresh and vital cell in a human body. In the processes of metabolism, the old and the rotten are incessantly eliminated to be replaced by the fresh and living ... According to this standard, then, is the society of our nation flourishing, or is it about to perish? I cannot bear to answer. As for those old and rotten elements, I shall leave them to the process of natural selection. ... I only, with tears, place my plea before the young and vital youth, in the hope that they will achieve self-awareness, and begin to struggle.

What is the struggle? It is to exert one's intellect, discard resolutely the old and the rotten, regard them as enemies and as the flood or savage beasts, keep away from their neighborhood and refuse to be contaminated by their poisonous germs. Alas! Do these words really fit the youth of our country? I have seen that, out of every ten youths who are young in age, five are old in physique; and out of every ten who are young in both age and physique, nine are old in mentality. Those with shining hair, smooth countenance, a straight back and a wide chest are indeed magnificent youths! Yet if you ask what thoughts and aims are entertained in their heads, then they all turn out to be the same as the old and rotten, like moles from the same hill. ... It is the old and rotten air that fills society everywhere. One cannot even find a bit of fresh and vital air to comfort those of us who are suffocating in despair.

China to borrow and reform in small ways like building arsenals and railroads while remaining Chinese at the core. It was the ideology of the "self-strengthening" movement.

3. Then, during the last decade of the Manchu dynasty, the *ti-yong* distinction came to be seen as inadequate. The *ti* itself was reinterpreted. The dominant view was that of Kang Youwei, who argued that Confucius had been a reformer and that Confucianism, properly understood, was a philosophy of change. This kind of thought was behind the rash of reforms of 1900–1911.

4. The fourth stage was a period of freedom and vigorous experimentation with new doctrines that began in 1914 and extended into the 1920s. It is called the May Fourth Movement after an incident in Beijing in 1919 in which thousands of students protested the settlement at Versailles that awarded former German possessions in Shandung to Japan. The powerful nationalism that led the students to demonstrate in the streets changed the complexion of Chinese thought. Instead of appealing to tradition, leading thinkers began to judge ideas in terms of their value in solving China's problems. It was also not accidental that this era of intellectual excitement corresponded almost exactly with the period of warlord rule—which afforded a breathing space between the ideological constraints of the old dynasty and those of the Nationalist and Communist eras that would follow.

Scholars who returned from abroad during the last years of Manchu rule often located in the safety of the treaty ports. During the May Fourth era, however, the center of advanced thought was Beijing. Cai Yuanpei (1868–1940), who had been minister of education under the republic, became the chancellor of Beijing University, and Chen Duxiu (1879–1942) became his dean of letters. Both men had had a classical education and had passed the traditional examinations. Cai joined the party of Sun Zhongshan and went to study in Germany. After the fall of Yuan Shikai, he made Beijing University into a haven for scholars who had returned from study in Japan or the West.

Chen Duxiu, a Francophile, had studied in Japan. In 1915 he launched *New Youth*, a magazine that played a role in the intellectual revolution of early-twentieth-century China comparable to the *cahiers* in the French Revolution or the pamphlets of Thomas Paine in the American Revolution. In his magazine Chen placed the blame for Chinese ills on the teachings of Confucius. He called for a generation of progressive, cosmopolitan, and scientific youth who would uphold the values of liberty, equality, and fraternity. (See Document, "Chen Duxiu's 'Call to Youth' in 1915.")

The greatest modern Chinese writer was Lu Xun (1881–1936). Like most other leading intellectuals of the period, he had been born in a scholar-official family. He went to Japan for eight years to study medicine but switched in mid-course to literature. His first work, *A Madman's Diary*, appeared in *New Youth* in 1918. Its protagonist is a pathetic figure whose madness takes the form of a belief that people eat people. Lu Xun's message was that only the vision of a madman could truly comprehend an abnormal and inhumane society.

As the May Fourth Movement developed, ideas propounded in Beijing quickly spread to the rest of China, especially to its urban centers. Protest demonstrations against imperialist privilege broke out in Shanghai, Wuhan, and Guangzhou, as they had in the capital. Nationalism and anti-imperialist sentiment were stronger than liberalism, although few thinkers did not speak out for democracy. Only members of an older generation of reformers, such as Kang Youwei, came full circle and, appalled by the slaughter of World War I and what they saw as Western materialism, advocated a return to traditional Chinese philosophies.

At the onset of China's intellectual revolution, Marxism had small appeal; Marx's critique of capitalist society did not fit Chinese conditions. More persuasive was the anarchism of Peter Kropotkin (1842–1921), who taught that mutual aid was as much a part of evolution as the struggle for survival. But after the Russian Revolution of 1917, Marxism-Leninism entered China. The Leninist definition of imperialism as the last crisis stage of capitalism had an immediate appeal, for it put the blame for China's ills on the West and offered "feudal" China the possibility of leapfrogging over capitalism to socialism. As early as 1919 an entire issue of *New Youth* was devoted to Marxism. Marxist study groups formed in Beijing and other cities. In 1919 a student from Hunan, Mao Zedong, who had worked in the Beijing University library, returned to Changsha to form a study group. Chen Duxiu was converted to Marxism in 1920. Instructed in organizational techniques by a Comintern agent, Chen and others formed the Chinese Communist Party in Shanghai in 1921; Zhou Enlai (1898–1976) formed a similar group in Paris during the same year. The numbers involved were small but grew steadily.

Nationalist China

GUOMINDANG UNIFICATION OF CHINA AND THE NANJING DECADE (1927–1937)

Sun Zhongshan had fled to Japan during the 1913–1916 rule by Yuan Shikai. He returned to Guangzhou in 1916, but despite his immense personal attractiveness as a leader he was a poor organizer, and his **Guomindang (GMD)**—or Nationalist Party—made little headway. For a time in 1922 he was driven out of Guangzhou by a local warlord. From 1923 Sun began to receive Soviet advice and support. With the help of Comintern agents like Michael Borodin, he reorganized his party on the Leninist model, with an

executive committee on top of a national party congress and, below this, provincial and county organizations and local party cells.

Since 1905 Sun had enunciated his "three principles of the people": nationality, livelihood, and rights. Sun's earlier nationalism had been directed against Manchu rule; it was now redirected against Western imperialism. The principle of people's livelihood was defined in terms of equalizing landholdings and nationalizing major industries. By "people's rights" Sun meant democracy, although he argued that full democracy must be preceded by a preparatory period of tutelage under a single-party dictatorship. Sun sent his loyal lieutenant Jiang Jieshi (Chiang Kai-shek) (1887–1975) to the Soviet Union for study. Jiang returned after four months with a cadre of Russian advisors and established a military academy at Huangpu to the south of Guangzhou in 1924. The cadets of Huangpu were to form a "party army." Sun died in 1925. By 1926 the Academy had graduated several thousand officers, and the GMD army numbered almost 100,000. The GMD had become the major political force in China, with 200,000 members; its leadership was divided between a left and a right wing.

Changes occurring within Chinese society spurred the growth of the party. Industries arose in the cities. Labor unions were organized in tobacco and textile factories. New ventures were begun outside the treaty ports, and chambers of com-

▲ **Jiang Jieshi (or Chiang Kai-shek) (1887–1975)** as a young revolutionary officer.
Brown Brothers.

merce were established even in medium-sized towns. Entrepreneurs, merchants, officials, journalists, and the employees of foreign firms formed a new and politically conscious middle class.

The quicksilver element in cities was the several million students at government, Catholic, and Protestant schools. In May 1925 students demonstrated against the treatment of workers in foreign-owned factories at Shanghai. Police in the international settlement fired on the demonstrators, killing thirteen and wounding fifty. The incident further inflamed national and anti-imperialist feelings. Strikes and boycotts of foreign goods were called throughout China. Those in Hong Kong lasted for fifteen months.

Under these conditions the Chinese Communist Party (CCP) also grew, and in 1926 it had about 20,000 members. The party was influential in student organizations, labor unions, and even within the GMD. By an earlier agreement Sun had permitted CCP members to join the GMD as individuals but had enjoined them from organizing CCP cells within the GMD. Moscow approved of this policy; it felt that the CCP was too small to accomplish anything on its own, and that by working within the GMD, its members could join in the "bourgeois, national, democratic struggle" against "imperialism and feudal warlordism." Zhou Enlai, for example, became deputy head of the political education department of the Huangpu Academy.

By 1926 the GMD had established a base in the area around Guangzhou, and Jiang Jieshi felt ready to march north against the warlord domains. He worried about the growing Communist strength, however, and before setting off he ousted the Soviet advisers and CCP members from the GMD offices in Guangzhou. The march north began in July. By the spring of 1927 Jiang's army had reached the Yangzi, defeating, and often absorbing, warlord armies as it advanced (see Map 28–2).

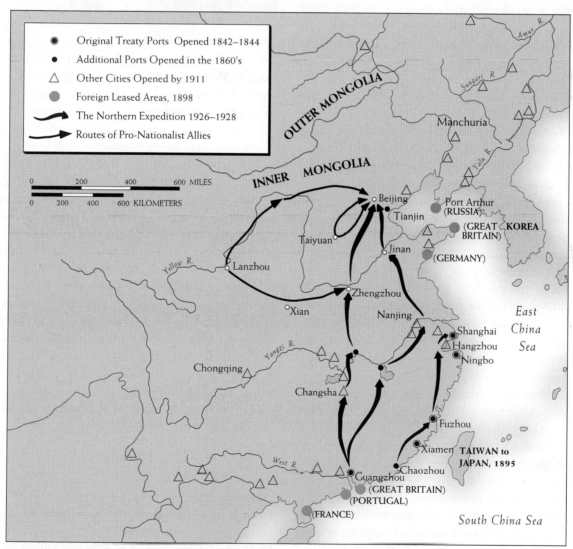

MAP 28–2 The Northern Expeditions of the Guomindang. These expeditions, from 1926 to 1928, unified most of China under the Nationalist (Guomindang) government of Jiang Jieshi, inaugurating the Nanjing decade. Warlord armies continued to hold power on the periphery.

After entering Shanghai in April 1927 Jiang carried out a sweeping purge of the CCP—against its members in the GMD, against its party organization, and against the labor unions that it had come to dominate. Hundreds were killed. The CCP responded by trying to gain control of the GMD left wing, which had established a government at Wuhan, and by armed uprisings. Both attempts failed. The surviving CCP members fled to the mountainous border region of Hunan and Jiangxi to the southwest and established the "Jiangxi Soviet." The left wing of the GMD, disenchanted with the Communists, rejoined the right wing at Nanjing, China's new capital. Jiang's army continued north, took Beijing, and gained the nominal submission of most northern Chinese warlords in 1928. By this time most foreign powers had recognized the Nanjing regime as the government of China.

Jiang Jieshi was the key figure in the Nanjing government. By training and temperament he believed in military force. He was unimaginative, strict, feared more than loved, and, amid considerable corruption, incorruptible. Jiang venerated Sun Zhongshan and his three "people's principles." The grandeur of Sun's tomb in Nanjing surpassed that of the Ming emperors. But where Sun, as a revolutionary, had looked back to the zeal of the Taiping rebels, Jiang, trying to consolidate his rule over provincial warlords, looked back to Zeng Guofan, who had put down the rebels and restabilized China. Like Zeng, Jiang was conservative and, though a Methodist, often appealed to Confucian values. The New Life Movement begun by Jiang in 1934 was an attempt to revitalize these values.

Jiang's power rested on the army, the party, and the government bureaucracy. The army was dominated by the Huangpu clique, which was personally loyal to Jiang, and by officers trained in Japan. After 1927 Soviet military advisors were replaced by German advisors, who reorganized Jiang's army along German lines with a general staff system. The larger part of GMD revenues went to the military, which was expanded into a modernized force of 300,000. Huangpu graduates also controlled the secret military police and used it against Communists and any others who opposed the government. The GMD was a dictatorship under a central committee. Jiang became president of the party in 1938.

The densely populated central and lower Yangzi provinces were the area of GMD strength. The party, however, was unable to control the outlying areas occupied by warlords, Communists, and Japanese. Some gains were made during the Nanjing decade: Jiang's armies defeated the northern warlords in 1930, put down a rebellion in the coastal province of Fujian in 1934, and extended their control over southern and southwest China two years later. But warlords ruled some areas until 1949. In 1931 Jiang attacked the Jiangxi Soviet. In 1934 the Communists were forced to abandon their mountain base and flee to the southwest and then to Shaanxi province in north-

The Long March. Mao Zedong led 100,000 Chinese Communist troops and personnel from the embattled Kiangsi Soviet in October 1934. They marched west and then north. About 10,000 reached the arid land of northern Shaanxi months later. They made Yenan their headquarters. In this picture, one carries a hoe. Have they come to work in a field?
Getty Images, Inc. Hulton Archive Photo.

western China. Of the 90,000 troops that set out on this epic **"Long March"** of 6,000 miles, only 20,000 survived. It was during this march that Mao Zedong wrested control of the CCP from the Moscow-trained, urban-oriented leaders and established his unorthodox view that a revolutionary Leninist party could base itself on the peasantry.

The Japanese had held special rights in Manchuria since the Russo-Japanese War of 1905. When Jiang's march north and the rise of Chinese nationalism threatened the Japanese position, field-grade officers of Japan's forces in Manchuria engineered a military coup in 1931, and in 1932 established a puppet state and proclaimed the independence of Manchuria. In the years that followed, Japanese army units moved south as far as the Great Wall. Chinese national sentiment demanded that Jiang resist, but Jiang, well aware of the disparity between his armies and those of Japan, felt that the internal unification of China should take precedence over war against a foreign power. On a visit to Xian in 1936 Jiang was captured by a northern warlord and held until he agreed to join with the CCP in a united front against Japan. In the following year, however, a full-scale war with Japan broke out, and China's situation again changed.

WAR AND REVOLUTION (1937–1949)

In 1937 the GMD controlled most of China and was recognized as its government, whereas the CCP survivors of the Long March had just begun to rebuild their strength in arid Shaanxi, an area too remote for Jiang's army to penetrate. But by 1949 CCP forces had conquered China, including border areas never under GMD rule, and Jiang and the GMD were forced to flee to Taiwan. What had happened?

The war with Japan was the key event. It began in July 1937 with an unplanned clash at Beijing and then spread. Battlefield victories soon convinced the Japanese military leaders to abandon negotiations in favor of a knockout blow. Beijing and Tianjin fell within a month, Shanghai was attacked in August, and Nanjing fell in December. During the following year the Japanese took Guangzhou and Wuhan and set up puppet regimes in Beijing and Nanjing. In 1940, frustrated by trying to work with Jiang, the leader of the left wing of the GMD and many of his associates joined the Japanese puppet government. Japan proclaimed its "New Order in East Asia," which was to replace the system of unequal treaties. It expected Jiang to recognize his situation as hopeless and to submit. Instead, in 1938 he relocated his capital to Chongqing, far to the west behind the gorges of the Yangzi. He was joined by thousands of Chinese, students and professors, factory managers and workers, who moved from occupied to free China.

Jiang's stubborn resistance to the Japanese won admiration from all sides. But the area occupied by the Japanese included just those eastern cities, railways, and densely populated Yangzi valley territories that had constituted the GMD base. The withdrawal to Chongqing cut the GMD off from most of the Chinese population; programs for modernization ended; and the GMD's former tax revenues were lost. Inflation increased geometrically, reducing the real income of officials, teachers, and soldiers alike. By the end of World War II and during the early postwar years salaries were paid in large packages of almost worthless money, which was immediately spent for food or goods possessing real value. Inflation led to demoralization and exacerbated the already widespread corruption.

The United States sent advisors and military equipment to strengthen Jiang's forces after the start of the Pacific War. The advisers, however, were frustrated by Jiang, who wanted not to fight the Japanese but to husband his forces for the anticipated postwar confrontation with the Communists. Within his own army a gap divided officers and men. Conditions in the camps were primitive, food poor, and medical supplies inadequate. The young saw conscription almost as a death sentence. Jiang's unwillingness to commit his troops against the Japanese also meant that the surge of anti-Japanese patriotism was not converted to popular support for the GMD.

For the Communists, the Japanese occupation was an opportunity. Headquartered at Yan'an, they consolidated their base in Shaanxi province. They began campaigns to promote literacy and production drives to promote self-sufficiency. Soldiers grew food so as not to burden the peasants. The CCP abandoned its earlier policy of expropriating lands in favor of reductions in rents and interest. (This change led to the widespread American view that the CCP were not Communists but agrarian reformers, despite their protests to the contrary.) The party took only those provincial and county offices needed to ensure their control and shared the rest with the GMD and other parties. It expanded village councils to include tenants and other previously excluded strata. But while compromising with other political and social groups, it strengthened the party internally.

Party membership expanded from 40,000 in 1937 to 1.2 million in 1945. Schools were established in Yan'an to train party cadres. Even as the party expanded, it maintained orthodoxy by a rectification campaign begun in 1942. Those tainted by liberalism, individualism, or other impure tendencies were criticized and made to confess their failings and repent at public meetings. Mao's thought was supreme. To the Chinese at large Mao represented himself as the successor to Sun Zhongshan, but within the Communist Party he presented himself as a theoretician in the line of Marx (1818–1883), Engels (1820–1895), Lenin (1870–1924), and Stalin (1879–1953).

Whereas the GMD ruled through officials and often in cooperation with local landlords, the Communists learned to operate at the grass-roots level. They infiltrated Japanese-controlled areas and also penetrated some GMD organizations and military units. CCP armies were built up from 90,000 in 1937 to 900,000 in 1945. These armies were supplemented by a rural people's militia and by guerrilla forces in nineteen

CHRONOLOGY

Modern China

Close of Manchu Rule	
1839–1842	Opium War
1850–1873	Taiping and other rebellions
1870s–1880s	Self-strengthening movement
1894–1895	Sino-Japanese War
1898	One hundred days of reform
1898–1900	Boxer Rebellion
1912	Republican revolution overthrows Qing dynasty
Warlordism	
1912–1916	Yuan Shikai president of Republic of China
1916–1928	Warlord era
1919	May Fourth incident
Nationalist China	
1924	Founding of Huangpu Military Academy
1926–1928	Jiang's march north and Guomindang reunification of China
1928–1937	Nanjing decade
1934–1935	Chinese Communists' Long March to Yan'an
1937–1945	War with Japan
1945–1949	Civil war and the establishment of the People's Republic of China

mountainous "base areas." By most accounts the Yan'an leadership and its party, army, and mass organizations possessed a cohesion, determination, and high morale that were conspicuously lacking in Chongqing.

But the strength of the Chinese Communists as of 1945 should not be overstated. Most Chinese villagers were influenced by neither the CCP nor the GMD, and although intellectuals in free China had become disaffected with the GMD, most did not positively support the CCP. When the war in the Pacific ended in 1945, China's future was unclear. The Soviet Union allowed CCP cadres to enter Manchuria, which it had seized during the last few days of the war, and blocked the entry of GMD troops until the following year. But even the Soviet Union recognized the GMD as the government of China and expected it to win the postwar struggle. The Allies directed Japanese armies to surrender to the GMD forces in 1945. The United States flew Jiang's troops from Chongqing to key eastern cities. His armies were by then three times the size of the Communists' and far better equipped.

A civil war broke out early in 1946. Both sides knew that the earlier united front had been a sham. Efforts by U.S. General George Marshall (1880–1959) to mediate were futile. Until the summer of 1947 GMD armies were victorious—even capturing Yan'an. But the tide turned in July as CCP armies went on the offensive in north China. They captured American military equipment left by the GMD forces, and by October 1948 the GMD forces had been driven from Manchuria. In January 1949 Beijing and Tianjin fell. By late spring CCP armies had crossed the Yangzi, taking Nanjing and Shanghai. A few months later all of China was in Communist hands. Many Chinese fled with Jiang to Taiwan or escaped to Hong Kong; they

▲ **Mao Zedong (1893–1976)** at his cave headquarters in Shaanxi province during World War II. He wears a padded winter jacket and writes with a Chinese brush. On his desk are the *Collected Works* of Lu Hsun.

Getty Images, Inc. – Taxi.

included not only GMD officials and generals, but entrepreneurs and academics as well. Not a few subsequently made their way to the United States.

In China apprehension was mixed with anticipation. The disciplined, well-behaved soldiers of the "Peoples' Liberation Army" were certainly a contrast to those of the GMD. As villages were liberated, lands were taken from landlords and given to the landless. In the cities crowds welcomed the CCP troops as liberators. The feeling was widespread that the future of China was once again in the hands of the Chinese.

MODERN JAPAN 1853–1945
Overthrow of the Tokugawa Bakufu (1853–1868)

From the seventeenth century into the nineteenth, the natural isolation of the islands of Japan was augmented by its policy of seclusion, making Japan into a little world of its own. The 260-odd domains were the states of this world, the *bakufu* in Edo was its hegemon, and the imperial court in Kyoto provided a sacerdotal or religious sanction for the *bakufu*-domain system. Then, in 1853 and 1854, the American ships of Commodore Perry came and forced Japan to sign a Treaty of Friendship, opening it to foreign intercourse. Fourteen years later the entire *bakufu*-domain system collapsed, and a new group of unusually talented leaders seized power. Seclusion, like the case of a watch, had been necessary to preserve the Tokugawa political mechanism. With the case removed, the jolt of the foreign intrusion caused the inner workings to fly apart.

It was surprising how little changed during the first four years after Perry. The *bakufu* attended to its affairs and the domains to theirs. The daimyo continued to spend every other year living in Edo. Political action consisted mainly of daimyo cliques trying to influence *bakufu* policy. The break came in 1858 when the *bakufu*, ignoring the imperial court's disapproval, was persuaded to sign a commercial treaty with the United States. In reaction, some daimyo, who wanted a voice in national policy making, criticized the treaty as contravening the hallowed policy of seclusion. Younger samurai, frustrated by their exclusion from office, started a movement to "honor the emperor." The *bakufu*, in turn, responded with a purge: Dissident daimyo were forced into retirement, while samurai critics were executed or imprisoned. The purge was effective until 1860, when the head of the *bakufu* council was himself assassinated by extremist samurai. His successors lacked the nerve to continue his tough policies, thus opening the way for a new kind of politics between 1861 and 1868.

In 1861 two domains, Chōshū and Satsuma, emerged to mediate, to heal the breach that had opened between the *bakufu* and the court. Chōshū was the first to come forth: Its officials traveled between Kyoto and Edo, proposing a policy that favored the *bakufu* but made concessions to the court. Next Satsuma sallied forth with a policy that made further concessions and ousted Chōshū as "the friend of the court." In response, the moderate reformist government of Chōshū adopted the pro-emperor policy of its extremist faction and, in turn, ousted Satsuma. Beaten in the diplomatic game, Satsuma seized the court in 1863 in a military coup, and the Chōshū radicals returned disgruntled to their domain.

Four points may be noted about the 1861–1863 diplomatic phase of domain action: (1) Even after 250 years of *bakufu* rule, several domains were still viable, autonomous units that could act when the opportunity arose; (2) the two domains that acted first and most of those that followed were large domains with many samurai—Chōshū had 10,000 samurai families and substantial financial resources; (3) both Satsuma and Chōshū had fought against the Tokugawa in 1600 and remembered an earlier independence; (4) by the 1861–1863 period, domain politics was no longer in the hands of daimyo and their high-ranking advisors. In both Satsuma and Chōshū, the new politics had opened decision-making to middle ranking samurai officials in a way that would have been impossible before 1853.

The 1863 Satsuma coup at the Kyoto court initiated a military phase of politics in which battles would determine every turning point. Events were complicated, for besides the court and the *bakufu*, there were more than 260 domains—somewhat like a circus with too many rings and sideshows. But most domains were too small to carry weight in national politics. Hereditary daimyo, for example, were influential mainly as *bakufu* officials. Of the larger domains, some were insolvent and others too closely associated with the *bakufu* to act independently. As long as Satsuma and Chōshū remained enemies, politics stalemated and the *bakufu* continued as hegemon. But when the two domains became allies in 1866, the *bakufu* was overthrown in less than two years.

The movement for a "union of court and camp" contributed to the *bakufu*'s downfall; daimyo, who earlier had criticized the *bakufu*, campaigned for a new conciliar rule in which they would participate together with the emperor. The movement came to nothing, but it led daimyo to withdraw support that might otherwise have gone to the *bakufu*. A second feature of this period was a strong antiforeignism. Samurai extremists assassinated foreigners as well as *bakufu* officials; one of their slogans was "expel the barbarians." Early on, Chōshū and Satsuma fired on foreign ships. But when Western gunboats bombarded those domains in retaliation, they immediately dropped their xenophobic slogan and set about buying rifles and gunboats.

Another aspect of the military phase of politics from 1863 to 1868 was the formation of new rifle units, commanded mostly by lower samurai. These units transformed political power in Japan. For example, Chōshū troops armed with Spencers and Minies—mostly surplus left over from the U.S. Civil War—defeated a traditionally armed but numerically superior *bakufu* army in mid-1866 with a numbing force.

A final development was a cultural shift in the way Japanese saw themselves. During the Tokugawa era they saw themselves as civilized Confucians and most of the rest of the world, China and Korea excepted, as barbarians. But in the face of superior Western technology, this view became untenable. In 1866 Fukuzawa Yukichi (1835–1901), a student of Western studies and a *bakufu* translator, introduced a Western theory of stages of history: The West, with its technology, science, and humane laws, was seen as "civilized and enlightened"; China, Japan, and countries like Turkey were seen as half civilized; other areas were seen as barbarian. This theory stood the traditional view almost on its head. Fukuzawa argued, furthermore, that technology was not detachable but grew out of the Western legal, political, economic, and educational systems. James Watt (1736–1819), he suggested, had been moved to invent the steam engine because inventions were protected by patents and inventors were rewarded with profits and honors. Fukuzawa argued further that Western systems required political freedoms and a citizenry with a spirit of independence. Fukuzawa's writings became immensely influential after the Restoration, eventually sparking the "Civilization and Enlightenment Movement" of the 1870s. (See Document, "A Japanese View of the Inventiveness of the West.")

Building the Meiji State (1868–1890)

Most attempts by non-Western nations to build modern states occurred during the twentieth century; the idea of a "developing nation" did not exist in the mid–nineteenth century. Yet Japan after the 1868 **Meiji Restoration** was just such a nation. (The years from 1868 to 1912 are referred to as the "Meiji period," after the era name that accompanied the accession of the new emperor.) It was committed to progress, by which it meant achieving wealth and power of the kind Western industrial nations possessed. In retrospect, we are aware that Japan had important assets that contributed to the attainment of these goals. But it also had liabilities, and they loomed large in the eyes of the Meiji leaders. There was no blueprint for progress. The government faced tough decisions as it advanced by trial and error. It also demanded that the Japanese people make sacrifices for the sake of the future.

The announcement of the restoration of rule by an emperor was made on January 3, 1868. In the battles that followed, Chōshū and Satsuma troops defeated those of the *bakufu*. In May, Edo surrendered to the imperial forces. Within months Edo Castle became the imperial palace and Edo was renamed Tokyo, the "eastern capital." A year later the last *bakufu* holdouts surrendered in Hokkaido. At the start the Meiji government was only a small group of samurai leaders from Chōshū, Satsuma, and a few other domains. These men controlled the youthful emperor through a handful of Kyoto nobles. They controlled their own domains through domain officials and the samurai commanders of the domain armies. They have been described, only half humorously, as twelve bureaucrats in search of a bureaucracy. But such a description belittles the vision with which they defined the goals of the new government.

CENTRALIZATION OF POWER

Their immediate goal was to centralize political power. What this entailed, concretely, was using the leverage of the Chōshū and Satsuma domain armies to abolish the domains. This was a ticklish operation in that many in these armies were loyal to their domain rather than to the young samurai leaders, who had left the domains to form the new central government. Nevertheless, by 1871 the young leaders had replaced the domains with prefectures controlled by the Tokyo government. To ensure a complete break with the past, each new pre-

▲ **Japan's first foreign mission**, headed by Prince Iwakura, Ambassador Extraordinary and Plenipotentiary, leaving Yokohama for the United States and Europe on December 23, 1871.
Scala/Art Resource, N.Y.

fectural governor was chosen from samurai of other regions. The first governor of the Chōshū area, for example, was a samurai of a former Tokugawa domain.

Having centralized political authority, in 1871 about half of the most important Meiji leaders went abroad for a year and a half—ostensibly to revise the unequal treaties but in fact to study the West. They traveled in the United States and Europe visiting parliaments, schools, and factories. On returning to Japan in 1872 they discovered that the stay-at-home officials were planning war with Korea. They quickly quashed the plan, insisting that the highest priority be given to domestic development. (See Document, "On Wives and Concubines.")

The second task of the Meiji leaders was to stabilize government revenues, which fluctuated with the price of rice since the land tax was collected mostly in grain. The government converted the grain tax to a money tax, shifting the burden of fluctuations onto the shoulders of the nation's farmers. But a third of the revenues still went to pay for samurai stipends, so in 1873 the government raised a conscript army and subsequently abolished the samurai class. The samurai were paid off in government bonds; but as the bonds fell during the inflation of the 1870s, most former samurai became impoverished. What had begun as a reform of government finance ended as a social revolution.

Some samurai rebelled. Those in the domains that had carried out the Restoration were particularly indignant at their treatment. The last and greatest uprising, in 1877 was by Satsuma samurai led by Saigō Takamori (1827–1877), who had broken with the government over the issue of Korea. When the uprising was suppressed in 1878, the Meiji government became militarily secure.

POLITICAL PARTIES

Other samurai opposed the government by forming political parties and campaigning for popular rights, elections, and a constitution. They drew heavily on liberal Western models that had become widely known through the "Civilization-and-Enlightenment" movement. National assemblies, they argued, were the means by which advanced societies tapped the energies of their peoples; parties in a national assembly would unite the emperor and the people, thereby curbing the arbitrary actions of the Satsuma-Chōshū clique. Samurai were the mainstay of the early party movement, despite its doctrines proclaiming all classes to be equal. During the mid-1870s there was some movement between the parties and the rebellions, but as the rebellions ended, the people's rights movement became more stable.

Then, with the government's formation of prefectural assemblies in 1878, what had been in fact unofficial pressure groups became true political parties. Many farmers joined, wanting their taxes cut; the poor joined too, hoping to improve their condition. The parties were given another boost after a political crisis in 1881, when the government promised a constitution and a national assembly within ten years. During the 1880s the parties had ups and downs. When poorer peasants rebelled, the parties temporarily dissolved to dissociate themselves from the uprisings. But as the date for national elections approached, the parties regrouped, regained strength, and the ties between party notables and local men of influence grew closer.

THE CONSTITUTION

The government viewed the party movement with distaste but was unsure how to counter it. The promise of a constitution had been one tactic. Itō Hirobumi (1841–1909), originally from Chōshū, went abroad to shop for a constitution that would serve the needs of the Meiji government. He found principles to his liking in Germany and brought home a German jurist to help adapt the conservative Prussian constitution of 1850 to Japanese uses. As promulgated in 1889, the Meiji Constitution was notable for the extensive powers granted to the emperor and for the severely limited powers it granted to the lower house in the **Diet** (the English term for Japan's bicameral national assembly).

The emperor was sovereign. According to the constitution, he was "sacred and inviolable." In Itō's commentaries the sacredness was defined in Shinto terms. As in Prussia, the emperor was given direct command of the armed forces. Yamagata Aritomo (1838–1922) had set up a German-type general staff system in 1878. The emperor had the right to name the prime minister and to appoint the cabinet. He could dissolve the lower house of the Diet and issue imperial ordinances when the Diet was not in session. The Imperial Household Ministry, which was outside the cabinet, administered the great wealth given to the imperial family during the 1880s—so that the emperor would never have to ask the Diet for funds. In every case, it was intended and understood that the Meiji leaders would act for the emperor in all of these matters. Finally, the constitution itself was presented as a gift from the emperor to his subjects.

The lower house of the Diet, in contrast, was given the authority only to approve budgets and pass laws. Both of these powers were hedged. The constitution stipulated that the previous year's budget would remain in effect if a new budget was not approved. The appointive House of Peers, the upper house of the Diet, had to approve any bill to become law. Furthermore, to ensure that the parties themselves would represent the stable and responsible elements of Japanese society, the vote was given only to adult males paying fifteen yen or more in taxes. In 1890 this was about 5 percent of the adult male population. In short, Itō had never intended to create a parliamentary system with full deliberative powers. What he

▲ **The Promulgation of the Meiji Constitution in 1889.** The emperor standing under the canopy, was declared "sacred and inviolable." Seated on the throne, at the left, is the empress.
Shosai Ginko (Japanese, act. 1874–1897). View of the Issuance of the State Constitution in the State Chamber of the New Imperial Palace, March 2, 1889 (Meiji 22), Ink and color on paper, 14 1/8 × 28 3/8 in. "The Metropolitan Museum of Art, Gift of Lincoln Kirstein, 1959 (JP3233-3235) Photograph © The Metropolitan Museum of Art.

devised was a constitutional system that included a parliament as one of its parts.

The government also created institutions designed to limit the future influence of the political parties. In 1884 it created a new nobility, honorable and conservative, with which to stock the future House of Peers. The nobility was composed of ex-nobles and the Meiji leaders themselves. Itō, born a lowly foot soldier in Chōshū, began in the new nobility as a count and ended as a prince. In 1885 he established a cabinet system and became the first prime minister, followed by Kuroda Kiyotaka (1840–1900) of Satsuma, and then by Yamagata Aritomo of Chōshū. In 1887 Itō established a privy council, with himself as its head, to approve the constitution he had written. In 1888 new laws and civil service examinations were instituted to insulate the imperial bureaucracy from the tawdry concerns of political parties. By this time the bureaucracy, which had begun as a loose collection of men of ability and of their protégés, had become highly systematized. Detailed administrative laws defined their functions and governed their behavior. They were well paid. In 1890 there were 24,000 officials; by 1908 there were 72,000.

Growth of a Modern Economy

The late Tokugawa economy was backward and not markedly different from the economies of other East Asian countries. Almost 80 percent of the population lived in the countryside at close to a subsistence level. Sophisticated but labor-intensive paddy-field techniques were used in farming. Taxes were high, as much as 35 percent of the product, and two thirds of the land tax was paid in kind. That is to say, money had only partially penetrated the rural economy. Japan had not developed factory production with machinery, steam power, or large accumulations of capital.

Early Meiji reforms unshackled the late Tokugawa economy. Occupations were freed, which meant that farmers could trade and samurai could farm. Barriers on roads were abolished, as were the monopolistic guilds that had restricted access to central markets. The abolition of domains threw open regional economies that had been partially self-enclosed. Most large merchant houses were too closely tied to daimyo finances and went bankrupt, but there rose a groundswell of new commercial ventures and of traditional agriculturally based industries.

Silk was the wonder crop. The government introduced mechanical reeling, enabling Japan to win markets previously held by the hand-reeled silk of China. About two thirds of Japanese silk production was exported, and not until the 1930s did cotton textiles become more important. Silk production rose from 2.3 million pounds in the post-Restoration era to 93 million in 1929.

A parallel unshackling occurred on the land. The land tax reform of the 1870s, although initially lowering taxes only slightly, created a powerful incentive for growth by giving farmers a clear title to their land and by fixing the tax in money. The freedom to buy and sell land led to a rise in tenancy from an estimated 25 percent in 1868 to about 44 percent at the turn of the century. Progressive landlords bought fertilizer and farm equipment. Rice production rose from 149 million bushels a year during 1880–1884 to 316 million during 1935–1937. More food, combined with a drop in the death rate—the result of better hygiene—led to population growth: from about 30 million in 1868 to 45 million in 1900 to 73 million in 1940. Because the farm population remained constant, the extra hands were available for factory and other urban jobs.

FIRST PHASE: MODEL INDUSTRIES

The development of modern industries was the government's greatest concern. They developed in four phases. The first, which lasted until 1881, was the era of model industries. With military strength a goal, the Meiji government expanded the arsenals and the shipyards that it had inherited from the Tokugawa. It also built telegraph lines, made a start on railroads, developed coal and copper mines, and established factories for textiles, cement, glass, tools, and other products. Every new industry begun during the 1870s was the work of the government; many were initiated by the Ministry of Industry, set up in 1870 under Itō. The quantitative output of these early industries was insignificant, however. Essentially they were pilot-plant operations that doubled as "schools" for technologists and labor.

Just as important to economic development was a variety of other new institutions such as banks, post offices, ports, roads, commercial laws, a system of primary and secondary schools, and a government university. They were patterned

◀ **Tomioka Spinning Mill.**
Begun by the government in 1870 as a model factory to show private entrepreneurs how to mechanize a traditional industry. It employed 210 women workers— many samurai daughters—and a French engineer. When its work was done, it was sold off to Mitsui in 1893.
Bettmann/Corbis.

after European and American examples, although the pattern was often altered to fit Japan's needs. For example, Tokyo Imperial University had a faculty of agriculture earlier than any university in Europe.

SECOND PHASE: 1880S–1890S

More substantial growth in the modern sector took place during the 1880s and 1890s. It was marked by the appearance of what would later become the great industrial combines known as *zaibatsu*. Accumulating capital was the greatest problem for would-be entrepreneurs. Iwasaki Yatarō (1834–1885) used political connections. After the Restoration he gained control of the ships that he had managed as a samurai official for the Tosa domain. He next acquired government ships that had been used to transport troops during the 1874 Taiwan Expedition and the 1877 Satsuma Rebellion. From these beginnings he built a shipping line to compete with foreign companies, started a bank, and invested in the enterprises that later became the Mitsubishi combine.

Shibusawa Eiichi (1840–1931) was another maverick entrepreneur. Born into a peasant family that made indigo dye, he became a merchant, joined the pro-emperor movement, then switched sides and became a retainer of the last shogun. He spent two years in France, and after 1868 entered the Finance Ministry. In 1873 he made the so-called heavenly descent from government to private business. Founding the First Bank, he showed a talent for beginning new industries with other people's money. His initial success was the Osaka Cotton Spinning Mill, established as Japan's first joint stock company in 1882. The investors profited hugely, and money poured in to found new mills; by 1896 the production of yarn had reached 17 million pounds, and by 1913 it was over ten times that amount. After the turn of the century cotton cloth replaced yarn as the focus of growth: Production rose more than 100-fold, from 22 million square yards in 1900 to 2,710 million in 1936.

Another area of growth was railroads. Before railroads, the bulk of Japan's commerce was carried by coastal shipping. It cost as much during the early Meiji period to transport goods

---

DOCUMENT   On Wives and Concubines

During the 1870s and 1880s leading Japanese thinkers introduced a wide range of Western ideas into their country. Among them were freedom and equality as rights inherent in human nature. Debating the questions of equality in marriage and the rights of wives, intellectuals voiced a radical criticism of concubinage and prostitution. As a consequence of these debates, laws were passed during the eighties and nineties that strengthened the legal status of wives. Mori Arinori (1847–1889), who had studied in the United States and England, wrote the following passage in 1874. He later became a diplomat and, between 1885 and 1889, the minister of education.

♦ Think of comparable instances in American or European history where new ideas led to dramatic social change? How long did the changes last and how deeply rooted did they become?

The relation between man and wife is the fundamental of human morals. The moral path will be achieved by establishing this fundamental, and the country will only be firmly based if the moral path is realized. When people marry, rights and obligations emerge between them so that neither can take advantage of the other.

There have hitherto been a variety of marriage practices [in our country] ... Sometimes there may be one or even several concubines in addition to the wife, and sometimes a concubine may become the wife. Sometimes the wife and the concubines live in the same establishment. Sometimes they are separated, and the concubine is the favored one while the wife is neglected ...

Taking a concubine is by arbitrary decision of the man and with acquiescence of the concubine's family. The arrangement, known as ukedashi, is made by paying money to the family of the concubine. This means, in other words, that concubines are bought with money. Since concubines are generally geisha and prostitutes patronized by rich men and nobles, many descendants in the rich and noble houses are the children of bought women. Even though the wife is superior to the concubine in households where they live together, there is commonly jealousy and hatred between them because the husband generally favors the concubine. Therefore, there are numerous instances when, the wife and the concubines being scattered in separate establishments, the husband repairs to the abode of the one with whom he is infatuated and wilfully resorts to scandalous conduct ...

Thus, I have here explained that our country has not yet established the fundamental of human morality, and I hope later to discuss how this situation injures our customs and obstructs enlightenment.

From Meiroku Zasshi, *Journal of the Japanese Enlightenment* trans. and with introduction by William Reynolds Braisted, assisted by Adachi Yasushi and Kikuchi Yūji (Cambridge, MA: Harvard University Press, 1976), pp. 104–105. © 1976 by the President and Fellows of Harvard College. Reprinted by permission of Harvard University Press.

DOCUMENT | A Japanese View of the Inventiveness of the West

Serious Japanese thinkers reacted to their country's weakness with proposals to adopt Western science and industry. But the "Civilization and Enlightenment Movement" of the 1870s had its lighter side as well. In 1871 the novelist Kanagaki Robun wrote a satire about a man with an umbrella, a watch, and eau de cologne on his hair, eating with a friend in a new beef restaurant. Before the Restoration, Buddhism had banned beef eating as a defilement. The comic hero, however, wonders, "Why we in Japan haven't eaten such a clean thing before." He then goes on to rhapsodize about Western inventions. See also "Liang Qichao Urges the Chinese to Reform" earlier in this chapter.

♦ What do pickled onions have to do with the marvels of Western technology?

In the West they're free of superstitions. There it's the custom to do everything scientifically, and that's why they've invented amazing things like the steamship and the steam engine. Did you know that they engrave the plates for printing newspapers with telegraphic needles? And that they bring down wind from the sky with balloons? Aren't they wonderful inventions! Of course, there are good reasons behind these inventions. If you look at a map of the world you'll see some countries marked "tropical," which means that's where the sun shines closest. The people in those countries are all burnt black by the sun. The king of that part of the world tried all kinds of schemes before he hit on what is called a balloon. That's a big round bag they fill with air high up in the sky. They bring the bag down and open it, causing the cooling air inside the bag to spread out all over the country. That's a great invention. On the other hand, in Russia, which is a cold country where the snow falls even in summer and the ice is so thick that people can't move, they invented the steam engine. You've got to admire them for it. I understand that they modeled the steam engine after the flaming chariot of hell, but anyway, what they do is to load a crowd of people on a wagon and light a fire in a pipe underneath. They keep feeding the fire inside the pipe with coal, so that the people riding on top can travel a great distance completely oblivious to the cold. Those people in the West can think up inventions like that, one after the other ... You say you must be going? Well, goodbye. Waitress! Another small bottle of *sake*. And some pickled onions to go with it!

From *Modern Japanese Literature*, D. Keene, ed. and trans. pp. 32–33. Copyright © 1956 Grove Press. Reprinted by permission of Grove/Atlantic, Inc.

fifty miles overland as it did to ship them to Europe. Railroads gave Japan an internal circulatory system, opening up hitherto isolated regions. In 1872 Japan had 18 miles of track; in 1894, 2,100 miles; and in 1934, 14,500 miles.

Cotton textiles and railroads were followed during the 1890s by cement, bricks, matches, glass, beer, chemicals, and other private industries. One can only admire the foresight and vigor of the bold entrepreneurs who pioneered in these industries. At the same time, the role of government in creating a favorable climate for growth should not be forgotten: The society and the polity were stable, the yen was sound, capital was safe, and taxes on industry were low. In every respect, the conditions enjoyed by Japan's budding entrepreneurs differed from those of China.

THIRD PHASE: 1905–1929

The economy continued to grow after the Russo-Japanese War in 1905 and spurted ahead during World War I. Light industries and textiles were central, but iron and steel, shipping, coal mining, electrical power, and chemicals also grew. An economic slump followed the war, and the economy grew slowly during the twenties. One factor was renewed competition from a Europe at peace; another was the great earthquake that destroyed Tokyo in 1923. Tokyo was rebuilt with loans, but they led to inflation. Agricultural productivity also leveled off during the twenties: It became cheaper to import foodstuffs from the newly acquired colonies of Taiwan and Korea than to invest in new agricultural technology at home.

By the twenties Japanese society, especially in the cities, was becoming modern. The Japanese ate better, were healthier, and lived longer. Personal savings rose with the standard of living. Urban workers opened postal saving accounts, drank beer, went to movies, and read newspapers. In 1890 31 percent of girls and 64 percent of boys went to primary schools; by 1905 the figures were 90 and 96 percent; and by 1925 primary school education was universal. Japan had done what no other non-Western nation had even attempted: It had achieved universal literacy. During the twenties, the thirties, and the war years increasing numbers of primary school graduates went on to middle and higher schools, or entered the new technical colleges. Nevertheless, an enormous cultural and social gap remained between the majority who had only a primary school education and the 3 percent who attended university. The gap would prove to be a basic weakness in the political democracy of the twenties.

It should also be noted that despite overall improvements in the condition of the Japanese, the human costs of growth were sometimes high. (See Document, "Natsume Sōseki on the Costs of Rapid Modernization.") Because textiles played a large role in the early phase of growth, well into the twentieth century more than half of the industrial labor force was women. They went to the mills after leaving primary school and returned to their villages before marrying. "Neither silk-reeling maids nor slops are kept for long," went the words of one song. Their working hours were long, their dormitories crowded, and their movements restricted. "Like the money in my employment contract, I remain sealed away," was another verse. Some contracted tuberculosis, the plague of late-nineteenth and early-twentieth-century Japan, and were sent back to their villages to die. The following verse bluntly captures the public attitude toward women factory workers:

> If a woman working in an office is a willow,
> A poetess is a violet,
> And a female teacher is an orchid,
> Then a factory woman is a vegetable gourd.[2]

FOURTH PHASE: DEPRESSION AND RECOVERY

A Japanese bank crisis in 1927, followed by the worldwide Great Depression in 1929, plunged Japan into unemployment and suffering. The distress was particularly acute in the rice-producing regions of the northeast. The political consequences of the Depression years were far-reaching. Yet most of Japan had recovered by 1933 and even the northeast by 1935, more rapidly than any other industrial nation.

An export boom and military procurements at home fueled the recovery. During the 1930s the production of pig iron, raw steel, and chemicals doubled. Japan could construct complete electric-power stations and became self-sufficient in machine tools and scientific instruments. Shipbuilding forged ahead; by 1937 Japan had a merchant fleet of 4.5 million tons, the third largest and certainly the newest in the world. Despite continued growth in cotton cloth during the 1930s, textiles slipped relative to the products of heavy industry. The quality of Japan's manufacturers also rose. The outcry in the West against Japanese exports at this time was not so much because of volume—a modest 3.6 percent of world exports in 1936—but because for the first time Japanese products had become competitive in terms of quality.

The Politics of Imperial Japan (1890–1945)

Parliaments began in the West and have functioned better there than in the rest of the world. For Japan to establish a constitution during the nineteenth century was a bold experiment. Even so cautious a constitution as that of Meiji in that age had

[2] E. Patricia Tsurumi, "Whose History Is It Anyway? And Other Questions Historians Should Be Asking," in *Japan Review* (1995) 6:17–38, p. 21. By permission of the International Research Center for Japanese Studies.

no precedent outside the West; most Western observers were skeptical of its chances for success. How are we now, in retrospect, to view the Japanese political experience after 1890?

One view is that because the Japanese were not ready for constitutional government, the militarism of the thirties was inevitable. In terms of an ideal democracy, Japanese society certainly had many weaknesses: a small middle class, weak trade unions, an independent military under the emperor, a strong emperor-centered nationalism, and so on. Still these weaknesses, others note, did not prevent the Diet from growing in importance, nor did they block the transfer of power from the bureaucratic Meiji leaders to political party leaders. The transfer fell short of full parliamentary government. Still, had it not been derailed by the Great Depression and other events, the advance toward parliamentary government might well have continued.

FROM CONFRONTATION TO THE FOUNDING OF THE SEIYŪKAI (1890–1900)

Two kinds of political history can be written about Japan under the Meiji Constitution. One would describe what the government did. It would include the drawing up of budgets, the building of modern military forces, the prosecution of wars, the formation of a banking system, the establishment of new universities, the reform of the tax system, and so on—all of those activities that characterize a modernizing state. The other kind of history would deal with politics, the struggles between different groups and bodies for power.

In 1890 the Meiji leaders—sometimes called *oligarchs*, the few who rule—were concerned with nation building, not politics. They saw the cabinet as "transcendental," as serving the emperor and nation above the ruck of partisan interests. They viewed the political parties as noisy, ineffective, and irresponsible. They saw the lower house of the Diet as a safety valve, a place to let off steam without interfering in the government's serious work of building a new Japan. But the oligarchs had miscalculated: The authority of the lower house to approve or turn down the budget made that body more powerful than they had intended. This drew the oligarchs, willy-nilly, into the political struggles they had hoped to avoid.

The first act of the parties in the new 1890 Diet was to slash the government's budget. Prime Minister Yamagata was furious but had to make concessions to get part of the cut restored. This pattern of applying pressure to the annual budget continued for almost a decade. Rising costs meant that the previous year's budget was never enough, and although the government tried to intimidate and bribe the parties, it failed. It even formed a government party and tried to win elections by enlisting the police and local officials for campaign support. The opposing political parties nevertheless maintained their control of the lower house. They were well-organized in the prefectures, where assemblies had begun in 1878, and

DOCUMENT | Natsume Sōseki on the Costs of Rapid Modernization

Natsume Sōseki (1867–1916) was one of the earliest of a series of great novelists to create a new literature in Japan after the turn of the century. Sōseki could often be humorous. One of his early works, I Am a Cat, looks at a Tokyo household from a feline perspective. He advocated ethical individualism as superior to state morality. He also wrote of human isolation in a changing society and of the dark side of human nature.

◆ What were the costs of Japan's rapid modernization? Was the uneasiness experienced by only a few advanced thinkers, or did it cut across the society? Was it different from alienation in the modern West?

The Civilization of Modern Japan

Let us set aside the question of the bragging about the new teachings acquired from the West, which are only superficially mastered. Let us suppose that in forty or fifty years after the Restoration, by the power of education, by really applying ourselves to study, we can move from teaching A to teaching B and even advance to C—without the slightest vulgar fame-seeking, without the slightest sense of vainglory. Let us further suppose that we pass, in a natural orderly fashion, from stage to stage and that we ultimately attain the extreme of differentiation in our internally developed enlightenment that the West attained after more than a hundred years. If, then, by our physical and mental exertions, and by ignoring the difficulties and suffering involved in our precipitous advance, we end by passing through, in merely one-half the time it took the more prosperous Westerners to reach their stage of specialization, to our stage of internally developed enlightenment, the consequences will be serious indeed. At the same time we will be able to boast of this fantastic acquisition of knowledge, the inevitable result will be a nervous collapse from which we will not be able to recover.

Passers-by

This is what your brother said. He suffers because nothing he does appears to him as either an end or a means. He is perpetually uneasy and cannot relax. He cannot sleep and so gets out of bed. But when he is awake, he cannot stay still, so he begins to walk. As he walks, he finds that he has to begin running. Once he has begun running, he cannot stop. To have to keep on running is bad enough, but he feels compelled to increase his speed with every step he takes. When he imagines what the end of all this will be, he is so frightened that he breaks out in a cold sweat. And the fear becomes unbearable.

I was surprised when I heard your brother's explanation. I myself have never experienced uneasiness of this kind. And so, though I could comprehend what he was saying, I could feel no sympathy for him. I was like a man who tries to imagine what it is like to have a splitting headache though he has never had one. I tried to think for a while. And my wandering mind hit upon this thing called "man's fate;" it was a rather vague concept in my mind, but I was happy to have found something consoling to say to your brother.

"This uneasiness of yours is no more than the uneasiness that all men experience. All you have to do is to realize that there is no need for you alone to worry so much about it. What I mean to say is that it is our fate to wander blindly through life."

Not only were my words vague in meaning but they lacked sincerity. Your brother gave me one shrewd, contemptuous glance; that was all my remarks deserved. He then said: "You know, our uneasiness comes from this thing called scientific progress. Science does not know where to stop and does not permit us to stop either. From walking to rickshaws, from rickshaws to horsedrawn cabs, from cabs to trains, from trains to automobiles, from automobiles to airships, from airships to airplanes—when will we ever be allowed to stop and rest? Where will it finally take us? It is really frightening."

"Yes, it is frightening," I said.

Your brother smiled. "You say so, but you don't really mean it. You aren't really frightened. This fear that you say you feel, it is only of the theoretical kind. My fear is different from yours. I feel in my heart. It is an alive, pulsating kind of fear."

First selection from M. Kosaka, *Japanese Thought in the Meiji Era.* Copyright © 1958 Pan-Pacific Press, pp. 447–448; second selection from E. McClellan, *Two Japanese Novelists: Soseki and Toson* (Chicago: University of Chicago Press, 1974) pp. 49–50.

---

enjoyed the support of the voters, mostly well-to-do landowners, who opposed the heavy land tax.

Unable either to coerce or defeat the opposing parties, and determined that his Meiji Constitution not fail, in 1900 Itō Hirobumi formed a new party. The party was called the Rikken Seiyūkai, or "Friends of Constitutional Government." The Seiyūkai was composed of ex-bureaucrats associated with Itō and politicians from the Liberal Party that a Tosa samurai, Itagaki Taisuke (1837–1919), had formed in 1881. For most of the next twenty years it was the most important party in Japan, providing parliamentary support for successive governments through its control of the lower house. This arrangement was satisfactory to both sides: Itō and subsequent prime ministers got the Diet support necessary for the government to function smoothly. The party politicians got cabinet posts and pork barrel legislation with which to reward their supporters. Itō had made the constitution work, but at the cost of relinquishing transcendental cabinets.

THE GOLDEN YEARS OF MEIJI

The years before and after the turn of the century represented the culmination of what the government had striven for since 1868. Economic development was under way. The unequal treaties were revised in two steps: Japan got rid of extraterritoriality in 1899 (by a treaty signed in 1894) and regained control of its own tariffs in 1911. However, it was events abroad that won Japan recognition as a world power.

The first event was a war with China in 1894–1895 over conflicting interests in Korea. From its victory Japan secured Taiwan, the Pescadores Islands, the Kwantung Peninsula in southern Manchuria, an indemnity, and a treaty giving it the same privileges in China as those enjoyed by the Western powers

(see Map 28–3). Russia, however, had its own expansionist plans and, obtaining French and German support, forced Japan to give up the Kwantung Peninsula, which included Port Arthur. Three years later, Russia took Kwantung for itself.

The second event was Japan's participation in 1900 in the international force that relieved the Boxers' siege of the foreign legations in Beijing. The Japanese troops were notable for their numbers and discipline.

The third event was the Anglo-Japanese Alliance of 1902. For Britain this alliance ensured Japanese support for its East Asian interests and warded off the likelihood of a Russo-Japanese agreement over spheres of influence in northeast Asia. For Japan the alliance meant it could fight Russia without fear that a third party would intervene.

MAP 28–3 Formation of the Japanese Empire.   The Japanese Empire grew in three stages: the Sino-Japanese War of 1894–1895, the Russo-Japanese War of 1904–1905, and Japanese conquests in Manchuria and nothern China after 1931.

▲ **Russo-Japanese War.** Japanese soldiers with flag and bayonets charge across a smoky field to engage Russian troops in the 1904–1905 Russo-Japanese War. Victory over Russia gave Japan Korea and a new international standing. The popularity of postcards, such as this one, reflected the new nationalism of Japan. Corbis-Bettmann.

The fourth event was the war with Russia that began in 1904, when Japanese torpedo boats launched a surprise attack on the Russian fleet at Port Arthur. On land, Japanese armies drove the Russians from their railway zones in Manchuria and seized Mukden in March 1905. The Russians sent their Baltic fleet to join the battle, but it was annihilated by Admiral Tōgō (1847–1934) at Tsushima Straits. After months of war, both countries were worn out; and on the home front, Russia was plagued by revolution. President Theodore Roosevelt (1858–1919) proposed a peace conference at Portsmouth, New Hampshire. The resulting treaty gave Japan the Russian lease on the southern portion of the Liaotung Peninsula (which it called the Kwantung Peninsula), the Russian railway in south Manchuria, the southern half of Sakhalin, and a recognition of Japan's "paramount interest" in Korea, which was annexed in 1910.

It is ironic that Japan, a country still not free of the system of unequal treaties, should itself have joined the imperialist scramble for colonies. Neither Japanese tradition, which had rarely looked to foreign expansion, nor Japan's economy, which was just beginning to build its modern industries and could not export capital, explains the desire for colonies. The explanation is simpler: Japan wanted equality with the great Western powers, and military power and colonies were the best credentials. Enthusiasm for empire was shared alike by political party leaders, most liberal thinkers, and conservative leaders.

RISE OF THE PARTIES TO POWER

The founding of the Seiyūkai by Itō in 1900 ended a decade of confrontation between the Diet and the government. The aging oligarch Itō soon found intolerable the day-to-day experience of dealing with party politicians, who, unlike the bureaucrats, neither obeyed him nor paid him the respect that he thought his due. He relinquished the presidency of the party to the noble Saionji Kinmochi (1849–1940) in 1903. Saionji also found it too much to bear and passed the post to Hara Takashi (1856–1921) in 1914. With Hara, the office found the man.

Hara was an outsider. Born a generation after the founding fathers of the Meiji state and in a politically unimportant northeastern domain, he began his political career as a newspaper reporter. He then entered the Foreign Office, eventually becoming ambassador to Korea, and then, in turn, an editor, a bank official, a company president, and a Diet member. He helped Itō to found the Seiyūkai. The most able politician in Japan, he was painstaking, patient, paternalistic, and perspicacious. His goals for Japan centered on the expansion of national wealth and power and were no different from those of Itō or Yamagata. But he felt that they should be achieved by party government, not oligarchic rule, and worked unceasingly to expand the power of his party. The years between 1905 and 1921 were marked by the struggle between these two alternative conceptions of government.

The struggle can be represented as a rising curve of party strength and a descending curve of oligarchic influence. The rising curve had two vectors: a buildup of the Seiyūkai party machine that enabled it to win elections and maintain itself as the majority (or plurality) party in the Diet, and the strengthening of the Diet vis-à-vis other elites within the government in Tokyo. For the former, Hara obtained campaign funds from industrialists and other moneyed interests. He also promoted pork barrel legislation in the Diet: Local constituencies that supported Seiyūkai candidates got new schools, bridges, dams, roads, or even railroad lines. Seiyūkai politicians established ties with local notables, who brokered the votes of their communities. When serving as home minister, Hara was even willing to call on the police and local officials to aid Seiyūkai election campaigns.

In co-opting other governmental elites, the Seiyūkai had mixed success. The party steadily increased its representation in the cabinet. It gained some patronage appointments in the central bureaucracy and in the newly formed colonial bureaucracy, although most bureaucrats remained professionals and resisted the intrusion of outside political appointees. Some career bureaucrats, however, developed working relations with the party and became partly politicized. In the House of Peers, and in the privy council, which ratified treaties, the Seiyūkai fared less well. By and large, these remained independent bodies. The Seiyūkai had no success in penetrating the military services. At most, it exercised some restraints on military budgets in time of peace.

The descending curve of weakening oligarchic control reflected the aging of the "men of Meiji." In 1900 Itō was the last oligarch to become prime minister. From 1901 to 1912 Katsura Tarō (1847–1913), a Chōshū general and Yamagata's protégé, and Saionji, Itō's protégé, took turns in the post. Both had Seiyūkai support. Toward the end of the period Katsura began to resent the fact that he, a grown man, had to go to Yamagata for every important decision. Changes within the elites also weakened the oligarchs. A younger generation of officers in the military services chafed at the continuing domination by the old Satsuma and Chōshū cliques. In the civil bureaucracy younger officials who had graduated from the law faculty of Tokyo Imperial University were achieving positions of responsibility. Proud of their ability, they saw the bureaucracy as an independent service and resisted oligarchic control almost as much as they resisted that of the parties.

The oligarchs did, however, maintain their power to act for the emperor in appointing prime ministers. With the deaths of Itō in 1909 and Yamagata in 1922 this vital function was taken over by Saionji and, later, by ex–prime ministers.

As the rising and descending curves approached each other, the political parties advanced. Several turning points were critical. One came in 1912. When the army's demands for a larger budget were refused, it withdrew its minister, causing Saionji's cabinet to collapse. Katsura formed a new cabinet and tried to govern using imperial decrees in place of Diet support. This infuriated the parties, and even the usually compliant Seiyūkai withdrew its support. Massive popular demonstrations broke out, a movement was organized for the "Protection of the Constitution," and party orators shouted "Destroy the Satsuma-Chōshū cliques" and "Off with Katsura's head." Katsura tried to counter the popular forces aligned against him by forming a second political party, to rival the Seiyūkai. The party became politically important during the 1920s, but Katsura was forced to resign in 1913. The lower house had brought down an oligarchic prime minister.

The curves finally crossed in 1918 when Hara became prime minister. It was the first time a politician who was not a Meiji founding father or a protégé of one had obtained the post. He enacted reforms but did nothing to remedy the parliamentary shortcomings of the Meiji Constitution.

Another development was the wave of liberalism that began during World War I and culminated in the period of party governments from 1924 to 1932. Japan had joined the Allies in World War I and came under the influence of democratic currents of thought from England and America. Scholars discussed revising the Meiji Constitution. Labor unions were organized, at first liberal and often Christian, and later Marxist. A social movement was launched to improve conditions in Japan's industrial slums and to pass social and labor legislation. The Kenseikai, which had been out of power since 1916, grew steadily more liberal and adopted several of the new social causes as its own, such as universal manhood suffrage. When Hara cut the tax qualification for voting from ten to three yen—a considerable extension of the franchise—the Kenseikai criticized the change as insufficient and the Seiyūkai as the perpetrator of class despotism.

During a brief interlude of nonparty cabinets between 1922 and 1924, the Kenseikai launched the Second Movement for the Protection of the Constitution. Liberal factions of the other big party, the Seiyūkai, joined in the movement, and the two parties formed a coalition government in 1924. For the next eight years the presidents of one or the other of the two major parties were appointed as prime ministers.

The cabinets (1924–1926) of Katō Kōmei are considered the peak of parliamentary power in prewar Japan. Born in 1860, Katō graduated from Tokyo Imperial University at the age of twenty-one and entered the Mitsubishi firm. He married the boss's daughter, spent time in England, and joined the Foreign Ministry, becoming foreign minister at forty. For a country that esteemed age, his rise was meteoric. He subsequently became a Diet member, a newspaper president, an ambassador to England, and, from 1914, president of the Kenseikai. Outspoken, cold, and haughty, Katō was widely respected, if not liked. He was an Anglophile who understood and advocated a British model of government. His ministry passed universal manhood suffrage, increased academic appointments to the House of Peers, and cut the military budget from 42 percent in 1922 to 29 percent in 1925. He also enacted social and labor legislation. In effect, he legalized the moderate socialist movement and outlawed revolutionary socialism. Katō's cabinet brought Japan close to a true parliamentary government, which, although not mandated by the Meiji Constitution, had not been banned by it either.

MILITARISM AND WAR (1927–1945)

The future of Japan's parliamentary government seemed assured during the mid-1920s. The economy was growing; society was stable; party leaders were experienced. Japan's international position was secure. By a decade later, however, party leaders had lost the gains of thirty-five years. By 1945 Japan had been defeated in a devastating war and was occupied by foreign troops for the first time in its history. How did this come about?

Put simply, a small shift in the balance of power among the governmental elites established by the Meiji Constitution had produced a major change in Japan's foreign policy. The parties had been the obstreperous elite between 1890 and 1926 and had advanced their influence by forcing the other elites to compromise. From the late 1920s the military became the obstreperous elite and did the same. Beginning in 1932 military men replaced party presidents as prime ministers. In 1937 Japan went to war with China; and by the end of 1941 Japan was allied with Germany and Italy, had clashed with the Soviet Union, and had gone to war with the United States.

From their inception, the military services in Japan had been constructed on different principles from Japan's civilian society. Soldiers were not samurai. The rifle companies of Satsuma and Chōshū had broken decisively with that tradition, and universal conscription had put the new military on a changed footing. But the armed services had their own schools, which inculcated the values of discipline, bravery, loyalty, and obedience. Soldiers saw themselves as the true heirs of those who had founded the modern Japanese state and the true guardians of Japanese tradition. They contrasted their loyalty to the emperor and their concern for all Japanese with the pandering to special interests by the political parties.

The military resented its diminished national stature during the 1920s, when military budgets were cut and the prestige of a military career had declined to the point where officers wore civilian clothes when off base. In particular, the fleet wing of the navy resented the decision by moderate admirals to accept a formula at the London Naval Conference of the Great Powers in 1930 that would weaken Japan's naval strength. But even during the liberal 1920s there had been no change in the constitutional position of the services; the general staffs remained directly responsible to the emperor. With the passing of the Meiji oligarchs, this meant they were responsible to no one but themselves.

A Crisis in Manchuria The new multilateral treaties (the 1921–1922 Washington Conference and the 1930 London Conference) that replaced the earlier system of bilateral treaties (such as the Anglo-Japanese Alliance) recognized the existing colonies of the victors in World War I but opposed new colonial ventures. The Western treaty powers were especially strong in support of the "open door" in China, which in their minds included Manchuria. Japan's position in Manchuria was ambiguous. Because Japan maintained its interests through a tame Chinese warlord, Manchuria was not, strictly speaking, a colony. But because Japan had gained its special position in Manchuria at the cost of 100,000 lives in the 1905 Russo-Japanese War, it saw its claim to Manchuria as similar to that of Western nations and their colonies.

From the late 1920s the Guomindang unification of China and the blossoming of Chinese nationalism threatened Japan's special position. Japanese army units tried to block the march north and murdered the Manchurian warlord when he showed signs of independence. In this crisis the party government in Tokyo equivocated, hoping to preserve a status quo that was crumbling before its eyes. The army saw Manchuria as a buffer between the Soviet Union and the Japanese colony of Korea and was unwilling to make concessions. So in 1931 the army provoked a crisis, took over Manchuria, and proclaimed it an independent state in 1932. When the League of Nations condemned Japan for violating the open door, Japan withdrew from the League in 1933.

The Great Depression Just as the crisis in Manchuria had called into question Japan's place in the international political order, so did the Great Depression cast doubts on the international economic order and on the *zaibatsu*. The *zaibatsu* were seen as rich capitalist profiteers in a country full of suffering and want, as the backers of the "established parties," and as internationalists at a time of rising nationalism.

Rural Japan was especially hard hit by the Depression. The real income of farmers fell by about a third between 1926 and 1931 and recovered only slowly. Our images of the depression in Japan, which may not be representative, come primarily from the northeast, where a crop failure in 1931 led to famine; children turned to begging for food from passing trains, and tenant farmers were forced to eat the inner bark of pine trees or to dig up the roots of wild plants. Urban workers suffered, too. The value of Japanese exports dropped 50 percent between 1929 and 1931. Workers' real income dropped from an index of 100 in 1929 to 69 in 1931. Unemployment rose to 3 million, and many factory workers returned to their villages, adding to the burden on the farm economy. Only the salaried middle class was better off as prices dropped.

As noted earlier, the government acted effectively to counter the depression. Going off the gold standard led to an export boom, and Japan came out of the depression faster than any other nation. By 1936 Japan's heavy industries were growing apace, and real wages were up. The recovery came too late to help the political parties, however; by 1936 political trends that had begun during the worst years of the depression had become irreversible.

The depression galvanized the political left and right. The political left was composed mainly of Socialist moderates who won eight Diet seats in 1928, eighteen in 1936, and thirty-seven in 1937. Supported by unionists and white-collar workers, they would reemerge as an even stronger force after World War II. There was also a radical left, consisting of many little Marxist parties and of the Japanese Communist Party, which had been founded in 1922. Although small and subject to growing governmental repression, the radical parties became influential in intellectual and literary circles during the twenties and thirties.

The Radical Right and the Military   The political right in pre–World War II Japan is difficult to define. Most Japanese, except for a few Marxist or Christian intellectuals, were imbued with an emperor-centered nationalism. The centrist parties were strongly nationalist and only weakly or sporadically liberal. During the 1930s, however, a new array of right-wing organizations went beyond the usual nationalism to challenge the status quo. Civilian ultranationalists used a combination of Shinto myths and Confucian values to attack the Western liberalism that had begun to enter Japan's urban society. Some bureaucrats looked to the example of Nazi Germany and argued for the exclusion of party politicians from government. Bureaucrats could run it better, serving the interests of all of the people. Military officers envisioned a "defense state" guided by themselves. They argued for military expansion and an autarchic colonial empire insulated from the uncertainties of the world economy. Young officers of the revolutionary right advocated "direct action" against the elites of

the parliamentary coalition and called for a second restoration of imperial power.

The last group precipitated political change. On May 15, 1932, junior army and navy officers attacked the Seiyūkai offices, the Bank of Japan, and the Tokyo police headquarters, and murdered Prime Minister Inukai. This attack occurred at the peak of right-wing agitation and the pit of the Depression. In these circumstances Saionji decided that it would be unwise to appoint another party president as the new prime minister; he chose instead a moderate admiral. For the next four years cabinets were led by moderate military men, but with continuing party participation. These cabinets were no more than a holding pattern; they satisfied neither the parties nor the radical young officers.

During 1936 and 1937 Japanese politics were buffeted by crosscurrents but continued to drift to the right. In the election of February 1936 the Minseitō, the successor to the Kenseikai, overturned the Seiyūkai-dominated Diet. It used as its slogan, "What shall it be, parliamentary government or Fascism?" A week later young officers responded with an attempted coup in Tokyo. Leading 1400 soldiers, they attacked government offices, killed cabinet ministers, although missing the prime minister, and occupied the Diet, the Army ministry, and other government buildings. They called for a cabinet made up of military men, but Saionji and other men about the emperor stood firm. The navy also opposed the rebellion, and within three days it was suppressed. It was the last "direct action" by the radical right in prewar Japan. The ringleaders were swiftly tried and executed, and generals sympathetic to them were retired. The officers in charge of the purge within the army were tough-minded technocrats, who throughout the budget cuts of the 1920s had advocated the further modernization of Japan's weaponry. They included General Tōjō Hideki (1884–1948), who would lead Japan into World War II.

Suppression of the radical young officers did not mean a withdrawal of the military from politics. On the contrary, the services interfered more than ever in the formation of cabinets, blocking whenever possible the appointment of party politicians or liberal bureaucrats. As a result, from 1936 on moderate prime ministers gave way to more outspokenly militaristic figures.

Opposition to militarism remained substantial nonetheless. In the 1937 election the prime minister, a former general whose political slogan was "Respect the gods and honor the emperor," tried to win control of the Diet by throwing government support to the Shōwakai, a Nazi-like party. It performed miserably at the polls, gaining only 40 Diet seats, while the two major centrist parties, which had joined in opposition to the government, won 354. The Japanese people were more level-

Tojo Hideki (1884–1948), prime minister at the time of the attack on Pearl Harbor in 1941 and one of the chief figures in the rise of Japanese militarism.
Corbis-Bettmann.

headed than their leaders. But the centrists' victory proved hollow, for, although a peacetime government could not rule without the Diet, the Diet could not oppose a government in wartime; by summer, Japan was at war in China.

The Road to Pearl Harbor   There were three critical junctures between the outbreak of war with China and the World War II campaign in the Pacific. The first was the decision in January 1938 to strike a knockout blow at the Nationalist Party (GMD) government in Nanjing. The war had begun the previous year when a skirmish broke out between Chinese and Japanese troops near Beijing and quickly spread. The Japanese army's leaders themselves disagreed on whether to continue. Many held that the only threat to Japanese interests in Korea and Manchuria was the Soviet Union, and that a long war in China was unnecessary and foolish. But as Japanese armies advanced, others on the general staff argued that the only way to end the war was to convince the Chinese Nationalists that fighting was hopeless. The general staff got its way, and the army quickly occupied most of the cities and railroads of eastern China. When Nationalist leader Jiang Jieshi (1887–1975) refused to give in, a stalemate ensued that lasted until 1945. China was never an active theater in the Pacific War.

The second critical decision was the signing of the **Tripartite Pact** with Germany and Italy in September 1940. Japan had long admired Germany. In 1936 it had joined Germany in the Anti-Comintern Pact directed against international communism. It also wanted an alliance with Germany against the Soviet Union. Germany insisted, however, that any alliance would also have to be directed against the United States and Britain. The Japanese would not agree; the Japanese navy, especially, saw the American Pacific fleet as its only potential enemy and was unwilling to risk being dragged into a German war. After Japanese troops were defeated by Russian troops in an undeclared miniwar from May to September 1939 on the Mongolian border, sentiment rose in favor of an alliance with Germany, but then Germany "betrayed" Japan by signing a nonaggression pact with the Soviet Union. Japan decided to improve its relations with the United States, but America insisted that Japan get out of China. By the late spring of 1940 German victories in Europe—the fall of Britain appeared imminent—again led military leaders in Japan to favor an alliance with Germany.

Japan signed the Tripartite Pact with three objectives in mind: to isolate the United States, to take over the Southeast Asian colonies of the countries defeated by Germany in Europe, and to improve its relations with the Soviet Union through the good offices of Germany. Japan achieved the last objective on its own when it signed a neutrality pact with the Soviet Union in April 1941. Two months later, Germany attacked the Soviet Union without consulting its ally Japan. It compounded this second "betrayal" by asking Japan to attack the Soviet Union in the east. Japan waited and watched. When the German advance was stopped short of Moscow, Japan decided to honor the neutrality pact and turn south. This decision marked, in effect, the end of Japan's participation in the Axis. Thereafter, it fought its own war in Asia. Yet instead of deflecting American criticism as intended, the Tripartite Pact, by linking Japan to Germany, led to a hardening of America's position on China.

The third and fatal decision was to go to war with the United States. In June 1940, following Germany's defeat of France, Japanese troops had moved into northern French Indochina. The United States retaliated by limiting strategic exports to Japan. When Japanese troops took southern Indochina in July 1941, the United States embargoed all exports to Japan; they cut Japanese oil imports by 90 percent, producing the "crisis of the dwindling stockpile." The navy's general staff warned that oil reserves would last only two years; after that the navy would lose its capability to fight. Its general staff pressed for the capture of the oil-rich Dutch East Indies. But it was too dangerous to move against Dutch and British colonies in Southeast Asia with the United States on its flank in the Philippines. The navy, therefore, planned a preemptive strike against the United States, and on December 7, 1941, it bombed Pearl Harbor. The Japanese decision for war wagered Japan's land-based air power, shorter supply lines, and what it saw as greater will power against American productivity. At the Imperial Conference where the all-or-nothing decision was taken, the navy's chief of staff compared the war with the United States to a dangerous operation that might save the life of a critically ill patient. In the end, of course, despite stunning initial victories, the war left Japan defeated and in ruins.

Japanese Militarism and German Nazism

Some of the salient features of Japanese militarism afford an interesting comparison with Nazi Germany. Both countries were late developers with elitist, academic bureaucracies and strong military traditions. Both had patriarchal family systems. The parliamentary systems of both were less well rooted than those of England, France, or the United States. Stricken by the Great Depression, both sought a solution in territorial expansion, justifying it in terms of being have-not nations. Both persecuted Socialists and then liberals. Both were modern enough in their military services, schools, governments, and communications to implement authoritarian regimes, but their values were not sufficiently modern or democratic to resist antiparliamentary forces.

The differences between the two countries are also striking. Despite the gap between its small educated elite and the rest of the population with only a middle-school education, and despite the cultural split between the more traditional rural areas and the Westernized cities, Japan was more homogeneous than Germany. It had no Catholic-Protestant split. It had no *Junker* class, nor was its socialist movement a serious contender for political power. The political process during the 1930s was also different. In Germany parliament ruled, so that to come to power the Nazis had to win an election. In this they were helped by the combination of the Great Depression and a runaway inflation that destroyed the German middle class and the centrist parties along with it. In Japan's constitutional system, the Diet was weaker. Control of the government was taken away from the Seiyūkai and Minseitō even while they continued to win elections. They remained strong at the polls partly because Japan did not suffer from inflation and the depression did not decimate its middle class.

The process by which the two countries went to war was also different. In Germany the Nazis rose as a mass party, created a totalitarian state, and then made war. The authority of the Nazi Party lasted until Hitler died in a Berlin bunker. In Japan there was neither a mass party nor a single group of leaders in continuous control of the government. The spiritual mobilization of the Japanese population, the implementation of controls over industry, and the formation of a nationalism so intense that university students could be mobilized as suicide (*kamikaze*) pilots all followed the outbreak of hostilities. In Japan it was not the totalitarian state that made war as much as it was war that made the state totalitarian.

The Allies depicted General Tōjō, the prime minister at the outbreak of war, as the Japanese Hitler. Yet when American planes began to bomb Japan in 1944, he was removed from office by the elder statesmen close to the emperor and succeeded by increasingly moderate prime ministers. The military, to be sure, continued to prosecute the war. Even after the devastation of the atomic bombs, the Imperial Conference on August 14, 1945, was divided three to three over the Allied ultimatum demanding unconditional surrender. The emperor broke the deadlock, saying that the unendurable must be endured. It was the only important decision that he had ever been allowed to make.

CHRONOLOGY

Modern Japan

Overthrow of Tokugawa Bakufu

1853–1854	Perry obtains Treaty of Friendship
1858	*Bakufu* signs commercial treaty
1861–1863	Chōshū and Satsuma mediate
1866	Chōshū defeats *bakufu* army
1868	Meiji Restoration

Nation Building

1868–1871	Shaping a new state
1871–1873	Iwakura mission
1873–1878	Social revolution from above
1877–1878	Satsuma Rebellion
1881	Promise of constitution
1889	Meiji Constitution promulgated
1890	First Diet session

Imperial Japan

1894–1895	Sino-Japanese War
1900	Seiyūkai formed
1904–1905	Russo-Japanese War
1910	Korea annexed

Era of Party Government

1918	Hara becomes prime minister
1925	Katō becomes prime minister
1925	Universal manhood suffrage passed

Militarism

1931	Japan takes Manchuria
1937	War with China
1941	Japan attacks Pearl Harbor
1945	Japan surrenders

Silk-weaving Mill in Japan.

Summary

China: the Nineteenth Century China's bureaucracy centered on the imperial court in Beijing. The court was concerned about governing China and, then, to protecting its land frontiers. For 2000 years, the only threats to China had come from beyond those frontiers. The expansion of imperial Russia reinforced this orientation. In the east, China was protected by the ocean. Even the Sino-Japanese pirates of the sixteenth century had been more a nuisance than a serious threat, and Europeans were initially viewed in the same light. The Opium War was fought in 1839–42, and other wars with European powers thereafter, but these were seen as "coastal incursions," which posed little threat to the Qing heartland. Far more serious were the Taiping and other rebellions, which seized villages, threatened gentry control of local society, and attacked officials at both district and provincial levels. For China, the important story of the nineteenth century was the success of gentry armies in suppressing these rebellions, a success using Western weapons but based on traditional values. Not until the very end of the century after Japan's defeat of China in 1895 and its defeat of Russia in 1905 did the Chinese begin substantial Westernizing reforms—and by then it was too late for the dynasty.

China: the Twentieth Century After the Qing fell in 1912, China was ruled for a decade and a half by regional warlords, a pattern not unlike the aftermaths of previous dynasties. But the ferment of the newly entering flood of Western ideas fed a growing nationalism. This nationalism permeated the Huangpu Military Academy that trained the officers of the Guomindang (or Nationalist) army; it lent legitimacy to the army's march north and to the establishment of the Nanjing government. By 1934, the Guomindang was winning; Communists were forced to abandon bases in south China and flee to the arid northwest. But then Japan invaded and occupied just those areas on which the Guomindang had depended. The Communists built up their army, extended their influence into "occupied China," and won the civil war that wracked China between 1945 and 1949.

The Transformation of Japan In contrast to China, the Tokugawa regime collapsed quickly—only 15 years after the arrival of Perry in 1853. With its collapse, an elaborate structure of vested interests was destroyed. Leon Trotsky once spoke of dislocations in history produced by modern weapons in countries with less advanced technologies. Traditional vested interests in Japan—represented by samurai rebellions using old-fashioned weapons—attempted to fight against the new reformist government in the decade after 1868, but they lost every battle. The new Meiji government began sweeping Westernizing reforms in every field. Economic growth went hand in hand with universal education. The emperor became the unifying symbol for traditional and conservative thinkers. The Diet (Japan's parliament) became the focus for progressives and liberals. A shifting balance between conservatives and liberals ensued, with parliamentary democracy making gains into the 1920s. But then the Great Depression and a crisis in Manchuria opened the way for the rise of militarism in the 1930s. One thing led to another and Japan went to war with the United States in 1941.

Review Questions

1. Which had the greater impact on China, the Opium War or the Taiping Rebellion?

2. How did the Qing (Manchu) dynasty recover from the Taiping Rebellion? Why was the recovery inadequate to prevent the overthrow of the dynasty in 1912?

3. Did the May Fourth Movement prepare the way for the Nationalist revolution? The Communist revolution? Or was it incidental to both?

4. After the Meiji Restoration, what steps did Japan's leaders take to achieve their goal of "wealth and power"?

5. What were the strengths and weaknesses of Japan's prewar parliamentary institutions? What led to the sudden rise of militarism during the thirties?

Key Terms

Boxers   (p. 840)

Diet   (p. 851)

Guomindang (GMD)   (p. 844)

Long March   (p. 846)

Meiji Restoration   (p. 849)

Taiping rebellion   (p. 836)

treaty ports   (p. 838)

Tripartite Pact   (p. 862)

zaibatsu   (p. 853)

Documents CD-ROM

East Asia Responds to the West

21.1 Lin Tse-hsü [Lin Zexu], Letter of Moral Admonition to Queen Victoria

21.2 "Use the Barbarians to Fight the Barbarians" (1842): Wei Yuan

21.3 "Why Are Western Nations Small and Yet Strong?": Feng Guifen

21.4 The Treaty of Nanking: Treaty of Peace, Friendship, Commerce, Indemnity, etc., Between Great Britain and China, August 29, 1842

21.5 The Abdication Decree (1912): Long Yu

21.6 Geisha: Glimpse of Unfamiliar Japan

21.8 Russo-Japanese War, 1904–1905, Imperial Rescript

Authoritarian and Totalitarian Experiments in Asia

24.1 Kita Ikki, Outline for the Reconstruction of Japan

24.2 Japanese Imperialism

24.3 Mao Tse-Tung: Report of an Investigation into the Peasant Movement in Hunan

24.4 "How to Be a Good Communist" (1939): Li Shaoqi

24.5 The New Communist State (1940–1950)

24.6 "From the Countryside to the City" (May 1949): Mao Zedong

24.7 The Failure of the Nationalist Government: The American Assessment (1949)

NOTE: *To learn more about the topics in this chapter, see the Suggested Readings at the end of the book.*

The twentieth century and first years of the new millennium saw global conflict and global interaction—made possible by advances in transportation and communication unprecedented in history.

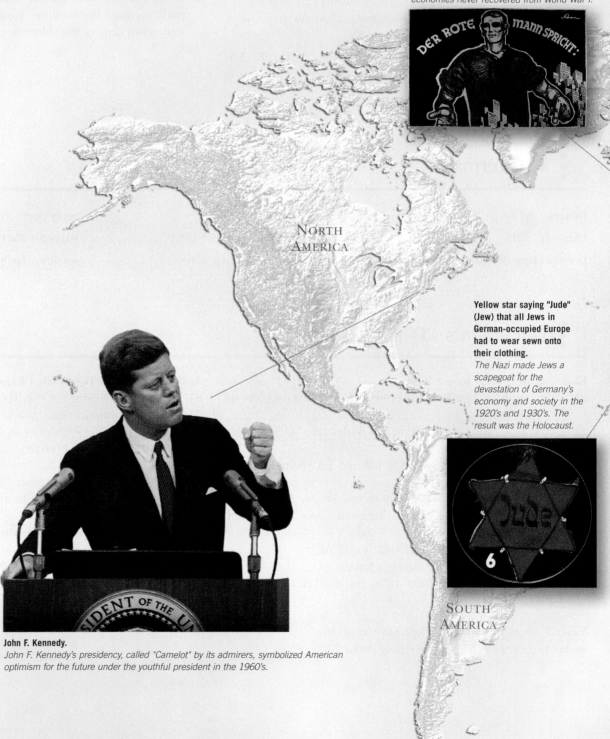

GLOBAL CONFLICT AND CHANGE

Austrian socialist poster from the 1920's.
Economic depression nurtured both socialism and fascism in the 1920's and 1930's throughout Europe, especially in Germany and Austria, whose economies never recovered from World War I.

DER ROTE MANN SPRICHT:

NORTH AMERICA

Yellow star saying "Jude" (Jew) that all Jews in German-occupied Europe had to wear sewn onto their clothing.
The Nazi made Jews a scapegoat for the devastation of Germany's economy and society in the 1920's and 1930's. The result was the Holocaust.

Jude
6

SOUTH AMERICA

SIDENT OF THE UN

John F. Kennedy.
John F. Kennedy's presidency, called "Camelot" by its admirers, symbolized American optimism for the future under the youthful president in the 1960's.

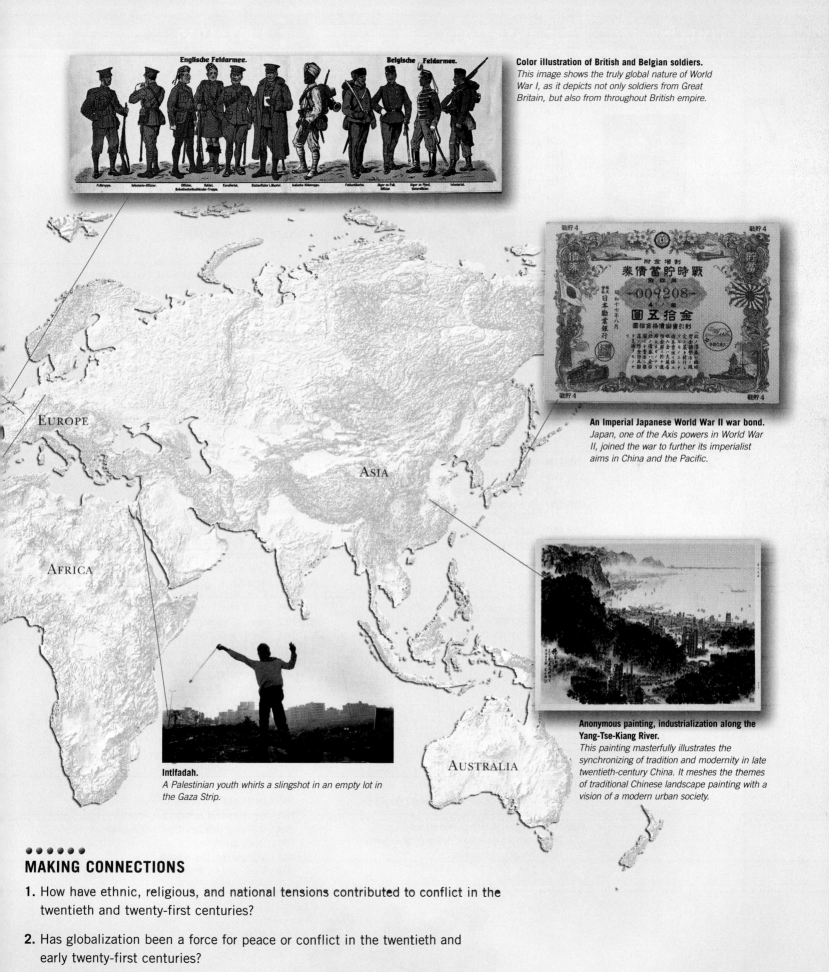

Color illustration of British and Belgian soldiers.
This image shows the truly global nature of World War I, as it depicts not only soldiers from Great Britain, but also from throughout British empire.

EUROPE

ASIA

AFRICA

An Imperial Japanese World War II war bond.
Japan, one of the Axis powers in World War II, joined the war to further its imperialist aims in China and the Pacific.

AUSTRALIA

Anonymous painting, industrialization along the Yang-Tse-Kiang River.
This painting masterfully illustrates the synchronizing of tradition and modernity in late twentieth-century China. It meshes the themes of traditional Chinese landscape painting with a vision of a modern urban society.

Intifadah.
A Palestinian youth whirls a slingshot in an empty lot in the Gaza Strip.

MAKING CONNECTIONS

1. How have ethnic, religious, and national tensions contributed to conflict in the twentieth and twenty-first centuries?

2. Has globalization been a force for peace or conflict in the twentieth and early twenty-first centuries?

PART 7

GLOBAL CONFLICT AND CHANGE

EUROPE

1914–1918	World War I
1917	Bolsheviks seize power, Russia
1919	Versailles Settlement
1922	Mussolini seizes power, Italy
1925	Locarno Pact
1933	Hitler comes to power
1936	Spanish Civil War begins
1938	Munich Conference
1939	World War II begins

1944	D-Day
1945	World War II ends
1948	Berlin blockade and airlift
1949	NATO treaty; Russia detonates atomic bomb
1953	Death of Stalin
1955	Warsaw Pact
1956	Soviets crush Hungarian revolt
1957	EEC founded
1958	Charles de Gaulle comes to power in France

▲ American World War II poster

◄ Pablo Picasso, Guernica, 1937

NEAR EAST/ INDIA

1922	British leave Egypt
\1922–1938	Mustafa Kemal first president of Turkey
1928	The Muslim Brotherhood founded by Hasan Al-Banna

1947	Indian Independence; creation of Pakistan
1948	Assassination of Mahatma Gandhi
1949	State of Israel founded
1953	Mosaddeq overthrown in Iran
1954–1970	Abdel Nasser leads Egypt
1956	Suez Crisis

Mao Tse-tung ►
with Nikita Khrushchev

EAST ASIA

1916–1928	Warlord era in China
1919	May 4th Movement in China
1925	Universal male suffrage in Japan
1928–1937	Nationalist government in China at Nanking
1931	Japan occupies Manchuria
1937–1945	Japan at war with China

1941	Japan attacks Pearl Harbor
1945	Japan surrenders after U.S. atomic bombs
1945–1949	Civil War in China; People's Republic founded
1950	N. Korea invades S. Korea
1952	U.S. ends occupation of Japan
1953–1972	Double-digit growth in Japan
1955	Liberal-Democratic Party formed in Japan
1959–1960	Sino-Soviet split

AFRICA

1919	W.E.B. DuBois holds first Pan-African Congress in Paris
1935	Mussolini invades Ethiopia

1942–1945	World War II engulfs North Africa
1955–1962	Wars of independence in French Algeria
1956	Sudan gains independence from Britain and Egypt
1956	Morocco and Tunisia gain independence from France
1957	Ghana an independent state under Kwame Nkrumah

THE AMERICAS

1917	U.S. enters World War I
1929	Wall Street Crash; the Great Depression begins
1930–1945	Vargas dictatorship in Brazil
1932	F.D. Roosevelt elected U.S. president
1938	Mexico nationalizes oil

1941	U.S. enters World War II
1945	Death of F.D. Roosevelt
1946	Perón elected president in Argentina
1954	U.S. Supreme Court outlaws segregation
1955	Perón overthrown
1956	Montgomery bus boycott
1959	Fidel Castro comes to power in Cuba

◄ Fidel Castro

1960 Paris Summit Conference collapses after U-2 incident
1961 Berlin Wall erected
1964 Khrushchev replaced as Soviet prime minister by Kosygin; as party secretary by Brezhnev
1968 Soviets invade Czechoslovakia
1972 British Impose direct rule on Northern Ireland
1972 Israeli Olympic athletes killed by Arab terrorists
1974 End of military rule in Greece
1974 Portuguese dictatorship deposed; democratic reforms begin

1977 Brezhnev president of USSR
1979 Margaret Thatcher becomes British prime minister
1980 Solidarity Movement in Poland
1981 Crackdown against Solidarity
1984–1985 Bitter strikes by miners in England
1984 Mikhail Gorbachev introduces *glasnost* in USSR

▲ Opening of the Berlin Wall, 1989

1989 Berlin Wall demolished
1990 Germany unified
1991 Failed coup in Soviet Union; Yeltsin emerges as leader of Russia
1991 Major replaces Thatcher as England's prime minister
1993 Czechoslovakia divides into two republics
1995 Dayton Peace Accords end war in Bosnia
1999 NATO military campaign against Serbia
2000 Putin elected president of Russia; overthrow of Milŏsevic in Yugoslavia

---

1966 Indira Gandhi becomes prime minister of India
1967 Israeli-Arab June War
1969 Golda Meir becomes prime minister of Israel
1969 Arafat elected P.L.O. chairman
1971 India-USSR friendship treaty
1973 Arab-Israeli October War
1972 Independence for Bangladesh
1973 OPEC oil embargo

1977 Menachem Begin becomes prime minister of Israel
1978 Iranian revolution under Khomeini's leadership
1979 Egyptian-Israeli Peace Treaty
1979 Iran takes U.S. hostages
1979 Soviets invade Afghanistan
1980–1988 Iran-Iraq War
1981 Hostages released in Iran
1981 Egypt's Sadat assassinated; succeeded by Hosni Mubarak
1982 Israel invades Lebanon
1984 Indira Gandhi assassinated

1989 Soviets leave Afghanistan
1989 Death of Khomeini
1990 Central Asian States become independent on fall of USSR
1990–1991 Gulf War
1991 Indian prime minister Rajiv Ghandi assassinated

Oil wells left burning ▶ by Iraqi troops in Kuwait

1959–1975 Vietnam War
1965–1976 Cultural Revolution devastates China
1968 Death of Ho Chi Minh, president of North Vietnam
1971 Lin Piao killed in China
1972 President Nixon visits China
1973 Economic growth slows in Japan

▲ Life in China during Cultural Revolution

1976 Death of Mao Tse-tung
1978–1989 New Economic policies of Teng Hsiao-p'ing in China
1978–1989 Vietnam occupies Cambodia
1980s Double-digit economic growth in South Korea and Taiwan

Tienanmen Square ▶

1988 Japan's GNP second in world
1989 Vietnam pledges to withdraw from Cambodia
1989 China crushes pro-democracy demonstrations in Beijing
1991–1992 Political scandals and plummeting stock market in Japan
1992 Kim Young Sam, civilian party leader, elected S. Korean president

---

1960 Belgian Congo granted independence as Zaire
1963 Kenya becomes an independent republic
1964 Zanzibar, the Congo, and Northern Rhodesia (Zambia) become independent republics
1965 Revolution in Kenya
1967–1970 Nigerian Civil War
1974 Drought and famine in Africa
1974 Emperor Haile Selassie of Ethiopia is deposed
1974–1975 Portugal grants independence to Guinea, Angola, Mozambique, Cape Verde

1980 Southern Rhodesia (Zimbabwe) gains independence from Britain
1984 Bishop Desmond Tutu awarded Nobel Peace Prize
1985 U.S. economic sanctions against South Africa result in more repression

1989 Conservative Botha government resigns in South Africa; DeKlerk becomes president
1992 Nelson Mandela freed from prison in South Africa
1994 Nelson Mandela elected president of South Africa

Nelson Mandela ▶

1960 Kennedy elected president
1962 Cuban Missile Crisis
1963 Kennedy assassinated
1964 Passage of Civil Rights Act
1965 U.S. expands Vietnam commitment
1968 Martin Luther King and Robert Kennedy assassinated; campus unrest
1968 Nixon elected
1970 Allende elected in Chile
1972 Nixon visits China and USSR; is reelected president
1973 Watergate scandal breaks
1973 Perón reelected, Argentina
1973 Chile's Allende overthrown
1974 Nixon resigns presidency

1979 Revolution in Nicaragua and El Salvador
1980 Iran hostage crisis
1980 Reagan elected president
1982 War between Argentina and Great Britain over Islas Malvinas (Falkland Islands)
1983 Argentine military government overthrown; elected government restored
1983 End of Mexican oil boom
1988 Major arms agreement between U.S. and USSR

1991 Gulf War
1992 Clinton elected president
1994 Revolt in Chiapas, Mexico
1998 Pope visits Cuba
2001 Terrorist attack on the World Trade Center in New York City and the Pentagon in Washington, D.C.

FREEDOM · FRATERNITY · FEDERATION

IMPERIAL FEDERATION. — MAP OF THE WORLD SHOWING THE EXTENT OF THE BRITISH EMPIRE IN 1886.

29

Imperialism and World War I

- Expansion of European Power and the "New Imperialism"

- Emergence of the German Empire

- World War I

- The Russian Revolution

- End of World War I

◄ THE BRITISH EMPIRE, 1886. The territories marked in red are the far-flung dominions of the empire; the black lines criss-crossing the oceans are the steamship routes that bind them together. Below, in the center, sits Britannia (the female personification of Britain) holding a trident, a potent symbol of British naval power. Surrounding her, the many different peoples of the empire stand or kneel in reverent gratitude for the freedom, fraternity, and federation she has bestowed upon them. The inset map shows the extent of the British Empire in 1786. The Granger Collection, New York.

GLOBAL PERSPECTIVE

Imperialism and the Great War

The outburst of European imperialism in the last part of the nineteenth century brought Western countries into contact with almost all the inhabited areas of the world and intensified their activity in places where they had already been interested. The growth of industry, the increased ease of transportation and communication, and the development of a world economic system all tended to bring previously remote and isolated places into the orbit of the West. By the time of the outbreak of World War I, European nations had divided Africa among themselves for exploitation, as the advent of steamships and railroads in the late nineteenth century allowed them to penetrate the African interior for the first time. The vast subcontinent of India had long been a British colony, producing primary products such as raw cotton that fed British industry. Much of China had fallen under European control after American "gunboat diplomacy" and the "Opium War" destabilized Chinese imperial rule in the nineteenth century. Indo-China was under French rule. The islands of the Pacific had been divided among Western powers. Much of the Middle East was under the nominal control of the Ottoman Empire, which was in its death throes and under European influence. The Monroe doctrine made Latin America a protectorate of the United States. Japan, pushed out of its isolation, had itself become an imperial power at the expense of China and Korea. What all of the Western imperial powers, as well as Japan, had in common was a need to extract raw materials from their colonies to feed their industries. Their colonies in turn were to serve as markets for Western manufactured goods, even at the expense of indigenous manufactures, as in the case of India's ancient cloth weaving industry. This, as well as the prestige that colonies afforded, helps explain why nations were so determined to obtain and retain colonies.

The emergence of a new, powerful German state at the center of Europe upset the old balance of power and threatened the peace established in 1815. Germany's Chancellor Bismarck, however, created a new system of alliances that preserved the peace for as long as he remained in power. The new German emperor, William II, abandoned this policy of restraint and sought greater power and influence for his country. The result was a system of alliances that divided Europe into two armed camps and greatly increased the chances of a general war. What began as yet another Balkan War involving the European powers became a world war that profoundly influenced the rest of the world. As the terrible war of 1914–1918 dragged on, the real motives that had driven the European powers to fight gave way to public affirmations of the principles of nationalism and self-determination. Peoples under colonial rule took seriously the public statements, and sometimes the private promises, made to secure their cooperation in supplying the war effort and sought to win their independence and nationhood. For the most part they were disappointed by the peace settlement. The establishment of the League of Nations and the system of mandates in place of open colonial rule did not change much. The British Empire inherited vast territories from the defeated German and the defunct Ottoman Empires and was larger than ever. The French retained and expanded their holdings in Africa, the Pacific, and the Middle East. The Americans added to the islands they controlled in the Pacific. Japanese imperial ambitions were rewarded at the expense of China.

A glance at the new map of the world could give the impression that the old imperial nations, especially Britain and France, were more powerful than ever. However, that impression would be superficial and misleading. The great Western European powers paid an enormous price in lives, money, and will for their victory in the war. Colonial peoples pressed for the rights that Western nations proclaimed as universal but denied to their colonies; influential minorities in the countries that ruled them sympathized with colonial aspirations for independence. Tension between colonies and their ruling nations was one cause of the instability in the world created by the Paris treaties of 1919.

THINK AHEAD
- Why were Western powers eager to obtain colonies?
- Why is World War I a turning point in history?
- How did World War I alter the relationship between imperial powers and colonized peoples?

DURING THE SECOND HALF OF THE NINETEENTH century, and especially after 1870, Europe exercised unprecedented influence and control over the rest of the world. North and South America, as well as Australia and New Zealand, almost became part of the European world as great streams of European immigrants populated them. Until the nineteenth century, Asia (with the significant exception of India) and most of Africa had gone their own ways, having little contact with Europe. But in the latter part of that century, almost all of Africa was divided among a number of European nations (see Chapter 27). Europe also imposed its economic and political power across Asia (see Map 29–1 and Chapter 28). By the next century, European dominance had brought every part of the globe into a single world economy. Events in any corner of the world had significant effects thousands of miles away.

These developments might have been expected to lead to greater prosperity and good fortune. Instead, they helped foster competition and hostility among the great powers of Europe and to bring on a terrible war that undermined Europe's strength and its influence in the world. The peace settlement, proclaimed as "a peace without victors," disillusioned idealists in the West. It treated Germany almost as harshly as Germany would have treated its foes if it had been victorious. The new system also failed to provide realistic and effective safeguards against a return to power of a vengeful Germany. The withdrawal of the United States into a disdainful isolation from world affairs destroyed the basis for keeping the peace on which the hopes of Britain and France relied. The frenzy for imperial expansion that had seized Europeans in the late nineteenth century had done much to destroy Europe's peace and prosperity and its dominant place in the world.

Expansion of European Power and the "New Imperialism"

The explosive developments in nineteenth-century science, technology, industry, agriculture, transportation, communication, and military weapons provided the chief sources of European power. They enabled a few Europeans (and Americans) to impose their will on other peoples many times their number by force. Institutional as well as material advantages allowed Westerners to have their way. The growth of national states that commanded the loyalty, service, and resources of their inhabitants to a degree previously unknown permitted the European nations to deploy their response in the most effective way. The Europeans also possessed another, less tangible weapon: the belief that their civilization and way of life were superior to all others. It gave them a confidence that often took the form of a cultural arrogance that fostered the expansionist mood.

The expansion of European influence was not new. Spain, Portugal, France, Holland, and Britain had controlled overseas territories for centuries, but by the mid–nineteenth century only Great Britain retained extensive holdings. The first half of the century was generally hostile to colonial expansion. Even the British had been sobered by their loss of the American colonies. The French acquired Algeria and part of Indochina, and the British made some additional gains in Canada, India, Australia, and New Zealand. However, the doctrine of free trade was dominant, and it opposed political interference in other lands.

After 1870, however, the European states swiftly spread their control over perhaps 10 million square miles and 150 million people, about a fifth of the world's land area and a tenth of its population. The movement has been called the **New Imperialism** (Map 29–1).

THE NEW IMPERIALISM

The word imperialism has come to be used so loosely as to become almost meaningless. It may be useful to offer a definition that might be widely accepted: "The policy of extending a nation's authority by territorial acquisition or by the establishment of economic and political hegemony over other nations."[1] Previous imperialisms had taken the form either of seizing land and settling it with the conqueror's people or of establishing trading centers to exploit the dominated area. The New Imperialism introduced new devices.

The usual pattern of the New Imperialism was for the European nation to invest capital in the "backward" country—to build productive enterprises and improved means of transportation and employ many natives in the process—and thereby transform its entire economy and culture. To guarantee their investments, the European states would make favorable arrangements with the local government either by enriching or threatening the rulers. If these arrangements proved inadequate, the dominant power established different degrees of political control ranging

---

[1] *American Heritage Dictionary of the English Language* (New York: Houghton Mifflin, 1969), p. 660.

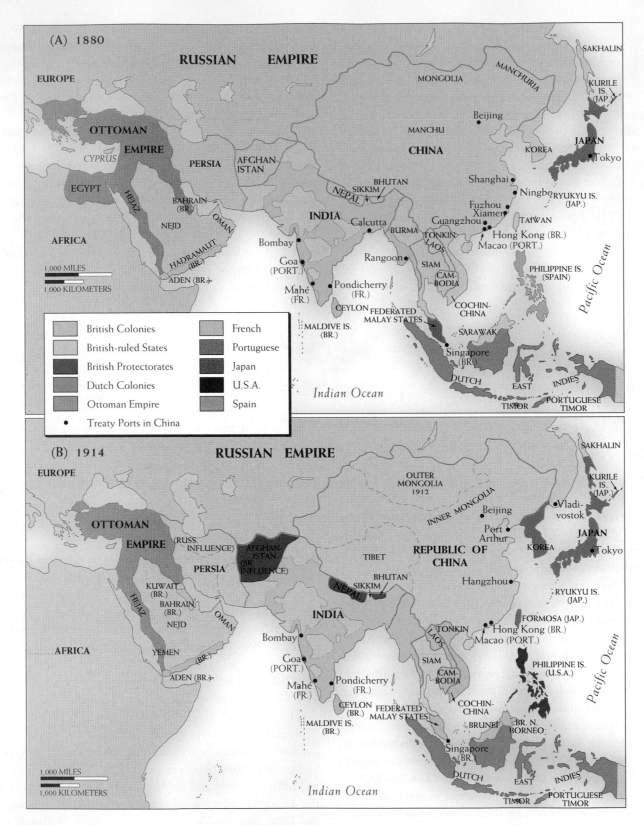

MAP 29–1 Asia 1880–1914. As in Africa (see Maps 27–2 and 27–3), the late nineteenth century saw imperialism spread widely and rapidly in Asia. Two new powers, Japan and the United States, joined the British, French, and Dutch in extending control both to islands and to the mainland and in exploiting an enfeebled China.

Knitting the World. An advertisement for the Singer Sewing Machine Company shows a seamstress knitting together the two halves of the western hemisphere. By the late nineteenth century, U.S. firms created a global demand for their goods. Singer sewing machines came with instruction booklets printed in 54 languages. Of the fifteen factories making the machines, only seven were in the United States.
Hartman Center for Sales. Advertising and Marketing History.

from full annexation as a colony, to protectorate status (whereby the local ruler was controlled by the dominant European state and maintained by its military power), to "spheres-of-influence" status (whereby the European state received special commercial and legal privileges without direct political involvement).

MOTIVES FOR THE NEW IMPERIALISM: ECONOMIC INTERPRETATION

There is still no agreement about the motives for the New Imperialism. The most widespread interpretation has been economic, most typically in the form given by the English radical economist J. A. Hobson and later adapted by Lenin. As Lenin put it, "Imperialism is the monopoly stage of capitalism,"[2] the last stage of a dying capitalist system. According to this interpretation, competition inevitably leads to the elimination of inefficient capitalists and, therefore, to monopoly. Powerful industrial and financial capitalists soon run out of profitable areas of investment in their own countries and persuade their governments to gain colonies in "backward" countries. Here they can find higher profits from their investments, new markets for their products, and safe sources of the needed raw materials.

The facts do not support this viewpoint. The European powers did invest considerable capital abroad, but not in the model of Hobson and Lenin. Britain, for example, made heavier investments abroad before 1875 than during the next two decades. Only a small percentage of British and European investments overseas, moreover, went to the new colonial areas. Most went into Europe itself or into older, well-established areas like the United States, Canada, Australia, and New Zealand. Moreover, investments in the new areas were not necessarily put into colonies held by the investing country.

The facts are equally discouraging for those who emphasize the need for new markets and raw materials. Colonies were not usually important markets for the great imperial nations, and all were forced to rely on areas that they did not control as sources of vital raw materials. It is not even clear that control of

the new colonies was particularly profitable. Some individuals and companies, of course, made great profits from particular colonial ventures but could rarely influence national policy. Although economic motives certainly played a part, understanding the New Imperialism requires a search for further motives.

CULTURAL, RELIGIOUS, AND SOCIAL INTERPRETATIONS

Advocates of imperialism put forth various justifications for their practices. Some argued that the advanced European nations had a responsibility to bring the benefits of their higher culture and superior civilization to the people of "backward" lands. (See Document, "Social Darwinism and Imperialism." Few people were influenced by such arrogant arguments, although many shared the intellectual assumptions behind them. Religious groups argued for the responsibility of Western nations to bring the benefits of Christianity to the heathen with more extensive efforts and aid from their governments. Politicians and diplomats argued for imperialism as a tool of social policy. In Germany, for instance, people suggested that imperial expansion might serve to deflect public interest from domestic politics and social reform. But Germany acquired few colonies, and such considerations were negligible. Another common and apparently plausible justification was that colonies would provide a good place to settle surplus population. In fact, most European emigrants went to North and South America and Australia.

STRATEGIC AND POLITICAL INTERPRETATIONS: THE SCRAMBLE FOR AFRICA

Strategic and political considerations seem to have been more important in bringing on the New Imperialism. The scramble for Africa in the 1880s, discussed in more detail in Chapter 27, is one example (see Maps 27–2 and 27–3). Britain was the only great power with extensive overseas holdings on the even of the scramble. The completion of the Suez Canal in 1869 made Egypt vitally important to the British because it sat astride the shortest route to India. Britain purchased a major, but not a controlling, interest in the canal in 1875. When Egypt's stability was threatened by internal troubles in the 1880s, the British established a protectorate. Then, to protect Egypt, they advanced into the Sudan.

France became involved in North Africa in 1830 by sending a naval expedition to Algeria to attack the pirates based there. Before long, French settlers arrived and established a colony. By 1882 France was in full control of Algeria and had taken over Tunisia to keep out Italy. Soon lesser states like Belgium, Portugal, Spain, and Italy were also scrambling for African colonies.

[2] V. I. Lenin, *Imperialism, the Highest Stage of Capitalism* (New York: International Publishers, 1939), p. 88.

DOCUMENT | Social Darwinism and Imperialism

One of the intellectual foundations of the New Imperialism was the doctrine of social Darwinism, a pseudoscientific application of Darwin's ideas about biology to nations and races. The impact of social Darwinism was substantial. In the selection that follows, an Englishman, Karl Pearson (1857–1936), attempts to connect concepts from evolutionary theory—the struggle for survival and the survival of the fittest—to the development of human societies.

> ◆ How does the author connect Darwin's ideas to the concept of human progress? Is it reasonable to equate biological species with human societies, races, or nations? How do the author's ideas justify imperial expansion? What arguments can you make against the author's assertions?

History shows me one way, and one way only, in which a state of civilisation has been produced, namely, the struggle of race with race, and the survival of the physically and mentally fitter race. This dependence of progress on the survival of the fitter race, terribly black as it may seem to some of you, gives the struggle for existence its redeeming features; it is the fiery crucible out of which comes the finer metal. You may hope for a time when the sword shall be turned into the ploughshare, when American and German and English traders shall no longer compete in the markets of the world for raw materials, for their food supply, when the white man and the dark shall share the soil between them, and each till it as he lists. But, believe me, when that day comes mankind will no longer progress; there will be nothing to check the fertility of inferior stock; the relentless law of heredity will not be controlled and guided by natural selection. Man will stagnate. ... The path of progress is strewn with the wreck of nations; traces are everywhere to be seen of the hecatombs of inferior races, and of victims who found not the narrow way to the greater perfection. Yet these dead peoples are, in very truth, the stepping stones on which mankind has arisen to the higher intellectual and deeper emotional life of today.

From Karl Pearson, *National Life from the Standpoint of Science*, 2nd ed. (Cambridge, UK: Cambridge University Press, 1907), pp. 21, 26–27, 64.

By the 1890s their intervention had led Britain to expand northward from the Cape of Good Hope into what is now Zimbabwe. Britain may have had significant strategic reasons for protecting the Suez and Cape routes to India, but France and the smaller European nations did not. Their motives were political as well as economic, for they equated status as a great power (Britain was the chief model) with the possession of colonies. They therefore sought colonies as evidence of their own importance.

Bismarck appears to have pursued an imperial policy, however brief, from coldly political motives. In 1884 and 1885 Germany declared protectorates over southwestern Africa, Togoland, the Cameroons, and East Africa. None of these places was particularly valuable or strategically important. Bismarck acquired colonies chiefly to improve Germany's diplomatic position in Europe and tried to turn France from hostility against Germany by diverting the French toward colonial interests. German colonies in Africa could also be used to persuade the British to be reasonable.

THE IRRATIONAL ELEMENT

Germany's annexations started a wild scramble by the other European powers to claim what was left of Africa. By 1890 almost all of the continent was parceled out. Great powers and small expanded into areas neither profitable nor strategic for reasons less calculating and rational than Bismarck's. "Empire in the modern period," D. K. Fieldhouse observed, "was the product of European power: Its reward was power or the sense of power.[3]

Such motives were not new. They had been well understood by the Athenian spokesman at Melos in 416 B.C.E., whose words were reported by Thucydides: "Of the gods we believe and of men we know clearly that by a necessity of their nature where they have the power they rule."

In Asia the emergence of Japan as a great power with claims on China and Korea frightened the other powers interested in China. The Russians were building a railroad across Siberia to Vladivostok and were afraid of any threat to Manchuria. Together with France and Germany, they applied diplomatic pressure that forced Japan out of the Liaotung Peninsula and its harbor, Port Arthur; all pressed feverishly for concessions in China. Fearing that China, its markets, and its investment opportunities would soon be closed to its citizens, the United States in 1899 proposed the "open door policy," which opposed foreign annexations in China and allowed entrepreneurs of all nations to trade there on equal terms. The support of Britain helped win acceptance of the policy by all the powers except Russia.

The United States had only recently emerged as a force in international affairs. Victory in the Spanish-American War of

[3] *The Colonial Empires* (New York: Delacorte, 1966), p. 393.

British Fort at Alexandria, Egypt. ➤ The opening of the Suez Canal in 1869 sharply reduced the time needed for travel from Europe to the Far East, and, for Great Britain, from England to its colony in India. Britain acquired a financial interest in the canal, giving it a strategic interest in Egypt. In 1882 Britain made Egypt a protectorate in order to secure the canal.

Hulton/Corbis/Bettmann.

THE DEVILFISH IN EGYPTIAN WATERS.

▲ **John Bull.** An American cartoonist in 1888 depicted John Bull (England) as the octopus of imperialism, grabbing land on every continent. Notice the hand at the left poised over Egypt.

The Granger Collection, N.Y.

1898 brought an informal protectorate over Cuba and the annexation of Puerto Rico; it thus drove Spain completely from the Western Hemisphere. The Americans also purchased the Philippine Islands and Guam, and Germany acquired the other Spanish islands in the Pacific. The Americans and the Germans also divided Samoa between them. What was left of the Pacific Islands was soon taken by France and England. Hawaii was annexed in 1898. This outburst of activity made the United States an imperial and Pacific power.

By 1900 most of the world had thus come under the control of the industrialized West. The greatest remaining vulnerable area was the Ottoman Empire, but its fate was closely tied up with European developments and must be treated in that context.

Emergence of the German Empire

FORMATION OF THE TRIPLE ALLIANCE (1873–1890)

Prussia's victories over Austria and France and its creation of a large, powerful German Empire in 1871 revolutionized European diplomacy. The sudden appearance of a vast new state that brought together most of the German people to form a nation of great and growing population, wealth, industrial capacity, and military power posed new problems.

The balance of power created at the Congress of Vienna was altered radically. Britain retained its position and so did Russia, even though it was somewhat weakened by the Crimean War. Austria, however, had lost ground, and its position was further threatened by the forces of nationalism within the Austro-Hungarian Empire. French power and prestige were badly damaged by the Franco-Prussian War and the German annexation of Alsace-Lorraine. The French were both afraid of their powerful new neighbor and resentful of their defeat and their loss of territory and of France's traditional position as the dominant Western European power.

BISMARCK'S LEADERSHIP (1873–1890)

Until 1890 Otto von Bismarck (1815–1898) continued to guide German policy. He insisted after 1871 that Germany was a satisfied power and wanted no further territorial gains, and he meant it. He wanted to avoid a new war that might undo his achievement. He tried to assuage French resentment by cultivating friendly relations and by supporting French colonial aspirations. He also prepared for the worst. If France could not be conciliated, it must be isolated. Bismarck sought to prevent an alliance between France and any other European power—especially Austria or Russia—that would threaten Germany with a war on two fronts.

War in the Balkans Bismarck's first move was to establish the Three Emperors' League in 1873. It brought together the three great conservative empires of Germany, Austria, and Russia. The league collapsed when Russia went to war with Turkey in 1877 as a result of uprisings in the Ottoman Balkan provinces. The tottering Ottoman Empire was preserved chiefly by the competing aims of those powers who awaited its demise. Ottoman weakness encouraged Serbia and Montenegro to come to the aid of their fellow Slavs in Bosnia and Herzegovina. Soon the rebellion spread to Bulgaria.

Then Russia entered the fray and created a major international crisis. The Russians hoped to expand at Ottoman expense and to achieve their most cherished goal: control of Constantinople and the Dardanelles. Russian intervention also reflected the influence of the **Pan-Slavic movement**, which sought to bring all the Slavic peoples, even those under Austrian or Ottoman rule, under the protection of Holy Mother Russia.

Before long the Ottoman Empire was forced to ask for peace. The Treaty of San Stefano of March 1878 was a Russian triumph, but a short-lived one. The Slavic states in the Balkans were freed of Ottoman rule, and Russia itself obtained territory and a heavy monetary indemnity. But the terms of the Russian victory alarmed the other great powers. Austria feared that the new Slav states in the Balkans and the powerful increase in Russian influence there would threaten its own Balkan provinces. The British were alarmed by the damage the Russian settlement would do to the European balance of power and especially by possible Russian control of the Dard-

anelles. Disraeli (1804–1881) was determined to resist, and British public opinion supported him. A popular song gave the language a new word for superpatriotism—jingoism:

> We don't want to fight.
> But by jingo if we do,
> We've got the men,
> We've got the ships,
> We've got the money too!
> The Russians will not have Constantinople!

Congress of Berlin Even before San Stefano, Disraeli had sent a fleet to Constantinople. After the magnitude of Russia's appetite was known, Britain and Austria forced Russia to agree to an international conference at which the provisions of San Stefano would be reviewed by the other great powers. The resulting Congress of Berlin met in June and July of 1878 under the presidency of Bismarck.

The decisions of the Congress were a blow to Russian ambitions. Bulgaria lost two thirds of its territory and was deprived of access to the Aegean Sea. Austria-Hungary was given Bosnia and Herzegovina to "occupy and administer," although those provinces remained formally under Ottoman rule. Britain received Cyprus, and France gained permission to occupy Tunisia. These privileges were compensation for the gains that Russia was permitted to keep. Germany asked for nothing, but the Russians were bitterly disappointed. The Three Emperors' League was dead.

The major trouble spot now was in the south Slavic states of Serbia and Montenegro. They deeply resented the Austrian occupation of Bosnia and Herzegovina, as did many of the natives of those provinces. The south Slavic question, no less than the estrangement between Russia and Germany, was a threat to the peace of Europe.

German Alliances with Russia and Austria Bismarck could ignore the Balkans, but not the breach in his eastern alliance system. With Russia alienated, he concluded a secret treaty with Austria in 1879. The resulting Dual Alliance provided that if either Germany or Austria were attacked by Russia, the ally would help the attacked party. If either was attacked by someone else, each promised at least to maintain neutrality. The treaty was renewed every five years until 1918. As the central point in German policy, it was criticized at the time; some have judged it mistaken in retrospect. It appeared to tie the German fortunes to those of the troubled Austro-Hungarian Empire and thus to borrow trouble. It also isolated the Russians and pushed them to alliances in the West.

Bismarck was aware of these dangers but discounted them. He never allowed the alliance to drag Germany into Austria's Balkan quarrels. He made it clear to the Austrians that the alliance was purely defensive and that Germany would never attack Russia.

Bismarck expected the news of the Austro-German negotiations to frighten Russia into seeking closer relations with Germany, and he was right. Russian diplomats soon approached him, and by 1881 he had renewed the Three Emperors' League on a firmer basis. Although it did not resolve all conflicts, it helped preserve peace.

The Triple Alliance   In 1882 Italy, ambitious for colonial expansion and annoyed by the French preemption of Tunisia, asked to join the Dual Alliance. At this point Bismarck's policy was a complete success. He was allied with three of the great powers and friendly with Great Britain, which held aloof from all alliances. France was isolated and no threat. Although the Three Emperors' League was allowed to lapse, the Triple Alliance (Germany, Austria, and Italy) was renewed for another five years in 1887. To restore German relations with Russia, Bismarck negotiated the Reinsurance Treaty that same year, in which both powers promised to remain neutral if either was attacked. All seemed smooth, but a change in the German monarchy soon overturned Bismarck's system.

In 1888 William II (r. 1888–1918) came to the German throne. Like many Germans of his generation, he was filled with a sense of Germany's destiny as the leading power of Europe. To achieve a "place in the sun," he and his contemporaries wanted a navy and colonies like Britain's. These aims, of course, ran counter to Bismarck's limited continental policy. In 1890 William used a disagreement over domestic policy to dismiss Bismarck.

During Bismarck's time, Germany was a force for European peace and was increasingly understood to be so. This position would not have been possible without its great military power. But it also required the leadership of a statesman who could exercise restraint and make a realistic estimate of what his country needed and what was possible.

FORGING THE TRIPLE ENTENTE (1890–1907)

Franco-Russian Alliance   Almost immediately after Bismarck's retirement, his system of alliances collapsed. His successor, General Leo von Caprivi (1831–1899), refused the Russian request to renew the Reinsurance Treaty, which he considered incompatible with the Austrian alliance. Political isolation and the need for foreign capital unexpectedly drove the Russians toward France. The French, who were even more isolated, were glad to pour capital into Russia if it would help produce an alliance and security against Germany. In 1894 the Franco-Russian alliance was signed.

Britain and Germany   Britain now became the key to the international situation. Colonial rivalries pitted the British against the Russians in Central Asia and against the French in Africa.

Traditionally, Britain had also opposed Russian control of Constantinople and the Dardanelles and French control of the Low Countries. There was no reason to think that Britain would soon become friendly with its traditional rivals or abandon its usual friendliness toward the Germans. Yet within a decade of William II's accession, Germany had become the enemy in the minds of the British. The problem lay in the foreign and naval policies of the German emperor and his ministers.

At first Germany tried to win the British over to the Triple Alliance, but when Britain clung to "splendid isolation," German policy changed. The idea was to demonstrate Germany's worthiness as an ally by withdrawing support and even making trouble for Britain.

The Germans began to exert pressure against Britain in Africa by barring British attempts to build a railroad from Capetown to Cairo. They also openly sympathized with the Boers of South Africa in their resistance to British expansion. In 1896 William insulted the British by sending a congratulatory telegram to Paul Kruger (1825–1904), president of the Transvaal, for repulsing a British raid "without having to appeal to friendly powers for assistance."

In 1898 William's dream of a German navy began to achieve reality with the passage of a naval law providing for nineteen battleships. In 1900 a second law doubled that figure. The architect of the new navy was Admiral Alfred von Tirpitz (1849–1930), who openly proclaimed that Germany's naval policy was aimed at Britain. His "risk" theory argued that Germany could build a fleet strong enough, not to defeat the British, but to inflict enough damage to make the British navy inferior to those of other powers like France or the United States. The threat posed by the German navy did more to antagonize British opinion than anything else.

▲ **Guerrillas.** Boer guerrillas pose near a railroad during their struggle against the British in the Boer War.
Culver Pictures, Inc.

Bismarck and the Kaiser. Bismarck and the young Kaiser William II meet in 1888. The two disagreed over many issues, and in 1890 William dismissed the aged chancellor.

German Information Center.

As the German navy grew and German policies seemed to become more threatening, the British were alarmed enough to abandon their traditional attitudes and policies.

Entente Cordiale   The first breach in Britain's isolation came in 1902 when an alliance was concluded with Japan to help defend British interests in the Far East against Russia. Next, Britain in 1904 concluded a series of agreements with the French, collectively called the Entente Cordiale. It was not a formal treaty and had no military provisions, but it settled all outstanding colonial differences between the two nations. The Entente Cordiale was a long step toward aligning the British with Germany's great potential enemy.

First Moroccan Crisis   At this point Germany decided to test the new understanding between Britain and France and to press for colonial gains. In March 1905 William II landed at Tangier, challenged the French predominance there in a speech in favor of Moroccan independence, and by implication asserted Germany's right to participate in Morocco's destiny. Germany's chancellor, Prince Bernhard von Bülow (1849–1929), intended to show France how weak it was and how little it could expect from Britain; he also hoped to gain significant colonial concessions.

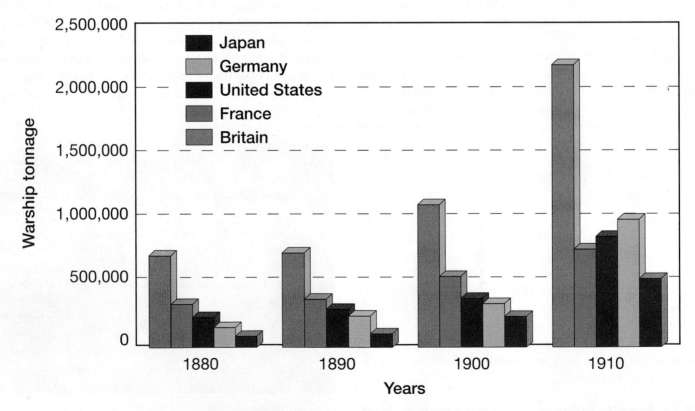

Figure 29–1 Warship Tonnage of the World's Navies 1880–1910.   Naval strength was the primary index of power before World War I. The United States held onto third place in the naval arms race, while Germany and Japan made significant gains.

Paul Kennedy, *Rise and Fall of the Great Powers* (New York: Random House, 1987), p. 203.

The Germans might well have achieved their aims, but they demanded an international conference to exhibit their power more dramatically. The conference met in 1906 at Algeciras in Spain. Austria sided with its German ally, but Spain, Italy, and the United States voted with Britain and France. The Germans had overplayed their hand, and the French were confirmed in their position in Morocco. German bullying had, moreover, driven Britain and France closer together. In the face of a possible German attack on France, Sir Edward Grey (1862–1933), the British foreign secretary, without making a firm commitment, authorized conversations between the British and French general staffs. Their agreements became morally binding as the years passed. By 1914 French and British military and naval plans were so mutually dependent that the two countries were effectively, if not formally, allies.

British Agreement with Russia   Britain's new relationship with France was surprising. But hardly anyone believed that the British whale and the Russian bear would ever be allies. The Russo-Japanese War of 1904–1905 made such a development seem even less likely because Britain was allied with Russia's enemy. But Britain had behaved with restraint, and the Russians were chastened by their humiliating defeat. The defeat had also led to the Russian Revolution of 1905, which left Russia weak and reduced British apprehensions. The British were also concerned that Russia might again drift into the German orbit.

With French support, the British made overtures to the Russians and in 1907 concluded an agreement with them that settled Russo-British quarrels in Central Asia and Persia and opened the door for wider cooperation. The Triple Entente, an informal but powerful association of Britain, France, and Russia, was now ranged against the Triple Alliance. Because Italy was unreliable, Germany and Austria-Hungary stood surrounded by two great land powers and Great Britain.

William II and his ministers had turned Bismarck's nightmare of the prospect of a two-front war with France and Russia into a reality and had made it more horrible by adding Britain to the hostile coalition. Bismarck's alliance system had been intended to maintain peace, but the new one increased the risk of war and made the Balkans, where Austrian and Russian ambitions clashed, a likely spot for it. Bismarck's diplomacy had left France isolated and impotent; the new arrangement found France associated with the two greatest powers in Europe, apart from Germany. The Germans could rely only on Austria, where troubles made it more likely to need aid than to provide it.

World War I
THE ROAD TO WAR (1908–1914)

The situation in the Balkans was exceedingly complicated. The weak Ottoman Empire controlled the central strip running west from Constantinople to the Adriatic. North and south of it were the independent states of Romania, Montenegro, Serbia, and Greece; Bulgaria, while technically still part of the empire, was legally autonomous and practically independent. The Austro-Hungarian Empire included Croatia and Slovenia and since 1878 had "occupied and administered" Bosnia and Herzegovina.

Except for the Greeks and the Romanians, most of the inhabitants of the Balkans spoke variants of the same Slavic language and felt a cultural and historical kinship with one another and with Russia. For centuries they had been ruled by Austrians, Hungarians, or Turks, and the growing nationalism that characterized late-nineteenth-century Europe made many of them eager for liberty or at least autonomy. The more radical among them longed for a union of the south Slavic, or Yugoslav, peoples in a single nation. They looked to independent Serbia as the center of the new nation and hoped to detach all the Slavic provinces (especially Bosnia, which bordered on Serbia) from Austria. Serbia was to unite the Slavs at the expense of Austria, as Piedmont had united the Italians and Prussia the Germans.

In 1908 a group of modernizing reformers called the Young Turks overthrew the Ottoman government. This threatened to revive the empire and to interfere with the plans of the European jackals to pounce on the Ottoman corpse. These events precipitated the first of a series of Balkan crises that would eventually lead to world war.

The Bosnian Crisis   In 1908 the Austrian and Russian governments decided to act before Turkey became strong enough to resist. They agreed to call an international conference in which each of them would support the other's demands. Russia would agree to the Austrian annexation of Bosnia and Herzegovina, and Austria would support Russia's request to open the Dardanelles to Russian warships.

Austria, however, declared the annexation unilaterally before any conference was called. The British, ever concerned about their own position in the Mediterranean, rejected the Russian demand. The Russians, feeling betrayed by the British, were humiliated and furious. Their "little brothers," the Serbs, were enraged by the loss of Bosnia, which they had hoped one day to include in an independent south Slavic nation led by themselves. The Russians were too weak to do anything but accept the new situation. The Germans had not been warned in advance of Austria's plans and were unhappy because the action threatened their relations with Russia. But Germany felt so dependent on the Dual Alliance that it assured Austria of its support. Austria had been given a free hand, and to an extent German policy was being made in Vienna. It was a dangerous precedent. At the same time, the failure of Britain and France to support Russia strained the Triple Entente and made it harder for them to oppose Russian interests again if they wanted to retain Russian friendship.

Second Moroccan Crisis The second Moroccan crisis, in 1911, emphasized the French and British need for mutual support. When France sent in an army to put down a rebellion, Germany took the opportunity to "protect German interests" in Morocco as a means of extorting colonial concessions in the French Congo. To add force to their demands, the Germans sent the gunboat *Panther* to the port of Agadir, allegedly to protect German citizens there. Once again, as in 1905, the Germans went too far. The *Panther's* visit to Agadir alarmed Britain. For some time Anglo-German relations had been deteriorating, chiefly because of the naval race, but negotiations failed to persuade William II and Tirpitz to slow down naval construction.

In this atmosphere, the British heard of the *Panther's* arrival in Morocco. They mistakenly believed that the Germans meant to turn Agadir into a naval base on the Atlantic. The crisis passed when France yielded some insignificant bits of the Congo and Germany withdrew from Morocco. The main result was to increase British fear of, and hostility to, Germany and to draw Britain closer to France. Specific plans were now formulated for a British expeditionary force to help defend France against German attack. The British and French navies agreed to cooperate. If France were attacked by Germany, Britain had to help defend the French, for its own security was inextricably tied up with that of France.

The Balkan Wars After the second Moroccan crisis, Italy feared that the recognition of the French protectorate in Morocco would encourage France to move into Libya. Consequently, in 1911 Italy attacked the Ottoman Empire to anticipate the French, defeated the faltering Turks, and obtained Libya and the Dodecanese Islands in the Aegean. The Italian victory encouraged the Balkan states to try their luck. In 1912 Bulgaria, Greece, Montenegro, and Serbia attacked the Ottoman Empire and won easily (see Map 29–2). After this First Balkan War the victors fell out among themselves. The Serbs and the Bulgarians quarreled about the division of Macedonia, and in 1913 a Second Balkan War erupted. This time Turkey and Romania joined Greece and Serbia against Bulgaria, which lost much of what it had gained since 1878.

The alarmed Austrians were determined to limit Serbian gains and especially to prevent the Serbs from obtaining a port on the Adriatic. An international conference sponsored by Britain in early 1913 resolved the matter in Austria's favor and called for an independent kingdom of Albania. But Austria felt humiliated by the public airing of Serbian demands. At first the Serbs defied the powers and stayed in Albania. Under Austrian pressure they withdrew, but in September 1913, after the Second Balkan War, the Serbs reoccupied sections of Albania. In mid-October Austria unilaterally issued an ultimatum to Serbia, which again withdrew from Albania. During this crisis many Austrians had wanted an all-out attack on Serbia to remove its threat once and for all. In Russia, Pan-Slavic sentiment pressed Czar Nicholas II (r. 1894–1917) to take a firm stand, but Russia nonetheless once again let Austria have its way.

The lessons learned from this crisis profoundly influenced behavior in the final crisis of 1914. The Russians had, as in 1908, been embarrassed by their passivity, and their allies were now more reluctant to restrain them. The Austrians were embarrassed by the results of accepting an international conference and were determined not to do it again. They had seen

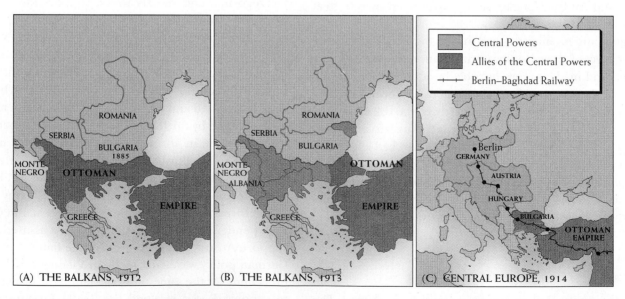

MAP 29–2 The Balkans, 1912–1913. Two maps show the Balkans before (a) and after (b) the two Balkan Wars; note the Ottoman retreat. In (c) we see the geographical relationship of the Central Powers and their Bulgarian and Turkish allies.

that better results might be obtained from a threat of direct force; they and their German allies did not miss the lesson.

SARAJEVO AND THE OUTBREAK OF WAR (JUNE–AUGUST 1914)

The Assassination   On June 28, 1914, a young Bosnian nationalist shot and killed the Austrian Archduke Francis Ferdinand (1863–1914), heir to the throne, and his wife as they drove through the Bosnian capital of Sarajevo. The assassin was a member of a conspiracy hatched by a political terrorist society called Union or Death, better known as the Black Hand. The chief of intelligence of the Serbian army's general staff had helped plan the crime. Even though his role was not actually known at the time, it was generally believed that Serbian officials were involved. The glee of the Serbian press supported that belief.

Germany and Austria's Response   The assassination was condemned throughout Europe. To those Austrians who had long favored an attack on Serbia as a solution to the empire's Slavic problem, the opportunity seemed irresistible. But it was never easy for the Dual Monarchy to make a decision. Conrad von Hotzendorf (1852–1925), chief of the Austrian general staff, urged an attack as he had often done before. Count Stefan Tisza (1861–1918), speaking for Hungary, resisted. Count Leopold Berchtold (1863–1942), the Austro-Hungarian foreign minister, knew that German support would be required if Russia should decide to protect Serbia. He also knew that nothing could be done without Tisza's approval and that only German support could persuade the Hungarians to accept a war. The question of peace or war, therefore, had to be answered in Berlin.

William II and Chancellor Theobald von Bethmann-Hollweg (1856–1921) readily promised German support for an attack on Serbia. It has often been said that they gave the Austrians a "blank check," but their message was firmer than that. They urged the Austrians to move swiftly, while the other powers were still angry at Serbia. They also indicated that a failure to act would be taken as evidence of Austria-Hungary's weakness and uselessness as an ally. Therefore, the Austrians never wavered in their determination to attack Serbia. They hoped, with the protection of Germany, to fight a limited war that would not bring on a general European conflict. However, they were prepared to risk even the latter. The Germans also knew that they risked a general war, but they hoped to "localize" the fight between Austria and Serbia.

These calculations proved to be incorrect. Bethmann-Hollweg hoped that the Austrians would strike swiftly and present the powers with a fait accompli while the outrage of the assassination was still fresh. He also hoped that German support would deter Russian involvement. Failing that, he was prepared

Assassination of the Archduke. Above: The Austrain Archduke Franz Ferdinand and his wife in Sarajevo on June 28, 1914. Later in the day the royal couple were assassinated by young revolutionaries trained and supplied in Serbia, igniting the crisis that led to World War I, Below: Moments after the assassination the Austrian police captured one of the assassins.
Brown Brothers.

for a continental war that would bring rapid victory over France and allow a full-scale attack on the Russians, who were always slow to bring their strength into action. This policy depended on British neutrality, and the German chancellor convinced himself that the British could be persuaded to stand aloof.

However, the Austrians were slow to act. They did not even deliver their deliberately unacceptable ultimatum to Serbia until July 24, when the general hostility toward Serbia had begun to subside. Serbia further embarrassed the Austrians by returning so soft and conciliatory an answer that even the mercurial German emperor thought it removed all reason for war.

CHRONOLOGY

Coming of World War I

1871	End of the Franco-Prussian War; creation of the German Empire; German annexation of Alsace-Lorraine
1873	Three Emperors' League (Germany, Russia, and Austria-Hungary)
1875	Russo-Turkish War
1878	Congress of Berlin
1879	Dual Alliance between Germany and Austria
1881	Three Emperors' League is renewed
1882	Italy joins Germany and Austria in Triple Alliance
1888	William II becomes German emperor
1890	Bismarck dismissed
1894	Franco-Russian alliance
1898	Germany begins to build battleship navy
1902	British alliance with Japan
1904	Entente Cordiale between Britain and France
1904–1905	Russo-Japanese War
1905	First Moroccan crisis
1907	British agreement with Russia
1908–1909	Bosnian crisis
1911	Second Moroccan crisis; Italy attacks Turkey
1912–1913	First and Second Balkan Wars
1914	Outbreak of World War I

But the Austrians were determined not to turn back. On July 28 they declared war on Serbia, even though they could not field an army until mid-August.

The Triple Entente's Response The Russians, previously so often forced to back off, responded angrily to the Austrian demands on Serbia. The most conservative elements of the Russian government feared that war would bring on revolution as it had in 1905. But nationalists, Pan-Slavs, and most of the politically conscious classes in general demanded action. The government ordered partial mobilization, against Austria only. This policy was militarily impossible, but its purpose was diplomatic: to pressure Austria to hold back its attack on Serbia.

Mobilization of any kind, however, was dangerous because it was generally understood to be equivalent to an act of war. It was especially alarming to General Helmuth von Moltke (1848–1916), head of the German general staff. The possibility that the Russians might start mobilization before the Germans could move would upset the delicate timing of Germany's only battle plan—the **Schlieffen Plan**, which required an attack on France first—and would endanger Germany. From this point on, Moltke pressed for German mobilization

and war. The pressure of military necessity mounted until it became irresistible.

The Western European powers were not eager for war. France's president and prime minister were on their way back from a visit to Russia when the crisis flared up again on July 24. The Austrians had, in fact, timed their ultimatum precisely, so that these two men would be at sea at the crucial moment. Had they been in Paris they might have attempted to restrain the Russians. But the French ambassador to Russia gave the Russians the same assurances that Germany had given its ally. The British worked hard to avoid trouble by traditional means: a conference of the powers. Austria, still smarting from its humiliation after the London Conference of 1913, would not hear of it. The Germans privately supported the Austrians but were publicly conciliatory in the hope of keeping the British neutral.

Soon, however, Bethmann-Hollweg realized what he should have known from the first: If Germany attacked France, Britain must fight. Until July 30 his public appeals to Austria for restraint were a sham. Thereafter, he sincerely tried to persuade the Austrians to negotiate and to avoid a general war, but it was too late. While Bethmann-Hollweg was urging restraint on the Austrians, Moltke was pressing them to act. The Austrians wondered who was in charge in Berlin, but they could not retreat without losing their own self-respect and that of the Germans.

On July 30 Austria ordered mobilization against Russia. Bethmann-Hollweg resisted the enormous pressure to mobilize, not because he had any further hope of avoiding war but because he wanted Russia to mobilize against Germany first and appear to be the aggressor. Only thus could he win the support of the German nation for war, especially the pacifistic Social Democrats. His luck was good this time. The news of Russian general mobilization came only minutes before Germany would have mobilized in any case. The Schlieffen Plan went into effect. The Germans invaded Luxembourg on August 1 and Belgium on August 3. The latter invasion violated the treaty of 1839, in which the British had guaranteed Belgian neutrality. This factor undermined the considerable sentiment in Britain for neutrality and united the nation against Germany. Germany then invaded France, and on August 4 Britain declared war on Germany.

The Great War had begun. As Sir Edward Grey put it, the lights were going out all over Europe. They would come on again, but Europe would never be the same.

STRATEGIES AND STALEMATE (1914–1917)

Throughout Europe jubilation greeted the outbreak of war. No general war had been fought since Napoleon, and the horrors of modern warfare were not yet understood. The dominant memory was of Bismarck's swift and decisive campaigns, in which costs and casualties were light and the rewards great.

Both sides expected to take the offensive, force a battle on favorable ground, and win a quick victory. The Triple Entente powers—or the Allies, as they came to be called—had superior numbers and financial resources as well as command of the sea (see Figure 29–1). Germany and Austria, the Central Powers, had the advantages of internal lines of communication and of having launched their attack first.

After 1905 Germany's only war plan was the one developed by Count Alfred von Schlieffen (1833–1913), chief of the German general staff from 1891 to 1906 (see Map 29–3). It aimed to outflank the French defenses by sweeping through Belgium to the Channel, then wheeling to the south and east to envelop the French and crush them against the German fortresses in Lorraine. In the east the Germans planned to stand on the defensive against Russia until France had been beaten, a task they thought would take only six weeks.

The apparent risk, besides the violation of Belgian neutrality and the consequent alienation of Britain, lay in weakening the German defenses against a direct attack across the frontier. Yet Schlieffen is said to have uttered the dying words, "It must come to a fight. Only make the right wing strong." The execution of his plan, however, was left to Helmuth von Moltke, the nephew of Bismarck's most effective general. Moltke was a gloomy and nervous man who lacked the talent of his illustrious uncle and the theoretical daring of Schlieffen. He added divisions to the left wing and even weakened the Russian front for the same purpose. The consequence of this hesitant strategy was the failure of the Schlieffen Plan by a narrow margin.

The War in the West   The French had also put faith in the offensive, but with less reason than the Germans. They badly underestimated the numbers and the effectiveness of the German reserves and set too much store on the importance

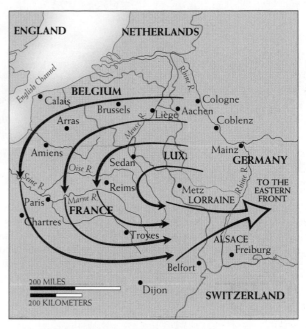

MAP 29–3 The Schlieffen Plan of 1905.   Germany's grand strategy for quickly winning the war against France in 1914 is shown by the wheeling arrows on the map. The crushing blows at France were, in the original plan, to be followed by the release of troops for use against Russia on Germany's Eastern Front. But the plan was not adequately implemented, and the war on the Western Front became a long contest instead.

The Western Front. French troops advancing on the Western Front. This scene of trench warfare characterizes the 20th century's first great international conflict. The trenches were protected by barbed wire and machine guns, which gave defenders the advantage.
Hulton/Corbis-Bettmann.

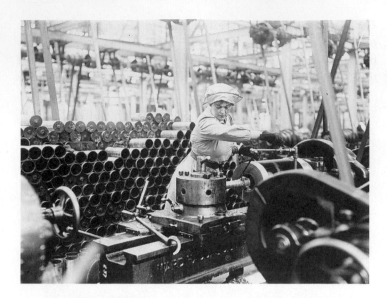

Women Munitions Workers in England. The First World War demanded more from the civilian populations than had previous wars, resulting in important social changes. The demands of the munitions industries and a shortage of men (so many of whom were in uniform) brought many women out of traditional roles at home and into factories and other war work.

Hulton Getty Picture Collection/Tony Stone Images.

of the courage and spirit of their troops, which proved insufficient against modern weapons, especially the machine gun. The French offensive on Germany's western frontier failed totally. In a sense this defeat was better than a partial success because it released troops for use against the main German army. As a result, the French and the British were able to stop the Germans at the Battle of the Marne in September 1914.

Thereafter, the war in the west became one of position instead of movement. Both sides dug in behind a wall of trenches protected by barbed wire that stretched from the North Sea to Switzerland. Strategically placed machine-gun nests made assaults difficult and dangerous. Both sides, nonetheless, attempted massive attacks initiated by artillery bombardments of unprecedented and horrible force and duration. Still, the defense was always able to prevent a breakthrough.

The War in the East   In the east the war began auspiciously for the Allies. The Russians advanced into Austrian territory and inflicted heavy casualties, but Russian incompetence and German energy soon reversed the situation (see Map 29–4). A junior German officer, Erich Ludendorff (1865–1937), under the command of the elderly General Paul von Hindenburg (1847–1934), destroyed or captured an entire Russian army at the Battle of Tannenberg; he also defeated the Russians at the Masurian Lakes. In 1915 the Central Powers pressed their advantage in the east and drove into the Baltic states and western Russia, inflicting over 2 million casualties in a single year. Russian confidence was badly shaken, but the Russian army stayed in the field.

As the battle lines hardened, both sides sought new allies. Turkey (because of its hostility to Russia) and Bulgaria (the enemy of Serbia) joined the Central Powers. Italy seemed an especially valuable prize, and both sides bid for its support with promises of a division of the spoils of victory. Because

John Singer Sargent, *Gassed*, 1918–1919.   Many new weapons were used extensively for the first time in the Great War of 1914–1918, including machine guns, barbed wire, tanks, airplanes, and several kinds of poison gas. The Germans were the first to employ gas as a weapon, firing a nonlethal kind of tear gas at the Russians on the Eastern Front in January 1915. By April, they had learned how to use the poison gas chlorine against the Allies on the Western Front. *Gassed*, by the American painter John Singer Sargent, can be compared to ancient Greek friezes depicting mythical battles. There is, however, an important difference in treatment: While Greek sculptures always portray an element of heroism along with death and suffering, Sargent's painting reveals only the horror of battle.

Imperial War Museum, London.

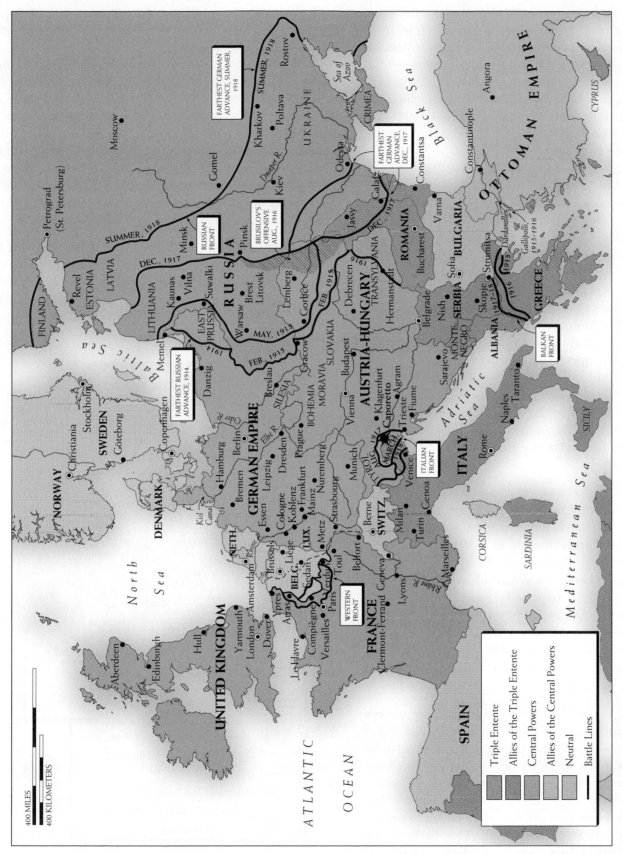

MAP 29–4 World War I in Europe. Despite the importance of military action in the Far East, in the Middle East, and at sea, the main theaters of activity in World War I were in the European areas shown here.

Legend:
- Triple Entente
- Allies of the Triple Entente
- Central Powers
- Allies of the Central Powers
- Neutral
- Battle Lines

400 MILES
400 KILOMETERS

FARTHEST GERMAN ADVANCE, SUMMER, 1918

FARTHEST GERMAN ADVANCE, DEC., 1917

RUSSIAN FRONT

BRUSILOV'S OFFENSIVE AUG., 1916

FARTHEST RUSSIAN ADVANCE, 1914

BALKAN FRONT

ITALIAN FRONT

WESTERN FRONT

SUMMER, 1918

DEC., 1917

MAY, 1915

FEB., 1915

1914

what the Italians wanted most was held by Austria, the Allies could make the more attractive promises. In a secret treaty of 1915 the Allies agreed to deliver to Italy most of *Italia Irredenta* (i.e., the Trentino, the South Tyrol, Trieste, and some of the Dalmatian Islands) after victory. By the spring of 1915 Italy was engaging Austrian armies. Although the Italian campaign distracted the Central Powers, it never produced significant results. Romania joined the Allies in 1916 but was quickly defeated and driven from the war.

In the Far East, Japan honored its alliance with Britain and entered the war. The Japanese quickly overran the German colonies in China and the Pacific and used the opportunity to improve their own position against China.

In 1915 the Allies undertook to break the deadlock in the fighting by going around it. The idea came chiefly from Winston Churchill (1874–1965), First Lord of the British Admiralty. He proposed an attack at Gallipoli on the Dardanelles and the swift capture of Constantinople. This policy would knock Turkey from the war, bring help to the Balkan front, and ease communication with Russia. Success depended on timing, speed, and daring leadership, but all of these qualities were lacking. The execution of the attack was inept and overly cautious. Troops were landed and, as resistance continued, the Allied commitment increased. Before the campaign was abandoned the Allies lost almost 150,000 men and diverted three times that number from more useful fighting.

Return to the West   Both sides turned back to the west in 1916 (see Map 29–5). General Erich von Falkenhayn (1861–1922), who had succeeded Moltke in September 1914, sought success by an attack on the French stronghold of Verdun. The commander of Verdun, Henri Pétain (1856–1951), became a hero. "They shall not pass" became a slogan of national defiance. The Allies tried to end the impasse by launching a major offensive along the River Somme in July. Once again, the superiority of the defense was demonstrated. The only result was enormous casualties on both sides. On all fronts the losses were great and the results meager. The war on land dragged on with no end in sight.

The War at Sea   As the war continued, control of the sea became more important. The British ignored the distinction between war supplies (which were contraband according to international law) and food or other peaceful cargo, which was not subject to seizure. They imposed a strict blockade meant to starve out the enemy, regardless of international law. The Germans responded with submarine warfare meant to destroy British shipping and to starve the British. They declared the waters around the British Isles a war zone, where even neutral ships would not be safe. Both policies were unwelcome to neutrals, and especially to the United States, which conducted ex-

tensive trade in the Atlantic, but the sinking of neutral ships by German submarines was both more dramatic and more offensive than Britain's blockade.

In 1915 the British liner Lusitania was torpedoed by a German submarine. Among the 1200 drowned were 118 Americans. President Woodrow Wilson (1856–1924) warned Germany that a repetition would not be accepted, and the Germans desisted rather than further anger the United States. This development gave the Allies a considerable advantage. The German fleet that had cost so much money and had caused so much trouble played no significant part in the war. The only battle it fought was at Jutland in the spring of 1916. The battle resulted in a standoff and confirmed British domination of the surface of the sea.

America Enters the War   In December 1916 President Wilson attempted to bring about a negotiated peace, but neither side was willing to give up its hopes for total victory. The war seemed likely to continue until one or both sides reached

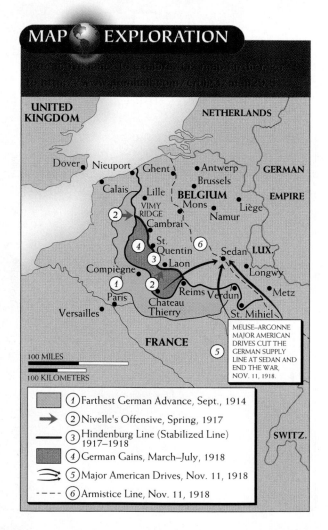

MAP 29–5 The Western Front 1914–1918.   This map shows the crucial Western Front in detail.

▲ **Gallipoli.** Australian and New Zealand troups huddle in scattered clumps on a hillside near Gallipoli
Getty Images Inc. – Hulton Archive Photos.

exhaustion. Two events early in 1917 changed the situation radically. On February 1 the Germans announced the resumption of unrestricted submarine warfare, which led the United States to break off diplomatic relations. On April 6 the United States declared war on Germany.

One of the deterrents to an earlier American intervention had been the presence of autocratic tsarist Russia among the Allies. Wilson could conceive of the war only as an idealistic crusade "to make the world safe for democracy." That problem was resolved in March of 1917 by a revolution in Russia that overthrew the tsarist government.

The Russian Revolution

The March Revolution in Russia was neither planned nor led by any political faction. It was the result of the collapse of the monarchy's ability to govern. Military and domestic failures produced massive casualties, widespread hunger, strikes by workers, and disorganization in the army. The peasant unrest that had plagued the countryside before 1914 did not subside during the conflict. All political factions were discontented.

In early March 1917 strikes and worker demonstrations erupted in Petrograd, as Saint Petersburg had been renamed. The ill-disciplined troops in the city refused to fire on the demonstrators, and the tsar abdicated on March 15. The government of Russia fell into the hands of members of the Duma, who formed a provisional government composed chiefly of Constitutional Democrats with Western sympathies. The various Socialists, including both Social Revolutionaries and Social Democrats of the Menshevik wing, also began to organize the workers into councils called **soviets**. Initially, they allowed the provisional government to function without actually supporting it. But they became estranged as the Constitutional Democratic Party failed to control the army or to purge "reactionaries" from the government.

In this climate the provisional government decided to remain loyal to the existing Russian alliances and to continue the war against Germany. Its fate was sealed when a new offensive in the summer of 1917 collapsed. Disillusionment with the war, shortages of food and other necessities at home, and the growing demand by the peasants for land reform undermined the government, even after its leadership had been taken over by the moderate Socialist Alexander Kerensky (1881–1970).

Machine-gunners. U.S. infantrymen (known as "doughboys") ▶ lie prone among smoke and broken trees while reinforcing French troops near the Marne.
Library of Congress.

DOCUMENT | Lenin Establishes His Dictatorship

After the Bolshevik coup in October, elections for the Constituent Assembly were held in November. The results gave a majority to the Social Revolutionary Party and embarrassed the Bolsheviks. Using his control of the Red Army, Lenin closed the Constituent Assembly in January 1918, after it had met for only one day, and established the rule of a revolutionary elite and his own dictatorship. Here is the crucial Bolshevik decree.

♦ What reasons does Lenin give for closing the legitimately elected Constituent Assembly? What other reasons might he have had? What were the soviets? Did they have a legitimate claim to the monopoly of political power? Was the dissolution of the assembly a temporary or permanent measure? What defense can be made for the Bolsheviks' action? Is it enough to justify that action?

... The Constituent Assembly, elected on the basis of lists drawn up prior to the October Revolution, was an expression of the old relation of political forces which existed when power was held by the compromisers and the Cadets. When the people at that time voted for the candidates for the Socialist-Revolutionary Party, they were not in a position to choose between the Right Socialist-Revolutionaries, the supporters of the bourgeoisie, and the Left Socialist-Revolutionaries, the supporters of Socialism. Thus, the Constituent Assembly, which was to have been the crown of the bourgeois parliamentary republic, could not become an obstacle in the path of the October Revolution and the Soviet power.

The October Revolution, by giving the power to the Soviets, and through the Soviets to the toiling and exploited classes, aroused the desperate resistance of the exploiters, and in the crushing of this resistance it fully revealed itself as the beginning of the socialist revolution ... the majority in the Constituent Assembly which met on January 5 was secured by the party of the Right Socialist-Revolutionaries, the party of Kerensky, Avksentyev and Chernov. Naturally, this party refused to discuss the absolutely clear, precise and unambiguous proposal of the supreme organ of Soviet power, the Central Executive Committee of the Soviets, to recognize the program of the Soviet power, to recognize the "Declaration of Rights of the Toiling and Exploited People," to recognize the October Revolution and the Soviet power. ...

The Right Socialist-Revolutionary and Menshevik parties are in fact waging outside the walls of the Constituent Assembly a most desperate struggle against the Soviet power. ...

Accordingly, the Central Executive Committee resolves: The Constituent Assembly is hereby dissolved.

Ever since April the Bolsheviks had been working against the provisional government. The Germans, in their most successful attempt at subversion, had rushed the brilliant Bolshevik leader V. I. Lenin (1870–1924) in a sealed train from his exile in Switzerland across Germany to Petrograd in the hope that he would cause trouble for the revolutionary government. The Bolsheviks demanded that all political power go to the soviets, which they controlled. The failure of the summer offensive encouraged them to attempt a coup, but it failed. Lenin fled to Finland, and his chief collaborator, Leon Trotsky (1877–1940), was imprisoned.

An abortive right-wing countercoup gave the Bolsheviks another chance. Trotsky, released from prison, led the powerful Petrograd Soviet. Lenin returned in October, insisted to his doubting colleagues that the time was ripe to take power, and by the extraordinary force of his personality persuaded them to act. Trotsky organized the coup that took place on November 6 and that concluded with an armed assault on the provisional government. The Bolsheviks, almost as much to their own astonishment as to that of the rest of the world, had come to rule Russia. (See Document, "Lenin Establishes His Dictatorship.")

The victors moved to fulfill their promises and to assure their own security. The provisional government had decreed an election for late November to select a Constituent Assembly. The Social Revolutionaries won a large majority over the Bolsheviks. When the assembly gathered in January, it met for only a day before the Red Army, controlled by the Bolsheviks, dispersed it. All other political parties also ceased to function in any meaningful fashion. In November and January the Bolshevik government promulgated decrees that nationalized the land and turned it over to its peasant proprietors. Factory workers were put in charge of their plants. Banks were taken from their owners and seized for the state, and the debt of the tsarist government was repudiated. Property of the church reverted to the state.

The Bolshevik government also took Russia out of the war, which they believed benefited only capitalism. They signed an

Petrograd Munitions Workers Demonstrating in 1917.
The barely-legible slogan at the top of the banner
reads, "Victory to the Petrograd Workers!"
RIa-Novosti/Sovfoto/Eastfoto.

armistice with Germany in December 1917. On March 3, 1918, they accepted the Treaty of Brest-Litovsk, by which Russia yielded Finland, Poland, the Baltic states, and the Ukraine. Georgian territory in the Transcaucasus region went to Turkey. The Bolsheviks also agreed to pay a heavy war indemnity. These terms were a terribly high price to pay for peace, but Lenin had no choice. The Bolsheviks needed time to impose their rule on a devastated and chaotic Russia.

Until 1921 the New Bolshevik government confronted massive domestic resistance. A civil war erupted between the "Red" Russians supporting the revolution and the **"White" Russians**, who opposed the Bolshevik triumph. In the summer of 1918 the tsar and his family were murdered. Loyal army officers continued to fight the revolution and received aid from the Allies. However, led by Trotsky, the Red Army eventually overcame the domestic opposition. By 1921 Lenin and his supporters were in firm control.

End of World War I

MILITARY RESOLUTION

The Treaty of Brest-Litovsk brought Germany to the peak of its success. The Germans controlled eastern Europe and its resources, especially food. By 1918 they were free to concentrate their forces on the Western Front. This turn of events would probably have been decisive had it not been balanced by American intervention. Still, American troops would not arrive in significant numbers for about a year, and both sides tried to win the war in 1917. An Allied attempt to break through in the west failed disastrously, bringing heavy losses to the British and the French and causing a mutiny in the French

army. The Austrians, supported by the Germans, defeated the Italians at Caporetto and threatened to overrun Italy, before they were checked with the aid of Allied troops. The deadlock continued, but time was running out for the Central Powers.

In 1918 the Germans, persuaded chiefly by Ludendorff—second in command to Hindenburg, but the real leader of the army—decided to gamble everything on one last offensive. The German army pushed forward and even reached the Marne again but got no farther. They had no more reserves, and the entire nation was exhausted. The Allies, on the other hand, were bolstered by the arrival of American troops in ever-increasing numbers. They launched a counteroffensive that was irresistible. As the Austrian fronts in the Balkans and Italy collapsed, the German high command knew that the end was imminent.

Ludendorff was determined that peace should be made before the German army could be thoroughly defeated in the field and that the responsibility should fall on civilians. For some time he had been the effective ruler of Germany under the aegis of the emperor. He now allowed a new government to be established on democratic principles and to seek peace immediately. The new government, under Prince Max of Baden (1867–1928), asked for peace on the basis of the **Fourteen Points** that President Wilson had declared as the American war aims. These were idealistic principles, including self-determination for nationalities, open diplomacy, freedom of the seas, disarmament, and establishment of a League of Nations to keep the peace. Wilson insisted that he would deal only with a democratic German government because he wanted to be sure he was dealing with the German people and not merely their rulers.

OVERVIEW Casualties of the Major Belligerents in World War 1

During World War I, Europeans turned the vast military and industrial power they had created in the nineteenth century against themselves. The result was an unprecedented slaughter that killed millions of soldiers and sailors and wounded many millions more. These casualties represented not only a waste of human life and talent but also the loss of consumers and producers. So traumatic were the losses that most Europeans were horrified at the prospect of another war. (In percentage terms, the French dead alone were the equivalent of the total populations—every man, woman, and child—of the states of Massachusetts, Connecticut, and Rhode Island.) The casualties of World War I help explain why the leaders of Britain and France sought to avoid another by adopting a policy of appeasement toward Hitler's demands in the late 1930s. No responsible statesman, they believed, would inflict another such slaughter on the nations of Europe.

Country	Killed	Wounded	Total Killed as Percentage of Population
Austria-Hungary	1.1 million	3.62 million	1.9
Belgium	38,000	44,000	0.5
Britain	723,000	1.16 million	1.6
Bulgaria	88,000	152,000	1.9
France	1.4 million	2 million	3.4
Germany	2 million	4.2 million	3.0
Italy	578,000	947,000	1.6
Romania	250,000	120,000	3.3
Russia	1.8 million	1.45 million	1.1
Serbia	278,000	138,000	5.7
Turkey	804,000	400,000	3.7
United States	114,000	205,000	0.1

The disintegration of the German army forced William II to abdicate on November 9, 1918. The majority branch of the Social Democratic Party proclaimed a republic to prevent the establishment of a soviet government under the control of their radical Leninist wing, which had earlier broken away as the Independent Socialist Party. Two days later this Republican, Socialist-led government signed the armistice that ended the war by accepting German defeat. The German people were, in general, unaware that their army had been defeated in the field and was crumbling. No foreign soldier stood on German soil. Many Germans expected a negotiated and mild settlement. The real peace embittered the German people, many of whom came to believe that Germany had not been defeated but had been tricked by the enemy and betrayed—even stabbed in the back—by Republicans and Socialists at home.

The victors rejoiced, but they also had much to mourn. The casualties on all sides came to about 10 million dead and twice as many wounded. The economic and financial resources of the European states were badly strained. The victorious Allies, formerly creditors to the world, became debtors to the new American colossus, itself barely touched by the calamities of war.

The old international order, moreover, was dead. Russia was ruled by a Bolshevik dictatorship that preached world revolution and the overthrow of capitalism everywhere. Germany was in chaos. Austria-Hungary had disintegrated into a swarm of small states competing for the remains of the ancient empire. These kinds of change stirred the colonial territories ruled by the European powers; overseas empires would never again be as secure as they had seemed before the war. Europe was no longer the center of the world, free to interfere when it wished or to ignore the outer regions if it chose. Its easy confidence in material and moral progress was shattered by the brutal reality of four years of horrible war. The memory of that war lived on to shake the nerve of the victorious Western powers as they confronted the new conditions of the postwar world.

SETTLEMENT AT PARIS

The Peacemakers The representatives of the victorious states gathered at Versailles and other Parisian suburbs in the first half of 1919. Wilson speaking for the United States, David Lloyd George (1863–1945) for Britain, Georges Clemenceau (1841–1929) for France, and Vittorio Emanuele Orlando (1860–1952) for Italy made up the Big Four. Japan, now recognized for the first time as a great power, also had an important part in the discussions.

Wilson's idealism came into conflict with the more practical war aims of the victorious powers and with many of the secret treaties that had been made before and during the war. The British and French people had been told that Germany would be made to pay for the war. Russia had been promised control of Constantinople in return for recognition of the French claim to Alsace-Lorraine and British control of Egypt. Romania had been promised Transylvania at the expense of Hungary. Some of the agreements contradicted others; Italy and Serbia had competing claims to the islands and shore of the Adriatic. During the war the British had encouraged Arab hopes of an independent Arab state carved out of the Ottoman Empire; those plans conflicted with the Balfour Declaration (1917), in which the British seemed to accept Zionism and to promise the Jews a national home in Palestine. Both of these plans conflicted with an Anglo-French agreement to divide the Near East between themselves.

The continuing national goals of the victors presented further obstacles to an idealistic "peace without victors." France was keenly conscious of its numerical inferiority to Germany and of the low birthrate that would keep it inferior. Naturally, France was eager to achieve a settlement that would permanently weaken Germany and preserve French political and military superiority. Italy sought the acquisition of Italia Irredenta ("unredeemed Italy"); Britain looked to its imperial interests; Japan pursued its own advantage in Asia; and the United States insisted on freedom of the seas, which favored American commerce, and on its right to maintain the Monroe Doctrine.

Finally, the peacemakers of 1919 faced a world still in turmoil. The greatest immediate threat appeared to be the spread of bolshevism. While Lenin and his colleagues were distracted by civil war, the Allies landed small armies in Russia to help overthrow the Bolshevik regime. Communist governments were established in Bavaria and Hungary. Berlin also experienced a dangerous Communist uprising led by the "Spartacus group" (Communist extremists). The Allies were sufficiently worried by these developments to allow and to support suppression of these Communist movements by right-wing military forces. They even permitted an army of German volunteers to operate against the Bolsheviks in the Baltic states.

The fear of the spread of communism played a part in the thinking of the diplomats at Versailles, but it was far from dom-

▲ **Versailles.** The German delegation signs the peace treaty ending the First World War in the Hall of Mirrors of the Palace of Versailles on June 28, 1919. This painting by Sir William Orpen completed in 1921, now hangs in the Imperial War Museum in London. U.S. President Woodrow Wilson is seated in the center, holding a clutch of papers.
Museum, London/Bildarchiv Preussischer Kulturbesitz.

inant. The Germans kept playing on such fears as a way of getting better terms, but the Allies, especially the French, would not hear of it. Fear of Germany remained the chief concern for France; attention to interests that were more traditional and more immediate governed the policies of the other Allies.

The Peace The Paris settlement consisted of five separate treaties between the victors and the defeated powers. Formal sessions began on January 18, 1919, and the last treaty was signed on August 10, 1920. The notion of "a peace without victors" became a mockery when the Soviet Union (as Russia was now called) and Germany were excluded from the peace conference. The Germans were simply presented with a treaty and compelled to accept it, which fully justified their complaint that the treaty had not been negotiated but dictated. The principle of national self-determination was violated many times, as it was unavoidable. Nevertheless, the diplomats of the small nations were angered by their exclusion from decision making. The undeserved adulation accorded Wilson on his arrival

Peacemakers. The Allies promoted Arab efforts to secure independence from Turkey in an effort to remove Turkey from the war. Delegates to the peace conference of 1919 in Paris included British Colonel T. E. Lawrence, who helped lead the rebellion against Turkey, and representatives from the Middle East. Prince Feisal, the third son of King Hussein, stands in the foreground of this picture; Lawrence is in the middle row, second from the right; and Brigadier General Nuri Pasha Said of Baghdad is second from the left.

Corbis-Bettmann.

gradually turned into equally undeserved scorn. He had not abandoned his ideals lightly but had merely given way to the irresistible force of reality.

The League of Nations Wilson put great faith in a new instrument for peace and justice, the **League of Nations**. Its covenant was an essential part of the peace treaty. The league was not intended as an international government, but as a body of sovereign states that agreed to pursue common policies and to consult in the common interest, especially when war threatened. In that case the members promised to submit the matter to arbitration, to an international court, or to the League Council. Refusal to abide by this agreement would justify league intervention in the form of economic and even military sanctions.

But the league was unlikely to be effective because it had no armed forces at its disposal. Action required the unanimous consent of its council, consisting of Britain, France, Italy, the United States, Japan, and four other states that had temporary seats. The Covenant of the League bound its members to "respect and preserve" the territorial integrity of all its members, which was generally seen as a device to ensure the security of the victorious powers. The exclusion from the League Assembly of Germany and the Soviet Union further undermined the league's claim to even-handedness.

Colonies Another provision of the covenant dealt with colonial areas. They were to be placed under the "tutelage" of one of the great powers under league supervision and encouraged to advance toward independence. Because there were no teeth in this provision, little advance was made. Provisions for disarmament were equally ineffective. Members of the league remained fully sovereign and continued to pursue their own national interests.

Germany In the West, the main territorial issue was the fate of Germany (see Map 29–6). Although a united Germany was less than fifty years old, no one seems to have thought of undoing Bismarck's work and dividing it into its component parts. The French would have liked to set up the Rhineland as a separate buffer state, but Lloyd George and Wilson would not permit that. Still, they could not ignore France's need for protection against a resurgent Germany. France received Alsace-Lorraine and the right to work the coal mines of the Saar for fifteen years. Germany west of the Rhine, and fifty kilometers east of it, was to be a demilitarized zone; Allied troops could stay on the west bank for fifteen years. In addition to this physical barrier to a new German attack, the treaty provided that Britain and the United States would guarantee to aid France if it were attacked by Germany. Such an attack was made more unlikely by the permanent disarmament of Germany. Its army was limited to 100,000 men on long-term service; its fleet was all but eliminated; and it was forbidden to have war planes, submarines, tanks, heavy artillery, or poison gas. As long as these provisions were observed, France would be safe.

The East The settlement in the East ratified the collapse of the great defeated empires that had ruled it for centuries. Germany's frontier lost much of Silesia and part of Prussia. East Prussia was cut off from the rest of Germany by a corridor carved out to give the revived state of Poland access to the sea. The Austro-Hungarian Empire disappeared. Most of its German-speaking people were gathered in the small Republic of Austria, cut off from the Germans of Bohemia and forbidden to unite with Germany. The Magyars occupied the much-reduced kingdom of Hungary.

MAP 29–6 World War I Peace Settlement in Europe and the Middle East.   The map of central and eastern Europe, as well as that of the Middle East, underwent drastic revision after World War I. The enormous territorial losses suffered by Germany, Austria-Hungary, the Ottoman Empire, Bulgaria, and Russia were the other side of the coin represented by gains for France, Italy, Greece, and Romania and by the appearance, or reappearance, of at least eight new independent states from Finland in the north to Yugoslavia in the south. The mandate system for former Ottoman territories outside Turkey proper laid foundations for several new, mostly Arab, states in the Middle East.

The Czechs of Bohemia and Moravia joined with the Slovaks and Ruthenians to the east to form Czechoslovakia, and this new state also included several million unhappy Germans. The southern Slavs were united in the kingdom of Serbs, Croats, and Slovenes, or Yugoslavia. Italy gained the Trentino and Trieste. Romania gained Transylvania from Hungary and Bessarabia from Russia. Bulgaria lost territory to Greece and Yugoslavia. Finland, Estonia, Latvia, and Lithuania became independent states, and much of Poland was carved out of formerly Russian soil. Similarly, in the Caucasus, the new nations of Georgia, Armenia, and Azerbaijan took advantage of the turmoil following the Russian revolution to enjoy a period of independence from 1918 to 1921. Autonomy was also achieved by Ukraine and Russia during this brief period.

The old Ottoman Empire also disappeared. The new Republic of Turkey was limited to little more than Constantinople and Asia Minor. Palestine and Iraq came under British control and Syria and Lebanon under French control as mandates of the League of Nations. Germany's former colonies in Africa were divided among Britain, France, Belgium, and South Africa. The German Pacific possessions went to Australia, New Zealand, and Japan.

In theory, the mandate system was meant to have the "advanced nations" govern the former colonies in the interests of the native peoples until they became ready to govern themselves. They were thus divided into three categories—A, B, and C—in descending order of their readiness for independence. In practice, most mandated territories were treated as colonies by the powers under whose "tutelage" they came. Not even one Class A mandate had achieved full independence twenty years after the signing of the treaty. Colonialism was to remain a problem even after World War II.

Reparations   Perhaps the most debated part of the peace settlement dealt with reparations for the damage done by Germany during the war. Before the armistice the Germans promised to pay compensation "for all damages done to the civilian population of the Allies and their property." The Americans judged that the amount would be between $15 billion and $25 billion and that Germany would be able to pay that amount. However, France and Britain, worried about repaying their war debts to the United States, were eager to have Germany pay the full cost of the war, including pensions to survivors and dependents. There was general agreement that Germany could not afford to pay such a sum, whatever it might be, and no sum was fixed at the conference. In the meantime Germany was to pay $5 billion annually until 1921. At that time a final figure would be set, which Germany would have to pay within thirty years. The French did not regret the outcome. Either Germany would pay and be bled into impotence, or Germany would refuse to pay and justify French intervention.

To justify these huge reparations, the Allies inserted the notorious Clause 231, the **war guilt clause**, into the treaty:

> The Allied and Associated Governments affirm, and Germany accepts, the responsibility of Germany and her allies for causing all the loss and damage to which the Allied and Associated Governments and their nationals have been subjected as a consequence of the war imposed upon them by aggression of Germany and her allies.

The Germans, of course, bitterly resented the charge. They had lost territories containing millions of Germans and great quantities of badly needed natural resources; they were presented with an astronomical and apparently unlimited reparations bill. To add insult to injury, they had to admit to a war guilt that they did not feel. Finally, they had to accept the entire treaty as it was written by the victors, without any opportunity for negotiation. Germany's Chancellor Philipp Scheidemann (1865–1939) spoke of the treaty as the imprisonment of the German people and asked, "What hand would not wither that binds itself and us in these fetters?" But there was no choice. The Social Democrats and the Catholic Center Party formed a new government, and their representatives signed the treaty. These parties formed the backbone of the Weimar government that ruled Germany until 1933; they never overcame the stigma of accepting the Treaty of Versailles.

EVALUATION OF THE PEACE

Few peace settlements have been more attacked than the one negotiated in Paris in 1919. It was natural that the defeated powers should have objected to it, but the peace was soon bitterly criticized in the victorious countries as well. Many of the French thought that it failed to provide adequate security for France, because it tied that security to promises of aid from the unreliable Anglo-Saxon countries. In England and the United States, liberals complained that the treaty violated the idealistic and liberal aims and principles that the Western leaders had professed. It was not a peace without victors. It did not end imperialism but attempted to promote the national interests of the winning nations. It violated the principles of national self-determination by leaving significant pockets of minorities outside the borders of their national homelands.

The most influential critic was John Maynard Keynes (1883–1946), a brilliant British economist who took part in the peace conference. When he saw the direction it was taking, he resigned in disgust and wrote a book called *The Economic Consequences of the Peace* (1920). It was a scathing attack, especially on reparations and the other economic clauses of the treaty. It was also a skillful assault on the negotiators, particularly on Wilson, who was depicted as a fool and a hypocrite. Keynes argued that the Treaty of Versailles was both immoral and unworkable. He called it a Carthaginian peace, referring to the utter destruction of Carthage by Rome after the Third Punic War (149–146 B.C.E.). He argued that such a peace would bring economic ruin and war to Europe unless it were repudiated. Keynes had a great effect on the British, who were already suspicious of France and glad of an excuse to withdraw from continental affairs. The decent and respectable position came to be one that aimed at revision of the treaty in favor of Germany.

Even more important was the book's influence in the United States. It fed the traditional tendency toward isolationism and gave powerful weapons to Wilson's enemies. Wilson's own political mistakes helped prevent American ratification of the treaty. Consequently, America was out of the League of Nations and not bound to defend France. Britain, therefore, was also free from its obligation to France. France was left to protect itself without adequate means to do so for long.

Many of the attacks on the Treaty of Versailles are unjustified. It was not a Carthaginian peace. Germany was neither dismembered nor ruined. Reparations could be and were scaled down, and until the great world depression of the 1930s the Germans recovered a high level of prosperity. Complaints against the peace should also be measured against the peace the victorious Germans had imposed on Russia at Brest-Litovsk and their plans for a European settlement in case of victory. Both were far more severe than anything enacted at Versailles. The attempt at achieving self-determination for nationalities was less than perfect, but it was the best solution Europe had ever accomplished in that direction.

The peace, nevertheless, was unsatisfactory in important ways. The elimination of the Austro-Hungarian Empire, however inevitable that might seem, created serious problems. Economically it was disastrous, for it separated raw materials from manufacturing areas and producers from their markets by new boundaries and tariff walls. In hard times, this separation created friction and hostility that aggravated other quarrels also created by the peace treaties. Poland and especially Czechoslovakia contained unhappy German minorities. Czechoslovakia itself was a collection of nationalities that did not find it easy to live together as a nation. Disputes over territories in eastern Europe promoted further tension. The peace was inadequate on another level as well. It rested on a defeat that Germany did not admit. The Germans believed they had been cheated rather than defeated. The high moral principles proclaimed by the Allies also undercut the validity of the peace, for it plainly fell far short of those principles.

Finally, the great weakness of the peace was its failure to accept reality. Germany and Russia were inevitably to play an important part in European affairs, yet they were excluded from the settlement and from the League of Nations. Given the many discontented parties, the peace was not self-enforcing, yet no satisfactory machinery for enforcing it was established. The league was never a serious force for this purpose. It was left to France, with no guarantee of support from Britain and no hope of help from the United States, to defend the new arrangements. Finland, the Baltic states, Poland, Romania, Czechoslovakia, and Yugoslavia were created or strengthened as a barrier to the westward expansion of Russian communism and as a threat in the rear to deter German revival. Most of these states, however, would have to rely on France in case of danger. France was simply not strong enough for the task if Germany were to rearm.

The tragedy of the Treaty of Versailles was that it was neither conciliatory enough to remove the desire for change, even at the cost of war, nor harsh enough to make another war impossible. A lasting peace required enforcing German disarmament while the more obnoxious clauses of the peace treaty were revised. Such a policy demanded continued attention to the problem, unity among the victors, and far-sighted leadership; none of these was present in adequate supply during the next two decades.

Summary

The New Imperialism European imperialism in the last part of the nineteenth century brought the Western countries into contact with most of the world. By 1914, European nations had divided Africa among themselves and controlled large parts of Asia and the islands of the Pacific. Much of the Middle East was under the nominal control of the Ottoman Empire, which was in its death throes and under European influence. The Monroe Doctrine made Latin America a protectorate of the United States. Japan had become an imperial power at the expense of China and Korea.

British soldiers release a message-carrying pigeon.

World War I The emergence of a new, powerful German state at the center of Europe upset the old balance of power. Bismarck, however, preserved the peace for as long as he remained in power. The new German emperor, William II, abandoned the policy of restraint and sought more power and influence for his country. The result was a system of alliances that divided Europe into two armed camps. What began as yet another Balkan War involving the European powers became a world war that influenced the rest of the world. As the terrible war of 1914–1918 dragged on, the real motives that had driven the European powers to fight gave way to public affirmations of the principles of nationalism and self-determination.

The Peace Settlement The peoples under colonial rule took these statements seriously and sought to win their own independence and nationhood. For the most part they were disappointed by the peace settlement. The British and French Empires were larger than ever. The Americans added to the islands they controlled in the Pacific. Japanese imperial ambitions were rewarded at the expense of China.

However, the old imperial nations, especially Britain and France, had paid an enormous price in lives, money, and will for their victory in the war. Colonial peoples pressed for the rights that were proclaimed as universal by the West but denied to their colonies; influential minorities in the countries that ruled them sympathized with colonial aspirations for independence. Tension between colonies and their ruling nations was a cause of instability in the world created by the Paris treaties of 1919.

Review Questions

1. What role did Bismarck envisage for the new Germany after 1871? How successful was he in carrying out his vision? Was he wise to tie Germany to Austria-Hungary?

2. Why and in what stages did Britain abandon "splendid isolation" at the turn of the century? Were the policies it pursued instead wise ones, or should Britain have followed a different course?

3. How did developments in the Balkans lead to the outbreak of World War I? What was the role of Serbia? Of Austria? Of Russia? What was the aim of German policy in July 1914? Did Germany want a general war?

4. Why did Germany lose World War I? Could Germany have won, or was victory never a possibility? Assess the settlement of Versailles. What were its benefits to Europe, and what were its drawbacks? Was the settlement too harsh or too conciliatory? Could it have secured lasting peace in Europe? How might it have been improved?

5. Why was Lenin successful in establishing Bolshevik rule in Russia? What role did Trotsky play? Was it wise policy for Lenin to take Russia out of the war?

Key Terms

Fourteen Points   (p. 891)

Italia Irredenta   (p. 888)

League of Nations   (p. 894)

mobilization   (p. 884)

New Imperialism   (p. 873)

Pan-Slavic movement   (p. 878)

reparations   (p. 895)

Schlieffen Plan   (p. 884)

war guilt clause   (p. 895)

White Russians   (p. 891)

Documents CD-ROM

NOTE: *To learn more about the topics in this chapter, see the Suggested Readings at the end of the book.*

30

Depression, European Dictators, and the American New Deal

- After Versailles: Demands for Revision and Enforcement

- Toward the Great Depression in Europe

- The Soviet Experiment

- The Fascist Experiment in Italy

- German Democracy and Dictatorship

- The Great Depression and the New Deal in the United States

◄ WEIMAR GERMANY. In this painting, which reflects the mood of social and political disillusionment that prevailed in much of Europe in the 1920s, George Grosz satirized conservative and right-wing groups in Weimar Germany, including the army, the courts, the newspapers, and the Nazi Party.

Grosz George (1893–1959) © VAGA, NY. Stuetzen der Gesellschaft (Pillars of Society), 1926. Oil on canvas, 2000,0 × 108,0 cm. Photo: Joerg P. Anders. Nationalgalerie, Staatliche Museen zu Berlin, Berlin, Germany.

The Interwar Period

The two decades between the great wars marked a period of immense political and economic transition around the globe. Many regions endured political turmoil and economic instability, followed by the establishment of militaristic authoritarian regimes. In Italy, it was the Fascists; in Germany, the Nazis; in the Soviet Union, Stalin's regime. Spain too came under the rule of a military dictator who rose to power with the assistance of the Nazis. Many Europeans, battered by the global economic crisis of the 1930s and, in the case of Germany, the harsh terms of the Treaty of Versailles, believed that only strong leaders could lead their countries to prosperity again in the global competition for resources and territory. In East Asia, Japan came into the grip of a right-wing militaristic government. China saw over twenty years of civil war and revolution that would culminate with the rise to power of the communists under Mao. Most of Latin America came under the sway of dictators or governments heavily influenced by the military. With the exception of Russia (and later China), all of these governments were right-wing. In fact, the Russian Revolution was a pivotal factor in the rise of right-wing and fascist dictators, who often justified their power on the basis of their firm opposition to the "Red Menace" and the growing popularity enjoyed by socialism and communism in many European countries during the economic crisis of the 1930s. To many observers in the late 1930s, the day of liberal parliamentary democracy appeared to be ending. The disruptions arising from World War I and the social and economic turmoil of the depression seemed to pose problems that liberal governments could not address. Only the radical medicine of socialism, communism, or right-wing dictatorships seemed capable of resolving the crisis. Some countries, such as France in the mid-1930s, were brought to the brink of civil war by the deep divisions between the right and left in their populations. Spain became engulfed in the civil war that brought General Francisco Franco (1892–1975) to power in 1939.

The interwar period also departed from the nineteenth-century ideal of *laissez-faire* economics, in which central governments assumed little responsibility for guiding the economies of their countries. The German inflation of the early 1920s, the worldwide financial collapse of the late 1920s,

the vast unemployment of the early 1930s, and the agricultural crisis of both decades, roused demands for government action. One reason for these demands was simply that more governments throughout the world were responsible to mass democratic electorates. Governments that failed to adequately address the problems were put out of office. This happened to the Republicans in the United States, the Socialist and Liberal parties in Germany, the left-wing parties in Japan, and various political parties in Latin America that failed to deal with the depression. Paradoxically, many democratic electorates actually turned themselves over to politically authoritarian regimes as they searched for social and economic stability.

Extreme forms of nationalism in both Europe and Japan also spawned authoritarianism. The authoritarian governments of Germany, Italy, and Japan all had agendas of nationalistic aggression. They shared the nineteenth-century conviction that territorial expansion was essential to national prestige and economic security. As a result they were prepared to move wherever they saw fellow nationals living outside their borders (a legacy of the creation of nation-states in the eighteenth and nineteenth centuries) or where they could establish dominance over other peoples and thus become imperial powers. Japan moved against Manchuria and later other parts of Asia. Italy invaded Ethiopia. Germany sought union with German-speaking peoples in Austria and Czechoslovakia and then sought to expand throughout eastern Europe. In turn, those actions challenged the dominance of Great Britain and the vital security interests of the United States. By the end of the 1930s the authoritarian regimes and the liberal democracies stood on the brink of a major confrontation.

THINK AHEAD

◆ Why did many people in the 1930s lose faith in liberal democracy and *laissez-faire* economics?

◆ What led many countries to adopt authoritarian regimes during this period?

◆ What was the relationship between extreme nationalism and the outbreak of World War II?

IN THE TWO DECADES THAT FOLLOWED THE CONCLUSION OF the Paris settlement, the Western world saw a number of experiments in politics and economic life. Two broad factors accounted for these experiments. First, the war, the Russian Revolution, and the peace treaty had transformed the political face of Europe. New political regimes had emerged in the wake of the collapse of the monarchies of Germany, Austria-Hungary, and Russia. These new governments immediately faced the problems of postwar reconstruction, economic dislocation, and nationalistic resentments. Most of these nations also included large groups who questioned the legitimacy of their governments.

Second, beginning in the early twenties, economic dislocations that led to the economic downturn that became known as the Great Depression began to spread across the world. It occurred through the combination of financial turmoil in the more advanced industrial nations and a collapse of commodity prices in the commodity-exporting countries. Faced with political instability and economic crisis, governments contrived various political and economic responses. In Europe these efforts often produced authoritarian regimes. In the United States the response to the depression led to a much-increased role for the federal government in the life of the nation.

After Versailles: Demands for Revision and Enforcement

The Paris settlement fostered both resentment and discontent. Those resentments counted among the chief political factors in Europe for the next two decades. Germany had been humiliated. The arrangements for reparations led to endless haggling over payments. Various national groups in the successor states of the Austro-Hungarian Empire felt that injustice had been done in their particular cases of self-determination. There were demands for further border adjustments. On the other side, the victorious powers, and especially France, often believed that the provisions of the treaty were being inadequately enforced. Consequently, throughout the 1920s and into the 1930s demands either to revise or to enforce the Paris treaties contributed to domestic political turmoil across the Continent. All too many political figures were willing to fish in these troubled international waters for a large catch of domestic votes.

Toward the Great Depression in Europe

Three factors combined to bring about the intense severity and the extended length of the **Great Depression**. First, a financial crisis stemmed directly from the war and the peace settlement. To this was added a crisis in the production and distribution of goods in the world market. These two problems became intertwined in 1929, and as far as Europe was concerned they reached the breaking point in 1931. Finally, both of these difficulties became worse than they might have been because no major Western European country or the United States provided strong, responsible economic leadership.

FINANCIAL TAILSPIN

As one of the chief victors in the war, France was determined to collect reparations from Germany. The United States was no less determined that its allies repay the wartime loans it had extended to them. The European allies also owed various debts to each other. German reparations were to provide the means of repaying the American and other allied debts. Most of the money that the Allies collected from each other also went to the United States.

▲ **Death on the Western Front.** One of the last American soldiers killed on the Western Front in November 1918. The carnage of World War I was one of the main causes of European weakness and instability in the 1920s and 1930s.
American Stock/Archive Photos.

The quest for payment of German reparations caused one of the major diplomatic crises of the 1920s; the crisis itself resulted in further economic upheaval. In early 1923 the Allies—France in particular—declared Germany to be in technical default of its reparation payments. On January 11, to ensure receipt of the hard-won reparations, French troops occupied the Ruhr mining and manufacturing district. The **Weimar Republic** ordered passive resistance that amounted to a general strike in the largest industrial region of the nation. Confronted with this tactic, the French government sent French civilians to run the German mines and railroads. France got its way. The Germans paid, but its victory cost France dearly. The English were alienated by the French heavy-handedness and took no part in the occupation. Britain became more suspicious of France and more sympathetic to Germany. The cost of the Ruhr occupation, moreover, vastly increased French as well as German inflation and damaged the French economy.

The political and economic turmoil of the Ruhr invasion led to international attempts to ease the German payment of reparations. The most famous of these were the Dawes Plan of 1924 and the Young Plan of 1929, both devised by Americans. At the same time, large amounts of American investment capital were pouring into Europe. However, by 1928 this lending decreased as American money became diverted into the booming New York stock market. The crash of Wall Street in October 1929—the result of virtually unregulated financial speculation—saw the loss of large amounts of money. Credit sharply contracted in the United States as numerous banks failed. Thereafter, little American capital was available for investment in Europe.

As the credit for Europe began to run out, a major financial crisis struck the Continent. In May 1931 the Kreditanstalt collapsed. The Kreditanstalt was a primary lending institution and major bank for much of central and eastern Europe. The German banking system consequently came under severe pressure and was saved only through government guarantees. As the German difficulties increased, U.S. president Herbert Hoover (1874–1964) announced in June 1931 a one-year moratorium on all payments of international debts. The Hoover moratorium was a prelude to the end of reparations. The Lausanne Conference of the summer of 1932 brought, in effect, the era of reparations to a close. The next year the debts owed to the United States were settled either through small token payments or simply through default.

PROBLEMS IN AGRICULTURAL COMMODITIES

The 1920s witnessed a contraction in the market demand for European goods relative to the Continent's productive capacity. This problem originated both within and outside Europe. In both instances the difficulty arose from agriculture. Better methods of farming, improved strains of wheat, expanded tillage, and more extensive transport facilities all over the globe vastly increased the quantity of grain. World wheat prices fell to record lows. Although this helped consumers, it decreased the income of European farmers. At the same time, higher industrial wages raised the cost of the industrial goods that farmers or peasants used. Consequently, they also had great difficulty paying off their mortgages and normal annual operation debts. These problems were especially acute in central and eastern Europe and abetted farmers' disillusionment with liberal politics. German farmers, for example, would become prime supporters of the National Socialist Workers Party (Nazis).

Outside Europe similar problems affected other producers of agricultural commodities. The prices they received for their products plummeted. Government-held reserves reached record levels. This glut of major world commodities involved the supplies of wheat, sugar, coffee, rubber, wool, and lard. The people who produced these goods in underdeveloped nations could no longer make enough money to buy finished goods from industrial Europe. As world credit collapsed, the economic position of these commodity producers worsened. Commodity production had simply outstripped world demand.

The results of the collapse in the agricultural sector of the world economy and the financial turmoil were stagnation and depression for European industry. Coal, iron, and textiles had depended largely on international markets. Unemployment spread from these industries to those producing finished consumer goods. Persistent unemployment in Great Britain and,

▲ **Jarrow Crusade.** In what was known as the "Jarrow Crusade" during the autumn of 1936 a group of approximately 200 protesters marched from the town of Jarrow in northeastern England to London to demonstrate their need for employment and the plight of their town where the previous year the shipyard had been closed.
Getty Images, Inc./Hulton Archive Photos.

to a lesser extent, in Germany during the 1920s had created "soft" domestic markets. The policies of reduced spending with which the governments confronted the depression further weakened domestic demand. By the early 1930s the depression was feeding on itself.

DEPRESSION AND GOVERNMENT POLICY

The depression did not mean absolute economic decline or total unemployment. However, the economic downturn spread potential as well as actual insecurity. People in nearly all walks of life feared the loss of their own economic security and lifestyles. The depression also frustrated normal social and economic expectations. Even the employed often seemed to make no progress; and their anxieties created a major source of social discontent.

The governments of the late 1920s and the early 1930s were not particularly well suited in either structure or ideology to confront these problems. The electorates demanded action. The government response depended largely on the severity of the Depression in a particular country and on the self-confidence of the nation's political system.

Great Britain and France undertook moderate political experiments. In 1924 the Labour Party in Great Britain established itself as a viable governing party by forming a short-lived government. It again formed a ministry in 1929. Under the pressure of the Depression and at the urging of King George V (r. 1910–1936), the Labour prime minister Ramsay Mac-Donald (1866–1937) organized a National Government, which was a coalition of the Labour, Conservative, and Liberal Parties. It remained in power until 1935, when a Conservative ministry led by Stanley Baldwin (1867–1947) replaced it.

The most important French political experiment was the **Popular Front** Ministry, which came to office in 1936. It was composed of Socialists, Radicals, and Communists—the first time that Socialists and Communists had cooperated in a ministry. The Popular Front addressed major labor problems in the French economy. By 1938 various changes in the cabinet in effect brought the Popular Front to an end.

The political changes in Britain and France were only of domestic significance. But the political experiments of the 1920s and 1930s that reshaped world history and civilization involved the establishment of a Soviet government in Russia, a Fascist regime in Italy, and a Nazi dictatorship in Germany.

The Soviet Experiment

The consolidation of the Bolshevik Revolution in Russia established the most extensive and durable of all twentieth-century authoritarian governments. The Communist Party of the Soviet Union retained power from 1917 until the end of 1991, and its presence influenced the political history of Europe

and much of the rest of the world, as did no other single factor. Unlike the Italian Fascists or the German National Socialists, the Bolsheviks seized power violently through revolution. For several years they confronted armed opposition, and their leaders long felt insecure about their hold on the country. The Communist Party was neither a mass party nor a nationalistic one. Its early membership rarely exceeded more than 1 percent of the Russian population. The Bolsheviks confronted a much less industrialized economy than that in Italy or Germany. They believed in and practiced the collectivization of economic life attacked by the right-wing dictatorships. The Marxist-Leninist ideology was broader than the nationalism of the Fascists and the racism of the Nazis. Communism was an exportable commodity. The Communists regarded

Lenin. Anxiety over the spread of the Bolshevik Revolution was a fundamental factor of European politics during the 1920s and 1930s. Images like this Soviet portrait of Lenin as a heroic revolutionary conjured fears among people in the rest of Europe of a political force determined to overturn their social, political, and economic institutions.

Gemalde von A. M. Gerassimow, "Lenin as Agitator"/Bildarchiv Preussischer Kulturbesitz.

their government and their revolution not as part of a national history but as epoch-making events in the history of the world and the development of humanity. (See Document, "A Communist Woman Demands a New Family Life.") Fear of communism and determination to stop its spread became one of the leading political forces in Western Europe and the United States for most of the rest of the century. Policies flowing from that opposition would influence their relationships with much of the rest of the world.

WAR COMMUNISM

Within the Soviet Union the Red Army under the organizational genius of Leon Trotsky (1879–1940) had suppressed internal and foreign military opposition to the new government. Within months of the revolution, a new secret police, known as *Cheka*, appeared. Throughout the civil war Lenin (1870–1924) had declared that the Bolshevik Party, as the vanguard of the revolution, was imposing the dictatorship of the proletariat. Political and economic administration became highly centralized. All major decisions flowed from the top in a nondemocratic manner. Under the economic policy of **"War Communism,"** the revolutionary government confiscated and then operated the banks, the transport facilities, and heavy industry. The state also forcibly requisitioned grain and shipped it from the countryside to feed the army and the workers in the cities. The fact of the civil war permitted suppression of possible resistance to this economic policy.

War Communism helped the Red Army defeat its opponents. The revolution had survived and triumphed. The policy, however, generated domestic opposition to the Bolsheviks, who in 1920 numbered only about 600,000 members. The alliance of workers and peasants forged by the slogan of "Peace, Bread, and Land" had begun to dissolve. Many Russians were no longer willing to make the sacrifices demanded by the central party bureaucrats. In 1920 and 1921 serious strikes occurred. Peasants were discontented and resisted the requisition of grain. In March 1921 the navy mutinied at Kronstadt. The Red Army crushed the rebellion with grave loss of life. Each of these incidents suggested that the proletariat itself was opposing the dictatorship of the proletariat. Also, by late 1920 it had become clear that further revolution would not sweep across the rest of Europe. For the time being the Soviet Union would constitute a vast island of revolutionary socialism in the larger sea of worldwide capitalism.

THE NEW ECONOMIC POLICY

Under these difficult conditions Lenin made a crucial strategic retreat. In March 1921, following the Kronstadt mutiny, he outlined the **New Economic Policy**, normally referred to as NEP. Apart from what he termed "the commanding heights"

of banking, heavy industry, transportation, and international commerce, considerable private economic enterprise was allowed. In particular, peasants could farm for a profit. They would pay taxes like other citizens, but they could sell their surplus grain on the open market. The NEP was consistent with Lenin's earlier conviction that the Russian peasantry held the key to the success of the revolution. After 1921 the countryside did become more stable, and a secure food supply seemed assured for the cities. Similar free enterprise flourished within light industry and domestic retail trade. By 1927 industrial production had reached its 1913 level. The revolution seemed to have transformed Russia into a land of small family farms and privately owned shops and businesses.

STALIN VERSUS TROTSKY

The NEP had caused sharp disputes within the Politburo, the highest governing committee of the Communist Party. The partial return to capitalism seemed to some members nothing less than a betrayal of sound Marxist principles. These frictions increased as Lenin's firm hand disappeared. In 1922 he suffered a stroke and never again dominated party affairs; in 1924 Lenin died. In the ensuing power vacuum, an intense struggle for leadership of the party commenced. Two factions emerged. One was led by Trotsky; the other by Joseph Stalin (1879–1953), who had become general secretary of the party in 1922. Shortly before his death Lenin had criticized both men. He was especially harsh toward Stalin. However, the general secretary's base of power lay with the party membership and with the daily management of party affairs. Consequently, he was able to withstand the posthumous strictures of Lenin.

Each faction wanted to control the party, but the struggle was fought over the question of Russia's path toward industrialization and the future of the Communist revolutionary movement. Trotsky, speaking for what became known as the left wing, urged rapid industrialization and looked to voluntary collectivization of farming by poor peasants as a means of increasing agricultural production. Trotsky further argued that the revolution in Russia could succeed only if new revolutions took place elsewhere. Russia needed the skills and wealth of other nations to build its own economy. As Trotsky's influence within the party began to wane, he also demanded that party members be permitted to criticize the policies of the government and the party. Trotsky, however, was a latecomer to the advocacy of open discussion. When in control of the Red Army, he had been an unflinching disciplinarian.

A right-wing faction opposed Trotsky. Although its chief ideological voice was that of Nikolai Bukharin (1888–1938), the editor of *Pravda*, the official party paper, Stalin was its true political manipulator. In the mid-1920s this group pressed for the continuation of Lenin's NEP and a policy of relatively slow industrialization.

DOCUMENT | A Communist Woman Demands a New Family Life

While Lenin sought to consolidate the Bolshevik Revolution against internal and external enemies, there existed within the young Soviet Union a vast utopian impulse to change and reform virtually every social institution that had existed before the revolution or those Communists associated with capitalist society. Alexandra Kollontai (1872–1952) was a spokesperson of the extreme political left within the early Soviet Union. There had been much speculation on how the end of bourgeois society might change the structure of the family and the position of women. In this passage written in 1920 Kollontai states one of the most radically utopian visions of this change. During the years immediately after the revolution, extreme rumors circulated in both Europe and America about sexual and family experimentation in the Soviet Union. Statements such as this fostered such rumors. Kollontai herself later became a supporter of Stalin and a Soviet diplomat.

♦ Why did Kollontai see the restructuring of the family as essential to the establishment of a new kind of Communist society? Would these changes make people loyal to that society? What changes in society does the kind of economic independence she seeks for women presuppose? What might childhood be like in this society?

There is no escaping the fact: the old type of family has seen its day. It is not the fault of the Communist State, it is the result of the changed conditions of life. The family is ceasing to be a necessity of the State, as it was in the past; on the contrary, it is worse than useless, since it needlessly holds back the female workers from more productive and far more serious work. ... But on the ruins of the former family we shall soon see a new form rising which will involve altogether different relations between men and women, and which will be a union of affection and comradeship, a union of two equal members of the Communist society, both of them free, both of them independent, both of them workers. No more domestic "servitude" of women. No more inequality within the family.

No more fear on the part of the woman lest she remain without support or aid with little ones in her arms if her husband should desert her. The woman in the Communist city no longer depends on her husband but on her work. It is not her husband but her robust arms which will support her. There will be no more anxiety as to the fate of her children. The State of the Workers will assume responsibility for these. Marriage will be purified of all its material elements, of all money calculations, which constitute a hideous blemish on family life in our days. ...

The woman who is called upon to struggle in the great cause of the liberation of the workers—such a woman should know that in the new State there will be no more room for such petty divisions as were formerly understood: "These are my own children, to them I owe all my maternal solicitude, all my affection; those are your children, my neighbour's children; I am not concerned with them. I have enough to do with my own." Henceforth the worker-mother, who is conscious of her social function, will rise to a point where she no longer differentiates between yours and mine; she must remember that there are henceforth only our children, those of the Communist State, the common possession of all the workers.

The Worker's State has need of a new form of relation between the sexes. The narrow and exclusive affection of the mother for her own children must expand until it embraces all the children of the great proletarian family. In place of the indissoluble marriage based on the servitude of woman, we shall see rise the free union, fortified by the love and mutual respect of the two members of the Workers' State, equal in their rights and in their obligations. In place of the individual and egotistic family there will arise a great universal family of workers, in which all the workers, men and women, will be, above all, workers, comrades.

From Alexandra Kollontai, *Communism and the Family*, as reprinted in Rudolf Schlesinger, ed. and trans., *The Family in the USSR* (London: Routledge and Kegan Paul, 1949), pp. 67–69. Reprinted by permission.

Stalin was the ultimate victor in these intraparty rivalries. Unlike the other early Bolshevik leaders, he had not spent a long exile in Western Europe. He was much less an intellectual and internationalist. He was also much more brutal. His handling of various recalcitrant national groups within Russia after the revolution had shocked even Lenin. Stalin's power lay in his command of bureaucratic and administrative methods. He was neither a brilliant writer nor an effective public speaker; however, he mastered the crucial, if dull, details of party structure, including admission and promotion. That mastery meant that

he could draw on the support of the lower levels of the party apparatus when he clashed with other leaders.

In the mid-1920s Stalin supported Bukharin's position on economic development. In 1924 he also enunciated, in opposition to Trotsky, the doctrine of "socialism in one country." He urged that socialism could be achieved in Russia alone. Russian success did not depend on the fate of the revolution elsewhere. Stalin thus nationalized the previously international scope of the Marxist revolution. He cunningly used the apparatus of the party and his control over the Central Committee of the Communist Party to edge out Trotsky and his supporters. By 1927 Trotsky had been removed from all his offices, ousted from the party, and exiled to Siberia. In 1929 he was expelled from Russia and eventually moved to Mexico, where he was murdered in 1940 by one of Stalin's agents. With the removal of Trotsky, Stalin was firmly in control of the Soviet state. It remained to be seen where he would direct its course and what "socialism in one country" would mean in practice.

DECISION FOR RAPID INDUSTRIALIZATION

While the capitalist economies of Western Europe floundered during the depression, the Soviet Union registered tremendous industrial advance. As usual in Russia, the direction and impetus came from the top. Stalin far exceeded his tsarist predecessors in the intensity of state coercion and terror he brought to the task. Russia achieved its stunning economic growth during the 1930s only at the cost of literally millions of human lives and the degradation of millions more. Stalin's economic policy clearly proved that his earlier rivalry with Trotsky had been a matter of political power rather than one of substantial ideological difference.

Through 1928 Lenin's NEP, as championed by Bukharin with Stalin's support, had steered Soviet economic development. Private ownership and enterprise were permitted to flourish in the countryside to ensure enough food for the workers in the cities. A few farmers, the *kulaks*, had become prosperous. They probably numbered less than 5 percent of the rural population. During 1928 and 1929 they and other farmers withheld grain from the market because prices were too low. Food shortages occurred in the cities and caused potential unrest. The goals of the NEP were no longer being fulfilled. Sometime during these troubled months, Stalin came to a momentous decision: Russia must industrialize rapidly to match the economic and military power of the West. Agriculture must be collectivized to produce sufficient grain for food and export and to free peasant labor for the factories. This program, which basically embraced Trotsky's earlier economic position, unleashed a second Russian revolution. The costs and character of "socialism in one country" now became clear.

Agricultural Policy   In 1929 Stalin ordered party agents into the countryside to confiscate any hoarded wheat. The *kulaks* bore the blame for the grain shortages. As part of the general plan to erase the private ownership of land and to collectivize farming, the government undertook a program to eliminate the *kulaks* as a class. A *kulak*, however, soon came to mean any peasant who opposed Stalin's policy. In the countryside, peasants and farmers at all levels of wealth resisted stubbornly. They were determined to keep their land. They wreaked their own vengeance on the policy of **collectivization** by slaughtering more than 100 million horses and cattle between 1929 and 1933. The situation in the countryside amounted to open warfare. The peasant resistance caused Stalin to call a brief halt to the process in March 1930. He justified the slowdown on the grounds of "dizziness from success."

Soon thereafter, the drive to collectivize the farms was renewed with vehemence, and the costs remained high. As many as 10 million peasants were killed, and millions of others were sent forcibly to collective farms or labor camps. Initially, because of the turmoil on the land, agricultural production fell. There was famine in 1932 and 1933. Milk and meat remained in short supply because of the livestock slaughter.

◀ **Kulaks.** During Stalin's drive to collectivize agriculture wealthy peasants known as Kulaks became the object of his wrath. Here a group of mostly peasant women demonstrate against the kulaks.
AP Wide World Photos.

Yet Stalin persevered. The *kulaks* were uprooted from their farms and sent to Siberia or other regions far from their homes. Peasants who remained had their lands incorporated into large collective farms. The state provided the machinery for these units through machine-tractor stations. The state thus retained control over major farm machines, a monopoly that was a powerful weapon.

Collectivization dramatically changed Russian farming. In 1928 approximately 98 percent of Russian farmland consisted of small peasant holdings. Ten years later, despite all the opposition, over 90 percent of the land had been collectivized, and the quantity of farm produce directly handled by the government had risen by 40 percent. The government now had primary direction over the food supply. The farmers and peasants could no longer determine whether there would be stability or unrest in the cities. Stalin and the Communist Party had won the battle of the wheat fields, but they had not solved the problem of producing enough grain. That difficulty has plagued the former Soviet Union to the present day.

Five-Year Plans The revolution in agriculture had been undertaken for the sake of industrialization. The increased grain supply was to feed the labor force and provide exports to finance the imports required for industrial development. The industrial achievement of the Soviet Union between 1928 and World War II was one of the most striking accomplishments of the twentieth century. Russia made a more rapid advance toward economic growth than any other nation in the Western world has ever achieved during any similar period of time. By even the conservative estimates of Western observers, Soviet industrial production rose approximately 400 percent between 1928 and 1940. The production of iron, steel, coal, electrical power, tractors, combines, railway cars, and other heavy machinery was emphasized. Few consumer goods were produced. The labor for this development was supplied internally. Capital was raised from the export of grain, even at the cost of internal shortage. The technology was generally borrowed from already industrialized nations.

The organizational vehicle for industrialization was a series of Five-Year Plans first begun in 1928. The State Planning Commission, or Gosplan, oversaw the program. It set goals of production and organized the economy to meet them. Coordinating all facets of production was immensely difficult and complicated. Deliveries of materials from mines or factories had to be assured before the next unit could carry out its part of the plan. There was many a slip between the cup and the lip. The troubles in the countryside were harmful. A vast program of propaganda was undertaken to sell the Five-Year Plans to the Russian people and to elicit cooperation. The industrial labor force, however, soon became subject to regimentation similar to that being imposed on the peasants. By the close of

▲ **Soviet Propaganda Poster.** An enormous propaganda effort accompanied the Soviet Five-Year Plans. This poster proclaims, "For the betterment of the Soviet people we are building an electricity plant."
Bildarchiv Preussischer Kulturbesitz.

the 1930s the accomplishment of the three Five-Year Plans was truly impressive and probably allowed the Soviet Union to survive the German invasion. Industries that had never existed in Russia now challenged and in some cases, such as tractor production, surpassed their counterparts in the rest of the world. Large, new industrial cities had been built and populated by hundreds of thousands of people.

Many non-Russian contemporaries looked at the Soviet economic experiment quite uncritically. While the capitalist world lay in the throes of the depression, the Soviet economy had grown at a pace never realized in the West. The American writer Lincoln Steffens (1866–1936) reported after a trip to Russia, "I have seen the future and it works." Beatrice Webb (1858–1943) and Sydney Webb (1859–1947), the British Fabian Socialists, spoke of "a new civilization" in the Soviet Union. These and other similar writers ignored the shortages in consumer goods and the poor housing. More important, they seem to have had little idea of the social cost of the Soviet achievement. Millions of people had been killed and millions more uprooted. The total picture of suffering and human loss during those years will probably never be known; the deprivation and sacrifice of Soviet citizens far exceeded anything described by Marx and Engels in relation to nineteenth-century industrialization in Western Europe.

THE PURGES

Stalin's decisions to industrialize rapidly and to move against the peasants aroused internal political opposition because they were departures from the policies of Lenin. In 1929 Stalin forced Bukharin, the fervent supporter of the NEP and his own former ally, off the Politburo. Little detailed information is known about further opposition, but it does seem to have existed among lower level party followers of Bukharin and other previous opponents of rapid industrialization. Sometime in 1933 Stalin began to fear that he would lose control over the party apparatus and that effective rivals might emerge. These fears were probably produced as much by his own paranoia as by real plots. Nevertheless, they resulted in the **Great Purges**, among the most mysterious and horrendous political events of this century. The purges were not understood at the time and are still not fully comprehended today.

On December 1, 1934, Sergei Kirov (1888–1934), the popular party chief of Leningrad (formerly Saint Petersburg and Petrograd) and a member of the Politburo, was assassinated. In the wake of the shooting thousands of people were arrested, and still more were expelled from the party and sent to labor camps. At the time it was believed that Kirov had been murdered by opponents of the regime. Direct or indirect complicity in the crime became the normal accusation against those whom Stalin attacked. It now seems practically certain that Stalin himself authorized Kirov's assassination to forestall any threat from the Leningrad leader.

The purges after Kirov's death were just the beginning of a larger process. Between 1936 and 1938 spectacular show trials were held in Moscow. Previous high Soviet leaders, including former members of the Politburo, publicly confessed political crimes. They were convicted and executed. It is still not certain why they made their palpably false confessions. Still other leaders and lower level party members were tried in private and

shot. Thousands of people received no trial at all. The purges touched persons in all areas of party life. It is inexplicable why some were executed, others sent to labor camps, and still others left unmolested. After the civilian party members had been purged, the prosecutors turned against the army. Important officers, including heroes of the civil war, were killed. Within the party itself, hundreds of thousands of members were expelled, and applicants for membership were removed from the rolls. The exact numbers of executions, imprisonments, and expulsions are unknown but certainly ran into the millions.

The trials and purges astonished observers from outside the Soviet Union. Nothing quite like this phenomenon had ever been seen. Political murders and executions were not new, but the absurd confessions were novel. The scale of the political turmoil was also unprecedented. The Russians themselves did not believe or comprehend what was occurring. There existed no national emergency or crisis. There were only accusations of sympathy for Trotsky or of complicity in Kirov's murder or of other nameless crimes. If a rational explanation is to be sought, it probably must be found in Stalin's concern for his own power. In effect, the purges created a new party structure absolutely loyal to him. The "old Bolsheviks" of the October Revolution were among his earliest targets. They and others active in the first years of the revolution knew how far Stalin had moved from Lenin's policies. New, younger party members replaced those executed or expelled. The newcomers knew little of old Russia or of the ideals of the original Bolsheviks. They had not been loyal to Lenin, Trotsky, or any Soviet leader except Stalin himself.

◀ **Party Congress, 1936.** By the mid-1930s Stalin's purges had eliminated many leaders and other members from the Soviet Communist Party. This photograph of a meeting of a party congress in 1936 shows a number of the surviving leaders with Stalin, who sits fourth from the right in the front row. To his left is Vyacheslav Molotov, long-time foreign minister. The first person on the left in the front row is Nikita Khrushchev, who headed the Soviet Union in the late 1950s and early 1960s.
Itar-Tass/Sovfoto/Eastfoto.

Despite the flagrant violence and widespread repression of the Soviet experiment, it found many sympathizers throughout the world. Some people did not know of its repression; others ignored those events. The Soviet Union almost immediately after the Bolshevik seizure of power had fostered the organization of Communist parties subservient to Moscow influence throughout the world. Others who were not formally members of these parties often sympathized with what they believed or hoped were the goals of the Soviet Union. During at least the first fifty years of its existence the Soviet Union managed to capture the imagination of some intellectuals in the West and in other parts of the globe who hoped for a utopian egalitarian transformation of society. During much of the 1930s, to these and other people, the Soviet Union also appeared as an enemy to the fascist experiments in Italy and Germany. The Marxist ideology championed by the Soviet Union appeared to many people living in the European colonial empires as a vehicle for freeing themselves from the colonial situation. The Soviet Union welcomed and trained many such anticolonial leaders and offered other support to their causes. In the wake of the collapse of the Soviet Union at the close of the century and what is now known about its repression it is difficult to understand the power its presence exercised over many people's political imaginations around the world, but that attraction was one of the most fundamental factors in world politics from the 1920s through at least the early 1970s.

The Fascist Experiment in Italy

The first authoritarian political experiment in Western Europe that arose in part from fears of the spread of bolshevism occurred in Italy. The general term *fascist*, which has been used to describe the various right-wing dictatorships that arose between the wars, was derived from the Italian Fascist movement of Benito Mussolini (1883–1945).

While scholars still dispute the exact meaning of *fascism* as a political term, the governments regarded as fascist were antidemocratic, anti-Marxist, antiparliamentary, and frequently anti-Semitic. They hoped to hold back the spread of bolshevism, which seemed a real threat at the time. They sought a world that would be safe for the middle class, small businesses, owners of moderate amounts of property, and small farmers. The Fascist regimes rejected the political inheritance of the French Revolution and of nineteenth-century liberalism. (See Document, "Mussolini Heaps Contempt on Political Liberalism.") Their adherents believed that normal parliamentary politics and parties sacrificed national honor and greatness to petty party disputes. They wanted to overcome the class conflict of Marxism and the party conflict of liberalism by consolidating the various groups and classes within the nation for great national purposes. As Mussolini declared in 1931, "The fascist conception of the state is all-embracing, and outside of the state no human or spiritual values can exist, let alone be desirable."[1] Fascist governments were usually single-party dictatorships characterized by terrorism and police surveillance. These dictatorships were rooted in the base of mass political parties.

RISE OF MUSSOLINI

The Italian *Fasci di Combattimento* ("Band of Combat") was founded in 1919 in Milan. Most of its members were war veterans who felt that the sacrifices of World War I had been in vain. They resented Italy's failure to gain the city of Fiume, toward the northern end of the Adriatic Sea, at the Paris conference. They feared socialism, inflation, and labor unrest.

Their leader or **Duce**, Benito Mussolini, was the son of a blacksmith. After having been a schoolteacher and a day laborer, he became active in Italian Socialist politics and by 1912 had become editor of the socialist newspaper *Avanti*. In 1914 Mussolini broke with the Socialists and supported Italian entry into the war on the side of the Allies. His interventionist position lost him the editorship of *Avanti*. He then established his own paper, *Il Popolo d'Italia*. Later he served in the army and was wounded. In 1919 Mussolini was just another Italian politician. His *Fasci* organization was one of many small political groups in a country characterized by such entities. As a politician, Mussolini was an opportunist par excellence. He could change his ideas and principles to suit every new occasion. Action for him was always more important than thought or rational justification. His one real rule was political survival.

Postwar Italian politics was a muddle. During the war the Italian Parliament had virtually ceased to function. Ministers had ruled by decree. However, many Italians were dissatisfied with the parliamentary system as it then existed. They felt that Italy had emerged from the war as less than a victorious nation, had not been treated as a great power at the peace conference, and had not received the territories it deserved. The main spokesman for this discontent was the extreme nationalist writer Gabriele D'Annunzio (1863–1938). In 1919 he captured Fiume with a force of patriotic Italians. The Italian army, enforcing the terms of the Versailles Treaty, eventually drove him out. D'Annunzio had provided the example of the political use of a nongovernmental military force. Removing him from Fiume made the parliamentary ministry seem unpatriotic.

Between 1919 and 1921 Italy was also wracked by social turmoil. Numerous industrial strikes occurred, and workers occupied factories. Peasants seized uncultivated land from large estates. Parliamentary and constitutional government seemed incapable of dealing with this unrest. The Socialist Party had captured a plurality of seats in the Chamber of Deputies in 1919.

---

[1] Quoted in Denis Mack Smith, *Italy: A Modern History* (Ann Arbor: University of Michigan Press, 1959), p. 412.

DOCUMENT | Mussolini Heaps Contempt on Political Liberalism

The political tactics of the Italian Fascists wholly disregarded the liberal belief in the rule of law and the consent of the governed. In 1923 Mussolini explained why the Fascists so hated and repudiated these liberal principles. Note his emphasis on the idea of the twentieth century as a new historical epoch requiring a new kind of politics and his undisguised praise of force in politics.

◆ Who would be some nineteenth-century liberal political leaders included in Mussolini's attack? Why might Mussolini's audience have been receptive to these views? What events or developments within liberal states allowed Mussolini to portray liberalism as so corrupt and powerless?

Liberalism is not the last word, nor does it represent the definitive formula on the subject of the art of government. ... Liberalism is the product and the technique of the nineteenth century. ... It does not follow that the Liberal scheme of government, good for the nineteenth century, for a century, that is, dominated by two such phenomena as the growth of capitalism and the strengthening of the sentiment of nationalism, should be adapted to the twentieth century, which announces itself already with characteristics sufficiently different from those that marked the preceding century. ...

I challenge Liberal gentlemen to tell if ever in history there has been a government that was based solely on popular consent and that renounced all use of force whatsoever. A government so con-structed there has never been and never will be. Consent is an ever-changing thing like the shifting sand on the sea coast, it can never be permanent: It can never be complete. ... If it be accepted as an axiom that any system of government whatever creates malcontents, how are you going to prevent this discontent from overflowing and constituting a menace to the stability of the State? You will prevent it by force. By the assembling of the greatest force possible. By the inexorable use of this force whenever it is necessary. Take away from any government whatsoever force—and by force is meant physical, armed force—and leave it only its immortal principles, and that government will be at the mercy of the first organized group that decides to overthrow it. Fascism now throws these lifeless theories out to rot. ... The truth evident now to all who are not warped by [liberal] dogmatism is that men have tired of liberty. They have made an orgy of it. Liberty is today no longer the chaste and austere virgin for whom the generations of the first half of the last century fought and died. For the gallant, restless and bitter youth who face the dawn of a new history there are other words that exercise a far greater fascination, and those words are: order, hierarchy, discipline. ...

Know then, once and for all, that Fascism knows no idols and worships no fetishes. It has already stepped over, and if it be necessary it will turn tranquilly and step again over, the more or less putrescent corpse of the Goddess of Liberty.

From Benito Mussolini, "Force and Consent" (1923), as trans. in Jonathan F. Scott and Alexander Baltzly, eds., *Readings in European History Since 1814* (New York: F. S. Crofts, 1931), pp. 680–682.

A new Catholic Popular Party had also done well. Both appealed to the working and agrarian classes. However, neither party would cooperate with the other, and parliamentary deadlock resulted. Under these conditions, many Italians honestly—and still others conveniently—believed that a Communist revolution might break out.

Initially, Mussolini was uncertain which way the political winds were blowing. He first supported the factory occupations and land seizures. Never one to be concerned with consistency, however, he soon reversed himself. He had discovered that many upper-class and middle-class Italians who were pressured by inflation and who feared property loss had no sympathy for the workers or the peasants. They wanted order rather than some vague social justice that might harm their own interests. Consequently, Mussolini and his Fascists took direct action in the face of the government inaction. They formed local squads who terrorized Socialist supporters. They attacked strikers and farm workers and protected strikebreakers. Conservative land and factory owners were grateful to the terrorists. The officers and institutions of the law simply ignored these crimes. By early 1922 the Fascists controlled the local government in many parts of northern Italy.

In 1921 Mussolini and thirty-four of his followers had been elected to the Chamber of Deputies. Their importance grew as the local Fascists gained more direct power. The Fascist movement now had hundreds of thousands of supporters. In October 1922 the Fascists, dressed in their characteristic black shirts, began a march on Rome. Intimidated, King Victor Emmanuel III (r. 1900–1946) refused to authorize using the army against the marchers. No other single decision so ensured a Fascist seizure of power. The cabinet resigned in protest. On October 29 the monarch telegraphed Mussolini in Milan and asked him to become prime minister. The next day Mussolini arrived in Rome by sleeping car and, as head of the government, greeted his followers when they entered the city.

Technically, Mussolini had come into office by legal means. The monarch did have the power to appoint the prime minister. Mussolini, however, had no majority in the Chamber of

Mussolini and the Black Shirts. Mussolini poses with supporters the day after the Black Shirt March on Rome intimidated the King of Italy into making him prime minister.

Bildarchiv Preussischer Kutturbesitz.

Deputies. Behind the legal façade of his assumption of power lay the months of terrorist disruption and intimidation and the threat of the Fascists' October march itself.

THE FASCISTS IN POWER

Mussolini had not really expected to be appointed prime minister. He moved cautiously to consolidate his power. He succeeded because of the impotence of his rivals, his own effective use of his office, his power over the masses, and his sheer ruthlessness. On November 23, 1922, the king and Parliament granted Mussolini dictatorial authority for one year to bring order to the lower levels of the government. Wherever possible, Mussolini appointed Fascists to office. Late in 1924, at Mussolini's behest, Parliament changed the election law. Previously parties had been represented in the Chamber of Deputies in proportion to the popular vote cast for them. According to the new election law, the party that gained the largest popular vote (with a minimum of at least 25 percent) received two thirds of the seats in the chamber. Coalition government, with all its compromises and hesitations, would no longer be necessary. In the election of 1924 the Fascists won a great victory and complete control of the Chamber of Deputies. They used that majority to end legitimate parliamentary life. A series of laws passed in 1925 and 1926 permitted Mussolini, in effect, to rule by decree. In 1926 all other political parties were dissolved, and Italy was transformed into a single-party, dictatorial state.

The Italian dictator made one important domestic departure that brought him significant political dividends. Through the Lateran Accord of February 1929 the Roman Catholic Church and the Italian state made peace with each other. Ever since the armies of Italian unification had seized papal lands in the 1860s the church had been hostile to the state. The popes had remained virtual prisoners in the Vatican after 1870. The agreement of 1929 recognized the pope as the temporal ruler of Vatican City. The Italian government agreed to pay an indemnity to the papacy for confiscated land. The state also recognized Catholicism as the religion of the nation, exempted church property from taxes, and allowed church law to govern marriage. The Lateran Accord brought further respectability to Mussolini's authoritarian regime.

German Democracy and Dictatorship
THE WEIMAR REPUBLIC

The Weimar Republic was born from the defeat of the imperial army, the revolution of 1918 against the Hohenzollerns, and the hopes of German Liberals and Social Democrats. Its name derived from the city in which its constitution was written and promulgated in August 1919. While the constitution was being debated, the republic, headed by the Social Democrats, accepted the humiliating terms of the Versailles Treaty. Although its officials had signed only under the threat of an Allied invasion, the republic was nevertheless permanently associated with the national disgrace and the economic burdens of the treaty. Throughout the 1920s the government of the republic was required to fulfill the economic and military provisions imposed by the Paris settlement. It became all too easy for nationalists and military figures whose policies had brought on the tragedy and defeat of the war to blame the young republic and the Socialists for the results of the conflict. In Germany, more than in other countries, the desire to revise the treaty was closely related to a desire to change the mode of domestic government.

The Weimar Constitution was a highly enlightened document. It guaranteed civil liberties and provided for direct election, by universal suffrage, of the **Reichstag** and the president. It also, however, contained certain crucial structural flaws that eventually allowed it to be overthrown. Seats in the Reichstag were allotted according to a complicated system of proportional representation. This made it relatively easy for small political parties to gain seats and resulted in shifting party combinations that led to considerable instability. Ministers were technically responsible to the Reichstag, but the president appointed and removed the chancellor, the head of the cabinet. Perhaps most important, Article 48 allowed the president, in an emergency, to rule by decree. The constitution thus permitted the possibility of presidential dictatorship.

The new government suffered major and minor humiliations as well as considerable economic instability. In March 1920 the right-wing Kapp Putsch, or armed insurrection, erupted in Berlin. Led by a conservative civil servant and supported by army officers, the attempted coup failed, but only after government officials had fled the city and workers had carried out a general strike. In the same month, strikes took place in the Ruhr mining district. The government sent in troops. Such extremism from both the left and the right would haunt the republic for all its days. In May 1921 the Allies presented a reparations bill for 132 billion gold marks. The German Republican government accepted this preposterous demand only after new Allied threats of occupation. Throughout the early 1920s there were numerous assassinations or attempted assassinations of important Republican leaders. Violence was the hallmark of the first five years of the republic.

Invasion of the Ruhr and Inflation   Inflation brought on the major crisis of this period. The financing of the war and continued postwar deficit spending generated an immense rise in prices. Consequently, the value of German currency fell. By early 1921 the German mark traded against the American dollar at a ratio of 64 to 1, compared with a ratio of 4.2 to 1 in 1914. The German financial community contended that the value of the currency could not be stabilized until the reparations issue had been solved. In the meantime, the printing presses kept pouring forth paper money, which was used to redeem government bonds as they fell due.

The French invasion of the Ruhr in January 1923, to secure the payment of reparations, and the German response of passive economic resistance produced cataclysmic inflation. The Weimar government paid subsidies to the Ruhr labor force, who had laid down their tools. Unemployment soon spread from the Ruhr to other parts of the country, creating a new drain on the treasury and also reducing tax revenues. The

▲ **Inflation in Germany.**   During the German inflation of 1923 currency literally was not worth the paper upon which it was printed. Here German children play with batches of worthless banknotes.
Bettmann/Hulton Deutsch Collection.

printing presses by this point had difficulty providing enough paper currency to keep up with the daily rise in prices. Money was literally not worth the paper it was printed on. Stores were unwilling to exchange goods for the worthless currency, and farmers withheld produce from the market.

The moral and social values of thrift and prudence were thoroughly undermined. Middle-class savings, pensions, and insurance policies were wiped out, as were investments in government bonds. Simultaneously, debts and mortgages could not be paid off. Speculators in land, real estate, and industry made great fortunes. Union contracts generally allowed workers to keep up with rising prices. Thus inflation was not a disaster for everyone. To the middle class and the lower middle class, however, the inflation was still one more trauma coming hard on the heels of the military defeat and the peace treaty. Only when the social and economic upheaval of these months is grasped can one understand the later German desire for order and security at almost any cost.

Hitler's Early Career   Late in 1923 Adolf Hitler (1889–1945) made his first significant appearance on the German political scene. The son of a minor Austrian customs official, he had gone to Vienna, where his hopes of becoming an artist were soon dashed. He lived off money sent by his widowed mother and later off his Austrian orphan's allowance. He also painted postcards for further income and later found work as a day laborer. In Vienna he encountered Mayor Karl Lueger's (1844–1910) Christian Socialist Party, which prospered on an ideology of anti-Semitism and from the social anxieties of the lower middle class. Hitler absorbed the rabid German nationalism and extreme anti-Semitism that flourished in Vienna. He came to hate Marxism, which he associated with Jews. During World War I Hitler fought in the German army, was wounded, rose to the rank of corporal, and won the Iron Cross for bravery. The war gave him his first sense of purpose.

After the conflict, Hitler settled in Munich. There he became associated with a small nationalistic, anti-Semitic political party that in 1920 adopted the name of National Socialist German Workers Party, better known simply as the **Nazis**. In the same year the group began to parade under a red banner with a black swastika. It issued a platform, or program, of Twenty-Five Points. Among other things, this platform called for the repudiation of the Versailles Treaty, the unification of Austria and Germany, the exclusion of Jews from German citizenship, agrarian reform, the prohibition of land speculation, the confiscation of war profits, state administration of the giant cartels, and the replacement of department stores with small retail shops. Originally the Nazis had called for a broad program of nationalization of industry in an attempt to compete directly with the Marxist political parties for the vote of the workers. As the tactic failed, the Nazis redefined the meaning of the word *socialist* in the party name, so that it suggested a nationalistic outlook. In 1922, Hitler said

> Whoever is prepared to make the national cause his own to such an extent that he knows no higher ideal than the welfare of his nation; whoever has understood our great national anthem, *Deutschland, Deutschland, über Alles* ["Germany, Germany, over All"], to mean that nothing in the wide world surpasses in his eyes this Germany, people and land, land and people—that man is a Socialist.[2]

This definition, of course, had nothing to do with traditional German socialism. The "socialism" that Hitler and the Nazis had in mind was not state ownership of the means of production but the subordination of all economic enterprise to the welfare of the nation. It often implied protection for small economic enterprises. Increasingly, over the years, the Nazis discovered that their social appeal was to the lower middle class, which found itself squeezed between well-organized big business and Socialist labor unions or political parties. The Nazis tailored their message to this troubled economic group.

Soon after the promulgation of the Twenty-Five Points, the storm troopers, or **SA** (*Sturm Abteilung*), were organized under the leadership of Captain Ernst Roehm (1887–1934). It was a paramilitary organization that initially provided its members with food and uniforms and, later in the decade, with wages. In the mid-1920s the SA adopted its famous brown-shirted uniform. The storm troopers were the chief Nazi instrument for terror and intimidation before the party came into control of the government. They were a law unto themselves. The organization constituted a means of preserving military discipline and values outside the small army permitted by the Paris settlement. The existence of such a private party army was a sign of the potential for violence in the Weimar Republic and the widespread contempt for the law and the institutions of the republic.

The social and economic turmoil following the French occupation of the Ruhr and the German inflation gave the fledgling party an opportunity for direct action against the Weimar Republic, which seemed incapable of providing military or economic security. By this time, because of his immense oratorical skills and organizational abilities, Hitler personally dominated the Nazi Party. On November 9, 1923, Hitler and a band of followers, accompanied by General Erich Ludendorff (1865–1937), attempted an unsuccessful putsch at a beer hall in Munich. When the local authorities crushed the rising, sixteen Nazis were killed. Hitler and Ludendorff were arrested and tried for treason. The general was acquitted. Hitler used the trial to make himself into a national figure. In his defense, he condemned the republic, the Versailles Treaty, the Jews, and the weakened condition of his adopted country. He was convicted and sentenced to five years in prison. He actually spent only a few months in jail before being paroled. During this time, he dictated *Mein Kampf* ("My Struggle"). Another result of the brief imprisonment was his decision to seize political power by legal methods.

The Stresemann Years   The officials of the republic were attempting to repair the damage from the inflation. Gustav Stresemann (1878–1929) was responsible primarily for reconstruction of the republic and for its achievement of a sense of self-confidence. Stresemann abandoned the policy of passive resistance in the Ruhr. The country simply could not afford it. Then, with the aid of banker Hjalmar Schacht (1877–1970), he introduced a new German currency. The rate of exchange was 1 trillion of the old German marks for one new Rentenmark. Stresemann also moved against challenges from both the left and the right. He supported the crushing of both Hitler's abortive putsch and smaller Communist disturbances. In late November 1923, after four months as chancellor, he resigned to become foreign minister, a post he held until his death in 1929. In that office he continued to influence the affairs of the republic.

---

[2] Alan Bullock, *Hitler: A Study in Tyranny*, rev. ed. (New York: Harper & Row, 1964), p. 76.

In 1924 the Weimar Republic and the Allies renegotiated the reparation payments. The Dawes Plan lowered the annual payments and allowed them to fluctuate according to the fortunes of the German economy. The last French troops left the Ruhr in 1925. The same year, Field Marshal Paul von Hindenburg (1847–1934), a military hero and a conservative monarchist, was elected president of the republic. He governed in strict accordance with the constitution, but his election suggested that German politics had become more conservative. Conservative Germans seemed reconciled to the republic. This conservatism was in line with the prosperity of the latter 1920s. Foreign capital flowed into Germany, and employment, which had been poor throughout most of the postwar years, improved smartly. Giant industrial combines spread. The prosperity helped to establish broader acceptance and appreciation of the republic.

In foreign affairs, Stresemann pursued a conciliatory course. He fulfilled the provisions of the Versailles Treaty even as he attempted to revise it by diplomacy. He was willing to accept the settlement in the West but was a determined, if sometimes secret, revisionist in the East. He aimed to recover German-speaking territories lost to Poland and Czechoslovakia and possibly to unite with Austria, chiefly by diplomatic means. The first step, however, was to achieve respectability and economic recovery. That goal required a policy of accommodation and "fulfillment," for the moment at least.

Locarno These developments gave rise to the Locarno Agreements of October 1925. The spirit of conciliation led foreign ministers Austen Chamberlain (1863–1937) for Britain and Aristide Briand (1862–1932) for France to accept Stresemann's proposal for a fresh start. France and Germany both accepted the western frontier established at Versailles as legitimate. Britain and Italy agreed to intervene against the aggressor if either side violated the frontier or if Germany sent troops into the demilitarized Rhineland. Significantly, no such agreement was made about Germany's eastern frontier, but the Germans made treaties of arbitration with Poland and Czechoslovakia, and France strengthened its ties with those countries. France supported German membership in the League of Nations and agreed to withdraw its occupation troops from the Rhineland in 1930, five years earlier than specified at Versailles.

Germany was pleased to have achieved respectability and a guarantee against another Ruhr occupation, as well as the possibility of revision in the east. Britain enjoyed playing a more even-handed role. Italy was glad to be recognized as a great power. The French were happy, too, because the Germans voluntarily accepted the permanence of their western frontier, which was also guaranteed by Britain and Italy, and France maintained its allies in the east.

The Locarno Agreements brought new hope to Europe. Germany's entry into the League of Nations was greeted with enthusiasm. Chamberlain, Briand, and Stresemann all received the Nobel Peace Prize in 1925 and 1926. The spirit of Locarno was carried even further when the leading European states, Japan, and the United States signed the Kellogg-Briand Pact in 1928, renouncing "war as an instrument of national policy."

CHRONOLOGY

Major Political Events of the 1920s and 1930s

1919 August	Constitution of the Weimar Republic promulgated
1920	Kapp Putsch in Berlin
1921 March	Kronstadt mutiny leads Lenin to initiate his New Economic Policy
1922 October	Fascist march on Rome leads to Mussolini's assumption of power
1923 January	France invades the Ruhr
November	Hitler's Beer Hall Putsch
1924	Death of Lenin
1925	Locarno Agreements
1928	Kellogg-Briand Pact; first Five-Year Plan launched in USSR
1929 January	Trotsky expelled from USSR
February	Lateran Accord between the Vatican and the Italian state
October	New York stock market crash
November	Bukharin expelled from his offices in the Soviet Union; Stalin's central position thus affirmed
1930 March	Bruning government begins in Germany
	Stalin calls for moderation in his policy of agricultural collectivization because of "dizziness from success"
September	Nazis capture 107 seats in German Reichstag
1931 August	National Government formed in Britain
1932 March 13	Hindenberg defeats Hitler for German presidency
May 31	Franz von Papen forms German Cabinet
July 31	German Reichstag election
November 6	German Reichstag election
December 2	Kurt von Schleicher forms German Cabinet
1933 January 30	Hitler made German chancellor
February 27	Reichstag fire
March 5	Reichstag election
March 23	Enabling Act consolidates Nazi power
1934 June 30	Blood purge of the Nazi Party
August 2	Death of Hindenburg
December 1	Assassination of Kirov leads to the beginning of Stalin's purges
1936 May	Popular Front government in France
July–August	Most famous of public purge trials in Russia

The joy and optimism were not justified. France had merely recognized its inability to coerce Germany without help. Britain had shown its unwillingness to uphold the settlement in the east. Austen Chamberlain declared that no British government ever would "risk the bones of a British grenadier" for the Polish corridor. Germany was not reconciled to the eastern settlement. It maintained clandestine military connections with the Soviet Union and planned to continue to press for revision.

In both France and Germany, moreover, the conciliatory politicians represented only a part of the nation. In Germany especially, most people continued to reject Versailles and regarded Locarno as only an extension of it. When the Dawes Plan ran out in 1929 it was replaced by the Young Plan, which lowered the reparation payments, put a term on how long they must be made, and removed Germany entirely from outside supervision and control. The intensity of the outcry in Germany against the continuation of any reparations showed how far the Germans were from accepting their situation. Despite these problems, war was by no means inevitable. Europe, aided by American loans, was returning to prosperity. German leaders like Stresemann would certainly have continued to press for change, but there is little reason to think that they would have resorted to force, much less to a general war. Continued prosperity and diplomatic success might have won the loyalty of the German people for the Weimar Republic and moderate revisionism, but the Great Depression of the 1930s brought new forces to power.

DEPRESSION AND POLITICAL DEADLOCK

The outflow of foreign, and especially American, capital from Germany that began in 1928 undermined the economic prosperity of the Weimar Republic. The resulting economic crisis brought parliamentary government to a halt. In 1928 a coalition of center parties and the Social Democrats governed. All went reasonably well until the Depression struck. Then the coalition partners differed sharply on economic policy. The Social Democrats refused to reduce social and unemployment insurance. The more conservative parties, remembering the inflation of 1923, insisted on a balanced budget. The coalition dissolved in March 1930. To resolve the parliamentary deadlock in the Reichstag, President von Hindenburg appointed Heinrich Brüning (1885–1970) as chancellor. Lacking a majority in the Reichstag, the new chancellor governed through emergency presidential decrees, as authorized by Article 48 of the constitution. The party divisions in the Reichstag prevented the overriding of the decrees. The Weimar Republic was transformed into a presidential dictatorship.

German unemployment rose from 2,258,000 in March 1930 to over 6,000,000 in March 1932. There had been persistent unemployment during the 1920s, but nothing of such magnitude or duration. The economic downturn and the parliamentary deadlock worked to the advantage of the more extreme political parties. In the election of 1928 the Nazis had won only 12 seats in the Reichstag, and the Communists had won 54 seats. Two years later, after the election of 1930, the Nazis held 107 seats and the Communists 77.

The power of the Nazis in the streets was also on the rise. The unemployment fed thousands of men into the storm troopers, which had 100,000 members in 1930 and almost 1 million in 1933. The SA freely and viciously attacked Communists and Social Democrats. For the Nazis, politics meant the capture of power through terror and intimidation as well as through elections. Decency and civility in political life vanished. Nazi rallies resembled secular religious revivals. The Nazis paraded through the streets and the countryside. They gained powerful supporters and sympathizers in the business, military, and newspaper communities. Some intellectuals were also sympathetic. The Nazis transformed this discipline and enthusiasm born of economic despair and nationalistic frustration into impressive electoral results.

HITLER COMES TO POWER

For two years Brüning continued to govern through the confidence of Hindenburg. The economy did not improve, and the political situation deteriorated. In 1932 the eighty-three-year-old president stood for reelection. Hitler ran against him and forced a runoff. The Nazi leader garnered 30.1 percent of the vote in the first election and 36.8 percent in the second. Although Hindenburg was returned to office, the vote convinced him that Brüning had lost the confidence of conservative German voters. In May 1932 he dismissed Brüning and appointed Franz von Papen (1878–1969) in his place. The new chancellor was one of a small group of extremely conservative advisers on whom the aged Hindenburg had become increasingly dependent. Others included the president's son and several military figures. With the continued paralysis in the Reichstag, their influence over the president amounted to control of the government. Consequently, the crucial decisions of the next several months were made by only a handful of people.

Papen and the circle around the president wanted to draw the Nazis into cooperation with them without giving Hitler effective power. The government needed the popular support on the right that only the Nazis seemed able to generate. The Hindenburg circle decided to convince Hitler that the Nazis could not come to power on their own. Papen removed the ban on Nazi meetings that Brüning had imposed and then called a Reichstag election for July 1932. The Nazis won 230 seats and polled 37.2 percent of the vote. Hitler would only

Hitler. Hitler's mastery of the techniques of mass politics and propaganda— including huge staged rallies like this one in 1938—was an important factor in his rise to power.
Bildarchlv Preussischer Kulturbesitz.

enter the Cabinet if he were made chancellor. Hindenburg refused. Another election was called in November, partly to wear down the Nazis' financial resources. The Nazis gained only 196 seats, and their percentage of the popular vote dipped to 33.1 percent. The advisers around Hindenburg still refused to appoint Hitler to office.

In early December 1932 Papen resigned, and General Kurt von Schleicher (1882–1934) became chancellor. People were now afraid of civil war between the extreme left and the far right. Schleicher decided to try and fashion a broad-based coalition of conservative groups and trade unionists. The prospect of such a coalition, including groups from the political left, frightened the Hindenburg circle even more than the prospect of Hitler. They did not trust Schleicher's motives, which have never been clear. Consequently, they persuaded Hindenburg to appoint Hitler chancellor. To control him and to see that he did little mischief, Papen was named vice chancellor, and other traditional conservatives were appointed to the Cabinet. On January 30, 1933, Adolf Hitler became the chancellor of Germany.

Hitler had come into office by legal means. All the proper forms and procedures had been observed. This was important, for it permitted the civil service, the courts, and the other agencies of the government to support him in good conscience. He had forged a rigidly disciplined party structure and had mastered the techniques of mass politics and propaganda. He understood how to touch the raw social and politi-

cal nerves of the electorate. His support appears to have come from across the social spectrum. Pockets of resistance appeared among Roman Catholic voters in the country and small towns. Otherwise, support for Hitler was particularly strong among farmers, war veterans, and the young, who had especially suffered from the insecurity of the 1920s and the Depression of the early 1930s. Hitler promised them security against Communists and Socialists, effective government in place of the petty politics of the other parties, and an uncompromising nationalist vision of a strong, restored Germany.

Much blame was once assigned to German big business for the rise of Hitler. However, there is little evidence that business contributions made any crucial difference to the Nazis' success or failure. Hitler's supporters were frequently suspicious of business and giant capitalism. They wanted a simpler world, one in which small property would be safe from both socialism and large-scale capitalist consolidation. These people looked to Hitler and the Nazis rather than to the Social Democrats because the latter, although concerned with social issues, never appeared sufficiently nationalistic. The Nazis won out over other conservative nationalistic parties because, unlike those conservatives, the Nazis did address the problem of social insecurities.

HITLER'S CONSOLIDATION OF POWER

Once in office, Hitler moved with almost lightning speed to consolidate his control. This process had three facets: the capture of full legal authority, the crushing of alternative political

The Nazis Pass Their Racial Legislation

Anti-Semitism was a fundamental tenet of the Nazi Party and became a major policy of the Nazi government. This comprehensive legislation of September 15, 1935, carried anti-Semitism into all areas of public life and into some of the most personal areas of private life as well. It was characteristically entitled the Law for the Protection of German Blood and Honor. Hardly any aspect of Nazi thought and action shocked the non-German world as much as this policy toward the Jews.

◆ How would this legislation have affected the normal daily interaction between Jews and non-Jews in Germany? Why are there specific prohibitions against mixed marriages and sexual relations between Jews and non-Jews? How does this legislation separate German Jews from the symbols of German national life?

Imbued with the knowledge that the purity of German blood is the necessary prerequisite for the existence of the German nation, and inspired by an inflexible will to maintain the existence of the German nation for all future times, the Reichstag has unanimously adopted the following law, which is now enacted:

Article I: (1) Any marriages between Jews and citizens of German or kindred blood are herewith forbidden. Marriages entered into despite this law are invalid, even if they are arranged abroad as a means of circumventing this law.

(2) Annulment proceedings for marriages may be initiated only by the Public Prosecutor.

Article II: Extramarital relations between Jews and citizens of German or kindred blood are herewith forbidden.

Article III: Jews are forbidden to employ as servants to their households female subjects of German or kindred blood who are under the age of forty-five years.

Article IV: (1) Jews are prohibited from displaying the Reich and national flag and from showing the national colors.

(2) However, they may display the Jewish colors. The exercise of this right is under state protection.

Article V: (1) Anyone who acts contrary to the prohibition noted in Article I renders himself liable to penal servitude.

(2) The man who acts contrary to the prohibition of Article II will be punished by sentence to either a jail or penitentiary.

(3) Anyone who acts contrary to the provisions of Articles III or IV will be punished with a jail sentence up to a year and with a fine, or with one of these penalties.

Article VI: The Reich Minister of Interior, in conjunction with the Deputy to the Führer and the Reich Minister of Justice, will issue the required legal and administrative decrees for the implementation and amplification of this law.

Article VII: This law shall go into effect on the day following its promulgation, with the exception of Article III, which shall go into effect on January 1, 1936.

From *Documents of German History*, Louis L. Snyder, ed. and trans. Copyright © 1938 Rutgers the State University, pp. 427–428. Reprinted by permission of Rutgers University Press.

groups, and the purging of rivals within the Nazi Party itself. On February 27, 1933, a mentally ill Dutch Communist set fire to the Reichstag building in Berlin. The Nazis quickly turned the incident to their own advantage by claiming that the fire proved the existence of an immediate Communist threat against the government. To the public, it seemed plausible that the Communists might attempt some action against the state now that the Nazis were in power. Under Article 48, Hitler made the Emergency Decree suspending civil liberties and proceeded to arrest Communists or alleged Communists. This decree was not revoked as long as Hitler ruled Germany.

In early March another Reichstag election took place. The Nazis still received only 43.9 percent of the vote. However, the arrest of the newly elected Communist deputies and the political fear aroused by the fire meant that Hitler could control the Reichstag. On March 23, 1933, the Reichstag passed an Enabling Act that permitted Hitler to rule by decree. There-

after, there were no legal limits on his exercise of power. The Weimar Constitution was never formally repealed or amended. It had simply been supplanted by the February Emergency Decree and the March Enabling Act.

Perhaps better than anyone else, Hitler understood that he and his party had not inevitably come to power. His potential opponents had stood divided between 1929 and 1933. He intended to prevent them from regrouping. In a series of complex moves, Hitler outlawed or undermined various German institutions that might have served as rallying points for opposition. In early May 1933 the offices, banks, and newspapers of the free trade unions were seized, and their leaders arrested. The Nazi Party itself, rather than any government agency, undertook this action. In late June and early July, the other German political parties were outlawed. By July 14, 1933, the National Socialists were the only legal party in Germany. During the same months the Nazis had taken control of the governments of the individual federal states in Germany. By the close of 1933 all major institutions of potential opposition had been eliminated.

The final element in Hitler's personal consolidation of power involved the Nazi Party itself. By late 1933 the SA, or storm troopers, consisted of approximately 1 million active members and a larger number of reserves. The commander of this party army was Ernst Roehm, a possible rival to Hitler himself. The German army officer corps, on whom Hitler depended to rebuild the national army, were jealous of the SA leadership. Consequently, to protect his own position and to shore up support with the regular army, on June 30, 1934, Hitler ordered the murder of key SA officers, including Roehm. Others killed between June 30 and July 2 included the former chancellor Kurt von Schleicher and his wife. The exact number of purged victims is unknown, but it has been estimated to have exceeded 100. The German army, which was the only institution in the nation that might have prevented the murders, did nothing. A month later, on August 2, 1934, President Hindenburg died. Thereafter, the offices of chancellor and president were combined. Hitler was now the *Führer*, or sole ruler of Germany and of the Nazi Party.

THE POLICE STATE

Terror and intimidation had helped propel the Nazis to office. As Hitler consolidated his power, he oversaw the organization of a police state. The chief vehicle of police surveillance was the **SS** (Schutzstaffel), or security units, commanded by Heinrich Himmler (1900–1945). This group had originated in the mid-1920s as a bodyguard for Hitler and had become a more elite paramilitary organization than the larger SA. In 1933 the SS had approximately 52,000 members. It was the instrument that carried out the blood purges of the party in 1934. By 1936 Himmler had become head of all police matters in Germany.

The police character of the Nazi regime was all-pervasive, but the people who most consistently experienced its terror were the German Jews. Anti-Semitism had been a key plank of the Nazi program—anti-Semitism based on biological racial theories stemming from late-nineteenth-century thought rather than from religious discrimination. Before World War II the Nazi attack on the Jews went through three stages of increasing intensity. In 1933, shortly after assuming power, the Nazis excluded Jews from the civil service. For a time they also attempted to enforce boycotts of Jewish shops and businesses. The boycotts won relatively little public support. In 1935 the Nuremberg Laws robbed German Jews of their citizenship. All persons with at least one Jewish grandparent were defined as Jews. The professions and the major occupations were closed to Jews. Marriage and sexual intercourse between Jews and

▲ **Anti-Jewish Policies.** Soon after seizing power, the Nazi government began harassing German Jewish businesses. Non-Jewish German citizens were urged not to buy merchandise from shops owned by Jews.
Bildarchiv Preussischer Kulturbesitz.

non-Jews were prohibited. Legal exclusion and humiliation of the Jews became the order of the day. (See Document, "The Nazis Pass Their Racial Legislation.")

The persecution of the Jews increased again in 1938. Business careers were forbidden. In November 1938, under orders from the Nazi Party, thousands of Jewish stores and synagogues were burned or otherwise destroyed. The Jewish community itself had to pay for the damage that occurred on this **Kristallnacht** because the government confiscated the insurance money. In all manner of other ways, large and petty, the German Jews were harassed. This persecution allowed the Nazis to inculcate the rest of the population with the concept of a master race of pure German "Aryans" and also to display their own contempt for civil liberties.

OVERVIEW   Political Tyranny of the 1920s and 1930s

Although political tyranny was not new to Europe, several factors in the 1920s and 1930s combined to give dictators of the right and the left unique power. The regimes set up by Mussolini in Italy, Stalin in the Soviet Union, and Hitler in Germany shared the following characteristics:

1. Well-organized, highly disciplined political parties, mass based in Italy and Germany, restricted membership in the Soviet Union

2. Nationalism

3. Programs that promised to cure social, political, and economic frustrations and end the pettiness of everyday politics

4. A monopoly over mass communications and propaganda

5. Highly effective instruments of terror and police power

6. Real or imagined national, class, or racial enemies who could be demonized to whip up mass support

7. Command over modern technology and its capacity for immense destruction

After the war broke out, Hitler decided in 1942 to destroy the Jews in Europe. It is thought that over 6 million Jews, mostly from eastern European nations, died as a result of that staggering decision, unprecedented in its scope and implementation.

WOMEN IN NAZI GERMANY

The Nazis believed in separate social spheres for men and women. Men belonged in the world of action, women in the home. The two spheres should not mix. Women who sought to liberate themselves and to adopt roles traditionally followed by men in public life were considered symptoms of cultural decline. Respect for women should arise from their function as wives and mothers. (See Document, "Hitler Rejects the Emancipation of Women.")

These attitudes stood in direct conflict with many of the social changes that German women, like women elsewhere in Europe, had experienced during the first three decades of the twentieth century. German women had become much

Nazi Party Rally.   Young women among an enthusiastic crowd extend the Nazi salute at a party rally in 1938. Nazi ideology encouraged women to favor traditional domestic roles over employment in the workplace and to bear many children. The onset of the war, however, forced the government to recruit workers.
Bildarchiv Preussischer Kulturbesitz.

DOCUMENT | Hitler Rejects the Emancipation of Women

According to Nazi ideology, women's place was in the home producing and rearing children and supporting their husbands. In this speech, Hitler urges this view of the role of women. He uses anti-Semitism to discredit those writers who had urged the emancipation of women from their traditional roles and occupations. Hitler returns here to the "separate spheres" concept of the relationship of men and women. His traditional view of women was directed against views that were associated with the Soviet experiment during the interwar years. Contrast this Nazi outlook on women and the family with the Bolshevik position described by Alexandra Kollontai in the document earlier in the chapter. Ironically, once World War II began, the Nazi leadership demanded that women leave the home and work in factories to support the war effort.

◆ What are the social tasks Hitler assigns to women? Why does he associate the emancipation of women with Jews and intellectuals? How does he attempt to subordinate the lives of women to the supremacy of the state?

The slogan "Emancipation of women" was invented by Jewish intellectuals and its content was formed by the same spirit. In the really good times of German life the German woman had no need to emancipate herself. She possessed exactly what nature had necessarily given her to administer and preserve; just as the man in his good times had no need to fear that he would be ousted from his position in relation to the woman. …

If the man's world is said to be the State, his struggle, his readiness to devote his powers to the service of the community, then it may perhaps be said that the woman's is a smaller world. For her world is her husband, her family, her children, and her home. But what would become of the greater world if there were no one to tend and care for the smaller one? How could the greater world survive if there were no one to make the cares of the smaller world the content of their lives? No, the greater world is built on the foundation of this smaller world. This great world cannot survive if the smaller world is not stable. Providence has entrusted to the woman the cares of that world which is her very own, and only on the basis of this smaller world can the man's world be formed and built up. The two worlds are not antagonistic. They complement each other, they belong together just as man and woman belong together.

We do not consider it correct for the woman to interfere in the world of the man, in his main sphere. We consider it natural if these two worlds remain distinct. To the one belongs the strength of feeling, the strength of the soul. To the other belongs the strength of vision, of toughness, of decision, and of the willingness to act. In the one case this strength demands the willingness of the woman to risk her life to preserve this important cell and to multiply it, and in the other case it demands from the man the readiness to safeguard life. …

So our women's movement is for us not something which inscribes on its banner as its programme the fight against men, but something which has as its programme the common fight together with men. For the new National Socialist national community acquires a firm basis precisely because we have gained the trust of millions of women as fanatical fellow-combatants, women who have fought for the common life in the service of the common task of preserving life. …

Whereas previously the programmes of the liberal, intellectualist women's movements contained many points, the programme of our National Socialist Women's movement has in reality but one single point, and that point is the child, that tiny creature which must be born and grow strong and which alone gives meaning to the whole life-struggle.

From J. Noakes and G. Pridham, eds., *Nazism, 1919–1945*, Vol. 2, *State, Economy and Society, 1933–39: A Documentary Reader*, Exeter Studies in History No. 8. University of Exeter Press, 1984, pp. 449–450.

more active and assertive. More of them worked in factories or were independently employed, and they had begun to enter the professions. Under the Weimar constitution, they voted. Throughout the Weimar period there was also a lively discussion of women's emancipation. For the Nazis these developments were signs of cultural weakness. They generally urged a much more traditional role for women in their new society. Nazi writers portrayed women as wives and mothers first and foremost.

The Nazis' point of view was supported by women of a generally conservative outlook and women who were following traditional roles as housewives, confirming the choices these women had made about how to lead their lives. In a period of high unemployment, the Nazi attitude also appealed to many men because it discouraged women from competing with them in the workplace. Such competition had begun during World War I, and many Nazis considered it symptomatic of the social confusion that had followed the German defeat.

The Nazi discussion of the role of women was also deeply rooted in Nazi racism. Nazi writers argued that the superiority of the pure German race depended on the purity of the blood of each and every individual. It was the special task of German mothers to preserve racial purity. Hitler particularly championed this view of women. They were to breed strong sons and daughters for the German nation. Nazi journalists often compared the role of women in childbirth to that of men in battle. Each served the state in particular social and gender roles. In both cases, the good of the nation was superior to that of the individual.

Most Nazis who discussed the role of women relegated them to the home. They also generally attacked feminist outlooks. Women were encouraged to bear many children, because the Nazis believed the declining German birth rate was the result of emancipated women who had spurned their natural and proper roles as mothers. The Nazis established special medals for women who bore large families. They also sponsored schools that taught women how to care for and rear children.

The Nazis also saw women as educators of the young and thus the special protectors of German cultural values. Through cooking, dress, music, and stories, mothers were to instill a love for the nation. As consumers for the home, women were to aid German-owned shops, to buy German-produced goods, and to avoid Jewish merchants.

The Nazis realized that in the midst of the Depression many women would need to work, but the party urged them to pursue employment that the Nazis considered natural to their character. These tasks included agriculture, teaching, nursing, social work, and domestic service. Nonetheless, despite some variation in the early and mid-1930s, the percentage of women employed in Germany changed little from the Weimar to the Hitler years: It was 37 percent in 1928 and the same again in 1939. Thereafter, because of the war effort, many more women were recruited into the German workforce.

The Great Depression and the New Deal in the United States

The United States emerged from the First World War as a major world power. However, it retreated from that role when the Senate refused to ratify the Versailles Treaty and subsequently failed to join the League of Nations. In 1920 Warren Harding (1865–1923) became president and urged a return to what he termed "normalcy," which meant minimal involvement abroad and conservative economic policies at home. Business interests clearly remained in the ascendent, with the federal government taking a relatively inactive role in national

economic life. Indeed, government inactivity was the virtual creed of Harding's successor, President Calvin Coolidge (1872–1933).

The first seven or eight years of the decade witnessed remarkable American prosperity. New electrical appliances such as the radio, phonograph, washing machine, and vacuum cleaner appeared on the market. Large-scale advertising campaigns attempted to persuade consumers to purchase such items. Real wages rose for many groups of workers. Industry grew at a robust rate. Automobile manufacturers assumed a major role in national economic life. Henry Ford's (1863–1947) Model T exemplified the determination of the automobile industry to produce for a mass market. Increasing numbers of factories became mechanized. Engineers and efficiency experts were the heroes of the business world. For most of the 1920s the New York stock market boomed. All of this remarkable activity stood in marked contrast to the various economic dislocations occurring in Europe.

The material prosperity appeared, however, in a sharply divided society. Segregation remained a basic fact of life for black Americans throughout the South and to a lesser degree in other areas of the country. The Ku Klux Klan, which sought to terrorize blacks, Roman Catholics, and Jews, enjoyed a resurgence. The Prohibition Amendment of 1919 (repealed in 1933) forbade the manufacture and transport of alcoholic beverages. In the wake of this divisive national policy, major criminal operations arose to supply liquor and to disrupt the stability of civic life. Many immigrants came from Mexico and Puerto Rico. They settled in cities where their labor was desired, but where they were often not welcomed or assimilated. Finally, the wealth of the nation was overwhelmingly concentrated in relatively few hands.

ECONOMIC COLLAPSE

In March 1929 Herbert Hoover became president, the third Republican in as many elections. On October 29, 1929, the New York stock market crashed. The other financial markets also went into a tailspin. During the next year the stock market continued to fall. The banks that had loaned people money with which to speculate in the market suffered great losses.

The financial collapse of 1929 triggered the Great Depression in America, although there were other underlying domestic causes. During the 1920s manufacturing firms had not made sufficient capital investment. The disproportionate amount of profits going to about 5 percent of the U.S. population had by the end of the decade begun to undermine the purchasing power of other consumers. Furthermore, agriculture had been in trouble for years. Finally, the economic difficulties in Europe and Latin America, which predated those in

Unemployed Workers. The Great Depression brought unprecedented unemployment to the United States. In 1930 unemployed workers were photographed standing outside the Municipal Lodging House in New York City.

Corbis-Bettmann.

the United States, meant foreigners were less able to purchase products produced in the United States.

The most pervasive problem of the Great Depression was the spread of unemployment. Joblessness hit poor unskilled workers most rapidly but then worked its way up the job ladder to touch factory and white-collar workers. As unemployment spread, small retail businesses suffered. In the major American manufacturing cities, hundreds of thousands of workers could not find jobs. The price of corn fell so low in some areas that it was not profitable to harvest the crop. By the early 1930s banks across the country began to fail, and people lost their savings.

The federal government was not really equipped to address the emergency. There was no tradition of federal action to alleviate economic distress. President Hoover organized economic conferences in Washington and encouraged the Federal Reserve to make borrowing easier. He supported the ill-advised Hawley-Smoot Tariff Act of 1930, with which Congress had hoped to protect American industry by a high tariff barrier. But fundamentally Hoover believed relief was a

matter for local government and voluntary organizations. In many areas the local relief agencies had actually run out of money by 1931.

New Role for Government

The election of 1932 was one of the most crucial in American history. Franklin Delano Roosevelt (1882–1945), in accepting the Democratic nomination, pledged his party to a "new deal for the American people." He overwhelmingly defeated Hoover, and quickly set about redirecting federal policy toward the Depression.

Roosevelt had been born into a moderately wealthy New York family. A distant cousin of Theodore Roosevelt (1858–1919), he had been educated at Harvard College and Columbia Law School. After serving in World War I as assistant secretary of the navy, in 1920 he ran as the Democratic vice presidential candidate. The next year, however, he was struck with polio and his legs became paralyzed. With extraordinary determination he went on to be elected governor of New York in 1928. As the newly elected president he attempted to convey to the nation the same kind of optimistic spirit that had informed his own personal struggle of the 1920s.

Roosevelt's first goal was to give the nation a sense that the federal government was acting to meet the economic challenge. The first 100 days of his administration became legendary. Coming into office at the height of the crisis in the banking system, he immediately closed all the banks and permitted only sound institutions to reopen. Congress convened in a special session and rapidly passed a new banking act. Shortly thereafter, Congress enacted the Agricultural Adjustment Act and the Farm Credit Act to aid the farm sector of the economy. To provide jobs, Roosevelt's administration sponsored the Civilian Conservation Corps. The Federal Emergency Relief Act provided funding for state and local relief agencies. To restore confidence, Roosevelt began making speeches, known as his "fireside chats," to the American people.

Roosevelt's most ambitious program was the National Industrial Recovery Act (NIRA), which established the National Recovery Administration (NRA). This agency attempted to foster codes written by various industries to regulate wages and prices. It was hoped that competition might be thus regulated to protect jobs and assure production.

The NIRA and other New Deal legislation, such as the Wagner Act of 1935, which established the National Labor Relations Board and the Fair Labor Standards Act of 1938, provided a larger role in the American economy for organized labor. It became easier for unions to organize. Union membership grew rapidly and steadily. American unionism took on a new character during these years. Previously, most unions

The Works Progress Administration was one of the chief ▶ New Deal agencies designed to create public works projects that would generate employment, as with this group repairing a street.
Corbis/Bettmann.

had organized by craft and had been affiliated with the American Federation of Labor. The major union gains of the 1930s, however, occurred through the organization of whole industries composed of workers in various crafts in a single union. The most important of these organizations were the United Mine Workers and United Automobile Workers. These new unions organized themselves into the Congress of Industrial Organizations. The CIO and the AFL were rivals until they merged in the 1950s. These new strong industrial labor organizations introduced a powerful new force into the American economic scene.

In 1935 the U.S. Supreme Court declared the NRA unconstitutional. Thereafter, Roosevelt deemphasized centralized economic planning. There were no fewer federal agencies—indeed, their number increased—but they operated in general independence from each other.

Through New Deal legislation, the federal government was far more active in the economy than it had been in the past. The government itself attempted to provide relief for the unemployed in the industrial sector. The major institution of the relief effort was the **Works Progress Administration**. Created in 1935, the WPA began a massive program of large public works.

The programs of the New Deal years also involved the federal government directly in economic development rather than turning such development over to private enterprise. Through the Tennessee Valley Authority (TVA), the government became directly involved in the economy of the four states of the Tennessee river valley. The TVA built dams and then produced and sold hydroelectricity. Never had the government undertaken so extensive an economic role. Another major new function for the government was providing security for the elderly, through the establishment of the Social Security Administration in 1935.

Hence, in one area of American life after another, it was decided that individual voluntary effort could not provide sufficient personal economic security and that the government must act to do so. These actions established a mixed economy in the United States—that is, one in which the federal government would play an ongoing active role alongside the private sector.

The New Deal changed much of American life. Yet despite its programs and new initiatives, it did not solve the unemployment problem. Indeed, in the late 1930s the economy began to falter again. It was the entry of the nation into World War II that brought the U.S. economy to full employment.

However, the New Deal did preserve American democracy and capitalism. The experience of the United States under the New Deal stood in marked contrast to the economic and political experiments taking place in Europe. Many businesspeople found Roosevelt far too liberal and his policies too activist. Nonetheless, the New Deal fundamentally preserved capitalism in a democratic setting, where, in contrast to Europe, there was a broad spectrum of political debate—much of it highly critical of the administration. The United States had demonstrated that a nation with a vast industrial economy could confront its gravest economic crisis and still preserve democracy.

Telephone Operator.

Summary

Postwar Problems   The Versailles settlement bred political discontent and resentment throughout Europe among both victors and the defeated. In the 1920s there were endless wrangles over reparations between Germany and the Allied powers. After World War I, Europe never recovered its prewar prosperity or stability. The onset of the Great Depression in 1929 caused severe problems in both Europe and the United States and led to the Nazi seizure of power in Germany and FDR's New Deal in the United States.

The Soviet Union   The Bolsheviks had expected communist revolutions to break out across Europe. When that did not happen, they were forced to consolidate their regime within Russia. Lenin's New Economic Policy gave the state control over heavy industry, transportation, and international commerce but allowed for small-scale private enterprise and peasant farms. Stalin abandoned this policy to push for rapid industrialization. He abolished private enterprise, collectivized agriculture, and eliminated his opponents in a series of purges in which millions were imprisoned or killed. Despite the violence and oppression, Marxist parties around the world were subservient to the Soviet Union as the world's only communist state and the enemy of fascism.

Fascist Italy   Benito Mussolini came to power in Italy in 1922. Many Italians were dissatisfied with the terms of the Versailles Treaty and frightened by the social unrest that followed World War I. Mussolini promised order and a strong state. Although he achieved power by legal means, he soon transformed Italy into a single-party dictatorship. In 1929 he came to terms with the Catholic Church by negotiating the Lateran Accord, which recognized the pope as the independent ruler of Vatican City.

Nazi Germany   The postwar Weimar Republic in Germany was buffeted by social, political, and financial instability. Many Germans refused to accept Germany's defeat in World War I or the terms of the Versailles Treaty. Rampant inflation destroyed the savings of the middle class. The Great Depression brought financial collapse and massive unemployment. Many Germans looked to Adolf Hitler and the Nazi Party for solutions. Once Hitler came to power in 1933, he quickly established a one-party dictatorship based on police terror, propaganda, racial anti-Semitism and the cult of Hitler as supreme leader. The Jews, in particular, were persecuted. Hitler also formed an alliance with the German army and began a program of rapid rearmament.

The United States   The United States emerged from World War I as a world power, but retreated into isolation during the 1920s. The prosperity of the 1920s ended in the Great Depression. Franklin Delano Roosevelt's New Deal greatly expanded the power of the federal government in social and economic affairs and preserved capitalism in a democratic setting.

Review Questions

1. Explain the causes of the Great Depression. Why was it more severe and why did it last longer than previous economic downturns? Could it have been avoided?

2. How did Stalin achieve supreme power in the Soviet Union? Why did he decide that Russia had to industrialize rapidly? Why did this require the collectivization of agriculture? Was the policy a success? How did it affect the Russian people? What were the causes of the great purges?

3. Why was Italy dissatisfied and unstable after World War I? How did Mussolini achieve power? What were the characteristics of the Fascist state?

4. Why did the Weimar Republic collapse in Germany? Discuss Hitler's rise to power. Which groups in Germany supported Hitler and why were they pro-Nazi? How did he consolidate his power?

5. Compare the authoritarian regimes in the Soviet Union, Italy, and Germany. What characteristics did they have in common? What role did terror play in each?

6. Why did the United States economy collapse in 1929? What policies did Roosevelt use to combat the Depression? How did his policies affect the role of the federal government in national life?

Key Terms

collectivization   (p. 908)

Duce   (p. 911)

fascism   (p. 911)

Führer   (p. 920)

Great Depression   (p. 903)

Great Purges   (p. 910)

Kristallnacht   (p. 920)

Mein Kampf   (p. 915)

Nazis   (p. 915)

New Economic Policy (NEP)   (p. 906)

Popular Front   (p. 905)

Reichstag   (p. 914)

SA   (p. 915)

SS   (p. 920)

War Communism   (p. 906)

Weimar Republic   (p. 904)

Works Progress Administration   (p. 925)

Documents CD-ROM

Authoritarian and Totalitarian Experiments in Europe
23.3 John Scott, Behind the Urals
23.4 Nadezhda Mandelstam, Hope Against Hope

23.5 The Rise of Benito Mussolini
23.6 Adolf Hitler

NOTE: *To learn more about the topics in this chapter, see the Suggested Readings at the end of the book.*

◄ ATOM BOMB. The detonation of atomic bombs over Hiroshima and Nagasaki, Japan in August 1945 revealed the deadly potential of modern technology to wipe out human civizilation. Corbis-Bettmann.

World War II

The second great war of the twentieth century (1939–1945) grew out of the unsatisfactory resolution of the first. In retrospect, the two wars appear to some people to be one continuous conflict—a kind of twentieth-century Thirty Years' War—with the two main periods of fighting separated by an uneasy truce. To others, that point of view distorts the situation by implying that the second war was the inevitable result of the first and its inadequate peace treaties.

The latter opinion seems more sound. Whatever the flaws of the treaties of Paris, the world suffered an even more terrible war than the first as a result of failures of judgment and will on the part of the victorious democratic powers. The United States, which had become the wealthiest and potentially the strongest nation in the world, disarmed almost entirely and withdrew into a shortsighted and foolish isolation; it could play no important part in restraining the angry and ambitious dictators who brought on the war. Britain and France refused to face the reality of the threat the Axis powers posed until the most deadly war in history was required to put it down. If the victorious democracies had remained strong, responsible, and realistic, they could have remedied whatever injustices or mistakes arose from the treaties without endangering the peace.

Equally important, however, was the unwillingness of the victorious powers to adjust the peace treaties from World War I, especially to lessen the burden on the devastated German economy, even in the face of the obvious inability of Germany to pay the enormous war reparations the victors demanded. Here too, the isolationism of the United States played a pivotal role, as the government insisted that its allies in World War I, France and Britain, whose economies were also struggling after the war, repay their debts to the United States. France and Britain, in turn, sought to fund their war debts using reparations extracted primarily from Germany, whose economy was also burdened by the occupation of the Ruhr Valley and the ensuing loss of some of its best industrial infrastructure and resources. A vicious cycle ensued, which the advent of the Great Depression only exacerbated. The inability of the democratic German government of the Weimar Republic to negotiate a better deal from the inflexible victors

of World War I added to the perception of ordinary Germans that it was weak and inept and thus contributed to its downfall. One of the legacies of World War II was a realization on the part of the Western World of the dangers excessively high foreign debts can pose to the world order, as poor countries, unable to repay or renegotiate their debt structures, can be tempted to secede from international institutions and invade their neighbors in an effort to salvage their economies and shore up their governments.

The second war itself was plainly a global war. The Japanese occupation of Manchuria in 1931, while not technically a part of that war, was a significant precursor. Italy attacked Ethiopia in 1935. Italy, Germany, and the Soviet Union intervened in the Spanish Civil War (1936–1939). Japan attacked China in 1937. European colonies or former colonies, such as Australia and other South Pacific islands, the Philippines, and regions of the Middle East and North Africa became theaters of war or, like India, were drawn into the conflict by helping to supply the combatants. Men and women from all the inhabited continents thus took part. The use of atomic weapons brought the frightful struggle to a close, but what are called conventional weapons did almost all the damage while state-sponsored genocide, such as the Holocaust, killed millions of civilians. The world reached a level of destructiveness that threatened the very survival of civilization, even without the use of atomic or nuclear devices.

The aftermath of World War II, and the analysis on the part of the victors of the causes of the conflict, led to the creation of the United Nations, an international organization designed to forestall future conflict through improved international diplomacy. Imperfect as the United Nations is, most scholars agree that it has helped preserve world peace.

THINK AHEAD

◆ What was the relationship between World War I and World War II? Why was the isolationism of the United States after World War I such an important factor in the advent of World War II?

◆ Why was World War II truly a global war?

◆ What lessons did the world learn from the experience of World War I and World War II?

THE MORE IDEALISTIC SURVIVORS OF THE FIRST World War, especially in the United States and Great Britain, thought of it as "the war to end all wars" and "a war to make the world safe for democracy." Only thus could they justify the awful slaughter, expense, and upheaval. How appalled they would have been had they known that only twenty years after the peace treaties a second great war would break out that would be more truly global than the first. In this war the democracies would be fighting for their lives against militaristic, nationalistic, authoritarian, and totalitarian states in Europe and Asia. Great Britain and the United States would be allied with the Communist Soviet Union. The defeat of the militarists and dictators would not bring the longed-for peace, but a Cold War in which the European states became second-class powers, subordinate to the two new great powers, partially or fully non-European: the Soviet Union and the United States.

Again the Road to War (1933–1939)

World War I and the Versailles Treaty had only a marginal relationship to the world depression of the 1930s. But in Germany, where the reparations settlement had contributed to the vast inflation of 1923, economic and social discontent focused on the Versailles settlement as the cause of all ills. Throughout the late 1920s Adolf Hitler and the Nazi Party had never ceased denouncing Versailles as the source of all Germany's trouble; the economic woes of the early 1930s seemed to bear them out.

Nationalism and attention to the social question, along with party discipline, had been the sources of Nazi success. They continued to influence Hitler's foreign policy after he became chancellor in early 1933. Moreover, the Nazi destruction of the Weimar Republic and of political opposition meant that German foreign policy lay in Hitler's own hands. Consequently, it is important to know his goals and the plans he had for achieving them. (See Document, "Hitler Describes His Goals.")

HITLER'S GOALS

From first to last, Hitler's racial theories and goals held the central place in his thought. He meant to go far beyond Germany's 1914 boundaries, which were the limit of the vision of his predecessors. He intended to bring the entire German people (*Volk*), understood as a racial group, together into a single nation. The new Germany would include all the Germanic parts of the old Habsburg Empire, including Austria. This virile and growing nation would need more space to live (**Lebensraum**), which would be taken from the Slavs, a lesser race, fit only for servitude. The new Germany would be purified by the removal of the Jews, the most inferior race in Nazi theory. The plan always required the conquest of Poland and the Ukraine as the primary areas for the settlement of Germans and for the provision of badly needed food. However, neither *Mein Kampf* nor later statements of policy were blueprints for action. Hitler was a brilliant improviser who exploited opportunities as they arose. But he never lost sight of his goal, which would almost certainly require a major war.

DESTRUCTION OF VERSAILLES

When Hitler came to power, Germany was too weak to permit the direct approach to his goals. The first problem was to shake off the fetters of Versailles and to make Germany a formidable military power. In October of 1933 Germany withdrew from an international disarmament conference and also from the League of Nations. These acts alarmed the French but were merely symbolic. In January of 1934 Germany made a nonaggression pact with Poland that was of greater concern, for it put into question France's chief means of containing the Germans. At last, in March 1935 Hitler formally renounced the disarmament provisions of the Versailles Treaty with the formation of a German air force, and soon he reinstated conscription, which aimed at an army of half a million men.

His path was made easier because the League of Nations was ineffective at keeping the peace. In September 1931 Japan occupied Manchuria, provoking an appeal to the League of Nations by China. The league responded by sending out a commission under the Earl of Lytton (1876–1951). The Lytton Report condemned the Japanese for resorting to force, but the powers were unwilling to impose sanctions. Japan withdrew from the league and kept control of Manchuria.

The league formally condemned Hitler's decision to rearm Germany, but it took no steps to prevent it. France and Britain felt unable to object because they had not carried out their own promises to disarm. Instead, they met with Mussolini (1883–1945) in June 1935 to form the so-called Stresa Front and agreed to maintain the status quo in Europe by force if necessary. But Britain was desperate to maintain superiority at sea. Contrary to the Stresa accords and at the expense of

| **Hitler Describes His Goals**

From his early career, Hitler had certain long-term general views and goals. They were set forth in his Mein Kampf, *which appeared in 1925, and included consolidation of the German* Volk *("People"), provision of more land for the Germans, and contempt for such "races" as Slavs and Jews. Here are some of Hitler's views.*

◆ What is the basic principle on which Hitler's policy is founded? How does he justify his plans for expansion? What reasons does he give for hostility to France and Russia? What is the basis for Hitler's claim of a right of every man to own farmland? Was that a practical goal for Germany in the 1930s? Was there any way for Hitler to achieve his goals without a major war?

The National Socialist movement must strive to eliminate the disproportion between our population and our area—viewing this latter as a source of food as well as a basis for power politics—between our historical past and the hopelessness of our present impotence. …

The demand for restoration of the frontiers of 1914 is a political absurdity of such proportions and consequences as to make it seem a crime. Quite aside from the fact that the Reich's frontiers in 1914 were anything but logical. For in reality they were neither complete in the sense of embracing the people of German nationality, nor sensible with regard to geomilitary expediency. …

As opposed to this, we National Socialists must hold unflinchingly to our aim in foreign policy, namely, to secure for the German people the land and soil to which they are entitled on this earth. …

… The soil on which some day German generations of peasants can beget powerful sons will sanction the investment of the sons of today, and will some day acquit the responsible statesmen of blood-guilt and sacrifice of the people, even if they are persecuted by their contemporaries. …

Much as all of us today recognize the necessity of a reckoning with France, it would remain ineffectual in the long run if it represented the whole of our aim in foreign policy. It can and will achieve meaning only if it offers the rear cover for an enlargement of our people's living space in Europe. …

If we speak of soil in Europe today, we can primarily have in mind only Russia and her vassal border states. …

… See to it that the strength of our nation is founded, not on colonies, but on the soil of our European homeland. Never regard the Reich as secure unless for centuries to come it can give every scion of our people his own parcel of soil. Never forget that the most sacred right on this earth is a man's right to have earth to till with his own hands, and the most sacred sacrifice the blood that a man sheds for this earth.

French security needs, Britain soon made a separate naval agreement with Hitler, allowing him to rebuild the German fleet to 35 percent of the British navy.

ITALY ATTACKS ETHIOPIA

The Italian attack on Ethiopia underscored the impotence of the League of Nations and the timidity of the Allies. Using a border incident as an excuse, Mussolini attacked Ethiopia in October 1935. His real intent was to avenge a humiliating defeat that the Italians had suffered in 1896, to begin the restoration of Roman imperial glory, and perhaps to divest Italians from the corruption of the Fascist regime and Italy's economic troubles.

The League of Nations condemned Italian aggression and voted economic sanctions. It imposed an arms embargo that limited loans and credits to and imports from Italy. But Britain and France were afraid of alienating Mussolini, so they refused to place an embargo on oil, the one economic sanction that could have prevented Italian victory. Even more important, the British

▲ **Invasion of Ethiopia.** Amid a crowd of Ethiopians, Italian troops astride donkeys advance on the ancient city of Gondar.
Getty Images Inc.-Hulton Archive Photos.

did not prevent the movement of Italian troops and munitions through the Suez Canal. This wavering policy was disastrous. The League of Nations and collective security were totally discredited, and Mussolini turned to Germany. By November 1, 1936, he could speak publicly of a Rome-Berlin "Axis."

REMILITARIZATION OF THE RHINELAND

The Ethiopian affair also influenced Hitler's evaluation of the strength and determination of the Western powers. On March 7, 1936, he took his greatest risk yet, sending a small armed force into the demilitarized Rhineland. This was a breach not only of the Versailles Treaty but also of the Locarno Agreements of 1925, agreements that Germany had voluntarily made. It also removed one of the most important elements of French security. France and Britain had every right to resist. The French especially had a claim to retain the only element of security left after the failure of the Allies to guarantee France's defense. Yet Britain and France made only a feeble protest with the League of Nations. British opinion would not support France. The French themselves were paralyzed by internal division and by military planning that was exclusively defensive. Both countries were further weakened by a growing pacifism.

A Germany that was rapidly rearming and had a defensible western frontier presented a completely new problem to the Western powers. Their response was the policy of **appeasement**. It was based on the assumption that Germany had real grievances, that Hitler's goals were limited and ultimately acceptable,

and that the correct policy was to negotiate and make concessions before a crisis could lead to war. Behind this approach was the general horror of another war. Memories of the last war were still fresh, and the prospect of aerial bombardment was terrifying. A firmer policy, moreover, would have required rapid rearmament. But British leaders especially were reluctant to pursue this path because of the expense and widespread belief that the arms race had been a major cause of the last war. As Germany armed, the French huddled behind their defensive wall, the Maginot Line, and the British hoped for the best.

THE SPANISH CIVIL WAR

The new European alignment that found the Western democracies on one side and the Fascist states on the other was made clearer by the Spanish Civil War, which broke out in July 1936. In 1931 the Spaniards had established a democratic republic. Elections in February 1936 brought to power a government ranging from Republicans of the left to Communists and anarchists. The defeated groups, especially the Falangists, the Spanish version of Fascists, would not accept defeat at the polls. In July, General Francisco Franco (1892–1975) led an army from Spanish Morocco against the republic (see Map 31–1).

Thus began a civil war that lasted almost three years, killed hundreds of thousands, and provided a training ground for World War II. Germany and Italy aided Franco with troops and supplies. The Soviet Union sent equipment and advisers to the

▲ **Pablo Picasso, *Guernica*, 1937.** Oil on Canvas. 11′5″ × 25′5³/₄″. The Spain Civil War divided Europe, with Fascist Italy and Nazi German assisting Franco, and Soviet Russia aiding the republic. Before its end in 1939, the war in Spain took some 500,000 lives. On April 26, 1937, planes from the German Condor Legion bombed the Basque town of Guernica, killing some 1,000 men, women and children and destroying about 70 percent of the buildings. It was the most effective aerial bombardment of a city up to that time, and its purpose was simply to create terror.

Museo Nacional Centro de Arte Reina/Sofia/© 1998 Estate of Pablo Picasso/Artists Rights Society (ARS), New York.

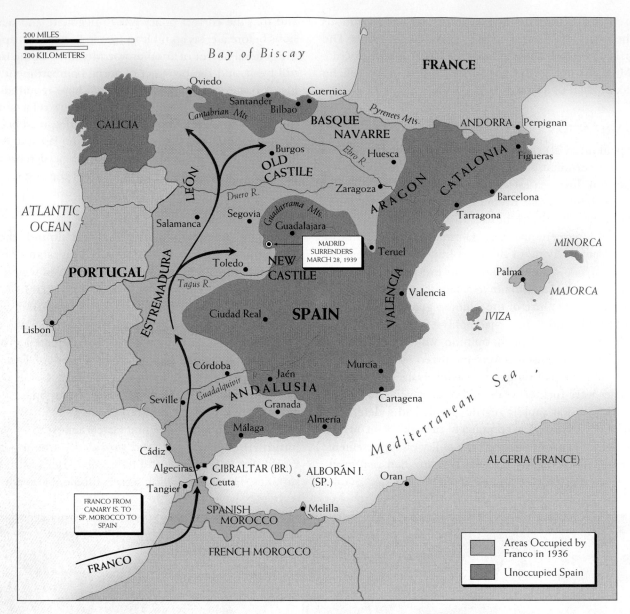

MAP 31–1 The Spanish Civil War, 1936–1939. The purple area on the map shows the large portion of Spain quickly overrun by Franco's insurgent armies during the first year of the war. In the following two years progress came more slowly for the Fascists as the war became a kind of international rehearsal for the coming World War II. Madrid's fall to Franco in the spring of 1939 had been preceded by that of Barcelona a few weeks earlier.

Republicans. Liberals and leftists from Europe and America volunteered to fight in the Republican ranks against fascism.

The civil war, fought on blatantly ideological lines, profoundly affected world politics. It brought Germany and Italy closer together, leading to the Rome-Berlin **Axis** Pact. The Axis powers were joined in the same year by Japan in the Anti-Comintern Pact, ostensibly against communism but really a new and powerful diplomatic alliance. In Western Europe, the appeasement mentality reigned. Although international law permitted the sale of weapons and munitions to the legitimate Republican government, France and Britain forbade the export of war materials to either side. The United States passed new neutrality legislation to the same end. By early 1939 the Fascists had won effective control of Spain.

AUSTRIA AND CZECHOSLOVAKIA

Hitler made good use of his new friendship with Mussolini. In 1934 Mussolini, not yet allied with Hitler, had frustrated a Nazi coup in Austria by threatening military intervention. In 1938 the new diplomatic situation encouraged Hitler to try again. He seems to have hoped to achieve his goal by propaganda, bullying, and threats, but the Austrian Premier, Kurt von Schuschnigg (1897–1977), refused to collapse. On March 9 the premier announced a plebiscite for March 13, in which the Austrian people could decide whether to unite with Germany for themselves. Hitler dared not let the plebiscite take place and invaded Austria on March 12. Mussolini made no objection, and Hitler marched into Vienna to the cheers of his Austrian sympathizers.

The *Anschluss*, or union of Germany and Austria, had great strategic significance, especially for Czechoslovakia, one of the bulwarks of French security. The Czechs were now surrounded by Germany on three sides.

The very existence of Czechoslovakia was an affront to Hitler. It was democratic and pro-Western; it had been created as a check on Germany and was allied both to France and the Soviet Union. It also contained about 3.5 million ethnic Germans who lived in the Sudetenland near the German border. These Germans had been the dominant class in the old Austro-Hungarian Empire, and they resented their new minority position. Supported by Hitler, they agitated for privileges and autonomy within the Czech state. The Czechs made many concessions; Hitler's motivation, however, was not to improve the lot of the Sudeten Germans but to destroy Czechoslovakia.

The French, as usual, deferred to British leadership. The British prime minister was Neville Chamberlain (1869–1940), a man thoroughly committed to the policy of appeasement. He was determined not to allow Britain to go to war again. He pressured the Czechs to make further concessions to Germany, but no concession was enough.

On September 12, 1938, Hitler made a provocative speech that led to rioting in the Sudetenland, and the declaration of martial law by the Czech government. German intervention seemed imminent. Chamberlain sought to appease Hitler at Czech expense and thus to avoid war. At Hitler's mountain retreat, Berchtesgaden, on September 15 Chamberlain accepted the separation of the Sudetenland from Czechoslovakia. Moreover, he and the French premier, Edouard Daladier (1884–1970), threatened to desert the Czechs if they did not agree. A week later Chamberlain flew again to Germany only to find that Hitler had raised his

MAP 31–2 Partitions of Czechoslovakia and Poland, 1938–1939. The immediate background of World War II is found in the complex international drama unfolding on Germany's eastern frontier in 1938 and 1939. Germany's expansion inevitably meant the victimization of Austria, Czechoslovakia, and Poland. With the failure of the Western powers' appeasement policy and the signing of a German-Soviet pact, the stage for the war was set.

DOCUMENT | Winston Churchill Warns of the Effects of the Munich Agreement

Churchill delivered a speech on the Munich Agreement before the House of Commons on October 5, 1938. Following are excerpts from it.

> ◆ What was decided at Munich? Why were the representatives of Czechoslovakia not at the meeting? Why did Chamberlain think the meeting was successful? Munich was the high point of the policy called "appeasement." How would its advocates defend this policy? Churchill was a leading opponent of appeasement. What are his objections to it?

The Chancellor of the Exchequer [Sir John Simon] said it was the first time Herr Hitler had been made to retract—I think that was the word—in any degree. We really must not waste time after all this long Debate upon the difference between the positions reached at Berchtesgaden, at Godesberg and at Munich. They can be very simply epitomized, if the House will permit me to vary the metaphor. One pound was demanded at the pistol's point. When it was given, £2 were demanded at the pistol's point. Finally, the dictator consented to take £17s. 6d. and the rest in promises of good will for the future. ...

I do not grudge our loyal, brave people, who were ready to do their duty no matter what the cost, who never flinched under the strain of last week—I do not grudge them the natural, spontaneous outbursts of joy and relief when they learned that the hard ordeal would no longer be required of them at the moment; but they should know the truth. They should know that there has been gross neglect and deficiency in our defenses; they should know that we have sustained a defeat without a war, the consequences of which will travel far with us along our road; they should know that we have passed an awful milestone in our history, when the whole equilibrium of Europe has been deranged, and that the terrible words have for the time being been pronounced against the Western democracies: "Thou art weighed in the balance and found wanting." And do not suppose that this is the end. This is only the beginning of the reckoning. This is only the first sip, the first foretaste of a bitter cup which will be proffered to us year by year unless, by a supreme recovery of moral health and martial vigor, we arise again and take our stand for freedom as in the olden time.

demands: He wanted cession of the Sudetenland in three days and its immediate occupation by the German army.

MUNICH

France and Britain prepared for war. At the last moment Mussolini proposed a conference of Germany, Italy, France, and Britain. It met on September 29 at Munich. Hitler received almost everything he had demanded. The Sudetenland, the key to Czech security, became part of Germany, thus depriving the Czechs of any chance of self-defense (see Map 31–2). In return, the rest of Czechoslovakia was spared. Hitler promised, "I have no more territorial demands to make in Europe." Chamberlain told a cheering crowd that he had brought "peace with honour. I believe it is peace for our time." (See Document, "Winston Churchill Warns of the Effects of the Munich Agreement.")

Even in the short run, the appeasement of Hitler at Munich was a failure. Soon Poland and Hungary also tore bits of territory from Czechoslovakia, and the Slovaks demanded autonomy. Finally, on March 15, 1939, Hitler broke his promise and occupied Prague, putting an end to Czech independence and to illusions that his only goal was to restore

Germans to the Reich. Munich remains an example of short-sighted policy that helped bring on a war in disadvantageous circumstances as a result of the very fear of war and the failure to prepare for it.

Hitler's occupation of Prague discredited appeasement in the eyes of the British people. In the summer of 1939 a Gallup Poll showed that three quarters of the British public believed it worth a war to stop Hitler. Although Chamberlain himself had not lost all faith in his policy, he felt the need to respond to public opinion, and he responded to excess.

It was apparent that Poland was the next target of German expansion. In the spring of 1939 the Germans put pressure on Poland to restore the formerly German city of Danzig and to allow a railroad and a highway through the Polish Corridor to connect East Prussia with the rest of Germany. When the Poles would not yield, the pressure mounted. On March 31 Chamberlain announced a Franco-British guarantee of Polish independence. Hitler did not take the guarantee seriously. He had come to hold the Western leaders in contempt. He knew that both countries were unprepared for war and that many of their populations were opposed to war for Poland.

Agreement at Munich. On September 29–30, 1938, Hitler met with the leaders of Britain and France at Munich to decide the fate of Czechoslovakia. The Allied leaders abandoned the small democratic nation in a vain attempt to appease Hitler and avoid war. Hitler sits in the center of the picture. To his right is British Prime Minister Neville Chamberlain.
Ullstein Bilderdienst.

Belief in the Polish guarantee was further undermined by the inability of France and Britain to get effective help to the Poles. The French, still dominated by the defensive mentality of the Maginot Line, had no intention of attacking Germany's western front. The only way to defend Poland was to bring Russia into the alliance against Hitler, but a Russian alliance posed many problems. Each side was profoundly suspicious of the other. The French and British were hostile to Russia's Communist ideology, and since Stalin's purge of the officer corps of the Red Army, they questioned the military value of an alliance with Russia. Besides, the Russians could not help Poland without the right to cross Romania and enter Poland. Both nations, suspicious of Russian intentions—and with good reason—refused to grant these rights. As a result, Western negotiations with Russia were slow and cautious.

THE NAZI-SOVIET PACT

The Russians also had good reason to hesitate. They resented being left out of the Munich Agreement. They were annoyed by the low priority that the West seemed to give to negotiations with Russia, compared with the urgency with which they dealt with Hitler. They feared, rightly, that the Western powers meant them to bear the burden of the war against Germany. As a result, they opened negotiations with Hitler, and on August 23, 1939, the world was shocked to learn of a Nazi-Soviet non-aggression pact. Its secret provisions, which were easily guessed and soon carried out, divided Poland between the two powers

and allowed Russia to annex the Baltic states and to take Bessarabia from Romania. The most bitter ideological enemies had become allies; Communist parties in the West changed their line overnight from the ardent advocacy of resistance to Hitler to a policy of peace and quiet.

The Nazi-Soviet pact sealed the fate of Poland, and the Franco-British commitment guaranteed a general war. On September 1, 1939, the Germans invaded Poland. Two days later Britain and France declared war on Germany. World War II had begun.

World War II (1939–1945)

World War II was truly global. Fighting took place in Europe and Asia, the Atlantic and the Pacific Oceans, the Northern and Southern Hemispheres. The demand for the fullest exploitation of material and human resources for increased production, the use of blockades, and the intensive bombing of civilian targets made the war of 1939 even more "total"— that is, comprehensive and intense—than that of 1914.

GERMAN CONQUEST OF EUROPE

The speed of the German victory over Poland astonished everyone, not least the Russians, who hastened to collect their share of the booty before Hitler could deprive them of it. On September

CHRONOLOGY

Coming of World War II

1919 June	Versailles Treaty
1923 January	France occupies the Ruhr
1925 October	Locarno Agreements
1931 Spring	Onset of Great Depression in Europe
1933 January	Hitler comes to power
October	Germany withdraws from League of Nations
1935 March	Hitler renounces disarmament, starts an air force, and begins conscription
October	Mussolini attacks Ethiopia
1936 March	Germany reoccupies and remilitarizes the Rhineland
July	Outbreak of Spanish Civil War
October	Formation of the Rome-Berlin Axis
1938 March	Anschluss with Austria
September	Munich Conference and partition of Czechoslovakia
1939 March	Hitler occupies Prague; France and Great Britain guarantee Polish independence
August	Nazi-Soviet pact
September 1	Germany invades Poland
September 3	September 3 Britain and France declare war on Germany

17 they invaded Poland from the east, dividing the country with the Germans. They then absorbed Estonia, Latvia, and Lithuania into the Soviet Union. In November 1940 the Russians invaded Finland, but the Finns fought back fiercely. Although they were finally compelled to yield territory and bases to Russia, they retained their independence. Russian difficulties in Finland may well have encouraged Hitler to invade the Soviet Union in June 1941, just twenty-two months after the 1939 treaty.

Meanwhile, the western front was quiet. The French remained behind the Maginot Line while Hitler and Stalin swallowed Poland and the Baltic states. Britain hastily rearmed and imposed the traditional naval blockade. Cynics in the West called it the phony war, or Sitzkrieg, but Hitler shattered the stillness in the spring of 1940. In April, without warning and with swift success, the Germans invaded Denmark and Norway. Hitler now had both air and naval bases closer to Britain. A month later a combined land and air attack struck Belgium, the Netherlands, and Luxembourg. German air power and armored divisions were irresistible. The Dutch surrendered in a few days, and the Belgians, although aided by the French and the British, surrendered less than two weeks later. The British and French armies in Belgium were forced to flee to the English Channel to seek escape from the beaches of Dunkirk. By the heroic effort of hundreds of Britons manning small boats, over 200,000 British and 100,000 French soldiers were saved, but casualties were high and much valuable equipment was abandoned.

The Maginot Line ran from Switzerland to the Belgian frontier. Until 1936 the French had expected the Belgians to continue the fortifications along their German border. After Hitler remilitarized the Rhineland without opposition, the Belgians lost faith in their French alliance and returned to neutrality, leaving the Maginot Line exposed on its left flank. Hitler's swift advance through Belgium therefore circumvented France's main line of defense. The French army, poorly and hesitantly led by generals who lacked a proper understanding of how to use tanks and planes, collapsed. Mussolini, eager to claim the spoils of victory when it was clearly safe to do so, attacked France on June 10, though without success. Less than a week later the new French government, under the ancient hero of Verdun, Henri Philippe Pétain (1856–1951), asked for an armistice. In two months Hitler had accomplished what Germany had failed to achieve in four years of bitter fighting in the previous war.

The terms of the armistice, signed June 22, 1940, allowed the Germans to occupy more than half of France, including the Atlantic and English Channel coasts. To prevent the French from fleeing to North Africa to continue the fight, and even more to prevent them from turning their fleet over to Britain, Hitler left southern France unoccupied. Pétain set up a dictatorial regime at the resort city of Vichy and collaborated with the Germans to preserve as much autonomy as possible.

Most of the French were too stunned to resist. Many thought that Hitler's victory was certain and saw no alternative to collaboration. A few, most notably General Charles de Gaulle (1890–1969), fled to Britain, where they organized the French National Committee of Liberation, or "Free French." The Vichy government controlled most of French North Africa and the navy. But the Free French began operating in central Africa and from London radioed messages of hope and defiance to France. As expectations of a quick German victory faded, a French Resistance movement arose.

BATTLE OF BRITAIN

Hitler expected the British to come to terms. He was prepared to allow Britain to retain its empire in return for a free hand for Germany in Europe. If there was any chance that the British would consider such terms, that chance disappeared when Winston Churchill (1874–1965) replaced Chamberlain as prime minister in May 1940.

One of Churchill's greatest achievements was establishing a close relationship with the American president Franklin D. Roosevelt (1882–1945), who found ways to help the British despite strong political opposition. In 1940 and 1941, before the United States was at war, America sent military supplies, traded destroyers for leases on British naval bases, and even convoyed ships across the Atlantic to help the British survive.

As Britain remained defiant, Hitler was forced to contemplate an invasion, which required control of the air. The first strikes by the German air force (*Luftwaffe*), directed against

▲ **Churchill and Roosevelt.** The close cooperation between Prime Minister Winston Churchill of Britain and President Franklin Roosevelt of the United States helped to assure the effective alliance of their two countries in World War II.
UPI/Corbis-Bettmann.

the airfields and fighter planes in southeastern England, began in August 1940. Had these attacks continued, Germany might soon have gained control of the air and, with it, the chance of a successful invasion. In early September, however, seeking revenge for British bombing raids on German cities, the Luftwaffe made London its major target. For two months, London was bombed every night. Much of the city was destroyed, and about 15,000 people were killed, but the theories of victory through air power alone proved vain. Casualties were much less than expected, and the bombings made the British people more resolute.

Moreover, the Royal Air Force (RAF), aided by the newly developed radar and an excellent system of communications, inflicted heavy losses on the Luftwaffe. Hitler lost the Battle of Britain in the air and was forced to abandon his plans for invasion.

GERMAN ATTACK ON RUSSIA

Operation Barbarossa, the code name for the invasion of Russia, was aimed at knocking Russia out of the war before winter could set in. Success depended in part on an early start, but here Hitler's Italian alliance proved costly. Mussolini was jealous of Hitler's success and annoyed at German condescension.

Consequently, Mussolini launched an attack against the British in Egypt and drove them back some sixty miles.

Battle of Britain. A rubble-strewn street in London after the city had experienced a night of German bombing. Despite many casualties and widespread devastation, the German bombing of London did not break British morale or prevent the city from functioning.
The Granger Collection, N.Y.

Encouraged by this success, he also invaded Greece. But in North Africa the British counterattacked and drove into Libya, and the Greeks also repulsed the Italians. In March 1941 the British sent help to the Greeks, and Hitler was forced to divert his attention to the Balkans and to Africa. General Erwin Rommel (1891–1944), later to earn the title "The Desert Fox," went to Africa and soon drove the British back into Egypt. In the Balkans the German army swiftly occupied Yugoslavia and crushed Greek resistance, but the price was a delay of six weeks for Barbarossa (see Map 31–3). This proved to be costly the following winter in the Russian campaign.

Operation Barbarossa was launched against Russia on June 22, 1941, and it almost succeeded. Stalin panicked. He had not fortified his frontier or ordered his troops to withdraw when attacked. Two thousand planes were destroyed on the ground. By November Hitler had gone farther into Russia than had Napoleon: The German army stood at the gates of Leningrad, on the outskirts of Moscow, and on the Don River. Of the 4.5 million troops with which the Russians had begun the fighting, they had lost 2.5 million; of their 15,000 tanks, only 700 were left. A German victory seemed imminent.

But the Germans could not deliver the final blow. In August there was a delay in their advance to decide on a course of action. One plan was to take Moscow before winter. Such a plan might have brought victory, for Moscow was Russia's transportation hub. Hitler, however, diverted significant forces to the south. By the time he was ready to return to the offensive near Moscow, it was too late. Winter struck the German army, which was not equipped to face it. Given precious time, Stalin was able to restore order and fortify the city. Even more important, troops had arrived from Siberia, where they had been placed to check a possible Japanese attack. In November and December the Russians counterattacked. The war had turned into one of attrition, and the Germans began to have visions of Napoleon's retreat.

HITLER'S EUROPE

The demands and distractions of war and Hitler's defeat prevented him from fully carrying out his plans. Therefore, it is hard to be sure what his intentions were, but the measures he took before his death give evidence of a regime probably unmatched in history for carefully planned terror and inhumanity. To give Lebensraum to the Germans at the expense of people he deemed inferior, Hitler established colonies of Germans in Poland, driving the local people from their land and using them as cheap labor. He had worse plans for Russia. The Russians would be driven to Central Asia and Siberia, where they would be kept in check by frontier colonies of German war veterans. Germans would settle the more desirable lands of European Russia.

Hitler's long-range plans included Germanization as well as colonization. In lands inhabited by people racially akin to the

MAP 31–3 Axis Europe 1941. On the eve of the German invasion of the Soviet Union, the Germany-Italy Axis bestrode most of Western Europe by annexation, occupation, or alliance—from Norway and Finland in the north to Greece in the south and from Poland to France. Britain, the Soviets, a number of insurgent groups, and, finally, the United States had before them the long struggle of conquering this Axis "fortress Europe."

Germans, like Scandinavia, the Netherlands, and Switzerland, the natives would be absorbed into the German nation. Such peoples would be reeducated and purged of dissenting elements, but there would be little or no colonization. He even had plans, only slightly realized, of adopting selected people from those he considered the lesser races into those he considered the master race.

Hitler regarded the conquered lands merely as a source of plunder. From eastern Europe he removed everything useful, including entire industries. In Russia and Poland the Germans simply confiscated the land. In the west the conquered

countries were forced to support the occupying army at a rate several times the real cost. The Germans used the profits to strip the conquered peoples of most necessities. The Nazis were frank about their policies. One of Hitler's high officials said, "Whether nations live in prosperity or starve to death interests me only insofar as we need them as slaves for our culture."[1]

[1] Quoted by Gordon Wright, *The Ordeal of Total War, 1939–1945* (New York: Harper & Row, 1968), p. 117.

Nazi Terror. In this vivid poster, the artist Ben Shahn (1898–1969) memorialized the destruction of Lidice. The Czechoslovakian town was obliterated by the Nazis on June 11, 1942, in vengeance for the resistance by Czechs against their Nazi rulers.
The Granger Collection, N.Y.

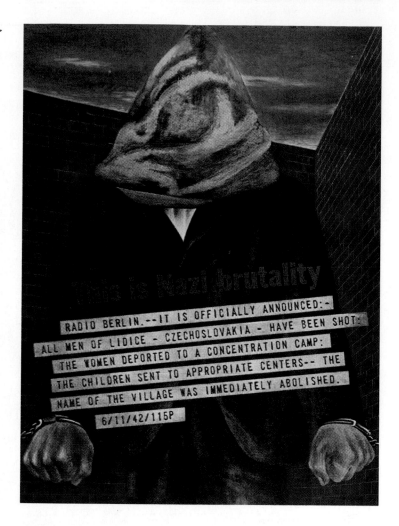

RACISM AND THE HOLOCAUST

The most horrible aspect of the Nazi rule in Europe arose from the inhumanity and brutality inherent in Hitler's racial doctrines. He considered the Slavs *Untermenschen*, subhuman creatures like beasts who need not be treated as people. In Poland the upper and professional classes were either jailed, deported, or killed. (See Document, "Oskar Rosenfeld Describes the Food Supply in the Lodz Ghetto.") Schools and churches were closed; marriage was controlled to keep down the Polish birthrate; and harsh living conditions were imposed. In Russia things were even worse. Hitler spoke of his Russian campaign as a war of extermination. Heinrich Himmler (1900–1945), head of Hitler's elite SS guard, formed extermination squads to eliminate 30 million Slavs to make room for the Germans. Some 6 million Russian prisoners of war and deported civilian workers may have died under Nazi rule.

Hitler had special plans for the Jews. He meant to make all Europe *Judenrein* ("free of Jews"). For a time he thought of sending them to Madagascar but later decided on the "final solution of the Jewish problem": extermination. The Nazis built extermination camps in Germany and Poland and used the latest technology to kill millions of men, women, and children just because they were Jews. Before the war was over, 6 million Jews had died in what has come to be called the **Holocaust**. Only about a million remained alive, mostly in pitiable condition (see Map 31–4).

◀ **Roundup of Warsaw Jews.** World War II resulted in the near-total destruction of the Jews of Europe, victims of the Holocaust spawned by Hitler's racial theories of the superiority and inferiority of particular ethnic groups. Hitler placed special emphasis on the need to exterminate the Jews, to whom he attributed particular wickedness. This picture shows a roundup of Jews in Warsaw, where there was a large Jewish population, ultimately on their way to concentration or death camps.
Corbis-Bettmann.

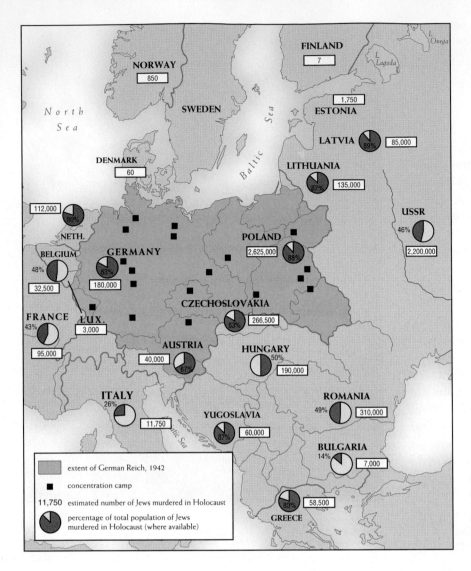

MAP 31–4 The Holocaust. The Nazi policy of ethnic cleansing—targeting Jews, Gypsies, political dissidents, and "social deviants"—began with imprisoning them in concentration camps, but by 1943 the *Endlösung*, or Final Solution, called for the systematic extermination of "undersirables".

THE ROAD TO PEARL HARBOR

The war took on truly global proportions in December 1941. The Japanese were already at war with China, and between the outbreak of that war in 1937 and the opening of the World War II campaign in the Pacific, there were three critical junctures. The first was the decision in January 1938 to destroy the Chinese Nationalist Party government in Nanjing. The army quickly occupied most of the cities and railroads of eastern China, killing over 300,000 people and brutally raping 7,000 women (known today as the Rape of Nanjing), but Jiang Jieshi (Chiang Kai-shek) refused to give in. The result was a stalemate that lasted until 1945. China was never a major theater of the war in the Pacific.

The second critical decision was the Tripartite Pact with Germany and Italy in September 1940. Japan had long admired Germany. In 1936 it had joined Germany in the Anti-Comintern Pact directed against international Communism. It also wanted an

alliance with Germany against the Soviet Union. Germany insisted, however, that any alliance also be directed against the United States and Britain, to which the Japanese would not agree. The Japanese navy, especially, was not interested in being dragged into a German war. After an undeclared miniwar with Russia from May to December 1939 on the Mongolian border, sentiment rose for an alliance with Germany, but then Germany "betrayed" Japan by signing a nonaggression pact with the Soviet Union. For a time Japan decided to improve its relations with the United States, but America insisted that Japan get out of China. By the late spring of 1940 German victories in Europe—the fall of Britain appeared imminent—again led the Japanese military to favor an alliance with Germany.

When Japan signed the Tripartite Pact it had three objectives: to isolate the United States, to take over the Southeast Asian colonies of Britain, France and the Netherlands, and to improve its relations with the Soviet Union through the good offices of Germany.

DOCUMENT | Oskar Rosenfeld Describes the Food Supply in the Lodz Ghetto

Tens of thousands of Jews were relocated to ghettos in Poland. These were cities sealed off from the rest of the world. Entrances and exits were closely guarded by the German Nazi occupiers. Maintaining the food supply was an enormous challenge for these communities of imprisonment. Oskar Rosenfeld, a professional journalist and one of the inhabitants of Lodz who, along with others, maintained a chronicle of the life of the ghetto, discussed the food supply in the early summer of 1943. Rosenfeld died in 1944, as did most of the people who had lived in the Lodz ghetto.

♦ Why would the cares of everyday life have seemed, as Rosenfeld asserts, more of a burden than the psychological burden of life in the ghetto? What steps had the inhabitants of the ghetto been required to take to look after their own food supply? Why were potatoes more important for nutrition than vegetables? How does this passage suggest what Rosenfeld terms "the nightmare of the ghetto"?

In general; one can say that people have grown accustomed to living surrounded by barbed wire and tolerate that state as almost natural, as a thing ordained by fate. For, in comparison with the cares of everyday life, the constant psychic constraints seem less burdensome. . . .

Since the offices of food supply are unable to provide the 85,000 inhabitants of the ghetto with the fresh vegetables they need; the gardeners are required to surrender a portion of their produce to the population. . . . In the early morning hours one can see groups of people, with agricultural tools in their hands and on their shoulders, marching through the streets to till the soil—heading out to the vegetable gardens. . . . No such figures were to be seen previously, just as there were no vegetable and potato beds on the grounds of the ghetto. The ghetto has been reconstructed; and as a result, we are supplied with vegetables not only by the [German] Ghetto Administration, but also by our own soil. . . .

During this first week, the month of June was a good friend to the ghetto dwellers. It brought them the most precious food that can be wished for in the ghetto: potatoes. When the carts appeared in the streets whether horse drawn or in hand carts—passersby halted and stared hopefully at the round fruits of the earth. What do the hungry care whether the potatoes are first or second quality as long as there are potatoes? . . . Suddenly, the potato shipments stopped. Potatoes were replaced by vegetables—spinach, lettuce, red beets, carrots, radishes—too little to fill empty stomachs: And since no more potatoes came in during the second half of June the allocated supplies had already been consumed, hunger and despair loomed in the horizon once again. The end of this month of June is reminiscent of last year's "starvation" June. . . .

The first truckloads of green vegetables are now rolling through the streets, causing renewed hope. Just hold out for a few more weeks, and then there will be potatoes again—the fresh young potatoes, not the sort of which half has to be thrown into the trash as unfit for consumption. This thought can be read on the face in the ghetto. . . . Ultimately, no one escapes the nightmare of the ghetto.

From Luchan Dobroszycki, *The Chronicle of the Lodz Ghetto*, copyright © 1984 Yale University Press, pp. 355–357. Reprinted by permission of Yale University Press.

The last objective was reached when Japan signed a neutrality pact with the Soviet Union in April 1941. Two months later Germany attacked the Soviet Union, without consulting Japan. It compounded this second "betrayal" by asking Japan to attack the Soviet Union in the east. Japan waited and watched. When the German advance faltered, Japan decided to honor the neutrality pact and turn south. This, in effect, was the end of Japan's participation in the Axis. Thereafter, it fought its own war in Asia. Yet instead of deflecting American criticism as intended, the pact, by linking Japan to Germany, hardened America's position on China.

The third and fateful decision was to go to war with the United States. In June 1941, following Germany's defeat of France, Japanese troops had occupied northern French Indochina. The United States retaliated by limiting strategic exports to Japan. In July 1941 Japanese troops took southern Indochina, and the United States embargoed all exports to Japan, cutting Japanese oil imports by 90 percent. The navy pressed for the capture of the oil-rich Dutch East Indies, but it would be too dangerous to move against Dutch and British colonies in Southeast Asia with the United States on its flank in the Philippines. The navy, therefore, planned a preemptive strike against the United States. The Japanese decision for war wagered Japan's land-based air power, shorter supply lines, and what it saw as greater will power against American productivity. At the Imperial Conference where the all-or-nothing decision was taken, the navy's chief of staff compared the war with the United States to a dangerous operation that might save a critically ill patient.

◀ **Pearl Harbor.** The successful Japanese attack on the American base at Pearl Harbor in Hawaii on December 7, 1941, together with simultaneous attacks on other Pacific bases, brought the United States into war against the Axis powers. For Japan, it was the opening phase of a campaign to capture European and American colonies in Southeast Asia.

U.S. Army Photograph.

AMERICA'S ENTRY INTO THE WAR

On Sunday morning, December 7, 1941, even while Japanese representatives were discussing a settlement in Washington, Japan launched an air attack on Pearl Harbor, Hawaii, the chief American naval base in the Pacific. The next day, the United States and Britain declared war on Japan. Three days later, Germany and Italy declared war on the United States.

THE TIDE TURNS

The potential power of the United States was enormous, but America was ill prepared for war (see Figure 31–1). Although conscription had been introduced in 1940, the army was tiny, inexperienced, and poorly supplied. American industry was not ready for war. The Japanese swiftly captured Guam, Wake Island, and the Philippines (see

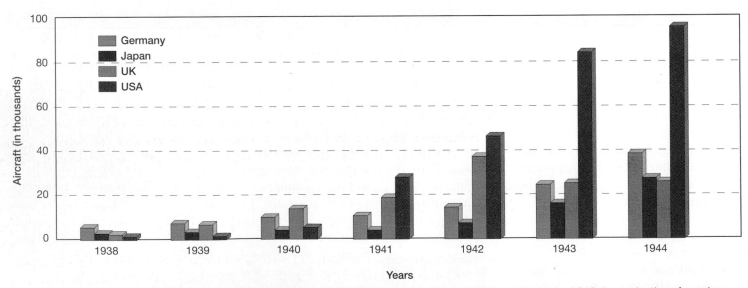

Figure 31–1 Production of Military Aircraft. Though at first the United States lagged behind Germany and Japan, by 1943, its production of warplanes and other weapons outstripped its enemies.

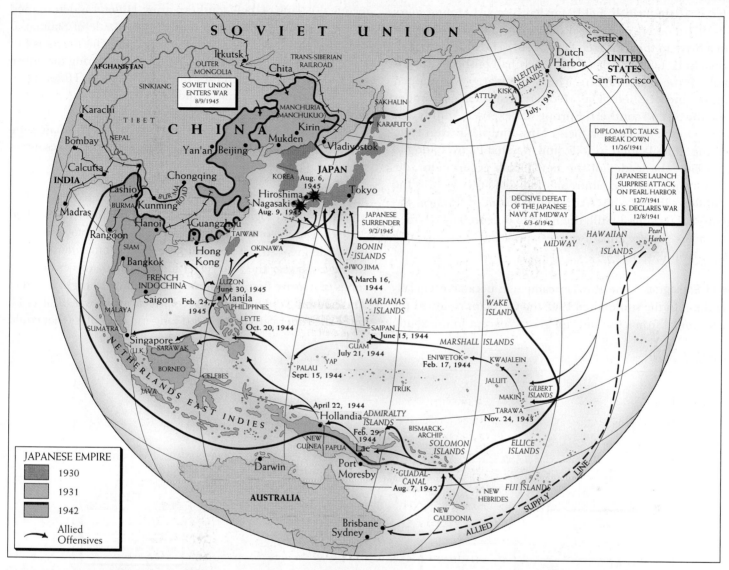

MAP 31–5 The War in the Pacific. As in Europe, the Allies initially had trouble recapturing areas that the Japanese had quickly seized early in the war. The map shows the initial expansion of the Japanese and the long struggle of the Allies to push them back to their homeland and defeat them.

Map 31–5). They also attacked Hong Kong, Malaya, Burma, and Indonesia. By the summer of 1942, the Japanese Empire stretched from the western Aleutian Islands south almost to Australia, and from Burma east to the Gilbert Islands in the mid-Pacific.

In the same year, the Germans almost reached the Caspian Sea in their drive for Russia's oil fields. In Africa, Rommel drove the British back toward the Suez Canal and was finally stopped at El Alamein, only seventy miles from Alexandria. Relations between the democracies and their Soviet ally were not close; German submarines were threatening British sup-

plies; the Allies were being thrown back on every front, and the future looked bleak.

The tide turned at the Battle of Midway in June 1942. A month earlier, both sides had suffered massive losses in the Battle of the Coral Sea, but greater U.S. ship production made such trade-offs unprofitable for Japan. At Midway, American planes destroyed four Japanese aircraft carriers. Soon American Marines landed on Guadalcanal in the Solomon Islands and began to reverse the momentum of the war. The war in the Pacific was far from over, but Japan was checked sufficiently to allow the Allies to concentrate their efforts first in the West.

Allied Landings in Africa, Sicily, and Italy In November 1942, an Allied force landed in French North Africa. Even before that landing, the British Field Marshal Bernard Montgomery (1887–1976), after stopping Rommel at El Alamein, had begun a drive to the west (see Map 31–6). The American general Dwight D. Eisenhower (1890–1969) had pushed eastward through Morocco and Algeria. The German army was trapped in Tunisia and crushed. The Mediterranean was now under Allied control, and southern Europe was exposed. In July and August 1943 the Allies took Sicily. Mussolini was driven from power, the Allies landed in Italy, and Marshal Pietro Badoglio (1871–1956), the leader of the new Italian government, declared war on Germany. Churchill had spoken of Italy as the "soft underbelly" of the Axis, but German resistance was tough and determined. Still, the need to defend Italy strained the Germans' energy and resources and left them vulnerable on other fronts.

Battle of Stalingrad The Russian campaign became especially demanding. In the summer of 1942 the Germans resumed the offensive on all fronts but did not get far, except in the south.

Their goal there was the oil fields near the Caspian Sea, and they got as far as Stalingrad on the Volga, a key point for protecting the flank of their southern army. Hitler was determined to take the city and Stalin to hold it. The Battle of Stalingrad raged for months with unexampled ferocity. The Russians lost more men than the Americans lost in combat during the entire war, but their heroic defenses prevailed. Because Hitler again overruled his generals and would not allow a retreat, an entire German army was lost.

Stalingrad marked the turning point of the Russian campaign. Thereafter, as the German military and material resources dwindled, the Russians advanced westward inexorably.

Strategic Bombing In 1943 the Allies also gained ground in production and logistics. The industrial might of the United States began to come into full force. New technology and tactics made great strides in eliminating the submarine menace. In the same year the American and British air forces began a series of massive bombardments of Germany by night and day. This bombing did not have much effect on the war until 1944. Then the Americans introduced long-range fighters that could

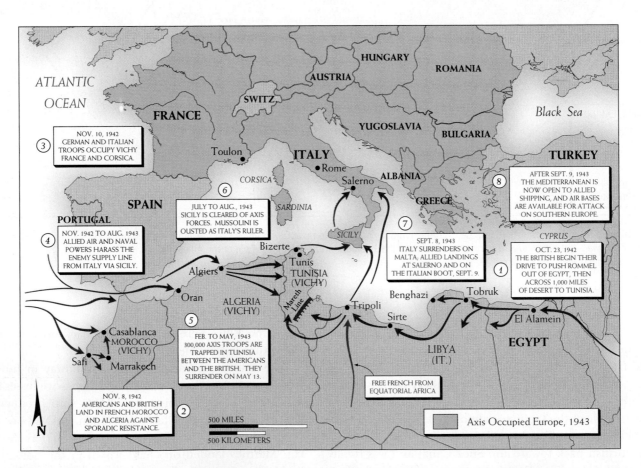

MAP 31–6 North African Campaigns, 1942–1945. Control of North Africa was important to the Allies if they were to have access to Europe from the south. The map diagrams this theater of the war from Morocco to Egypt and the Suez Canal.

▲ **Stalingrad.** Russian soldiers, in their heroic defense of Stalingrad, dug trenches from building to building in the city. The German defeat at Stalingrad in February 1943 marked the turning point of the Russian campaign. Thereafter the Russians advanced inexorably westward. Archive Photos.

protect the bombers and allow accurate missions by day. By 1945 the Allies could bomb at will.

DEFEAT OF NAZI GERMANY

On June 6, 1944 (D-Day), in one of greatest amphibious assaults ever attempted, Allied troops landed in force on the coast of Normandy (see Map 31–7). By the beginning of September France had been liberated.

All went smoothly until December, when the Germans launched a counterattack called the Battle of the Bulge through the Forest of Ardennes. However, it was their last gasp. The Allies recovered the momentum and pushed eastward. They crossed the Rhine in March 1945, and German resistance crumbled. This time there could be no doubt that the Germans had lost the war on the battlefield.

In the east, the Russians were within reach of Berlin by March 1945. Because the Allies insisted on unconditional surrender, the Germans fought on until May. Hitler committed suicide in an underground hideaway in Berlin on May 1, 1945. The Russians occupied Berlin by agreement with their Western allies. The Third Reich had lasted a dozen years instead of the millennium predicted by Hitler.

FALL OF THE JAPANESE EMPIRE

The war in Europe ended on May 8, 1945, and by then victory over Japan was in sight (see also Chapter 28). The original Japanese attack on the United States had been a calculated risk against the odds. The longer the war lasted, the greater the impact of American superiority in industrial production and human resources. Beginning in 1943 American forces began a campaign of "island hopping," selecting major bases and places strategically located along the enemy supply line. Starting from the Solomons, they moved northeast toward the Japanese homeland. American bombers launched a terrible wave of bombings that destroyed Japanese industry and disabled the Japanese navy. But still the Japanese government, dominated by a military clique, refused to surrender.

Confronted with Japan's determination, the Americans made plans for a frontal assault on the Japanese homeland, which, they calculated, would cost unacceptable American casualties and even greater losses for the Japanese. At this point, science and technology presented the Americans with another choice. Since early in the war a secret program had been in progress. Its staff was working to use atomic energy for military purposes.

On August 6, 1945, an American plane dropped an atomic bomb on the city of Hiroshima. More than 70,000 of its 200,000 residents were killed. Two days later the Soviet Union declared war on Japan and invaded Manchuria. The next day a second atomic bomb fell, this time on Nagasaki. Even then the Japanese were prepared to face an invasion rather than give up. It was only the unprecedented intervention of Emperor Hirohito (r. 1926–1989) that forced the government to surrender on August 14. Even then, the Cabinet made the condition that Japan could keep its emperor. President Harry Truman (1884–1972), who had come to office on April 12, 1945, on the death of Franklin D. Roosevelt, accepted the condition. Peace was formally signed on September 2, 1945.

THE COST OF WAR

World War II was the most terrible war in history. Military deaths are estimated at 15 million, and at least as many civilians were killed. If deaths linked indirectly to the war are included, as many as 40 million may have died. Most of Europe and significant parts of Asia were devastated. Yet the end of so terrible a war brought little opportunity for relaxation. The dawn of the Atomic Age that brought a dramatic end to the war made people conscious that another major war might destroy humanity. Everything depended on the conclusion of a stable peace, but even as the fighting ended, the victors began to quarrel.

The Domestic Fronts

World War II represented an effort of total war by all the belligerents. Never before in world history had so many men and women and so many resources been devoted to military effort. One result was the carnage that occurred on the battlefields and at sea. Another was an unprecedented organization of civilians on the various home fronts. Each domestic effort and experience was different, but almost no one escaped the impact of the conflict. Shortages, propaganda campaigns, and new political developments were ubiquitous. In this section we look at the home fronts of the principal European belligerents.

GERMANY: FROM APPARENT VICTORY TO DEFEAT

Hitler had expected to defeat all his enemies by rapid strokes, or *blitzkrieg*. Such campaigns would scarcely have affected Germany's society and economy. During the first two years of the war, in fact, Hitler demanded few important sacrifices from the German people. Spending on domestic projects continued, and food was plentiful; the economy was not on a full wartime footing. The failure to knock out the Soviet Union changed everything. Because enough food could no longer be imported from the east, Germany had to mobilize for total war, and the government demanded major sacrifices.

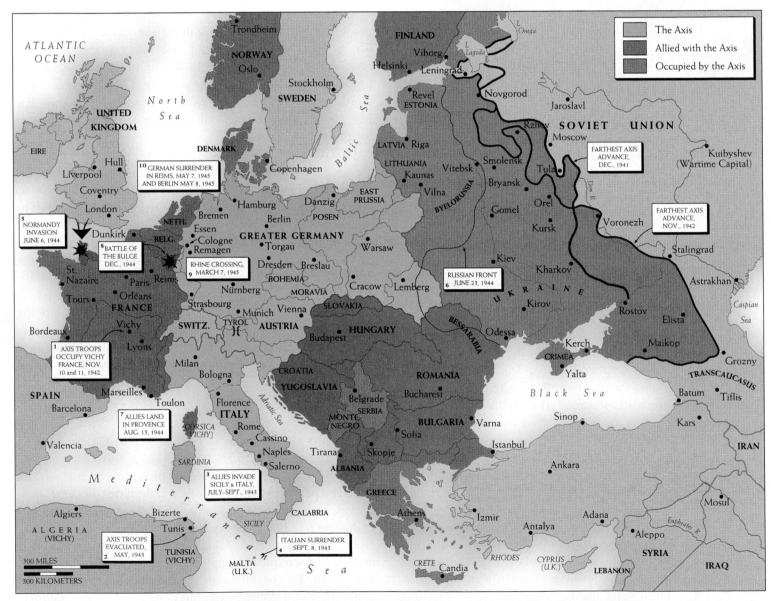

MAP 31–7 Defeat of the Axis in Europe, 1942–1945. Here we see some major steps in the progress toward Allied victory against Axis Europe. From the south through Italy, the west through France, and the east through Russia, the Allies gradually conquered the continent to bring the war in Europe to a close.

A great expansion of the army and military production began in 1942. As minister for armaments and munitions, Albert Speer (1905–1981) guided the economy, and Germany met its military needs instead of making consumer goods. Major German business enterprises aided the growth of wartime production. Between 1942 and late 1944 the output of military products tripled, but as the war went on the army absorbed more men from industry, hurting the production of even military goods.

Beginning in 1942 everyday products became scarce. Prices and wages were controlled, but the standard of living of German workers fell, Burdensome food rationing began in April 1942, and shortages were severe until the Nazi government seized food from occupied Europe. To preserve their own home front, the Nazis passed on the suffering to their defeated neighbors.

By 1943 there were also serious labor shortages. The Nazis required German teenagers and retired workers to work in the factories, and increasing numbers of women joined them.

To achieve total mobilization the Germans closed retail businesses, raised the maximum age of women eligible for compulsory service, shifted non-German domestic workers to wartime industry, moved artists and entertainers into military service, closed theaters, and reduced such basic public services as mail and railways. Finally, the Nazis forced thousands of people from conquered lands to labor in Germany.

Hitler assigned women a special place in the war effort. The celebration of motherhood continued, with an emphasis on women who were the mothers of important military figures. Films portrayed ordinary women who became especially brave and patriotic during the war and remained faithful to their husbands who were at the front. Women were thereby depicted as mothers and wives who would send their sons and husbands off to war. The government portrayed other wartime activities of women as the natural fulfillment of their maternal roles. As air raid wardens they protected their families; as factory workers in munitions plants they aided their sons on the front lines. Women working on farms were providing for their

▲ **D-Day.**   Allied troops landed in Normandy on D-Day, June 6, 1944. This photograph, taken two days later, shows long lines of men and equipment moving inland from the beach to reinforce the troops leading the invasion.
Archive Photos.

▲ **Bombing of Cologne.** The Allied campaign of aerial bombardment did terrible damage to German cities. This photograph shows the devastation it delivered to the city of Cologne on the Rhine.
UPI/Corbis-Bettmann.

soldier sons and husbands; as housewives they were helping to win the war by conserving food and managing their households frugally. Finally, by their faithful chastity, German women were protecting racial purity. They were not to marry or to engage in sexual relations with men who were not Germans. German women were thus supposed to demonstrate the kind of service and courage required by the war.

The war years also saw an intensification of political propaganda on the domestic front beyond what occurred in other countries. Hitler and other Nazis genuinely believed that weak domestic support had led to Germany's defeat in World War I, and they were determined that this would not happen again. Nazi propaganda blamed the outbreak of the war on the British and its prolongation on the policies of Germany's opponents. It also stressed the might of Germany and the inferiority of its foes.

Propaganda Minister Josef Goebbels (1897–1945) used radio and films to boost the Nazi cause. Movies of the collapse of Poland, Belgium, Holland, and France demonstrated German military might. Throughout the conquered territories the Nazis used the same mass media to frighten inhabitants about

▲ **Hiroshima.** This photo, taken a few days after an atomic bomb was dropped, poignantly captures the total devastation wreaked on the city.
Corbis-Bettmann.

Youth rally. Members of the Nazi German Women's Youth Movement perform calisthenics.

Getty Images Inc. – Hulton Archive Photos.

the possible consequences of an Allied victory. Later in the war the ministry broadcast exaggerated claims of Nazi victories. As the German armies were checked on the battlefield, especially in Russia, propaganda became a substitute for victory. To stiffen German resolve, the propaganda also aimed to frighten the German population about the consequences of defeat.

After May 1943, when the Allies began their major bombing offensive over Germany, the German people had much to fear. One German city after another endured heavy bombing, fires, and destruction. But the bombing did not undermine German morale—on the contrary, it may have confirmed the general fear of defeat at the hands of such savage opponents and increased German resistance.

World War II brought increased power to the Nazi party in Germany. Every area of the economy and society came under the direct influence or control of the party. The Nazis were determined that they, rather than the traditionally honored German officer corps, would profit from the new authority flowing to the central government because of the war effort. Throughout the war years there was virtually no serious opposition to Hitler or his ministers. In 1944 a small group of army officers made an attempt to assassinate Hitler; the effort failed, and there was no significant popular support for this act.

The war brought great changes to Germany, but what transformed the country afterward was the experience of defeat accompanied by vast physical destruction, invasion, and occupation. Hitler and the Nazis had brought the nation to such a complete and disastrous end that only a new kind of state with new political structures could emerge.

FRANCE: DEFEAT, COLLABORATION, AND RESISTANCE

In France the Vichy government cooperated closely with the Germans for a variety of reasons. Some of the collaborators believed that the Germans were sure to win and wanted to be on the victorious side. A few sympathized with the ideas and plans of the Nazis. Many conservatives regarded the French defeat as a judgment on what they saw as the corrupt, secularized, liberal Third Republic. But most of the French were not active collaborators and remained helpless and demoralized by defeat and German power.

Many conservatives and extreme rightists saw the Vichy government as a device to reshape the French national character and halt the decadence they associated with political and religious liberalism. The Roman Catholic clergy, who had lost power and influence under the Third Republic, gained status under Vichy. The church supported Pétain; his government supported religious education. Vichy adopted the church's views of the importance of family and spiritual values. Divorce was forbidden during the first three years of marriage and difficult thereafter; large families were rewarded.

The Vichy regime embraced an intense, chauvinistic nationalism. It encouraged the long-standing prejudice against foreigners working in France and persecuted those who were not regarded as genuinely and thoroughly French. The chief victims were French Jews. Anti-Semitism was not new in France, as the Dreyfus affair had demonstrated. Even before Germany undertook Hitler's "final solution" in 1942, the French had begun to remove Jews from government, education, and publishing. In 1941 the Germans began to intern Jews living in occupied France; soon they carried out killings and imposed large fines collectively on the Jews of the occupied zone. In the spring of 1942 the Germans began deporting Jews, ultimately over 60,000, to the extermination camps of eastern Europe. The Vichy government had no part in these decisions, but it made no protest, and its own anti-Semitic policies facilitated the process.

A few Frenchmen had fled to join de Gaulle's Free French forces soon after the defeat of 1940. Serious internal resistance to the German occupiers and to the Vichy government, however, developed only late in 1942. The Germans attempted to force young people in occupied France to work in German factories; some of them fled and joined the Resistance, but the total number of resisters was small. Many were deterred by fear. Some disliked the violence that resistance inevitably entailed. As long as it appeared that the Germans would win the war, moreover, resistance seemed imprudent and futile. In all, less than 5 percent of the adult French population appear to have been involved.

By early 1944 the tide of battle had shifted. An Allied victory appeared inevitable, and the Vichy government was clearly doomed. Only then did an active Resistance assert itself. General de Gaulle urged the French people to resist their conquerors and their lackeys in the Vichy government. Within France, Resistance groups joined forces to plan for a better day. From Algiers on August 9, 1944, the Committee of National Liberation declared the authority of Vichy illegitimate. Soon French soldiers joined in the liberation of Paris and established a government for Free France. On October 21, 1945, France voted to adopt a new constitution as the basis of the Fourth Republic. The French people had experienced defeat, disgrace, deprivation, and suffering. Hostility and bitter quarrels over who had done what during the occupation and the Vichy period divided them for decades.

GREAT BRITAIN: ORGANIZATION FOR VICTORY

On May 22, 1940, the British Parliament gave the government emergency powers. The government could now institute compulsory military service, food rationing, and various controls over the economy.

Churchill and the British war cabinet moved as quickly as possible to mobilize the nation. By the end of 1941 British production had already surpassed Germany's. To meet the heavy demands on the labor force, factory hours were extended, and women were brought into the workforce in great numbers. Unemployment disappeared, and the working classes had more money to spend than they had enjoyed for many years. To avoid inflation caused by increased demand for an inadequate supply of consumer goods, savings were encouraged, and taxes raised to absorb the excess purchasing power.

The bombing "blitz" conducted by the German Luftwaffe against British targets in the winter and spring of 1940 to 1941 was the most immediate and dramatic experience of the war for the British people. The German air raids killed thousands and destroyed the homes of many more. Many families removed their children to the countryside. Gas masks were issued to thousands of city dwellers, who were frequently compelled to take shelter from the bombs in the London subways.

After the spring of 1941 Hitler needed most of his air force for the Russian front, but the bombing of Britain continued, killing more than 30,000 people. Terrible as it was, this toll was much smaller than the number of Germans killed by Allied bombing later in the war. In England as in Germany, however, the bombing did not break the people's spirit but seems to have made them more determined.

During the worst months of the "blitz" the remarkable speeches of Winston Churchill cheered and encouraged the British people. He united them with a sense of common suffering and purpose. They were called upon to make many

sacrifices: Transportation facilities were strained simply from carrying enough coal for domestic heating and for running factories. Food and clothing for civilians were in short supply, and the government adopted strict rationing to achieve a fair distribution. Every scrap of land was farmed, increasing the productive portion by almost 4 million acres. Gasoline was in short supply, so private vehicles almost disappeared.

The British established their own propaganda machine to influence the Continent. The British Broadcasting Company (BBC) sent programs to every country in Europe in the local language to encourage resistance against the Nazis. At home the government used the radio to unify the nation. Soldiers at the front heard the same programs as their families at home.

For most of the population, strangely enough, the standard of living improved over the course of the war. The general health of the nation also improved for reasons that are still not clear. These gains should not be exaggerated, but many connected them with the active involvement of the government in the economy and the lives of the citizens. This wartime experience may have contributed to the Labour Party's victory in 1945; many feared that a return to Conservative rule would bring a return to the economic misery of the 1930s.

THE UNITED STATES: AMERICAN WOMEN AND AFRICAN AMERICANS IN THE WAR EFFORT

In the United States, the withdrawal of millions of men from the workforce and their induction into the armed forces created a demand for new workers, especially in the burgeoning defense industries. In part, it was filled by millions of women leaving the home to enter the labor force, some of them taking jobs in defense plants doing work usually done only by men. Economic pressures caused by the Great Depression of the 1930s had already brought many more women into the workforce than had been common before. Most came from poor families and worked in white-collar jobs to support themselves or to help their families eke out a living. Even so, the heavy burden of housework and the widespread hostility to the idea of women working outside the home kept the vast majority of women at home.

America's entry into the war changed things quickly. The need for vast amounts of equipment to wage the war called for and attracted new groups to seek work in the many enlarged and newly created factories. African Americans from the South came to Northern and Western cities to seek well-paying jobs, and women, too, came forward in greater numbers than ever before. Prejudices of various kinds had kept them from many opportunities, but the needs of war overcame such prejudice. In October 1942, President Roosevelt made the new situation clear: "In some communities employers dislike to hire women. In others they are reluctant to hire Negroes. We can no longer afford to indulge such prejudice."

Many women already working moved over to jobs in the defense industries; others entered the work force for the first time, lured less by wages than by patriotism. Their brothers and boyfriends were risking their lives for their country and its ideals of freedom and democracy. They were eager to do their part to support them, to be, in the words of a current song, the woman "behind the man behind the gun." Another popular song, "Rosie the Riveter," told of a young woman working in an aircraft factory to provide protection for her boyfriend in the Marines. Rosie came to be one of the best known symbols of the war effort when she appeared on the cover of the *Saturday Evening Post*. With her rivet gun on her lap she stamped on a copy of Hitler's *Mein Kampf*, the hated symbol of the enemy's evil.

THE SOVIET UNION: "THE GREAT PATRIOTIC WAR"

No nation suffered greater loss of life or more extensive physical destruction during World War II than the Soviet Union. Perhaps as many as 16 million people were killed, and vast numbers of Soviet troops were taken prisoner. Hundreds of cities and towns and well over half the industrial and transportation facilities of the country were devastated. The Germans sent thousands of Soviet prisoners to work in factories in Germany as forced labor. The Germans also confiscated grain supplies and drew mineral resources and oil from the Soviet Union to serve their own war effort.

Stalin (1879–1953) conducted the war as virtual chief of the armed forces, and the State Committee for Defense provided strong central coordination. In the decade before the war, Stalin had already made the Soviet Union a highly centralized nation; he had attempted to manage the entire economy centrally through the Five-Year Plans, the collectivization of agriculture, and the purges. The country was thus on what amounted to a wartime footing long before the conflict erupted. When the war began, millions of citizens entered the army, but the army did not grow in influence at the expense of the state and the Communist Party—that is, Stalin.

Soviet propaganda differed from that of other nations. Because the Soviet government distrusted the loyalty of its citizens, it confiscated radios to prevent the people from listening to German propaganda. In large cities the government erected large loudspeakers to broadcast to the people in place of radios. Soviet propaganda emphasized Russian patriotism, not Marxist class conflict. The struggle was called "The Great Patriotic War." As in other countries, writers and playwrights helped sustain public support for the war. Sometimes they drew on Communist themes, but they also portrayed the common Soviet citizen as contributing to a great patriotic struggle.

Great Russian novels of the past reappeared; more than half a million copies of Tolstoy's *War and Peace* were published dur-

ing the siege of Leningrad. Other authors wrote straightforward propaganda fostering hatred of the Germans. Serge Eisenstein (1898–1948), the great filmmaker, produced a vast epic entitled *Ivan the Terrible*, which glorified one of the most brutal tsars of Russia's past. Musicians, such as Dimitri Shostakovich (1906–1975), wrote scores that sought to contribute to the struggle and evoke heroic emotions. The most important of these was Shostakovich's Seventh Symphony, also known as the "Leningrad Symphony."

Stalin even made peace with the Russian Orthodox Church. He pursued friendly relations with church leaders and allowed them to enter the Kremlin. Stalin hoped that this new policy would give him more support at home and permit the Soviet Union to be viewed more favorably in those parts of eastern Europe where the Orthodox Church predominated.

Within occupied portions of the western Soviet Union, an active resistance movement arose against the Germans. The swiftness of the German invasion had stranded thousands of Soviet troops, some of whom escaped and carried on irregular resistance warfare behind enemy lines. Stalin supported partisan forces in lands held by the enemy for two reasons: He wanted to cause as much difficulty as possible for the Germans; and the Soviet-sponsored resistance reminded the peasants in the conquered regions that the Soviet government, with its policies of collectivization, had not disappeared. Stalin feared that the peasants' hatred of the Communist government might lead them to collaborate with the invaders. When the Soviet army moved westward toward the end of the war, it incorporated the partisans into the regular army.

As the Soviet armies reclaimed the occupied areas and then moved across eastern and central Europe, the Soviet Union established itself as a world power second only to the United States. Stalin had been a reluctant belligerent, but he emerged a major victor. In that respect, the war and the extraordinary patriotic effort and sacrifice it generated consolidated the power of Stalin and the party more effectively than had the political and social policies of the previous decade.

Preparations for Peace

The split between the Soviet Union and its wartime allies that followed the war and began to emerge as it ended should cause no surprise. As the self-proclaimed center of world communism, the Soviet Union was openly dedicated to the overthrow of the capitalist nations, although this message was muted when the occasion demanded. On the other side, the Western allies were no less open about their hostility to communism and its chief purveyor, the Soviet Union.

Although cooperation against a common enemy and strenuous propaganda efforts in the West helped improve Western feeling toward the Soviet ally, Stalin remained suspicious and

Home front. Russian women apply grease to howitzer shells at a munitions plant during World War II.
Getty Images Inc. – Hulton Archive Photos.

critical of the Western war effort. Likewise, Churchill never ceased planning to contain the Soviet advance into Europe. For some time Roosevelt seems to have hoped that the Allies could continue to work together after the war, but even he was losing faith by 1945. Differences in historical development and ideology, as well as traditional conflicts over political power and influence, soon dashed hopes of a mutually satisfactory peace settlement and continued cooperation to uphold it.

THE ATLANTIC CHARTER

In August 1941, even before America entered the war, Roosevelt and Churchill had met off Newfoundland and agreed to the Atlantic Charter. A broad set of principles in the spirit of Wilson's Fourteen Points, it provided a theoretical basis for the peace they sought. When Russia and the United States joined Britain in the war, the three powers entered a purely military alliance in January 1942, leaving all political questions aside. The first political conference was the meeting of foreign ministers in Moscow in October 1943. The ministers reaffirmed earlier agreements to fight on until the enemy surrendered unconditionally and to continue cooperating after the war in a united-nations organization.

TEHRAN

The first meeting of the three leaders took place at Tehran, the capital of Iran, in 1943. Western promises to open a second front in France the next summer (1944) and Stalin's agreement to join in the war against Japan (when Germany was defeated) created an atmosphere of goodwill in which to discuss a postwar settlement. Stalin wanted to retain what he

had gained in his pact with Hitler and to dismember Germany. Roosevelt and Churchill made no firm commitments.

The most important decision was for the Western Allies to attack Germany from Europe's west coast instead of from southern Europe by way of the Mediterranean. This decision meant, in retrospect, that Soviet forces would occupy eastern Europe and control its destiny. At Tehran in 1943 the Western allies did not foresee this clearly, for the Russians were still fighting deep within their own frontiers, and military considerations were paramount everywhere.

By 1944 the situation was different. In August, Soviet armies were in sight of Warsaw, which had risen in expectation of liberation. But the Russians turned south into the Balkans, allowing the Polish rebels to be annihilated. The Russians gained control of Romania and Hungary, gaining advances of which centuries of expansionist tsars had only dreamed. Alarmed by these developments, Churchill went to Moscow and met with Stalin in October. They agreed to share power in the Balkans on the basis of Soviet predominance in Romania and Bulgaria, Western predominance in Greece, and equality of influence in Yugoslavia and Hungary. These agreements were not enforceable without American approval, and the Americans were known to be hostile to such un-Wilsonian devices as "spheres of influence."

The three powers easily agreed on Germany's disarmament and denazification and on its division into four zones of occupation by France and the Big Three (the USSR, Britain, and the United States). Churchill, however, began to balk at Stalin's plan to dismember Germany and objected to his demand for reparations in the amount of $20 billion as well as for forced labor from all the zones, with Russia to get half of everything. These matters were left to fester and cause dissension in the future.

The settlement of eastern Europe remained a problem. Everyone agreed that the Soviet Union deserved neighboring governments that were friendly, but the West insisted that they also be independent, autonomous, and democratic. The Western leaders, and especially Churchill, were not eager to see eastern Europe fall under Russian domination. They, especially Roosevelt, were also truly committed to democracy and self-determination.

However, Stalin knew that independent, freely elected governments in Poland and Romania would not be safely friendly to Russia. He had already established a subservient government in Poland at Lublin in competition with the Polish government in exile in London. Under pressure from the Western leaders, however, Stalin agreed to reorganize the government and to include some Poles friendly to the West. He also signed a Declaration on Liberated Europe, promising self-determination and free democratic elections. Stalin was never free of the fear that the Allies might still make an arrangement with Germany and betray him. Yet he appeared eager to avoid conflict before the war with Germany was over, and he probably thought it worth endorsing some meaningless principles as the price of continued harmony. In any case, he wasted little time violating these agreements.

Big Three at Potsdam. This photograph shows the "Big Three" at Potsdam. By the summer of 1945 only Stalin remained of the original leaders of the major Allies. Roosevelt and Churchill had been replaced by Harry Truman and Clement Attlee.
Corbis-Bettmann.

YALTA

The next meeting of the Big Three was at Yalta in the Crimea in February 1945. The Western armies had not yet crossed the Rhine, and the Soviet army was within 100 miles of Berlin. The war with Japan continued, and no atomic explosion had yet taken place. Roosevelt, faced with an invasion of Japan and prospective heavy losses, was eager to bring the Russians into the Pacific war as soon as possible.

As a true Wilsonian, Roosevelt also suspected Churchill's determination to maintain the British Empire and Britain's colonial advantages. The Americans thought that Churchill's plan to set up British spheres of influence in Europe would encourage the Russians to do the same and lead to friction and war. To encourage Russian participation in the war against Japan, Roosevelt and Churchill made extensive concessions to Russia in Asia. Again in the tradition of Wilson, Roosevelt stressed a United Nations organization: "Through the United Nations, he hoped to achieve a self-enforcing peace settlement that would not require American troops, as well as an open world without spheres of influence in which American enterprise could work freely."[2] Soviet agreement on these points seemed well worth concessions elsewhere.

POTSDAM

The Big Three met for the last time in the Berlin suburb of Potsdam in July 1945. Much had changed since the last conference. Germany was defeated, and news of the successful exper-

MAP 31–8 Territorial Changes in Europe After World War II. The map shows the shifts in territory that followed the defeat of the Axis. No treaty of peace formally ended the war with Germany.

[2] Robert O. Paxton, *Europe in the Twentieth Century* (New York: Harcourt Brace Jovanovich, 1975), p. 487.

imental explosion of an atomic weapon reached the American president during the meetings. The cast of characters was also different: President Truman replaced Roosevelt; and Clement Attlee (1883–1967), leader of the Labour Party, replaced Churchill during the conference. Previous agreements were reaffirmed, but progress on undecided questions was slow.

Russia's western frontier was moved far into what had been Poland and included part of German East Prussia (see Map 31–8). In compensation, Poland was allowed "temporary administration" over the rest of East Prussia and Germany east of the Oder-Neisse river line, a condition that became permanent.

In effect, Poland was moved about 100 miles west, at the expense of Germany, to accommodate the Soviet Union. The Allies agreed that Germany would be divided into occupation zones until the final peace treaty was signed, and the country remained divided until the end of the Cold War more than forty years later.

A Council of Foreign Ministers was established to draft peace treaties for Germany's allies. Growing disagreements made the job difficult, and it was not until February 1947 that Italy, Romania, Hungary, Bulgaria, and Finland signed treaties. The Russians signed their own agreements with the Japanese in 1956. These disagreements were foreshadowed at Potsdam.

Navajo Language Used as Code.

Summary

The Coming of War The second great war of the twentieth century (1939–1945) grew out of the unsatisfactory resolution of the first. In retrospect, the two wars appear to some people to be one continuous conflict, with the two main periods of fighting separated by an uneasy truce. To others, that point of view distorts the situation by implying that the second war was the inevitable result of the first and its inadequate peace treaties.

The latter opinion seems more sound. Whatever the flaws of the treaties of Paris, the world suffered an even more terrible war than the first as a result of failures of judgment and will on the part of the victorious democratic powers. The United States, which had become the wealthiest and potentially the strongest nation in the world, disarmed almost entirely and withdrew into foolish isolation; it could play no important part in restraining the ambitious dictators who would bring on the war. Britain and France refused to face the threat posed by the Axis powers until the most deadly war in history was required to put it down. If the victorious democracies had remained strong, responsible, and realistic, they could have remedied whatever injustices or mistakes arose from the treaties without endangering the peace.

World War II The second war itself was plainly a world war. The Japanese occupation of Manchuria in 1931 was a precursor. Italy attacked Ethiopia in 1935. Italy, Germany, and the Soviet Union intervened in the Spanish Civil War (1936–1939). Japan attacked China in 1937. These developments revealed that aggressive forces were on the march around the globe and that the defenders of the world order lacked the will to stop them. The formation of the Axis among Germany, Italy, and Japan guaranteed that the war would be fought around the world. There were fighting and suffering in Asia, Africa, the islands of the Pacific, and Europe. The use of atomic weapons brought the struggle to a close, but what are called conventional weapons did almost all the damage. The survival of civilization was threatened even without the use of nuclear devices.

This was ended not with unsatisfactory peace treaties but with no treaty at all in the European area where it had begun. The world quickly split into two unfriendly camps: the Western led by the United States, and the Eastern led by the Soviet Union. This division hastened the liberation of former colonial territories.

Review Questions

1. What were Hitler's foreign policy aims? Was he bent on conquest in the East and dominance in the West, or did he simply want to return Germany to its 1914 boundaries?

2. Why did Britain and France adopt a policy of appeasement in the 1930s? What were its main features? Did the appeasers buy the West valuable time to prepare for war by their actions at Munich in 1938?

3. How was Hitler able to defeat France so easily in 1940? Why was the air war against Britain a failure? Why did Hitler invade Russia? Why did the invasion ultimately fail? Could it have succeeded?

4. Why did Japan attack the United States at Pearl Harbor? What was the significance of American intervention in the war? Why did the United States drop atomic bombs on Japan? Did President Truman make the right decision when he ordered the bombs used?

5. What impact did World War II have on the civilian population of Europe? How did experiences on the domestic front of Great Britain differ from those of Germany and France? What impact did "The Great Patriotic War" have on the people of the Soviet Union? Did participation in World War II solidify Stalin's hold on power?

6. What was Hitler's "final solution" to the Jewish problem? Why did Hitler want to eliminate Slavs as well? Some historians have looked at the twentieth century and have seen a period of great destruction as well as of great progress. Was the twentieth century truly a "century of Holocaust"? Discuss the ramifications of these questions.

Key Terms

Anschluss (p. 935)

appeasement (p. 933)

Axis (p. 934)

blitzkrieg (p. 948)

Holocaust (p. 941)

Lebensraum (p. 931)

Luftwaffe (p. 938)

Documents CD-ROM

World War II
25.1 Adolf Hitler, The Obersalzberg Speech
25.2 The Atlantic Charter

25.3 The Rape of Nanjing
25.4 Hiroshima and Nagasaki
25.6 The Charter of the United Nations

NOTE: *To learn more about the topics in this chapter, see the Suggested Readings at the end of the book.*

32

The West Since World War II

- The Cold War Era

- European Society in the Second Half of the Twentieth Century and Beyond

- American Domestic Scene Since World War II

- The Soviet Union to 1989

- 1989: Year of Revolutions in Eastern Europe

- The Collapse of the Soviet Union

- The Collapse of Yugoslavia and Civil War

- Challenges to the Atlantic Alliance

◀ FRANK O. GEHRY, *GUGGENHEIM MUSEUM BILBAO*, SPAIN, 1997.
Hailed as a masterpiece in 1997, Frank Gehry's *Guggenheim Museum Bilbao, Spain*, has become a beacon of artistic innovation and cultural cooperation at the turn of the millennium, providing a model for new forms of political and cultural thought. Just as the museum's billowing forms expand conceptions of what a building is—combining a puzzle of individual parts into an elegantly unified whole—so must 21st-century Europe aspire to combine diversity and unity under the banner of pluralistic democracy. This is a not an easy task, as recent conflicts in war-torn Yugoslavia and Chechnya and acts of terror in Madrid and elsewhere challenge the West's resolve.
Javier Bauluz Stringer/AP/Wide World Photo.

GLOBAL PERSPECTIVE

The West Since 1945

The history of the West since the end of World War II has been full of paradoxes. Europe, which gave birth to Western civilization and remained its center from the eighteenth century until the war, declined in world influence. During the four decades immediately after the war, the United States and the Soviet Union rose to predominance and replaced Western Europe as the major powers on the world scene. Consequently, while the traditional center of Western influence exerted little power, both new great Western powers came to exert more political and military power than any other previous nation of continental Europe. But they did so in conflict with each other.

Immediately after 1945 the nations of the West entered the Cold War. That ideological, economic, and military rivalry between the United States and the Soviet Union dominated political struggles throughout the world for more than half a century. It divided Europe between NATO and Warsaw Pact military forces and forced nations outside of Europe, in Asia, Africa, and Latin America, to side with one or the other of the superpowers. Hence the Cold War too became a world war that had an important impact on non-Western nations that at times became theaters of conflict in which indigenous civil wars melded into the struggle between the United States and the Soviet Union, as in the case of Cuba, Angola, Korea, and Vietnam. A neutral stance in this conflict became extremely difficult for any nation to sustain.

In the later 1980s, however, the Cold War unexpectedly ended as the Soviet Union and the nations of Eastern Europe, their economies exhausted from failed experiments in central planning and repression, experienced enormous internal political changes and began the difficult transition to democracy and capitalism. These changes have clearly opened a new epoch of Western history. The United States has emerged from the Cold War as the single remaining superpower. Western Europe has achieved a new level of economic and political unity under the auspices of the European Union, although its peoples and governments are hesitant to press the process too far too rapidly. The economic success of the European Union has inspired other regional global treaties to promote free markets, including NAFTA (North Atlantic Free Trade Association), as well as the global WTO (World Trade Organization). Europe has also been more ambitious than the United States in promoting international organizations such as the World Court designed to discipline countries that oppress their neighbors or threaten world peace. Eastern Europe and the former Soviet Union are experiencing economic turmoil and political uncertainty. Although some Eastern European countries such as Poland, the Czech Republic, and Hungary are better prepared than others to join the European Union, the shared aspiration of all Eastern European nations to become EU members bodes well for the future of this region. Except for Latvia, Estonia, and Lithuania, newly independent former regions of the Soviet Union such as Ukraine, Georgia, and Belarus have an even more difficult path ahead of them in developing their economies and societies. Together with the Islamic countries, such as Uzbekistan, Turkmenistan, and Kazakhstan, these countries face added difficulties from the legacy of repressive authoritarian government and centrally planned economies. The security of Europe's eastern borders will depend on the success of these Eastern European nations and former Soviet republics in making the transition to democracy.

Another important factor in the history of both the United States and Europe since World War II has been the rising immigration from the rest of the world. Germany has seen the influx of significant numbers of *gastarbeiters* (guest workers) from Turkey, while France, Italy, and Spain receive more immigrants from North Africa and the Middle East, many from their former colonies. The United States, with its long history as an immigrant nation, has been more comfortable dealing with the influx of non-European immigrants, but struggles persist over language, cultural identity, and assimilation. Europe, less accustomed to non-European immigration, has found it even more difficult to accommodate immigrants whose religions, languages, and appearance differ from those of Europeans.

THINK AHEAD

- What was the Cold War, and why can we rightly call it a world war?
- How has the relationship between the United States and Europe changed since World War II? How might it develop in the future?
- How has immigration changed the face of Europe since 1945?

IN THE MORE THAN HALF A CENTURY SINCE THE CONCLUSION of World War II, Europe's influence on the world scene has been transformed. The destruction and financial strains of the war left Europe exhausted and incapable of exercising the kind of power it had formerly exerted. Almost immediately after the war, the Cold War developed between the United States and the Soviet Union. Europe along with other parts of the world became a divided and contested territory, with America dominant in Western Europe and the Soviets dominant in Eastern Europe. The European powers themselves could not determine the outcome of that struggle for world dominance between the superpowers. Furthermore, less than five years after the war Europeans began to lose control of their overseas empires.

Within both the world context and the more narrow Western context, the greatest change that took place after 1945 was the emergence of the United States as a fully active great power. The American retreat from leadership that occurred in 1919 was not repeated. The decision by the United States to take an activist role in world affairs touched virtually every aspect of the postwar world. As a result of this acceptance of a leadership role, American domestic politics and its foreign policy became intertwined as in no previous period of American history.

Europe did not stagnate in this situation. Rather its society continued to develop in new directions. Population, agricultural production, and general consumption increased, especially in Western Europe. As in virtually every other part of the world, Europe experienced the impact of American culture through military alliances, trade, tourism, and popular entertainment. Europeans also began to build structures for greater economic cooperation.

Yet for forty-five years after the Second World War, Europe remained divided between a Western region generally characterized by democracies and an Eastern region characterized by Communist Party authoritarian states dominated by the Soviet Union. From the late 1970s onward there were political stirrings and economic stagnation in Eastern Europe and the Soviet Union. These culminated in 1989 with revolutions throughout Eastern Europe and in 1991 with the collapse of Communist government in the Soviet Union itself. Since those events Europeans have been seeking to forge a new political direction. The movement toward unification, most particularly of the currency, continues in Western Europe. But the several nations that emerged from the former Soviet Union continue to experience political confusion and economic stagnation. The attacks of September 11, 2001, on the United States and the international events flowing therefrom have challenged the post–World War II Western alliance.

The Cold War Era

INITIAL CAUSES

The tense relationship between the United States and the Soviet Union that dominated world history during the second half of the twentieth century originated in the closing months of World War II. In part, the new coldness between the Allies arose from the mutual feeling that each had violated previous agreements. The Russians were plainly asserting permanent control of Poland and Romania under puppet Communist governments. The United States, on the other hand, was taking a harder line on the extent of German reparations to the Soviet Union.

In retrospect, however, it appears unlikely that friendlier styles on either side could have avoided a split that rested on basic differences of ideology and interest. The Soviet Union's attempt to extend its control westward into central Europe and the Balkans and southward into the Middle East was a continuation of the policy of tsarist Russia. It had been Britain's traditional role to restrain Russian expansion into these areas;

the United States inherited that task as Britain's power waned. The alternative was to permit a major change in the balance of power in the world in favor of a huge, traditionally hostile nation. That nation, dedicated in its official ideology to the overthrow of nations like the United States, was governed by Stalin (1879–1953), an absolute dictator, who had repeatedly demonstrated his capacity for the most amazing deceptions and the most horrible cruelties. Few nations would be likely to take such risks.

In the aftermath of World War II, however, the Americans made no attempt to roll back Soviet power where it already existed. This was true even though American military forces were the greatest in their history, American industrial power was unmatched in the world, and America had a monopoly on atomic weapons. In less than a year from the war's end, the Americans reduced their forces in Europe from 3.5 million to half a million. The speedy withdrawal reflected pressure to "get the boys home," but it was also fully in accord with America's peacetime plans and goals. These goals included support for self-determination, autonomy, and democracy in the political sphere; and free trade, freedom of the seas, no barriers to investment, and the Open Door in the economic sphere. As the strongest, richest nation in the world—the one with the greatest industrial plant and the strongest currency—the United States would benefit handsomely if an international order based on such goals were established.

American hostility to colonial empires created tensions with France and Britain, but these stresses were minor. The main conflict was with the Soviet Union. From the Soviet perspective, extending the borders of the USSR and dominating the formerly independent states of Eastern Europe would provide needed security and would compensate the Soviet people for the fearful losses they had endured in the war. The Soviets could thus see American resistance to their expansion as a threat to their security and their legitimate aims. American objections over Poland and other states could be seen as attempts to undermine regimes friendly to Russia and to encircle the Soviet Union with hostile neighbors.

The growth in France and Italy of large Communist parties plainly taking orders from Moscow led the Americans to believe that Stalin was engaged in a great worldwide plot to subvert capitalism and democracy. In the absence of reliable evidence about Stalin's intentions, it is impossible to know for certain if these suspicions were justified, but most people in the West considered them plausible.

AREAS OF EARLY COLD WAR CONFLICT

The new mood of hostility among the former allies appeared quickly. In February 1946 both Stalin and his foreign minister, Vyacheslav Molotov (1890–1986), gave public speeches in which they spoke of the Western democracies as enemies. A month later Churchill (1874–1965) delivered a speech in Fulton, Missouri, in which he spoke of an Iron Curtain that had descended on Europe, dividing a free and democratic West from an East under totalitarian rule. He warned against Communist subversion and urged Western unity and strength to counter the new menace. In this atmosphere, difficulties grew.

The attempt to deal cooperatively with the problem of atomic energy was an early victim of the **Cold War**. The Americans put forward a plan to place the manufacture and control of atomic weapons under international control, but the Russians balked at proposed requirements for on-site inspection and for limits on veto power in the United Nations. The plan fell through. The United States continued to develop its own atomic weapons in secrecy, and the Russians did the same. By 1949, with the help of information obtained by Soviet spies in Britain and the United States, the Soviet Union had exploded its own atomic bomb, and the race for nuclear weapons was on.

The resistance of Westerners to what they increasingly perceived as Soviet intransigence and Communist plans for subversion and expansion took clearer form in 1947. Since 1944

civil war had been raging in Greece between the royalist government restored by Britain and insurgents supported by the Communist countries, chiefly Yugoslavia. In 1947 Britain informed the United States that it was financially no longer able to support the Greeks. On March 12 President Truman (1884–1972) asked Congress for legislation that would provide funds to support Greece and also Turkey, which was under Soviet pressure to yield control of the Dardanelles, and Congress complied. In what became known as the Truman Doctrine, the American president advocated a policy of supporting "free people who are resisting attempted subjugation by armed minorities or by outside pressures," by implication anywhere in the world.

American aid to Greece and Turkey took the form of military equipment and advisers. For Western Europe, where the menacing growth of Communist parties was fueled by postwar poverty and hunger, the Americans devised the European Recovery Program. Named the **Marshall Plan** after George C. Marshall (1880–1959), the secretary of state who introduced it, this program provided broad economic aid to European states on condition only that they work together for their mutual benefit. The Soviet Union and its satellites were invited to participate. Finland and Czechoslovakia were willing, and Poland and Hungary showed interest. The Soviets, however, forbade them to take part.

The Marshall Plan helped restore prosperity to Western Europe and set the stage for Europe's unprecedented postwar economic growth. It also led to the waning of Communist strength in the West and to the establishment there of solid democratic regimes.

From the Western viewpoint, this policy of "containment" was a new and successful response to the Soviet and Communist challenge. Stalin may have considered it a renewal of the old Western attempt to isolate and encircle the USSR. His answer was to replace all multiparty governments behind the Iron Curtain with thoroughly Communist regimes completely under his control. He also called a meeting of all Communist parties around the world at Warsaw in the autumn of 1947. There they organized the Communist Information Bureau (Cominform), a revival of the old Comintern, dedicated to spreading revolutionary communism throughout the world.

In February 1948 a more dramatic and brutal display of Stalin's new policy took place in Prague. The Communists expelled the democratic members of what had been a coalition government and murdered Jan Masaryk (1886–1948), the foreign minister and son of the founder of Czechoslovakia, Thomas Masaryk (1850–1937). President Eduard Benes (1884–1948) was forced to resign, and Czechoslovakia was brought fully under Soviet rule.

These Soviet actions, especially those in Czechoslovakia, increased American determination to go ahead with its own arrangements in Germany. The Russians swiftly dismantled German industry in the eastern zone, but the Americans chose to try to make Germany self-sufficient, which meant restoring rather than destroying its industrial capacity. To the Soviets the restoration of a powerful industrial Germany, even in the western zones only, was frightening and unacceptable.

Disagreement over Germany produced the most heated postwar debate. When the Western powers agreed to go forward with a separate constitution for the western sectors of Germany in February 1948, the Soviets walked out of the joint Allied Control Commission. In the summer of that year the Western powers issued a new currency in their zone. Berlin, although well within the Soviet zone, was governed by all four powers. The Soviets chose to seal the city off by closing all railroads and highways to West Germany. Their purpose was to drive the Western powers out of Berlin.

The Western allies responded to the Berlin Blockade with an airlift of supplies to the city that lasted almost a year. In May 1949 the Russians were forced to back down and to open access to Berlin. The incident greatly increased tensions and suspicions between the opponents. It hastened the separation of Germany into two states, a situation that prevailed for forty years. West Germany formally became the German Federal Republic in September 1949, and the eastern region became the German Democratic Republic a month later.

NATO AND THE WARSAW PACT

Meanwhile, the nations of Western Europe had been coming closer together. The Marshall Plan encouraged international cooperation. In March 1948 Belgium, the Netherlands, Luxembourg, France, and Britain signed the Treaty of Brussels, providing for cooperation in economic and military matters. In April 1949 these nations joined Italy, Denmark, Norway, Portugal, and Iceland to sign a treaty with Canada and the United States that formed the North Atlantic Treaty Organization (NATO). NATO committed its members to mutual assistance in case any of them was attacked. For the first time in history the United States committed itself to defend allies outside the Western Hemisphere. NATO formed the West into a bloc. A few years later West Germany, Greece, and Turkey joined the alliance (see Map 32–1).

Soviet relations with the states of Eastern Europe were governed by a series of bilateral treaties providing for close ties and mutual assistance in case of attack. In 1949 the Council of Mutual Assistance (COMECON) was formed to integrate the economies of these states. Unlike the NATO states, the Eastern alliance system was under direct Soviet domination through local Communist parties controlled from Moscow and overawed by the presence of the Red Army. The Warsaw Pact of May 1955, which included Albania, Bulgaria, Czechoslovakia, East Germany, Hungary, Poland, Romania, and the Soviet Union, merely gave formal recognition to a system that already existed. Europe stood divided into two unfriendly blocs.

In 1953 Stalin died; later that year an armistice was concluded in Korea (see Chapter 33). Both events produced hope that international tensions might lessen, but the rivalry of power and polemics soon resumed.

CRISES OF 1956

The events of 1956 had considerable significance both for the Cold War and for what they implied about the realities of European power in the postwar era.

Suez   In July 1956 President Gamal Abdel Nasser (1918–1970) of Egypt nationalized the Suez Canal. Great Britain and France feared that this action would close the canal to their supplies of oil in the Persian Gulf. In October 1956 war broke out between Egypt and Israel. The British and French seized the opportunity to intervene; however, the United States refused to support their action. The Soviet Union protested vehemently. The Anglo-French forces had to be withdrawn, and control of the canal remained with Egypt.

▲ **Berlin Airlift.** The Allied airlift in action during the Berlin Blockade. Every day for almost a year Western planes supplied the city until Stalin lifted the blockade in May 1949.
Bildarchiv Preussischer Kulturbesitz.

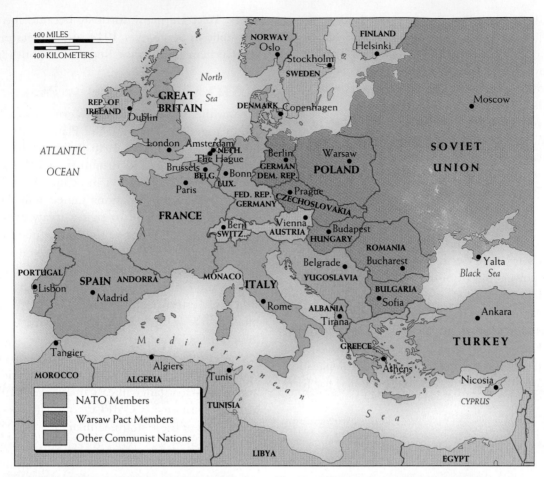

MAP 32–1 Major Cold War European Alliance Systems. The North Atlantic Treaty Organization, which includes both Canada and the United States, stretches as far east as Turkey. By contrast, the Warsaw Pact nations were the contiguous Communist states of Eastern Europe, with the Soviet Union, of course, as the dominant member.

The Suez intervention proved that without the support of the United States the nations of Western Europe could no longer undertake meaningful military operations to impose their will on the rest of the world. It also appeared that the United States and the Soviet Union had restrained their allies from undertaking actions that might have resulted in a wider conflict. The fact that neither of the superpowers wanted war constrained both Egypt and the Anglo-French forces.

Poland   The autumn of 1956 also saw important developments in Eastern Europe that demonstrated similar limitations on independent action among the Soviet bloc nations. When the prime minister of Poland died, the Polish Communist Party leaders refused to choose as his successor the person selected by Moscow. Considerable tension developed. The Soviet leaders even visited Warsaw to make their opinions known. In the end, Wladyslaw Gomulka (1905–1982) emerged as the new Communist leader of Poland. He was the choice of the Poles, and he proved acceptable to the Soviets because he promised continued economic and military cooperation and most par-

ticularly continued Polish membership in the Warsaw Pact. Within those limits he halted the collectivization of Polish agriculture and improved the relationship between the Communist government and the Polish Roman Catholic Church.

Uprising in Hungary   Hungary provided the second trouble spot for the Soviet Union. (See Document, "The Church and the Communist Party Clash over Education in Hungary.") In late October demonstrations of sympathy for the Poles occurred in Budapest. The Communist government moved to stop the demonstrations, and street fighting erupted. A new ministry headed by former premier Imre Nagy (1896–1958) was installed by the Hungarian Communist Party. Nagy was a Communist who sought a more independent position for Hungary. He went much further in his demands than Gomulka and directly appealed for political support from non-Communist groups in Hungary. Nagy called for the removal of Soviet troops and the ultimate neutralization of Hungary. He even called for Hungarian withdrawal from the Warsaw Pact. These demands were wholly unacceptable to the Soviet Union.

In early November Soviet troops invaded Hungary; deposed Nagy, who was later executed; and imposed Janos Kadar (1912–1989) as premier.

THE COLD WAR INTENSIFIED

The events of 1956 ended the era of fully autonomous action by the European nation-states. In different ways and to differing degrees, the two superpowers had demonstrated the new political realities. After 1956 the Soviet Union began to talk about "peaceful coexistence" with the United States. In 1958 negotiations began between the two countries for limitations on the testing of nuclear weapons. However, in the same year the Soviet Union also announced that the status of West Berlin had to be changed and the Allied occupation forces withdrawn. The demand was refused. In 1959 tensions relaxed sufficiently for several Western leaders to visit Moscow and for Soviet Premier Nikita Khrushchev (1894–1971) to tour the United States. A summit meeting was scheduled for May 1960

DOCUMENT | The Church and the Communist Party Clash over Education in Hungary

Throughout Eastern Europe, the Roman Catholic Church became one of the strongest opponents of the postwar Communist Party governments. It raised issues relating to church schools, free worship, participation in church-sponsored organizations, and the erection of new church buildings. One of the harshest clashes took place in Hungary. Following are two statements that illustrate the opposing positions of the church and the party. Cardinal Mindszenty (1892–1975) was later imprisoned and became one of the most well known political prisoners in Eastern Europe.

◆ How does Mindszenty relate the position of church-supported schools to the nature and rights of parenthood? How does he compare the actions of the Communist Party to those of Hitler? How does the Minister of Public Worship set party members against the church? How does he attempt to place loyalty to the party above private beliefs? What does the Communist Party fear from religious education and participation in religious activities on the part of its members of their children?

Statement of Josef Cardinal Mindszenty, May 20, 1946

The right of the Church to have schools is entirely in concord with the right of parents to educate their children. What is incumbent upon the parents in all questions of natural life is incumbent upon the Church with regard to the supernatural life. Parents are prior to the state, and their rights were always and still are, acknowledged by the Church. The prerogative of parents to educate their children cannot be disputed by the state, since it is the parents who give life to the child. They feed the child and clothe it. The child's life is, as it were, the continuation of theirs. Hence it is their right to demand that their children are educated according to their faith and their religious outlook.

It is their right to withhold their children from schools where there religious convictions are not only disregarded but even made the object of contempt and ridicule. It was this parental right which German parents felt was violated when the Hitler government deprived them of their denominational schools. The children came home from the new schools like little heathens, who smiled derisively or laughed at the prayers of their parents.

You Hungarian parents will likewise feel a violation of your fundamental rights if your children can no longer attend the Catholic schools solely because the dictatorial State closes down our schools by a brutal edict or renders their work impossible.

Statement of the Hungarian Communist Minister of Public Worship, June 7, 1950

We must start a vast work of enlightenment, and in the first place explain to our party colleagues and also to all workers that any father who sends his child to religion classes, places it in the hands of the enemy and entrusts his soul and thinking to the enemies of peace and imperialistic warmongers.

A part of our working people believes that participation of children in religious instruction is a private matter which has nothing to do with the political conviction of their parents. They are wrong. To send children to a reactionary pastor for religious instruction, is a political movement against the People's Democracy, whether intentional or not. …

In carrying out the basic principles, religion within the party is no private matter, but we must take a difference between plain party members and party officials, and must not in any case make party membership dependent on the fact whether our party members are religious. In the first place, we must expect from our party officials, our leading men, that they do not send their children to religious instruction courses, do not take part in religious ceremonies and train their wives in the spirit of communistic conception.

Also, we must patiently endeavor to enlighten our members, and ensure through training and propaganda that they realize; "In going to Church, taking part in processions, sending our children to religious instruction, we unconsciously further the efforts of clerical reaction."

From Colman J. Barry, O.S.B., *Readings in Church History* © 1965 by The Missionary Society of Saint Paul the Apostle in the State of New York. Used by permission of Paulist Press, Inc.

in Paris, and American President Dwight D. Eisenhower (1890–1969) was to go to Moscow.

Just before the gathering, the Soviet Union shot down an American U-2 aircraft that was flying reconnaissance over Soviet territory. Khrushchev demanded an apology from President Eisenhower, who accepted responsibility but refused to apologize. Khrushchev then refused to take part in the summit conference, and Eisenhower's trip to the Soviet Union was canceled.

The Soviet actions to destroy the possibility of the summit conference on the eve of its opening were not simply the result of the American spy flights. The Soviets had long been aware of the American flights but chose to protest at this time for two reasons. Khrushchev had hoped that the leaders of Britain, France, and the United States would be sufficiently divided over the future of Germany so that a united Allied front would be impossible. (The divisions did not come about as he had hoped.) Consequently, the conference would have been of little use to him. Second, by 1960 the Communist world itself had become split between the Soviets and the Chinese. The latter accused the Russians of lacking revolutionary zeal. Khrushchev's action was, in part, a response to those charges

Cuban Missile Crisis of 1962. The American ambassador to the United Nations displayed photographs to persuade the world of the threat to the United States less than one hundred miles from its own shores.
Corbis/Bettmann.

and proof of the hard-line attitude of the Soviet Union toward the capitalist world.

The abortive Paris conference opened the most difficult period of the Cold War. In 1961 the new U.S. president, John F. Kennedy (1917–1963), and Premier Khrushchev met in Vienna. The conference was inconclusive, but Kennedy left wondering if the two nations could avoid war. Throughout 1961 thousands of refugees from East Germany had fled to West Berlin. This outflow was a political and economic embarrassment to East Germany. In August 1961 the East Germans erected a concrete wall along the border between East and West Berlin. Henceforth, until November 1989, it was possible to cross only at designated checkpoints and with proper papers.

A year later the Cuban Missile Crisis brought the most dangerous days of the Cold War. The Soviet Union placed missiles in Cuba, a nation friendly to Soviet aims lying less than 100 miles from the United States. The United States blockaded Cuba, halted the shipment of new missiles, and demanded the removal of existing installations. After a tense week the Soviets backed down and the crisis ended.

DÉTENTE AND AFTERWARD

In 1963 the two powers concluded a Nuclear Test Ban Treaty. This agreement marked the start of a lessening in the sharp tensions between the United States and the Soviet Union that had commenced just after the end of World War II. In 1968 the Soviet Union invaded Czechoslovakia to block its growing independence and to overthrow the government of its rela-

CHRONOLOGY

Major Dates in the Era of the Cold War

1948	Berlin Blockade
1949	Formation of the North Atlantic Treaty Organization (NATO)
1950	Outbreak of the Korean War
1953	Death of Stalin
1956 July	Egypt seizes the Suez Canal
October	Anglo-French attack on the Suez Canal; Hungarian Revolution
1957	Treaty of Rome establishes the European Economic Community (EEC)
1960	Paris Summit Conference collapses
1961	Berlin Wall erected
1962	Cuban Missile Crisis
1963	Russian-American Test Ban Treaty
1968	Russian invasion of Czechoslovakia
1975	Helsinki Accords
1979	Russian invasion of Afghanistan
1981	Military crackdown on Solidarity Movement in Poland
1985	Reagan-Gorbachev summit
1987	Major American-Soviet Arms Limitation Treaty
1989	Berlin Wall comes down
1991	Soviet Union dissolves

tively liberal leader, Alexander Dubcek (1921–1974). Although deplored by the United States, this action led to no renewal of tensions. During the presidency of Richard Nixon (1913–1994) the United States embarked on a policy of detente, or reduction of tension, with the Soviet Union. This policy involved trade agreements and mutual reduction of strategic armaments. The Soviet invasion of Afghanistan in 1979, although not directly affecting Europe, hardened relations between Washington and Moscow, and the U.S. Senate refused to ratify the Strategic Arms Limitation Treaty of 1979.

The administration of President Ronald Reagan (1911–2004) initially slowed arms limitation negotiations and successfully deployed a major new missile system in Europe. The United States also launched a new arms proposal, known as the Strategic Arms Defense Initiative, to create a system that would use highly developed technology in space to defend against nuclear attack. The proposal was controversial at home but played a major role in arms negotiations between the United States and the Soviet Union. One of the purposes of the Reagan arms buildup was simply to outspend the Soviet Union and force it to exhaust its own financial resources and continue to starve consumer industries.

President Reagan and Soviet leader Mikhail S. Gorbachev (b. 1931) held a friendly summit meeting in 1985, the first East-West summit in six years. Other meetings followed. Arms negotiations continued until, in December 1987, the United States and the Soviet Union agreed to dismantle over 2,000 medium-

and shorter-range missiles. The treaty provided for mutual inspection. This action represented the most significant agreement since World War II between the two superpowers.

Thereafter, the political upheavals in Eastern Europe and the Soviet Union overwhelmed the issues of the Cold War. The Soviet Union abandoned its support for Communist governments in Eastern Europe. By the close of 1991 the Soviet Union itself had collapsed and been replaced by the Commonwealth of Independent States. The era of the Cold War had concluded in a manner that virtually no one had predicted.

European Society in the Second Half of the Twentieth Century and Beyond

The sharp division of Europe into a democratic West and Communist East for most of the second half of the twentieth century makes generalizations about social and economic developments difficult. Prosperity in the West contrasted with shortages in the Eastern economies, which were managed to benefit the Soviet Union. Most of the developments discussed in this chapter took place in Western Europe.

TOWARD WESTERN EUROPEAN UNIFICATION

Since 1945, the nations of Western Europe have taken unprecedented steps toward economic cooperation. The process of economic integration has not been steady, nor is it completed. The collapse of the Soviet Union and the emergence of new

Soviet Invasion of Czechoslovakia. In the summer of 1968 Soviet tanks rolled into Czechoslovakia, ending that country's experiment in liberalized communism, known as the Prague spring. This picture shows defiant, flag-waving Czechs passing a Soviet tank in the immediate aftermath of the invasion.
Hulton Archive Photos/Getty Images, Inc.

President Ronald Reagan and Premier Mikhail Gorbachev confer at a summit meeting in December 1989.
AP/Wide World Photos.

free governments in Eastern Europe have further complicated an already difficult process.

The Marshall Plan and NATO gave the involved countries new experience in working with each other and demonstrated the productivity, efficiency, and simple possibility of cooperative action. In 1950 France, West Germany, Italy, and the "Benelux" countries (Belgium, the Netherlands, and Luxembourg) organized the European Coal and Steel Community. Its success reduced the suspicions of government and business groups about the concept of coordination and economic integration.

It took more, however, to draw European leaders toward further unity. The unsuccessful Suez intervention and the resulting diplomatic isolation of France and Britain persuaded many Europeans that only through unified action could they significantly influence the two superpowers or control their own destinies. Consequently, in 1957, through the Treaty of Rome, the six members of the Coal and Steel Community agreed to form a new organization: the **European Economic Community**. The members of the Common Market, as the EEC soon came to be called, sought to achieve the eventual elimination of tariffs, a free flow of capital and labor, and similar wage and social benefits in all the participating countries. The chief institutions of the EEC were a Council of Foreign Ministers and a High Commission composed of technocrats. The former came to be the dominant body.

The Common Market was a stunning success. By 1968 all tariffs among the six members had been abolished well ahead of the planned schedule. Trade and labor migration among the members grew steadily. Moreover, nonmember states began to copy the Community and seek membership. In 1959 Britain, Denmark, Norway, Sweden, Switzerland, Austria, and Portugal formed the European Free Trade Area. However, by 1961 Great Britain had decided to seek Common Market membership. Twice—in 1963 and 1967—France vetoed British membership on the grounds that Britain was too closely tied to the United States and its policies to support the EEC wholeheartedly.

Nevertheless, the Common Market survived and continued to prosper. In 1973 Great Britain, Ireland, and Denmark became members. Discussions continued on further steps toward integration, including proposals for a common currency. Throughout the late 1970s, however, and into the 1980s momentum slowed. Norway and Sweden, with relatively strong economies, declined to join. Although in 1982 Spain, Portugal, and Greece applied for membership and were eventually admitted, there continued to be sharp disagreements and a sense of stagnation within the Community.

Finally, the leaders of the Community reached an important decision in early 1988. They targeted the year 1992 for achieving a virtual free-trade zone throughout the Community, entailing the elimination of remaining trade barriers and other restrictive trade policies. In 1991 the leaders of the Community signed the Treaty of Maastricht, which made a series of specific institutional proposals that would lead to a unified currency and a strong central bank. This treaty was submitted to referendums in a number of European states. It failed to be adopted in Denmark and only narrowly passed in France, making clear that it could not be enforced without wider popular support. When the treaty went into effect in November 1993, the European Community was renamed the **European Union (EU)**.

The troubles of the Maastricht Treaty illustrate a new phase in the process of European unity. Until recently the process of establishing greater unity has been carried out primarily by political leaders and by bureaucrats in the individual governments and the Community High Commission in Brussels. As the prospect of unity becomes imminent, however, the people of Europe have begun to raise issues about the democratic nature of the emerging political entity they are being asked to join. They are clearly in favor of some kind of close cooperation and perhaps union, but they are unwilling to see it set forth only by politicians and bureaucrats. They wish to see a wider European market, but they want that market to be genuinely free and not overregulated. Finally, the European Community, now the European Union, has recently had to deal with how it should relate to the newly independent states in Eastern Europe.

The Euro. Some thousand people stand around a huge euro symbol in a park in Frankfurt's banking district in Germany, January, 1, 1997. AP/Wide World Photos.

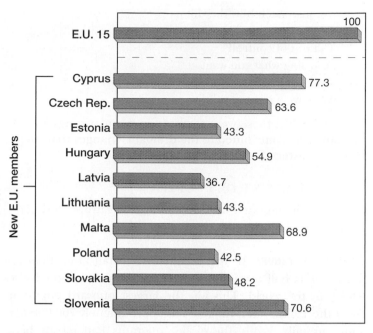

Figure 32–1 Gross National Product of Existing EU Members and New Member States, 2004. The cost of absorbing new EU members, many of which have standards of living that are far lower, will be high but the economic potential is great.

The most striking recent element of the expanding momentum of economic cooperation was the adoption of a common currency, the **euro**. Twelve nations including Austria, Belgium, Finland, France, Germany, Greece. Ireland, Italy, Luxembourg, the Netherlands, Portugal, and Spain constitute the region using this new currency. In January 1, 1999, the currencies of these nations were fixed according to the value of the euro. In January 2002 the national currencies of these nations were replaced by new coins and notes denominated in the euro. Such a widespread common currency is unprecedented in European history.

In 2004 the European Union embraced the largest expansion in its history. Ten new members entered the Union. They were Cyprus, the Czech Republic, Estonia, Hungary, Latvia, Lithuania, Malta, Poland, Slovakia, and Slovenia. On one day the Union came to include an additional seventy-five million people with nine languages This expansion will present enormous challenges because the economies in these nations, most of whom are from the former Eastern Soviet block, are much less developed (see Figure 32–1). They come to the Union in hopes that membership will foster prosperity; their needs will place new political strains on the existing structures. They will be permitted to adopt the euro only when their economies have become sufficiently strong.

Students and Popular Music

Nothing so characterized both student and youth culture in the second half of the twentieth century as rock music, which first emerged in the 1950s. Now part of the fabric of contemporary European life, rock music abounds on radio and television. The lyrics of the Beatles, the British rock group that became wildly popular on both sides of the Atlantic in the 1960s, may have become the most widely dispersed poetry in history. Rock appealed across national and cultural borders. It did as much to create a more uniform European culture as advertising or the economic freedom provided by the European Economic Community.

Rock music became part of a continuing critique of contemporary society. Many lyrics emphasized the need for love, the anguish of isolation, a desire for sexual liberation, and hopes for community and peace. During the 1960s rock music in the West was an integral feature of the antiwar movement, student rebellions that rocked both Europe and the United States, and a vehicle for expressing discontent with the older generation. In the 1970s and 1980s it emerged as a major vehicle for cultural and political criticism in Eastern Europe and the Soviet Union. Rock stars came to symbolize daring and even heroism. Their music emphasized subjectivity and individualism. Lyrics directly criticized Communist governments, as in this example from "Get Out of Control," sung at a rock concert in Leningrad in 1986:

> We were watched from the days of kindergarten.
> Some nice men and kind women
> Beat us up. They chose the most painful places
> And treated us like animals on the farm.
> So we grew up like a disciplined herd.
> We sing what they want and live how they want
> And we look at them downside up, as if we're trapped.

We just watch how they hit us
Get out of control!
Get out of control!
And sing what you want
And not just what is allowed
We have a right to yell![1]

Sentiments like these were common in popular songs and undoubtedly contributed to the dramatic changes that swept through Eastern Europe.

THE MOVEMENT OF PEOPLES

Many people migrated from, to, and within Europe during the half century following World War II.

External Migration   In the decade and a half after 1945 approximately half a million Europeans each year settled elsewhere in the world. This was the largest outward migration since the 1920s, when the rate was approximately 700,000 persons annually. While the earlier migrants had mostly been from rural areas, the later migrants often included educated city dwellers.

Decolonization in the postwar period contributed to an inward flow of European colonials from overseas (see Chapter 34). The most dramatic example of this phenomenon was the more than 1 million French colonials who moved to France after the end of the Algerian War. British citizens returned from various parts of the British Empire; Dutch came back to the Netherlands from Indonesia; and Portuguese returned from Africa.

Decolonization also provoked a migration of non-European inhabitants of the former colonies to Europe. Great Britain, for example, received thousands of immigrants from India and Pakistan, and from its former African and Caribbean colonies. France received many immigrants from its former colonies in Indochina and the Arab world. This influx caused social tension and conflict. In Great Britain, for example, during the 1980s there were angry clashes between the police and non-European immigrants. France has had similar difficulties, which have contributed to the emergence there of the National Front, an extreme right-wing group led by Jean-Marie LePen (b. 1928). This group has drawn strength from the racial and ethnic tensions that have developed as a tight job market provokes resentment among some working-class voters toward North African immigrants.

As a result of this external migration into Europe, large Islamic populations now exist in several European nations and have become political factors in France and Germany.

[1] Quoted in Artemy Troitsky, *Back in the USSR: The True Story of Rock in Russia* (Boston: Faber & Faber, 1987), p.127, as cited in Sabrina P. Rimet, *Social Currents in Eastern Europe: The Sources and Meaning of the Great Transformation* (Durham, N.C.: University Press, 1991), p. 239.

▲ **Decolonization.** A tearful Frenchman in Marseilles witnesses the storage of flags of defeated regiments after the Algerian War.
Getty Images Inc./Hulton Archive Photos.

Internal Migration   World War II and its aftermath created a vast refugee problem. Millions of people were displaced from their homes. Many cities in Germany and in central and eastern Europe had been bombed or overrun by invading armies. Hundreds of thousands of foreign workers had been moved into Germany to contribute to the war effort. There were thousands of prisoners of war. Some of these people were returned to their homeland willingly; others, unwillingly. Changes in borders after the war also caused many people to move or be moved. For example, Poland, Czechoslovakia, and Hungary sent millions of ethnic Germans to Germany. Hundreds of thousands of Poles left from territory taken over by the Soviet Union. An estimated 3 million East Germans migrated to West Germany.

Once the Cold War set in, Soviet domination made it impossible for Eastern Europeans to migrate to other parts of Europe, whether for political or economic reasons. As a result, until the collapse of the Soviet empire, most internal migration in Europe after the immediate postwar years occurred outside the Communist bloc.

The major motivation for internal migration from the late 1950s onward was economic opportunity. The prosperous nations of northern and Western Europe had jobs that paid good wages and provided excellent benefits, often financed in part by the governments. Thus, there was a flow of workers from the poorer countries of Turkey, Greece, Yugoslavia, Italy, Spain, and Portugal into the wealthier countries of France, West Germany, Switzerland, and the Benelux nations. The establishment of the European Economic Community in 1957 facilitated this movement.

The migration of workers into northern Europe snow-balled after 1960. Several hundred thousand workers entered France and Germany each year. Virtually all these migrants settled in cities. They were usually welcomed during years of prosperity and resented later when European economies began to slow in the mid-1980s. In Germany during the early 1990s, they were attacked.

In the late 1980s politics again became a major factor in European migration. The pressure of thousands of refugees seeking to escape from Eastern Europe to the West con-tributed to the collapse of the Communist governments of Eastern Europe in 1988 and 1989. Since 1989 people from all over Eastern Europe have migrated to the West. The civil war in the former Yugoslavia has also created many refugees. Europe has been in recession, however, and the new migrants are generating tension, resentment, and strife. Several nations have taken legal and administrative steps to restrict migration.

THE NEW MUSLIM POPULATION

Well into the twentieth century the European relationship with most of the Muslim world was either at arm's length or colonial-ist. Muslims from the Ottoman Empire, the greatest Muslim state, rarely traveled in Europe, and few Europeans traveled in the empire. Europeans encountered Muslims mainly as subjects, in colonies, such as Algeria, Egypt, the Indian subcontinent, sub-Saharan Africa, and the East Indies. In all of these regions from at least the mid–nineteenth century onward, Christian mission-aries often clashed with Muslim religious teachers.

At the same time most Europeans, with the exception of a few minority communities in the Balkans and the former Soviet Empire, regarded themselves and their national cul-tures as either Christian or secular. Indeed, until recently most Europeans paid little attention to Islam.

That indifference began to change in the 1960s and had dis-solved by the end of the twentieth century as a sizable Muslim population settled in Europe. This highly diverse immigrant community had become an issue in Europe even before the events of September 11, 2001, discussed later in this chapter.

The immigration of Muslims into Europe and particularly Western Europe arose from two chief sources: European eco-nomic growth and decolonization. As the economies of West-ern Europe began to recover in the quarter century after World War II, a labor shortage developed. To fill this demand, Western Europe imported laborers, many of whom came from Muslim nations. For example, Turkish "guest workers" were invited to move to West Germany—on a temporary basis, it was presumed—in the 1960s, and Britain welcomed Pakistanis. The aftermath of decolonization and the quest for a better life led Muslims from East Africa and the Indian subcontinent to settle in Great Britain. The Algerian war brought many

▲ **Violence Against Foreign Workers.** Youthful right-wing rioters clashed with police and threw firebombs in Rostock, Germany, in August 1992. Much of the violence was directed against foreign workers.
Reuters/Corbis-Bettmann

Muslims from North Africa into France. Today there are approximately 1.3 million Muslims in Great Britain, 3.2 mil-lion in Germany, and 4.2 million in France. Smaller but still significant numbers have settled in Italy, Spain, Sweden, Den-mark, and the Netherlands, nations that had previously had generally homogeneous populations.

These Muslim immigrant communities share certain social and religious characteristics. Originally, many Muslims came to Europe expecting they would eventually return to their homes, an expectation their host countries shared. Neither the immigrants nor the host nations gave much thought to assimilation. Moreover, except for Great Britain, where all immigrants from the Commonwealth may vote immediately upon settling there, European governments made it difficult for Muslim, or any other, immigrants to take part in civic life. Unlike the United States, few European countries had any experience in dealing with large-scale immigration. The vari-ous Muslim communities have therefore generally remained unassimilated and self-contained. This apartness has provided internal community support for Muslim immigrants but pre-vented them from fully engaging with the societies in which they live. Many of their children have not learned European languages well, and Muslim women tend to remain strictly confined to their homes.

But the world around these communities has changed. Many of the largely unskilled jobs that the immigrants origi-nally filled have disappeared. Most of the Muslim immigrants to Europe, unlike many who have settled in the United States and Canada, were neither highly skilled nor professionally educated. As a result, they and their adult children who may have grown up in Europe find it difficult to get jobs in the

Muslim Women Wearing Headscarves, France. The presence of foreign-born Muslims whose labor is necessary for the prosperity of the European economy is a major issue in contemporary Europe. Many of these Muslims, such as these women, live in self-contained communities.

Figaro Magazine/Torregano/Getty Images, Inc.

modern service economy. Furthermore, as European economic growth has slowed, European Muslims have become the target of politicians, such as Le Pen in France, who seek to blame the immigrants for a host of problems from crime to unemployment.

The radicalization of parts of the Islamic world has also touched the Muslim communities in Europe. Although Turkish Muslims living in Germany come from a nation that has been secularized since the 1920s and thus tend to be less religiously observant than Pakistani Muslims dwelling in Great Britain, Muslims from both countries have been involved in radical Islamic groups, and some belonged to organizations involved in the September 11, 2001, attack on the United States. By contrast, the French government has exerted more control over its Muslim community.

Nonetheless, European Muslims are not a homogeneous group. They come from different countries, have different class backgrounds, and espouse different Islamic traditions. Many European Muslims and Muslim clerics disagree strongly with each other. Some emphasize a more traditional message; others preach a more radical one that is highly critical of the West. At the same time, these Muslim communities so often now marked by deep poverty and unemployment have become a major concern for European social workers who disagree among themselves about how their governments should respond to them.

NEW PATTERNS IN THE WORK AND EXPECTATIONS OF WOMEN

In the decades since World War II the work patterns and social expectations of women have changed markedly. In all social ranks women have begun to assume larger economic and political roles. Women have entered the learned professions and are filling more major managerial positions than ever before in European history. (See Document, "Simone de Beauvoir Urges Economic Freedom for Women.")

FEMINISM

Certain more or less traditional patterns continue to describe the position of women in both family and economic life. Despite enormous gains during the second half of the twentieth century, and despite the collapse of those authoritarian governments whose social policies inhibited the advancement of women into the mainstream of society, gender inequality remained a major characteristic of the social life of Europe at the opening of the twenty-first century.

Since World War II, European feminism, although less highly organized than American feminism, has set forth a new agenda. The most widely read postwar work on women's issues was undoubtedly Simone de Beauvoir's (1908–1986) *The Second Sex*, published in 1949. In that work, de Beauvoir explored the difference being a woman rather than a man had made in her life. She was part of the French intellectual establishment and thus wrote from a privileged position. Over the years, however, she and other European feminists argued that at all levels, European women experienced distinct social and economic disadvantages. In the courts, for example, divorce and family laws favored men. European feminists also called attention to the social problems that women faced, including spousal abuse.

More Married Women in the Workforce The number of married women in the workforce has risen sharply. Both middle-class and working-class married women have sought jobs outside the home. Because of the rather low birthrate in the 1930s, there were few young single women to be employed just after the war. Married women entered the job market to replace them. Some factories changed their work shifts to accommodate the needs of married women. Consumer conveniences and improvements in health care also made it easier for married women to enter the work force by reducing the demands of child care on their time.

In the twentieth century children were no longer expected to make substantial contributions to family income. They spent much of their time in compulsory schools. When families need more income than one worker can provide, both parents work. Even without financial necessity, both parents are now likely to work when both are motivated to pursue careers.

Simone de Beauvoir Urges Economic Freedom for Women

Simone de Beauvoir was the single most important feminist voice of mid–twentieth-century Europe. In The Second Sex, *published in France in 1949, she explored the experience of women coming of age in a world of ideas, institutions, and social expectations shaped historically by men. Much of the book discusses the psychological strategies that modern European women had developed to deal with their status as "the second sex." Toward the end of her book, de Beauvoir argues strongly that economic freedom and advancement for women are fundamental to their personal fulfillment.*

♦ Why does de Beauvoir argue that the achievement of civic rights must be accompanied by economic freedom for women? Why does the example of the small number of professional women illustrate issues for European women in general? How does she indicate that even professional women must overcome a culture in which the experience of women is fundamentally different from that of men? Do de Beauvoir's comments seem relevant for women at the opening of the twenty-first century? What similarities do you see with the views of Priscilla Wakefield (Chapter 20 and Mary Wollstonecraft (Chapter 22)?

According to French law, obedience is no longer included among the duties of a wife, and each woman citizen has the right to vote; but these civil liberties remain theoretical as long as they are unaccompanied by economic freedom. ... It is through gainful employment that woman has traversed most of the distance that separated her from the male; and nothing else can guarantee her liberty in practice. Once she ceases to be a parasite, the system based on her dependence crumbles; between her and the universe there is no longer any need for a masculine mediator. ...

When she is productive, active, she regains her transcendence; in her projects she concretely affirms her status as subject; in connection with the aims she pursues, with the money and the rights she takes possession of, she makes trial of and senses her responsibility. ...

There are ... a fairly large number of privileged women who find in their professions a means of economic and social autonomy. These come to mind when one considers woman's possibilities and her future ... [E]ven though they constitute as yet only a minority; they continue to be the subject of debate between feminists and antifeminists. The latter assert that the emancipated women of today succeed in doing nothing of importance in the world and that furthermore they have difficulty in achieving their own inner equilibrium. The former exaggerate the results obtained by professional women and are blind to their inner confusion. There is no good reason ... to say they are on the wrong road; and still it is certain that they are not tranquilly installed in their new realm: as yet they are only halfway there. The woman who is economically emancipated from man is not for all that in a moral, social, and psychological situation identical with that of man. The way she carried on her profession and her devotion to it depends on the context supplied by the total pattern of her life. For when she begins her adult life she does not have behind her the same past as does a boy; she is not viewed by society in the same way; the universe presents itself to her in a different perspective. The fact of being a woman today poses peculiar problems for an independent human individual.

New Work Patterns   In the late twentieth century the work pattern of European women displayed much more continuity than it did in the nineteenth century. Single women entered the workforce after their schooling and continued to work after marriage. They might withdraw from the workforce to care for young children but return when the children begin school. Several factors created this new pattern, but women's increasing life expectancy is one of the most important.

When married women died relatively young, child rearing filled much of their lives. The lengthening life-span has meant that child rearing occupies much less of women's lives. Consequently, women throughout the Western world have new concerns about how they will spend those years when they are not involved with rearing children. The age at which women have

decided to bear children has risen. Women have tended to bear children in their early twenties in Eastern Europe and in their late twenties in Western Europe. In urban areas, childbearing occurs later and the birthrate is lower than elsewhere.

Many women have begun to limit sharply the number of children they bear or to forgo childbearing and child rearing altogether. Both men and women continue to expect to marry, but the new careers open to women and the desire of couples to maintain as high a standard of living as possible have contributed to a declining birthrate.

Women in the New Eastern Europe   Many paradoxes surround the situation of women in Eastern Europe now that it is no longer governed by Communists. Under communism women

Simone de Beauvoir, here with her companion the philosopher, Jean Paul Sartre, was the major femminist writer in post-war Europe.

Getty Images Inc./Hulton Archive Photos.

generally enjoyed social equality as well as a broad spectrum of government-financed benefits. A significant proportion (normally well over 50 percent) of women worked in these societies both because they could and because it was expected of them. There were, however, no significant women's movements since they, like all independent associations, were frowned on.

The new governments of the region are free but have so far shown little concern toward women's issues. The economic difficulties the new governments face may endanger the funding of various health and welfare programs that benefit women and children. For example, a free market economy may not allow Eastern European women the extensive maternity benefits they used to enjoy. Moreover, the high proportion of women in the workforce could leave them more vulnerable than men to the region's economic troubles. Women may well find themselves being laid off before men and hired for new jobs later than men.

American Domestic Scene Since World War II

Three major themes have characterized the postwar American experience—an opposition to the spread of communism, an expansion of civil rights to blacks and other minorities at home, and a determination to achieve ongoing economic growth. Virtually all of the major postwar political debates and social divisions have arisen from these issues.

TRUMAN AND EISENHOWER ADMINISTRATIONS

The foreign policy of President Harry Truman was directed against Communist expansion in Europe and East Asia. He enunciated the Truman Doctrine in regard to Greece and Turkey and initiated the Marshall Plan for European reconstruction. As will be discussed more fully in the next chapter, he led the United States to support the UN intervention against aggression in Korea. Domestically, the Truman administration pursued what may be regarded as a continuation of the New Deal. However, Truman encountered considerable opposition from conservative Republicans. The major achievement of those Republicans was the passage in 1947 of the Taft-Hartley Act, which limited labor union activity. Truman won the 1948 election against great odds. Through policies he termed the Fair Deal, he sought to extend economic security.

Those efforts, however, were frustrated as fear of a domestic Communist menace swept much of the country. Senator Joseph McCarthy (1909–1957) of Wisconsin led the campaign against the perceived Communist danger within the ranks of American citizens and government agencies. The patriotism and loyalty of scores of prominent Americans were challenged. That development, a frustration with the war in Korea, and perhaps the natural weariness of the electorate after twenty years of Democratic Party government led to the election of war hero Dwight Eisenhower in 1952.

In retrospect, the Eisenhower years now seem a period of calm after the war years of the 1940s and before the turmoil of the 1960s. Eisenhower, personally popular, ended the Korean War. The country was generally prosperous. Home building increased dramatically, and the vast interstate highway system was initiated. The president was less activist than either Roosevelt or Truman had been.

Beneath the apparent quiet of the Eisenhower years, however, stirred several forces that would lead to the disruptions of the 1960s. One of them flowed from the injustices of segregation and racial inequality. Another flowed from the long-term implications of some of the major foreign policy commitments the Eisenhower administration made in its effort to oppose the advance of communism. One of those commitments led to American involvement in Vietnam; indeed, that involvement began under Eisenhower.

CIVIL RIGHTS

In 1954 the United States Supreme Court, in the decision of *Brown* v. *Board of Education of Topeka*, declared unconstitutional the segregation of the black and white races. Shortly thereafter the Court ordered the desegregation of schools. For the next ten years the struggle over school integration and civil rights for black Americans stirred the nation. Southern states attempted to resist school desegregation. In 1957 Eisenhower sent troops into Little Rock, Arkansas, to integrate the schools, but resistance continued in other Southern states.

While the battle raged over the schools, American blacks began to protest segregation in other areas. In 1955 the Reverend Martin Luther King Jr. (1929–1968) organized a boycott in Montgomery, Alabama, against segregated buses. The Montgomery bus boycott marked the beginning of the use of civil disobedience to fight racial discrimination in the United States. Drawing on the ideas of Henry David Thoreau (1817–1862) and the experience of Mohandas Gandhi (1869–1948) in India, the leaders of the civil rights movement went to jail rather than obey laws they considered unjust. The civil rights struggle continued well into the 1960s. One of its most dramatic moments was the 1963 march on Washington by tens of thousands of supporters of civil rights legislation. The greatest achievements of the movement were the Civil Rights Act of 1964, which desegregated public accommodations, and the Voting Rights Act of 1965, which cleared the way for black Americans to vote. This legislation as well as ongoing protests against housing and job discrimination brought black citizens nearer to the mainstream of American life than they had ever been.

However, much yet remained undone. In 1967 major race riots occurred in several American cities, resulting in signifi-

▲ **Martin Luther King Jr.**, pictured here with his wife Coretta, was the most prominent civil rights leader in the United States. Here he leads a protest march in 1965.
Battmann–Corbis.

cant loss of life. Those riots, followed by the assassination of Martin Luther King Jr., in 1968, weakened the civil rights movement. Despite new efforts to fight discrimination, the movement lacked a major national leader. Not until the late 1980s did a new leader emerge in the person of the Reverend Jesse Jackson (b. 1941), who raised new issues of racial equality and promoted drives that led to the registration of many black voters. There was, however, little follow-up to this campaign.

Race relations continue to plague the social life of the United States. Although black Americans have more access to education and public office, especially in urban areas, they lag behind other Americans economically and in their prospects for good health. Furthermore, as other groups, particularly Latino Americans, began to enter the political process in the 1980s and raise issues on behalf of their own communities, racial relations became more complicated. In 1992 one of the most destructive riots in American history—triggered by a court decision relating to the treatment of black Americans by the police—devastated parts of Los Angeles. The presidential campaigns of 1992 and 1996 were conspicuous for the absence of discussion of minority issues.

NEW SOCIAL PROGRAMS

The advance of the civil rights movement in the late 1950s and early 1960s represented the cutting edge of a new advance of political liberalism. In 1960 John F. Kennedy narrowly won the presidential election. He saw himself as attempting to set the country moving again after the years of Eisenhower torpor. Kennedy defined his aims as seeking to move toward a New Frontier. One goal was to put a man on the moon. He also attempted unsuccessfully to expand medical care under the social security program. In the civil rights movement, however, he basically reacted rather than led.

Nevertheless, the reaction to Kennedy's assassination in 1963 provided the occasion for his successor, Lyndon Johnson (1908–1973), to press for activist legislation. Johnson set forth a bold domestic program known as the War on Poverty, which established major federal programs to create jobs and provide job training. Furthermore, new entitlements were added to the social security program, including Medicare, which provides medical services for the elderly and disabled. Johnson's drive for what he termed the Great Society brought to a close the era of major federal initiatives that had begun under Franklin Roosevelt. The liberal impulse remained alive in American politics, but by the late 1960s the electorate had begun to become much more conservative.

THE VIETNAM WAR AND DOMESTIC TURMOIL

Johnson's activist domestic vision quickly was overshadowed by the U.S. involvement in Vietnam (to be considered more fully in the next chapter). By 1965 Johnson had decided to

Kent State Protest. The clash between protesting students and the Ohio National Guard at Kent State University was the most violent moment in the protests against the U.S. involvement in Vietnam. AP/Wide World Photos.

send tens of thousands of Americans to Vietnam. This policy led to the longest of American wars. At home, the war and particularly the draft provoked vast public protests. Most young American men who were drafted went into the armed forces, but significant numbers, especially college and university students, resisted. Large-scale protests involving civil disobedience, often patterned after those of the civil rights movement, erupted on campuses throughout the country. In some cases units of the National Guard were sent to restore calm. At Kent State University in Ohio in 1970 the National Guard killed four protestors. In all these respects, the Vietnam War divided the nation as had no conflict since the Civil War.

The national unrest led Lyndon Johnson to decide not to seek reelection in 1968. Richard Nixon led the Republicans to victory. His election marked the beginning of an era of American politics dominated by conservative policies. Nixon campaigned on a platform of law and order. He also stressed his former experience in foreign policy as vice president (under Eisenhower). Perhaps the most important act of his administration was his reestablishment of diplomatic relations with the People's Republic of China. Initially, Nixon's policies toward Vietnam were no more successful than those of Johnson. Half of the casualties in the war occurred under his administration. Nonetheless, he concluded the war in 1972. That same year he was reelected, but soon thereafter the Watergate scandal began to erode his administration.

THE WATERGATE SCANDAL

On the surface, the Watergate scandal involved only the burglary of the Democratic Party national headquarters by White House operatives in 1972. The deeper issues related to questions of the extent of presidential authority and the right of the government to intrude into the personal lives of citizens. In 1973 Congress established a committee to investigate the scandal. Testimony before that committee revealed that President Nixon had recorded conversations in the White House. The Special Prosecutor, who had been appointed to investigate the charges, finally gained access to the tapes in the summer of 1974 through a decision of the Supreme Court. In the meantime the Judiciary Committee of the House of Representatives voted three articles of impeachment against Nixon. Shortly thereafter, certain of the newly released tapes revealed that Nixon had ordered federal agencies to try to cover up White House participation in the burglary. After this revelation, Nixon became the only American president to resign.

The Watergate scandal further shook public confidence in the government. It was also a distraction from the major problems facing the country, especially inflation, which had resulted from fighting the war in Vietnam while expanding federal domestic expenditures. The subsequent administrations of Gerald Ford (1974–1977, b. 1913) and Jimmy Carter (1977–1981, b. 1924) battled inflation and high interest rates without significant success. Furthermore, the Carter administration became bogged down in the Iran hostage crisis of 1980 after Iranians took more than forty Americans hostage and held them for over a year.

THE TRIUMPH OF POLITICAL CONSERVATISM

In 1980 Ronald Reagan was elected president by a large majority and reelected four years later. Reagan was the first fully ideological conservative to be elected in the postwar era. Reagan sought to reduce the role of the federal government in American life. The chief vehicle to this end was a major tax cut and reform of the taxation system. The consequence of America's vastly increased defense spending and the tax policy was the largest fiscal deficit in American history. However, inflation was controlled, and the American economy experienced its longest peacetime expansion.

The straightforward conservatism of the Reagan administration proved offensive to many Americans who had traditionally supported a liberal political and social agenda. His policies were regarded as hostile to blacks and women. High officials were involved in scandals, particularly the sale of arms to Iran in exchange for the promised release of American hostages in Lebanon. Despite these difficulties, Reagan left office as probably the most popular and successful of the post–World War II American presidents.

In 1988 Vice President (under Reagan) George Bush (b. 1924) was elected to succeed Reagan. He was immediately confronted by the major changes that Gorbachev was carrying out in the Soviet Union and the extraordinary transformations occurring in Eastern Europe that are discussed later in this chapter. Bush kept the NATO alliance strong and close to the United States at a time when observers had begun to question its utility. In 1989 he sent troops into Panama to oust its dictator, Manuel Noriega (b. 1940). In the summer of 1990, in response to the invasion of Kuwait by Iraq, he initiated the largest mobilization of American troops since the Vietnam War. Using the United Nations, he forged a broad worldwide coalition against Iraq's aggression. In early 1991 the coalition launched Operation Desert Storm and forced Iraq out of Kuwait.

The victory in the Persian Gulf War was the high point of the Bush presidency. Thereafter, he stumbled in the face of the serious economic problems confronting the nation. In 1992 the Democratic nominee, Governor William Clinton (b. 1946) of Arkansas, won the election.

The Clinton presidency encountered difficulties almost from the beginning. During his first two years in office he tried to bring about a dramatic change in health care finance and delivery. This effort ultimately failed and left the Clinton presidency with a reputation for being poorly managed.

In 1994, in one of the most far-reaching changes in recent American politics, the Republican Party won majorities in both houses of Congress. The new Republican-controlled Congress undertook major changes in the funding of welfare, taxation, and government regulation. This Congress continued the conservative redirection of federal policy that had begun with the election of Ronald Reagan.

The presidential election of 1996 saw the reelection of President Clinton and of a Republican-dominated Congress and Senate. Scandals plagued both parties. The House of Representatives censured and fined Newt Gingrich, the Speaker of the House. A personal sexual scandal and allegations of perjury plagued President Clinton during 1998, although the Republicans lost seats in the House of Representatives in that year's election. In the wake of the election loss, Gingrich resigned from the House, and President Clinton was impeached. He was acquitted in early 1999 by the Senate. In terms of policy, Clinton was seen as moving the Democractic Party into a more conservative stance.

The presidential election of 2000 between Texas governor George W. Bush (the son of the former president) and Vice President Al Gore was the closest in modern American history. Gore won a majority of the popular vote but failed to win a majority in the electoral college. The pivotal electoral votes depended on which candidate carried Florida, where the final vote count was disputed for more than a month after the November election. After complicated legal disputes over how, or indeed whether, to recount the Florida vote, the U.S. Supreme Court voted 5 to 4 to halt the recount, which resulted in Bush being declared the winner in Florida and thus in the presidential election as well.

On September 11, 2001, a surprise terrorist attack on New York City and Washington, D.C., transformed the political life of the United States. As the nation rallied to respond, a period of remarkable bipartisan cooperation followed. In October 2001, the United States began a war against terrorism with air attacks against terrorist positions in Afghanistan. U.S. forces also attacked the forces of the extremist Islamic Taliban regime in Afghanistan, which had tolerated the presence of Islamic terrorists within the part of Afghanistan that was under its control. In 2003 as a second step in the response to the terrorist threat the United States invaded Iraq, an event fully discussed in the last section of this chapter and in Chapter 34.

In 2004 President Bush successfully overcame the challenge of Democratic candidate John Kerry to achieve re-election with a majority of both the popular and electoral college vote. His re-election would appear to provide a strong base for his attempting to secure his conservative legislative agenda while continuing the existing directions of his foreign policy.

The Soviet Union to 1989

The major themes of Soviet history after 1945 were the rivalry with the United States for world leadership, the rivalry with China for the leadership of Communist nations, the effort to sustain Soviet domination of Eastern Europe, and a series of unsuccessful attempts to reform the Stalinist state, which ended in 1991 with the collapse of the Soviet Union.

The Soviet Union emerged from World War II as a major world power, but Stalin did little or nothing to modify the repressive regime he had fostered. The police remained ever present. The cult of personality around Stalin expanded, and the central bureaucracy continued to grow. Heavy industry was still favored in place of production for consumers. Agriculture continued to be troubled. Stalin's personal authority over the party and the nation remained unchallenged. In foreign policy he solidified Soviet control over Eastern Europe for the purposes of both Communist expansion and Soviet national security. The Soviet army assured subservience to the goals of the Soviet Union. Such continued to be the situation until Stalin died on March 6, 1953.

THE KHRUSHCHEV YEARS

No single leader immediately replaced Stalin, but by 1956 Nikita Khrushchev became premier, remaining in that position until 1964. He never enjoyed the extraordinary powers of Stalin.

In 1956, at the Twentieth Congress of the Communist Party, Khrushchev made a secret speech (later published outside the

Soviet Union) in which he denounced Stalin and his crimes against Socialist justice during the purges of the 1930s. (See Document, "Khrushchev Denounces the Crimes of Stalin: The Secret Speech.") The speech caused shock and consternation in party circles and opened the way for limited, but genuine, internal criticism of the Soviet government. By 1958 all of Stalin's former supporters were gone, but none had been executed.

Under Khrushchev, intellectuals were somewhat freer to express their opinions. This so-called thaw in the cultural life of the country was closely related to the premier's interest in the opinions of experts on problems of industry and agriculture. He often went outside the usual bureaucratic channels in search of information and new ideas. Novels such as Aleksandr Solzhenitsyn's (b. 1918) *One Day in the Life of Ivan Denisovich* (1963) could be published. However, Boris Pasternak (1890–1960), the author of *Dr. Zhivago*, was not permitted to accept the Nobel Prize for literature in 1958. The intellectual liberalization of Soviet life during this period looked favorable largely in comparison with what had preceded it and continued to seem so later when freedom of expression declined again in the two decades after Khrushchev's fall.

In economic policy Khrushchev made moderate efforts to decentralize economic planning and execution. During the late 1950s he often boasted that Soviet production of consumer goods would overtake that of the West. Steel, oil, and electric power production continued to grow, but the consumer sector including housing improved only marginally. The ever-growing defense budget and the space program that successfully launched the first human-engineered earth satellite, *Sputnik*, in 1957 made major demands on the nation's productive resources.

▲ **The Kitchen Debate.** One of the most famous incidents of the Cold War was a spontaneous debate between Nikita Khrushchev and Vice President Richard Nixon at a trade fair in Moscow. Because it took place at a display of kitchen appliances, it was sometimes called the Kitchen Debate.
Elliott Erwitt/Magnum Photos, Inc.

Khrushchev strongly redirected Stalin's agricultural policy. He recognized that despite the collectivization of the 1930s the Soviet Union could not feed its own people. Khrushchev removed many of the most restrictive regulations on private cultivation. The machine-tractor stations were abandoned. Existing collective farms were further amalgamated. The government undertook an extensive "virgin lands" program to extend wheat cultivation by hundreds of thousands of acres. This policy initially increased grain production to new records. The applied farming techniques, however, proved inappropriate for the soil, and the new lands soon underwent severe erosion. The agricultural problem continued to grow over the decades. By the 1970s the Soviet Union imported vast quantities of grain from the United States and other countries. United States grain imports constituted a major facet of the policy of detente.

By 1964 high Communist Party leaders and many people lower in the party had concluded that Khrushchev had tried to do too much too soon and had done it too poorly. His foreign policy, culminating in the back-down over the Cuban Missile Crisis, appeared a failure. On October 16, 1964, after defeat in the Central Committee of the Communist Party, Khrushchev resigned. Leonid Brezhnev (1906–1982) eventually emerged as his successor.

BREZHNEV

Domestically the Soviet government became markedly more repressive after 1964. Intellectuals enjoyed less and less freedom and had little direct access to the government leadership. In 1974 the government expelled Solzhenitsyn. Jewish citizens of the Soviet Union were harassed. Bureaucratic obstacles impeded emigration to Israel.

The internal repression gave rise to a dissident movement. Certain Soviet citizens dared to criticize the regime in public and to carry out small demonstrations against it. They accused the Soviet government of violating the human rights provisions of the 1975 Helsinki Accords. The dissidents included prominent citizens, such as the Nobel Prize–winning physicist Andrei Sakharov (1921–1989). The Soviet government responded with further repression.

In foreign policy the Brezhnev years witnessed attempts both to reach accommodation with the United States and to continue to expand Soviet influence and maintain Soviet leadership of the Communist movement. Nonetheless, growing Soviet spending on defense, and particularly on naval expansion, put ongoing pressures on the consumer side of the economy.

In December 1979 the Soviet Union invaded Afghanistan. A Soviet presence had already existed in that country, but for reasons that still remain unclear, the Soviet government felt required to send in troops to ensure its influence in Central Asia. The Afghanistan invasion, in addition to exacerbating tensions with the United States, tied the hands of the Soviet government in its own sphere of influence in Eastern Europe. There seems

DOCUMENT | Khrushchev Denounces the Crimes of Stalin: The Secret Speech

In 1956 Khrushchev denounced Stalin in a secret speech to the Party Congress. The New York Times published a text of that speech smuggled from Russia.

◆ What are the specific actions on the part of Stalin that Khrushchev denounced? Why does Khrushchev pay so much attention to Stalin's creation of the concept of an "enemy of the people"? Why does Khrushchev draw a distinction between the actions of Stalin and those of Lenin?

Stalin acted not through persuasion, explanation, and patient cooperation with people, but by imposing his concepts and demanding absolute submission to his opinion. Whoever opposed this concept or tried to prove his viewpoint and the correctness of his position was doomed to removal from the leading collective [group] and to subsequent moral and physical annihilation. ...

Stalin originated the concept of "enemy of the people." This term automatically rendered it unnecessary that the ideological errors of a man or men engaged in a controversy be proved; this term made possible the usage of the most cruel repression violating all norms of revolutionary legality, against anyone who in any way disagreed with Stalin, against those who were only suspected of hostile intent, against those who had bad reputations.

This concept "enemy of the people" actually eliminated the possibility of any kind of ideological fight or the making of one's views known on this or that issue, even those of a practical character. In the main, and in actuality, the only proof of guilt used, against all norms of current legal science, was the "confession" of the accused himself; and, as a subsequent probing proved, "confessions" were acquired through physical pressures against the accused. ...

Lenin used severe methods only in the most necessary cases, when the exploiting classes were still in existence and were vigorously opposing the revolution, when the struggle for survival was decidedly assuming the sharpest forms, even including civil war.

Stalin, on the other hand, used extreme methods and mass repressions at a time when the revolution was already victorious, when the Soviet State was strengthened, when the exploiting classes were already liquidated and Socialist relations were rooted solidly in all phases of national economy, when our party was politically consolidated and had strengthened itself both numerically and ideologically. It is clear that here Stalin showed in a whole series of cases his intolerance, his brutality and his abuse of power. Instead of proving his political correctness and mobilizing the masses, he often chose the path of repression and physical annihilation, not only against actual enemies, but also against individuals who had not committed any crimes against the party and the Soviet Government. ...

From The New York Times, *5 June 1956, pp. 13–16.*

---

little doubt that the Soviet hesitation to react more strongly to events in Poland during the 1980s, which are discussed in the next section, stemmed in part from having committed military resources to Afghanistan and from the broad condemnation the invasion provoked from some Western European Communist Parties and from the governments of nations not aligned with the West. The Soviet government also clearly lost internal support as its army became bogged down and suffered steady losses.

COMMUNISM AND SOLIDARITY IN POLAND

In early July 1980 the Polish government raised meat prices. The result was hundreds of protest strikes across the country. On August 14 workers occupied the Lenin shipyard at Gdansk. The strike soon spread to other shipyards, transport facilities, and factories connected with the shipbuilding industry. The most important leader to emerge from among the strikers was Lech Walesa (b. 1944). The strike leaders refused to negotiate with the government through any of the government-controlled unions. The Gdansk strike ended on August 31 after the government promised the workers the right to organize an independent union. Less than a week later the Polish Communist head of state was replaced; later that year the Polish courts recognized Solidarity as an independent union, and the state-controlled radio—for the first time in thirty years—broadcast a Roman Catholic Mass.

In the summer of 1981, for the first time in any European Communist state, secret elections for the Polish party congress permitted real choices among the candidates. Poland remained a nation governed by a single party, but real debate was temporarily permitted within the party congress. This extraordinary Polish experiment came to a rapid close in late 1981. General Wojciech Jaruzelski (b. 1923) became head of the party, and the army moved into the center of Polish events. In December 1981 martial law was declared. The government arrested several Solidarity leaders. Martial law would continue until late in the 1980s.

By the time of Brezhnev's death in 1982, the entire Soviet system had grown rigid and seemed hardly capable of meeting the needs of its people or pursuing a successful foreign policy. Until

Mujahidin, or Muslim guerrilla warriors, with a captured Soviet armored vehicle in January 1980 near Afghanistan's border with Pakistan. The Soviet invasion of Afghanistan in 1979 met with fierce resistance and sparked a sharp response from the United States, which halted sales of wheat to the Soviet Union and boycotted the Olympic Games held in Moscow in 1980.
C. Spengler/Sygma

the middle of the 1980s, however, no observers expected rapid change in the Soviet Union or its satellites. The nations of Eastern Europe were expected to continue with one-party governments, their aspirations for self-determination smothered, and only limited possibilities for independent political action. What had lasted forty years, it was assumed, would endure into the future. No one anticipated the vast changes that were imminent.

GORBACHEV ATTEMPTS TO REDIRECT THE SOVIET UNION

Both of Brezhnev's immediate successors, Yuri Andropov (1914–1984) and Constantin Chernenko (1911–1985), died after holding office for short periods. In 1985 Mikhail S. Gorbachev (b. 1931) came to power. In what proved to be the last great attempt to reform the Soviet system and eliminate its repressive Stalinist heritage, he immediately set about making the most remarkable changes that the Soviet Union had witnessed since the 1920s. His

reforms unloosed forces that within seven years would force him to retire and end both Communist rule and the Soviet Union as it had existed since the Bolshevik Revolution of 1917.

Initially, Gorbachev and his supporters challenged the way the party and bureaucracy had traditionally managed the Soviet government and economy. Under the policy of *perestroika*, or restructuring, they proposed major economic and political reforms. The centralized economic ministries were reduced in size. A larger role was allowed for private enterprise on the local level. By early 1990, in a clear abandonment of traditional Marxist ideology, Gorbachev had begun to advocate private ownership of property. He and his advisors considered policies to liberalize the economy and move it rapidly toward a free market. Despite these organizational changes the Soviet economy, instead of growing, stagnated and even declined. Shortages of food, consumer goods, and housing became chronic. In a pattern that has continued to characterize Russian political life, old-fashioned Communists blamed these results on the abandonment of centralized planning. Democratic critics blamed overly slow reform and urged a more rapid move to a free market economy.

Gorbachev also allowed, within the Soviet context, an extraordinarily broad public discussion and criticism of Soviet history and Soviet Communist Party policy. This development was termed *glasnost*, or openness. Certain Communist figures from the 1920s, such as Bukharin (1888–1938), who had been executed by Stalin, once again received official public recognition for their positive contributions to Soviet history. Within factories, workers were permitted to criticize party officials and the economic plans of the party and the government. Censorship was relaxed and free expression encouraged. Dissidents were released from prison. In the summer of 1988 Gorbachev presided over a party congress that witnessed full debates. In 1988 a new constitution permitted openly contested elections. After real political campaigning, a novel experience for the Soviet Union, the Congress of People's Deputies was elected in 1989 and then formally elected Gorbachev as president.

The Soviet Union was a vast empire of diverse peoples and nationalities. Some of those groups had been conquered under the tsars; others, such as the Baltic states, had been incorporated into the Soviet Union under Stalin. Glasnost quickly brought to the fore the discontents of all such peoples, no matter how or when they had been incorporated into the Soviet state. Gorbachev proved particularly inept in addressing these ethnic complaints.

1989: Year of Revolutions in Eastern Europe

In 1989 Soviet domination and Communist rule in Eastern Europe came to an abrupt end. None of these revolutions could have taken place without the refusal of the Soviet Union to intervene militarily as it had done in 1956 and 1968. For the first time since the end of World War II the peoples of Eastern Europe could shape their own political destiny without the almost certain military intervention of the Soviet Union. Once they realized the Soviets would stand back, thousands of ordinary citizens denounced Communist Party domination and asserted their desire for democracy.

The generally peaceful character of most of these revolutions was not inevitable. It may, in part, have resulted from the shock with which much of the world responded to the violent repression of prodemocracy protesters in Beijing's Tienanmen Square by the People's Republic of China in the late spring of 1989. The Communist Party officials of Eastern Europe and the Soviet Union clearly decided at some point in 1989 that they could not offend world opinion with a similar attack on democratic demonstrators.

SOLIDARITY REEMERGES IN POLAND

During the mid-1980s, Poland's government relaxed martial law. By 1984 several leaders of Solidarity had been released from prison and began again to work for free trade unions and democratic government. An active underground press and several new dissenting political organizations emerged. Poland's economy continued to deteriorate, demonstrating the inability of Communist governments to deliver economic growth and prosperity.

During 1987 the government released the last of its Solidarity prisoners in a sweeping amnesty. In 1988 new strikes occurred that even the leaders of Solidarity had not anticipated. This time the Communist government failed to reimpose control. Solidarity was legalized.

Jaruzelski, with the tacit consent of the Soviet Union, repealed martial law and promised free elections to a parliament with increased powers. When elections were held in 1989, the Communists lost overwhelmingly to Solidarity candidates. Late in the summer Jaruzelski, unable to find a Communist who could forge a majority coalition in parliament, turned to Solidarity. On August 24, 1989, after negotiating with Lech Walesa, Jaruzelski named Tadeusz Mazowiecki (b. 1927) the first non-Communist prime minister of Poland since 1945. The appointment was made with the express approval of Gorbachev.

HUNGARY MOVES TOWARD INDEPENDENCE

Hungary had for some time shown the greatest national economic independence of the Soviet Union in Eastern Europe. The Hungarian government had emphasized the production of food and consumer goods. It had also permitted a small stock exchange. In early 1989, as events unfolded in Poland, the Hungarian Communist government began to take other independent actions. In January its parliament permitted independent political parties. Soon thereafter the government permitted free travel

between Hungary and Austria, opening the first breach in the Iron Curtain. Thousands of East Germans then moved into Austria through Hungary. From Austria they went to West Germany.

In May 1989 Premier Janos Kadar (1912–1989), who had been installed after the Soviet intervention in 1956, was voted from office by the parliament. Thousands of people gave an honorary burial to the body of Imre Nagy, who had been executed in 1958. The Hungarian Communist Party changed its name to the Socialist Party and permitted the emergence of other opposition political parties. In October, Hungary promised free elections. By 1990 a coalition of Democratic parties controlled the Parliament and governed the country.

THE BREACH OF THE BERLIN WALL AND GERMAN REUNIFICATION

In the autumn of 1989 popular demonstrations erupted in many East German cities. The most important occurred in Leipzig. The streets filled with people demanding democracy and an end to Communist Party rule.

Gorbachev told the leaders of the East German Communist Party that the Soviet Union would no longer support them. With startling swiftness, the Communist leaders of the East German government resigned, making way for a younger generation of Communist Party leaders. These new leaders, who remained in office for just weeks, promised political and economic reform. They convinced few East Germans, however, and the emigration to the West continued. In November 1989, in one of the most emotional moments in European history since 1945, the government of East Germany ordered the opening of the Berlin Wall. Tens of thousands of East Berliners crossed into West Berlin to

▲ **The Fall of the Berlin Wall.** The most dramatic moment in the weeks of the collapse of communist regimes in eastern Europe occurred in November 1989 when crowds destroyed the Berlin Wall, the most prominent symbol of the Cold War divisions in Europe.
A.Avarkian/Time Life Pictures/Getty Images, Inc.

celebrate, to visit families, and to shop with money provided by the West German government. Shortly thereafter, free travel began between East and West Germany. By early 1990 the Communist government of East Germany, after failing to reorganize itself, had been swept away in free elections.

The revolution in East Germany had broad ramifications for international relations. The citizens of the two Germanies were determined to reunify. With the collapse of Communist Party government in East Germany, there was no longer a viable distinction between them. Late in 1989 the ministers of the European Economic Community accepted in principle the unification of Germany. By February 1990 reunification had become a foregone conclusion, accepted by the United States, the Soviet Union, Great Britain, and France.

THE VELVET REVOLUTION IN CZECHOSLOVAKIA

Late in 1989, in "the velvet revolution," Communist rule in Czechoslovakia quickly unraveled. In November, under popular pressure from street demonstrations and well-organized political opposition, the Communist Party began to retreat from office. The patterns were similar to those occurring elsewhere. The old leadership resigned, and younger Communists replaced them. The changes they offered were inadequate.

The popular new Czech leader who led the forces against the party was Václav Havel (b. 1936), a playwright of international

▲ **Statue of Lenin.** The collapse of Communist Party governments in Eastern Europe and Soviet Union was the most important political event of the closing years of the twentieth century. It was accompanied by the destruction of the public symbols of those governments. Throughout the region gigantic statues of Communist Party leaders were torn down. Here, Hungarians explore a toppled statue of Lenin.
Sygma.

standing whom the government had frequently imprisoned. Havel and the group he represented, which called itself Civic Forum, negotiated changes with the government. These included an end to the political dominance of the Communist Party (which had been written into the constitution), inclusion of non-Communists in the government, elimination of traditional Marxist education, removal of travel restrictions, and relaxation of censorship.

Early in December the tottering Communist government admitted that the invasion of 1968 had been a mistake. The Soviet Union and other Warsaw Pact states did likewise. Shortly thereafter Civic Forum succeeded in forcing the resignation of Gustav Husak (b. 1913), who had been president of Czechoslovakia since 1968, and in guaranteeing a free election for his successor. In late December 1989 Havel was elected president.

VIOLENT REVOLUTION IN ROMANIA

The most violent upheaval of 1989 occurred in Romania, where President Nicolae Ceausescu (1918–1989) had governed without opposition for almost a quarter century. Romania was a one-party state with total centralized economic planning. Ceausescu, who had been at odds with the Soviet government for some time, maintained his Stalinist regime in the face of Gorbachev's reforms. He was supported by an army and a security force loyal to him. He had also placed his closest relatives in major political positions where they personally profited through corrupt practices.

On December 15 troubles erupted in the city of Timisoara in western Romania. The security forces sought to arrest a clergyman who had tried to protect the rights of ethnic Hungari-

▲ **Václav Havel.** President Václav Havel of the Czech Republic led the revolution that overthrew the Communist government of his nation and has since become a powerful advocate of political democracy and moderation in Eastern Europe.
Giles Bassignac/Liaison Agency, Inc.

ans within Romania's borders. Over the next two days the Romanian security forces fired on demonstrators in Timisoara. Casualties ran into at least the hundreds. A few days later demonstrators in Bucharest publicly shouted against Ceausescu at a major rally, and by December 22 the city was in full revolt. Fighting, with many casualties, broke out between the army, which supported the revolution, and the security forces loyal to Ceausescu. The revolutionaries gained control of the television station and broadcast reports of the spreading revolution. Ceausescu and his wife attempted to flee the country but were captured, tried, and executed by firing squad on December 25. His death ended the shooting between the army and security forces. The provisional government in Bucharest announced that the first free elections since the end of World War II would take place in the spring of 1990.

The Collapse of the Soviet Union

Gorbachev clearly believed, as shown by his behavior toward Eastern Europe in 1989, that the Soviet Union could no longer afford to support Communist governments in that region or intervene to uphold their authority. He was beginning to advance a similar view of the nature of the authority of the Communist Party within the Soviet Union.

RENUNCIATION OF COMMUNIST POLITICAL MONOPOLY

In early 1990 Gorbachev formally proposed to the Central Committee of the Soviet Communist Party that the party abandon its monopoly of power (see Document "Gorbachev Proposes the Soviet Communist Party Abandon Its Monopoly on

---

DOCUMENT | **Gorbachev Proposes that the Soviet Communist Party Abandon Its Monopoly of Power**

On February 5, 1990, President Mikhail Gorbachev proposed to the Central Committee of the Soviet Communist Party that it abandon its position as the single legal party as provided in Article 6 of the Soviet constitution. His proposal followed similar actions by several of the Communist Parties of Eastern Europe. From the time of Lenin through Brezhnev, the Soviet Communist Party portrayed itself as the sole vanguard of the revolution. Gorbachev argued that it should abandon that special role and compete for political power with other political parties. Within two years, the party was no longer in power, Gorbachev had resigned, and the Soviet Union no longer existed.

◆ Why did Gorbachev argue that the Soviet Communist Party must reform itself? To what extent did his speech call for the abandonment of traditional Communist Party goals? How did he think the Soviet Communist Party could function in a pluralistic political system?

The main thing that now worries Communists and all citizens of the country is the fate of *perestroika*, the fate of the country and the role of the Soviet Communist Party at the current, probably most crucial, stage of revolutionary transformation.

[It is important to understand] . . . that the party will only be able to fulfill the mission of political vanguard if it drastically restructures itself, masters the art of political work in the present conditions and succeeds in cooperating with forces committed to *perestroika*.

The crux of the party's renewal is the need to get rid of everything that tied it to the authoritarian–bureaucratic system, a system that left its mark not only on methods of work and inter-relationships within the party, but also on ideology, ways of thinking and notions of socialism.

The [newly proposed] platform says: our ideal is a humane, democratic socialism, expressing the interests of the working class and all working people; and relying on the great legacy of Marx, Engels and Lenin, the Soviet Communist Party is creatively developing socialist ideals to match present-day realities and with due account for the entire experience of the 20th century.

The platform states clearly what we should abandon. We should abandon the ideological dogmatism that became ingrained during past decades, outdated stereotypes in domestic policy and outmoded views on the world revolutionary process and world development as a whole.

We should abandon everything that led to the isolation of socialist countries from the mainstream of world civilization. We should abandon the understanding of progress as a permanent confrontation with a socially different world. . . .

The party's renewal presupposes a fundamental change in its relations with state and economic bodies and the abandonment of the practice of commanding them and substituting for their functions.

The party in a renewing of society can exist and play its role as vanguard only as a democratically recognized force. This means that its status should not be imposed through constitutional endorsement.

The Soviet Communist Party, it goes without saying, intends to struggle for the status of the ruling party. But it will do so strictly within the framework of the democratic process by giving up any legal and political advantages, offering its program and defending it in discussions, cooperating with other social and political forces, always working amidst the masses, living by their interests and their needs.

From *The New York Times*, 6 February 1990, p. A16.

Power"). After intense debate the Committee adopted his proposal, abandoning the Leninist position that only a single elite party could act as the vanguard of the revolution and forge a new Soviet society.

Gorbachev confronted challenges from three major political forces by 1990. One consisted of those groups—considered conservative in the Soviet context—whose members wanted to maintain the influence of the Communist Party and the Soviet army. They were deeply disturbed by the country's economic stagnation and political and social disorder. They still appeared to control significant groups in the economy and society. During late 1990 and early 1991 Gorbachev, who himself seems to have been disturbed by the nation's turmoil, began to appoint members of these factions to key positions in the government. In other words, Gorbachev seemed to be making a strategic retreat. He apparently believed that only these more conservative forces would give him the support he needed.

Gorbachev made this calculation because he was now facing opposition from members of a second group, those who wanted much more extensive and rapid change. Their leading spokesman was Boris Yeltsin (b. 1931). He and those supporting him wanted to move quickly to a market economy and a more democratic government. Like Gorbachev, Yeltsin had risen through the Communist Party and then become disillusioned with its policies. Throughout the late 1980s he had been critical of Gorbachev. In 1990 he was elected president of the Russian Republic, the largest and most important of the Soviet Union's constituent republics. In the new political climate, that position gave him a firm political base from which to challenge Gorbachev's authority and increase his own.

The third force was regional unrest. Some of the republics of the Soviet Union had experienced considerable discontent in the past, but it had been repressed by the military or the Communist Party. Initially, the greatest unrest came from the three Baltic republics of Estonia, Latvia, and Lithuania.

During 1989 and 1990 the parliaments of the Baltic republics tried to increase their independence, and Lithuania actually declared independence. Discontent also arose in the Soviet Islamic republics in Central Asia. Riots broke out in Azerbaijan and Tajikistan. Throughout 1990 and 1991 Gorbachev sought to negotiate new constitutional arrangements between the republics and the central government. His failure to do so may have been the most important reason for the rapid collapse of the Soviet Union.

THE AUGUST 1991 COUP

The turning point in all of these events came in August 1991 when the conservative forces that Gorbachev had brought into the government attempted a coup. Armed forces occupied Moscow, and Gorbachev himself was placed under house arrest while on vacation in the Crimea. The forces of political and economic reaction—led by people who, at the time, were associated with Gorbachev—had at last attempted to seize control. Boris Yeltsin denounced the coup and asked the world to help maintain the Soviet Union's movement toward democracy.

Within two days the coup collapsed. Gorbachev returned to Moscow, but in humiliation, having been victimized by the groups to whom he had turned for support. One of the largest public demonstrations in Russian history, perhaps the largest, celebrated the failure of the coup in Moscow. From that point on, Yeltsin steadily became the dominant political figure in the nation. In the months immediately after the coup the Communist Party, compromised by its participation in the coup, totally collapsed. The constitutional arrangements between the central government and the individual republics were revised. On December 25, 1991, the Soviet Union ceased to exist, Gorbachev left office, and the Commonwealth of Independent States came into being (see Map 32–2).

THE YELTSIN YEARS

As president of Russia, Boris Yeltsin was the head of the largest and most powerful of the new states. His popularity was high both in Russia and in the Commonwealth in 1992, but by 1993 he faced serious economic and political problems. Opposition to Yeltsin personally and to his economic and political reforms grew in the Russian parliament. Its members were mostly former Communists who wanted to slow or halt the movement toward reform. The impasse between the president and the parliament crippled the government. In September 1993 Yeltsin suspended parliament, which responded by deposing him. Parliament's leaders tried to provoke popular uprisings

▲ **Chechnya.** A Chechen fighter points his rifle at the head of a Russian prisoner of war outside the Chechen capital Grozny in August 1996. AP/Wide World Photos.

MAP 32–2 The Commonwealth of Independent States.   In December 1991 the Soviet Union broke up into its fifteen constituent republics. Eleven of these were loosely joined in the Commonwealth of Independent States. Also shown is the autonomous region of Chechnya, which has waged two bloody wars with Russia in the last decade.

against Yeltsin in Moscow. The military, however, backed Yeltsin and eventually surrounded the parliament building with troops and tanks. On October 4, 1993, after pro-parliament rioters rampaged through Moscow, Yeltsin ordered the tanks to attack the parliament building, crushing the revolt.

These actions temporarily consolidated Yeltsin's position and authority. The major Western powers, deeply concerned by the turmoil in Russia, supported him. The crushing of parliament left Yeltsin far more dependent than before on the military, and the country's continuing economic problems bred unrest. In the December elections, for example, radical nationalists openly intolerant of non-Russian ethnic groups and advocating rebuilding Russia's empire made an uncomfortably strong showing, nearly capturing more seats in the new parliament than supporters of Yeltsin. In 1994 the central government found itself at war in the province of Chechnya, a conflict from which the central government eventually emerged as the loser. This conflict

demonstrated the very limited capacity of the government to exercise its authority when faced with significant resistance.

The parliamentary elections of late 1995 saw the Communist Party reassert its political presence as it achieved control of over one third of the seats in the Russian parliament. The Communist leadership claimed that it did not intend to return to its former authoritarian ways. The parliamentary elections represented a major rebuff to the Yeltsin government, which had become increasingly unpopular. Yet by very deft political actions, Yeltsin defeated the Communist Party candidate for the presidency in the summer of 1996.

Thereafter Russian politics remained highly confused. (See Document, "Aleksandr Solzhenitsyn Ponders the Future of Russian Democracy.") President Yeltsin, who suffered from poor health, faced steady opposition in the Russian parliament. The economic life of the nation remained stagnant at best. In 1998 Russia defaulted on its debt payments. Political assassinations

DOCUMENT | Aleksandr Solzhenitsyn Ponders the Future of Russian Democracy

Aleksandr Solzhenitsyn, the foremost Russian novelist of his generation, was one of the most outspoken critics of the Communist government of the Soviet Union. He was expelled from the country in 1974 and lived for many years in the United States. After the collapse of the Soviet Union and the Soviet Communist government, he returned to live in Russia. In recent years, he has been highly critical of the new Russian government. In January 1997, he outlined his criticism in The New York Times.

◆ What are Solzhenitsyn's chief criticisms of the structure of the new Russian government? Why does he not consider it democratic? Why does he emphasize the necessity of establishing structures of local self-government? Why does he believe corruption could undermine democracy in Russia? Have events in Russia since 1997 alleviated those concerns?

What is known today as "Russian democracy" masks a Government of a completely different sort. *Glasnost*—freedom of the press—is only an instrument of democracy, not democracy itself. And to a great extent freedom of the press is illusory, since the owners of newspapers erect strict taboos against discussion of issues of vital importance, while in the outlying parts of the country newspapers get direct pressure from the province authorities.

Democracy in the unarguable sense of the word means the rule of the people—that is a system in which the people are truly in charge of their daily lives and can influence the course of their own historical fate. There is nothing of the sort in Russia today.

In August 1991, the "councils of people's deputies," though only window dressing under the rule of the Communist Party, were abolished throughout the country. Since then, the united resistance of the President's machine, the Government, State *Duma* [Parliament], leaders of the political parties and majority of governors has prevented the creation of any agencies of local self-government.

Legislative assemblies do exist at the regional level but are entirely subordinate to the governors, if only because they are paid by the province's executive branches. (The election of governors is only a recent development and far from widespread; most governors were appointed by the President.)

There exists no legal framework or financial means for the creation of local self-government; people will have no choice but to achieve it through social struggle. All that really exists is the government hierarchy, from the President and national Government on down.

... The Constitution of 1993, which was passed hastily and not in a manner to inspire confidence, groans under the weight of the President's power. The rights it allocates to the State *Duma* are exceedingly constrained.

... This system of centralized power cannot be called a democracy.

It could be said that throughout the last 10 years of frenetic reorganization our Government has not taken a single step unmarked by ineptitude. Worse, our ruling circles have not shown themselves in the least morally superior to the Communists who preceded them. Russia has been exhausted by crime, by the transfer into private hands of billions of dollars' worth of the nation's wealth. Not a single serious crime has been exposed, nor has there been a single public trial. The investigatory and judicial systems are severely limited in both their actions and their resources.

The destructive course of events over the last decade has come about because the Government, while ineptly imitating foreign models, has completely disregarded the country's creativity and particular character as well as Russia's centuries-old spiritual and social traditions. Only if those paths are freed up can Russia be delivered from its near fatal condition.

---

occurred. The economic downturn contributed to further political unrest. In the face of these problems, Yeltsin resigned the presidency just as the new century opened. His resignation made the premier, Vladimir Putin, acting president. Putin was elected president in his own right in March 2001. Putin renewed the war against the rebels in Chechnya, which resulted in heavy casualties and enormous destruction there, but also strengthened Putin's political support in Russia itself. After the terrorist attacks on the United States, Putin extended cooperation with the American assault on Afghanistan largely because the Russian government was afraid that Islamic extremism would spread beyond Chechnya

to other regions in Russia and to the largely Muslim nations that bordered Russia in Central Asia and the Caucasus.

The Chechen war spawned one of the major acts of recent terrorism. In September 2004, a group of Chechens captured an elementary school in Beslan, a community in the Russian republic of North Ossetia (in the north Caucasus) on the opening day of the term. Approximately 1,200 students, teachers, and parents were held hostage for several days. When government troops stormed the school, approximately 330 of the hostages were killed.

In the wake of this event and as part of his determination that the central Russian government will dominate the economy and political life, Putin has pursued policies of strong governmental centralization. Power has been taken away from local political units and placed in the hands of central government. The central government has also moved against citizens who have accumulated great wealth in the past decade. Overall it must be concluded that the future of democratic processes face great difficulty in Russia.

The Collapse of Yugoslavia and Civil War

Yugoslavia was created after World War I. Its borders included six major national groups—Serbs, Croats, Slovenes, Montenegrins, Macedonians, and Bosnians (Muslims)— among whom there have been ethnic disputes for centuries (see Map 32–3). The Croats and Slovenes are Roman Catholic and use the Latin

alphabet. The Serbs, Montenegrins, and Macedonians are Eastern Orthodox and use the Cyrillic alphabet. The Bosnians are Islamic. Most members of each group reside in a region with which they are associated historically—Serbia, Croatia, Slovenia, Montenegro, Macedonia, and Bosnia-Herzegovina—and these regions constituted individual republics within Yugoslavia. Many Serbs, however, lived outside Serbia proper.

Yugoslavia's first Communist leader, Marshal Tito (1892–1980), had acted independently of Stalin in the late 1940s and pursued his own foreign policy. He succeeded in muting ethnic differences by encouraging a cult of personality around him and by complex political power sharing. After his death serious economic difficulties undermined the authority of the central government, and Yugoslavia gradually dissolved into civil war.

In the late 1980s the old ethnic differences came to the fore again in Yugoslav politics. Nationalist leaders—most notably Slo-

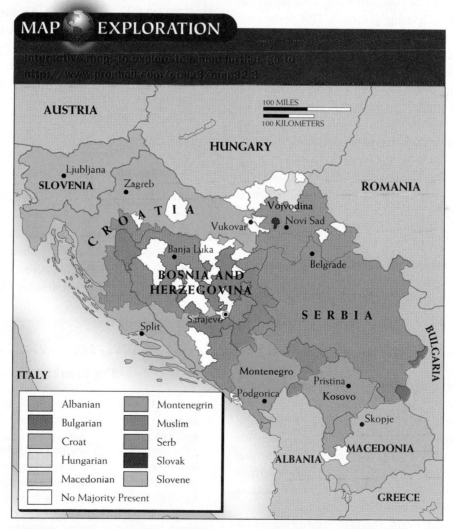

MAP 32–3 The Ethnic Composition in the Former Yugoslavia. The rapid changes in Eastern Europe during the close of the 1980s intensified long-standing ethnic tensions in the former Yugoslavia. This map shows where Yugoslavia's ethnic population lived in 1991, before internal conflicts escalated.

Destruction of Sarajevo. An elderly parishioner walks through the ruins of St. Mary's Roman Catholic Church in Sarajevo. The church was destroyed by Serb shelling in May 1992.
Reuters/Corbis-Bettmann.

bodan Milošević (b. 1941) in Serbia and Franjo Tudjman (b. 1922) in Croatia—gained increasing authority. The Serbs contended that Serbia did not exercise sufficient influence in Yugoslavia and that Serbs living in Yugoslavia, but outside Serbia, encountered systematic discrimination, especially from Croats. Ethnic tension and violence soon resulted. During the summer of 1990, in the wake of the changes in the former Soviet bloc nations, Slovenia and Croatia declared independence from the central Yugoslav government and were soon recognized by several European nations, including, most importantly, Germany. Recognition from the full European community soon followed.

From this point on, violence escalated steadily. Serbia—concerned about Serbs living in Croatia and about the loss of lands and resources there—was determined to maintain a unitary Yugoslav state that it would dominate. Croatia was equally determined to secure independence. Croatian Serbs demanded safeguards against discrimination and violence, providing the Serbian army with a pretext to move against Croatia. By June 1991 full-fledged war had erupted between the two republics. Serbia accused Croatia of reviving fascism, while Croatia accused Serbia of maintaining a Stalinist regime. At its core, however, the conflict is ethnic; as such, it highlights the potential for violent ethnic conflict within the former Soviet Union.

The conflict took a new turn in 1992 as Croatian and Serbian forces determined to divide Bosnia-Herzegovina. The Muslims in Bosnia—who had lived alongside Serbs and Croats for generations—soon became crushed between the opposing forces. The Serbs in particular, pursuing a policy called "ethnic cleansing," a euphemism redolent of some of the worst horrors of World War II, killed or forcibly moved many Bosnian Muslims.

More than any other single event, the unremitting bombardment of Sarajevo, the capital of Bosnia-Herzegovina, brought the violence of the Yugoslav civil war to the attention of the world. The United Nations attempted unsuccessfully to mediate

the conflict and imposed sanctions, which had little influence. Early in 1994, however, a shell exploded in the marketplace in Sarajevo, killing dozens of people. Thereafter, NATO forced the Serbs to withdraw their artillery from around Sarajevo.

The events of the civil war came to a head in 1995 when NATO forces carried out strategic air strikes. Later that year under the leadership of the United States, the leaders of the warring forces completed a peace agreement in Dayton, Ohio. The agreement was of great complexity but recognized an independent Bosnia. The terms of the agreement have been enforced by the presence of NATO troops, including many from the United States.

In the late 1990s Serbian aggression against ethnic Albanians in the province of Kosovo again provoked a NATO response. For months the world watched as the Serbian military drove Albanians from Kosovo where the Albanians constituted the majority of the population. Casualties, atrocities, and deaths were daily occurrences. These tactics resembled those that had been used earlier in the decade in Bosnia. In early 1999 NATO intervened and launched an air attack against the Serbian forces that was the largest military action in Europe since the close of World War II. Belgrade was repeatedly bombed. As a result, the Serbian army withdrew from Kosovo, and NATO ground forces entered the province to protect the ethnic Albanians. In 2000 a revolution overthrew the regime of Slobodan Milošević, and the new Yugoslav government handed him over in June 2001 to the International War Crimes Tribunal at the Hague for trial as a war criminal.

Challenges to the Atlantic Alliance

NATO has continued to exist following the collapse of the Soviet Union and has moved to expand its membership to include Poland, the Czech Republic, and Hungary. Yet the exact present purpose of NATO remains ill defined. Although initially taking a reluctant role in settling the civil war in the former

CHRONOLOGY

The Breakup of Yugoslavia

June 1991	Slovenia declares independence.
June 1991	Croatia declares independence.
April 1992	War erupts in Bosnia and Herzegovina after Muslims and Croats vote for independence.
November 1995	Peace agreement reached in Dayton, Ohio.
January 1992	Macedonia declares independence.
April 1992	Serbia and Montenegro proclaim a new Federal Republic of Yugoslavia.
March 1998	War breaks out in Kosovo, a province of Serbia.
March 1999	NATO bombing of Serbia begins
2000	Milošević Regime overthrown.

◀ **President George W. Bush and British Prime Minister Tony Blair.** The United States and Great Britain led the coalition against Iraq. Here Prime Minister Tony Blair and President George W. Bush address a joint press conference on November 7, 2001.

R. Bowner/AP Wide World Photos.

Yugoslavia, NATO eventually attempted to assume the role of internal peacekeeper in the new Europe. The role was not welcomed by all NATO members or the broad European publics.

The sense of drift in the purpose of NATO and the inward looking tendency of continental Europe manifested itself in new and unexpected ways after the September 11, 2001, attacks by al Qaeda on the United States. Initially Europeans deeply sympathized with the tragedy and loss of life experienced by Americans. After all many Europeans as well as many other non-Americans died in the collapse of the Twin Towers. NATO aircraft patrolled the skies of the United States. Not long thereafter, however, a significant split developed as the United States government of President George W. Bush responded to the terrorist assault.

The September 11 attacks on the United States transformed and redirected American foreign policy into what the administration of President George W. Bush termed "a war on terrorism." In late 2001, the United States attacked the Taliban government of Afghanistan, rapidly overthrowing it. The defeat of the Taliban destroyed al Qaeda's Afghan bases, but not its leadership, which appears to have survived, although it was dispersed and remains in hiding.

Following the Afghan campaign, the Bush administration set forth a policy of preemptive strikes and intervention against potential enemies of the United States. The administration argued that the danger of weapons of mass destruction—then believed to have been developed by governments such as that of Iraq—falling into the hands of international terrorist organizations posed so severe a danger to the security of the United States that the nation could not wait to respond to an attack but must stand prepared to take preemptive action. This argument, which aroused controversy both at home and abroad, marked a major departure from previous United States foreign policy.

The sharpest and thus far lasting division arose in the months immediately before and in the months subsequent to

the American invasion of Iraq in 2003. The American invasion, which will be discussed more fully in Chapter 34, received the support of numerous European governments including most notably the United Kingdom, Italy, Poland, Bulgaria, and Spain. Other traditional European allies of the United States, however, most particularly, France and Germany, sharply criticized American decision-making and actions. Popular political opinon across Europe dissented vocally from American policy.

Once the invasion had been carried out and the occupation commenced, terrorists struck in Europe itself. On March 11, 2004, at least 190 people were killed in commuter train bombings in Madrid, Spain. The Madrid bombings were the largest act of terrorism against civilians in Europe since World War II. The al Qaeda–sponsored attack demonstrated that such terrorist attacks can directly influence European political processes. The terrorist attack occurred just before the Spanish election, in which the Spanish government, which had supported the American invasion of Iraq, was voted from office. The new Spanish government announced that it would withdraw Spanish troops from the conflict.

As this book goes to press, profound divisions continue to exist between the United States and many of its historic postwar allies. Many Europeans see themselves, their values, and their emerging political community as different from Americans and their values and political community. The long-term relationship will no doubt be worked through on many issues beyond the immediate one of Iraq. More than likely, external events and the wider conflict between the West and radical political Islam will be the determining factors characterizing the Atlantic alliance, as was the division between a democractic West and a communist Eastern block in the past.

▲ **Terrorist Bombing Madrid.**   Police search for clues from the debris of one of the trains destroyed in the terrorist attack of March 11, 2004. AP/Wide World photos.

Internet Cafe in Amsterdam.

Summary

The Cold War　U.S.-Soviet cooperation did not survive World War II. After 1945 Europe was divided into a Soviet-dominated zone in the East (the Warsaw Pact) and a U.S.-led zone in the West (NATO). U.S.-Soviet rivalry played itself out around the world from the 1950s to the 1980s, although gradually a spirit of détente arose between the two powers, especially under President Ronald Reagan and Soviet leader Mikhail Gorbachev. The Cold War ended with the collapse of Communist rule in Eastern Europe in 1989 and the disappearance of the Soviet Union in 1991.

Postwar European Society　Since World War II, European society has been marked by a rise in prosperity and consumerism, more rights and opportunities for women, moves toward political and economic unification symbolized by the adoption of a common currency, the euro, in 2002 and the publication of a draft constitution for a united Europe in 2003.

The United States　The major themes in postwar American history were opposition to Communism at home and abroad, the expansion of civil rights to African Americans, and economic prosperity. Politically, the relatively liberal years from the late 1950s through the 1970s were succeeded by a growing conservatism especially under the presidencies of Ronald Reagan, George Bush, and George W. Bush. Even the Democratic President Bill Clinton was more a centrist than a liberal. After the terrorist attacks of September 11, 2001, the United States embarked on a war on terrorism that led to wars in Afghanistan and Iraq.

Eastern Europe　The failure of the Communist regimes in Eastern Europe and the Soviet Union to produce economic prosperity or political liberalization led to their growing unpopularity. Soviet economic difficulties led Mikhail Gorbachev to institute liberal reforms that led to the collapse of the communist rule first in Eastern Europe, then in the Soviet Union itself. The disappearance of the Soviet Union led to independence for much of the former Soviet empire. Russia itself has experienced social, economic, and political turmoil under presidents Boris Yeltsin and Vladimir Putin.

In the former Yugoslavia, the end of Communist rule led to dismemberment and civil war. In the 1990s the NATO powers, led by the United States, intervened to halt the fighting and end a pattern of ethnic atrocities.

Review Questions

1. What were the causes of the Cold War? How did the United States and the Soviet Union each react to what it perceived to be the other's hostility? What was the effect of the Cold War on Europe?

2. How did the outcome of World War II affect Europe's position in the world? What were the factors behind the movement toward European unification? How successful has this movement been?

3. What were the chief characteristics of Western European society in the decades since 1945? What was the experience of Eastern Europe during the same period and why was it different?

4. What were the most important developments in the domestic history of the United States between 1945 and 1968? How did the Vietnam War affect American society? When did the shift to political conservatism occur in the United States? What did it mean for the role of the federal government?

5. Describe the Soviet economy between 1945 and 1990. Did it meet the needs of the Soviet people? What were the causes for the collapse of the Soviet Union? What role did Gorbachev play in that process?

6. Describe the collapse of Communist rule in Eastern Europe. Why was it a relatively bloodless revolution? What problems have followed the collapse of Communist rule?

7. Was the old Yugoslavia a national state? Why did it break apart and slide into civil war? How did the West respond to this crisis?

8. How did the American response to the attacks of September 11, 2001, cause significant rifts in the NATO alliance? Why do some European nations feel able to dissent from the U.S. position in the Middle East when they rarely did so during the Cold War?

Key Terms

Cold War   (p. 962)

Euro   (p. 969)

European Economic Community   (p. 968)

European Union   (p. 968)

glasnost   (p. 980)

Marshall Plan   (p. 962)

perestroika   (p. 980)

Documents CD-ROM

The Cold War

26.1 The Soviet Victory: Capitalism versus Communism (February 1946): Joseph Stalin

26.2 "An Iron Curtain Has Descended Across the Continent" (March 1946): Sir Winston Churchill

26.3 The Truman Doctrine (March 1947): Harry Truman

26.4 The Marshall Plan (June 1947): George C. Marshall

26.7 Henry A. Myers, "East Berliners Rise Up Agaisnt Soviet Oppression," A Personal Account

26.8 "The Victory of Communism Is Inevitable!": Speech to the 22nd Communist Party Congress (1962): Nikita Khrushchev

Race, Ethnicity, and Conflict in the Twentieth Century

28.3 Martin Luther King, Jr.

Contemporary Issues in World History

29.1 A United Germany in a United Europe (June 5, 1990): Helmuth Kohl

29.2 The Reconciliation of France and Germany (September 24, 1990): Francois Mitterand

29.3 Ethnic Cleansing in Northwestern Bosnia: Three Witness

29.6 Saddam's Invasion of Kuwait: Two Rationales

29.7 "We Wage a War to Save Civilization Itself" (2001). George W. Bush

NOTE: *To learn more about the topics in this chapter, see the Suggested Readings at the end of the book.*

33

East Asia

The Recent Decades

- Japan
- China
- Taiwan
- Korea
- Vietnam

◀ BRIDGE OVER HUANGPU RIVER IN SHANGHAI. Note the juxtaposition of new (the bridge and ramps) and old (industrial sites not yet replaced by modern factories).
China Tourism Press/Xie Guang Hui/Getty Images/Image Bank.

GLOBAL PERSPECTIVE

Modern East Asia

Before World War II, only Europe, the United States, and Japan had successfully combined the ingredients needed for modern economic growth. It was as though these countries had a magic potion that the rest of the world lacked. Industrialization in East Asia during recent decades made clear that there was no magic potion: The West and Japan just got there first. The industrialization of East Asia raises issues that will powerfully affect future relations among nations.

One question is whether high-wage nations will be able to compete with those low-wage nations that have found the formula for growth. Until recently, the advanced nations were satisfied with their share of world trade. They sold the products of their heavy industries and advanced technologies and bought raw materials and the labor-intensive products of light industries. They assumed that their technological advantage was permanent, and that they could always stay sufficiently ahead of the less-developed nations to maintain high wages for their workers. This assumption has now been challenged. Since the 1960s, Taiwan, South Korea, Hong Kong, and Singapore have not only achieved modern economic growth but have also moved rapidly into high technology—well before their wages reached Western levels. This has made them formidable competitors in precisely those areas in which the West has considered itself preeminent. European nations have responded, in part, by adopting protectionist policies, while the United States, with some exceptions, has kept its market open. By doing so, the United States during the 1990s regained competitiveness, but at the cost of holding down wages, drastic corporate restructuring, relocating jobs abroad, and accumulating huge trade deficits. Will it be willing to continue paying this price? China, the most recent East Asian industrializer, is moving toward higher levels of technology and will possess the economic advantages of cheap labor for decades. If it succeeds in its development goals, the impact on high-wage nations will be massive.

A second issue raised by East Asian economic growth concerns natural resources. An oil crisis occurred in the early 1970s when demand outran supply. There were shortages at the pumps, a steep rise in the price of oil, and a transfer of wealth from industrial to oil-rich nations. Experts pointed out that the world's reserves were dwindling. Market forces, however, uncovered new sources of supply and the crisis faded, yet oil reserves are still being used up faster than ever as demand rises. At some point demand will again outstrip supply, and as oil and gas prices soared in 2004, some economists suggested that the point is near at hand. It is likely that in the future the management of trade and allocation of scarce resources such as oil will become even more important in international relations than is true today.

A third issue is population. Japan's population quadrupled in the course of its industrialization and then began to level off without a need for draconian measures. Its pattern resembled that of the advanced nations of the West. China, in contrast, already had a huge population when it began its recent industrialization under Deng. Since it could ill afford a further quadrupling, it adopted extremely tough policies to limit births. Still, by 2030, its populatin may peak at 1.6 billion. Whether other less-developed nations in the world follow the Japanese or Chinese pattern will depend on their particular circumstances, but for many, the Chinese model seems unavoidable.

A fourth issue concerns the political consequences of economic growth. The recent history of Taiwan and South Korea suggests that East Asian dictatorships can evolve toward democracy as standards of living rise. Will the same thing happen in China? As Chinese become caught up in the material benefits of their market economy, will the Chinese Communist Party relax or lose its monopoly on government? It will take decades for China to reach a Taiwanese level of well-being. Also, postwar Taiwan and South Korea were less thoroughly authoritarian to begin with and were strongly influenced by the United States. It is too early to tell.

A final issue, the dark companion of industrial and population growth, is pollution. As long as most of the world remained underdeveloped, the industrial nations assumed that their wastes would harmlessly vanish into the vast reaches of surrounding lands and seas. But as populations encroach on forested lands, and Eastern Europe, India, Russia, and East Asia industrialize, pollution has become more threatening. Even apart from disasters such as Minamata and Chernobyl, automobile fumes, industrial effluents, chimney gases, pesticides, garbage, and sewage cause lakes to die, forests to wither, and level of toxins to rise. In some areas the damage appears near irreversible.

THINK AHEAD

- How does the industrialization of East Asia affect future relations among the nations of the world?

- What is the impact of East Asian economic growth on the world's natural resources? On pollution?

- Does recent history suggest that the Chinese government will become more democratic as its citizens become more prosperous?

THE HISTORY OF EAST ASIA SINCE THE END OF World War II may be divided into two phases (see Map 33–1). In the first from 1945 to 1980, several East Asian nations became Communist but achieved only a small improvement in the lives of their peoples. In stark contrast, the nations that used a mixture of state guidance and market-oriented economies made the region as a whole the most dynamic in the postwar world. Japan led the way, achieving economic growth that has often been spoken of as miraculous but can more sensibly be described as single-minded. Japan also developed into a robust parliamentary democracy with freedoms comparable to those of Western Europe or the United States.

Taiwan and South Korea began their economic development a decade or two later and from a much lower level, and though lacking the political freedom of Japan, they attained stunning economic growth, as did the tiny British colony of Hong Kong and the even tinier ex-British colony of Singapore. Viewing the progress of these countries, it would appear that the values of the East Asian heritage—hard work, frugality, family orientation, thirst for education, and concern for getting ahead—lead almost automatically to economic development if given half a chance.

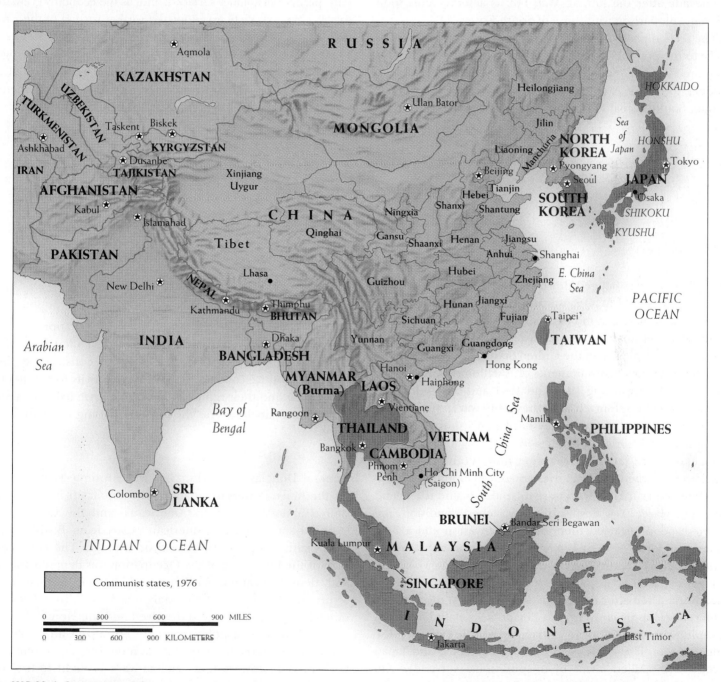

MAP 33–1 Contemporary Asia.

The Communist nations—China, North Korea, and Vietnam—did less well. China was wracked by continuous political convulsions. Despite gaining undisputed political authority over a vast area comparable to that of the Qing Empire, the government was unable to tap the energies and talents of its people. The contrast between the low productivity of the Chinese in China and the remarkable productivity of the same people in Hong Kong and Taiwan was startling.

Vietnam, plagued by wars during these early decades, did not develop at all. North Korea, where most of the industry of Japan's prewar colony was located, did slightly better during the decade after the Korean War, but its achievements soon paled in comparison with those of South Korea.

The second phase of postwar East Asian history was from the 1980s to the present. During the 1980s, those nations that had prospered earlier continued to grow. Japan's per capita product, for a time, zoomed past that of Germany and France. Taiwan, South Korea, Hong Kong, and Singapore (sometimes referred to as the "tiger" economies) also achieved amazing advances (see Figure 33–1). Growth went hand in hand with social stability and an increasingly varied cultural life. Especially notable were advances in democracy in Taiwan and South Korea. But during the 1990s, a recession rippled through East Asia and growth halted or slowed. Japan was especially hard hit.

The most remarkable positive changes occurred in China, which, even while maintaining a Communist dictatorship, launched a market economy. The result was explosive growth and an export boom. It began in southeastern coastal areas and then spread to the rest of the nation. Long suppressed entrepreneurial abilities surfaced, and, as the economy grew, the society changed. Vietnam adopted a weaker version of the same policy. It permitted private enterprises and opened its markets to some foreign capital. Only North Korea resisted the changes sweeping the rest of the Communist world. The rigidities of its singular brand of communism took their toll, and as it entered the twenty-first century, its people suffered hunger and misery.

Japan

For Japan, already bogged down in its occupation of China, the decision in 1941 to go to war with the United States and its allies was a desperate gamble. By all objective measures—steel production, oil, machine tools, heavy chemicals, shipping—Japan was far weaker than the United States. The Japanese military, however, misread statements of isolationist sentiment in the United States during 1940 and 1941 and concluded that Americans had no stomach for a drawn-out war in the western Pacific. In terms of strategy, they bet Japan's shorter lines of supply against American productivity.

By early 1945, Japanese was poor, hungry, and ill-clothed. Cities were burned out, factories scarred by bombings; shipping had been sunk, railways were dilapidated, and trucks and cars were scarce. Yet, despite their wretched condition, the Japanese people steeled themselves for invasion and a final battle in defense of their homeland. Then, in early August, atomic bombs were dropped on Hiroshima and Nagasaki, and the Soviet Union declared war on Japan and invaded Manchuria. Even after these disasters, opinion at the imperial conference, hastily convened to decide on a national policy, was split, with three favoring surrender and three for continuing the war. The emperor broke the deadlock, and Japan accepted the Allied terms of unconditional surrender. On August 15, the emperor broadcast Japan's surrender to the Japanese people, saying that the "unendurable must be endured."

After years of wartime propaganda, the Japanese reacted with shock to the fact of surrender, deep sadness at having lost the war, relief that the bombing was over, and apprehension about what would come next. They expected a harsh and vindictive occupation, but when they found it constructive, they turned to positive cooperation. Their receptivity to new democratic ideas and their repudiation of militarism led one Japanese writer to label the era "the second opening of Japan."

THE OCCUPATION

General Douglas MacArthur was the Supreme Commander for the Allied Powers in Japan. His headquarters in Tokyo was staffed almost entirely by Americans, and the Occupation forces themselves were American, apart from British Commonwealth troops on the island of Shikoku. The chief concern of the first phase of the Occupation was demilitarization and democratization. Civilians and soldiers abroad were returned to Japan and the military was demobilized. Ultranationalist organizations were dissolved and the Home Ministry was abolished. The police were decentralized and political prisoners were freed. Following the model of the Nuremberg trials in Germany, wartime leaders were brought to trial for "crimes against humanity." In addition, 210,000 officers, businessmen, teachers, and officials—the leaders of wartime Japan—were removed from office. The thoroughness of these reforms reflected the Occupation view that Japanese society had been tainted by feudal and militaristic values and that Japan's leaders had been joined in a huge conspiracy to wage aggressive war.

As a part of democratization, Shinto was disestablished as the state religion, labor unions were encouraged, and the holding companies of zaibatsu combines were dissolved. The old educational system, which had forced students at an early age to choose either an elite or a mass track, was changed to a single-track system that kept open longer the option of continuing in school. The most radical undertaking was a land reform that expropriated landlord holdings and sold them to landless tenants at a fractional cost. The effect, ironically, was to create a countryside of politically conservative small farmers. Needless to say, some of these reforms merely accelerated changes already under way in Japan, and all of the reforms depended on the cooperation—at times enthusiastic and at times reluctant—of Japanese officials.

Of all the Occupation reforms, none was more important than the new constitution, written by the Government Section of MacArthur's headquarters and passed into law by the Japanese Diet. It fundamentally changed Japan's polity in five respects:

1. A British-style parliamentary state was established in which the cabinet became a committee of the majority party or coalition in the Diet. This broke with the Meiji Constitution, which had permitted the emperor or those who acted in his name to appoint prime ministers without regard for the Diet. The new constitution also added an American-style independent judiciary and a federal system of prefectures with elected governors and local leaders.

2. Women were given the vote.

3. The rights to life, liberty, the pursuit of happiness, a free press, and free assembly were guaranteed. These were joined by newer rights, such as academic freedom, collective bargaining, sexual equality in marriage, and minimal standards of wholesome and cultural living.

4. Article 9, the no-war clause, stipulated, "The Japanese people forever renounce war as a sovereign right of the nation" and will never maintain "land, sea, and air forces" or "other war potential." This article would make Japan into something unique in the world: a major power without commensurate military strength.

5. The constitution defined a new role for the emperor as "the symbol of the state deriving his position from the will of the people with whom resides sovereign power."

The Japanese people accepted the new constitution and embraced democracy with uncritical enthusiasm. The no-war

▲ **Emperor Hirohito and General MacArthur.** The two men met at the U.S. Embassy in Tokyo in 1945. MacArthur felt the emperor contributed to the stability of Japan and made the work of the Occupation easier. The emperor was glad to be of use and relieved he was not hanged as a war criminal.
Corbis/Bettmann.

clause was viewed by most as the guarantee of a peaceful future. Although it did not preclude the formation of a Self-Defense Force, it acted as a brake on military expenditures, which half a century later were only about 1 percent of Japan's gross domestic product. The Japanese had been readied for the changed status of the emperor by his speech on January 1, 1946, in which he renounced all claims to divinity. The Occupation saw to it that the emperor traveled about Japan in a manner appropriate to his new status as a symbol of the state. No one who saw this mild, rumpled-looking, and inarticulate man mistook him for a Shinto god. By the late 1960s most, though not all, Japanese had come to feel a considerable affection for Emperor Hirohito, who, they felt, had shared in their wartime and postwar hardships. They were saddened by his death in 1989. (See Document, "Two Views of the 'Symbol Emperor.'")

By the end of 1947, most of the planned reforms had been carried out. To create a climate in which the new democracy could take root and flourish, the Occupation in its second phase turned to Japan's economic recovery. It dropped plans to deconcentrate big business further, encouraged the Japanese government to curb inflation, and cracked down on Communist unions which used strikes for political ends. The United States also gave Japan $2 billion in economic aid.

The outbreak of the Korean War in 1950 marked the start of the third and final phase of the Occupation. The American military, fully engaged in the peninsular war, no longer had time for Japan. Consequently, Japanese officials began to look to the Cabinet and the Diet for policy decisions, not to the occupying forces. By the time Japan regained its sovereignty in April 1952, the effect of the changeover was hardly noticeable in the daily life of the Japanese people. On the same day as the peace treaty, Japan signed a security treaty with the United States that provided for American bases and committed the United States to Japan's defense. Although attacked by the political left, the security treaty became the cornerstone of Japan's minimalist defense policy.

PARLIAMENTARY POLITICS

In 1945, Japan had a parliamentary potential that harked back to the rise of party power in the Diet between 1890 and 1932. It also had an authoritarian potential compounded of those factors that had led to the rise of militarism. Had the country been occupied by the Soviet Union, the efficiency of its bureaucracy, its wartime economic planning organs, its educated and disciplined workforce, and its receptivity to change after defeat would doubtless have made Japan a model Communist state. Occupied by the United States, the parliamentary potential emerged.

CHRONOLOGY

Japan Since 1945

1945	Japan surrenders
1946	Peace and security treaties
1948–1954	Yoshida ministries
1950–1953	Korean War
1955	Liberal and Democratic Parties merge
1955–1973	Double-digit economic growth
1972	Japan recognizes the People's Republic of China
1973–1989	Economic growth continues at slower pace
1990	Bubble bursts and recession begins
1991	Socialists lose Diet seats
1994–1996	Non-LDP coalitions govern; LDP-led coalitions reestablished
2001	Koizumi Junichirō becomes prime minister
2003	Japan sends troops to Iraq

Japan's postwar politics can be divided into three periods. The first, from 1945 to 1955, was the continuation of prewar party politics as modified to fit the new political environment. Two conservative parties and a socialist party emerged. The Liberals and the Democrats—the conservative parties—were the successors to the two mainstream prewar parties. They resumed their struggle for power in the early postwar elections. The Japanese Socialist Party, which won 26 percent of the vote in 1947, was the heir of the moderate prewar Socialist Party, which had received 9 percent of the vote in 1937.

For most of this first decade, the Liberals held power under Prime Minister Yoshida Shigeru (1878–1967). Before the war, Yoshida had been an ardent imperialist but had favored close ties with Britain and the United States and opposed the rise of militarism. After the war, as president of the Liberal Party, he cooperated closely with MacArthur and worked to rebuild Japan's economy. Probusiness and anti-Communist, he was so autocratic in his dealings with bureaucrats and lesser politicians that he was nicknamed "one-man Yoshida."

The long second period from 1955 to 1993 has been called the one-and-a-half party system. The "one" party was the Liberal Democratic Party (**LDP**), formed by a merger of the two conservative parties in 1955. It held power throughout this period. The "half party," so called because it was permanently out of power, was the Japanese Socialist Party. It had split in two in 1951 and come back together in 1955.

What did one-party rule for thirty-eight years mean? One-party rule is not usually associated with representative government. In the immediate postwar years, the strength of the conservatives was simply the continuation of prewar constituencies, that is to say, the network of ties between local men of influence, prefectural assemblymen, and Diet politicians, and their ties to business and the bureaucracy. From the 1960s onward, the LDP became identified as the party that was rebuilding Japan and maintaining Japan's security through close ties with the United States. It was widely recognized as more able than other parties. Despite the cozy relationships that developed between the LDP and business, periodic scandals, and a widespread distrust of politicians, the Japanese people voted to keep it in power. Rule by a single party for such a long period provided for an unusual continuity in government policies. Within the larger pattern of the LDP hegemony, several trends were notable:

1. From 1955 to 1960, Japanese politics was marked by ideological strife. The LDP was led by wartime figures who had been purged after the war but had resumed their political careers. These leaders rather high-handedly modified several Occupation reforms, recentralized the police, strengthened central government controls over education, and even considered a revision of the constitution. The opposition was led by Marxist Socialists, many of whom

had been persecuted during the war. The Socialists branded LDP rule as the "tyranny of the majority," since legislation was often passed by "snap votes," and warned of the revival of authoritarianism. Diet sessions were marked by confrontation, rancor, and occasional violence. After 1960, confrontation politics declined. Adopting a "low posture," the new LDP prime minister dropped controversial political issues and drew up a plan to double the national income in ten years. These moves inaugurated a more peaceful era. As prosperity grew during the seventies and eighties, ideological confrontation declined further. In many areas a consensus emerged as LDP consulted opposition politicians before presenting bills to the Diet.

2. Another trend was a steady decline in the LDP popular vote from 63 percent in 1955, to 55 percent in 1963, to 43 percent in 1976. The decline mirrored Japan's economic growth: Farmers, small shopkeepers, and others, who traditionally voted for the LDP, became a smaller part of the population, while unionized laborers and white-collar workers, who tended to vote for the Socialists, increased. By the late seventies, the conservatives faced the possibility that they would have to form a coalition to stay in power. But in the 1979 election the steady twenty-year decline in the LDP popular vote came to an end. For the next fourteen years the party enjoyed a stable majority in the powerful Lower House of the Diet—though not always in the Upper House—and maintained its rule.

3. Although it received less than half of the popular vote, the LDP maintained its Diet majority because its opposition fragmented: In 1960, non-Marxist members broke from the Socialist Party to form a competing Democratic Socialist Party. In 1964, the Value Creating Society (Sōka Gakkai), a Nichiren Buddhist sect that grew to include almost one tenth of the Japanese population, formed the Clean Government Party (Kōmeitō). The Japanese Communist Party, which became less militant after the end of the Korean War, also gained ground and during the 1970s received almost 10 percent of the popular vote. Competition at the polls between candidates of these smaller opposition parties benefited the larger LDP.

The third and recent era of politics began in 1993. The notable feature of this era was the decline and fall of the left. The Japanese Socialist Party had been the principal opposition party for almost fifty years. But the end of the Cold War, the worldwide rejection of Marxism, the decline of labor union membership and militancy, and the widespread Japanese view that Socialist politicians had little to contribute to their recession-ridden country signaled the demise of socialism in Japan. In the 1993 election the Socialists dropped from 136 to 70 seats in the Lower House of the Diet. In 1994, hungry for a taste of power after decades in the wilderness, they set aside their principles and joined the LDP in a coalition government. In the 1996 general election, voters showed their disapproval by stripping the Socialists of all but 26 seats; in the 2000 election the total dropped further to 19 seats. The Communist Party also slumped. In the 2003 election, Socialists and Communists together garnered less than 5 percent of the seats in the 480 member Lower House.

The collapse of the left inaugurated an era of multiparty conservative politics. The players were the LDP, still the largest party, a shifting number of smaller conservative parties, and the Clean Government Party. Japanese electoral politics during the 1990s was punctuated by scandals and factional strife, but the single overriding issue was the economy. In 1993 the LDP lost 52 of its 275 seats, a consequence of its failure to end the recession. In its place, a non-LDP Conservative coalition held power between 1994 and 1996. But the crisis continued. In 1996 the voters turned again to the LDP in the hope that its more seasoned politicians might be able to deal with the lagging economy. With ups and downs, since that time the LDP has maintained its hegemony, since 2001 under the leadership of the popular Koizumi Junichirō. In the election of 2003 opposition politicians joined in the Democratic Party, which rose to 177 seats in the Lower House. Japanese editorials asked: Would the LDP stay in power indefinitely or did the rise of the Democrats point toward a future two-party system?

ECONOMIC GROWTH

The extraordinary story of the economic rise of East Asia after World War II began with Japan. Japanese productivity in 1945 was about the same as it had been in 1918. By 1955 it had recovered to prewar levels, but just as growth was expected to moderate, it forged ahead and continued at a double-digit pace for almost two decades. Shipbuilding, machine tools, steel, heavy chemicals, automobiles, and consumer electronics and optics led the way. Before the war, "made in Japan" had meant cheap, ten-cent-store goods. By the late 1970s Sony, Toyota, Honda, Panasonic, Toshiba, Seiko, and Canon were known throughout the world for the quality of their products.

Several factors explain this growth. An infrastructure of banking, marketing, and manufacturing skills had carried over from prewar Japan. The international situation was also favorable: Oil was cheap, access to raw materials and export markets was easy, and under American sponsorship Japan gained early entry into the World Bank, the International Monetary Fund, and other international organizations. A rate of savings close to 20 percent helped reinvestment. This reflected a traditional frugality but was also a modern necessity in view of inadequate pensions.

A revolution in education contributed as well. In the prewar years education for most Japanese ended with middle school and only 2 or 3 percent of students went to university. By the early

Middle School Students in Japanese Literature Class. Girls and boys wear school uniforms and study together. Desks are pushed together to accomodate large classes. The teacher is dressed like a businessman.
Charles Gupton/Getty Images Inc.–Stone Allstock.

1980s, almost all middle school graduates went on to high school, and a rising percentage of high school graduates went on to higher education. Even more telling is the fact that by the early eighties Japan was graduating more engineers than the United States, and that virtually all of them were employed in productive, nonmilitary industries. (At the time, the total number of lawyers in Japan roughly equaled a single year's graduating class from American law schools.) This upgrading of human capital and channeling of its best minds into productive careers enabled Japan to tap the huge backlog of technology that had developed in the United States during and after the war years. It proved far cheaper to license or buy technology than to invent it. After "improvement engineering," Japan sold its products to the world.

Another factor was an abundance of high-quality, cheap labor. Following a postwar baby boom, the population in 1950 was 83 million; by 2004 it rose to 127 million. It is expected to stabilize and then decline early in the twenty-first century. Immediately after the war about 47 percent of Japan's labor force was in agriculture; by 2005 only a tiny fraction worked on the land. Until the mid-1960s more labor was available than jobs, which kept wages low. Labor organization proved no bar to economic growth. Industrial workers in Japan during the immediate postwar decades were more highly unionized than those in the United States, but the basic component of labor organization was the company-based union, rather than a trade union. Company-based unions regularly engaged in spring offensives and marched with red flags on May Day, but

they also took great pains not to impair their companies' productivity. Since the 1980s the strength of unions has declined. In 2005, about one fifth of the labor force belonged to unions.

The government aided manufacturers with tariff protection, foreign exchange, and special depreciation allowances. Industries in advanced technologies benefited from cheap loans, subsidies, and products from government research laboratories. Small budgets for defense spending and welfare kept corporate taxes low. The Finance Ministry and the Ministry of Trade and Industry encouraged the Bank of Japan to back private banks in refinancing Japan's industries. Critics who spoke of "Japan Inc." as though Japan were a single gigantic corporation overstated the case: Competition between companies within Japan was fierce, but government was more supportive of business than it was regulative.

By 1973 the Japanese economy had become "mature." Double-digit growth gave way to 4 percent growth. Labor became more expensive, research budgets grew as the backlog of cheap technology declined, welfare costs rose, and tough but costly antipollution policies were implemented. Behind the statistic of slower growth was a change in the composition of the economy: Smokestack industries declined while service industries, pharmaceuticals, specialty chemicals, scientific equipment, computers, and robots grew. Japan's trade, hitherto balanced, began to generate huge surpluses. The surpluses were mainly due to the growing appetite of world markets for Japanese products but were also a result of protectionist policies. These policies led to friction and to demands from the United States and Europe for their abolition.

Sluggish growth, or no growth at all, characterized the nineties. Convinced that their boom would never end, Japanese had bid up the price of corporate shares and land to unrealistic levels—several times those of Europe and America. In 1991 the "bubble" burst: The price of land and stocks plummeted. Japanese who had bought shares of stock or real estate at exaggerated prices were hard hit; banks that had made housing or margin loans incurred huge losses. As banks and individuals retrenched, the economy slowed. Thousands of small companies went bankrupt, large companies restructured and cut their research budgets, some workers were laid off or retired early, and fewer new graduates were hired. Unemployment rose from the usual 1.5 percent to more than 5 or 6 percent, and hidden unemployment was even higher.

As Japan entered the twenty-first century, newspapers asked why the Japanese government dilly-dallied, taking only palliative measures. One explanation was the magnitude of the problem: Financial bureaucrats recoiled at the enormous costs of refinancing bank debt in the face of an already unbalanced budget. Another was the absence of a national consensus in favor of a bailout. Although corporations had been hurt by the recession, most individual Japanese, still protected by lifetime employment, were unwilling to shoulder new taxes. Instead,

▲ **Nissan Motors Assembly Line.** An almost completely automated assembly line at Nissan Motors' Zama factory. The high cost of labor in Japan makes such robot-intensive production economical.
Reuters/Susumu Takahashi/Archive Photos.

they increased their savings and hoped that Japan would muddle through. In this situation, no political party dared come out in favor of heavier taxes or a bailout of the banks.

Some economists predicted a gray future for Japan. Certainly, high labor costs made competition with China and other Asian neighbors difficult. Equally ominous to Japanese prospects was the rapidity of its neighbors' advance into high technology.

Others lamented the recession but saw the downturn as a necessary correction of speculative excesses. Japanese industry had emerged leaner and more competitive after the "oil shocks" of 1972 and 1979 and would do so again. They noted, too, that the recession was anomalous in that while domestic consumption sank, exports rose, and Japan's favorable balance of trade grew. In 2003 Japan's trade surplus with the United States was over $66 billion—reflecting the American appetite for Japanese cars. Even Japan's redoubtable management skills seemed exportable: Nissan's Tennessee plant took 17.37 hours to assemble an automobile, while at General Motors' the average was 26.75. Equally notable was Japan's determination to maintain its lead in flat screens, fermentation chemistry, robotics, and materials research, and to become a world force in biotechnology, medical instruments, and airplanes. New science and engineering buildings on the Tokyo University campus dwarf the prewar brick buildings of the faculties of law, letters, economics, and education.

An export-led recovery began in 2002. The recovering American economy and the soaring Chinese economy were critical. Japanese economists began to speak of the "complementarity" of Japanese and Chinese markets. In 2004 a new phase was marked by the rise of consumer spending and stock valuations. Continuing recovery was linked to the world economy.

Slower growth notwithstanding, at the dawn of the third millennium Japan's economic weight loomed large. Its economy was second only to the United States, and almost equal to the economies of Germany and France put together. Or, in another perspective, its economy was slightly larger than the economies of the rest of Asia combined. See Figure 33–1 and the Overview table on p. 1002, which compare Japanese productivity with other countries.

Of course, such figures cannot be taken at face value. Per capita product does not equate simply with standard of living. Costs are high in Japan, as in other developed nations. Goods in other Asian nations cost less to produce and are cheaper. Exchange rates also make a difference. China's GDP (Gross Domestic Product) would score higher if it did not hold down the value of its currency to encourage exports. Still, after all qualifications, the fact remains that Japan achieved a near European level of affluence through the peaceful development of human resources in a free society.

SOCIETY AND CULTURE

The triple engines of change—Occupation reforms, economic growth, and rapid expansion of higher education—transformed Japanese society. In 1945, almost half of the population lived in villages organically rooted in the past; half a century later most Japanese lived in cities, more than a quarter in the Tokyo-Osaka industrial corridor. As in the United States and Europe, a tiny percentage of the population produced the food for the rest. Families changed, too. In 1945 the three-generation extended family of grandparents, parents, and children was considered standard, and most marriages were arranged. Fifty years later the nuclear family of parents and children was the norm, and most marriages were "love matches." From the 1950s and 1960s, companies and government offices built huge apartment blocks for their

A Comparison of Japan with Germany and France in the Year 2005 (IMF Estimates)		
	GDP (in billions)	Population (in millions)	Per Capita GDP
Germany	$2,769	83	$33,575
France	$2,052	64	$33,111
Total	$4,821	147	$32,796 (average)
Japan	$4,759	127	$37,241

Figure 33–1

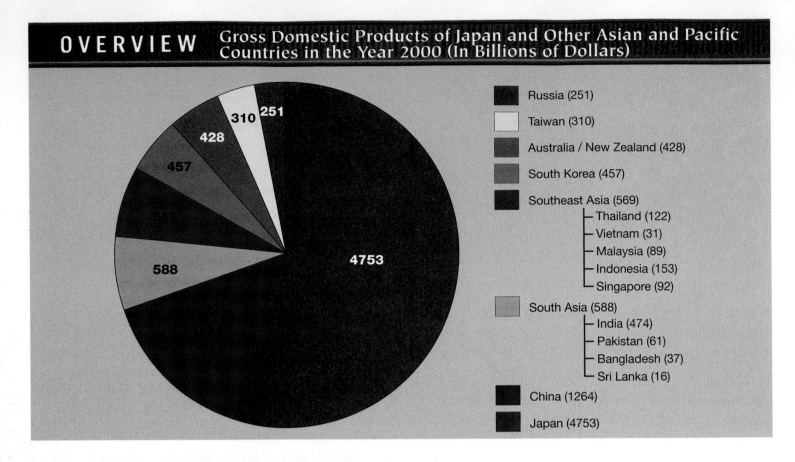

OVERVIEW Gross Domestic Products of Japan and Other Asian and Pacific Countries in the Year 2000 (In Billions of Dollars)

Russia (251)

Taiwan (310)

Australia / New Zealand (428)

South Korea (457)

Southeast Asia (569)
— Thailand (122)
— Vietnam (31)
— Malaysia (89)
— Indonesia (153)
— Singapore (92)

South Asia (588)
— India (474)
— Pakistan (61)
— Bangladesh (37)
— Sri Lanka (16)

China (1264)

Japan (4753)

employees on the edges of cities. The apartments were small, but wives welcomed life without mothers-in-law. In the 1960s and 1970s, larger apartments, called "mansions" in Japanese, were built in cities and purchased by middle- and higher-income families; only the rich could afford city houses. As incomes rose, people bought rice cookers, washing machines, dryers, televisions, computers, and other electronic equipment. Consumerism was constrained only by the small size of living units.

The status of women rose. Occupation reforms had given women the vote, legal equality, and an equal share of the family inheritance. Women's colleges gained the right to award degrees, and women enrolled in hitherto all-male universities, including the former imperial universities. Rising incomes and smaller families enabled parents to give all their children a higher education. Coed excursions to ocean beaches or ski slopes became commonplace. Most women worked for a few years after completing their education and married later: The average age of marriage rose from 24 in 1970 to 28 in 2002. Wives usually stayed at home while their children were small, but many returned to work when their children entered middle school. In 1980, almost twice as many wives stayed at home than worked, while in 2002 more wives worked than stayed at home. A working wife had a greater say in household matters. With the shift toward nuclear families, wives became household authority figures, at least during the long hours that their husbands worked and commuted. Greater eco-

nomic leeway also made divorce an option: The number tripled to European levels between 1970 and 2002.

In the new Japan, getting ahead depended on education. Middle school was compulsory, virtually everyone went on to high school, and of these, by the year 2005, over half, about the same percent as in the United States, went on to some form of higher education. The pressure to enter good schools started in kindergarten. Mothers routinely compared children's test scores and sent their children to after-school tutoring classes. Examinations determined admissions at every level, even for the cram schools that prepped failed candidates to retake university entrance examinations. Magazine articles regularly lamented the excesses of Japan's "examination society." They claimed that Japan's lockstep education was appropriate to the needs of assembly-line production, but not to the needs of "the information age." But little was done to change the system. A few students rebelled against their parents or bullied their schoolmates, but most students realized that the pressure to excel was for their own good and limited their rebellion to reading violent and sadistic *manga* (comics).

On the positive side, the enormous prewar gap between the tiny educated elite and the masses with only a middle school education disappeared. Whatever the reality, more than 90 percent of Japanese saw themselves as middle class. This consciousness was the social base for the new democracy and for

▲ **Body Language.** Japanese businessmen exchange business cards in Tokyo. A businesswoman stands and observes. An almost diplomatic formality governs such occasions.
Getty Images, Inc.

the growing number of voters who described themselves as independents. More education also explains Japan's tremendous consumption of newspapers, magazines, and books. Bookstores stocked every variety of books imaginable: serious fiction, mysteries, histories, poetry, science fiction, romances, cookbooks, translations, as well as books on investing, self-improvement, and home repairs.

In prewar Japan, the claims of the individual vis-à-vis the family, community, and state were often weak. Postwar prosperity brought greater personal autonomy. Public opinion polls of workers showed a desire for more meaningful work and a larger sphere of independence apart from their job. Small pleasures did not replace duties but became an expected part of everyday life. The young, who took affluence for granted, met with friends at coffeehouses or McDonald's, watched American movies or Japanese *anime*, and frequently traveled abroad.

Attitudes toward minorities, about 2 percent of the population, improved during the postwar decades. The Ainu of Hokkaido, long despised and neglected, had mostly died off or been absorbed into the majority population during the prewar century. In the postwar years, the 20,000 or 30,000 who maintained or regained an ethnic identity formed political organizations, got the support of leftist parties, and obtained welfare legislation. A larger problem was the *burakumin* or outcast communities, which were especially numerous in western Japan. Though physically indistinguishable from other Japanese, their members were shunned as marriage partners and frequently barred from good jobs. Political and legal action improved their condition, though social prejudices persisted. A less tractable problem was the 900,000 Koreans in Japan. By

the 1980s, most had been born and educated in Japan but were not citizens, since citizenship was determined by blood, not birthplace. Early on, many supported North Korea, though few wished to live there. As South Korea industrialized, Japanese Koreans were no longer seen as the people of a backward nation, but they were still viewed as separate from Japanese and suffered social and occupational prejudices.

As the new millennium began, the most serious social problem facing Japan was the aging of its population. In 1980, there were five workers for every retired person; by 2010 and for several decades thereafter, there will be fewer than two. Corporate pensions were underfunded, private savings were inadequate, and government and public pensions (the Japanese equivalent of Social Security) added to government deficits. A recurring question was how the old will be supported and how they will vote in elections. This problem, of course, is not unique to Japan. All developed nations have experienced a shift from high to lower fertility and mortality, but the imbalance is particularly severe in Japan, Italy, and Germany, where wartime population losses and postwar baby booms skewed age group distribution.

Japan is crowded and would be more livable with fewer people. Some see today's low birthrate as an opportunity to reduce population. The prospective problem of too few workers, they argue, might be solved by raising the retirement age, starting pensions later, and tapping the reservoir of nonworking, middle-aged women. Ironically, in recession Japan, where graduates had trouble finding jobs and companies already carried excess workers, the immediate problem was too few jobs, not too few workers. Despite this, during the past decade, Japanese from Brazil and Peru and illegal immigrants

◄ **Comic Book.** Raised from childhood in the arts of *ninja*, the young heroine Azumi slays evil men. The popularity of this *Bigu Komikku* (Big Comic) led to a movie (*anime* or animated) version. Was this the Japanese model for "Kill Bill?" Japan has specialized comics for every cohort—for children, teenage boys, teenage girls, and adults.
Clive Streeter © Dorling Kindersley.

DOCUMENT | Two Views of the "Symbol Emperor"

The murkiest aspect of Japan's prewar emperor-centered ideology was the juxtaposition of the emperor as a modern monarch and the emperor as a living deity, ultimately descended from the sun goddess. In the first selection, former Prime Minister Yoshida Shigeru, a product of Meiji Japan, basically accepts the prewar ideology but argues that because in fact the emperor exercised little power before World War II, nothing was changed by the postwar constitution. In the second selection, Nobel Prize winner Ōe Kenzaburō, a humanistic and slightly leftist novelist, recognizes that the emperor has been stripped of his former authority but worries about a revival of his Shinto identity.

♦ What does Yoshida mean by "as naturally," and why does Ōe call the prewar emperor an "absolute ruler"?

1.

In regard to the question of the Imperial structure of government, as it existed in Japan, I pointed out that the Meiji Constitution had originated in the promises made to the Japanese people by the Emperor Meiji at the beginning of his reign, and there was little need to dwell on the fact that democracy, if we were to use the word, had always formed part of the traditions of our country, and was not—as some mistakenly imagined—something that was about to be introduced with the revision of the Constitution. As for the Imperial House, the idea and reality of the Throne had come into being among the Japanese people as naturally as the idea of the country itself; no question of antagonism between Throne and people could possibly arise; and nothing contained in the new Constitution could change that fact. The word "symbol" had been employed in the definition of the Emperor because we Japanese had always regarded the Emperor as the symbol of the country itself—a statement which any Japanese considering the issue dispassionately would be ready to recognize as an irrefutable fact.

2.

Japan's emperor system, which had apparently lost its social and political influence after the defeat in the Pacific War, is beginning to flex its muscles again, and in some respects it has already recouped much of its lost power—with two differences: first, the Japanese today will not accept the prewar ideology-cum-theology that held the emperor to be both absolute ruler and living deity. Nevertheless, imperial rites performed quite recently were done in such a manner as to impress upon us that the emperor's lineage can be traced to a deity; I am referring here to the rituals associated with the present emperor's enthronement and the so-called Great Thanksgiving Service that followed it. These ceremonies provoked little objection from either the government or the people, indeed most Japanese seemed to take it all very much for granted.

---

from other parts of Asia have come in large numbers to take the lowly jobs that Japanese despise. Many illegals are deported, but larger numbers arrive.

The postwar transformation of Japanese society might be expected to have produced deep cultural strains and social dislocations. At the margin, these did occur. The growth among the urban poor of "new religions" such as the Value Creating Society was interpreted by some as an attempt to re-create a sense of community within an increasingly impersonal urban society. One aberrant apocalyptic cult released nerve gas in a Tokyo subway in 1995, leaving the Japanese shocked that something so "un-Japanese" could happen. White-collar workers, or "salary men," spent hours commuting to work in crowded buses and trains. In Japan's corporate world *karoshi*, or death from overwork, has become a recognized phenomenon.

Yet the ability of the society—family, school, office, and workshop—to absorb strains and lend support to the individual was impressive. Lifetime employment—only slightly affected by the bursting of the bubble—gave both workers and salaried employees a sense of security. Even during the long recession, layoffs were the exception. Japanese wives, according to public opinion polls, felt they were better off than their American counterparts. Of children born in Japan, about 1 percent were to unwed mothers; in the United States the figure was thirty times greater. Infant mortality was the lowest in the world and longevity the highest. Japan also had far less crime. Even big cities were safe at night. Drugs were not a problem. Effective gun control had predictable results: in 2002, 24 persons, mostly gang members, were killed by guns in Japan; the figure for the United States was almost 10,000. In 2000 the prison population in the United States was thirty times greater than that of Japan. Despite crowded housing and omnipresent social pressures, by most objective measures Japanese society was stable and healthy.

Japanese culture has also remained vital. The traditional arts flourished—poetry, painting, pottery, fabrics, tea ceremony, flower arrangement, the Kabuki and Nō drama. The best artists were designated as Living National Treasures and held in respect. In architecture, literature, painting, and dance, the prewar tradition of vigorous experiments with new or hybrid forms continued. The awareness of nature, so evident in films like Kurosawa Akira's *Rashomon* or *The Seven Samurai,* carried over to television dramas. Films by Itami Jūzo (*Tampopo*) and Suo Masayuki (*Shall We Dance*) combined humor and social satire. Symphony orchestras in Japan's major cities played Mozart and Stravinsky as well as native compositions with haunting passages played on the Japanese flute and zither. Clothing designers competed in Tokyo, New York, and Paris. College students formed rock bands, listened to jazz, and read Japanese science fiction along with the writings of serious novelists. Postwar Japan amply supports an argument for parallelism between economic and cultural dynamics.

JAPAN AND THE WORLD

At the start of the new millennium, Japan had three sets of critical international relationships: with the world, East Asia, and the United States. With the world, Japan was a trading partner and, as it described itself, a "UN nation." It gave more foreign aid to developing countries than did other nations. It was a member of major international economic organizations. Its economy depended on free trade, and it worked assiduously to ensure the requisite conditions. A second set was with its East Asian neighbors. For reasons of history and proximity, Japan was extraordinarily sensitive (and at moments insensitive) to developments in Korea, Taiwan, China, and the Russian Far East. Newspapers covered these nations in detail. Japan's relations with China, South Korea, and Taiwan have improved during recent decades. Toward China, Japan felt a growing ambivalence. They appreciated Chinese imports of Japanese goods, which had rescued the Japanese economy, but they worried that China's growing military strength was affecting the political balance in East Asia, if not posing a future threat.

The third critical relationship was with the United States. The two countries were political allies, major trading partners, and were linked by mutual security concerns. The 1952 security treaty, several times amended, remained the cornerstone of all Japanese defense planning. In recent years Japan has moved toward more positive military cooperation—within the limits of its constantly reinterpreted "peace constitution." When terrorists struck at the United States in September 2001, Prime Minister Koizumi spoke out in support of the United States and against terrorism. The Diet passed new laws permitting the Self-Defense Forces, for the first time, to play an active, noncombat role in a war zone in support of U.S. forces. In 2003 Japan sent troops to Iraq. In an East Asia in which China and Russia have atomic weapons and North Korea, a rogue nation, threatens to develop them, Japanese feel increasingly vulnerable. If Japan's trust in the U.S. "nuclear umbrella" ever wavered, it would become a nuclear power overnight.

China

The story of China after 1949 might begin with the four Ma's: Malthus, Marx, Ma Yinchu, and Mao Zedong. Malthus had claimed that population would expand geometrically whereas food would increase only arithmetically. Marx rejected the Malthusian hypothesis, along with classical economics, as myths of the capitalist stage of history. Professor Ma Yinchu (1882–1982), the chancellor of Beijing University, published in 1957 *New Principles on Chinese Population,* in which he argued that unchecked population growth would impede capital accumulation and depress living standards. Mao Zedong, faithfully following the teachings of Marx, purged Professor Ma and closed down population institutes at Chinese universities. What followed was a population increase from 550 million in 1949 to nearly a billion in 1981. Real growth occurred in the Chinese economy during the 1960s and 1970s, but the gains were eaten up by the extra mouths. In the face of this crisis, in 1981 the Chinese government adopted a national policy of one child per family. It recognized that the policy ran contrary to the deep-rooted Chinese sense of family but argued that without it, China's future would be bleak. Thereafter the increase slowed but the population still crossed the 1.3 billion mark in 2005.

SOVIET PERIOD (1950–1960)

Civil war in China ended in 1949 as the last of Jiang Jieshi's troops fled to Taiwan. The People's Republic of China was proclaimed in October. The following year, China entered into an alliance with the Soviet Union. The decade that followed is often called the "Soviet period" because the Soviet model was adopted for the government, the army, the economy, and higher education.

CHRONOLOGY

China Since 1949

1949	Communist victory; People's Republic of China
1950	Sino-Soviet alliance; China invaded Tibet
1953	First Five-Year Plan
1958	Great Leap Forward
1960–1963	Sino-Soviet split
1965–1976	Cultural Revolution
1972	Nixon visit to Beijing
1976	Mao Zedong dies
1978	Deng Xiaoping in power
1989	Tienanmen Square incident
1997	Deng Xiaoping dies
1998–2001	China's economy grows while rest of Asia in recession

The first step taken by the Communist government was military consolidation. Even after the republic was proclaimed, Chinese armies continued to push outward, conquering vast areas with non-Chinese populations. Tibet, for example, was seized in 1950. Once subdued, the areas inhabited by Tibetans, Uighur Turks, Mongols, and other minorities were designated autonomous regions. They were occupied by the Chinese army and were settled by a growing number of Chinese immigrants. Although their governments were staffed mainly by members of the indigenous populations, they were tightly controlled by the Chinese Communist Party.

Political consolidation followed. The most powerful elite was the Communist Party. Its members held the key levers of power in the government, army, and security forces. Mao was both party chairman and head of state. He ruled through the Standing Committee of the Political Bureau (Politburo) of the party's Central Committee. Below the Politburo were regional, provincial, and district committees with party cells in every village, factory, school, and government office. The party expanded from 2.7 million members in 1947 to 17 million in 1961. Party members were exhorted to energize and enforce the local enactment of government policies.

Economic reconstruction began immediately. An attempt was made to integrate the industries in Manchuria and former treaty ports with the rest of China. Huge numbers of workers were mobilized to build new bridges, dams, roads, and railways. China's first five-year plan for economic development began in 1953. The Soviet Union sent financial aid as well as engineers and planners.

Rural society underwent two fundamental changes: land redistribution and then collectivization. In the early fifties, party cadres visited villages and held meetings at which landlords were denounced and forced to confess their crimes. Some were rehabilitated, others were sent to labor camps, and hundreds of thousands—some scholars estimate several million—were killed. Their holdings were redistributed to the landless, and local responsibilities formerly borne by landlord gentry were shifted to associations dominated by former tenant farmers. Then in 1955 and 1956, before the new landowners had time to put down roots as private landowners, all lands were seized by the state and collectivized. The timing was important: There was the earlier example of the Soviet Union, where collectivization came six years after redistribution; it was resisted by the *kulaks*, who had had time to put down roots.

During the early 1950s, intellectuals and universities also became a target for thought reform; the Chinese slang term was **brainwashing**. This involved study and indoctrination in Marxism, group pressure to produce an atmosphere of insecurity and fear, which would be followed by confession, repentance, and reacceptance by society. The indoctrination was intended to strengthen party control. But beyond this was the optimistic belief that the inculcation of correct moral doctrines could mobilize human energies on behalf of the state—perhaps a belief with distant Confucian roots. In 1956 Mao felt that intellectuals had been adequately indoctrinated and, concerned lest creativity be stifled, he said in a speech, "Let the hundred flowers bloom"—a reference to the lively discourse among the many schools of philosophy in ancient Zhou China. To his surprise, intellectuals responded with a torrent of criticism that did not spare the Communist Party. Mao thereupon reversed his position, sending many leading writers and intellectuals to labor camps.

By the late 1950s Mao was disappointed with the results of collectivization and the first five-year plan. In 1958 he abandoned a second plan (and the Soviet model) in favor of a mass mobilization to unleash the productive energies of the people. He called it the **Great Leap Forward**. One slogan was "Hard work for a few years and happiness for a thousand." Campaigns were organized to accomplish vast projects; iron smelters were built in "backyards" and instant industries were the order of the day. In the countryside, village-based collective farms gave way to communes of 30,000 persons or more. The results were disastrous. Homemade iron was unusable, instant industries failed, and agricultural production plummeted. Scholars estimate that between 1958 and 1962 as many as 20 to 30 million Chinese starved to death. To control the damage, communes were broken into production brigades in 1959, and two years later these were further broken into production teams of forty households. But even these actions could not overcome the ills of low incentives and collective responsibility; through the 1970s agricultural production fell.

It was also during these years that Sino-Soviet relations deteriorated. Disputes arose over borders. China was dissatisfied with the level of Soviet aid. It was also embarrassed by the Soviet debunking of Stalin's cult of personality, since within China Mao was still venerated as the "great helmsman." For its part, the Soviet Union condemned the Great Leap Forward as leftist fanaticism and resented Mao's view of himself, after Stalin's death, as the foremost theoretician and exponent of world communism. In 1960, the Soviet Union halted economic aid and withdrew its engineers from China, and by 1963 the split was visible to the outside world. Each country deployed about a million troops along their mutual border. Had relations between the two Communist giants been amicable, these troops, deployed elsewhere, might have changed the course of history in Southeast Asia and Eastern Europe. The Sino-Soviet split was arguably the single most important development in postwar international politics.

The years between 1960 and 1965 saw conflicting trends. The utter failure of the Great Leap Forward led some Chinese leaders to turn away from Mao's reckless radicalism toward more moderate policies. Mao kept his position as the head of the party but was forced to give up his post as head of state to another veteran Communist official. Yet even as the government moved toward realistic goals and stable bureaucratic management, General Lin Biao (1908–1971) reestablished within the army the party committees and procedures for ideological indoctrination which had lapsed after the failure of the Great Leap Forward. A new mass movement was also begun to transform education.

THE GREAT PROLETARIAN CULTURAL REVOLUTION (1965–1976)

In 1965, Mao once again emerged to dominate Chinese politics. Mao the revolutionary had never been able to make the transition to Mao the ruler of an established state. When he looked at the Chinese Communist Party and the government bureaucracy, he saw a new privileged elite; when he looked at younger Chinese, he saw a generation with no experience of revolution. Mao feared that the Chinese revolution—his revolution—would end up as a Soviet-style bureaucratic communism run for the benefit of officials, so he called for a new revolution to create a truly egalitarian culture.

Obtaining army support, Mao urged students and teenaged youth to form bands of Red Guards. In the early feverish phase of the **Cultural Revolution**, the guards invoked Mao's sayings contained in the "Little Red Book" almost as holy scripture. Mass rallies were held. One rally in Beijing was attended by "millions" of youths, who then made "long marches" back to their home provinces to carry out Mao's program. Universities were shut down as student factions fought among themselves. Teachers were beaten, imprisoned, and subjected to such extremes of humiliation that many committed suicide. Books and artworks were destroyed in a campaign against "the four olds." Stone Buddhas that had endured since the Song dynasty were smashed or defaced. Things foreign also came under attack. Homes were ransacked for foreign books, and Chinese who had studied abroad were persecuted. Even the borrowing of foreign technology was denigrated as "sniffing after the farts of foreigners and calling them sweet." Red Guards attacked local party headquarters and beat to death persons they regarded as reactionaries, including some party cadres. High officials were purged. The crippled apparatus of party and government was replaced by revolutionary committees. Chinese today recall these events as a species of mass hysteria that defies understanding.

Eventually Mao tired of the violence and near anarchy. In 1968 and 1969 he called in the army to take over the revolutionary committees. In 1969, a new Central Committee, composed largely of military men, was established, and General Lin Biao was named as Mao's successor. Violence came to an end as millions of students and intellectuals were sent to the countryside to work on farms. In 1970 and 1971 the revolutionary

▲ **Everyday Life in China During the Cultural Revolution.** School children parading during the Cultural Revolution with red banners proclaiming "Long live Chairman Mao." This peaceful scene belies the violence that often marked this period.
Corbis.

committees were reconstituted as party committees. Worsening relations with the Soviet Union also made China's leaders desire greater stability at home. In 1969, a pitched battle had broken out between Chinese and Russian troops over an island in the Ussuri River. After this encounter, the Chinese built bomb shelters in their main cities. It was just at this time that President Nixon began to withdraw U.S. troops from Vietnam. When he proposed a renewal of ties, China quickly responded. Nixon visited Beijing in 1972, opening a new era of diplomatic relations.

The second phase of the Cultural Revolution between 1969 and 1976 was moderate only in comparison with what had gone before. On farms and in factories, ideology was still seen as an adequate substitute for economic incentives. Universities reopened, but students were admitted by class background, not by examination. In 1971, Lin Biao was purged. According to the official account of his death, Lin had tried to kill Mao and seize the government, but when his coup failed, he died in a plane crash while attempting to escape to the Soviet Union. Lin's place was taken by the so-called Gang of Four, which included Mao's wife and was abetted by the aging Mao. Class struggle was revived, and an official campaign was launched attacking the rightist "political swindlers" Lin Biao and Confucius.

CHINA AFTER MAO

Political Developments   Mao's death in 1976 brought immediate changes. Within four weeks the Gang of Four and their radical supporters had been arrested. In their place, Deng Xiaoping 1904–1997) emerged as the dominant figure in Chinese politics. Twice purged for rightist tendencies—once during the Cultural Revolution he was paraded around Beijing wearing a dunce cap—Deng was determined that such things not happen again. He ousted his enemies, rehabilitated those purged during the Cultural Revolution, and put his supporters in power. Portraits and statues of Mao were removed from most public places in August 1980. After the lunacy of the Cultural Revolution, the establishment of a normal Communist dictatorship came as a welcome relief. The people began to enjoy a measure of security and the prospect of better lives.

There continued, however, a tension between the determination of the ruling party to maintain its grip on power and its desire to obtain the benefits of some liberalization. The tension was most visible in China's intellectual life. The government's repudiation of the Cultural Revolution had led to an outpouring of stories, plays, and reports. In *Nightmare* by Xu Hui, the mother of a son killed during the Cultural Revolution asks, "Why? Why? Can anyone tell me why?" Liu Binyan wrote of corrupt officials who had "degenerated into parasitical insects that fed off the people's productivity and the socialist system." But criticism of Deng's rule was not allowed. Writers were regularly enjoined to be "led by the Communist Party and guided by Marx-Leninism." When a writer in 1983 overstepped the invisible line separating what was permissible from what was not, a short campaign was launched against "spiritual pollution." In 1985 and 1987 as well, the government organized campaigns against "capitalist thinking" and "bourgeois democracy."

Universities returned to normal in 1977. Entrance examinations were reinstituted, purged teachers were returned to their classrooms, and scientists and scholars were sent to study in Japan and the West. During the late seventies and eighties students still spent one afternoon a week discussing party directives or the writings of Deng Xiaoping. But far more influential was the new openness within China and the growing contacts with the wider world as scholars returned from the West. Students became aware of the prosperity achieved by Japan, Hong Kong, and Taiwan. They began to demand greater freedoms and even political democracy. During the late 1980s, the ferment that marked Eastern Europe and the Soviet Union under Gorbachev also appeared in China: it was as if a new virus had entered the Communist world.

The new spirit came to a head in April and May of 1989, when hundreds of thousands of students, workers, and people from all walks of life demonstrated for democracy in Tienanmen Square in Beijing and in dozens of other cities. Hunger strikes were held. Students published prodemocracy newspapers. Banners proclaimed slogans, among them "Give us freedom or give us death." A twenty-seven-foot polystyrene-and-plaster Goddess of Democracy and Freedom was erected in the square. At first, government leaders could not agree on how to respond, but the hardline faction led by Deng won out and in early June sent in tanks and troops. Hundreds of students were killed, and leaders who did not escape abroad were jailed. The

event defined the political climate in China in the years that followed: No challenge to Communist Party rule was tolerated, though considerable freedom was allowed in other areas of life.

Economic Growth In the economic sphere, China's leaders repudiated the policies of Mao. After taking power, Deng said in a speech (or is said to have said) that "to be rich is glorious." His greatest achievement in the years after 1978 was to demonstrate in China the superiority of market incentives to central planning. In 1985, Hu Yaobang, the General Secretary of the CCP, expressed a similarly realistic view, that China "had wasted twenty years" on "radical leftist nonsense."

In China's villages, as the farm family once again became the basic unit of production, grain production rose from about 300 million tons in the 1980s to more than 500 million

▲ **Goddess of Democracy and Freedom.** Student activists construct a "Goddess of Democracy and Freedom," taking the Statue of Liberty as their model. The goddess was in place in Tienanmen Square shortly before tanks drove students from the square in June 1989.
Reuters/Ed Nachtrieb/Archive Photos.

in the late 1990s. A local leader commented, "When people work for themselves, they work better." Then, as farmers living near cities found it much more profitable to abandon grains in favor of specialty crops such as fruit or the feedgrains required by China's rising consumption of meat, grain production declined to 431 million tons in 2003. Farm family incomes continued to rise, though still only a third of those of city dwellers. Worried about rising imports of grains and future self-sufficiency, in 2003 the government announced agricultural subsidies to promote grain production.

State-operated enterprises were the surviving portion of the old, centrally planned, command economy. As late as 1982, their output was 74 percent of total industrial production. Over half ran at a loss, and because they employed twice the labor needed to run them efficiently, they were a constant drain on China's state-owned banks. Their workers were paid little and had little incentive to work hard, since they enjoyed the security of the so-called "iron ricebowl." In 1999 the government announced a plan to sell off these enterprises. The state ownership required by China's constitution would give way to public (that is to say, private) ownership. The costs would be high—defaulted loans, bankruptcies, unemployed workers, and a sudden rise in pensioners—but the drain on the state budget would end. In 1997 their share of total industrial production had been 40 percent; by 2003 it declined to 31 percent; most of the decline, however, was due to rapid growth in the market sector of the economy.

The main driver of the economy was the free market sector. Between 1980 and 1994 the Chinese economy grew at double-digit rates and, after 1995, in the high single digits. Exports rose from $7 billion in 1975 to $183 billion in 1997 to $436 billion in 2003. The surge in new enterprises began in special economic zones established along the border with Hong Kong and quickly spread along the coast. Shanghai, with a population of 14 million, became a city of industrialists and skyscrapers, and the site of China's first stock exchange. Shandong Province in the northeast attracted huge investments from Japan, South Korea, and the United States, and achieved stunning growth, as did Manchuria, another industrial heartland. As entrepreneurs, cities, and local governments joined in, the tide of enterprise swept inland. Wuhan, a major communications hub and automobile manufacturer in central China, averaged growth of 16 or 17 percent during the early 1990s. Yet in the hinterlands large regions lagged behind and clamored for government assistance. To achieve growth, however, the government was willing to tolerate personal and regional inequities.

The factors that fueled this growth were clear: a huge surplus of good quality, cheap labor, a savings rate of 35–40 percent, a level of protectionism higher than other Asian nations, large investments from abroad, and open world markets. China, in effect, successfully used tariffs to shield its markets,

Cheap Labor. Wages at this Beijing shirt factory are low by Western standards but high by Chinese standards. This is not a sweatshop but a modern factory. Should Western nations leave the production of textiles to low-wage nations? What of steel or micro electronics?
A. Raney/Photo Edit.

while making use of cheap labor to flood foreign markets with goods and build up its currency reserves –which in 2003 were second only to those of Japan. China joined the World Trade Organization in 2001; since then its protectionism has become less blatant.

Social Change During the Mao years, farmers had been tied to their village collective. Cities were closed to those without residence permits. City dwellers, whether they worked in factories, hospitals, schools, newspapers, or government offices, were members of "units." Units, like company towns, provided their members with jobs, housing, food, child care, medical services, and pensions. Party cadres controlled the units and, through them, every aspect of their members' lives. Block organizations exercised surveillance over the inhabitants and reported infractions of socialist morality to the authorities.

Under Deng, controls were loosened. The police became less active—except against political dissidents, censorship was reduced, and ties with the outside world were allowed to develop. The unit also diminished in importance as food became widely available in free markets and apartments were sold to their inhabitants on easy terms. Private housing brought with it the freedom to change jobs. As workers with higher salaries began to provide for their own needs, life became freer and more enjoyable. The market economy placed a premium on individual decisions and initiatives.

The new prosperity and changing mores became increasingly visible. The blue Mao uniforms of the 1960s were followed by suits, however ill-fitting, and later, for the young, blue jeans,

Shanghai Street scene. Bikers and cars move in separate lanes. New highrise buildings are in the background. Note the three-wheel bike transporting lumber in the foreground.
Jeff Greenberg/PhotoEdit.

sneakers, and colorful jackets. By the 1990s, innovative Chinese designers were holding fashion shows in Shanghai and Beijing. Young people associated freely, and in urban areas earlier taboos against public displays of affection were relaxed. The household treasures of the 1960s, radios and bicycles, gave way to stoves and refrigerators in the 1970s, and, in the next decade, to washing machines and color televisions. Crowds gathered around displays of motorbikes in department stores. By the early nineties, motorbikes and privately owned cars competed in crowded streets with the ceaseless flow of bicycles. Private restaurants opened, and travel for pleasure became commonplace. In 1988, most passengers on domestic airline flights were foreign; ten years later, most were Chinese.

The estimated Chinese per capita GDP, as measured by the exchange value of its currency, was about $1933 in 2005. This is low. But as measured in purchasing power, the figure is closer to $6,000. The awareness of most Chinese that their living standard has improved sharply over the past two decades shapes their attitudes.

The new wealth, quite naturally, was unevenly distributed. The more successful entrepreneurs bought houses, cars, microwaves, computers, and cell phones. They traveled abroad and sent their children to private schools. As their lifestyle became more Western, they were sometimes called China's new middle class, but in fact they constituted an upper class. Other city dwellers also participated in the new prosperity, but many barely scraped by and unemployment remained high. Among the rural 70 percent of the population, the pace of change has been slower. In prosper-

ous belts near cities, the number of large brick houses and tractors impressed foreign visitors. But in the hinterlands, apart from the most enterprising, hardship remained the rule. In the West envy is green. In China the envy and resentment by have-nots toward the newly affluent are called the "red-eye disease."

China and the World   From the 1950s to the 1970s, China isolated itself from the rest of the world. The Sino-Soviet split defined its relations to the north. The Cold War defined its relations with Japan, South Korea, Taiwan, and the United States. (See Document, "U.S. Foreign Policy: A Chinese Dissident's View.") China gave aid to North Vietnam during the Vietnamese War but then, as Vietnamese anti-Chinese sentiments reasserted themselves, turned around and briefly invaded Vietnam in 1979. In some measure China's relations with its neighbors reflected its internal political turmoil. The turmoil ended during the 1980s and changes set in. Economic growth gave China some leeway. Trade ties with the non-Communist world led China to look outward and adopt more moderate policies.

In the 1990s, foreign relations improved across the board. Relations with Russia became amicable. China welcomed increased trade and investment from Taiwan and South Korea, despite its fear of Taiwan's growing independence, despite its continuing, if increasingly reluctant, support of North Korea. China also worked to improve its ties with Southeast Asia.

China's relations with the United States were complicated. Both during and after the Cold War, U.S. military alliances with Japan, South Korea, and Taiwan, and its ties to the non-Communist nations of Southeast Asia acted as the main countervailing force to Chinese hegemony in the region. China resented the U.S. presence in what it considered—in Middle Kingdom fashion—its own proper sphere of influence. The first step toward a new relationship was President Nixon's visit to China in 1972. The United States extended diplomatic recognition to China in 1979.

Since the 1980s, exports to the United States have been vital to China's economic growth and became more so during the 1990s as the rest of East Asia slipped into recession. China's exports to the United States increased from $62 billion in 1997 to $152 billion in 2003; its imports from the United States increased from $13 to $34 billion. The United States was unhappy with this imbalance and has protested Chinese piracy of hundreds of millions of dollars' worth of U.S. movies, computer software, and CDs each year.

The United States was also critical of Chinese human rights abuses, nuclear testing, and arms sales to Iran and Pakistan. The United States, nonetheless, hoped that a deeper Chinese engagement with the United States and the rest of the world would lead to better relations. Deng's successor, Premier Jiang Zemin, visited the United States in 1997 and President Clinton returned the visit the following year, strengthening U.S.-Chi-

| **U.S. Foreign Policy: A Chinese Dissident's View**

Wei Jingsheng, a Chinese advocate of democratic rights, was deported to the United States in late 1997. A year later, in The New York Times *op-ed page essay, he criticized U.S. policy as pandering to Chinese tyranny.*

◆ Should U.S. foreign policy be used to promote human rights even in poor countries with cultural traditions different from the West? Or should the United States avoid interference in the domestic politics of other nations and aim primarily at furthering American economic and security goals? What can foreign policy achieve? Where should the balance be struck?

China's Diversionary Tactics

One year ago, after 18 years in a Chinese prison, I was "released" and sent here. A Chinese official said that if I ever set foot in China again, I would immediately be returned to prison. ...

The State Department, in a report last January, used my forced exile as evidence that China was taking "positive steps in human rights" and that "Chinese society continued to become more open." These "positive steps" led the United States and its allies to oppose condemnation of China at a meeting of the United Nations Commission on Human Rights in April. In the months that followed, President Clinton and other Western leaders traveled to China, trumpeting increased economic ties and muting criticism on human rights.

Thus, without fear of sanction, the Chinese Government intensified its repression in 1998. Once the leaders achieved their diplomatic victories, they turned to their main objective: the preservation of tyrannical power. This year, about 70 people are known to have been arrested. ...

Li Peng, the speaker of the National People's Party Congress, declared recently, "If an organization's purpose is to promote a multiparty system in China and to negate the leadership prerogatives of the Chinese Communist Party, then it will not be permitted to exist."

This statement clearly shows that the Communist Party's primary objective is to sustain its tyranny, and to do so it must deny the people basic rights and freedoms. We must measure the leaders' progress on human rights not by the "release" of individuals but by the people's ability to speak, worship and assemble without official interference and persecution.

nese ties. In 2000, the U.S. House of Representatives voted to give China a permanent most-favored nation status, opening the way for China's admission to the World Trade Organization in 2001. When terrorists destroyed the World Trade Center in September 2001, China saw this as an opportunity to move against pro-independence Muslim groups in its own western provinces and gave verbal backing to the U.S. campaign against terrorism. A generational change in Chinese leadership occurred when Hu Jintao became General Secretary of the CCP in 2002 and premier in 2003. Apart from a slightly more open style of governance, it is not clear what the change will mean. Since 2003 China has cooperated with the United States, Japan, and South Korea, to restrain the development of nuclear weapons by North Korea.

Taiwan

Taiwan is a mountainous island less than 100 miles off the coast of central China. A little larger than Belgium or Massachusetts, it has a population of 22.8 million. Originally a distant and backward part of the Qing empire, it became a Japanese colony in 1895 as a spoil of the Sino-Japanese War.

The Japanese found it relatively easy to rule since the Taiwanese lacked a modern sense of national identity and were accustomed to rule by officials who came from across the seas and spoke a language they could not understand. (Standard Chinese and the Fujian dialect spoken by Taiwanese are mutually unintelligible.) The Japanese colonial government quickly suppressed opium and bandits and eradicated epidemic diseases. It built roads and railroads, reformed the land system, and introduced improvements in agriculture. Before 1895 education had been the privilege of a tiny elite; sixty years later, 71 percent of school-age children attended the "common schools" established by the Japanese. (In the Dutch East Indies and French Indochina the figure was about 10 or 15 percent.) Light industries were introduced, and during the thirties, textiles, chemicals, ceramics, and machine tools. Though mostly owned by Japanese and run in their interest, more benefits seem to have accrued to the local population than was the case in Korea, another Japanese colony.

Anticolonial feelings rose slowly. During the twenties Taiwanese petitioned for political reforms and greater personal freedoms. The Japanese made a few concessions, but after the China war began in 1937, they reverted to strict controls and assimilationist policies. At the end of the war the Taiwanese were happy to see the Japanese leave and welcomed Guomindang officials as liberators. The new officials, however, viewing the Taiwanese as Japanese collaborators, looted the economy and ruled harshly. When Taiwanese protested in February 1947, the Guomindang put down the demonstrators and over several months killed almost 10,000 Taiwanese, many of them community leaders. By the time Jiang Jieshi (Chiang Kai-shek) and 2 million more military and civilian mainlanders fled to the island in 1949, its economy and society were in disarray. Mainlanders looked down on the Taiwanese, who in turn hated their new rulers and in private often compared them unfavorably to the Japanese.

In the mid-fifties order was restored, and rapid economic growth followed. Heavy industries were put under state control; other former Japanese industries were sold to private parties. With the outbreak of the Korean War in 1950, U.S. aid became substantial. Foreign investment was welcomed. Light industries were followed by consumer electronics, steel, and petrochemicals, then computers and semiconductors. From the late eighties, investments in China began. By the late nineties, Taiwan was the world's largest producer of monitors, keyboards, motherboards, and computer mice; it was second in notebook PCs and fourth in integrated circuits. Some of these were actually manufactured in Taiwanese-owned plants in mainland China. Estimated per capita product in 2005 was $13,900 (or nearer to $25,000 in purchasing power), many times that of mainland China.

Until 1987, government was authoritarian, martial law was in effect, and opposition parties were banned. The GMD (Guomindang) maintained that its government, the Republic of China, was the legitimate government of all China. Posters on Taipei billboards proclaimed the official goal of eventually reconquering the mainland. As the self-proclaimed government of all of China, a minority of GMD mainlanders was able to dominate the Taiwanese population.

Social changes began during the 1960s. Education advanced, as rising numbers entered universities. Taiwanese and mainlanders began to intermarry. A new middle class emerged, and Taiwanese began to enter the GMD. Jiang Jieshi died in 1975, a year before Mao. Under his son Jiang Jingguo, who was president from 1978 to 1988, Taiwan inched toward representative government. In 1987 martial law ended and opposition parties formed.

After Jiang Jingguo's death, Taiwan moved steadily in the direction of representative government. First, in 1996, a non-mainlander was elected president. Li Denghui, though a member of the GMD, was born in Taiwan, graduated from a Taiwanese high school, and then went on to Kyoto Imperial University, and Cornell. Li described the March 1996 election in which he became president as "the first free election in 5000 years of Chinese history." During the election China attempted to intimidate the voters by firing missiles into the waters off Taiwan. The voters reacted by giving Li a substantial majority of their votes. Then,

four years later in 2000, the candidate of an opposition party, Chen Shuibian, was elected as Li's successor. Also a Taiwanese, Chen was born in poverty, rose to become a corporate lawyer and, in 1994, mayor of Taipei. His election, which ended fifty years of GMD rule, was hailed by one scholar as "the first peaceful transition of power from one political party to another in Taiwanese history, and probably in all of Chinese history."

Since 1949 the Communist government in Beijing had claimed that Taiwan was a province of China unlawfully controlled by a "bandit" government. It did not rule out taking Taiwan by force. It also maintained that its relation with the island was a matter of internal Chinese politics and refused diplomatic ties with any nation maintaining such ties with Taiwan. For almost thirty years, from the outbreak of the Korean War in 1950 until 1979, Taiwan was a protégé of the United States, which ignored the mainland and supported Taiwan's claim to be the legitimate government of China. In 1979, however, the United States broke off relations with Taipei and recognized Beijing as the legitimate government of a China that included Taiwan. The United States, nevertheless, continued informal relations with Taiwan, and continued to trade with it and sell it arms. Curiously, it was during the years of diplomatic limbo after the 1979 break that Taiwan's economy grew and its society became democratic.

At the onset of the twenty-first century, both China and the United States were apprehensive about Taiwan. China worried that a democratically elected government would give Taiwan a claim to legitimacy in the eyes of the world. It also worried that Taiwan's prosperity would make its peoples less willing to

▲ **Parade in Taiwan.** Women cadets, probably from ROTC-like organizations in colleges, march in modern Taipei. In the background is a monumental edifice with a Pagoda-like roof, the Jiang Jieshi (Chiang Kai-shek) Memorial Hall.
Paul W. Liebhardt.

rejoin the mainland—a view lent credence by public opinion polls in Taiwan. It spoke of using force to retake the island. The United States feared that within a decade or two China would have the military power to do just that. It cautioned President Chen not to speak of independence. He replied that a declaration of independence was unnecessary since Taiwan already functioned as an independent state. Many in the U.S. Congress felt that the United States could not stand by and see this prosperous and democratic state, which it had helped to create, be forcibly taken over by China.

Korea

Korea and Vietnam, the other two countries in the East Asian zone of civilization, both became colonies. Vietnam became a part of French Indochina in 1883; Korea was annexed by Japan in 1910. In both countries, the imposition of colonialism on a people with a high indigenous culture and a strong sense of national identity engendered a powerful anticolonial nationalism. After World War II, both were divided into a Communist north and a non-Communist south, Korea immediately and Vietnam years later. Both experienced civil war. In each instance the United States entered the conflicts to stem the spread of communism. Never before had the United States fought in countries about which it knew so little.

Korea as a Japanese Colony

The social ills and political and economic weaknesses that had characterized the Choson dynasty in 1800 continued through the nineteenth century. As the century drew to a close, a three-cornered rivalry arose among China, Japan, and Russia, with Korea as the prize. Japan won. Defeating China in the Sino-Japanese War (1894–1895) and Russia in the Russo-Japanese War (1904–1905), it made Korea a protectorate in 1905 and annexed it in 1910.

Annexation was followed by changes designed to make Korea into a model colony. A land survey and land tax reform clarified land ownership. As public hygiene was enforced, infectious diseases dropped sharply, and the population grew from 14 million in 1910 to 24 million in 1940. Attendance at common schools increased from 20,000 in 1910 to 1.2 million in 1939, while attendance at higher common schools, girls' higher schools, and trade schools also rose. New money was issued and banks established. As in Taiwan, a huge investment was made in roads, railways, and telegraph lines. The 1920s saw further investments in areas such as hydroelectric power, nitrogenous fertilizer plants, and mining. Most large-scale industries were Japanese-owned, but Korean entrepreneurs began textile mills, shipping lines, and small industries. Even excluding mining and transport, employment in industry rose from 385,000 in 1932 to 1,322,000 in 1943. The colonial trans-formation was not just a matter of economics. Koreans who studied at Japanese universities came into contact with the full range of political, social, literary, and artistic currents of the modern world and brought their new knowledge back to Korea. By the 1930s a modern culture was forming in Korea's cities. In sum, by carrying out a truncated version of Meiji-type reforms, the Japanese had made Korea into something vastly different from what it had been in 1910.

Being a Japanese colony was nonetheless a hard road to modernity. The colonial government was authoritarian. Its goal was to make Korea into a part of Imperial Japan—albeit a subordinate one; any benefits to Koreans were incidental. Education was Japan-oriented and instruction was given in Japanese. The land tax reform primarily benefited landowners. Japanese and Korean land companies bought up former crown lands, and tenancy rose from 42 percent in 1913 to 69 percent in 1945. The Japanese in Korea received better salaries, medical care, education, and jobs than their Korean counterparts. Whether in government, banking, or industry, Koreans were mainly relegated to the lower echelons. To be sure, this was true in all colonies, but it particularly rankled in Korea because it was an older culture and racially close to Japan. The colonial regime, moreover, suppressed all nationalist movements and political opposition, denying Koreans the experience of self-government. Many who became politically active fled to China or the Soviet Union. The police, half of whom were Koreans, earned a reputation for brutality and were hated by the populace. After 1937, the Japanese policy of "assimilation" grew even harsher: Koreans were pressured to adopt Japanese names, drafted to fight in Japan's wars, and sent to labor in factories in Japan. Only "Comfort women were recruited, sometimes forcibly, to service Japanese troops." Only in recent years has this bitter colonial legacy begun to subside.

North and South

Immediately upon Japan's defeat in 1945, Soviet troops occupied the North, and U.S. forces occupied Korea south of the Thirty-Eighth Parallel. There had been a promise of unification, but two separate states developed. In the South, the United States initially sought to encourage the formation of a democratic, self-governing nation but settled for the anti-Communist and somewhat authoritarian government of Syngman Rhee (1875–1965), a longtime nationalist leader whose party won the May 1948 election. With Rhee's installation as the first president of the Republic of Korea, the United States formally ended its military government of Korea. Many of Rhee's officials and officers had formerly served in the colonial government or the Japanese military. His government was strongly supported by Conservative Koreans and by the million or so Koreans who had fled the North.

In the North, the Russians established a Communist government under Kim Il Sung (1912–1994). Kim had worked with the Chinese Communists during the 1930s and subsequently with the Soviet Union. When the South held elections in 1948, the North hurriedly followed suit. In September, the Democratic People's Republic of Korea was established. Not a few of its officers and officials had fought on the Communist side in the Chinese Civil War. At the end of 1948 the Soviet Union withdrew its troops from North Korea. During 1949 and early 1950 the United States withdrew most of its troops from the South. The withdrawal was part of a larger American disengagement from continental Asia after the Communist victory in China. The United States also briefly dissociated itself from the Chinese Nationalist regime on Taiwan as a part of its policy of "letting the dust settle."

CIVIL WAR AND U.S. INVOLVEMENT

On June 25, 1950, North Korea invaded the South in an attempt to reunite the Korean peninsula. Kim Il Sung, the North Korean leader, had received Stalin's permission for the invasion and a promise from Mao to send Chinese troops in case the United States entered the war. He planned for a quick victory before the United States had time to intervene. But the Cold War had already begun in Europe, and the invasion, coming four months after the signing of the Sino-Soviet Alliance, was seen by the United States as an act of aggression by world communism. The United States rushed troops from Japan to South Korea and obtained United Nations backing for its action. It also sent naval forces to the Taiwan Straits to protect Taiwan, and, over the next several years, entered into military alliances with South Korea, Japan, Taiwan, the Philippines, and the non-Communist states of Southeast Asia. This marked a major turn in postwar American foreign policy.

During the first months of the war, the unprepared American and South Korean forces were driven southward into a small area around Pusan on the southeastern rim of the peninsula (see Map 33–2). But then, amphibious units led by the United Nations commander General Douglas MacArthur landed at Inchon in the middle of Korea's western coast, and drove back the North Korean armies beyond the Thirty-Eighth Parallel deep into North Korea. In midwar, American policy had shifted from the containment of communism to a rollback.

The UN forces in Korea were half American and two fifths Korean; the rest were contingents from Britain, Australia, Turkey, and twelve other nations. In the final phase of the war, China sent in "volunteers" to rescue the beleaguered North Korean forces. Chinese troops pushed the overextended UN forces back to a line close to the Thirty-Eighth Parallel. After months of fierce fighting, the war became stalemated in 1951 and ended with an armistice on July 27, 1953. Thereafter the two Koreas maintained a hostile peace. On each side of the heavily guarded border were about 600,000 troops. The 142,000 American casualties made the war the fourth largest in U.S. history.

RECENT DEVELOPMENTS

In the decades that followed, North Korea remained a closed, authoritarian state with a planned economy. It stressed heavy industry, organized its farmers in collectives, and totally controlled education and the media. Most Japanese industries in Korea before 1945 had been in the North, giving it an early edge. But from the 1970s the Northern economy became sluggish. Shortages of food, clothing, and other necessities were chronic. The cult of personality surrounding "the great leader" Kim Il Sung went beyond that of even Stalin or Mao. The Korean Communist Party was Marxist-Leninist, but

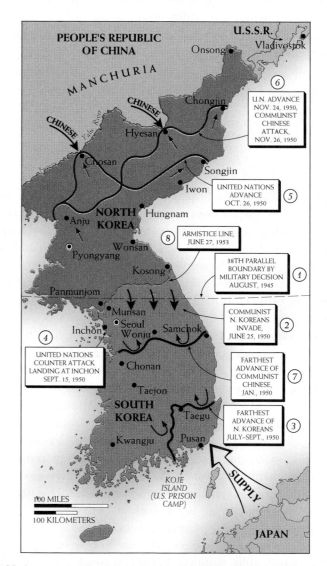

MAP 33–2 Korea, 1950–1953. This map indicates the major developments in the bitter three-year struggle that followed the North Korean invasion of South Korea in 1950.

the kinship terminology used to describe the fatherly leader, the mother party, and the familial North Korean state gave the official state philosophy an almost Confucian coloration. Kim designated his son, "the beloved leader" Kim Jong-il (b. 1942), as his successor, and when the father died in 1994, the son became the leader of North Korea—the only instance of hereditary succession in a Communist state.

In South Korea, Rhee remained in office until 1960, when at age eighty-five he was forced to retire in the wake of massive student demonstrations. There followed twenty-seven years of rule by two generals. The first, Park Chung-hee, seized power in a military *coup d'état* in 1961. Shedding his uniform, he then won a controlled election and became a civilian president. His rule was semiauthoritarian: Opposition parties were legal and active but their leaders were often jailed. Students were able to mount protest demonstrations but were usually blocked by riot police and frequently tear-gassed. Still, South Koreans could read non-Communist foreign books and magazines and travel abroad. Many Koreans approved of Park's economic policies but came to resent his use of police and intelligence agencies to sustain his rule. Park was assassinated by his intelligence chief in 1979. Another general, Chun Doo-hwan, seized power the following year, transformed himself into a civilian president, and ruled until 1987 in the pattern established by his predecessor.

At the inception of Park's rule, unemployment had been rife and poverty widespread. Park and his successor Chun were determined to promote economic growth. Emphasizing science and technology, they supported business and swiftly expanded higher education. Management drew on skills learned during the colonial era; labor was disciplined, hard-working, and cheap. The United States gave large amounts of aid and provided an open market for Korean exports. The result was double-digit growth. Especially notable was the growth of *chaebol* such as Hyundai or Daewoo, which resembled the Mitsui or Mitsubishi *zaibatsu* of prewar Japan. The policies of the two leaders, and their successors after 1987, were successful beyond their expectations. Korea's gross national product has risen product dramatically (see Figure 33–2.)

With an estimated per capita product in 2005 of $14,362 (with a purchasing power of over $19,000), South Korea has moved into the ranks of developed nations and become the world's eleventh largest economy. The country's voice in world affairs grew with its economy.

In 1987, an era of increasingly democratic politics began. Ironically, the industrialization and urbanization wrought by the two generals created an affluent and educated middle class that was no longer willing to tolerate authoritarian rule. A crisis occurred in the early summer of 1987 when a student activist drowned in a bathtub at the headquarters of the Korean CIA. In protest, half a million civilians demonstrated in the streets of Seoul. As Chun's term ended, a free election was held in

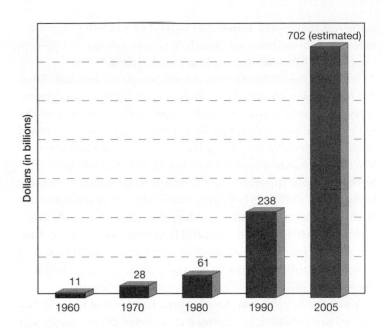

Figure 33–2 South Korean Gross National Product 1960–2005.

December. Although the two main opposition parties split the antigovernment vote and Chun's hand-picked successor, Roh Tae-woo, became president, most Koreans saw the election as an opening to democracy. This was confirmed four years later when Kim Young-sam, a moderate politician, was elected president. He purged the generals who had supported Park and Chun, replaced them with officers willing to work with party governments, and launched investigations of his predecessors' finances. Though one reporter commented that corruption was as Korean as *kimchee* (a traditional dish of spicy, pickled cabbage), the hundreds of millions of dollars in secret bank accounts uncovered by investigators astonished even the Koreans. In 1995 Chun and Roh and several top *chaebol* leaders were arrested. Chun and Roh were also charged with ordering the killing of hundreds of political demonstrators in Kwangju in 1980. They were sent to prison but later released.

Further evidence of the durability of representative government in South Korea followed. Kim Dae-jung was elected president in 1997, the first election of an opposition leader. A long-time prodemocracy campaigner, Kim had earlier been the target of assassination attempts and once condemned to die. He was pro-labor, a populist, a Catholic, and an idealist. He took office with high hopes but encountered difficulties that proved insurmountable. The economy sagged; layoffs and fear of further job losses left public opinion unsettled. Kim adopted a "sunshine policy" of openness, reconciliation, and material aid toward North Korea. His efforts to reduce tensions on the peninsula earned him a Nobel Peace Prize in 1998, but it later came out that North Korea had agreed to a summit only after receiving a bribe from the South. When North Korea failed to reciprocate Kim's overtures, Kim's popularity fell.

In December 2002 another opposition politician, Roh Moo-hyun, was elected president. Roh was younger, more liberal, and represented a younger generation with no memory of the Korean War. He was backed by a minority party and resented by the conservative majority party in the National Assembly. In March, 2004, the conservatives voted to impeach him. The Korean people apparently felt the impeachment improper, for in the April election they gave Roh's URI Party a majority of National Assembly seats. In May, the Constitutional Court overturned the impeachment and Roh returned to office. Critical of the United States and open to closer relations with China and the government in the north, Roh's presidency opened the possibility of new international relations.

Since the Korean War, South Korea had been allied with the United States, which guaranteed its defense. North Korea was backed by the Soviet Union and China, the latter asserting that their solidarity was "as close as lips and teeth." But after the collapse of the Soviet Union, Russia lost interest in its former ally. China continued to offer support but was more attracted by the allure of a vibrant South Korea, with which it estab-

lished diplomatic relations in 1992. Since then, South Koreans have invested billions in China, trade between the two nations has flourished, and in 1995 the Chinese president visited Seoul. North Korea was increasingly an orphan.

The North Korean record was poor. Not only was its economy a shambles, but its government had also engaged in assassinations, counterfeiting, drug smuggling, and kidnapping. Using a Pakistan connection, it also began to develop nuclear weapons. When charged with this in 2003, it first denied and then boasted of the development. The United States, China, South Korea and Japan moved to persuade North Korea to renounce nuclear weapons. Even China did not want a nuclear North Korea on its doorstep. As of 2004, the future of negotiations and of the North Korean state was unclear. Would North Korea be able to extract blackmail payments from richer states to sustain its miserable population? Would it respond to overtures from the new regime in South Korea, and haltingly follow China toward a market economy? Would it subsist as a threadbare totalitarian state, or collapse like East Germany?

Vietnam

THE COLONIAL BACKDROP

The Nguyen dynasty that reunited Vietnam in 1802 was still vigorous in 1858 when France began its conquest of the area, but it proved no match for France. France completed its conquest of Vietnam and Cambodia in 1883, formed the Indochinese Union in 1887, and added Laos to the Union in 1893.

In many ways Indochina was a classic example of colonial rule: a people of one race and culture, for the sake of economic benefits and national glory, controlling and exploiting a people of another race and culture in a far-off land. To obtain access to the country's natural resources, the French built harbors, roads, and a railway linking Saigon, Hanoi, and southern China. They established rubber plantations in the Mekong Delta and tea plantations in the highlands. They also introduced modern mining technology for the extraction of coal and built breweries, rice and paper mills, and glass and cement factories for local consumption. All were dominated by the French or, in smaller enterprises, by Chinese. Workers were paid very low wages. Except as laborers, the only role for Vietnamese in the economy was as landlords. In the South, 3 percent of landowners owned 45 percent of the land and received 60 percent of the crop grown by their tenants. Although irrigation works in the Mekong Delta quadrupled the area of rice fields, the consumption of rice by peasants declined. The skewed distribution of wealth meant that there developed no indigenous middle class, apart from the landlords and Chinese merchants whose commercial acumen was resented by Vietnamese. The French also did little to educate the Vietnamese: in 1939, over 80 percent of the population

▲ **The Two Kims.** South Korean President Kim Dae-jung traveled to Pyongyang in June 2000 to promote his "sunshine policy." As he departs he hugs Kim Jong-il, the North Korean leader. But when the North Korean leader failed to respond with a visit to Seoul or with an easing of tensions, sunshine turned to rain, and Kim Dae-jung's popularity sagged.

Koren Pool/Yonhap/AP/Wide World Photos.

was illiterate, possibly a higher percentage than in the early nineteenth century under the Nguyen.

During the early decades of French rule, the Vietnamese made futile attempts to restore the dynasty. By the early twentieth century, Vietnamese nationalists in exile in China, Japan, and France had formed political parties. But when they tried to organize within Vietnam, the parties were suppressed and their leaders jailed or executed. Under the French, only clandestine parties survived. The most skilled organizer of such parties was Ho Chi Minh (1892–1969), who had participated in the founding of the French Communist Party in 1920, studied in Moscow in 1923, and worked under the Comintern agent Mikhail Borodin in Canton in 1925. Ho founded the Revolutionary Youth League of Vietnam in 1925 and sent its cadres to China and the Soviet Union for training. He then founded the Indochinese Communist Party in 1930. When the Popular Front gained power in France (1936–1938), opposition parties were tolerated in Vietnam and Ho's party emerged the strongest. After 1938 the French again suppressed all opposition groups. Shortly before the outbreak of the Pacific War, the Japanese occupied Vietnam. For their own convenience, until March 1945 they ruled through the Vichy French puppets. Ho, who in 1941 had formed the **Viet Minh** (League for the Independence of Vietnam) as a popular

▲ **Hanoi 1954.** Cheering crowds watch a victory parade after Geneva Accords end war with the French. Like the later "Vietnam War," this was seen as a war of liberation.
Corbis/Bettman.

front organization to resist the Japanese, proclaimed the Democratic Republic of Vietnam after Japan's defeat in 1945 and became the preeminent nationalist leader in his country.

There followed three cycles of war and almost three decades of peace.

THE ANTICOLONIAL WAR

The first war lasted from 1946 to 1954. On one side was the Viet Minh, led by Ho. It was controlled by Communists but also included some representatives of Nationalist parties. On the other side were the French, who had reoccupied Vietnam immediately after the war, and their conservative Vietnamese allies. The French tried to legitimize their rule by setting up in 1948 a puppet government under Bao Dai, the last in the line of Nguyen emperors. After years of war, the French lost a major battle at Dien Bien Phu in 1954 and, with it, the will to continue what critics at home called the "dirty war." They departed in defeat.

A conference at Geneva divided the country into a Communist North and a non-Communist South. In the South, Ngo Dinh Diem, a Nationalist leader who had not collaborated with the French, came to power and established the Republic of Vietnam. Much of his political support came from the 900,000 Vietnamese who had fled from the North.

THE VIETNAM WAR

The second cycle of war, from 1959 to 1975, involved the United States. During the 1940s, in line with its wartime anticolonial position, the United States had urged the French to reach an accommodation with Ho Chi Minh. But after the rise of Communist China and the outbreak of the Korean War, it came to see French actions in Vietnam as an attempt to stem the tide of communism—a view encouraged by the French. It recognized the French-sponsored government of Bao Dai and gave $4 billion in aid between 1950 and 1954. When the French withdrew, it transferred its support to Diem.

Fighting began with guerrilla attacks against Southern troops in the late 1950s (see Map 33–3). Some said these were a local response to Diem's suppression of his political enemies, while others, including North Vietnam after the war, said they were directed from the North. Local incidents eventually turned into a full-scale war between the North and the South. The North received material aid from the Soviet Union and China, although, unlike the Korean War, China sent no "volunteers" to fight in Vietnam. The South was aided by the United States, whose forces increased from 600 military advisers in 1961, to 16,000 troops in 1963, 70,000 in 1965, and over half a million in 1969. Despite such massive support, South Vietnam—and the United States— lost the war. The reasons for the defeat were several.

1. The South was difficult to govern. In comparison to the North, the region had been less deeply influenced by

Chinese culture. It was ethnically diverse, with Chinese, Cambodians, and Chams as well as Vietnamese. In religion, it was divided among several varieties of Buddhists, Catholics, and two powerful "new religions," the Cao Dai in the eastern provinces and the Hoa Hao in the western provinces. The two millenarian sects possessed private armies, and though opposed to the Communists, they stood apart from the South Vietnamese government, at times warring among themselves. Throughout this era, the inability of successive Southern governments to unify their fragmented society was a basic weakness in their struggles with the Communist North.

2. All too often corrupt, the South Vietnamese government inspired little loyalty in its citizens.

3. Ho Chi Minh was a national hero to many South Vietnamese as well as to Northerners. Even non-Communists sometimes viewed the United States as the successor to the French—despite its total lack of colonial ambitions in Southeast Asia—and supported Communist guerrillas as the heirs of the earlier anticolonial struggle.

4. Both the Communist guerrillas in the South and the North Vietnamese troops fought better than the soldiers of the South Vietnamese government.

5. In the jungle terrain of Vietnam, the technological edge of the United States was blunted. A greater tonnage of bombs was dropped on supply trails in Cambodia than on Japan in World War II, yet supplies continued to flow to the South.

At the beginning, the U.S. government saw the war, like the earlier war in Korea, as a part of the broader struggle against world communism. After the gravity of the Sino-Soviet split became apparent, the government saw it more narrowly as a war to halt the spread of Chinese communism. Few in the United States understood the depth of the traditional Viet-

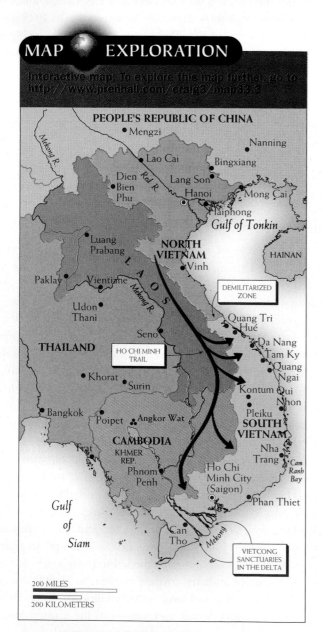

MAP 33–3 Vietnam and its Southeast Asian Neighbors. The map identifies important locations associated with the war in Vietnam.

▲ **Ho Chi Minh (1892–1969).** Ho became a Communist in France in 1920, studied in Moscow, and founded the Indochinese Communist Party in 1930. He fought, in succession, against the Japanese, French, and Americans. He did not live to see the Communist victory in 1975.

Corbis/Bettmann.

namese ambivalence toward China which would resurface shortly after the war. As the war dragged on and casualties mounted, opposition to the war grew and public opinion became divided. In 1968, Lyndon Johnson said he would not run for reelection. When Richard Nixon became president, he called for the "Vietnamization" of the war and began to withdraw American troops. In January 1973, a ceasefire was arranged in Paris, and two months later the last U.S. troops left. Fighting broke out anew between North and South, the South Vietnamese forces collapsed in 1975, and the country was reunited under the Hanoi government in the North. Saigon was renamed Ho Chi Minh City.

In the mid-1970s, few areas of the world were as devastated as Vietnam and its neighbors. After unifying the country, Hanoi sent many thousands of those associated with the former South Vietnamese government to labor camps, collectivized its agricultural lands, and in 1976 began a five-year plan for the economy. Several hundred thousand Vietnamese and ethnic Chinese fled by boat or across the Chinese border.

WAR WITH CAMBODIA

Vietnam's third cycle of war was with Cambodia, its neighbor to the west. Pol Pot (1926–1998) and the Communist **Khmer Rouge** ("Red Cambodia") had come to power in 1975. During the next three years, his government evacuated cities and towns, abolished money and trade, banned Buddhism, and executed or caused to die of starvation an estimated 1 million persons, roughly 15 percent of the Cambodian population. Schoolteachers and the educated were singled out as special targets.

Clashes occurred between Khmer Rouge troops and Vietnamese troops along their common border. Vietnam was Cambodia's historical enemy, as China was Vietnam's. In response to the clashes, Pol Pot purged the Khmer Rouge of pro-Vietnamese elements. In 1978, Vietnam retaliated by invading and occupying most of Cambodia and setting up a puppet government. Most Cambodians accepted Vietnamese rule: They feared Pol Pot more than they hated Vietnam. But Cambodia was unable to completely suppress Pol Pot's guerrilla forces.

In its international relations, the unified Vietnam of 1975 became an ally of the Soviet Union and gave the Soviets a naval base at Cam Ranh Bay in return for economic, military, and diplomatic support. But relations with China took a turn for the worse. Vietnam had long feared Chinese domination and resented China's invitation to Nixon in 1972, when American troops were still fighting on its soil. China, in turn, felt its wartime aid had not been duly appreciated, resented Vietnam's treatment of its ethnic Chinese, and feared an expansionist Vietnam allied with the Soviet Union. In 1979, China decided to "teach Vietnam a lesson" and invaded four Northern provinces. Seasoned Vietnamese troops repelled the invaders, but losses were heavy on both sides. For years there-

after China supported Pol Pot's guerrillas and maintained pressure on Vietnam's northern border with occasional shellings and attacks.

RECENT DEVELOPMENTS

During the late 1980s, the situation changed. The collapse of the Soviet Union destroyed Vietnam's primary international relationship. Vietnam's leaders also became aware that victories in wars were hollow as long as their people remained destitute.

In 1989, Vietnam withdrew from its costly occupation of Cambodia in favor of a UN-sponsored government made up of contending Cambodian factions. One of these factions, led by the pro-Vietnamese Communist leader Hun Sen, staged a coup in 1997 and took over the government. His rule was strengthened when Pol Pot died in 1998 and the Khmer Rouge collapsed.

By the mid-1990s, Vietnam's relations with China had improved and trade opened across their border. China's landlocked Yunnan province began to use the port of Haiphong as an outlet for its products. The collapse of the Khmer Rouge had removed the obstacle to better relations. In 1995, Vietnam joined ASEAN (Association of Southeast Asian Nations)—an important advance in its relations with its closest and richer neighbors—and reestablished diplomatic relations with the

▲ **Skulls.** A worker cleans a skull excavated from a mass grave in Cambodia. The Khmer Rouge, under Pol Pot, murdered about one sixth of the Cambodian population. Doctors, teachers, and other educated people were especially targeted.
AP Wide World Photos.

United States. It moved toward "normal" relations with the rest of the world.

At home, the Hanoi dictatorship maintained its grip on the nation. The Communist government monopolized political power, controlled the army, police, and media, and supported a large sector of state-run industries. But it also permitted the start of a market economy (the *doi moi* reforms). In place of collective agriculture, farmers were allowed to keep the rice they grew, and as a result Vietnam went from conditions of near starvation to become the world's second largest exporter of rice. Garment manufacturing, food processing, and the production of other consumer goods grew apace. Between 1991 and 1996 the economy achieved an average growth of over 8 percent and received more offers of foreign investment than it could absorb. By 1996, shops in Vietnam were full of food and goods, when only ten years earlier there had been famine in some areas. In these reforms the South played a critical role as the engine of the economy. It also served as a model—slightly more liberal, pluralistic, and cosmopolitan—that even most North Vietnamese saw as desirable.

But as the new millennium dawned, all was not rosy. The economy had grown apace but so had population. With 82 million persons, Vietnam was one of the world's most densely populated nations. More than half had been born after the end of the Vietnam War. Hanoi's population, which was 130,000 in the 1930s, reached about 4 million; Ho Chi Minh City's (Saigon), less than a million in the 1970s, grew to 4.5 million. A high percentage of labor was agricultural, and in the countryside barter was not uncommon. The gap in the standard of living between urban and rural Vietnamese also grew. In 2005, Vietnam's estimated per capita income was over $600 (as measured by purchasing power, it was over $2,500). Foreign investors were drawn to Vietnam by cheap labor but put off by shortages, delays, red tape, and financial bottlenecks.

Beijing, China.

Summary

Japan   The U.S.-led occupation after World War II established a democratic government and set Japan on the way to its remarkable postwar prosperity. By the twenty-first century, Japan had the second largest economy in the world. Politically, the conservative Liberal Democratic Party has remained dominant, despite occasional electoral losses. Socially Japan has remained stable with the world's highest longevity rate.

China   Communist rule was established in 1949. Until his death in 1976, Mao Zedong remained in control of China. Mao broke with the Soviet Union in the 1950s and launched the disastrous Cultural Revolution in 1965. After his death, China opened its economy to free-market reforms. The result has been surging economic growth and rising prosperity. Politically, however, the Communist Party has blocked democratic reform, even using force in 1989 to crush prodemocratic demonstrations.

Taiwan   The Nationalist Party set up a separate state in Taiwan under U.S. protection after their defeat in the Chinese civil war in 1949. Since then Taiwan has evolved into a prosperous democratic state. The Chinese government, however, insists that Taiwan is an integral part of China. The status of Taiwan could lead to conflict between the United States and China.

Korea   The postwar occupation of Korea by the Soviets and the United States led to its division into the Communist state of North Korea and the pro-Western South Korea. This division survived the Korean War of 1950–1953. The prosperity of democratic South Korea contrasts with the poverty and hunger of North Korea. Although contacts between the two Koreas have increased, the North remains a closed society.

Vietnam   From the end of World War II until the 1970s, Vietnam was almost continuously involved in war, first against the reimposition of French colonial rule, then against the United States and its South Vietnamese allies. North Vietnam's victory over the South in 1975 reunified the country, but Vietnam remains relatively poor, only slowly moving toward economic liberalization.

Review Questions

1. Is postwar Japan better understood in terms of a return to the liberalism of the 1920s, or as a fresh start based on Occupation reforms? Why did the Occupation of Japan go so smoothly and the recent American occupation of Iraq so poorly?

2. How long would it take and at what rate of growth, for China's economy to catch up to Japan's? To reach the present Japanese per capita income? What obstacles do you see to such growth?

3. Is China from 1949 until the death of Mao better understood as an outgrowth of its earlier history, or as a Commu-

nist state comparable, for example, to the old Soviet Union? And to what would you compare China since Deng?

4. Examine the precolonial and colonial eras of Korea and Vietnam. How did these background factors shape the period after World War II?

5. How did the Cold War affect the postwar histories of Korea and Vietnam?

6. If you were the U.S. secretary of state, what long-term China policy would you propose to the president?

Key Terms

brainwashing   (p. 1006)

Cultural Revolution   (p. 1007)

Great Leap Forward   (p. 1006)

Khmer Rouge   (p. 1019)

LDP   (p. 998)

Viet Minh   (p. 1017)

Documents CD-ROM

World War II
25.5 "Tojo Makes Plea of Self Defense"

The Cold War
26.5 Korea: The Thirty-Eighth Parallel
26.6 General Douglas MacArthur, Report to Congress, April 19, 1951: "Old Soldiers Never Die"

Decolonization
27.7 Views of a Viet Cong Official
27.8 An American Prisoner of War

Contemporary Issues in World History
29.4 Deng Xiaoping, A Market Economy for Socialist Goals

NOTE: *To learn more about the topics in this chapter, see the Suggested Readings at the end of the book.*

CHAPTER 34

Postcolonialism and Beyond

Latin America, Africa, Asia, and the Middle East

- Beyond the Postcolonial Era

- Latin America Since 1945

- Postcolonial Africa

- Central, South, and Southeast Asia

- The Postcolonial Middle East

◄ BAGHDAD, APRIL 2003. American forces pull down a statue
of Iraqi leader Saddam Hussein in Al Ferdous Square,
Baghdad. Onlookers cheer and wave. One man points the sole
of his shoe at Hussein in a sign of disrespect.
Markus Matzel/Das Fotoarchiv/Peter Arnold, Inc.

Democratization, Globalization, and Terrorism

The three decades since the 1970s have witnessed two remarkable political and economic developments: democratization and globalization. The advances wrought by these two processes met their most severe challenge on September 11, 2001, when terrorists associated with the al Qaeda terrorist network hijacked U. S. airliners and crashed them into the World Trade Center in New York City and the Pentagon in Washington, D. C., killing thousands of people.

Since 1970, on one continent or another, democratic political rights have expanded. Authoritarian regimes of both the right and the left have been reformed or collapsed. Democracies have replaced dictatorships, military juntas, or one-party Communist autocracies. Progress has not been uniform, but more and more people everywhere aspire to have a voice in how they are governed. This process of political change, usually termed democratization, involves expanding the number of people who participate in the political processes, and the orderly change in, or confirmation of, executive and legislative leaders through elections. Although there are still many autocracies and authoritarian states, never before have so many nations around the world seen such an extension of democratic government.

An unprecedented series of economic linkages, generally termed globalization, has accompanied the spread of democracy. This process has included the forging of new trade and manufacturing agreements, such as NAFTA, among the leading industrial nations. Globalization has reduced trade barriers, including tariffs and other regulations that have hindered the circulation of goods, services, and labor among nations. The emergence of such worldwide trading networks has led to the consolidation of economic enterprises as owners of capital seek to locate their centers of production in the most advantageous labor and resource markets. The great corporations of the United States, Europe, and Asia now operate in a multinational setting.

Globalization's supporters believe that it will produce more goods and services at a lower cost to consumers than a highly regulated economy could. Its critics argue that globalization will concentrate power in the hands of unregulated corporations and that governments have surrendered too much of their authority to regulate the economy, preserve the environment, and protect workers. The critics also believe that the new economic structures mean that poor nations, many of them the emerging nations discussed in this chapter, become poorer so that rich nations can become richer. Globalization rode the wave of prosperity that seems to have crested in the late 1990s. It remains to be seen what will occur in the more difficult times of our present decade.

The debate over globalization has made both its admirers and detractors more aware of the vast areas of deep poverty that persist around the world, especially in South and Central America, the Caribbean, Africa, and much of Asia—regions that still struggle with the legacy of European colonialism. Most of these regions were poor long before globalization gathered momentum, but the enormous and widely advertised prosperity of so much of the Northern Hemisphere has made the poorer regions more conscious of their poverty and, especially in Africa and the Middle East, ripe for political extremism. Among Muslims, such extremism has often come to be associated with Islamic fundamentalism (political Islamism). As the most prosperous nation and the last remaining superpower, the United States has become the target of those opposed to globalization.

The economic, military and diplomatic involvement of the United States in other regions of the globe has led some people to view it as an imperial power and to attack it using terrorist tactics. Its strong support for the state of Israel, the festering Israeli-Palestinian conflict, and, most recently, the U. S. invasion of Iraq, have also convinced many in the Muslim world that the United States is the enemy of Islam and that they are justified in using terrorist tactics to attack it. Within the United States, as well as across the world, debate continues over the future role of the United States and whether the United States can best protect the interests of its citizens and the peace and prosperity of the world through unilateral and preemptive invasions such as that of Iraq or through greater cooperation with international bodies such as the United Nations.

THINK AHEAD

◆ What are the arguments of the proponents and opponents of globalization?

◆ How has the legacy of European colonialism affected the Middle East, Asia, and Africa?

◆ Why has the United States become a prime target for terrorists? What is the debate over how the United States should best respond to this threat?

THE SIX DECADES SINCE WORLD WAR II SAW Europe eclipsed by the rise of the two superpowers—the United States and the Soviet Union—and then witnessed the collapse of the Soviet Union (see Chapter 32). Elsewhere in the world, especially in the less developed regions, the post–World War II decades witnessed the end of Western colonialism and challenges to European and superpower imperialism. New nations emerged in Africa and Asia.

Two developments in non-Western regions have particularly impacted the entire world and will continue to do so during the foreseeable future. First, as explored in the previous chapter, East Asia, Japan, and more recently, China have emerged as major political and economic powers. Second, the rise of radical political Islam as a result of developments in the postcolonial Middle East now presents a political and military challenge across much of the globe.

The waning of colonial and imperial dominance of the many by the few and the emergence of new powerful forces from the previous colonial world must be set within a larger historical perspective, however. Since the sixteenth century the various non-European portions of the globe had been drawn steadily into the European sphere of economic and political influence. Those areas to be treated here—Latin America, Africaa, Southwest and Central Asia, South and Southeast Asia, and the Middle East—were often subjected, exploited, and colonized by European powers. The period of colonialism that began in earnest in the seventeenth century was a fateful, but relatively brief, episode in world history. The last significant colonial holdings were given their independence in the 1960s.

Beyond the Postcolonial Era

It may be argued that, especially with the passing of apartheid in South Africa, the postcolonial era has also ended. At present we who live in the West are witnessing waves of economic growth, much like those of the early 1990s in much of East Asia; the forging of new political alignments, both regional and transregional; internal struggles to build political systems that allow the development of civil society and limit the domination of corrupt oligarchic or dictatorial regimes; and, most dramatically, the determination of forces arising from radical Islam to confront the influence on the rest of the world of the West in general and the United States in particular.

Since 1945 two distinct developments occurred in the postcolonial world. The first—in a process that is generally termed *decolonization*—was the emergence of the various parts of Africa and Asia from the direct government and administration of foreign powers, and the organization of those previous colonial dependencies into independent states. Included in this category are India, Pakistan, most Arab states, the Latin American nations, and the new nations of Africa (see Map 34–1).

As the process of decolonization took place and new nations then established themselves with greater or lesser degress of stability, there have been four stages in their relationship to the strong Western nations. First, until the breakup of the Soviet Union, its rivalry with the United States manifested itself on every continent and added to the tensions and turmoil of the era. New emerging nations tended to be under the patronage of one of the superpowers (or, less often, that of China). That bipolar division of the former colonial world has ended.

▲ **Protest.** The globalization of the world economy has sparked hostile political reaction. Numerous groups attend World Trade Organization meetings to protest the development of previously untouched parts of the world, which they claim result in environmental damage and in expanded wealth for the developed nations and frequent unemployment and poverty elsewhere.
AP Wide World Photos.

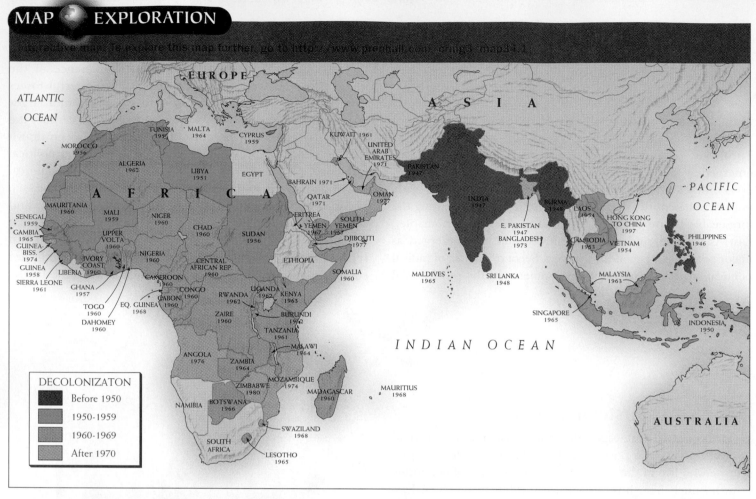

MAP 34–1 Decolonization Since World War II. The Western powers' rapid retreat from imperialism after World War II is graphically shown on this outline map covering half the globe—from West Africa to the Southwest Pacific.

Second, in the years since the end of the Cold War and collapse of the Soviet Union, the character of the world economy, including issues of both trade and resource allocation, has led to new modes of economic interdependence, now usually termed *globalization*, that remain ill-defined and troublesome, whether they relate to automobile production, oil reserves, trade restrictions, or international debt.

Third, the ideas of civil society and participatory government, often symbolized by the democracies of the United States, Western Europe, and Japan, have gained ground even in those regions where autocratic, authoritarian regimes have been the only forms of government, at least since colonial times. In all three kinds of interaction, change has often outpaced peoples' and leaders' awareness of it. The world looks different today from just thirty, let alone fifty, years ago. The rhetoric of decolonization is still used, but it is applied to different realities.

These stages of development which seemed relatively steady and peaceful, however, have given way to a fourth, largely unanticipated set of developments, in which forces of religious life have reasserted themselves throughout much of the world. A central question for the present era is whether to see the global variety of cultural and religious traditions as a creative or divisive force in the twenty-first century and beyond. One much discussed contemporary model for understanding the complex international scene today is that of the "West versus the Rest," in which the post-Enlightenment Western world and its ethos are seen as the hope of the future, while all other civilizational traditions of religion and culture are depicted as rallying points for opposition to the spread of Western-style "modernity." In this model, the future is seen as involving less conflict and competition between national states (a state of affairs that has existed in Europe and spread around the globe since 1800). Instead, this model sees a **clash of civilizations** coming increasingly to dominate world affairs.[1] This analysis pits Islamic, Western Christian, Eastern Orthodox, Buddhist, Hindu, Confucian, and other religio-cultural traditions or "civilizations" against one another in a resurgence of religious,

[1] See Samuel P. Huntington, "The Clash of Civilizations?" *Foreign Affairs* 72, 3 (Summer 1993): pp. 22–49, and a vast array of articles around the world written in response to this provocative and simplistic piece. This article was followed by a whole book devoted to the so-called "Huntington thesis": *The Clash of Civilizations and the Remaking of World Order* (New York: 1996), in which Huntington somewhat refined his ideas.

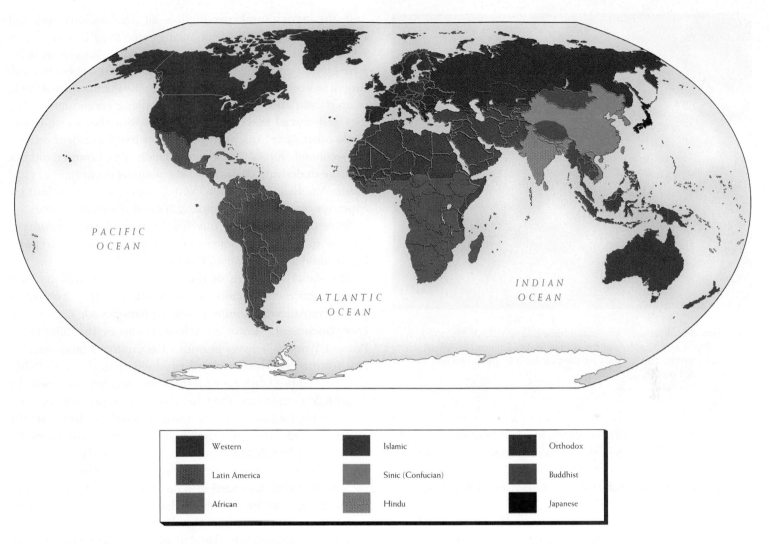

MAP 34–2   Major civilizations of the contemporary world.

ethnic, and cultural chauvinism that portends new bloodletting and international conflict (see Map 34–2). This analysis has received much confirmation for many observers in the wake of international political developments following the attacks of September 11, 2001, on the United States.

Other observers believe this model misconstrues and overplays the importance of religious resurgence and the degree of fundamental difference in values and goals of the major religio-cultural traditions or worldviews of humankind. They would urge that much of the purpose and value of studying the varied traditions of world culture and their modern representatives and derivatives is to be able to take a more nuanced and balanced view of the modern world as a domain in which many cultural and religious and political traditions will continue to compete, but one in which people of all backgrounds and types must get along. Population control, the environment, political accommodation, food supply, public health, and the like must become the focus of shared international concern and effort; our common need for solutions to such transnational, planetwide problems must take precedence over wide "civilizational" differences. That the task will not be easy is evident from any review of the troubled history of the last half century.

However, if we seek to understand the larger global scene, we must at least recognize the persistent influence of the great religions and moral traditions of humankind, however we may interpret that influence. In particular, Buddhist, Christian, and Islamic faith and values continue to claim the allegiance of major sectors of our globe, not only in Africa and Asia, but also in Europe and the Americas. No longer can we assume that secular rationalism will easily monopolize ideology during the process of material modernization. Rather we can expect a pluralistic global community in which diverse traditions must coexist and learn from one another.

▲ **Clash of Civilizations.** American hostages in blindfolds are paraded by their Iranian captors at the United States Embassy in Tehran, Iran in November, 1979, following the overthrow of the American supported regime.
Corbis–Bettmann.

In the remainder of this chapter, we shall examine the traditionally examined areas of postcolonial political and economic development and then conclude with an extensive consideration of the political and cultural conflict emerging from the contemporary Middle East.

Latin America Since 1945

During the second half of the twentieth century and beyond, the nations of Latin America (see Map 34–3) experienced divergent paths of political and economic change. Their leaders tried repeatedly to alleviate their people's dependence on the more developed portions of the globe. At best, these efforts have had mixed results; at worst, they have led to repression and tragedy.

Before World War II the states of Latin America had been economically dependent on the United States and Western Europe. Beginning in the 1950s a shift occurred in those dependent relationships without any significant change in the general situation of dependency. The United States loomed larger than ever; the Soviet Union also for a time came to play a far larger economic and political role. In that respect Latin America, like so many other parts of the world, dwelled in the shadow of the rival superpowers and became an arena for confrontations between them.

The economic life of the region reflected those new facts of dependence. Attempts were made to expand the industrial base

and the agricultural production of the various national economies. Virtually all the financing came from U.S. and Western European banks or from Soviet subsidies. Enormous debts were contracted to Western banks, and these debts made Latin American economies virtual prisoners to the fluctuations of world interest rates and the international banking community. Subsidies and special market arrangements with the Soviet Union made other Latin American nations no less dependent on outside economic forces. These new relationships, however, did not alter the underlying character of the national economies of most Latin American countries, which remain overwhelmingly exporters of agricultural commodities and mineral resources.

Since the 1970s, Latin America shipped massive amounts of cocaine to the United States and Europe; this has led to political turmoil and civil war in Colombia.

The social structures of the Latin American nations have become more complicated since World War II. A culture of poverty remains the dominant social characteristic of the area. (See Document, "Lourdes Arizpe Discusses the Silence of Peasant Women.") Even periods of economic boom, such as that fostered in Mexico by oil production in the late 1970s, have proved brief and have almost inevitably been followed by decline. Migration into the cities from the countryside has created tremendous urban overcrowding and slums inhabited by the desperately poor (see Figure 34–1). In many countries the standards of health and nutrition have fallen. The growth of service industries in the cities has also fostered the emergence of a professional, educated middle class, often possessed with a strong desire to imitate the affluent lifestyle of their social counterparts in the United States and Western Europe. This new professional middle class has displayed little taste for radical politics, major social reform, or revolution. They and the more traditional landed and industrial elites were willing, especially during the 1960s and 1970s, to support military governments pledged to maintain order and the status quo.

Political events in Latin America led to the establishment of authoritarian governments of both the left and the right and

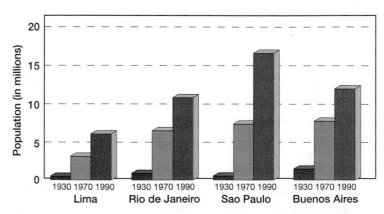

Figure 34–1 Population of major South American cities, 1930–1990.

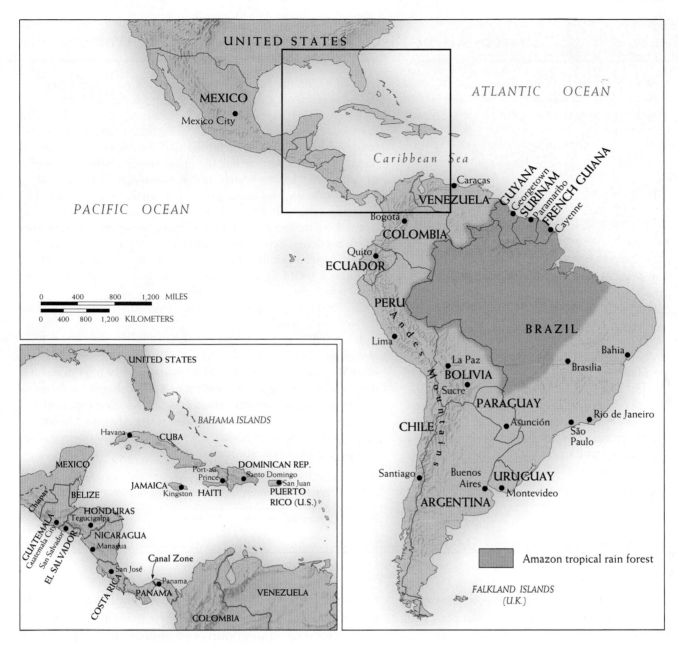

MAP 34–3 Contemporary Central and South America.

to a retreat from the ideal and model of parliamentary democracy. Only Mexico, Colombia, Venezuela, and Costa Rica remained parliamentary states throughout this period. Elsewhere, two paths of political development were followed. In Cuba and Nicaragua, and for a short time in Chile, revolutionary socialist governments with close ties to the Soviet Union were established. Elsewhere, often in response to the fear of revolution or Communist activity, military governments held power for long periods, sometimes punctuated with brief interludes of civilian rule. Such were the situations in Chile, Brazil, Argentina, Bolivia, Peru, and Uruguay. Governments of both the left and the right engaged in repression, suspending civil liberties, and arresting enemies.

These political changes fostered new roles for two traditional Latin American institutions: the military and the Roman Catholic Church. The armies of the various nations have played key political roles since the wars of independence, but toward the close of the twentieth century they frequently assumed the direct government of nations rather than use indirect influence. In the clash between the forces of social revolution and reaction, many Roman Catholic priests and bishops protested social and economic inequalities and attacked the repression of

DOCUMENT | Lourdes Arizpe Discusses the Silence of Peasant Women

Lourdes Arizpe, a Mexican anthropologist, wrote extensively on the plight of peasant women in the 1970s. In this passage she discusses how the lives and history of Mexican peasant women are shrouded in silence. Though her remarks are directed toward the situation in Mexico, they may well apply to peasant women in other cultures as well.

> What are the factors that Arizpe cites as leading to the historical silence of peasant women? Why does she believe it is important for such women to learn to speak with their own voices? How do the stereotypes of Mexican peasant women both contribute to and arise from the silence? Why does she believe peasant women to be the most marginalized of all women?

History has imposed a greater silence on peasant women than on any other social group. Perhaps it is the solitude of the plains or the obligatory circumspection of their gender or merely political repression, but circumstances combine to force them to live in a secret world. Doubtless there are those who would assert that their tie to nature leads them to express themselves with actions rather than words. But the male peasant lives in the natural world without being silenced.

Silence, when not deliberate (although, how can we be sure it isn't?) could be anger or wisdom or, simply, a gesture of dignity. When there is no one worth talking to, I stay silent. If someone doesn't want to recognize my existence, I stay silent. In the spectrum of invisibility that history has imposed on women, perhaps the most invisible of the invisibles have been the peasants.

When direct expression is not permitted, the possibility of knowledge is lost and we fill that disturbing vacuum with phantoms. It is therefore not surprising that the Mexican mentality is filled with myths and stereotypes about peasant women. There is the submissive Indian woman who is a product of condescending maternalism; the wild woman both fantasized about and feared by men; the brazen hussy of melodramatic soap operas; the faint-hearted but treacherous small-town woman invented by the urban mind. Silence is also created by everyone's desire to hear what they want to hear rather than listen to what women are trying to say.

Today it seems that everyone mouths concerns about peasant women without any sincere interest.

… What is important today is to create opportunities for peasant women to speak.

It is not that they have never spoken, only that their words have never been recognized. Because their words are discomforting when they denounce exploitation; disturbing when they display a deep understanding of the natural world not shared by their city sisters; strange when they describe an integrating vision of the universe; and because, being women's words, they are not important to androcentric [male-centered] history. Of all the marginalized peoples, peasant women are the most marginalized.

Lourdes Arizpe, "Peasant Women and Silence," trans. by Laura Beard Milroy in *Women's Writing in Latin America: An Anthology* by Sara Castro-Klarén, Sylvia Malloy, and Beatriz Sarlo. Copyright © 1992 by Westview Press. Reprinted by permission of Westview Press.

---

opposition forces. Certain Roman Catholic theologians combined traditional Christian ideas of concern for the poor with Marxist ideology to formulate what came to be known as a **liberation theology**. Generally speaking, the Vatican has attacked this Latin American theological initiative, and as a result its impact has diminished.

During the last decade and a half, Latin America has changed significantly. Several nations, including Argentina, Chile, and Brazil, like the rest of the world, have moved toward democratization. In a departure from earlier policies there has been a strong tendency throughout the continent to allow private markets rather than the state to address economic issues. Yet these changes have remained tenuous, as several nations have had difficulty paying their foreign debts and protecting the value of their currency. In most nations, the military keeps a watchful eye on democratic developments and remains apprehensive about disorder. The end of the Cold War brought to a close one source of external political challenge, but the internal social problems of these nations have continued to raise major difficulties for their governments. Several nations have faced new sources of disorder in the post–Cold War era from powerful drug-producing cartels that have challenged the authority of governments.

REVOLUTIONARY CHALLENGES

There were four major attempts among the nations of Latin America to establish genuinely revolutionary governments pursuing major social and economic change. They occurred in Cuba in 1959, in Chile in 1970, in Nicaragua in 1979, and in Peru in the 1980s. Each involved some form of Marxist political organization, and with the exception of the Shining Path revolutionary movement in Peru, each revolutionary government pursued a close relationship with the Soviet Union. All three had immense symbolic importance not only in Latin America, but also anywhere the colonial influence of Europeans and the economic dominance of the United States once prevailed. The establishment of these governments provoked active resistance and intervention by the United States. It also encouraged opposition to social and political change by traditional elites throughout Latin America.

The Cuban Revolution   Cuba had remained a colony of Spain until the Spanish-American War of 1898. Thereafter, it achieved independence within a sphere of U.S. influence, which took the form of economic domination and occasional military intervention. The fluctuating governments of the island had been both ineffective and corrupt. During the 1950s Fulgencio Batista (1901–1973), a dictator supported by the U.S. government, ruled Cuba.

Historically, Cuba had been politically restive. During the 1940s university student groups led antigovernment agitation. Among the students thus politicized in those years was Fidel Castro Ruz (b. 1926), the son of a wealthy landowner. On July 26, 1953, he and others attacked a government army barracks. The revolutionary movement that he thereafter came to lead in exile took its name from that date: the Twenty-Sixth of July Movement. In 1956 Castro and a handful of followers set sail on a yacht from Mexico and landed in Cuba. They took refuge in the Sierra Maestra Mountains, from which they organized guerrilla attacks on Batista's supporters. By late 1958 Castro's forces were positioned to topple Batista, who fled Cuba on New Year's Day in 1959. By the middle of January, Castro had arrived in Havana as the revolutionary victor.

Castro undertook the most extensive political, economic, and social reconstruction in recent Latin American history. He rejected parliamentary democracy and governed Cuba as a dictator. For approximately the first decade of the revolution he ruled in a personal manner; by the early 1970s, although Castro continued to dominate, executive power was vested in a council. The revolutionary government carried out major land redistribution. In some cases, groups of relatively small landowners were established. On other parts of the island, large state farms became the model.

The Cuban Revolution spurned an industrial economic model and concentrated on improving the agricultural sector. Despite an attempt to turn toward more mixed agriculture, the production of sugar kept its leading role, and the Cuban economy remained monocultural.

Efforts to expand sugar production were disappointing, because too much was attempted too quickly by people who had had too little experience in raising and processing sugar cane. The sugar industry came to depend on large Soviet subsidies and on the Soviet Bloc nations for its market. In that respect, the Cuban economy did not escape the cycle of external dependence.

In foreign affairs, the Cuban Revolution was characterized by a sharp break with the United States and a close relationship with the Soviet Union. Shortly after achieving power, Castro

▲ **Fidel Castro,** waving to cheering crowds acknowledging his triumph over the Batista regime on January 1, 1959.
UPI/Corbis-Bettmann.

aligned himself with the Cuban Communist Party and thereafter with the Soviet Bloc. The United States, under both Republican and Democratic administrations, was hostile toward Castro and toward the presence of a Communist state less than 100 miles from the Florida mainland. In 1961 the United States and Cuban exiles launched the unsuccessful Bay of Pigs invasion. The close Cuban relationship to the Soviet Union prepared the ground for the missile crisis of 1962, which is generally regarded as the most dangerous incident of the entire Cold War. Thereafter followed about a decade of cool relations between Cuba and the United States without overt hostility. During the late 1970s and the 1980s a dialogue of sorts was undertaken between Cuba and the United States, but formal diplomatic relations have not resumed. Mutual distrust continues.

With the collapse of the Soviet Union and the end of the Cold War, the future of Castro's Cuba has become uncertain. Cuba remains the only state closely associated with the former Soviet Bloc that has not experienced substantial political or economic reform. The subsidies that flowed from the Soviet Union to support the Cuban economy are no longer available, however, creating a shortage of everyday consumer goods. The Marxist political and economic ideology stands discredited throughout the world, but the aging Castro's leadership appears to remain intact, at least for the moment. Cuba must soon confront the need for new political leadership or a successor to Castro. It must also confront the need for economic reform and find a new role for itself in a Latin American order in which the issues of the Cold War are no longer relevant. One hint of the perception of the need for a new direction came in 1998 when the Castro government permitted a highly publicized visit from Pope John Paul II and allowed the public celebration of Mass.

Throughout the Cold War, Cuba assumed an importance far greater than its size might suggest. After 1959 it served as a center for the export of Communist revolution throughout Latin America and, after it sent troops to Angola in the late 1970s, in Africa as well. A key policy of the U.S. government, pursued with differing intensities and strategies under different administrations, was to prevent a second Cuba or Communist-dominated state in Latin America. That goal led to direct and indirect intervention in other revolutionary situations and to support for authoritarian governments in Latin America that were dedicated to resisting Marxist revolution.

Chile Until the 1970s Chile was the single most enduring model of parliamentary democracy in Latin America. It had experienced political turmoil and governments of the left and the right, but its parliamentary structures had remained in place. During the 1960s, however, as economic life became more difficult and class relationships deteriorated, Chilean politics became more polarized. Unemployment and labor unrest rose alarmingly. There was profound resentment of the economic domination of Chile by large U.S. corporations.

The situation came to a head in 1970 when Salvador Allende (1908–1973), the candidate of the left-wing political coalition and a Marxist, was elected president with a plurality of the votes. His coalition did not control the Chilean congress, nor did it have the support of the military. For a few months the center and right-wing political groups took a watch-and-wait attitude. Allende nationalized some businesses. The congress blocked policies related to land redistribution, wage improvement, and resistance to foreign economic influence, so Allende began to expropriate foreign property, much of which belonged to U.S. corporations, by decree. This policy frightened the Chilean owners of small and medium-sized businesses. Workers were dissatisfied with the relatively modest effect that socialization had on their daily lives. Inflation ballooned. Despite the expropriation of large estates and the reorganization of agriculture, harvests were poor.

In the autumn of 1973 Allende found himself governing a nation in turmoil without significant domestic political support and with many foreign enemies. He proved unwilling to make significant political compromises. In the wake of strikes and disorder, the army became hostile. The government of the United States was deeply disturbed by the Allende experiment and by the prospect of a Marxist nation on the western coast of South America. The Nixon administration actively supported the discontent within the Chilean army. In mid-September 1973 an army coup overthrew Allende, who was killed in the presidential palace. Chile's short-lived experiment in Marxist socialism ended.

Thereafter, for fifteen years Chile was governed by a military junta, whose most important member, General Augusto Pinochet (b. 1915), served as president. The military govern-

ment pursued a close relationship with the United States and a policy of strong resistance to Marxism in the hemisphere. It also suggested a state-directed free-market economy and reversed the expropriations of the Allende years. After a brief period of economic improvement, inflation and unemployment resumed. The rule of the Chilean military was marked by harsh political repression.

In a referendum held in late 1988, Chileans rejected Pinochet's bid for another term as president. Democratization has been relatively smooth. Civilian governments have investigated the political repression of the Pinochet years and uncovered thousands of cases of torture and murder. The government nonetheless moved slowly, not wishing to provoke the army or revisit the most controversial era of the nation's history. In 1999, while in Great Britain for a medical consultation, General Pinochet was arrested when the government of Spain sought to extradite him to that country to stand trial for the disappearances of Spanish citizens under his rule. Pinochet was ultimately returned to Chile where he was judged too sick to stand trial. Attempts have continued, however, to bring him before some kind of judicial forum.

The Sandinista Revolution in Nicaragua In the summer of 1979 a Marxist guerrilla force, the **Sandinistas**, overthrew the corrupt dictatorship of the Somoza family in Nicaragua. The Somozas had governed Nicaragua more or less as their own personal preserve since the 1930s with moderate, but rarely enthusiastic, support from the United States. The Sandinistas established a collective government that pursued social and economic reform and reconstruction. The movement—with Roman Catholic priests on its leadership council—epitomized the new political and social forces in Latin America. The exact direction of the revolutionary government remained unclear because it confronted significant domestic political opposition and direct military challenge from the contra guerrilla movement.

The government of the United States, particularly under the Reagan administration (1981–1989), was hostile to the Sandinistas. It provided both direct and indirect aid to the opposition guerrillas and criticized the Sandinistas. The U.S. government feared the spread of Marxist revolutionary activity in Central America, a fear reinforced by the close ties between the Sandinistas and the Soviet Union. For the United States, the Sandinista government represented a Central American version of Castro's Cuba.

The rule of the Sandinistas came to a relatively quick end. In early 1990, after a negotiated peace settlement with the contras, they lost the presidential election to an opposition coalition that also captured control of the National Assembly. A floundering economy and U.S. aid had contributed to the electoral victory. Nicaraguans were also tired of the civil war that had shaken the country for a decade. The Sandinistas relinquished power peacefully, and a democratic government supported by the United States has remained in control despite persistent economic weaknesses.

PURSUIT OF STABILITY UNDER THE THREAT OF REVOLUTION

Argentina In 1955 the Argentine army revolted against the excesses and corruption of the Perón dictatorship, and Juan Perón (1895–1974) went into exile. Two decades of economic stagnation and social unrest followed. Neither the army nor the civilian political leaders could forge the kind of political coalition involving the working class that Perón had created. Nor could any of the post-Perón governments cope with unemployment and inflation. In 1973 Perón was recalled from exile in a desperate and futile attempt to restore the fragile stability of a generation earlier. He died about a year later.

By 1976 the army had undertaken direct rule. There was widespread repression; thousands of citizens simply disappeared, never to be heard of again. The leading army officers played something like a game of musical chairs as they moved in and out of an ever-changing ruling junta. In April 1982 General Leopoldo Galtieri (b. 1926), in an effort to score a political success, launched a disastrous invasion of the Islas Malvinas (Falkland Islands). Argentina was decisively defeated by Britain, and the military junta was thoroughly discredited.

In 1983 civilian rule was restored, and Argentina set out on the road to democratization. The major political figure responsible for this achievement was President Raul Alfonsín (b. 1927). Under his leadership, many of the former military figures responsible for the years of repression received prison sentences. Civilian courts took over the role formerly assigned to military tribunals. Alfonsín also sought to turn more real political authority over to the Argentine congress. In all respects Argentina has provided the most extensive example in Latin America of the restoration of democratic practices after military rule. Peaceful elections and transitions of governments have occurred for almost two decades.

The Argentine government easily survived a brief attempted military coup in 1990. Thereafter its major difficulties have been economic. There is rising labor discontent. Many businesses and industries, such as telephone communications, formerly owned by the government have been privatized. Argentina has thus attempted to encourage foreign investment to sustain economic growth. Nonetheless, in 2001 it became clear that Argentina would be unable to repay its foreign debts. Rising unemployment, a currency devaluation, and drastic cuts in basic government services have led to political turmoil.

Brazil In 1964 the military assumed the direct government of Brazil and did not fully relinquish it until the mid-1980s. The military government stressed order and used repression to maintain it. The army itself, however, was divided about the wisdom of the military's move into the political realm. Many officers were concerned that the corruption of everyday politics would undermine the army reputation and sap its esprit de corps. They also feared that respect for the army would come to depend on its success in the political arena. Consequently, within the army itself, certain forces sought to restore a more nearly normal or democratic government. In 1985 civilian government returned under the military's watchful eye.

The military government fostered denationalized industrial development. Non-Brazilian corporations were invited to spearhead the drive toward industrialization. In this respect Brazil opted for an industrial model, but an industrialism guided and dominated from the outside. One result was the accumulation of a massive foreign debt, the servicing and repayment of which have become perhaps Brazil's most important national problem. The relative success of the government's industrialization policy also made Brazil the major industrialized nation in Latin America, which has had a huge impact on the Brazilian rain forest. Subsidies and tax incentives have made the clearing of the Amazon rain forest especially profitable for large landholders involved in cattle ranching. By 1998, 12 percent of Brazil's rain forest had been cleared.

The great question now is how the social changes wrought by industrialism, such as growing urbanization, will be able to receive political accommodation. In Brazil, as in Argentina, the economic and social pressures of the society have spawned conditions ripe for political agitation. It was just that possibility that in the past had led so many citizens—within both the traditional and the new professional elites—to support authoritarian government.

Poverty. A young boy takes a break from sorting garbage at a dump in the outskirts of Sao Paulo, Brazil in 1999.
AP/Wide World Photos.

The civilian government of President Fernando Collor de Mello that came to office in 1990, like numerous other governments in the region, advocated privatization. He and his advisors favored allowing market forces to stimulate growth. They also attempted to contain inflation. During 1992, however, President Collor was impeached by the Brazilian Senate on charges of corruption and using his office to enrich himself. In 1995 Fernando Henrique Cardoso won the presidency, and he has pursued economic policies led by technocrats in hopes of achieving economic growth along with democratic stability.

In 1995, Fernando Henrique Cardoso won the presidency and was re-elected to a second term. He pursued economic policies led by technocrats in hopes of achieving economic growth along with economic stability. By 2003, however, Brazil's economic growth had sharply slowed and required international assistance. In 2003 in the wake of the economic turmoil, Luiz Inácio Lula da Silva became the first person from a working class background to achieve election to the Brazilian presidency. Thus far he has attempted to combine socialist concern for social services along with an austere economic policy.

Mexico Institutionally, Mexico has undergone relatively few political changes since World War II. In theory at least, the government continued to pursue the goals of the revolution. Power remained firmly in the control of the Partido Revolucionario Institucional (PRI), which until the late 1980s had maintained the appearance of stability.

Yet shifts had occurred under this apparently stable surface. The government retreated from some of the aims of the revolu-

Zapatistas. Named after the revolutionary hero Emiliano Zapata (depicted on the banner, see Chapter 26) the Zapatistas demanded rights for the impoverished Native American population of Mexico, especially in the southern state of Chiapas where this photograph was taken in 1997.
AP/Wide World Photos.

tion and appeared conservative when compared to Marxist Cuba or Allende's Chile. In the early 1950s certain large landowners were exempted from the expropriation and redistribution of land. The Mexican government maintained open relations with Cuba and the other revolutionary regimes of Latin America but also resisted any intrusion of Marxist doctrines into Mexico. When necessary, it arrested political malcontents.

Mexico experienced an oil boom from 1977 to 1983. Oil revenues brought immense new wealth into the nation, but the world oil glut burst that bubble. The aftermath revealed the absence of any policy of stable growth. Like so many other states in the region, Mexico amassed large foreign debts and, in doing so, surrendered real economic independence.

In 1988 the PRI encountered a major challenge at the polls. Opposition candidates received much of the vote in a hotly contested election. Whether the election results were honestly reported may never be known. The PRI remained in power, but with the knowledge that it would not be able to dominate the political scene in the manner it had for over half a century. Thereafter, the internal leadership of the party began to move toward greater decentralization in the way the party was run. The newly elected president, Carlos Salinas, moved rapidly to privatize economic enterprise. He also favored free-trade agreements. The most important of these was the North American Free Trade Agreement (NAFTA), which created a vast free-trade area among Mexico, Canada, and the United States. Under Salinas' policies the economic growth rate of Mexico became the best it had been in ten years. In 1991 Salinas came to a new accommodation with the Roman Catholic Church, thus moving away from the traditional anticlericalism that had characterized Mexican politics. By 1991 the PRI appeared to have regained its former political ascendancy.

The situation was largely a façade, however. Beginning in 1994 Mexico underwent a series of political shocks. Its government had to call out troops to quell armed rebellion in Chiapas. During the election of that year, the leading candidate of the PRI was assassinated, and party members were openly charged with complicity in the deed. Party corruption received increasing publicity. Early in 1995 Mexico suffered a major economic downturn, and the peso was sharply devalued. Only loans from the United States saved the economy. Ernesto Zedillo, elected president in 1994, blamed Salinas and his family for the situation, and Salinas went into exile abroad. Thereafter Mexico entered a period of political uncertainty and economic austerity; further unrest occurred in Chiapas. In the election of 2000 the PRI candidate for president lost to Vicente Fox. For the first time in seventy years the PRI were out of power. A genuinely new party system may be developing in Mexico, an eventuality that will become clear only in subsequent elections.

CONTINUITY AND CHANGE IN RECENT LATIN AMERICAN HISTORY

The most striking aspect of the history of the past six decades in Latin America is its tragic continuity with the region's previous history. Revolution has brought moderate social change, but at the price of authoritarian government, economic stagnation, and dependence on different foreign powers. Real independence has not been achieved. Throughout the region for much of the period, parliamentary democracy has been fragile at best; it was the first element of national life to be sacrificed to the conflicting goals of socialism, economic growth, or resistance to revolution.

The recent trends toward democratization and market economics may mark a break in that pattern, however. The region might well enjoy healthy economic growth if inflation can be contained and investment fostered. The challenge—difficult both politically and economically—will be to see that the fruits of any new prosperity are shared in a way that prevents new political resentment and turmoil. Furthermore, as in the past, economic turmoil far from Latin America may have an adverse impact on its destiny. Each time such turmoil has occurred, the governments of Latin America, like the current government of Mexico, have found themselves economically dependent upon either the United States or European governments and bankers.

Postcolonial Africa

Africa represents the clearest example of continuity between arbitrary colonial territories and emergent independent states. Most of its modern nations are direct inheritors of their colonial predecessors' boundaries, just as the former colonial capitals have typically become the new national capitals of independent Africa. Despite the obvious reasons for such continuity from colonial into postcolonial times, it is remarkable that the colonial frontiers, which had little to do with the boundaries of traditional tribal territories or indigenous empires and states, should have managed to persist so consistently. If nationalism was a European export to the rest of the world, Africa provides striking examples of how attractive it can be as a motive for supratribal and transregional state formation.[2]

The rise of African nationalism can generally be dated to the period between the two world wars, when previously fragmented or regional opposition to European colonial occupation began to be replaced by larger scale anti-imperialist movements. In World War II the important roles that Africa was called on to play with its natural and human resources, as well as the experience of thousands of Africans abroad, proved a catalyst for African nationalism. After the war, Europe was also largely disposed to give up its colonial empires (see Chapter 32).

[2] We are especially indebted to Roland Oliver, *The African Experience* (London and New York, 1991), pp. 227–264, for many of the broader interpretations put forward in the current section.

THE TRANSITION TO INDEPENDENCE

The nearly six decades since World War II have seen a previously European-dominated continent become a huge array of independent states. In 1950, apart from Egypt, only Liberia, Ethiopia, and white-controlled South Africa were sovereign states. By 1980 no African territory (except for two tiny Spanish holdings on the Moroccan coast) was ruled by a European state, although South Africa and Namibia continued to be white-dominated. Native sons, such as Kwame Nkrumah (1909–1972) in the Gold Coast (modern Ghana), Jomo Kenyatta (1893–1978) in Kenya, Julius Nyerere (b. 1922) in Tanganyika (later Tanzania), and Patrice Lumumba (1925–1961) in the Congo became symbols of African self-determination and freedom from foreign domination. (See Document, "Pan-African Congress Demands Independence.")

The actual transition from colonial administrative territories to independent national states was less fraught with conflict and bloodshed than one might have expected. All in all, relatively few cases involved extended violent conflict with colonial powers, although those were ferocious. The most protracted and bloody wars of independence from European overlords were the guerrilla struggles fought in French Algeria from 1955 to 1962; in Portuguese Angola and Mozambique

▲ **Ethnic Conflict.** Rwandan refugees carry their belongings as they stream out of the Mugunga refugee camp in Zaire (Congo) back toward Rwanda in one of the many ethnic conflicts that tore apart central Africa in the 1990s.

David Guttenfelder/AP Wide World Photos.

For more than two centuries before World War II European powers had dominated or directly ruled large parts of Africa. Before World War II nationalist political movements came to the fore in a number of these colonial empires. After the war, nationalist movements burgeoned throughout most of the colonial world.

The costs of fighting World War II meant the European powers had less wealth with which to govern their colonies. In addition, the principles of the victorious Allies in Europe were inconsistent with colonialism, as was the foreign policy of the United States, now the dominant Western power.

In the following passage, representatives to the 1945 Fifth Pan-African Congress meeting in Manchester, England, set forth their demand for freedom.

> ◆ What are the social and political goals these African leaders demanded? How did World War II help to allow such goals to be voiced? Why did these leaders believe they deserved to resort to force?

Declaration to the Colonial Powers

The delegates believe in peace. How could it be otherwise, when for centuries the African peoples have been the victims of violence and slavery? Yet if the Western world is still determined to rule mankind by force, then Africans, as a last resort, may have to appeal to force in the effort to achieve freedom, even if force destroys them and the world.

We are determined to be free. We want education. We want the right to earn a decent living; the right to express our thoughts and emotions, to adopt and create forms of beauty. We demand for Black Africa autonomy and independence so far and no further than it is possible in this One World for groups and peoples to rule themselves subject to inevitable world unity and federation.

We are not ashamed to have been an age-long patient people. We continue willingly to sacrifice and strive. But we are unwilling to starve any longer while doing the world's drudgery, in order to support by our poverty and ignorance a false aristocracy and a discarded imperialism.

We condemn the monopoly of capital and the rule of private wealth and industry for private profit alone. We welcome economic democracy as the only real democracy.

Therefore, we shall complain, appeal and arraign. We will make the world listen to the fact of our condition. We will fight in every way we can for freedom, democracy, and social betterment.

Molefi Kete Asante and Abus S. Abarry, *African Intellectual Heritage: A Book of Sources* (Philadelphia: Temple University Press, 1996), pp. 520–521.

from 1961 to 1975; and in Democratic Republic of Congo (formerly the Belgian Congo, then Zaire), Zambia (formerly Northern Rhodesia), and Zimbabwe (formerly Southern Rhodesia) from 1960 to 1980. Usually, however, the transfer of power was relatively peaceful.

Sadly, the same cannot be said of the internal conflicts that often arose after colonial withdrawal and frequently resulted in part from the colonial powers' earlier failure to develop sufficient economic and political infrastructures in their territories. Much of the instability in emergent African states has been a legacy of both the colonial powers' generally minimal efforts to prepare their colonial subjects for self-government and the haphazard nineteenth-century division of the continent into often arbitrary colonial units (see Chapter 27). With the departure of European colonial administrations, the establishment of new African governments created a host of difficulties and often succeeded only after substantial civil strife and even full-scale civil war.

None of the nascent African states had enough educated, trained, and experienced native citizens to staff the political, administrative, economic, and social apparatuses of a sovereign country, and this alone made for difficult times after independence. Corruption among new officials proved rife; military coups often provided the only stable governance available; the attempt to implement planned economies on a socialist model often brought economic catastrophe; and tribal and regional revolts led to civil wars.

Most dangerous and costly to the new states were the separatist struggles, civil wars, and even border wars between new states that grew out of the independence struggles. The Nigerian civil war of 1967–1970, in which more than a million people died from the fighting and the associated famine, was an especially bloody example (see next section). Other new nations caught for periods in open warfare have been Morocco and the western Sahara; Libya and Chad; South African-held Namibia; Ethiopia and Eritrea; Kenya, Uganda, and Tanzania; Rawanda and Burundi; Somalia; and the Sudan. These conflicts were not only bloody and frequent; they also ratified rather than repudiated the postcolonial state divisions.

Every African state has had a different experience and history since World War II; here we will briefly examine only two examples, Nigeria and South Africa.

Nigeria The modern Republic of Nigeria is the most populous state in Africa, with about 100 million inhabitants in 1995. It was formed when the British joined their protectorates of Northern Nigeria and Southern Nigeria in 1914. Nigeria achieved independence in 1960 and ratified a republican constitution in 1964 that federated the three major provincial regions—the Eastern, Western, and Northern—under a national government based in Lagos, the former British administrative capital. Nigeria's largest ethnic and linguistic groups are the major ones of the same three regions or provinces: Igbo (Ibo) in the Eastern, Yoruba in the Western, and Hausa and Fulani in the Northern. Although these languages have been recognized since 1980 as acceptable for federal business, the official Nigerian language is English.

Nowhere was the aftermath of independence bloodier than in Nigeria, which was, at its inception, arguably the most powerful and potentially successful state in independent Africa. The three-province federation fixed in the 1964 constitution soon proved unworkable, and a 1966 coup d'état brought a military government into power. Its leader, an Ibo, was himself assassinated within seven months, and Lieutenant Colonel Yakubo Gawon (b. 1934) took over amid ethnic unrest that ended in massacres in the fall of 1966. Gawon's government subdivided the three provinces into states, three each in the Western and Eastern Provinces, and six in the Northern. Efforts were made into early 1967 to resolve differences with the Eastern states. But in May 1967, the Eastern Province's assembly empowered its leader, Lieutenant Colonel Odumegwu Ojukwu (b. 1933), to form a new, independent state of Biafra out of the three states of the Eastern Province. Ojukwu was an Ibo nationalist but aspired to control lands beyond those of the Ibos—in particular, those containing the important off-shore oil reserves of the Eastern Province. The new Biafran state was able to gain recognition from several African states; secure arms and support from France, South Africa, and Portugal; and develop successful worldwide propaganda depicting Biafra as a small, brave, mostly Christian country fighting for its survival against a hostile, oppressive, mostly Muslim central government.

The ensuing two and a half years saw a tragic and bloody civil war pitting elements of independent Africa's best national army against each other and bringing widespread death and destruction. The larger federal forces slowly chipped away at the Biafran state. The estimated death toll soared above a million before the Biafrans surrendered in January 1970. Out of this brutal conflict, however, came an increased sense of Nigerian unity, along with a major role for the military in Nigerian politics. The struggle also contributed to the development of African diplomacy and of international aid efforts in Africa, both of which were to be hallmarks of African affairs in the next two decades.[3]

Gawon was overthrown by another military commander in 1975. In the ensuing years Nigeria has been plagued by political instability at the top, with its leadership passing usually from one military ruler to another, except for the interlude of the four-year Second Republic under President Usman Aliyu Shagari (b. 1925), a Fulani Muslim from the north whose rule ended in a military coup in 1983. A decade later, the military regime nullified the 1993 election of Yoruba leader Moshood Abiola to the presidency. This debacle ended in a coup by General Sani Abacha, who instituted four years of repressive and brutal military rule. Abiola was imprisoned for four years and the Nigerian playwright and environmental activist Kenule "Ken" Saro-Wiwa (b. 1941) was executed in 1995.

One of the most distinguished Nigerians of recent times, the Nobel laureate writer Wole Soyinka (b. 1934), led protest demonstrations against the military government in 1994 and later went into exile, where in 1996 he helped found a seventeen-member National Liberation Council dedicated to creating a government in exile. Abacha died in June 1998 and was replaced by General Abubakar, who has reversed some of Abacha's repressive actions. Abiola died in July while still in prison. There followed however, some hopeful signs: Soyinka was able to return from exile in October 1998 to a hero's welcome, and some political prisoners were released by Abubakar thereafter. Finally, military rule was replaced as promised in 1999 by civilian government under an elected president, Olusegun Obasanjo, and a new constitution was ratified and implemented. The elections took place in 2003, and there is considerable hope that democratic rule will continue. Problems of religious communal animosities and ethnic divisions remain, but for the first time in sixteen years, the 1999 elections brought a duly constituted civilian rule to Nigeria. There is now some hope that the old corruption and poor management may give way to a democratic government that will not relapse into old ways.

South African One of the most tragic chapters in the history of modern Africa at long last has been closed: that of white minority rule in South Africa, with its radical separation of white from nonwhite peoples in all areas of life as official government policy for nearly fifty years. In the rest of East and southern Africa, minority white-settler governments tried in vain in the postwar period to put down African independence movements or efforts to create participatory multiracial states. Only in South Africa did they manage, until the 1990s, to sustain a white supremacist and separatist political reality in the face of internal resistance and outside pressure.

From the time the Afrikaner-led National Party (NP) came to power in 1948, the Union of South Africa was governed according to the avowedly racist policy of *apartheid* ("apartness"). Until the dismantling of this policy after 1991, the white minority (in 1991, 5.4 million persons) ran the country,

---

[3] Oliver, *African Experience*, pp. 235–236.

Nelson Mandela. On May 10, 1994, Nelson Mandela was sworn in as president of South Africa, bringing an end to the apartheid, white minority government that had imprisoned him for twenty-seven years.

David Brauchli/AP/Wide World Photos.

maintaining economic and political control and privilege. Its 31 million blacks, 3.7 million "coloreds" (of mixed blood), and 1 million Indians were kept strictly segregated—treated, at best, as second-class citizens or, in the case of blacks, as noncitizens or even nonhumans. This system was maintained chiefly by repression, most visibly direct military and police action, to quell dissent and enforce apartheid laws. Only in the past decade was this changed and apartheid officially dismantled as a principle of state.

The history of apartheid and its passing is a bloody and tortured, but finally triumphant one. In part as a result of worldwide opposition to apartheid, South Africa saw itself become increasingly isolated from the 1960s onward. Meanwhile, the rest of Africa—including other white-run states like Rhodesia (now Zimbabwe)—progressed to majority, African rule. In 1961 South Africa withdrew from the British Commonwealth of Nations. In the sixties and seventies the government created three tiny "independent homelands" for blacks inside the country, allowing the white minority to treat blacks as immigrant "foreigners" in the parts of South Africa where most had to work. The international community refused to recognize the homelands, or "Bantustans." South Africa's isolation was further dramatized when two anti-apartheid black leaders, the Zulu chief Albert Luthuli in 1960 and the Anglican bishop Desmond Tutu in 1984, were awarded the Nobel Prize for their work against apartheid.

By 1978, as Pieter Botha (b. 1916) came to power, apartheid was failing: The homelands were economic and political catastrophes; the country was in an inflationary recession, skilled whites were emigrating; and with other white colonial regimes on the way out, South Africa was becoming an international pariah. In the 1980s the struggle between the white minority and the black majority intensified, and Botha's concessions on issues such as interracial marriage and public-transportation segregation could not calm the situation. Internal opposition to apartheid grew, and calls for a boycott of South Africa brought increasing international pressure. Threats from guerrilla forces prompted the government to send its troops on preemptive raids on guerrilla bases in neighboring countries.

Beginning in 1986 many nations responded to Desmond Tutu's call and imposed economic sanctions against the government. Anti-apartheid movements in the United States and elsewhere had convinced companies and individuals to liquidate investments in South Africa. Strikes by black workers in 1987 led the government to declare a state of emergency, but the resulting violent confrontation created widespread support among Western nations for a complete trade embargo.

In June 1988 more than 2 million black workers went on strike to protest new repressive labor laws and a ban on political activity by trade unions and anti-apartheid groups. President Botha resigned in August 1989. His replacement, F. W. de Klerk (b. 1936), began to dismantle white-only rule and the official structures of apartheid. In February 1990 de Klerk announced radical changes, and a series of landmark government actions followed: the lifting of the ban on the African National Congress (ANC), the main anti-apartheid organization; the release of ANC leader Nelson Mandela after twenty-seven years of imprisonment; and the repeal of the Separate Amenities Act, the legal basis for segregation in public places. In early 1991 de Klerk announced plans to end all apartheid laws, and in June the race registration law was repealed. In March 1992, in a whites-only referendum in which over 85 percent of voters turned out, 67.8 percent voted to grant constitutional equality to all races. De Klerk and Mandela, despite terrorist attempts from both black and white extremists to derail the talks, were able to bring their own and eighteen other parties to endorse a new interim constitution. This constitution was to be implemented once national elections could be held in which all citizens of South Africa would be enfranchised. (For their leadership, Mandela and de Klerk shared the Nobel Peace Prize for 1993.)

Despite continued violence the elections were held in April 1994. The ANC won 63 percent of the vote, the NP 20 percent, and other parties the remainder, thus relegating apartheid's ugly racist ideology to the slag heap of history. The nonracial constitution of December 1996 offered a new basis for the future, but despite the rising political hope, substantial mineral resources, and the highest GNP in Africa, the new state still faces huge problems: one of the world's most extreme income inequalities; insufficient education and economic infrastructure, rampant black poverty; high unemployment; militant extremist groups, woefully inadequate public services in much of the country; potentially severe water-supply and water-quality problems; and difficulties in attracting enough foreign investment fast enough to fulfill Mandela's promises of a new era of economic and social progress. The new government of Thabo Mbeki, elected to succeed Mandela in 1999 for a five-year term, is now striving to continue the new democratic experiment and trying to deal with the huge social and economic problems that the majority of the population face. The daunting obstacles to be surmounted will, however, no longer include a state system that holds the majority of the population in social, economic, and political bondage.

The new independent states of Africa have been anything but models. And any ideas of a union or unions of nations have either failed (the uniting of Zanzibar and Tanganyika in the new state of Tanzania is a notable exception) or remain pure conjectures about an uncertain future. Nevertheless Africa did not revert to tiny tribal and regional political units. And, it must be noted, some struggles—such as those in the Darfur region of Sudan, Somalia, Rwanda, Sierra Leone, Angola, and Liberia—are still ongoing, their human consequences catastrophic, and their ultimate outcomes not clear.

THE AFRICAN FUTURE

Most African states have not achieved peace and prosperity. However, the last fifty-plus years have seen radical change and development that would have been unimaginable before. After decades of struggles and trials, the prospects for future government stability are not entirely bleak. Economic problems still loom extremely large, but even in that sphere some progress is being made after decades of failed socioeconomic planning and development schemes. In any case, every African state is different; each faces unique problems and must draw on its unique resources if it is to be successful in the present century. The often heavy burdens of the past—be they regional rivalries and hatreds, religious and linguistic divisions, major economic and social policy mistakes in early independence, or the crippling experience of apartheid—still present formidable hurdles.

Probably even more serious are those problems with which almost all of Africa's new nations still have to contend: overpopulation, poverty, disease (especially HIV/AIDS), famine, lack of professional and technical expertise, and general economic underdevelopment. In particular, the explosive growth of new urban centers at the expense of rural areas has disrupted the continent's traditionally agrarian-based societies, age-old family and tribal allegiances, religious values, and sociopolitical systems. The challenge for African nations in the twenty-first century is how to build a civil society and achieve economic health and political stability in the face of internal divisions, exploding population growth, and world-market competition.

Central, South, and Southeast Asia—The Islamic Heartland

The lands today dominated or significantly marked by Islamic culture and containing either Muslim majority populations or major Muslim minority numbers stretch from North and West Africa to the Philippines. More specifically, they are found in the Arab world from Morocco to Iraq and the Gulf, in the Balkans and Turkish-speaking world of Turkey and the former Soviet Central Asian republics, in Persian-speaking Iran and parts of Central Asia, in western China, and in South and Southeast Asia. India, Bangladesh, Pakistan, and Indonesia have the four largest Muslim populations in the world, the first three having about 132, 109, and 125 million Muslims, respectively, and the last more than 180 million. The Muslims of the entire Arab world number no more than 250 million. The various nations of this huge region of Central, South, and Southeast Asia illustrate the many different ways in which Islamic faith and practice may manifest themselves and affect political life.

TURKEY

Turkey, a non-Arab country, represents a modernist republican experiment that has managed to allow a civil society and a democratically elected government to be the norm, despite struggles over the place of religion in society and lapses into military rule. However, the Turkish military has repeatedly deposed elected governments and supervised the selection of new leadership. Economically, Turkey has certainly had its difficulties, but along with Israel it is still the most economically advanced Middle Eastern country in the region. With the creation of new Turkic-language-speaking states in Central Asia after the breakup of the Soviet Union, Turkey is making a bid, and may succeed, to strengthen its ties with this underdeveloped part of the world and to be a major factor in its emergence over the next generation. (See Document, "A Modernist Muslim Poet's Eulogy for His Mother.")

Geographically and culturally Turkey is part of both Europe and Asia. Istanbul, its main commerical and cultural center, is located in continental Europe. In recent years, Turkey, already a member of NATO, has sought admission into the European Union.

Turkey also participates in several significant European cultural events such as the European soccer competition and the widely watched (in Europe at least) Eurovision song contest. In coming years, the issue of Turkish membership in the European Union will be contested because many across Europe are skeptical about admitting an overwhelmingly Muslim nation

DOCUMENT | A Modernist Muslim Poet's Eulogy for His Mother

The following is a poem drawn from the autobiography of Aziz Nesin, That's How It Was but Not How It's Going to Be (1966). Nesin (b. 1915) is a prolific Turkish writer, political commentator, and social critic whose writing career began in 1946 with his publication of a satirical weekly paper. The following poem is a eulogy for his long-dead mother, a reflection on the deprivations she endured, and a determined promise to ensure women a better life in the future. It reflects the widespread feeling among secular modernists in Turkey and elsewhere that one of the hallmarks of modernity is the emancipation of women. The final two lines repeat the original Turkish title of Nesin's book.

> ◆ What is the impact of addressing the poem to his own mother rather than to some other female figure? What specific things is Nesin criticizing in the poem?

A Vow to My Mother's Memory

All mothers, the most beautiful of mothers,
You are the most beautiful of the beautiful,
At thirteen you married;

At fifteen you gave me birth.
You were twenty-six,
You died before you lived.
I owe you this heart overflowing with love.
I don't even have your picture;
It was a sin to have a photograph taken.
You saw neither movie, nor play.
Electricity, gas, water, stove,
Nor even a bedstead were found in your home.
You could never bathe in the sea,
You couldn't read nor write.
Your lovely eyes
Looked at the world from behind a black veil.
When you were twenty-six
You died, before you lived—
Henceforward, mothers will not die before they live.
That's how it was,
But not how it's going to be!

Aziz Nesin, *Istanbul Bay: The Autobiography of Aziz Nesin, Part I*, p. 9. Copyright © 1977 Center for Middle Eastern Studies. Reprinted by permission.

---

ino the Union and about the less than stellar Turkish human-rights record. Up to now, the longtime persecution of the ten- to twelve–million strong Kurdish minority in Turkey has been a sticking point for European acceptance of the idea of admitting Turkey to the European Union. Human-rights violations such as imprisonment of journalists, repression of the Kurdish language, and freedom of speech, as well as serious indebtedness to the International Money Fund have worked against Turkey's case for EU admission also. In addition, various Islamist parties have emerged in Turkey that have complicated the political landscape. It remains to be seen whether Turkey will align itself more with Europe, the Middle East, or Central Asia in the years ahead, even though it is making a strong effort to join Europe while reaching out to Central Asia.

IRAN AND ITS ISLAMIC REVOLUTION

Iran, the most important state of central Asia, was ruled from 1925 to 1941 as a monarchy by a former army commander, Reza Khan, who had come to power by military takeover and governed under the old Persian title Shah Reza Pahlavi. He attempted to introduce modernist economic, educational, and governmental reforms [not unlike his contemporary in Turkey, Atatürk (1881–1938), although his reforms were aimed at creating not a parliamentary, popularly based state, but a highly centralized monarchy]. By the time Russian and

British forces deposed Reza in 1941 and installed his son, Muhammad Reza, as shah, the power of the Shi'ite religious leaders, or *ulama*, had been muted and a strong, centralized state established. The son, like his father, sought to ground the legitimacy of Pahlavi rule on the ancient, pre-Islamic imperial dynasties of greater Iran, especially that of the Achaemenids (see Chapter 4). He continued his father's basically secularist state building from the end of World War II until 1978, with one interruption from 1951 to 1953. Those two years saw Muhammad Mosaddeq (1881–1967) come to power through a nationalist revolution, only to be overthrown in a counterrevolution that succeeded through covert American and British support (and thereby made American motives and actions vis-à-vis Iran greatly suspect in the eyes both of the Iranian masses and politicians).

In the 1960s Muhammad Reza Shah was finally forced by popular opposition, led by educated elites of the secular left and *ulama* of the religious right, to institute land reform and other socialist or populist reforms. However, his cavalier attitude toward, and his violent repressive measures against, the leftist and especially the religious opposition alienated the Iranian masses. For all of the modernizing and the military and economic buildup that the shah initiated, his reign failed to narrow the gap between the wealthy elites and the poor masses. The fact that fully half of Iran's 60-odd million inhabitants are

▲ **Khomeini.** The bearded ayatollah waves to a cheering throng in Tehran, Iran in February 1979.

Reuters/Corbs-Bettmann.

non-Persian-speaking Turks, Kurds, Arabs, and other minorities did little to help him consolidate and strengthen his nationalistic Iranian monarchy.

Finally, in 1978 religious leaders and secularist revolutionaries joined forces to end the shah's long regime with a revolution fueled by Shi'ite Islamic feeling and symbolism. In 1979 the constitution of a new Islamic republic was adapted under the guidance of the Shi'ite religious leader, or *ayatollah*, Ruhollah Khomeini (1902–1989). Subsequent years have seen a protracted war with Iraq (1980–1988) and the institution of repressive and violent measures against enemies of the new regime not unlike those used under the shah. Still, the new state—with religious leaders exercising a degree of influence over politics not seen since early Safavid times in the sixteenth century—has survived. Khomeini and his successors, Hashemi Rafsanjani (b. 1934) and Ali Khameini (b. 1939), however, were not free of or untainted by politics. They had to struggle to find a new formula for combining Muslim values and norms with twentieth-century *realpolitik*, and this will continue to be a major challenge for their successors.

The immediate successor to Rafsanjani, Mohammad Khatami, was elected to the presidency in 1997 by a resounding majority in the first real national leadership election since the 1979 revolution. Khatami, a moderate cleric himself as well

as former minister of culture with a reputation as a relative liberal among the major figures in Iranian politics, has tried to steer Iran on a moderate and more liberal course. Many think his election and administration represent a key step in Iran's movement after its watershed revolution toward a more stable government and more internationally engaged and accepted power in the Middle Eastern and Indian Ocean sphere. The wide ranging reforms that people expected from Khatami have failed to materialize. There have been sporadic and unsuccessful student protests against the clerical government. In 2003, Shirin Ebadi, an Iranian lawyer, won the Nobel Peace Prize for her efforts to improve the status of women in Iran.

AFGHANISTAN AND THE FORMER SOVIET REPUBLICS

North of Iran, 40 million Central Asian Muslims predominate in the broad region that stretches across the south-central reaches of the former USSR between the Crimea and China, and 30 million or more Muslims live in Chinese Central Asia. These people have had to sustain their religious and intellectual traditions in the face of Russian and Chinese cultural, linguistic, and political imperialism. In the 1980s both Soviet and Chinese Muslims appeared to be asserting themselves. The 1979 Soviet invasion and occupation of Afghanistan, whose people had close ties to the Muslim peoples in the Soviet Union, reflected the potential importance of this movement. The phased withdrawal of Soviet forces from Afghanistan in 1988 looked surprisingly like the U.S.

▲ **Iranian Women in New Roles.** In the offices of the first Iranian women's daily newspaper, *Rooznameh Zan.* Despite the reactionary adoption of a conservative dress code for women after the 1978 Iranian revolution, women in Iran today are pursuing a variety of careers and taking an active part in public discourse. This is not to argue that women's equality is being implemented, but only that women will not likely be suppressed for much longer in Iranian society.

Eslami Rad/Liaison Agency, Inc.

Afghan Women. Shortly after the Taliban were driven out of Kabul in November 2001, several Afghan women, one unveiled, venture out in the street.
Reuters/Corbis-Bettmann.

withdrawal from South Vietnam in 1974. It was soon followed by a much more momentous about-face in the form of the collapse of the Soviet Union in 1990 into many separate states, most of which remain loosely connected through the Commonwealth of Independent States (CIS). The Central Asian republics within the Commonwealth include Kazakhstan, Kyrgyzstan, Tajikistan, Turkmenistan, and Uzbekistan and the Caucasian republics of Armenia, Azerbaijan, Georgia, and Moldova. Suddenly the Central Asian Islamic republics of the former USSR found themselves effectively independent states, yet with little of the infrastructure to manage such a transition. The great challenge is whether they and their sister states of the commonwealth can attain political viability without being destroyed by economic collapse or ethnic or regional conflict first.

The Soviet invasion of Afghanistan produced a major unexpected result. Thousands of Muslims, mostly fundamentalist in outlook, had arrived in Afghanistan to oust the Soviets and their Afghan puppets. Conservative Arab states and the United States supported this effort, which succeeded by the late 1980s. The conservative Arab states saw the Afghan War as an opportunity both to resist the expansion of Soviet influence into their sphere and to divert the energies of their own religious extremists. The United States saw the Afghan War as another round in the Cold War. The militant Muslim fundamentalists saw it as a religious struggle against an impious Western power.

After the Soviets withdrew, a power vacuum in Afghanistan lasted almost a decade. By 1998, however, rigorist Muslims known as the *Taliban* had seized control of the country. They imposed their own version of Islamic law, which involved strict regimentation of women and public executions and mutilations for criminal offenses. The Taliban also allowed groups of Muslim terrorists known as *al Qaeda*, which means "Base," to establish training camps in their country. The terrorists who attacked the United States on September 11, 2001, came from these camps. As will be seen later in the chapter, one response of the United States to those attacks was a military campaign against the Taliban government of Afghanistan.

INDIA

India, a largely Hindu state, and Pakistan, a largely Muslim state, gained independence in 1947 after the British agreed to a partition of the subcontinent. Much of their subsequent history has been one of mutual antagonism. This was born out of the Hindu-Muslim communal violence and the disputes over Kashmir and other areas that accompanied the partition. The tragedy of the massive displacement of Muslims from the new India and of Hindus and Sikhs from the new Pakistan (about 8 million people in each case) was and is still immense for millions of families and individuals. The two states still have not resolved their major differences, including their conflicting claims to Kashmir. Their rivalry has been exacerbated recently by a new round of saber rattling, this time a nuclear one begun by five Indian underground nuclear tests carried out in mid-May 1998, which were closely followed by similar Pakistani tests two weeks later. Since that time there have been a number of crises between the two nations in which there have been fears of a nuclear exchange.

Bereft of its spiritual and material father, Mohandas Gandhi (1869–1948), after his assassination in 1948 at the hands of a Hindu fanatic, India has been directed for most of its existence by the leaders of Gandhi's Congress Party. First came Gandhi's follower and nationalist colleague, Jawaharlal Nehru (1889–1964), who developed India's famous theory of political neutrality vis-à-vis world alignments, such as that of the superpowers in the Cold War. Nehru's long leadership carried India through the critical organizational period of early independence and not only Pakistani disputes but also a brief Himalayan war with China in 1962. His secularist, reconciliatory policies reduced the communal hatreds, religious zealotry, and regional tensions of the postpartition era, and he also made progress in the huge task of economic development of the overpopulated, underdeveloped new nation. His government oversaw the nuts-and-bolts internal work of damping such potentially divisive movements as Sikh religious separatism and of forging a national federation from states divided by religious, cultural, and political history as well as by languages. In this era Hindi and English were set as the national languages, and fourteen major regional languages, each associated with a state, were recognized for regional official use.

Nehru's resolute opposition to caste privilege also helped improve equality of citizenship beyond universal suffrage.

Nehru was succeeded by another Congress leader, Lal Bahadur Shastri (1904–1966), who saw India through a debilitating nine-month war and standoff with Pakistan in 1965. His successor was Nehru's daughter, Indira Gandhi (1917–1984; prime minister, 1966–1977, 1980–1984; no familial relation to Mohandas Gandhi). She carried on most of her father's policies and similarly managed to steer a tricky course of neutralism during the Cold War and its East–West tensions. India's 1971 victory over Pakistan and the subsequent creation of Bangladesh to replace East Pakistan cemented for some years her often shaky political control; this war and the subsequent development, with Russian help, of an atomic bomb confirmed India as the major power in South Asia. The failure of her efforts to reduce national poverty and improve India's general economic health soon overcame her postwar popularity. After her efforts to assume virtual dictatorial power in the face of calls for her resignation, in 1977 she and the Congress Party were ousted by the voters for three years. She was reelected prime minister in an amazing turnaround and served until her resolute efforts to quell Sikh separatism brought about her assassination in 1984 by two Sikhs from her own palace guard.

Indira Gandhi's son, Rajiv Gandhi (1944–1991), was elected prime minister after her, and his handling of the thorny Sikh issue was generally applauded. Indications that he and Prime Minister Bhutto might work together to resolve some of the old India-Pakistan hostilities were also promising. Charges of corruption in his government led to his party's temporary fall and the prime ministership of V.P. Singh (b. 1931), who worked in his brief period of leadership to defuse Hindu-Sikh and Hindu-Muslim communal tensions. Singh's resignation gave Gandhi as leader of the Congress Party a chance in the national and state elections of 1991, but during the campaign he was assassinated by a Sri Lankan Tamil suicide bomber. Because no party won the subsequent national vote, the leader of the Congress Party, P. V. Narasimha Rao, was asked to form a government. He and the Congress managed afterwards to make substantial economic progress and, despite failures such as the 1992 radical Hindu riot and attack on the Babri Mosque in Ayodhya, to keep the lid generally on a wide variety of communal and separatist problems, from the Sikhs in the Punjab to Muslims in Kashmir and the south, Hindu extremists, and Uttarakhand separatists in the Himalayas. In 1997, Vice President K. R. Narayanan, a former academic and foreign service officer, assumed the presidency. He and his party were displaced in 2004 by an unexpected Congress Party victory.

India's problems remain large. Poverty and disease, including plague outbursts, remain serious problems. Separatist movements based on regional linguistic affinity, such as that of

▲ **Hindu Militants.** Hindu militants attack a Muslim mosque in Ayodhya, India, December 6, 1992. The razing of this mosque at the hands of a mob led by Hindu communalist extremists touched off a wave of Hindu-Muslim violence in India. The Hindus claimed the mosque, built some 500 years ago, occupied the site of what had originally been a Hindu temple and sought to have a new temple built once the mosque was cleared away.

Sunil Malhotra/Reuters/Corbis-Bettmann.

the Tamil peoples of the south, or religious affinity, such as that of the Sikhs of the Punjab, have pulled at the unity of the Indian state. Industrialization and agricultural modernization have recently made great strides, yet the neutralizing force of runaway population growth has yet to be countered enough to ensure a brighter future for India's masses. India's population is now at about 1 billion and growing at nearly 2 percent per year. The growing strength of militant Hindu nationalists and fundamentalists and new outbreaks of communal violence between Hindus and India's large Muslim minority pose serious threats to the country's political stability. As the world's largest functioning democracy, India will be an important model of representative government and pluralistic society if it succeeds in staying together and solving or even reducing its harshest problems—overpopulation and mass poverty.

PAKISTAN AND BANGLADESH

The architect and first president of Pakistan, Muhammad Ali Jinnah (1876–1948), oversaw the creation of a Muslim state comprising the widely separated East and West Pakistan in the two predominantly Muslim areas of northwest India and East Bengal. New constitutions, war with India, religious versus secularist ideological strife, repeated military rule, and consistent return to the ballot box have marked the often baffling pendulum swings of the new nation in its first half century. In 1971 East Pakistan seceded and became the new Islamic nation of Bangladesh. Indian and Bangladeshi relations have been troubled since then. However, the main political division in the subcontinent remains that between India and Pakistan.

Pakistan's groping efforts to create a fully Islamic society and to solve its massive economic problems have been hampered by periodic lapses into dictatorship. Such lapses are usually punctuated by bloodshed and military coups, the most recent being that which brought the military leader Zia ul-Haqq (1924–1988) to power in 1977. The elections of November 1988, following his death in a suspicious air crash, opened the door to the possible success of parliamentary government rule. The new prime minister, Benazir Bhutto (b. 1953), was the daughter of the man whom Zia ul-Haqq overthrew and executed. She was also the first female leader of a major Islamic state in the twentieth century. Her time in office was cut short by the president's dismissal of her government in August 1990.

Benazir returned to the prime ministership, only to be deposed by the president on charges of corruption in 1996 and convicted in 1999. The successor government did not last long, for in 1999, General Parviz Musharraf, Chief of Army Staff, took over as chief executive of Pakistan and has continued to govern since that time. Of all central Asian governments, that of Pakistan has confronted the most direct challenge from radical Islam.

INDONESIA AND MALAYSIA

The new East Indies state of Indonesia came into being in 1949 as a nominal republic succeeding the long Dutch and brief Japanese colonial dominions in the East Indies. The much smaller territory of Malaya received its independence from British colonial rule in 1957 as a federation under a rotating monarch; it was later joined by the states of Sarawak and Sabah in northern Borneo, forming the federation of Malaysia. Each of these two new sovereign states faces different challenges.

Indonesia, the largest Muslim country in the world (about 178 million of its estimated 200 million people are Muslim), is trying to achieve a consensus among its disparate and scattered parts. It must determine how Muslim religious faith is to be reconciled with secularist government. The overriding problem for Malaysia (population 20 million) has been the cleft between the largely Chinese (32 percent) and partly Indian (9 percent) non-Muslim minority on the one hand, and the largely Muslim majority of Malay and other indigenous peoples (59 percent) on the other. Both nations have rich cultural traditions and natural resources; it remains to be

◀ **Tsunami.** On December 26, 2004 a powerful earthquake off the northwestern coast of Sumatra unleashed a massive *tsunami* (Japanese, "harbor wave") that devasted a vast section of the Indian Ocean from Thailand to Tanzania (a distance of over 4,000 miles). Over 200,000 people were killed and a great number left homeless by this natural disaster, one of the most calamitous in modern history. Indonesia alone lost over 160,000 people, the worst-hit area being Acheh province in northern Sumatra, a separatist region that has battled government authorities for centuries (see Chapter 27).

seen how each will choose to preserve them while meeting the demands of modern global politics and participation in the global economy. An important part of the future of Islam as a global religious and cultural tradition, as well as the future of these two Asian states, is at stake.

The Postcolonial Middle East

Today no other part of the postcolonial world so dominates international concern and conflict as the Middle East. The issues have arisen as a result of the new nations established in the region since World War I, the Arab-Israeli conflict, the rise of political Islamism, and the military intervention of the United States in Iraq.

New Nations in the Middle East

The modern Middle East arose as a result of the slow collapse of the Ottoman Empire and the subsequent intervention in the region by Western powers during World War I and the Versailles Peace Conference. Those powers in effect carved out new nations and protectorates in the Middle East. Saudi Arabia, Iraq, and Egypt became sovereign states after World War I, and Lebanon and Syria were officially given their independence by France during World War II. Yet these states became truly independent of European control only after World War II. In l948 Great Britain abandoned its protectorate over Palestine and the United Nations recognized the state of Israel. During the late l940s and thereafter, other Arab states gained independence: Jordan in 1946; Libya in 1951; Morocco and Tunisia in 1956; Algeria in 1962; and, by 1971, Yemen, Oman, and the small Arabian Gulf states. (See Map 34–4.)

As elsewhere in the developing world, these states have sought political self-determination amidst political instability and autocratic rule. All share the classical Arabic written language (*fusha*) whereas the spoken colloquial language ('*amiyya*) varies from country to country and even city to city. Various attempts to create pan-Arab alliances or federations have all failed primarily because regional differences and political interests have overcome the common cultural denomitators. The heritage of these efforts to establish an Arab nationalism remains important today.

In the wake of World War II, many of the foremost leaders of Arab nationalism, such as Gamal Abdul Nasser of Egypt (1918–1970), were sympathetic to socialism or the Soviet Union. Because socialism and communism were Western ideologies, left-leaning Arab nationalism was no less Western in its orientation than were nationalists friendly to the United States. Moreover, Soviet communism was overtly atheistic and hence doubly offensive to devout Arab Muslims.

Nationalism forged by nondemocratic Middle Eastern governments, usually traditional monarchies or authoritarian regimes dominated by the military, brought different results to the various Arab nations. Oil made Saudi Arabia wealthy and powerful and the Gulf states, such as Kuwait, rich, but not powerful. Other states, such as Jordan, Syria, and Egypt, which lacked oil, remained burdened by large impoverished populations.

Arab governments defining themselves according to the values of nationalism worked out arrangements with local Muslim authorities. For example, the Saudi royal family turned over its educational system to adherents of a rigorist, puritanical form of Islam called *Wahhabism* (see Chapter 27) while modernizing the country's infrastructure. The Egyptian government attempted to play different Islamic groups off against one another. These governments retained the support of prosperous, devout middle-class Muslims while doing little about the plight of the poor. In general, Muslim religious leaders were highly critical of the Soviet Union and its influence in the region. Consequently, for many in the Middle East today the memory of secular Arab nationalism remains the memory of an example of a failed secular approach to politics and to Arab self-identity.

The Arab-Israeli Conflict

Nowhere in the affairs of the Middle East has the influence of the superpowers and Europe been more sharply felt than in the 1948 creation of the state of Israel in the former British mandate territory of Palestine. This event was the achievement of the world Zionist movement founded in 1897 by Theodor Herzl (1860–1904) in Europe. The British Balfour Declaration of 1917, issued during the middle of World War I and thus reflecting British wartime goals and concerns, had already favored the establishment of a national homeland for the Jews in Palestine. Even in 1920, however, there were only about 60,000 Jews and ten times that number of Arabs in Palestine. As some voices at the time, such as the American fact-finding Mission, the 1919 King-Crane Commission sent by the American president Woodrow Wilson foresaw, and time would bear out, trouble lay ahead. (See Document, "Recommendations of the King-Crane Commission.")

The interwar years saw increasing Jewish settlement and growing communal conflict poorly mediated by the often contradictory policy of the British. Immigration of Jews, largely from Eastern Europe, increased in the 1920s and 1930s until Britain tried in 1936 to restrict it severely—an effort that tragically prevented many European Jews from escaping the Nazi Holocaust. Because of the Nazi attempt to exterminate European Jewry, after the war the Zionist movement received a tremendous boost among Jews worldwide and from the Allied nations, who felt the need to atone for the indescribable horror of the Holocaust by helping to secure a refuge for Jews from around the world.

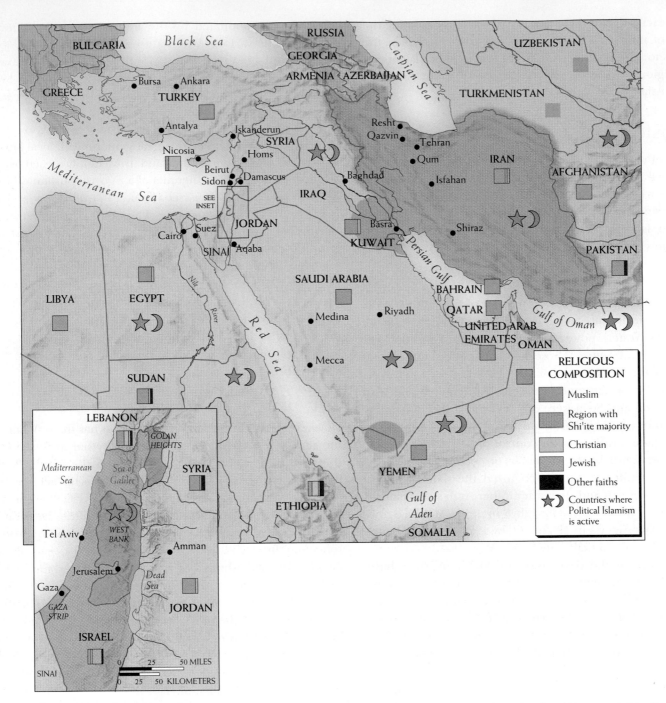

MAP 34–4 The Modern Middle East and the Distribution of Major Religious Communities.   The inset shows Israel and the occupied territories.

The concept of return to the Holy Land had a long history in Judaism. However, translating the concept into the creation of a national state was difficult because, for centuries, the land, administered by the Ottoman Empire, had been the home of Arabic-speaking Palestinians, primarily Muslims, but also Christians and Jews, all of whom were without voice in the matter of the fate of their own land over march of the twentieth century. The Palestinians have understandably not been able to see why they should be displaced and persecuted, whether because of another people's historic religious attachment to the land or as reparation for Europe's sins against the Jews. On the other hand, especially in the light of nineteenth- and twentieth-century European anti-Semitic persecutions, Jews themselves felt the desperate need for a homeland where they might be safe and to which Jews everywhere might flee from future persecutions and the nagging anti-Semitism that still rears its ugly head around the globe. For the last 50 years, Arabs and Israelis motivated by two deeply held views have clashed, and with each year, an equitable solution acceptable to all parties seems less likely.

In 1945 Britain found itself beset in Palestine by Jews seeking to settle there and by Jewish underground and terrorist organizations aiming to oust the British. In 1947 the British washed their hands of the problem, and the United Nations called for partition of the former mandate territory into a Jewish and an Arab state. The existing Arab states refused to accept the UN resolution, but in May 1948 Jews in Palestine proclaimed the independent state of Israel anyway. This declaration led to the Israeli-Arab war of 1948–1949, in which Syria, Iraq, Lebanon, Jordan, Egypt, and Saudi Arabia attacked Israel but lost to the better-armed, better trained, and more resolute Israelis, ceding not only the UN-proposed Israeli territory, but also a substantial portion of that designated by the UN for a Palestinian state. In addition to the plight of Palestinians subjected to Israeli rule or occupation, the creation of Israel also produced a massive Palestinian refugee problem that has yet to be resolved by anyone—the Arab nations, Israel itself, the United Nations, or other interested parties. Over the half-century since 1948, nearly seventy-five per cent of the Palestinians in the world have been refugees from their homeland; the war of 1967 and the later aftermaths of two *intifadahs* only added additional refugees to the original ones.

Since 1948 there has been, at best, an armed truce between Israel and its neighbors and, at worst, open warfare. The Arab nations and the Palestinian people displaced by the new state have generally not wanted to accept Israel's right to exist as a state, and Israel (with the support of the United States) has taken aggressive measures, often in defiance of world opinion and international law regarding **occupied territories**, to ensure its survival. The most serious military confrontations were the Suez Crisis of 1956, when Israel (and briefly France and England) invaded the Sinai; the 1967 June war (often referred to as the "Six Day War"), when Israel occupied the Sinai, the Golan Heights, and the West Bank (of the Jordan River); the October war of 1973, or the Yom Kippur war, when the Egyptians and Syrians staged a surprise attack on Israel in the Sinai and the Golan that ended in a standoff; and the Israeli invasions of Lebanon in 1978 and 1982 in the context of the Lebanese-Syrian conflict and the professed determination of Israel to extirpate anti-Israeli terrorist refuges.

Ever since the fall of 2000, the region has spiraled into an abyss of violence with repeated Israeli military assaults on towns and refugee camps in the West Bank and Gaza and regular Palestinian extremist suicide attacks on mainly civilian targets.

▲ **Confrontation.** An Israeli settler in prayer shawl carries his American M16 assault rifle past a group of Palestinians in Hebron, who sit in front of a shuttered shop where a large Star of David has been painted.
Kevin Lamarque/Getty Images, Inc./Hulton Archive Photos.

Most recently, the highly provocative construction by Israel of a massive "separation wall" through the West Bank is currently (2004) asserting Israeli control over still more Palestinian West-Bank territory, ostensibly in the name of increased Israeli security from suicide bombings. The virtual pull-back of the United States from any serious effort at bringing either Israel or the Palestinians back into negotiations has now left the future of the region in still greater danger and uncertainty.

Simultaneously, in a cycle of violence familiar from Northern Ireland to Vietnam, the frustrations of an embattled Israel have made it increasingly ready to meet terrorist atrocities with preemptive military actions and violent reprisals, both at home and abroad. Israel has responded to extremist terrorist attacks and civilian resistance such as the ***Intifadah***, or uprising (literally, "shaking"), in the occupied territories with air and commando raids on Arab states thought to support Palestinian terrorism; with repressive, even punitive, measures against the Palestinian populations in the occupied territories; and generally with a hard-line stance against negotiation over the status of the territories seized in 1967.

Arab and some non-Arab states have been equally intransigent about recognizing Israel's right to exist, have supported guerrilla groups attacking Israel, and have refused until recently to deal directly with Israel to reach a long-term Middle East solution. Egypt was the first notable exception to this policy. In the late 1970s, under Gamal Abdel Nasser's successor, President Anwar Sadat (1918–1981), and through the

DOCUMENT | The King-Crane Commission Report, August 28, 1919

In the postwar peace settlements, following World War One, it proved impossible to reconcile the claims of the Arabs, the Zionists, the British and the fact-finding French. The American President Woodrow Wilson sent a fact-finding mission to the region to determine what the people of the region really wanted. The King-Crane Commission was headed by Henry C. King, the president of Oberlin College and Charles R. Crane, a businessman and philanthropist.

The commission spent several weeks in the Middle East meeting with representatives of the various ethnic, religious, and national communities.

Although the findings eventually had no influence of policy in the region, the commission's report is remarkable because it captured in a systematic way the uncertain political mood in the Middle East immediately following World War I. As the following section reveals, the United States was held in high regard in the region. The report also anticipated some of the problems relating to Arab-Jewish relations.

◆ What are some of the major political issues highlighted by the commission? Why did the commission find such a positive attitude towards the United States?

A. We recommend, as most important of all, and in strict harmony with our Instructions, that whatever foreign administration (whether of one or more Powers) is brought into Syria, should come in not at all as a colonising Power; in the old sense of that term, but as a Mandatory under the League of Nations with a clear consciousness that "the well-being and development," of the Syrian people form for it a "sacred trust." . . .

(5) The period of "tutelage" should not be unduly prolonged, but independent self-government should be granted as soon as it can safely be done; remembering that the primary business of governments is not the accomplishment of certain things, but the development of citizens. . . .

E. We recommend, in the fifth place, serious modification of the extreme Zionist programme for Palestine of unlimited immigration of Jews, looking finally to making Palestine distinctly a Jewish state. . . .

If, however, the strict terms of the Balfour Statement are adhered to—favouring "the establishment in Palestine of a national home for the Jewish people," "it being clearly understood that nothing shall be done which may prejudice the civil and religious rights of existing non-Jewish communities in Palestine"—it can hardly be doubted that the extreme Zionist programme must be greatly modified. For a national home for the Jewish people is not equivalent to making Palestine into a Jewish State; nor can the erection of such a Jewish State be accomplished without the grave trespass upon the civil and religious

▲ Bomb attack. Israeli policeman inspect the wreckage of an Israeli bus following a suicide bomb attack near Yagur junction east of Haifa in northern Israel, April 10th, 2002. The military wing of the Palestinian Islamist Hamas movement claimed responsibility for the suicide attack, which killed at least 10 people and injured another 20.

Getty Images, Inc.-Agence France Presse.

mediation of U.S. President Jimmy Carter (b. 1924), Egypt entered into direct negotiations with Israel's prime minister Menachem Begin (1913–1994). The two countries reached an agreement—the Camp David Accords—in 1978, and in 1979 signed a formal peace treaty. Sadat was assassinated in 1981 by Egyptian Muslim extremists, but the treaty has held up under his successor, Husni Mubarak (b. 1928).

Nonetheless, despite the Egyptian-Israeli accords, violence and political impasse—tragic, morally debilitating, and materially draining for all the peoples of the area—continued through the 1980s and 1990s and has only accelerated since 2000. Recent Israeli military actions in the occupied territories were provoked by, but in turn have brought on, more Palestinian terrorist bombings in Israel and abroad.

Added to this bleak history and current struggle is the ugly legacy of hate instilled in many on both sides over the past fifty years. Arabs and even many Muslims outside the Arab world have come to label non-Israeli Jews, Israelis, and both religious and political Zionists as oppressors and enemies, making virtually no distinction among them. Many Israelis and some Jews around the world have similarly vilified all Arabs and Muslims. In many ways

rights of existing non-Jewish communities in Palestine. . . . Then it is to be remembered that the non-Jewish population of Palestine—nearly nine-tenths of the whole emphatically against the entire Zionist programme. The tables show that there was no one thing upon which the population of Palestine were more agreed than upon this. To subject a people so minded to unlimited Jewish immigration, and to steady financial and social pressure to surrender the land, would be a gross violation of the principle just quoted, and of the people's rights, though it kept within the forms of law. It is to be noted also that the feeling against the Zionist programme is not confined to Palestine, but shared very generally by the people throughout Syria, as our conferences clearly showed. More than seventy-two percent—1.350 in all the petitions in the whole of Syria were directed against the Zionist programme. Only two requests—those for a united Syria and for independence had a larger support. ...

In view of all these considerations, and with a deep sense of sympathy for the Jewish cause, the Commissioners feel bound to recommend that only a greatly reduced Zionist programme be attempted by the Peace Conference, and even that, only very gradually initiated. This would have to mean that Jewish immigration should be definitely limited, and that the project for making Palestine distinctly a Jewish commonwealth should be given up. ... Nevertheless, upon the face of the returns, America was the first choice of 1,152 of the petitions presented—more than sixty per cent-while no other Power had as much as fifteen per cent for first choice.

And the conferences showed that the people knew the grounds upon which they registered their choice for America. They declared that their choice was due to knowledge of America's record; the unselfish aims with which she had come into the War; the faith in her felt by multitudes of Syrians who had been in America; the spirit revealed in American educational institutions in Syria, especially the College in Beirut, with its well-known and constant encouragement of Syrian national sentiment; their belief that America had no territorial or colonial ambitions, and would willingly withdraw when the Syrian State was well established as her treatment both of Cuba and the Philippines seemed to them to illustrate; her genuinely democratic spirit; and her ample resources.

From the point of view of the desires of the "people concerned," the Mandate should clearly go to America.

U.S. government

Arab-Israeli and Muslim-Jewish relations are at an all-time low, and it may require a generation or more to displace the prejudice, stereotyping, and hatred so long accumulated. The human crisis is far from over, even if peace were to arrive tomorrow.

Some events of recent years gave at least brief hope for an eventual resolution to the conflict. In 1991, in the wake of the Gulf War that followed Iraq's invasion of Kuwait, the parties to the Arab-Israeli conflict began peace negotiations. The negotiations ended with the 1993 Middle East Peace Agreement, also known as the Oslo Agreement, which raised hopes for a negotiated settlement and the creation of an independent Palestinian state alongside the Jewish state of Israel.

In fact, there has been little substantive progress made in the eleven years since the 1993 agreement. Jordan and Egypt did agree in 1994 to a peace treaty with Israel, but some other Arab states—foremost among them Syria—have still not been willing to negotiate with Israel, and Israel has preferred to keep developing settlements and roads in such a way as to preclude any contiguous territory with which to form a viable state. Extremists on both sides have tried to put up obstacles to the success of the peace initiative. In early 1994 an American-born Israeli Jewish fanatic machine-gunned worshipers in a mosque in Hebron. In November 1995 another Jewish Israeli extremist assassinated Prime Minister Yitzhak Rabin for trying to make peace and to allow the eventual creation of even a circumscribed Palestinian state. Then, in the run-up to the Israeli elections of May 29, 1996, called in the wake of Rabin's death, Palestinian extremists carried out a series of savage bombings on buses and in crowded shopping areas. The subsequent victory in the elections of a Likud conservative hard-liner, Benjamin Netanyahu (b. 1949), over Rabin's Labor successor, Shimon Peres, by a margin of less than 1 percent of the vote, cast new uncertainty on peace prospects.

The leadership on both sides proved not to be up to serious progress to implement the ideals of the Oslo Agreement. The Netanyahu regime repeatedly took hard-line stands and even provocative actions such as the determined expansion of Jewish West Bank settlements. To the latter end, new roads and building projects were implemented to divide further the Palestinian population in the occupied territories. Other actions included curtailment of water supplies to Palestinian areas and public declarations of Israel's determination to retain all of Jerusalem and much of the territories even in the face of international censure. Nor did the Palestinian Authority created by the 1993 peace agreement prove any better. Under the leadership of Yasser Arafat (1929–2004), it grew steadily more corrupt, ineffective, and out of touch with its constituencies, and the suffering of the masses in the West Bank and Gaza in particular only grew steadily worse after the agreement. Despite the efforts of the Palestinian and Israeli security forces, Palestinian guerrillas of the extremist wing of the resistance organization Hamas have been able to slaughter Israeli civilians in daylight bombings, even during religious holidays such as Passover, in a sustained effort to torpedo the already shaky **peace process**. These terrorist attacks have led Israel to seal its borders often, resulting in the loss of livelihood for thousands of Arabs in the occupied territories who normally work in Israel proper, and this has exacerbated the already dire plight of Gaza in particular, keeping thousands of Palestinian families in poverty and starvation and in turn feeding the extremist resistance groups.

The Netanyahu era ended after a scandal involving the prime minister himself, and in March 2000, Ariel Sharon became prime minister, Sharon is the former army general charged with responsibility for the camp massacres by Christian militias operating in the 1982–1983 Israeli invasion of south Lebanon. His administration has been marked by an escalation of violence on both sides. Sharon, however, has also proposed that Israel withdraw from Gaza and close Israeli settlements in that region, a proposal that has proved controversial on both sides. His government has also begun to erect a fence separating Israeli and Palestinian territory. Arafat died in late 2004. His passing may present a new opportunity for negotiations in the region with the Palestinians now led by Mahmoud Abbas, who was elected to Palestinian presidency in January 2005.

MIDDLE EASTERN OIL

The oil wealth of the Arab and Iranian world has been another significant factor in the recent history the region. Oil, or black gold, has been both a blessing and a curse for the people and countries of the Middle East. Ever since the discovery of oil in Iran in 1908 but especially after Saudi Arabia's first oil production in 1939, the world demand for oil has surged. In the mid 1970s, oil became a major bargaining chip in international diplomacy that the Arab and other oil-rich Third World states—such as Venezuela, Nigeria, Iran, and Indonesia—have used to their advantage. In the Arab countries of North Africa and especially of Arabia and the Gulf, oil production and wealth have changed every aspect of life. Oil has propelled formerly peripheral and virtually unknown countries of the Sahara or the Arabian deserts into major roles in the world of international banking and finance. Oil has also boosted the damaged self-confidence of the Arab world after a century and a half of Western domination. A testimony to the global importance of Middle Eastern oil was the

willingness of the United States and European nations to form a coalition with some Arab countries and to commit massive forces to the region to expel Iraq from Kuwait after Iraq's invasion of its neighbor in 1990. Though the economic benefits of oil are all too obvious, this resource has not necessarily had the corresponding political remuneration for people in the Middle East. Because of its importance to the world economy, the Middle East has been subject to considerable foreign involvement, whether from Europe, the United States, or the former Soviet Union which has sometimes been detrimental to its political development. The most famous example of this feature is the 1953 CIA backed coup in Iran which overthrew the popular government of Muhammad Mossadeq who had sought to nationalize the Iranian oil industry. In 2000, Madeline Albright, then the U.S. Secretary of State, apologized to the Iranian nation for the role of the United States in this coup and for the negative effects it may have had on Iranian political development.

THE RISE OF POLITICAL ISLAMISM

The increase in the global importance of the oil-producing states of the Middle East has coincided with a new round of Muslim efforts in the Middle East and elsewhere to revive pristine Muslim values and standards and to reform the perceived evils and failures in Muslim societies. In the spirit, and often in the footsteps, of earlier Muslim resurgents such as those of the eighteenth century in India, Arabia, and Africa, many Muslims have sought to return to the "fundamentals" of Islamic life, faith, and society. They see this as a means of rejuvenation, of social and economic as well as political justice, and of defense against the encroachment of foreign, usually Western secularist and materialist, values and norms. Indeed, a major new element in twentieth-century Muslim revivalism is its consciousness of being a viable response to the destructive influence of Western-style "modernity" on the mores, values, and religious faith and practice of Muslim peoples.

Much of the appeal of Islamist groups everywhere is their willingness and ability to address the needs of the underclasses in Middle Eastern, North African, and Asian cities and countries. Many Muslims around the world may generally agree with the critique of modern society that these movements present but are most often in strong disagreement with the proposed solution to the current economic and cultural predicament. Where government after government of Muslim-majority countries has failed to provide social services such as housing, medical care, education, and jobs, the Islamist groups have succeeded under the banner of a just, moral Muslim societal ideal. While the world press, and especially the U.S. press, have heard only of the relatively small fringe groups of Islamist extremists, Muslims at the grass-roots level have seen the major Islamist groups in the dictatorships or military regimes under which most of them live providing services for which the state has long abdicated its responsibility.

Such Muslim fundamentalism—or, to give it a more correct name, "Islamist reformism"—motivated many of the revolutionaries who overthrew the government of Muhammed Reza Shah (r. 1941–1978) in Iran in 1978, as discussed earlier in the chapter. It is also seen in the Muslim Brethren movement in Egypt and elsewhere, in the Welfare Party in Turkey, and in many other groups, from Morocco to the Persian Gulf, and also outside the Middle East proper. All such Islamist groups see themselves as tradiotionalist—whether radical, conservative, or liberal/moderate—in that they feel their approach is one that is true to basic Muslim values and norms. The political actions of the reformist groups range from revolutionary action (Iran) to democratic participation (Turkey) to complete political quietism (the Tablighi international revivalist movement begun in Pakistan). Whether these movements will bring lasting change to Islamic societies is an open question for the Muslim world generally and the Middle East in particular. There is no question, however, of their present-day attraction and influence.

The background to modern Islamist reform lies in the European expansion over much of the globe in just a few centuries. This expansion brought far more social and political change than religious or even cultural change to the Islamic world. It saw the emergence globally of European-style nationalism and the idea of the nation-state; of post-Enlightenment ideals of individual liberties and rights and representative government; and of the concept of one's religious faith and affiliation as a strictly private, "religious" matter and one's citizenship as a public, "secular" matter. Such ideas proved revolutionary, or at the least disruptive, in the Islamic world, especially in this century.

The twentieth century in Islamic parts of the world presents a checkered history of autocratic governments generally at least as far removed from their citizenries as any of the medieval or premodern, often foreign (primarily Turkish) dynasties that had ruled Arab, Persian, Indian, or other regions of the Muslim-majority world. Experiments with European-style parliamentary government have only rarely taken hold in the Islamic world (or the rest of the Third World); nor have either liberal democratic or Marxist-socialist political and social ideals proven viable for the long term. Even so, until recently little of the political discourse in Islamic lands has given serious attention to specifically *Islamic* alternatives.

With the rise and postcolonial independence of many national states and the flourishing of diverse nationalisms, politics became often theoretically as well as actually divorced from Islamic religious tradition and its norms. This breach occurred in overt ways that it had not before, however large the actual gap always was between the religious ideals of government as guardian of the Sharī'ah order on the one hand and the political realities of governing as power politics on the other. Where leaders had previously claimed Muslim faith and allegiance,

some, such as the Arab nationalists of the post–World War I era, came to espouse secular ideologies and to ignore religion except to use it as a political weapon. And used as a weapon it was; in the late twentieth and early twenty-first centuries as in those earlier, Islamic religious allegiance has commonly been invoked to bolster a ruler's claim to legitimacy and often to cloak in pious garb much more mundane objectives and programs.

In short, the recent past has seen no realization of an "ideal" Islamic state in which religious and political authority are conjoined. If anything, the gap has widened typically between Islamic norms and ideals on the one hand and political and social realities on the other. Even in the postrevolutionary Islamic Republic of Iran there has been a clear division between political necessity and reality and religious values and standards. However sincerely the latter are claimed as the basis of state policy and procedure, no one can miss the frequent stretching of those standards to justify pragmatic political decisions. Nonetheless, the ideals championed in the Iranian Revolution proved a powerful counterweight to the secular ideas of Arab nationalism.

When we look at the Islamist movements of recent decades, we find that the calls for a congruence of religion and politics in the Islamic world trace less to some kind of ideal model of a religious state or so-called **theocracy** than to a sorely felt need for simple social and political justice, such as that which Islam (or any of the other great religious traditions) has always demanded for individuals and groups alike. The cries for a "jihad" of Muslims are aimed less often outward than inward, less at foreign "devils" and more at domestic tyrants, corruption, and social and economic injustice. Indeed, perhaps the most international and widely influential of all contemporary Islamic revivalist or reform movements, that of the Tabligh-i Jama'at, is even explicitly apolitical in its tenets; it looks to convert the individual person of faith to true submission (*islam*) rather than lip service: Reform of the world begins with oneself.

As for those reform movements that are avowedly political, be they activist but nonviolent (the majority) or extremist and violent (the minority), they live upon the deep sense of socioeconomic and political injustice that citizens of most Islamic countries (like most other Third-World countries) rightfully feel. Such feelings can, however, go over the edge and end in extremism and even terrorism. Osama Bin Laden, the dispossesed Saudi millionare who founded and has led his own violent movement, al Qaeda, from the 1990s to the present, stunned the world, and especially the United States, with suicide attacks using civilian airliners to destroy the World Trade Center towers and part of the Pentagon building on September 11, 2001. His motive was primarily to get revenge for the American military presence in Saudi Arabia, the American-led blockade of Iraq, and the American support of Israel against the Palestinians. (See Document, "Jihad Against Jews and Crusaders: World Islamic Front Statement, 1998.")

DOCUMENT | **Jihad Against Jews and Crusaders: World Islamic Front Statement, 1998**

Usama Bin Laden is one the leaders of the al Qaeda terrorist organization that was responsible for the attacks on September 11th. He came from a privileged background in Saudi Arabia and eventually volunteered to oust the Soviet Union from Afghanistan in the 1980s. Their success in driving out the Soviets convinced Bin Laden and like minded individuals that a similar "holy war" should be implemented in the rest of the Islamic world. Their goal was to recreate an Islamic state that would replace the quasi-Islamic and secular governments of the Middle East. Because a vast majority of Muslims do not agree with their political views and their terrorist tactics, they started increasingly to couch their rhetoric in xenophobic terms. Utilizing anti-American and anti-Semitic statements, Bin Laden and his followers hoped to grab the attention of Muslims around the world by commenting on prominent political issues and problems in the region. In 1998, Bin Laden issued a legal proclamation, based on his questionable and invalid interpretation of the Islamic faith, that called for the killing of Americans. When this proclamation was first issued it did not garner considerable attention nor did it inspire many Muslims around the world.

♦ On what religious authority does Bin Laden rest his claims? How does Bin Laden hope to ignite a mass revolution and support for his agenda?

The Arabian Peninsula has never—since Allah made it flat, created its desert, and encircled it with seas—been stormed by any forces like the crusader armies spreading in it like locusts, eating its riches and wiping out its plantations. All this is happening at a time in which nations are attacking Muslims like people fighting over a plate of food. In the light of the grave situation and the lack of support, we and you are obliged to discuss current events, and we should all agree on how to settle the matter.

No one argues today about three facts that are known to everyone; we will list them, in order to remind everyone:

First, for over seven years the United States has been occupying the lands of Islam in the holiest of places, the Arabian Peninsula, plundering its riches, dictating to its rulers, humiliating its people, terrorizing its neighbors, and turning its bases in the Peninsula into a spearhead through which to fight the neighboring Muslim peoples. If some people have in the past argued about the fact of the occupation, all the people of the Peninsula have now acknowledged it. The best proof of this is the Americans' continuing aggression against the Iraqi people using the Peninsula as a staging post, even though all its rulers are against their territories being used to that end, but they are helpless. Second, despite the great devastation inflicted on the Iraqi people by the crusader-Zionist alliance, and

despite the huge number of those killed, which has exceeded 1 million ... despite all this, the Americans are once against trying to repeat the horrific massacres, as though they are not content with the protracted blockade imposed after the ferocious war or the fragmentation and devastation.

So here they come to annihilate what is left of this people and to humiliate their Muslim neighbors.

Third, if the Americans' aims behind these wars are religious and economic, the aim is also to serve the Jews' petty state and divert attention from its occupation of Jerusalem and murder of Muslims there. The best proof of this is their eagerness to destroy Iraq, the strongest neighboring Arab state, and their endeavor to fragment all the states of the region such as Iraq, Saudi Arabia, Egypt, and Sudan into paper statelets and through their disunion and weakness to guarantee Israel's survival and the continuation of the brutal crusade occupation of the Peninsula.

All these crimes and sins committed by the Americans are a clear declaration of war on Allah, his messenger, and Muslims. And ulema have throughout Islamic history unanimously agreed that the jihad is an individual duty ...

On that basis, and in compliance with Allah's order, we issue the following fatwa to all Muslims:

The ruling to kill the Americans and their allies—civilians and military—is an individual duty for every Muslim who can do it in any country in which it is possible to do it, in order to liberate the al-Aqsa Mosque and the holy mosque [Mecca] from their grip, and in order for their armies to move out of all the lands of Islam, defeated and unable to threaten any Muslim. This is in accordance with the words of Almighty Allah, "and fight the pagans all together as they fight you all together", and "fight them until there is no more tumult or oppression, and there prevail justice and faith in Allah."

This is in addition to the words of Almighty Allah: "And why should ye not fight in the cause of Allah and of those who, being weak, are ill-treated (and oppressed)?—women and children, whose cry is: 'Our Lord, rescue us from this town, whose people are oppressors; and raise for us from thee one who will help!'"

We—with Allah's help—call on every Muslim who believes in Allah and wishes to be rewarded to comply with Allah's order to kill the Americans and plunder their money wherever and whenever they find it. We also call on Muslim ulema, leaders, youths, and soldiers to launch the raid on Satan's U.S. troops and the devil's supporters allying with them, and to displace those who are behind them so that they may learn a lesson.

U.S. government translation

Terrorist Attack. On September 11, 2001 a terrorist attack targeted the World Trade Center Towers in New York City. In this photograph the first of the twin towers is in flames as the second plane heads directly toward the second tower. In a very brief time both towers collapsed with the loss of nearly 3,000 lives.

Masatomo Kuriya, Corbis/Sygma.

These carefully executed and massively destructive attacks have led the United States into still heavier military involvement in the Middle East and Central Asia. In October 2001, the United States attacked the Taliban government of Afghanistan, rapidly overthrowing it. The defeat of the Taliban destroyed al Qaeda's Afghan bases, but not its high-profile leadership, which appears to have survived, although it was dispersed and remains in hiding. Whether this military response to the threat of terrorism is successful remains to be seen. What is clearer, however, is that the ongoing war on terrorism is radically changing the security needs of the United States. The U.S. military is transferring many of its troops and bases that were previously located in Western Europe and East Asia closer to the Middle East. It would appear that American troops will not soon leave this part of the world.

Further United States intervention followed in 2003 with the invasion of Iraq.

IRAQ AND UNITED STATES INTERVENTION

The modern nation of Iraq was established after World War I. For millennia, this area was home to powerful empires. More recently, it was part of the Ottoman Empire. Iraq as such had never been a distinct political unit and until 1921 was primarily a geographic term, referring to today's southern Iraq. Postwar imperial concern and the potential of oil under Iraqi soil motivated the British government to oversee the creation of Iraq which they felt would best protect their interests in the region. Given the disparate ethnic and religious groups in the country, the British could not identify a suitable leader within Iraq. Instead, the British imported a politician from Arabia named Faysal ibn Husayn and crowned him king of the

Taliban fighters brandish machine-guns and rocket launchers near the Tora Bora mountains in Afghanistan, the site of a major battle with U.S. forces in late 2001.

Knutt Mueller/Das Fotoarchiv/Peter Arnold, Inc.

▲ **Kuwaiti Oil Wells in Flames.** A Kuwaiti looks at one of the more than six hundred oil wells left burning by Iraqi troops as they retreated during the Gulf War in 1991. The willingness of the United States and Europe to commit massive forces to expel Iraq from Kuwait reflects the global importance of the region's oil wealth.
Will Burgess/Reuters/Corbis-Bettmann.

Hashemite Monarchy of Iraq. Until 1958, the monarchy ruled Iraq with the help of British advisors. A consortium of foreign oil companies, largely British, dominated the Iraqi oil industry and the British army maintained their military bases in Iraq.

Many Iraqis came to resent this arrangement and the foreign presence in their country. A bloody coup d'état in 1958 under the leadership of Abd al-Karim Qasem brought a violent end to the monarchy. By this time, Iraqis had developed a distinct sense of national identity that was highly critical of foreign involvement in Iraq affairs. By 1979, the Ba'ath party was the dominant force in Iraq policy. That year Saddam Hussein started his tyrannical reign. Shortly after he took power he invaded Iran and initiated the tragic and bloody Iran-Iraq War (1980–1988). He also invaded and occupied Kuwait in 1990. An international military coalition under the leadership of the United States (Operation Desert Storm) expelled the Iraqi army from Kuwait. During the 1990s, Iraq was an international pariah subject to extensive economic sanctions monitored by the United Nations. The Iraqi government eventually expelled the United Nations inspectors in 1998, and the United Nations was unable to reinsert them for almost five years.

The United States government adopted a policy of regime change in Iraq during the last years of the Clinton administration though it did little to carry out that policy. In the wake of 9/11, however, the Bush administration became convinced that the government of Saddam Hussein had to be removed and with it any threat of Iraqi weapons of mass destruction. During late 2002 and early 2003 the United States and British governments sought to obtain passage of the United Nations Security Council resolutions that would require Iraq to disarm on its own or to face disarmament by military force. The efforts to obtain an effective United Nations Security Council resolution failed primarily because the governments of France and Russia threatened to veto the measure. In the face of the United Nations's failure to pass a resolution, the United States, Great Britain, and Australia, backed by the support of a coalition of over forty other nations, called the "Coalition of the Willing," invaded Iraq in the middle of March 2003. After three weeks of fighting, the Coalition succeeded in removing the government of Saddam Hussein from power. The announced goals of the invasion, in addition to toppling the Iraqi regime, were to destroy Iraq's capacity to manufacture or deploy weapons of mass destruction and to bring consensual government to the Iraqi people.

The invasion of Iraq was undertaken with considerable international opposition most notably from France, Germany and Russia. It also provoked large antiwar demonstrations in the United States and other parts of the world. The war has created strains within the European Union and NATO. It also marks a new era in relations between the United States and Europe and also with the rest of the world.

Currently, it is immensely difficult to ensure peace and stability in Iraq. Many Iraqis have resisted the occupation of Iraq by foreign forces and historical factors militate against a un unified government. The unpreparedness of the Americans and their allies to deal with the chaos of post-war Iraq has exacer-

▲ **Traffic Cop.** A U.S. marine directs Iraqi civilians in the northern city of Kirkuk in April 2003.
Sebastian Bolesch/Das Fotoarchiv/Peter Arnold, Inc.

bated matters. At the same time, the American-led Coalition for Authority had a difficult time formulating a clear policy amidst a difficult and dangerous situation which has laid the American government open to criticism in the region and around the world. The failure to find weapons of mass destruction in Iraq led to wide questioning of the rationale for the war. Throughout Iran an insurgency has been launched against the Coalition forces and against Iraqis, particularly those in the security services, which had cooperated with the Coalition and the recently installed Iraqi government. In the United States itself, President George W. Bush secured re-election in 2004 and commenced his second term indicating that he will continue to pursue his existing policies in the Middle East. In late January 2005, an election was held in Iraq under conditions of insurgent attacks to elect the Assembly that will write a new constitution. With voter turnout much higher than had been widely anticipated, the election received widespread praise even from critics of American policy. The challenges of securing ever wider internal support for the construction of democratic processes now confront the emerging Iraqi government and American policy makers.

Summary

The Postcolonial World   Since 1945 the European colonial empires have disappeared from Africa and Asia and have been replaced by a multitude of independent states. These states have had to adjust their political and economic relations first to one or other of the superpowers during the Cold War and then, since the disappearance of the Soviet Union, to the West.

Women with Cellular
Phone in Bangladesh.

Latin America   Most Latin American countries remain politically and economically dependent on the United States. Except in Cuba, no revolutionary movement has been able to overturn the traditional structure of Latin American society. Despite social and economic problems, Argentina and Brazil have managed to move from military rule to stable democratic, civilian government. In Mexico, the long dominance of the PRI ended in 2000.

Africa   Independent Africa has faced severe problems: overpopulation, poverty, the absence of an educated middle class, tribal and class conflict, arbitrary boundaries, disease, economic dependence, and political instability. While Nigeria has remained mired in ethnic and religious strife and has experienced a succession of military dictatorships, South Africa has emerged as a stable, multi-ethnic democracy with the end of white rule in the 1990s. The challenge for Africa as a whole is to build a truly civil society and achieve economic health and political stability.

The Middle East   Oil and Muslim reaction to the creation of the State of Israel have dominated the history of the Middle East since the 1940s. While the possession of vast deposits of oil has made some Middle Eastern governments wealthy, it has not led to the creation of prosperous democratic societies. The existence of Israel has inflamed the Middle East for more than five decades. Although efforts by the United States to sponsor an Arab-Israeli peace have made some progress, the cycle of terror and retaliatory violence has persisted, and it is unclear whether a lasting peace between Israel and its neighbors can be achieved or a viable Palestinian state created.

Political Islamism, although not a monolithic movement, has proved increasingly disruptive to the region and the entire Islamic world.

In the wake of the terrorist attacks of September 11, 2001, the United States overthrew the Taliban regime in Afghanistan and Saddam Hussein in Iraq. The United States finds itself increasingly embroiled in a chaotic and unstable region of the world.

Review Questions

1. Are the nations of Latin America still economically dependent on the United States and Western Europe? Why is this so? How did the superpower rivalry of the Cold War affect Latin America? How successful has the worldwide trend toward democratization been in Latin America? Describe the transition from military rule to civilian democracy in Brazil, Argentina, and Chile. Has Mexico made a similar transition?

2. What factors contributed to the spread of decolonization in sub-Saharan Africa? Why were the newly independent states so fragile? Has postcolonial Nigeria lived up to its potential? Why is Nigeria's record significant for Africa as a whole? Describe the apartheid regime in South Africa. Why was it dismantled in the 1990s? What problems does the new South Africa face?

3. Compare and contrast the role of Islam in Turkey, Iran, Pakastan, and Malaysia. How does the profound influence of Islam in this and other regions of the world suggest the power of religious tradition in modern politics and society?

4. What have been the major factors in the creation of the modern Middle East? How have interventions by European powers and the United States affected this region? Compare and contrast the role of religion and nationalism in the Middle East.

5. Explain the origin and course of the Arab-Israeli conflict? What have been the major turning points? Have there been moments when the conflict might have reached a peaceful resolution?

6. Describe the origins and character of political Islamism. Why has it taken so radical a political course? Why was the Soviet invasion of Afghanistan an important event in its development? Why has the United States become the primary target of political Islamism? Describe the course of the responses of the United States to the attacks of September 11, 2001.

Key Terms

apartheid   (p. 1037)

ayatollah   (p. 1041)

clash of civilizations   (p. 1026)

globalization   (p. 1026)

Intifadah   (p. 1047)

liberation theology   (p. 1030)

occupied territories   (p. 1047)

peace process   (p. 1050)

political Islamism   (p. 1050)

Sandinistas   (p. 1032)

theocracy   (p. 1051)

Documents CD-ROM

Decolonization
27.3 Frantz Fanon, The Wretched of the Earth
27.4 Kwame Nkrumah, I Speak of Freedom: A Statement of African Ideology
27.5 Israel's Proclamation of Independence
27.6 Palestinian Declaration of Independence

Race, Ethnicity, and Conflict in the Twentieth Century
28.2 "The Struggle Is My Life" (1961): Nelson Mandela

28.4 Keith B. Richburg, A Black Man Confronts Africa
28.5 Alain Destexhe, Rwanda and Genocide in the Twentieth Century
28.6 U.N. Declaration of Human Rights

Contemporary Issues in World History
29.5 Pope John Paul II, Centesimus Annus
29.8 Henry A. Myers, "Now, in the Twenty-First Century"

NOTE: *To learn more about the topics in this chapter, see the Suggested Readings at the end of the book.*

Glossary

absolutism Term applied to strong centralized continental monarchies that attempted to make royal power dominant over aristocracies and other regional authorities.

Acropolis The religious and civic center of Athens. It is the site of the Parthenon.

Afrikaans The new language, derived from Dutch, that evolved in the seventeenth-and eighteenth-century Cape Colony.

agape Meaning "love feast." A common meal that was part of the central ritual of early Christian worship.

agora The Greek marketplace and civic center. It was the heart of the social life of the polis.

agricultural revolution The innovations in farm production that began in the eighteenth century and led to a scientific and mechanized agriculture.

amir/emir An Islamic military commander.

Amitabha Buddha The Buddhist Lord of the Western Paradise, or Pure Land.

Annam The Chinese term for Vietnam.

Anschluss Meaning "union." The annexation of Austria by Germany in March 1938.

anti-Semitism Prejudice, hostility, or legal discrimination against Jews.

apartheid "Apartness," the term referring to racist policies enforced by the white-dominated regime that existed in South Africa from 1948 to 1992.

apostolic primacy The doctrine that the popes are the direct successors to the Apostle Peter and as such heads of the church.

appeasement The Anglo-French policy of making concessions to Germany in the 1930s to avoid a crisis that would lead to war. It assumed that Germany had real grievances and Hitler's aims were limited and ultimately acceptable.

Areopagus The governing council of Athens, originally open only to the nobility. It was named after the hill on which it met.

Arianism The belief formulated by Arius of Alexandria (ca. 280–336 C.E.) that Jesus was a created being, neither fully man nor fully God, but something in between.

aristocratic resurgence Eighteenth-century aristocratic efforts to resist the expanding power of European monarchies.

Aryans The Indo-European speakers who invaded India and Iran in the second and first millenia B.C.E.

assignats Government bonds based on the value of confiscated church lands issued during the early French Revolution.

Atman-Brahman The unchanging, infinite principle of reality in Indian religion.

Atomists School of ancient Greek philosophy founded in the fifth century B.C.E. by Leucippus of Miletus and Democritus of Abdera. It held that the world consists of innumerable, tiny, solid, indivisible, and unchangeable particles called atoms.

Augustus The title given to Octavian in 27 B.C.E. and borne there–after by all Roman emperors.

Ausgleich Meaning "compromise." The agreement between the Habsburg Emperor and the Hungarians to give Hungary considerable administrative autonomy in 1867. It created the Dual Monarchy, or Austria-Hungary.

Axis The alliance between Nazi Germany and fascist Italy. Also called the Pact of Steel.

ayan Ottoman notables.

ayatollah A major Shi'ite religious leader.

bakufu "Tent government." The military regime that governed Japan under the shōguns.

bazaari The Iranian commercial middle class.

bhakti Hindu devotional movements.

bishop Originally a person elected by early Christian congregations to lead them in worship and supervise their funds. In time, bishops became the religious and even political authorities for Christian communities within large geographical areas.

Black Death The bubonic plague that killed millions of Europeans in the fourteenth century.

Black Legend The argument that Spanish treatment of native Americans was uniquely inhumane.

blitzkrieg Meaning "lightning war." The German tactic early in World War II of employing fast-moving, massed armored columns supported by airpower to overwhelm the enemy.

bodhisattva A "Buddha to be" who postpones his own nirvana until he has helped all other beings become enlightened.

Bolsheviks Meaning the "majority." Term Lenin applied to his faction of the Russian Social Democratic Party. It became the Communist Party of the Soviet Union after the Russian Revolution.

Boxers A nationalistic Chinese religious society that attacked foreigners and their encroachments on China in the late nineteenth century.

boyars The Russian nobility.

Brahmanas Texts dealing with the ritual application of the Vedas.

brainwashing The Communist practice of forced indoctrination of individuals in Marxist thought followed by confession of errors, repentance, and reacceptance by society. It was particularly favored in China under Mao.

Bronze Age The name given to the earliest civilized era, c. 4000 to 1000 B.C.E. The term reflects the importance of the metal bronze, a mixture of tin and copper, for the peoples of this age for use as weapons and tools.

caliphate The true line of succession to Muhammad.

calpulli The wards into which the Aztec capital, Tenochtitlan, was divided.

cantonments The segregation of areas in which Europeans lived in British-ruled India from those areas inhabited by native Indians.

Catholic Emancipation The grant of full political rights to Roman Catholics in Britain in 1829.

catholic Meaning "universal." The body of belief held by most Christians enshrined within the church.

caudillo Latin American strongman, or dictator, usually with strong ties to the military.

censor Official of the Roman republic charged with conducting the census and compiling the lists of citizens and members of the Senate.

Censorate The branch of the imperial Chinese government that acted a watchdog, reporting instances of misgovernment directly to the emperor and remonstrating when it considered the emperor's behavior improper.

Chartism The first large-scale European working-class political movement. It sought political reforms that would favor the interests of skilled British workers in the 1830s and 1840s.

chiaroscuro The use of shading to enhance naturalness in painting and drawing.

chicha A maize beer brewed by the *mamakuna* for the Inca elite.

civilization A form of human culture marked by urbanism, metallurgy, and writing.

clash of civilizations Political theory, most often identified with Harvard political scientist Samuel P. Huntington, which contends that conflict between the world's religio-cultural traditions or "civilizations" increasingly dominates world affairs.

Cold War The ideological and geographical struggle between the United States and its allies and the USSR and its allies that began after World War II and lasted until the dissolution of the USSR in 1989.

collectivization The bedrock of Stalinist agriculture, which forced Russian peasants to give up their private farms and work as members of collectives, large agricultural units controlled by the state.

conquistadores Meaning "conquerors." The Spanish conquerors of the New World.

Consulate French government dominated by Napoleon from 1799 to 1804.

Convention French radical legislative body from 1792 to 1794.

corvée A French labor tax requiring peasants to work on roads, bridges, and canals.

Counter-Reformation The sixteenth-century reform movement in the Roman Catholic Church in reaction to the Protestant Reformation.

Creoles Persons of European descent who were born in the Spanish colonies.

Crusades Religious wars directed by the church against infidels and heretics.

Cultural Revolution A movement launched by Mao between 1965 and 1976 against the Soviet-style bureaucracy that had taken hold in China. It involved widespread disorder and violence.

culture The ways of living built up by a group and passed on from one generation to another.

cuneiform A writing system invented by the Sumerians that used a wedge-shaped stylus, or pointed tool, to write on wet clay tablets that were then baked or dried (cune*us* means "wedge" in Latin). The writing was also cut into stone.

Curia The papal government.

daimyo Japanese territorial lord.

Daoism A Chinese philosophy that teaches that wisdom lies in becoming one with the *Tao*, the "way," which is the creative principle of the universe.

debt peonage A system that forces agricultural laborers (peons) to work and live on large estates (haciendas) until they have repaid their debts to the estate's owner.

deism A belief in a rational God who had created the universe, but then allowed it to function without his interference according to the mechanisms of nature and a belief in rewards and punishments after death for human action.

Delian League An alliance of Greek states under the leadership of Athens that was formed in 478–477 B.C.E. to resist the Persians.

demesne The part of a manor that was cultivated directly for the lord of the manor.

dependency theory Theory that contends that after the states of Latin America achieved independence in the early-mid nineteenth century they remained economically and culturally dependent on Europe, and later, the United States.

devshirme The system under the Ottoman Empire that required each province to furnish a levy of Christian boys who were raised as Muslims and became soldiers in the Ottoman army.

dharma Moral law or duty.

diaspora Dispersion of an originally homogeneous people or culture. Among the many diasporas in world history, some of the most famous are the Jewish, the Chinese, the African, the Irish, and the Armenian.

Diet The bicameral Japanese parliament.

Diet of Worms The meeting of the representative (diet) of the Holy Roman Empire presided over by the Emperor Charles V at the Germain city of Worms in 1521 at which Martin Luther was ordered to recant his ninety-five theses. Luther refused and was declared outlaw although he was protected by the Elector of Saxony and other German princes.

diffusion The spread of ideas, objects, or traits from one culture to another.

divine right of kings The theory that monarchs are appointed by and answerable only to God.

domestic or putting-out system of textile production Method of producing textiles in which agents furnished raw materials to households whose members spun them into thread and then wove cloth, which the agents then sold as finished products.

Duce Meaning "leader." Mussolini's title as head of the Fascist Party.

Duma The Russian parliament, after the revolution of 1905.

dynastic cycle The term used to describe the rise, decline, and fall of China's imperial dynasties.

ego According to Freudian theory, the part of the mind that mediates between the impulses of the id and the asceticism of the superego and allows the personality to cope with the inner and outer demands of its existence.

empiricism The use of experiment and observation derived from sensory evidence to construct scientific theory or philosophy of knowledge.

enclosures The consolidation or fencing in of common lands by British landlords to increase production and achieve greater commercial profits. It also involved the reclamation of waste land and the consolidation of strips into block fields.

encomienda The grant by the Spanish crown to a colonist of the labor of a specific number of Indians for a set period of time.

Enlightenment The eighteenth-century movement led by the *philosophes* that held that change and reform were both desirable through the application of reason and science.

Epicureans School of philosophy founded by Epicurus of Athens (342–271 B.C.E.). It sought to liberate people from fear of death and the supernatural by teaching that the gods took no interest in human affairs and that true happiness consisted in pleasure, which was defined as the absence of pain.

equestrians Literally "cavalrymen" or "knights." In the earliest years of the Roman Republic, those who could afford to serve as mounted warriors.

Estado Novo The "new state" based on political stability and economic and social progress supposedly established by the dictator Getulio Vargas after 1937.

Etruscans A people of central Italy who exerted the most powerful external influence on the early Romans.

Eucharist Meaning "thanksgiving." The celebration of the Lord's Supper. Considered the central ritual of worship by most Christians. Also called Holy Communion.

euro The common currency created by the EEC in the late 1990s.

European Economic Community (EEC) The economic association formed by France, Germany, Italy, Belgium, the Netherlands, and Luxembourg in 1957. Also known as the Common Market.

European Union The new name given to the EEC in 1993. It included most of the states of Western Europe.

Fabians British socialists in the late nineteenth and early twentieth century who sought to achieve socialism through gradual, peaceful, and democratic means.

family economy The basic structure of production and consumption in preindustrial Europe.

fascism Political movements that tend to be antidemocratic, anti-Marxist, antiparliamentary, and often anti-Semitic. Fascists were invariably nationalists and exhalted the nation over the individual. They supported the interests of the middle class and rejected the ideas of the French Revolution and nineteenth-century liberalism. The first fascist regime was founded by Benito Mussolini (1883–1945) in Italy in the 1920s.

fealty An oath of loyalty by a vassal to a lord, promising to perform specified services.

feudal society The social, political, military, and economic system that prevailed in the Middle Ages and beyond in some parts of Europe.

fief Land granted to a vassal in exchange for services, usually military.

Fourteen Points President Woodrow Wilson's (1856–1924) idealistic war aims.

Führer Meaning "leader." The title taken by Hitler when he became dictator of Germany.

gentry In China, a largely urban, landowning class that represented local interests and functioned as quasi-bureaucrats under the magistrates.

ghazis Warriors who carried Islam by force of arms to pagan groups.

ghettos Separate communities in which Jews were required by law to live.

glasnost Meaning "openness." The policy initiated by Mikhail Gorbachev in the 1980s of permitting open criticism of the policies of the Soviet Communist Party.

globalization Term used to describe the increasing economic and cultural interdependence of societies around the world.

Glorious Revolution The largely peaceful replacement of James II by William and Mary as English monarchs in 1688. It marked the beginning of constitutional monarchy in Britain.

Golden Horde Name given to the Mongol rulers of Russia from 1240 to 1480.

Grand Mufti The chief religious authority of the Ottoman Empire. Also called "the Shaykh of Islam."

Great Depression A prolonged worldwide economic downturn that began in 1929 with the collapse of the New York Stock Exchange.

Great Leap Forward Mao's disastrous attempt to modernize the Chinese economy in 1958.

Great Purges The imprisonment and execution of millions of Soviet citizens by Stalin between 1934 and 1939.

Great Reform Bill (1832) A limited reform of the British House of Commons and an expansion of the electorate to include a wider variety of the propertied classes. It laid the groundwork for further orderly reforms within the British constitutional system.

Great Schism The appearance of two and at times three rival popes between 1378 and 1415.

Great Trek The migration between 1835 and 1847 of Boer pioneers (called *voortrekkers*) north from British-ruled Cape Colony to establish their own independent republics.

guild An association of merchants or craftsmen that offered protection to its members and set rules for their work and products.

Guomingdang (GMD) China's Nationalist Party, founded by Sun Yat-sen.

hacienda Large landed estates in Spanish America.

hadith A saying or action ascribed to Muhammad.

Hajj The pilgrimage to Mecca that all Muslims are enjoined to perform at least once in their lifetime.

Harappan Term used to describe the first civilization of the Indus Valley.

harem The wives, concubines, female relatives, and servants in a Muslim household – usually confined to a section of a house or palace.

Hegira The flight of Muhammad and his followers from Mecca to Medina in 622 C.E. It marks the beginning of the Islamic calendar.

heliocentric theory The theory, now universally accepted, that the earth and the other planets revolve around the sun. First proposed by Aristarchos of Samos (310–230 B.C.E.).

Helots Hereditary Spartan serfs.

heretics People who publicly dissent from officially accepted dogma.

hieroglyphics The complicated writing script of ancient Egypt. It combined picture writing with pictographs and sound signs. Hieroglyph means "sacred carvings" in Greek.

Hindu Term applied to the diverse social, racial, linguistic, and religious groups of India.

Holocaust The Nazi extermination of millions of European Jews between 1940 and 1945. Also called the "final solution to the Jewish problem."

Holy Roman Empire The revival of the old Roman Empire, based mainly in Germany and northern Italy, that endured from 870 to 1806.

home rule The advocacy of a large measure of administrative autonomy for Ireland within the British Empire between the 1880s and 1914.

hoplite phalanx The basic unit of Greek warfare in which infantrymen fought in close order, shield to shield, usually eight ranks deep.

Huguenots French Calvinists.

humanism The study of the Latin and Greek classics and of the Church Fathers both for their own sake and to promote a rebirth of ancient norms and values.

humanitas The Roman name for a liberal arts education.

id According to Freudian psychoanalysis, the part of the mind that consists of amoral, irrational, driving instincts for sexual gratification, aggression, and physical and sensual pleasure.

The Iliad and the Odyssey, The Epic poems by Homer about the "Dark Age" heroes of Greece who fought at Troy. The poems were written down in the eighth century B.C.E. after centuries of being sung by bards.

imams Islamic prayer leader.

impact of modernity The effect of western political, economic, and social ideas and institutions on traditional societies.

imperator Under the Roman Republic, it was the title given to a victorious general. Under Augustus and his successors, it became the title of the ruler of Rome, meaning "emperor."

imperium In ancient Rome, the right to issue commands and to enforce them by fines, arrests, and even corporal and capital punishment.

import substitution The replacement of imported goods with those manufactured domestically.

Indo-European A widely distributed language group that includes most of the languages spoken in Europe, Persian, Sanskrit, and their derivatives.

Indo-Greeks Bactrian rulers who broke away from the Seleucid Empire to found a state that combined elements of Greek and Indian civilizations.

indulgences Remission of the temporal penalty of punishment in purgatory that remained after sins had been forgiven.

Industrial Revolution Mechanization of the European economy that began in Britain in the second half of the eighteenth century.

intifadah Literally, "shaking." Uprisings by the Palestinians against Israeli occupation.

Islam Meaning "submission." The religion founded by the prophet Muhammad.

Islamic fundamentalism A movement among many Muslims to return to the "fundamentals" of Islamic faith, life, and society.

Italia Irredenta Meaning "unredeemed Italy." Italian-speaking areas that had been left under Austrian rule at the time of the unification of Italy.

jacobins The radical republican party during the French Revolution that displaced the Girondins.

Jains An Indian religious community that teaches compassion for all beings.

Janissaries Elite Ottoman troops who were recruited through the *devshirme.*

jatis The many subgroups that make up the Hindu caste system.

jihad "Struggle in the path of God." Although not necessarily implying violence, it is often interpreted to mean holy war in the name of Islam.

July Monarchy The French regime set up after the overthrow of the Bourbons in July 1830.

Junkers The noble landlords of Prussia.

junzi The Confucian term for a person who behaves ethically, in harmony with the cosmic order.

Ka'ba A black meteorite in the city of Mecca that became Islam's holiest shrine.

Kabuki A realistic form of Japanese theater similar to English Elizabethan drama.

Kalahari A large desert in southwestern Africa that partially isolates southern Africa from the rest of he continent.

kamikaze "Divine winds" which sank a portion of the invading Mongol fleet in Japan in 1281.

karma The Indian belief that every action has an inevitable effect. Good deeds bring good results; evil deeds have evil consequences.

Khmer Rouge Meaning "Red Cambodia." The radical Communist movement that ruled Cambodia from 1975 to 1978.

kleindeutsch Meaning "small German." The argument that the German-speaking portions of the Habsburg Empire should be excluded from a united Germany.

Kristallnacht Meaning "crystal night" because of the broken glass that littered German streets after the looting and destruction of Jewish homes, businesses, and synagogues across Germany on the orders of the Nazi Party in November 1938.

La Reforma the nineteenth-century Mexican liberal reform movement that opposed Santa Ana's dictatorship and sought to foster economic progress, civilian rule, and political stability. It was strongly anti-clerical.

laissez-faire French phrase meaning "allow to do." In economics, the doctrine of minimal government interference in the working of the economy.

latifundia Large plantations for growing cash crops owned by wealthy Romans.

LDP The Liberal Democratic Party. A conservative party that has dominated postwar Japanese politics.

League of Nations The association of sovereign states set up after World War I to pursue common policies and avert international aggression.

Lebensraum Meaning "living space," The Nazi plan to colonize and exploit Eastern Europe.

Legalism The Chinese philosophical school that argued that a strong state was necessary in order to have a good society.

levée en masse The French revolutionary conscription (1792) of all males into the army and the harnessing of the economy for war production.

liberalism In the nineteenth century, support for representative government dominated by the propertied classes and minimal government interference in the economy.

liberation theology The effort by certain Roman Catholic theologians to combine Marxism with traditional Christian concern for the poor.

Logos Divine reason, or fire, which according to the Stoics, was the guiding principle in nature.

Long Count A Mayan calendar that dated from a fixed point in the past.

Long March The flight of the Chinese communists from their Nationalist foes to northwest China in 1934.

Luftwaffe The German air force in World War II.

madrasa An Islamic college of higher learning.

Magna Carta The "Great Charter" limiting royal power that the English nobility forced King John to sign in 1215.

Magna Graecia Meaning "Great Greece" in Latin, it was the name given by the Romans to southern Italy and Sicily because there were so many Greek colonies in the region.

Magyars The majority ethnic group in Hungary.

Mahabharata **and** *Ramayana* The two classical Indian epics.

Mahayana The "Great Vehicle" for salvation in Buddhism. It emphasized the Buddha's infinite compassion for all beings.

manakuna Inca women who lived privileged but celibate lives and had important economic and cultural roles.

Mandate of Heaven The Chinese belief that Heaven entrusts or withdraws a ruler's or a dynasty's right to govern.

Manichaeism A dualistic and moralistic view of reality in which good and evil, spirit and matter warred with each other.

mannerism A style of art in the mid to late sixteenth century that permitted artists to express their own "manner" or feelings in contrast to the symmetry and simplicity of the art of the High Renaissance.

manor Village farms owned by a lord.

Marshall Plan The U.S. program, named after Secretary of State George C. Marshall, that provided economic aid to Europe after World War II.

Marxism The theory of Karl Marx (1818–1883) and Friedrich Engels (1820–1895) that history is the result of class conflict, which will end in the inevitable triumph of the industrial proletariat over the bourgeoisie and the abolition of private property and social class.

Meiji restoration The overthrow of the Tokugawa *bakufu* in Japan in 1868 and the transfer, or "restoration," of power to the imperial government under the Emperor Meiji.

Mein Kampf Meaning "My Struggle." Hitler's statement of his political program, published in 1924.

Mensheviks Meaning the "minority." Term Lenin applied to the majority moderate faction of the Russian Social Democratic Party opposed to him and the Bolsheviks.

mercantilism Term used to describe close government control of the economy that sought to maximize exports and accumulate as much precious metals as possible to enable the state to defend its economic and political interests.

Mesoamerica The part of North America that extends from the central part of modern Mexico to Central America.

Mesopotamia Modern Iraq. The land between the Tigris and Euphrates Rivers where the first civilization appeared around 3000 B.C.E.

Messiah The redeemer whose coming Jews believed would establish the kingdom of God on earth. Christians considered Jesus to be the Messiah (Christ means Messiah in Greek).

mestizos Persons of mixed Native American and European descent.

Mexica The Aztecs name for themselves.

mfecane A period of widespread warfare and chaos among Bantu peoples in east-central Africa during the early nineteenth century.

millets Within the Ottoman Empire, ethnic communities that administered their own educational, charitable, and judicial affairs.

Minoan The Bronze Age civilization that arose in Crete in the third and second millennia B.C.E.

mita The Inca system of forced labor in return for gifts and ritual entertainments.

Mitimaqs Communities whom the Incas forced to settle in designated regions for strategic purposes.

mobilization The placing of a country's military forces on a war footing.

monotheism The worship of one universal God.

Moors The Spanish and Portuguese term for Muslims.

Mughals Descendants of the Mongols who established an Islamic empire in India in the sixteenth century with its capital at Delhi.

mujtahid A Shi'ite religious-legal scholar.

mulattos Persons of mixed African and European descent.

Mycenaean The Bronze Age civilization of mainland Greece that was centered at Mycenae.

mystery religions The cults of Isis, Mithras, and Osiris, which promised salvation to those initiated into the secret or "mystery" of their rites.

nacionalismo A right-wing Argentine nationalist movement that arose in the 1930s and resembled European fascism.

National Studies A Japanese intellectual tradition that emphasized native Japanese culture and institutions and rejected the influence of Chinese Confucianism.

nationalism The belief that one is part of a nation, defined as a community with its own language, traditions, customs, and history that distinguish it from other nations and make it the primary focus of a person's loyalty and sense of identity.

natural selection According to Darwin, the process in nature by which only the organisms best adapted to their environment tend to survive and transmit their genes, while those less adapted tend to be eliminated.

Nazis The German Nationalist Socialist Party.

neocolonial economy An economic relationship between a former colonial state and countries with more developed economies in which the former colony exports raw materials to and imports manufactured goods from the more developed nations.

Neo-Daoism A revival of Taoist "mysterious learning" that flourished as a reaction against Confucianism during the Han dynasty.

Neolithic Revolution The shift beginning 10,000 years ago from hunter-gatherer societies to settled communities of farmers and artisans. Also called the Age of Agriculture, it witnessed the invention of farming, the domestication of plants and animals, and the development of technologies such as pottery and weaving. "Neolithic" comes from the Greek words for "new stone."

New Economic Policy (NEP) A limited revival of capitalism, especially in light industry and agriculture, introduced by Lenin in 1921 to repair the damage inflicted on the Russian economy by the Civil War and War Communism.

New Imperialism The extension in the late nineteenth and early twentieth centuries of Western political and economic dominance to Asia, the Middle East, and Africa.

Nicene Creed A statement of Christian belief, formulated by the council of Christian bishops at Nicaea in 324 C.E., that rejected Arianism in favor of the doctrine that Christ is both fully human and fully divine.

Nilotic Africa The lands along the Nile River.

ninety-five theses Document posted on the door of Castle Church in Wittenberg, Germany on October 31, 1517 by Martin Luther protesting, among other things, the selling of indulgences.

Nirvana In Buddhism the attainment of release from the wheel of *karma*.

Nō play A highly stylized form of Japanese drama in which the chorus provides the narrative line as in classical Greek plays.

oba Title of the king of Benin.

obsidian A hard volcanic glass that was widely used in Mesoamerica.

occupied territories Land occupied by Israel as a result of wars with its Arab neighbors in 1948-1949, 1967, and 1973.

Old Regime Term applied to the pattern of social, political, and economic relationships and institutions that existed in Europe before the French Revolution.

orthodox Meaning "holding the right opinions." Applied to the doctrines of the Catholic Church.

orthopraxy The correct practice of a religion.

Ottoman Empire The imperial Turkish state centered in Constantinople that ruled large parts of the Balkans, North Africa, and the Middle East until 1918.

padishah Meaning "emperor." One of the titles of the Ottoman monarchs.

Paleolithic Age The earliest period when stone tools were used, from about 1,000,000 to 10,000 B.C.E. From the Greek meaning "old stone."

Panhellenic ("all-Greek") The sense of cultural identity that all Greeks felt in common with each other.

pan-Islamism The movement that advocates that the entire Muslim world should form a unified political and cultural entity.

Pan-Slavic movement The movement to create a nation or federation that would embrace all the Slavic peoples of Eastern Europe.

Papal States Territory in central Italy ruled by the pope until 1870.

parlement French regional court dominated by hereditary nobility. The most important was the Parlement of Paris, which claimed the right to register royal decrees before they could become law.

parliamentary monarchy A state headed by a monarch but whose power is shared with a national representative body.

pastoralists People whose way of life centers on the raising and herding of livestock; nomads.

patricians The hereditary upper class of early Republican Rome.

peace process Efforts, chiefly by the United States, to broker a peace between the State of Israel and the PLO.

Peloponnesian Wars The protracted struggle between Athens and Sparta to dominate Greece between 465 and Athens' final defeat in 404 B.C.E.

peninsulares Native-born Spaniards who immigrated from Spain to settle in the Spanish colonies.

perestroika Meaning "restructuring." The attempt in the 1980s to reform the Soviet government and economy.

Perónism An authoritarian, nationalist movement founded in Argentina in the 1940s by the dictatore Juan Perón.

pharaoh The god-kings of ancient Egypt. The term originally meant "great house" or palace.

Pharisees The group that was most strict in its adherence to Jewish law.

philosophes The eighteenth-century writers and critics who forged the new attitudes favorable to change. They sought to apply reason and common sense to the institutions and societies of their day.

Phoenicians The ancient inhabitants of modern Lebanon. A trading people, they established colonies throughout the Mediterranean.

pipiltin Aztec bureaucrats and priests.

pirs Shi'ite holy men.

plantation economy The economic system stretching between Chesapeake Bay and Brazil that produced crops, especially sugar, cotton, and tobacco, using slave labor on large estates.

plebeians The hereditary lower class of early Republican Rome.

plenitude of power The teaching that the popes have power over all other bishops of the church.

pochteca Aztec merchants.

pogroms Organized riots against Jews in the Russian Empire.

polis The basic Greek political unit. Usually, but incompletely, translated as "city-state," the Greeks thought of the *polis* as a community of citizens theoretically descended from a common ancestor.

political Islamism Political movement that seeks to return to the fundamentals of Islamic life through rejuvenation of Muslim faith and society and the rejection of Western, Materialist, and secularist values and norms.

polytheism The worship of many gods.

Popular Front A government of all left-wing parties that took power in France in 1936 to enact social and economic reforms.

populares Roman politicians who sought to pursue a political career based on the support of the people rather than just the aristocracy.

positivism the philosophy of Auguste Comte that science is the final, or positive, stage of human intellectual development because it involves exact descriptions of phenomena, without recourse to unobservable operative principles, such as gods or spirits.

Pragmatic Sanction The legal basis negotiated by the Emperor Charles VI (r. 1711–1740) for the Habsburg succession through his daughter Maria Theresa (r. 1740–1780).

PRI The Institutional Revolutionary Party, which emerged from the Mexican revolution of 1911 and governed Mexico until the end of the twentieth century.

Proletarianization The process whereby independent artisans and factory workers lose control of the means of production and of the conduct of their own trades to the owners of capital.

Ptolemaic system The pre-Copernican explanation of the universe, which placed the Earth at the center of the universe.

Punic Wars Three wars between Rome and Carthage for dominance of the western Mediterranean that were fought from 264 B.C.E. to 146 B.C.E.

Pure Land Buddhism A variety of Japanese Buddhism that maintained that only faith was necessary for salvation.

puritans English Protestants who sought to "purify" the Church of England of any vestiges of Catholicism.

Qanun Ottoman administrative law.

Quechua The Inca language.

quipu Knotted string used by Andean peoples for recordkeeping.

Qur'an Meaning "a reciting." The Islamic bible, which Muslims believe God revealed to the prophet Muhammad.

racism The pseudoscientific theory that biological features of race determine human character and worth.

raj The years from 1858 to 1947 during which India was governed directly by the British Crown.

raja An Indian King.

Ramadan The month each year when Muslims must fast during daylight hours.

Reconquista The Christian reconquest of Spain from the Muslims from 1000 to 1492.

Reformation The sixteenth-century religious movement that sought to reform the Roman Catholic Church and led to the establishment of Protestantism.

regular clergy Monks and nuns who belong to religious orders.

Reichstag The German parliament, which existed in various forms, until 1945.

Reign of Terror The period between the summer of 1793 and the end of July 1794 when the French revolutionary state used extensive executions and violence to defend the Revolution and suppress its alleged internal enemies.

relativity Theory of physics, first expounded by Albert Einstein in 1905, in which time and space exist not separately, but rather as a combined continuum.

Renaissance The revival of ancient learning and the supplanting of traditional religious beliefs by new secular and scientific values that began in Italy in the fourteenth and fifteenth centuries.

reparations The requirement incorporated into the Versailles Treaty that Germany should pay for the cost of World War I.

repartimiento A labor tax in Spanish America that required adult male native Americans devote a set number of days a year to Spanish economic enterprises.

revisionism The advocacy among nineteenth-century German socialists of achieving a humane socialist society through the evolution of democratic institutions, not revolution.

SA The Nazi parliamentary forces, or stormtroopers.

Sahara The world's largest desert. It extends across Africa from the Atlantic to the eastern Sudan. Historically, the Sahara has hindered contact between the Mediterranean and sub-Saharan Africa.

Sahel An area of steppe and semidesert that borders the Sahara.

samsara The endless cycle of existence, of birth and rebirth.

samurai Professional Japanese warriors.

Sandinistas The Marxist guerrilla force that overthrew the Somoza dictatorship in Nicaragua in 1979.

sans-culottes Meaning "without breeches." The lower-middle classes and artisans of Paris during the French Revolution.

satraps Governors of provinces in the Persian Empire.

savannah An area of open woodlands and grassy plains.

Schlieffen Plan Germany's plan for achieving a quick victory in the West at the outbreak of World War I by invading France through Belgium and Luxembourg.

Scholasticism Method of study based on logic and dialectic that dominated the medieval schools. It assumed that truth already existed; students had only to organize, elucidate, and defend knowledge learned from authoritative texts, especially those of Aristotle and the Church Fathers.

Scientific Revolution The sweeping change in the scientific view of the universe that occurred in the West in the sixteenth and seventeenth centuries.

scramble for Africa The late nineteenth-century takeover of most of Africa by European powers.

secular clergy Parish clergy who did not belong to a religious order.

serfs Peasants tied to the land they tilled.

Shahanshah "King of kings," the title of the Persian ruler.

Shari'a Islamic religious law.

Shi-a The minority of Muslims who trace their beliefs from the caliph Ali who was assassinated in 661 C.E.

Shintō "The way of the gods." The animistic worship of the forces of nature that is the indigenous religion of Japan.

Shōgun A military official who was the actual ruler of Japan in the emperor's name from the late 1100s until the mid-nineteenth century.

Silk Road Trade route from China to the West that stretched across Central Asia.

Sophists Professional teachers who emerged in Greece in the mid-fifth century B.C.E. who were paid to teach techniques of rhetoric, dialectic, and argumentation.

soviets Workers' and soldiers' councils formed in Russia during the Revolution.

spinning jenny A machine invented in England by James Hargreaves around 1765 to mass-produce thread.

SS The chief security units of the Nazi state.

Steppe peoples Nomadic tribespeople who dwelled on the Eurasian plains from eastern Europe to the borders of China and Iran. They frequently traded with or invaded more settled cultures.

Stoics A philosophical school founded by Zeno of Citium (335–263 B.C.E.) that taught that humans could only be happy with natural law.

streltsy Professional troops who made up the Moscow garrison. They were suppressed by Peter the Great.

studia humanitatis During the Renaissance, a liberal arts program of study that embraced grammar, rhetoric, poetry, history, philosophy, and politics.

stupa A Buddhist shrine.

suffragettes British women who lobbied and agitated for the right to vote in the early twentieth century.

Sufi A movement within Islam that emphasizes the spiritual and mystical.

sultan A Muslim royal title that means "authority."

Sunna Meaning "tradition." The dominant Islamic group whose followers are called Sunnis.

superego According to Freud, the part of the mind that embodies the external moral imperatives and expectations imposed on the personality by society and culture.

Swahili A language and culture that developed from the interaction of native Africans and Arabs along the East African coast.

symposion The carefully organized drinking party that was the center of Greek aristocratic social life. It featured games, songs, poetry, and even philosophical disputation.

syncretism Blending or fusion of different systems of religious or philosophical beliefs.

Table of Ranks An official hierarchy established by Peter the Great in imperial Russia that equated a person's social position and privileges with his rank in the state bureaucracy or army.

taille The direct tax on the French peasantry.

Taiping rebellion A nineteenth-century revolt against China's Manchu dynasty that was inspired by quasi-Christian ideas and that led to enormous suffering and destruction before its collapse in 1868.

Tennō "Heavenly emperor." The official title of the emperor of Japan.

tetcutin Subordinate Aztec lords.

tetrarchy Diocletian's (r. 306–337 C.E.) system for ruling the Roman Empire by four men with power divided territorially.

theocracy A state ruled by religious leaders who claim to govern by divine authority.

Theravada The "Way of the Elders." A school of Buddhism that emphasized the monastic ideal.

Thermidorean Reaction The reaction against the radicalism of the French Revolution that began in July 1794. Associated with the end of terror and establishment of the Directory.

Third Estate The branch of the French Estates General representing all of the kingdom outside the nobility and the clergy.

three-field system A medieval innovation that increased the amount of land under cultivation by leaving only one-third fallow in a given year.

tlatoani An Aztec ruler.

transubstantiation The doctrine that the entire substances of the bread and wine are changed in the Eucharist into the body and blood of Christ.

treaty ports Chinese ports ruled by foreign consuls where foreigners enjoyed commercial privileges and immunity from Chinese laws.

Trekboers White livestock farmers in Cape Colony.

tribunes Roman officials who had to be plebeians and were elected by the plebeian assembly to protect plebeians from the arbitrary power of the magistrates.

Tripartite Pact The alliance between Japan and Nazi Germany and Fascist Italy that was signed in 1940.

ulama "Persons with correct knowledge." The Islamic scholarly elite who served a social function similar to the Christian clergy.

Umma The Islamic community.

"unequal treaties" Agreements imposed on China in the nineteenth century by European powers, the United States, and Japan that granted their citizens special legal and economic privileges on Chinese soil.

Upanishads Vedic texts most concerned with speculation about the universe.

Urdu-Hindi A language that combines Persian-Arabic and native Indian elements. Urdu is the Muslim version of the language. Hindi is the Hindu version.

uzama An order of hereditary chiefs in Benin.

varnas The four main classes that form the basis for Hindu caste relations.

vassal A person granted an estate or cash payments in return for accepting the obligation to render services to a lord.

Vedas The sacred texts of the ancient Aryan invaders of India. The Rig Vedas are the oldest materials in the Vedas.

vernacular The everyday language spoken by the people as opposed to Latin.

Viet Minh The Communist-dominated popular front organization formed by Ho Chi Minh to establish an independent Vietnamese republic.

Wahhabis Followers of Ibn Abd al-Wahhab (1703-1792) who sought to combat the excesses of popular and Sufi piety in Islam and looked to the Qur'an and the traditions of the Prophet as the sole authoritative guidance in religion.

War Communism The economic policy adopted by the Bolsheviks during the Russian Civil War to seize the banks, heavy industry, railroads, and grain.

war guilt clause Clause of the Versailles Treaty, which assigned responsibility for World War I solely to Germany.

water frame A water-powered device invented by Richard Arkwright to produce a more durable cotton fabric. It led to the shift in the production of cotton textiles from households to factories.

Weimar Republic The German democratic regime that existed between the end of World War I and Hitler's coming to power in 1933.

White Russians Those Russians who opposed the Bolsheviks (the "Reds") in the Russian Civil War of 1918–1921.

Works Progress Administration (WPA) New Deal program created by the Roosevelt administration in 1935 that provided relief for the unemployed in the industrial sector during the Great Depression in the United States.

yangban Elite Korean families of the Choson period.

zaibatsu Large industrial combines that came to dominate Japanese industry in the late nineteenth century.

Zen A form of Buddhism, which taught that Buddha was only a man and exhorted each person to attain enlightenment by his or her own efforts.

Zionism The movement to create a Jewish state in Palestine (the Biblical Zion).

Zoroastrianism A quasi-monotheistic Iranian religion founded by Zoroaster (ca. 628–551 B.C.E.) who preached a message of moral reform and exhorted his followers to worship only Ahura Mazda, the Wise Lord.

Suggested Readings

CHAPTER 1

General Prehistory

P. BOGUCKI, *The Origins of Human Society* (1999). An excellent summary of recent scholarship on the earliest origins of human societies.

F. BRAY, *The Rice Economies: Technology and Development in Asian Societies* (1986). Still the best authority on the origins of rice cultivation and its effect on the develepment of ancient Asia.

M. EHRENBERG, *Women in Prehistory* (1989). An account of the role of women in early times.

C. FREEMAN, *Egypt, Greece and Rome: Civilizations of the Ancient Mediterranean* (2004). Good comparative study of Egypt with Greece and Rome.

D. C. JOHNSON and M. R. EDEY, *Lucy: The Beginning of Mankind* (1981). An account of the African origins of humans.

S. M. NELSON, ed., *Ancient Queens: Archaeological Explorations* (2003). Reassesses women rulers and female power in the ancient world.

S. M. NELSON and M. ROSEN-AYALON, *In Pursuit of Gender: Worldwide Archaeological Approaches* (2002). Essays on gender and the archaeology of the ancient world.

D. L. NICHOLS and T. H. CHARLTON, eds., *The Archaeology of CityStates: Cross-cultural Approaches* (1997). One of a growing body of books and essay collections employing cross-cultural and comparative approaches to world history and archaeology.

M. OLIPHANT, *The Atlas of the Ancient World: Charting the Great Civilizations of the Past* (1992). An excellent comprehensive atlas of the ancient world.

P. L. SHINNIE, *Ancient Nubia* (1996). A study of the African state most influenced by Egyptian culture.

Near East

M. E. AUBER, *The Phoenicians and the West* (1996). A new study of an important sea-going people who served as a conduit between East and West.

BEN-TOR, ed., *The Archaeology of Ancient Israel* (1992). A useful and up-to-date survey.

J. BOTTÉRO, *Everyday Life in Ancient Mesopotamia* (2001). Interesting vignettes of ancient Mesopotamian life.

H. CRAWFORD, *Sumer and the Sumerians* (1991). A discussion of the oldest Mesopotamian civilization.

I. FINKELSTEIN and N. A. SILBERMAN, *The Bible Unearthed: Archaeology's New Vision of Ancient Israel and the Origin of its Sacred Texts* (2001). An interesting discussion of the insights of recent archaeological finds on the history of the Bible and ancient Israel.

G. LEICK, *Mesopotamia: The Invention of the City* (2002). Good discussion of the urban history of ancient Mesopotamia.

J. N. POSTGATE, *Early Mesopotamia* (1992). An excellent study of Mesopotamian economy and society from the earliest times to about 1500 B.C.E., helpfully illustrated with drawings, photos, and translated documents.

D. B. REDFORD, *Akhenaten* (1987). A study of the controversial religious reformer.

W. F. SAGGS, *The Might That Was Assyria* (1984). A history of the northern Mesopotamian Empire and a worthy companion to the author's account of the Babylonian Empire in the south.

M. VAN DE MIEROOP, *A History of the Ancient Near East, ca. 3000–323 B.C.* (2004). An up-to-date comprehensive survey of ancient Near Eastern history.

India

D. P. AGRAWAL, *The Archaeology of India* (1982). A fine survey of the problems and data. Detailed, but with excellent summaries and brief discussions of major issues.

C. CHAKRABORTY, *Common Life in the Rigveda and Atharvaveda—An Account of the Folklore in the Vedic Period* (1977). An interesting attempt to reconstruct everyday life in the Vedic period from the principal Vedic texts.

J. R. MCINTOSH, *A Peaceful Realm: The Rise and Fall of the Indus Civilization* (2002). Discusses what archaeologists have managed to unearth so far regarding Harrapan civilization.

W. D. O'FLAHERTY, *The Rig Veda: An Anthology* (1981). An excellent selection of Vedic texts in prosaic but very careful translation, with helpful notes on the texts.

J. E. SCHWARTZBERG, ed., *A Historical Atlas of South Asia* (1978). The definitive reference work for historical geography. Includes chronological tables and substantive essays.

R. THAPAR, *Early India: From the Origins to A.D. 1300* (2003). A comprehensive introduction to the early history of India.

China

M. LOEWE and E. SHAUGHNESSY eds., *The Cambridge History of Ancient China: From the Origins of Civilization to 221 B.C.* (1999). A comprehensive and authoritative history of ancient China.

K. C. CHANG, *The Archeology of Ancient China*, 4th ed. (1986). The standard work on the subject.

K. C. CHANG, *Art, Myth, and Ritual, The Path to Political Authority in Ancient China* (1984). A study of the relation between shamans, gods, agricultural production, and political authority during the Shang and Zhou dynasties.

N. DI COSMO, *Ancient China and its Enemies: The Rise of Nomadic Power in East Asian History* (2002). An excellent study of the relationship between China and nomadic peoples that was a powerful force in shaping Chinese and Central Asian history.

C. Y. HSU, *Western Chou Civilization* (1988).

D. N. KEIGHTLEY, *The Origins of Chinese Civilization* (1983).

M. E. LEWIS, *Sanctioned Violence in Early China* (1990).

X. Q. LI, *Eastern Zhou and Qin Civilizations* (1986). This work includes fresh interpretations based on archaeological finds.

Americas

R. L. BURGER, *Chavín and the Origins of Andean Civilization* (1992). A lucid and detailed account of the rise of civilization in the Andes.

M. D. COE and R. KOONTZ, *Mexico: From the Olmecs to the Aztecs* (2002). Good survey of ancient Mexico.

D. Drew, *The Lost Chronicles of the Maya Kings* (1999). Fine introduction to the history of Maya civilization.

V. W. Fitzhugh and A. Crowell, *Crossroads of Continents: Cultures of Siberia and Alaska* (1988). Covers the area where the immigration from Eurasia to the Americas began.

R. Ford, ed., *Prehistoric Food Production in North America* (1985). Examines the origins of agriculture in the Americas.

P. D. Hunt, *Indian Agriculture in America: Prehistory to the Present* (1987). Includes a discussion of preconquest agriculture.

A. Knight, *Mexico: From the Beginning to the Spanish Conquest* (2002). First of a three-volume comprehensive history of Mexico.

C. Morris and A. Von Hagen, *The Inka Empire and Its Andean Origins* (1993). An overview of Andean civilization with excellent illustrations.

M. Moseley, *The Incas and Their Ancestors: The Archaeology of Ancient Peru* (1992). An overview of Peruvian archaeology.

J. A. Sabloff, *The New Archaeology and the Ancient Maya* (1990). A lively account of recent research in Maya archaeology.

I. Silverblatt, *Moon, Sun, and Witches: Gender Ideologies and Class in Inca and Colonial Peru* (1987). A controversial but thought-provoking discussion of Incan ideas about gender.

CHAPTER 2

China

R. Berstein, *Ultimate Journey: Retracing the Path of an Ancient Buddhist Monk who Crossed Asia in Search of Enlightenment* (2001). Discusses the diffusion of Buddhism from India to China.

H. G. Creel, *What Is Taoism? And Other Studies in Chinese Cultural History* (1970).

W. T. de Bary et al., *Sources of Chinese Tradition* (1960). A reader in China's philosophical and historical literature. It should be consulted for the later periods as well as for the Zhou.

H. Fingarete, *Confucius—The Secular as Sacred* (1998).

Y. L. Fung, *A Short History of Chinese Philosophy*, ed. by D. Bodde (1948). A survey of Chinese philosophy from its origins down to recent times.

A. Graham, *Disputers of the Tao* (1989).

D. Hawkes, *Ch'u Tz'u: The Songs of the South* (1985).

D. C. Lau, trans., *Lao-tzu, Tao Te Ching* (1963).

D. C. Lau, trans., *Confucius, The Analects* (1979).

C. Li, ed., *The Sage and the Second Sex: Confucianism, Ethics, and Gender* (2000). A good introduction to gender and ethics in Confucian thought.

B. I. Schwartz, *The World of Thought in Ancient China* (1985).

A. Waley, *Three Ways of Thought in Ancient China* (1956). An easy yet sound introduction to Confucianism, Daoism, and Legalism.

A. Waley, *The Book of Songs* (1960).

B. Watson, trans., *Basic Writings of Mo Tzu, Hsun Tzu, and Han Fei Tzu* (1963).

B. Watson, trans., *The Complete Works of Chuang Tzu* (1968).

H. Welch, *Taoism, The Parting of the Way* (1967).

India

A. L. Basham, *The Wonder That Was India*, rev. ed. (1963). Still unsurpassed by more recent works. Chapter VII, "Religion," is a superb introduction to the Vedic Aryan, Brahmanic, Hindu, Jain, and Buddhist traditions of thought.

W. N. Brown, *Man in the Universe: Some Continuities in Indian Thought* (1970). A penetrating yet brief reflective summary of major patterns in Indian thinking.

W. T. de Bary et al., *Sources of Indian Tradition* (1958). 2 vols. Vol. I, *From the Beginning to 1800*, ed. and rev. by Ainslie T. Embree (1988). Excellent selections from a variety of Indian texts, with good introductions to chapters and individual selections.

P. Harvey, *An Introduction to Buddhism* (1990). Chapters 1–3 provide an excellent historical introduction.

T. J. Hopkins, *The Hindu Religious Tradition* (1971). A first-rate, thoughtful introduction to Hindu religious ideas and practice.

K. Klostermaier, *Hinduism: A Short History* (2000). A relatively compact survey of the history of Hinduism.

J. M. Koller, *The Indian Way* (1982). A useful, wide-ranging handbook of Indian thought and religion.

R. H. Robinson and W. L. Johnson, *The Buddhist Religion*, 3rd ed. (1982). An excellent first text on the Buddhist tradition, its thought and development.

R. C. Zaehner, *Hinduism* (1966). One of the best general introductions to central Indian religious and philosophical ideas.

Israel

A. Bach, ed., *Women in the Hebrew Bible: A Reader* (1999). Excellent introduction to the ways in which biblical scholars are exploring the role of women in the Bible.

Bright, *A History of Israel* (1968), 2nd ed. (1972). One of the standard scholarly introductions to biblical history and literature.

W. D. Davies and L. Finkelstein, eds., *The Cambridge History of Judaism*. Vol. I, *Introduction: The Persian Period* (1984). Excellent essays on diverse aspects of the exilic period and later.

J. Neusner, *The Way of Torah: An Introduction to Judaism* (1979). A sensitive introduction to the Judaic tradition and faith.

The Oxford History of the Biblical World, M. D. Coogan, ed. (1998).

Greece

The Cambridge Companion to Greek and Roman Philosophy, D. Sedley ed., (2003).

G. B. Kerferd, *The Sophistic Movement* (1981). An excellent description and analysis.

J. Lear, *Aristotle: The Desire to Understand* (1988). A brilliant yet comprehensible introduction to the work of the philosopher.

T. E. Rihil, *Greek Science* (1999). Good survey of Greek science incorporating recent reseach on the topic.

J. M. Robinson, *An Introduction to Early Greek Philosophy* (1968). A valuable collection of the main fragments and ancient testimony to the works of the early philosophers, with excellent commentary.

G. Vlastos, *The Philosophy of Socrates* (1971). A splendid collection of essays illuminating the problems presented by this remarkable man.

G. Vlastos, *Platonic Studies*, 2nd ed. (1981). A similar collection on the philosophy of Plato.

G. Vlastos, *Socrates, Ironist and Moral Philosopher* (1991). The results of a lifetime of study by the leading interpreter of Socrates in our time.

Comparative Studies

(Increasingly world historians are looking at ancient civilizations in relationship to each other rather than as isolated entities to try to understand commonalities and differences in social and cultural development.)

W. DONIGER, *Splitting the Difference: Gender and Myth in Ancient Greece and India* (1999).

G. E. R. LLOYD, *The Ambitions of Curiosity: Understanding the World in Ancient Greece and China* (2002).

G. E. R. LLOYD, *The Way and the Word: Science and Medicine in Early China and Greece* (2002).

T. MCEVILLEY, *The Shape of Ancient Thought: Comparative Studies of Greek and Indian Philosopies* (2002).

CHAPTER 3

The Rise of Greek Civilization

P. CARTLEDGE, *The Spartans* (2003). A readable account of this enigmatic people.

J. CHADWICK, *The Mycenaean World* (1976). A readable account by a man who helped decipher Mycenaean writing.

R. DREWS, *The Coming of the Greeks* (1988). A fine discussion of the Greeks' arrival as part of the movements of the Indo-European peoples.

J. V. FINE, *The Ancient Greeks* (1983). An excellent survey that discusses historical problems and the evidence that gives rise to them.

M. I. FINLEY, *World of Odysseus*, rev. ed. (1965). A fascinating attempt to reconstruct Homeric society.

P. GREEN, *Xerxes at Salamis* (1970). A lively and stimulating history of the Persian War.

D. HAMEL, *Trying Neaira* (2003). A lively account of the events surrounding a famous jury trial that sheds interesting light on Athenian society in the fourth century B.C.E.

V. D. HANSON, *The Western Way of War* (1989). A brilliant and lively discussion of the rise and character of the hoplite phalanx and its influence on Greek society.

V. D. HANSON, *The Other Greeks* (1995). A revolutionary account of the Greek invention of the family farm and its centrality for the shaping of the *polis.*

D. KAGAN, *The Great Dialogue: A History of Greek Political Thought from Homer to Polybius* (1965). A discussion of the relationship between the Greek historical experience and political theory.

W. K. LACEY, *The Family in Ancient Greece* (1984).

J. F. LAZENBY, *The Defense of Greece, 490–479 B.C.* (1993). A new and valuable study of the Persian Wars.

J. F. MCGLEW, *Tyranny and Political Culture in Ancient Greece* (1993). A recent account of political developments in the Archaic period.

O. MURRAY, *Early Greece* (1980). A lively and imaginative account of the early history of Greece to the end of the Persian War.

A. M. SNODGRASS, *The Dark Age of Greece* (1972). A good examination of the archaeological evidence.

B. S. STRAUSS, *The Battle of Salamis: The Naval Encounter That Saved Greece and Western Civilization* (2004). A lively account of the major naval battle of the Persian Wars and its setting.

A. G. WOODHEAD, *Greeks in the West* (1962). An account of the Greek settlements in Italy and Sicily.

W. J. WOODHOUSE, *Solon the Liberator* (1965). A discussion of the great Athenian reformer.

S. G. MILLER, *Ancient Greek Athletics* (2004). The most complete and most useful account of the subject.

Classical and Hellenistic Greece

W. BURKERT, *Greek Religion* (1987). An excellent study by an outstanding student of the subject.

J. R. LANE FOX, *Alexander the Great* (1973). An imaginative account that does more than the usual justice to the Persian side of the problem.

Y. GARLAN, *Slavery in Ancient Greece* (1988). An up-to-date survey.

P. GREEN, *Alexander to Actium: The Historical Evolution of the Hellenistic Age* (1990). A remarkable synthesis of political and cultural history.

C. D. HAMILTON, *Agesilaus and the Failure of Spartan Hegemony* (1991). An excellent biography of the king who was the central figure in Sparta during its domination in the fourth century B.C.E.

N. G. L. HAMMOND, *Philip of Macedon* (1994). A new biography of the founder of the Macedonian Empire.

N. G. L. HAMMOND AND G. T. GRIFFITH, *A History of Macedonia*, Vol. 2, *550–336 B.C.* (1979). A thorough account of Macedonian history that focuses on the careers of Philip and Alexander.

R. JUST, *Women in Athenian Law and Life* (1988). An account of women's place in Athenian society.

D. KAGAN, *The Peloponnesian War* (2003). A narrative history of the war.

B. M. W. KNOX, *The Heroic Temper: Studies in Sophoclean Tragedy* (1964). A brilliant analysis of tragic heroism.

D. M. LEWIS, *Sparta and Persia* (1977). A valuable discussion of relations between Sparta and Persia in the fifth and fourth centuries B.C.E.

A. A. LONG, *Hellenistic Philosophy: Stoics, Epicureans, Sceptics* (1974). An account of Greek science in the Hellenistic and Roman periods.

R. MEIGGS, *The Athenian Empire* (1972). A fine study of the rise and fall of the empire, making excellent use of inscriptions.

J. J. POLLITT, *Art and Experience in Classical Greece* (1972). A scholarly and entertaining study of the relationship between art and history in classical Greece, with excellent illustrations.

J. J. POLLITT, *Art in the Hellenistic Age* (1986). An extraordinary analysis that places the art in its historical and intellectual context.

E. W. ROBINSON, *Ancient Greek Democracy* (2004). A stimulating collection of ancient sources and modern interpretations.

D. M. SCHAPS, *Economic Rights of Women in Ancient Greece* (1981).

B. S. STRAUSS, *Athens After the Peloponnesian War* (1987). An excellent discussion of Athens' recovery and of the nature of Athenian society and politics in the fourth century B.C.E.

B. S. STRAUSS, *Fathers and Sons in Athens* (1993). An unusual synthesis of social, political, and intellectual history.

V. TCHERIKOVER, *Hellenistic Civilization and the Jews* (1970). A fine study of the impact of Hellenism on the Jews.

G. VLASTOS, *Socrates, Ironist and Moral Philosopher* (1991). The results of a lifetime of study by the leading interpreter of Socrates in our time.

CHAPTER 4

Iran

M. BOYCE, *Zoroastrians: Their Religious Beliefs and Practices* (1979). The most recent survey, organized historically and based on extensive research.

M. BOYCE, ed. and trans., *Textual Sources for the Study of Zoroastrianism* (1984). Well-translated selections from a broad range of ancient Iranian materials.

J. M. COOK, *The Persian Empire* (1983). Survey of the Achaemenid period.

J. CURTIS, *Ancient Persia* (1989). Excellent portfolio of photographs of artifacts and sites, with a clear historical survey of the arts and culture of ancient Iran.

W. D. DAVIES AND L. FINKLESTEIN, ed., *The Cambridge History of Judaism*, Vol. 1, Introduction; "The Persian Period". Good articles on Iran and Iranian religion as well as Judaism.

J. DUCHESNE-GUILLEMIN, trans., *The Hymns of Zarathushtra*, trans. by M. Henning (1952, 1963). The best short introduction to the original texts of the Zoroastrian hymns.

R. N. FRYE, *The Heritage of Persia* (1963, 1966). A first-rate survey of Iranian history to Islamic times: readable but scholarly.

R. GHIRSHMAN, *Iran* (1954). Good material on culture, society, and economy as well as politics and history.

W. W. MALANDRA, trans. and ed., *An Introduction to Ancient Iranian Religion: Readings from the Avesta and Achaemenid Inscriptions* (1983). Helpful especially for texts of inscriptions relevant to religion.

India

A. L. BASHAM, *The Wonder That Was India*, rev. ed. (1963). Excellent material on Mauryan religion, society, culture, and history.

A. L. BASHAM, ed., *A Cultural History of India* (1975). A fine collection of historical-survey essays by a variety of scholars. See Part I, "The Ancient Heritage" (Chapters 2–16).

N. N. BHATTACHARYYA, *Ancient Indian History and Civilization: Trends and Perspectives* (1988). Covers Mauryan and Gupta times as well as earlier periods, with chapters on political systems, cities and villages, ideology and religion, and art.

W. T. DE BARY et al., COMP., *Sources of Indian Tradition*, 2nd ed. (1958). Vol. I: *From the Beginning to 1800*, ed. and rev. by Ainslie T. Embree (1988). Excellent selections from a wide variety of Indian texts, with good introductions to chapters and selections.

B. ROWLAND, *The Art and Architecture of India: Buddhist/Hindu/Jain*, 3rd rev. ed. (1970). The standard work, lucid and easy to read. Note Part Three, "Romano-Indian Art in North-West India and Central Asia."

V. A. SMITH, ed., *The Oxford History of India*, 4th rev. ed. by Percival Spear et al. (1981), pp. 71–163. A dry, occasionally dated historical survey. Includes useful reference chronologies.

R. THAPAR, *Ashoka and the Decline of the Mauryans* (1973). The standard treatment of Ashoka's reign.

R. THAPAR, *A History of India, Part I* (1966), pp. 50–108. Three chapters that provide a basic survey of the period.

S. WOLPERT, *A New History of India*, 2nd ed. (1982). A basic survey history. Chapters 5 and 6 cover the Mauryans, Guptas, and Kushans.

Greek and Asian Dynasties

A. K. NARAIN, *The Indo-Greeks* (1957. Reprinted with corrections, 1962). The most comprehensive account of the complex history of the various kings and kingdoms.

F. E. PETERS, *The Harvest of Hellenism* (1970), pp. 222–308. Helpful chapters on Greek rulers of the Eastern world from Seleucus to the last Indo-Greeks.

J. W. SEDLAR, *India and the Greek World: A Study in the Transmission of Culture* (1980). A basic work that provides a good overview.

D. SINOR, ed., *The Cambridge History of Early Inner Asia* (1990). See especially Chapters 6 and 7.

CHAPTER 5

P. BOHANNAN AND P. CURTIN, *Africa and Africans*, rev. ed. (1971). An enjoyable and enlightening discussion of African history and prehistory and of major African institutions (e.g., arts, family life, religion).

R. BULLIET, *The Camel and the Wheel* (1990). Explains why the camel was chosen over the wheel as a means of transport in the Sahara.

P. CURTIN, S. FEIERMANN, L. THOMPSON, AND J. VANSINA, *African History* (1978). Probably the best survey history. The relevant portions are chapters 1, 2, 4, 8, and 9.

T. R. H. DAVENPORT, *South Africa: A Modern History*, 3rd rev. ed. (1987). Chapter 1 gives excellent summary coverage of prehistoric southern Africa, the Khoisan peoples, and the Bantu migrations.

B. DAVIDSON, *The African Past* (1967). A combination of primary-source selections and brief secondary discussions trace sympathetically the history of the diverse parts of Africa.

P. GARLAKE, *The Kingdoms of Africa* (1978). A lavishly illustrated set of photographic essays that provide a helpful introduction to the various historically important areas of precolonial Africa.

E. GILBERT AND J. REYNOLDS, *Africa in World History* (2004). The best new survey of African history, placing it in a global context.

R. W. JULY, *Precolonial Africa: An Economic and Social History* (1975). A very readable, topically arranged study. See especially "The Savannah Farmer," "The Bantu," "Cattle-men," and "The Traders" chapters.

H. LOTH, *Woman in Ancient Africa*, trans. by S. Marnie (1987). An interesting survey of legal, familial, cultural, and other aspects of women's roles.

R. OLIVER, *The African Experience* (1991). A masterly, balanced, and engaging sweep through African history. The chapters on prehistory and early history are outstanding summaries of the results and implications of recent research.

I. VAN SERTIMA, *Black Women in Antiquity* (1984, 1988). Studies of queens, goddesses, matriarchy, and other aspects of the role and status of women in Egyptian, Ethiopian, and other African societies of the past.

CHAPTER 6

From Republic to Empire

R. BAUMANN, *Women and Politics in Ancient Rome* (1995). A Study of the role of women in roman public life.

A. H. BERNSTEIN, *Tiberius Sempronius Gracchus: Tradition and Apostasy* (1978). A new interpretation of Tiberius's place in Roman politics.

T. J. CORNELL, *The Beginnings of Rome: Italy and Rome from the Bronze Age to the Punic Wars, c. 1000–264 B.C.* (1995). A consideration of the royal and early republican periods of Roman history.

T. CORNELL AND J. MATTHEWS, *Atlas of the Roman World* (1982). Much more than the title indicates, this book presents a comprehensive view of the Roman world in its physical and cultural setting.

J-M. DAVID, *The Roman Conquest of Italy* (1997). A good analysis of how Rome united Italy.

A. GOLDSWORTHY, *Roman Warfare* (2002). A good military history of Rome.

A. GOLDSWORTHY, *In the Name of Rome: The Men Who Won the Roman Empire* (2004). The story of Rome's greatest generals in the republican and imperial periods.

E. S. GRUEN, *Diaspora: Jews Amidst Greeks and Romans* (2002). A fine study of Jews in the Hellenistic and Roman world.

E. S. GRUEN, *The Hellenistic World and the Coming of Rome* (1984). A new interpretation of Rome's conquest of the eastern Mediterranean.

W. V. HARRIS, *War and Imperialism in Republican Rome, 327–70 B.C.* (1975). An analysis of Roman attitudes and intentions concerning imperial expansion and war.

A. KEAVENEY, *Rome and the Unification of Italy* (1988). The story of how Rome organized her defeated opponents.

S. LANCEL, *Carthage, A History* (1995). Includes a good account of Rome's dealings with Carthage.

J. F. LAZENBY, *Hannibal's War: A Military History of the Second Punic War* (1978). A careful and thorough account.

F.G.B. MILLAR, *The Crowd in Rome in the Late Republic* (1999). A challenge to the view that only aristocrats counted in the late republic.

M. PALLOTTINO, *The Etruscans*, 6th ed. (1974). Makes especially good use of archaeological evidence.

H. H. SCULLARD, *A History of the Roman World 753–146 B.C.*, 4th ed. (1980). An unusually fine narrative history with useful critical notes.

G. WILLIAMS, *The Nature of Roman Poetry* (1970). An unusually graceful and perceptive literary study.

Imperial Rome

W. BALL, *Rome in the East: The Transformation of an Empire* (2001). A thorough account of the influence of the East on Roman history.

T. BARNES, *The New Empire of Diocletian and Constantine* (1982).

K. R. BRADLEY, *Slavery and Society at Rome* (1994). A study of the role of slaves in Roman life.

P. BROWN, *The Rise of Western Christendom: Triumph and Diversity, 200–1000* (1996). A vivid picture of the spread of Christianity by a master of the field.

A. FERRILL, *The Fall of the Roman Empire, The Military Explanation* (1986). An interpretation that emphasizes the decline in the quality of the Roman army.

K. GALINSKY, *Augustan Culture* (1996). A work that integrates art, literature, and politics.

A. H. M. JONES, *The Later Roman Empire*, 3 vols. (1964). A comprehensive study of the period.

D. KAGAN, ed., *The End of the Roman Empire: Decline or Transformation?* 3rd ed. (1992). A collection of essays discussing the problem of the decline and fall of the Roman Empire.

J. E. LENDON, *Empire of Honor, The Art of Government in the Roman World* (1997). An original and path-breaking interpretation.

E. N. LUTTWAK, *The Grand Strategy of the Roman Empire* (1976). An original and fascinating analysis by a keen student of modern strategy.

R. MACMULLEN, *Roman Social Relations, 50 B.C. to A.D. 284* (1981).

R. MACMULLEN, *Corruption and the Decline of Rome* (1988). A study that examines the importance of changes in ethical ideas and behavior.

R. W. MATHISON, *Roman Aristocrats in Barbarian Gaul: Strategies for Survival* (1993). An unusual slant on the late empire.

J.F. MATTHEWS, *Laying Down the Law: A Study of the Theodosian Code* (2000). A study of the importance of Roman law as a source for the understanding of Roman history and civilization.

W. A. MEEKS, *The Origins of Christian Morality: The First Two Centuries.* An account of the shaping of Christianity in the Roman Empire.

F. MILLAR, *The Emperor in the Roman World, 31 B.C.–A.D. 337* (1977). A study of Roman imperial government.

F. MILLAR, *The Roman Empire and Its Neighbors*, 2nd ed. (1981).

H. M. D. PARKER, *A History of the Roman World from A.D. 138 to 337* (1969). A good survey.

M. I. ROSTOVTZEFF, *Social and Economic History of the Roman Empire*, 2nd ed. (1957). A masterpiece whose main thesis has been much disputed.

V. RUDICH, *Political Dissidence Under Nero, The Price of Dissimulation* (1993). A brilliant exposition of the lives and thoughts of political dissidents in the early empire.

E. T. SALMON, *A History of the Roman World, 30 B.C. to A.D. 138* (1968). A good survey.

R. SYME, *The Roman Revolution* (1960). A brilliant study of Augustus, his supporters, and their rise to power.

R. SYME, *The Augustan Aristocracy* (1985). An examination of the new ruling class shaped by Augustus.

L. A. THOMPSON, *Romans and Blacks* (1989).

CHAPTER 7

D. BODDE, *China's First Unifier* (1938). A study of the Qin unification of China, viewed through the Legalist philosopher and statesman LiSi.

T. T. CH'U, *Law and Society in Traditional China* (1961). Treats the sweep of Chinese history from 202 B.C.E. to 1911 C.E.

T. T. CH'U, *Han Social Structure* (1972).

A. COTTERELL, *The First Emperor of China* (1981). A study of the first Qin emperor.

R. COULBORN, *Feudalism in History* (1965). One chapter interestingly compares the quasi feudalism of the Zhou with that of the Six Dynasties period.

J. K. FAIRBANK, E. O. REISCHAUER, AND A. M. CRAIG, *East Asia: Tradition and Transformation* (1989). A fairly detailed single-volume history covering China, Japan, and other countries in East Asia from antiquity to recent times.

J. GERNET, *A History of Chinese Civilization* (1982). A survey of Chinese history.

D.A. GRAFF AND R. HIGHAM, *A Military History of China* (2002).

C. Y. HSU, *Ancient China in Transition* (1965). On social mobility during the Eastern Zhou era.

C. Y. HSU, *Han Agriculture* (1980). A study of the agrarian economy of China during the Han dynasty.

J. LEVI, *The Chinese Emperor* (1987). A novel about the first Qin emperor based on scholarly sources.

M. LOEWE, *Everyday Life in Early Imperial China* (1968). A social history of the Han dynasty.

J. NEEDHAM, *The Shorter Science and Civilization in China* (1978). An abridgment of the multivolume work on the same subject with the same title—minus Shorter—by the same author.

S. OWEN, ed. and Trans., *An Anthology of Chinese Literature: Beginnings to 1911* (1996).

I. ROBINET, *Taoism: Growth of a Religion* (1987).

M. SULLIVAN, *The Arts of China* (1967). An excellent survey history of Chinese art.

D. TWITCHETT AND M. LOEWE, eds., *The Ch'in and Han Empires, 221 B.C.E.–C.E. 220* (1986). Vol. 1 of *The Cambridge History of China*.

Z. S. WANG, *Han Civilization* (1982).

B. WATSON, *Ssu-ma Ch'ien, Grand Historian of China* (1958). A study of China's premier historian.

B. WATSON, *Records of the Grand Historian of China*, Vols. 1 and 2 (1961). Selections from the *Shiji* by Sima Qian.

B. WATSON, *The Columbia Book of Chinese Poetry* (1986).

F. WOOD, *The Silk Road: Two Thousand Years in the Heart of Asia* (2003). A lively narrative combined with photographs and paintings.

A. WRIGHT, *Buddhism in Chinese History* (1959).

Y. S. YU, *Trade and Expansion in Han China* (1967). A study of economic relations between the Chinese and their neighbors.

CHAPTER 8

General

P. BOL, *This Culture of Ours* (1992). An insightful intellectual history of the Tang through the Song dynasties.

J. CAHILL, *Chinese Painting* (1960). An excellent survey.

J. K. FAIRBANK AND M. GOLDMAN, *China: A New History* (1998). The summation of a lifetime engagement with Chinese history.

F. A. KIERMAN JR., AND J. K. FAIRBANK, eds., *Chinese Ways in Warfare* (1974). Chapters by different authors on the Chinese military experience from the Zhou to the Ming.

Sui and Tang

P. B. EBREY, *The Aristocratic Families of Early Imperial China* (1978).

D. MCMULLEN, *State and Scholars in T'ang China* (1988).

S. OWEN, *The Great Age of Chinese Poetry: The High T'ang* (1980).

S. OWEN, trans. and ed., *An Anthology of Chinese Literature: Beginnings to 1911* (1996).

E. G. PULLEYBLANK, *The Background of the Rebellion of An Lu-shan* (1955). A study of the 755 rebellion that weakened the central authority of the Tang dynasty.

E. O. REISCHAUER, *Ennin's Travels in T'ang China* (1955). China as seen through the eyes of a ninth-century Japanese Marco Polo.

E. H. SCHAFER, *The Golden Peaches of Samarkand* (1963). A study of Tang imagery.

SO. TEISER, *The Ghost Festival in Medieval China* (1988). On Tang popular religion.

D. TWITCHETT, ed., *The Cambridge History of China*, Vol. III: *Sui and T'ang China, 589–906 Part 1*, (1979).

G. W. WANG, *The Structure of Power in North China During the Five Dynasties* (1963). A study of the interim period between the Tang and the Song dynasties.

A. F. WRIGHT, *The Sui Dynasty* (1978).

Song

B. BIRGE, *Women, Property, and Confucian Reaction in Song and Yuan China (960–1366)* (2002). The rights of women to property—whether in the form of dowries or inheritances—were considerable during the Song but declined thereafter.

C. S. CHANG AND J. SMYTHE, *South China in the Twelfth Century* (1981). China as seen through the eyes of a twelfth-century Chinese poet, historian, and statesman.

E. L. DAVIS, *Society and the Supernatural in Song China* (2001).

J. W. HAEGER, ed., *Crisis and Prosperity in Song China* (1975).

R. HYMES, *Statesmen and Gentlemen* (1987). On the transformation of officials into a local gentry elite during the twelfth and thirteenth centuries.

R. HYMES, *Way and Byway: Taoism, Local Religion, and Models of Divinity in Sung and Modern China* (2002).

M. ROSSABI, *China Among Equals* (1983). A study of the Liao, Qin, and Song Empires and their relations.

W. M. TU, *Confucian Thought, Selfhood as Creative Transformation* (1985).

K. YOSHIKAWA, *An Introduction to Song Poetry*, trans. by B. Watson (1967).

Yuan

T. T. ALLSEN, *Mongol Imperialism* (1987).

J. W. DARDESS, *Conquerors and Confucians: Aspects of Political Change in Late Yuan China* (1973).

DE RACHEWILTZ, trans., *The Secret History of the Mongols: A Mongolian Epic Chronicle of the Thirteenth Century* (2003). A new translation of a key historical work on the life of Genghis.

H. FRANKE AND D. TWITCHETT, eds., *The Cambridge History of China*, Vol. VI: *Alien Regimes and Border States, 710–1368* (1994).

J. D. LANGLOIS, *China Under Mongol Rule* (1981).

R. LATHAM, trans., *Travels of Marco Polo* (1958).

H. D. MARTIN, *The Rise of Chingis Khan and His Conquest of North China* (1981).

D. MORGAN, *The Mongol Empire and its Legacy* (1999). Genghis, the several khanates, and the aftermath of empire.

P. RATCHNEVSKY, *Genghis Khan, His Life and Legacy* (1992). The rise to power of the Mongol leader, with a critical consideration of historical sources.

CHAPTER 9

M. ADOLPHSON, *The Gates of Power: Monks, Courtiers, and Warriors in Premodern Japan* (2000). A new interpretation stressing the importance of temples in the political life of Heian and Kamakura Japan.

B.L. BATTEN, *To the Ends of Japan: Premodern Frontiers, Boundaries, and Interactions.* (2003). An interesting treatment of Heian Japan, topic by topic.

C. BLACKER, *The Catalpa Bow* (1975). An insightful study of folk Shinto.

R. BORGEN, *Sugawara no Michizane and the Early Heian Court* (1986). A study of a famous courtier and poet.

D. M. BROWN, ed., *The Cambridge History of Japan: Ancient Japan* (1993). This series of six volumes sums up several decades of research on Japan.

D. BROWN AND E. ISHIDA, eds., *The Future and the Past* (1979). A translation of a history of Japan written in 1219.

The Cambridge History of Japan, D.M. BROWN, ed.; Vol. 1, *Ancient Japan*, W. McCullough and D. H. Shively eds; Vol. 2, *Heian Japan*, K. Yamamura, ed. Vol. 3, *Medieval Japan*. Fine multi-author works.

M. Collcutt, *Five Mountains* (1980). A study of the monastic organization of medieval Zen.

T.D. Conlon, *State of War: The Violent Order of Fourteenth Century Japan* (2003). Compare Conlon's account with those of Souyri and Friday.

P. Duus, *Feudalism in Japan* (1969). An easy survey of the subject.

W. W. Farris, *Population, Disease, and Land in Early Japan, 645–900* (1985). An innovative reinterpretation of early history.

W. W. Farris, *Heavenly Warriors: The Evolution of Japan's Military, 500–1300* (1992).

W. W. Farris, *Sacred Texts and Buried Treasures* (1998). Studies of Japan's prehistory and early history, based on recent Japanese research.

K. F. Friday, *Samurai, Warfare and the State in Early Medieval Japan* (2004). Weapons and warfare in Japan from the tenth to fourteenth centuries.

A. E. Goble, *Go Daigo's Revolution* (1996). A provoking account of the 1331 revolt by an emperor who thought emperors should rule.

J. W. Hall, *Government and Local Power in Japan, 500–1700: A Study Based on Bizen Province* (1966). A splendid and insightful book.

J. W. Hall and T. Toyoda, *Japan in the Muromachi Age* (1977). Another collection of essays.

D. Keene, ed., *Anthology of Japanese Literature from the Earliest Era to the Mid-Nineteenth Century* (1955).

D. Keene, ed., *Twenty Plays of the No Theatre* (1970).

T. Lamarre, *Uncovering Heian Japan: An Archeology of Sensation and Inscription* (2000). The "archeology" in the title refers to digging into literature.

I. H. Levy, *The Ten Thousand Leaves* (1981). A fine translation of Japan's earliest collection of poetry.

J. P. Mass and W. Hauser, eds., *The Bakufu in Japanese History* (1985). Topics in *bakufu* history from the twelfth to the nineteenth centuries.

I. Morris, trans., *The Pillow Book of Sei Shonagon* (1967). Observations about the Heian court life by the Jane Austen of ancient Japan.

S. Murasaki, *The Tale of Genji*, trans. by A. Waley (1952). A comparison of this translation with that of Seidensticker is instructive.

S. Murasaki, *The Tale of Genji*, trans. by E. G. Seidensticker (1976). The world's first novel and the greatest work of Japanese fiction.

R. J. Pearson et al., eds., *Windows on the Japanese Past: Studies in Archaeology and Prehistory* (1986).

D. L. Philippi, trans., *Kojiki* (1968). Japan's ancient myths.

J. Piggot, *The Emergence of Japanese Kingship* (1997).

E. O. Reischauer, *Ennin's Diary, the Record of a Pilgrimage to China in Search of the Law and Ennin's Travels in T'ang China* (1955).

E. O. Reischauer and A. M. Craig, *Japan: Tradition and Transformation* (1989). A more detailed work covering the sweep of Japanese history from the early beginnings through the 1980s.

H. Sato, *Legends of the Samurai* (1995). Excerpts from various tales and writings.

D. H. Shively and W. H. McCullough, eds., *The Cambridge History of Japan: Heian Japan* (1999).

D. T. Suzuki, *Zen and Japanese Culture* (1959).

H. Tonomura, *Community and Commerce in Late Medieval Japan* (1992).

R. Tsunoda, W. T. de Bary, and D. Keene, comps., *Sources of the Japanese Tradition* (1958). A collection of original religious, political, and philosophical writings from each period of Japanese history. The best reader. A new edition should be out soon.

H. P. Varley, *Imperial Restoration in Medieval Japan* (1971). A study of the 1331 attempt by an emperor to restore imperial power.

A. Waley, trans., *The No Plays of Japan* (1957). Medieval dramas.

K. Yamamura, ed., *Cambridge History of Japan: Medieval Japan* (1990).

Chapter 10

Iran

M. Boyce, *Zoroastrians: Their Religious Beliefs and Practices* (1979). A detailed survey by the current authority on Zoroastrian religious history. See Chapters 7–9.

M. Boyce, ed. and trans., *Textual Sources for the Study of Zoroastrianism* (1984). A valuable anthology with an important introduction that includes Boyce's arguments for a revision of the dates of Zoroaster's life (to between 1400 and 1200 B.C.E.).

R. N. Frye, *The Heritage of Persia* (1963). Still one of the best surveys, Chapter 6 deals with the Sasanid era.

R. Ghirshman, *Iran* (1954 [orig. ed. 1951]). An introductory survey of similar extent to Frye, but with differing material also.

R. Ghirshman, *Persian Art: The Parthian and Sasanid Dynasties* (1962). Superb photographs, and a very helpful glossary of places and names. The text is minimal.

Geo Widengran, *Mani and Manichaeism* (1965). Still the standard introduction to Mani's life and the later spread and development of Manichaeism.

India

A. L. Basham, *The Wonder That Was India* (1963). The best survey of classical Indian religion, society, literature, art, and politics.

W. T. de Bary et al., comp., *Sources of Indian Tradition*, 2nd ed. (1958), Vol. I, *From the Beginning to 1800*, ed. and rev. by Ainslie T. Embree (1988). Excellent selections from a wide variety of Indian texts, with good introductions to the text selections.

S. Dutt, *Buddhist Monks and Monasteries of India* (1962). The standard work. See especially Chapters 3 ("Bhakti") and 4 ("Monasteries Under the Gupta Kings").

D. G. Mandelbaum, *Society in India* (1972). 2 vols. The first two chapters in Volume I of this study of caste, family, and village relations are a good introduction to the caste system.

B. Rowland, *The Art and Architecture of India: Buddhist/Hindu/Jain*, 3rd rev. ed. (1970). See the excellent chapters on Sungan, Andhran, and other early Buddhist art (6–8, 14), the Gupta period (15), and the Hindu Renaissance (17–19).

V. A. Smith, *The Oxford History of India*, 4th rev. ed. (1981). See especially pages 164–229 (the Gupta period and following era to the Muslim invasions).

R. Thapar, *A History of India, Part I* (1966), pp. 109–193. Three chapters covering the rise of mercantilism, the Gupta "classical pattern," and the southern dynasties to ca. 900 C.E..

P. Younger, *Introduction to Indian Religious Thought* (1972). A sensitive attempt to delineate classical concerns of Indian religious thought and culture.

Chapter 11

O. Grabar, *The Formation of Islamic Art* (1973). A critical and creative interpretation of major themes in the development of distinctively Islamic forms of art and architecture.

A. HOURANI, *A History of the Arab Peoples* (1991). A masterly survey of the Arabs down through the centuries and a clear picture of many aspects of Islamic history and culture that extend beyond the Arab world.

H. KENNEDY, *The Prophet and the Age of the Caliphates: The Islamic Near East from the Sixth to the Eleventh Century* (1986). The best survey of early Islamic history.

I. LAPIDUS, *A History of Islamic Societies* (1988). A comprehensive overview of the rise and development of Islam all over the world.

F. E. PETERS, *Muhammad and the Origins of Islam* (1994). A balanced analysis of the life of Muhammad.

F. RAHMAN, *Major Themes of the Qur'an* (1980). The best introduction to the basic ideas of the Qur'an and Islam, seen through the eyes of a perceptive Muslim modernist scholar.

F. SCHUON, *Understanding Islam* (1994). Compares the Islamic worldview with Catholic Christianity. A dense, but intellectually stimulating, discussion.

M. SELLS, *Approaching the Qur'an. The Early Revelations* (1999). A fine introduction and new translations of some of the more common earlier Qur'anic revelations.

B. STOWASSER, *Women in the Qur'an, Traditions and Interpretation* (1994). An outstanding systematic study of statements regarding women in the Qur'an.

CHAPTER 12

K. ARMSTRONG, *Muhammad: A Biography of the Prophet* (1992). Strong on religion.

R. BARTLETT, *The Making of Europe, 950–1350* (1992). A study of the way immigration and colonial conquest shaped the Europe we know.

M. BLOCH, *Feudal Society*, Vols. 1 and 2, trans. by L. A. Manyon (1971). A classic on the topic and as an example of historical study.

P. BROWN, *Augustine of Hippo: A Biography* (1967). Late antiquity seen through the biography of its greatest Christian thinker.

J. H. BURNS, *The Cambridge History of Medieval Political Thought c. 350–c. 1450* (1991). The best scan.

R. H. C. DAVIS, *A History of Medieval Europe: From Constantine to St. Louis* (1972). Unsurpassed in clarity.

R. FLETCHER, *The Barbarian Conversion: From Paganism to Christianity* (1998). Up-to-date survey.

J. B. GLUBB, *The Great Arab Conquests* (1995). Jihadists.

G. GUGLIELMO, ed., *The Byzantines* (1997). Updates key issues.

D. GUTAS, *Greek Thought, Arabic Culture* (1998). A comparative intellectual history.

G. HOLMES, Ed., *The Oxford History of Medieval Europe* (1992). Overviews of Roman and northern Europe during the "Dark Ages."

B. LEWIS, *The Middle East: A Brief History of the Last 2,000 Years* (1995)

C. MANGO, *Byzantium: The Empire of New Rome* (1980).

J. MARTIN, *Medieval Russia 980–1584* (1995). A concise narrative history.

R. MCKITTERICK, ed., *Carolingian Culture: Emulation and Innovation* (1994). Fresh essays.

J.J. NORWICH, *Byzantium: The Decline and Fall* (1995).

J.J. NORWICH, *Byzantium: The Apogee* (1997). The whole story in two volulmes.

R.I. PAGE, *Chronicles of the Vikings: Records, Memorials, and Myths* (1995). Sources galore.

F. ROBINSON, ed., *The Cambridge Illustrated History of the Islamic World* (1996). Spectacular.

S. RUNCIMAN, *Byzantine Civilization* (1970). Succinct, comprehensive account by a master.

P. SAWYER, *The Age of the Vikings* (1962). Old but solid account.

C. STEPHENSON, *Medieval Feudalism* (1969). Excellent short summary and introduction.

L. WHITE JR., *Medieval Technology and Social Change* (1962). Often fascinating account of how primitive technology changed life.

H. WOLFRAM, *The Roman Empire and Its Germanic Peoples* (1997). Challenging, but most rewarding.

CHAPTER 13

The Islamic Heartlands

L. AHMED, *Women and Gender in Islam. Historical Roots of a Modern Debate* (1992). A good historical survey of the status of women in Middle Eastern societies.

J. BERKEY, *The Formation of Islam. Religion and Society in the Near East 600–1800* (2002). An interesting new synthesis foducing on political and religious trends.

C. E. BOSWORTH, *The Islamic Dynasties: A Chronological and Genealogical Handbook* (1967). A handy reference work for dynasties and families important to Islamic history in all periods and places.

M. A. COOK, *Commanding Right and Forbidding Wrong in Islamic Thought* (2001). A masterful anaylsis of the development of Islamic law.

P. K. HITTI, *History of the Arabs*, 8th ed. (1964). Still a useful English resource, largely for factual detail. See especially Part IV, "The Arabs in Europe: Spain and Sicily."

A. HOURANI, *A History of the Arab Peoples* (1991). The newest survey history and the best, at least for the Arab Islamic world.

S. K. JAYYUSI, ed., *The Legacy of Muslim Spain*, 2 vols. (1994). A comprehensive survey of the arts, politics, literature, and society by experts in various fields.

B. LEWIS, ed., *Islam and the Arab World* (1976). A large-format, heavily illustrated volume with many excellent articles on diverse aspects of Islamic (not simply Arab, as the misleading title indicates) civilization through the premodern period.

D. MORGAN, *The Mongols* (1986). A recent and readable survey history.

J. J. SAUNDERS, *A History of Medieval Islam* (1965). A brief and simple, if sketchy, introductory survey of Islamic history to the Mongol invasions.

India

W. T. DE BARY et al., comp., *Sources of Indian Tradition*, 2nd ed. (1958), Vol. I, *From the Beginning to 1800*, ed. and rev. by Ainslie T. Embree (1988). Excellent selections from a wide variety of Indian texts, with good introductions to chapters and individual selections.

S. M. IKRAM, *Muslim Civilization in India* (1964). The best short survey history, covering the period 711 to 1857.

R. C. MAJUMDAR, gen. ed., *The History and Culture of the Indian People*, Vol. VI, *The Delhi Sultanate*, 3rd ed. (1980). A comprehensive political and cultural account of the period in India.

F. ROBINSON, ed., *The Cambridge History of India, Pakistan, Bangladesh, Sri Lanka, Nepal, Bhutan, and the Maldives* (1989). A very helpful quick reference source with brief but well-done survey essays on a wide range of topics relevant to South Asian history down to the present.

A. WINK, *Al-Hind: The Making of the Indo-Islamic World*, Vol. 1 (1991). The first of five promising volumes to be devoted to the Indo-Islamic world's history. This volume treats the seventh to eleventh centuries.

Southeast Asia

L. ANDAYA, *The World of Maluku: Eastern Indonesia in the Early Modern Period* (1993). A comprehensive view of the formation of what is now Indonesia.

B. W. ANDAYA AND L. ANDAYA, *A History of Malaysia* (1982). A good overiview of Indonesia's smaller but critical northern neighbor.

J. SIEGEL, *Shadow and Sound: The Historical Thought of a Sumatran People* (1979). An excellent analysis tracing the relation between foreign influences and local practice.

CHAPTER 14

B. S. BAUER, *The Development of the Inca State* (1992). An important new work that emphasizes archaeological evidence over the Spanish chronicles in accounting for the emergence of the Inca Empire.

F. F. BERDAN, *The Aztecs of Central Mexico: An Imperial Society* (1982). An excellent introduction to the Aztecs.

R. E. BLANTON, S. A. KOWALEWSKI, G. FEINMAN, AND J. APPEL, *Ancient Mesoamerica: A Comparison of Change in Three Regions* (1981). Concentrates on ancient Mexico.

K. O. BRUHNS, *Ancient South America* (1994). A clear discussion of the archaeology and civilization of the region with emphasis on the Andes.

R. L. BURGER, *Chavín and the Origins of Andean Civilization* (1992). A detailed study of early Andean prehistory by one of the leading authorities on Chavín.

R. M. CARMACK, J. GASCO, AND G. H. GOSSEN, *The Legacy of Mesoamerica: History and Culture of a Native American Civilization* (1996). A survey of Mesoamerica from its origins to the present.

I. CLENDINNEN, *Aztecs: An Interpretation* (1995). A fascinating attempt to reconstruct the Aztec world.

M. D. COE, *Breaking the Maya Code* (1992). The story of the remarkable achievement of deciphering the ancient Maya language.

M. D. COE, *The Maya* (1993). The best introduction.

M. D. COE, *Mexico from the Olmecs to the Aztecs* (1994). A wide-ranging introductory discussion.

G. CONRAD AND A. A. DEMAREST, *Religion and Empire: The Dynamics of Aztec and Inca Expansionism* (1984). An interesting comparative study.

S. D. GILLESPIE, *The Aztec Kings* (1989).

R. HASSIG, *Aztec Warfare.*

J. HYSLOP, *Inka Settlement Planning* (1990). A detailed study.

M. LEÓN-PORTILLA, *Fifteen Poets of the Aztec World* (1992). An anthology of translations of Aztec poetry.

M. E. MILLER, *The Art of Mesoamerica from Olmec to Aztec* (1986). A well-illustrated introduction,

C. MORRIS AND A. VON HAGEN, *The Inka Empire and Its Andean Origins* (1993). A clear overview of Andean prehistory by a leading authority. Beautifully illustrated.

M. E. MOSELY, *The Incas and Their Ancestors: The Archaeology of Peru* (1992). Readable and thorough.

J. A. SABLOFF, *The Cities of Ancient Mexico* (1989). Capsule summaries of ancient Mesoamerican cultures.

J. A. SABLOFF, *Archaeology and the Maya* (1990). A look at changing views of the ancient Maya.

L. SCHELE and M. E. MILLER, *The Blood of Kings* (1986). A rich and beautifully illustrated study of ancient Maya art and society.

R. S. SHARER, *The Ancient Maya*, 5th ed. (1994). A classic. Readable, authoritative, and thorough.

M. P. WEAVER, *The Aztecs, Maya, and Their Predecessors* (1993). A classic textbook.

CHAPTER 15

L. B. ALBERTI, *The Family in Renaissance Florence*, trans. by R. N. Watkins (1962). A contemporary humanist, who never married, explains how a family should behave.

E. AMT, ed., *Women's Lives in Medieval Europe: A Source-book* (1992). Outstanding collection of sources.

H. BARON, *The Crisis of the Early Italian Renaissance*, Vols. 1 and 2 (1996). New edition of an old, major work, setting forth the civic dimension of Italian humanism.

G. BARRACLOUGH, *The Origins of Modern Germany* (1963). Penetrating political narrative.

S. BRAMLY, *Discovering the Life of Leonard da Vinci* (1991). The man and the genius.

G. BRUCKER, *Renaissance Florence* (1983). Still one of the best introductions.

G. BULL, *Michelangelo: A Biography* (1995). Recent life in full.

J. BURCKHARDT, *The Civilization of the Renaissance in Italy* (1867). The famous classic that still has as many defenders as detractors.

S. FLANAGAN, *Hildegard of Bingen, 1098–1179: A Visionary Life* (1995). A most interesting German woman.

E. HALLAM, ed., *Chronicles of the Crusades (1989).* All nine!

D. HERLIHY, *Medieval Households* (1985). Survey of Middle Ages that defends the medieval family against modern caricatures.

D. HERLIHY AND C. KLAPISCH-ZUBER, *Tuscans and Their Families* (1985). Important work based on unique demographic data that gives the reader an appreciation of quantitative history.

G. HOLMES, *Renaissance* (1996). An expert's take on the subject.

J. C. HOLT, *Magna Carta*, 2nd ed. (1992). The famous document and its interpretation by succeeding generations.

J. HUIZINGA, *The Waning of the Middle Ages: A Study of the Forms of Life, Thought, and Art in France and the Netherlands in the Dawn of the Renaissance* (1924). A classic study of "mentality" at the end of the Middle Ages.

L. JARDINE, *Worldly Goods: A New History of the Renaissance* (1996). The material side of the Renaissance.

M. KING, *Women of the Renaissance* (1991). Women's presence and creativity.

W. H. MCNEILL, *Plagues and Peoples* (1976). The Black Death in a broader context.

R. I. MOORE, *The Formation of a Persecuting Society: Power and Deviance in Western Europe, 950–1250* (1987). A sympathetic look at heresy and dissent.

T. NOONAN, *Contraception: A History of Its Treatment by the Catholic Theologians and Canonists* (1967). A fascinating account of medieval theological attitudes toward sexuality and sex-related problems.

J. RILEY-SMITH, ed., *Oxford Illustrated History of the Crusades* (1995) Lucid, gorgeous, and up-to-date.

J. WEISHEIPL, *Friar Thomas* (1980). Biography of Saint Thomas Aquinas, both the man and the theologian.

CHAPTER 16

M. BRECHT, *Martin Luther: His Road to Reformation, 1483–1521* (1985). Best on young Luther.

C. BROWN, et al., *Rembrandt: The Master and His Workshop* (1991) A great master's art and influence.

R. BRIGGS, *Witches and Neighbors: A History of European Witchcraft* (1996). A readable introduction.

E. DUFFY, *The Stripping of the Altars* (1992). Strongest argument yet that there was no deep reformation in England.

H. O. EVENNETT, *The Spirit of the Counter Reformation* (1968). The continuity and independence of Catholic reform.

HANS-JÜRGEN GOERTZ, *The Anabaptists* (1996). Best treatment of minority Protestants.

O. P. GRELL AND A. CUNNINGHAM, *Health Care and Poor Relief in Protestant Europe* (1997) The civic side of the Reformation.

M. HOLT, *The French Wars of Religion, 1562–1629* (1995). Scholarly appreciation of religious side of the story.

J. C. HUTCHISON, *Albrecht Durer* (1990). The life behind the art.

H. JEDIN, *A History of the Council of Trent*, Vols. 1, 2 (1957–1961). Comprehensive, detailed, and authoritative.

M. KITCHEN, *The Cambridge Illustrated History of Germany* (1996). Comprehensive and accessible.

A. KORS AND E. PETERS, eds., *European Witchcraft, 1100–1700* (1972). Classics of witch belief.

W. MACCAFFREY, *Elizabeth I* (1993). Magisterial study.

G. MATTINGLY, *The Armada* (1959). A masterpiece, novel-like in style.

D. MCCOLLOCH, *The Reformation* (2004). No stone unturned, with English emphasis.

H. A. OBERMAN, *Luther: Man Between God and Devil* (1989). Authoritative biography

J. W. O'MALLEY, *The First Jesuits* (1993). Extremely detailed account of the creation of the Society of Jesus and its original purposes.

S. OZMENT, *The Age of Reform 1250–1550: An Intellectual and Religious History of Late Medieval and Reformation Europe* (1980). Broad, lucid survey.

S. OZMENT, *When Fathers Ruled: Family Life in Reformation Europe* (1983). Effort to portray the constructive side of Protestant thinking about family relationships.

S. OZMENT, *The Bürgermeister's Daughter: Scandal in a Sixteenth Century German Town* (1996). What a woman could do at law in the sixteenth century.

G. PARKER, *The Thirty Years' War* (1984). Large, lucid survey.

J. H. PARRY, *The Age of Reconnaissance* (1964). A comprehensive account of explorations from 1450 to 1650.

W. PRINZ, *Durer* (1998). Latest biography of Germany's greatest painter.

J. J. SCARISBRICK, *Henry VIII* (1968). The best account of Henry's reign.

G. STRAUSS, ed. and trans., *Manifestations of Discontent in Germany on the Eve of the Reformation* (1971). A rich collection of sources for both rural and urban scenes.

H. WUNDER, *He Is the Sun, She Is the Moon: Women in Early Modern Germany* (1998). Best study of early modern women.

CHAPTER 17

J. ABUN-NASR, *A History of the Maghrib in the Islamic Period* (1987). The most recent North African survey. Pages 59–247 are relevant to this chapter.

D. BIRMINHAM, *Central Africa to 1870* (1981). Chapters from the *Cambridge History of Africa* that give a brief, lucid overview of developments in this region.

P. BOHANNAN AND P. CURTIN, *Africa and Africans*, rev. ed. (1971). Accessible, topical approach to African history, culture, society, politics, and economics.

P. D. CURTIN, S. FEIERMANN, L. THOMPSON, AND J. VANSINA, *African History* (1978). An older, but masterly survey. The relevant portions are Chapters 6–9.

R. ELPHICK, *Kraal and Castle: Khoikhoi and the Founding of White South Africa* (1977). An incisive, informative interpretation of the history of the Khoikhoi and their fateful interaction with European colonization.

R. ELPHICK AND H. GILIOMEE, *The Shaping of South African Society, 1652–1820* (1979). A superb, synthetic history of this crucial period.

J. D. FAGE, *A History of Africa* (1978). Still a readable survey history.

M. HISKETT, *The Development of Islam in West Africa* (1984). The standard survey study of the subject. Of the relevant sections (Chapters 1–10, 12, 15), that on Hausaland, which is treated only in passing in this text, is noteworthy.

R. W. JULY, *Precolonial Africa: An Economic and Social History* (1975). Chapter 10 gives an interesting overall picture of slaving in African history.

R. W. JULY, *A History of the African People*, 3rd ed. (1980). Chapters 3–6 treat Africa before about 1800 area by area; Chapter 7 deals with "The Coming of Europe."

I. M. LEWIS, Ed., *Islam in Tropical Africa* (1966), pp. 4–96. Lewis's introduction is one of the best brief summaries of the role of Islam in West Africa and the Sudan.

D. T. NIANI, ed., *Africa from the Twelfth to the Sixteenth Century, UNESCO General History of Africa*, Vol. IV (1984). Many survey articles cover the various regions and major states of Africa in the centuries noted in the title.

R. OLIVER, *The African Experience* (1991). A masterly, balanced, and engaging survey, with outstanding syntheses and summaries of recent research.

J. A. RAWLEY, *The Transatlantic Slave Trade: A History* (1981). Impressively documented, detailed, and well-presented survey history of the Atlantic trade; little focus on African dimensions.

A. F. C. RYDER, *Benin and the Europeans: 1485–1897* (1969). A basic study.

JOHN K. THORNTON, *The Kingdom of Kongo: Civil War and Transition, 1641–1718* (1983). A detailed and perceptive analysis for those who wish to delve into Kongo state and society in the seventeenth century.

M. WILSON AND L. THOMPSON, eds., *The Oxford History of South Africa*, Vol. I., *South Africa to 1870* (1969). Relatively detailed, if occasionally dated, treatment.

CHAPTER 18

I. BERLIN, *Many Thousands Gone: The First Two Centuries of Slavery in North America* (1998); *Generations of Captivity: A History of African American Slaves* (2003). Two volumes representing the most extensive and important recent treatment of slavery in North America.

R. BLACKBURN, *The Making of New World Slavery from the Baroque to the Modern 1492–1800* (1997). An extraordinary work.

B. COBO, *History of the Inca Empire* (1979). A major discussion.

N. D. COOK, *Born to Die: Disease and New World Conquest, 1492–1650* (1998) A survey of the devastating impact of previously unknown diseases on the native populations of the Americas.

P. D. CURTIN, *The Atlantic Slave Trade: A Census* (1969). Remains a basic work.

D. B. DAVIS, *The Problem of Slavery in Western Culture* (1966). A brilliant and far-ranging discussion.

H. L. GATES JR. AND W. L. ANDREWS, eds., *Pioneers of the Black Atlantic: Five Slave Narratives from the Enlightenment 1772–1815* (1998). An anthology of autobiographical accounts.

S. GRUZINSKI, *The Conquest of Mexico: The Incorporation of Indian Societies into the Western World, 16th–18th Centuries* (1993). Interprets the experience of Native Americans, from their own point of view, during the time of the Spanish conquest.

L. HANKE, *Bartolomé de Las Casas: An Interpretation of His Life and Writings* (1951). A classic work.

R. HARMS, *The Diligent: A Voyage through the Worlds of the Slave Trade* (2002). A powerful narrative of the voyage of a French slave trader.

J. HEMMING, *The Conquest of the Incas,* (1970). A lucid account of the conquest of the Inca Empire and its aftermath.

J. HEMMING, *Red Gold: The Conquest of the Brazilian Native Americans, 1500–1760* (1978). A careful account with excellent bibliography.

H. KLEIN, *The Middle Passage: Comparative Studies in the African Slave Trade* (1978). A far-ranging overview of the movement of slaves from Africa to the Americas.

M. LEON-PORTILLA, ed., *The Broken Spears: The Aztec Account of the Conquest of Mexico* (1961). A collection of documents recounting the experience of the Aztecs from their own point of view.

P. MANNING, *Slavery and African Life: Occidental, Oriental, and African Slave Trades* (1990). An admirably concise economic-historical synthesis of the evidence, with multiple tables and statistics to supplement the magisterial analysis.

A. PAGDEN, *Lords of All the World: Ideologies of Empire in Spain, Britain, and France* c. 1500–c. 1800 (1995). An effort to explain the imperial thinking of the major European powers.

S. B. SCHWARTZ, *Sugar Plantations in the Formation of Brazilian Society: Bahia, 1550–1835* (1985). A broad-ranging study of the emergence of the plantation economy.

I. K. STEELE, *The English Atlantic, 1675–1740s: An Exploration of Communication and Community* (1986). An exploration of culture and commerce in the transatlantic world.

S. J. STEIN, *Peru's Indian Peoples and the Challenge of Spanish Conquest: Huamanga to 1640* (1983). A work that examines the impact of the conquest of the Inca empire over the scope of a century.

H. THOMAS, *Conquest: Montezuma, Cortés, and the Fall of Old Mexico* (1993). A splendid modern narrative of the event with careful attention to the character of the participants.

H. THOMAS, *The Slave Trade: The Story of the Atlantic Slave Trade: 1440–1870* (1999). A sweeping narrative overview.

J. THORNTON, *Africa and Africans in the Making of the Atlantic World, 1400–1680* (1992). A discussion of the role of Africans in the emergence of the transatlantic economy.

N. WACHTEL, *The Vision of the Vanquished: The Spanish Conquest of Peru Through Indian Eyes, 1530–1570* (1977). A presentation of Incan experience of conquest.

CHAPTER 19

China

D. BODDE AND C. MORRIS, *Law in Imperial China* (1967). Focuses on the Qing dynasty (1644–1911).

T. BROOK, *The Confusions of Pleasure: Commerce and Culture in Ming China* (1988).

C. S. CHANG AND S. L. H. CHANG, *Crisis and Transformation in Seventeenth Century China: Society, Culture, and Modernity* (1992).

P. CROSSLEY, *Translucent Mirror: History and Identity in Qing Imperial Ideology* (1999).

W. T. DE BARY, *Learning for One's Self: Essays on the Individual in Neo-Confucian Thought* (1991). A useful corrective to the view that Confucianism is simply a social ideology.

M. C. ELLIOTT, *The Manchu Way: The Eight Banners and Ethnic Identity in Late Imperial China* (2001). The latest word; compare to Crossley above.

M. ELVIN, *The Pattern of the Chinese Past: A Social and Economic Interpretation* (1973). A controversial but stimulating interpretation of Chinese economic history in terms of technology. It brings in earlier periods as well as the Ming, Qing, and modern China.

J. K. FAIRBANK, ed., *The Chinese World Order: Traditional China's Foreign Relations* (1968). An examination of the Chinese tribute system and its varying applications.

H. L. KAHN, *Monarchy in the Emperor's Eyes: Image and Reality in the Ch'ien-lung Reign* (1971). A study of the Chinese court during the mid-Qing period.

P. KUHN, *Soulstealers: The Chinese Sorcery Scare of 1768* (1990).

LI YU, *The Carnal Prayer Mat*, trans. by P. Hanan (1990).

F. MOTE AND D. TWITCHETT, eds., *The Cambridge History of China: The Ming Dynasty 1368–1644*, Vols. VI (1988) and VII (1998).

S. NAQUIN, *Peking Temples and City Life, 1400–1900* (2000).

S. NAQUIN AND E. S. RAWSKI, *Chinese Society in the Eighteenth Century* (1987).

J. B. PARSONS, *The Peasant Rebellions of the Late Ming Dynasty* (1970).

P. C. PERDUE, *Exhausting the Earth, State and Peasant in Hunan, 1500–1850* (1987).

D. H. PERKINS, *Agricultural Development in China, 1368–1968* (1969).

E. RAWSKI, *The Last Emperors: A Social History of Qing Imperial Institutions* (1998).

M. RICCI, *China in the Sixteenth Century: The Journals of Matthew Ricci, 1583–1610* (1953).

W. ROWE, *Hankow* (1984). A study of a city in late imperial China.

G. W. SKINNER, *The City in Late Imperial China* (1977).

J. D. SPENCE, *Ts'ao Yin and the K'ang-hsi Emperor: Bondservant and Master* (1966). An excellent study of the early Qing court.

J. D. SPENCE, *Emperor of China: A Self-Portrait of K'ang-hsi* (1974). The title of this readable book does not adequately convey the extent of the author's contribution to the study of the early Qing emperor.

J. D. SPENCE, *Treason by the Book* (2001). An account of the legal workings of the authoritarian Qing state that reads like a detective story.

L. A. STRUVE, trans. and ed., *Voices from the Ming-Qing Cataclysm* (1993). A reader with translations of Chinese sources.

F. WAKEMAN, *The Great Enterprise* (1985). On the founding of the Manchu dynasty.

Japan

M. E. BERRY, *Hideyoshi* (1982). A study of the sixteenth-century unifier of Japan.

M. E. BERRY, *The Culture of Civil War in Kyoto* (1994). On the Warring States era.

H. BOLITHO, *Treasures Among Men: The Fudai Daimyo in Tokugawa Japan* (1974). A study in depth.

H. BOLITHO, *Bereavement and Consolation: Testimonies from Tokugawa Japan* (2003). Instances of how Tokugawa Japanese handled the death of a child.

C. R. BOXER, *The Christian Century in Japan, 1549–1650* (1951).

The Cambridge History of Japan; Vol. 4 J.W. Hall (ed.), *Early Modern Japan* (1991). A multi-author work.

M. CHIKAMATSU, *Major Plays of Chikamatsu*, trans. by D. Keene (1961).

R. P. DORE, *Education in Tokugawa Japan* (1965).

G. S. ELISON, *Deus Destroyed: The Image of Christianity in Early Modern Japan* (1973). A brilliant study of the persecutions of Christianity during the early Tokugawa period.

J. W. HALL AND M. JANSEN, eds., *Studies in the Institutional History of Early Modern Japan* (1968). A collection of articles on Tokugawa institutions.

J. W. HALL, K. NAGAHARA, AND K. YAMAMURA, eds., *Japan Before Tokugawa* (1981).

S. HANLEY, *Everyday Things in Premodern Japan: The Hidden Legacy of Material Culture* (1997).

H. S. HIBBETT, *The Floating World in Japanese Fiction* (1959). An eminently readable study of early Tokugawa literature.

M. JANSEN, ed., *The Nineteenth Century*, Vol. 5 in *The Cambridge History of Japan* (1989).

K. KATSU, *Musui's Story* (1988). The life and adventures of a boisterous, no-good samurai of the early nineteenth century. Eminently readable.

D. KEENE, trans., *Chushingura, the Treasury of Loyal Retainers* (1971). The puppet play about the forty-seven rōnin who took revenge on the enemy of their former lord.

O.G. LIDIN, *Tanegashima: The Arrival of Europe in Japan* (2002). The impact of the musket and Europeans on sixteenth-century Japan.

M. MARUYAMA, *Studies in the Intellectual History of Tokugawa Japan*, trans. by M. Hane (1974). A seminal work in this field by one of modern Japan's greatest scholars.

J.L. MCCLAIN, et. al., *Edo and Paris: Urban Life and the State in the Early Modern Era* (1994). Comparison of city life and government role in capitals of Tokugawa Japan and France.

K. W. NAKAI, *Shogunal Politics* (1988). A brilliant study of Arai Hakuseki's conceptualization of Tokugawa government.

P. NOSCO, ed., *Confucianism and Tokugawa Culture* (1984). A lively collection of essays.

H. OOMS, *Tokugawa Village Practice: Class, Status, Power, Law* (1996).

A. RAVINA, *Land and Lordship in Early Modern Japan* (1999). A sociopolitical study of three Tokugawa domains.

I. SAIKAKU, *The Japanese Family Storehouse*, trans. by G. W. Sargent (1959). A lively novel about merchant life in seventeenth-century Japan.

G. B. SANSOM, *The Western World and Japan* (1950).

J. A. SAWADA, *Confucian Values and Popular Zen* (1993). A study of *Shingaku*, a popular Tokugawa religious sect.

C. D. SHELDON, *The Rise of the Merchant Class in Tokugawa Japan* (1958).

T. C. SMITH, *The Agrarian Origins of Modern Japan* (1959). On the evolution of farming and rural social organization in Tokugawa Japan.

P. F. SOUYRI, *The World Turned Upside Down: Medieval Japanese Society* (2001). After a running start from the late Heian period, an analysis of the overthrow of lords by their vassals.

R. P. TOBY, *State and Diplomacy in Early Modern Japan: Asia in the Development of the Tokugawa Bakufu* (1984).

C. TOTMAN, *Tokugawa Ieyasu: Shōgun* (1983).

C. TOTMAN, *Green Archipelago, Forestry in Preindustrial Japan* (1989).

H. P. VARLEY, *The Ō'nin War: History of Its Origins and Background with a Selective Translation of the Chronicle of Ō'nin* (1967).

K. YAMAMURA AND S. B. HANLEY, *Economic and Demographic Change in Preindustrial Japan, 1600–1868* (1977).

Korea

T. HATADA, *A History of Korea* (1969).

W. E. HENTHORN, *A History of Korea* (1971).

KI-BAIK LEE, *A New History of Korea* (1984).

P. LEE, *Sourcebook of Korean Civilization*, Vol. I (1993).

Vietnam

J. BUTTINGER, *A Dragon Defiant, a Short History of Vietnam* (1972).

NGUYEN DU, *The Tale of Kieu* (1983).

N. TARLING, ed., *The Cambridge History of Southeast Asia* (1992).

K. TAYLOR, *The Birth of Vietnam* (1983).

A. B. WOODSIDE, *Vietnam and the Chinese Model* (1988).

CHAPTER 20

F. ANDERSON, *The Crucible of War: The Seven Years' War and the Fate of Empire in British North America, 1754–1766* (2000) A splendid narrative and analysis.

J. BLUM, *Lord and Peasant in Russia from the Ninth to the Nineteenth Century* (1961). Remains a thorough and wide-ranging discussion.

P. BURKE, *The Fabrication of Louis XIV* (1992). Examines the manner in which the public image of Louis XIV was forged in art.

P. BUSHKOVITCH, *Peter the Great: The Struggle for Power, 1671–1725* (2001). Replaces previous studies.

L. COLLEY, *Britons: Forging the Nation, 1707–1837* (1992) A major study of the making of British nationhood.

P. DEANE, *The First Industrial Revolution,* (1999). A well-balanced and systematic treatment.

J. DE VRIES, *European Urbanization 1500–1800* (1984). The most important and far-ranging of recent treatments of the subject.

W. Doyle, *The Old European Order, 1660–1800* (1992). The most thoughtful treatment of the subject.

R. J. W. Evans, *The Making of the Habsburg Monarchy, 1550–1700: An Interpretation* (1979). Places much emphasis on intellectual factors and the role of religion.

D. Fraser, *Frederick the Great: King of Prussia* (2001) Excellent on both Frederick and eighteenth-century Prussia.

E. Hobsbawm, *Industry and Empire: The Birth of the Industrial Revolution* (1999). A survey by a major historian of the subject.

K. Honeyman, *Women, Gender and Industrialization in England, 1700–1850* (2000). Emphasizes how certain work or economic roles became associated with either men or women.

O. H. Hufton, *The Poor of Eighteenth-Century France, 1750–1789* (1975). A brilliant study of poverty and the family economy.

L. Hughes, *Russia in the Age of Peter the Great* (1998). An excellent account.

D. I. Kertzer and M. Barbagli, *The History of the European Family: Family Life in Early Modern Times, 1500–1709* (2001). A series of broad-ranging essays covering the entire Continent.

S. King and G. Timmons, *Making Sense of the Industrial Revolution: English Economy and Society, 1700–1850* (2001). Examines the Industrial Revolution through the social institutions that brought it about and were changed by it.

M. Kishlansky, *A Monarchy Transformed: Britain 1603–1714* (1996) An excellent synthesis.

P. Langford, *A Polite and Commercial People: England 1717–1783* (1989). An excellent survey of mid-eighteenth-century Britain covering social history as well as politics, the overseas wars, and the American Revolution.

A. Lossky, *Louis XIV and the French Monarchy* (1994). The most recent major analysis.

F. E. Manuel, *The Broken Staff: Judaism Through Christian Eyes* (1992). An important discussion of Christian interpretations of Judaism.

M. A. Meyer, *The Origins of the Modern Jew: Jewish Identity and European Culture in Germany, 1749–1824* (1967). A general introduction organized around individual case studies.

D. Underdown, *Fire from Heaven: Life in an English Town in the Seventeenth Century* (1992). A lively account of how a single English town experienced the religious and political turmoil of the century.

D. Valenze, *The First Industrial Woman* (1995). An elegant work exploring the manner in which industrialization transformed the work of women.

J. West, *Gunpower, Government, and War in the Mid–Eighteenth Century* (1991). A study of how warfare touched much government of the day.

CHAPTER 21

S. S. Blair and J. Bloom, *The Art and Architecture of Islam, 1250–1800* (1994). A fine survey of the period for all parts of the Islamic world.

R. Canfield, ed., *Turko-Persia in Historical Perspctive* (1991). A good general collection of essays.

K. Chelebi, *The Balance of Truth* (1957). A marvelous volume of essays and reflections by probably the major intellectual of Ottoman times.

W. T. de Bary et al., comp., *Sources of Indian Tradition*, 2nd ed. (1958), Vol. I, *From the Beginning to 1800*, ed. and rev. by Ainslie T. Embree (1988). Excellent selections from a wide variety of Indian texts, with good introductions to chapters and individual selections.

S. Faroqi, *Towns and Townsmen of Ottoman Anatolia* (1984). Examines the changing balances of economic power between the urban and rural areas.

C. H. Fleischer, *Bureaucrat and Intellectual in the Ottoman Empire: The Historian Mustafa Ali (1541–1600)* (1986). A major study of Ottoman intellectual history.

G. Hambly, *Central Asia* (1966). Excellent survey chapters (9–13) on the Chaghatay and Uzbek (Shaybanid) Turks.

R. S. Hattox, *Coffee and Coffee-Houses: The Origins of a Social Beverage in the Medieval Near East* (1985). A fascinating piece of social history.

M. G. S. Hodgson, *The Gunpowder Empires and Modern Times*, Vol. 3 of *The Venture of Islam*, 3 vols. (1974). Less ample than Vols. 1 and 2 of Hodgson's monumental history, but a thoughtful survey of the great post-1500 empires.

S. M. Ikram, *Muslim Civilization in India* (1964). Still the best short survey history, covering the period from 711 to 1857.

H. Inalcik, *The Ottoman Empire: The Classical Age 1300–1600* (1973). An excellent, if dated, survey with solid treatment of Ottoman social, religious, and political institutions.

H. Inalcik, *An Economic and Social History of the Ottoman Empire, 1300–1914* (1994). A masterly survey by the dean of Ottoman studies today.

C. Kafadar, *Between Two Worlds: The Construction of the Ottoman State* (1995). A readable analysis of theories of Ottoman origins and early development.

N. R. Keddie, ed., *Scholars, Saints, and Sufis: Muslim Religious Institutions in the Middle East Since 1500* (1972). A collection of interesting articles well worth reading.

M. Mujeeb, *The Indian Muslims* (1967). The best cultural study of Islamic civilization in India as a whole, from its origins onward.

G. Necipoglu, *Architecture, Ceremonial, and Power: The Topkapi Palace in the Fifteenth and Sixteenth Centuries* (1991). A superb analysis of the symbolism of Ottoman power and authority.

L. Pierce, *The Imperial Harem: Women and Sex in the Ottoman Empire* (1993). Ground-breaking study on the role of women in the Ottoman Empire.

D. Quatarert, *An Economic and Social history of the Ottoman Empire 1300–1914* (1994). The authoritative account of Ottoman economy and society.

J. Richards, *The Mughal Empire*, Vol. 5 of *The New Cambridge History of India* (1993). A impressive synthesis of the varying interpretations of the Mughal India.

S. A. A. Rizvi, *The Wonder That Was India*, Vol. II (1987). A sequel to Basham's original *The Wonder That Was India*; treats Mughal life, culture, and history from 1200 to 1700.

F. Robinson, *Atlas of the Islamic World Since 1500* (1982). Brief, excellent historical essays, color illustrations with detailed accompanying text, and chronological tables, as well as precise maps, make this a refreshing general reference work.

R. Savory, *Iran Under the Safavids* (1980). A solid and readable survey.

S. J. Shaw, *Empire of the Gazis: The Rise and Decline of the Ottoman Empire, 1280–1808*, Vol. I of *History of the Ottoman Empire and Modern Turkey* (1976). A solid historical survey with excellent bibliographic essays for each chapter and a good index.

CHAPTER 22

D. BEALES, *Joseph II: In the Shadow of Maria Theresa, 1741–1780* (1987). The best treatment in English of the early political life of Joseph II.

M. BIAGIOLI, *Galileo Courtier: The Practice of Science in the Culture of Absolutism* (1993). A major revisionist work that emphasizes the role of the political setting on Galileo's career and thought.

D. D. BIEN, *The Calas Affair: Persecution, Toleration, and Heresy in Eighteenth-Century Toulouse* (1960). Classic treatment of the famous case.

T. C. W. BLANNING, *The Culture of Power and the Power of Culture: Old Regime Europe 1660–l789* (2002). The strongest treatment of the relationship of eighteenth-century cultural changes and politics.

R. DARNTON, *The Literary Underground of the Old Regime* (1982). Classic essays on the world of printers, publishers, and booksellers.

P. DEAR, *Revolutionizing the Sciences: European Knowledge and Its Ambitions, 1500–1700* (2001). A broad-ranging study of both the ideas and institutions of the new science.

I. DE MADARIAGA, *Catherine the Great: A Short History* (1990). A good brief biography.

S. GAUKROGER, *Francis Bacon and the Transformation of Early-Modern Philosophy* (2001). An excellent, accessible introduction.

J. GLEIXK, *Isaac Newton* (2003) The best brief biography.

D. GOODMAN, *The Republic of Letters: A Cultural History of the French Enlightenment* (1994). Concentrates on the role of salons.

I. HARRIS, *The Mind of John Locke: A Study of Political Theory in Its Intellectual Setting* (1994). The most comprehensive recent treatment.

J. L. HEILBRON, *The Sun in the Church: Cathedrals as Solar Observatories* (2000). A remarkable study of the manner in which Roman Catholic cathedrals were used to make astsronomical observations and calculations.

K. J. HOWELL, *God's TwoBooks: Copernican Cosmology and Biblical Interpretqation in Early Modern Science* (2003) Best introduction to early modern issues of science and religion.

J. MELTON, *The Rise of the Public in Enlightenmen Europe* (2001). A superb overview of the emergence of new institutions which made the expression of a broad public opinion possible in Europe.

T. MUNCK, *The Enlightenment: A Comparative Social History 1721–1794* (2000). A clear introduction to the social background making possible the spread of Enlightenment thought.

S. MUTHU, *Enlightenment against Empire* (2003) A study of philosophes who criticized the European empires of their day.

D. OUTRAM, *The Enlightenment* (1995). An excellent brief introduction.

R. PORTER, *The Creation of the Modern World: The Untold Story of the British Enlightenment* (2001) A superb, lively overview.

P. RILEY, *The Cambridge Companion to Rousseau* (2001). Excellent accessible essays by major scholars.

E. ROTHCHILD, *Economic Sentiments: Adam Smith, Condorcet, and the Enlightenment* (2001). A sensitive account of Smith's thought and its relationship to the social questions of the day.

S. SHAPIN, *The Scientific Revolution* (1996). An important revisionist survey emphasizing social factors.

L. STEINBRÜGGE, *The Moral Sex: Woman's Nature in the French Enlightenment* (1995). Emphasizes the conservative nature of Enlightenment thought on women.

P. ZAGORIN, *How the Idea of Religious Toleration Came to the West* (2003) An excellent exploration of the rise of toleration.

CHAPTER 23

R. ANSTEY, *The Atlantic Slave Trade and British Abolition, 1760–1810* (1975). A standard overview that emphasizes the role of religious factors.

B. BAILYN, *The Ideological Origins of the American Revolution* (1967). An important work illustrating the role of English radical thought in the perceptions of the American colonists.

K. M. BAKER, *Inventing the French Revolution: Essays on French Political Culture in the Eighteenth Century* (1990). Important essays on political thought before and during the revolution.

K. M. BAKER AND C. LUCAS, eds., *The French Revolution and the Creation of Modern Political Culture*, 3 vols. (1987). A splendid collection of important original articles on all aspects of politics during the revolution.

R. J. BARMAN, *Brazil: The Forging of a Nation, 1798–1852* (1988). The best coverage of this period.

C. BECKER, *The Declaration of Independence: A Study in the History of Political Ideas* (1922). Remains an important examination of the political and imperial theory of the Declaration.

J. F. BERNARD, *Talleyrand: A Biography* (1973). A useful account.

L. BETHELL, *The Cambridge History of Latin America*, Vol. 3 (1985). Contains an extensive treatment of independence.

R. BLACKBURN, *The Overthrow of Colonial Slavery, 1776–1848* (1988). A major discussion quite skeptical of the humanitarian interpretation.

T. C. W. BLANNING, ed., *The Rise and Fall of the French Revolution* (1996). A wide-ranging collection of essays illustrating the debates over the French Revolution.

J. BROOKE, *King George III* (1972). The best biography.

R. COBB, *The People's Armies* (1987). The major treatment in English of the revolutionary army.

O. CONNELLY, *Napoleon's Satellite Kingdoms* (1965). The rule of Napoleon and his family in Europe.

E. V. DA COSTA, *The Brazilian Empire* (1985). Excellent coverage of the entire nineteenth-century experience of Brazil.

D. B. DAVIS, *The Problem of Slavery in the Age of Revolution, 1770–1823* (1975). A transatlantic perspective on the issue.

F. FEHÉR, *The French Revolution and the Birth of Modernity* (1990). A wide-ranging collection of essays on political and cultural facets of the revolution.

A. FORREST, *The French Revolution and the Poor* (1981). A study that expands consideration of the revolution beyond the standard social boundaries.

M. GLOVER, *The Peninsular War, 1807–1814: A Concise Military History* (1974). An interesting account of the military campaign that so drained Napoleon's resources in western Europe.

J. GODECHOT, *The Counter-Revolution: Doctrine and Action, 1789–1804* (1971). An examination of opposition to the revolution.

A. GOODWIN, *The Friends of Liberty: The English Democratic Movement in the Age of the French Revolution* (1979). A major work that explores the impact of the French Revolution on English radicalism.

L. HUNT, *Politics, Culture, and Class in the French Revolution* (1986). A series of essays that focus on the modes of expression of the revolutionary values and political ideas.

W. W. KAUFMANN, *British Policy and the Independence of Latin America, 1802–1828* (1951). A standard discussion of an important relationship.

E. KENNEDY, *A Cultural History of the French Revolution* (1989). An important examination of the role of the arts, schools, clubs, and intellectual institutions.

M. KENNEDY, *The Jacobin Clubs in the French Revolution: The First Years* (1982). A careful scrutiny of the organizations chiefly responsible for the radicalizing of the revolution.

M. KENNEDY, *The Jacobin Clubs in the French Revolution: The Middle Years* (1988). A continuation of the previously listed study.

H. KISSINGER, *A World Restored: Metternich, Castlereagh and the Problems of Peace, 1812–1822* (1957). A provocative study by an author who became an American secretary of state.

G. LEFEBVRE, *The Coming of the French Revolution* (trans. 1947). A classic examination of the crisis of the French monarchy and the events of 1789.

G. LEFEBVRE, *Napoleon*, 2 vols., trans. by H. Stockhold (1969). The fullest and finest biography.

J. LYNCH, *The Spanish American Revolutions, 1808–1826* (1986). An excellent one-volume treatment.

P. MAIER, *American Scripture: Making the Declaration of Independence* (1997). Stands as a major revision of our understanding of the Declaration.

G. MASUR, *Simón Bolívar* (1969). The standard biography in English.

S. E. MELZER AND L. W. RABINE, eds., *Rebel Daughters: Women and the French Revolution* (1992). A collection of essays exploring various aspects of the role and image of women in the French Revolution.

M. MORRIS, *The British Monarchy and the French Revolution* (1998). Explores the manner in which the British monarchy saved itself from possible revolution.

R. MUIR, *Tactics and the Experience of Battle in the Age of Napoleon* (1998). Examines the wars from the standpoint of the soldiers in combat.

H. NICOLSON, *The Congress of Vienna* (1946). A good, readable account.

T. O. OTT, *The Haitian Revolution, 1789–1804* (1973). An account that clearly relates the events in Haiti to those in France.

R. R. PALMER, *Twelve Who Ruled: The Committee of Public Safety During the Terror* (1941). A clear narrative and analysis of the policies and problems of the committee.

R. R. PALMER, *The Age of the Democratic Revolution: A Political History of Europe and America, 1760–1800*, 2 vols. (1959, 1964). An impressive survey of the political turmoil in the transatlantic world.

C. PROCTOR, *Women, Equality, and the French Revolution* (1990). An examination of how the ideas of the Enlightenment and the attitudes of revolutionaries affected the legal status of women.

A. J. RUSSELL-WOOD, ed., *From Colony to Nation: Essays on the Independence of Brazil* (1975). A series of important essays.

P. SCHROEDER, *The Transformation of European Politics, 1763–1848* (1994). A fundamental treatment of the diplomacy of the era.

T. E. SKIDMORE AND P. H. SMITH, *Modern Latin America*, 4th ed. (1997). A very useful survey.

A. SOBOUL, *The Parisian Sans-Culottes and the French Revolution, 1793–94* (1964). The best work on the subject.

A. SOBOUL, *The French Revolution* (trans. 1975). An important work by a Marxist scholar.

D. G. SUTHERLAND, *France, 1789–1825: Revolution and Counterrevolution* (1986). A major synthesis based on recent scholarship in social history.

T. TACKETT, *Religion, Revolution, and Regional Culture in Eighteenth-Century France: The Ecclesiastical Oath of 1791* (1986). The most important study of this topic.

T. TACKETT, *Becoming a Revolutionary: The Deputies of the French National Assembly and the Emergence of a Revolutionary Culture (1789–1790)* (1996). The best study of the early months of the revolution.

J. M. THOMPSON, *Robespierre*, 2 vols. (1935). The best biography.

D. K. VAN KEY, *The Religious Origins of the French Revolution: From Calvin to the Civil Constitution, 1560–1791* (1996). Examines the manner in which debates within French Catholicism influenced the coming of the revolution.

M. WALZER, ed., *Regicide and Revolution: Speeches at the Trial of Louis XVI* (1974). An important and exceedingly interesting collection of documents with a useful introduction.

I. WOLOCH, *The New Regime: Transformations of the French Civic Order, 1789–1820s* (1994). An important overview of just what had and had not changed in France after the quarter century of revolution and war.

G. WOOD, *The Radicalism of the American Revolution* (1991). A major interpretation.

CHAPTER 24

I. BERLIN, *Generations of Captivity: A History of African-American Slaves* (2003) A major work.

D. BLACKBOURN, *The Long Nineteenth Century: A History of Germany, 1780–1918* (1998). An outstanding survey.

D. G. CREIGHTON, *John A. MacDonald* (1952, 1955). A major biography of the first Canadian prime minister.

D. DONALD, *Lincoln* (1995). Now the standard biography.

R. B. EDGERTON, *Death or Glory: The Legacy of the Crimean War* (2000). Multifaceted study of a badly mismanaged war that transformed many aspects of European domestic politics.

M. HOLT, *The Rise and Fall of the American Whig Party: Jacksonian Politics and the Onset of the Civil War* (2003) An extensive survey of the Jacksonian era.

R. KEE, *The Green Flag: A History of Irish Nationalism* (2001). A vast survey.

W. LACQUER, *A History of Zionism* (1989). The most extensive one-volume treatment.

M. B. LEVINGER, *Enlightened Nationalism: The Transformation of Prussian Political Culture, 1806–1848* (2002). A major work based on the most recent scholarship.

J. M. McPHERSON, *The Battle Cry of Freedom: The Civil War Era* (1988). An excellent one-volume treatment.

D. MORTON, *A Short History of Canada* (2001). Useful popular history.

J. P. PARRY, *The Rise and Fall of Liberal Government in Victorian Britain* (1994). An outstanding study.

A. PLESSIS, *The Rise and Fall of the Second Empire, 1852–1871* (1985). A useful survey of France under Napoleon III.

D. M. POTTER, *The Impending Crisis, 1848–1861* (1976) A penetrating study of the coming of the American Civil War.

A. SKED, *Decline and Fall of the Habsburg Empire 1815–1918* (2001). A major, accessible survey of a difficult subject.

D. M. SMITH, *Cavour* (1984). An excellent biography.

C. P. STACEY, *Canada and the Age of Conflict* (1977, 1981). A study of Canadian foreign relations.

D. WETZEL, *A Duel of Giants: Bismarck, Napoleon III, and the Origins of the Franco-Prussian War* (2001). Broad study based on most recent scholarship.

CHAPTER 25

M. ADAS, *Machines as the Measure of Men: Science, Technology, and Ideologies of Western Dominance* (1989). The best single volume on racial thinking and technological advances as forming ideologies of European colonial dominance.

A. ASCHER AND P. A. STOLYPIN, *The Search for Stability in Late Imperial Russia* (2000). A broad-ranging biography based on extensive research.

I. BERLIN, *Karl Marx: His Life and Environment*, 4th ed. (1996). A classics volume that remains an excellent introduction.

JANET BROWNE, *Charles Darwin*, 2 vols. (2002) An eloquent, accessible biography.

J. BURROW, *The Crisis of Reason: European Thought, 1848–1914* (2000). The best overview available.

A. D. CHANDLER JR., *The Visible Hand: Managerial Revolution in American Business* (1977). Remains the best discussion of the innovative role of American business.

A. CLARKE, *The Struggle for the Breeches: Gender and the Making of the British Working Class* (1995). An examination of the manner in which industrialization made problematical the relationships between men and women.

W. CRONIN, *Nature's Metropolis: Chicago and the Great West, 1848–1893* (1991) The best examination of any major American nineteenth-century city.

P. GAY, *Freud: A Life for Our Time* (1988). The new standard biography.

R. F. HAMILTON, *Marxism, Revisionism, and Leninism: Explication, Assessment, and Commentary* (2000). A contribution from the perspective of a historically minded sociologist.

S. HAHN, *A Nation under Our Feet: Black Political Struggles in the Rural South from Slavey to the Great Migration* (2003). A major synthesis.

A. HOURANI, *Arab Thought in the Liberal Age 1789–1939* (1967). A classic account, clearly written and accessible to the nonspecialist.

D. I. KERTZER AND M. BARBAGLI, eds., *Family Life in the Long Nineteenth Century, 1789–1913: The History of the European Family* (2002). Wide-ranging collection of essays.

J. T. KLOPPENBERG, *Uncertain Victory: Social Democracy and Progressivism in European and American Thought* (1986). An extremely important comparative study.

J. KÖHLER, *Zarathustra's Secret: The Interior Life of Friedrich Nietzsche* (2002). A controversial new biography.

L. KOLAKOWSKI, *Main Currents of Marxism: Its Rise, Growth, and Dissolution*, 3 vols. (1978). Especially good on the last years of the nineteenth century and the early years of the twentieth.

P. KRAUSE, *The Battle for Homestead, 1880–1892* (1992). Examines labor relations in the steel industry.

D. LANDES, *The Wealth and Poverty of Nations: Why Some Are So Rich and Some So Poor* (1998). A major international discussion of the subject.

M. MCGERR, *A Fierce Discontent: The Rise and Fall of the Progressive Moevement in America l870–1920* (2003). The best recent synthesis.

E. MORRIS, *Theodore Rex* (2002). Major survey of Theodore Roosevelt's presidency and personality.

A. PAIS, *Subtle Is the Lord: The Science and Life of Albert Einstein* (1983). Remains the most accessible scientific biography.

J. RENDALL, *The Origins of Modern Feminism: Women in Britain, France and the United States, 1780–1860* (1985). A well-informed introduction.

R. SERVICE, *Lenin: A Biography* (2002). Based on new sources and will no doubt become the standard biography.

R. M. UTLEY, *The Indian Frontier and the American West, 1846–1890* (1984). A broad survey of the pressures of white civilization against Native Americans.

D. VITAL, *A People Apart: The Jews In Modern Europe, l789–1939* (1999). A deeply informed survey.

CHAPTER 26

S. ARROM, *The Women of Mexico City, 1790–1857* (1985). A pioneering study.

E. BERMAN, ed., *Women, Culture, and Politics in Latin America* (1990). Useful essays.

L. BETHELL, ed., *The Cambridge History of Latin America*, 8 vols. (1992). The single most authoritative coverage, with extensive bibliographical essays.

V. BULMER-THOMAS, *The Economic History of Latin America Since Independence* (1994). A major study in every respect.

E. B. BURNS, *The Poverty of Progress: Latin America in the Nineteenth Century* (1980). Argues that the elites suppressed alternative modes of cultural and economic development.

E. B. BURNS, *A History of Brazil* (1993). The most useful one-volume treatment.

D. BUSHNELL AND N. MACAULAY, *The Emergence of Latin America in the Nineteenth Century* (1994). A survey that examines the internal development of Latin America during the period.

R. CONRAD, *The Destruction of Brazilian Slavery, 1850–1889* (1971). A good survey of the most important problem in Brazil in the second half of the nineteenth century.

R. CONRAD, *World of Sorrow: The African Slave Trade to Brazil* (1986). An excellent survey of the subject.

E. V. DA COSTA, *The Brazilian Empire: Myths and Histories* (1985). Essays that provide a thorough introduction to Brazil during the period of empire.

H. S. FERNS, *Britain and Argentina in the Nineteenth Century* (1968). Explains clearly the intermeshing of the two economies.

M. FONT, *Coffee, Contention, and Change in the Making of Modern Brazil* (1990). Extensive discussion of the problems of a single-commodity economy.

R. GRAHAM, *Britain and the Onset of Modernization in Brazil* (1968). Another study of British economic dominance.

S. H. HABER, *Industry and Underdevelopment: The Industrialization of Mexico, 1890–1940* (1989). Examines the problem of industrialization before and after the revolution.

G. HAHNER, *Emancipating the Female Sex: The Struggle for Women's Rights in Brazil, 1850–1940* (1990). An extensive examination of a relatively understudied issue in Latin America.

C. H. HARING, *Empire in Brazil: A New World Experiment with Monarchy* (1958). Remains a useful overview.

J. HEMMING, *Amazon Frontier: The Defeat of the Brazilian Indians* (1987). A brilliant survey of the experience of Native Americans in modern Brazil.

R. A. HUMPHREYS, *Latin America and the Second World War*, 2 vols. (1981–1982). The standard work on the topic.

F. KATZ, ed., *Riot, Rebellion, and Revolution in Mexico: Social Base of Agrarian Violence, 1750–1940* (1988). Essays that put the violence of the revolution in a longer context.

A. KNIGHT, *The Mexican Revolution*, 2 vols. (1986). The best treatment of the subject.

S. MAINWARING, *The Catholic Church and Politics in Brazil, 1916–1985* (1986). An examination of a key institution in Brazilian life.

M. C. MEYER AND W. L. SHERMAN, *The Course of Mexican History* (1995). An excellent survey.

M. MORNER, *Adventurers and Proletarians: The Story of Migrants in Latin America* (1985). Examines immigration to Latin America and migration within it.

J. PAGE, *Perón: A Biography* (1983). The standard English treatment.

D. ROCK, *Politics in Argentina, 1890–1930: The Rise and Fall of Radicalism* (1975). The major discussion of the Argentine Radical Party.

D. ROCK, *Argentina, 1516–1987: From Spanish Colonization to Alfonsin* (1987). Now the standard survey.

D. ROCK, ed., *Latin America in the 1940s: War and Postwar Transitions* (1994). Essays examining a very difficult decade for the continent.

R. M. SCHNEIDER, *"Order and Progress": A Political History of Brazil* (1991). A straightforward narrative with helpful notes for further reading.

T. E. SKIDMORE, *Black into White: Race and Nationality in Brazilian Thought* (1993). Examines the role of racial theory in Brazil.

P. H. SMITH, *Argentina and the Failure of Democracy: Conflict Among Political Elites. 1904–1955* (1974). An examination of one of the major political puzzles of Latin American history.

S. J. STEIN AND B. H. STEIN, *The Colonial Heritage of Latin America: Essays on Economic Dependence in Perspective* (1970). A major statement of the dependence interpretation.

D. TAMARIN, *The Argentine Labor Movement, 1930–1945: A Study in the Origins of Perónism* (1985). A useful introduction to a complex subject.

H. J. WIARDA, *Politics and Social Change in Latin America: The Distinct Tradition* (1974). Excellent essays that stress the ongoing role of Iberian traditions.

J. D. WIRTH, ed., *Latin American Oil Companies and the Politics of Energy* (1985). A series of case studies.

J. WOLFE, *Working Women, Working Men: São Paulo and the Rise of Brazil's Industrial Working Class, 1900–1955* (1993). Pays particular attention to the role of women.

J. WOMACK, *Zapata and the Mexican Revolution* (1968). A classic study.

CHAPTER 27

General Works

S. COOK, *Colonial Encounters in the Age of High Imperialism* (1996). A good introduction to the imperial enterprise in Africa and Asia.

D. K. FIELDHOUSE, *The West and the Third World. Trade, Colonialism, Dependence and Development* (1999). Addresses whether colonialism was detrimental or beneficial to colonized peoples.

P. HOPKIRK, *The Great Game: The Struggle for Empire in Central Asia* (1992). Focuses on the political and economic rivalries of the imperial powers.

India

A. AHMAD, *Islamic Modernism in India and Pakistan, 1857–1964* (1967). The standard survey of Muslim thinkers and movements in India during the period.

C. A. BAYLY, *Indian Society and the Making of the British Empire, The New Cambridge History of India*, II. 1 (1988). One of several major contributions of this author to the ongoing revision of our picture of modern Indian history since the eighteenth century.

A. GHOSH, *In an Antique Land. History in the Guise of a Traveler's Tale* (1992). An anthropologist traces the footsteps of a premodern slave traveling with his master from North Africa to India. A gripping tale of premodern life in the India Ocean basin and also of contemporary Egypt.

R. GUHA, ed., *Subaltern Studies: Writings on South Asian History and Society* (1982). Essays on the colonial period that focus on the social, political, and economic history of "subaltern" groups and classes (hill tribes, peasants, etc.) rather than only the elites of India.

S. N. HAY, ed., "Modern India and Pakistan," Part VI of Wm. Theodore de Bary et al., eds., *Sources of Indian Tradition*, 2nd ed. (1988). A superb selection of primary-source documents with brief introductions and helpful notes.

F. ROBINSON, ed., *The Cambridge Encyclopedia of India, Pakistan, Bangladesh, Sri Lanka, Nepal, Bhutan, and the Maldives* (1989). A fine collection of survey articles by various scholars, organized into topical chapters ranging from "Economies" to "Cultures."

Central Islamic Lands

J. J. DONAHUE AND J. L. ESPOSITO, eds., *Islam in Transition: Muslim Perspectives* (1982). An interesting selection of primary-source materials on Islamic thinking in this century.

W. CLEVELAND, *A History of the Modern Middle East*, 3rd ed. (2004). A balanced and well-organized overview of modern Middle Eastern history.

A. DAWISHA, *Arab Nationalism in the Twentieth Century. From Triumph to Despair* (2003). A good overview of the development of Arab nationalism.

S. DERINGIL, *The Well-Protected Domains: Ideology and the Legitimation of Power in the Ottoman Empire, 1876–1909* (1998). An impressive study on nationalism and reform in the Ottoman Empire.

D. F. EICKELMAN, *Knowledge and Power in Morocco: The Education of a Twentieth-Century Notable* (1985). A fascinating study of traditional Islamic education and society in the twentieth century through a social biography of a Moroccan religious scholar and judge.

A. HOURANI, *Arabic Thought in the Liberal Age, 1798–1939* (1967). The standard work, by which all subsequent scholarship on the topic is to be judged.

N. R. KEDDIE, *An Islamic Response to Imperialism* (1968). A brief study of al-Afghani, the great Muslim reformer, with translations of a number of his writings.

B. LEWIS, *The Emergence of Modern Turkey*, 2nd ed. (1968). A concise but thorough history of the creation of the Turkish state, including nineteenth-century background.

J. O. VOLL, *Islam; Continuity and Change in the Modern World* (1982). Chapters 1–6. An interpretive survey of the Islamic world since the eighteenth century. Its emphasis on eighteenth-century reform movements is especially noteworthy.

Africa

A. A. BOAHEN, *Africa Under Colonial Domination, 1880–1935* (1985). Vol. VII of the *UNESCO General History of Africa*. Excellent chapters on various regions of Africa in the period. Chapters 3–10 detail African resistance to European colonial intrusion in diverse regions.

W. CARTEY AND M. KILSON, eds., *The Africa Reader: Colonial Africa* (1970). Original source materials give a vivid picture of African resistance to colonial powers, adaptation to foreign rule, and the emergence of the African masses as a political force.

P. CURTIN, S. FEIERMANN, L. THOMPSON, AND J. VANSINA, *African History* (1978). The relevant portions are Chapters 10–20.

B. DAVIDSON, *Modern Africa: A Social and Political History* (1989). A very useful survey of African history.

J. D. FAGE, *A History of Africa* (1978). The relevant chapters, which give a particularly clear overview of the colonial period, are 12–16.

B. FREUND, *The Making of Contemporary Africa: The Development of African Society Since 1800* (1984). A refreshingly direct synthetic discussion and survey that take an avowedly, but not reductive, materialist approach to interpretation.

T. PAKENHAM, *The Scramble for Africa* (1991). An excellent analysis of the imperialist age in Africa.

A. D. ROBERTS, ed., *The Colonial Moment in Africa: Essays on the Movement of Minds and Materials, 1900–1940* (1986). Chapters from *The Cambridge History of Africa* treating various aspects of the colonial period in Africa, including economics, politics, and religion.

CHAPTER 28

China

P. M. COBLE, *The Shanghai Capitalists and the Nationalist Government, 1927–1937* (1980).

L. E. EASTMAN, *The Abortive Revolution: China Under Nationalist Rule, 1927–1937* (1974).

L. E. EASTMAN, *Seeds of Destruction: Nationalist China in War and Revolution, 1937–1949* (1984).

M. ELVIN AND G. W. SKINNER, *The Chinese City Between Two Worlds* (1974). A study of the late Qing and Republican eras.

J. W. ESHERICK, *The Origins of the Boxer Rebellion* (1987).

S. ETŌ, *China's Republican Revolution* (1994).

J. K. FAIRBANK AND M. GOLDMAN, *China, a New History* (1998). A survey of the entire sweep of Chinese history; especially strong on the modern period.

J. K. FAIRBANK AND D. TWITCHETT, eds., *The Cambridge History of China.* Like the premodern volumes in the same series, the volumes on modern China represent a survey of what is known. Volumes 10–15, which cover the history from the late Qing to the People's Republic, have been published, and the others will be available soon. The series is substantial. Each volume contains a comprehensive bibliography.

J. FITZGERALD, *Awakening China: Politics, Culture, and Class in the Nationalist Revolution* (1996).

C. HAO, *Chinese Intellectuals in Crisis: Search for Order and Meaning, 1890–1911* (1987).

W. C. KIRBY, ed., *State and Economy in Republican China* (2001).

P. A. KUHN, *Rebellion and Its Enemies in Late Imperial China: Militarization and Social Structure, 1796–1864* (1980). A study of how the Confucian gentry saved the Manchu dynasty after the Taiping Rebellion.

P. KUHN, Origins of the Modern Chinese State (2002).

J. LEVENSON, *Liang Ch'i-ch'ao and the Mind of Modern China* (1953). A classic study of a major Chinese reformer and thinker.

LU XUN, *Selected Works* (1960). Novels, stories, and other writings by modern China's greatest writer.

S. NAQUIN, *Peking: Temples and City Life, 1400–1900* (2000).

E. O. REISCHAUER, J. K. FAIRBANK, AND A. M. CRAIG, *East Asia: Tradition and Transformation* (1989). A detailed text on East Asian history. Contains ample chapters on Japan and China and shorter chapters on Korea and Vietnam.

H. Z. SCHIFFRIN, *Sun Yat-sen, Reluctant Revolutionary* (1980). A biography.

B. I. SCHWARTZ, *Chinese Communism and the Rise of Mao* (1951). A classic study of Mao, his thought, and the Chinese Communist Party before 1949.

B. I. SCHWARTZ, *In Search of Wealth and Power: Yen Fu and the West* (1964). A fine study of a late-nineteenth-century thinker who introduced Western ideas into China.

J. D. SPENCE, *The Gate of Heavenly Peace: The Chinese and Their Revolution, 1895–1980* (1981). Historical reflections on twentieth-century China.

J. D. SPENCE, *The Search for Modern China* (1990). A thick text but well written.

M. SZONYI, *Practicing Kinship: Lineage and Descent in Late Imperial China* (2002).

S. Y. TENG AND J. K. FAIRBANK, *China's Response to the West* (1954). A superb collection of translations from Chinese thinkers and political figures, with commentaries.

T. H. WHITE AND A. JACOBY, *Thunder Out of China* (1946). A view of China during World War II by two who were there.

Japan

G. AKITA, *Foundations of Constitutional Government in Modern Japan* (1967). A study of Itō Hirobumi in the political process leading to the Meiji constitution.

G. C. ALLEN, *A Short Economic History of Modern Japan* (1958).

A. E. BARSHAY, *The Social Sciences in Modern Japan: the Marxian and Modernist Traditions* (2004). Different interpretations of history.

J. R. BARTHOLOMEW, *The Formation of Science in Japan* (1989). The pioneering English-language work on the subject.

W. G. BEASLEY, *Japanese Imperialism, 1894–1945* (1987). Excellent short book on subject.

G. M. BERGER, *Parties Out of Power in Japan, 1931–1941* (1977). An analysis of the condition of political parties during the militarist era.

G.L. BERNSTEIN, *Recreating Japanese Women, 1600–1945* (1991).

The Cambridge History of Japan, The Nineteenth Century, M.B. Jansen, ed. (1989); *The Twentieth Century,* P. Duus, ed. (1988). Multi-author works.

A. M. CRAIG, *Chōshū in the Meiji Restoration* (2000). A study of the Chōshū domain, a Prussia of Japan, during the period 1840–1868.

A. M. CRAIG AND D. H. SHIVELY, eds., *Personality in Japanese History* (1970). An attempt to gauge the role of individuals and their personalities as factors explaining history.

P. Duus, *Party Rivalry and Political Change in Taisho Japan* (1968). A study of political change in Japan during the 1910s and 1920s.

P. Duus, *The Abacus and the Sword, the Japanese Penetration of Korea, 1895–1910* (1995). A thoughtful analysis.

S. Ericson, *The Sound of the Whistle: Railroads and the State in Meiji Japan* (1996). An economic and social history of railroads, an engine of growth and popular symbol.

Y. Fukuzawa, *Autobiography* (1966). Japan's leading nineteenth-century thinker tells of his life and of the birth of modern Japan.

A. Garon, *The State and Labor in Modern Japan* (1987). A fine study of the subject.

C. N. Gluck, *Japan's Modern Myths: Ideology in the Late Meiji Period* (1988). A brilliant study of the complex weave of late Meiji thought.

A. Gordon, *The Evolution of Labor Relations in Japan: Heavy Industry, 1853–1955* (1985). A seminal work.

B. R. Hackett, *Yamagata Aritomo in the Rise of Modern Japan, 1932–1922* (1973). History as seen through the biography of a central figure.

I. Hall, *Mori Arinori* (1973). A biography of Japan's first minister of education.

T. R. H. Havens, *The Valley of Darkness: The Japanese People and World War II* (1978). Wartime society.

C. Iriye, *After Imperialism: The Search for a New Order in the Far East, 1921–1931* (1965). (Also see other studies by this author.)

D. M. B. Jansen and G. Rozman, eds., *Japan in Transition from Tokugawa to Meiji* (1986). Contains fine essays.

W. Johnston, *The Modern Epidemic: A History of Tuberculosis in Japan* (1995). A social history of a disease.

E. Keene, Ed., *Modern Japanese Literature, An Anthology* (1960). A collection of modern Japanese short stories and excerpts from novels.

F. Y.T. Matsusaka, *The Making of Japanese Manchuria, 1904–1932* (2001). On railroad strategies in empire building.

J. W. Morley, ed., *The China Quagmire* (1983). A study of Japan's expansion on the continent between 1933 and 1941. (For diplomatic history, see also the many other works by this author.)

R. H. Myers and M. R. Peattie, eds., *The Japanese Colonial Empire, 1895–1945* (1984).

T. Najita, *Hara Kei in the Politics of Compromise, 1905–1915* (1967). A study of one of Japan's greatest party leaders.

K. Ohkawa and H. Rosovsky, *Japanese Economic Growth: Trend Acceleration in the Twentieth Century* (1973).

M. Ravina, *The Last Samurai: The Life and Battles of Saigo Takamori* (2004). Unlike the movie, this account of the Satsuma uprising is historical.

G. Shiba, *Remembering Aizu* (1999). A stirring autobiographical account of a samurai youth whose domain lost in the Meiji Restoration.

K. Smith, *A Time of Crisis: The Great Depression and Rural Revitalization* (2001). An intellectual history of village movements during the 1930s.

J. J. Stephan, *Hawaii Under the Rising Sun* (1984). Japan's plans for rule in Hawaii.

R. H. Spector, *Eagle Against the Sun: The American War with Japan* (1985). A narrative of World War II in the Pacific.

E. P. Tsurumi, *Factory Girls: Women in the Thread Mills of Meiji Japan* (1990). A sympathetic analysis of the key component of the Meiji labor force.

W. Wray, *Mitsubishi and the N. Y. K., 1870–1914* (1984). The growth of a shipping *zaibatsu*, with analysis of business strategies, the role of government and imperialist involvements.

CHAPTER 29

L. Albertini, *The Origins of the War of 1914*, 3 vols. (1952, 1957). Discursive but invaluable.

V. R. Berghahn, *Germany and the Approach of War in 1914* (1973). A work similar in spirit to both of Fischer's (see below) but stressing the importance of Germany's naval program.

R. Bosworth, *Italy and the Approach of the First World War* (1983). A fine analysis of Italian policy.

S. B. Fay, *The Origins of the World War*, 2 vols. (1928). The most influential of the revisionist accounts.

F. Fischer, *Germany's Aims in the First World War* (1967). An influential interpretation that stirred a great controversy in Germany and around the world by emphasizing Germany's role in bringing on the war.

F. Fischer, *War of Illusions* (1975). A long and diffuse book that tries to connect German responsibility for the war with internal social, economic, and political developments.

D. Fromkin, *Europe's Last Summer: Who Started the Great War in 1914?* (2004). A lively account that fixes on the final crisis in July 1914.

J. N. Horne, *Labour at War: France and Britain, 1914–1918* (1991). An examination of a major issue on the home fronts.

J. Joll, *The Origins of the First World War* (1984). A brief but thoughtful analysis.

P. Kennedy, *The Rise of the Anglo-German Antagonism 1860–1914* (1980). An unusual and thorough analysis of the political, economic, and cultural roots of important diplomatic developments.

W. L. Langer, *European Alliances and Alignments*, 2nd ed. (1966). A splendid diplomatic history of the years 1871–1890.

W. L. Langer, *The Diplomacy of Imperialism* (1935). A continuation of the previous study for the years 1890–1902.

D. C. B. Lieven, *Russia and the Origins of the First World War* (1983). A good account of the forces that shaped Russian policy.

A. Mombauer, *The Origins of the First World War. Controversies and Consensus* (2002). A fascinating survey of the debate over the decades and the current state of the question.

R. Pipes, *A Concise History of the Russian Revolution* (1996). A one-volume version of a scholarly masterpiece.

Z. Steiner, *Britain and the Origins of the First World War* (1977). A perceptive and informed account of the way British foreign policy was made in the years before the war.

H. Strachan, *The First World War* (2004). A fine one-volume account of the war.

A. J. P. Taylor, *The Struggle for Mastery in Europe, 1848–1918* (1954). Clever but controversial.

S. R. Williamson, Jr., *Austria-Hungary and the Origins of the First World War* (1991). A valuable study of a complex subject.

CHAPTER 30

W. S. Allen, *The Nazi Seizure of Power: The Experience of a Single German Town, 1930–1935*, rev. ed. (1984). A classic treatment of Nazism in a microcosmic setting.

J. BARNARD, *Walter Reuther and the Rise of the Auto Workers* (1983). A major introduction to the new American unions of the 1930s.

K. D. BRACHER, *The German Dictatorship* (1970). A comprehensive treatment of both the origins and the functioning of the Nazi movement and government.

A. BULLOCK, *Hitler: A Study in Tyranny*, rev. ed. (1964). The best biography.

M. BURLEIGH AND W. WIPPERMAN, *The Racial State: Germany 1933–1945* (1991). Emphasizes the manner in which racial theory influenced numerous areas of policy.

R. CONQUEST, *The Great Terror: Stalin's Purges of the Thirties* (1968). The best treatment of the subject to this date.

G. CRAIG, *Germany, 1866–1945* (1978). A major survey.

I. DEUTSCHER, *The Prophet Armed* (1954), *The Prophet Unarmed* (1959), and *The Prophet Outcast* (1963). Remains the major biography of Trotsky.

I. DEUTSCHER, *Stalin: A Political Biography*, 2nd ed. (1967). The best biography in English.

B. EICHENGREEN, *Golden Fetters: The Gold Standard and the Great Depression, 1919–1939* (1992). A remarkable study of the role of the gold standard in the economic policies of the interwar years.

E. EYCK, *A History of the Weimar Republic*, 2 vols. (trans. 1963). The story as narrated by a liberal.

M. S. FAUSOLD, *The Presidency of Herbert Hoover* (1985). An important treatment.

G. FELDMAN, *The Great Disorder: Politics, Economics, and Society in the German Inflation, 1914–1924* (1993). The best work on the subject.

S. FITZPATRICK, *Stalin's Peasants: Resistance and Survival in the Russian Village After Collectivization* (1994). A pioneering study.

P. FUSSELL, *The Great War and Modern Memory* (1975). A brilliant account of the literature arising from World War I during the 1920s.

J. K. GALBRAITH, *The Great Crash* (1979). A well-known account by a leading economist.

R. GELLATELY, *The Gestapo and German Society: Enforcing Racial Policy, 1933–1945* (1990). A discussion of how the police state supported Nazi racial policies.

H. J. GORDON, *Hitler and the Beer Hall Putsch* (1972). An excellent account of the event and the political situation in the early Weimar Republic.

R. HAMILTON, *Who Voted for Hitler?* (1982). An examination of voting patterns and sources of Nazi support.

J. HELD, ed., *The Columbia History of Eastern Europe in the Twentieth Century* (1992). Individual essays on each country.

P. KENEZ, *The Birth of the Propaganda State: Soviet Methods of Mass Mobilization, 1917–1929* (1985). An examination of the manner in which the Communist government inculcated popular support.

B. KENT, *The Spoils of War: The Politics, Economics, and Diplomacy of Reparations, 1918–1932* (1993). A comprehensive account of the intricacies of the reparations problem of the 1920s.

D. LANDES, *The Unbound Prometheus: Technological Change and Industrial Development in Western Europe from 1750 to the Present* (1969). Includes an excellent analysis of both the Great Depression and the few areas of economic growth.

B. LINCOLN, *Red Victory: A History of the Russian Civil War* (1989). An excellent narrative account.

M. MCAULEY, *Bread and Justice: State and Society in Petrograd, 1917–1922* (1991). A study that examines the impact of the Russian Revolution and Leninist policies on a major Russian city.

D. J. K. PEUKERT, *Inside Nazi Germany: Conformity, Opposition, and Racism in Everyday Life* (1987). An excellent discussion of life under Nazi rule.

R. PIPES, *The Unknown Lenin: From the Secret Archives* (1996). A collection of previously unpublished documents that indicated the repressive character of Lenin's government.

P. PULZER, *Jews and the German State: The Political History of a Minority, 1848–1933* (1992). A detailed history by a major historian of European minorities.

L. J. RUPP, *Mobilizing Women for War: German and America Propaganda, 1939–1945* (1978). Although concentrating on a later period, it includes an excellent discussion of general Nazi attitudes toward women.

A. M. SCHLESINGER, JR., *The Age of Roosevelt*, 3 vols. (1957–1960). The most important overview.

D. M. SMITH, *Mussolini's Roman Empire* (1976). A general description of the Fascist regime in Italy.

D. M. SMITH, *Italy and Its Monarchy* (1989). A major treatment of an important neglected subject.

A. SOLZHENITSYN, *The Gulag Archipelago*, 3 vols. (1974–1979). A major examination of the labor camps under Stalin by one of the most important contemporary Russian writers.

R. J. SONTAG, *A Broken World, 1919–1939* (1971). An exceptionally thoughtful and well-organized survey.

A. J. P. TAYLOR, *English History, 1914–1945* (1965). Lively and opinionated.

H. A. TURNER JR., *German Big Business and the Rise of Hitler* (1985). An important major study of the subject.

H. A. TURNER JR., *Hitler's Thirty Days to Power* (1996). A narrative of the events leading directly to the Nazi seizure of power.

L. YAHIL, *The Holocaust: The Fate of European Jewry, 1932–1945* (1990). A major study of this fundamental subject in twentieth-century history.

CHAPTER 31

A. ADAMTHWAITE, *France and the Coming of the Second World War, 1936–1939* (1977). A careful account making good use of the French archives.

E. R. BECK, *Under the Bombs: The German Home Front, 1942–1945* (1986). An interesting examination of a generally unstudied subject.

R. S. BOTWINICK, *A History of the Holocaust*, 2nd ed., 2002. A brief but broad and useful account of the causes, character and results of the Holocaust.

A. BULLOCK, *Hitler: A Study in Tyranny*, rev. ed. (1964). A brilliant biography.

W. S. CHURCHILL, *The Second World War*, 6 vols. (1948–1954). The memoirs of the great British leader.

A. CROZIER, *The Causes of the Second World War*, 1997. An examination of what brought on the war.

R. B. FRANK, *Downfall: The End of the Imperial Japanese Empire*, 1998. A thorough, well-documented account of the last months of the Japanese empire and the reasons for its surrender.

J. L. GADDIS, *We Now Know: Rethinking Cold War History* (1998). A fine account of the early years of the Cold War making use of new evidence emerging since the collapse of the Soviet Union.

J. L. GADDIS, P. H. GORDON, E. MAY, eds., *Cold War Statesmen Confront the Bomb: Nuclear diplomacy Since 1945* (1999). A collection of essays discussing the effect of atomic and nuclear weapons on diplomacy since WW II.

M. GILBERT, *The Holocaust: A History of the Jews of Europe During the Second World War* (1985). The best and most comprehensive treatment.

A. IRIYE, *Pearl Harbor and the Coming of the Pacific War* (1999). Essays on how the Pacific war came about, including a selection of documents.

J. KEEGAN, *The Second World War* (1990). A lively and penetrating account by a master military historian.

I. KERSHAW, *Hitler: 1889–1936: Hubris* (1999) and *Hitler: 1936–1945: Nemesis* (2001). An outstanding two-volume biography.

W. F. KIMBALL, *Forged in War: Roosevelt, Churchill, and the Second World War,* (1998). A study of the collaboration between the two great leaders of the West based on a thorough knowledge of their correspondence.

W. MURRAY AND A. R. MILLETT, *A War to be Won: Fighting the Second World War,* (2000). A splendid account of the military operations in the war.

R. OVERY, *Why the Allies Won* (1997). An anlysis of the reasons for the victory of the Allies with special emphasis on technology.

N. RICH, *Hitler War Aims,* 2 vols. (1973–1974). The best study of the subject in English.

H. THOMAS, *The Spanish Civil War,* 3rd ed. (1986). The best account in English.

P. WANDYCZ, *The Twilight of French Eastern Alliances,* 1926–1936 (1988). A well-documented account of the diplomacy of central and eastern Europe in a crucial period.

G. L. WEINBERG, *A World at Arms: A Global History of World War II* (1994). A thorough and excellent narrative account.

CHAPTER 32

B. S. ANDERSON AND J. P. PINSSER, *A History of Their Own: Women in Europe from Prehistory to the Present,* Vol. 2 (1988). A broad-ranging survey.

R. BERNSTEIN, *Out of the Blue: The Story of September 11, 2001 from Jihad to Ground Zero* (2002). An excellent account by a gifted journalist.

A. BROWN, *The Gorbachev Factor* (1996). An important commentary by an English observer.

D. CALLEO, *Rethinking Europe's Future* (2003) A daring book by an experienced commentator.

J. L. GADDIS, *What We Know Now* (1997). Examines the Cold War in light of newly released documents.

D. J. GARROW, *Bearing the Cross: Martin Luther King, Jr. and the Southern Leadership Conference 1955–1968* (1986). The best work on the subject.

W. HITCHCOCK, *Struggle for Europe: The Turbulent History of a Divided Continent, 1945–2002* (2003). The best overall narrative now available

D. KEARNS, *Lyndon Johnson and the American Dream* (1976). A useful biography.

J. KEEP, *The Last of the Empires: A History of the Soviet Union, 1956–1991* (1995). A clear narrative.

M. MANDELBAUM, *The Ideas That Conquered the World: Peace, Democracy, and Free Markets* (2002). An important analysis by a major commentator on international affairs.

J. MANN, *The Rise of the Vulcans: The History of Bush's War Cabinet* (2004). An account of the major foreign policy advisors behind the invasion of Iraq.

R. MANN, *A Grand Delusion: America's Descent into Vietnam* (2001). The best recent narrative.

J. McCORMICK, *Understanding the European Union: A Concise Introduction* (2002) Outlines the major features.

N. NAIMARK, *Fires of Hatred: Ethnic Cleansing in Twentieth-Century Europe* (2002). A remarkably sensitive treatment of a tragic subject.

R. SAWKA AND ANNE STEVENS, eds., *Contemporary Europe* (2000). A collection of essays on major topics.

G. STOKES, ed., *From Stalinism to Pluralism: A Documentary History of Eastern Europe Since 1945* (1996). An important collection of documents that are not easily accessible elsewhere.

M. WALKER, *The Cold War and the Making of the Modern World* (1994). A major survey.

CHAPTER 33

China

R. BAUM, *Burying Mao: Chinese Politics in the Age of Deng Xiaoping* (1996).

A. CHAN, R. MADSEN, J. UNGER, *Chen Village under Mao and Deng* (1992).

J. CHANG, *Wild Swans: Three Daughters of China* (1991). An intimate look at recent Chinese society through three generations of women. Immensely readable.

J. FENG, *Ten Years of Madness: Oral Histories of China's Cultural Revolution* (1996).

J. FEWSMITH, *China Since Tiananmen: The Politics of Transition* (2001). Focus is on the rise to power of Jiang Zemin and Chinese politics during the nineties.

B. M. FROLIC, *Mao's People: Sixteen Portraits of Life in Revolutionary China* (1987).

T. GOLD, *State and Society in the Taiwan Miracle* (1986). The story of economic growth in postwar Taiwan.

M. GOLDMAN, *Sowing the Seeds of Democracy in China: Political Reform in the Deng Xiaoping Era* (1994).

A. IRIYE, *China and Japan in the Global Setting* (1992).

D. M. LAMPTON, *Same Bed, Different Dreams: Managing U.S.–China Relations, 1989–2000* (2001).

H. LIANG, *Son of the Revolution* (1983). An autobiographical account of a young man growing up in Mao's China.

K. LIEBERTHAL, *Governing China, from Revolution Through Reform* (2004).

B. LIU, *People or Monsters? and Other Stories and Reportage from China After Mao* (1983). Literary reflections on China.

R. MACFARQUHAR AND J. K. FAIRBANK, eds., *The Cambridge History of China,* Vol. 14, *Emergence of Revolutionary China* (1987), and Vol. 15, *Revolutions Within the Chinese Revolution, 1966–1982* (1991).

L. PAN, *Sons of the Yellow Emperor: A History of the Chinese Diaspora* (1990). A pioneer study that treats not only Southeast Asia but the rest of the world as well.

M. R. RISTAINO, *Port of Last Resort: The Diaspora Communities of Shanghai* (2001).

T. SAICH, *Governance and Politics of China* (2004).

H. WANG, *China's New Order* (2003). Translation of a work by a Qinghua University professor, a liberal within the boundaries of what is permissable in China.

G. WHITE, ed., *In Search of Civil Society: Market Reform and Social Change in Contemporary China* (1996).

M. WOLF, *Revolution Postponed: Women in Contemporary China* (1985).

ZHANG X. AND SANG Y., *Chinese Lives: An Oral History of Contemporary China* (1987).

Japan

G. L. BERNSTEIN, *Haruko's World: A Japanese Farm Woman and Her Community* (1983). A study of the changing life of a village woman in postwar Japan.

T. BESTOR, *Neighborhood Tokyo* (1989). A portrait of contemporary urban life in Japan.

G. L. CURTIS, *The Logic of Japanese Politics: Leaders, Institutions, and the Limits of Change* (1999).

G. L. CURTIS, *Policymaking in Japan: Defining the Role of Politicians* (2002).

M. H. CUSUMANO, *The Japanese Automobile Industry* (1985). A neat study of the postwar business strategies of Toyota and Nissan.

R. P. DORE, *City Life in Japan* (1999). A classic, reissued.

R. P. DORE, *Land Reform in Japan* (1959). Another classic.

S. GARON, *Molding Japanese Minds: The State in Everyday Life* (1997).

S. M. GARON, *The Evolution of Civil Society from Meiji to Heisei* (2002). That is to say, from the mid–nineteenth century to the present day.

A. GORDON, ed., *Postwar Japan as History* (1993).

H. HIBBETT, ed., *Contemporary Japanese Literature: An Anthology of Fiction, Film, and Other Writing Since 1945* (1977). Translations of postwar short stories.

Y. KAWABATA, *The Sound of the Mountain* (1970). Sensitive, moving novel by Nobel author.

J. NATHAN, *Sony, the Private Life* (1999). A lively account of the human side of growth in the Sony Corporation.

D. OKIMOTO, *Between MITI and the Market* (1989). A discussion of the respective roles of government and private enterprise in Japan's postwar growth.

S. PHARR, *Losing Face: Status Politics in Japan* (1996).

E. F. VOGEL, *Japan as Number One: Lessons for America* (1979). While dated and somewhat sanguine, this remains an insightful classic.

Korea and Vietnam

B. CUMINGS, *Korea, The Unknown War* (1988).

B. CUMINGS, *The Origins of the Korean War* (Vol. 1, 1981; Vol. 2, 1991).

B. CUMINGS, *The Two Koreas: On the Road to Reunification?* (1990).

C. J. ECKERT, *Korea Old and New, A History* (1990). The best short history of Korea, with extensive coverage of the postwar era.

C. J. ECKERT, *Offspring of Empire: The Koch'ang Kims and the Colonial Origins of Korean Capitalism, 1876–1945* (1991).

G. M. T. KAHIN, *Intervention: How America Became Involved in Vietnam* (1986).

S. KARNOW, *Vietnam: A History.* rev. ed. (1996).

L. KENDALL, *Shamans, Housewives, and Other Restless Spirits: Women in Korean Ritual and Life* (1985).

K. B. LEE, *A New History of Korea* (1984). A translation by E. Wagner and others of an outstanding Korean work covering the full sweep of Korean history.

T. LI, *Nguyen Cochinchina: South Vietnam in the Seventeenth and Eighteenth Centuries* (1998).

D. MARR, *Vietnam 1945: The Quest for Power* (1995).

C. W. SORENSEN, *Over the Mountains Are Mountains* (1988). How peasant households in Korea adapted to rapid industrialization.

A. WOODSIDE, *Vietnam and the Chinese Model* (1988). Provides the background for Vietnam's relationship to China.

CHAPTER 34

Latin America

P. BAKEWELL, *A History of Latin America: c. 1450 to the Present* (2003). An up-to-date survey.

A. CHOMSKY et al., *The Cuba Reader: History, Culture, Politics* (2004). Very useful, broad-ranging anthology.

J. DOMINGUEZ AND M. SHIFTER, *Contructing Democratic Governance in Latin America* (2003). Contains individual country studies.

G. JOSEPH et al. , *The Mexico Reader: History, Culture, Politics* (2003). Excellent introduction to major issues.

P. LOWDEN, *Moral Opposition to Authoritarian Rule in Chile* (1996). A discussion of Chilean politics from the standpoint of human rights.

J. PRESTON AND S. DILLON, *Opening Mexico: The Making of a Democracy* (2004). Excellent analysis of recent developments in Mexico.

H. WIRARDA, *Democracy and Its Discontents: Development, Interdependence, and U.S. Policy in Latin America* (1995). A useful overview.

Africa

B. DAVIDSON, *Let Freedom Come* (1978). Remains a thought commentary of African independence.

R. W. JULY, *A History of the African People,* 5th ed. (1995). Provides a careful and clear survey of post–World War I history and consideration of nationalism.

J. HERBST, *States and Power in Africa* (2000). Relates current issues of African state-building to those before to the colonial era.

J. H. LATHAM, *Africa, Asia, and South America Since 1800: A Bibliographic Guide* (1995). A valuable tool for finding materials on the topics in this chapter.

N. MANDELA, *Long Walk to Freedom: The Autobiography of Nelson Mandela* (1995). Autobiography of the African leader who transformed South Africa.

L. THOMPSON, *A History of South Africa* (2001). The best survey.

N. VAN DE WALLE, *African Economies and the Politics of Permanent Crisis, 1979–1999* (2001). Exploration of difficulties of African economic development.

India and Pakistan

O. B. JONES, *Pakistan: Eye of the Storm* (2003). Best recent introduction.

R. RASHID, *Taliban: Militant Islam, Oil and Fundamentalism in Central Asia* (2001). Analysis of radical Isalmist regime in Afghanistan.

R. W. STERN, *Changing India: Bourgeois Revolution on the Subcontinent* (2003). Overview of forces now changing Indian society.

S. WOLPERT, *A New History of India* (2003). The closing chapters of this fine survey history are particularly helpful in orienting the reader in postwar Indian history until the mid-1980s.

Islam and the Middle East

A. AHMED, *Discovering Islam. Making Sense of Muslim Hisotry and Society*, rev. ed. (2003). An excellent and readable overivew of Islamic–Western relations.

J. ESPOSITO, *The Islamic Threat: Myth or Reality*, 2nd ed. (1992). A useful corrective to some of the polemics against Islam and Muslims today.

J. J. ESPOSITO, ed., *The Oxford Encyclopedia of Islam* (1999). A thematic survey of Islamic history, particularly strong in the Modern Era.

D. FROMKIN, *A Peace to End All Peace: The Fall of the Ottoman Empire and the Creation of the Modern Middle East* (2001). Very good on the impact of World War I on the region.

G. FULLER, *The Future of Political Islam* (2003). A very good overview of Islamist ideology by a former CIA staff member.

J. KEAY, *Sowing the Wind: The Seeds of Conflict in theMiddle East* (2003). A balanced account.

N. R. KEDDIE, *Modern Iran. Roots and Results of Revolution* (2003). Chapters 6–12 focus on Iran from 1941 through the first years of the 1978 revolution and provide a solid overview of history in this era.

G. KEPEL, *Jihad: The Trail of Political Islam* (2002). An extensive treatment by a leading French scholar of the subject.

Credits

Chapter 13, page 349: Bodleian Library, University of Oxford.

Chapter 14, page 373: Getty Images, Inc. - Photodisc.

Chapter 15, page 401: Musee Conde, Chantilly.

Part 4, page 432, top to bottom, left to right: Emanuel de Witte, "Interior of the Portugese Synagogue on Amsterdam," 1680. Oil on canvas, 43-1/2 × 39" (110.5 × 99.1 cm). © Rijksmuseum, Amsterdam; Library of Congress; The Granger Collection.

Part 4, page 433, top to bottom, left to right: Pawel Wojcik © Dorling Kindersley; Dorota and Mariusz Jarymowicz © Dorling Kindersley; Royal Ontario Museum/Corbis; Corbis/Bettmann.

Part 4 Timeline, page 434, top to bottom, left to right: Elizabeth I (1558-1603) standing on a map of England in 1592. An astute politician in both foreign and domestic policy, Elizabeth was perhaps the most successful ruler of the sixteenth century. By courtesy of the National Portrait Gallery, London; Sultan Muhammad (active ca. 1501-1545), "Allegory of Worldly and Otherworldly Drunkenness". Leaf from a manuscript of a "Divan" by Hafiz, folio 137r. Opaque watercolor, ink and gold on paper. 11 3/8 × 8 1/2 in. (28.9 × 21.6 cm). Promised Gift of Mr. and Mrs. Stuart Cary Welch, Jr. in honor of the students of Harvard University and Radcliffe College. Partially owned by The Metropolitan Museum of Art and The Arthur M. Sackler Museum, Harvard University, 1988. Copyright 1989, Metropolitan Museum of Art; Library of Congress; The Bridgeman Art Library International Ltd; © Archivo Iconografico, S. A./Corbis.

Part 4 Timeline, page 435, top to bottom, left to right: Bridgeman-Giraudon/Art Resource, NY; Francis Wheatley (RA) (1747-1801) "Evening", signed and dated 1799, oil on canvas, 17 1/2 × 21 1/2 in. (44.5 × 54.5 cm), Yale Center for British Art, Paul Mellon Collection/Bridgeman Art Library (B1977.14.118); Getty Images Inc. - Stone Allstock; Japan Airlines Photo; Unidentified Artist. The Emperor Ch'ien Lung (1736-1795) as a Young Man. Colors on silk. H. 63-1/2 in. W. 30-1/2 in. © The Metropolitan Museum of Art, Rogers Fund, 1942. (42.141.8). Photograph © 1980 The Metropolitan Museum of Art; Embassy of Kenya; © Hulton-Deutsch Collection/CORBIS.

Chapter 16, page 437: The Granger Collection.

Page 474 (top): Getty Images, Inc.- Photodisc.

Chapter 17, page 477: Max Alexander © Dorling Kindersley

Chapter 18, page 501: North Wind Picture Archives.

Chapter 19, page 529: Tai Chin, "Fisherman on an Autumn River", (1390-1460). Painting. Ink and color on paper. 18-1/8 × 291-1/4 in. (46 × 740 cm). Courtesy of the Freer Gallery of Art, Smithsonian Institution, Washington, D.C.

Chapter 20, page 571: The Granger Collection.

Chapter 21, page 609: Copyright The British Museum.

Part 5, page 632, top to bottom, left to right: © The Wallace Collection, London; © Dorling Kindersley, Courtesy of the Museu da Cidade, Lisbon.

Part 5, page 633, top to bottom, left to right: © James A. Sugar/CORBIS; © The Wallace Collection, London; Francisco de Goya, "Los fusilamientos del 3 de Mayo, 1808" 1814. Oil on canvas, 8'6" × 11'4". © Museo Nacional del Prado, Madrid; Antoine Jean Gros (1771-1835), "Napoleon in the Plague House at Jaffa". 1804. Oil on Canvas. Louvre, Paris, France. Reunion des Musees Nationaux/Art Resource, NY.

Part 5 Timeline, page 634, top to bottom, left to right: Anonymous, France, 18th century, "Seige of the Bastille, 14 July, 1789." Obligatory mention of the following: Musee de la Ville de Paris, Musee Carnavalet, Paris, France. Bridgeman-Giraudon/Art Resource, NY; Bildarchiv Preubischer Kulturbesitz; Corbis/Bettmann; Bettmann/Corbis; The Granger Collection, New York.

Part 5 timeline, page 635, top to bottom, left to right: "Col. James Todd on elephant Indian painting" ca. 1880. E.T. Archive, Victoria and Albert Museum; © Hulton-Deutsch Collection/CORBIS; © Christie's Images/Corbis.

Chapter 22, page 637: Réunion des Musées Nationaux/Art Resource, NY.

Chapter 23, page 665: Erich Lessing/Art Resource, NY.

Chapter 24, page 699: Museum of the City of New York/Hulton/Archive.

Part 6, page 732, top to bottom, left to right: Bridgeman Art Library, London/SuperStock; Linda Whitwam © Dorling Kindersley.

Part 6, page 733, top to bottom, left to right: © Dorling Kindersley, Courtesy of the Selimiye Barracks / Florence Nightingale Museum, Istanbul; Mita Arts Gallery, Tokyo; Ray Moller/Dorling Kindersley © Royal Pavilion Museum and Art Galleries, Brighton; Woodfin Camp & Associates.

Part 6 Timeline, page 734, top to bottom, left to right: Bildarchiv Preubischer Kulturbesitz; Bildarchiv Preubischer Kulturbesitz; Corbis/Bettmann; © Hulton-Deutsch Collection/CORBIS; Library of Congress.

Part 6 Timeline, page 735, top to bottom, left to right: Bildarchiv Preubischer Kulturbesitz; Shosai Ginko (Japanese, act. 1874-1897), View of the Issuance of the State Constitution in the State Chamber of the New Imperial Palace, March 2, 1889 (Meiji 22), Ink and color on paper, 14 1/8 × 28 3/8 in. The Metropolitan Museum of Art, Gift of Lincoln Kirstein, 1959 (JP3233-3235) Photograph © The Metropolitan Museum of Art; Corbis/Bettmann; The Granger Collection.

Chapter 25, page 737: Reunion des Musees Nationaux/Art Resource, NY.

Chapter 26, page 773: Diego Rivera (1866-1957), "The Flower Carrier (formerly "The Flower Vendor". 1935.Oil and tempera on Masonite. 48 in. × 47 3/4 in. (121.92 cm × 121.29 cm) San Francisco Museum of Modern Art. Albert M. Bender Collection, Gift of Albert M. Bender in memory of Caroline Walter. © Banco de Mexico Diego Rivera & Frida Kahlo Museums Trust. Av. Cinco de Mayo No. 2, Col. Centro, Del. Cuauhtemoc 06059, Mexico, D.F. Reproduction authorized by the Instituto Nacional de Bellas Artes y Literatura.

Chapter 27, page 799: Getty Images Inc. - Hulton Archive Photos.

Page 828 (top): © Werner Forman/Art Resource, NY.

Chapter 28, page 831: Courtesy United States Naval Academy Museum

Part 7, page 866, top to bottom, left to right: Peter Wilson © Dorling Kindersley; Corbis/Bettmann; Andy Crawford/Dorling Kindersley © Imperial War Museum, London.

Part 7, page 867, top to bottom, left to right: Andy Crawford / Dorling Kindersley © Imperial War Museum, London; Matthew Ward © Dorling Kindersley; Aurora & Quanta Productions Inc; Art Resource, N.Y.

Part 7 Timeline, page 868, top to bottom, left to right: The Granger Collection; Pablo Picasso , 'Guernica' 1937, Oil on canvas.

11'5 1/2 × 25'5 3/4. Museo Nacional Centro de Arte Reina Sofia/ © 2004 Estate of Pablo Picasso/Artists Rights Society (ARS), New York; Getty Images Inc. - Hulton Archive Photos; Corbis/Bettmann.

Part 7 Timeline, page 869, top to bottom, left to right: Corbis/Sygma; Corbis/Bettmann; Corbis/Bettmann; Getty Images Inc. - Hulton Archive Photos; AP/Wide World Photos.

Chapter 29, page 871: Corbis/Bettmann.

Chapter 30, page 901 Underwood & Underwood/Corbis.

Chapter 31, page 929: Corbis/Bettmann.

Chapter 32, page 959: Peter Arnold, Inc.

Chapter 33, page 993: Getty Images Inc. - Stone Allstock.

Chapter 34, page 1023: AP Wide World Photos.

Index

NOTE: *Italic page numbers refer to illustrations and maps.*

World History Documents CD-ROM

SINGLE PC LICENSE AGREEMENT AND LIMITED WARRANTY

READ THIS LICENSE CAREFULLY BEFORE OPENING THIS PACKAGE. BY OPENING THIS PACKAGE, YOU ARE
AGREEING TO THE TERMS AND CONDITIONS OF THIS LICENSE. IF YOU DO NOT AGREE, DO NOT OPEN THE
PACKAGE. PROMPTLY RETURN THE UNOPENED PACKAGE AND ALL ACCOMPANYING ITEMS TO THE PLACE YOU
OBTAINED THEM.

1. **GRANT OF LICENSE AND OWNERSHIP:** THE ENCLOSED COMPUTER PROGRAMS <<AND DATA>> ("SOFTWARE")
ARE LICENSED, NOT SOLD, TO YOU BY PEARSON EDUCATION, INC. PUBLISHING AS PEARSON PRENTICE HALL
("WE" OR THE "COMPANY") AND IN CONSIDERATION OF YOUR PURCHASE OR ADOPTION OF THE ACCOMPANYING
COMPANY TEXTBOOKS AND/OR OTHER MATERIALS, AND YOUR AGREEMENT TO THESE TERMS. WE RESERVE ANY
RIGHTS NOT GRANTED TO YOU. YOU OWN ONLY THE DISK(S) BUT WE AND/OR OUR LICENSORS OWN THE SOFT-
WARE ITSELF. THIS LICENSE ALLOWS YOU TO USE AND DISPLAY YOUR COPY OF THE SOFTWARE ON A SINGLE
COMPUTER (I.E., WITH A SINGLE CPU) AT A SINGLE LOCATION FOR ACADEMIC USE ONLY, SO LONG AS YOU COM-
PLY WITH THE TERMS OF THIS AGREEMENT. YOU MAY MAKE ONE COPY FOR BACK UP, OR TRANSFER YOUR COPY
TO ANOTHER CPU, PROVIDED THAT THE SOFTWARE IS USABLE ON ONLY ONE COMPUTER.

2. **RESTRICTIONS:** YOU MAY NOT TRANSFER OR DISTRIBUTE THE SOFTWARE OR DOCUMENTATION TO ANY-
ONE ELSE. EXCEPT FOR BACKUP, YOU MAY NOT COPY THE DOCUMENTATION OR THE SOFTWARE. YOU MAY
NOT NETWORK THE SOFTWARE OR OTHERWISE USE IT ON MORE THAN ONE COMPUTER OR COMPUTER TER-
MINAL AT THE SAME TIME. YOU MAY NOT REVERSE ENGINEER, DISASSEMBLE, DECOMPILE, MODIFY, ADAPT,
TRANSLATE, OR CREATE DERIVATIVE WORKS BASED ON THE SOFTWARE OR THE DOCUMENTATION. YOU MAY
BE HELD LEGALLY RESPONSIBLE FOR ANY COPYING OR COPYRIGHT INFRINGEMENT THAT IS CAUSED BY YOUR
FAILURE TO ABIDE BY THE TERMS OF THESE RESTRICTIONS.

3. **TERMINATION:** THIS LICENSE IS EFFECTIVE UNTIL TERMINATED. THIS LICENSE WILL TERMINATE AUTO-
MATICALLY WITHOUT NOTICE FROM THE COMPANY IF YOU FAIL TO COMPLY WITH ANY PROVISIONS OR LIMI-
TATIONS OF THIS LICENSE. UPON TERMINATION, YOU SHALL DESTROY THE DOCUMENTATION AND ALL
COPIES OF THE SOFTWARE. ALL PROVISIONS OF THIS AGREEMENT AS TO LIMITATION AND DISCLAIMER OF
WARRANTIES, LIMITATION OF LIABILITY, REMEDIES OR DAMAGES, AND OUR OWNERSHIP RIGHTS SHALL SUR-
VIVE TERMINATION.

4. **LIMITED WARRANTY AND DISCLAIMER OF WARRANTY:** COMPANY WARRANTS THAT FOR A PERIOD OF 60
DAYS FROM THE DATE YOU PURCHASE THIS SOFTWARE (OR PURCHASE OR ADOPT THE ACCOMPANYING TEXT-
BOOK), THE SOFTWARE, WHEN PROPERLY INSTALLED AND USED IN ACCORDANCE WITH THE DOCUMENTA-
TION, WILL OPERATE IN SUBSTANTIAL CONFORMITY WITH THE DESCRIPTION OF THE SOFTWARE SET FORTH
IN THE DOCUMENTATION, AND THAT FOR A PERIOD OF 30 DAYS THE DISK(S) ON WHICH THE SOFTWARE IS DE-
LIVERED SHALL BE FREE FROM DEFECTS IN MATERIALS AND WORKMANSHIP UNDER NORMAL USE. THE COM-
PANY DOES NOT WARRANT THAT THE SOFTWARE WILL MEET YOUR REQUIREMENTS OR THAT THE OPERATION
OF THE SOFTWARE WILL BE UNINTERRUPTED OR ERROR-FREE. YOUR ONLY REMEDY AND THE COMPANY'S
ONLY OBLIGATION UNDER THESE LIMITED WARRANTIES IS, AT THE COMPANY'S OPTION, RETURN OF THE DISK
FOR A REFUND OF ANY AMOUNTS PAID FOR IT BY YOU OR REPLACEMENT OF THE DISK. THIS LIMITED WARRAN-
TY IS THE ONLY WARRANTY PROVIDED BY THE COMPANY AND ITS LICENSORS, AND THE COMPANY AND ITS LI-
CENSORS DISCLAIM ALL OTHER WARRANTIES, EXPRESS OR IMPLIED, INCLUDING WITHOUT LIMITATION, THE
IMPLIED WARRANTIES OF MERCHANTABILITY AND FITNESS FOR A PARTICULAR PURPOSE. THE COMPANY DOES
NOT WARRANT, GUARANTEE OR MAKE ANY REPRESENTATION REGARDING THE ACCURACY, RELIABILITY, CUR-
RENTNESS, USE, OR RESULTS OF USE, OF THE SOFTWARE.

5. **LIMITATION OF REMEDIES AND DAMAGES:** IN NO EVENT, SHALL THE COMPANY OR ITS EMPLOYEES,
AGENTS, LICENSORS, OR CONTRACTORS BE LIABLE FOR ANY INCIDENTAL, INDIRECT, SPECIAL, OR CONSE-
QUENTIAL DAMAGES ARISING OUT OF OR IN CONNECTION WITH THIS LICENSE OR THE SOFTWARE, INCLUD-
ING FOR LOSS OF USE, LOSS OF DATA, LOSS OF INCOME OR PROFIT, OR OTHER LOSSES, SUSTAINED AS A
RESULT OF INJURY TO ANY PERSON, OR LOSS OF OR DAMAGE TO PROPERTY, OR CLAIMS OF THIRD PARTIES,
EVEN IF THE COMPANY OR AN AUTHORIZED REPRESENTATIVE OF THE COMPANY HAS BEEN ADVISED OF THE
POSSIBILITY OF SUCH DAMAGES. IN NO EVENT SHALL THE LIABILITY OF THE COMPANY FOR DAMAGES WITH
RESPECT TO THE SOFTWARE EXCEED THE AMOUNTS ACTUALLY PAID BY YOU, IF ANY, FOR THE SOFTWARE OR
THE ACCOMPANYING TEXTBOOK. BECAUSE SOME JURISDICTIONS DO NOT ALLOW THE LIMITATION OF LIA-
BILITY IN CERTAIN CIRCUMSTANCES, THE ABOVE LIMITATIONS MAY NOT ALWAYS APPLY TO YOU.

6. **GENERAL:** THIS AGREEMENT SHALL BE CONSTRUED IN ACCORDANCE WITH THE LAWS OF THE UNITED
STATES OF AMERICA AND THE STATE OF NEW YORK, APPLICABLE TO CONTRACTS MADE IN NEW YORK, EX-
CLUDING THE STATE'S LAWS AND POLICIES ON CONFLICTS OF LAW, AND SHALL BENEFIT THE COMPANY, ITS
AFFILIATES AND ASSIGNEES. THIS AGREEMENT IS THE COMPLETE AND EXCLUSIVE STATEMENT OF THE
AGREEMENT BETWEEN YOU AND THE COMPANY AND SUPERSEDES ALL PROPOSALS OR PRIOR AGREEMENTS,
ORAL, OR WRITTEN, AND ANY OTHER COMMUNICATIONS BETWEEN YOU AND THE COMPANY OR ANY REPRE-
SENTATIVE OF THE COMPANY RELATING TO THE SUBJECT MATTER OF THIS AGREEMENT. IF YOU ARE A U.S.
GOVERNMENT USER, THIS SOFTWARE IS LICENSED WITH "RESTRICTED RIGHTS" AS SET FORTH IN SUBPARA-
GRAPHS (A)-(D) OF THE COMMERCIAL COMPUTER-RESTRICTED RIGHTS CLAUSE AT FAR 52.227-19 OR IN SUB-
PARAGRAPHS (C)(1)(II) OF THE RIGHTS IN TECHNICAL DATA AND COMPUTER SOFTWARE CLAUSE AT DFARS
252.227-7013, AND SIMILAR CLAUSES, AS APPLICABLE.

SHOULD YOU HAVE ANY QUESTIONS CONCERNING THIS AGREEMENT OR IF YOU WISH TO CONTACT THE COM-
PANY FOR ANY REASON, PLEASE CONTACT IN WRITING: LEGAL DEPARTMENT, PRENTICE HALL, 1 LAKE STREET,
UPPER SADDLE RIVER, NJ 07450 OR CALL PEARSON EDUCATION PRODUCT SUPPORT AT 1-800-677-6337.